The comprehensive *Cambridge Guide to American Theatre* covers American theatre from its earliest history to the present, with special attention given to contemporary theatre throughout the United States. In addition to some 2,300 compact entries on people, venues, plays, and other theatrical phenomena, almost 100 topical entries are provided, covering theatre in several major U.S. cities and such disparate subjects as Asian-American theatre, theatre architecture, female and male impersonation, magic, costume, Shakespeare on the American stage, unions, Hispanic theatre, stage lighting, and dramatic theory. The entries, arranged alphabetically, provide information not only on mainstream topics but also on marginalized and alternative theatre, popular forms (such as circus, vaudeville, and burlesque), and key plays from the U.S. theatrical annals. In fact, the breadth of the *Guide*'s coverage helps to redefine the domain of the American theatre.

Over 80 experts in the field have contributed entries to the *Guide*. Useful cross references are provided throughout, linking one essay to another, and approximately 1,000 additional sources are suggested for further reading, both in the entries and in a supplemental bibliography. The entries are also illuminated by 170 illustrations. A biographical index, a special feature of the *Guide,* lists dates and major occupations for more than 3,000 individuals mentioned in the text.

The *Cambridge Guide to American Theatre* will be a useful reference work, both in the United States and around the world, for all those associated with or interested in the theatre.

CAMBRIDGE GUIDE TO
AMERICAN THEATRE

Cambridge Guide to

AMERICAN THEATRE

Edited by

DON B. WILMETH
Brown University

and

TICE L. MILLER
University of Nebraska, Lincoln

CAMBRIDGE
UNIVERSITY PRESS

Published by the Press Syndicate of the University of Cambridge
The Pitt Building, Trumpington Street, Cambridge CB2 1RP
40 West 20th Street, New York, NY 10011-4211, USA
10 Stamford Road, Oakleigh, Melbourne 3166, Australia

First published 1993

Printed in the United States of America

Library of Congress Cataloging-in-Publication Data
Cambridge guide to American theatre / edited by Don B. Wilmeth and Tice L. Miller.
p.   cm.
Includes bibliographical references (p.   ) and index.
ISBN 0-521-40134-8 (hc)
1. Theatre – United States – Dictionaries.
I. Wilmeth, Don B.   II. Miller, Tice L.
PN2220.C35   1993
792'.0973 – dc20   92-35030
CIP

A catalog record for this book is available from the British Library

ISBN 0-521-40134-8 hardback

Contents

Preface and Acknowledgments

The *Cambridge Guide to American Theatre* is, in the best sense of the word, a spinoff from the earlier *Cambridge Guide to World Theatre,* edited by Martin Banham. Prof. Banham has been our greatest supporter from the beginning, and has offered numerous useful suggestions and answered all of our queries quickly and helpfully; indeed, the present *Guide* began by our gathering the U.S. entries from his world guide to form a nucleus for our subsequent work. However, few of the entries from the parent volume appear as they did in 1988; most have been revised or updated, with more suggestions for additional reading. The American *Guide,* though following the basic format of the world guide, has several additional features, including more extensive bibliographical assistance (both throughout the text and in a supplemental list by DBW at the end) and a Biographical Index that provides dates and major occupations (keyed to entries in the text) for a majority of individuals mentioned but without their own entries.

The American *Guide* has been designed to offer scholars, students, and general readers a comprehensive view of the history and present practice of the theatre in the United States. We hope it will be a useful reference source for concise, carefully selected, and authoritative information on a broad spectrum of topics relating to American theatre from its earliest history to the present (early 1992), beginning with a detailed Introduction. There has been a conscious effort to be sensitive to contemporary theatre. In addition, although a one-volume format necessarily limits the contents (and has dictated the inclusion of a large number of relatively brief entries), there has been a concerted effort to cover American theatre in the broadest possible terms; indeed, the editors' goal, in part, is to help redefine, through the variegated coverage of the *Guide,* just what American theatre is. Consequently, we have included numerous topics that often fall outside of what was once considered theatre – such as circus, magic, vaudeville, burlesque, and folk festivals. There are entries not only on these popular forms but also on numerous marginalized groups and artists, including gay/lesbian theatre, African-American, Asian-American, and Nuyorican, among others. Although in all these instances the coverage has by necessity often been slighter than wished, we nevertheless believe users of the *Guide* will find many categories covered that have too frequently been omitted from similar reference works.

We have included overviews on several major cities – Boston, Philadelphia, Los Angeles, Seattle, San Francisco, Chicago, and Minneapolis – that have both an active past and present history of theatre. (New York's theatrical history permeates the volume as a whole.) In addition, we have tried to include major companies (and in some cases venues) throughout the country, thus truly providing national coverage.

We have also included entries on certain specific plays and musicals; these do not provide detailed plot synopses or textual analyses (since this is not a guide to drama as literature), but rather give brief stage histories, touch on themes, and offer just enough information on plot or structure to lead the user to the next step – which, in most instances, will be to read the actual script. Users should note that, unless indicated otherwise, the dates given for plays refer to first performances.

On the assumption that there are more guides to film than to the stage, actors whose careers primarily have been on the screen have been omitted (with some obvious exceptions). Although the names of many foreign theatre artists can be found scattered through the *Guide,* only those who have settled in the United States, are of seminal importance, and/or spent a large portion of their career working on U.S. stages have their own entries. If one wishes to trace the activities of an individual who is mentioned in the text but does not have a major entry, it is often possible to do so via this volume's Biographical Index (by DBW). This index is quite exhaustive, although some minor figures have been omitted, as has one major one – William Shakespeare, who is cited so often that listing him would add pages to the index. Note that we have made every reasonable effort, including personal contact, to locate dates for those names included in this index, but in some instances this has been difficult or impossible. We would welcome for future editions any missing dates provided by users of this *Guide.*

Entries have been written by over 80 contributors, whose initials appear beneath their entries. (A list of contributors is provided in the front matter of this volume, matching initials against names.) Contributors are ultimately responsible for the reliability of their individual entries, although the editors have attempted to verify any questionable fact. We are extraordinarily grateful for the excellent work of this army of scholars, researchers, and writers, without which this *Guide* would not have been possible. We have tried, within the limitations of a reference work and the constraints of our general style, to allow contributors to speak with their own voices and, when appropriate, to express their own points of view. Indeed, on occasion more than one contributor has dealt with overlapping subjects, and thus several points of view are represented – a situation that we consider an asset rather than a liability.

Our contributors have carefully chosen details and emphases to highlight the importance of each entry's inclusion. Attributions for all quotations, although not always included in the *Guide,* were indeed supplied by the contributors, thus making it possible for us to verify their accuracy when necessary. To balance the brevity of most individual entries, we have listed full-length sources when available (and a few serial essays, if of particular usefulness). It should be stressed, however, that the authority for each entry is its contributor, whereas frequently the sources have been added by the editors; inclusion of a source does not necessarily indicate its quality or trustworthiness, though such judgments have often been applied.

The most difficult stage in the evolution of a reference work of this sort is, of course, the selection of individual entries. Our various lists went through many phases, with input from numerous individuals, most named below. Names and topical entries were added up to the last minute. Ultimately, however, we are responsible for all choices, and our contributors and advisors cannot be held accountable for some obvious oversight. Such discoveries are unavoidable, for a one-volume guide can only be selective, and editors admittedly often divulge their own predilections, despite a concerted effort for balance and objective coverage of essentials. What is most regretted is the necessary exclusion of a sizable number of worthy candidates, especially theatre academics and writers.

We have tried to make the *Guide* accessible in many ways. In addition to the aforementioned Biographical Index, there is a List of Topical Entries at the beginning of the *Guide,* intended to direct readers to more comprehensive entries of interest. One may begin on the macro level by reading the Introduction (in part or in whole), then move on to a subtopic within the history (e.g., musical theatre), and end up checking entries for specific plays, companies, and venues cross-referenced in that entry. Alternatively, starting at the micro level, an entry for a specific individual or play might lead to entries on certain cities or performance categories. Cross-referencing, shown in boldface type, is extensive but not exhaustive; topics are cross-referenced when they can in some obvious way enlighten a specific entry. Entries are listed alphabetically, on a letter-by-letter basis. (We have used the spelling "theatre" throughout, except where it appears as Theater in a proper name.)

Illustrations have been selected for the theatrical content they convey rather than for decorative purpose. Rather than nontheatrical portraits of individuals, for example, we have chosen to portray actors on stage or in a particular role. An effort has been made to represent all phases and periods of American theatre, including popular forms such as the circus and vaudeville. With some significant iconographical exceptions, we have favored illustrations that are rarely reproduced.

The editors and contributors are indebted to too many librarians and archivists to enumerate here; however, without their expertise this volume would have been impossible. Specifically, we are grateful to the following for special assistance and advice: Jason Anthony, Hollis Ashby, Charlene Baldridge, Daniel Y. Bauer, John Lee Beatty, Mary Bing, Lee Breuer, Pat Brown, Sarah Brown, David Carlyon, Bridget Carpenter, Rosemary Cullen, Tracy Davis, Kate Davy, Michael Bigelow Dixon, Pat Douglas, Geraldine Duclow, Andrew Edmonson, Layne Ehlers, the late Maurice Evans, John Frick, Jan Geidt, George Goodwin, John Guare, Paul Hamilton, John Heidger, Rosaline Heinz, Mary C. Henderson, Ann Holmes, Norris Houghton, Jorge Huerta, Erin Hurley, C. Lee Jenner, Barbara A. Jeppesen, Toni Kotite, Pebble Kranz, James Lapine, Elizabeth Lecompte, Tracy Leipold, Cathy Linberg, Nancy Lindeman, Romulus Linney, Lucille Lortel, John R. Lucas, Nobu McCarthy, Don McDaniel, Emily Mann, Laurence Maslon, Jeffrey Mason, Cleveland Morris, Christine Murray, Kent Neely, Brian Nelson, Stephen Nunns, Scott Perrin, Tom Postlewait, Joseph R. Roach, Trish Sandberg, David Savran, Jim Seacat, Marian Seldes, Laurence Senelick, Ann Stonehouse, Antigone Trimis, Judy Via, Paula Vogel, Ronald Wainscott, Gloria Waldman, Stephen Weeks, Ken Werther, David Wheeler, Margaret Wilkerson, and George Woodyard. Richard E. Kramer has been especially generous in his assistance. Judy Wilmeth deserves special mention for her critical and objective eye, and for her support throughout the preparation of the *Guide.*

At Cambridge University Press, Sarah Stanton served as initiator and early advisor; throughout the process she has always been available for advice and counsel. In the New York office, Julie Greenblatt, our press editor, has supported our effort every inch of the way, responding to an endless stream of queries and holding our hands when discouragement threatened to set in. With Michael Gnat we were fortunate to have a superb production editor, not only perspicacious but knowledgeable about the theatre as well; his suggestions have made this a better and more accessible guide. Thanks go also to Susan Cutrofello for her keen eye as a proofreader.

Finally, we are very much in the debt of all those before us who contributed to the study of American theatre history, and especially to those responsible for the important standard theatre references that enabled the present volume, such as Gerald Bordman, George Bryan, Stanley Green, Otis Guernsey, Samuel Leiter, J. P. Wearing, and John Willis.

Contributors

AA	Arnold Aronson	AEG	A. E. Green	LM	Laurence Maslon
GSA	Gordon S. Armstrong	SG	Spencer Golub	NMcC	Nellie McCaslin
		EH	Erin Hurley	RM	Richard Moody
JA	James Aikens	EGH	Errol G. Hill	TLM	Tice L. Miller
SMA	Stephen M. Archer	FH	Foster Hirsch	WJM	Walter J. Meserve
AB	Alec Baron	MCH	Mary C. Henderson	KN	Kent Neely
DB	David Bradby	RAH	Roger A. Hall	BO	Bobbi Owen
FB	Frances Bzowski	TH-S	Tori Haring-Smith	MEO	M. Elizabeth Osborn
JLB	John L. Bracewell	CLJ	C. Lee Jenner	HFP	Hilary F. Poole
LAB	Larry Brown	RJ	Ricky Jay	NP	Naima Prevots
MB	Misha Berson	EK	Eileen Kearney	TP	Thomas Postlewait
MBan	Martin Banham	JK-D	James Kotsilibas-Davis	ER	Elizabeth Ramirez
RKB	Rosemarie K. Bank			JER	Joel E. Rubin
LDC	Larry D. Clark	MK	Margaret M. Knapp	MR	Maarten Reilingh
MC	Marvin Carlson	NK	Nicolás Kanellos	AS	Alisa Solomon
TC	Thomas Connolly	PK	Philip Kolin	AHS	Arthur H. Saxon
GD	Geraldine Duclow	REK	Richard E. Kramer	LS	Laurence Senelick
JD	John Degen	FHL	Felicia H. Londré	LSh	Louis Sheaffer
JDo	Jill Dolan	GL	George Latshaw	MS	Maxine S. Seller
PAD	Peter A. Davis	SL	Stephen Langley	NS	Nahma Sandrow
WD	Weldon Durham	TL	Thomas Leabhart	RAS	Robert A. Schanke
KME	Kathryn Marguerite Ervin	BM	Bogdan Mischiu	PT	Peter Thomson
		BCM	Brenda C. Murphy	BBW	Barry B. Witham
RE	Ronald Engle	BMcC	Bruce A. McConachie	DBW	Don B. Wilmeth
AF	Angelika Festa			DJW	Daniel J. Watermeier
KF	Kathy Fletcher	BMcN	Brooks McNamara	GW	George Woodyard
LF	Lisa Fusillo	DM	Dorothy Mandel	RW	Ron West
MF	Mark Fearnow	DMcD	Douglas McDermott	RHW	Ronald H. Wainscott
SF	Scott Fosdick	JDM	Jeffrey D. Mason	SW	Stanley Weintraub

Topical Entries

Introduction: Survey from the beginning to the present

1. To the Civil War The early history of the American theatre is largely one of the transference of European traditions, primarily those of provincial England, and a gradual development toward self-identity, which did not reach its full potential until after WW I. Early settlers in the colonies, many representing the same antitheatre element that existed in England, through the exigencies of the times diverted their energies into other and more complex channels than entertainment. As actors in the real-life drama of survival in hostile surroundings, colonists, with some notable exceptions, reflected Benjamin Franklin's attitude: "After the first cares for the necessities of life are over, we shall come to think of the embellishments."

The earliest records of theatre in the New World were not English in origin at all; indeed, the initial dramatic performances were the **Native American rituals** performed by Indians of the North and South. Early in the 16th century the Spanish discovered Aztec performances in Mexico that blended song, dance, comic byplay, and animal imitations; warlike tribes in the U.S. Northeast, though less inclined to organized theatricals, had variegated revels; and tribes in the Pacific Northwest created elaborate stage effects for dramatizations of tribal mythology. More complex theatre, however, is tenuously documented as having occurred in Spanish as early as 1538 in the Southwest and Mexico and by 1606 in French, in what is now Canada.

With the establishment of the first settlement (Jamestown, VA, 1607) in what would become the U.S., two traditions were quickly established among the English-speaking residents. The Southern colonies, especially the Royalist colony of Virginia, were more congenial to the theatre; Puritan New England and Quaker-dominated Pennsylvania were vehemently against this frivolous pastime, although William Penn's efforts were inevitably overturned by regal veto, the King and his court being strong supporters of the theatre in England. Nonetheless, in various colonies between 1700 and 1716 laws were passed against the theatre with some effect. In Massachusetts, Increase Mather expressed the typical Puritan attitude when he wrote in 1687 that "there is much discourse of beginning Stage-Plays in New England. The last year Promiscuous Dancing was openly practised." Despite such outcries, there were local amateur theatricals from an early date. A nonextant piece called *Ye Bare and Ye Cubb,* the first recorded play in English presented in the colonies, was written by one William Darby of Accomac Country, VA, and performed in 1665 by Darby, Cornelius Wilkinson,

and Philip Howard in Cowles Tavern, though this is the last recorded performance in Virginia until 1702. In 1687 a **Boston** innkeeper named John Wing attempted to outfit a room in his establishment for theatrical use, but to no avail: Attitudes like Mather's and the protests of Judge Samuel Sewall ended the brief experiment. There is evidence, however, that three years later a Harvard College student, Benjamin Colman, wrote the first play (*Gustavus Vasa*) by an American to be acted in the colonies. In Virginia students at William and Mary College offered in 1702 the recitation of a "pastoral colloquy" before the governor. Other colloquies of this sort were offered at other institutions of higher learning. Between 1699 and 1702 a Richard Hunter petitioned for permission to produce plays in New York, then a town of 4,436 people; it was granted, but no more is known. On 6 May 1709, however, the Governor's Council in New York forbade "play acting and prize fighting," with no rationale provided.

Early evidence of professional efforts is scattered and imprecise. The British vagabond player Anthony (Tony) Aston is generally credited as the first professional actor in America; in 1703, in his early 20s, he acted in "Charles Town," SC, writing that he "turn'd *Player* and *Poet,* and wrote one Play on the Subject of the Country." He then claims to have gone to New York. His play is unknown, and in 1704 he returned to London. In 1715, the first known play written and published in America appeared. Written by Governor Robert Hunter of New York, *Androboros* is a satire on the citizens of that city and the New York Senate. There is no record of performance.

For the next 35 years theatrical activity was sporadic. In 1716, in Williamsburg, VA, the most advanced town in the colonies to promote theatre, William Levingston, who ran a dancing school, built a theatre that was operated by his indentured servants William and Mary Stagg until Levingston's death in 1729. In 1724 a makeshift playhouse (The New Booth) was built in the Society Hill section of **Philadelphia** for "roap dancing" and the traditional clown pieces called Pickleherring. The 1730s marks the advancement of Charleston as a theatrical center and the erection of a theatre in Dock Street in 1736. During the same period there was limited activity in New York: In 1730 an amateur production of *Romeo and Juliet* was presented, the first **Shakespeare on the American stage;** in 1732 a space above a commercial establishment was turned into a playing space; and in 1735 at "The New Theatre" (a converted warehouse in Pearl Street) a season of recent English plays, including *The Beaux' Stratagem,* was presented.

A sustained record of professional theatre in Philadelphia, which quickly became America's theatrical center until about 1825, dates from 1749 and is associated with the activities of the first professional company known in the colonies under **Walter Murray and Thomas Kean,** about whom we know virtually nothing. In August they performed in Plumstead's Warehouse, converted for use as a playhouse; by February they were performing in New York in a converted building in Nassau Street. In October 1751 they opened a new, crudely built wooden playhouse in Williamsburg, played in Maryland the following year as The Virginia Company of Comedians, and then drifted into obscurity. They had, however, as historian Hugh F. Rankin indicates, acted "as an advance agent for those to follow, whetting the appetite of the colonials for the drama and upon occasion wearing down religious and moralistic opposition."

The next chapter in the history of theatre in America is the story of one company, The London Company of Comedians (renamed in 1763 The **American Company** of Comedians), and their total dominance of the theatrical scene for 50 years, beginning in 1752 under the leadership of **Lewis Hallam, Sr.,** and continuing from 1758 under **David Douglass,** who married Hallam's widow. The Hallam Company, sent to America on speculation by Lewis's eldest brother William, who remained in London, arrived in Williamsburg with a completely professional company of 12 adults and three children, a complete repertoire of plays, and basic scenery and costumes. Operating on a sharing system, the company began their first season at Kean's old playhouse on 16 September with *The Merchant of Venice;* in July 1754 they moved to New York, carrying with them a letter of endorsement from Governor Dinwiddie to the governor of New York. Until October 1754 they played in New York, Philadelphia, Annapolis, and Charleston, spending the next three years in Jamaica, where Lewis Hallam died in 1755. Douglass, an erstwhile actor and printer, brought the company back to New York in 1758, and within six years had added "American" to their name. Despite continued opposition from all quarters (Puritan, Quaker, Lutheran, Presbyterian, Baptist), Douglass, with **Lewis Hallam, Jr.,** as leading man, took his company up and down the East Coast, building new theatres or revamping old buildings, and introducing significant new British plays to the public. In the early 1760s Douglass even attempted an invasion of New England, first in Newport, RI, in 1761, and the next year in Providence – both stops a challenge to his ingenuity. In order to avoid criticism, he advertised his plays as "moral dialogues," and in Providence called his makeshift playhouse a "schoolhouse." Literally drummed out of town, Douglass returned to New York, where he opened the temporary Chapel of Beekman Street Theatre in 1761, followed in 1766 and 1767 by the construction of two more important and permanent theatres.

The first permanent theatre on the American continent, the **Southwark Theatre** (1766), which stood until 1912, also was the scene for the first professionally produced play by a native author: Thomas Godfrey's *The Prince of Parthia,* a heroic tragedy in blank verse set in Parthia near the beginning of the Christian era – and thus in no way American in subject matter – premiered on 24 April 1767. It was sheer chance that this play earned its historic position, for a play called *The Disappointment* by Thomas Forrest was to receive that honor but was abruptly withdrawn because it contained "personal reflections unfit for the stage." Douglass's second major venture, the **John Street Theatre,** opened 7 December 1767, predominating among **New York City theatres** for 30 years.

On 20 October 1774 the Continental Congress forbade all extravagance and dissipation, including stage entertainments; Douglass and his company returned to the West Indies the following year. Other than military theatricals, theatre ceased during the hostilities, though plays – many little more than political satire in dialogue form and the majority unperformed – were written during the period, including those by **Mercy Otis Warren, Hugh Henry Brackenridge,** and **Robert Munford.** Also written were anonymous pieces such as *The Blockheads,* inspired by the performance in Boston of General John Burgoyne's farce *The Blockade of Boston,* as well as John Leacock's *The Fall of British Tyranny* (both 1776). The real activity, however, took place among the military on both sides. In 1775 the John Street was renamed the Theatre Royal and presented a long series of dramatic productions performed by the British military, until their evacuations in 1783. The same was true in other major cities, such as Boston, where a theatre was organized in Faneuil Hall during 1775–7, and Philadelphia, where a Captain Delancey and Captain John André, later involved with Benedict Arnold, were leaders of a theatrical group under General William Howe. Despite edicts to the contrary, the Continental Army also performed: At Valley Forge, for example, Washington's troops presented Addison's *Cato* in 1778.

After the Revolution, in 1782, professionals began to return. Lewis Hallam, Jr., brought back the Old American Company from Jamaica in 1784, picking up where they had left off in 1774. Along with **John Henry,** they were the major actors of the day, joined soon by **Thomas Wignell.** On 16 April 1787 the reinstated company offered the first professional production of a native American comedy on an American subject: **Royall Tyler**'s *The Contrast,* which, among other firsts, introduced Jonathan the stage **Yankee,** the prototype of many subsequent Yankees and the first native type to be developed. With the elimination of all repression, Philadelphia was stimulated as a theatre center due to the efforts of Wignell and Alexander Reinagle, a musician, who in 1794 opened the superior **Chestnut Street Theatre** with a new group of actors. After this period of reestablishment, the 1790s became a decade of rapid expansion. Wignell erected theatres in Baltimore (1794) and Washington (1800); in 1792 **John Hodgkinson** joined the Old American Company; with the repealing of restrictive laws in New England, Boston and Providence became important centers, especially with the opening of

Boston's **Federal Street Theatre** in 1794, followed two years later by the Haymarket; and other scattered activity spread theatre throughout the young country, including French-speaking theatres in Charleston (1794) and in New Orleans (1791, though not part of the U.S. until 1803). In 1798 New York kept pace with Philadelphia with the opening of the **Park (New) Theatre** where **William Dunlap,** whose drama *The Father* had been performed at the John Street in 1789, initially became a partner of Lewis Hallam, Jr., and John Hodgkinson but ultimately assumed the management, recording a career of ups and downs, ending in bankruptcy in 1805. After a brief period of management by actor **Thomas Abthorpe Cooper, Stephen Price,** America's first professional manager, took control in 1809 and, by encouraging appearances by **international stars,** beginning with **George Frederick Cooke** in 1810, helped undermine the **stock company** system. Actors such as Cooper and **John Howard Payne** (remembered primarily as a playwright) exploited the starring possibilities, and – after the uncertainties of the War of 1812 – a steady flow of actors from England appeared, including in the 1820s Edmund Kean, **Junius Brutus Booth, William B. Wood, William Warren, Sr., Tyrone Power, Laura Keene,** Charles Kean, and **John Brougham,** to mention only a few.

More significant than foreign imports of stars and plays was the slow Americanization of the theatre, which accelerated during the first half of the 19th century. Native-born stars began to emerge in the 1820s, beginning with **Edwin Forrest,** America's first great actor and the first native-born performer to create excitement abroad. In his footsteps came Augustus A. Addams, **McKean Buchanan,** John R. Scott, J. Hudson Kirby, and, most significantly, **John E. McCullough, E. L. Davenport,** and **James Murdoch** (and, toward the end of this period, great actors like Edwin Booth and Joseph Jefferson III). Among the actresses of the period, none received more acclaim than Forrest's contemporary, **Charlotte Cushman,** who by midcentury was the dominating tragic actress on the American stage and an international star. Other actresses of note during the first half of the century include **Mary Ann Duff, Josephine Clifton, Clara Fisher, Maggie Mitchell, Lotta Crabtree, Adah Isaacs Menken,** and **Anna Cora Mowatt,** remembered today for her play *Fashion* (1845), the most significant native comedy of manners of its time. Its central character is Trueman, another Yankee in the tradition of *The Contrast's* Jonathan; such roles were the specialty of numerous significant American comic actors, including **James H. Hackett, George Handel Hill, Danforth Marble,** and Joshua Silsbee (as well as the later **John E. Owens** and **Denman Thompson**).

Parallel with the emergence of American-born actors is the growth of native plays and native characters. As a result of a playwriting contest sponsored first in 1828 by Forrest for "the best tragedy, in five acts, of which the hero, or principal character shall be an original of the country," 200 plays were submitted overall and nine prizes were awarded, four retained in his repertoire. The first

winner, **John Augustus Stone**'s *Metamora,* which echoes back to Major Robert Roger's 1766 play *Ponteach* and other early dramatic efforts to write plays about the noble red man, became the most durable of the dozens of Indian plays written and performed for the next half-century [see **Native Americans portrayed**]. Stone was one of a number of notable playwrights of the period from Philadelphia; others included **James Nelson Barker, Robert Montgomery Bird, Richard Penn Smith, Mordecai Manuel Noah, Robert T. Conrad,** and **Samuel Woodworth.**

In addition to the Indian and the Yankee, a minor native character was the stage Negro, the first appearing in John Murdock's *The Triumphs of Love* (1795) and culminating in the many versions of *Uncle Tom's Cabin* beginning in 1852. Related to the dramatic development of African-American characters is the phenomenal popularity of the blackface **minstrel show** stimulated by **Thomas D. Rice** in the late 1820s. Two additional types emerged before the Civil War: the tough city lad, Mose the fire b'hoy, as depicted in **Benjamin Baker**'s *A Glance at New York* (1848); and the stout-hearted frontiersman, beginning with Col. Nimrod Wildfire in **James K. Paulding**'s *The Lion of the West* (1831). In addition to the development of native types, American drama up to midcentury was dominated by the burlesques and dramas of immigrant playwright-actors like John Brougham and **Dion Boucicault.** Advancements in writing techniques were made by **George Henry Boker,** arguably the period's best writer of romantic drama in the English-speaking world (in particular his *Francesca da Rimini* [1855]), though Bird's romantic plays as performed by Forrest were more popular.

As the U.S. expanded its territory, enterprising theatre entrepreneurs took small companies into the Ohio and Mississippi Valley, beginning in 1815 when **Samuel Drake** went from Albany, NY, into **frontier** settlements in Kentucky, Ohio, and Tennessee. **James H. Caldwell** established a first-rate English-speaking theatre in New Orleans by 1819. The names **Noah Ludlow** and **Sol Smith** were familiar ones along the rivers and in the wild; combining forces they established the first real theatre in St. Louis in 1835. **Chicago**'s first theatre dates from 1847. During the same period William **Chapman** was operating his Mississippi Floating Theatre (see **showboats**). By midcentury, thanks to the gold rush, theatre came to California. The first theatrical performance by professional actors was given in **San Francisco** in 1850, and by 1862 the Salt Lake Theatre (UT) was established. The star system was unequivocally aided by this westward expansion, for Western managers paid higher salaries than in the East to attract the best talent available.

By 1800 a definite shift of influence from Philadelphia to New York had begun. Philadelphia's population in 1820 was 63,802, New York's 123,706; by 1840 it was 93,655 to 312,710, and by midcentury New York boasted almost half a million people. The Chestnut Street Theatre, managed by William Warren and William B. Wood, began to lose dominance in Philadelphia in 1811, followed in 1828 by the **Arch Street Theatre** and the **Walnut Street Theatre** (renovated from a **circus** to a theatre in 1811). Philadelphia could not support three major theatres, and in 1828–9 all three went bankrupt. The country was rapidly changing, with a growing urban lower-class audience on the rise, significant emigrations on the horizon, an active revolt against English domination of the stage in motion, and a major civil war around the corner. Gradually playwrights were able to gain a living writing plays, encouraged by the copyright law of 1856. The number and quality of playhouses increased, gas **stage lighting** was introduced in 1816, native **scenic design**ers were gaining recognition, and greater realism – given impetus by the 1846 presentation of Charles Kean's *King John* – was sought. The Lafayette Theatre, built in New York in 1826, boasted of border lights and equipment for aquatic and equestrian drama [see **animals as performers**]. The second Park opened in 1821 with a capacity of 2,500, topped by the 3,500 of the first **Bowery Theatre** in 1826. The **Chatham Garden Theatre** opened in 1825; what became **Barnum's American Museum** began operation in 1841, as did the famous **Boston Museum**, which operated a most successful stock company for almost 50 years beginning in 1843; the **Astor Place Opera House** opened in 1847; Brougham's Lyceum in 1850. Some of the more successful managements up to midcentury fought the growing trends of stars and long runs: for example, **William Mitchell** at the **Olympic Theatre** in New York during 1839–50. **William E. Burton**, who leased Palmo's Opera House in 1848 and opened it as **Burton's Chamber Street Theatre**, followed suit, dominating as the fashionable New York theatre until the emergence of the **Wallack's** stock company beginning in 1853.

By the Civil War the American theatre had undeniably established a strong, individualistic mainstream tradition, relatively free of foreign influence, despite strong impulses from new European migrations to America. After a brief curtailment of growth, the American theatre would experience a great period of prosperity following the War Between the States, lasting until about 1915.   DBW

2. The Civil War to the First World War The Civil War only disrupted theatrical activities in the East, and by early 1862 the theatres in New York, Boston, and Philadelphia were open and thriving. Such patriotic pieces as **Charles Gayler**'s *Bull Run; or, the Sacking of Fairfax Courthouse* (1861) appeared in New York at the New Bowery Theatre three weeks after the actual battle. Into the 1880s Wallack's continued as the leading New York playhouse, offering a steady diet of old and new British comedies with a superb acting company that included **Mme. Elizabeth Ponisi, Rose Coghlan, Henry J. Montague,** and **Charles Coghlan**. William Warren remained a fixture at the Boston Museum until his retirement in 1883, offering a wide range of comic roles, classic as well as contemporary. **Mrs. John Drew** managed a talented company at the Arch Street Theatre in Philadelphia during 1861–92, establishing the careers of her son, John Drew, and her daughter, Georgina Drew Barrymore [see **Drew–Barrymore**].

At the beginning of the decade, Edwin Forrest and Charlotte Cushman reigned as the leading tragedians in America, although Forrest's position was being challenged by **Edwin Booth,** the son of English-born tragedian J. B. Booth. Young Booth had served his apprenticeship in California (1852–6) and returned east in 1856 to establish himself as a star. Success the following year in Boston and New York made him an actor to watch. In the fall of 1862 he played in New York at the same time as Forrest, inviting comparison with the older actor. Cultivated theatre patrons had long abandoned Forrest and found Booth's quiet, unassuming, intellectual, and refined style more suitable for their ideal of a "temple of the arts." Booth's slight but handsome physique (dark hair and eyes) made him the ideal late Victorian tragedian as Forrest's muscular physique had attracted patrons 30 years earlier. Critic Nym Crinkle (**Andrew C. Wheeler**) thought Booth's Hamlet resembled a 19th-century gentleman more than a 16th-century courtier. While his most famous role was Hamlet – which he played for 100 performances at the **Winter Garden Theatre** during the 1864–5 season – he excelled in other roles requiring intellectual rather than emotional or physical force: Iago, Richard II, Shylock, Cardinal Richelieu (in Bulwer-Lytton's play), and Bertuccio in Tom Taylor's *The Fool's Revenge*. Booth departed from tradition in building his own theatre (**Booth's**, 1869) with neither a raked and grooved stage, an apron, nor proscenium doors. A better actor than manager, he succumbed to the financial panic of 1873 and lost the theatre through bankruptcy. Considered by historians as America's finest actor, Booth spent the last two decades of his life successfully touring as a star.

Booth was not the only actor challenging theatrical traditions: **Matilda Heron** became an overnight success in 1857 with her portrayal of Marguerite Gautier in Dumas's *The Lady of the Camellias* (called *Camille* in New York), exhibiting a style of acting marked by excessive emotional display and a seeming lack of technique and control. For the next half-century, the style attracted such actresses as **Lucille Western, Clara Morris,** and **Mrs. Leslie Carter. Joseph Jefferson III** also broke with the traditional school in the 1860s with his portrayal of **Rip Van Winkle** in Boucicault's dramatization. After presenting it in London (1865) for 170 performances, Jefferson brought it to New York in 1866, and in the title role established himself as the leading comedian of his age, as Booth was the leading tragedian. Jefferson endowed Rip with charm, humor, and pathos: His quiet, even casual, style seemed free of all staginess, with nothing forced or unnatural. In 1874 **Frank Mayo** idealized the frontiersman in **Frank H. Murdoch**'s drama *Davy Crockett;* like Jefferson, Mayo underplayed the emotional points and offered a style of acting that seemed natural to his audiences.

Dramatic tastes changed significantly in the 1860s: The historical costume dramas of Stone, Bird, Knowles, and Bulwer-Lytton began to go out of fashion; more popular were melodramas that offered adventure, romance, and obligatory sensational events. In **Augustin Daly**'s most successful melodramas, suspense and novel disasters abound:

Frank Keenan, Blanche Bates, and Robert Hilliard in Belasco's *The Girl of the Golden West* (1905). Courtesy: Robinson Locke Collection.

a man tied to railroad tracks facing an approaching train (*Under the Gaslight*, 1867); the heroine stranded on a steamship about to explode (*A Flash of Lightning*, 1868); or the rescue of a man bound to a log entering a sawmill (*The Red Scarf*, 1868). These dramas had broad emotional appeal and played to a large popular audience.

The excitement over *Camille* and the new French drama resulted in numerous adaptations. There was good reason for these French plays achieving instant popularity: They dealt with contemporary events and discussed subjects formerly considered taboo (adultery, for example). **Dion Boucicault** made a profession out of Anglicizing French plays; Augustin Daly was responsible in part or whole for 44 adaptations of French drama, in addition to borrowing others from the German and English theatres. While the Dramatic Copyright Law of 1856 improved the playwright's legal rights, it was not until the International Copyright Agreement was accepted by the U.S. in 1891 that managers found it as profitable to produce native plays as foreign ones.

American social comedies and dramas in the 1870s reflected the important topics of the day: stock speculation, social climbing, the winning of the West, divorce and the family, and, in a romantic way, the Civil War. Daly's big hit of 1875, *The Big Bonanza,* poked fun at those who naively attempted to make a "killing" on Wall Street. **Bronson Howard** offered a more serious treatment of the subject in *The Banker's Daughter* (1878), and in *Young Mrs. Winthrop* (1883) he touched upon the subjects of money, social status, and divorce. In *The Henrietta* (1887) Howard suggested that the country's obsession with making money was leading to moral decline. (This theme was explored by **David Belasco** and **Henry C. DeMille** in *Men and Women* [1890], and exploited by **Clyde Fitch** in *The Climbers* [1901]; a better play of the genre, **Langdon Mitchell**'s *The New York Idea* [1906], satirizes divorce and social customs among the wealthy.) Historians have regarded Bronson Howard as the first professional playwright in America because he successfully made a living from his

plays. His biggest hit, **Shenandoah** (1889), used the Civil War as a background for an essentially romantic plot, as did **William Gillette**'s spy stories *Held by the Enemy* (1886) and **Secret Service** (1896), Belasco's *The Heart of Maryland* (1895), and Fitch's *Barbara Frietchie* (1899).

The frontier and the winning of the West provided countless plots and characters, including Davy Crockett and the American cowboy. Daly set his **Horizon** (1871) in the West, as did **Bret Harte** for *Two Men of Sandy Bar* (1876), **Joaquin Miller** for *The Danites* in the Sierras (1887), **Bartley Campbell** for **My Partner** (1879), **Augustus Thomas** for *Arizona* (1899), and Belasco for *The Girl of the Golden West* (1905). **William Vaughn Moody**'s *The Great Divide* (1906) contrasts the East and the West in what some historians regard as the first modern American play.

In the final years of the 19th century a more realistic treatment of subject began to replace melodrama. Playwrights rejected long-held conventions dearly loved by audiences – including romantic plots, spine-chilling rescues, and happy endings – in favor of a truthful depiction of life. The farce-comedies of **Edward Harrigan** in the 1870s and '80s offered a theatrical but authentic portrait of life among the recent immigrants in New York; **William Dean Howells** called Harrigan the American Goldoni, and championed his plays. In the 1890s, the increased interest in Ibsen offended traditionalists like **William Winter** and **John Ranken Towse**, but the new drama was defended by critics Howells, **Hamlin Garland**, and **James G. Huneker**. James A. Herne's *Margaret Fleming* (1890) presented a realistic portrait of the consequences of a husband's infidelity and avoided a happy ending. Herne's more conventional **Shore Acres** (1892) maintained the externals of realism but returned in character and plot to sentimental melodrama, and was similar in style to Denman Thompson's *The Old Homestead* (1886). Augustus Thomas also combined the trappings of realism and local color in *Alabama* (1891), *Arizona* (1899), *The Witching Hour* (1907), and *The Copperhead* (1918). More important are **Edward Sheldon**'s

Salvation Nell (1908), *The Nigger* (1909), and *The Boss* (1911), which deal with social problems in a realistic framework.

The public's demand for popular entertainment was insatiable. **Adah Isaacs Menken**'s *Mazeppa* (1861) thrilled the masculine element of the audience as she gave the illusion of riding nude on the back of a wild horse. *The Black Crook* (1866) created a vogue for elaborate musical spectacle, owing much of its success to a Parisian ballet troupe of one hundred "beautiful girls" in flesh-colored tights. **Lydia Thompson**'s "British Blondes" Burlesque Company from London drew crowded houses in New York for seven months (1868–9) [see **burlesque**]. French companies presented the new *opéra bouffe* of Jacques Offenbach to New York audiences in the late 1860s, and **Maurice Grau** formed a company in the 1870s to present French operettas and French stars. *Evangeline* (1874) offered an American version of *opéra bouffe;* written by Edward E. Rice and J. C. Godwin, it featured a scantily clad female chorus, elaborate scenery, and comedian **Nat Goodwin.** The success of the **Kiralfy** brothers' *Around the World in Eighty Days* (1875) set the standard for large-scale spectacular theatre for the next two decades. The comic operettas of **Gilbert and Sullivan** found an audience in this country after the huge success of *HMS Pinafore* in 1878–9. **Charles Hoyt**'s "musical trifle," *A Trip to Chinatown* (1890), offered songs, dances, and risqué comedy in addition to a thin plot and ran for 650 performances. A decade later, an English import, *Florodora* (1900), survived for 505 performances and made famous its sextet of chorus girls. **Florenz Ziegfeld** inaugurated his *Follies* **revue** in 1907, featuring beautiful girls, elaborate costumes and sets, and leading comedians; over the years he discovered such talents as **Fannie Brice, W. C. Fields, Eddie Cantor,** and **Bert Williams.**

Operetta continued its hold on American **musical theatre** into the 1920s. **Victor Herbert** gained success with European-styled pieces and is regarded as America's first important composer of operetta. The proper setting for operetta remained in Central Europe with Franz Lehar's memorable *The Merry Widow* (1907), and with operettas by **Rudolf Friml** and **Sigmund Romberg.**

Specialists such as **Lotta Crabtree** charmed New York audiences during 1867–91 with her singing, dancing, and banjo playing. A master of the quick costume change, she played both Little Nell and the Marchioness in John Brougham's dramatic version of *The Old Curiosity Shop,* and six roles in *The Little Detective.* **George L. Fox** drew packed houses to the Olympic Theatre (1868) with the pantomime *Humpty Dumpty,* which he was to perform 1,268 times in New York alone. **Eddie Foy** gained fame in the 1890s by clowning in such musical pieces as *Sinbad the Sailor* (1891) and *Ali Baba* (1892). **Tony Pastor** presented the top speciality acts at his **vaudeville** theatres in the 1870s and '80s, including the Four Cohans, **Lillian Russell,** and the **Weber and Fields** comedy duo. **George M. Cohan** would move from vaudeville to the musical stage, establishing himself as a star in 1904–5 in his own *Little Johnny Jones.* Lillian Russell became a leading star on the American musical stage. Weber and Fields opened their own Music Hall in 1896, which for seven years was regarded as one of Broadway's brightest attractions. The future of the speciality acts in the 20th century, however, lay with **B. F. Keith** and **Edward F. Albee,** businessmen who introduced continuous vaudeville and organized the industry into a giant national circuit, gaining a near monopoly over it.

Economics and public taste after the Civil War dictated a change in the theatrical order. Although Wallack and Burton had been strong managers, the most powerful force in the theatre had been the actor as star. Realism and the demand for artistic unity made the rise of the modern director inevitable. During the 1869–70 season, Augustin Daly leased the **Fifth Avenue Theatre** and began developing his own company. He hired actors by type rather than by lines of business; often cast plays without regard to tradition, lines of business, or possession of parts; rehearsed each play with careful attention to interpretation, blocking, costuming, and scenery; and, while he opposed the star system, developed a succession of stars including **Agnes Ethel, Fanny Davenport, Clara Morris,** and **Ada Rehan.** At his own **Daly's Theatre** in the 1880s, he featured a quartet of actors including John Drew, Ada Rehan, **Mrs. G. H. Gilbert,** and **James Lewis.** Known as the home of light comedy in New York, Daly's displaced Wallack's as the most fashionable playhouse in the city. In 1884 he toured his company to London – the first American to do so – and later to Paris and Germany. Four years later he produced *The Taming of the Shrew* at Stratford-upon-Avon in the Shakespeare Memorial Theatre. Historians consider him the first American *régisseur* in the style of the Duke of Saxe-Meiningen.

A. M. Palmer tightly controlled every aspect of his productions at the **Union Square Theatre** (1872–83), the **Madison Square Theatre** (1884–91), and Wallack's old theatre (renamed Palmer's, 1888–96). Whereas Daly's Theatre was known as the home of comedy, Palmer's featured "polite melodrama," which he mounted with taste and care. With the assistance of **A. R. Cazauran,** Palmer built a strong company by hiring established actors such as Agnes Ethel, Clara Morris, **Kate Claxton, Rose Eytinge,** Charles R. Thorne, Jr., and **James O'Neill.** His most popular successes included Kate Claxton in *The Two Orphans* (1874); **Richard Mansfield** in *A Parisian Romance* (1883); and premieres of Clyde Fitch's *Beau Brummell* (1890) and Augustus Thomas's *Alabama* (1891).

Steele MacKaye also saw himself as an all-powerful manager who shaped every aspect of his productions. He designed the elevator stage at the Madison Square Theatre (1880), which allowed for an entire setting to be shifted in 40 seconds. He also built the **Lyceum Theatre** (1884–5) and taught the Delsarte system of expression. In 1887 he directed his own *Paul Kauvar,* which demonstrated his skill in handling crowd scenes in the Meiningen manner; but MacKaye remains a controversial figure in the American theatre because he failed to finish most of his projects.

Through staging, lighting, and scenery, David Belasco attempted to create the illusion of real life.

He served as stage manager of the Madison Square and Lyceum theatres in the 1880s, after which he turned to producing in 1895. Also a successful playwright, Belasco excelled in writing sentimental melodramas, which he tailored for specific stars and interpolated with enough contemporary thought to make them seem modern. He starred Mrs. Leslie Carter in *Zaza* (1899); **Blanche Bates** in *Madame Butterfly* (1900); Bates and **George Arliss** in *Sweet Kitty Bellairs* (1903); **David Warfield** in *The Return of Peter Grimm* (1911); and a replica of a Child's restaurant in *The Governor's Lady* (1912). Belasco used publicity to make stars out of his actors and is credited by some historians with being the most successful of American *régisseurs;* but while he involved himself directly in producing theatre, his business methods were little different from other commercial producers.

By the mid-1870s the resident stock company and repertory system had become unprofitable to maintain and were rapidly being replaced by "combination companies." A play would open in New York, run until attendance lagged, then be transported in its entirety – actors, sets, properties – from city to city. The number of such "combination" companies steadily increased until the *New York Dramatic Mirror* reported nearly 100 companies on the road during the 1876–7 season. MacKaye's *Hazel Kirke* (1880) was sent out in three road companies while still running in New York. Interest in local plays, companies, and actors was replaced by interest in touring attractions. Theatrical trade papers in New York, such as *Dramatic News* (1875) and *Dramatic Mirror* (1879), were established to cater to this interest.

Touring in America promised financial rewards for **international stars** and native actors alike. Adelaide Ristori made the first of several American tours in 1866, acting in Italian except for her last visit in 1884–5. The English actress Adelaide Neilson made her first of two American appearances in 1872. Tommaso Salvini made his American debut in 1873 and returned four more times, playing with American actors in bilingual performances. **Henry E. Abbey** brought Sarah Bernhardt to the U.S. in 1880 for her first tour of seven months, which covered 50 cities and 156 performances. In 1883 Abbey also brought Henry Irving, Ellen Terry, and the Lyceum Company for the first of several visits; Irving's carefully mounted productions set a new standard for the American stage. Eleonora Duse imported her natural style of acting to New York for the first of four visits in 1893 and, on her last international tour in 1924, died in Pittsburgh.

All major American stars toured. After the loss of his theatre in 1873, Edwin Booth spent the last two decades of his life touring in Shakespearean and pseudoromantic plays, including two seasons (1887–9) with **Lawrence Barrett. John Mc-Cullough,** an actor in the Forrest tradition, gave up management of the **California Theatre** (1875) to tour for the next nine seasons. Of the new generation of actors, Richard Mansfield toured in such eccentric parts as Baron Chevrial in *A Parisian Romance* (1883) and in the title roles in *Prince Karl* (1886), *Dr. Jekyll and Mr. Hyde* (1887), *Richard III* (1889), *Beau Brummel* (1890), and *Cyrano de Bergerac*

(1898). Mansfield introduced **Shaw** to an American audience as Bluntschli in *Arms and the Man* (1894), and later as Dick Dudgeon in *The Devil's Disciple* (1897). **Otis Skinner** had learned his trade in Booth's and Daly's companies and scrambled to play roles such as Hajj in *Kismet* (1911), which would best showcase his talents. **E. H. Sothern** made a hit with Edward Rose's romantic drama *The Prisoner of Zenda* (1895), and later acted Shakespeare together with his second wife, **Julia Marlowe.** The public's loss of interest in the traditional repertory and the demand for new plays left Mansfield and his generation scrambling to find suitable vehicles in which to star.

Establishing herself in the 1880s as a star in light comedy and melodrama, **Mrs. Minnie Maddern Fiske** adjusted better to the demands of the new drama. She encouraged the production of **Ibsen on the American stage** by acting Nora in *A Doll's House* (1894), the title role in *Hedda Gabler* (1903), Rebecca West in *Rosmersholm* (1907), and Mrs. Alving in *Ghosts* (1927). She also created the title character in Edward Sheldon's *Salvation Nell* (1908). Probably more effective in comedy, Mrs. Fiske was praised for her psychological truthfulness and simplicity of effects. Critics associated her in style with Duse. She and her husband, **Harrison Grey Fiske,** leased the **Manhattan Theatre** in 1903 and established an acting company, allowing them to remain independent of the Theatrical Syndicate.

Arnold Daly, like Mansfield, brought Shaw's plays before an American public. In 1903 he directed and starred in the American premiere of *Candida,* which ran for 133 performances. In 1904–5 he organized a company that produced *You Never Can Tell, The Man of Destiny, How He Lied to Her Husband,* a revival of *Candida,* and *Mrs. Warren's Profession;* the last was considered an immoral play and led to Daly's arrest [see **censorship**]. Although acquitted, he soon lost the zeal for dramatic reform and reverted to performing in standard works.

The growing power of the businessman in the American theatre can be evidenced in the 1890s with the demise of Palmer's and Daly's companies, and the rise of the Frohman brothers as New York's leading producers. **Daniel Frohman** had assumed control of the Lyceum Theatre from Steele MacKaye in 1885 and established a stock company and acting school, which lasted from 1887 until 1902. His company included such stellar performers as E. H. Sothern, **Virginia Harned,** Mary Mannering, **William Faversham, Henrietta Crosman, Henry Miller, Georgia Cayvan,** Herbert Kelcey, and James H. Hackett. He minimized risks and maximized profits by producing bright new plays by established writers, including Belasco and DeMille's *The Charity Ball* (1889); Henry Arthur Jones's *The Dancing Girl* (1891); Pinero's *Trelawny of the Wells* (1898); and Fitch's *The Moth and the Flame* (1898). **Charles Frohman** established two companies at Proctor's in 1890 to produce and tour new plays. In 1893 he built the **Empire Theatre,** which quickly gained the reputation of being a "star factory." He hired John Drew from Daly's company in 1892 and added William Gillette to his stable of stars, including **Maude Adams,** Ethel Barrymore, and **Henry E. Dixey.** His numerous hits include Belasco and **Franklin Fyles**'s *The Girl I Left Behind Me* (1893); James M. Barrie's *The Little Minister* (1897) and *Peter Pan* (1905), both starring Maude Adams; and William Gillette's *Sherlock Holmes* (1899).

Charles Frohman is best known for organizing in 1896 a theatrical trust comprising three partnerships: Frohman and Al Hayman; the booking firm of **Marc Klaw** and **Abraham L. Erlanger**; and Philadelphia theatre owners S. F. Nixon and J. Fred Zimmerman. Called the **Syndicate,** this trust gained a monopoly over the American theatre by controlling bookings, theatre buildings, and talent. In 1896 they either operated or directly controlled 33 first-class houses from coast to coast, and by 1903 had extended their holdings to 70. At the height of their power, they had exclusive rights to book over 700 theatres. The canceling of engagements, double bookings, broken contracts, and general disorganization that characterized theatre of the 1880s were eliminated. For 15 years Frohman and the Syndicate tightly controlled the American theatre and ran it on "big business" principles. They judged a play's worth solely on its ability to generate a profit. The **Shuberts**' (Lee, Sam, and Jacob J.) "Independent Movement" in 1900 challenged the position of the Syndicate: They also gained control over theatres from coast to coast; offered attractive bookings to independent managers; and began producing their own shows. Fierce competition between the two groups resulted in an oversupply of attractions and theatres; cities built separate theatres for Syndicate and Independent productions. **Economic** disaster was averted by an agreement between the two parties in 1914. Charles Frohman went down in the *Lusitania* in 1915, and afterward the Syndicate declined in power. The **Shubert Organization** has remained a vital force in the 20th-century American theatre.

Critics **Walter Prichard Eaton, Norman Hapgood, Brander Matthews,** John Ranken Towse, and William Winter denounced the Syndicate's purely commercial policy in the early 1900s and envisaged a national theatre supported by either public or private funds. Interest in the idea grew with the *Arena* publishing the symposium "A National Art Theatre for America" in 1904. Four years later **Heinrich Conried** announced plans for such a company in New York, and despite his death the following year, money was raised and the **New Theatre** opened under **Winthrop Ames**'s direction on 6 November 1909 with Julia Marlowe and E. H. Sothern in *Antony and Cleopatra*. The lack of a well-trained company and the New Theatre's poor acoustics contributed to its demise in 1911, although the project may have been doomed from the start: 20th-century theatre problems could not be solved with 19th-century solutions. This attempt to create an art theatre did express dissatisfaction with the triteness of the American stage, an attitude reinforced through visits in the 1910s by such foreign companies as the Irish Players of the Abbey Theatre (1911), **Max Reinhardt**'s company in *Sumurun* at the **Casino Theatre** (1912), Granville Barker's productions at Wallack's Theatre for the New Stage Society of New York (1915), and Jacques Copeau's Vieux-Colombier Company at the Old Garrick Theatre (1917). These companies demonstrated that theatre could be more than manufactured entertainment for mass tastes and could touch the human mind and spirit in an important way. **William A. Brady,** a commercial producer, presented Edward Sheldon's *The Boss* (1911) and Shaw's *Major Barbara* (1915). Amateur theatre groups were organized throughout the country, inspired by artists such as Maurice Browne of the Chicago Little Theatre (1912). In New York, the **Washington Square Players** (1914), led by **Lawrence Langner** and Edward Goodman, produced the plays of Ibsen, **Chekhov,** and Shaw, as well as important new works by American writers. In 1916 the **Provincetown Players** presented *Bound East for Cardiff,* the first **O'Neill** play to be staged. The same year, in Detroit, **Sheldon Cheney** founded *Theatre Arts,* a magazine dedicated to the art of the theatre. In 1919, members of the recently defunct Washington Square Players founded the **Theatre Guild,** the first U.S. professional art theatre. Led by Lawrence Langner, **Philip Moeller, Theresa Helburn,** and others, the Guild became an important theatre offering professional productions of plays not normally seen in the commercial theatre.   TLM

3. The First World War to the 1960s
After WW I, **Actors' Equity** demanded improved working conditions in the theatre and pushed for unionization of the acting profession; this resulted in an actors' strike in 1919. Stagehands had first organized themselves into a **union** in 1886, and later had affiliated with the American Federation of Labor (1894). After several unsuccessful attempts, performers formed Actors' Equity in 1913. Producers, including George M. Cohan and the Shuberts, fought the union and were joined by many actors who considered themselves artists not laborers; but on 6 August 1919, Equity went on strike, demanding official recognition and a closed shop for legitimate performers. They were supported by the stagehands and musicians, and by the AFL. The Theatre Guild met Equity's terms immediately, but all other producers resisted, and their plays closed. On 6 September, the producers capitulated and signed contracts that stipulated minimum contracts, improved rehearsal conditions, higher pay, and better working conditions.

In 1920 the Provincetown Players brought Eugene O'Neill's first full-length play, **Beyond the Horizon,** to Broadway, where it ran for 111 performances and won a Pulitzer Prize. Critics **George Jean Nathan** and Ludwig Lewisohn touted play and author as important new forces in the American theatre. O'Neill followed with *The Emperor Jones* (1920), an expressionistic drama that featured **Charles Gilpin** and the scenery of **Cleon Throckmorton,** and *Anna Christie* (1921), starring **Pauline Lord.** Working quickly, within three years he had added *The Straw* (1921) and *The First Man* (1922), dominating the American theatre of the 1920s as no playwright had in previous decades.

Popular successes in the 1920s include **Avery Hopwood** and **Mary Roberts Rinehart**'s *The Bat* (1920), which ran over two years, and Anne Nichols's *Abie's Irish Rose* (1922), which received

John Barrymore in Arthur Hopkins's production of *Hamlet*. Courtesy: Culver Service Collection.

scathing reviews but survived for 2,327 performances. Hopwood made a fortune writing such risqué fluff as *The Gold Diggers* (1919) and *The Demi-Virgin* (1921). The *Ziegfeld Follies* began to look dated in the 1920s, but gaining in popularity were all-Negro revues, such as **Noble Sissle** and **Eubie Blake**'s *Shuffle Along* (1921), and *Blackbirds* (1928), a compendium of songs and dances that made a star of hoofer **Bill "Bojangles" Robinson.** Musical comedy survived because of pretty chorus girls and memorable songs by **Vincent Youmans, George Gershwin, Cole Porter,** and **Richard Rodgers,** and such superb performers as **W. C. Fields, Al Jolson, Ed Wynn, Fanny Brice, Bert Williams, Will Rogers, Bert Lahr,** and **Jimmy Durante. George and Ira Gershwin** created a new jazz style with hits such as *Lady, Be Good!* (1924), *Tip-Toes* (1925), and *Funny Face* (1927). The **Marx Bros.** clowned in such vehicles as *The Cocoanuts* (1925) by **George S. Kaufman** and **Irving Berlin,** and *Animal Crackers* (1928) by Kaufman, **Morrie Ryskind,** and others, after which they took their buffoonery to Hollywood.

Operetta remained popular, with long runs for Rudolf Friml's *Rose-Marie* (1924) and Sigmund Romberg's *The Student Prince* (1924) and *The Desert Song* (1926). *Show Boat* (1928), by **Jerome Kern** and **Oscar Hammerstein II,** broke new ground by drawing on American musical traditions and by better integrating the book, music, songs, and dances; **Joseph Urban** designed the show, adding to his reputation for creating opulent sets for opera, theatre, and the *Ziegfeld Follies*.

Although the New Theatre had failed to create a more artistic American stage in the early 1910s, efforts continued into the 1920s. **Arthur Hopkins, Robert Edmond Jones,** and John Barrymore [see **Drew–Barrymore**] combined forces in 1920 to present Shakespeare's *Richard III,* and two years later to revive *Hamlet* in a somewhat untraditional interpretation by Barrymore. The production ran 101 performances, and Barrymore repeated his success in London (1925). In 1923, the **Moscow Art Theatre**'s acting company visited New York. Critics pretended not to notice that the company performed in Russian as they praised its ensemble training. Although the Stanislavsky system of acting was not unknown in the U.S., demonstration of the MAT work to New York audiences had lasting impact. Two members of the company, **Richard Boleslavski** and Maria Ouspenskaya, remained in America to teach in the **American Laboratory Theatre.** In 1924 **Walter Hampden** organized his own company at the Colonial (later the Hampden) Theatre and for five years offered Shakespeare, Ibsen, Rostand, and other less commercial playwrights. **Eva Le Gallienne** leased the 50-year-old **Fourteenth Street Theatre** in 1926, gathered together a company of veterans and newcomers, and opened with Chekhov's *The Three Sisters;* few critics showed interest, but Le Gallienne kept her **Civic Repertory Theatre** intact for six years, presenting 34 plays, most of which would have been fiscally impossible on Broadway.

Under the guidance of Lawrence Langner, the Theatre Guild emerged in the 1920s as America's most artistic producing organization. The company – which at one time included **Alfred Lunt and Lynn Fontanne, Dudley Digges,** Helen Westley, **Lee Simonson,** and **Philip Moeller** – presented a number of important world premieres, including Shaw's *Heartbreak House* (1920) and **Elmer Rice**'s expressionistic *The Adding Machine* (1923). In 1925 they opened their own Guild Theatre with a production of Shaw's *Caesar and Cleopatra*. During 1920–30 the Guild offered 67 different productions, 15 the work of American playwrights.

American comedy became more worldly in the 1920s with George S. Kaufman, replacing its penchant for folksy, romantic, and sentimental nonsense with witty and irreverant stabs at native society and culture. Kaufman and **Marc Connelly**'s *Dulcy* (1921) elevated Lynn Fontanne to stardom and was the first of their collaborations, which included *To the Ladies* (1922), *Merton of the Movies* (1922), and *Beggar on Horseback* (1924), the last an expressionistic satire on American business. Kaufman collaborated successfully with other writers, including **Edna Ferber** and **Moss Hart,** while Connelly enjoyed his greatest triumph with *The Green Pastures* (1930), which played for 640 performances. **George Kelly** attracted attention in 1922 with *The Torchbearers,* a satire on the Little Theatre movement [see **community theatre**], before writing his highly popular comedy *The Show-Off* two years later and his Pulitzer Prize–winning *Craig's Wife* in 1925. **Philip Barry** and **S. N. Behrman** wrote fashionable comedies with wit and style, albeit a streak of sentimentality. Behrman's *The Second Man* (1927) featured Alfred Lunt and Lynn Fontanne in a comedy about an artist's choice between two women. Barry's *Paris Bound* (1927) and *Holiday* (1928) presented a charming portrait of the wealthy just before the stock market crash of 1929. His best play, *The Philadelphia Story* (1939), allowed **Katharine Hepburn** to dazzle in a light-hearted treatment of life among the wealthy. The best American farce of the 1920s was **Ben Hecht** and **Charles MacArthur**'s *The Front Page* (1928), a cynical and satirical look at big-city life in Chicago.

Serious drama probed the romantic assumptions underlying American life. War received a realistic and truthful depiction in **Maxwell Anderson** and **Laurence Stalling**'s *What Price Glory* (1924), which George Jean Nathan thought superior to every other play inspired by WW I. In the same year, O'Neill's *Desire Under the Elms* offered a

Jeanne Eagels as Sadie Thompson in *Rain* (1922–3). Photo: White. Courtesy: Ward Morehouse Collection.

Freudian interpretation of New England puritanism that relied for much of its power on Robert Edmond Jones's highly symbolic setting. The prolific O'Neill with mixed success examined other aspects of American life in *The Fountain* (1925), *The* **Great God Brown** (1926), and **Strange Interlude** (1928), the last a nine-act, five-hour dramatic novel that ran for 432 performances and won a Pulitzer. The same year, Maxwell Anderson and Harold Hickerson's *Gods of the Lightning* brought the Sacco and Vanzetti murder case before a New York audience. **Sidney Howard** dissected the American way of life in **They Knew What They Wanted** (1924), *Lucky Sam McCarver* (1925), *Ned McCobb's Daughter* (1926), and *The* **Silver Cord** (1927), the last about excessive maternal devotion. **Robert Sherwood** attracted attention in 1927 with *The* **Road to Rome,** a bittersweet reenactment of Hannibal's march, starring **Jane Cowl.**

At the end of the decade, radio and motion pictures emerged as rivals for the American theatre audience. Radio had grown from its first regular broadcasts in 1920 to a full-scale entertainment industry by 1930. Motion pictures added sound with *The Jazz Singer* in 1927, which made it possible to film stage plays and show them for a fraction of the cost of a theatre ticket. Between 1920 and 1930 theatres outside New York decreased in number from 1,500 to 500, many converting to film, as the professional theatre in America became almost exclusively located in Manhattan. The Depression was radically to reduce what was left: During the 1927–8 Broadway season, the number of stage productions reached a record of 280; by 1939–40 this had been reduced to 80.

The American theatre in the 1930s directly reflected the nation's political and economic crises. Leftist theatre groups proliferated, including the New Playwrights' Theatre (1926), Workers' Drama League (1929), Workers' Laboratory Theatre (1930), League of Workers' Theatres (1932), and **Theatre Union** (1933), among the most active. They were founded by writers such as Michael Gold and **John Howard Lawson,** who returned from Russia ea-

ger to form a theatre of the left. **Clifford Odets**'s inflammatory **Waiting for Lefty** (1935) drew its early sponsorship from the League of Workers' Theatres. The Theatre Union gained an early success with *Peace on Earth* (1933), an antiwar piece, and **Stevedore** (1934), a play dealing with the relationship between black and white workers. Left-wing theatre remained a short-lived phenomenon of the 1930s, as its writers and artists were absorbed into the mainstream of American theatre and films. Many were blacklisted during the McCarthy Hearings in the 1950s.

The Harlem Renaissance of the 1920s generated a new interest in black literature, which continued in the 1930s. Plays about blacks by whites – **Paul Green**'s **In Abraham's Bosom,** Marc Connelly's *Green Pastures,* and O'Neill's *The Emperor Jones* – had been more successful than those by blacks until W. E. B. Du Bois, **Langston Hughes,** and others organized black companies. Hughes's **Mulatto** (1935) was the most successful play by an **African-American** playwright in the 1930s.

Politically sensitive but more concerned with artistic ideals, the **Group Theatre** began in 1931 as a palace revolt within the Theatre Guild, led by younger members **Harold Clurman, Cheryl Crawford,** and **Lee Strasberg.** They were joined by 28 actors, including **Franchot Tone, Morris Carnovsky,** Clifford Odets, **Sanford Meisner,** and **Stella Adler,** to set up a summer colony in Connecticut. Under the tutelage of Strasberg, the Group sought an acting technique for realistic plays. After a summer of work and analysis, the Group Theatre produced Paul Green's *The* **House of Connelly** (1931), followed by John Howard Lawson's *Success Story* (1932) and **Sidney Kingsley**'s **Men in White** (1933). They discovered playwright Clifford Odets and produced his **Awake and Sing!** and *Waiting for Lefty,* both in 1935. They gave **William Saroyan** a hearing in 1939 with **My Heart's in the Highlands** before running into financial problems in 1941 and disbanding.

In 1935 the **Federal Theatre** was organized by the Works Progress Administration to create jobs for out-of-work theatre people. Mrs. **Hallie Flanagan** of the Vassar Experimental Theatre was appointed first director and charged with locating the unemployed and putting them to work. This, the first subsidized producing agency in U.S. history, was disbanded by the government in 1939 on grounds of leftist infiltration. The Federal Theatre made several distinctive contributions to the American Theatre, including the **Living Newspaper** productions. African-American units of the Federal Theatre offered new plays by black authors but are remembered mainly by the "voodoo" *Macbeth* (1936), directed by **Orson Welles,** and the *Swing Mikado* (1938).

The **censorship** and closing of the Federal Theatre's production of **Marc Blitzstein's** *The Cradle Will Rock* (1937) led to the resignations of Welles and **John Houseman,** and to their creation of the **Mercury Theatre.** Welles, who had demonstrated a remarkable originality as a director both with Marlowe's *Doctor Faustus* (1937) and the earlier *Macbeth,* directed an impressive modern-dress *Julius Caesar* (1937) with fascist costumes and **Abe Feder's** lighting.

The depressed economy sharply reduced the number of Broadway productions, prompting five playwrights – Robert Sherwood, Maxwell Anderson, Sidney Howard, S. N. Behrman, and Elmer Rice – to join together in 1938 to form their own producing organization, the **Playwrights' Company.** Opening with Sherwood's *Abe Lincoln in Illinois* (1938), they presented Anderson's *Knickerbocker Holiday* (1938), Rice's *American Landscape* (1938), and Behrman's *No Time for Comedy* (1939), launching an ambitious program that would survive until 1960. Together with the Theatre Guild, they set the standard for Broadway production in the late 1930s.

The successful musicals of the 1930s tended to be both stylish and topical. George S. Kaufman and Howard Dietz's *The Band Wagon* (1931) offered brilliant artistry: directing by **Hassard Short,** dancing by **Fred and Adele Astaire,** and such memorable songs as "Dancing in the Dark" and "The Beggar Waltz." *Of Thee I Sing* (by the Gershwins, George S. Kaufman, and Morrie Ryskind, 1931) satirized the supreme court, president, vice-president, diplomatic corps, and the general humbug of American elections. In 1935, *Porgy and Bess* arrived on Broadway, making famous such songs as "Summertime" and "It Ain't Necessarily So." In the 1940–1 season, *Pal Joey* (by Richard Rodgers and **Lorenz Hart**), and *Lady in the Dark* (by Moss Hart, Ira Gershwin, and **Kurt Weill**) offered more mature subjects and a worldly tone. *Pal Joey* showcased Gene Kelly, and *Lady in the Dark* had superb performances by **Gertrude Lawrence** and Danny Kaye.

The Depression gripped the nation spiritually as well as economically, and set the tone for serious drama. O'Neill wrote *Mourning Becomes Electra* (1931), a six-hour play based on the *Oresteia;* Philip Moeller directed, Robert Edmond Jones designed, and **Alla Nazimova, Alice Brady,** and Earle Larimore starred. Two years later *Tobacco Road* opened for a seven-year run, based on Erskine Caldwell's steamy novel of Georgia backwoods'

poor white trash, starring Henry Hull as Jeeter Lester. In 1935 *Awake and Sing!*, Sidney Kingsley's **Dead End,** and Maxwell Anderson's **Winterset** offered a somber picture of the American dream. **Lillian Hellman's** *The Children's Hour* (1934) and *The Little Foxes* (1939), **John Steinbeck's** *Of Mice and Men* (1937), and **Thornton Wilder's** epic *Our Town* (1938) suggested the anxiety underlying American life.

Bad economic times produced some of America's best comic writing. O'Neill penned a domestic comedy in 1933, *Ah, Wilderness!*, which critics thought sentimental and moralistic but reassuring. **Sam and Bella Spewack's** *Boy Meets Girl* (1935) provided a light-hearted spoof of Hollywood. **Clare Boothe's** *The Women* (1936) was a bitchy satire on idle and wealthy urban women. The Kaufman and Hart collaborations, *You Can't Take It with You* (1936) and *The Man Who Came to Dinner* (1939), were the funniest American comedies since *The Front Page,* and have remained classics. **Rachel Crothers** returned from Hollywood in 1937 to write *Susan and God,* a satire on the efforts of a wife to reform her alcoholic husband. *My Heart's in the Highlands* and *The Time of Your Life* (both 1939) established William Saroyan as an important playwright. **Howard Lindsay** and **Russel Crouse's** *Life with Father* (1939), starring Lindsay and Dorothy Stickney, became a smash hit that ran for 3,216 performances, then a record. James Thurber and **Elliott Nugent's** *The Male Animal* appeared the same season and satirized intellectual as well as romantic notions of the nation.

America's favorite acting couple, Alfred Lunt and Lynn Fontanne, remained popular throughout the 1930s, playing comedy with elegance, grace, and perfect teamwork. **Katharine Cornell** and **Helen Hayes** were considered the first ladies of the American stage for their beauty and ability to play classical as well as modern roles. Other important actresses included **Tallulah Bankhead,** Eva Le Gallienne, **Ruth Gordon,** and Katharine Hepburn. Except for Alfred Lunt and John Barrymore (before he went to Hollywood), the American stage lacked distinguished males: The better younger players were opting for a career in films.

Broadway prospered during WW II. Irving Berlin's *This Is the Army* (1942), Rodgers and Hammerstein's *Oklahoma!* (1943) and *Carousel* (1945), and **Leonard Bernstein's** *On the Town* (1944) set the pace for musical entertainment. Much of America's serious drama depicted the war as simple melodrama, including Moss Hart's *Winged Victory* (1943), Maxwell Anderson's *Storm Operation* (1944), and James Gow and **Arnaud D'Usseau's** *Tomorrow the World* (1943), which were antifascist. In the spring of 1945, **Tennessee Williams's** *The Glass Menagerie* opened on Broadway to excellent notices, with fine performances by **Laurette Taylor, Eddie Dowling,** and **Julie Haydon.** Comedies offered little more than escape, except Thornton Wilder's *Skin of Our Teeth* (1942), which preached survival in a strange theatrical style. More typical were Joseph Kesselring's off-beat farce *Arsenic and Old Lace* (1941), **John van Druten's** sentimental *I Remember Mama* (1944), and **Mary Coyle Chase's** fantastic *Harvey* (1944).

The immediate postwar period saw renewed activity by established writers, including O'Neill's *The Iceman Cometh* (1946), Hellman's *Another Part of the Forest* (1946), Maxwell Anderson's *Anne of the Thousand Days* (1948), Clifford Odets's *The Country Girl* (1950), and Kingsley's **Darkness at Noon** (1951), adapted from Arthur Koestler's novel. At the time of O'Neill's death in 1953, his reputation was in decline; a reevaluation of his work began with **José Quintero**'s 1956 revival of *The Iceman Cometh* at **Circle in the Square: Jason Robards, Jr.**'s portrayal of Hickey drew widespread praise and launched his career. Later that year, O'Neill's **Long Day's Journey into Night** premiered at the same theatre under Quintero's direction and was hailed as the playwright's greatest work. *A **Moon for the Misbegotten*** followed in 1957 and *A Touch of the Poet* in 1958. In 1959, the Coronet Theatre in New York was renamed in O'Neill's honor.

Popular successes at the time reflected the public's continued interest in the war and its own idealism. **Garson Kanin**'s comedy **Born Yesterday** (1946) made a star of **Judy Holliday.** Other hits included William Wister Haines's melodrama *Command Decision* (1947); **Norman Krasna**'s farce *John Loves Mary* (1947); Thomas Heggen and **Joshua Logan**'s comedy **Mister Roberts** (1947), starring **Henry Fonda;** Donald Bevan and Edmund Trzcinski's thriller *Stalag 17* (1951); and Herman Wouk's courtroom drama *The Caine Mutiny Court Martial* (1954).

After the war, Tennessee Williams, **Arthur Miller,** and **William Inge** emerged as the major new playwrights. *A Streetcar Named Desire* (1947), with stellar performances by **Marlon Brando, Jessica Tandy,** Karl Malden, and **Kim Hunter,** solidified the reputation Williams established with *The Glass Menagerie* and won both the Pulitzer Prize and the Critics' Circle Award. In 1947, Miller's *All My Sons* drew respectable notices and won the Drama Critics Award; two years later his **Death of a Salesman,** under **Elia Kazan**'s direction and with a brilliant performance by **Lee J. Cobb,** duplicated Williams's success. Williams and Miller depicted a society that had grown decadent, obsessed with materialism and power. Williams wrote with compassion and poetic insight about people unable to cope who seek escape through booze, drugs, daydreams, and sex. His post-1950 plays include *The Rose Tattoo* (1951), **Cat on a Hot Tin Roof** (1955), *Orpheus Descending* (1957), **Sweet Bird of Youth** (1959), and *The **Night of the Iguana*** (1961); later his reputation suffered from such lesser pieces as *The Milk Train Doesn't Stop Here Anymore* (1963), *Vieux Carré* (1977), and *Clothes for a Summer Hotel* (1980). Arthur Miller focused more on the larger social and political issues in *The **Crucible*** (1953), *A View from the Bridge* (1956), and *Incident at Vichy* (1964); his latest plays were not well received in the U.S. Inge's reputation has not worn as well as those of his two colleagues. In 1950 **Come Back, Little Sheba** established him as an important playwright and promoted the career of actress **Shirley Booth.** Inge would enjoy meteoric success with hits *Picnic* (1953), **Bus Stop** (1955), and *The Dark at the Top of the Stairs* (1957) before

his star faded in the 1960s; his plays now seem sentimental and contrived.

After the war, Rodgers and Hammerstein continued their mastery of the musical with **South Pacific** (1949), **The King and I** (1951), and their last major collaboration, *The Sound of Music* (1959). This was a golden age of the American musical. Hits by other composers include Berlin's **Annie Get Your Gun** (1946) and **Call Me Madam** (1950); **Harburg** and Saidy's **Finian's Rainbow** (1947); **Lerner and Loewe**'s **Brigadoon** (1947) and **My Fair Lady** (1956); Cole Porter's **Kiss Me Kate** (1948); **Frank Loesser**'s **Guys and Dolls** (1950); Bernstein's **Wonderful Town** (1953) and **West Side Story** (1957); and **Jule Styne**'s *Gypsy* (1959). The American musical possessed energy and style and was recognized as the nation's most original contribution to world theatre.

Comedy grew tame and unadventuresome in the 1950s, relying on stock plots and comic devices. Ronald Alexander's domestic comedy **Time Out for Ginger** was a minor hit the same year (1952) **George Axelrod**'s sex farce, *The Seven Year Itch,* ran for 1,141 presentations and made a star of Tom Ewell. Another smash hit, **John Patrick**'s *The Teahouse of the August Moon* (1953), endured for 1,027 performances and won both the Critics' Circle and Pulitzer Prize. **Samuel Taylor**'s two hits, *Sabrina Fair* (1953) and *Pleasure of His Company* (1958), reminded audiences of Philip Barry and S. N. Behrman. George S. Kaufman and Howard Teichmann cowrote a mild satire about American business methods, *The Solid Gold Cadillac* (1953). Sidney Kingsley's farcical *Lunatics and Lovers* (1954) offered audiences a screwball comedy with Buddy Hackett. Thornton Wilder's *The **Matchmaker,*** which later served as the book for **Hello, Dolly!,** opened in 1955; likewise **Jerome Lawrence** and **Robert E. Lee**'s 1956 **Auntie Mame** was later transformed into the musical *Mame.* In 1959, **Paddy Chayevsky**'s *The Tenth Man* provided mysticism and love in a plot that threatened to turn serious.

In the work of the **Actors Studio,** the postwar American theatre found an acting style in which to interpret the realistic plays of Williams, Miller, and Inge. Elia Kazan, **Robert Lewis,** and Cheryl Crawford founded the Studio in 1947, joined by Lee Strasberg a year later. Strasberg's system of acting based on Stanislavsky's writings became known as the Method and attracted a generation of actors including Marlon Brando and **Geraldine Page.** Kazan became the prominent director of his age, mounting important premieres for all three playwrights. As if to underscore the passing of an era, in 1958 Lunt and Fontanne gave their farewell performance in *The Visit.*

In the 1920s, Robert Edmond Jones had set the standard for American stage scenery by evolving a style of simplified sets that suggested rather than reproduced reality. His successor, **Jo Mielziner,** dominated American stage design from 1930 until his death in 1976. Mielziner used transparent scenery in a cinematic way to complement the poetic quality of plays by Williams and Miller. **Ming Cho Lee** followed Mielziner as the major influence upon more contemporary stage design in a style that features collage, textured surfaces, and scaffolding. Other important scenic artists of the postwar era include **Boris Aronson, Oliver Smith, Jean Rosenthal, Santo Loquasto,** and **Eugene Lee.**

After WW II, high production costs on Broadway and efforts to establish professional theatre outside of New York resulted in the **Off-Broadway** and regional theatre movements. Off-Broadway recorded its first major success in 1952 with José Quintero's revival of Williams's **Summer and Smoke** at the Circle in the Square. The production reclaimed the play (which had earlier failed on Broadway) and made a star of Geraldine Page. Judith Malina and Julian Beck opened The **Living Theatre** in 1951; **Norris Houghton** and T. Edward Hambleton founded the Phoenix in 1953; and **Joseph Papp** created the most important Off-Broadway theatre, the **New York Shakespeare Festival,** in 1954. Outside New York, in 1947 **Margo Jones** founded Theatre '47 in Dallas, and Nina Vance the **Alley Theatre** in Houston. In 1950 **Zelda Fichandler** and Edward Mangum created the **Arena Stage** in Washington, DC. Two years later **Herbert Blau** and **Jules Irving** established the Actors' Workshop in San Francisco. In 1955, the **American Shakespeare Festival** opened in Stratford, CT, joining the **Oregon Shakespeare Festival** (founded in 1935) as a major summer company dedicated to the production of Shakespeare's plays [see **Shakespearean festivals**].
TLM

4. 1960 to the present During the three decades between 1960 and 1990 American theatre changed profoundly. Most important, it decentralized: For the first time since resident repertory theatres disappeared in the late 19th century, theatre people could hope to conduct respectable careers independently of New York, while audiences in other regions gained consistent access to professional theatre.

Faced with mounting competition from television as well as rising production costs that discouraged risk and, by extension, inflated theatre tickets to luxury items, the Broadway commercial stage faded as the creative and economic heart of American theatre. Since the turn of the century, Broadway had been the sole locus of generating and casting new works, disseminated after their New York runs to other locales through Broadway's extension, "the road." Whereas 327 companies toured the country in 1900, by the 1990s the road had virtually disappeared, replaced by a network of nonprofit, institutional theatres established in population centers throughout the country. Nonprofit theatres were also linked with, and even founded as, adjuncts to theatre degree programs at universities and colleges, a practice that has since spread abroad.

Together with the **alternative theatre**s that sprang up Off- and Off-Off Broadway and beyond, these regional theatres soon initiated most new American plays plus a significant percentage of musicals, formerly Broadway's special preserve. As the number of stable institutional theatres grew, expanding and diversifying their repertoires, the number of Broadway houses and productions in them shrank. Whereas 54 Broadway theatres presented an average of 146 productions per season in the 1930s, only 36 theatres offering 63 shows remained by 1964, a trend that continued. Also diminished was the sample of people prepared to buy expensive tickets for an ever narrower and more conservative range of fare dominated by small-cast comedies, blockbuster musicals, and imports of British hits.

Alterations in the circumstances of production were accompanied by equally extensive ones in other areas of theatre and drama, advanced in the late 1950s and early '60s by a new theatrical generation with priorities at odds with those of the establishment. Socially committed and aesthetically radical, these pioneers were sympathetic to Bertolt Brecht's Epic Theatre, Antonin Artaud's Theatre of Cruelty, and the neo-Dadaist Happenings of the art world. Inspired by director-theoreticians Peter Brook and Jerzy Grotowski, they would try to renew the stage by stripping away accumulated conventions to reach an essence, what Brook and Grotowski called a "holy" core.

In the process, the style, structure, and conventions of new American plays were retooled, as were subject matter and creative methodology. New genres of theatre and interpretive strategies proliferated, among them cross-disciplinary hybrids such as dance-theatre and **performance art;** docudrama, the hyperreal, and simulations; environmental theatre; guerilla theatre; structuralist theatre; poststructuralist or deconstructive theatre; choreodrama; and **New Vaudeville.** With them came altered criteria for actors, directors, and designers. Similarly, orthodox theatre **architecture** evolved or was abandoned for found environments and other untraditional spaces; arena and thrust stages became widespread, as did both "black box" and flexible arrangements that combined familiar and novel features.

Meanwhile, the demographics of theatre expanded on stage and in the audience to include members of minority groups along with their cultural priorities, perspectives, and styles. At first heard only on the fringe, the voices of African Americans, Latinos, Asians, gays, and women would soon reach Broadway, where they would win Tony Awards and Pulitzer Prizes, the highest mainstream theatrical honors. This multicultural attitude extended to artistic and intellectual approaches from other countries, to which American theatre became more open than at any previous time in its history.

In tandem with such challenges to the status quo was a financial revolution with social implications affecting the place of theatre in American life. Government, foundation, corporate, and individual donations joined the box office and private investment in the **economic** structure of the industry. As part of his Great Society program, President Lyndon B. Johnson personally rammed the 1965 bill creating the National Endowment for the Arts (NEA) through the legislature. The government was back in show business for the first time since the **Federal Theatre Project** of the Roosevelt administration during the Great Depression of the 1930s was killed after four years by Congressional reactionaries in a fever of communist witch-hunting. The NEA would fund state arts councils, which in turn spawned municipal counterparts.

This diversification of income sources signaled a growing acceptance of theatre as a cultural resource worthy of charitable support like museums, symphony orchestras, and libraries. Labor-intensive and handmade in an age of assembly-line technology, theatre was becoming a vulnerable art form, increasingly unable to earn its own way and, therefore, in need of society's commitment to preserve it.

The ideological foundations of many of the transformations discussed above combined a diluted version of existentialism and absurdism with the post-Marxian, post-Freudian views of the New Left, plus liberal political theory and smatterings of Zen Buddhism and other Eastern systems of thought. The unconsoling visions of the existential and the absurd captured the temper of an exhausted, postwar Europe better than they did that of the continental U.S., which had escaped invasion and was soon enjoying rapid economic expansion. These philosophies, moreover, ran contrary to a deeply entrenched belief, central to the country's self-image, in the purposeful unfolding of individual and national progress. Turning away from realism and its psychological acting approaches, emerging American playwrights like **Edward Albee, Arthur Kopit,** and **John Guare** embraced the absurdist stylistic vocabulary, but discarded most of the existentialist content. What remained surfaced through such thinkers as Erich Fromm and Martin Buber as a faith in the redeeming power of interpersonal love.

Purged of Fromm and Buber's theological arguments and eroticized by New Left pundits, love became the buzzword of 1960s idealists. In support of the civil rights movement and in rebellion against the escalating Vietnam War, the children of this generation, armed with flowers, would muster love to challenge the leadership of the nation and the prevailing mores of their society, which they believed hypocritical, soullessly commercial, and militaristic. "All you need is love," sang the Beatles in the anthem of the era, a popular entertainment version of Fromm. In a New Left take on this sentiment, the **Living Theatre** enacted its signature "love pile" of embracing spectators and performers, and the nude actors of the **Performance Group** moved among audience members to caress them.

The chief representatives of the New Left were Herbert Marcuse, Norman O. Brown, and R. D. Laing, who, together with allied social thinkers such as Erving Goffman, Eric Berne, Marshall McLuhan, and Claude Lèvi-Strauss, articulated a rationale for social, political, and aesthetic agendas of the 1960s. All neo-Romantic stances, they attack reason, handmaiden of the science that promised utopia but delivered the tools for world annihilation; instead they promoted intuition, emotion, and sensuality as antidotes to the pathology of the postindustrial world. Theory and social practice meshed as the youthful counterculture – liberated by relaxed obscenity laws and improved birth control methods – dropped out of society, turned on

to sex and drugs, and tuned in to rock and roll, a phenomenon reflected in plays like Jack Gelber's *The **Connection*** (1959), Dale Wasserman's *One Flew Over the Cuckoo's Nest* (1963), the hippie musical ***Hair*** (1967), the Performance Group's *Dionysus in '69* (1968), Robert Patrick's ***Kennedy's Children*** (1970), and **Michael Weller**'s ***Moonchildren*** (1972).

Recalling a familiar American motif, the free expression of individuality was equated with present satisfaction and a bright future; hostile forces dictating conformity were linked with the past. Taking up this theme, the new generation rejected their parents' material dream along with the competitive instincts and hierarchical structures that accompanied it.

In the theatre, these ideas supported experiments of theatre artists who formed or refocused their companies in the late 1950s and the '60s, among them such diverse talents as Judith Malina and Julian Beck (the Living Theatre), **Joseph Chaikin (the Open Theatre)**, Peter Schumann (**Bread and Puppet Theatre**), **Richard Schechner,** and **Andre Gregory** (the Manhattan Project). Like the Group Theatre of the 1930s, most would organize their companies and create their plays communally, a principle they extended to **collective** playwriting and to the stage itself, where the ensemble, not individual actors, starred. Whatever their differences, all would discard psychological acting for the presentational, realistic, and naturalistic dramaturgy for theatricalist idioms, and long-standing conventions of decorum for nudity and obscenity. Operating largely outside the commercial system, they reexamined traditional relationships between actor and character, stage and auditorium, theatre and other arts, and theatre and life.

"Theatre and life are one," wrote Peter Brook in *The Empty Space* (1968), and in this era they often were. Political demonstrators coopted dramatic techniques, producing events with an eye to television, for over 50 million sets were in America by 1960. John Cage used the chance procedures and recordings of everyday noise in his compositions; choreographers like Merce Cunningham and Ann Halprin created dances from everyday behavior and presented them in everyday locales; and in his Happenings, **Allan Kaprow** blurred the distinction between life and art, artist and audience. Simultaneously, activist theatre companies such as the Living Theatre, the Bread and Puppet Theatre, El Teatro Campesino, and the **San Francisco Mime Troupe** took to the streets, theatricalizing the environment.

Sociology and psychology, among other disciplines, also cross-pollinated with theatre. Analysts adapted actor-**training** techniques to therapy, while companies interested in renewing the actor's craft lifted sensitivity-training techniques from psychology. Such groups also explored the games theories of human behavior popularized by Goffman and Berne and adapted for the theatre by Viola Spolin. Her techniques of transformational acting came to both the mainstream and alternative theatres, through not only her influential book, *Improvisation for the Theatre* (1963), but also the work of her son **Paul Sills,** who in the 1950s practiced his mother's

Andrea Snow and Sharon Lockwood in the San Francisco Mime Troupe's *The Dragon Lady's Revenge*. Courtesy: San Francisco Mime Troupe.

theories at **Chicago**'s Compass and **Second City** improvisational theatres, then went on in the 1960s to originate another new genre, Story Theatre.

Centered in the Greenwich Village district of Manhattan where rents were then low and a bohemian atmosphere friendly to the arts prevailed, the kindred Off-Broadway movement had begun in the 1950s as a low-overhead but still commercial venue for work with scant Broadway potential: classics, revivals of neglected American plays, and American premieres of recent European plays by innovative writers like Genêt and Brecht. By 1960, however, the same economic pressures that would cripple Broadway had infected Off-Broadway, giving rise to the next wave of alternative theatres. By the late 1970s only a few Off-Broadway producers still functioned, and today only a handful of the once numerous little playhouses of no more than 299 seats still attempt to operate commercially. Operating costs tripled while capacity remained static; consequently fare grew more conservative. Revues, improvisational comedy troupes, and small-scale musicals like *The Fantasticks* (1960, now in its fourth decade) became staples, while more daring work shifted to Off-Off Broadway (OOB).

Off-Off Broadway became what Off-Broadway was not – a forum devoted to new American plays, a laboratory for cutting-edge critical theory, and a home for the artistic expression of heterodox social and political thought. Newcomers, many of them more interested in process than in creating a lasting work of art, improvised stages in lofts, church basements, coffeehouses, parks, and garages.

The Off-Off Broadway movement was spurred on in 1959 with **Caffe Cino,** which began presenting plays by such new writers as **Maria Irene Fornés, Terrence McNally,** and **Jean-Claude van Itallie. La MaMa,** founded in 1961 by **Ellen Stewart,** has continued to be the most durable of the 1960s venues (although its future in the early 1990s was in doubt), producing new playwrights in addition to providing a platform for young directors, among them **Tom O'Horgan, Wilford Leach,** and **Andrei Serban.** Others followed rapidly: Al Carmines's **Judson Poets' Theatre** (1961), **Wynn Handman**'s **American Place Theatre** (1964), Ralph Cook's Theatre Genesis (1964), and New York's **Public Theater** (1967), the developmental arm of the **New York Shakespeare Festival,** arguably the most important producing organization of the postwar era.

As the 1970s approached, experimental theatre turned away from the public art of the '60s toward inner visions that were apolitical, antihistorical, and self-reflexive. Individualistic where their predecessors were communitarian, **Richard Foreman**'s Ontological-Hysteric Theatre (1968), **Robert Wilson**'s Byrd Hoffman School of Birds (1969), and **Lee Breuer** with the **Mabou Mines** (1970) mediated on formalist concerns more closely akin to developments in music, dance, and art than to conventional theatre. Like **Gertrude Stein** before them, they were fascinated by their own creative processes and the pictures screened in their imaginations. Together with such allied performance artists as **Ping Chong, Laurie Anderson,** and **Meredith Monk,** this group represents what is called Theatre of Images. This rubric reflects the strongly visual, even painterly, qualities of their productions together with a corresponding disruption of language as rational discourse, reversing the time-honored authority of the word over spectacle, mind over sensory perception. Neither are Theatre of Images plays driven by coherent linear plots; rather they operate spacially and, like music, enlarge on motifs. Nor do actors inhabit characters; instead they function performatively, like kinetic sculpture in surreal dreamscapes. The Theatre of Images leaves spectators, like visitors to a contemporary art gallery, to make what they will of what they individually see.

Wilson's work is mystical and operatic, Foreman's rigorously cerebral, whereas Breuer's juxtaposes icons of popular and elite culture. All exploit multiple media as well as postmodern, deconstructive strategies. These methods have passed to 1980s imagists such as **JoAnne Akalaitis, Elizabeth LeCompte** with the **Wooster Group, Martha Clarke** in her dance-theatre, and writer-director **John Jesurun,** who applies sculptural and cinematic ideas to theatre.

The self-dramatizing impulse of the Theatre of Images is akin to the art world performances of the 1960s and '70s in which the materials of artists such as California's **Chris Burden** were their own bodies. In the name of immediacy, Burden variously crawled on glass and stuck pins in his stomach. A gentler strain appears in today's numerous autobiographical monologists, among whom **Spalding Gray** is king. Others followed in the 1980s, emerging from the performance clubs of the East Village to play at P.S. 122, **Dance Theatre Workshop,** the Kitchen, Franklin Furnace, and other showcases for prickly fringe art, with the lucky few moving on to the **Brooklyn Academy of Music**'s New Wave Festival and **Lincoln Center**'s counterpart, Serious Fun, and occasionally to Broadway, where **Lily Tomlin** and Whoopi Goldberg have performed **one-person** shows italicizing race, gender, and self. While this trend reflects both the enterprise of actor-writers in a shrinking market and a liking for alternative career paths inherited from the 1960s, it also suggests the spirit of the narcissistic era that writer Tom Wolfe has called the "Me Generation."

Only a decade from its inception, the OOB movement of the 1970s had grown enough to warrant a collective service organization, the Off-Off Broadway Alliance (OOBA), later succeeded by the **Alliance of Resident Theatres/New York.** By 1974–5 there were 150 OOB theatres, which had produced 548 plays that season. After the mid-1970s, however, OOB took a more conservative turn: The reaction of social and aesthetic forces with erotic energy that had enlivened the 1960s artistic scene slowed just as inflation rose and the national economy slumped.

The sensibilities of Caffe Cino and La MaMa playwrights like Tom Eyen, Robert Heide, **Rochelle Owens, Ronald Tavel,** and Paul Foster no longer seemed to capture the post-Vietnam times. The Bread and Puppet Theatre retreated to Vermont (1970) and the Open Theatre disbanded (1973), as did the Performance Group (1979) and the Manhattan Project, the Judson Poets' Theatre (1981), Theatre Genesis, and others. In their stead arose not-for-profit theatres with long-term institutional goals and more traditional artistic tastes. The **Circle Repertory Company** (1969), **Playwrights Horizons** (1971), Ensemble Studio Theatre (1971), and Second Stage (1979) emphasized the work of American playwrights like **A. R. Gurney, Tina Howe, Romulus Linney, Ronald Ribman,** or **Christopher Durang,** whose 1970s works had relatively familiar dramaturgic genes. Others, such as the **Chelsea Theatre Center,** the **Manhattan Theatre Club,** the **Acting Company,** and the Dodger Theatre (1978) mixed new American plays with premieres of foreign plays or freshly interpreted standards. At first outsiders, these groups would become fixtures of the mainstream theatre. Ironically, three nonprofit theatres, all specializing in revivals, have moved to homes in Broadway playhouses: the Circle in the Square, Uptown, the **Roundabout Theatre Company,** and the brand new National Actors Theatre, founded by actor Tony Randall in the fall of 1991.

In addition to the theatrical movements outlined above, theatre of the 1960s and '70s embraced racial causes, gender issues, antiwar sentiments, and the interests of many other constituencies as diverse as the deaf (**National Theatre of the Deaf,** 1967),

former prison inmates (The Family, 1972), and the elderly (Tale Spinners, 1975). Here minority artists found regular employment, while long-disenfranchised audiences could now see plays by one of their own in which the destinies of characters like themselves were central rather than background to the American saga.

African-American theatre has won the most prominent place in both nonprofit and commercial arenas. Whereas in 1948 black novelist and playwright **James Baldwin** moved to France to escape racism at home, in 1990 **August Wilson** collected his second Pulitzer Prize for Drama. While Broadway had long mounted musicals and revues by and about African Americans, commercial productions of legitimate plays were rare and runs short. Black drama awaited the moral and political momentum of the emerging civil rights movement. The first great crossover was **Lorraine Hansberry**'s play A *Raisin in the Sun* (1959), which ran on Broadway for 530 performances and won the New York Drama Critics' Circle Award – a first not only for an African American but also for a woman. It would make both a profit and the careers of the original and later cast members, including Sidney Poitier, **Ossie Davis, Ruby Dee, Claudia McNeil,** Diana Sands, and Louis Gossett, Jr. Its director, **Lloyd Richards,** went on to open establishment doors for numerous other black artists; he also affected national arts policy as head of the influential **National Playwrights Conference** and of one of the country's most prestigious theatrical training grounds, the Yale School of Drama, together with its professional arm, the **Yale Repertory Theatre.**

Other commercial hits would follow *Raisin,* among them Ossie Davis's *Purlie Victorious* (1961), but the mood of African-American drama now became militant, discouraging white, male, commercial producers. Until the mid-1980s, musicals remained the chief Broadway outlet for black talent, and remains a major one today.

The new, increasingly confrontational black drama took its cue more from Malcolm X's Black Power movement than from Martin Luther King's dream of integration. Baldwin's *Blues for Mister Charlie* (1964) dealt with the death of a civil rights worker, anticipating the fierce plays of LeRoi Jones (**Amiri Baraka**) and **Ed Bullins,** both of whom saw theatre as the artistic arm of radical politics and orthodox dramaturgy as an aspect of white oppression. Writing unsparingly of their dual experiences as women in a man's world and blacks in a white society, playwrights **Adrienne Kennedy** and **Ntozake Shange** developed unique dramatic forms that owed more to poetry than to theatrical precedent.

At the same time, the Johnson Administration's poverty programs made government funds available to bolster black theatre companies like Amiri Baraka's Spirit House in Newark, NJ, support augmented after 1965 by the new NEA. With both public and private monies to support their growth, troupes sprang up nationwide, most important among them the **Free Southern Theatre** (New Orleans), New **Lafayette Theatre** (Harlem), **Negro Ensemble Company** (the East Village), Concept East (Detroit), and Black Arts/West (San Francisco). By 1968 there were 40 such groups, and when the first National Black Theatre Festival convened in Winston-Salem, NC, in 1989, some 200 theatres were represented.

Douglas Turner Ward, Lonne Elder, Joseph A. Walker, Philip Hayes Dean, Sonia Sanchez, Derek Walcott, Leslie Lee, Richard Wesley, and **Ron Milner** were among the new playwrights. So were **Alice Childress,** the first black woman to have a play professionally produced in America (*Trouble in Mind,* 1952); **Charles Gordone,** whose *No Place to Be Somebody* (1970) won the first Pulitzer Prize in Drama awarded to an African-American dramatist; and **Charles Fuller,** who won the second for *A Soldier's Play* in 1981. Their achievements would ease the way for the present generation of playwrights, including August Wilson, **Suzan-Lori Parks,** and **George C. Wolfe.**

Other racial minorities also found theatre an effective tool for dealing with discrimination and asserting their place in the national mosaic. **Hanay Geiogamah**'s Native American Theatre Ensemble evolved out of the American Indian Movement of the late 1960s, as did **Spiderwoman** (1975), a feminist theatre founded by Muriel Miguel and her sisters, Cuna/Rappahannock Indians. **Luis Valdéz** established **El Teatro Campesino** on a flatbed truck beside the picket lines of California's Chicano and Filipino grape pickers, then embraced the larger dilemma of **Chicano**s caught between Mexican and American cultures. New York theatres, such as **INTAR,** the **Repertorio Español,** and the **Puerto Rican Traveling Theatre,** have expanded the opportunities for Latino actors and directors. Together with programs for Latino writers at the NYSF and several regional theatres, such companies have nurtured enough able playwrights – Lynne Alvarez and **Eduardo Machado** among them – to fill a recent anthology of contemporary **Hispanic-American** plays.

Except for such pseudo-Oriental plays by white authors as *Teahouse of the August Moon* or musicals like *The King and I* and *Flower Drum Song,* Asians were theatrically near-invisible until 1965 when the **East West Players** were established in **Los Angeles,** followed by the Asian-American Workshop in **San Francisco** and the **Pan Asian Repertory** in New York. Today **Asian-American** playwrights are regularly produced in the subsidized theatre, including Frank Chin, **Philip Kan Gotanda,** Jessica Hagedorn, and James Yoshimura. The first Broadway accolades went to Chinese-American playwright **David Henry Hwang** for his *M. Butterfly.*

Gay theatre groups were formed in the 1960s following the efforts of activists to gain recognition and respect for the homosexual lifestyle. While some gay theatre has existed for its own subculture, Mark Crowley's *The Boys in the Band* (1968) ran for 1,000 performances Off-Broadway. The acceptance of homosexual subjects by mainstream audiences gained momentum in the 1980s. **Harvey Fierstein**'s *Torch Song Trilogy* (1982) won the Drama Critics' Award and Tony for best play, followed the next season by the hit **Jerry Herman**/Fierstein musical *La Cage Aux Folles.* **Gay and lesbian theatre** companies formed an alliance in 1978, with 28 groups identified across the country in 1981.

Predominantly camp performances of the late 1960s and '70s have faded and been replaced by a sober response to **AIDS,** the fatal disorder that has hit the performing arts community particularly hard. Plays such as Larry Kramer's *The Normal Heart* (1985), William M. Hoffman's *As Is* (1985), or Paula Vogel's *The Baltimore Waltz* (1991) abandon the earlier celebratory posture for one of grief for the dead and rage with a sluggish official response to the epidemic. In 1987 Kramer shifted his focus from the stage to the streets, founding ACT-UP (AIDS Coalition to Unleash Power) and utilizing theatricalized civil disobedience to promote political action. In recognition of its efforts, ACT-UP received a Bessie Award, the Tony of performance art.

On the heels of the women's liberation movement – itself an offspring of civil rights initiatives – women's and **feminist theatre**s were widely established in the 1970s, and women began to enter the professional theatre in unprecedented numbers, not only as actresses, but as everything from artistic directors to stage managers and critics. By the 1980s the value of women to establishment theatre was acknowledged in Pulitzer Prizes to **Beth Henley, Marsha Norman,** and **Wendy Wasserstein,** raising by fifty percent the total number of the prizes to women playwrights since their inception in 1918. In 1982 **Ellen Burstyn** became the first woman president of the Actors' Equity Association, followed by **Colleen Dewhurst** in 1984, the same year that **Heidi Landesman** won the Tony for her sets for *Big River,* the first such award to a woman designer. Another landmark was the inauguration in Buffalo, NY, of an International Women's Playwrights Conference (1988), which drew some 291 women representing 34 nations.

Unlike the Pulitzer winners, many playwrights with feminist sensibilities held unorthodox views of dramatic structure, characterization, and other theatrical verities, among them Shange, Fornés, and Kennedy, as well as Eve Merriman, **Megan Terry, Corinne Jacker, Karen Malpede, Rosalyn Drexler,** and **Susan Yankowitz.** Their homes were the activist, feminist companies on the fringe. Regional groups included Boston's Caravan Theatre (1965), the Rhode Island Feminist Theatre (1973), the **Omaha Magic Theatre** (1968), **At the Foot of the Mountain** (1974), the Washington Area Feminist Theatre (1972), and Circle of the Witches (1973). In New York the New Feminist Repertory was founded in 1969, followed by Women's Interart Theatre (1971), the New York Feminist Theatre Troupe (1973), the Women's Experimental Theatre (1976), the New Cycle Theatre (1977), and the **Women's Project** (1978). By 1980 the number of such women's theatres had grown to 110.

Although women in performance art were initially hostile to theatre, by the 1980s the genre had attracted a sizable number of theatre people, particularly feminists: For example, Robbie McCauley, an African American, deals with issues of race and gender; **Rachel Rosenthal** often explores attitudes to the female body, as does **Karen Finley; and Holly Hughes** looks at lesbian sexuality. All of their work is in part autobiographical, all centered on the performer rather than production values, all both formally and thematically experimental.

In addition to **ethnic,** gender, and sexual diversification, the late 1960s also saw a proliferation of anti-American plays as the nation turned against the Vietnam War. The San Francisco Mime Troupe, Yale Repertory Theatre, and the Living Theatre all performed agit-prop, antiwar material, as would the Bread and Puppet Theatre, the Performance Group, La MaMa ETC, the Open Theatre, and others. Among the antiwar plays were **Robert Lowell**'s *The Old Glory* (1964), Megan Terry's *Viet Rock* (1966), Joseph Heller's *We Bombed in New Haven* (1968), and **David Rabe**'s Vietnam trilogy: *The Basic Training of Pavlo Hummel* (1968), *Sticks and Bones* (1971), and *Streamers* (1976). Most Vietnam plays look at the home front rather than battlefield trauma, with Amlin Gray's *How I Got That Story* (1979) a partial exception.

Arising at the same time were docudramas inspired by the work of German playwrights Rolf Hochhuth and Peter Weiss, who used oral history and the public record to indict corrupt official acts. Daniel Berrigan drew on courtroom transcripts for *The Trial of the Catonsville Nine* (1971), a government prosecution of Berrigan and fellow draft opponents, while **Eric Bentley** exploited Congressional annals for *Are You Now Or Have You Ever Been* (1972), his look at the 1950s McCarthy hearings. Following in this tradition is **Emily Mann**'s *Execution of Justice* (1982), a montage of perspectives on the murder of a gay, San Francisco councilman, Harvey Milk. A related group of protest plays responded to fears of Apocalypse in the age of nuclear warfare, among them **Sam Shepard**'s *Icarus's Mother* (1965), Edward Albee's *Box* (1968), Tennessee Williams's *The Red Devil Battery Sign* (1975), and the Mabou Mines's *Dead End Kids* (1982).

Stimulated by large grants – beginning in 1959 with the Ford Foundation followed by the Rockefeller Foundation and others, and including support from the NEA – the regional theatre movement had begun to gain significant momentum by the mid-1960s. It built on the initiatives of small, pioneer companies, all begun by neophyte directors opposed to Broadway's commercial standards and in search of somewhere else to work. In 1961 Ford created the **Theatre Communications Group** (TCG) to assist the **resident nonprofit** sector. Important regional companies followed: the **Guthrie Theatre** in **Minneapolis** and the **Seattle Repertory** (both founded in 1963); the **Actors Theatre of Louisville,** KY, and **Trinity [Square] Repertory Company** of Providence, RI (both 1964); **Long Wharf** in New Haven, CT (1965); Yale Repertory Theatre (1966); and the **American Conservatory Theatre** in San Francisco (1966). Cultural centers – among them Lincoln Center in New York, **John F. Kennedy Center** in Washington, DC, and the Music Center in Los Angeles – were built with theatres as part of their complexes. By 1992 these modest beginnings had grown into a network of some 229 theatres nationwide. Most called themselves resident repertory companies, although in most cases only management was resident and shows were rarely produced in rotating rep, which proved prohibitively expensive. Initially, the repertoires of these theatres were biased toward the conservatively interpreted classics and standards favored by establishment board members and subscribers; but by the early 1970s more risk-taking and production of new plays seemed possible – though in the unsure atmosphere of the economy in the 1990s there has been a return to safer, less experimental fare in many regional theatres.

While in New York the new theatre evolved downtown and elsewhere, the Broadway of the 1960s and '70s remained lively, although each year it owed more to products developed elsewhere. Its dominant playwrights were **Neil Simon** and Edward Albee, who from different angles would both explore deteriorating family personal relationships and the inability of individuals to maintain community. Simon's long list of comedies reached a climax with his Pulitzer Prize–winning *Lost in Yonkers* (1991). Albee emerged as the 1960s' major dramatist with *Who's Afraid of Virginia Woolf?* (1962) after early successes with a series of one-act plays. He won the Pulitzer Prize in 1966 for *A Delicate Balance,* but has had little success since then.

Rock music and **nudity** went mainstream in the 1960s when the counterculture musical *Hair* (1967) transferred from the Public Theater to Broadway, where it remained a cultural as well as an artistic event and spawned a wave of imitations. Traditional musical forms, however, continued to dominate, represented by *Camelot* (1960), *Fiddler on the Roof* (1964), *Hello, Dolly!* (1964), *Funny Girl* (1964), *Man of La Mancha* (1965), *Mame* (1966), and *Cabaret* (1966).

Dominating musical theatre since the mid-1970s is **Stephen Sondheim.** Though one of his latest efforts, *Assassins,* was not successful, he is nevertheless widely regarded as the most original and innovative composer-lyricist now writing in the American theatre. For most of his career he worked closely with director **Harold Prince,** a major force in the development of the American musical. By the mid-1980s, the choreographer-director had been elevated to a new position of power as the American musical had become less dependent upon a book than on a concept or theme. The best known of the new breed were the late **Bob Fosse** and **Michael Bennett,** the latter responsible for developing the longest running show on Broadway, *A Chorus Line* (1973). Today, only director-choreographer **Tommy Tune** retains a reputation comparable to his predecessors.

Much of the best drama of the 1970s and '80s came from Off-Broadway and from the trio of Sam Shepard, **Lanford Wilson,** and **David Mamet,** who have produced some of the most resonant American dramas of the post-1960s decades. Shepard's plays appear realistic on the surface, belying their vivid theatricality and close relationship with the absurd. His characters struggle toward some kind of transcendental experience; his plays depend not on well-made plots but on highly personal images to which the audience must find connections. Wilson's lyrical prose suggests the influence of Tennessee Williams. Arguably his best play, *Fifth of July* (1978) became a metaphor for an entire generation coming to terms with its own failed idealism. Mamet uses language brilliantly to depict the spiritual emptiness that lies at the core of contemporary American life, though whereas Wilson is a lyric realist and Shepard takes a mythic tone, Mamet's signature is a terse and profane urban vernacular that brings to mind the crisp, hard-driving, and quick-changing phrases of 1920s Chicago jazz.

Mamet's career, in fact, began in Chicago at the St. Nicholas theatre, which he helped to found in 1974. During the 1960s and '70s, anchored by the older **Goodman Theatre** and encouraged by the brainy irreverence of Second City, **Chicago** developed a nationally acclaimed alternative enclave of husky Off-Loop companies (**Body Politic,** the **Organic Theatre, Victory Gardens,** St. Nicholas, **Steppenwolf**). Although still not as theatrically active as New York, Chicago has become a major U.S. theatre center of the 1990s.

Since 1970, transfers of London successes have often fleshed out Broadway seasons, among them Peter Shaffer's *Equus* and *Amadeus;* David Storey's *The Changing Room* and *Home;* Tom Stoppard's *Travesties* and *The Real Thing;* Andrew Lloyd Webber and Tim Rice's *Jesus Christ Superstar* and *Evita,* as well as Webber's *Cats* and *Phantom of the Opera;* Harold Pinter's *The Homecoming* and *Betrayal;* and plays by David Hare, Simon Gray, Caryl Churchill, and others. The Royal Shakespeare Company, which has visited several times, is especially remembered for *The Life and Adventures of Nicholas Nickleby* in 1980, a production whose staging approaches owed something to the theatricalist styles of the American experimental theatre of the 1960s and '70s and influenced subsequently dramaturgy, staging approaches, and box office prices (with its top $100 ticket, a new Broadway high).

The American theatre from the mid-1980s into the 1990s depended less on Broadway than at any time this century, and more on the resident nonprofit theatres both in and outside of New York. New plays now originated regularly at such theatres as the New York Shakespeare Festival, Playwrights Horizons, Chicago's Steppenwolf Theatre Company and Goodman Theatre, the Yale Repertory Theatre, **American Repertory Theatre** at Harvard, **Mark Taper Forum** in Los Angeles, Actors Theatre of Louisville, and New Haven's Long Wharf Theatre, among many others. The *Best Plays of 1984–5* reported that 6 of their 10 best plays did not originate on Broadway. In 1992, for the first time, the Pulitzer Prize for Drama (for 1991) was awarded to a play that had not been produced in New York City (Robert Schenkkan's *The Kentucky Cycle*).

High costs continued to make producing in Manhattan a risky business. During the 1984–5 season, for example, a new musical, *Grind,* lost its entire investment of $4,750,000; in 1992 a comparable production lost closer to $7,000,000. The

New York Times reported that a revival of *Arsenic and Old Lace* in 1986 cost $700,000 compared to the original amount in 1941 of $37,000. Even Off-Broadway plays cost up to $400,000 to produce. Ticket prices of $40–60 for Broadway had become the norm. Nevertheless, the 1991–2 Broadway season recorded a new high in ticket sales ($292 million), and more productions were presented than in any of the preceding five years.

Production values in the American theatre of the 1980s remained high. The Broadway musical, though less dependent on American products, had no equal, with a wide array of talented young performers including **Bernadette Peters, Mandy Patinkin,** Ben Vereen, and Tommy Tune. Prevalent was a serious problem resulting from the dearth of composers and writers who could attract a large enough audience to reward investors, a situation that had not abated in the early 1990s. A new generation of talented actors, among them **Judith Ivey,** John Lithgow, **Meryl Streep, William Hurt,** Pamela Reed, Lindsay Crouse, **Kevin Kline, Mary Beth Hurt, Glenn Close, Stockard Channing,** and **Swoosie Kurtz,** promised distinguished performances in the future, although a number by 1990 had devoted more energy to films and television than to the stage. However, the theatre still was not attracting the younger playgoer: One estimate placed the average age of the Broadway audience at 44. High ticket prices, the appeal of films (and videos), and material that failed to attract a younger generation were undoubtedly major reasons for this condition. With electronic media radically changing how we received information, the future of the American stage seemed to depend in part on the work of such innovators as Foreman, Robert Wilson, **Peter Sellars,** and others, though even these original artists had yet to attract large followings.

Theatrical trends in the early 1990s were difficult to ascertain. On the one hand, the AIDS epidemic had transformed theatrical depiction of the disease and its effect from the first-generation plays of the 1980s that openly named the scrounge (*The Normal Heart, As Is*) to those of the early 1990s that only indirectly refer, or have no allusion, to AIDS, such as McNally's *Lips Together, Teeth Apart,* Scott McPherson's *Marvin's Room,* or **Craig Lucas**'s **Prelude to a Kiss.** At the other topical and tone extremes were **participatory** and escapist entertainments typified by *Shear Madness, Nunsense, Forever Plaid, Tony n' Tina's Wedding, Song of Singapore,* and *Catskills on Broadway.*

If trends were not apparent, what was obvious was the devastating effect of the economic recession on all theatrical venues, from Broadway to nonprofit regional theatres. Broadway had few strong seasons in the late 1980s and early '90s: Even a nonmusical Broadway production cost over $1 million to produce. (It cost $900,000 to move *Prelude to a Kiss* 36 blocks from Circle Rep to Broadway.) In recent years nonprofit theatre has seen declining growth rates in support from individuals, corporations, and private foundations; government funding has also eroded.

The nonprofit sector, including major regional companies, though still more adventurous than much of commercial Broadway or Off-Broadway, tended toward less experimental and more proven fare in the late 1980s and early '90s. A sign of the times was the resignation or dismissal of an unusually large number of artistic directors, often for economic reasons (or the failure to keep an operation fiscally sound). A trend toward attempted **censorship** through conservative elements of Congress and control of the National Endowment for the Arts, as well as so-called "political correctness," created moments of tension and concern, as well as a debate that continues. Even the commercial theatre experienced new crises. Outcries were heard over the casting of a British actor in the Eurasian lead of Broadway's *Miss Saigon* and the use of non-Hispanic actors in the Chilean play *Death and the Maiden* by Ariel Dorfman. In reality, such controversy indicates a growing awareness of our pluralistic, multicultural society, and the idea of nontraditional casting is now a fact in many theatre companies, though this battle is not yet completely won.

The British musical invasion (*Cats, Les Misérables, Phantom of the Opera, Miss Saigon*) has continued, and few original American musicals of note were produced. (The much-anticipated *Nick and Nora* opened and closed quickly early in 1992.)

Even successful American efforts, such as *The **Will Rogers Follies,*** demonstrated no notable innovations, echoing back to a mythic American past. In 1992 musical production was most notable for revivals or revamping of earlier music: *Man of La Mancha, Guys and Dolls, The **Most Happy Fella, Jelly's Last Jam*** (music by Jelly Roll Morton), and *Crazy for You,* the last loosely based on Gershwin's *Girl Crazy*.

The deaths of such influential and committed artists as Joseph Papp, **William Ball, José Ferrer,** and Colleen Dewhurst marked the end of an era of great growth in the American theatre. Yet some encouragement for the future was to be found, for example, in the maturation of John Guare (***Six Degrees of Separation***), the continuing productivity of August Wilson, the inauguration of Tony Randall's National Actors Theatre (not an entirely successful venture as of this writing), the efforts of the **Broadway Alliance,** and the large number of new talents that continued to be heard throughout the U.S. theatrical network.   CLJ   DBW

For general sources and reference works on American theatre, see the Bibliography at the end of the *Guide*. Where possible, specific sources are suggested with appropriate entries.

A

Aarons, Alexander A. (1891–1943) and **Alfred E. Aarons** (1865–1936) Producers, theatrical managers. Alfred began as a theatrical callboy in Philadelphia, then moved in 1890 to New York, where he managed the Standard Theatre, **Koster and Bial**'s, the Manhattan Roof Garden, and the **Broadhurst Theatre.** He also wrote songs for several undistinguished musicals and produced a number of musicals and plays.

Alexander, Albert's son, produced several of the **Gershwins**' most successful shows of the 1920s and '30s, including *Lady Be Good* and *Girl Crazy.* With **Vinton Freedley** he built the **Alvin Theatre** in New York in 1927, but lost it in financial reverses five years later. He worked in Hollywood for several years in a variety of production jobs with MGM and RKO.   MK

Abbey, Henry Edwin (1846–96) Impresario known early in his career for presenting costly entertainments to audiences outside major theatre centers and, from 1880, for his success in booking the best European actors, actresses, and opera singers for U.S. engagements [see **international stars**], for which he became known as "The Napoleon of the Managers." The partnership of Abbey, John B. Schoeffel, and **Maurice Grau** managed theatres in New York, **Boston,** and **Philadelphia,** as well as the tours of domestic and international stars. With backing from **Charlotte Crabtree,** Abbey and Schoeffel leased the Park Theater, New York (1877), bringing together there **William H. Crane** and **Stuart Robson,** a starring tandem that flourished until 1889. The partnership took over the Metropolitan Opera House, New York (1883), but, despite assembling a brilliant company of singers, experienced heavy losses in two seasons. Their management of the Metropolitan Opera House from 1891 until Abbey's death in 1896 was distinctive for the great stars they hired.   WD

> See: R. Hossalla, "Henry E. Abbey, Commercial Manager," PhD diss., Kent State U, 1972.

Abbott, George (1887–) Director, playwright, and actor. In his 1963 autobiography (*Mister Abbott*), Abbott praises his Harvard drama teacher **George Pierce Baker** in a way that defines his own theatrical creed: "Professor Baker gave you no nonsense about inner meanings and symbolism; he turned your whole thoughts and energies into the practical matter of how to make a show." Taking Baker's lessons to heart, Abbott became the most practical showman in Broadway history. As performer, coauthor, play doctor, and director of over 130 productions, Abbott has entertained audiences more often and over a longer period of time than anyone else. He first acted on a Broadway stage in 1913; in the fall of 1989 he directed a workshop production of a new musical called *Frankie.* As both director and coauthor his specialties are racy contemporary melodrama (*Broadway,* 1926); split-second farce (*Three Men on a Horse,* 1935); and peppy musicals with vigorous choreography (*On Your Toes,* 1936; *Damn Yankees,* 1955). Gangsters, bookies, gold diggers, politicians, baseball heroes, hoofers, and hookers populate his work, providing colorful slices of Americana. Despite the occasional suggestion of sexual daring (as in *Coquette* [1927] and *New Girl in Town* [1957], his musical version of *Anna Christie*) and of political conflict (*The Pajama Game,* 1954; *Fiorello!* 1959), the typical Abbott show is archly conservative. The famed "Abbott touch" always kept his shows spinning at a brisk clip, but Abbott downplays his technique, claiming that all he does is make actors "say their final syllables."   FH

Abe Lincoln in Illinois by **Robert E. Sherwood.** Biographical play in 12 scenes; winner of the Pulitzer Prize for 1938–9. Sherwood's play featured **Raymond Massey** as Lincoln in a loosely constructed work held together only by the presence of the central character in each of its episodes, sketching the life of Lincoln from 22-year-old student of grammar to grim-faced president-elect. The highly praised production was directed by **Elmer Rice** and was the first project of the newly formed **Playwrights' Company;** the play opened on 15 October 1938 at the **Plymouth Theatre** in New York and ran for 472 performances. A screen version starring Massey was released in 1940.   MF

Abie's Irish Rose The story of the mixed-up marriage between a Jewish boy and an Irish girl, written and produced by Anne Nichols (c. 1891–1966); opened at the Fulton Theatre on 23 May 1922. Although critics panned it as an ethnic burlesque, audiences loved the heartwarming story, and it made a fortune for its author-producer. Called "the million dollar play," it set a 14-year record of 2,327 consecutive performances (closing in 1927). Its success continued as a play (revived 1937, 1954), a film (1928, 1946), a radio show (1940s), and a TV sitcom ("Bridget Loves Bernie," 1970s). Nichols wrote numerous forgettable plays, vaudeville sketches, and musicals before and after *Abie's Irish Rose*'s phenomenal success.   FB

Abraham, F[ahrid] Murray (1939–) Actor and teacher. Often cast as villains, Abraham is an accomplished comedian. First appearing on stage in Ray Bradbury's *The Wonderful Ice Cream Suit* (Los Angeles, 1965) and on Broadway in Robert Shaw's *The Man in the Glass Booth* (1969), he is best known for the film *Amadeus* (Academy Award for his Salieri, 1984). An acting teacher at Brooklyn College, he received an Obie for *Uncle Vanya* (1983) and New York's Mayor's Award of Honor for Art and Culture (1988). Recent appearances include *A Midsummer Night's Dream* (**New York Shakespeare Festival**, 1988), *Waiting for Godot* (**Lincoln Center**, 1988), *King Lear* (**American Repertory**, 1991), and a revival of **Mamet**'s *A Life in the Theater* (**Jewish Repertory Theatre**, 1991).   REK

Academic theatre Study of theatrical production techniques, as opposed to dramatic literature, has flourished in colleges and universities only in this century, although the beginnings of college dramatics predate the nation's founding. Although the earliest student-produced plays and shows are incompletely documented, the first indication of such dramatic interest is found in a Harvard University President's diary in 1698. Students of William and Mary in Virginia staged a "pastoral colloquy" in 1702, whereas most of New England, permeated by Puritan influence, considered theatre in any form to be vicious, ungodly, and unworthy of study. Cotton Mather in 1723 referred to texts as "Satan's Library" and "empty and vicious pieces of poetry." Nevertheless, the diary of one Nathaniel Ames, a Harvard student, lists productions of such plays as *Cato, The Orphan, The Recruiting Officer,* and *The Drummer* during 1758–9.

Harvard's professors saw in the drama a valuable tool for instruction; by 1781 the faculty wrote scripts to be "exhibited" as "academical exercises." Commencement plays and dialogues were somewhat regularly included, and a few literary societies produced what might be termed extracurricular plays. Similarly, Yale enjoyed theatrical productions as extracurricular activities, seemingly unmolested by college authorities. So, too, the College of Philadelphia (later the University of Pennsylvania) saw student-acted productions from its foundation in 1755. The staging of *The Masque of Alfred* during Christmas holidays (1756–7) may well have inspired the student Thomas Godfrey to compose the first American tragedy to be produced, *The Prince of Parthia* [see **Introduction**, §1].

The early 19th century saw 168 colleges founded, mostly church-sponsored. Orthodox religion re-established its dominance of American cultural life, but the people of the new nation grew steadily more tolerant toward the theatre. Harvard's Hasty Pudding Club, founded in 1795, began theatrical production in 1844 with *Bombastes Furioso*. Faculties, it would seem, preferred tragedy; the students, if left to their own resources, gravitated toward farce, satire, and comedy. Still no classroom study of theatre can be found in this period.

After the Civil War, students began to form organizations for the express purpose of presenting plays. The Thalian Dramatic Association, founded at Brown University in 1866, was one of the earliest of these producing agencies. Such clubs frequently flourished, died out when the leadership graduated, and were in turn replaced by others. Benefit performances were common, the proceeds being turned over to some campus activity or other, but rarely for the production budgets. Nevertheless, productions increased in quantity, as did all other extracurricular aspects of college life.

Harvard again led the way; the Hasty Pudding Club initiated musical burlesques, influencing many other campuses to do the same. As the production of foreign-language scripts increased, Harvard produced, after six months' rehearsal, *Oedipus Rex* in May 1881, probably the first Greek tragedy done in the original in the U.S. The continuing use of the drama by foreign-language departments no doubt helped raise the respectability of the theatre in the public eye.

The beginnings of formalized classroom instruction in theatrical techniques, leading to departments of theatre and drama, are somewhat vague. In 1886 William O. Partridge, a Columbia University Professor, pleaded for such departments, but most historians have dated the beginnings of formal theatre instruction from **George Pierce Baker**'s "English 47, English – the Technique of the Drama," called the "most celebrated academic course in America." Baker offered this course to graduate students in English at Harvard beginning in 1905, continuing almost without interruption until 1923–4, adding 47a in 1916 as an advanced course. In 1912 he added his 47 Workshop, essentially an acting and producing agency to stage plays written in his classes.

Certainly others had preceded him, most notably Thomas Dickinson's instructions in staging at Baylor in 1901–2. Frederick H. Koch had produced staged readings at the University of North Dakota as early as 1905–6. Harry Bainbridge Gough at De-Pauw University and Paul M. Pearson at Swarthmore similarly advanced the academic theatre. Later pioneers such as E. C. Mabie at Iowa and Alexander Drummond at Cornell began to influence their campuses and, after WW I, the nation. Another professor of influence was **Brander Matthews**, who wrote several books on dramatic theory and founded a Dramatic Museum at Columbia. Playwright **Hatcher Hughes** taught playwriting at Columbia; Donald Clive Stuart fostered theatre at Princeton, as did Samuel Eliot of Smith.

The first department of theatre in the U.S. was founded in 1914 at the Carnegie Institute of Technology (now Carnegie–Mellon) in Pittsburgh. Thomas Wood Stevens and **B. Iden Payne** produced plays there for the College Theatre. Later George Pierce Baker founded a more influential postgraduate Department of Drama at Yale in 1925. Annual meetings of university educators interested in theatrical production led to the founding of the American Educational Theatre Association in 1936, attracting some eighty members; the same organization, later called the American Theatre Association, dealt with some 1,600 theatre departments in the U.S. until its dissolution in 1986, replaced by the Association for Theatre in Higher Education.

Even colleges without theatre departments offer productions today. In 1977 the National Endowment for the Arts estimated that some 2,500 colleges and universities presented 30,000 presenta-

The Acting Company (1985–6) in Maria Irene Fornés's *Drowning* (inspired by a Chekhov short story and part of an evening of seven plays all based on Chekhov), directed by Robert Falls. Photo: Diane Gorodnitzki. Courtesy: The Acting Company.

tions of 7,500 scripts for an estimated audience of nine million.

Theatre production and curriculum followed in secondary or high schools in America only a few years after its arrival on college campuses. First presented to raise money for some worthy cause, high-school plays became recognized by some as an end in their own right as early as 1912. Few states offer separate certification for high-school teachers of drama, but the growth of dramatic activity at the secondary-school level has been impressive. By the beginning of the 1980s, the NEA reported some 30,000 high-school theatre programs in the U.S., offering about 150,000 performances annually to a total of 45 million audience members; 92.2% of American high schools are engaged in some sort of theatrical endeavor.

American students thus may encounter live theatre at any level of their education. Even in primary schools, much **children's theatre** is presented, although figures are inexact. Course work in drama or theatre is more commonly encountered at the high-school level, as are more fully mounted productions, often extracurricularly. A student wishing to specialize in theatre vocationally may select from thousands of U.S. college programs, usually pursuing a Bachelor of Arts or Bachelor of Fine Arts degree. Similarly, Master of Arts or Master of Fine Arts (the latter considered a terminal degree, comparable to the doctorate) are offered nationwide, and about 40 Doctor of Philosophy degrees in theatre are available. Such programs are usually less concerned with production techniques than with the historical and theoretical aspects of theatre. SMA

See: B. Hobgood, ed., *Master Teachers of Theatre,* Carbondale, IL, 1988; K. R. Wallace, ed., *History of Speech Education in America,* New York, 1954.

Acconci, Vito (1940–   ) Bronx-born **performance art**ist, poet, sculptor who also works in video and installations. Educated in private Cath-

olic schools, he studied literature at Holy Cross College and the University of Iowa (MA, 1964). In his 1960s and '70s videotapes and body-art performances (*Following Piece* [1969], *Trademarks* [1970], *Conversions* [1971], and *Seedbed* [1972]), Acconci dramatized visions of failure and aggression, the politics of the body, language, space, and time. His sculptural installations (such as *Adjustable Wall Bra,* 1990) and architectural designs for parks and playgrounds investigate the political and psychological subtexts of meeting places. Acconci's work is influenced by Catholicism, action painting, minimalism, pop art, psychology, feminism, sociology of language, and the political strategies used during the Vietnam War (self-immolation, surveillance, and boundary protection). AF

Ackerman, P. Dodd (1876–1963) Designer and scenic artist whose studio provided 78 sets for Broadway in the 1920s and '30s, including *Five Star Final* (1930), a tripartite setting that was one of the first examples of simultaneous settings on Broadway. AA

Across the Continent; or, Scenes from New York Life and the Pacific Railroad by **James J. McCloskey.** This sensational melodrama premiered at the Park Theatre, Brooklyn, 28 November 1870. Oliver Doud Byron starred as Joe Ferris, an outcast gambler known as "The Ferret." Byron's wife, Kate Crehan, older sister of **Ada Rehan,** played a small role. New York's seedy Five Points area provided the primary setting, but the popularity of the last act at a western railroad station inspired a rash of frontier plays. Indians, led by villainous John Adderly, attacked Ferris and his friends, who were saved by the bravery of Ferris, a clever telegraph ploy, and a trainload of Army troops. RAH

Acting Company John Houseman and Margot Harley organized the first graduating class of the Drama Division of Juilliard School into a permanent repertory troupe (originally, City Center Acting Company), which began performing at the City Center in New York in 1972. Since 1980 it has functioned as the touring arm of the **John F. Kennedy Center for the Performing Arts** in Washington, DC; headquartered in New York, under the artistic direction of **Zelda Fichandler** (as of 1991), it continues primarily as a touring company with members selected nationally by auditions and molded into an ensemble. Actors perform a variety of roles, classical and modern. The 1988–9 repertoire included: *Boy Meets Girl*, *The Phantom Tollbooth*, and *Love's Labour's Lost*. In 1991 it was reported that the Acting Company had performed over 67 plays in 46 states before two million people. Alumni of the company include **Kevin Kline, Patti LuPone, William Hurt,** and **Christopher Reeve.** TLM

Actors' Equity Association Oldest of the major actors' **unions,** founded by 122 actors in 1913. After years of unscrupulous exploitation, working without a standard agreement or minimum wage, actors by 1895 began to combat these conditions, first with the Actors' Society. After the Society's dissolution in 1912, Actors' Equity, under the leadership of its first president, **Francis Wilson,** began to fight for support from other labor organizations in order to negotiate successfully a basic contract acceptable to all producers. In 1919, the Association of Actors and Artistes of America, formed and chartered by the American Federation of Labor that year, recognized Equity as the union representing actors in the theatre. A 30-day strike in August 1919 spread to eight cities, closed 37 plays, and prevented the opening of 16 others. Despite efforts by the **Producing Managers' Association** to negate Equity's effort with their own Actors' Fidelity Association, a five-year contract with Equity was signed by most producers. Over the next decade Equity gained a union shop agreement (1924), adopted provisions to protect actors in dealing with agents (1929), guaranteed members a minimum wage (1933), and established minimum rehearsal pay (1935). Today Equity has grown into a work force of over 39,000 actors and stage managers with headquarters in New York City and regional offices in Los Angeles, Chicago, and San Francisco. Though Equity has caused controversy with some rulings, the union has generally fought social injustice, making strong efforts for ethnic minorities, women, and performers with disabilities. In 1991 **Ron Silver** was elected its president. DBW

See: A. Harding, *The Revolt of the Actors,* New York, 1929.

Actors' Fund of America Founded in 1882 in response to the needs of aged actors and as a result of a campaign by **Harrison Grey Fiske** in his *New York Dramatic Mirror,* this charitable organization counted among its incorporators **Edwin Booth, Joseph Jefferson III, Lawrence Barrett, A. M. Palmer, P. T. Barnum,** and **Edward Harrigan,** with **Lester Wallack** its first president. Large gifts, beginning with $500 from Edwin Booth, and leg-

acies have assured the Fund's future, making it, as **Brooks Atkinson** noted, "scrupulous and merciful." A retirement home for many former troupers, first located on Staten Island and now in Englewood, NJ, was established in 1902. Ten presidents have led the Fund, including such theatrical notables as Palmer, **Daniel Frohman, Vinton Freedley,** and, until her death, Nedda Harrigan Logan, who took office in 1980. DBW

See: L. Simon, *The History of The Actors' Fund of America,* New York, 1972.

Actors Studio, The Founded in 1947 by **Group Theatre** alumni **Elia Kazan, Cheryl Crawford,** and **Robert Lewis,** the Actors Studio is a unique workshop for professional actors. It is not a school; it charges no tuition; and once an actor is accepted (by a rigorous audition process) he or she becomes a member for life, for the Studio's basic assumption is that there is no terminal degree for an actor. Under **Lee Strasberg,** who joined the Studio in 1949 and who from 1951 until his death in February 1982 was its strong-willed artistic director, the Studio became renowned as the high temple of the Method. The popular notion of the Studio as a place where the mumble, scratch, and slouch are tokens of integrity derives from films directed by Elia Kazan (*A Streetcar Named Desire,* 1951; *On the Waterfront,* 1954; *East of Eden,* 1955) which feature moody, verbally inarticulate, spectacularly neurotic performances by such Studio members as **Marlon Brando** and James Dean.

Those who admire the Studio's naturalistic style praise it for psychological revelation. Opponents attack the Studio as a place where self-indulgence, mannerism, and inaudibility are encouraged as actors examine their own emotions at the expense of the character or the play. Even Studio detractors, however, admit that the Method is a useful technique for the requirements of realistic film acting. The Studio's achievements continue to be hotly debated but its influence is undeniable; its Method has come to be identified as the quintessential American style. In 1963, after years of hesitation, the Studio formed its own short-lived theatre on Broadway; but its enduring legacy is the films directed by Kazan and the vibrant film performances of its many illustrious members, from Brando, Dean, and Montgomery Clift to **Dustin Hoffman, Robert de Niro, Al Pacino,** Shelley Winters, **Geraldine Page,** and Frank Corsaro, who is the Studio's present artistic director. FH

See: D. Garfield, *A Player's Place: The Story of The Actors Studio,* New York, 1980; F. Hirsch, *A Method to Their Madness: The History of the Actors Studio,* New York, 1984; S. Vineberg, *Method Actors: Three Generations of an American Acting Style,* New York, 1991.

Actors Theatre of Louisville One of the leading regional theatres, located in Louisville, KY, most noted for encouraging and producing original scripts. Richard Block and Ewel Cornett founded the Actors Theatre in 1964. Although successful, Block was replaced at his request in 1969 by **Jon Jory,** who had previously worked at the **Cleveland Play House** and had cofounded New Haven's **Long Wharf Theatre.**

Chekhov's *The Seagull* as staged at the Actors Theatre of Louisville as part of its 1989 "Classics in Context" series. Photo: David Talbott. Courtesy: Actors Theatre of Louisville.

Jory's appointment and leadership proved beneficial. By 1970–1, season tickets accounted for 95% of the house's capacity. In 1972 the company moved to their present location, the old Bank of Louisville Building. A $1.7 million conversion of the building resulted in the Pamela Brown Theatre (capacity 641) and the Victor Jory Theatre (capacity 160).

In 1977 the Actors Theatre achieved international acclaim by initiating the Humana Festival of New American Plays. Scripts such as *The Gin Game* and *Crimes of the Heart* premiered at the Actors Theatre, moved to Broadway, and won Pulitzer Prizes for Drama. Other new plays produced included *Extremities* and *Executive of Justice*. In 1986 ATL initiated the Classics in Context Festival, which presents works from world literature supported by films, lectures, and exhibits. The 20th Century Project and the Bingham Signature Shakespeare project are recent innovations.

Jory and the Actors Theatre have received numerous awards and prizes as a result of their work. In 1978 they received the **Margo Jones** Award for achievement in regional theatres; the next year the **Shubert** Foundation's James N. Vaughn Award for encouraging new scripts. In 1980 they received a special Antoinette Perry (Tony) Award.   SMA

Adams, Edwin (1834–77) Actor. He made his debut in Boston in 1853, and after almost a decade of acting in support of such stars as **Joseph Jefferson III** and **E. A. Sothern,** he had his first important New York engagement in 1863 with **Kate Bateman**'s company. During the Civil War, he established himself as a traveling star especially distinguished for his playing of romantic or light comedy characters in such vehicles as *The Lady of Lyons* and *Narcisse.* In 1869, **Edwin Booth** selected him to play Mercutio opposite his Romeo for the opening of **Booth's Theatre.** He was subse-

quently featured at Booth's Theatre in several roles, including the dual roles of Phidias and Raphael in *The Marble Heart* and most notably the title role in a dramatization of Tennyson's *Enoch Arden,* perhaps his favorite characterization. In 1876, following a starring tour of Australia, Adams returned to the U.S. gravely ill. He made his last appearance at the **California Theatre** in San Francisco on 27 May 1876.   DJW

Adams (Kiskadden), Maude (1872–1953) Actress, daughter of Salt Lake City star Annie Adams. At five Maude was starring as Little Schneider in *Fritz, Our German Cousin* in San Francisco. Her adult career began at 16 with a New York debut at the **Star Theatre** in *The Paymaster.* In 1890 she began an association with producer **Charles Frohman** that lasted until 1915. A box-office favorite until 1932 (despite an early retirement during 1918–31), she emerged in 1897 as a star, capitalizing on her eternal youthfulness and whimsey, as Lady Babbie in *The Little Minister,* a character rewritten for her by James Barrie. She also starred in U.S. productions of his *Quality Street* (1901), *Peter Pan* (1905), *What Every Woman Knows* (1908), *The Legend of Leonora* (1914), and *A Kiss for Cinderella* (1916). Other parts included Rostand's *L'Aiglon,* the strutting hero in his *Chantecler,* and **Shakespeare**'s Viola, Juliet, and Rosalind. In the 1920s she was a lighting consultant for General Electric. In 1931 she toured with **Otis Skinner** in *The Merchant of Venice.* During 1937–50 she taught theatre at Stephens College, Missouri.   DBW

See: A. Patterson, *Maude Adams: A Biography,* New York, 1907; P. Robbins, *Maude Adams: An Intimate Portrait,* New York, 1956.

Adding Machine, The by **Elmer Rice.** First directed by **Philip Moeller** for the **Theatre Guild,** this seminal American expressionistic play opened

19 March 1923 with **Dudley Digges** in the leading role. Although not a commercial success, the play influenced an ensuing wave of expressionistic drama. Like the German experiments that inspired it, Rice's play journeys through a series of stylized settings designed imaginatively by **Lee Simonson;** unlike European prototypes, this play has an antihero at its center. Mr. Zero is a bigoted, self-centered, fully Americanized, and stupid man who is nonetheless victimized by advancing technology and the big-business ethic. RHW

Ade, George (1866–1944) Playwright and librettist. Born and educated in Indiana, Ade made a name for himself as a reporter in Chicago before turning his talents to the theatre. His most popular librettos, *The Sultan of Sulu* (1902) and *The Sho-Gun* (1904), were influenced by **Gilbert and Sullivan,** but he is best remembered for two dramatic comedies of small-town life, *The **County Chairman*** (1903) and *The College Widow* (1904). The latter introduced the subject of collegiate adventures and the game of college football to the American stage. Because he had an outstanding ear for current slang and a keen eye for characterizing the everyday residents of his native mid-America, his more than a dozen plays and librettos, although seldom revived, illuminate the social record of the turn of the 20th century. LDC

Felix Adler, most famous of the grotesque white-faced clowns. Courtesy: Don B. Wilmeth.

Adler, Celia (1890–1979) Actress-daughter of actors **Jacob Adler** and Dina Stettin, raised by stepfather Sigmund Feinman, another actor. She began acting as a child and spent her life in **Yiddish theatre** in New York and on tour. Associated with intellectually ambitious troupes such as the **Yiddish Art Theatre,** she demonstrated qualities of sensitivity and emotional vulnerability. NS

Adler, Felix (1895–1960) The American **circus's** most famous grotesque white-face clown (in drag), recognized by his oversized red nose (which lit up), his grossly padded rear, exaggerated yellow shoes, minuscule hat, and tiny umbrella. In the tradition of **Dan Rice,** Adler worked with a piglet that he fed with a bottle. He was also one of the first great producing clowns, developing routines for the entire troupe of **Ringling** clowns. DBW

Adler, Jacob (1855–1926) **Yiddish** actor who began his career in theatre as a young man with a small company in Riga, Latvia, and by the 1880s became, in London and then New York, one of its stars. As actor and producer (especially at the Grand Theatre), he identified himself with serious emotional roles and with **Jacob Gordin's** *The Jewish King Lear* (1892). Also famous for love affairs, for most of his career he was married to Sara Adler and often costarred with her. Of their seven children, six became actors. Especially talented were **Celia,** famous on the Yiddish stage, and **Luther** and **Stella,** famous on the English-language stage. NS

See: L. Rosenfeld, *Bright Star of Exile: Jacob Adler and the Yiddish Theatre,* New York, 1977.

Adler, Luther (Lutha) (1903–84) New York–born actor and director whose 1908 Bowery stage debut began a 13-year apprenticeship in his father's **Yiddish theatre.** Adler's first Broadway role in *Humoresque* (1923) was followed by roles in *The Monkey Talks* (1925); *Money Business* (1926); *We Americans* (1926); *The Music Master* (1927); **Street Scene** (1929); and *Red Dust* (1929), among others. Joining the **Group Theatre** in 1932, Adler made important acting contributions including Don Fernando in *Night Over Taos* (1932); Sol Ginsberg in *Success Story* (1933); Julian Vardaman in *Alien Corn* (1933); and Moe Axelrod in **Awake and Sing!** (1935). His premiere role was Joe Bonapart in **Odets's** **Golden Boy** (1937). In later years Adler appeared in revivals and replaced stars **Paul Muni** (1946) and **Zero Mostel** (1965, **Fiddler on the Roof**). Director of *Angel Street* (1955), A **View from the Bridge** (1960), and a national tour of *Jane Eyre* (1943–4), Adler produced *A Flag Is Born* (1966). His last appearances included General St. Pé in *Waltz of the Toreadors* (1969) and Gregory Solomon in *The **Price*** (1970). GSA

Adler, Richard (1923–), composer; and **Jerry Ross** (Jerold) (1926–55), lyricist. Adler attended the University of North Carolina and served in the Navy before turning to composing; Ross appeared in Yiddish stage productions as a child, then attended New York University. Together, they first contributed songs to the revue **John Murray Anderson's Almanac** (1953). Their best-known work was for the musicals *The **Pajama Game*** (1954) and **Damn Yankees** (1955). Both shows had contemporary settings and benefited from **George Abbott**'s fast-paced direction and **Bob Fosse**'s choreography. The Adler–Ross songs were unpretentious, often humorous, pop tunes. After Ross's death Adler wrote for television and concert orchestras as well as contributing to the musical stage with shows such as *Kwamini* (1961) and *Music Is* (1976). He also produced, notably a 1973 revival of *The Pajama Game* with a multiracial cast, and the musical *Rex* (1976). Adler's memoirs, *You Gotta Have Heart* (with Lee Davis) appeared in 1990.   MK

Adler, Stella (1903–92) Actress and teacher. Daughter of the Yiddish actor-producer **Jacob Adler,** Stella grew up surrounded by great plays and bravura acting. Always interested in the technique of acting, she studied with **Richard Boleslavski** at the **American Laboratory Theatre** in the 1920s even after she had become an established performer. She joined the **Group Theatre** in 1931 because she believed in its founder, **Harold Clurman,** whom she married. A tall, statuesque blonde with imperial carriage and mid-Atlantic diction, Adler ironically had her greatest theatrical success playing downtrodden Depression-era housewives in the Group's productions of **Clifford Odets**'s *Awake and Sing!* (1935) and *Paradise Lost* (1935). Her last appearance on a New York stage was in 1945 in *He Who Gets Slapped,* but since 1949, when she founded the Stella Adler Conservatory, she had served the theatre as a teacher. Reminiscing about her famous acting family and her husband, recalling her experiences studying with Stanislavsky in Paris in 1934, rising from her thronelike chair to demonstrate an action, continuing to flay the memory of her archrival **Lee Strasberg,** issuing threats and portents, and regaling students with advice about life as well as art, Adler was a witty, exhilarating teacher. Countering Strasberg's Method with its focus on self, she urged students to transcend their own experiences by developing their imaginations and by investigating the play's circumstances rather than their own.   FH

See: S. Adler, *The Technique of Acting,* New York, 1988.

Adonis, a two-act musical burlesque by William Gill. Opened 4 September 1884 at the Bijou Theatre, New York, running 603 performances. This self-described "respectful perversion" of the Pygmalion myth, which borrowed existing melodies from sources as diverse as Beethoven and David Braham, sees a statue of Adonis (**Henry E. Dixey**) brought to life, pursued by women, reduced to disguises, and finally electing to return to stone. The longest-running hit of its day, it made a matinee idol of Dixey, who revived it throughout his career.   JD

African-American theatre African-American theatre had a dual origin. First came the indigenous theatre consisting of folktales, songs, music, dance, and mimicry that blacks performed in cabins, at camp meetings, and in open parks like Congo Square in New Orleans. African in spirit, these

Henry Dixey as the statue brought to life in *Adonis*. Courtesy: Don B. Wilmeth.

expressions were transformed by the American environment [see **ethnic theatre**]. Then came the **African Theatre** in imitation of white playhouses and scripted dramas that **William Henry Brown** established in 1821. Though Brown began with **Shakespeare,** he also staged a sketch on slavery and his own play *The Drama of King Shotaway* (1823). His theatre produced two notable Shakespearean actors in **James Hewlett** and **Ira Aldridge.**

The African Theatre had no successors in antebellum America except for two plays written by the ex-slave **William Wells Brown** and read by him on abolitionist platforms. One, *The Escape; or, A Leap for Freedom* (1858), survives. Black indigenous expressions, however, were by the 1840s adopted by white comedians and fashioned into blackface minstrelsy that caricatured blacks on Southern plantations. Ironically, the now-disdained **minstrel show** opened the professional stage to African-Americans. Billed as authentic Negroes, black minstrels inherited the burnt-cork stereotype characters created by whites and gave them validity. At the same time, black performers were polishing acting skills in short farces that were added to their shows. Ernest Hogan, **Billy Kersands,** and **Sam Lucas** were three leading black minstrels, while noteworthy black troupes included Charles B. Hicks's Georgia Minstrels (1865), Callender's Original Georgia Minstrels (1872), and Haverly's Colored Minstrels (1878). Since black playgoers were segregated in an upper gallery section in most theatres, these shows played primarily to white audiences; yet their success ensured perpetuation of the genre into the first decades of the 20th century.

Vying for popularity with the minstrels were ubiquitous "Tom shows" based on the dramatization of *Uncle Tom's Cabin* (1852). Despite the novel's intent to eradicate slavery, stage versions seen throughout the land for 80 years reinforced the theatrical image of blacks as ignorant, submissive, happy-go-lucky creatures. Tom shows also began to employ blacks as slave characters and in plantation choruses, but eventually the play was denounced by black leaders.

Black companies of higher caliber emerged after the Civil War. Anna and Emma Hyers, classically trained prodigies from Sacramento, CA, toured the country in *opéra bouffe* and original musicals such as *Out of Bondage* (1877). The Astor Place Company of Colored Tragedians under **J. A. Arneaux** came into being in 1884 with a Shakespearean repertoire, and in 1889 Theodore Drury gave the first performance of his Opera Company. Professional concert artists and solo readers like **Henrietta Vinton Davis** appeared across the country.

In the popular theatre a shift in the minstrel pattern occurred with white-produced shows. Sam Jack's *Creole Show* (1891–7) introduced women in the lineup and as a dancing chorus. John W. Isham added a story line to olio specialities in *The Octoroons* (1895) and operatic selections for the finale of *Oriental America* (1896). This last production prepared Broadway for the invasion of original black musicals such as *A Trip to Coontown* (1898) by the multitalented **Bob Cole** and Billy Johnson, and *In Dahomey* (1902) by **Bert Williams** and George Walker. Teamed with these star performers were the composer Will Marion Cook, who wrote the operetta *Clorindy; or, The Origin of the Cake Walk* (1898), the playwright Jesse Shipp, and the versatile brothers James W. and **J. Rosamond Johnson.**

Also prominent at this time were long-lasting road companies in vaudeville, notably Sissieretta Jones's Black Patti Troubadours and Gus Hill's The Smart Set, which was later acquired by brothers Salem Tutt Whitney and J. Homer Tutt.

In straight drama, William Edgar Easton wrote two historical plays on the Haitian revolution: *Dessalines* (1893) and *Christophe* (1911), which were produced by Henrietta Vinton Davis. Scott Joplin composed his opera *Treemonisha* (1911), but it remained unproduced for decades. In 1897 Bob Cole organized a stock company and training school at Worth's Museum in New York. Others followed, urged on by black critics Sylvester Russell of the *Freeman* (Indianapolis) and Lester Walton of the New York *Age,* who felt that resident companies in African-American theatres would encourage dramatic plays, provide regular employment to black actors, and permit open seating. In 1906 Robert Motts of Chicago started the Pekin Stock Company, whose success spawned other Pekins in Cincinnati, OH, and Savannah, GA. In New York the Negro Players were formed in 1912, and the **Lafayette Players** in 1915. Some of these companies staged original musicals and dramas; others contented themselves with popular Broadway revivals.

Blacks first appeared on Broadway in dramatic roles in *Three Plays for a Negro Theatre* (1917) by the white writer Ridgely Torrence. This auspicious start, cut short by America's imminent entry into WW I, was confirmed by **Charles Gilpin**'s stunning performance for the **Provincetown Players** in *The Emperor Jones* (1920). However, the commercial success of *Shuffle Along* (1921) brought a resurgence of black musicals that stirred critics to rail against the pervasive image of black song-and-dance clowns on the professional stage. W. E. B. Du Bois, editor of *The Crisis,* urged formation of a nationwide movement of little theatres presenting plays "about us, by us, for us, and near us." His magazine and *Opportunity* sponsored playwriting competitions and published prizewinning entries. W. Richardson's one-act *The Chip Woman's Fortune* (1923) was the earliest nonmusical black play seen on Broadway. In the years ahead, black college drama professors like **Randolph Edmonds, Owen Dodson,** and **Thomas D. Pawley** would begin writing and directing original plays with their students.

Three dramas by white playwrights demonstrated the reach of black histrionic talent. **Paul Green**'s *In Abraham's Bosom* (1926) shared Pulitzer Prize honors with an experienced cast including the gifted **Rose McClendon; Dorothy and Dubose Heyward**'s 1927 hit *Porgy* inspired the operatic version by **George Gershwin** (*Porgy and Bess*); and **Marc Connelly**'s *The Green Pastures* (1930) with De Lawd magnificently played by **Richard B. Harrison** earned a Pulitzer Prize and a five-year run. The 1930s witnessed an upsurge of socially relevant plays like Hall Johnson's *Run Little Chillun* (1933), **Langston Hughes**'s *Mulatto* (1935), and *Stevedore* (1934) by white authors Paul Peters and George Sklar. The short-lived **Federal Theatre Project,** through its Negro Units in 22 cities, sponsored black playwrights and productions including Theodore Browne's *Natural Man* (1937) in Seattle, Theodore Ward's *Big White Fog* (1938) in Chicago, and **Orson Welles**'s production of the "voodoo" *Macbeth* (1936) in Harlem.

In the 1940s the American Negro Theatre made steady progress in training and production at its Harlem-based Library Theatre until its successful *Anna Lucasta* (1944) transferred to Broadway and caused the breakup of the company. **Richard Wright**'s *Native Son* (1941), imaginatively staged by Orson Welles, revealed the driving, versatile talent of **Canada Lee** as Bigger Thomas, and Theodore Ward's *Our Lan'* (1946), a moving historical drama about newly freed slaves seeking a homestead, showed well **Off-Broadway** but lost its appeal when altered for a bigger house. **Paul Robeson**'s record-breaking *Othello* (1943) belongs to this decade.

After WW II the civil rights movement gained momentum. Plays such as Louis Peterson's *Take a Giant Step* (1953) on Broadway, William Branch's *In Splendid Error* (1954), **Alice Childress**'s *Trouble in Mind* (1955), and **Loften Mitchell**'s *A Land Beyond the River* (1957) at the Greenwich Mews Theatre Off-Broadway dealt unambiguously with the racial problem and used racially mixed casts. Companies like **Joseph Papp**'s **New York Shakespeare Festival** began to cast black actors in traditionally white roles. The trend toward integration was reflected in **Lorraine Hansberry**'s award-winning drama *A Raisin in the Sun* (1959) and **Ossie Davis**'s satiric comedy *Purlie Victorious* (1961). Nevertheless, the slow pace of social reform, coupled with a controversial Vietnam War, triggered unrest on college campuses and in black urban communities. African-American theatre revealed this frustration in a series of revolutionary dramas led by **Amiri Baraka**'s *Dutchman* (1964). As government and foundation funds were hurriedly released to ameliorate conditions in inner cities, black theatres mushroomed nationwide, generating a crop of new playwrights and productions and opening opportunities for directors, designers, and technicians. The search for a black identity led to experimentation with new dramatic forms. In 1969 **Lonnie Elder**'s *Ceremonies in Dark Old Men* just missed and **Charles Gordone**'s *No Place to Be Somebody* captured the Pulitzer Prize. Other significant playwrights of the period were **Ed Bullins,** Phillip Hayes Dean, **Adrienne Kennedy, Ron Milner,** Charlie Russell, Joseph Walker, and Richard Wesley.

Among the few theatre groups to survive when funding was withdrawn were the **Negro Ensemble Company** of New York and the Inner City Cultural Center in Los Angeles. African-American theatre had gained immeasurably from this period of upheaval but had made little headway in the Broadway commercial theatre, which responded by staging a number of extravagant revivals and adaptations of white musicals with black casts, such as *Hello, Dolly!* (1967), *The Wiz* (1975), and *Timbuktu!* (1978). Only *The Great White Hope* (1968) by white playwright Howard Sackler, with a bravura performance by **James Earl Jones** as prizefighter Jack Jefferson, merits attention. Both Sackler and Jones received top awards for their work. Important black productions of the 1970s and early '80s include **Ntozake Shange**'s *For Colored Girls . . .* (1976), **Vinnette Carroll**'s *Your Arms Too Short to Box with God* (1976), Phillip Hayes Dean's monodrama *Paul Robeson* (1978), and **Charles Fuller**'s Pulitzer Prize–winning *A Soldier's Play* (1981). The most important voice to emerge in the 1980s was that of **August Wilson,** who, in close collaboration with director **Lloyd Richards,** has written and staged a series of plays chronicling black life in the decades of the 20th century. Five plays have so far been produced, with two of them, *Fences* (1983) and *The Piano Lesson* (Broadway, 1990), winning Pulitzer Prizes.   EGH

> See: E. Hill, ed., *The Theatre of Black Americans,* 1980, reprinted, New York, 1987; L. Mitchell, *Black Drama: The Story of the American Negro in the Theatre,* New York, 1967; C. W. and B. J. Molette, *Black Theatre: Premise and Presentation,* Bristol, IN, 1986; L. C. Sanders, *The Development of Black Theater in America: From Shadows to Selves,* Baton Rouge, LA, 1988; A. Woll, *Black Musical Theatre from Coontown to Dreamgirls,* Baton Rouge, LA, 1989. See additional sources in the bibliography at the end of the *Guide.*

African Theatre The first African-American company was founded on 21 September 1821 by **William Henry Brown** at his **African Grove** apartments located behind City Hospital, lower Broadway. The company opened with a cut version of *Richard III.* In the succeeding two years it moved to two locations on Mercer Street before being forced to disband by the police. In its repertoire was Brown's *The Drama of King Shotoway,* the earliest known play by a black writer, which dealt with the insurrection of the Caribs of St. Vincent. From this company came the internationally acclaimed actor **Ira Aldridge.**   EGH

African Grove A pleasure garden (c. 1816–23) situated on Thomas Street, lower Broadway. It served the black population of the area with ice cream, tea, ale, wine, and evening entertainment after the fashion of Vauxhall and **Chatham** gardens, which did not admit blacks. It was started by **William Henry Brown,** who went on to establish the **African Theatre** (1821) with actors drawn from performers at the garden. This was the first African-American theatre company of record.   EGH

After the Fall by **Arthur Miller** opened 23 January 1964 at the ANTA-Washington Square Theatre in New York. Directed by **Elia Kazan,** the **Lincoln Center** Repertory Company cast included **Jason Robards, Jr.,** as Quentin, the tortured lawyer who comes to terms with the evil of his own nature during the course of this memory play; Barbara Loden as his second wife Maggie, a character based on Miller's own second wife Marilyn Monroe; Patricia Roe as Quentin's first wife Louise; and **Hal Holbrook,** Zohra Lampert, Salome Jens, Paul Mann, Faye Dunaway, Ralph Meeker, **David Wayne,** and Barry Primus. It ran for 59 performances. A successful revival and its London premiere occurred at Britain's National Theatre in 1990.   BCM

Agents The gradual demise of the **stock company** resident in its own theatre late in the 19th century gave rise not only to the commercialization of American theatrical production in the guise of the "combination system," but also to the emergence of brokers who eventually formed agencies to furnish actors, designers, stagehands, and other necessary personnel to independent managers and producers. Their services frequently included booking touring shows as well as New York productions. Theatre managers from around the country went to them every summer to secure stars and attractions for their seasons.

The first dramatic agency was probably founded in 1859 in New York, but others followed in Chicago and major theatrical centers. The most important agency to emerge was the H. S. Taylor Theatre Booking Agency in New York, which was sold in 1888 to **Klaw** and **Erlanger** and became their base for organizing the Theatrical **Syndicate** eight years later.

Reaction to the Syndicate led to the formation of independent agencies to handle performers and specialty acts; surviving its monopoly, these agencies became and remained a force in the 20th century. The most enduring has been the William Morris Agency founded by Viennese-born William Morris, who entered show business as an assistant to a leading agent of foreign vaudeville acts in America. Morris formed his own agency c. 1900, eventually building his roster to include **Al Jolson, Eddie Cantor, Will Rogers,** Charlie Chaplin, and many others, charging 10% of clients' earnings. The William Morris Agency, still in existence, no longer dominates the field and has competition from several large agencies (notably International Creative Management) and many independents.

Press agents are the descendants of the 19th-century "advance men" of touring "duplicate" companies that emanated mainly from New York. As employees of managers (producers), they arrived in each town on the itinerary usually a day before the show, provided information and lithographs (later photographs) to local newspapers, posted bills, distributed free tickets for favors given, checked on box-office procedures, and arranged for the company's stay in town. Many came from the ranks of journalists, and a sizable number graduated into the ranks of producers and general managers. After several decades of wrangling over working conditions and division of labors, press agents became independent and combined with company and house managers to form the Association of Theatrical Press Agents and Managers (ATPAM) in 1938. Although their function remains historically the same – to create as much publicity (preferably free) for the show for a fee – they no longer handle any business details.   MCH

Ah, Wilderness! Eugene O'Neill's lone comedy which opened on 2 October 1933 proved to be enduring and revivable especially in university and community theatres. **Philip Moeller** directed and **Robert Edmond Jones** designed the long-running **Theatre Guild** production, which starred **George M. Cohan** (making a rare appearance in another's play) and Elisha Cook in the leading role of young Richard. Celebrating coming to terms with adolescent urges, the comedy is a surprisingly nostalgic and sentimental look at the years of O'Neill's youth. Apparently, the playwright was pining wistfully for the gentle childhood and supportive family life he never experienced.   RHW

Ahmanson Theatre see **Center Theatre Group**

AIDS in the American theatre An ever-growing menace through the 1980s, the scourge of AIDS (acquired immune deficiency syndrome) had personally affected virtually everyone active in the American theatre by 1990. The deaths of leading artists such as Broadway choreographer **Michael Bennett** and writer-director-performer **Charles Ludlam** alter the course of theatre history; so does the loss of many artists who do not live long enough to attain fame. Producers and playwrights across the country confront fear, rage, and grief – their own and that of their communities – through their work. They are driven to commemorate lost colleagues and take a stand against the homophobia in their society. The result is not only an ever-growing body of "AIDS plays," but also a much wider range of work darkened by the shadow of the disease.

AIDS is now woven into the fabric of every kind of theatre, from Broadway comedies (**Richard Greenberg**'s *Eastern Standard,* **Wendy Wasserstein**'s *The Heidi Chronicles*) to the performance art of **Karen Finley** and **Spalding Gray.** It is an unspoken presence in **Craig Lucas**'s *Prelude to a Kiss,* the story of a young lover whose beautiful wife comes to inhabit the body of a dying man.

Plays that deal directly with AIDS are almost always personal responses to devastation. *The Normal Heart,* a barely fictionalized account of an activist's struggles, dramatizes the ferocious will of Larry Kramer, its author. William M. Hoffman wrote *As Is* – which, like the Kramer play, opened in New York in 1985 – as a way of coping with the death of friends. Harry Kondoleon has made public the autobiographical ground of *Zero Positive,* which depicts the moment when the main character learns he carries the virus that causes AIDS.

Noted American playwrights **Lanford Wilson, Harvey Fierstein, Christopher Durang, Terrence McNally,** and **A. R. Gurney** have also dealt explicitly with the epidemic. In the early 1990s major AIDS plays include Cheryl West's *Before It Hits Home,* which shows the disease at work in the black community; Paula Vogel's poetic tribute to her dead brother, *The Baltimore Waltz;* Tony Kushner's epic *Angels in America;* and Scott McPherson's metaphorically oriented play *Marvin's Room,* in which illness and dying are dealt with in universal terms, never mentioning AIDS. MEO

See: M. E. Osborn, ed., *The Way We Live Now: American Plays and the AIDS Crisis,* New York, 1990.

Aiken, George L. (1830–76) Playwright. Aiken is known for one play: *Uncle Tom's Cabin; or, Life Among the Lowly,* a dramatization of Mrs. Stowe's novel, presented at Troy, NY, on 27 September 1852, with Aiken in the part of George Harris. In response to audience demand for more episodes from the novel, Aiken prepared a sequel, *The Death of Uncle Tom; or, the Religion of the Lowly,* and in mid-November combined the two plays into one drama of six acts, now the standard version.

G. C. Howard [see **Howard family**], manager of the company and Aiken's cousin, rewarded the 22-year-old actor-playwright with a bonus of forty dollars and a gold watch for the "week of extra work" required to devise a role (Eva) for his four-year-old daughter Cordelia.   RM

Ain't Supposed to Die a Natural Death With book, music, and lyrics by the multitalented Melvin Van Peebles, this two-act 1971 musical, depicting the seamier side of black life in an urban ghetto during the troublesome 1960s, ran for 325 performances on Broadway. It captured several awards, including Drama Desk Awards to the author and to the director **Gilbert Moses,** a Tony Award to actress Minnie Gentry, and a Grammy Award for its recorded music.   EGH

Akalaitis, JoAnne (1937–) American actress, director, and founding member of the avant-garde group **Mabou Mines.** Her experimental works have been performed at major art centers and festivals throughout the U.S. and Europe, including the New York **Public Theater,** The Kitchen (NYC), the Walker Art Center (Minneapolis), the

Mark Taper (Los Angeles), Théâtre St. Denis (France), Teatro Goldoni (Italy), and the National Galerie (Berlin). During 1983–4 she directed a controversial production of Beckett's *Endgame* with music by her former husband Philip Glass at the American Repertory Theatre. A champion of German writer Franz Xaver Kroetz, she has directed a number of his plays, including productions in 1984 and 1990 of *Through the Leaves*. Other recent productions include *Green Card* (Joyce, 1988), *The Screens* (Guthrie, 1989), and, at the Public Theater, *Cymbeline* (1989), *Henry IV, Parts l and 2* (1991), and *'Tis Pity She's a Whore* (1992). In 1990 Akalaitis was named artistic director of the **New York Shakespeare Festival;** in 1991 she assumed control of day-to-day operations. DBW

Akins, Zoë (1886–1958) Prolific playwright, scenarist, and adapter of French and Hungarian plays, began her career with an experimental *vers libre* drama, *The Magical City* (1916). Her early sophisticated comedies and wistful tragedies about worldly and slightly jaded women were followed by a rash of typical popular comedies. Her first and best hit was *Déclassée* (1919). Others which had either critical or popular success were *Papa* (1919), *Greatness: A Comedy* (1921; also called *The Texas Nightingale*), *Daddy's Gone A-Hunting* (1921), and *The Greeks Had a Word for It* (1929; later filmed as *The Golddiggers*). In 1935, in a controversial decision, Akins received the Pulitzer Prize for her adaptation of Edna Ferber's *The Old Maid.* Her successful screenplays include *Morning Glory* (1932) and *Camille* (1937). FB

See: R. Mielech, "The Plays of Z. A. Rumbold," Unpub. diss., Ohio State U, 1974.

Albee, Edward (1928–) American playwright. Albee made a spectacular debut with four one-act plays in an absurdist style (*The Zoo Story,* written 1958; *The Death of Bessie Smith,* 1959; *The Sandbox,* 1959; and *The American Dream,* 1960), and capped his reputation with the Broadway productions of *Who's Afraid of Virginia Woolf?* (1962) and an audacious and belligerent metaphysical mystery, *Tiny Alice* (1964). He was greeted as the leader of a new theatrical movement, and his name was linked with those of **Tennessee Williams, Arthur Miller,** and **William Inge** as a major American playwright. Refusing, however, to capitalize on the qualities that made *Virginia Woolf* so powerful – the lacerating wit and incendiary character conflict – Albee has pursued an increasingly rarefied style, one that is emotionally and sexually evasive and that often forsakes dramatic impact for mandarin elegance. Despite critical and commercial defeats, Albee has continued to write prolifically in three forms: adaptations (**Carson McCullers**'s *Ballad of the Sad Café* [1963], **James Purdy**'s *Malcolm* [1965], Giles Cooper's *Everything in the Garden* [1967], and Nabokov's *Lolita* [1980]); short chamber plays that are musical in their repetitions and juxtapositions of image and motif (*Box and Quotations from Mao-Tse Tung,* 1968; *Listening,* 1975, and *Counting the Ways,* 1976); and full-length plays in which ordered lives are invaded and transformed. His settings may appear realistic, but Albee is at heart a fabulist; like the imaginary child in *Virginia Woolf,* surreal surprises hover over most of his work. In his wisest play, *A Delicate Balance* (awarded the Pulitzer Prize in 1966), Harry and Edna carry a mysterious psychic plague into their best friends' living room. The title character in *The Lady from Dubuque* (1979) is an angel of death. Talking sea creatures emerge from the water to confront sedate picnickers in *Seascape* (which won the Pulitzer Prize in 1975).

Albee's mainstream reputation is now at a low ebb. His last Broadway production (in 1983), *The Man Who Had Three Arms,* was decimated by the critics; recent plays, such as *Marriage Play* (1987), which did not have a U.S. premiere until 1992 in his own staging (coproduced by the **Alley** and the **McCarter Theatre**), and *Three Tall Women* (1991) premiered out of New York, several at the English Theater in Vienna. In the long run, however, Albee will surely reclaim his place as an important stylist, a writer of wit and sensibility. FH

See: C. Green, *Edward Albee: An Annotated Bibliography,* New York, 1980; A. Paolucci, *From Tension to Tonic: The Plays of Edward Albee,* Carbondale, IL, 1972.

Albee, Edward F[ranklin] (1857–1930) **Vaudeville** producer and executive. The great-grandson of one of the original Minute Men, Albee, born in Maine, left home in 1876 to join a circus, serving first as common roustabout and later as ticket seller. In 1885 Albee joined **B. F. Keith** in **Boston,** where Keith had opened a dime museum in a vacant store in 1883. With business poor, Albee supposedly suggested the exploitation of light opera at variety theatre prices, leading to a pirated, condensed version of **Gilbert and Sullivan**'s *The Mikado* presented five times a day with the slogan "Cleanliness, Courtesy and Comfort," Keith and Albee quickly built a vaudeville empire, with Albee largely responsible for planning the theatre structures that formed the Keith circuit. In 1900 they founded the Vaudeville Managers' Protective Association, followed in 1906 with the **United Booking Office,** both designed virtually to monopolize first-class vaudeville. After Keith's death in 1914 and his son's in 1918, Albee controlled the Keith Circuit, asserting power over his performers with his own in-house union, the National Vaudeville Artists (1916). The Keith circuit, dominating Eastern vaudeville, merged with other circuits in 1927 to form the Keith–Albee Orpheum Corporation, controlling 700 theatres in the U.S. and Canada and booking some 15,000 performers. Less a showman than a builder, Albee continued the policy of clean, family fare after his partner's death, eschewing coarseness and enforcing his standards with fines and blacklisting. Groucho Marx (see **Marx Bros.**) opined that "Albee was the owner of a large cotton plantation and the actors were his slaves." A year before his death, Albee's empire was subsumed by RKO (the Radio–Keith–Orpheum Corporation) led by Joseph P. Kennedy. DBW

See: R. Snyder, *The Voice of the City: Vaudeville and Popular Culture in New York,* New York, 1989.

Costume design by Theoni V. Aldredge for the final scene of *A Chorus Line*. Courtesy: Theoni V. Aldredge.

Albertson, Jack (1910–81) Character actor, vaudeville song-and-dance man, and straight man to such comics as **Phil Silvers,** Milton Berle, and **Bert Lahr.** His first stage success, as replacement for **Eddie Foy,** was in a Broadway revival of *The Red Mill* (1946). He first gained serious notice in a West Coast production of *Waiting for Godot* (1957). Subsequently he won a Tony (and later an Academy Award) as the father in *The Subject Was Roses* (1964), played with "a fine mixture of truculence and self-pity," wrote critic Howard Taubman. Albertson's last stage appearance, on Broadway in 1972, was as the irascible former vaudevillian, Willie Clark, in *The Sunshine Boys.* Though a frequent film actor, his final major credit was in the TV series "Chico and the Man" (1974–6).   DBW

Alcazar Theatre Name of four different **San Francisco** playhouses:
1. A distinctive Moorish structure erected in 1885 on O'Farrell St. as a lecture/music hall, but that soon housed a popular resident stock company (including young **Maude Adams**) under the able management of Fred **Belasco** (brother of David). This theatre perished in the 1906 earthquake.
2. Rebuilt New Alcazar on Sutter St., operating under that name from 1907 to 1911.
3. In 1912 a third was built on O'Farrell, offering a wide range of productions (housed local **Federal Theatre** unit in 1936–7). It was known as the Alcazar up to 1939, then again from 1952 until its demolition in 1961.
4. Last Alcazar opened in 1976, in an old Geary St. hotel; it was torn down in 1982 despite community efforts to save it.   MB

Aldredge, Theoni V. (1932–) Greek-born costume designer. Aldredge studied and then worked at the **Goodman Theatre** in Chicago before coming to New York in 1958. From 1962 onward she was a principal designer for the **New York Shakespeare Festival.** From the mid-1970s she had been part of the collaborative team – **Michael Bennett, Robin Wagner,** and **Tharon Musser** – that produced *A Chorus Line* and *Dreamgirls,* among others. Aldredge designed landmark productions such as *Who's Afraid of Virginia Woolf?* and *Hair* (prior to Broadway), and also designs for ballet, opera, television, and film, including *Network* and *The Great Gatsby.* She is an excellent collaborative artist, and her designs are integrated with and supportive of the direction and overall visual statement of a production. Costumes for the elegant but troubled and short-lived musical *Nick & Nora* (1991) were designed by her.   AA

Aldrich, Louis see *My Partner*

Aldrich, Richard Stoddard (1902–86) Producer. Born in Boston and educated at Harvard (1925), Aldrich learned his trade as business manager of the Jitney Players (1923, 1924, 1927) and general manager of **Richard Boleslavski**'s **American Laboratory Theatre** (1926–8) before beginning producing on Broadway (1930). His more than 35 Broadway plays included a revival of Shaw's *Pygmalion* (1945) starring his second wife, **Gertrude Lawrence;** *Caesar and Cleopatra* (1949) with Sir Cedric Hardwicke and Lilli Palmer; and *Goodbye, My Fancy* (1948) and *The Moon Is Blue* (1951), which ran for 226 and 924 performances, respectively. Aldrich also presented the Old Vic at the **Century Theatre** (1946), the Habimah Players from Tel Aviv, and the Dublin Gate Theatre company (1948). He was a successful **summer stock** theatre producer, operating four theatres and packaging shows for the strawhat circuit.   TLM

Aldridge, Ira (1807–67) African-American actor who, starting with the **African Theatre** in New

Ira Aldridge as Mungo, the slave of a West Indian planter, in Isaac Bickerstaffe's *The Padlock,* written in 1768 and first performed by Aldridge in the 1820s. Courtesy: Don B. Wilmeth.

York, moved to England at the age of 17, and became a touring provincial actor in Britain and Ireland for over 25 years. In 1833 he replaced the mortally ill Edmund Kean as Othello at London's Covent Garden Theatre to a mixed press, and in 1852 began a series of highly successful appearances in Europe and Russia, receiving several decorations from heads of state. His return to London's West End in 1865 was widely praised. Aldridge played over 40 roles, black and white, many of them Shakespearean. Equally brilliant in tragedy and comedy, he often performed Othello and Mungo (in Bickerstaffe's comic operetta *The Padlock*) on the same bill. He introduced psychological realism in acting in the 1850s well before his European counterparts. He died while on an engagement in Lódz, Poland, in 1867.   EGH

See: H. Marshall and M. Stock, *Ira Aldridge, The Negro Tragedian,* London, 1958, new ed., 1968; H. Marshall, *Further Research on Ira Aldridge,* Carbondale, IL, 197?.

Alexander (née Quigley), Jane (1939–)
Actress who gained stardom as the white mistress of the black boxing champion in *The Great White Hope* (1968), a role she first created at the **Arena Stage** in Washington, DC. A New Englander dedicated to regional theatre, to which she returns

frequently, she was critically acclaimed as Lavinia in *Mourning Becomes Electra* at the **American Shakespeare Festival** Theatre in 1971 and at the Eisenhower in Washington, DC, and the Huntington Hartford in Los Angeles in 1972. Other New York theatre appearances include *Six Rms Riv Vu* (1972), *First Monday in October* (1978), **William Gibson**'s *Monday After the Miracle* (1982), *Shadowlands* (1990), and *The Visit* (1992), the last directed by her second husband, **Edwin Sherin.**   DBW

Alison's House Suggested by the life of Emily Dickinson, **Susan Glaspell**'s three-act realistic drama studies the family of a famous poet 18 years after her death as the survivors wrestle with problems of familial responsibility and an artist's position in society. **Eva Le Gallienne** created the errant niece in the **Civic Repertory Theatre** production, which opened 1 December 1930 and moved uptown to the Ritz [see **Walter Kerr Theatre**] in May after winning a Pulitzer Prize. More conventional than Glaspell's earlier work, the play is self-consciously literary, but achieves an eerie sense of timelessness within its turn-of-the-century setting.   KF

Allen, Fred (né John Florence Sullivan)
(1894–1956) Comedian and humorist, remembered for his radio appearances, his stinging observations of American life, and his pronounced nasal intonation. Allen began his career as a comic vaudeville juggler (1911), appearing under several names. After touring Australia/New Zealand, he gained praise as Fred Allen from *Variety* for "probably the brightest talk ever heard on a vaudeville stage," headlining at The **Palace.** He chronicled this phase of his career in *Much Ado About Me* (1956). Prior to beginning his radio career (1932), his dour appearance and stand-up patter were featured in musical **revue**s including *The Passing Show of 1922, The Greenwich Village Follies,* and *Three's a Crowd* (1930).   DBW

See: R. Taylor, *Fred Allen: His Life & Wit,* Boston, 1989.

Allen, Gracie see Burns, George

Allen, Jay Presson (née Jacqueline Presson) (1922–)
Writer and producer. Known for adaptations, Allen wrote *The Prime of Miss Jean Brodie* (stage, 1966; screen, 1969), *Forty Carats* (1968), *Tru* (1989), and *The Big Love* (1991), which she directed. Allen wrote screenplays for ***Cabaret*** (1972) and ***Deathtrap*** (1982), producing the latter and "Family" (TV, 1976–80).   REK

Allen, Viola (1869–1948)
Actress who made her stage debut in *Esmeralda* in New York in 1882. In 1884 **John McCullough** engaged her to play his daughter in *Virginius,* then made her his leading lady. In subsequent seasons she played opposite W. E. Sheridan, the Italian Tommaso Salvini, and **Joseph Jefferson.** For four years she was leading lady in **Charles Frohman**'s Empire Stock Company. An intelligent and appealing actress, sometimes thought to be overtechnical, she was, until her retirement in 1918, a popular touring star,

highly regarded for such portrayals as Viola, the double roles of Hermione and Perdita, and Dolores (*In the Palace of the King*).   FHL

Allen, Woody (né Allen Stewart Konigsberg) (1935–)

Actor, playwright, and director who since 1970 has devoted his considerable talent to screenwriting and film direction. His play *Don't Drink the Water* debuted on Broadway in 1966 at the **Morosco Theatre;** it was followed in 1969 by *Play It Again, Sam* (**Broadhurst**), in which he also played the role of Allan Felix, and in 1981 by *The Floating Light Bulb* (**Lincoln Center**).   DBW

> See: E. Lax, *Woody Allen: A Biography,* New York, 1991.

Alley Theatre, The

Established as an amateur organization in Houston, TX, by Mr. and Mrs. Robert Altfeld and Nina Vance, who became artistic head, the theatre began production in November 1947 in a rented 87-seat dance studio, the name inspired by a narrow alleyway that led to the studio. Its second home, an attic-fan manufacturing plant converted to a 231-seat arena theatre, opened on 8 February 1949 with a production of *The Children's Hour* utilizing professional actors. In 1954 the theatre became fully professional. The current building, which opened in November 1968, was named after Nina Vance following her death in 1980. Pat Brown, an actress-director appointed artistic head in 1981, attempted to fill the two theatres in the complex (one seating 824 and another arena-style holding 296) with more adventurous and experimental fare than its previous conservative offerings. Under Brown, a landmark exchange in June 1983 with the Stephen Joseph Theatre in Scarborough, England, was initiated; in July 1985 they presented Alan Ayckbourn's *Season's Greetings* at New York's Joyce Theatre. After Brown's departure in 1988, Gregory Boyd became artistic director in 1989.   DBW

All God's Chillun Got Wings

by **Eugene O'Neill.** In a controversial production directed by **James Light** for Experimental Theatre, Incorporated, at the Provincetown Playhouse, this bitter but sympathetic drama of miscegenation was threatened by the authorities before premiering on 15 May 1924. Centering on the sad marriage of a black man struggling for dignity and a white woman who ultimately falls into madness, this domestic tragedy brought **Paul Robeson** to national attention and featured Mary Blair as the frail wife who cannot cope with ostracism and denigration. Much furor was vented and ink spilt over whether Robeson actually kissed Blair's white hand.   RHW

Alliance of Resident Theatres/New York (ART/New York)

131 Varick Street, Room 904, NYC 10013. Incorporated in 1972 for the purpose of promoting artistic growth and excellence in the New York City nonprofit theatre by providing services and advocacy for this community, ART/New York has over 100 theatre and associate members. In addition to numerous management, real estate, intern, and marketing projects and services, ART has evolved a "City Advocacy Plan" and provides numerous publications, including *Theatre Times,* a trade newspaper devoted to the New York nonprofit theatre.   DBW

Alliance Theatre Company

The largest resident professional theatre in the southeast, the Alliance Resident Theatre began in 1968 as a division of the Atlanta (Georgia) Arts Alliance, an organization that included the Atlanta Opera and the Atlanta Ballet. In 1970 it adopted its present name. Currently operating on a six-million-dollar annual budget with 22,000 subscribers, the Alliance has its home (two theatres: an 826-seat proscenium house; a 200-seat flexible space) in the Robert W. Woodruff Arts Center.   LAB

All My Sons

by **Arthur Miller** opened on 29 January 1947 at the Coronet Theatre in New York, directed by **Elia Kazan,** with a cast including Ed Begley, Beth Merrill, **Arthur Kennedy,** and Karl Malden, and a set designed by **Mordecai Gorelik.** It won the New York Drama Critics' Circle Award, running for 328 performances. In 1987 a Broadway production won the Tony for Best Revival. The tightly structured, Ibsenist play depicts the effects on a midwestern family of the dawning awareness that the father, Joe Keller, knowingly shipped faulty engine parts that caused the deaths of young pilots during World War II – including, indirectly, that of his son. Miller's play drives inexorably toward Keller's understanding that his moral responsibility reaches beyond providing for his family.   BCM

Alswang, Ralph (1916–79)

Set, costume, and lighting designer, director, and producer. Alswang began his career in 1942 with *Comes the Revelation.* After serving in the Air Force he returned to Broadway with *Home of the Brave.* Subsequent designs included *The Rainmaker* (1954), *Sunrise at Campobello* (1958), and *A Raisin in the Sun* (1959). He also served as designer and consultant to several theatres, including the Uris Theatre in New York and the Garden State Arts Center, NJ.   AA

Alternative theatre

One of the terms developed to describe theatrical work growing out of the burgeoning cultural movement of the 1960s and '70s. As the name suggests, alternative theatre defined itself against dominant work – whether in commercial, political, or aesthetic terms – and sought to challenge the status quo as it was represented by mainstream middle-class theatre. Early on, alternative theatres aligned themselves with particular social movements: For instance, the **Free Southern Theatre** in Louisiana, New Feminist Theater in New York, and **El Teatro Campesino** in California not only responded to but were part of the civil rights, feminist, and farmworkers' movements, respectively. As such, they sought out new audiences, hoping to reflect and represent the experiences of those whose voices were never heard on mainstream stages.

These theatres, and a spate of others like them (there were more than 100 **feminist theatre**s in the U.S. in the early 1970s), by definition rejected the values of commercial theatre. More interested in helping to forge political movements than in earning a profit by selling entertainment, they redefined the relationship between spectator and performer, developed new performance styles and, perhaps most important, attracted a new army of theatre workers – the term itself revealing new attitudes toward the process of theatrical production. Few of those drawn to work in these political theatres were theatre professionals; instead, the theatres were staffed by constituents of the political movements. Thus, alternative theatres often established programs to train people as actors – and for virtually every other theatrical task. More often than not, plays presented by alternative theatres were developed through group improvisation or, at the very least, were written specifically for the group by company members. As part of its alternative impulse, the alternative theatre rejected the mainstream theatre's definition of a script as a commercial property, as well as its rigid divisions of labor. In the alternative theatre, scripts often were not even written down. Meanwhile, company members not only acted but painted scenery, hung lights, played musical instruments, and helped round up an audience.

Although most of the specific issue-related theatres died out by the 1980s, another strand of the alternative theatre movement persisted. While groups like the Free Southern Theatre or the **Living Theatre** primarily looked outward, concentrating on theatre's role in changing society through its direct engagement of social issues, others looked inward, searching for ways of changing society by offering spectators new ways of seeing and of thinking about themselves and their place in the world. These theatres, often politically radical as well, concentrated more on new aesthetic forms, new styles of creating work, and new approaches to acting.

The **Open Theatre,** for instance, which began in 1963 (and closed 10 years later), concentrated on developing what director **Joseph Chaikin** described as the actor's "presence" – that is, the performer, rather than the character, was to be the central focus of his theatre. The realism of the conventional theatre was to be replaced by self-conscious attention to the unique qualities of live performance.

Over the past two decades, techniques pioneered by these early alternative theatres – such as the acting exercises of the Open Theatre or the **collective** structure of feminist theatres – were adopted and adapted by new alternative theatres. While these theatres also defined themselves in opposition to the mainstream, that definition tended to become more and more aesthetic, if only because the social movements of the 1960s and '70s and the counterculture that had grown up with them had themselves faded away. In urban centers like New York, the countercultural life was less possible in the 1980s than in the turbulent decades before: rents had skyrocketed, making it difficult for alternative theatre artists to support themselves at odd jobs while spending the bulk of their time making theatre; the avant-garde was getting commodified, bringing alternative theatre mainstream media attention and audiences.

Thus, many of the alternative theatres that remained in the 1980s, and those that started up,

were more interested in artistic exploration than in political commitment. The formalism of **Robert Wilson,** for instance, can be counted as part of the alternative theatre in this sense, as can the often autobiographical but still highly formal work of **Richard Foreman,** the **Wooster Group,** and **Mabou Mines.**

Many of these theatres remain active in the 1990s, and a new generation of alternative theatre artists has grown up under their influence. In the absence of a vibrant countercultural movement, however, this new generation more often finds itself working in fragmented ways – experimental directors like **Anne Bogart** and **Peter Sellars,** for example, do not work consistently with the same company. Also, nowadays the term "alternative theatre" tends to describe a physical space – such as New York's **Dance Theatre Workshop** and Performance Space 122, or San Francisco's Life on the Water – where alternative works can be booked.   AS

See: M. V. Heuvel, *Performing Drama/Dramatizing Performance,* Ann Arbor, 1991; J. Schevill, *Break Out!,* Chicago, 1973; T. Shank, *American Alternative Theater,* New York, 1982; E. van Erven, *Radical People's Theatre,* Bloomington, IN, 1988.

Alvin Theatre see **Neil Simon Theatre**

AMAS Musical Theatre A multiracial, not-for-profit, **Off-Off Broadway** company specializing in new American musicals for family audiences; founded in 1969 by Rosetta Burton Le Noire, Mara Kim, and Gerta Grunen to counter divisive aspects of the Civil Rights Movement. Under Le Noire's artistic direction, AMAS (Latin for "you love") promotes ecumenical understanding by bringing people of different races together for a common artistic goal. AMAS's greatest success has been **Loften Mitchell**'s revue *Bubbling Brown Sugar* (1975), which transferred to Broadway (1976) and London (1977).   CLJ

Ambassador Theatre 215 West 49th St., NYC [Architect: Herbert J. Krapp]. Built in 1921, when prime sites in the theatre district were being rapidly used up, the **Shuberts'** architect was forced to design the new 1,100-seat theatre diagonally across the plot to make maximum use of the area. The Ambassador was intended to house operettas, the Shuberts' perennial theatrical product, but it was leased for nonmusicals as well. In 1935, the playhouse was sold and thereafter it was used for live and film presentations as well as a radio and television studio. In 1956, it was reacquired by the Shuberts, who returned it to legitimate roles.   MCH

Amberg, Gustav (1844–1921) Theatre manager. A native of Prague, Amberg managed German-speaking theatres during the 1870s in Cincinnati and Detroit. In 1879, together with **Heinrich Conried** and Mathilde Cottrelly, he founded the **Thalia Theater** (old Bowery Theatre), which became the preeminent German theatre in New York, engaging German stars Ludwig Barnay (1883–8), Adolf Sonnenthal (1884), and Ernst Possart (1887–8). In 1883 Amberg became sole manager of the Thalia. Disbanding the company in 1888, he opened the Amberg Theatre (later Irving Place) until financial failure in 1891. He worked for the **Shubert Organization** in his final years.   RE

Amen Corner, The First produced by Howard University in 1955, this domestic drama by **James Baldwin** reached Broadway a decade later via a year's run in **Los Angeles** (1964–5). The play portrays an overly zealous pastor of a Harlem storefront church who, lacking compassion, can neither forgive her wayward, dying husband nor accept her son's piano-playing career. Critical reaction found the play dated in light of the revolutionary black drama then in vogue.   EGH

Amend, Karle Otto (1885–1944) Though primarily known as a scenic artist – his Amend Scenic Studios was one of the major scenic houses in the 1920s and early '30s – Amend was also a designer and created the sets for **Earl Carroll**'s *Vanities* (1926–32). He began as a performer in his native Ohio and was first identified as a scene painter in 1912. In WW I he was an innovator in camouflage techniques.   AA

> See: K. Amend, *Behind the Scenes* (exhibition catalogue), New York, 1981.

America Hurrah by **Jean-Claude van Itallie**. Three short plays made up this evening of theatre that opened at New York's Pocket Theatre on 7 November 1966. (Earlier versions of *Interview* and *Motel* had been previously produced under different titles.) *Interview,* directed by **Joseph Chaikin**, satirizes the dehumanizing aspects of job-hunting in American business. *TV* and *Motel,* both directed by Jacques Levy, explore other aspects of commercialism and materialism while registering protest against the Vietnam War. The production was hailed for the freshness of its nonrealistic devices, especially the actors presented as grotesque puppets in *Motel,* and for the ensemble acting.   FHL

American Academy of Dramatic Arts The first and oldest conservatory of professional acting training in the U.S. Located in New York City, the Academy was founded in 1884 as The Lyceum Theatre School of Acting by Franklin Haven Sargent. In 1974 it opened a campus in the Los Angeles area. A nonprofit educational institution, AADA offers an associate degree and a Certificate of Advance Studies in Actor Training. Selected third-year students are invited to be members of a production company. The Academy's stated purpose is "To provide a broad and practical education to those desiring to make acting their profession." Distinguished alumni include **Jason Robards, Jr., Lucille Lortel, Ruth Gordon, Hume Cronyn, Colleen Dewhurst, Anne Bancroft,** and **Garson Kanin.**   TLM

American Buffalo Winner of a **Joseph Jefferson [III]** Award (Chicago), an Obie, and a New York Critics' Circle Award, **David Mamet**'s two-act drama, appearing shortly after *Sexual Perversity in Chicago,* established the writer as a serious new American playwright. In its 1975 **Chicago** pre-

miere as a coproduction of **Goodman** Stage 2 and Mamet's own St. Nicholas company, it was the first of many Mamet plays to be directed by **Gregory Mosher.** Its first Broadway production two years later, directed by **Ulu Grosbard** and starring Robert Duvall as Teach, ran for 135 performances at the **Ethel Barrymore Theatre.** Al Pacino played Teach in a celebrated revival at the **Long Wharf Theatre** (New Haven) in 1980, which moved to **Off-Broadway** in 1982 and Broadway in 1983, with a stop at the **John F. Kennedy Center** in between. On the surface, the drama concerns the bungled heist of an old nickel by three lowlifes based in a Chicago pawnshop. At a deeper level, we are encouraged to view the language of American business and power politics as an insidious force that infiltrates and destroys human relationships.   SF

American Company, The Most prominent theatre company in the American colonies. Founded in 1752 by London theatre manager William **Hallam** and his brother Lewis, it was originally known as the London Company of Comedians. Reorganized in 1758 by **David Douglass,** it assumed the name The American Company of Comedians in 1763, probably to avoid trouble during the anti-importation movement in the post–French and Indian War depression. Touring until 1774, the company went to Jamaica for the duration of the war. Upon their return in 1784, they regained their preeminent position, playing major cities along the eastern seaboard. In 1792 the company was reorganized under Lewis Hallam, Jr., and **John Henry,** continuing at New York's **Park Theatre** until 1806. [See also **Introduction, §1.**]   PAD

American Conservatory Theater (ACT) (previously Theatre) A noncommercial regional repertory company that combines performing with a training school. Founded in 1965 by **William Ball,** ACT has made its home in San Francisco since 1967. Ball attracted critical notice in 1958 with an **Off-Broadway** staging of **Chekhov**'s *Ivanov.* Subsequent productions throughout the U.S. and Canada made him one of the most promising young directors in America. In 1965 he established ACT at the Pittsburgh Playhouse as an experimental and educational company with a more "dashing style" than he saw elsewhere. Arrangements quickly soured, and Ball took ACT on the road for much of 1966, settling permanently in San Francisco for a January 1967 opening. Playing in two theatres, the downtown Geary and the Marine Memorial, the 50-member company offered 15 plays during the 1967–8 season, including *A Flea in Her Ear, The Three Sisters, The Devil's Disciple,* **Little Murders,** *A* **Delicate Balance,** and *Hamlet.* The late **Allen Fletcher** joined ACT in 1970 to head the Conservatory training program, now with some 70 acting students annually. The company ran up deficits of $900,000 in 1973, which required reductions in the size of the company and its repertoire. Ball was succeeded in 1987 by Edward Hastings, who announced his own resignation in 1991, to be replaced in 1992 by Carey Perloff, artistic director of New York's Classic Stage Company. As a result of earthquake damage, during 1990–1 ACT resituated around the corner from the Geary to the Palace of Fine Arts Theater. TLM

> See: J. R. Wilk, *The Creation of an Ensemble: The First Years of the American Conservatory Theatre* [*sic*], Carbondale, IL, 1986.

American Dream, The One-act play by **Edward Albee** produced **Off-Broadway** in January 1961 (with the unsuccessful one-act opera *Bartleby,* replaced by his *The Death of Bessie Smith*) for 370 performances. Based in part on the earlier *The Sandbox,* this play featured the same characters, Mommy and Daddy, offering a sketch that shows their vapid lives while caricaturing American values and types. The title character, a muscular and handsome young man, is emasculated by his adopted parents. As C. W. E. Bigsby notes, Albee offers no alternative to the inhumane and venal family, "an icon of the American system." Albee's play proved immediately popular, however, especially with students, and was produced often in university theatres, along with other Albee one-acts (and often in concert with Ionesco short plays). DBW

American Indians see **Native-American ritual/theatre; Native Americans portrayed on stage**

American Jewish Theatre Most recently located on New York's West 26th St., this nonprofit theatre, founded in 1974 by Stanley Brechner, produces or coproduces classics, new plays, and musicals that deal with Jewish ideas and culture. It has also developed its own material with its Deborah Project (a group of Jewish women writers). Outstanding productions have included **Paddy Chayefsky**'s *The Tenth Man;* **Peretz Hirschbein**'s *The Green Fields;* a critically acclaimed revival of the musical *The Rothschilds* (**Bock, Harnick,** and Yellen), which transferred to **Circle in the Square** (Downtown) in April 1990; and a revised version of *Rags* (1991), a 1986 musical flop. DBW

American Laboratory Theatre (ALT) Inspired by the first American appearance of the **Moscow Art Theatre** in January 1923, the American Laboratory Theatre (originally called the Theatre Arts Institute) was founded in New York six months later by a group of wealthy American patrons as a school for training young actors in the Stanislavsky system. Providing a well-rounded three-year program, the school was a significant first step in translating Stanislavsky's ideas about truth in acting into an American idiom. There were courses in mime, ballet, fencing, phonetics, and corrective gymnastics, but the school's focus was the classes taught by **Richard Boleslavski** and Maria Ouspenskaya, two impassioned émigrés from Stanislavsky's company.

During 1925–30, with Boleslavski as its artistic director, the Lab sponsored a theatre, modeled on the Moscow Art but advertised as America's first native, creative theatre. Most of its productions, however, were of new and revived European plays rather than the original American drama its charter promised. The Lab (disbanded in 1933) and its

theatre were an important link between the historic appearance of Stanislavsky's company and the establishment in 1931 of America's first true theatrical collective, the **Group Theatre,** cofounded by **Harold Clurman, Lee Strasberg,** and **Cheryl Crawford,** who had listened intently to Boleslavski's inspiring lectures. FH

American National Theatre and Academy (ANTA) Chartered in 1935 as a tax-exempt, self-supporting "people's" theatre, ANTA languished until after World War II, when a Board of Directors, infused with theatre personalities and entertainment industry leaders, raised money to help ANTA acquire the Guild Theater (1950), renamed the ANTA Playhouse. Noncommercial works, such as *The Tower Beyond Tragedy,* **Robinson Jeffers**'s adaptation of Aeschylus' *Oresteia,* and revivals, such as *Twentieth Century* (1932) by **Ben Hecht** and **Charles MacArthur,** were featured. In 1963 ANTA built the Washington Square Theatre, which temporarily housed the Repertory Theatre of **Lincoln Center.** WD

American Negro Theatre Founded in Harlem by Abram Hill and **Frederick O'Neal** in 1940 to provide a permanent company for black theatre artists displaced by the demise of the **Federal Theatre Project.** Using the 135th Street Library theatre, the company enjoyed initial success with Hill's *On Striver's Row* (1940) and Theodore Browne's *Natural Man* (1941), but began to disintegrate after Philip Yordan's *Anna Lucasta* (1944) moved to Broadway, played 957 performances, and became an international hit. The theatre closed in 1950. EGH

American Place Theatre 111 West 46th St., NYC [Architect: Richard D. Kaplan]. Founded as a producing organization dedicated to the presentation of new American plays by living authors, the American Place Theatre started at St. Clement's Church on West 46th Street. Its founders were **Wynn Handman** and Reverend **Sidney Lanier,** the vicar of the church. In 1971, an underground complex of theatres, offices, and workrooms at the rear of the Stevens building on the Avenue of the Americas was presented to the group through changes in the building and zoning laws that permitted the builder of an office skyscraper to add extra stories if a theatre was also added within the structure. The company pays $5.00 per year (25-year lease) for this space. Handman continues as artistic director (he was assisted by Julia Miles, who ran the Women's Project [now **Women's Project and Productions**] there [1978–87]). The company mounts full-scale productions as well as numerous works-in-progress during its 10-month season. MCH

American Repertory Theatre The first company of this name, founded in 1946 by **Eva Le Gallienne** with **Margaret Webster** and **Cheryl Crawford,** was located in an obsolete theatre on Columbus Circle. Despite a notable company of actors and the objective to become New York's version of Britain's Old Vic or the Comédie-

Adrian Hall's 1991 production of *King Lear* at the American Repertory Theatre, with F. Murray Abraham as Lear and Stephanie Roth as Cordelia. Photo: Richard Feldman. Courtesy: ART.

Française, it was defunct by 1948. The second company of this name (ART) under **Robert Brustein** began an association in 1980 with Harvard University. Dedicated to neglected works from the past, new American plays, and innovative classical productions, the theatre has staged controversial productions (such as *Endgame* [1984–5], disclaimed by Beckett), innovative direction, and experimental work, such as the 1985 production of portions of **Robert Wilson**'s *the CIVIL WarS* and Wilson's 1991 staging of Ibsen's *When We Dead Awaken*. It has also mounted inaugural productions, such as **Marsha Norman**'s *'night, Mother* (1982) and the 1985 Tony Award–winning musical *Big River,* later seen in New York. In 1986 ART received a special Tony Award and a National Endowment for the Arts Ongoing Ensemble Award.   DBW

American Shakespeare Theatre Founded in Stratford, CT, in 1951 as the American Festival Theatre under the guidance of **Lawrence Langner,** its name was changed in 1972. Designed by Edwin Howard, the octagonal shaped theatre reminiscent of the exterior of the original Globe Theatre, with a thrust stage and an auditorium seating about 1,500, opened on 12 July 1955 with *Julius Caesar* as part of an eight-week season. Under a series of artistic directors, approximately 75 productions have been staged, including non-Shakespearean works beginning with **Shaw**'s *Caesar and Cleopatra* in 1963. In 1959 special spring performances for students were added. Among the better known actors to have appeared here are **Morris Carnovsky, Jessica Tandy, Katharine Hepburn, Kate Reid, James Earl Jones, Christopher Plummer,** and **Alfred Drake.** In 1977 the Connecticut Center for the Performing Arts was established to expand the season to include guest artists and touring companies. The most recent full summer season was 1979, followed by sporadic production and finally virtual inactivity since 1982. In January of that year the theatre filed for bankruptcy with a debt of almost $2 million. A proposed solution to its financial woes has yet to lead to full-time operation, despite a brief summer season (as The American Festival Theatre) in 1989 by a company from the **American Conservatory Theater.**   DBW

See: R. Cooper, *The American Shakespeare Theatre: Stratford, 1955–1985,* Washington, DC, 1986.

American Theatre Camp St., New Orleans. English-language theatre was successfully established in New Orleans with the American Theatre, which flourished during 1824–40. A substantial brick structure, the house was built by **James H. Caldwell,** who served as its manager for eight years before leasing it to others. Caldwell and his successors assembled competent companies, provided novelties along with the standard repertory, and brought in whatever stars were available each season. After he had launched his larger and more opulent **St. Charles,** Caldwell disposed of the "pretty little playhouse" on Camp, which was rebuilt as the Camp St. Exchange in 1840.   MCH

See: J. Kendall, *The Golden Age of the New Orleans Theater,* Baton Rouge, 1952.

American Shakespeare [Festival] Theatre in 1957. Courtesy: Michael Gnat.

American Theatre Company A showcase theatre company founded in 1968 in New York City by Alice Scudder Emerick and Richard Kuss. The group is important because of its distinctive revival of American classics such as **Charles A. Hoyt**'s *A Texas Steer* (1890), **William Vaughn Moody**'s *The Faith Healer* (1910), **Rachel Crothers**'s *He and She* (1920), and **Robert Munford**'s *The Patriots* (1776). Directors Kuss and Ellis Santone and scenic artist Charles Gillette were volunteers; no administrators were paid, but some actors were. Unable to sustain the cost of increasing professionalization, the company ceased production in 1978. WD

Ames, Winthrop (1871–1937) Producer and director. Ames, a wealthy Bostonian, was a leader in the art theatre movement. At **Boston**'s Castle Square Theatre (1904–7), at New York's ill-fated **New Theatre** (1909–11), and finally at the two theatres he built: the **Little Theatre** (1912, West 44th St.) – "a little Pullman car of a place," he called it – and the **Booth** (West 45th St.).

Ames was the first American to make a serious study of the European art theatres. In 1907 he visited 64 theatres, saw 53 productions in Paris, London, Berlin, Vienna, and Munich, and kept a detailed notebook including 154 sketches of scenic innovations. In 1912 Ames introduced the "new stagecraft" to New York by bringing over **Reinhardt**'s production of *Sumurun*. He also encouraged **Norman Bel Geddes**'s experiments in stage lighting at his two theatres.

Ames prepared minutely detailed prompt scripts ("mother copies," he called them) for his productions, and the results always reflected his lively imagination and impeccable taste. Most notable: Galsworthy's *The Pigeon* (1912), Schnitzler's *The Affairs of Anatol* (1912, starring John Barrymore [see **Drew–Barrymore**]), **Shaw**'s *The Philanderer* (1913), *Snow White* (1913, his own adaptation), Maeterlinck's *The Betrothel* (1918), and **Kaufman** and **Connelly**'s *Beggar on Horseback* (1924). RM

Anania, Michael (1951–) Resident set designer for the Paper Mill Playhouse (NJ) since 1985 where his productions include *Windy City* (1985). He has designed several of the Broadway musical revivals at the New York City Opera such as *A Little Night Music* (1990) and *The Most Happy Fella* (1991). In addition he has designed at **Central City Opera House** and the Lake George Opera Festival. Working in these venues he has established a reputation as a creator of large-scale and romantic settings. He has also designed on Broadway and for many regional theatres. AA

Anderson, John (Hargis) (1896–1943) Drama critic. Born in Pensacola, FL, and educated at the University of Virginia (1918), Anderson worked as a reporter, feature writer, and a columnist for the *New York Post* (1918–24), serving as drama critic during 1924–8. From 1928 to 1937 he wrote the dramatic column for the *New York Evening Journal,* and for the *Journal-American* from 1937 until his death. Anderson's forte was an astute eye and vivid prose that communicated theatrical excitement to his readers. His books include *Box Office* (1930) and *The American Theatre* (1938). TLM

Anderson, John Murray (1886–1954) Producer, designer, and director. After beginning his theatrical career as a producer of pageants and civic masques, Anderson applied the new stagecraft of Gordon Craig and his followers to the American **revue** when he presented the *Greenwich Village Follies* (1919). The show's success, due largely to its simple, imaginative, and beautiful scenery and costumes, launched an annual series of revues that rivaled the *Ziegfeld Follies* in the taste and artistry of its *mise-en-scène.* The *Greenwich Village Follies* were also noted for their "ballet ballads," poems and stories set to music and dance. Anderson was soon in demand as a designer, director, and producer. Over the next 30 years he was primarily known as a facile director of musicals, nightclub floor shows, and circuses. Among his musical theatre productions were two editions of the revue *Murray Anderson's Almanac* (1929 and 1953). His autobiography was published in 1954. MK

Anderson, Judith (née Frances Margaret Anderson–Anderson) (1898–1992) First Australian-born actress appointed DBE (1960). She consistently excelled in powerful, tragic roles. Failing in her planned singing career, she turned to acting, made her debut in Sydney in 1915, followed by a two-year tour with an American stock company. Her first New York appearance was in 1918; her first substantial success was as Elise in *Cobra* (1924), followed by the Unknown One in *As You Desire Me* (1931) and Lavinia in *Mourning Becomes Electra* (1932). In 1936 she was Gertrude to John Gielgud's Hamlet in New York; in 1937 she made her London debut (Old Vic) as Lady Macbeth opposite Laurence Olivier (repeated with **Maurice Evans,** New York, 1941). She played the title role in **Robinson Jeffers**'s adaptation of Euripides' *Medea* in 1947 (revived in 1974). At the Old Vic in 1960 she appeared as Irina Arkadina in *The Seagull.* In 1970, with minimal success, she toured as Hamlet. In 1984 she appeared regularly on the television daytime drama *Santa Barbara.* The same year a theatre on New York's **Theatre Row** (West 42nd St.) was named after her. DBW

Anderson, Laurie (1947–) Chicago-born **performance art**ist, composer, and musician whose work addresses mass audiences and explores popular music idioms. As a child, she studied the violin and attended special art classes. She studied art history at Barnard College, sculpture at Columbia University (MFA, 1972), and wrote for major art journals. Her work is influenced by Sol LeWitt, John Cage, Fluxus, Conceptual Art, and popular culture. Supported by voice filters, loops, and sequencers that manipulate the pitch and texture of her natural voice, Anderson's media image emphasizes androgyny and explores the ambiguities of language and sound. Her work ranges from *Automotive* (1972), scored for car horns; a Fluxus-inspired street performance, *Duets on Ice* (1974), in which she played a prepared violin while standing in blocks of melting ice; to *Empty Places* (1988–90), a concert with media images, projections, songs, storytelling, and stand-up comedy. Her multimedia event, *United States* (1978–83) was recorded by Warner Bros., and a section of it, *O Superman* (1980), became a hit in the U.S. and in Britain.   AF

Anderson, Mary (1859–1940) Actress. At 16, in 1875, she made her debut as Juliet at **Macaulay's Theatre** in Louisville, and this quickly led to other engagements. Her major assets were her classical physical beauty and a rich, expressive voice. She made her New York debut in 1877. W. S. Gilbert wrote a short play, *Comedy and Tragedy*, for her. Americans proudly called her "Our Mary."

During her 14-year career on both sides of the Atlantic, she played 18 leading roles, including such favorites as Rosalind and Galatea in *Pygmalion and Galatea*. She was also the first actress to double the roles of Hermione and Perdita. In 1890 at the height of her career, she retired from the stage, settled in England, and married Antonio de Navarro. She returned to the stage during WW I, however, appearing in various benefit performances. Her memoirs were published as *A Few Memories* (1896) and *A Few More Memories* (1930).   FHL DJW

Anderson, Maxwell (1888–1959) Playwright and dramatic theorist whose prolific career spanned three decades, although the bulk of his critically acclaimed work came in the 1930s. He won the Pulitzer Prize for **Both Your Houses** (1933), the Drama Critics' Circle Award for **Winterset** (1935, the first such award ever given), and another for *High Tor* (1937). He gained a reputation as an antiwar dramatist, and **What Price Glory** (1924), coauthored with **Lawrence Stallings,** pioneered by bringing onstage the realistic, salty language of men at war. Other Anderson plays with wartime settings or themes include *Valley Forge* (1934), *Key Largo* (1939), *Candle in the Wind* (1941), and *The Eve of St. Mark* (1942).

Anderson turned frequently to the lives of monarchs and other political leaders for the subject matter of his dramas. Important examples include **Elizabeth the Queen** (1930), *Mary of Scotland* (1933), **Knickerbocker Holiday** (1938, a musical written in collaboration with **Kurt Weill**), *Joan of Lorraine* (1947), *Anne of the Thousand Days* (1948), and *Barefoot in Athens* (1951). Anderson also successfully adapted others' work for the stage. Examples are **Lost in the Stars** (1949, also in collaboration with Weill), and *The Bad Seed* (1954). Anderson never tired of attempting to justify the use of blank verse in modern drama, and with *The Essence of Tragedy* (1939) became the first American playwright to publish a detailed theory of tragedy. An astute businessman, he was one of the founders of the **Playwrights' Company** (1938).   LDC

See: L. Avery, ed., *Dramatist in America: Letters of Maxwell Anderson, 1912–1958,* Chapel Hill, NC, 1977; A. Shivers, *The Life of Maxwell Anderson,* New York, 1983.

Anderson, Robert W[oodruff] (1917–) New York–born and Harvard-educated playwright, Robert Anderson first drew attention by winning the National Theatre Conference prize with *Come Marching Home* (1945). After an eight-year hiatus during which he taught playwriting and adapted 36 plays and several novels for the Theatre Guild of the Air, he burst upon Broadway with the long-running **Tea and Sympathy** (1953). This sensitive study of a young man's growth from innocence into experience is still considered his outstanding work. He was the only new playwright ever elected to membership (1953) in the **Playwrights' Company,** which produced three of his plays: *All Summer Long* (1953), *Tea and Sympathy,* and *Silent Night, Lonely Night* (1959). His play *The Days Between* (1965) helped inaugurate the American Playwright's Theatre. He proved that an evening of one-act plays was still viable Broadway fare with *You Know I Can't Hear You When the Water's Running* (1967) and *Solitaire/Double Solitaire* (1970). Anderson adapted several of his plays to film, including the autobiographical **I Never Sang for My Father** (1968), the screenplay for which earned him a 1970 Academy Award nomination.   LDC

See: T. Adler, *Robert Anderson,* Boston, 1978.

And Miss Reardon Drinks a Little by **Paul Zindel** opened at the **Morosco Theatre** 25 February 1971 following his Pulitzer Prize–winning *The Effect of Gamma Rays on Man-in-the-Moon Marigolds* (1971). Originally written as a one-act (1966), the full-length version deals with three sisters who are all schoolteachers: one an inebriated realist, another a hardened administrator, and the third a disturbed waif who is the catalyst for the play's debate about whether she should be institutionalized. The cast included **Estelle Parsons** as the drunken Catherine Reardon, Nancy Marchand as the strict Ceil Adams, and **Julie Harris** as the disturbed Anna Reardon. The play ran 108 performances.   KN

André Regarded as one of **William Dunlap**'s best plays; first produced by the Old **American Company** at New York's **Park Theatre,** 30 March 1798. Based on an incident from the American Revolution concerning the capture and execution of a British spy, Dunlap's sympathetic treatment of Major André was a source of criticism at a time when the U.S. was about to pass the infamous Anti-Sedition Act of 1798. It was Dunlap's first attempt at writing native drama and was praised for its structure, though only modestly received. Five years later, Dunlap presented a musical version titled *Glory of Columbia.*   PAD

Angelou, Maya (née Marguerite Johnson) (1928–) Best known as an autobiographer, Angelou writes, acts, and directs. Her performances include *Porgy and Bess* (1954–5 European tour), *The Blacks* (1960), and *Look Away* (1973), which earned her a Tony nomination. Her plays, including *Cabaret for Freedom* (with Godfrey Cambridge, 1960), *Ajax* (1974), *And Still I Rise* (1976), and *King* (1990), examine racism and survival, often through music. She is credited as the first professional black woman film director and screenwriter.   TH-S

Anglin, Margaret (1876–1958) Actress. Daughter of the Speaker of the Canadian Parliament, she trained at **Charles Frohman**'s **Empire Theatre** School, made her debut in 1893, and toured opposite **James O'Neill** and **Richard Mansfield.** She became leading lady of the Empire company opposite **Henry Miller** (1899–1905), and under their own management (1905–8), they produced *The Great Divide* by **William Vaughn Moody.** She then devoted herself to classical plays in productions designed by **Livingston Platt** in the manner of Edward Gordon Craig. Highlights were her summer productions of *Antigone, Electra,* and *Medea* in the Hearst Amphitheatre at the University of California, Berkeley (1910, 1913, and 1915), and her tour in *The Taming of the Shrew, Twelfth Night, As You Like It,* and *Antony and Cleopatra* (1913–14). Except for a few revivals of her Greek productions, she appeared in modern plays from 1915 to 1943. In 1911 she married the actor Howard Hull. A large, commanding woman, she lacked warmth and charm but was unsurpassed at tears and dark interior emotions.   DMcD

Animal Crackers A musical farce by **George S. Kaufman** and **Morrie Ryskind** starring the **Marx Bros.,** with music and lyrics by Bert Kalmar and Harry Ruby, opened on Broadway 23 October 1928 and ran 191 performances. Groucho and Zeppo played an African explorer and his secretary, and Chico and Harpo played musicians, all attending a house party in a Long Island mansion. The character of Chandler was based on **Otto H. Kahn,** financier and "angel," and one scene parodied the spoken interior monologues of **O'Neill**'s *Strange Interlude,* which was still running when *Animal Crackers* opened. Paramount released the film version, with screenplay by Ryskind, in 1930.   JDM

Animal impersonation may be the earliest form of acting: Tribal shamans disguised themselves as animal divinities to ensure successful hunts, evoke fertility spirits, or propitiate malign influences. New Mexicans preserved such an aboriginal deer dance to the 20th century. However, the portrayal of animal characters in the theatre was not common until after the French Revolution, when, as a by-blow of Rousseau's ideas, the noble savage was held to exist even under the skin of an ape. The sensitive anthropoid in Gabriel and Rouchefort's panto**mime** *Jocko; or, the Ape of Brazil* (1825) was one of the most successful tearjerkers of all time. Skilled performers like the Englishman Gouffe and the Italo-French Gabriel **Ravel** and Joseph Marzetti (d. 1864) popularized Jocko and his epigone Pongo throughout early 19th-century America. Such impersonation remained a speciality of European acrobat families (Martinetti, Lauri), who regularly played comic animals, especially two-man mules and horses, in pantomime and vaudeville.

Perhaps because she changed both species and sex, **Maude Adams** failed as the lead in *Chantecler* (1910), Edmond Rostand's metamorphosis of barnyard fowl and forest creatures into alexandrine-spouting humanoids. American realism was chary of the genre and relegated it to **children's theatre.**

Maude Adams in James Barrie's *Peter Pan,* pictured with the dog, Nana. Souvenir program, 1906. Courtesy: Don B. Wilmeth.

The most familiar and enduring examples are imports: Nana, the St. Bernard nursemaid in J. M. Barrie's *Peter Pan* (1904), the anthropomorphized dog and cat in Maeterlinck's *The Blue Bird* (1908), and the grateful lion in **Shaw**'s *Androcles and the Lion* (1913).

Still, a strain of antirealism on the modern American stage has fostered nonillusionistic impersonations, starting with the mammoth and dinosaur in **Thornton Wilder**'s *The Skin of Our Teeth* (1942), and devolving into the amphibious lizards of **Albee**'s *Seascape* (1975) and Mikhail Baryshnikov as the cockroach in Kafka's *Metamorphosis,* adapted by Steven Berkoff. Musical comedy also welcomed it: Caroline the cow in *Gypsy* (1959) is a stallmate of Imogene the cow in *The Wizard of Oz* (1903), whom L. Frank Baum considered a more stageworthy beast than Toto. The bulldog Tige in *Buster Brown* (1905) was well characterized by a human (George Ali), as were Snoopy the beagle in *You're a Good Man, Charlie Brown* (1969), the phallic wolf in *Into the Woods* (1988), and **T. S. Eliot**'s *Cats.* Horses have been variously portrayed: by characters with hobby-horse suits round their waists in Anouilh's *Becket* (1961) and **Arthur Kopit**'s *Indians* (1968), and by mimes in leotards and cagelike masks in Peter Shaffer's *Equus* (1976).

These functions have been largely assumed by the animated cartoon, for the antics of Felix the Cat, Mickey Mouse, and Bugs Bunny can be more flexible and fantastical than any living embodiment. Only **Bert Lahr** as the Cowardly Lion in the film of *The Wizard of Oz* (1938) seems to have transcended the limitations of the form.   LS

Animals as performers The heyday of the performing animal followed the Age of Enlightenment and the rise of the equestrian **circus:** "Animaux savants" were believed to rival the noble savage as an exemplum of natural perfectibility. Hippodrama, in which trained horses took leading roles, became extremely popular. The hit play was H. M. Milner's *Mazeppa; or, The Wild Horse of Tartary* (1831), in which the young prince, stripped down to fleshings, is strapped to a horse set loose on a treadmill and attacked by stuffed vultures. In the U.S., the title role was usually taken by a woman, most notoriously by **Adah Isaacs Menken.** Another prime example was **Bannister**'s *Putnam, the Iron Son of '76* (1844), with its famous run on horseback down the rocky steps of Horse Neck. Although hippodrama fell into desuetude by midcentury, new technology created concurrent tracks that enabled a horse race to be the climax of Charles Bernard's *The County Fair* (**Union Square Theatre,** New York, 1889) and Lew Wallace's *Ben-Hur* (1899).

Dog drama, a subspecies of melodrama in which a canine saves the victim and identifies the villain, throve in Bowery theatres before the Civil War: One of its principal purveyors was Mary Hewins, who could rewrite any standard play to star a troupe of trained mongrels. **Vaudeville** became a hospitable milieu for animal acts from Fink's Mules to Swain's Cats and Rats; Consul the chimpanzee (d. 1904) was an international star in his own right. Owing to high costs and danger, horses, elephants, and lions, common in European variety houses, made only rare appearances in American vaudeville. However, **Siegfried and Roy,** German trainers, currently stage a successful **magic** show with wild beasts in Las Vegas revues. In today's theatre, live animals are seen, if at all, in musical comedy (e.g., Sandy in *Annie,* 1977): The biggest laugh in **Billy Rose**'s *Jumbo* (1935) came when **Jimmy Durante,** with the title character on a lead, walked nonchalantly past a cop; asked where he was taking the elephant, Durante replied, "Elephant? What elephant?"   LS

Anisfeld, Boris Izrailevich (1879–1973) Bessarabian-born painter and designer. As a member of the "World of Art" group he worked with Diaghilev's *Ballets Russes* and the Pavlova Ballet before coming to the U.S. in 1918. An exhibition of his paintings toured the country that year, and in 1919 he began an extended association with the Metropolitan Opera. Known for his brilliant use of color, he helped introduce unit settings and folk motifs into the vocabulary of the New Stagecraft in America. His production of the world premiere of Prokofiev's *The Love for Three Oranges* (1921) at the Chicago Opera is one of his best known. In 1928 he joined the faculty of the School of the Art Institute of Chicago and taught there for more than 30 years.   AA

Anna Christie In a wonderfully moody production directed by **Arthur Hopkins** and designed by **Robert Edmond Jones,** this **Eugene O'Neill** drama was a perfect vehicle for emotional actress **Pauline Lord** and character actor George Marion as Anna and Chris, respectively. Originally written and produced as the failed *Chris Christophersen* in 1920, the revision opened a long run at the Vanderbilt Theatre on 2 November 1921. Anna, one of O'Neill's most fully drawn women, is a desperate prostitute who finally finds family and love only to lose them and regain them uneasily and uncertainly in the final scene. Although the play received the Pulitzer Prize, O'Neill eventually denied its importance, claiming that audiences and critics mistakenly took the conclusion for a happy one. Nonetheless, *Anna Christie* was unusually explicit in both language and situation for its time and helped to free the New York stage for yet grittier subject matter as the decade progressed. The play was the basis for the **Bob Merrill–George Abbott** musical *New Girl in Town* (1973).   RHW

Anna Lucasta Three-act drama by Philip Yordan; opened **Off-Broadway** at the 135th Street Library Theatre in Harlem (16 June 1944) for 19 performances, then moved to Broadway's Mansfield Theatre (30 August 1944) for 957 performances, becoming one of the first serious Off-Broadway plays to receive significant critical attention. Abram Hill and Harry Wagstaff Gribble of Harlem's newly founded (1940) **American Negro Theatre** adapted the script about a Polish-American family's struggles in a small Pennsylvania town to focus on the wayward daughter of a black working-class family. The production, which featured **Earle Hyman, Canada Lee, Frederick O'Neal,** and Hilda Simms, served to recognize and validate the **African-American** voice on Broadway.   EK

Annie Two-act musical comedy, music by **Charles Strouse,** lyrics by **Martin Charnin,** book by Thomas Meehan. Opened 21 April 1977 at New York's **Alvin Theatre,** running 2,377 performances. Based on Harold Gray's classic comic strip, this heartwarming musical of kids, dogs, and Christmas in the 1930s follows Little Orphan Annie's pursuit of her real parents, culminating in adoption by Daddy Warbucks. Pointedly old-fashioned in an age of musicals striving to be sophisticated and up-to-date, its unabashed sentimentality, played without camp, won wide appeal. Initially unable to find a Broadway producer, the show first appeared in 1976 at the **Goodspeed Opera House,** East Haddam, CT. There it caught the attention of **Mike Nichols,** who nurtured it and produced it on Broadway, where it won both the Tony and Drama Critics' Circle awards for Best Musical. *Annie II,* a sequel focusing on *Annie*'s villain, Miss Hannegan, closed before reaching Broadway in 1990.   JD

See: M. Charnin, *Annie: A Theatre Memoir,* New York, 1977.

Annie Get Your Gun Two-act musical comedy, music and lyrics by **Irving Berlin,** book by Herbert and **Dorothy Fields.** Opened 16 May 1946 at the **Imperial Theatre,** New York, running 1,147 performances. **Richard Rodgers** and **Oscar Hammerstein II,** who produced the show, had originally engaged **Jerome Kern** to write the score;

Ethel Merman in *Annie Get Your Gun* (1946). Courtesy: New York Public Library of the Performing Arts.

but after Kern's death in 1945, they turned to Irving Berlin. An old-fashioned star vehicle, it tells, amid show-business trappings, the story of the rivalry and romance between **Annie Oakley** (**Ethel Merman**) and Frank Butler (Ray Middleton), competing sharpshooters in **Buffalo Bill**'s **Wild West exhibition,** a setting providing the occasion for lavish production numbers. Of the fourteen songs introduced (among them "There's No Business Like Show Business"), nine featured Merman and three of the remaining five her leading man. A successful American tour (starring **Mary Martin**) and London production (starring Dolores Gray) followed. For a major 1966 revival at **Lincoln Center** (again starring Merman), Berlin replaced one of the two songs not sung by Annie or Frank with a new contrapuntal duet for the two of them. A perennial favorite, *Annie Get Your Gun* was the most successful musical in the long careers of both Berlin and Merman.   JD

ANTA see **American National Theatre and Academy**

Anthony, Joseph (né Deuster) (1912–   ) Actor and director. Born in Milwaukee, Anthony attended the University of Wisconsin and **Pasadena Playhouse** School (1931–5). He made his acting debut in a West Coast production of *Mary of Scotland,* after which he appeared in New York with the **Federal Theatre** in 1937, and later in numerous roles including Richters in *Skipper Next to God* (1948), Casanova in *Camino Real,* and Prince Bounine in *Anastasia* (1954). In 1948 he made his New York directing debut with *Celebration.* Working in both films and the theatre, Anthony established himself as one of America's premiere directors. His stage credits include *The Rainmaker* (1954), *The Lark* (1955), *The Most Happy Fella* (1956), *Winesburg, Ohio* (1958), *The Best Man* (1960), *Mary, Mary* (1961), *Romulus* (1962), *110 in the Shade* (1963), *Slow Dance on the Killing Ground* (1964), and *Finishing Touches* (1973). In 1976 he was appointed Professor of Theatre Arts at SUNY–Purchase.   TLM

Antin, Eleanor (1935–   ) New York–born conceptual and **performance art**ist who also works in photography, video, and film. Antin studied writing and art at City College of New York (BA, 1958) and acting at New York's Tamara Daykarhanova School (1955–7). Early conceptual performances were *Carving: A Traditional Sculpture* (1972), *Representational Painting* (1972), and *100 Boots* (1973). Antin developed fictional-autobiographical personae, such as a king, a nurse, a black movie star, or a black ballerina. In *My Life with Diagelev* (1981–5), Antin (who is white) toured as a black Russian dancer, reading from her memoirs. In *The Last Night of Rasputin* (1989), she screened her film about prerevolutionary Russia and reminisced about her fictional life as the black dancer Eleanora Antinova.   AF

Antoon, A[lfred] J[oseph] (1944–92) Director who originally studied for the priesthood, but graduated from Boston College in 1968 with a theatre degree. In 1972–3 he had two award-winning productions on Broadway – *That Championship Season* and a *Much Ado About Nothing* set in a turn-of-the-century America – both transfers from the **New York Shakespeare Festival,** for which since 1971 he did much of his finest work, making updatings of Shakespeare a specialty. Other recent productions included **Gurney**'s *The Art of Dining* (1979) and *Song of Singapore* (1991), his last effort before his death from AIDS.   CLJ

Anything Goes Two-act musical comedy, music and lyrics by **Cole Porter,** which opened 21 November 1934 at New York's **Alvin Theatre,** running 420 performances. Conceived as a vehicle to feature stars **Ethel Merman, William Gaxton,** and **Victor Moore,** the original book by **Guy Bolton** and **P. G. Wodehouse** dealt with a group of eccentric characters involved in a shipwreck; but upon the sinking of the *SS Morro Castle,* the book was hastily rewritten by **Howard Lindsay** and **Russel Crouse** (their debut as playwrights) to treat romantic complications involving society folk and con men aboard a transatlantic liner. One of the most popular musicals of the 1930s, it introduced many Porter standards – the title song, plus "I Get a Kick Out of You," "All Through the Night," and "You're the Top." The show has proven extremely durable. A version successfully produced Off-Broadway in 1962, with the book revised by Guy Bolton and songs from other Porter shows interpolated into the score, became a staple of the amateur repertoire. A 1987 Broadway revival at Lincoln Center's **Vivian Beaumont Theatre** – with book yet again revised by Timothy Crouse and John Weidman and new interpolations as well as some restorations to the original score – ran 804 performances, won a Tony Award, and had a successful national tour.   JD

Any Wednesday Two-act comedy by Muriel Resnik; opened on Broadway at the **Music Box Theatre** (18 February 1964) for 982 performances, starring Sandy Dennis (Tony Award) and a young Gene Hackman. Set in New York's Upper East Side, the play addresses personal and business ethics as an arrogant, married business tycoon supports his daffy, innocent, tax-deductible young mistress, losing both wife and mistress in the end. Audiences appreciated the mature subject matter, which acknowledged the many gray areas regarding ethics. EK

Apollo Theatre Historic showplace of black entertainers at 125th Street, Harlem, New York. Originally a burlesque theatre, this two-balconied, 1,700-seat theatre became the mecca of black show business when it was taken over in 1935 by Frank Schiffman and Leo Brecher. Now-famous big bands, instrumentalists, singers, dancers, and stand-up comedians all graced the Apollo stage, some making their first public appearance at the regular Wednesday amateur night show. The theatre was closed in 1977 and later reopened as a television studio for the black cable market. The building was granted landmark status in 1983. Its future as a venue for live entertainment is currently in jeopardy. EGH

See: J. Schiffman, *Uptown: The Story of Harlem's Apollo Theatre,* New York, 1971; J. Schiffman, *Harlem Heyday,* New York, 1984.

Architecture, theatre The earliest American colonial performance venues were temporary structures and converted rooms in inns or private homes fitted, at best, with a curtained raised stage and some seats. The first recorded playhouse was built by William Levingston in Williamsburg, VA, between 1716 and 1718; absolutely no evidence as to what its interior may have been like survives. It is known, however, that from its beginnings the American playhouse was influenced by its English counterpart. At first this meant a box, pit, and gallery arrangement for the auditorium, a simple proscenium stage, perhaps with a wing-and-groove scenic system, and, at least in the 18th century, an apron with proscenium doors.

There are records of **New York City theatre** spaces in 1732 and 1735. These were followed in 1736 by the Dock Street Theatre in Charleston, SC, built to house amateur productions. The first "professional" theatre in colonial America was Plumstead's Warehouse in **Philadelphia,** made into a performing space by the company of **Walter Murray and Thomas Kean** in 1749 as they began their American tour. In New York, they performed at the Nassau Street Theatre in 1750. A notice for this theatre in 1751 mentioned 10 boxes – the first record of such a seating arrangement. Also in 1751, a crude playhouse was quickly erected in Williamsburg for the Murray–Kean Company, though again little detail is known.

A more professional period began with the arrival in Yorktown in 1752 of **Lewis Hallam**'s London Company of Comedians, who bought and renovated Murray and Kean's Williamsburg playhouse, creating a box, pit, and gallery structure with some sort of balcony. As the company toured New York, Philadelphia, and Charleston over the next two years, they converted or reconstructed existing theatres. Notably, in New York, they built a new Nassau Street Theatre on the site of the old one – probably the first American theatre based specifically on English theatre architecture. Under

David Douglass, who took over the Company of Comedians in 1758, the troupe traveled through the major East Coast theatre centers, building or renovating theatres in the English tradition at each stop. The two most notable of these theatres were the **Southwark,** built just outside Philadelphia in 1766, and the **John Street** in New York, opened in 1767. Both these theatres were relatively well equipped, with a flat-wing and groove system for scenery, a green front-cloth behind the proscenium, oil lamps, and basic audience amenities. The John Street is described in Jonathan's famous speech from **Royall Tyler**'s *The Contrast,* which premiered there in 1787. Both theatres no doubt compared favorably with English provincial theatres at the time, if not the better London counterparts.

Plays and other entertainments were banned by the Continental Congress in 1774, putting a temporary end to most theatre construction. Activity resumed after the Revolution, and theatres of varying degrees of sophistication were erected in Richmond, Norfolk, Alexandria, Annapolis, Boston, Providence, Portland (ME), Baltimore, Charleston, New Orleans, Newport, New York, and other cities, several of these under the management of **Thomas Wade West;** but it was in the last decade of the century that a golden age of theatre architecture began, with architectural style and production facilities equalled to those of England. The **Chestnut Street Theatre,** perhaps designed by John Inigo Richards, opened in Philadelphia in 1794 and was, at the time, the most sophisticated theatre in the country; in 1816 it would become the first theatre in the world illuminated by gaslight [see **stage lighting**]. The **Federal Street Theatre** in Boston also opened in 1794, and 1798 saw the opening of the **Park Theatre** in New York. These three were similar in all respects to contemporary English playhouses. They were relatively large – the Park seated 2,000 – and contained curved benches in the pit and three tiers of boxes and galleries. The stage machinery, though not elaborate, was up-to-date and allowed for the sort of spectacle that was becoming popular at the turn of the century. The **National Theatre** opened in Washington, DC, in 1800. Meanwhile, the Olympic Theatre, built to house a **circus,** opened in Philadelphia in 1809 but was renovated as a legitimate house in 1811, re-opening as the **Walnut Street Theatre,** which still stands. Also in 1811 came the worst theatre disaster to that time: The Richmond Theatre burned, killing 71 spectators including the governor of Virginia (see **fires**).

By 1815 theatre began to follow the general westward expansion of the U.S., and makeshift theatres are documented in Ohio, Kentucky, Indiana, and Tennessee. Facilities were primitive. A contemporary account describes a stage 10 ft wide and 8 ft deep that became crowded with the introduction of scenery. There was evidence of a theatre in Detroit in 1816, St. Louis records a theatre in 1827, **Chicago** in 1837 (the first Chicago building exclusively for theatre was on Randolph Street in 1847). New Orleans, too, had become a thriving theatre center with French performances by 1791. The Camp Street or **American Theatre** (1824) in New Orleans had gaslight two years before any theatre in New York, and the **St. Charles Theatre** (1835) was one of the most elegant in the country. A unique development were the floating theatres on the Ohio and Mississippi Rivers. **Noah Ludlow** may have created the first as early as 1817, but the first **showboat** specifically designed as such was built by William Chapman in 1831 and based in Pittsburgh; it seated about 200 spectators. Spanish-language productions in California were performed in missions, but the first English-language productions and the first theatre structures date from the Mexican–American War. A Monterey lodging house that still stands was converted into a theatre by soldiers in 1848 and is considered California's first theatre. Playhouses appeared in Sacramento in 1849 and **San Francisco** in 1850.

After 1800 New York rapidly developed as the nation's largest city and the center of theatrical activity. Through the first half of the 19th century several theatres were built in lower Manhattan including the second Park (1821); the **Bowery** (1826), which was the largest in the country with a 3,500-seat capacity and the first New York theatre with gaslight; the Italian Opera House (1833), which was the first American opera house; and the **Astor Place Opera House** (1847), site of the infamous anti-Macready riots of 1849. **Boston,** which had been a latecomer to the theatre circuit, added the Washington Street Theatre and the **Tremont Theatre** in 1827 to the existing Federal Street Theatre. Throughout the 19th century almost every city of any size built an "opera house," which was not necessarily intended for opera, but was a multiuse performance space that could house a range of traveling entertainments and even nonperformance activities such as conventions. These spaces were loosely based on European models; it was even possible to buy published plans showing how to design such a structure.

Throughout this period, the theatres were typified by increasing size and elegance and greater refinement in stage machinery. Exteriors were often done in some version of Greek or Roman revival, creating a sense of dignity and sophistication as well as becoming the most imposing edifices in the cities. The frequent fires that plagued theatres had the one benefit of allowing a fairly steady renewal and renovation of the structures. The New Park, for example, had a 45-ft proscenium opening and a 70-ft-deep stage; it seated 2,500 in an auditorium with a raked pit, three tiers of boxes, and a surrounding gallery. When the Bowery Theatre was rebuilt after the fire of 1845, it had a seating capacity of 4,000 and a stage depth and width of 126 ft, making it one of the largest legitimate theatres in the world. (The Academy of Music, an opera house that opened in New York in 1854, seated 4,500.)

Huge theatres typified by the Bowery were appropriate for large-scale melodrama and spectacle, but as gentlemanly melodrama and realism began to dominate, the trend was reversed. A greater intimacy and a more detailed form of scenery was now required. **Steele MacKaye**'s remodeling of the **Madison Square Theatre** is the best documented of the changes these new trends wrought. For greater intimacy MacKaye reduced the theatre to a 700-seat capacity and eliminated the forestage and the orchestra pit – the orchestra was housed above the proscenium arch. Most notably, he installed an elevator stage with two levels, which allowed one scene to be set on the "offstage" level while another was being played; the elevator could be raised or lowered in 40 seconds. Though lacking the technical sophistication, **Wallack's Theatre** and **Daly**'s **Fifth Avenue Theatre** continued this trend as the center of the New York theatre district moved north up Broadway.

American theatre architecture in the second half of the 19th century followed the trend in Europe. The box, pit, and gallery configuration was replaced by a more luxurious orchestra seating area and balconies. Boxes remained as decorative appendages in American theatres into the early 20th century, but the orchestra eventually became the preferred seating area as individual upholstered chairs with armrests became common after the Civil War. The proscenium or picture-frame stage was the norm, and this sort of theatre, often elaborately decorated, continued to be built through the 1920s. Because the theatre builders were more often interested in business than theatre, "nonessential" spaces – lobbies, dressing rooms, and space between rows of seats – were minimal to nonexistent. The 1930s Depression put a virtual end to theatre construction in the U.S. until after World War II.

Richard Wagner's Festspielhaus in Bayreuth, Germany, is often considered the first modern theatre because of its fan-shaped auditorium design and lack of boxes, creating a "democratic" seating arrangement. Though this 1876 theatre would eventually have a profound influence on 20th-century theatre architecture, it had little immediate impact on American playhouse design. Toward the end of the 19th century, however, a conscious rethinking of theatre architecture began to emerge, and many fanciful theatres were proposed, even if virtually none were built. One of the most extravagant was Steele MacKaye's Spectatorium, designed for the World's Columbian Exposition in Chicago in 1893. It was to hold 10,000 spectators for a pageant chronicling the life of Columbus. The theatre was actually started, but never completed because of the financial crisis of 1893.

In terms of innovation and influence, the closest American counterpart to the Bayreuth Festspielhaus was the Chicago **Auditorium Theatre** designed by Dankmar Adler and Louis Sullivan in 1886. It was virtually the first theatre in the U.S. to address problems of sightlines and acoustics. The upper and lower balconies could be closed off by means of a hinged ceiling, and the rear of the auditorium closed by a hanging curtain. Thus the seating capacity ranged from 2,500 to 4,000, and all seats had unobstructed views of the stage; side galleries, as at Bayreuth, were abolished. The acoustics achieved a perfection unmatched in previous American theatre architecture. In addition, the theatre contained its own electrical generating plant and air cooling system. Adler and Sullivan expressed patriotic and democratic sentiments in their speeches and writings, and saw the Auditorium Theatre as an example of American architecture.

The trends toward intimacy, technical sophistication, and a scientific approach to acoustical and visual design reached a pinnacle with **Winthrop Ames**'s Little Theatre (1912) in New York. Seating only 299 spectators in a Continental dish-style auditorium, the stage had a revolve and 35 traps. The auditorium ceiling could be lowered to change the angle of lighting. Although a balcony was added in 1919 to enlarge the seating capacity, the theatre was still a financial failure.

The antiquarian movement of the 19th century led to a re-examination of the original staging of classical plays. This, coupled with new movements in European theatre, led to the exploration of new stage spaces and configurations. Drawing on Greek and Elizabethan precedents, the thrust stage emerged as a popular alternative to the proscenium. Some of the first efforts in that direction in the U.S. were the projects for "dome theatres" by **Norman Bel Geddes.** First described in 1914 and revised in various ways over the years, Bel Geddes's theatres tended to be a variant of a Greek theatre with a curved stage partially surrounded by curved auditorium seating, all architecturally unified under a single domed structure. A related form of theatre was being used in Germany by **Max Reinhardt.** At roughly the same time, several universities began to create makeshift thrust theatres in an attempt to recreate Elizabethan conditions for the staging of Shakespeare. A notable permanent example was the theatre at Sarah Lawrence College, built in 1952 with a trapezoidal apron in front of a picture-frame stage. However, the real triumph of the thrust stage in North America came with **Tyrone Guthrie**'s Festival Theatre in Stratford, Ontario (1953–7), designed in collaboration with **Tanya Moiseiwitsch.** The general pattern of this theatre was repeated at the **Guthrie Theatre** (1963) in **Minneapolis** and at several theatres around the country built in the 1960s and '70s. It incorporated a stepped thrust stage surrounded on three sides by a curved, stepped auditorium and a balcony. The design could accommodate 1,400 spectators but in a relatively intimate arrangement in which no spectator was more than 80 ft from the stage.

The theatre-in-the-round or arena stage has held a great fascination for theatre architects through the 20th century, but it has rarely been a successful venture. One of the earliest examples was a makeshift arena stage at Teacher's College in New York in 1914. Bel Geddes's Theatre No. 14 (1922), another visionary project never constructed, proposed a method for arena staging. The University of Washington in **Seattle** began experimenting with arena staging in 1932, culminating in the Penthouse Theatre (1940) with a seating capacity of 185. There are several other examples from the 1950s and '60s, the most successful being **Margo Jones**'s Theatre '47, The **Alley Theatre** (1949), the Playhouse Theatre in Houston (1950), New York's **Circle in the Square** (1951), and the **Arena Stage** (1961). However, in order to incorporate the scenic demands of the repertoire, these and other arena-type theatres sometimes resort to closing off a section of audience to create a scenic space, thus turning the theatres into a form of thrust stage.

More common since the 1960s is the flexible-space theatre, sometimes known as a "black box."

Most often associated with colleges or the studio space for an arts complex, these have no fixed seating and can be reconfigured for each production in virtually any style desired. The trend toward environmental production in the late 1960s and '70s encouraged the development of such spaces, and several were designed by environmental designer Jerry Rojo.

Unlike almost all other periods of theatre history, in which the type of performance and the shape of the theatre evolved simultaneously, the mid-20th century in the U.S. accommodated a conglomeration of styles and shapes. The increasingly popular thrust stage could not work well for opera, for instance, or certain forms of drama. Arena and flexible staging, while successful in some cases, was unacceptable in others. At the same time, civic pride was leading many cities to construct municipal theatres or even more elaborate arts centers. Since few cities could afford to build the complete range of theatres necessary for the different demands of modern performance, compromises were evolved. **George Izenour** was the champion of the multiuse space, a single auditorium that could be used or mechanically adapted for a wide range of performances. The Loeb Drama Center in Cambridge or the Civic Center in El Paso, TX, are examples. Although a few were successful, most proved less than ideal and often were compromised by acoustical or mechanical difficulties or proved inadequate for some or all the activities for which they were intended. The **Vivian Beaumont Theatre** (1965) at Lincoln Center (designed by Eero Saarinen and **Jo Mielziner**), for example, was an attempt to combine a proscenium and a thrust stage in a flexible format. It is generally considered an unsuccessful compromise and has been plagued by sightline and acoustic problems.

The most successful theatres of the latter half of the 20th century have been modified thrust stages unencumbered by excessive mechanical devices and intended for single-use purposes. Economics has also reduced the construction of completely new theatres since the 1970s, and most recent new theatres – coming full circle from colonial times – are renovations of structures intended for other uses, often in fairly simple thrust or end-stage arrangements, such as the **Milwaukee Repertory** Theatre created out of an abandoned power station. Also, the frequently good acoustics and intimacy of many older picture-frame theatres are being recognized and restored. As opposed to the postwar years, no one is advocating any sort of ideal theatre structure.

AA

See: M. C. Henderson, *The City & the Theatre,* Clifton, NJ, 1973; G. C. Izenour, *Theater Design,* New York, 1977; B. McNamara, *The American Playhouse in the Eighteenth Century,* Cambridge, MA, 1969; B. McNamara, J. Rojo, R. Schechner, *Theatres, Spaces, Environments,* New York, 1975; W. C. Young, *Famous American Playhouses, 1716–1971,* 2 vols., Chicago, 1973.

Arch Street Theatre 609–615 Arch St., **Philadelphia** [Architect: William Strickland]. Believing that Philadelphians would support a newer, more elegant playhouse than the **Chestnut,** a group of

Arch Street Theatre, Philadelphia. Courtesy: The Free Library of Philadelphia.

citizens pledged the money to build the Arch Street Theatre and leased it to **William B. Wood,** late of the rival theatre. It opened in 1828, but Wood did not last long as manager, and it passed to other hands. Starting in 1861, it enjoyed its most prosperous and famous period when **Mrs. John Drew** became manageress. For nearly a decade, she maintained a peerless company of actors in excellent productions. In 1879, Mrs. Drew was forced to accede to the "combination system," in which each play is individually cast and presented for as long a run as it has the public's interest. After she retired from the theatre's management in 1892, it was often closed. Before it was demolished in 1936, the theatre had been used by German and **Yiddish** companies. MCH

Ardrey, Robert (1908–80) Playwright, best known for allegorical plays of the 1930s, especially *Casey Jones* (1938), examining job enslavement, and *Thunder Rock* (1939), which explored Americans' quandary over the brewing war in Europe. Although produced by the **Group Theatre** with direction by **Elia Kazan,** *Thunder Rock* was more popular in Europe. RHW

See: P. M. Rodney, "Robert Ardrey: A Biographical and Critical Analysis," PhD diss., Case Western Reserve, 1980.

Arena Stage 6th St. and Maine Ave., NW, Washington, DC [Architect: Harry Weese]. In 1950, a group of six associated with George Washington University founded a theatrical company, Arena Stage, under the guidance of Professor Edward Mangum. They opened their first season in a moviehouse, presenting their plays "in the round." When most of the original group drifted away to other pursuits, **Zelda Fichandler,** one of the founding members, took over the reins of leadership and remained its director until 1991. In 1956, the company moved into an old brewery and gradually built an audience. In 1961, sharing the management with her husband Thomas, Mrs. Fichandler moved into a new modern theatre with the help of grants from the Ford Foundation and others. In Phase II of its development (1970), a 500-seat, modified-thrust-stage playhouse (the Kreeger) joined the 800-seat mainstage; later, a cabaret theatre (the Old Vat Room) was added. In 1991 Doug Wager, who had been associated with Arena in various capacities since 1974, succeeded Fichandler. The Arena Stage Company supports a full company of actors, directors, and designers and presents new American and European plays along with musicals and classical revivals. MCH

See: L. Maslon, *The Arena: The First Forty Years,* Washington, DC, 1991.

Arent, Arthur (1904–72) Playwright remembered for his work with the **Federal Theatre**

Liviu Ciulei's production of Molière's *Don Juan* (in Richard Nelson's translation) at the Arena Stage (1978–9 season). Photo: George de Vincent. Courtesy: Arena Stage.

Project. He and a research team created **Living Newspapers,** volatile, imaginative attempts to confront important social and political issues. His best-known work includes an exposé of utilities, *Power* (1937), which expressed the urgent need for affordable electric power for the ordinary and poor consumers; and *Triple-A Plowed Under* (1936), about the economic vicissitudes of farmers and the agricultural way of life during the Depression. **One-Third of a Nation** (1938), a scathing examination of the plight of the poor and substandard housing (emblemized by a burning tenement designed by **Howard Bay**), was the most dynamic of all Living Newspapers. After the demise of the Federal Theatre Project, Arent moved into film, radio, and television.   RHW

Aria da Capo by **Edna St. Vincent Millay** was first directed by the author and produced by the **Provincetown Players** in New York (5 December 1919). The title of the one-act refers to a song in three parts and reflects its structure: A sequence in which two shepherds play out the consequences of greed and territoriality is framed by ironic displays of trivial interaction using *commedia dell'arte* characters. Poetic language and stylized props serve as counterpoint to the play's antiwar message, which proved popular after WW I. The piece was subsequently produced by many little theatres across the country.   KF

Arkansas Repertory Theatre In 1976 Arkansas Rep held its first performances in a former Methodist church, its home for the next 12 years. Besides eight main-stage productions per season, the company mounts an extensive touring series and an Arts-in-Education program for middle and secondary schools. It was one of four theatres in the nation to participate in CULTURE, conducting drama workshops within state prisons. In 1988 the company moved to new facilities in downtown Little Rock.   LAB

Arkin, Alan (1934–   ) Actor and director who began with St. Louis's improvisational Compass Players (1959) and made his New York debut with **Chicago**'s **Second City** (1961) and his legitimate debut in Joseph Stein's *Enter Laughing* (Tony, 1963). He appeared in *Luv* (1964) before directing Livings's *Eh?* (**Circle in the Square**, 1966), *Little Murders* (Obie, 1969), and *The Sunshine Boys* (1972). Arkin's films include *The Russians Are Coming, The Russians Are Coming* (1966), *Wait Until Dark* (1967), *Catch-22* (1970), and *The In-Laws* (1979). *Halfway Through the Door*, Arkin's autobiography, appeared in 1979. His son Adam is also an actor.   REK

Ark Theatre Not-for-profit, **Off-Off Broadway** company founded in 1976 by a married team, Donald Marcus and Lisa Milligan, later joined by Bruce Daniel. They favored an eclectic and offbeat repertoire of old and new plays such as *Idle Hands* (1979), an adaptation of Chekhov's *Platonov*. Before the theatre failed after the 1985–6 season, it had produced plays by such fresh American talents as **A. R. Gurney, Julie Taymor,** and Lynne Alvarez.   CLJ

Arlen, Harold (1905–86) Composer who began in the entertainment field as a nightclub performer and rehearsal pianist. During the early 1930s he wrote songs for Harlem's Cotton Club and for Broadway revues; he also appeared in vaudeville. Starting in the mid-1930s he worked in both theatre and film, contributing songs to the Broadway revue *Life Begins at 8:40* (1934), writing the score for the **Ed Wynn** musical *Hooray for What!* (1937) and composing the sound track for the film *The Wizard of Oz* (1939). While continuing his career in Hollywood, Arlen also wrote the scores for the Broadway musicals *Bloomer Girl* (1944), *St. Louis Woman* (1946), *House of Flowers* (1954), *Jamaica* (1957), and *Saratoga* (1959). Many of Arlen's songs, such as "Stormy Weather," were written in an African-American blues style.   MK

See: E. Jablonski, *Harold Arlen: Happy With the Blues,* Garden City, NY, 1961.

Arliss, George (né George Augustus Arliss-Andrews) (1868–1946) British-born character actor and playwright whose greatest successes occurred in the U.S. after 1901. Arliss, immediately recognizable due to his distinctive features (long, narrow face, pointed nose, habitual monocle, and charming voice), spent 40 years perfecting the playing of villains, great historical leaders, and wise old men with an apparent effortlessness that concealed his polished technique. Louis Parker, author of his best known vehicle, *Disraeli* (1911), said Arliss could "express more with one finger than most actors can express with their entire bodies." His most notable stage roles, in addition to Disraeli, were in *The Second Mrs. Tanqueray* (1901) with Mrs. Pat Campbell, *The Darling of the Gods* (1902) with **Blanche Bates**, *Hedda Gabler* (1904) and *Rosmersholm* (1907) with **Mrs. Fiske**, *Paganini* (1915), *The Green Goddess* (1921), *Old English* (1924), and his last formal stage appearance as Shylock (1928). In 1923 he returned to London after a 22-year absence to appear in Archer's *The Green Goddess*. His successful film career began in 1920, and during the '30s he made over 20 films, portraying among other characters such historical figures as Voltaire, Rothschild (Meyer and Nathan), Cardinal Richelieu, and Wellington. He wrote or collaborated on six plays and wrote two important autobiographies: *Up the Years from Bloomsbury* (1927) and *My Ten Years in the Studio* (1940).   DBW

Armstrong, Will Steven (1930–69) Set and costume designer. After assisting **Jo Mielziner, Donald Oenslager,** and **Boris Aronson,** Armstrong began his career at the **Williamstown Theatre Festival,** designing its first 30 productions. His major productions included *Ivanov* (1958), for which he won an Obie; *Carnival* (1962) for which he won a Tony; *The Lion in Winter* (1966); and *Forty Carats* (1968). He also designed for the **American Shakespeare Festival,** Phoenix Theatre, and the New York City Opera. Much of his work was typified by an attempt to break through the proscenium.   AA

Arneaux, J. A. (1855–?) African-American actor. Born in Georgia of a white French father and a black mother, Arneaux received a good postsecondary education in northern cities and in Paris. A journalist by profession, he took to the stage, first as a song-and-dance artist at **Tony Pastor**'s Metropolitan Theatre on Broadway, then as a legitimate actor and manager of the Astor Place Company of Colored Tragedians, the leading black dramatic troupe in America in the 1880s. Based in New York, the company also performed to great acclaim in both Philadelphia and Providence, RI. Arneaux's roles included Iago, Macbeth, and Pythias, but his favorite part in which he excelled was Richard III, being ranked with Macready, **Edwin Booth,** and **Lawrence Barrett.** EGH

Arnone, John (1949–) Designer. Intending to be an actor, Arnone was a cofounder of the Lion Theatre Company in New York with director **Garland Wright.** He began to design sets for the company, including the highly successful *Vanities* (1976). Employing styles ranging from elaborate detail, such as the miniature city for *New Jerusalem* (1978), to stark symbolism, Arnone has become associated with directors **JoAnne Akalaitis, Des McAnuff,** and Len Jenkin. He has also designed for film and television, including "The Days and Nights of Molly Dodd" and "Tales from the Darkside." AA

Aronson, Boris (1898–1980) Russian-American painter, sculptor, and set designer. Aronson remains as perhaps the most respected American designer of the mid-20th century. He was born in Russia and studied with Aleksandra Ekster, a constructivist designer with the Kamerny Theatre. He left Russia for Berlin in 1922, and in 1923 emigrated to the U.S., where his first assignments were for the Unser Theatre and the **Yiddish Art Theatre.** By the 1930s he was designing major shows on Broadway and working with the **Group Theatre.** His early work reflected not only the influences of Ekster but of Marc Chagall and Nathan Altman, who designed for the Moscow Jewish Theatre. The cubist-fantastic style characteristic of Chagall's paintings can be seen in much of Aronson's early work and even in later works, such as the acclaimed 1959 set for *J.B.*

Despite his enormous output and critical success for plays by **William Saroyan, Tennessee Williams, Clifford Odets,** and others, and hit musicals including *South Pacific,* he did not achieve widespread recognition until he teamed up with director **Harold Prince** on the 1964 musical *Fiddler on the Roof.* This was followed by six more musicals, including *Cabaret* and *A Little Night Music.* This collaboration seemed to bring out Aronson's creativity. His designs ranged from realistic detail for plays like *Awake and Sing!* to technological fantasies such as *Company* that used steel, plexiglass, and projections. His constructivist influences could be seen throughout his work. His sets always had a strong sense of line and form and a generally subtle but evocative use of color used symbolically to support the mood of the play. For the 1940 production of Ballet Theatre's *The Great*

American Goof, Aronson employed, for the first time, a technique he called "Projected Scenery" – a method of projecting colored slides on neutral, abstract shapes in order to create and change the mood and space of a piece. This technique was displayed in the 1947 exhibition of his work at the Museum of Modern Art, aptly titled "Painting with Light." AA

See: F. Rich with L. Aronson, *The Theatre Art of Boris Aronson,* New York, 1987.

Aronson, Rudolph (1856–1919) Impresario, theatre manager, composer. After studying music in Berlin and Paris, Aronson presented a series of orchestral concerts in New York. In 1882 he opened the **Casino Theatre,** where for 12 seasons he mounted lavish productions of European and British comic operas, most notably *Erminie,* which tallied some 1,200 performances in the decade after its premiere in 1886. Among the many performers who attained stardom at the Casino were **Lillian Russell, Francis Wilson, De Wolf Hopper,** and **Jefferson De Angelis.** Aronson also introduced New Yorkers to the pleasures of the roof garden, as he brought his comic operas to the Casino's roof during the summer months. After leaving the Casino, he managed the Bijou Theatre for several years, and was the proprietor of the Metropole Hotel at his death. He also composed more than 150 musical works and left an autobiography, *Theatrical and Musical Memoirs* (New York, 1913). MK

Aronstein, Martin (1936–) A prolific lighting designer, Aronstein has designed over 150 Broadway productions. He began his professional career in 1960 with the **New York Shakespeare Festival** and continued his association with it ever since. He has also designed extensively for regional theatres. Major productions include *Tiny Alice, Play It Again, Sam, Ain't Supposed to Die a Natural Death,* In the Boom Boom Room, and *Promises, Promises.* AA

Around the World in Eighty Days, Jules Verne's 1873 novel of Phileas Fogg's travels, has served as the basis for several Broadway musicals. One early version by Hungarian brothers Imre, Bolossy, and Arnold **Kiralfy,** opening 28 August 1875 (the third that year alone) at New York's Academy of Music, became one of the staples of 19th-century popular musical theatre, revived in New York alone at least six times between 1876 and 1888. The production, loaded with sumptuous ballets, processions, and specialty song-and-dance acts, consisted of 18 scenes designed to display scenic exoticism and special effects. There was a distinctly Asian feel to Fogg's journey; critics singled out the scenes from Borneo, Calcutta, and the Taj Mahal as especially impressive. The sinking of the steamship constituted a particularly special effect. Like *The Black Crook* before it, this extravaganza proved extremely durable, with more than a half-dozen revivals through the rest of the century.

A freely adapted version with 1,200 performers was staged at New York's *Hippodrome* in the 1911–12 season. Another *Around the World* [sic], with book by **Orson Welles** and songs by **Cole Porter,** opened 31 May 1946 at the Adelphi Theatre, New York, under the aegis of the **Mercury Theatre.** It lasted only 75 performances. This extravaganza, with 34 songs and a huge cast, featured Welles as the villain pursuing Fogg in a wide range of disguises and sufficient outrageous presentational gimmicks that most critics' reviews evoked comparisons to *Hellzapoppin.* The Porter score produced no standards, but the show, an extraordinary star turn for Welles, did include a magic show and a train wreck.   JD

Arrow Maker, The, by California native Mary Austin, was the final production of New York's **New Theatre** (1911). The three-act drama of Native American life was set in the Sierras prior to the white occupation of California. George Foster Platt's direction, which emphasized authentic costumes, folk songs, chants, and dances, failed to mask from critical view the play's turgid language and trite situations. Austin's vituperative criticism of the company's handling of her script further impeded her efforts to get her plays produced on Broadway. The play was later popular with amateur groups and high schools. [See also **Native Americans portrayed.**]   WD

Arsenic and Old Lace by Joseph Kesselring. A **Lindsay–Crouse** production and Kesselring's only Broadway success; opened at the Fulton Theatre, 10 January 1941 (1,444 performances). Directed by **Bretaigne Windust,** it starred **Josephine Hull** and Jean Adair as Aunt Martha and Aunt Abby, two of the nicest maiden ladies who ever invited the minister to tea but who were, in reality, homicidal maniacs poisoning 13 men in "one of the blandest murder games ever played in Brooklyn," wrote **Brooks Atkinson.** Brilliantly revived in 1986 at the **46th Street Theatre,** this hilarious murder-farce-comedy starred **Jean Stapleton** and Polly Holliday as the bizarre sisters; Abe Vigoda replaced Boris Karloff's Jonathan, **William Hickey** portrayed the strange Dr. Einstein (Edgar Stehli), and Tony Roberts assayed the blustering nephew Mortimer Brewster (Allyn Joslyn).   GSA

Artef Yiddish acronym for Workers' Theater Group; began in New York in 1925 as a dramatic studio/collective under the auspices of the communist daily *Freiheit* (Freedom) (see **Yiddish theatre**). Several more cohorts of actors entered in successive studios and studied together until assimilated into the performing nucleus. Like other Soviet-influenced groups of the period, Artef's members were committed to spreading radical politics through expressionist, even agitprop, productions that stressed stylized groupings and mass movement. The press outside the Yiddish community praised its colorful vitality in repertory adapted from the Yiddish canon or translated into Yiddish from contemporaneous American and Soviet plays, some 80 productions in all. After a last major effort in 1939, Artef performed only sporadically until 1953.   NS

Arthur, Julia (née Ida Lewis) (1869–1950) Canadian-born actress who played the leading feminine roles in about 200 plays, including the first Lady Windermere in America (1893). From her success in 1891 in F. R. Giles's *The Black Masque* at the **Union Square Theatre** until her first retirement in 1899, after her marriage to millionaire Benjamin P. Cheney, Arthur attained acclaim in numerous Shakespearean roles as well as contemporary parts. During 1895–7 she appeared at London's Lyceum under Henry Irving. She was most successful in roles featuring unbridled temperament, pathos, and tears. After a 15-year retirement she returned to the stage; her last appearance was on tour in 1924 in *Saint Joan.*   DBW

Asch, Sholom (1880–1957) Polish-born playwright and novelist who wrote in Yiddish. His plays mainly concern the conflict between orthodox and emancipated Jew, and he achieved early fame and notoriety with *The God of Vengeance* (1907), closed down by the police for immorality when produced on Broadway in 1923. Other notable plays include *Downstream* (1904), *The Messiah Period* (1906), *Sabatai Zevi* (1908), *Wealthy Reb Shloime* (1913), and *Mottke the Thief* (1917). Several of his novels were dramatized and performed by **Maurice Schwartz.**   AB

Asian-American theatre This term could apply to the work of all American theatre artists of Asian ancestry – from the avant-garde spectacles of **Ping Chong** to the Broadway playmaking of **David Henry Hwang.** More often, however, it refers to a contemporary movement of **ethnic**-identified theatre that has yielded several regional companies and provided encouragement, training, and professional exposure to scores of Asian-American actors, directors, and, perhaps most significantly, playwrights. Whether it has also produced a unified aesthetic or political outlook is open to debate.

Historically, artists of Asian extraction have been performing in the U.S. for over a century; but until recently an intricate nexus of social and cultural factors kept them marginalized or excluded from mainstream theatre, and impeded the development of Asian-American stage literature.

Traditional operas, puppet shows, and acrobatic displays were imported from China as early as the 1850s. Exotic and baffling to many Westerners, these vivid spectacles were welcomed by the masses of Chinese laborers who emigrated to California to mine gold, build the railroad, and start up Chinatowns. Tung Hook Tong was, in 1852, probably the first such opera company to tour nationally. Other Chinese performers played extended runs in San Francisco; some eventually toured in variety and vaudeville.

Anti-Chinese sentiment flared in the economically depressed 1870s [see *My Partner* regarding contemporary stage caricatures of Chinese], and in 1882 Congress passed the Asian Exclusion Act to stem immigration. Related racial violence drove many Chinese from California to other regions of the country. The new Chinatowns soon had their own amateur opera clubs, and by 1900 there were professional Chinese opera houses in New York,

Chinese Theatre on Jackson Street, Chinatown, in turn-of-the-century San Francisco. Courtesy: Michael Gnat.

Portland (OR), and Boston as well as **San Francisco.**

Interest in traditional performance gradually diminished, and by the 1930s many Chinatown theatres had become Chinese-language cinemas. By then a large contingent of Japanese (and a smaller number of Filipinos) had also settled in the U.S., mostly in the West. However, apart from the variety artists who imitated such Caucasian celebrities as **Fred Astaire, Sally Rand,** and Bing Crosby in Chinatown nightclubs during the 1930s and '40s, few Asian Americans appeared in Western-style live entertainment. The American theatre continued periodically to produce shows with Asian themes – from *The First Born* (a 19th-century melodrama set in San Francisco's Chinatown), to **Gilbert and Sullivan**'s *Mikado,* to the post–World War II Broadway hits *Teahouse of the August Moon* and *The King and I.* But Asiatic actors were usually relegated to playing stock character maids, cooks, vamps, and spies, while Caucasians played the "Oriental" leads. (The same was often true in Hollywood films.)

The differences between Western and Asian drama kept some Asian immigrants away from theatre, as did language barriers and moral qualms about show business. Moreover, Japanese Americans were virtually banished from all public life when the Government interned them in relocation camps during WW II. But as third- and fourth-generation Asian Americans appeared, the stereotyping and casting practices remained. The 1949 **Rodgers–Hammerstein** musical *Flower Drum Song* was the first (and for many years the only) professional New York production set in a modern Asian-American milieu.

In 1965, finding little meaningful stage or screen work, Alberto Isaacs, Mako, and other Asian-American actors and directors created **East West Players** in **Los Angeles.** It was the thick of the civil rights era, and EWP was a self-help venture, talent showcase, and declaration of ethnic pride. Unlike contemporary **African-American** ensembles, however, EWP had no repertoire of new plays or stable of writers to draw on; at first it staged classics and scripts set in Asia (*Rashomon*).

In 1973 two sister ensembles were formed: the Asian Exclusion Act (now Northwest Asian American Theatre) in **Seattle** and the activist Asian American Theatre Workshop in San Francisco. AATW (later renamed the Asian American Theatre Company) caused the bigger splash, with new plays high on its agenda – plays exploding the old media images of Asians and aggressively revealing the frustrations and contradictions of Asian-American experience. In this vein, cofounder Frank Chin's hip, nervy scripts garnered immediate national attention: first *Chickencoop Chinaman* and later his *Year of the Dragon* and *Gee, Pop!* Chin was the first Asian-American dramatist to have a "legit" production in New York (*Chickencoop Chinaman,* 1972, **American Place Theatre**).

In 1977 actor-director **Tisa Chang** founded New York's **Pan Asian Repertory Theatre,** the fourth regional outlet for Asian-American drama. This loose network of subscription theatres boosted the careers of many fine Asian-American actors, including John Lone, Mako, Nobu McCarthy, Dennis Dun, and Joan Chen, and introduced works by dozens of U.S. writers with ancestral roots in Japan, China, Korea, the Philippines, and other Asian countries. Repeated themes include the Japanese-American WW II internment, generational clashes between Asian-bred immigrants and their Americanized children, the history and persistence of racism, the mythic reverberations from Asian cultures. Realism laced with satiric surrealism is the predominant style, but much variety exists. Noteworthy texts include: Velina Hasu Houston's *Tea* (the courtship of a black GI and a Japanese war bride); **Philip Kan Gotanda**'s memory play *Song for a Nisei Fisherman;* Wakako Yamauchi's *And the Soul Shall Dance* (set on a Depression-era farm); Laurence Yep's *Pay the Chinaman* (about Chinese con men in early California); Ric Shiomi's *Yellow Fever* (detective tale with an ethnic twist); and Ernest Abuba's *An American Story* (about a mixed-raced family in San Diego).

A few Asian-American playwrights have "crossed over" into mainstream venues. Most prominently, **David Henry Hwang**'s early works (*F.O.B., Dance and the Railroad*) debuted at New York's **Public Theater,** and his *M. Butterfly* won a Tony on Broadway. **Berkeley Repertory Theatre, Eureka Theatre, Manhattan Theatre Club, Mark Taper Forum,** and **Los Angeles Theatre Center** have mounted scripts by Hwang, Gotanda, Houston, and others.

Not all dramatists of Asian descent have worked within the Asian-American theatre axis; some prefer not to affix any ethnic labels to their work. The many linked with the movement have, however, kept involved in it long after finding success in other realms. In 1990 Hwang and **B. D. Wong** led a protest by Asian-American artists over the casting of a white actor (Jonathan Pryce) in a major Eurasian role in the Broadway musical *Miss Saigon,* igniting a vigorous public debate about the meaning of "nontraditional" casting and muticulturalism.

As their ranks continue to swell, Asian Americans have repudiated the notion that they are a "silent, invisible" minority by actively participating in all areas of popular culture; and while some critics now decry ethnic-specific cultural expression as a "balkanization" of the arts, Asian-American drama leaders defend its ongoing importance. East West Players artistic director Nobu McCarthy commented in 1991, "Our artists should graduate and perform shoulder-to-shoulder with white artists in the mainstream. But first we must discover who *we* are, before we become the mainstream." MB

See: M. Berson, ed., *Between Worlds: Contemporary Asian American Plays,* New York, 1990; F. Chine et al., eds., *Aiiieeee! An Anthology of Asian American Writers,* New York, 1975; E. Kim, *Asian American Literature,* Philadelphia, 1982.

As Is by William M. Hoffman, the first AIDS play on the commercial stage, opened at **Circle Repertory Company** on 10 March 1985. Directed by **Marshall Mason,** it moved to Broadway's **Lyceum Theatre** on 1 May and ran seven months. The play explores the victimization of an AIDS patient who is abandoned by lover and family, before his ex-lover accepts him "as is." Infused with bitter gallows humor, but less strident than Larry Kramer's *The Normal Heart* (1985), the play balances specific personal issues and broad political concerns. It garnered three Tony nominations, an Obie, and a Drama Desk Award.   HFP

Asolo State Theatre Founded in 1960 by students and faculty of Florida State University, AST became an official state theatre in 1965 and fully professional in 1966. Besides a full repertory season of classic and original plays, current programs include an acting conservatory and an educational touring theatre for schools in the Sarasota area. In 1989 the company moved to new facilities in the Asolo Center for the Performing Arts. The original Asolo Theatre was built in Asolo, Italy, in 1798 and brought to Sarasota in 1949.   LAB

Association of Producing Artists (APA) Founded in 1960 by **Ellis Rabb** in an attempt to create a collective of theatre artists offering a wide range of material in a repertory structure, APA spent its first four seasons, in addition to touring, with residencies at Princeton, Milwaukee's Fred Miller Theatre, the **Folksbiene** Theatre in New York City, and at the University of Michigan. In 1964 it joined the **Off-Broadway** Phoenix Theatre, which had been organized in 1953 by **T. Edward Hambleton** and **Norris Houghton** (with **Stuart Vaughan** as artistic director, 1958–62) and had presented notable productions of standard plays and new works, including *Once Upon a Mattress* (1959) and **Kopit**'s *Oh Dad, Poor Dad* (1962). For five years the APA at the Phoenix presented a wide range of plays, most notably *Man and Superman* (1964); *You Can't Take It with You* (1965); *Right You Are* (1966); *The Show-Off* (1967); *Pantagleize* (codirected by Rabb and **John Houseman**), *The Misanthrope,* and *Exit the King* (1968); and *Cock-a-Doodle Dandy* and *Hamlet* (1969). Several seasons were spent at NYC's **Lyceum Theatre** prior to APA's dissolution in 1970.   DBW

Association of Theatrical Press Agents and Managers (ATPAM) see **agents**

Astaire (né Austerlitz), Fred (1899–1987) and **Adele** (1898–1981) Dancers, singers, and actors. As children the Astaires spent 10 years in **vaudeville,** where they perfected their dancing and teamwork. In 1917 they made their New York **musical theatre** debut in *Over the Top.* Influenced by the ballroom dancing of Vernon and Irene Castle, the Astaires also studied with Broadway choreographer and director **Ned Wayburn.** Their dances were fluid, stylish, and often witty, in keeping with the frothy musicals in which they appeared. After featured roles in several shows, the Astaires were the stars of *Lady, Be Good!* (1924), for which **George and Ira Gershwin** wrote the score. The successful partnership with the Gershwins was repeated with *Funny Face* (1927). They starred with **Marilyn Miller** in *Smiles* (1930), and made their last appearance as a team in the **Howard Dietz–Arthur Schwartz** revue, *The Band Wagon* (1931). After Adele's retirement, Fred appeared alone in *The Gay Divorcee* (1932) before leaving for Hollywood and a career in musical films. Critics generally considered Adele to be the stronger dancer and more vivid personality of the partnership. Equally popular in England, the Astaires brought several of their American successes to the London stage during the 1920s.   MK

See: F. Astaire, *Steps in Time,* New York, 1959; S. Green and B. Goldblatt, *Starring Fred Astaire,* New

York, 1973; J. Mueller, *Astaire Dancing,* New York, 1985; T. Satchell, *Astaire: The Biography,* London, 1987.

As Thousands Cheer, music and lyrics by **Irving Berlin,** sketches by **Moss Hart,** opened 3 September 1933 at New York's **Music Box Theatre,** running 400 performances. A topical **revue** treating life during the Depression, it took the novel form of a newspaper, with each segment representing a section or column (comics, society pages, lonelyhearts column, etc.). The connection might be far-fetched, as when "weather report" became the excuse for **Ethel Waters** to introduce "Heat Wave," or an occasion for opulence, as in the rotogravure section's "Easter Parade." Most of the skits were lighthearted, although there were some serious overtones; one headline was "Unknown Negro Lynched by Frenzied Mob," which yielded the wrenching "Supper Time." Given a lavish production by **Sam H. Harris,** the show featured, in addition to Miss Waters, **Marilyn Miller,** Clifton Webb, and Helen Broderick. A revised and localized version, retitled *Stop Press,* was presented in London in 1935. JD

Astor Place Opera House Broadway, East 9th St. and Astor Pl., NYC. In their pursuit of operatic pleasure, well-to-do New Yorkers built the Astor Place close to an exclusive enclave on Lafayette Street settled by the Astors and their friends; but opera did not remain long the house's principal fare, and the 1,800-seat theatre was given over to other entertainments. In 1849, during an engagement by the English star William Macready, a riot was triggered from a long-smouldering feud between Macready and the American star **Edwin Forrest,** which was also fed by anti-English sentiment among the Irish denizens of the Bowery area. The militia was called in to quell the riot, and the order was given to fire at the crowd. When the smoke had cleared, at least 22 (possibly as many as 31) people had died and 150 were wounded. A recent play by **Richard Nelson** (*Two Shakespearean Actors*) deals with the Macready–Forrest rivalry. In 1852, the theatre was renamed the New York to rid it of its tainted past, but in 1854 it was sold at auction to the Mercantile Library Association; thereafter it was known as Clinton Hall until it was torn down in 1891. MCH

Astor Place Opera House riot, 1849. Courtesy: Library of Congress.

See: R. Moody, *The Astor Place Riot,* Bloomington, IN, 1955.

Atkinson, (Justin) Brooks (1894–1984) Drama critic. Educated at Harvard University where he attended **George Pierce Baker**'s Workshop 47, Atkinson taught English for a year (1917–18) at Dartmouth College and worked as a reporter on the Springfield (MA) *Daily News.* A year later, he began a four-year stint as assistant drama critic to **H. T. Parker** on the *Boston Daily Evening Transcript.* In 1922 he became book review editor for the *New York Times,* succeeding **Stark Young** as the paper's theatre critic in 1926. When war broke out in 1941, he took an overseas assignment, later receiving a Pulitzer Prize (1947) for his reports on the Soviet Union. After the war (1946) he returned to reviewing the Broadway theatre. The most respected critic of his generation, Atkinson offered commonsense opinions in a graceful style, and was known for both his fairness and candor. He thought that the theatre should reach out and relate to the world outside of the art; therefore he did not mingle with theatre people or attend rehearsals, believing that his reviews were for the "average guy who goes to the theatre." At his retirement in 1960, the Mansfield Theatre was renamed in his honor. His many books include *Broadway Scrapbook* (1948), *Brief Chronicles* (1966), *Broadway* (1970), and *The Lively Years: 1920–1973.* TLM

At the Foot of the Mountain (AFOM) Founded in 1974, this **feminist theatre** company produced resident work and touring productions by other such companies from its base in **Minneapolis.** Administered initially by playwright **Martha Boesing,** director Phyllis Jane Rose, and producer Jan Magrane, the company evolved from a grass-roots collective of mostly white, middle-class women into a multicultural theatre supported by community audiences and various grants. Early productions included *Raped,* a revision of Brecht's *The Exception and the Rule,* and *The Story of a Mother,* scripted collaboratively by Boesing and the company. JDo

Auditorium Theatre 50 East Congress Parkway, Chicago [Architects: Sullivan and Adler]. Set within a multipurpose building encompassing a hotel, offices, and stores, the Auditorium was intended to be supported by the commercial enterprises in the complex. Designed by the experimental firm of Dankmar and Adler, it introduced no stunningly new concepts architecturally but was provided with near-perfect acoustics and sightlines, a flexible auditorium and stage, and striking interior decoration. It opened in 1899 and was in use as an opera house and theatre until 1942, when it was largely abandoned. Once threatened with destruction, it was restored and reopened in 1967 after a civic campaign was launched to save it. Today it is used for Broadway road shows, dance companies, and pop concerts. MCH

Aunt Dan and Lemon by **Wallace Shawn.** Produced in New York (**Public Theater**) in 1985 (and London), this mediation on Nazi atrocities also explores the playwright's relationships with his audience in provocative monologues by Lemon (Leonora), a reclusive young English woman in her 20s, existing on fruit juices and memories of Aunt Dan (Danielle, played by **Linda Hunt**), an Oxford don. Before dying, Dan corrupts Lemon's concept of public and private morality with her reminiscences of Mindy, a high-priced prostitute and Dan's lesbian lover who strangled her arms-dealer lover during oral sex. In a thin plot, Dan's verbal tirades corrupt Lemon and lead to her second-hand embrace of Henry Kissinger, the policies of violence that rot our society, and to a defence of Nazi death camps. GSA

Auntie Mame by **Jerome Lawrence and Robert E. Lee,** adapted from Patrick Dennis's novel, opened at the **Broadhurst Theatre** on 31 October 1956 and ran for 639 performances. Seen through the eyes of young Patrick Dennis, the play presents the multiple aspects of his aunt Mame Dennis's character and her ability to convert adversity into success. Mame's flamboyant nature drives the play, which nearly replaces plot with a series of vignettes spanning 1928–46. Rosalind Russell gave her major career performance as Mame in both the play and the 1958 Warner Bros. film, which won an Academy Award for Best Comedy. *Mame,* the musical adaptation by Lawrence, Lee, and **Jerry Herman,** opened 24 May 1966 at the **Winter Garden,** ran for 1,508 performances, and was revived in 1983.
RW

Autumn Garden, The, by **Lillian Hellman** departs from the author's characteristic use of strong theatrical moments and sharply defined moral issues to explore the empty lives and unhappy relationships of spiritless middle- and upper-class people. Opening 7 March 1951 at the Coronet Theater, the play was directed by **Harold Clurman** and featured a fine ensemble cast. **Fredric March** appeared as a failed painter whose return to his boyhood home triggers melancholy self-recognition in his friends. Jane Wyatt played his dissatisfied wife. **Brooks Atkinson** found that the play followed "perhaps unintentionally in the Chekhov tradition of character description, aimlessness, and mood."
KF

Awake and Sing! by **Clifford Odets.** Along with *Golden Boy,* this play represents Odets at his best and as the voice for his company, the **Group Theatre,** which first produced it 19 February 1935 under the direction of **Harold Clurman.** Set in a Bronx apartment designed by **Boris Aronson,** the naturalistic presentation of this study of a Depression-era Jewish family depicts Bessie, a domineering mother played by **Stella Adler,** trying to control a family in upheaval, especially restless children: unhappily pregnant Hennie (Phoebe Brand) and starry-eyed Ralph (Jules [John] Garfield) who serves as protagonist of the play and effects the escape of his sister. As her lover Moe puts it, "Make a break or spend the rest of your life in a coffin." The children's grandfather Jacob, who adds a Marxist flavor to the proceedings, sacrifices himself in order to fulfill Ralph's dreams, symbolized by the mail plane periodically flying overhead.
RHW

Awards, theatrical Various professional theatre and other organizations support excellence with many awards, usually given annually. Among the more significant are the following:
1. **Actors' Equity** annually presents the St. Clair Bayfield Award to honor an outstanding performer (selected by several New York drama critics) in a nonfeatured role in a Shakespearean production in greater New York. It has also taken over the presentation of the Clarence Derwent Awards, founded in 1945 by **Derwent** to recognize the best actor and actress appearing in nonfeatured roles, and now given by Actors' Equity to promising newcomers.
2. The American Academy and Institute of Arts and Letters established their Medal for Good Speech in 1924 to recognize correct utterance in the use of language on the stage and in radio and television. The Academy also recognizes a composer, lyricist, or librettist with the **Marc Blitzstein** Award for Musical Theatre. The **Richard Rodgers** Production Award is given to those who are not already established in the field.
3. The American College Theatre Festival gives several annual awards: (a) the ACTF Award for theatrical design excellence; (b) the ANTA West Award for an original script written by a student; (c) the David Library of the American Revolution Award for Playwriting on American Freedom and Americana; (d) the **Lorraine Hansberry** Playwriting Award for scripts on the black experience; (e) the Columbia/Embassy Television Playwriting Award; (f) the National Student Playwriting Award; (g) the Irene Ryan Winners Circle Acting Awards; and (h) the Jane Chambers Playwriting Award (addressing women's experiences).
4. The American Society for Theatre Research gives the Barnard Hewitt Award for best theatre book of the year, as well as a young scholar's award.
5. The Association for Theatre in Higher Education (ATHE) annually gives an Award of Merit for distinguished service to the educational theatre, the ATHE Citation for Distinguished Service to the Theatre, and other awards to published essays and books on production or pedagogy.
6. Brandeis University Creative Arts Awards, begun in 1957, recognize outstanding artistic contributions during a lifetime of distinguished achievement.
7. Columbia University Graduate School of Journalism. Among the Pulitzer Prizes awarded annually is the prize of $1,000 for a distinguished play written by an American, preferably dealing with American life.
8. The Daniel Blum *Theatre World* Awards, founded in 1945, recognize "promising personalities who have appeared throughout the season."
9. The Drama Desk Award honors outstanding achievement in the Broadway or **Off-Broadway** scene in several categories.
10. The **Drama League** of America annually gives its Distinguished Performance Award.
11. The **Dramatists Guild** annually awards the Elizabeth Hull–Kate Warriner Award to a playwright dealing with a controversial subject in a script produced in New York City.
12. The **George Jean Nathan** Awards, begun

in 1959, honor the author of "the best piece of drama criticism published during the previous year."

13. The **Helen Hayes** Awards, given annually in Washington, DC, recognize all aspects of theatrical production, including new scripts, which are awarded the **Charles MacArthur** Award.

14. The **John F. Kennedy Center** for the Performing Arts bestows the Kennedy Center Honors, a national tribute to excellence and life achievement in the performing arts. It also sponsors the College of Fellows of the American Theatre.

15. John Simon Guggenheim Memorial Foundation Fellowships have included Fellows in Drama since 1928 and Fellows in Stage Design and Production since 1926.

16. The **Joseph Jefferson [III]** Awards are presented annually in Chicago to promote theatrical excellence.

17. The Joseph Maharam Foundation, Inc. established the Maharam Theatrical Design Awards in 1965 to honor scenic and costume design in Broadway and **Off-Broadway** shows.

18. The **Jujamcyn Theaters** Award recognizes regional theatres that have made outstanding contributions.

19. The League of New York Theatres and Producers, Inc. sponsors the **Antoinette Perry** Awards (Tonys), given annually since 1947 for "Distinguished Achievement in the Theatre" – awards being presented for each of several aspects of production on Broadway.

20. **Los Angeles** Drama Critics' Circle Awards are given annually for outstanding production work in that city.

21. The **Margo Jones** Awards, established 1961, are given annually to "the producing manager of an American or Canadian theatre whose policy of presenting new dramatic works continues most faithfully in the tradition of Margo Jones."

22. The National Theatre Conference recognizes and encourages excellence in theatre with their **Paul Green** Foundation Awards. The Conference also gives the Barrie and Bernice **Stavis** Award for emerging writers.

23. The New England Theatre Conference Awards, founded 1957, annually honor outstanding creative achievement in the American theatre.

24. The New York Drama Critics' Circle Awards, established 1936, annually honor outstanding productions.

25. Outer Critics' Circle Awards, begun 1950, annually honor outstanding achievement in the professional theatre, in addition to the **John Gassner** Award for an outstanding new playwright.

26. The **Shubert** Foundation Award, established 1945, annually recognizes a published work in the field of theatre in the U.S.

27. The Society of Stage Directors and Choreographers (SSDC) Award of Merit for outstanding achievement in the performing arts is awarded infrequently.

28. The Theatre Library Association since 1968 has annually recognized a published work in the field of theatre in the U.S. with the George Freedley Memorial Award.

29. The *Variety* New York Drama Critics' Poll, begun in 1939, annually recognizes outstanding achievement in a variety of categories.

30. The *Village Voice* **Off-Broadway** Awards (Obies), founded in 1956, recognize theatrical achievement in the Off-Broadway theatre.

31. William Shakespeare Awards for Classical Theatre (Wills) are presented by the **Shakespeare Theatre** in Washington, DC, to individuals for preservation of the vitality of classical theatre.

32. The **Zeisler** Award for distinguished service to **resident nonprofit professional theatre** was established in 1986 by **Jon Jory** to honor senior artists. The award rotates to honor a director, actor, designer, or administrator.   SMA

See: *Awards, Honors & Prizes*, Detroit, 1989.

Axelrod, George (1922–) New York–born playwright, director, and producer whose reputation rests on two plays: *The Seven Year Itch,* a 1952 three-act comedy that starred Tom Ewell as a Walter Mitty–like imaginative publisher who, while a summer bachelor, dreams of romantic involvement with the girl upstairs (Marilyn Monroe in the film version); and *Will Success Spoil Rock Hunter?* (1955), a Hollywood spoof with Walter Matthau and Orson Bean. Axelrod produced *A Visit to a Small Planet* (1957) and directed a number of comedies, including **Neil Simon**'s *The Star-Spangled Girl* (1966).   DBW

Ayers, Lemuel (1915–55) Scenic and costume designer. From the late 1930s until his death, Ayers designed some of Broadway's most memorable plays and musicals including *Oklahoma!* (1943), *Kiss Me, Kate* (also coproduced; 1948), *Camino Real* (1953), and *The Pajama Game* (1954). Ayers developed a painterly, almost whimsical style, but was also capable of evocative realism as in *Angel Street* (1941), which had an unusually shallow set painted on black velour.   AA

Azenberg, Emanuel (1934–) American producer, called by the *New York Times* one of Broadway's "most successful producers and one of its outspoken critics." Although he works closely with the **Shubert Organization,** in the mid-1980s he essentially left the Broadway establishment by walking out on the League of American Theatres and Producers. Although he has been producing in New York since 1961 (almost 40 Broadway plays in 30 years), his greatest successes have been since 1982. His single major client has been **Neil Simon,** all of whose plays since 1972 have been produced by Azenberg. Recent productions have included *Biloxi Blues,* a revival of *Joe Egg,* **Sondheim**'s *Sunday in the Park with George,* and Simon's *Lost in Yonkers* (1991). In 1990 he ventured into film by producing Stoppard's *Rosencrantz and Guildenstern Are Dead.*   DBW

B

Babe, Thomas (1941–) Playwright-director, educated at Harvard, Cambridge (England), and Yale Law School (JD, 1972). He has been identified through most of his career with the **New York Shakespeare Festival,** beginning with his first professionally produced play, *Kid Champion* (1974), about the downfall of a rock star, and including *Rebel Women* (1976), *A Prayer for My Daughter* (1978), *Taken in Marriage* (1979, with **Meryl Streep**), *Salt Lake City Skyline* (1980), and *Buried Inside Extra* (1982–3), directed by **Joseph Papp.** Recent plays have been produced first in Los Angeles (including *Demon Wine* at the **Los Angeles Theatre Center**); since the late 1980s Babe has turned more attention to directing.   DBW

Babes in Arms Two-act musical comedy, music by **Richard Rodgers,** lyrics by **Lorenz Hart,** book by Rodgers and Hart; opened 14 April 1937 at the **Sam S. Shubert Theatre,** New York, and ran 289 performances. The classic "Hey, kids, let's put on a show" musical, it told of a group of show-business youths, left alone by their touring parents, trying to raise enough money to avoid being sent to a state farm. The low-budget production was appropriately cast with young, generally unknown performers, among them **Alfred Drake.** The score contributed more Rodgers and Hart standards than any other – including "Where or When," "My Funny Valentine," "Johnny One-Note," and "The Lady Is a Tramp" – and **George Balanchine**'s choreography contributed an early example of the subsequently popular "dream ballet."   JD

Babes in Toyland Two-act musical fantasy, music by **Victor Herbert,** words by Glen Mac-Donough; opened 13 October 1903 at the old **Majestic Theatre,** New York, for a run of 192 performances. Following the earlier 1903 success of their extravagant musical version of *The Wizard of Oz,* producer Fred Hamlin and director **Julian Mitchell** commissioned this fairy-tale musical, which first appeared in Chicago in June and, after its New York run, toured the country for years. The libretto tells the story of Alan and Jane, who, fleeing their wicked uncle, arrive in Toyland, meet a bevy of Mother Goose characters, and have myriad adventures. The great appeal of the show lay in lavish scenic spectacle (a fearsome spider's forest, the Moth Queen's flowery palace) and Herbert's classic score ("Toyland," "The March of the Toys"). The show was Victor Herbert's first great popular success.   JD

Bacall, Lauren (née Betty Joan Perske) (1924–) Actress-singer who, after graduating from the **American Academy of Dramatic Arts,** appeared in walk-on roles on Broadway before leaving for Hollywood and a 25-year film career. She returned to Broadway in 1959 in the comedy *Goodbye Charlie,* and also starred in *Cactus Flower* (1965). In 1970 she made her musical comedy debut in *Applause,* for which she received a Tony Award. After several films, she returned again to the musical stage in *Woman of the Year* (1981). While expressing reservations about her limited singing voice, critics praised Bacall's magnetism, energy, and humor. Her critically acclaimed autobiography (*By Myself*) appeared in 1978.   MK

Bacon, Frank (1864–1922) Actor and dramatist. A native of California, Bacon emphasized Yankee character parts in melodramas such as ***Ten Nights in a Barroom*** and in comedy sketches, mainly in the **San Francisco** area, until the 1906 earthquake, when he departed for New York. There he performed in such plays as *Alabama, Pudd'nhead Wilson,* and **Winchell Smith**'s *The Fortune Hunter.* In *Lightnin'* (1918), written in collaboration with Smith, Bacon achieved his greatest acting success as Lightnin' Bill Jones, a charming rascal and ne'er-do-well who enjoys tall tales and strong drink. Dependent upon Bacon's acting, which he interrupted to participate in the 1919 actors' strike, the plays ran for three years, breaking all existing records with 1,291 performances.   WJM

Bailey, Pearl [Mae] (1918–90) Actress-singer of black and Creek Indian ancestry whose career began in 1933 after winning an amateur contest in Philadelphia and reached its apogee in 1967 with the title role in an all-black ***Hello, Dolly!*** featuring Cab Calloway, for which she received a special Tony Award. "Pearlie Mae" considered herself a singer and humorist, not an actress, and even though she was a top nightclub attraction from 1946 on, she appeared in five Broadway musicals (including *Dolly*): *St. Louis Woman* (1946), *Arms and the Girl* (1950), *Bless You All* (1950), and *House of Flowers* (1954). Of her films, notable were *Carmen Jones* in 1954 (as Frankie) and ***Porgy and Bess*** in 1959 (as Maria). Bailey wrote two volumes of memoirs: *The Raw Pearl* (1968) and *Pearlie Mae: Talking to Myself* (1971).   DBW

Bainter, Fay (1891–1968) Prominent on the New York stage in the 1920s and '30s, Bainter, formerly a child actress in Los Angeles, was notable for wife, understanding mother, or faithful friend roles. After her New York debut in *The Rose of Panama* (1912), she appeared in scores of parts on Broadway, in **summer stock,** and on tour, ranging from Ming Toy in *East Is West* (1918) to Mary Tyrone in a national tour (1957–8) of *Long Day's Journey into Night.* Reprising her role in a 1953 touring production, she is remembered best for her final film performance as the grim Mrs. Amelia Tilford in *The Children's Hour* (1961).   DBW

Baker, Belle (née Bella Becker) (1895–1957) Vaudeville singer who introduced 163 songs, including "Blue Skies" (1926), written for her by **Irving Berlin.** A product of New York's Lower East Side Jewish ghetto, Baker, one of vaudeville's "red-hot mamas" and equally adept at comedy or pathos, earned a 1913 billing at The **Palace.** By 1917 her receipts topped all name performers in New York's **Keith** theatres. As late as 1932 she introduced one of her biggest hits, "All of Me."   DBW

Baker, Benjamin A. (1818–90) Playwright. "Uncle Ben Baker" deserted his prompter's post at William **Mitchell's Olympic** Theatre and, for Mitchell's benefit, wrote *A Glance at New York in 1848,* which opened on 15 February 1848 starring **F. S. Chanfrau** as Mose. Encouraged by the "shouts of delight from the Bowery B'hoys in the pit," and a run of 74 performances, Baker created more adventures for Mose: *New York as It Is* (1848), *Mose in California* (1849), and *Mose in China* (1850).   RM

Baker, George Pierce (1866–1935) Educator. A year after graduating from Harvard University in 1887, Baker returned as an instructor in the English Department. In 1905, he began offering a course in playwriting entitled English 47. Three years later he founded the Harvard Dramatic Club and served as its sponsor. And in 1912 he established Workshop 47 as a laboratory theatre for plays written in English 47. The program and Baker's growing reputation attracted to Harvard such promising talents as **Eugene O'Neill, Sidney Howard,** Thomas Wolfe, **Edward Sheldon,** and **Philip Barry.** He resigned and moved to Yale in 1925 as head of its first Department of Drama, retiring in 1933. Beginning in 1927 he worked to establish the National Theatre Conference, and served as its first president in 1932. He is remembered as a teacher and mentor to the generation of American playwrights who came to the front in the 1920s. His ideas about the craft of playwriting are set forth in *Dramatic Technique* (1919).   TLM

See: W. Kinne, *George Pierce Baker and the American Theatre,* Cambridge, MA, 1954.

Baker, Josephine (née Freda Josephine McDonald) (1906–75) Entertainer who left her indigent family in St. Louis at the age of 16 to play in all-black revues in Philadelphia and New York. Her outrageous comic antics had a succès de scandale in Paris in *La Revue Nègre* (Théâtre des Champs-Elysées, 1925). Some celebrated her as a combination of "boxing kangaroo, sen-sen gum and racing

cyclist"(*Candide*), while moralists condemned her as the decline of the West made flesh. "La Baker's" rubber-limbed Charlestons and black bottoms and her cincture of phalliform bananas became fixtures of Parisian night life. Her repertory of American classics ("Always"), French nostalgia ("La Petite Tonkinoise"), and the signature tune "J'ai Deux Amours" were sung in a thin soprano. After WW II, during which she had worked for the Resistance, she made many "farewell tours" to raise money for the orphans she housed on her estate in Milandes. She returned to the U.S. in 1948 and 1951 and was active for civil rights, though as a performer she never equaled her success abroad. Needy and ailing, she died during the run of a revue at the Paris Bobino.   LS

See: L. Haney, *Naked at the Feast,* New York, 1981; P. Rose, *Jazz Cleopatra,* New York, 1989.

Baker, Paul (1911–   ) Educator/director. A Texan who studied with **George Pierce Baker** at Yale, Baker taught 29 years at Baylor University, staging controversial productions (Hamlet played by three actors) in a venue with three stages surrounding the audience. As first head of the **Dallas Theater Center** (1959–early '80s), Baker staged over 60 new scripts and American premieres at DTC, receiving the first **Rodgers** and **Hammerstein** Award for theatrical contribution in the Southwest (1961).   DBW

Balaban and Katz Theatre Circuit In 1916 A. J. (1889–1962) and Barney (1888–1971) Balaban combined their Chicago movie theatres with those of Sam Katz (1892–1961), presenting thematic musical revues designed by Frank Cambria and staged by **Vincent Minnelli.**   DMcD

See: C. Balaban, *Continuous Performance,* New York, 1942.

Balanchine, George (né Georgi Balanchivadze) (1904–83) Russian-born ballet dancer-choreographer and theatre choreographer. Recognized as one of the leading figures in 20th-century dance, Balanchine is credited with establishing the American balletic style. In addition to his work in ballet, Balanchine also contributed to American musical theatrical **dance,** choreographing such shows as *The Ziegfeld Follies* (1935), *On Your Toes* (1936), *Babes in Arms* (1937), and *Song of Norway* (1937). Balanchine's theatrical choreography is considered to have been well integrated in the shows, and he never demanded the insertion of a ballet segment. His dances interpreted the essence and feeling of the musical score within the context of the script.   LF

See: F. Mason, *I Remember Balanchine,* New York, 1991; B. Taper, *Balanchine,* 2d ed., New York, 1983.

Baldwin, James [Arthur] (1924–87) African-American novelist, essayist, and playwright. The most widely read of contemporary black authors, Baldwin wrote two plays. In *The Amen Corner* (produced at Howard University in 1954 and on Broadway in 1965) a fanatical woman pastor tries unsuccessfully to turn her son against the father whose love she has rejected. Despite a convincing performance by **Beah Richards,** the play was coolly received by leading critics. In ***Blues for Mr. Charlie*** (1964) Baldwin examined racial attitudes in the murder of an angry black youth by a white bigot. The writing is often shrill, characters' motivations are questionable, and the author's viewpoint remains ambivalent.   EGH

> See: J. Campbell, *Talking at the Gates,* New York, 1991; L. Pratt, *James Baldwin,* Boston, 1978; C. Sylvander, *James Baldwin,* New York, 1980.

Baldwin Theatre Built as Baldwin's Academy of Music on Market St., this 1,969-seat **San Francisco** theatre opened on 6 March 1876 with *Richard III* starring Barry Sullivan. Part of the six-story Baldwin Hotel, its elegant accoutrements included red velvet seats, gilt decorations, and crystal chandeliers. It was managed until 1882 by the inveterate **Thomas Maguire,** who produced numerous plays by his young assistants, **David Belasco** and **James Herne,** and maintained a stock company with popular actor **James O'Neill** among its leading men. Until it burned in 1895 [see **fires**], the Baldwin hosted many great touring stars and companies of the day and was a favorite of San Francisco's social set.   MB

Ball, William (1931–91) Flamboyant, charismatic actor-director, described by director Tom Moore as alternately "a genius, a tyrant, a benevolent dictator and a madman." Ball, founder in 1965 of the **American Conservatory Theatre** in Pittsburgh, brought the company to **San Francisco** in 1967, almost single-handedly reviving legitimate theatre in that city. In 1986 he resigned amid financial and artistic controversy, leaving behind a career record of over 300 productions, 87 which he directed (including legendary productions of *The Taming of the Shrew* [1976] and *Cyrano de Bergerac* [1974] – both subsequently televised). Prior to ACT, Ball had acted with regional companies and Shakespeare festivals, and in the late 1950s and early '60s directed several award-winning **Off-Broadway** productions and in 1964 directed two plays for **Lincoln Center** (at the **ANTA** Theatre, Washington Square). His book, *A Sense of Direction: Some Observations on the Art of Directing,* was published in 1984.   DBW

Ballard, Lucinda (1908–) Costume designer. An assistant to scenic designers **Norman Bel Geddes** and **Claude Bragdon** early in her career, Ballard has been an active designer (principally of costumes) for theatre, film, and ballet. She received the first Tony Award for Costume Design for the plays *Happy Birthday, Another Part of the Forest,* ***Street Scene,*** *John Loves Mary,* and *The Chocolate Soldier* in the 1947 Broadway season. She also won a Tony in 1961 for *The Gay Life* and the 1945 Donaldson Award for *The* ***Glass Menagerie.*** In recent years she has supervised the costumes for revivals of productions she originally designed.   BO

Balsam, Martin (1919–) Film and stage actor. Born in New York City, Balsam has specialized in major supporting roles, almost always sympathetic. He made his professional debut in *The Play's the Thing* at the Red Barn, Locust Valley, NY (August 1941) and on Broadway as Mr. Blow in *Ghost for Sale* at Daly's Theatre (1941). His awards include the Outer Circle Award and a *Variety* poll citation for performances in *You Know I Can't Hear You When the Water's Running* (1967) and an Academy Award as best supporting actor in *A Thousand Clowns* (1965).   SMA

Bancroft, Anne (née Anna Maria Luisa Italiano) (1931–) Stage and film actress who made her Broadway debut as Gittel Mosca in *Two for the Seesaw* (1958). She secured her stardom with such roles as Annie Sullivan in *The* ***Miracle Worker*** (1959) and Mother Courage in *Mother Courage and Her Children* (1963). Other substantial Broadway roles were in *The Devils* (1965), *A Cry of Players* (1968), *Golda* (1977), and *Duet for One* (1981). Her awards include Tonys for Gittel Mosca and Annie Sullivan. She received the Oscar for best actress for *The Miracle Worker* (1962). Married to film director Mel Brooks, she has appeared in several of his films. At the time of her debut, she was described as "the most engaging gamin to light up a stage"; later, critics spoke glowingly of "her guts and her spirit, the elegance of her style, and the passion of her playing."   SMA

> See: W. Holtzman, *Seesaw: A Dual Biography of Anne Bancroft and Mel Brooks,* Garden City, NY, 1979.

Bandmann, Daniel (1840–1905) German-born actor who first acted in 1857–8 at the Altes Stadt Theatre, NYC, and then in Germany and Central Europe (1859–62). He first acted in English at **Niblo's Garden,** New York (15 January 1863) as Shylock. Thereafter he toured the world with a company recruited and rehearsed by costar Louise Beaudet. After settling on his ranch near Missoula, MT (1886), he played only short seasons each fall. He married Mary T. Kelly in 1892 and retired. His most prominent roles were Hamlet, Shylock, Narcisse, Richelieu, and Dr. Jekyll (in his own adaptation). He acted in the traditional style, featuring rhetorical declamation and striking poses. In 1885 he published *An Actor's Tour* (Boston).   DMcD

Banker's Daughter, The One of **Bronson Howard**'s most popular plays, first produced at the **Union Square Theatre** in 1878 for a run of 137 performances and revived many times over the next four decades. The story of Lilian, who, despite her love of young Routledge, marries an older (and wealthier) man in order to protect her family's failing fortunes, appealed to an audience still recovering from the devastating effects of the financial panic of 1873. The play was also the focus of a lecture Howard delivered in 1886 entitled *An Autobiography of a Play,* in which he details the extraordinary evolution of the work from its original manifestation in 1873 as *Lilian's Last Love* to the 1879 revision, *The Old Love and the New.* The lecture, published in 1914, provides a remarkable insight into Howard's writing process, and helped establish him as America's first true professional playwright.   PAD

Bankhead, Tallulah (1902–68) Stage and film actress noted for her vibrant energy, sultry voice, explosive speech, and impetuous behavior. The daughter of one of the most famous political families of Alabama, she debuted on Broadway in 1919 and achieved fame in 1923 in London in *The Dancers.* She returned to the U.S. in 1923 for film work and reappeared on Broadway in 1933. After a revival of *Rain,* she was widely acclaimed as Regina in *The Little Foxes* (1939) and won the New York Drama Critics Circle Award for best actress as Sabina in *The Skin of Our Teeth.* She won the best actress award from the New York Film Critics in 1944 for *Lifeboat.* She published her autobiography, *Tallulah,* in 1952. Her final stage appearance was in *The Milk Train Doesn't Stop Here Anymore* (1964, **Brooks Atkinson Theatre**).   SMA

> See: B. Dennis, *Tallulah, Darling,* New York, 1972; B. Gill, *Tallulah,* New York, 1972.

Bannister, Nathaniel (Harrington) (1813–47) Actor and dramatist who began his career in New York and Philadelphia before going to New Orleans in 1834, where he married the widow of **John Augustus Stone** and established his reputation as a playwright. After 1837 the Bannisters performed regularly in New York. The author of at least 40 plays ranging through ancient history (*Gaulantus the Gaul,* 1836), national incidents (*The Maine Question,* 1839), romantic comedy (*The Gentleman of Lyons,* 1838), and moral dilemmas (*The Destruction of Jerusalem,* 1837), Bannister wrote mainly to please the public. His popular spectacle, *Putnam, the Iron Son of '76* (1844), opened with 78 performances and exploited the considerable feats of Black Vulture, a horse [see **animals as performers**]. The most distinctive actor-dramatist of his time, with six published plays, Bannister was a thoughtful and well-read man, an innovator who enriched theatre managers and died young and a pauper.   WJM

Baraka, Amiri (né Everett LeRoi Jones) (1934–   ) **African-American** poet, essayist, and playwright. Assumed his new name and mission in the 1960s when he became leader of the black arts revolutionary movement that viewed theatre as a weapon in the struggle for black liberation. He has produced some 20 plays, many of them one-acts, that powerfully dramatize social and racial problems in expressive forms and with unnerving frankness. Hailed for his "fierce and blazing talent," condemned for his blatant antiwhite posture, Baraka was notwithstanding the most prominent American dramatist of the 1960s with such plays as the Obie Award–winning *Dutchman* (1964), *The Slave* (1964), *A Black Mass* (1966), and *Slave Ship* (1967). He founded the Black Arts Repertory Theatre/School in Harlem (1965–6) and Spirit House in Newark, NJ (1966), where his plays were produced. Baraka's earlier writings and speeches had a profound influence on the younger generation of playwrights. He later rejected black nationalism for revolutionary socialism as shown in his play *The Motion of History* (1975). His autobiography was published in 1984.   EGH

> See: K. Benston, *Baraka: The Renagade and the Mask,* New Haven, 1976; W. Sollors, *Amiri Baraka/LeRoi Jones: The Quest for a "Populist Modernism,"* New York, 1978.

Barbette (né Vander Clyde) (1904–73) Aerialist, born near Austin, TX. He made his circus debut dressed as a girl as one of the Alfaretta Sisters, but soon developed his own single act, under the name Barbette. At the Paris Alhambra (1923) his elegant trapeze artistry became a sensation when he snatched off his blond wig at the end to reveal that the slender aerial queen was male (see **female/male impersonation**). He was taken up by Jean Cocteau, who devoted an essay to him and used him dressed in a Chanel evening gown in his film *Blood of a Poet.* After a triumphant career in Europe, Barbette contracted a chill at Loew's State, New York (1938); when this developed into a crippling bone disease, he became a popular trainer.   LS

Barefoot in the Park Second Broadway script by **Neil Simon,** opening at the **Biltmore Theatre** 23 October 1963 and running 1,530 performances. One of his most successful works, it provided actor Robert Redford's first major role. Corrie and Paul Bratter's newlywed misadventures show Simon's thematic conviction that harmony demands moderation and compromise rather than change. Using a stairway as a running gag, characters develop more fully than in his first script, *Come Blow Your Horn.*   RW

Barker, James Nelson (1784–1858) Playwright, poet, and politician. Born into a politically and socially influential American family, Barker combined his love of country with his love of theatre. Among his plays are *America* (1805); *Tears and Smiles* (1807), a patriotic comedy; *The Embargo* (1808), a defence of Jefferson's Embargo Act; *The Indian Princess* (1808), the first produced American play about Pocahontas; and *Marmion; or, The Battle of Flodden Field* (1812), in which England's treatment of 16th-century Scotland was transferred to America. Barker's greatest achievements are his 11 essays on drama in the *Democratic Press* (18 December 1816–19 February 1817) and his remarkable tragedy of New England intolerance, *Superstition; or, The Fanatic Father* (1824), in which the villain protagonist, a clergyman, mistakes his own passions for the Word of God. Thereafter, Barker, an avid supporter of Andrew Jackson, absorbed himself in politics, contributing to literature with poetry rather than plays.   WJM

> See: P. Musser, *James Nelson Barker,* Philadelphia, 1929.

Barker, Richard (1834?–1903) British-born director. Originally a performer, Barker joined the staff of London's Savoy Theatre and came to the U.S. as director of the "official" production of **Gilbert and Sullivan**'s *The Mikado* (1885). He went on to direct other works in America, ranging from operetta to extravaganza. A skillful stager of musicals, Barker became, in an age of transatlantic star performers, the first transatlantic director. He frequently returned to the U.S. to direct operetta and comic opera.   JD

Barnabee, Henry Clay (1833–1917) Musical comedy actor. A passionate amateur singer, he worked as a retail clerk in Boston until 1865 when he became a Lyceum (see **Chautauqua and Lyceum**) entertainer. He made his professional stage debut in Boston the following year and later headed his own concert company. He was a founding member of the **Boston Ideal Opera Company** (1879) and their successors, The Bostonians (1887). A tenor, he specialized in such **Gilbert and Sullivan** roles as Sir Joseph Porter and Bunthorne, but he was also noted for his Dr. Dulcamera in Donizetti's *The Elixir of Love*. He created the role of the Sheriff of Nottingham in *Robin Hood* by **Harry Bache Smith** and **Reginald De Koven**. In 1913 his autobiography, *My Wanderings,* appeared.
    DMcD

Barnes, Clive Alexander (1927–) London-born and Oxford-educated dance and drama critic who first established his credentials as a dance critic for *Dance and Dancers* (1950–) and for *The Times* (1961–5). In 1965 he came to the U.S. as dance critic for the *New York Times,* adding the drama post in 1967. A decade later he was replaced as drama critic, and within the year (1977) resigned from the *Times* to become dance/drama critic for the *New York Post.* Noted for his clever style, Barnes wrote of *Agnes of God*: "Some plays are so concerned with being theatrical that they forget to be dramatic." He has been accused of being pro-British and of supporting the avant-garde more than the Broadway theatre.   TLM

Barnes, Djuna (1892–1982) Avant-garde playwright, primarily a poet, who wrote many short plays (1916–26), some published under the name Lydia Steptoe and several produced by the **Provincetown Players.** A theatre reviewer for *Theatre Guild Magazine* (1929–31), she is best remembered for her blank-verse tragedy *The Antiphon* (publ. 1958), a semiautobiographical work concerning a bitter childhood conveyed in enigmatic, Joycean language. Its only production was in Swedish at Stockholm's Royal Dramaten Theatre (1961).
    TH-S

See: L. Kannenstine, *The Art of Djuna Barnes,* New York, 1977; M. Broe, *Silence and Power,* Carbondale, IL, 1991.

Barnes, Howard (1904–68) Drama critic. Born in London of American parents, Barnes graduated from Yale in 1925 and studied at Queen's College, Oxford, and the Sorbonne in Paris. He joined the *New York World* as an assistant film critic, switching to the *New York Herald-Tribune* in 1928 as theatrical reporter and dramatic editor under **Percy Hammond,** then from 1936–42 as assistant drama critic and film critic under **Richard Watts, Jr.** He was chief drama critic from 1942 until his retirement in 1951. Barnes's prose style glittered. *Death of a Salesman,* he wrote, "has majesty, sweep and shattering dramatic impact."   TLM

Barnum, P[hineas] T[aylor] (1810–91) Entrepreneur and showman, a hard-headed businessman of great personal integrity whose *modus operandi* used deceit and innovative methods of publicity to promote both popular and high culture. Starting as a shopkeeper and editor of a weekly newspaper in Danbury, CT, he moved to New York in 1834 and the next year commenced as a showman by exhibiting an ancient black woman he claimed was 160 years old and George Washington's nurse. In 1841 he purchased a museum (see **Barnum's American Museum**), where he mixed freak shows with "moral" drama and brought out the midget Tom Thumb (Charles Stratton), whose European appearances in 1844 made Barnum and the notion of "humbug" notorious. In 1849 the Museum became a stock company, and the next year he organized the American tour of the Swedish soprano Jenny Lind, who received $1,000 a night. Barnum retired in 1855, but soon resumed his business. He did not enter the **circus** trade until 1871, merging with James A. Bailey in 1881 to create "The Greatest Show on Earth," a combination of circus, menagerie, and sideshow; the acquisition of the elephant Jumbo was his greatest feat there. Throughout his busy life, Barnum regularly issued versions of his life story and optimistic philosophy, including his *Autobiography* (1854), *The Humbugs of the World* (1865), and *Struggles and Triumphs* (1869 [the best version: ed. G. S. Bryan, 2 vols., 1927]).   LS

See: N. Harris, *Humbug, the Art of P. T. Barnum,* Boston, 1973; A. H. Saxon, *P. T. Barnum: The Legend and the Man,* New York, 1989.

Barnum's American Museum Broadway and Ann St., NYC. In 1841, **P. T. Barnum,** America's greatest showman, bought Scudder's Museum and quickly turned it into a city landmark. As part of the price of admission to see real and fake curiosities and an assortment of human freaks and oddities, Barnum provided concerts and light entertainment in a Lecture Room. In 1849, this was expanded into a full-scale theatre for dramatic performances. In 1850, the seating was increased to 3,000 for the presentation of *The* **Drunkard,** the temperance drama. Thereafter, Barnum presented a series of moral plays in a moral manner with a stock company of actors of unimpeachable morality. In 1865, the museum and theatre burned to the ground. Although he moved to 559 Broadway, Barnum's second venture never achieved the success of the first, and was destroyed by **fire** after only a few years of operation.   MCH

Barr (né Baer), Richard (Alphonse) (1917–89) Producer-director and president of the League of American Theaters and Producers for 21 years, best known for bringing early works by **Edward Albee** to the American public by coproducing (with **Clinton Wilder**) *The Zoo Story, The American Dream,* and *The Death of Bessie Smith.* These were followed by all of Albee's major plays, including *Who's Afraid of Virginia Woolf?,* Albee's first Broadway production, which, due to Barr's initiative, established preview performances in New York (1962). Barr also championed other young playwrights: Alone and in partnership, he pro-

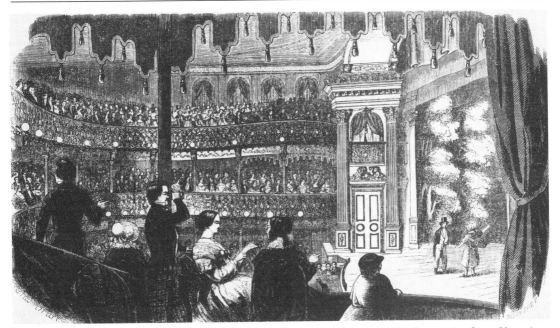

The Lecture Room, a euphemism for "theatre," at Barnum's American Museum. Wood engraving from *Gleason's Pictorial,* 29 Jan. 1853. Courtesy: Laurence Senelick.

duced early works by **Lanford Wilson,** William Hanley, **Terrence McNally,** Jack Richardson, **John Guare, A. R. Gurney, Amiri Baraka** (as LeRoi Jones), **Jean-Claude Van Itallie,** and **Paul Zindel.** He also presented American premieres of works by Beckett and Ionesco.   DBW

Barratt, Watson (1884–1962) Scene designer. Barratt began as a magazine illustrator but became the staff designer for the **Shubert brothers** with *Sinbad* (1918). His work included various Shubert **revue**s, including *The Passing Show, Artists and Models,* and *Greenwich Village Follies.* Musicals included *Florodora* (1920), *The Last Waltz* (1921), *Blossom Time* (1922), and *The Student Prince* (1924). In the late 1930s he began to work on more serious productions, including *The Time of Your Life* (1939).   AA

Barrett, Lawrence (1838–91) Actor and manager who made his debut as Murad in *The French Spy* in Detroit in 1853 and his first important New York appearances in 1857 as a member of **William E. Burton**'s Metropolitan Theatre Company. He subsequently was a member of Boston's **Howard Athenaeum** Company (1858–61). Barrett was associated with **Edwin Booth** throughout his career. In 1863 he acted with Booth at the **Winter Garden Theatre,** and in 1871–2 at **Booth's Theatre** he was the leading supporting actor, appearing most notably as Adrian de Mauprat to Booth's celebrated Richelieu, but also alternating Othello and Iago with him. At Booth's Theatre, Barrett also starred as James Harebell in **W. G. Wills**'s *The Man O'Airlie* (one of his most acclaimed roles), as Leontes in a spectacular production of *The Winter's Tale,* and as Cassius with Booth's Brutus in a lavish revival of *Julius Caesar.* This last production was later toured by Barrett under the management of **Jarrett** and **Palmer.** Although a professional disagreement estranged them for the next seven years, Booth and

Lawrence Barrett as Cassius in *Julius Caesar.* Courtesy: Don B. Wilmeth.

Barrett were reconciled in 1880, and their relationship continued to be close for the rest of their lives. Barrett managed Booth's last starring tours (1886–91), and for the last three seasons they made nationwide "joint starring" tours. Barrett managed the **California Theatre** in **San Francisco** (1866–70, with **John McCullough**) and the Variety Theatre in New Orleans (1871–3). In 1884–5 he leased Henry Irving's Lyceum Theatre during the latter's first American tour. Generally, however, Barrett spent most of his career as a touring star with his own company. He was also keenly interested in encouraging American drama and dramatists, commissioning numerous original plays and adaptations during his career. He presented **W. D. Howells**'s first full-length play, *Counterfeit Presentment* (1877), and William Young's *Pendragon* (1881) and *Ganelon* (1888), and successfully revived **George Henry Boker**'s *Francesca da Rimini* (1883).

Slender with a sensitive face, deep-set expressive eyes, and an unusual vocal range, Barrett was regarded as a studious, sometimes compelling, but also overly technical actor. His most successful roles after Harebell were Lanciotto in *Francesca da Rimini,* Hernani, Cassius, and (late in his career) Othello.   DJW

> *See:* M. Bailey, "Lawrence Barrett," PhD diss., U of Michigan, 1942.

Barry, Philip (James Quinn) (1896–1949) A popular dramatist of the 1920s and '30s, Barry got his start with two plays written in **George Pierce Baker**'s Workshop 47 at Harvard: *A Punch for Judy* (1921) and *You and I* (1923), a Broadway success. Focusing on the problems of family relations, romance, sexual intrigue, and professional vocation, he developed a modern comedy of manners: *In a Garden* (1925), ***Paris Bound*** (1927), ***Holiday*** (1928), *The Animal Kingdom* (1932), and The ***Philadelphia Story*** (1939), which starred **Katharine Hepburn.** These plays regularly feature the "Barry girl," a well-heeled if somewhat spoiled young woman who rejects the smug conventions associated with materialist culture and upper-class society. Barry's protagonists, male and female, struggle to serve the liberal ideals of personal integrity, tolerance, art, and freedom. Less well-received were his quasi-allegorical plays on metaphysical themes: *Hotel Universe* (1930), *The Joyous Season* (1934), *Here Come the Clowns* (1938, perhaps his best serious play), and *Liberty Jones* (1941). Productions in the 1940s were only moderately successful, even though Hepburn acted in *Without Love* (1942), and **Tallulah Bankhead** starred in *Foolish Notion* (1945). His last play, *Second Threshold* (1951), was finished posthumously by **Robert E. Sherwood**.   TP

> *See:* J. P. Roppolo, *Philip Barry*, New York, 1965; B. Gill's introduction in P. Barry, *State of Grace: Eight Plays*, New York, 1975.

Barrymore see **Drew–Barrymore family**

Barter Theatre Founded in 1933 in Abingdon, VA, when Robert Porterfield and company admitted Depression-strapped patrons to the Opera House for 30¢ or any usable item, especially food. The uniqueness of the company's location and business approach, the quality of its ensemble acting, the generosity of the Abingdon community, and the inspired leadership of Porterfield and his successors, Rex Partington and Pearl Price Hayter, have sustained production for more than 50 years. Barter Theatre has toured the mid-Atlantic states, and the company has been named the State Theatre of Virginia.   WD

Barton, James (1890–1962) Comedian, dancer, singer, and character actor. Barton, who began in vaudeville and burlesque, graduated to revues and musicals as a top hoofer ("the man with the laughing feet") and in 1934 replaced Henry Hull as the crude, degenerate Jeeter Lester in ***Tobacco Road,*** a role he played 1,899 times. Other notable roles included Hickey in *The Iceman Cometh* (1946) and the hard-drinking westerner Ben Rumson in *Paint Your Wagon* (1951).   DBW

Barton, Lucy (1891–1971) Educator, costume designer, author of the classic text *Historic Costume for the Stage* (1936, 1961). She considered a career as a performer while studying at the Carnegie Institute of Technology, but turned instead to costuming, subsequently working for the costume house Van Horn and Son (Philadelphia) before beginning teaching. In 1947 Barton was appointed costumer and professor at the University of Texas, where she remained until retirement in 1961. Although she designed numerous plays and **pageants** and wrote other books, she is best remembered for teaching on the art of costume and establishing the first baccalaureate program in costume design.   BO

***Basic Training of Pavlo Hummel, The* David Rabe**'s first professionally produced play. Part of his Vietnam Trilogy, Obie Award–winning *Pavlo* premiered at the **Public Theater** on 2 May 1971 and ran for 363 performances. William Atherton played Pavlo, Joe Fields was Sergeant Tower, and Albert Hall was Ardell, Pavlo's spectral companion. A 1977 revival on Broadway starred **Al Pacino**. In a blend of fantasy, flashback, and military drills and rituals, Rabe depicts the foolish heroics of Pavlo from boot camp to his meaningless death in a Saigon whorehouse. Pavlo's love of violence is symptomatic of America's Vietnam mentality for Rabe.   PCK

Bat, The Three-act mystery-drama written by **Avery Hopwood** and **Mary Roberts Rinehart,** based on her novel, *The Circular Staircase*. It opened on 23 August 1920 at the **Morosco Theatre** and continued for 867 performances – at the time the second-longest-running show in Broadway history. A model of its genre, the play starred **Effie Ellsler** as Cornelia Van Gorder, but May Vokes captured the hearts of the audience as the hysterical maid, Lizzie. It has been revived, filmed, and televised several times.   FB

Bateman family Hezekiah Linthicum Bateman (1812–75), manager, first relied on his child-prodigy daughters before managing London's Lyceum Theatre, where he brought Henry Irving to prominence in *The Bells* (1871) and then in *Hamlet* (1874, for 200 performances).

His wife, **Sidney,** (1823–81) wrote *Self* (1856), assumed the Lyceum management at her husband's death, and later managed Sadler's Wells (1879).

Daughters **Kate** (1843–1917) and **Ellen** (1844–1936) began performing Shakespeare in New York (1849) when they were six and five, then in London (1851). Kate played Portia, Richmond, and Lady Macbeth; Ellen played Shylock, Richard III, and Macbeth. Later, Kate played in *Leah, the Forsaken* (1862, New York; 1863, London) and appeared with Irving; Ellen retired.

Daughters **Virginia** (1853–1940) and **Isabel** (1854–1934) made their London debuts in 1865, then joined Irving. Virginia married Edward Compton and was the mother of Fay Compton and Compton McKenzie. Isabel comanaged Sadler's Wells before becoming Reverend Mother General of the Community of St. Mary the Virgin at Wantage (1898).   RM

Bates, Blanche (1873–1941) Actress. Daughter of Frank Bates, manager of noted **stock companies** in Portland and **San Francisco,** she made her debut in the latter (1893) after an early marriage and a brief career as a schoolteacher. By 1895 she had become a leading lady there. A successful tour opposite **James O'Neill** (1899–1900) brought her to New York and the attention of **David Belasco,** who starred her as Cho-Cho-San in *Madame Butterfly* (1900), Cigarette in *Under Two Flags* (1901), Yo-San in *The Darling of the Gods* (1902), and Minnie in *The Girl of the Golden West* (1905). She retired in 1926. Full of power and humor, she portrayed a liberated woman who was always energetic, resourceful, and faithful.   DMcD

Bates, Kathy (1948–) Memphis-born actress, trained at Southern Methodist University, who received instant general popularity with her Academy Award–winning performance in Stephen King's *Misery* (1990). For the 15 previous years, however, beginning with her New York debut as Joanne in *Vanities* (1976), Bates had established a solid theatrical reputation, in particular with her critically acclaimed performances in *'night Mother* (1982–3) and *Frankie and Johnny in the Clair de Lune* (1987–8). **Otis Guernsey** described Bates's Obie-winning performance in the latter as "toughness warring with vulnerability, bitterness with wistfulness." Other credits include *Goodbye Fidel; Fifth of July; Come Back to the Five and Dime, Jimmy Dean, Jimmy Dean;* and *The Art of Dining.*   DBW

Battle, Hinton (1956–) German-born African-American performer and actor, trained as a dancer (former soloist with the Dance Theatre of Harlem), whose Broadway debut as the Scarecrow in *The Wiz* (1975) was followed by **Bob Fosse**'s *Dancin'* (1978). Since then he has thrice received the Tony Award for Featured Actor in a Musical (*Sophisticated Lady* [1981], *The Tap Dance Kid* [1984], and *Miss Saigon* [1991]). Only in *Miss Saigon* has he not demonstrated his elegant dancing style, instead gaining critical acclaim for the "grit and passion" of his portrayal as the marine John, the hero's best friend, and for his rousing, revivalist Act II show-stopper "Bui-Doi."   DBW

Bay, Howard (1912–86) Stage and film designer whose designs included *The Little Foxes, Show Boat, The Music Man, Finian's Rainbow,* and *Man of La Mancha.* Although he became associated with the sentimental musicals of the 1940s and '50s, which were very painterly in style, he virtually began his career with a superrealistic tenement set for the **Federal Theatre Project**'s *One Third of a Nation.* Bay believed that a designer "must not polish a single style," but rather must be adaptable to any situation; he was thus known as a pragmatist and for his ingenious solutions to design problems. During 1965–82 Bay taught at Brandeis University. He authored the well-respected book *Stage Design* (1974).   AA

Bayes, Nora (née Eleanor or Leonora Goldberg) (1880–1928) Vaudeville singer-comedienne who, despite an undistinguished voice, was a major star in America and England, praised for her ability to dramatize or "put over" a song. She introduced such standards as "Shine on Harvest Moon," "Has Anybody Here Seen Kelly?" and George M. Cohan's "Over There" (1917), the most famous song of WW I. Her second husband of five, Jack Norworth, was her stage partner during 1908–13 (the billing was "Nora Bayes, Assisted and Admired by Jack Norworth"). Star of numerous **revue**s and musicals, she had a theatre named after her in 1918 (later the Forty-fourth Street Theatre). She was known for her egocentricism and temperament. Bayes nonetheless devoted much time and money to charities, especially those concerned with children (three of whom she adopted), and earned as much as $5,000 a week touring.   DBW

Beaton, Cecil (1904–80) British-born theatrical set and costume designer, photographer, and writer, knighted in 1972, whose neoromantic style is best known in this country through his costume designs for the Broadway and film versions of *My Fair Lady* (1956). He won Oscars for that and for *Gigi* (1958). He also created exuberant designs for films and ballet from the 1940s through the '60s.   DBW

See: H. Vickers, *Cecil Beaton, A Biography,* Boston, 1985.

Beatty, Clyde (Raymond) (1903–65) Animal trainer, quintessential **circus** showman. Beatty was born in the U.S. (unusual for circus animal trainers) and developed the "American style" jungle act (gun and whip in hand, challenging animals to attack). He began as a solo act in 1922 (with polar bears) in the Gollmar Circus; from 1926 until the Depression he was with the Hagenbeck–Wallace show. In 1930 Beatty appeared with 40 jungle-bred big cats in a mixed animal act (lions and tigers together). In 1936 he founded his own circus (with 500 employees by the 1950s). In all, Beatty trained some 2,000 lions and tigers, as well as bears, leopards, pumas, and jaguars. He wrote or coauthored *The Big Cage* (1933), *Jungle Performers* (1941), and *Facing the Big Cats* (1965).   DBW

John Lee Beatty's design for Terrence McNally's *Lips Together, Teeth Apart*. Photo: Keith Meyers. Courtesy: *New York Times* Pictures.

Beatty, John Lee (1948–   ) Designer, educated at Brown and Yale. Active since the early 1970s with the **Manhattan Theatre Club** and **Circle Repertory Company,** among others, by the mid-1980s Beatty had become the most prolific designer in New York, having as many as six shows running simultaneously. A master of poetic or lyric realism, he designed the premieres of virtually all the plays of **Lanford Wilson** and several by **Beth Henley.** His ability to create evocative settings through deceptive simplicity has worked well for many new plays at the **New York Shakespeare Festival** and many regional theatres, as well as for **McNally**'s *Lips Together, Teeth Apart* (1991) and *Ain't Misbehavin'* (1978) and several other small musicals. He is also known for playful and theatrical settings, such as the caricature environment for *Song of Singapore* (1991) and the shows by magicians **Penn and Teller.**   AA

Beaufort, John David (1912–92) Journalist and drama critic. Born in Edmonton, Alberta, Beaufort came to the U.S. in 1922. Beginning with the *Christian Science Monitor* in 1930, he served as film and drama critic (1939–43, 1951–62), drama critic (1971–4), and contributing drama critic (1975–92). Noted for balanced criticism, Beaufort wrote of *A Raisin in the Sun* (1959) that it overcomes "a fairly obvious plot by the authenticity of its dialogue, its candor, honesty of character delineation, and lack of special pleading."   TLM

Beck, Julian see **Living Theatre**

Bedford, Brian (1935–   ) Since his 1959 U.S. acting debut in Peter Shaffer's *Five Finger Exercise,* this British-born actor has devoted his career to U.S. and Canadian stages, winning NY awards in *The Knack* (Obie, 1965) and *School for Wives* (Tony, 1971). His most recent New York roles were Alceste in **Circle in the Square**'s production of *The Misanthrope* (1982–3) and the British actor Macready in **Richard Nelson**'s *Two Shakespearean Actors* (1992). In addition to periodic New York engagements he has been seen (primarily in Shakespeare or Molière) at the **John F. Kennedy Cen-**

ter, the **Old Globe Theatre** (San Diego), and the **Shakespeare Theatre at the Folger.** Since 1975 he has had starring roles in National Tours of *Equus, Deathtrap, Whose Life Is It Anyway?, The Real Thing,* and his own one-man show based on Shakespeare's life and works, *The Lunatic, The Lover & The Poet.*   DBW

Beggar on Horseback by **George S. Kaufman** and **Marc Connelly,** based on Paul Apel's *Hans Sonnenstösser's Höllenfahrt,* opened on Broadway 12 February 1924 and ran 224 performances. Neil McRae (Roland Young) is a penniless composer who must choose between marrying the girl he loves or Gladys Cady, the brassy daughter of a rich manufacturer whose money could guarantee Neil the artistic freedom he craves. Most of the action involves an extended dream sequence done in an expressionistic style: Neil dreams that he marries Gladys, but after her social calendar and her father's business dehumanize him, he kills her entire family, who refuse to die but return to try him, find him guilty of writing "highbrow" music, and sentence him to labor in the Cady Consolidated Art Factory.   JDM

Behrman, S[amuel] N[athaniel] (1893–1973) Playwright. Though Behrman came from a middle-class family, his plays are typically set in genteel upper-class drawing rooms. Dramatizing conflicts of conscience and values among wealthy, privileged characters, Behrman produced a steady series of urbane and curiously impersonal high comedies such as *The Second Man* (1927), *Biography* (1932), *End of Summer* (1936), *No Time for Comedy* (1939), and *But for Whom Charlie* (1964). Two recurrent character types haunt his salons: fashionable, tolerant matrons (often played, charmingly, by **Ina Claire**) and cynically detached self-made artists and sybarites. Not quite problem plays or plays of ideas in the Shavian mold, Behrman's discussion dramas (notably weak in story and structure) chart the progress of his well-spoken characters toward a position of wordly compromise, a sophisticated *via media.* The **Theatre Guild** presented most of Behrman's work, and his smart comedies have

David Belasco's *The Darling of the Gods* at the Belasco Theatre (1902), with Blanche Bates and George Arliss. Photo: Byron. Courtesy: Museum of the City of New York.

come to be identified as the Guild's prevailing house style.   FH

See: K. Reed, *S. N. Behrman,* Boston, 1975.

Belasco, David (1853–1931) Director, playwright, and manager. A **San Francisco** native, he made his acting debut there (1872) and toured the west as a supporting player, settling at San Francisco's **Baldwin Theatre** as stage manager and playwright (1878–82). There he collaborated with **James A. Herne** in writing and producing, and first worked with Gustave Frohman, who brought him to New York as stage manager and resident dramatist for the new **Madison Square Theatre** (1882). In 1884 he moved to **Daniel Frohman**'s **Lyceum Theatre,** performing the same tasks until 1890, when he became an independent producer. His long apprenticeship involved the staging of scores of productions and the writing, alone or in collaboration, of more than three dozen plays. The first play of which he was sole author was *May Blossom* (1884), but his first successes were in collaboration with **Henry C. DeMille,** beginning with *The Wife* (1887). Until 1902 Belasco produced plays for booking by the Theatrical **Syndicate.** His most notable productions in this period were *Madame Butterfly* (1900), *Under Two Flags* (1901), *The Auctioneer* (1901), and *Du Barry* (1901). He broke with the Theatrical Syndicate in a dispute over fees, leased a theatre from **Oscar Hammerstein,** and entered into the richest phase of his career (1902–15). During this period he did 42 original productions and revivals in New York City and on tour. The most famous were *The*

Darling of the Gods (1902), *The **Girl of the Golden West*** (1905), *The Rose of the Rancho* (1906), *The **Easiest Way*** (1909), and *The Governor's Lady* (1912). He also built a new theatre (1907) and kept both houses active for the rest of the period. Though he was responsible for another 35 productions between 1915 and his retirement in 1930, his influence had waned, and his work was treated condescendingly.

Though prodigiously active as a playwright, affixing his name to some 70 works, none still holds the stage. Even in playwriting his greatest contribution was in creating and managing stage effects. In collaborating with DeMille, Belasco would pace the stage, describing scenes and effects while DeMille took notes. DeMille would then write out the dialogue, which Belasco would polish during rehearsals. As a producer Belasco did nothing that had not been done before, but he did it more elaborately and carefully. Desiring to be realistic without being unpleasant, he combined a scenic realism, which demanded solid, three-dimensional pieces and actual objects whenever possible [see **scenic design**], with melodramatic action and sentimental idealization of character. Working with the designer Louis Hartmann and the technicians John H. and Anton Kliegl, he pioneered the use of electric lights to create mood [see **stage lighting**]. He selected talented but relatively unknown performers (**Blanche Bates, Mrs. Leslie Carter, Frances Starr,** and **David Warfield**) whom he cast to type in vehicles created for them. Each piece was rehearsed for 10 weeks (rather than the normal 4), so that as nearly as possible the leading performers were playing carefully derived extensions of their own personalities on stage. Belasco's memoir, *The Theatre Through Its Stage Door,* was published in 1919.   DMcD

> See: L. Marker, *David Belasco: Naturalism in the American Theatre,* Princeton, NJ, 1975; C. Timberlake, *The Life & Work of David Belasco: The Bishop of Broadway,* New York, 1954; W. Winter, *The Life of David Belasco,* New York, 1925.

Belasco Theatre NYC theatre at 111 West 44th Street. Designed by architect George Keister, it opened on 16 October 1907 with a production of *A Grand Army Man,* starring **David Warfield** and directed by the new theatre's owner, producer **David Belasco.** (Until 1910 the theatre was called the Stuyvesant, to avoid confusion with another house bearing Belasco's name.) The theatre, which cost $750,000 to erect, was elaborately decorated. The stage and backstage areas were unusually well equipped, and the lighting system – a special interest of Belasco's – was considered to be particularly innovative. In 1909 Belasco added a penthouse, which contained offices and a lavish apartment for himself. Belasco continued to produce at the theatre until his death in 1931. Among his spectacularly conceived productions in the house were *The Return of Peter Grimm* (1911), with David Warfield; *The Governor's Lady* (1912), in which an accurate replica of a Child's Restaurant was built onstage; and a memorable 1922 presentation of *The Merchant of Venice,* with Warfield as Shylock. After Belasco's death the theatre was leased, at various times, to **Katharine Cornell, Elmer Rice,** the **Group Theatre,** and the National Broadcasting Company, which used it as a radio playhouse in the early 1950s. It became a legitimate house again in 1953. The Belasco, which seats approximately 1,000 spectators, is currently owned by the **Shubert Organization.** Tony Randall's classical repertory company, the National Players, was housed in the Belasco in 1991.   BMCN

Bel Geddes, Barbara (1922–   ) Actress, known best today for her continuing role as Eleanor Ewing in the television series "Dallas" (1978–84, 1985–91). Daughter of **Norman Bel Geddes,** she made her first stage appearance in 1940 in summer stock, followed by her Broadway debut as the fledgling actress in *Out of the Frying Pan.* Of a dozen other New York appearances, most important are *Deep Are the Roots* (**Clarence Derwent** Award), *The Moon Is Blue* (1951), *Cat on a Hot Tin Roof* (1955), *Mary, Mary* (1961), and *Finishing Touches* (1973). From a naïve ingenue Bel Geddes has matured into a sympathetic character actress.   DBW

Bel Geddes, Norman (1893–1958) Set and industrial designer who pioneered the use of lenses in **stage lighting** equipment. Bel Geddes is probably better known for his industrial designs ranging from cars to stoves; he is sometimes called "the father of streamlining." The number of his designs for the theatre was small in comparison to his contemporaries, but they were often visionary and influential. His most ambitious design was for an unrealized project based on *The Divine Comedy.*

Sectional drawing of *The Miracle,* staged by Max Reinhardt with designs by Norman Bel Geddes in 1924 at the Century [New] Theatre, which was turned into a cathedral. Original in *Scientific American.* Courtesy: Don B. Wilmeth.

The set was to include 70-ft towers and a performance area some 100 ft wide. His visionary designs are suggestive, emblematic, and possessed of towering grandeur, thus creating a theatrical sense of space. Most of his **scenic design**s that were executed were detailed and naturalistic, such as *Dead End,* because of the demands of the theatre at the time. He is best known for transforming the Century Theatre [the renamed **New Theatre**] into a cavernous gothic cathedral for **Max Reinhardt's** production of *The Miracle.* Bel Geddes also had projects for innovative theatre spaces that altered the traditional audience–performer relationship. His autobiography, *Miracle in the Evening,* was published in 1960.   AA

Bellamy, Ralph (1904–91) Actor born in Chicago. After touring with William Owen (1921) he worked steadily in provincial theatre, directing his own stock company. He debuted in New York in 1929 as Ben Davis in *Town Boy* and made his film debut in *The Secret Six* (1931, with Clark Gable and Jean Harlow). By 1943 he had made 84 pictures and thereafter alternated between film and theatre (*State of the Union,* 1945; *Detective Story,* 1949), with frequent work in television. In 1958 he won the New York Drama Critics' Award, the Delia Austrian Award, and a Tony for his Franklin Delano Roosevelt in *Sunrise at Campobello.* Between 1952 and 1964 he served four terms as President of Actors' Equity. His reminiscences, *When the Smoke Hit the Fan,* appeared in 1979.   SMA

Bellew, Kyrle (1855–1911) English-born actor, son of a popular preacher and public reader, Bellew served in the British navy and merchant marine. Emigrating to Australia (1870), he abandoned gold mining for the stage (1874). His English debut was in Brighton (30 August 1875). Subsequently, he acted with the Bancrofts and with Henry Irving. He was a fixture in New York at **Wallack's Theatre** during 1885–7 and from 1902 until his death. Noted for his graceful bearing and beautiful voice, he excelled in polite comedy.   DMcD

Bells Are Ringing Two-act musical, music by **Jule Styne**, words by **Betty Comden** and **Adolph Green**; opened 29 November 1956 at the **Sam S. Shubert Theatre,** New York, and ran 924 performances. Written as a star vehicle for **Judy Holliday,** the libretto, which tells the story of a switchboard operator at an answering service, gave Holliday an opportunity to create a wide range of vocal characterizations as she became involved in the lives of clients, ultimately falling in love with one (Sydney Chaplin, in his debut). One of the few musicals of its day not based on a source from another medium, *Bells Are Ringing* was deftly tailored to the talents of its performers and provided a couple of enduring standards – the ballads "Just in Time" and "The Party's Over."   JD

Ben-Ami, Jacob (1890–1977) Russian-born actor and director who achieved critical acclaim on both Yiddish- and English-speaking stages. Born in Minsk, he worked with the Hirshbein Troupe in Odessa, the Vilna Troupe, and, for a short period, the Fineman Art Theatre in London. Ben-Ami emigrated to New York in 1912 and joined **Maurice Schwartz**'s Irving Place Theatre in 1918. Dissatisfied with the superficial quality of **Yiddish theatre,** Ben-Ami sought to modernize the repertoire. Differences with Schwartz in 1919 led him to found his own **Jewish Art Theatre,** where he discarded the old starring system and offered works by Sholom Aleichem, Tolstoi, and Hauptmann. (Schwartz reorganized as the **Yiddish Art Theatre.**) Discovered by **Arthur Hopkins,** in 1920 he was given his first English-speaking role as Peter Krumback in *Samson and Delilah.* His Broadway acting career extended to 1972 and included Michael Cape in **O'Neill**'s *Welded* (1924), Arthur Kober in *Evening Song* (1934), and Forman in *The Tenth Man* (1959). He was a member of **Eva Le Gallienne**'s **Civic Repertory Theatre** (1929–31), portraying a memorable Trigorin in *The Seagull.* He acted and directed for the **Theatre Guild** and toured his Yiddish productions to Africa and South America.   TLM   AB

Benchley, Robert (1889–1945) Humorist, actor, drama critic, and professional celebrity. Educated at Harvard University, Benchley wrote for the *New York Tribune* and *Vanity Fair* before becoming dramatic editor of the old *Life* (1920–9) and of the *New Yorker* (1929–40). His short humorous sketches on minor problems of the middle class appeared in *Life, Liberty,* and other popular magazines. Many of these were recycled into vaudeville sketches, and later into short films in which Benchley appeared. In the 1930s, he appeared in numerous feature films. A charter member of the Algonquin Round Table and of the New York Drama Critics Circle, Benchley was noted for his sophisticated wit and urbanity.   TLM

See: B. Rosmond, *Robert Benchley: His Life and Good Times,* Garden City, NY, 1970.

Ben Greet Players see **Greet Players**

Ben-Hur by William Young. This dramatization of Lew Wallace's historical novel opened to wide acclaim on 29 November 1899 at the **Broadway Theatre.** One of several religious dramas at that time, it represented a pinnacle of spectacular stage realism. It played through the season and in road

Act II, Tableau 1 (between decks of the Roman Trireme, "Astrea") of *Ben-Hur,* directed by Ben Teal. Photo: Joseph Byron (for a souvenir program). Courtesy: Don B. Wilmeth.

companies until movie realism displaced it. The play followed Ben-Hur, a Jew, through numerous conflicts with Messala, a Roman. The hero survived an ordeal as galley slave and defeated Messala in a grueling chariot race. He found his mother and sister, whose leprosy was healed by Jesus; was reunited with his lost love, Esther; and became a devout Christian. The lavish spectacle included 120,000 sq ft of scenery. The chariot race – the highlight of the presentation – featured treadmills for eight horses and two chariots, a moving wall to convey motion, a fan to simulate wind in the charioteers' faces, and a rolling panorama of spectators. Two film versions followed (1925, 1959). RAH

> See: A. N. Vardac, *Stage to Screen*, Cambridge, MA, 1949.

Bennett, Michael (né Di Figlia) (1943–87) Choreographer and director who began his Broadway career as a dancer, creating his first choreography for *A Joyful Noise* (1966). Bennett served as both director and choreographer for *Promises, Promises* (1968) and *Coco* (1969). In the early 1970s he teamed with **Harold Prince** and **Stephen Sondheim** in the creation of two "concept musicals," *Company* (1970) and *Follies* (1971), for which Bennett served as choreographer and codirector. He next directed and choreographed the more traditional *Seesaw* (1973), followed by the critically acclaimed *A Chorus Line* (1975). A concept musical about the lives of Broadway's chorus dancers, *A Chorus Line*'s brilliant dance sequences were the most vivid element of the production. Bennett went on to direct and choreograph *Ballroom* (1978) and *Dreamgirls* (1981). Illness forced him to withdraw as director of the London production of *Chess* (1986). As a choreographer, Bennett most often employed a precise, rhythmic, but emotionally expressive style of jazz dance admirably suited to contemporary characters and situations. MK

> See: K. Kelly, *One Singular Sensation: The Michael Bennett Story*, New York, 1990; K. Mandelbaum, *A Chorus Line and the Musicals of Michael Bennett*, New York, 1989.

Bennett, Richard (1873–1944) Actor, born in Deacon's Mills, IN, who first appeared on the stage at the Standard Theatre, **Chicago**, in 1891, and made his debut on Broadway at **Niblo's Garden** in *The Limited Mail*. His first London appearance was as Jefferson Ryder in *The Lion and the Mouse* in 1906, and his film career began in 1913. Among his more successful roles were He in *He Who Gets Slapped*, Judge Gaunt in **Winterset**, Tony in *They Knew What They Wanted*, and Robert Mayo in *Beyond the Horizon*. Bennett excited considerable controversy by berating audiences and critics, even stopping shows to lecture the audience. Three of his daughters, Constance, Barbara, and Joan, had successful film careers. SMA

> See: J. Bennett & L. Kibbee, *The Bennett Playbill*, New York, 1970.

Bennett, Robert Russell (1894–1981) Orchestrator, conductor, and composer, Bennett was the son of musicians. He began as a music copyist and orchestrated **Cole Porter**'s first hit song, "An Old Fashioned Garden" (1919). Although he set out to be a serious composer, Bennett spent most of his career arranging the scores for some 300 Broadway musicals, including *Show Boat, Oklahoma!, South Pacific,* and *My Fair Lady.* Noted for the speed of his arrangements, he turned out as many as 80 pages of music a day. Bennett also scored over 30 Hollywood films and served as musical director for NBC television. MK

Benny, Jack (né Benjamin Kubelsky) (1894–1974) Comedian, born in Chicago to Polish immigrants, who entered variety in 1911 as the violinist half of Salisbury and Benny and first interjected gags in his fiddling while entertaining fellow naval trainees. As a solo act he played **vaudeville, nightclubs,** and **Earl Carroll**'s *Vanities*, evolving a persona of prissiness and musical ineptitude. In 1929 he moved permanently to Hollywood to make films, and in 1932 initiated his hugely popular radio career, developing the superb comic timing and traits of vanity and avarice that later transferred successfully to television (1950–65). On retiring from TV, he performed **one-person** shows and, at the time of his death, was rehearsing for the film of **Neil Simon**'s *The Sunshine Boys*. LS

> See: J. and J. Benny, *Sunday Nights at Seven*, New York, 1991; I. Fein, *Jack Benny: An Intimate Biography*, New York, 1976; *Jack Benny Checklist*, Los Angeles, 1970.

Bentley, Eric (Russell) (1916–) English-born drama critic, translator, editor, playwright, educator, and director. Educated at Oxford and Yale (PhD, 1941), Bentley gained recognition in the late 1940s for his translations of **Brecht**'s plays. He worked in both the U.S. and European theatre, codirecting the German-language premiere of *The Iceman Cometh* in Zurich (1950) and directing his translation of *The Good Person of Setzuan* in New York (1956). Drama critic of the *New Republic* during 1952–6, Bentley also held distinguished academic positions as **Brander Matthews** Professor of Dramatic Literature at Columbia University (1952–69), **Katharine Cornell** Professor of Theatre at SUNY–Buffalo (1977–82), and professor of comparative literature, University of Maryland (1982–). He is a noted translator of Brecht, Pirandello, and Schnitzler, author of 10 original plays, and author or editor of numerous books, including *The Playwright as Thinker* (1946), *The Life of the Drama* (1964), *The Brecht Commentaries 1943–1980* (1981), and *Thinking About the Playwright* (1987). TLM

Berghof, Herbert (1909–90) Austrian-born actor, director, and teacher who studied with Aleksandër Moisiu, **Max Reinhardt, Lee Strasberg,** and at the **Actors Studio** (charter member). His professional debut was in *Don Carlos* (Vienna, 1927), and he was introduced to the New York theatre world as director of *From Vienna* (1939). He first appeared on Broadway in 1940, codirecting and performing in *Reunion in New York*. He staged the first U.S. production of *Waiting for Godot* (1956). Berghof taught acting at Columbia University, the New School for Social Research, the **Neighborhood Playhouse,** and the American Theatre Wing. In 1945 he founded the Herbert Berghof Studio, which he directed with his wife, **Uta Hagen.** In 1946 he founded the HB Playwrights Foundation, where he gave his last performance in August 1990 in his production of Strindberg's *Easter.*   SMA

Berkeley, (William Enos) Busby (1895–1976) Dance director in theatre and film who claimed that he had no dance or music training, yet became one of the foremost dance directors of his time, particularly in film. *A Connecticut Yankee* (1927) marked Berkeley's debut as a dance director-choreographer. Berkeley set a precedent in *The Street Singer* (1929) by being choreographer, director, and producer (with J. J. **Shubert**). Best remembered for his work in film, Berkeley developed camera techniques that used unique lighting effects and extravagant stage sets as well as animations and his famous "overhead shots." These elements of Berkeley's brilliance and inventiveness were integrated into his **dance** sequences. He authored *The Busby Berkeley Book.*   LF

Berkeley Repertory Theatre A popular **resident nonprofit** company founded (1968) in Berkeley, CA, by actor-director Michael Leibert and known for consistently high production standards. Based first in a tiny College Ave. storefront, it was distinguished by a strong acting ensemble and a repertoire accenting classics and familiar modern works. In 1980 it relocated to a handsome new 400-seat facility downtown. Leibert left in 1983; the current head, Sharon Ott (1984), no longer maintains a permanent company but offers vigorous productions of more daring contemporary plays, plus classics reinterpreted via bold directorial and design concepts. In 1986 a "Parallel Season" of new works was instituted, airing scripts by **Philip Kan Gotanda, José Rivera,** and other noteworthy American writers.   MB

Berlin, Irving (né Israel Baline) (1888–1989) Composer and lyricist. With his family he emigrated to America from Russia at age 2. He received little formal education and held a variety of jobs before publishing his first song in 1907. Four years later his "Alexander's Ragtime Band" became an international sensation, launching a vogue for popular songs written in a ragtime or pseudo-ragtime rhythm. Berlin wrote his first complete Broadway score for *Watch Your Step* (1914). After contributing songs to other musical comedies and revues, he created the score for an all-soldier show, *Yip, Yip Yaphank* (1918), and in the following year wrote several songs for *The Ziegfeld Follies.* During 1921–4 Berlin and producer **Sam H. Harris** offered a series of *Music Box Revues,* which introduced many of Berlin's standards, such as "What'll I Do?" and "All Alone." His other shows of the 1920s were *The Cocoanuts* (1925) and *The Ziegfeld Follies* (1927).

In the 1930s Berlin responded to a trend toward treating social and political issues in musicals by creating the score to *Face the Music* (1932), a satire on police corruption. He also included in his score for the revue *As Thousands Cheer* (1933) the song "Supper Time," a lament about the lynching of a southern black.

After spending several years writing for Hollywood films, Berlin returned to Broadway with the score for *Louisiana Purchase* (1940), and an updated all-soldier show, *This Is the Army* (1942). Four years later Berlin wrote the music for *Annie Get Your Gun,* proving that he, like **Rodgers** and **Hammerstein,** could write a score in which the song grew naturally out of the dramatic action. In 1950 he wrote the songs for *Call Me Madam,* and 12 years later Broadway heard his final score, written for *Mr. President* (1962).

One of America's most successful composers of popular music, Berlin's most memorable contributions to the musical stage were individual songs rather than complete scores. Rarely interested in experimentation or innovation, Berlin's strength was his ability to adapt to changing musical styles and to reflect in his music the thoughts, feelings, and aspirations of average Americans.   MK

See: L. Bergreen, *As Thousands Cheer: The Life of Irving Berlin,* New York, 1990.

Berlin, Pamela (1952–) Director who, after directing canonical works and operas at regional theatres, served for two years as literary manager of Ensemble Studio Theatre. She has developed and premiered important new works in New York, notably *To Gillian on Her 37th Birthday* (1983), *Elm Circle* (1984), *Crossing Delancey* (1985), *Steel Magnolias* (1987), and Elaine Berman's *Peacetime* (1992). She made her Broadway debut with *The Cemetery Club* (1990). She is a graduate of Radcliffe and Southern Methodist University.   TH-S

Berman, Eugene (1899–1972) Set and costume designer and painter. Born in St. Petersburg, Russia, lived in Paris 1918–39, then the U.S. Berman first visited Italy in 1922, and his studies of Italian landscape and Renaissance and baroque theatrical design influenced him greatly. His wispy, almost surreal sketches are filled with such architectural elements as arches and colonnades and have a strong sense of proportion, all reminiscent of Piranesi. In the 1920s he was classed with a group of artists known as neoromantics. Most of his designs were for ballet and opera, and he worked frequently with **George Balanchine.** Berman's design for Anthony Tudor's *Romeo and Juliet* with American Ballet Theatre is considered one of his best.   AA

See: *The Theatre of Eugene Berman,* New York (MoMA), 1947.

Bernard, John (1756–1828) British actor-manager who had an extensive career in the U.S. Born in Portsmouth, he played provincial theatres before his debut at London's Covent Garden in *The Beaux' Stratagem* in 1787. **Wignell** brought him to Philadelphia's **Chestnut Street Theatre,** where he remained until 1803, thence moving to Boston's **Federal Street Theatre,** which he comanaged during 1806–10. He then toured the U.S. and

Canada extensively, returning in 1819 to England, where he died in poverty. He describes his career as a leading low comedian in two books, *Retrospections of America, 1797–1811* (1887) and *Retrospections of the Stage* (1832).   SMA

Bernard (né Barnett), Sam (1863–1927) English-born comedian who as a boy appeared in U.S. variety (1876–84). Later, with a specialty in German dialect (developed at dime museums and pleasure gardens), he appeared with **Weber & Fields,** first with their **burlesque** company and later at their Music Hall (until 1901). A long string of successes followed, most notably Mr. Hoggenheimer in *The Girl from Kay's* (1903), a role that was reprised in 1927 for his last appearance (*Piggy*).   DBW

Bernard, William Bayle (1807–75) Expatriate American playwright. Born in Boston, son of actor-manager **John Bernard,** Bernard moved to England in 1820, became involved in English theatre, and made his reputation as a writer of plays about America and an adaptor of American plays and fiction to English understanding. His adaptation of **James Kirk Paulding**'s *The Lion of the West* was entitled *The Kentuckian; or, A Trip to New York* (1833). Although several versions of *The Yankee Peddler* existed, Bernard's adaptation for **G. H. "Yankee" Hill** – *The Yankee Peddler; or, Old Times in Virginia* – became a popular vehicle. Bernard was also responsible for dozens of incidental farces.   WJM

Bernstein, Aline (1880–1955) Set and costume designer who became involved in theatre as a founding member of the **Neighborhood Playhouse** (1915). Her successful designs there, such as *The Little Clay Cart,* led to work with the **Theatre Guild** and on Broadway, and in 1926 actress **Eva Le Gallienne** asked her to design for a newly founded **Civic Repertory Theatre.** Bernstein first worked with producer **Herman Shumlin** on *Grand Hotel* and continued her association with him through the 1930s, most notably on the plays of **Lillian Hellman,** including *The **Little Foxes.*** Bernstein's early designs utilized adaptable unit sets, whereas some of her later work employed mechanical devices for a cinematic change of scenes. Bernstein founded the Costume Museum, which later was absorbed by the Metropolitan Museum of Art. Her autobiography, *An Actor's Daughter* [her father was Joseph Frankau], first appeared in 1941.   AA

See: C. Klein, *Aline,* New York, 1979.

Bernstein, Leonard (1918–90) Composer. Although his primary career was as a conductor of symphony orchestras, Bernstein wrote the scores for six musicals. In 1944 he composed the music for **Jerome Robbins**'s ballet "Fancy Free"; when this was expanded into the full-length musical *On the Town* (1944), Bernstein wrote the entire score. Critics complimented him for the fresh, lively sound of his music. Nine years passed before Broadway heard another Bernstein score. *Wonderful Town*

gave him the opportunity to write a nostalgic score full of pastiches of the "swing" music popular in the 1930s. In 1956 Bernstein wrote the music for *Candide,* a musical adaptation of the Voltaire novel. Although the show was not a commercial success, Bernstein's score, with its echoes of various classical composers and its dry, satiric sound, was recognized as one of the finest written for the Broadway stage. A 1974 revival of *Candide* proved to be more successful with audiences. Bernstein's most famous score, that for *West Side Story,* premiered in 1957. Critics praised the music for its ability to embody the tensions and passions of the show's teenage characters. Although his contributions to the Broadway stage were relatively few, Bernstein's musically sophisticated and inventive scores earned him a reputation as one of the foremost Broadway composers.   MK

See: Bernstein's *Findings,* New York, 1982; P. Gradenwitz, *Leonard Bernstein: The Infinite Variety of a Musician,* New York, 1987; J. Peyser, *Bernstein, A Biography,* New York, 1987.

Bettelheim, Edwin Sumner (1865–1938) Theatre journalist and critic. Born in Albany and educated at Cornell, Bettelheim edited the *Albany Mirror* before purchasing the [New York] *Dramatic Times* from **Leander Richardson** in 1888. This he consolidated with the *New York Dramatic News,* which he bought in 1896, to publish and edit the *New York Dramatic News and Dramatic Times* until 1919. Lee **Shubert, Charles B. Dillingham, George C. Tyler,** and **Channing Pollock** worked for Bettelheim early in their careers.   TLM

Beyond the Horizon Although this play opened with poorly staged trial matinees at the **Morosco Theatre** on 3 February 1920, **Eugene O'Neill**'s first Broadway production received the second Pulitzer Prize for Drama. When public and critical interest in the play were aroused, it settled in for a regular run that signaled momentous change in serious American drama. Directed by Homer Saint-Gaudens, assisted by **Richard Bennett** (who also played the leading role of Robert Mayo), O'Neill's tragic study of two struggling brothers would recur in variations throughout his work for decades. Here the brothers struggled over the love of Ruth (Helen Mackeller) and pitted Robert the artist, trapped on the farm but longing for unseen wonders of the sea, against Andrew (Edward Arnold), the prosaic farming brother who is content with the land but who, after losing Ruth, travels afar without appreciating what he sees at sea or in exotic lands. Robert and Ruth suffer a loveless marriage, and all three major characters are unfulfilled as the play ends with the death of Robert reaching for the rising sun. Like all of O'Neill's work, this play is autobiographical, exploring in part the rivalry, love, and frustration O'Neill experienced with his brother.   RHW

Big White Fog by Theodore Ward was presented for 10 weeks in 1938 by the Chicago unit of the **Federal Theatre Project.** It was the premiere production of the Negro Playwrights Company in New York in 1940, an event notable for its cast

(**Canada Lee,** Hilda Offley, and Frank Silvera) and the scenic design of Perry Watkins (first black member of the Union of Scenic Artists). The drama spans 10 years (1922–32) and examines the political options available to African Americans. The father in the household is actively involved in Garvey's nationalist movement in opposition to his brother (a capitalist) and, later, his son (a communist). Through the deterioration of the Garvey movement and the Depression, we see the family's cataclysmic struggle to survive.   KME

Bikel, Theodore (1924–) Austrian-born actor, folksinger, and past president of **Actors' Equity** (1973–82). Bikel apprenticed with the Habimah Theatre in Tel Aviv and appeared in several London stage productions before coming to the U.S. in 1954. A heavy-set character actor, Bikel has played many nationalities, most notably in *The Lark* (1955), *Fiddler on the Roof* (over 1,000 times since 1959), *The Sound of Music* (1959), and *Zorba* (1975). He has toured frequently, replaced actors in major roles, and returned to favorite vehicles on many occasions. A popular cabaret performer, described in 1989 as "a good-natured international troubadour," Bikel has also been a political activist for the performing arts, serving as officer of the International Federation of Actors and Associated Actors and Artistes of America.   DBW

Biloxi Blues Second work in **Neil Simon**'s "Brighton Beach Trilogy"; opened 28 March 1985 at the **Neil Simon Theatre,** running for 524 performances. Following *Brighton Beach Memoirs* by several years, the play relates the WW II boot-camp experience of Eugene Jerome, the semiautobiographical Simon. Through the interaction of six members of Jerome's basic training unit and their opposition to a sadistic, semipsychotic drill sergeant, Simon continued to illustrate the futility of uncompromising behavior. The actions of a persecuted Arnold Epstein and the indecisive Don Carney introduce the notion that life demands conscious choice, even if drastic consequences result.   RW

Biltmore Theatre 261 West 47th St., NYC [Architect: Herbert J. Krapp]. Still believing that theatres represented a solid real estate venture, the Chanin brothers, builders, erected the Biltmore with under 1,000 seats for serious plays and comedies. Unfortunately, the Depression robbed them of their theatrical empire. After a year during which it was rented to the **Federal Theatre Project,** the playhouse was sold to Warner Bros., who leased it to **George Abbott.** In the next 15 years, Abbott presented and often directed about a dozen or more of his own productions at the theatre. In 1951, the theatre was sold and became a CBS-TV studio. In 1961, with another owner, seats were added to it and it was reclaimed for legitimate production. Dark since 1987, it was sold at auction in 1988 and again in 1991.   MCH

Bingham, Amelia (1869–1927) Actress. While a student at Ohio Wesleyan University, she acted with the traveling company of Lloyd Bingham in the summer of 1890. A year later she married him and toured the Pacific Coast with **McKee Rankin.** Her New York debut was in December 1893. She became a star under **Charles Frohman**'s management (1897), but was her own producer for **Clyde Fitch**'s *The Climbers* (15 January 1901), whose Mrs. Sterling was her greatest role. She also played in stock companies and in vaudeville (1905–14). Her last appearance was in *The Pearl of Great Price* (New York, 1927).   DMcD

Biography Comedy by **S. N. Behrman** produced in 1932 by the **Theatre Guild** and directed by **Philip Moeller.** Marion Froude, a restless egoist, writes her biography for a magazine edited by Richard Kurt, a fierce young socialist. The politically conservative Leander Nolan, a former lover, fears her revelations will spoil his bid for a seat in the U.S. Senate, and he begs her to quash her story. She destroys her manuscript, then breaks with Kurt, whom she has grown to love. In opting for the middle way between conservatism and radicalism, Marion encapsulates the situation of many mainstream American playwrights of the 1930s.   WD

Birch, Patricia (1930?–) Modern dancer and theatre choreographer who joined the Martha Graham Dance Company in 1950, rising to soloist in 1955. She later danced for **Agnes de Mille** in the New York City Center revivals of *Brigadoon* (1955), *Carousel* (1954), and *Oklahoma!* (1958); and for **Jerome Robbins,** playing the role of "Anybody's" in the national company of *West Side Story* (1960). Her first theatrical choreography was *The Carefree Tree* (1956), and she only worked sporadically thereafter. Birch's choreography for *You're a Good Man, Charlie Brown* (1967) revitalized her career and led to a series of successes, including *The Me Nobody Knows* (1970), *Grease* (1972), and the revival of *Candide* (1974). It was in the choreography in *A Little Night Music* (1973) that Birch displayed her versatility, breaking from the usual form of flamboyant and spectacular dance numbers by crafting a subtle blend of **dance** and dialogue.   LF

Bird, Robert Montgomery (1806–54) Playwright whose major plays – *The Gladiator* (1831), *Oralloosa* (1832), and *The Broker of Bogota* (1834) – were prizewinners in **Edwin Forrest**'s playwriting contests and were performed by him. *Gladiator* and *Broker* were retained in Forrest's repertoire, with extraordinary profits for him and only $2,000 for Bird; *Pelopidas* (1830), another winner, was never produced. Discouraged by his bitter financial quarrels with Forrest, Bird turned to novels: *Hawks of Hawk Hollow* (1836) and *Nick of the Woods* (1837) are the best known.

Bird received his medical degree in 1827, practiced for a year, wrote two plays in 1827 (*The Cowled Lover* and *Caridorf*), and taught at Pennsylvania Medical College (1841–3). At his death his notebook outlined plans for 11 tragedies, 12 comedies, 33 melodramas, and 25 novels.   RM

See: C. Dahl, *Robert Montgomery Bird,* New York, 1963.

Ladies of the ballet preparing to "fly" in *The Black Crook* (1866). Courtesy: New York Public Library for the Performing Arts.

Black Crook, The Four-act musical extravaganza by Charles M. Barras, music by various composers. Opened 12 September 1866 at **Niblo's Garden,** running 474 performances. This first "monster hit" of the American **musical theatre** was born of disaster: A French ballet troupe – stranded in New York when the theatre they were to perform in burned down – was grafted onto a gothic Faustian melodrama (by stage-manager-turned-author Barras) that was scheduled for production at Niblo's. The resultant hybrid was a five-and-a-half-hour amalgam of scenic splendor, earnest melodramatics, and huge ballet interludes, all set to a melange of pseudoclassical and contemporary popular music. Beyond this range of attractions, the show was vilified in many quarters for the "near-nudity" of dancers in tights, which ensured the show's reputation as a succès de scandale. Grossing over $1,000,000 in its initial engagement, it toured the country and received regular Broadway revivals for the rest of the century.   JD

> *See:* J. Whitton, *The Naked Truth!: An Inside History of The Black Crook,* Philadelphia, 1897; L. G. Odom, "*The Black Crook* at Niblo's Garden," *The Drama Review* 26 (1982).

Blackface minstrelsy see **Minstrel show**

Blackstone, Harry (né Henri Bouton) (1885–1965) Though best known for his full-stage illusions, the "Great Blackstone" 's most impres-

sive feats were the vanishing bird cage (complete with bird) and the "Spirit Dancing Handkerchief" (both still performed by **Harry Blackstone, Jr.** [1935–]). During his long career he appeared in vaudeville, tab shows between movies, and (from 1914) full evenings in legitimate theatres. During WW II he took his show to 165 military posts under USO sponsorship; at the peak of his popularity he starred in his own radio show ("Blackstone – Magic Detective") and was hero of his own comic book. Among his more spectacular stage illusions were "Levitation of Princess Karnac" (which he inherited from **Kellar**), the "Vanishing Horse," "Sepoy Mutiny" (a cannon illusion), and sawing a woman in half with a buzz saw (with the victim in full view). Blackstone is still remembered for one of his trademarks – the production and distribution of rabbits to children in the audience. Blackstone's son, who first appeared with his father's show at age six months, presented a full-length **magic** show on Broadway in 1980; it had the longest run of any straight magic show in history (118 performances).   DBW

> *See:* H. Blackstone, Jr., with C. and R. Reynolds, *The Blackstone Book of Magic & Illusion,* New York, 1985.

Blaine, Vivian (Stapleton) (1923–) Singer-actress. After attending the **American Academy of Dramatic Arts,** she appeared in **nightclubs** and **summer stock** before making her Broadway debut as Miss Adelaide in *Guys and Dolls* (1950); as the forlorn fiancée of gambler Nathan Detroit, she stopped the show with "Adelaide's Lament." She also succeeded Shelley Winters in *A Hatful of Rain* (1955) and starred in the musical *Say, Darling* (1958) and the comedy *Enter Laughing* (1963).   MK

Blake, Eubie see **Sissle, Noble**

Blake, William Rufus (1805–63) Canadian-born actor, playwright, and manager, noted for his portrayal of old men on the American stage. With the possible exception of **William Burton,** he was without equal in this line. Blake made his New York debut at the **Chatham Garden Theatre** in 1824 and subsequently appeared with great success in the U.S. and Britain. In the 1820s and '30s he managed successively the **Tremont Theatre, Boston;** the **Walnut Street** in **Philadelphia;** and, with H. E. Willard, the **Olympic Theatre,** New York. Later he was principal comedian in the New York stock companies of Burton, **Laura Keene,** and **Lester Wallack.** His final appearance was as Sir Peter Teazle at the **Boston Theatre** on 21 April 1963; he died suddenly the next day.   DBW

Blanchard, Kitty (1847–1911) Actress whose first professional appearance was at age 10 at the National Theatre in Philadelphia. In the mid-1860s she became a popular comedienne in **Boston,** first with the Continental Theatre company and then with Selwyn's (later the Globe) Theatre company. In 1869 she married the leading man at Selwyn's, **Arthur McKee Rankin.** Together they toured nationwide for almost 20 years, most notably in the melodramas *The Two Orphans* and *The Dan-*

ites. In the 1890s, following a separation from her husband, Mrs. Rankin appeared in several **Charles Frohman** productions and in support of **Richard Mansfield** and E. M. and Joseph Holland. DJW

Blau, Herbert (1926–) Director and postmodern critic who, in *The Impossible Theater: A Manifesto* (1964), vowed "to talk up a revolution" and has. Blau's later critical work – *Take Up the Bodies: Theater at the Vanishing Point* and *Blooded Thought: Occasions of Theatre* (1982), *The Eye of Prey: Subversions of the Postmodern* (1987), and *The Audience* (1990) – propounds a Foucaultian "theatrum philosophicum" of the mind. Blau's central themes are "the self-abolishing [and self-observing] thought of theatre," the co-opting of theatrical performance by writing and the decentering of culture based in logocentric language via the complicating of thought's linguistic expression. Blau and **Jules Irving** pioneered stage work on Brecht and Beckett at **San Francisco** Actors Workshop, which they cofounded (1952), before becoming coartistic directors of the Repertory Theatre of **Lincoln Center** (1965). Resigning his position in 1967, following his controversial production of *Danton's Death* (which opened the **Vivian Beaumont Theatre**), Blau cofounded the California Institute of the Arts (1968), where he was in charge of actor training. His later work with KRAKEN (formerly the Oberlin Group) was rigorously physical and groupcreated. Blau continually promotes modes of seeing – authorship and spectatorship – that address and partially redress the new cultural subjects of division and pastiche. SG

Bleckner, Jeff (1943–) Director and television producer. Bleckner has directed for **Long Wharf, Arena Stage, La MaMa** (1970, Obie for **Shepard**'s *The Unseen Hand*), **Mark Taper Forum,** and **Yale Repertory.** For the **New York Shakespeare Festival** in 1971 he directed *Sticks and Bones* (Tony, Drama Desk, and NY Drama Critics' Circle awards) and *The Basic Training of Pavlo Hummel* (Obie, Drama Desk). He won television's Emmys for "Hill Street Blues" (1983) and "Concealed Enemies" (on "American Playhouse," 1984). REK

Blessing, Lee (1950–) Minneapolis-born playwright, trained at the University of Iowa Graduate Writer's Workshop and author of plays such as *Independence* (1984, **Actors Theater**), *Eleemosynary* (1988, TheatreWorks), *Cobb* (1989, **Yale Rep**), *Fortinbras* (1991, La Jolla Playhouse), and *Lake Street Extension* (1992, Ensemble Theater of Cincinnati). Made his Broadway debut with the two-character *A Walk in the Woods* (1987), in which a Soviet and an American diplomat privately attempt to reach a disarmament agreement. His strongest work to date, the play was subsequently produced on PBS's "American Playhouse" (1989) and in London (1988) and Moscow (1989). Blessing spent the 1992–3 season as Playwright-in-Residence at New York's Signature Theatre Company. CLJ

Blinn, Holbrook (1872–1928) San Francisco-born actor who first appeared onstage locally as a

child in *Streets of New York* (1878). After a year at Stanford University (1891–2), he made his New York debut in *The New South* (1893), and his first London appearance in *The Cat and the Cherub* (1897). He began playing leading parts for **Arnold Daly**'s Company (1907–8) and afterward with **Mrs. Fiske** (1908–11), portraying Jim Platt in *Salvation Nell* (1908) and Karsten Bernick in *Pillars of Society* (1901). In 1911 **Harrison Grey Fiske** featured him as Michael Regan in **Edward Sheldon**'s *The Boss*. During the 1913–14 season he produced a series of 30 one-acts at the Princess Theatre, acting in several. Other starring roles included Lord Illingworth in *A Woman of No Importance* (1916) with **Margaret Anglin;** Georges Duval in *The Lady of the Camellias* in an all-star revival (1917); and Pancho Lopez in *The Bad Man* (1920), a role that brought him recognition for his comic ability. Blinn was a versatile actor able to play a wide range of roles from the brutal Jim Platt to the aristocratic Georges Duval. TLM

Blitzstein, Marc (1905–64) Philadelphia-born composer, librettist, and adapter who studied at the Curtis Institute of Music and later trained with Nadia Boulanger in Paris and Arnold Schönberg in Berlin. He is best known as the composer-librettist for *The Cradle Will Rock* (1937), a prolabor operetta developed within the **Federal Theatre Project.** The controversial production, famously recounted in **John Houseman**'s *Run-through* (1972), was revived a few months later by **Orson Welles** and Houseman as part of the **Mercury Theatre**'s first season. He later translated and adapted Brecht's *The Threepenny Opera* (1952), an **Off-Broadway** success (2,611 performances). Other musical works included *Regina* (1949), based on **Lillian Hellman**'s *The Little Foxes,* and *Juno* (1959), based on Sean O'Casey's *Juno and the Paycock.* At the time of his death, a murder victim in Martinique, he was developing an opera about the Sacco and Vanzetti case. TP

See: E. A. Gordon, *Mark the Music: The Life and Work of Marc Blitzstein,* New York, 1989.

Blondin, Charles (né Jean-François-Emile Gravelet) (1824–97) French wire-walker and son of nomadic performers who studied with the **Ravel** family, taking his name from his tutor Jean Ravel Blondin and cultivating the bayonet springboard. Fame came in 1859 when, on a U.S. tour with the Ravels, he crossed Niagara Falls on a tightrope; he later repeated this feat blindfolded or pushing a man in a wheelbarrow, or stopping halfway across to cook an omelette. Much imitated, especially by "Female Blondins," he pursued his altitudinous profession until the age of 70. LS

Bloodgood (née Stevens), Clara (1870–1907) Actress. After appearing under **Charles Frohman**'s management, beginning with her debut in *The Conquerors* (1898), Bloodgood became a favorite of **Clyde Fitch,** appearing first in his *The Climbers* (1901), then in roles written for her – notably Jinny Austin in *The Girl with the Green Eyes* (1902) and Becky Warder, the consummate liar, in *The Truth* (1907). She also appeared as Violet Robinson in the American premiere of **Shaw**'s *Man and Superman* (1905). *The Truth,* a hit in London with Marie Tempest, was a disaster in New York but a succcess for Bloodgood on the road. Apparently suffering from depression, the actress shot herself in a Baltimore hotel room shortly before a performance. Fitch denied the suicide had been motivated by a dedication of *The Truth* to Tempest.   DBW

Bloomgarden, Kermit (1904–76) Producer. Born in Brooklyn and educated at New York University, Bloomgarden made his producing debut in 1940 with Albert Bein's *Heavenly Express,* which promptly closed. In 1945 he sponsored his first hit, *Deep Are the Roots,* a drama about racial conflict. This was followed in 1946 by **Lillian Hellman**'s *Another Part of the Forest,* beginning a long association with the playwright. Success continued with *Command Decision* (1947), *Death of a Salesman* (1949), *The Crucible* (1953), *A View from the Bridge* (1955), *The Diary of Anne Frank* (1955), *The Most Happy Fella* (1956), *Look Homeward, Angel* (1957), and *The Music Man* (1957). He presented Hellman's *Toys in the Attic* in 1960, but had few other productions of note until *The Hot l Baltimore* (1973) and the New York mounting of *Equus* (1974). Bloomgarden believed that producers should interfere as little as possible with artists except to "throw out sparks that will stimulate them to make better use of their own creativity."   TLM

> *See:* L. Doherty, "The Art of Producing: The Life and Work of Kermit Bloomgarden," PhD diss., City U of New York, 1989.

Blossom Time Three-act operetta, music by **Sigmund Romberg,** words by Dorothy Donnelly; opened 29 September 1921 at the **Ambassador Theatre,** New York, running 592 performances. Based on a popular Viennese operetta, this sentimental, highly fictionalized "biography" of Franz Schubert used Schubert's own music as the basis for its songs. Romberg, a house composer for the **Shubert**s who had written scores for 25 shows in seven years, was assigned to revise it for American production, largely on the strength of his successful adaptation of *Maytime* (1917). He and Donnelly drastically revised the original and created a smash success that was the second-longest-running musical of the 1920s (after Romberg's *The Student Prince*) and became a staple of road companies for the next 30 years.   JD

Blues for Mr. Charlie by **James Baldwin** was produced during the 1963–4 Broadway season and heralded the violence that would erupt as playwrights of the 1960s began to voice the anger of the African-American community. A searing analysis of attitudes and emotions based on the factual murder of Emmett Till, the play tells of the black son of a preacher who, returning home to the South, is found dead after an innocent conversation with a white woman. Set simultaneously in Blacktown and Whitetown USA, the play's characters speak to the audience in soliloquy and dialogue during the course of the trial to reveal the fears and hatreds burning in the deep South. The play ends on a somewhat hopeful note.   KME

Bock, Jerry (1925–) and **Sheldon Harnick** (1924–) Composer and lyricist, each of whom began writing for the Broadway musical stage in the 1950s; however, they did not work as collaborators until *The Body Beautiful* (1958). In the following year their show *Fiorello!* won the Pulitzer Prize for Drama. Among their other notable scores were *She Loves Me* (1963), *Fiddler on the Roof* (1964), *The Apple Tree* (1966), and *The Rothschilds* (1970), after which they ended their partnership. Writing in an era when most musicals had an exotic or period setting, Bock and Harnick were adept at varying their style to match the time and place of each show, while at the same time working within the traditional forms of Broadway show music.   MK

Body Politic Theatre Founded in 1966 by Chicago's Community Arts Foundation under the direction of Jim Shiflett and with help from **Paul Sills** and **Mike Nichols,** the Body Politic was the seminal theatre in the early development of **Chicago**'s Off-Loop theatre renaissance. Although it has long been a producing company, its major early contribution was as a host to many other companies, most notably the **Organic Theater.**   SF

Boesing, Martha (1936–) Playwright-director best known as founding manager of **At the Foot of the Mountain** Theatre (AFOM), a women's **collective** in **Minneapolis,** from which she resigned in 1984. Acting in Minneapolis theatre in the '60s, Boesing later started writing plays that deal primarily with women's personal and political issues. Her early plays with AFOM include *River Journal* (1975), and *Raped* (1976) and *The Story of a Mother* (1977), created collaboratively with the company. Boesing's nonrealist plays are often participatory ritual dramas. She has received NEA and Bush Foundation fellowships in playwriting.   JDo

Bogart, Anne (1951–) Director whose detailed stagings incorporate music, dance, and large-ensemble performance in original pieces and reinterpreted classics. Influenced by the international avant-garde, during 1980–8 she directed at universities and small theatres in New York and Europe, working with environmental frameworks to investigate political concerns. Most memorable are her *South Pacific* (1984), set in a mental institution; *1951* (with **Mac Wellman,** 1986) on the McCarthy years; *Cinderella/Cendrillon* (1988), reworking Massenet's opera; and her Obie-winning *No Plays, No Poetry* (1988), an original exploration of Brecht. Artistic Director of **Trinity Repertory Company** during 1989–90, she resigned over a budget dispute. After staging *Once in a Lifetime* (1990) at **American Repertory Theatre,** she returned to New York to free-lance and explore vaudeville, resulting in the cowriting (with Tina Landau) of *American Vaudeville,* which she directed at the **Alley** in March 1992. She was elected President of **Theatre Communications Group** in 1991, and in 1992 received an Obie for her direction of Paula Vogel's *Baltimore Waltz*. She is cofounder (with Tadashi Suzuki) of Saratoga International Theater Institute.   TH-S

Bogosian, Eric (1953–) Massachusetts-reared Obie Award–winning actor, playwright, and monologist, best known for the comedic gallery of profane and power-addicted American males he assembles in **one-person** shows like *Drinking in America* (1986), *Sex, Drugs & Rock and Roll* (1987), and his one full-length play, *Talk Radio* (1987; film version, 1988). Among fellow monologists, Bogosian's sensibility lies midway between the mainstream focus of **Lily Tomlin** and Richard Pryor and the experimental perspectives of **Spalding Gray** or **Laurie Anderson.**   CLJ

Boker, George Henry (1823–90) Playwright and poet. His principal play, *Francesca da Rimini* (1855), first performed by **E. L. Davenport** (Lanciotto), did not achieve major success until 1882 when **Lawrence Barrett** appeared as Lanciotto and **Otis Skinner** as Paolo. It was retained in Barrett's repertoire and was revived by Skinner (Lanciotto) in 1901. Boker wrote 10 other plays. The best known: *The World a Mask* (1851) and *The Bankrupt* (1855). Boker once confided to **Bayard Taylor** that he had no ambition to become "a mere playwright" but wanted to be "acknowledged as a poet." He wrote several volumes of poetry: *The Lesson of Life* (1848), *Poems of the War* (1864), and *The Will of the People* (1864).

Boker served as Minister to Turkey (1871–5), as Minister Plenipotentiary to Russia (1875–8), and President of Philadelphia's Union League (1878–84).   RM

See: E. Bradley, *George Henry Boker, Poet and Patriot,* Philadelphia, 1927.

Boland, Mary (1880–1965) Actress remembered for her fluttery matrons and zany mothers in film. Boland served her apprenticeship in stock and on tour. Her New York debut (1905) was in *Strongheart*. In the teens she was **John Drew**'s leading lady in nine **Frohman** productions. Initially cast in serious roles, her portrayal as the scatterbrained Mrs. Wheeler in *Clarence* (1919) established her as a flexible talent. During the 1920s she was one of America's most popular stage comediennes. Seen infrequently on stage after 1930, her final appearance in 1954 (as the mother in *Lullaby*) provoked one critic to state that she was as "overwrought and mercurial as ever."   DBW

Boleslavski (also Boleslavsky), Richard (né Boleslaw Ryszard Srzednicki) (1887–1937) An original member of the **Moscow Art Theatre**'s first Studio, he left Russia in 1920, joined the "Kachalov Group" (an MAT offshoot) in Prague (1921) and settled in the U.S. in 1922. Boleslavski's **Princess Theatre** lectures and his article "First Lesson of Acting" (October 1923) introduced Americans to the Stanislavskian concept of "concentration" in acting and were the basis of his book *Acting: The First Six Lessons* (1933). Boleslavski and

former MAT actress Maria Ouspenskaya cofounded the **American Laboratory Theatre** (ALT, 1923–30) where, with critic **John Mason Brown,** dancer Mikhail Mordkin, and composer Douglas Moore, they taught a full theatre curriculum. Boleslavski's development of the actor's expressive means and intellectual and cultural awareness linked the MAT tradition to the **Group Theatre,** though Boleslavski believed one of the founders and former student, **Lee Strasberg,** erroneously stressed affective memory over dramatic action in his teaching. Boleslavski had a varied NYC stage directing career (including the ALT subscription series begun in 1925), directed 15 major Hollywood films in the 1930s, and wrote two autobiographical books (published 1932).   SG

See: J. W. Roberts, *Richard Boleslavsky: His Life and Work in the Theatre,* Ann Arbor, MI, 1981.

Bolger, Ray (1904–87) Dancer and singer. After making his debut with a musical stock company in Boston, Bolger spent a few years in vaudeville before appearing on Broadway in *The Merry World* (1926). His loose-limbed, comic dancing style was featured in several **revue**s, including **George White**'s *Scandals of 1931*. He appeared in *Life Begins at 8:40* (1934) and created the part of Junior Dolan in **Rodgers** and **Hart**'s *On Your Toes* (1936), in which he performed **George Balanchine**'s choreography for the "Slaughter on Tenth Avenue" ballet. During the 1940s Bolger starred in such popular musicals as *By Jupiter* (1942) and *Three to Make Ready* (1946). In *Where's Charley?* (Tony, 1948), a musical version of *Charley's Aunt,* Bolger stopped the show with his rendition of "Once in Love with Amy." After a decade away from Broadway, Bolger returned to the musical stage in the 1960s for *All American* (1962) and *Come Summer* (1969), neither of which was a hit.   MK

Bolton, Guy (1883–1979) Librettist and playwright. He began writing plays in 1911, and soon after turned to writing librettos. In 1915 he joined composer **Jerome Kern** for the first of the **Princess Theatre** musicals, *Nobody Home.* The success of this modest and ingratiating musical comedy was repeated with *Very Good Eddie* (1915), *Have a Heart* (1917), *Oh, Boy!* (1917), and others. Bolton's Princess Theatre librettos were praised for their unusually coherent plots and well-developed characters. His career as a librettist spanned forty years, encompassing such hits as *Sally* (1920), *Lady, Be Good* (1924), *Oh, Kay!* (1926), and *Anything Goes* (1934). With lyricist **P. G. Wodehouse,** Bolton coauthored an autobiography, *Bring on the Girls* (1953).   MK

Bonstelle, Jessie (Laura) (1872?–1932) Director-actress, best known for directing the Detroit Civic Theatre. Born near Greece, NY, by age 9 she could recite 150 selections, mostly Shakespearean. After attending a convent school, Bonstelle entered a road company of *Bertha, the Beautiful Sewing Machine Girl* and later worked for **Augustin Daly** and the **Shubert**s. In 1910 she founded a repertory company in Detroit that ran for 14 years. In 1925 she opened the Bonstelle Playhouse and later organized the Detroit Civic Theatre. The Depression threatened the organization, for which she actively campaigned until the time of her death. Among the many stars she developed were **Katharine Cornell, Melvyn Douglas,** Frank Morgan, and William Powell. SMA

> *See:* W. L. Deam, "A Biographical Study of Miss Laura Justine Bonstelle-Stuart Together with an Evaluation of Her Own Contributions to the Modern Theatre World," PhD diss., U of Michigan, 1954.

Booth, Agnes (née Marion Agnes Land Rookes) (1846–1910) Australian-born actress, made her first American appearances in San Francisco where she married Harry Perry, a popular actor (1861). After her New York debut in 1865 (Florence Trenchard in *Our American Cousin*) she supported **Edwin Forrest** for a season. From 1866 to 1874 she was with the **Boston Theatre** Company under the management of **Junius Brutus Booth, Jr.,** whom she married in 1867. Following starring tours during 1847–76, she became leading actress with such New York stock companies as **Union Square, Park Theatre, Niblo's Garden,** and, during 1881–91, the **Madison Square** company. Her third marriage (1885) was to John B. Schoeffel, a prominent theatre manager. With a singularly rich, distinctive voice and expressive features, Mrs. Booth, a versatile actress, was best playing forceful, spirited women, like Cleopatra, Mrs. Ralston in Charles Young's *Jim, the Penman,* and the Duchess of Milford in *The Sporting Duchess.* She appeared last as Rose in an adaptation of *L'Arlesienne* (1897). DJW

Booth, Edwin Thomas (1833–93) Actor and manager who made his debut in 1849 at the **Boston Museum** as Tressel in support of his father's Richard III. Booth continued to act with his father accompanying him to California in 1852. When the elder Booth left California, Edwin remained, playing in **San Francisco** and Sacramento and touring various small towns and mining camps. During 1854–5, he toured with **Laura Keene** to Melbourne and Sydney, with a brief engagement in Honolulu on the return voyage. In 1856 he returned to the east, making starring engagements in Baltimore, Richmond, and **Boston.** He made his first major New York appearance at **Burton's Chambers Street Theatre** in May 1857. From this point until his retirement in 1891, his acting career was generally a series of unbroken successes. For 10 years (1864–74), Booth was involved in the management of several theatres, most notably the **Winter Garden** (1864–7) and his own **Booth's Theatre** (1869–74). His management was particularly distinguished by his carefully mounted, visually splendid productions of *Hamlet, Julius Caesar, The Merchant of Venice, Othello,* and *Richelieu.* However, after Booth lost his theatre in 1873 due to poor financial management, he abandoned management and spent the remainder of his career touring.

Early in his career (1861–2) Booth had starred in London (where his only child Edwina was born) and in Manchester and Liverpool. In 1881–2, at the

Edwin Booth as Hamlet (1870). Courtesy: Harvard Theatre Collection.

height of his powers, he played at London's Princess's Theatre and alternated Othello and Iago with Henry Irving at the Lyceum Theatre. He appeared in London again in 1883 and then toured the provincial circuit. In 1883 he also made a highly successful tour of several German cities. During 1886–91 he completed several extensive national tours in association with his close friend, **Lawrence Barrett.** Booth's last performance was as Hamlet at the **Brooklyn Academy of Music** in 1891.

Darkly handsome and gifted with a slender, graceful figure, a clear, musical voice and luminous, expressive eyes, he was the finest American tragedian of his time. At his best portraying brooding, melancholy characters like Brutus or Hamlet – his greatest characterization – or capturing darkly sinister personalities like Iago or Bertuccio (*The Fool's Revenge*), Booth was also successful in the playfully comic roles of Benedick and Petruchio, and especially as the wily, histrionic Cardinal Richelieu. Late in his career, his King Lear and Shylock were widely admired.

The hallmark of his acting style was a certain vocal, physical, and emotional restraint or "quietude"; this was the chief quality that distinguished his acting from the often violent excesses of the earlier romantic school to which his father, **Junius Brutus,** belonged. Mollie (Mary) Devlin, his first wife, called his style the "conversation, colloquial school." Booth, for example, spoke Shakespeare's verse or the lesser stuff of Edward Bulwer [Lytton] or **John Howard Payne** as if it were "natural conversation." An amateur Booth-watcher, Mary Isabella Stone, commented not only on the "naturalness" of Booth's speaking, but also on the richly suggestive, complex "tonalities" of "exquisite sarcasm," or of "sincere, friendly interest and sympathy," or of "mingled grief, astonishment, and anger." Booth's gestures, facial expressions, and movements were also regarded as "natural." He did not strain after effect. In one of his notes in Furness's *Variorium Othello,* he advises would-be Iagos to make sure "every movement, gesture, look, and tone should be in harmony," and, above all, to concentrate on "sincerely felt emotion." Perhaps because of his concentration on feeling, Booth reportedly lost his own personality in a role, creating vivid, completely different, believable characters.

Throughout his career, Booth diligently tried to better not only his art, but also the theatrical profession. He eagerly shared the stage with fellow stars, including not only Irving and Barrett, but also Bogumil Dawison, Tommaso Salvini, **Helena Modjeska, Charlotte Cushman,** and **Fanny Janauschek.** In 1888, he established The Players as a social and cultural **club** for actors and others interested in theatre. [See also **Introduction, §2.**]   DJW

> See: R. Lockridge, *Darling of Misfortune,* New York, 1932; E. Ruggles, *Prince of Players,* New York, 1953; C. H. Shattuck, *The Hamlet of Edwin Booth,* Urbana, IL, 1969; D. J. Watermeier (ed.), *Between Actor and Critic: Selected Letters of Edwin Booth and William Winter,* Princeton, NJ, 1971; D. J. Watermeier, *Edwin Booth's Performances: The Mary Isabella Stone Commentaries,* Ann Arbor and London, 1990; W. Winter, *The Life and Art of Edwin Booth,* New York, 1894.

Booth, John Wilkes (1839–65) American actor, brother of **Edwin.** He made his professional debut in 1855 at the Charles Street Theatre in Baltimore as Richmond in *Richard III,* and subsequently played supporting roles for several seasons, principally at the **Arch Street Theatre** in **Philadelphia** and the Richmond Theatre. By the early 1860s he was an established popular touring star, playing mainly in the midwestern and southern theatrical circuits. He was undoubtedly a talented, sometimes compelling, but also erratic and undisciplined actor, who was probably at his best playing romantic characters and melodramatic heroes and villains. His first New York appearance was as Richard III at the old **Wallack's Theatre** (1862); his last stage appearance was as Pescara in *The Apostate* at **Ford's Theatre** on 18 March 1865.

Almost a month later (14 April 1865) in the same theatre, Booth, a Southern sympathizer, assassinated Lincoln while the President was watching a performance of Tom Taylor's *Our American Cousin.* His motive may have been misguided patriotism or a desire for notoriety.   DJW   MB

> See: A. Clarke, *The Unlocked Book: A Memoir of John Wilkes Booth,* New York, 1938; A. Furtwangler, *Assassin on Stage: Brutus, Hamlet, and the Death of Lincoln,* Urbana, IL, 1991; S. Kimmel, *The Mad Booths of Maryland,* rev. ed., New York, 1969; G. Samples, *Lust for Fame,* Jefferson, NC, 1982 (the last is often unreliable).

Booth, Junius Brutus (1796–1852) Anglo-American actor who rose to stardom in London, but who spent the bulk of his career in America. Born in London, Booth tried various occupations before becoming an actor in 1813. After a continental tour in 1814–15, Booth performed at Brighton and Worthing before starring in 1817 at Covent Garden. Edmund Kean, concerned with a possible new rival, invited Booth to Drury Lane to play Iago to his Othello. After one performance, Booth retreated to Covent Garden, where he starred for a few months, then toured the provinces, playing London only occasionally. In 1821 he deserted his wife and child and emigrated to America with Mary Ann Holmes.

Booth bought a farm in Maryland and toured the U.S. until his death, except for visits to England in 1825–6 and 1836–7. He sired 10 children in Maryland, six of whom reached their majority. His London wife, Adelaide Dellanoy, learned of Booth's American family and in 1851 divorced Booth, who married Holmes a few weeks later.

As an actor, Booth was often compared to Kean, even accused of imitating him. Romantic, passionate, frequently seeming out of control, Booth gained such notoriety in the New World with his often aberrant behavior as to be billed "The Mad Tragedian." Heavy drinking complicated his situation, but Walt Whitman said of him, "The words fire, energy, *abandon,* found in him unprecedented meanings. I never heard a speaker or actor who could give such a string to hauteur or the taunt."

About 1852 Booth began construction on his farm of Tudor Hall, based on an English design – a structure that still stands. He played **San Francisco** and Sacramento in 1852, appeared for the last time in New Orleans, and died on a Mississippi River steamboat near Louisville. He is buried in Green Mount Cemetery in Baltimore.   SMA

> See: S. Archer, *Junius Brutus Booth: Theatrical Prometheus,* Carbondale, IL, 1992.

Booth, Junius Brutus, Jr. (1821–83) American actor and theatre manager who made his debut in 1834 at the Pittsburgh Theatre as Tressel to his father's Richard III. After over a decade of playing stock at various theatres, including New York's **Bowery** and Boston's **Howard Athenaeum,** he migrated to California in 1851 where he acted and managed several theatres in **San Francisco** until he returned east in 1864. At various times, he managed for his brother **Edwin,** the **Boston Theatre,** the **Walnut Street Theatre,** the **Winter Garden,** and for one season **Booth's Theatre.** He was a competent manager, but generally an undistinguished actor, although he was well regarded for his King John and Cassius. He married three women, all actresses: first Clementine DeBar, then Harriet Mace (d. 1859), and finally Agnes Land Perry (d. 1910) [see **Agnes Booth**], who was a successful leading actress for many years. Four of Junius's children pursued stage careers: Blanche DeBar, Marion, Junius Brutus III (d. 1887), and Sydney Barton Booth (1873–1937).   DJW

Booth, Shirley (née Thelma Booth Ford) (1907–92) Actress whose career began in 1919 with the Poli Stock Company. Her first New York appearance was in *Hell's Bells* (1925). She is best known for her haunting portrayal of the anguished and slovenly Lola in **Inge**'s *Come Back, Little Sheba* (1950), for which she received a Tony Award and, for the film version, an Academy Award. In addition she has appeared in such productions as *Goodbye, My Fancy* (1948), *A Tree Grows in Brooklyn* (1951), *The Time of the Cuckoo* (1952), *By the Beautiful Sea* (1954), *The Desk Set* (1955), *Juno* (1959), and *Look to the Lilies* and *Hay Fever* (1970). In 1972 she toured as Mrs. Gibson in *Mourning in a Funny Hat*. During the 1960s she played the comic strip character Hazel on television.   DBW

Boothe [Luce], Clare (1905–87) Playwright, journalist, and national political figure. Although she wrote several plays, none was as successful as *The Women* (1936), which was both praised and condemned for its vitriolic view of society women. A two-term congresswoman and an ambassador to Italy and Brazil, Luce often included current events in her dramas, such as *Kiss the Boys Goodbye* (1938), which she wrote as an allegory about fascism, and *Margin for Error* (1939), a comedy-melodrama that **Burns Mantle** labeled "the first successful anti-Nazi play to reach the stage." Still interested in women, Luce wrote a one-act, contemporary version of *A Doll's House* called *Slam the Door Softly* in 1971.   FB

> See: S. Shadagg, *Clare Boothe Luce: A Biography*, New York, 1970; W. Sheed, *Clare Boothe Luce*, New York, 1982.

Booth's Theatre Built for **Edwin Booth** at the corner of Sixth Avenue and Twenty-third Street in New York, it opened on 3 February 1869 with a production of *Romeo and Juliet*. The theatre was designed by the architectural firm of Renwick and Sands: James Renwick, Jr., was a distinguished architect among whose major buildings are St. Patrick's Cathedral, the Smithsonian Institution, and the Main Hall at Vassar College. Booth's Theatre was built of granite in an ornate Second Empire style. The building measured 150 ft (along 23rd St.) by 100 ft deep and rose to a height of 125 ft. Attached to the west end of the theatre was a five-story wing, the ground floor of which was for commercial shops, with three floors above for artist studios and apartments and the top floor reserved for Booth's private flat. The lavishly decorated and appointed auditorium followed the standard 19th-century horseshoe-shaped configuration, although it had a fairly narrow apron and a sunken orchestra pit similar to that designed for the Bayreuth Festspielhaus some seven years later. There were a number of other mechanical innovations in the design of the theatre, including a forced-air heating and cooling system, a set of hydraulic ramps that raised vertically moving bridges or platforms for changing scenery, a sprinkler system for fire protection, and an electrical spark ignition device that for the first time in the U.S. permitted both the auditorium and stage lights to be extinguished during performances.

Some of the finest Shakespearean productions of the era were mounted at the theatre during Booth's four-year tenure. After he lost control of it in 1873 – the result of poor financial management – Booth's

Booth's Theatre interior with set for first act of *Romeo and Juliet*. Watercolor by Charles W. Witham (1869). Courtesy: Museum of the City of New York.

Theatre was leased and managed by various individuals including **Junius Brutus Booth, Jr., Henry C. Jarrett** and Henry David Palmer, **Augustin Daly,** George Rignold, and **Dion Boucicault.** In 1883, the theatre was rebuilt as a department store, which in turn was razed in the 1960s.   DJW

Booth Theatre 222 West 45th St., NYC [Architect: Henry B. Herts]. Built by the **Shubert brothers** in partnership with producer **Winthrop Ames,** the Booth opened in 1913 with its sister house, the **Sam S. Shubert,** and completes the western wall of Shubert Alley, which originated as a fire passage behind the Hotel Astor. Winthrop Ames envisioned this small house, seating about 800, for his productions of intimate dramas and comedies, which have been its staple ever since. When Ames retired in 1932, the theatre reverted to the Shuberts, in whose possession it still remains. It has housed four Pulitzer Prize–winning productions: *You Can't Take It with You* (1936), *The Time of Your Life* (1939), *That Championship Season* (1972), and the musical *Sunday in the Park with George* (1984).   MCH

Born Yesterday Comedy written and directed by **Garson Kanin;** opened 4 February 1946 at New York's **Lyceum Theatre,** becoming an instant hit (1,642 performances). Set in Washington, DC, the play follows a boorish businessman intent on buying influence. He hires a *New Republic* writer to educate his wife, a beautiful ex–chorus girl, who lacks the appropriate social graces for the husband's purposes. The cast included Paul Douglas as the boorish husband, Gary Merrill as the writer, and **Judy Holliday** as the wife. Holliday, cast after screen actress Jean Arthur succumbed to stage fright in tryouts, enjoyed rave reviews and is often credited with the play's long success.   KN

Borscht belt Begun around the turn of the century, this term refers to a chain of some 500 resort hotels, bungalows, and summer camps in the Catskill and Adirondack mountains that catered to a largely New York Jewish clientele. Its name is derived from the popular red beet soup. After **vaudeville**'s decline, it became an important training ground for comedians (1930s). Dozens of prominent comics (Joey Adams, Danny Kaye, Red Buttons, Milton Berle, Jerry Lewis, etc.) began their careers as "social directors" or *tummlers* (funmakers) in these establishments. A 1991 Broadway show, *Catskills on Broadway,* featuring four comics, did much to capture the ambience of these venues and their humor.   DBW

See: J. Adams with H. Tobias, *The Borscht Belt,* New York, 1966; M. K. and H. Frommer, eds., *It Happened in the Catskills,* New York, 1991.

Bosco, Philip (Michael) (1930–) Largely unknown outside of the New York theatre (despite film and TV appearances), where many would cite him as the best working actor today – certainly an actor's actor – Bosco most recently has essayed such character roles as the apoplectic opera impresario in *Lend Me a Tenor* (Tony Award for best actor, 1989), Harpagon in **Circle in the Square**'s *The Miser* (1990), and a comic Italian-American gangster in *Breaking Legs* (1991). This tall, heavy-set actor, rarely unemployed since his professional debut in 1954 (in summer stock), is arguably one of our few classically adept actors, appearing frequently in Shakespeare, Ibsen, and **Shaw** (including roles in five productions with director **Stephen Porter,** among them Undershaft in *Major Barbara,* William in *You Never Can Tell,* and Burgoyne in *The Devil's Disciple*). An actor of rare intelligence, Bosco was a resident actor at **Arena Stage** in Washington, DC (1957–60), the **Shakespeare Festival** (Stratford, CT) (1962–4), and **Lincoln Center** Repertory Theatre (1966–9).   DBW

Boss, The, by Edward Sheldon; opened 9 January 1911 in Detroit and 30 January in New York for 88 performances. An effective and violent melodrama that pits a self-made, Irish-American, street-dirty labor boss against the WASPish and high-toned capitalist establishment. Caught in the middle are the poor families of the "fourth ward" and the capitalist's daughter who ministers to the ward. Boss "Shindy Mike" was played by **Holbrook Blinn,** who codirected with producer **William A. Brady; Emily Stevens** was the daughter. On the occasion of a successful revival (**Chelsea Theatre Center,** 1976), **Walter Kerr** noted that the obvious melodrama masked pioneering realistic subtleties.   MR

Boston This major New England city has never accorded theatre the courtesies that literature, art, and music have known. The great public library, the symphony, and the art museum satisfied the populace. The legacy of Puritanism and an enduring respect for the Lord's Day were not the only reasons that theatre failed early to be fully accepted here; Boston was a provincial city that held its prejudices dear. The drama was seen as something particularly foreign to the shores of Massachusetts Bay, and narrow-minded patriots kept alive the strictures of their Puritan forebears by opposing any British attempts to circumvent colonial prohibitions on the theatre. Any support of the theatre by Bostonians has been fitful; there was an abundance of theatres in the 19th century, but most genteel patrons would only resort to the theatre that called itself a "museum." After all, this was an era in which Oliver Wendell Holmes would not deign to read a novel on a Sunday, let alone frequent the playhouse. Yet by the 20th century, Bostonians accepted the city's status as a tryout town and were willing to preview New York attractions and eventually even support two major regional companies.

Theatre began in Boston with several false starts. In 1687 when John Wing tried to set up a theatre in his tavern, he incurred the wrath of Reverend Increase Mather and Judge Samuel Sewall, who stifled his attempt forthwith. Boston's next theatrical venture involved an abortive production of Otway's *The Orphan* (1750) by two English amateurs and sundry locals at The Coffee House on King (now State) Street. The performance was broken up by a crush of would-be spectators, and the ensuing melee caused the General Court to proscribe stage plays. This law exacerbated tensions between the colonists and the troops quartered in the city for the next 25 years, since the military, eager for dramatic diversions, claimed that the English Licensing Act of 1737 overruled any provincial provisions. In 1769 even the rumor that the garrison was contemplating a performance caused patriotic unrest. After the revolution broke out, sometime playwright General Burgoyne organized several performances for the benefit of his soldiers' widows and children. One of these, *The Blockage of Boston* (1775) at Faneuil Hall, was terminated by news of the battle of Bunker Hill. The *New England Chronicle* trumpeted the news of the ill-starred performance by labeling its audience "deluded wretches."

After the war, attempts were made to overturn the theatre ban. And, in 1792, speaking in the legislature, John Gardiner made the first recorded American defense of the theatre. Later that year **Joseph Harper**'s New Exhibition Room was opened on Board Alley (near present-day Hawley Street). Boston's first theatre had a capacity of 500 and was probably little more than a refurbished stable, featuring rope dancing, singing, recitation, and ballet in its opening performances. Plays masquerading as "moral lectures" came afterward; Garrick's *Lethe* and Otway's *Venice Preserv'd* were the first plays presented. Five months after the Room opened, public agitation arose over its allegedly foreign (most of the actors were British) and antidemocratic (most of the characters were lords and ladies) predisposition. Since the theatre ban was still on the book, the sheriff was dispatched to close the Room. His arrival during a performance of *The School for Scandal* caused an uproar: The audience tore down both Governor John Hancock's portrait and the Seal of the Commonwealth from the walls. The performance was stopped, but this law was never enforced again, and was finally repealed in 1797. The Board Alley theatre's brief success encouraged the construction of a permanent theatre, and in 1794 the **Federal St. Theatre,** an elegantly appointed house seating approximately 1,000, was constructed. Two years later the Haymarket opened near the heart of today's theatre district, the corner of Boylston and Tremont Streets. It was a much larger playhouse – one of the largest structures in the city – and a description exists of its crude technical capabilities.

The Haymarket barely survived the turn of the century, but during the next hundred years a building boom produced 21 theatres. The next significant one was the **Tremont** (1827), which hoped to cater to fashionable patrons unsatisfied by the program of only one theatre. Indeed, the growing sophistication of Boston audiences encouraged the proliferation, if not the success, of a variety of theatrical enterprises. The rivalry between the Federal and Tremont was so intense that both closed by midcentury.

The city's two most important theatres in the 19th century were the **Boston Museum** and the **Boston Theatre.** The former housed the best American **stock company** through the century's middle decade, and was the home of **William Warren,** arguably the greatest American comic actor, and the beloved Mrs. J. R. Vincent. The enormous Boston Theatre presented stock, opera, and variety performances as well as touring stars. The city had become a regular stop for English, American, and European tours early in the century – **George Frederick Cooke** first played Boston in 1811. Edmund Kean, chagrined by a poor turnout for his mistimed second visit (1821), arrogantly refused to go on; Bostonians repaid the insult four years later by running Kean out of town before he could even open. Other performers fared better: Boston was William Charles Macready's favorite American city, and Rachel had one of her most successful American stands there (1855).

Variety acts were popular from the first: A "learned pig" is reported to have entertained Bostonians at Bowen's Columbian Museum (1798), and 70 years later the ceiling of the **Howard Athenaeum** provided the setting for the first human fly act. The "Viennoise Children," the **Ravel**s, and performers of lesser quality held the stage for so much of the time that William W. Clapp, in his *Record of the Boston Stage* (1853), complained of "Thespis and Melpomene weeping over the tomb of legitimate drama" in Boston. The ascendancy of variety caused him to demand a new theatre that would present drama exclusively. Clapp's call went unheeded until well into the next century. By the time **Keith** and **Albee** began their dime "showstore" at the Gaiety Museum (1883), local stock had largely succumbed to the touring combination

companies. By 1894, when they opened the Colonial, the first all-vaudeville theatre, variety seemed triumphant. Nonetheless, the Broadway tryout system, pioneered at the Boston Theatre by playwright **Charles H. Hoyt** for *A Trip to Chinatown* (1891), reinvigorated the city's legitimate theatre throughout most of the following century.

The **Shubert**s gained a monopoly on the downtown houses by 1934, and anything playing in them was either headed for Broadway or on tour from it. They had to contend with the strictest local **censorship** in the country, which was no longer solely in the hands of the amateur Watch and Ward Society, but was now enforced by an official city censor. "Banned in Boston" became an infamous epithet; it was also, no doubt, attached to barely blue properties by wily press **agents.** Starting in 1915, every theatrical contract signed by producers and managers had a secret rider appended that prohibited everything from lascivious language to "all forms of muscle dancing by either sex." (This rider was finally overturned by ACLU pressure in 1965.) *Strange Interlude*'s consignment to nearby Quincy (1929) was the most notorious banning incident. The system's hypocrisy was transparent: At the "Old" Howard, strippers muscledanced with impunity.

In the meantime, the Little Theatre movement (see **community theatre**) made its impact on the city. A combination of forces from Mrs. Lyman Gale's Toy Theatre (1912) and the failed Castle Square Theater, which had presented **George Pierce Baker**'s Harvard prize plays (1911–17), were marshaled by Australian actor Henry Jewett to form a resident company. He managed to construct the Repertory Theatre of Boston (1925), but his death (1930) ended his endeavor.

Through the Depression and WW II, the New England Repertory and the Tributary Theatre of Boston struggled to keep local theatricals alive, and **Jerome Kilty**'s Brattle Theater Company briefly vitalized the local scene (1947–52). In 1957 Michael Murray's Charles Playhouse troupe created the first new legitimate performance space in Boston since Jewett's when they converted an old church into their own theatre, where they remained for 13 years. The 1960s found Harvard in Cambridge a proving ground for local artistry: Student productions of **Thomas Babe** and the late Timothy Mayer set standards that laid the groundwork for the careers of **Peter Sellars, Stockard Channing,** and many others. Across the river, **David Wheeler**'s Theatre Company of Boston gave the American premiere of Pinter's *The Dwarfs* (1966) and presented **Al Pacino** in *Richard III* (1973).

The 1970s were a transitional decade; by its end the tryout system was virtually dead. There were still artistically successful small theatres, most notably the Cambridge Ensemble, but many of the efforts of other experimental groups seemed forced. Encouraged by grants from a new state arts council, dozens of fringe companies indulged themselves until the Commonwealth's fiscal collapse in 1989. One tiny theatre that managed to survive and prosper through these years was the Lyric Stage, which celebrated its 17th season by transferring to a large new theatre (1991). In spite of the economy, there continue to be some 50 companies operating in and around Boston. The climax of the postwar era was the almost simultaneous arrival in town of two resident companies: The **American Repertory Company** (ART, 1980) and the Huntington Theatre (1982), sponsored by Harvard and Boston University, respectively. The ART is a technically dazzling director's theatre; the Huntington reveres the dramatic text above all else. The creation of the annual **Elliott Norton** Award (1982), bestowed by a committee of leading local critics (including Norton himself), is as much a tribute to the Dean of American drama critics as it is a reflection of Boston's sudden rebirth as a center of regional theatre. TC

See: W. Ball (on the Federal St. Theatre), *Bostonian Society Publications,* vol. 8 (1911); W. W. Clapp, Jr., *A Record of the Boston Stage,* 1853, reissued, New York, 1968; D. King (survey of Boston theatres), *Marquee,* vol. VI, no. 3 (1974); B. McNamara, *The American Playhouse in the 18th Century,* Cambridge, 1969; E. Norton, *Broadway Down East,* Boston, 1978; W. Reardon, "Banned in Boston," PhD diss., Stanford, 1953; E. Tompkins, *The History of the Boston Theatre 1854–1901,* Boston, 1908.

Boston Ideal Opera Company (The Bostonians) Comic opera company. Founded by Miss E. H. Ober in 1879 in order to present an "ideal" production of *HMS Pinafore,* the company, made up primarily of church choir singers from the Boston area, was noted for its high standards in both the singing and the mounting of comic operas. Although based in Boston, the company toured extensively. Reorganized as the Bostonians in 1887, the company announced its intention of encouraging the development of American comic opera. They launched the career of composer **Reginald De Koven** with their production of *Robin Hood* (1891) and performed the same service for **Victor Herbert** with *Prince Ananias* (1894). After a defection by several members of the troupe in 1898, the company declined, ending its existence in the 1904–5 season. MK

Boston Museum Tremont St. between Court and School Sts., Boston [Architect: Hammatt Billings, 1846]. In 1841, **Moses Kimball** opened the Boston Museum and Gallery of Fine Arts at the corner of Tremont and Bromfield Streets to offer a collection of curiosities to the public at a small admission charge. In combination with the museum was a "concert saloon," which in 1843 was transformed into a regular theatre with a stock company. In 1844, after the phenomenal success of *The Drunkard,* which played 100 performances, it provided a steady diet of moral plays, earning it the name of "deacon's theatre." In 1846 the entire enterprise was moved into its new building, and under a succession of astute managers, particularly R. M. Field, it housed the finest dramatic corps in America during the 1860s and '70s. Its most distinguished member, **William Warren the younger,** spent almost his entire career (1847–82) with it. The company was disbanded in 1894, and the theatre fell into the Theatrical **Syndicate**'s hands until it was razed in 1903. MCH

Boston Theatre, shown advertising the 1911 appearance of Sarah Bernhardt. Courtesy: Michael Gnat.

See: C. McGlinchee, *The First Decade of the Boston Museum,* Boston, 1940; E. Mammen, *The Old Stock Company School of Acting,* Boston, 1945.

Boston Theatre Designed by architect H. Noury and erected on Washington St. in 1854 through public subscription in response to the closing of the **Federal St.** and **Tremont** theatres; **Dion Boucicault** called it "the finest theatre in the world." A technical showplace, its seating capacity of 3,140 made it the largest theatre in the country. **Edwin Booth** made his first starring appearance there (1857), and **Joseph Jefferson III** first played **Rip Van Winkle** there (1869). By 1885 the theatre's well-regarded stock company operated independently and spent most of its time touring New England; it dissolved sometime in the late 1890s. **B. F. Keith** turned the theatre into a vaudeville and motion picture house after 1909. Sixteen years later it was torn down to make way for the Keith Memorial Theatre. TC

Both Your Houses A political farce by **Maxwell Anderson,** produced by the **Theatre Guild** on 6 March 1933 and directed by Worthington Miner. The production closed after 72 performances, but reopened on 12 June for 48 performances after its Pulitzer Prize was announced. The action hinges on the passage of an outlandish appropriations bill through Congress that pitted Sheppard Strudwick's idealistic freshman Congressman against the corrupted old guard, an ensemble distinguished by Walter C. Kelly's aging politico. The scenario was a plausible representation of contemporary Congressional politics. The dramaturgical machinery is apparent, but the dialogue is sharp and inspiring.   MR

Boucicault, Dion[ysius] (Lardner) (1820–90) Playwright, actor, and manager. Born in Ireland, Boucicault had a substantial reputation in English theatres before coming to America in 1853 as manager of the popular actress **Agnes Robertson** (1833–1916), his second wife (although he disclaimed the legitimacy of this marriage when he married Louise Thorndyke in 1885). Of the Boucicault children, **Darby George** (1859–1929) acted in American, Australian, and English theatres, and **Aubrey** (1869–1919) had a minor reputation on the English stage.

A month after landing in New York, this author of at least 22 plays, including *London Assurance* (1841), revealed his great energy by starring Miss Robertson in *The Young Actress,* his version of Edward Lancaster's *The Manager's Daughter.* During that fall season of 1853 New Yorkers saw seven plays by Boucicault. Before returning to England in 1860, Boucicault wrote 30 plays, seven of which were published. He lectured, although without great success, toured his theatre company frequently, and managed theatres in New Orleans (1855), Washington (1858), and New York (1859). He also expedited the enactment of a U.S. copyright law that gave playwrights "along with the right to present and publish the said composition, the sole right to act, perform or represent the same" (18 April 1856). His major contribution to American drama during these years is shown in two distinctive efforts: *The Poor of New York* (1857) and *The Octoroon* (1859).

During 1860–72 Boucicault lived in England and wrote at least 22 plays, the most important one for Americans being a rewrite of *Rip Van Winkle* (1865) for **Joseph Jefferson III.** His return to America in 1872 marked the beginning of a period during which he crossed the Atlantic a number of times. From 1877 to 1889 he published 13 essays in the *North American Review;* these explain his dramaturgy and are a major contribution to **dramatic theory** in America. A master of visual, aural, and theatrical effects, Boucicault pandered to popular tastes for his triumphant success in both England and America during 1855–75. Changes of taste left him confused, and his popularity declined during the last years of his life.   WJM

See: R. Hogan, *Dion Boucicault,* New York, 1969; F. Fawkes, *Dion Boucicault,* New York, 1979.

Bovasso, Julie (Julia Anne) (1930–91) Actor, playwright, director, producer. After acting at major regional theatres and in New York, she founded Tempo Playhouse (1953), producing, directing, and performing in American premieres of work by Genêt, Ionesco, Cocteau, and de Ghelderode. In 1956, she received Obies for Best Experimental Theatre and her performance in *The Maids.* She wrote several loosely structured satires that combine vaudeville, **circus,** and music in flamboyantly theatrical collages. At **La MaMa,** she premiered her *Moondreamers* (1968), *Gloria and Esperanza* (1969, Obies for script, direction, and performance), *Schubert's Last Serenade* (1971), and *Monday on the Way to Mercury Island* (1971). Her *Down by the River Where Waterlilies are Disfigured Everyday* premiered at *Trinity Repertory Company* (1971). Volatile and temperamental, she canceled her own shows and was dismissed from others. She was the first woman to direct at **Lincoln Center** and founded the Women's Theatre Council (later New York Theatre Strategy).   TH-S

Bowery Theatre 46–48 The Bowery, NYC [Architect: Ithiel Town; John Trimble]. When a sprinkling of wealthy and fashionable New York families began to settle near the Bowery, the link to the Boston Post Road, they decided to erect a playhouse more conveniently located for them than the **Park Theatre.** Pledging money and buying land on which Henry Astor's tavern had stood, they erected what came to be known as the Bowery Theatre, although it passed through a succession of names. Superior to the Park in appearance, both inside and out, it presented several seasons of drama, opera, and ballet before its audience left it to return to the older house. In 1830, **Thomas S. Hamblin** secured its lease and, for the next 20 years, dominated its policies. Hamblin's tenure included the highwater years for the playhouse, during which the greatest names of the American theatre (**J. B. Booth, Edwin Forrest,** the **Wallack**s, **Louisa Lane Drew, Frank Chanfrau**) appeared on its stage. Hamblin eventually bought the theatre, but bad times forced him to lose it. A succession of managers followed, who presented spectacle and melodrama to please the neighborhood.

The district surrounding the theatre became the haven for the newly arriving immigrant groups who poured into New York at midcentury, and the theatre began increasingly to reflect the new populations of the area, becoming the temple of entertainment for New York's Lower East Side. Until 1879 the dramatic fare was in English; thereafter it passed to German acting troupes, who renamed it the **Thalia;** then to Yiddish performers in 1891; next to Italian vaudevillians; and finally to

The Bowery Theatre as drawn in 1831. Courtesy: Mary C. Henderson.

Chinese vaudeville, which was playing at the time of its fiery demise (1929). It had burned and been rebuilt five times previously (1828, 1830, 1836, 1838, 1845; see **fires**), and each reconstruction had carried it further away from its original neoclassical facade into a strange mixture of architectural styles.   MCH

Boys from Syracuse, The Two-act musical comedy, music by **Richard Rodgers,** lyrics by **Lorenz Hart,** book by **George Abbott;** opened 23 November 1938 at the **Alvin Theatre,** New York, running 235 performances. A musical version of *The Comedy of Errors,* this fast-paced, bawdy romp was the first musical-comedy adaptation of **Shakespeare.** Chosen largely to trade on a striking resemblance between Hart's brother, Teddy, and comedian Jimmy Savo (they played the twin Dromios), Shakespeare's plot is closely followed, though laced with anachronism, contemporary slang, and such Rodgers and Hart classics as "This Can't Be Love" and "Falling in Love with Love." A 1963 Off-Broadway revival ran for 502 performances, proving the durability of the piece.   JD

Boys in the Band, The, by Mart Crowley was one of the first frank treatments of homosexuality in mainstream theatre. Combining sharp humor with emotional revelation, this portrait of a birthday party turned vicious opened **Off-Broadway** 14 April 1968 at Theatre Four, after having been produced by the Playwrights Unit, Vandam Theatre, in January 1968. It ran for 1,000 performances, traveled to London, and subsequently received numerous productions throughout the U.S. and Europe. A film version was released in 1970.   KF

Brackenridge, Hugh H[enry] (1748–1815) Author and playwright. Writing for his students at Maryland Academy, he did not consider his plays – *The Battle of Bunker's-Hill* and *The Death of General Montgomery in Storming the City of Quebec* (1777) – finished dramas. Both plays, composed in blank verse, emphasize patriotic virtue and stress the strong emotional qualities that characterized much of Brackenridge's writing. As teacher, judge, legislator, and chaplain in Washington's army, Brackenridge exhibited a belief in persuasive oratory in writing and a sense of mission.   WJM

See: C. Newlin, *The Life and Writings of Hugh Henry Brackenridge,* Princeton, NJ, 1932.

Brady, Alice (1892–1939) Stage and film actress and singer. Making her New York debut as a chorus girl in *The Mikado* at 18, she appeared in major **Gilbert and Sullivan** roles for the next two years, then as Meg in *Little Women* (1912). In 1914 she entered silent pictures for Famous Players Company. By 1923 she had made 32 films, but continued working in the theatre. In 1928 she joined the **Theatre Guild;** her most memorable stage role was as Lavinia in **O'Neill**'s *Mourning Becomes Electra.* She returned to films as a singer-actress in 1933.   SMA

Brady, William A[loysius] (1863–1950) Manager and producer. Born in San Francisco, Brady

made his first stage appearance in 1882, and his debut as a producer in 1888. He purchased the rights to *After Dark* from **Dion Boucicault** in 1899 and presented it at the **Bowery Theatre. Augustin Daly** sued him for plagiarizing the locomotive scene from *Under the Gaslight;* Brady eventually lost, but attained publicity by hiring prizefighter James J. Corbett to appear in the cast and later featuring him in several vehicles. In 1896 he leased the Manhattan Theatre, where he enjoyed several successes, including *Way Down East* in 1898. A year later he married actress **Grace George** and promoted her career. She opened his Playhouse in 1911 with *Sauce for the Goose,* and later appeared in *The School for Scandal* and **Shaw**'s *Major Barbara.* Brady managed the careers of numerous players including his wife's and his daughter, **Alice**'s. His more than 260 productions included *Street Scene* (1929), which ran for 600 performances and won a Pulitzer. Also a sports promoter and film pioneer, Brady was recognized as a "born gambler" with an "uncanny instinct for drama." Brady's memoir, *Showman,* was published in 1937.   TLM

Bragdon, Claude (1866–1946) A self-trained architect, Bragdon did not enter the theatre until 1919 as a designer for **Walter Hampden**'s productions. Though he worked for no one else, Bragdon's simplified settings and experiments with light were a major influence on the development of the New Stagecraft. Even before entering the theatre Bragdon worked on the development of what he called "color music" – an art form consisting primarily of light and sound. He produced several "Song and Light" shows in the mid-1910s, including one in New York's Central Park that attracted 150,000 spectators over five nights.   AA

Branch, William (1927–) African-American writer of protest plays beginning in the early 1950s. In *A Medal for Willie* (1951), a southern black woman rejects the medal posthumously awarded to her soldier son. In *In Splendid Error* (1954) abolitionist Frederick Douglass questions his reluctance to support the rebellion when he learns of John Brown's heroic sacrifice at Harper's Ferry. Branch has written other dramas about black leaders for the stage, television, and screen.   EGH

Brando, Marlon (1924–) Actor. Although his major reputation comes from his work as a film actor (*A Streetcar Named Desire, On the Waterfront, The Godfather*), it was as Stanley Kowalski in **Elia Kazan**'s stage production of **Tennessee Williams**'s *A Streetcar Named Desire* (1947), his final theatre role, that Brando first made his mark as an actor of moody intensity. Among his other limited stage appearances were *I Remember Mama* (1944), *Truckline* (1946), and *Candida* (1947). His style is often seen as the most famous product of the **Actors Studio** (see also **Lee Strasberg**). Brando is currently completing his autobiography.   MB

See: R. Schickel, *Brando: A Life in Our Times,* New York, 1991.

Bread and Puppet Theatre Founded in New York in 1961 by Peter Schumann, who had previ-

Bread and Puppet Theatre in *Uprising of the Beast,* Milan, Italy (1990). Photo: Tony D'Urson. Courtesy: Bread and Puppet Theatre.

ously organized the New Dance Group in Germany, Bread and Puppet has never been an orthodox group in manning, finance, or artistic policy. Not an ensemble but a loose association of performers under Schumann's firm direction, and supplemented as needed by amateurs, the company has so mistrusted the idea of purchasing entertainment that, whenever possible, it offers its services free. This principle is based on its founder's maxim, "theatre is like bread, more like a necessity" – an axiom enacted literally in the course of each performance by the giving of bread to the audience. Deeply involved in the contemporary reaction against what is perceived as the overintellectualization of Western culture, as epitomized in its powerful tradition of literary theatre, Schumann and his associates work with larger-than-life puppets to create a nonnarrative theatre that addresses contemporary issues – such as the Vietnam War – through disturbing visual images rather than words. In performances such as "The Cry of the People for Meat," and "The Domestic Resurrection Circus" (the latter presented each summer since 1974), religious iconography and political message are combined in an attempt to offer a critique of contemporary society in terms of its own values. After a four-year residence at Goddard College, in 1974 Schumann moved to a farm near Glover, VT, and the company nominally disbanded. In practice it has continued to regroup for summer festivals at Glover, and for specific commissions such as the 1975 "Anti-Bicentennial" at the University of California – an angry and moving elegy to the last Indian survivor of white genocide in the state.

More recently Schumann and his associates scripted plays such as Büchner's *Woyzeck* (New York, 1981) and toured Europe and Russia in 1990 with *Uprising of the Beast.*   AEG   DBW

> *See:* S. Brecht, *The Bread and Puppet Theatre,* New York, 1988.

Brecht in the American theatre Bertolt Brecht was a preeminent German dramatist, director, and poet whose plays, performance style, and theory of epic theatre have influenced Western theatre, primarily since WW II. In the early 1920s he developed the anti-illusionistic staging techniques evident in his highly successful *Die Dreigroschenoper* (1928, music by **Kurt Weill;** trans. as *The Threepenny Opera*) in Berlin. Influenced by the work of **Erwin Piscator,** Brecht's *Verfremdungseffekt* or "alienation effect" in acting and his theory of "non-Aristotelian" drama continue to stimulate intellectual debate.

The 1933 New York premiere of *The Threepenny Opera* at the **Empire Theatre** was unsuccessful. Brecht first visited the U.S. during October–December 1935 when his play *Mother* was produced by the New York **Theatre Union** at the **Civic Repertory Theatre.** Fleeing Nazi Germany in 1933, Brecht lived in Denmark, Sweden, Finland, and finally the U.S. Many of his major works were written in exile, including *Mother Courage and Her Children* (1938–9), *The Good Woman of Setzuan* (1938–40), and *The Caucasian Chalk Circle* (1944–5). He arrived in California in July of 1941 and settled in Santa Monica, where he worked on at least 50 film projects, mostly with other German refugees (Fritz Lang, Lion Feuchtwanger, Peter Lorre, Ferdinand Reyher), but received little recognition from Hollywood. *Hangmen Also Die* (1942), written for director Fritz Lang, was his only success. Intended for Broadway, Brecht's *The Caucasian Chalk Circle* remained unproduced during his American years. Unwilling to compromise in his writing to the tastes of Broadway, he was unsuccessful in collaborative efforts in New York, even with Erwin Piscator, who on several occasions expressed interest in producing his works. In 1945 Berthold Viertel directed *The Private Life of the Master Race* in Brecht's first New York production at City College's Pauline Edwards Theatre. The production, panned by reviewers, was apparently doomed by barely intelligible German accents, and rehearsals consumed by Brecht elaborating on his acting theories with cast and director. *Galileo* opened in Hollywood in July 1947 with **Charles Laughton** and moved to New York in December. Brecht appeared before the House Un-American Activities Committee one day before leaving the U.S. for Zurich on 31 October 1947. After his return to East Berlin in 1949 and the founding of the Berliner Ensemble at the Theater am Schiffbauerdamm with Helene Weigel, Brecht's "model" productions acquired an international reputation and were produced throughout the world. In 1954 **Marc Blitzstein**'s New York production of *The Threepenny Opera* with **Lotte Lenya** popularized Brecht's name in America, but it was primarily through the translation of his major plays and theory by **Eric Bentley** that Brecht became well known and frequently produced in university and regional theatres in the U.S., especially during the 1960s and '70s. RE

See: B. Brecht, *Arbeitsjournal 1938–1955*, Frankfurt/Main, 1973; J. K. Lyon, *Bertolt Brecht in America*, Princeton, NJ, 1980; K. Völker, *Brecht: A Biography*, New York, 1978.

Breuer, Lee (1937–) Actor, playwright, director, and founding member of the avant-garde theatre company **Mabou Mines.** Breuer, who calls himself a "reluctant radical," began his career in the early 1960s with the **San Francisco** Actors' Workshop, moving to Europe in 1965 to study with the Berliner Ensemble and the Polish Theatre Lab. For Mabou Mines he served as director, author, adapter, producer, and performer. His staging and adaptation of Beckett's work has earned him three Obie Awards. His trilogy *Animations* (*The **Red Horse*** [1970], *The B. Beaver* [1974], and *The Shaggy Dog* [1978]) was published in 1979, and *Sister Suzie Cinema* (Public Theater, 1980) in 1986. In 1988 he wrote and directed a gender-reversed adaptation of *King Lear* with **Ruth Maleczech** as Lear. Outside Mabou Mines his most notable effort has been *The Gospel at Colonus* (1983), which he conceived, adapted, and directed for the **Brooklyn Academy of Music**'s "Next Wave Festival" (performed later at Broadway's **Lunt–Fontanne**, Washington's **Arena Stage,** and in San Francisco), as was *The Warrior Ant* (1988), heard first in concert at **Lincoln Center** in 1986. In the 1980s, while serving as director of the directing program at the Yale School of Drama, his focus was on creating a new theatre that merges Asian and African arts with American performance techniques. DBW

Brice, Fanny (Fannie) (née Frances Borach) (1891–1951) Comedienne and singer whose gawky walk, repertoire of comic faces, and ability to sing both satiric and serious songs with equal success made her a star of **revue**s for over a quarter of a century. After serving an apprenticeship in amateur shows and burlesque, Brice appeared in **Ziegfeld**'s *Follies of 1910*. She remained with the *Follies* for six more editions through 1923, then switched to **Irving Berlin**'s *Music Box Revue* (1924). An attempt to star in a book musical, *Fioretta* (1929), was a failure. Brice appeared in four more revues: *Sweet and Low* (1930), *Billy Rose's Crazy Quilt* (1931), and two editions of *The Ziegfeld Follies* (1934, 1936) produced by the **Shubert**s after Ziegfeld's death. In most of her songs and sketches Brice affected a Yiddish accent that heightened her satirical treatment of such subjects as the ballet and silent film "vamps." The musical *Funny Girl* is loosely based on portions of Brice's career. MK

See: B. Grossman, *Funny Woman: The Life and Times of Fanny Brice*, Bloomington, IN, 1991.

Brig, The, by Kenneth H. Brown. This **Living Theatre** production, directed by Judith Malina and designed by Julian Beck, opened 15 May 1963 for 239 performances. The nonplay, with nondialogue and noncharacters, set in a Marine prison in 1957, details the brutal routine of one day. Critics loathed its impersonal violence, based on Brown's own experience, but the play toured Europe, was made into a film, and aired on U.S. and Canadian television. REK

Brigadoon Two-act musical with book and lyrics by **Alan Jay Lerner** and music by **Frederick Loewe;** opened at Broadway's **Ziegfeld Theatre** (13 March 1947) and ran for 581 performances, winning the Drama Critics' Award for Best Musical. It was revived six times at the New York City Center, and once at the **Majestic Theatre**, a 133-performance run beginning 16 October 1980. Originally staged by **Robert Lewis** and choreographed by **Agnes de Mille,** this romantic, escapist fantasy is set in the 18th-century Scottish village of Brigadoon, which magically remains untouched since it appears only once a century. With its well-integrated lyrical dialogue, songs, instrumentation, and dance, *Brigadoon* charmed postwar audiences and critics. Its songs include "Heather on the Hill" and "Almost Like Being In Love." EK

Brighton Beach Memoirs by **Neil Simon** opened on 27 March 1983 at the **Alvin Theatre** for 1,530 performances. Simon's return to semiautobiography, this first episode in the "Brighton Beach Trilogy" relates the early adolescence of Eugene Morris Jerome (Simon) as Depression-era stress shifts to that of pre–WW II. The play balances employment ordeals of the father, Jack, and elder brother, Stanley, and Eugene's adolescent anxieties against the repressed rivalry of the mother, Kate, and her boarding sister Blanche. Continuing Simon's theme of moderation, the play suggests the nurturing aspect of a family can stifle if carried to excess. RW

Brisson, Frederick (1913–84) Producer. Danish-born and English-educated, Brisson worked in Europe before emigrating to the U.S. in the late 1930s. After WW II, he began producing musicals and light comedy on Broadway, either independently or with various partners; these included *The Pajama Game* (1954), *Damn Yankees* (1955), *New Girl in Town* (1957), *The Pleasure of His Company* (1958), *Under the Yum Yum Tree* (1960), *Generation* (1965), *Coco* (1969), and *Twigs* (1971). However, Brisson also challenged Broadway audiences with Peter Shaffer's *Five Finger Exercise* (1959), Harold Pinter's *The Caretaker* (1962), and Tom Stoppard's *Jumpers* (1974). TLM

Broadhurst, George H[owells] (1866–1952) Playwright and theatre manager. Born in London, Broadhurst emigrated to America in 1886 and managed several regional theatres before gaining some success in New York with farce-comedies – *What Happened to Jones* (1897) and *Why Smith Left Home* (1899). Primarily concerned with commercial theatre, Broadhurst made his best contribution to American drama with *The Man of the Hour* (1906), a melodrama about a young mayor who successfully resists organized political corruption, and *Bought and Paid For* (1911), which exploits the problems of a wealthy, self-made man who counts his wife among his possessions. One of the better

writers of social melodrama before WW I, Broadhurst produced a number of successful plays and
eventually became known for his light musical
comedies. In 1918 a new Broadway venue was
named the **Broadhurst Theatre** in his honor.
WJM

Broadhurst Theatre 235 West 44th St., NYC
[Architect: Herbert J. Krapp]. Continuing their
custom to name playhouses after prominent theatrical personages, the **Shubert**s opened another of
their 1917-built theatres in honor of **George
Broadhurst**, an English-born playwright, who
enjoyed fleeting fame as the author of a string of
successful modern melodramas. Broadhurst also
often produced his own plays and managed the
house in tandem with the Shuberts. Seating about
1,200, its policy has alternated between musicals
and dramas. Among its more successful tenants
have been *Beggar on Horseback* (1924), *The Green
Hat* (with the young **Katharine Cornell**) (1925),
Broadway (1926), *Men in White* (1933), *The Petrified Forest* (1935), *Victoria Regina* (with **Helen
Hayes**) (1936), and the musicals *Fiorello!* (1959)
and *Cabaret* (1967). It remains a Shubert theatre.
MCH

Broadway by Philip Dunning and **George Abbott**, a wise-cracking, fast-paced melodrama of
nightclub life that opened 9 September 1926 and
ran for 601 performances, grossing more than $2
million for its youthful producer, **Jed Harris.** The
play's volatile combination of both deadly and
clownish gangsters, hard-boiled chorus girls, sly
cops, contemporary street slang, onstage violence,
and the triumph of true love proved a lasting
contribution to American popular culture, setting a
pattern repeated by Harris with *The Front Page*
(1928) and by Abbott in *Three Men on a Horse*
(1935). Film versions of *Broadway* were produced
in 1929 and 1942.   MF

Broadway, Off- and Off-Off see **Off
Broadway** and **Off-Off Broadway**

Broadway Alliance, The An experiment begun in 1990 as a result of agreements made by the
League of American Theaters and Producers, the
three major New York theatre organizations/own-
ers, and all the unions and guilds active on Broadway. As a result, the production of serious drama
is encouraged by the reduction of at least 25%
(salary, royalty, or personnel) and, initially, by a
top ticket price of $24 (though this was revised in
late 1991). The first production under the scheme
was **Steve Tesich**'s *The Speed of Darkness,* followed by Timberlake Wertenbaker's *Our Country's
Good* (both 1991).   DBW

Broadway Bound The conclusion of **Neil Simon**'s "Brighton Beach Trilogy"; opened at the
Broadhurst Theatre on 4 December 1986, running for 756 performances. The semiautobiographical play returns young Eugene Morris Jerome
(Simon) to Brighton Beach after WW II. The rising
radio-comedy-writing careers of Eugene and his
brother, Stanley – a close parallel to Simon's – is

balanced against the disintegration of their parents'
and grandparents' marriages. The brothers' success
lies in the way their strengths complement the
other's weaknesses. Each of the marital failures
illustrates Simon's thematic involvement with the
results of extreme behavior and unwillingness to
compromise. A TV version (no other Simon play
has received such a treatment), broadcast in March
1992, included **Anne Bancroft** and **Jerry Orbach.**
RW

Broadway Theatre Name borne by a succession of New York playhouses.
1. 356–8 Broadway, NYC [Architect: John M.
Trimble]. The first important New York theatre
to bear the name, this Broadway Theatre was
modeled on London's Haymarket, and with 4,500
seats was the largest theatre built before 1847, when
it opened its doors. Intended to replace the **Park
Theatre** in public favor, it never achieved the
prominence of the earlier theatre, although many
stars appeared on its stage. It was torn down in
1859.
2. Broadway and 41st St., NYC [Architect: J. B.
McElfatrick and Co.]. Built in 1888 when 41st
Street was still "uptown" for the rest of the city, it
was dedicated to musical comedy, operetta, and
spectacle. Later, when the new theatre district began to coalesce around 42nd Street, the theatre was
assimilated within its borders. Both **Edwin Booth**
and Sir Henry Irving made final appearances in
New York at the Broadway. Too large for the later
dramatic and musical fare, it was used for motion
pictures and vaudeville before being torn down in
1929.
3. 1681 Broadway, NYC [Architect: Eugene De
Rosa]. Opened as B. S. Moss's Colony Theatre in
1924, the playhouse seesawed between plays and
movies for more than 25 years. Renamed the
Broadway in 1930, it is a large 1,800-seat house,
well suited for musicals. Among its outstanding
tenants have been *This Is the Army* (1942), *Lady in
the Dark* (1943), *Gypsy* (1959), *Evita* (1979), and
Miss Saigon (1991). Since 1943, it has been a **Shubert** theatre.   MCH

Brooklyn Academy of Music (BAM) Incorporated in 1859, the original 1861 theatre on
Montague Street burned down in 1903. Herts and
Tallant's 1908 replacement, a neo-Renaissance
building with four auditoriums at 30 Lafayette
Street, was the first multiple-theatre facility in the
U.S. Then as now BAM was a center for all the
performing arts. In its heyday, opera singers Nellie
Melba and Marian Anderson played there, as did
conductor Arturo Toscanini, violinist Jascha Hei-
fetz, dancers Ruth St. Denis and Ted Shawn, and
many others.
   Under the direction of Harvey Lichtenstein, BAM
is now an energetic and resourceful not-for-profit
presenting organization and an anchor of urban
renewal in downtown Brooklyn. In addition to
traditional arts groups such as the Brooklyn Philharmonic and visiting theatre, opera, and dance
troupes, Lichtenstein has housed three legitimate
theatre companies: the Chelsea Theatre (1968–78),
the BAM Theatre Company (1977–9 under Frank

Dunlop; 1979–81 under David Hugh Jones), and the Dodger Theatre (1978–80). A friend of experimental arts, during the 1970s Lichtenstein began to present **Robert Wilson,** the **Living Theatre,** and the **Bread and Puppet Theatre,** among other theatrical pioneers. Since 1983, BAM's premiere program has been its Next Wave Festival, a prestigious, vanguard arts showcase featuring an international roster of progressive dance, music, theatre, and performance artists.   CLJ

Brooks Atkinson Theatre 256 West 47th St., NYC [Architect: Herbert J. Krapp]. When it opened in 1926, the third of the Chanin-built theatres was named after **Richard Mansfield,** one of the outstanding actors of a previous generation. After the playhouse reverted to the mortgage company early in the Depression, it was leased to a succession of managements. In 1931, the **Group Theatre** launched its initial venture, *The House of Connelly,* from its stage. In 1944, the theatre was sold to Michael Myerberg, who subsequently leased it to CBS-TV during 1950–60. Thereafter, it was returned to legitimate use and renamed the **Brooks Atkinson** after the recently retired and revered *New York Times* drama critic. In 1964, **Tallulah Bankhead** made her final stage appearance, in *The Milk Train Doesn't Stop Here Anymore,* from its stage. Three years later, the theatre passed to the control of the **Nederlander** Organization. In 1975, the comedy *Same Time, Next Year* became its longest-running tenant (three years).   MCH

Brothers, The, by Kathleen Collins. Directed by Billie Allen, featuring Seret Scott, Josephine Premice, and Trazana Beverly, this play premiered 31 March 1982 as part of the **Women's Project** at the **American Place Theatre.** The play, an investigation of the lives of an upwardly mobile African-American family from 1948 to 1968, reflects, distorts, and views through the women around them the lives of the brothers (never seen onstage).   KME

Brougham, John (1810–80) Irish-American playwright and actor whose reputation rests principally on his outlandish Indian burlesques: *Po-ca-hon-tas; or, the Gentle Savage* (1855), "An Original Aboriginal Erratic Operatic Semi-Civilized and Demi-Savage Extravaganza," and *Metamora; or, the Last of the Pollywogs* (1857). He poked fun at the stage version of the "noble savage," particularly that of **Edwin Forrest** in *Metamora; or, The Last of the Wampanoags.* Brougham had a facile pen – too facile he once admitted. He wrote 126 wide-ranging pieces – adaptations (*Dombey and Son,* 1848), gothic melodrama (*The Gunmaker of Moscow,* 1857), tearful melodrama (*Night and Morning,* 1855), sensational melodrama (*The Lottery of Life,* 1868), and social satire (*The Game of Love,* 1856) – but never with any "gall in his ink," according to one critic. As principal actor in most of his pieces, he was praised for his joviality, versatility, topical interpolations, and impromptu "before-the-curtain" speeches.

Born in Dublin, Brougham performed in amateur theatricals at Trinity College, appeared at London's Olympic (1830, with Madame Vestris) and

at Covent Garden; leased the Lyceum (1840); came to America (1842), appearing at the **Park** and touring the country; became stage manager at **Burton's Chambers Street Theatre** (1848); had two flings at management (at Brougham's Broadway Lyceum [1850–2] and the old **Bowery** [1856–7]); and was employed as actor-playwright at **Wallack's** for seven seasons – "the brightest part of my artist's life," he reported. He spent the Civil War years in London, returning in 1865 to continue as actor-playwright at the **Winter Garden** and at **Daly**'s **Fifth Avenue Theatre.**   RM

See: W. Winter, ed., *Life, Stories, and Poems of John Brougham,* Boston, 1881.

Broun, Heywood (1888–1939) Drama critic and columnist. Born in Brooklyn, Broun attended Harvard before pursuing a career in journalism on the *Morning Telegraph* (1910–11) and the *New York Tribune* (1911–21), including a short stint as drama critic (1915–16). For the *Tribune* he was war correspondent (1917) and literary editor (1918–21) before joining the *New York World* (1921); there he wrote on all subjects, including the theatre, and established his reputation as an important liberal voice. His vigorous defense of Sacco and Vanzetti (1927) cost him his job. Syndicated by Scripps–Howard newspapers during 1928–39, Broun's column remained committed to concerns of the political left. He was fired in 1939 after successfully establishing the American Newspaper Guild. Broun was a member of the Algonquin Round Table, the author of 13 books, and the father of actor and author Heywood Hale Broun.   TLM

See: R. O'Conner, *Heywood Broun: A Biography,* New York, 1975.

Brown, Arvin (1940–) Artistic director of the **Long Wharf Theatre** since 1967. His first production there was *Long Day's Journey into Night* (1966). Among his many Long Wharf productions that have enjoyed transfers to Broadway, *The National Health* (by Peter Nichols, 1974), **American Buffalo** (1981), and *A View from the Bridge* (1983) all received nominations before *A Day in the Death of Joe Egg* (Nichols, 1984) and *All My Sons* (1987) earned their Tony Awards. He has directed and lectured around the U.S. and worldwide. A lengthy interview with Brown appears in *The Director's Voice* (**Theatre Communications Group,** 1988).   MR

Brown, John Mason (1900–69) Drama critic. Educated at Harvard University, Brown began his journalist career on the *Louisville Courier-Journal* in 1917. During 1923–4 he reported on the European theatre for Boston and Louisville newspapers before becoming associate editor and drama critic for *Theatre Arts Monthly* (1924–8). In 1929 Brown moved to the *New York Evening Post* and established his column "Two on the Aisle," which remained popular throughout the 1930s. In 1941 he accepted a similar position on the *New York World-Telegram,* but the outbreak of the war prompted him to join the Navy in 1942. Two years later he became associate editor and drama critic of *Saturday*

Review, where his column "Seeing Things" remained a standard for 10 years. Brown wrote in an easy informal style that **John Simon** characterized as "chatty urbanity." His many books include *The Modern Theatre in Revolt* (1929), *Two on the Aisle* (1938), *Seeing Things* (1946), *Dramatis Personae* (1963), and *The Worlds of Robert E. Sherwood* (1965).   TLM

Brown, Lew see **DeSylva, B. G. "Buddy"**

Brown, "Colonel" T[homas] Allston (1836–1918) Dramatic editor, historian, and theatrical **agent**. Brown published *History of the American Stage* (1870) and *A History of the New York Theatre* (3 vols., 1903), and served for seven years as dramatic editor of the *New York Clipper* (1863–70), establishing it as a leading theatrical trade paper with up-to-date information on minstrel shows, circuses, ballet dances, music halls, and burlesques. He also worked as an advance man, business manager, advertising agent, and press agent, parlaying his knowledge of the road into *The Showman's Guide* (1st ed., 1868), containing names of principal halls, lists of distances, best routes, rent per night, seating capacities, and names of bill posters, newspapers, and hotels. Brown established his own dramatic agency in 1870 and continued managing until his retirement in 1906. While a colorful theatrical personality, "Colonel" Brown was not a first-rate historian, and his books contain numerous errors.   TLM

Brown, Tony see **Margolis, Kari**

Brown, William Henry (fl. 1820s) African-American theatre manager and playwright. An ex-West Indian seaman, Brown became the father of African-American theatre when he established the **African Theatre** in New York in 1821 with a repertoire including condensed versions of plays such as *Richard III, Pizarro, Tom and Jerry,* and *Obi; or, Three-Fingered Jack,* as well as pantomimes. Brown also wrote and produced the first African-American play, *The Drama of King Shotaway* (1823), based on personal experience of the 1795 Black Caribs' insurrection on St. Vincent. From his African Theatre emerged **James Hewlett**, the first black Shakespearean actor, and **Ira Aldridge,** black actor renowned in England and Europe in the 19th century. Brown may also have founded a theatre in Albany, NY, in 1823.   EGH

Brown, William Wells (1819–84) An escaped slave, Brown joined the abolitionist movement from his Boston home and wrote two antislavery plays that he read from lecture platforms. The first, *Experience; or, How to Give a Northern Man a Backbone* (1856), satirizes a proslavery northern preacher who recants after being sold into slavery and later released; the second, *The Escape; or, A Leap for Freedom* (1858), describes domestic life on a southern plantation as slaves plot their escape.   EGH

See: W. E. Farrison, *William Wells Brown, Author and Reformer,* Chicago, 1969.

Browne, Roscoe Lee (1925–) African-American actor of stage, screen, and television.

Browne was a world-class track star and college instructor before embarking on a stage career. An actor of controlled power, he is as comfortable in Shakespeare (he played seven seasons with the **New York Shakespeare Festival**) as in O'Neill (**Desire Under the Elms,** 1974). His film credits include the title role in *The Liberation of L. B. Jones* (1970), and he has made numerous appearances on television.   EGH

Bruce, Lenny (né Alfred Schneider) (1926–66) Stand-up comic who became a martyr to his cult image. After serving in the Navy during WW II, he studied acting under the GI bill and began as a **nightclub** comedian. Working out of small clubs in Greenwich Village, he first gained notoriety for his liberal use of four-letter words; gradually, he became noted for his savage attacks on establishment hypocrisy. As his act developed into intimate, improvisational harangues of the audience, he shocked the conventional and rejoiced the "hip" with his freewheeling satire of narcotics legislation, organized religion, sexual taboos, and race relations. Frequently arrested for drug abuse and blasphemy (the Home Office refused to let him perform in England), he sank into paranoia and died of an overdose of narcotics. After his death, he became a totem – in **Kenneth Tynan**'s words, "the man who went down on America's conscience" – and a play, *Lenny,* was devoted to him.   LS

See: L. Bruce, *How to Talk Dirty and Influence People,* Chicago, 1965.

Brustein, Robert (1927–) American critic, actor, director, and founder of the **Yale Repertory** and **American Repertory** theatres. He has served on the faculties of several universities, and was the Dean of the Yale Drama School during 1965–79, years recalled in his book *Making Scenes.* The author of nine other important books on theatre and society (most notably *The Theatre of Revolt* [1964], *The Third Theatre* [1968], *Revolution as Theatre* [1970], *Who Needs Theatre* [1986], and *Reimagining American Theatre* [1991]), Brustein has been one of the most respected and controversial critics, primarily as drama critic for *The New Republic* since 1959 (on a regular basis until 1968; he was also sometime critic for the London Sunday *Observer*). He received the **George Jean Nathan** Award for Dramatic Criticism in 1962 and 1987. In 1979 Brustein was unexpectedly released as Dean at Yale and moved to Harvard, where ART was established. At Yale and Harvard, he has supervised over 170 professional productions.   DBW

Brutus; or, The Fall of Tarquin One of the most popular works by an American in the first half of the 19th century, though written and first performed (3 December 1818) in London, where playwright **John Howard Payne** had been working as an actor and writer. Conceived as a vehicle for Edmund Kean's fiery acting style, the play suited many American tragedians over the next 70 years, including **Edwin Forrest** and **Edwin Booth,** who saw the blank-verse tragedy as a great leading role and symbolic of American nationalism. Payne's admitted use of several popular sources to tell the story of Brutus's defeat of Saxton Tarquin caused some to question his originality and validity as a playwright. PAD

Bryant, Dan (né Daniel Webster O'Brien) (1833–75) Minstrel and manager. After his debut (as dancer) at New York's Vauxhall Garden in 1843, Bryant graduated to blackface minstrelsy (1849) with "Sable Harmonists," and in 1850 joined Charley White at the Bowery's Melodeon Minstrel Hall. In 1857 Dan and his brothers Jerry and Neil founded Bryant's Minstrels – Jerry and Dan the "end men" and Neil interlocutor. Bryant's became New York's premiere **minstrel show** company. "Dixie," written by troupe member **Dan Emmett**, was introduced by them (1859), though Bryant was best known for his "rude and untutored" black character dance, "Essence of Old Virginny." Bryant, also a good Irish-dialect actor, appeared in that guise first in *Handy Andy* (1863). His natural inclination toward blackface comedy brought him back to minstrelsy in 1868. DBW

Brynner, Yul (1920?–85) Actor and singer whose early life is mired in contradictory accounts. After playing small roles in two Broadway plays, he made his musical theatre debut in *Lute Song* (1946). In 1951 he appeared as the imperious yet likable king in *The King and I,* a role that would be identified with him for the rest of his life. He revived the role on Broadway in 1977 and toured with it for several seasons. His biography was written by his son Rock in 1989. MK

Buchanan, McKean (1823–72) Actor. A cotton broker who began playing leading roles with the amateur Histrionic Association (New Orleans, 1848), he appeared in Bristol, England, and New York City the following year. He set off as a traveling star, playing all across the American South and West, the English provinces, and Australia. After 1860 he appeared opposite his daughter, Virginia. A large man (6' 4'' tall) with a powerful voice, he was frequently compared to **Edwin Forrest** and **John McCullough** in style, and he specialized in Shylock, Macbeth, Othello, Richard III, Lear, Richelieu, and Sir Giles Overreach. Critics either praised him or damned him extravagantly, and he was as often noted for his eccentric personal behavior as for his acting. DMcD

> See: W. Leman, *Memories of an Old Actor,* San Francisco, 1886; reprinted New York, 1969.

Bullins, Ed (1935–) African-American playwright who began writing fiction but, seeing **Baraka**'s plays on stage, felt drama was more effective in reaching black audiences. Since 1965 Bullins has written several dozen plays and is produced internationally. In 1967 he joined the New **Lafayette Theatre** as resident playwright, became its associate director, and edited its periodical *Black Theatre.* Among his best known plays are *Goin' a Buffalo* (1966), *In the Wine Time* (1968), *The Duplex* (1970), *In New England Winter* (1971), *The Fabulous Miss Marie* (1971), and *The Taking of Miss Janie* (1975). Bullins's experiments in form combine rhythmic, racy dialogue, black ritual, and jazz and blues music as integral elements of his dramaturgy. His work has been recognized by an Obie and in 1975 the New York Drama Critics' Circle Award. In 1982 Bullins moved to San Francisco, where he has had several new plays produced. EGH

Buloff, Joseph (1899–1985) Gifted **Yiddish theatre** actor and director first with the Vilna Troupe, where he distinguished himself in the title role of Ossip Dimov's *Yoshke Musikant,* then in America where he acted with **Maurice Schwartz**'s **Yiddish Art Theatre** and directed for the **Folksbiene** and others, forming the New York Art Theatre in 1934–5. He eventually moved to English-speaking roles on Broadway and was active in Israel during the 1950s and '60s. A posthumous volume of memoirs appeared in 1991. AB

Bunker-Hill see **Burk, John Daly**

Burden, Chris (1946–) Boston-born conceptual and **performance art**ist who also works in sculpture, assemblage, installation, video, and language art. He lived briefly in China, but spent most of his childhood and adolescence in Europe, where his father worked as engineer for the Ford Foundation. He studied architecture and physics at Pomona College (BA, 1969) and sculpture at the University of California at Irvine (MFA, 1971). His early 1970s body art performances must be seen in the context of minimalism, conceptual art, and American domestic and foreign politics. Important performances were *Five Day Locker Piece* (1971), *Shoot* (1971), and *Trans-fixed* (1974). All of Burden's work, including such recent installations as *Samson* (1985) and *Exposing the Foundations of the Museum* (1987), explore the institutional fantasies of power and technology. AF

Burgess, Neil (1846–1910) Boston-born actor who made his debut with Spalding's Bell Ringers in 1865. He gained attention in a dame role, Mrs. Benjamin Bibbs in *The Quiet Family,* and won stardom in 1879, touring extensively in a dramatization of Alice B. Neal's 1858 novel *The Widow Bedott Papers,* in which he played the garrulous, malapropistic "widdy-woman" wooed by seedy Deacon Sniffles. He equaled but did not surpass this success as Betsy Puffy in *Vim* (1882) and Aunt Abigail Prue in his own production of Charles Bernard's *The County Fair* (1888). Burgess's comic cross-dressing (see **female/male impersonation**) made him one of the richest actors in America, but his fortune evaporated in ill-advised speculations, and, as the **stock** system declined, he was reduced as of 1899 to playing tabloid versions of his best parts in vaudeville. LS

Buried Child Three-act drama by **Sam Shepard,** first performed on 27 June 1978 by San Francisco's **Magic Theatre** and produced at New York's **Theater for the New City** on 19 October 1978, later transferring to the Theatre de Lys. Important revivals include those in 1979 at **Yale Repertory**

Theatre and **Circle Repertory Theatre.** A London production opened at the Hampstead Theatre Club 19 June 1980. Shepard described his Pulitzer Prize–winning play as "a kind of test. I wanted to write a play about a family." **Mel Gussow**'s review of the two 1979 productions called it "a dirge for the decline of traditional values, a wake for the American dream, . . . a penetrating excavation into the essence of blood ties." Using powerful images within a tenuous narrative, the play – set in a shabby midwestern farmhouse – focuses on a young man's attempt to rediscover his heritage and his identity within a family in the grip of sordid secrets.   FHL

Burk, John Daly (c. 1776–1808) Playwright known for his patriotic spectacle, *Bunker-Hill; or, The Death of General Warren* (Boston, February 1797; New York, September 1797) and for his detailed account of the primitive staging: "Our twelve-minute battle . . . Charlestown on fire and Warren animating the Americans amidst the smoak [*sic*] and confusion produce an effect scarce credible." For 20 years *Bunker-Hill* became the American theatre's standard offering for the Fourth of July and for Evacuation Day (25 November).

Expelled from Dublin's Trinity College, Burk came to Boston in 1796, and in 1808 was killed in a duel. He edited two newspapers, practiced law, and wrote six other plays – *Female Patriotism; or, The Death of Joan of Arc* (1798) the best known – as well as a *History of Virginia* and *History of the Late-War in Ireland* (1799).   RM

See: C. Campbell (ed.), *Some Materials to Serve for a Brief Memoir of John Daly Burk,* Albany, 1868.

Burke, Billie (Mary William Ethelbert Appleton Burke) (1886–1970) Actress; quintessential flibbertigibbet on stage and screen. With a cameolike delicacy of feature and little-bird voice, Billie Burke will always be remembered as Glinda, the Good Witch, in the film *The Wizard of Oz* (1939). Daughter of a singing circus clown, Billie spent 1903–7 as a singer in England, returning to New York to star opposite John **Drew** in *My Wife.* Under **Charles Frohman**'s management, she became the toast of Broadway, pursued by such celebrities as Mark Twain, Enrico Caruso, and W. Somerset Maugham. In 1914 she married the showman **Florenz Ziegfeld.** After his death in 1932, burdened with his debt-ridden estate, she turned to films as a way to settle her husband's obligations.

Between 1917 and 1944 Burke starred in 12 plays on Broadway. Later she noted that she excelled only in light, gay things. "I often had cute plays but never a fine one." A lover of animals, she once had a menagerie comparable to a fair-sized zoo on her 22-acre New York estate. She wrote (with Cameron Shipp) two autobiographies: *With a Feather on My Nose* (1949) and *With Powder on My Nose* (1959).   DBW

Burlesque show A raucous and bawdy style of variety performance, partly inspired by **Lydia Thompson** and her British blondes, partly by

May Howard (Havill), Canadian-born burlesque performer who became star of her own company and by 1897 was the first "burlesque queen." This portrait first appeared in the New York *Police Gazette.* Courtesy: Laurence Senelick.

blackface **minstrel shows** and "leg shows" like *The Black Crook.* The manager **Michael B. Leavitt** is credited with its invention by creating Mme Rentz's Female Minstrels (Rentz from a popular circus), later the **Rentz–Santley** troupe (after Mabel Santley, its star). One of its earliest personalities was May Howard, who ran her own company in the 1880s.

Burlesque rapidly developed a tripartite structure: In Part One, dance and song rendered by a female company was intermingled with low comedy from male comedians; Part Two was an olio of specialities in which the women did not appear; and Part Three comprised a grand finale. "Clean" versions of these preponderantly female productions were widely sponsored by the Miner family. Sam T. Jack, who opened the first exclusively burlesque theatre in Chicago, pioneered "dirty" burlesque or "turkey show," which was especially popular in the Western honky-tonks. The Empire and Mutual Circuits or Wheels reveled in such maculose entertainment, while the Columbia Circuit booked only clean shows until 1925, when it too was forced by dwindling receipts to go dirty.

Leading entrepreneurs were the **Minsky** brothers: Abe, who brought belly dancers (known as "cootchers") and the illuminated runway from Paris; publicists Billy and Morton; and Herbert, who introduced opera. From the early 1900s to 1935, they molded the image of American burlesque at the Republic Theatre and the National Winter Garden, New York. By present-day standards, the offerings were tame, for the girls never disrobed completely; but the blatant double entendre in the dialogue between straight man and "talking woman," as well as runway interplay between strippers and audience, enraged moralists. The striptease (see also **nudity**), which achieved extraordinary invention and daring, entered burlesque in 1921 with "Curls" Mason, and Carrie Finnell performed the first tassel dance, twirling the fringe from her nipples. The most memorable personalities among the strippers were Millie De Leon, the urbane **Gypsy Rose Lee** (a protégée of gangster Waxy Gordon), and the indestructible **Anne Corio.** Among the comedians nurtured by the form were Sliding Billy Watson, **Billy "Beef Trust" Watson,** Al Shean [of **Gallagher and Shean**], **Willie Howard, Phil Silvers,** Abbott and Costello, and Jackie Gleason, while routines like "Floogle Street" became classics.

Changing times brought about an end to classic burlesque. New York courts banned the runway in 1934 and all burlesque in 1942, and the Burlesque Artists Association had its charter revoked in 1957. Go-go dancing, the Las Vegas–style revue, and television siphoned off the remaining talents, and revivals, like Corio's widely toured *This Was Burlesque,* tend to be steeped in nostalgia. The form has inspired **Arthur Hopkins**'s play *Burlesque* (1927), Ralph Allen's musical *Sugar Babies* (1979), and feminist dramas that stress the exploitation of the stripper as commodity. LS

See: R. C. Allen, *Horrible Prettiness: Burlesque and American Culture,* Chapel Hill, NC, 1991; S. Conner, *Steve Mills and the Twentieth Century American Burlesque Show,* New York, 1979; A. Corio, *This Was Burlesque,* New York, 1968; M. Minsky, *Minsky's Burlesque,* New York, 1986; B. Sobel, *Burleycue,* New York, 1931; I. Zeidman, *The American Burlesque Show,* New York, 1967.

Burn This by **Lanford Wilson** opened at the **Plymouth Theatre** on 14 October 1987 after performances at the **Mark Taper Forum,** the **Steppenwolf Theatre,** and the **Circle Repertory Company;** it closed after 437 performances. Structured as a contemporary, conventional romantic comedy, *Burn This* nevertheless is a serious exploration of passionate love and its relationship to death, creativity, and the decline of Western civilization. Directed by **Marshall W. Mason** and featuring **John Malkovich** and Joan Allen as the starcrossed lovers, *Burn This* provoked controversy for its excessive use of profanity, but was widely regarded as Wilson's most forceful play to date. DJW

Burnett, Frances Hodgson (1849–1924) Prolific English-born writer who dramatized and produced 13 of her novels, beginning with *Esmeralda* (1881). *The Real Little Lord Fauntleroy* (1888) was her greatest popular and financial success, both in London and New York. The unauthorized dramatization of this novel caused Burnett to promote the legal right of an author to control such dramatizations and resulted in the 1911 Copyright Act in England. Sentimental and upbeat, many of her books, such as *Fauntleroy, Esmeralda, A Lady of Quality, A Little Princess,* and *The Dawn of Tomorrow* made a successful transition from print to stage to film. Her autobiography, *The One I Knew the Best of All,* appeared in 1893. FB

See: V. Burnett, *The Romantick Lady: The Life Story of an Imagination,* New York, 1927; A. Thwaite, *Waiting for the Party: The Life of Frances Hodgson Burnett,* New York, 1974.

Burns, George (né Nathan Birnbaum) (1896–) and **Gracie Allen (née Grace Ethel Cecile Rosalie Allen)** (1895–1964) Burns and Allen were the paradigm of American male–female doubles acts, his wry underplaying setting in relief her staccato dizziness. Burns had been a trick roller skater, dance teacher, and song-and-dance man in vaudeville; Allen entered show business as a child in an Irish sisters act. They teamed up in 1923 and married in 1926, Burns playing the quizzical straight man to her Dumb Dora. "Lamb Chops," one version of their cross-talk act, was signed to a six-year contract in the **Keith** theatres (1926–32). They had their own radio show (1932–49) and moved successfully to television. After Allen's retirement in 1958, Burns, wielding his omnipresent cigar, continued to perform, a high point being his Carnegie Hall recital in 1976. LS

See: C. Blythe and S. Sackett, *Say Good Night, Gracie!,* New York, 1986; G. Burns with C. H. Lindsay, *I Love Her, That's Why,* New York, 1955; G. Burns, *Living It Up,* New York, 1977.

Burnside, R. H. (1870–1952) Producer, writer, composer, and director. Born into a theatrical family in Glasgow, Burnside learned his trade at the Savoy Theatre in London before his arrival in New York (1894) as stage director for **Lillian Russell.** He established his reputation conceiving and staging lavish spectacles at the **Hippodrome** (1909–23), and became known as the "man who made the girls disappear into water." He continued in this line until the 1940s when he staged revivals of **Gilbert and Sullivan.** TLM

Burrows, Abe (Abram S.) (1910–85) Playwright, librettist, "play doctor," and director. Born in New York City, Burrows moved to Hollywood in 1939 and divided his time between these two entertainment centers for the rest of his life. Following a successful career in radio (he was the chief writer for "Duffy's Tavern," for example), he first scored as a playwright in 1950 by coauthoring *Guys and Dolls* with Jo Swerling and **Frank Loesser.** This success (Tony, Drama Critics' Circle Award) propelled him during the next decade into several assignments as lyricist or librettist for musicals, including *Three Wishes for Jamie* (1952), *Can-Can* (1953), *Silk Stockings* (1955), *Say, Darling* (1958), *First Impressions* (1959), and *How to Succeed in Business Without Really Trying* (1961; Tony, Pulitzer Prize). He also adapted *Cactus Flower* from a French comedy by Barillet and Gredy for a successful 1965 Broadway production. He made his debut as a director with *Can-Can,* and soon became known for his ability to infuse stage comedies with the kind of wit and gentle humor that characterized his personality and allowed him to work harmoniously with testy writers when called upon as an unbilled "doctor" for shows in trouble. In 1991 a theatre at New York University was named after him.   LDC

Burstyn, Ellen (née Edna Rae Gillooly) (1932–   ) Actress, past president **Actors' Equity** (1982–5), and artistic director of the **Actors Studio.** Once a showgirl on Jackie Gleason's television show and now a champion of womens' status in American film and theatre, Burstyn, who has long striven to play roles that intrigued her irrespective of their size, has played significant parts in plays as disparate as *Same Time, Next Year* (1975, Tony), *84 Charing Cross Road* (1982), *Driving Miss Daisy* (1988), *Shirley Valentine* (1989), and *Shimada* (1992). She won an Academy Award for her sensitive portrayal in *Alice Doesn't Live Here Anymore* (1974).   DBW

Burton (né Jenkins), Richard (1925–84) Blessed with a golden voice and a larger-than-life stage presence, this Welsh-born actor never fulfilled his promise, instead turning with reckless abandon to a largely turbulent life of drinking, womanizing, and notoriety, marked by a series of chiefly inferior films. Nevertheless, Burton's mark on American theatre was noteworthy. Half of his total stage work, other than seasons with the Old Vic or at Stratford, England, occurred in the U.S.; after 1957 all of his theatre appearances, save one, were here. He first appeared on Broadway in *The Lady's Not for Burning* (1950), followed by *Legend of Lovers* (1951), *Time Remembered* (1957), *Camelot* (1960 and a 1980–1 tour), *Hamlet* (1964, dir. John Gielgud; a record run of 139 performances for the play), *Equus* (1976), and – in an attempt to rekindle some of his old box-office magic – *Private Lives* (1983) with his former wife, Elizabeth Taylor. His daughter, Kate, is a successful actress.   DBW

See: M. Bragg, *Richard Burton: A Life,* Boston, 1988.

Burton, William E[vans] (1804–60) British-born actor and manager who ran one of the best stock companies in the U.S., earning at the same time the reputation, according to **Laurence Hutton,** as the "funniest man who ever lived." Burton's first professional appearance was in 1831 at London's Pavilion Theatre, followed the next year with an engagement opposite Edmund Kean at the Haymarket Theatre. In 1834 he made his American debut at the **Arch Street Theatre.** In 1841 he entered management in New York at the National Theatre, short-lived due to the destruction by fire of the theatre seven weeks later. He also managed briefly the **Chestnut** and Arch Street theatres in Philadelphia, the Washington Theatre, and the Front Street Theatre in Baltimore. In 1848 he leased Palmo's Opera House, renamed **Burton's Chamber Street Theatre,** and in 1856, with increasing competition from **J. W. Wallack,** moved to The Metropolitan Theatre, Broadway, renamed Burton's New Theatre. He withdrew from manage-

William Burton's Toodles, drunk. Photo: Gurney, N.Y. Courtesy: Laurence Senelick.

ment in 1858. Burton's Theatres operated successfully during 1848–56 largely without visiting stars, boasting such company members as **Henry Placide, William Rufus Blake, George Holland, Charles Fisher, Lester Wallack,** and **John Brougham,** who also wrote numerous new pieces for Burton. Audiences, however, came primarily to see Burton perform such roles as Bob Acres, Tony Lumpkin, Bottom, Falstaff, and especially Timothy Toodles in his own *The Toodles,* Aminidab Sleek in Morris Barnett's *The Serious Family,* and Captain Cuttle in Brougham's stage version of Dickens's *Dombey and Son.* His last New York appearance was at **Niblo's Garden** in 1859. Burton also wrote plays (nonextant). His biography, by William L. Keese, was published in 1885.   DBW

See: R. C. Johnson, "The Theatrical Career of William E. Burton," PhD diss., Indiana U, 1967.

Burton's Chambers Street Theatre Chambers Street between Broadway and Centre Street, New York. In 1844, well-known Broadway restaurateur Signor Fernando Palmo took the fortune he made from his kitchens and invested it in a small opera house to bring Italian opera to New York. After two disastrous seasons, he returned to the kitchen, losing both his theatre and his money. For several years, Palmo's Opera House housed a variety of entertainments, but it enjoyed its greatest success when actor-manager **William E. Burton** took it over (1848–56). As Burton's Chambers Street Theatre, it presented farces, burlettas, and light comedy. When Burton joined the uptown exodus, the theatre was taken over by minstrel companies, then rented to the federal government as a courthouse. In 1876, it was demolished.   MCH

Bury the Dead by **Irwin Shaw.** This antiwar play in one act, produced by the short-lived Actors Repertory Company, was done first at left-wing fundraisers in March 1936, then opened on Broadway on 18 April 1936, where it ran for 97 performances. The 23-year-old Shaw applied the model of the "strike play" to the circumstances of the war "that is to begin tomorrow night." Despite the pleas of religious leaders, generals, and even their loved ones, six corpses of soldiers refuse to lie down and be buried. Shaw's skillful combination of argumentation, macabre humor, and montage produced an event that – in the words of **Brooks Atkinson** – "burrows under the skin of argument into the raw flesh of sensation."   MF

Bush, Anita (c. 1883–1974) African-American actress credited with founding the **Lafayette Players** (1915–32). Bush was a member of the [Bert] Williams and Walker company that toured Britain with their hit musical *In Dahomey* (1903–4). When the company disbanded she ran a dancing chorus for four years. In 1915 she formed the Anita Bush Stock Company to play weekly repertory at Harlem's Lincoln Theatre, transferring six weeks later to the rival **Lafayette Theatre,** whose name the players adopted. The company (which Bush left in 1920) produced a galaxy of well-known black actors, but its plays were invariably condensed Broadway material.   EGH

Bus Stop by **William Inge** opened on 2 March 1955 and ran for 478 performances. Directed by **Harold Clurman,** the cast was headed by **Kim Stanley** as Cherie, a down-on-her-luck nightclub singer who is stranded with fellow travelers at a tiny Kansas restaurant in the dead of night. This collection of misfits, each with a story to tell, created an ensemble production and a mood described as Chekhovian by **Louis Kronenberger.** The play is still frequently staged by amateur and professional groups. In making the film version (1956), director **Joshua Logan** and screenwriter **George Axelrod** transformed it into a one-woman show that featured Marilyn Monroe as Cherie.   MR

Button, Jeanne (1930–) Costume designer who, after training at the Carnegie Institute of Technology and Yale School of Drama, made her New York debut in 1963 with *Tambourines for Glory.* The designer of costumes for *The Robber Bridegroom* and *Wings,* among other productions, she received a Maharam Award for *MacBird.* Button has designed costumes for many regional theatres, notably the Great Lakes Shakespeare Festival and the **Yale Repertory Theatre,** as well as for television. She has extensive **Off-Broadway** credits, and has taught design at Yale, New York University, and (since 1990) Tulane.   BO

C

Cabaret Two-act musical, music and lyrics by **John Kander and Fred Ebb** (respectively), book by **Joe Masteroff;** opened 20 November 1966 at the **Broadhurst Theatre,** New York, running 1,165 performances. One of the early "concept" musicals in its concern with theme over linear narrative, this metaphor for a world ignoring the coming of Nazism is based on Christopher Isherwood's *Berlin Stories*. The stories of the doomed romances of an American writer and an English cabaret singer and of a German matron and a Jewish fruitseller are told in the context of the cabaret, the world of unreality that opens and closes the show, presided over by its sardonic Emcee (**Joel Grey**). The numbers in the cabaret serve not to advance the narrative, but to comment on the action and establish the general air of decadence. These Brechtian overtones are enhanced by the **Weill**-like music, some of it written to be sung by Weill's widow, **Lotte Lenya,** as Fraulein Schneider. *Cabaret* won Tony and Drama Critics' Circle awards as best musical, and was made into an Oscar-winning film (in revised form) by **Bob Fosse** in 1972. JD

Caffe Cino The Ur theatre of the **Off-Off Broadway** movement. Joseph Cino, a former dancer, opened his coffeehouse at 31 Cornelia Street in Greenwich Village in December 1958. Soon local poets were doing readings and actors were performing scenes. While the first play presented was a condensed version of Oscar Wilde's *The Importance of Being Earnest,* a new generation of dramatists whose sensibilities were at odds with the commercial mainstream soon made the Cino's 8 × 8-ft stage their home, paying the expenses of their brief runs by passing the hat. Robert Patrick, Paul Foster, Tom Eyen, **Lanford Wilson,** Robert Heide, **Maria Irene Fornés,** William M. Hoffman, **Megan Terry,** Leonard Melfi, Jeff Weiss, **John Guare,** and **Jean-Claude van Itallie** were among the regulars whose plays Joe Cino introduced with a whoosh of steam from the espresso machine as he swirled a black thrift-shop cape. While Cino imposed no artistic criteria, the quintessential Caffe Cino playwright was H. M. Koutoukas, whose plays had a tacky, high-camp glamour suited to an atmosphere that Patrick describes as a cross between "Lourdes and Sodom." The Cino burned down on Ash Wednesday, 1965. Although it did reopen, Joe Cino committed suicide under the influence of drugs in 1967. *Village Voice* critic Michael Smith tried to keep the coffeehouse going for awhile, but the spirit had died with Cino, the first Off-Off Broadway impresario. CLJ

Cage Aux Folles, La, see *La Cage Aux Folles*

Cahill, Marie (1870–1933) Brooklyn-born singer and comedienne who made her Broadway debut in *A Tin Soldier* (1886). After developing her exuberant performing style in featured roles, she scored a triumph with the song "Nancy Brown," which she interpolated into the score of *The Wild Rose* (1902). For the next 15 years she was one of Broadway's biggest attractions, starring and touring in a dozen musicals, including **Victor Herbert**'s *It Happened in Nordland* (1904). Despite objections from Herbert and others, she continued to interpolate vaudeville and specialty numbers into her shows. Her last performance was in *The New Yorkers* (1930). MK

Caius Marius Considered the best of **Richard Penn Smith**'s 20 plays, it was the second script to win **Edwin Forrest**'s famous playwriting contest. Its theme, of a populist leader fighting the established aristocracy, appealed to the Jacksonian critics. But the five-act, blank-verse tragedy, based on the life of the Roman general Caius Marius, was poorly received by audiences and dropped from Forrest's repertoire shortly after it opened at the **Arch Street Theatre** on 12 January 1831. PAD

Caldwell, James H. (1793–1863) British-born actor-manager who pioneered the theatre in the Mississippi valley. He made his debut in Manchester, England, and came to the U.S. in 1816 to perform in Charleston; but he soon began managing in Kentucky and assembled his own touring company. On New Year's Day, 1824, he opened the Camp Street or **American Theatre,** the first English-language house in New Orleans and the first U.S. theatre illuminated by gas. Caldwell built theatres for his companies in such cities as Mobile, Nashville, and Cincinnati, thus rising to dominate the Mississippi and Ohio river valleys. His success was such that in 1835 he opened the **St. Charles Theatre** with a first-rate company and visiting stars of the highest magnitude. Intense competition with **Ludlow** and **Sol Smith** fostered excellent theatre in the area, but in 1837 a financial panic ruined Caldwell, the St. Charles Theatre burned down in 1842, and by 1843 he could no longer successfully compete and so retired from the stage. He held several official positions in New Orleans, fled to New York at the beginning of the Civil War, and died there in 1863. SMA

See: P. S. Hostetler, "James H. Caldwell: Theatre Manager," PhD diss., LSU at Baton Rouge, 1964.

Caldwell, Zoë (Ada) (1934–) Australian-born actress and director whose professional debut was with the Union Theatre Company, Stratford-upon-Avon, England (1958–9); she made her London debut at the **Royal Court** in 1960. After seasons in Canada and Australia, her U.S. debut occurred in 1963 at the Tyrone **Guthrie Theatre** in Minneapolis, followed by her New York debut in 1965 as the Prioress in John Whiting's *The Devils.* While remaining active in regional theatre, she is best remembered for the Tony Award–winning title roles in *The Prime of Miss Jean Brodie* (1968) and *Medea* (1982). Her directing credits include *An Almost Perfect Person* (1977), *Richard II* (1979), *The Taming of the Shrew* and *Hamlet* (1985), and *Park Your Car in Harvard Yard* (1991). In 1988 she assumed the direction of the Glenda Jackson–**Christopher Plummer** *Macbeth.* A superb technician with great power on stage, she has avoided being typecast, while leaning toward work in the classics. The wife of producer **Robert Whitehead**, she was awarded the OBE in 1970. DBW

Calhern, Louis (né Carl Henry Vogt) (1895–1956) Actor-director. With his tall, distinguished figure, aristocratic face, and physical grace, Calhern was considered a real "pro," rising from burlesque bit player to elder statesman of films (he made 68). A matinee idol in the 1920s, he afterward made few stage appearances, though he was praised as the Colonel in *Jacobowsky and the Colonel* (1944), Justice Oliver Wendell Holmes in *The Magnificent Yankee* (1946), and *King Lear* (1950). DBW

California Theatre The most respected **San Francisco** playhouse of its day opened on Bush St. on 18 January 1869 with Bulwer-Lytton's *Money* – an apt choice because Bank of California honcho William C. Ralston bankrolled the luxurious 2,400-seat, $250,000 theatre for actors **John McCullough** and **Lawrence Barrett.** Under McCullough's extended management, a first-rate stock company supported top guest stars (**Modjeska, Edwin Booth, Boucicault**) and introduced such innovations to San Francisco as the box set. The theatre's fortunes fell after Ralston's death and McCullough's 1877 departure; it was torn down in 1888. The New California, on the same site, stayed active until the 1906 earthquake, though never recapturing its predecessor's glory. MB

Call, Edward Payson (1928–) Connecticut-born, University of Maryland–educated director who has established a distinguished career, mainly in regional theatre. He was production manager at **Circle in the Square** (1958–61) before seven "very formative years" at the **Guthrie Theatre** (1963–70); the first artistic director of the **Denver Center Theatre Company** (1979–83), which he developed on the Guthrie model; and artistic associate at the Arizona Theatre Company (1987–9), where he still directs. Call's free-lance credits include the **Mark Taper Forum, Arena Stage,** the **Vivian Beaumont, Old Globe, American Conservatory Theatre,** and **Long Wharf.** TLM

Call Me Madam Two-act musical comedy, music and lyrics by **Irving Berlin,** book by **Howard Lindsay** and **Russel Crouse;** opened 12 October 1950 at the **Imperial Theatre,** New York, running 644 performances. A straightforward star vehicle, the show follows the adventures of Sally Adams (**Ethel Merman**), a loud, brassy woman appointed ambassador to "Lichtenburg" as a political plum. Occasioned by President Truman's appointment of socialite hostess Perle Mesta as ambassador to Liechtenstein, the show sought to capitalize on the success of the earlier Berlin–Merman effort, ***Annie Get Your Gun*** (1946). The role so suited Merman that she made the 1953 film version, her only screen appearance in one of her stage roles. JD

Camelot Two-act musical, music by **Frederick Loewe,** words by **Alan Jay Lerner;** opened 3 December 1960 at New York's **Majestic Theatre,** running 873 performances. Based on T. H. White's *The Once and Future King,* this was Lerner and Loewe's attempt to repeat the success of their ***My Fair Lady*** (1956); it again featured Julie Andrews (Guinevere) playing opposite a nonsinging British actor (Welshman **Richard Burton** as King Arthur). The show was plagued by problems (both Lerner and director **Moss Hart** were hospitalized during rehearsals, and a newspaper strike shortened its run), but its title song became associated with the new Kennedy administration. It has received frequent professional revivals over the years, featuring actors playing King Arthur, most frequently Richard Harris. A critically acclaimed revival at New Jersey's Paper Mill Playhouse (1991) featured designs by **Michael Anania** and staging by Robert Johanson. Loewe retired after *Camelot,* effectively ending the successful Lerner and Loewe collaboration. JD

Camino Real by **Tennessee Williams** opened in New York on 19 March 1953, closing after 60 performances. The cast, directed by **Elia Kazan,** included **Eli Wallach,** Jo Van Fleet, Barbara Baxley, and Frank Silvera. In 1957 the play was directed by Peter Hall in London. It was revived at the **Circle in the Square** in 1960, directed by **José Quintero,** and at the **Vivian Beaumont** in 1970, directed by Milton Katselas with **Al Pacino** and **Jessica Tandy.** The play is an existential fantasy about romantic bohemians who have trouble surviving in a contemporary world pervaded by cynical self-interest, political oppression, and the loss of human feeling. BCM

Campbell, Bartley (1843–88) Playwright. Born in a suburb of Pittsburgh and privately educated, he turned to journalism and then to playwriting. The first of his 35 plays was *Through Fire* (1871). During 1872–6 he wrote and staged plays for R.

M. Hooley in **Chicago**. From 1876 until his mental breakdown in 1885 he was America's most popular melodramatist. His greatest success was the mining camp melodrama *My Partner* (1879), which became a starring vehicle for Louis Aldrich as Joe and Charles Parsloe as Wing Lee. Though Parsloe went on to other parts, Aldrich, having purchased the rights to the play for a paltry $10 a performance, played it for the rest of his career. Campbell's other outstanding plays were *The Galley Slave* (1879) and *The White Slave* (1881). DMcD

> See: N. Wilt, ed., *The White Slave and Other Plays*, Princeton, NJ, 1940.

Camp St. Theatre see **American Theatre**

Can-Can Two-act musical comedy with book (and direction) by **Abe Burrows** and music and lyrics by **Cole Porter;** opened at the **Sam S. Shubert Theatre** (7 May 1953) for 892 performances. Subsequently three revivals were short-lived: August 1959 in Central Park's Theatre-in-the-Park; May 1962 by Broadway's New York City Center Light Opera Company; and April 1981 in the **Minskoff Theatre**. The 1953 production, hailed for its dancing, garnered two Tony Awards: **Michael Kidd** (choreography) and **Gwen Verdon** (best supporting actress). Set in Paris in 1893, *Can-Can* demonstrates the alluring effect of provocative dancing at a shady nightclub on some straitlaced legal investigators. Songs include "C'est Magnifique" and "I Love Paris." EK

Candide Two-act "comic operetta," music by **Leonard Bernstein,** lyrics by **Richard Wilbur** (and others), book by **Lillian Hellman;** opened at the **Martin Beck Theatre,** New York, 1 December 1956, running 73 performances. The original *Candide,* directed by **Tyrone Guthrie,** is one of the most famous failures in Broadway history. This musical version of Voltaire's novel, an expensive nine-week flop, was recorded by Columbia Records after the show closed. The record, introducing the public to Bernstein's extraordinary score, became an all-time best-seller. The show persisted in concert versions until 1973, when **Harold Prince** staged an "environmental" production of a revised version, with a completely new book by Hugh Wheeler, in Brooklyn. Transferred to Broadway on 8 March 1974, the revision, with the action in and around the audience, played 704 performances and won the Drama Critics' Circle Award for Best Musical. The revised version has since entered the repertoire of the New York City Opera. JD

Cantor, Arthur (1920–) Producer and press representative. Cantor represented Broadway productions before coproducing **Chayefsky**'s *The Tenth Man* (1959) and Mosel's *All the Way Home* (Drama Critics' Circle Award, 1960). His productions include **Gardner**'s *A Thousand Clowns* (1962), Bolt's *Vivat! Vivat Regina!* (1972), *Private Lives* (1975), *St. Mark's Gospel* (1978), Thompson's *On Golden Pond* (1979), *Ian McKellen Acting Shakespeare* (1984), *Starlight Express* (1987), *A Room of One's Own*, *Caged*, and James Sherman's *Beau Jest* (all 1991).

Eve Bennett-Gordon as Cunegonde ("Glitter and Be Gay") in Leonard Bernstein's *Candide* at the Goodman Theatre (1984). Photo: Steve Leonard. Courtesy: Goodman Theatre.

Cantor owned the Coconut Grove and Tappanzee Playhouses, headed the theatre division of Mercury Records, and is joint managing director of London producers, H. M. Tennent, Ltd. Cantor cofounded Washington, DC's **Helen Hayes** Awards and is coauthor, with Stuart Little, of *The Playmakers* (1970). REK

Cantor, Eddie (1892–1964) Singer and comedian who, after spending his early years in **vaudeville** and English music halls, made his legitimate theatre debut in a London revue. His first American appearance was in *Canary Cottage* (1917). **Florenz Ziegfeld** hired Cantor for his cabaret show *The Midnight Frolic,* and then featured him in the *Ziegfeld Follies of 1917.* Cantor also appeared in the next two *Follies* (1918, 1919). Like **Al Jolson** he often appeared in blackface, a vestige of the American **minstrel show.** During his musical numbers he would skip across the stage and clap his hands while smirking his way through some slightly suggestive lyrics. Cantor also appeared in several *Follies* sketches as a timid but potentially hot-tempered young man. He switched to the **Shubert** management for a few years, after which Ziegfeld presented him in a book musical, *Kid Boots* (1923). Cantor appeared in two more Ziegfeld shows, the *Follies of 1927* (for which he collaborated on the libretto as well as being the star performer), and *Whoopee* (1928), a book musical. His final Broadway appearance was in *Banjo Eyes* (1941). In addition to his work in the theatre, Cantor appeared in numerous films and was a star of radio and television. He coauthored two autobiographies: *My Life Is in Your Hands* (1928) and *Take My Life* (1957) MK

Capalbo, Carmen (Charles) (1925–) Pennsylvania-born producer, writer, and director, influential in the seminal years of the **Off-Broadway** movement. After a year at the Yale School of Drama (1945–6), he began in 1946 to present revivals of neglected contemporary classics – O'Casey, **Odets, O'Neill** – first at the Cherry Lane Theatre in Greenwich Village, later at Broadway's tiny Bijou Theatre. His most important production was the 1955 revival of Brecht's *The Threepenny Opera,* produced with Stanley Chase at the Theatre de Lys. Starring **Lotte Lenya,** it won both Tony and Obie awards, ran a record 2,611 performances, and helped to restore Brecht's American reputation. CLJ

Capital Repertory Company A thriving not-for-profit regional theatre in Upstate New York, founded in 1980 by Michael Van Landingham and Oakley Hall III. After several seasons in the Catskill community of Lexington, the company relocated to Albany, the state capital. Its eclectic repertoire, which emphasizes 20th-century American drama, balances revivals of recent and older plays with premieres. CLJ

Caricature/caricaturists The caricature, long established in Europe as an instrument of journalistic ego deflation, appeared in America in the 19th century practiced by artists for large-circulation weeklies, Thomas Nast of *Harper's Weekly* foremost among them. Best defined as the art of exaggeration with a trace of venom, the caricature could range from gentle to gross distortion for the sake of comment. The comic illustrated magazine, which established the art of caricature in earnest, crossed the ocean with the arrival of Austrian Joseph Keppler and his publication of *Puck* in 1877. The caricature was and continues to be well-suited to the extravagances of the world of the theatre. Hardly an issue of *Puck* went by that did not feature a theatrical caricature; its success inspired imitations, and soon newspapers and established publications began routinely to include caricatures.

American caricaturists borrowed liberally from the styles and techniques of Dore, Daumier, and Hogarth, and from each other. The earliest theatrical caricatures appeared in *The Comic History of the Human Race* (1851), with representations of **Edwin Forrest** and **P. T. Barnum** among its targets. In 1868, W. J. Gladding drew twelve caricatures of leading players on the American stage, which were assembled and published by the Dunlap Society in 1897. Thereafter, theatrical caricatures appeared regularly on the pages of most newspapers and periodicals.

Among the best known artists was James Montgomery Flagg, whose work (on the gentle side of caricature) appeared in almost every popular magazine and newspaper. Ohioan Alfred J. Frueh drew

prolifically for the *St. Louis Post-Dispatch* and later for the *New York World* and *New Yorker;* his early caricatures were compiled for a book called *Stage Folk* (1922). William Auerbach-Levy also published his work in a range of New York newspapers and the *New Yorker* as well as in the book *Is That Me?* (1947). Artist Reginald Marsh augmented his living as a fine artist with a mixture of cartoon and caricature, which he called "cartoonicles," for the *New York News* in the 1920s. Peggy Bacon, frequently called the **Dorothy Parker** of pen and ink, contributed to the *New Yorker,* and Irma Selz provided caricatures for *Vanity Fair, Harper's Bazaar,* and the *New York Post* during her career. Sam Norkin has spent most of his career working for the *New York News* and is still active in the field. The dean of all theatrical caricaturists is **Al Hirschfeld,** who still contributes to the *New York Times.* Hirschfeld regards Miguel Covarrubias, who died in 1957, as one of the most influential of all theatrical caricaturists, and pays tribute to him for raising the standards of caricature drawing and honing it into an art. MCH

See: M. Henderson, *Broadway Ballyhoo,* New York, 1989.

Cariou, Len (1939–) Canadian-born actor, director, and singer. A classically trained actor whose early career was most closely associated with the Stratford (Ontario) Shakespeare Festival and the Tyrone **Guthrie Theatre** in Minneapolis, Cariou has received his greatest acclaim as a leading man in Broadway musicals. His first musical comedy appearance was in the role of Bill Sampson in *Applause* (1970). Critics praised Cariou's performance as Fredrik Egerman in *A Little Night Music* (1973), complimenting him for his acting ability and fine singing voice. Cariou returned to the musical stage in 1979 to portray the monomaniacal "Demon Barber of Fleet Street" in *Sweeney Todd.* His bravura performance in one of the musical theatre's most demanding roles earned him the Tony Award as best actor in a musical. A later musical role, that of Teddy Roosevelt in *Teddy and Alice* (1987), was less successful. In addition to performing, Cariou has directed several plays, and has served as Artistic Director of the Manitoba Theatre Centre. In 1991 he appeared on Broadway in **Steve Tesich**'s *The Speed of Darkness,* the first play produced under The **Broadway Alliance.** MK

Carle, Richard (1871–1941) Comedian, librettist, and lyricist. Carle made his musical theatre debut in *Niobe* (1891), and soon became a popular comedian and singer in such shows as *A Mad Bargain* (1893), *Excelsior, Jr.* (1895), and *Yankee Doodle Dandy* (1898). Unlike other comic opera performers, Carle's comic persona was that of a shrewd, worldly prankster rather than a butt or simpleton. Carle also wrote the scripts and lyrics for many of his shows. His last appearance was in *The New Yorkers* (1930). Although reviewers often criticized the double entendres in Carle's material, he toured constantly to appreciative audiences across America. MK

Carmen Jones by **Oscar Hammerstein II** opened in the **Broadway Theatre** 2 December 1943 and ran 502 performances. Set during WW II among black workers in a Southern parachute factory, it was based on the Meilhac–Halevy adaptation of Prosper Mérimée's *Carmen* but retained Georges Bizet's music almost intact. **Billy Rose,** producer and director, was known for spectacles and is credited for hiring **Howard Bay** (settings), **Raoul Pène du Bois** (costumes), and **Hassard Short** (color schemes and lighting). In 1991, Simon Callow directed a critically acclaimed revival at London's Old Vic Theatre. KN

Carnovsky, Morris (1897–92) Beginning his long acting career with the **Theatre Guild** in the 1920s, Carnovsky departed in 1931 to join the **Group Theatre.** Among his many distinguished performances with the Group were those in **Clifford Odets**'s *Awake and Sing!* (1935), *Paradise Lost* (1935), *Golden Boy* (1937), *Rocket to the Moon* (1938), and *Night Music* (1940). With his mobile face, leonine profile, and commanding voice, he played characters much older than himself. Like other Group members, Carnovsky developed his own version of the Method; he disagreed with **Lee Strasberg**'s emphasis on the actor's own emotions but believed that, used properly, the Method could help actors to create classic roles. Beginning in the mid-1950s, in a series of acclaimed Shakespearean interpretations, Carnovsky achieved a fusion of the Method's psychological realism with the demands of poetic style. For the **New York Shakespeare Festival** and various universities he performed Lear, Falstaff, Prospero, and Shylock. Like all the Group alumni he was a lifelong student of the art of acting and had continued to be active as both a performer and a teacher. In 1983, with lovely simplicity, he portrayed Firs in Chekhov's *The Cherry Orchard* at New Haven's **Long Wharf Theatre,** and in 1984 he published a book of reflections, *The Actor's Eye.* FH

Carousel Considered by many **Rodgers** and **Hammerstein**'s finest accomplishment; their second collaborative effort. The musical play in a prelude and two acts, based on Ferenc Molnár's *Liliom* (1921), was presented by the **Theatre Guild** at the **Majestic Theatre** 19 April 1945, running for 890 performances. It is frequently revived and now belongs in the repertoire of several opera companies. Molnár's fantasy was transferred from Budapest to a New England fishing village in the late 1800s, where the leading character, handsome bully Billy Bigelow (**John Raitt**), an amusement park talker, falls in love with Julie Jordan (Jan Clayton) but proves incapable of providing either her emotional or material needs. When she becomes pregnant, Billy, desperate for money, dies in a robbery attempt. He is allowed to return to earth to do one good deed, but his daughter (Bambi Linn) refuses the stolen star he offers her, and he returns to purgatory. As directed by **Rouben Mamoulian** and choreographed by **Agnes de Mille,** *Carousel* climbed new heights of creativity and musical inventiveness, with classics such as "If I Loved You," "June Is Bustin' Out All Over,"

"Soliloquy," and "You'll Never Walk Alone." A 1956 film starred Gordon MacRae and Shirley Jones. DBW

Carroll, Earl (1892–1948) Producer, theatre manager, and composer who began his theatrical career as a program seller in Pittsburgh. He tried his hand at songwriting and, after serving as a pilot in WW I, launched into theatrical producing with *The Lady of the Lamp* (1920). Three years later he inaugurated a **revue** series called the *Earl Carroll Vanities,* which continued annually through 1932, with sporadic editions thereafter. Although they featured established performers such as **W. C. Fields, Jack Benny,** and Milton Berle, the *Vanities* were most noted for their daring use of **nudity** in "living curtain" tableaux, and for Carroll's barrage of outrageous publicity stunts. He opened his own theatre in New York in 1923 but lost it in the Depression. In 1936 he left for Hollywood, where he was an associate producer at 20th Century–Fox. In 1938 he opened the Earl Carroll Theatre and Restaurant in Hollywood. MK

See: K. Murray, *The Body Beautiful: The Story of Earl Carroll,* Pasadena, CA, 1976.

Carroll, Vinnette (1922–) African-American actress, director, and teacher, noted for productions of original musical plays under her direction. University-educated Carroll received professional training from **Erwin Piscator, Lee Strasberg,** and **Stella Adler.** She taught drama at the High School for the Performing Arts in Manhattan and directed the Ghetto Arts Program in New York before becoming artistic director of the Urban Arts Corps in Greenwich Village, where several of her productions were conceived and staged. Her credits include an Obie for acting in Errol John's *Moon in a Rainbow Shawl* (1962), the Outer Critics' Circle Award for distinguished directing in 1971–2, and several Tony nominations. Memorable among her Broadway productions are *Don't Bother Me, I Can't Cope* (1972), written by Micki Grant and showing how blacks have used their music to cope with life's problems, and *Your Arm's Too Short to Box with God* (1977), based on stories taken from the Gospel of Matthew. Since 1980 Carroll has worked in Fort Lauderdale, FL, where she has established her own repertory company. EGH

Carter, Mrs. Leslie (1862–1937) Actress. Mrs. Carter and **David Belasco,** her tutor and director, discovered that striking beauty, emotional pyrotechnics, and a sensational divorce could make a star performer – first in *The Heart of Maryland* (1895, for a three-year run), in which she swung on the clapper of a bell to keep it from ringing, and then in such slightly lurid dramas as *Zaza* (1899), *Du Barry* (1901), and *Adrea* (1905). According to one critic, Mrs. Carter would "weep, vociferate, shriek, rant, become hoarse with passion, and finally flop and beat the floor."

Although after breaking with Belasco (1906) she continued to perform, on the road and sometimes under her own management, in *Camille, The Second Mrs. Tanqueray,* and *The Circle,* she never matched her successes with Belasco. RM

See: C. H. Harper, "Mrs. Leslie Carter: Her Life & Acting Career," PhD diss., U of Nebraska at Lincoln, 1978.

Casino Theatre Broadway and West 39th St., NYC [Architects: Francis Kimball and Thomas Wisedell]. Designed in a Moorish style complete with turret, the Casino was opened by **Rudolph Aronson** in 1882. During its long history, it presented musical shows of all varieties: comedies, operettas, comic operas, and **revue**s. In 1890, Aronson opened New York's first roof garden theatre atop the Casino, where light musical fare was served up with light after-theatre refreshments. The house is best remembered for *Florodora,* one of the most popular musical comedies of its day. The Casino was torn down in 1930.   MCH

Cassidy, Claudia (1905–   ) Drama critic. Born in Illinois, Cassidy spent her girlhood in Chicago and attended the University of Illinois in Urbana. She began her career as a drama and music critic with the *Chicago Journal of Commerce* in 1925, quickly gaining a reputation for being tough but fair. In 1941, she left the *Journal* to organize the music and drama departments of the new *Chicago Daily Sun* (now the *Sun-Times*). Within a year, she was hired by the *Tribune*. Until her retirement in 1965, Cassidy wrote a daily column, "On the Aisle," and contributed to the Sunday edition. She toured Europe during the summers, sending back to the *Tribune* her impressions of "Europe on the Aisle." Considered the most powerful **Chicago** critic, Cassidy was credited with stopping New York producers from sending weak companies on the road. Her major credo was that the "only way to judge a play is to wait and see if the theatre brings it to life."   TLM

See: J. C. C. Casey, "An Analysis of the Drama Reviews of Chicago's Claudia Cassidy, 1925–1965," PhD diss., U of Maryland, 1990.

Cat on a Hot Tin Roof **Tennessee Williams**'s Pulitzer Prize–winning drama, directed by **Elia Kazan,** opened 24 March 1955 at the **Morosco Theatre** with **Barbara Bel Geddes** as Maggie, Ben Gazzara as Brick, Burl Ives as Big Daddy, and **Mildred Dunnock** as Big Mama. It ran 694 performances. Kazan persuaded the playwright to alter the original ending by bringing Big Daddy back on stage and by making Maggie more sympathetic; thus the play had two different third acts (the reading and stage versions). In 1974 Williams combined the original and the Kazan-inspired revision for the **American Shakespeare Theatre** production starring Elizabeth Ashley, Keir Dullea, and Fred Gwynne as Big Daddy. A popular revival in 1990 starred Kathleen Turner with Charles Durning (Tony Award) as Big Daddy. The 1958 film version featured Ives's Big Daddy with Elizabeth Taylor and Paul Newman. The play was televised in 1976 with Robert Wagner, Natalie Wood, and Laurence Olivier and in 1984 with Jessica Lange, Tommy Lee Jones, and **Rip Torn.** Like other Williams's plays, *Cat* explores levels of love and mendacity – Maggie and Brick; Brick and Big Daddy; and Brick with his college (homosexual?)

friend Skipper. The ultimate victor is Maggie who, having finally gotten Brick into bed, hopes the lie about her pregnancy may come true.   PCK

Cawthorn, Joseph (1868–1949) Comedian. As a child, Cawthorn performed in minstrel shows and in English music halls. Returning to America, he appeared in comic operas as a "Dutch comic," speaking fractured English with a German accent. After early successes in such musicals as *Excelsior, Jr.* (1895) and *Miss Philadelphia* (1897), Cawthorn played leading roles in *The Fortune Teller* (1898), *Mother Goose* (1903), *The Free Lance* (1906), *Little Nemo* (1908), *The Slim Princess* (1911), and many other shows. During WW I he dropped his German accent. His last Broadway appearance was in *Sunny* (1925), which starred **Marilyn Miller.**   MK

Cayvan, Georgia (1858–1906) Actress who made her New York debut in 1880 as Dolly Dutton (*Hazel Kirke*); however, her forceful portrayal as Jocasta (*Oedipus Tyrannus,* 1881) brought her prominence. Thereafter, as a leading actress of the **Madison Square Theatre** and 1887–94 of the **Lyceum Theatre** Company, she acted love-torn heroines in numerous popular comedies and melodramas, such as **H. DeMille** and **Belasco**'s *The Wife,* Buchanan's *Squire Kate,* and Pinero's *The Amazons.* Following a season touring with her own company, she retired in poor health in 1897.   DJW

Cazuran, Augustus R. (1820–89) Playwright, journalist, and drama critic. Arriving in American from Ireland in 1848, Cazuran served as theatre critic for the *New York Herald,* fought for the North in the Civil War, and afterward wrote for the *Washington Chronicle,* in whose pages he reported Lincoln's assassination, having been in the audience at **Ford's Theatre.** Employed at the **Union Square Theatre** as play reader, translator, and adaptor, he was "ever useful," according to G. C. D. Odell. Although his original plays (such as *The Fatal Letter* [1884]) failed in the theatre, his adaptations were successful, including those of Thomas Hardy's *Far from the Madding Crowd* (1882) and Octave Feuillet's *A Parisian Romance* (1883), which made **Richard Mansfield** famous.   WJM

Céleste, Mme Céline (Céleste Keppler) (1811–82) French dancer, the majority of whose unusual career belongs to the English and U.S. theatres. Most works of reference accept her own claim that she was born in 1814, but her marriage in Baltimore in 1828, following her NY debut in 1827 at the Bowery, and the birth of a child in 1829 make that improbable. She had visited the U.S. with a Parisian dance troupe (1827–30), and had already divested herself of husband and child when she made her English debut in 1830. A graceful dancer and mime, she solicited from English playwrights pieces that either would allow her to remain speechless throughout or would accommodate her unrepentant French accent. Céleste became a wealthy woman and had several lucrative and wildly popular American tours as dancer and actress, often playing several roles in the same night (1834–43, 1851, 1865). Her most popular vehicle was *The French Spy*. PT

Censorship Earliest theatrical opposition in America stemmed from the moral predilections of the colonial Puritans, who viewed all idle behavior as ungodly and dangerous. Although also an expression of political opposition, their stated concern was the moral well-being of the community. Seventeenth-century legislation from most of the early colonies banned idle behavior and various forms of paratheatrical amusement. The first verifiable account of theatrical opposition was the unsuccessful court action brought against three actors from Virginia, who in 1665 attempted a production of *Ye Bare and Ye Cubb*.

By the early 18th century many colonies attempted legislation banning theatrical performances. Not until the Massachusetts Act of 1750 were any of these attempts successful, since White Hall, through the Board of Trade, maintained that such acts inhibited commerce. There followed a handful of censorship acts in New Hampshire, Rhode Island, New York, and Pennsylvania, culminating in the Continental Congress passing its own version in 1774. To declare these acts as simply moral refinements of the Puritan character ignores the vital political and economic role theatre played just prior to the Revolutionary War. In discouraging the playing of British plays and players, the rebellious colonials were expressing their mercantile resentment of all things British. The perception of British superiority over American theatre would continue to shape critical thinking and production for much of the 19th century.

Constitutionally guaranteed freedom of speech notwithstanding, the new nation continued its colonial traditions. The Alien and Sedition Acts of 1798 did little to promote the politically vital plays that had marked prerevolutionary drama. Although short-lived, the acts certainly contributed to the inconsistency of American drama in the early 19th century.

The early 19th century saw little direct intervention, though audience taste and a puritanical sensibility still prevailed. Shocked by a revealing costume, audiences walked out of a performance by the French dancer Madam Hutin in New York in 1827. By the 1830s provocative displays increased as theatres sought larger audiences from an increasing pool of semiliterate immigrants and the working class. Palmo's Opera House (see **Burton**'s) in 1847 introduced "living pictures" [*tableaux vivants*], largely composed of scantily clad women (see **nudity**); New York officials closed the production. In 1861 **Ada Isaacs Menken** premiered her controversial "nude" scene in a revival of *Mazeppa,* and New York audiences flocked to see *The Black Crook* in 1866 despite objections from local clergy and the press, which branded the large chorus of lightly dressed young women as unsuitable for public presentation. Not until 1872, when Anthony Comstock formed his Committees for the Suppression of Vice, was there a major effort to suppress morally objectionable material. Within a year the repressive Comstock Law was passed.

The rise of the powerful Theatrical **Syndicate**

resulted in an increased concern for commercial viability. A systematic suppression of noncommercial works hindered the arrival of realism and caused those few playwrights who attempted realistic works to modify or abandon their style. **James Herne,** whose *Margaret Fleming* was refused a professional venue in Boston and New York in 1890 for its unsuitable themes, exemplified the difficulty early realists had in overcoming the aesthetic demands of a strictly commercial theatre industry.

The frankness in theme and language that realism brought was a perpetual source for censorship in the early 20th century. In 1905, when **Arnold Daly** attempted a performance of *Mrs. Warren's Profession* in NYC, both he and his leading lady were arrested after opening night and the show closed. Similar action was brought against **Clyde Fitch**'s *Sapho* in 1900 and George Scarborough's *The Lure* in 1913. Curiously, the popular musical **revue**s, such as *The Ziegfeld Follies* and *The Passing Shows* of the **Shubert Organization,** were largely overlooked by censors, despite their increasing reliance upon (partial) female nudity.

The 1920s were a particularly tumultuous time. With popularity of **burlesque** and the early successes of such alternative theatrical venues as the **Provincetown Players,** there was a concomitant rise in censorship. **O'Neill**'s *Desire Under the Elms* and *Strange Interlude* were widely opposed on moral grounds (both banned in **Boston**), though it may have been the frankness of subject and the intense realism that caused the greatest concern. *What Price Glory* by **Anderson** and **Stallings** drew criticism for its realistic depiction of war, while **Mae West** was arrested, sentenced to 10 days in jail, and fined $500 for her play *Sex*. Partly as a result of this play, New York passed the infamous Wales Padlock Law in 1927. Local authorities could now arrest actors, lock theatres, and ban productions deemed indecent. Although rarely invoked, it remained on the books for 40 years and led many theatrical producers to modify their work to avoid prosecution.

By the 1930s a new wave of political censorship arose with the founding of the WPA's **Federal Theatre Project,** coming under attack from two fronts. Its unabashed propensity to address difficult social and political issues drew fire from the politicians in Washington, while its popular successes raised the ire of commercial producers, who viewed a subsidized theatre as unfair competition. Under pressure from the House Un-American Activities Committee, Congress disbanded the FTP in 1939. That same year, New York City cracked down on burlesque houses, closing the **Minsky Brothers**' theatres on 42nd Street.

In response to this increased pressure and the threat of more dire consequences during the McCarthy era, American producers in the 1940s and '50s generally censored themselves, agreeing to changes and rewrites as requested by local officials. At the same time, playwrights like **Williams, Saroyan, Hellman,** and **Miller** tested the boundaries of popular taste and legal morality while risking their careers in defiance of McCarthyism. Their work laid the foundation for the eventual disintegration of the old obscenity laws in the 1960s.

Central in this movement was **Edward Albee**'s *Who's Afraid of Virginia Woolf?* (1962), which was denied the Pulitzer Prize in 1963 in a celebrated case over symbolism and language. Theatre, in reflecting the social rebelliousness of the 1960s, soon challenged every theatrical taboo. The 1967 production of *Hair,* with its famous nude lineup, marked the end of the traditional censoring institutions. The Supreme Court's 1969 decision on the show's ban in Boston made the transition absolute.

In the 1970s a new form of aesthetic censorship began as playwrights demanded absolute fidelity to their scripts. Following the lead of Samuel Beckett, Albee stopped a production of *Virginia Woolf?* in 1972, and in 1975 he sued the **American Conservatory Theatre** for their interpretation of his play *Tiny Alice.* The past 20 years have also seen renewed calls for censorship from Christian fundamentalists. The National Federation for Decency, founded in 1976, began national boycotts against sponsors of films and television shows it declared indecent. Reconstituted in 1987 as the American Family Association, it led the 1989 attack on the NEA for its support of controversial artists and performers. PAD

See: N. Hentoff, *The First Freedom: The Tumultuous History of Free Speech in America,* New York, 1980; A. Laufe, *The Wicked Stage,* New York, 1978; A. Nielsen, *The Great Victorian Sacrilege,* Jefferson, NC, 1991.

Center Stage Founded in Baltimore by committee in 1963 and since designated the State Theatre of Maryland, it has grown from a theatre dominated by modern classics into one that balances classics with new works. The theatre courted controversy in 1971 with Daniel Berrigan, Jr.'s *The Trial of the Catonsville Nine,* based on nearby civil disobedience. Managed for most of its history by Peter Culman, the theatre thrived under the artistic directorship (1977–91) of Stan Wojewodski, Jr., replaced after his departure to the **Yale Rep** by Irene Lewis. Premieres include works by **Eric Overmyer** (*On the Verge*) and David Feldshuh (*Miss Evers' Boys*). In 1991 the theatre added the flexible Head Theater to its existing 541-seat main stage. SF

Center Theatre Group (Los Angeles) Founded in 1966 to serve as the umbrella organization for activities at both the Ahmanson Theatre and the **Mark Taper Forum,** which, with the Dorothy Chandler Pavilion, form the principal venues of the Music Center of Los Angeles County. Both were completed in April 1967, and are owned and operated as public trusts. **Gordon Davidson** serves as artistic director.

The 2,100-seat Ahmanson is a commercial theatre that typically mounts productions with wide appeal (five of **Neil Simon**'s plays have premiered here), and features well-known film and stage actors.

The nonprofit company at the smaller (750-seat) Taper, in its first 23 seasons (1967–90) presented 137 mainstage productions, 57 West Coast or American premieres, and 38 world premieres, including works by **Romulus Linney, A. R. Gur-**

ney, **Luis Valdez, Neil Simon, Lanford Wilson,** and **Jean-Claude van Itallie.**

In the 95-seat John Anson Ford Theatre in Hollywood, the company develops new plays through staged readings, workshops, and fully mounted productions, including *Sundays at the Itchey Foot* (1980), a literary cabaret.

Taper productions have won 8 Obies and 10 Tony Awards, and in 1977 the company received the special Tony for regional theatre. Artists have included directors **Tyrone Guthrie, Harold Clurman, Marshall W. Mason, Athol Fugard, Ellis Rabb, José Quintero, Robert Woodruff,** and Kenneth Branagh; designers **Ming Cho Lee, Peter Wexler, Tharon Musser,** and **Ralph Funicello;** and many well-known film and stage actors. JDM

Central City Opera House Built in 1876, during the Colorado gold rush, to take advantage of the continuous stream of talent in transit between San Francisco and the East Coast, the facility fell into disrepair by 1900, with the gold rush over. Willed to the University of Denver in 1931, it was restored in 1932, becoming home to an annual summer opera festival hosting world-renowned opera stars. The festival led to a revitalization of the Central City area, which has since become a popular tourist attraction. PAD

Century Theatre see **New Theatre**

Ceremonies in Dark Old Men Domestic tragicomedy by African-American playwright **Lonnie Elder.** Set in a Harlem barbershop that fronts for selling bootleg whiskey, the play exposes the survival strategies of those victimized because of their race. In a 1969 **Negro Ensemble Company** production, the play was mostly praised for its realism and objectivity by New York critics who proposed it as a Tony Award candidate. Dissenting voices thought it overlong, some characters inconsistent, and the ending predictable. EGH

Chaikin, Joseph (1935–) Director, actor, and producer. Born in Brooklyn and educated at Drake University, Chaikin made his New York debut in *Dark of the Moon* (1958). He joined The **Living Theatre** the following year and appeared in *Many Loves* and *Tonight We Improvise* (1959); *The Connection* and Brecht's *Jungle of Cities* (1961–2); and *Man Is Man* (1962). For the Writers' Stage (1964), he performed in Ionesco's *The New Tenant* and *Victims of Duty.* Chaikin founded The **Open Theatre** in 1964 as an experimental company to build and perform new scripts. The success of *America Hurrah!* in 1966 (1967 in London) established his reputation. His workshop approach to composition also produced *Terminal* and *The Serpent* in 1970, the latter a series of episodes on the history of murder. Chaikin has directed for the **New York Shakespeare Festival, Manhattan Theatre Club, Magic Theatre** of **San Francisco,** and **Mark Taper Forum** of **Los Angeles.** An articulate spokesman for the 1960s avant-garde movement, Chaikin has won numerous awards, including five Obies. After a stroke in 1984 resulted in aphasia,

Chaikin appeared in NYC for the first time in 1991 (**American Place**) in plays he coauthored with **Sam Shepard** (*The War in Heaven*) and **van Itallie** (*Struck Dumb*) that reflected that experience.   TLM

See: E. Blumenthal, *Joseph Chaikin,* Cambridge (UK)/ New York, 1984.

Champion, Gower (1921–80) Dancer, choreographer, and director who appeared as a dancer in *The Streets of Paris* (1939) and several other shows before turning to choreography with *Small Wonder* (1948). After dancing with his wife Marge in several Hollywood films, Champion returned to Broadway as the director and choreographer of *Bye Bye Birdie* (1960). The charm and energy of his staging led to further directing and choreography assignments for *Carnival* (1961), *Hello, Dolly!* (1964), *I Do! I Do!* (1966), *Irene* (1973), *Mack and Mabel* (1974), and others. Champion died just as his last show, *42nd Street,* was about to open in 1980. His initial directorial work evinced a fresh and inventive approach to staging a musical. *Carnival,* in particular, was praised for its imaginative, stylized production. Champion, along with **Bob Fosse** and **Michael Bennett,** made the choreographer-director the dominant figure in the musical theatre of the 1970s.   MK

Chaney, Stewart (1910–69) Scenic designer of many of the popular Broadway shows of the late 1930s and '40s, including *Life with Father* (1939) and *The Late George Apley* (1944). He became known for clever and stylish interiors, although he was capable of architectural and painterly settings. He wished to strike a balance between three-dimensional realism and artificial theatricality. *The Voice of the Turtle* (1943), simultaneously depicting three rooms of an apartment, including a kitchen sink with running water, was one of his most famous.   AA

Chanfrau, Frank (1824–84) New York–born actor. Inspired to become an actor by a performance of **Edwin Forrest,** he gained recognition through his ability to imitate Forrest, starting on a tour of theatres and cities across America that eventually led him to the **Olympic Theatre** in New York in 1848. As Mose the fire b'hoy in *A Glance at New York,* written for him by **Benjamin A. Baker,** Chanfrau became the "lion" of the town. Dressed in the red shirt, plug hat, and turned-up trousers of the New York fireman, Chanfrau was featured in several Mose plays, particularly *The Mysteries and Miseries of New York* by Henry W. Plunkett. Friends leased the **Chatham Theatre** for Chanfrau, who renamed it the National and continued to perform the role of Mose for about three and a half years. After this popularity, Chanfrau performed the title role 560 times in *Kit the Arkansas Traveller,* and played the lead character in **Thomas de Walden**'s *Sam* 783 times.   WJM

Chang, Tisa (1945?–) Chinese-American actor, director, and founder-artistic director of **Pan Asian Repertory Theatre.** Born in China, she graduated from Barnard College and studied with **Uta Hagen,** performed on Broadway, and first directed at **La MaMa** ETC. In 1977 she created Pan Asian Rep, with the intention of opening up more opportunities for **Asian-American theatre** artists. The many works she has directed there include new plays by R. A. Shiomi and Ernest Abuba (her husband), cross-cultural versions of classics (a bilingual Mandarin-English *A Midsummer Night's Dream*), and ambitious thematic projects (*Ghashiram Kotwal,* an Indian music-drama).   MB

Channing, Carol (1921–) Seattle-born and Bennington-educated singer and comedienne who made her Broadway debut in *No for an Answer* (1941). Critics praised her work in the revue *Lend an Ear* (1948), and in the following year she became a star with her larger-than-life performance as 1920s vamp Lorelei Lee in the musical version of *Gentlemen Prefer Blondes.* She succeeded Rosalind Russell in *Wonderful Town* (1954), appeared in the short-lived musical *The Vamp* (1955) and the revue *Show Girl* (1961), and toured with the Bernard **Shaw** play *The Millionairess* (1963) before starring in the long-running hit *Hello, Dolly!* in 1964. As matchmaker Dolly Gallagher Levi, Channing gave a warm, funny, and at times outrageous performance. In subsequent years, she was unable to find vehicles worthy of her unique talents. *Lorelei* (1974) lasted only a few months, and the play *Legends* (1986) closed before reaching Broadway.   MK

Channing, Stockard (née Susan Williams Antonio Stockard) (1944–) New York–born and Radcliffe-educated (BA, 1965) actress who began professional stage work in 1967 with the Theatre Company of Boston and, after a stint in California, made her Broadway debut in 1971. Despite some dozen major NYC appearances since, a failed TV series, and poorly received films (excepting *Grease*), it was not until her Tony Award–winning portrayal in *Joe Egg* (1985 Broadway revival) that her extraordinary stage talent began to be recognized. Other notable appearances include **Neil Simon**'s *They're Playing Our Song* (1980), **Guare**'s *The House of Blue Leaves* (1986 revival, as Bunny), Ayckbourn's *Woman in Mind* (1988, Drama Desk), **Gurney**'s *Love Letters* (1989), and especially Guare's *Six Degrees of Separation* (1990), in which she was critically acclaimed as Ouisa. Her most recent New York appearance was in Peter Hall's production of Guare's *Four Baboons Adoring the Sun* (1992) at the **Vivian Beaumont.** Gurney has said that Channing has the ability "to combine a sense of comedy with a sense of pathos to get at the ache underneath."   DBW

Chapman, John Arthur (1900–72) Drama critic. A native of Colorado, Chapman began his career with *The Denver Times* (1917–19) before moving to the New York *Daily News* (1920), where he became dramatic editor (1929) and replaced **Burns Mantle** as drama critic (1943), retiring in 1971. He wrote a popular column, "Mainly About Broadway," in the 1930s, and edited the *Best Plays* series during 1947–53. He was known as "Old Frostface" for his straightforward prose and no-nonsense demeanor.   TLM

Chapman family see showboats

Charles II; or, The Merry Monarch Considered by many to be **John Howard Payne's** most popular work, this three-act comedy, based on Alexander Duval's *La Jeunesse de Henri V* (1806), was a collaborative effort. Payne, who claimed to have penned the work while in Paris in 1823, was assisted by **Washington Irving** (much of the comic dialogue betrays his style), who had anonymously assisted on five other Payne plays. It opened on 27 May 1824 at London's Covent Garden. Popular on the American stage for much of the 19th century (in the repertoires of **Joseph Jefferson III** and **Fanny Kemble**), it was initially attributed to the English writer Thomas Dibdin and criticized for being a simplistic farce, dwelling on the romantic adventures of Rochester and King Charles II.   PAD

Charnin, Martin (1934–) Lyricist, director, and actor. After graduating from Cooper Union, he began to act and write lyrics, contributing lyrics to the **Off-Broadway** revue *Kaleidoscope* and playing Big Deal in **West Side Story** (both 1957). He wrote lyrics for a number of musicals, notably *Two by Two* (1970), *Annie* (1977), and *I Remember Mama* (1979). He also directed several plays and musicals, including *Sid Caesar and Company* (1989) and *Carnal Knowledge* (1990).   MK

Chase, Mary (Ellen) Coyle (1907–81) Playwright and screenwriter. Her first produced play, *Me Third* (1936), was written for the **Federal Theatre Project** in Denver. She continued writing plays throughout her career, most of which had limited success, ending with *Cocktails with Mimi* in 1974. In 1952 *Mrs. McThing,* starring **Helen Hayes,** was a hit on Broadway; but her most successful drama was *Harvey,* the name given a giant invisible rabbit, which won the Pulitzer Prize in 1944 and became one of the longest running plays on Broadway.   FB

See: P. Westbrook, *Mary Ellen Chase,* New York, 1965.

Chatham Theatre (Chatham Garden Theatre) Park Row between Pearl and Duane Sts., NYC [Architect: George Conklin]. In 1823, Hippolite Barrière, proprietor of the Chatham Gardens, decided to dispense light entertainment along with summer refreshments on the property. He erected a tent theatre, perhaps America's first summer playhouse; the following year, he built a permanent structure and was for several seasons a formidable rival to the **Park Theatre.** After 1827, its vogue passed, it presented everything from **Shakespeare** to equestrian drama to French opera under a succession of managers that failed to revive its fortunes. In 1832, it was converted to a Presbyterian chapel.   MCH

Chautauqua and Lyceum Prominent cultural, educational, and religious organizations of the late 19th–early 20th century, part of a movement initiated by evangelists traveling the "sawdust trail" along the western frontier in gospel tents, beginning in an organized fashion with the Millerites in 1842. Both Chautauqua and Lyceum ultimately offered theatrical or platform entertainment.

Chautauqua, founded by John Heyl Vincent and Lewis Miller, began in New York State during the summer of 1874 as a tent meeting on the shores of Lake Chautauqua. By 1884 Chautauqua had expanded beyond its original intent to offer only religious instruction, and began to include cultural edification of all sorts, including dramatic interpretation and stereoptican views. Experiments with summer Chautauqua circuits began in 1904, first organized by Keith Vawter and Roy J. Ellison; soon there were Chautauqua tents throughout the country, carried over established circuits (by 1912 there were over 1,000 independent Chautauquas) in the summer. Very soon, show business became part of the formula of the brown tents [see **tent show**] of Chautauqua – brown, in contrast to the white top of the **circus,** became a symbol of its quasi-cultural inspiration – and because of the extensive circuits, a good Chautauqua act could survive for years. Typically, a Chautauqua program combined elements of **vaudeville** (especially as vaudeville became more "refined") and dramatic sketches, in addition to the usual smattering of lectures and other "cultural" programming. Since early Chautauqua was generally hostile to traditional theatre, preference was given to platform performances, in particular the **one-person** show; as Victorian intolerance for the stage weakened, more actual drama was offered in Chautauqua. As early as 1904 the New York Chautauqua offered Ben Jonson's masque *The Sad Shepherd,* and in 1910 plays of Shakespeare were presented by the Nicholson Sylvan Players. The ultimate cause (of many) of Chautauqua's rather abrupt demise in the 1920s was the radio, although there is still an active program at the permanent home in New York.

Quite different from Chautauqua, the Lyceums, active as early as 1826, operated in the winter, in permanent venues, and in urban settings, in contrast to tent Chautauqua in rural areas. Although different institutions, both often shared a common pool of talent; but there was less pure entertainment in Lyceum. Still, with skilled promoters – in particular James Redpath in the last half of the 19th century – Lyceum prospered, with a less perceptible collapse than Chautauqua, continuing into the 1940s and gradually having its function usurped by college and university lecture, writer, and performance series. During its heyday, some of the great celebrities of the time appeared as Lyceum presentations, including Daniel Webster, Edgar Allan Poe, **Fanny Kemble, Charlotte Cushman,** Charles Dickens, and Mark Twain.   DBW

See: J. Gentile, *Cast of One,* Urbana, 1989; H. Harrison, *Culture Under Canvas,* New York, 1958; C. Horner, *The Life of James Redpath and the Development of the Modern Lyceum,* New York, 1926; F. Lorch, *The Trouble Begins at Eight,* Ames, IA, 1968; T. Morrison,

Lucian Pintillie's 1987–8 production at the Arena Stage of *The Cherry Orchard* with (left to right) Shirley Knight, Tana Hicken, and Rebecca Ellens. Photo: Joan Marcus. Courtesy: Arena Stage.

Chautauqua, Chicago, 1974; and W. Slout, *Theatre in a Tent,* Bowling Green, OH, 1972. DBW

Chayefsky, Paddy (1923–81) Playwright. A self-styled activist social critic, Chayefsky established himself as a writer during the heyday of live television drama, moved to the films with the highly honored *Marty* (1955), succeeded briefly as a Broadway playwright, and finally abandoned the legitimate stage to concentrate again on writing for the motion pictures. His Broadway plays were *Middle of the Night* (1956), *The Tenth Man* (1959; revived at Lincoln Center in 1989), *Gideon* (1961), and *The Passion of Josef D* (1964). His last play, *The Latent Heterosexual* (1968), was successfully produced in American regional professional theatres and at the Bristol Old Vic in England. The culmination of his film-writing career came with *Network* (1976). LDC

See: J. Clum, *Paddy Chayefsky,* Boston, 1976.

Chekhov on the American stage *The Seagull* was produced professionally in 1916 by the **Washington Square Players** in New York, but the **Moscow Art Theatre**'s 1923–4 touring productions first won over American critical opinion to Chekhov. Attempts to create an American ensemble Chekhov began with **Eva Le Gallienne**'s **Civic Repertory Theatre** productions of *Three Sisters* (the play's first English-language staging, 1926); *The Cherry Orchard* (1928), with guest artist **Alla Nazimova** as Ranevskaya and at the National Theatre (1944) with Le Gallienne as Ranevskaya and **Joseph Schildkraut** as Gaev; and *The Seagull* (1929), with the great Yiddish actor **Jacob Ben-Ami** as Trigorin. Former MAT actor Leo Bulgakov staged the **Yiddish Art Theatre**'s *Cherry Orchard* (1928) and A Cooperative Company's *Seagull* (1929). Actors **Franchot Tone** and **Morris Carnovsky** appeared in the first English-language production of *Uncle Vanya* (**Morosco Theatre,** 1929). MAT alumna Maria Germanova staged *Three Sisters* (1930) and appeared in the **American Lab-**oratory **Theatre** production at the **Longacre Theatre.**

Lee Strasberg's Method-inspired **Actors Studio** production of *Three Sisters* (Randall Jarrell's adapted translation) at the Morosco Theatre (1964) featured **Kim Stanley, Geraldine Page,** and Shirley Knight in the title roles and **Group Theatre** alumnus **Luther Adler** as Chebutykin. The cast floundered under Strasberg's desultory direction, the unequal charisma of the individual performers, and the general difficulty in translating studio exercises into stage performances.

The first Chekhov "star package" was **Jed Harris**'s 1930 **Cort Theatre** production of *Uncle Vanya* (designer, **Jo Mielziner**), with **Osgood Perkins** as Astrov and **Lillian Gish** as Elena. The 1938 *Seagull* (**Stark Young**'s translation) at the **Sam S. Shubert Theatre,** designed by **Robert Edmond Jones,** featured **Lynn Fontanne, Alfred Lunt, Uta Hagen,** and Sydney Greenstreet. The **Guthrie McClintic** *Three Sisters,* designed by Motley (**Ethel Barrymore Theatre,** 1942), starred **Judith Anderson, Katharine Cornell, Ruth Gordon,** and Edmund Gwenn. **Mike Nichols**'s 1973 staging of *Uncle Vanya* (**Circle in the Square**) offered **George C. Scott** as a lumbering Astrov, Nicol Williamson as a manic Vanya, and Julie Christie as a placid Elena.

The adaptation-as-star approach was exemplified by: *Fireworks on the James,* after Chekhov's unfinished *Platonov,* at the Provincetown Playhouse (1940); **Joshua Logan**'s *The Wisteria Trees,* which transplanted *The Cherry Orchard* to the American South (**Martin Beck Theatre,** 1950); and **Neil Simon**'s *The Good Doctor* (Broadway premiere 1973), one of many attempts to dramatize Chekhov's short stories. Experimental productions of Chekhov's plays have included **Tyrone Guthrie**'s arena staging of *Three Sisters* (Minneapolis Repertory Theatre) and **Ellis Rabb**'s modern-dress *Seagull* (**Association of Performing Artists,** 1962). Michael Schultz directed an all-black *Cherry Orchard* at the **Public Theater** (1973), the site of

Andre Gregory–The Manhattan Project's largely improvisatory *Seagull* (1974), for which the spectators shifted their seats with designer **Ming Cho Lee**'s three set changes. Thomas Pasatiri's operatic *Seagull* premiered at the Houston Grand Opera (1974) and was revived at the **John F. Kennedy Center,** Washington, DC (1978), where **Peter Sellars** also staged *The Seagull* (1985). Romanian **Andrei Serban**'s iconic *Cherry Orchard* at the **Vivian Beaumont Theatre** (1977) featured **Irene Worth, Raul Julia, Meryl Streep,** and a sparsely furnished **Santo Loquasto**–designed white set, backed by a cyclorama, exposing the play's epic and transitional historical moment. Praised for its individual tableaux and energetic *mise-en-scène* but criticized for its broad comic approach, Serban's staging pushed Chekhov through "the fourth wall" to a more universal poetic plane for American audiences. Serban's *Uncle Vanya* at **La MaMa** (1983), with **Joseph Chaikin** in the title role, was set in a vast interior space, while his *Three Sisters* (**American Repertory Theatre,** 1983) employed a mirrored stage backed by a painted drop of the theatre's rear wall to suggest the artificiality of the stage classic and theatrical presentation.

The Hungarian émigré Squat Theatre Company deconstructed *Three Sisters* (NYC, 1980; originally staged in Budapest, 1976) with audiotape, a prompter, and three hirsute, cigar-smoking men in white suits. Romanian Lucian Pintilie's *Seagull* (**Guthrie Theatre,** 1984) reversed play sequence and repeated scenes to accrete a new drama of play and memory on Radu Boruzescu's open play world set, dominated by a rustically Gothic tracking stage. Pintilie's *Cherry Orchard* at Washington's **Arena Stage** (1987–8 season) set a portion of the action in a "real" wheatfield. Peter Brook's international cast performed *The Cherry Orchard* as a timeless myth on carpets with simple furnishings at the **Brooklyn Academy of Music** (1988), and MAT artistic director Oleg Efremov's *Ivanov* (1990–1) was seen at the **Yale Repertory Theatre** with **William Hurt.** Recent imported productions of Chekhov include the (Moscow) Sovrenennik Theatre's *Three Sisters* (Goodwill Games, Seattle, 1990) and Eimuntas Nekrosius's brilliantly playful staging of *Uncle Vanya* for the State (Youth) Theatre of Lithuania (Joyce Theatre, NYC, 1991). SG

See: T. W. Clyman, ed., *A Chekhov Companion,* Westport, CT, 1985; V. Emeljanow, ed., *Chekhov: The Critical Heritage,* Boston, 1981; L. Senelick, *Anton Chekhov,* London, 1985.

Chekhov, Michael (Mikhail Aleksandrovich)

(1891–1955) Russian stage and film actor, director, and teacher for whom acting represented a "spiritual logic," designed to quell his chaotic soul and to reconcile humanity to inner pain. Chekhov (the playwright's nephew) joined the **Moscow Art Theatre**'s First Studio in 1912, working with Leopold Sulerzhitsky and Evgeny Vakhtangov. Chekhov's theatrical existentialism derived from Eastern and Western philosophy and from Rudolf Steiner's anthroposophy, which Chekhov first encountered in 1922. Steiner's eurythmy, "the science of visible speech" as the soul's "universal language," and Emile-Jacques Dalcroze's euryth-

mics, or musical kinesis, coalesced in Chekhov's "psychological gesture," the internal, archetypal physicalization of a spiritual-emotional state, from which characterization develops. Attacked for his mysticism and determined to save modern Russian theatrical culture from Soviet censorship, Chekhov emigrated in 1928. He came to New York in 1935 with the Moscow Art Players (formed in Paris, 1934) at Sol Hurok's invitation to perform a program of Russian classics. Chekhov's lectures on the creative process influenced and divided **Group Theatre** members. The Chekhov Theatre Studio, begun in 1936 at actress Beatrice Straight's family estate in England, relocated to Ridgefield, CT (1939) and NYC (1941), disbanding in 1942. During this period, the Studio Players were critically savaged for a Dostoyevski mélange entitled *The Possessed* (1939) and toured the U.S. (1940–2), and Chekhov successfully codirected *Twelfth Night* at Broadway's Little Theatre (1941). He worked in Hollywood (1943–55), instructing many "stars" and appearing in 11 films, including an Academy Award–nominated performance in Hitchcock's *Spellbound* (1945). Chekhov's books include *The Path of the Actor* (autobiography, 1928); *On the Actor's Technique* (in Russian, 1946); *To the Actor* (1953); *Michael Chekhov's To the Director and Playwright* (compiled by Charles Leonard, 1963); and *Michael Chekhov: Lessons for the Professional Actor* (compiled from his class lectures, 1941–2). In 1980, Straight and Robert Cole founded the Michael Chekhov Studio in NYC, where classes were taught by Chekhov's former pupils. An alternative group, the Michael Chekhov Study Center, headed by Eddie Grove, was formed in Los Angeles. SG

See: L. Black, *Mikhail Chekhov as Actor, Director, and Teacher,* Ann Arbor, MI, 1987; M. Kirby, ed., *The Drama Review* (Michael Chekhov Issue), 3 (Fall 1983).

Chelsea Theatre Center

After workshop productions in Manhattan churches during 1965–7, founder **Robert Kalfin** settled the not-for-profit theatre at the **Brooklyn Academy of Music** in 1968. There for nine seasons the Chelsea – run by an effective triumvirate of Yale School of Drama graduates (Kalfin as Artistic Director, Michael David as Executive Director, and Burl Hash as Productions Director) – produced sophisticated work that earned it a dozen commercial transfers and some 50 honors, including Tony, Obie, Drama Desk, and Drama Critics' Circle awards. Although the Chelsea mounted some revivals – notably Kleist's *The Prince of Homburg* and the **Hellman–Wilbur–Bernstein** musical version of Voltaire's *Candide* – it favored American premieres of adventurous modern plays, native and foreign. Among them: the uncut version of Genêt's *The Screens,* Allen Ginsberg's *Kaddish,* Handke's *Kaspar,* Bond's *Saved,* Storey's *The Contractor,* Isaac Bashevis Singer's *Yentl,* and Witkiewicz's *The Crazy Locomotive.* The Chelsea early supported the innovative and often militant plays of emerging **African-American** writers such as **Ed Bullins, Ron Milner,** and **Amiri Baraka,** and sponsored appearances by alternative groups such as the Iowa Theatre Lab, **El Teatro Campesino,** and the **San Francisco Mime Troupe.** David and Hash left when the Chelsea relocated to Manhattan in 1978, an unfortunate move that contributed to the theatre's failure in 1983. A 1986 effort to revive operations as a developmental workshop also failed.   CLJ

See: D. Napoleon, *Chelsea on the Edge: The Adventures of an American Theater,* Ames, IA, 1991.

Cheney, Sheldon (1886–1980) Critic and author who championed the modernist movement in the American theatre of the 1910s through his books *The New Movement in Theater* (1914) and *The Art Theater* (1916), and through **Theatre Arts** magazine, of which he was founding editor (1916–21). Cheney called for a nonnaturalistic aesthetic for the American stage, for a poetic and symbolic treatment of human experience that engaged rather than eliminated the imagination. A graduate of the University of California at Berkeley (1908), Cheney studied with **George Pierce Baker** at Harvard (1913), and later spent five years in Europe, touring and studying theatres. His 13 books on art history, architecture, and theatre include *The Theatre: 3000 Years of Drama, Acting and Stagecraft* (1929), considered the first comprehensive history of theatre written in this country.   TLM

Cherry Sisters A **vaudeville** sister act from Iowa. Originally there were five sisters – **Jessie** (c. 1836–1903), **Ella** (d. 1934), **Lizzie** (Elizabeth) (1869?–1936), **Addie** (Addie Rose Alma) (1859?–1942), and **Effie** (1879?–1944) – the latter two being the most active, appearing together as late as 1935. As amateurs they confused jeers with adulation, touring the Midwest for three years unofficially as the "world's worst actresses." In 1896 **Oscar Hammerstein** brought four (all but Jessie) to New York's **Olympia** Theatre, where, billed as the "Charming Cherry Sisters," but better known as the "vegetable sisters" because of the missiles tossed at them – provoked, they were told, by stars jealous of their talent – they began a successful career singing and reciting atrociously but with all seriousness (dancing, they believed, was immoral). Their peculiar act ("so bad it was great") made them a fortune.   DBW

Chestnut Street Theatre Chestnut near 6th St., Philadelphia [Architect: Inigo Richards?].

Chestnut Street Theatre, Philadelphia. Engraving by W. Ralph, after a drawing by S. Lewis; published in *New York Magazine* (1794). Courtesy: Cooper–Hewitt Museum of Decorative Arts and Design.

Prominent Philadelphians raised the capital to underwrite a theatre to replace the deteriorating **Southwark** and locate it in the center of the city. It was leased to **Thomas Wignell** and Alexander Reinagle, who set about assembling an acting company. Completed in 1793, its opening was delayed for a year because of an outbreak of yellow fever. A handsome, well-appointed house, the exterior continued to be improved upon from plans furnished by Benjamin Latrobe. By 1805, it was considered the finest playhouse with the best acting company in America. In 1816, gaslighting was introduced for the first time in a theatre, but in 1820 the playhouse burned down [see **fires**]. It was rebuilt in a version by William Strickland that bore little resemblance to the original. The theatre's most prosperous years occurred under the management of **William Warren** and **William Wood,** which ended in 1828. Thereafter, it went steadily downhill as new theatres were built and better acting companies arose to challenge it. In 1855, the theatre was demolished. A new theatre bearing the same name was built six blocks away but was unlike the original; it, too, was razed in 1917.   MCH

Chicago For much of its colorful history, Chicago theatre was buffeted between fire and New York City, forces that alternately impeded local activity and spurred greater accomplishment. The **fires** of the 19th century, the fire codes of the 20th century, and the competition from New York of both centuries provided challenges that ultimately strengthened and defined the character of local stage efforts, leading ultimately to an independent theatre community of considerable verve and originality.

Like other American cities, Chicago had been a thriving and multifaceted theatrical community in the period prior to the rise of the Theatrical **Syndicate** and the **Shubert**s, and it has been a leader in the movement to decentralize American theatre in the latter half of this century. The period in between the two flourishings was comparatively fallow in terms of local production, thereby making it easy to divide Chicago's theatrical history into three major periods: boom town, road town, and regional center.

The role of fire in the city's theatrical development also was considerable. The history of theatre in 19th-century Chicago is in large degree the history of theatres being built, burning down, and being replaced by bigger, fancier structures. Chicago's first theatre was built by **J. B. Rice** in 1847 and burned down three years later. It was rebuilt, only to be surpassed by more imposing structures – including **McVicker's Theatre, Hooley's Theatre,** The Woods, Crosby's Opera House, Aiken's Theater, and others – most of which were leveled by the Great Chicago Fire of 1871, and many of which were rebuilt with astounding rapidity. A series of fires shortly after the turn of the century were capped by the immense tragedy of the burning of the Iroquois Theatre on 30 December 1903, killing 600 holiday matinee patrons. That fire led to exceedingly restrictive fire codes that would stay in place for 70 years, severely hampering Chicago's entrance into the regional theatre movement. When *Sun-Times* critic Glenna Syse and others finally succeeded in convincing the Richard J. Daley administration to relax those codes in the early 1970s, there was an immediate emergence of many small storefront theatres of the type that still typifies theatre in that city.

Ironically, the first recorded performance for money in Chicago was an exhibition of fire-eating in a private home in 1834, when Chicago was a city of some 4,000 souls. As Chicago grew, one-man exhibitions were joined by **circus**es, which in turn were joined by J. B. Rice and the theatres mentioned above. The range of performance during the period before and after the 1871 fire included so-called legitimate theatre (comedy, satire, melodrama, and tragedy), as well as opera, ballet, pantomime, strolling players, **vaudeville, burlesque, minstrel shows,** and such singular attractions as Joseph Barton, Mlle. Zoe, **Buffalo Bill Cody,** and Texas Jack. Leading actors who performed in Chicago in the period included **Charlotte Cushman, Edwin Booth, James O'Neill,** and **Joseph Jefferson III.** The **stock companies** of the 1870s gave way to combination companies in subsequent decades.

By the end of the century, waves of immigrants had added foreign-language theatre to the mix of lower-priced entertainment available in the neighborhoods. (**Ibsen**'s *Ghosts* received its world premiere in Chicago in its original Norwegian.) In summer, the shore of Lake Michigan was dotted with musicals. Meanwhile, the Syndicate tightened its grip on commercial production in the big Loop theatres with fare that increasingly relied on star vehicles, machinery, and spectacular scenery.

As a reaction to the glossy values of the commercial stage, Chicago was an active participant in the Little Theatre movement [see **community theatre**]. Local leaders included The New Theater (begun in 1906), various companies led by Donald Robertson, Jane Addams's **Hull-House Players,** and the Chicago Little Theatre. Most featured serious European plays ignored by the commercial theatre. The leadership was idealistic, determinedly amateur, and poorly funded. Most of these art theatres did not survive the 1910s.

By 1920, Chicago had made the transition from boom town to road town. One way of plumbing the meaning of that change is to look at the role of the local critics. At the turn of the century, critics like Delancey Halbert, **Amy Leslie,** Lyman Glover, **Burns Mantle, Percy Hammond,** W. L. Hubbard, and Barrett Eastman were responsible for shaping a climate of opinion for theatre that was an exuberant mix of high and low culture, locally produced and imported, professional and amateur. By the 1920s, and into the decades that followed, the only significant role left to local critics – led in this period by Leslie, **Ashton Stevens,** and **Claudia Cassidy** – was to pass on the merits of shows coming from or heading to New York. The economies of scale enjoyed by touring productions – not to mention radio and movies – virtually eliminated significant local competition. The Hull-House Players continued in various incarnations, as did other small amateur theatres; but the only lasting local theatre of the period was the **Goodman,** which, founded in 1925 with high artistic ambitions, was itself reduced to a purely educational status by the Depression.

The seeds of Chicago's theatrical rebirth can be found in small amateur efforts. Viola Spolin, author of the still popular *Improvisation for the Theater* and other texts, got started as a recreational director inventing games for inner-city children in the 1920s and '30s. Spolin's methods for eliciting spontaneous behavior were passed on to her son, **Paul Sills,** who gave them practical use in a series of theatrical enterprises in the 1950s and '60s.

It was David Shepherd, a classmate of Sills at the University of Chicago and a collaborator in the Playwrights Theatre Club, who had the idea for a theatre that would combine *commedia dell'arte* techniques and German cabaret in a topical format. Following workshops given by Spolin, Sills and Shepherd opened the innovative but short-lived Compass Players in 1955, to be succeeded four years later by the **Second City,** a company whose members were greatly to influence the development of comedic theatre across the nation and, especially, on television.

In 1963 the theatre program at the Jane Addams Hull-House was revived by Robert Sickinger. His high artistic ideals, commitment to a community-based ethos, and progressive repertory set a new standard for local production and helped nurture a generation of young artists – including **David Mamet** – who would build the Chicago theatre in subsequent decades. For the most part, however, 1960s Chicagoan theatre comprised road shows, dinner theatre (which William Pullinsi claimed to have invented with the Candlelight Playhouse in suburban Summit), community and college productions, and a commercial but artistically ambitious effort at the Ivanhoe Theatre. What came to be known as the Off Loop movement began late in the decade with a pair of theatres on opposite sides of Lincoln Avenue. The Kingston Mines hosted a wide variety of work, from the fantastic to musical premieres such as *Grease*. Directly across the street, the **Body Politic** led the way, both with its own productions and by hosting other groups. It was at Body Politic that Paul Sills created Story Theater, and it was at Body Politic that Stuart Gordon landed with his **Organic Theater,** a group that had been closed down when it offered University of Wisconsin students a nude Peter Pan. The Organic went on to create a string of successful original productions, the most enduring of which was a science fiction comic book trilogy called *Warp!*

The most professional, big budget resident theatres in the 1970s were the north shore Academy Festival Theatre – perhaps most famous for Broadway-bound productions of *Moon for the Misbegotten* and *Morning's at Seven* – and the Goodman. The Goodman had turned professional under John Reich in 1969, and gained stability under William Woodman's directorship in the 1970s. With the relaxation of the fire code and the concomitant rise of the Off Loop scene (Northlight, **Victory Gardens,** and **Wisdom Bridge** all began in 1974), Woodman brought in young **Gregory Mosher** to start a vigorous Stage 2 series. In the meantime, David Mamet was making a mark by cofounding (also in 1974) the St. Nicholas Theater – the leading Off Loop theatre in the late 1970s – and writing *Sexual Perversity in Chicago* for the Organic. Mosher and Mamet first joined forces with *American Buffalo,* a coproduction of Stage 2 and St. Nicholas. They continued to work together throughout Mosher's ascension to leadership positions at the Goodman and New York's **Lincoln Center.**

A movement toward professionalization went hand-in-hand with a gradual shift in artistic approach as the 1970s progressed. The stylistic adventurousness of groups like Godzilla Rainbow and Pary Productions gave way to a pronounced naturalism typified by the acting of the **Steppenwolf Theatre Company** and director **Robert Falls**'s energetic productions at Wisdom Bridge. As Falls replaced Mosher at the Goodman, and *Daily News* critic **Richard Christiansen** – an early supporter of Mamet and Steppenwolf – moved to the powerful *Tribune,* this highly physical brand of naturalism became entrenched, to the point that it was referred to as "the Chicago style." This term primarily referred to actors, but it also had its exemplars in such playwrights as Mamet, James Yoshimura, Rick Cleveland, Claudia Allen, Dean Corrin, Charles Smith, Steve Carter, Alan Gross, and Jeffrey Sweet (as opposed to the less naturalistic writing of Lonnie Carter, John Logan, Nicholas Patricca, and Darrah Cloud). Writers of all stripes have found support at a variety of theatres specializing in new work, most notably Victory Gardens.

This naturalistic focus led to excellence as well as a certain lack of breadth: By the late 1980s, there was relatively little avant-garde work in Chicago and, with the exception of the Court Theater and The Shakespeare Repertory, few premodern productions. In the early 1990s, however, signs of a swing away from naturalism could be seen in the work of small groups like Theater Oobleck, as well as in the increasing success of director **Frank Galati,** whose productions bridged disparate genres and styles.

At its height in the late 1980s, membership in the League of Chicago Theatres topped 150 institutions. Recession reduced the field by 20%, but the volume of continuing activity ensured a degree of creative vitality for some years to come. That vitality encompassed musicals (at Marriott's Lincolnshire Theatre, Candlelight, and the Drury Lanes), ethnic theatre (at Angel Island, Black Ensemble, Chicago Theatre Company, ETA, Kuumba, and Latino Chicago), numerous improvisational comedy clubs, and the rise of midsized commercial venues (Apollo, Briar Street, Royal George, Wellington) that offered hope of a rising standard of living for local actors. Every other May the International Theatre Festival exposed Chicago to a wide spectrum of performance styles. Theatre programs at Northwestern, DePaul, Columbia, and Loyola – not to mention the state universities – provided a stream of talent for the creation of theatres that began with small budgets and large ambitions: Bailiwick, City Lit, Live Bait, Next, Pegasus, Raven, Remains, and others. Having survived fire and New York City, Chicago faced the continuing challenges of making art and finding an audience. SF

See: J. Coleman, *The Compass,* New York, 1990; J. C. Czechowski, "Art and Commerce: Chicago Theatre 1900–1920," PhD diss., U of Michigan, 1982; S. Fosdick, "The Press on Chicago Theater: Influencing an Emergent Style," PhD diss., Northwestern U, 1991; L. Glover, *The Story of a Theatre,* Chicago, 1898; W. Leonard, *Chicago Stagebill Yearbook,* Chicago, 1947; *Resetting the Stage: Theater Beyond the Loop 1960–1990,* exhibit catalog, Chicago Public Library Special Collections Dept, 1990; R. Sherman, *Chicago Stage – Its Records and Achievements,* Chicago, 1947; J. Sweet, *Something Wonderful Right Away,* New York, 1978.

Chicago Two-act "musical vaudeville," music by **John Kander,** lyrics by **Fred Ebb,** book by Ebb and **Bob Fosse;** opened at the **46th Street Theatre,** New York, 3 June 1975, running 898 performances. Based on Maurine Dallas Watkins's 1926 play of the same name, *Chicago* treats, in the form of a series of **vaudeville** acts, the glorification of criminals as celebrities, focusing on two "merry murderesses," Roxie Hart (**Gwen Verdon**) and Velma Kelly (**Chita Rivera**). Bob Fosse, following collaborative difficulties on *Pippin* (1972), not only directed and choreographed but took credit for shaping the book, a step toward his eliminating collaborators in *Dancin'* (1978) and *Big Deal* (1986). The vaudeville motif gave Fosse scope to recreate the popular dance forms, classic or sleazy, of the 1920s, while the score makes pointed allusions to memorable melodies from period **revue**s. *Chicago* marks a major achievement in Fosse's record as an *auteur* director-choreographer of "concept" musicals. JD

Chicano theatre Chicano theatre belongs to the larger category of Spanish-speaking theatre in the U.S. Its origins date from the arrival of the Spanish conquerors, including the priests interested in the spiritual conquest, in the 16th century. Dramatic performances were recorded in the Southwest as early as 1598, when Juan de Oñate's band of explorers performed an early religious play near El Paso, TX. Throughout the period of settlement and growth of the following centuries, the dominant Hispanic culture and language in the area gave attention to the theatre. During the 19th century, both **San Francisco** and **Los Angeles** were major centers of **Hispanic theatre** activity that sponsored visits by operatic companies even before the California gold rush. As the railroad linked major cities throughout the Southwest, especially Laredo, San Antonio, and El Paso, the ethnic communities with a strong sense of their heritage and traditions maintained local cultural activities and hosted traveling road companies en route to and from Mexico City.

By the 1920s Chicano theatre flourished from Los Angeles to Chicago. Productions of musical **revue**s and zarzuelas coincided with serious plays that addressed issues particular to Chicano communities. The problems of adapting culturally and linguistically to a predominantly Anglo culture were standard themes. The level of activity subsequently subsided during the Depression and WW II years, although it did not disappear entirely.

The more recent Chicano theatre movement co-incided with activism in the U.S. civil rights movement in the 1960s. In the summer of 1965, when **Luis Valdéz** joined César Chávez as he was organizing the farm workers' strike in the fields of Delano, CA – using politically orientated improvisational theatre to underscore the migrant workers' cause – he became the acknowledged father of the new direction in Chicano theatre. His *actos,* as they came to be called, were short agitprop pieces that dramatized the essence and spirit of the Chicano reality. The new Chicano theatre was, suddenly, a revolutionary theatre committed to social change. From this initial experience, Valdéz established **El Teatro Campesino** (Farm Workers' Theatre).

This group served as the model for a host of other Chicano theatre groups created throughout the West and Southwest, and extending across the country into Illinois, Indiana, and Wisconsin. Adrian Vargas created Teatro de la Gente (People's Theatre) in 1967. In 1971 **Jorge Huerta** developed the Teatro de la Esperanza (Theatre of Hope) in Santa Barbara, a group whose stability is second only to that of El Teatro Campesino. In 1972 Joe Rosenberg established the Teatro Bilingüe (Bilingual Theatre) in Kingsville, TX. At the peak of the movement, as many as 100 groups were functioning throughout the U.S. Rubén Sierra, Roberto D. Pomo, Romulus Zamora, and Manuel Pickett are but a few of the other major directors. A national network was established in 1971 to maintain linkages among the groups. Called TENAZ (El Teatro Nacional de Aztlán/National Aztlán Theatre), it has sponsored the annual festivals that bring together groups from all over the U.S. as well as from Latin America to learn about their common heritage and share their experiences. The road has not always been smooth: Differences in function and orientation were particularly evident at the fifth festival celebrated in 1974 in Mexico City, where Valdéz was severely criticized. Nevertheless, the festivals provided for a useful interchange and gave opportunity for fresh perspectives on techniques.

The farm-worker issue catapulted El Teatro Campesino into existence, but the themes captured in its Brechtian-style *actos* were many and varied. *Soldado razo* decried the mistreatment of Mexican-Americans in the Vietnam War; *Vendidos* depicted the worst of Chicago stereotypes. Valdéz's **Zoot Suit,** based on a historical episode of racial violence in East Los Angeles in the summer of 1943, opened in Los Angeles in 1978 as a tremendous critical and popular success – a record that unfortunately did not hold true when it opened months later as the first Chicano show to arrive on Broadway. After a period of reorganization in San Luis Obispo, the company has in more recent years staged Valdéz's *I Don't Have to Show You No Stinking Badges* and *Simply Maria* (1986) by Josefina Lopéz, a young Mexican woman raised in Los Angeles. The latter play builds on Valdéz's inherent sense of the comic while at the same time cutting into the pain and prejudice of cross-cultural living.

An entire generation of Chicano writers has picked up the cue, adding original notes derived from the rich traditions and folklore of the Chicano people.

Most plays are identified by author; others are the product of a group effort, a kind of *creación colectiva.* Teatro de la Esperanza was particularly active in the latter vein. Growing out of a student movement at Santa Barbara into a professional theatre group, it staged its first full-scale production, *Guadalupe* – a play that chronicled the exploitation of Chicanos in a small California community – in 1974. That success led to *La victima* (1976), another documentary experiment based on the deportation of Mexican workers alleged to be injurious to the American economy. Later plays include *Hijos: Once a Family* (1979), *Loteria de pasiones* (Lottery of Passions, 1984), and Lalo Cervantes's *Teodolo's Final Spin* (1988).

Among the women playwrights Estela Portillo Trambley is notable for her *Puente negro, Autumn Gold, Blacklight,* and *Sor Juana,* the last an impressive and stimulating work that captures both the intellect and the emotion of the 17th-century Mexican nun, herself a brilliant poet and playwright. Several writers who are not exactly Mexican-American are claimed by the movement. One is Milcha Sanchez-Scott, born to a Columbian father and an Indonesian-Chinese-Dutch mother, whose play **Roosters** (1987) deals with family conflicts and Chicano issues around a metaphor of cockfighting. Another is Arthur Giron, born of Guatemalan parents; his play *Money* chronicles the fast and vicious world of high finance and corporate foundations. Other important writers include Rubén Sierra and Carlos Morton.

The Chicano theatre is normally written and performed in the peculiar linguistic mixture typical of the Chicano population. Words and phrases in the two languages are constantly interchanged depending upon the context. Most groups perform in the "Spanglish" dialect most comfortable to their situation; some groups prefer to maintain the separation and will alternate performances in Spanish and English. Economic difficulties have dimmed some opportunities for Chicano theatre at the same time social issues have changed some of the needs. The effort to educate the majority population about Chicano issues while serving the interests of the Chicano population itself presents a major challenge, especially now that not as many groups are functioning as before. The publication of texts continues to be a high priority as a venue for encouraging production. From its humble beginnings the Chicano theatre has achieved an impressive level of accomplishment. GW

See: J. W. Brokaw, *Educational Theatre Journal,* Dec 1977; J. A. Huerta, *Chicano Theatre: Themes and Forms,* New York, 1982; J. A. Huerta, ed., *Necessary Theater: Six Plays about the Chicano Experience,* Houston, 1989; J. A. Huerta and N. Kanellos, *Nuevos Pasos: Chicano and Puerto Rican Drama,* Houston, 1979; M. E. Osborn, *On New Ground: Contemporary Hispanic-American Plays,* New York, 1987; E. C. Ramírez, *Footlights Across the Border: A History of Spanish-language Professional Theatre on the Texas Stage,* New York, 1990.

Children of a Lesser God

Children of a Lesser God Mark Medoff's two-act drama about a relationship between a hearing man and a deaf woman was inspired by Phyllis Frelich, a deaf actress he met in 1977. Medoff developed the play while heading the New Mexico

State University Drama Department and premiered it there as a workshop (April 1979). **Gordon Davidson** added the play to the fall 1979 season of Los Angeles's **Mark Taper Forum,** where **Emanuel Azenberg** saw the production and subsequently moved it to New York's **Longacre Theatre** (opening 30 March 1980 and running 887 performances). It won the Tony for best play and the Outer Critics' Circle and Drama Desk awards (1980). The play examines ideas about disabilities as the lead character confronts loving, then marrying, a woman who does not consider deafness an impairment nor speech an attribute.   KN

***Children's Hour, The* Lillian Hellman**'s first and longest running play "struck Broadway like a thunderbolt" when it opened at **Maxine Elliott**'s Theatre on 20 November 1934 for a run of 691 performances. Based on a real-life incident in Scotland, the play tells the story of two boarding school teachers whose lives are ruined by a malicious student who suggests they are lesbians. At the end, Martha (Anne Revere) kills herself when she faces the possibility of the truth of the accusation. Although the play was banned in **Boston** and London, critics compared Hellman to Ibsen and Strindberg and nominated the play for the Pulitzer Prize; however, the subject matter was too inflammatory, and the award was instead given to **Zoë Akins**'s *The **Old Maid**.* As a direct result, the New York Drama Critics' Circle Award was established. In 1952 the play had a moderately successful revival, running for 189 performances.   FB

Children's theatre In the U.S., children's theatre is a 20th-century movement, although dramatic activities for and by children were reported as early as the 18th and 19th centuries. It was not until 1903, however, that a theatre designed especially for youth was founded. This was the Children's Educational Theatre, established by Alice Minnie Herts, a recreation director at the Educational Alliance, a social settlement on New York's Lower East Side. Noting that theatre was one of the most popular activities for adults in the neighborhood, Herts suspected it might have the same appeal for children.

Herts's goals were threefold: to help young people learn the language and customs of their new country; to meet the social needs of the community by providing a place for families to gather; and to help people "create an idea from within rather than to impose one on them from without." These remain the major goals of children's theatre today.

The first season opened with a highly successful production of *The Tempest,* followed by *Ingomar, As You Like It,* and *The Forest Ring.* The reputation of the Children's Educational Theatre spread rapidly, and within the next few years plays for youth were reported in **Boston, Chicago, San Francisco, Los Angeles,** and other urban centers with large immigrant populations. All were under the auspices of community centers, with many of the scripts written by social workers because of the paucity of plays for young audiences. Although the Children's Educational Theatre was forced to close for financial reasons seven years after its founding, the popularity of the enterprise resulted in a restructuring called The Education Players. Unlike its forerunner, the players were adults, with children as spectators.

Meanwhile, drama classes and clubs were formed in New York settlements and libraries for the purpose of providing children with creative outlets: puppetry, acting, and the enjoyment of storytelling. Many of these activities were led by members of the Junior League, a women's organization dedicated to social service. Although a few private schools described dramatic programs and pageants, the theatre arts were not a part of the curriculum.

Broadway had never concerned itself with children's theatre, although a few such productions took place during these early years: *Peter Pan,* starring **Maude Adams** (1905) and *The Blue Bird* (1910) were the most notable. **Eva Le Gallienne**'s **Civic Repertory Theatre** presented *Alice in Wonderland,* and stock companies frequently offered plays suitable for family audiences. The latter could not be construed as children's theatre, however, as they were given in the evening at regular theatre prices rather than during school hours.

The next significant pioneering effort was made by **Winifred Ward** at Northwestern University in the early 1920s. By making a distinction between

Lillian Hellman's *The Children's Hour,* presented at Maxine Elliott's Theatre (1934). Courtesy: Michael Gnat.

children's theatre (which children enjoy as spectators) and creative drama (in which they participate informally), Ward provided guidance for educators and guidelines for producers. Teaching, writing, lecturing, and organizing leaders in the field resulted in the formation of a professional organization, now known as the American Alliance for Theatre and Education. The following decades saw the emergence of qualified educators on all levels and the introduction of university courses designed to prepare teachers, **community theatre** directors, and performers in this new branch of theatre. With this leadership came textbooks, playwrights for children's theatre, and conferences on regional and national levels. In 1935 Sara Spencer established the first publishing house devoted exclusively to plays for children; during the 1940s **Charlotte Chorpenning,** herself a playwright, laid down the first rules of writing for the child audience. **Clare Tree Major,** an actress, formed one of the first and longest lived professional touring companies performing for children and teenagers. Established in 1923, it lasted until her death in 1954.

The social upheaval of the 1960s affected children's theatre as it did all of the arts. With few exceptions, "Happenings," improvisation, **participatory theatre,** and musicals replaced the straight play. The success of the **Paper Bag Players,** a company founded in 1958, introduced a new and imaginative format that was imitated by a number of groups within the next few years. The "Bags'" 50-minute scripts were composed of 12–15 skits with little, if any, thematic connection. Short, sometimes satiric, but always humorous, they were developed by the company and the composer. The simplicity of this approach was the first step in the liberation of children's theatre from formal structure and familiar content.

With the 1970s and '80s subject matter hitherto taboo became acceptable: Plays dealing with death, divorce, prejudice, and unhappy endings were new choices for the child audience. Theatre-in-Education (TIE) focused on social issues ranging from racial conflict to child abuse and drugs. These programs were often left open-ended so as to stimulate discussion and follow-up activities, and were sponsored by schools for assembly programs because of their educational value.

Notable exceptions to these changes were ESIPA in Albany, NY, the first state in the country to mandate children's theatre; the Palo Alto Children's Theatre in California; and The **Children's Theatre Company** of Minneapolis, all of which had their own facilities. Rising costs of real estate and production made building prohibitive without generous subsidy and community support. Some companies formed alliances with adult theatres, whereas others toured, accepting residencies of a day to a month or more in a school where workshops were held during or after school hours for teachers. An **Actors' Equity** contract not only raised salaries but forced all union companies to provide adequate wages and working conditions. Practitioners now fell into three categories: community, educational, and professional. Money, still in short supply, despite government subsidy and foundation grants, continued to plague the move-

ment. By the end of the century, however, well-prepared performers, directors, teachers, playwrights, and research were major achievements. NMcC

See: R. Bedard & J. Tolch, eds., *Spotlight on the Child: Studies in the History of American Children's Theatre,* Westport, CT, 1989; N. McCaslin, *Theatre for Children in the United States: A History,* Norman, OK, 1971, and *Historical Guide to Children's Theatre in America,* Westport, 1987.

Children's Theatre Company, The
Minneapolis-based children's theatre company; one of the few in the U.S. with its own well-equipped facility. Founded in 1961 by John Clark Donahue, it is dedicated to providing theatre of the highest quality for young people and their families. In addition, classes in the performing arts offer unique opportunities for technical and theatre training. For several years it operated a fully accredited school of the arts. Although most of the productions are adaptations of children's classics, folktales, and fairy tales, many of the scripts are original. Unlike the majority of community theatres, performers are young adults.   NMcC

Childress, Alice
(1920–) African-American playwright. Born in Charleston, SC, and raised in Harlem, Childress opened the New York stage to black women writers when her play *Gold Through the Trees* (1952) was professionally produced **Off-Broadway.** She had for 12 years been an actress with the **American Negro Theatre,** and her most important play, *Trouble in Mind* (1955), voiced the protest of a veteran black actress against playing a stereotypical "darkie" role in a Broadway-bound production. It won the Obie Award for best original Off-Broadway play. Other notable plays by Childress that feature strong black women of compassion and dignity are *Wedding Band* (1966) and *Wine in the Wilderness* (1969). More recent works include the screenplay *A Hero Ain't Nothin' but a Sandwich* (1977), on teenage drug addiction, and *Moms* (1987), a play recalling the life of comedienne Jackie "Moms" Mabley.   EGH

Chip Woman's Fortune, The
One-act folk drama by **Willis Richardson** demonstrating the simple charity of the poor toward the poor in a southern community when the meager savings of a street collector of woodchips are shared to help a friend pay his debt. First produced in 1923 on a triple bill by the Ethiopian Art Players in Chicago, the play was taken to Washington, DC, then to Harlem's **Lafayette Theatre,** and finally to Broadway, where it was judged to be "unaffected and wholly convincing." It was the earliest nonmusical black play seen on Broadway.   EGH

Chodorov, Jerome
(1911–) and **Edward** (1904–88) Playwriting brothers who often collaborated, but not with each other. Edward's principal contributions are *Kind Lady* (1935), a **Grace George** mystery, and *Oh, Men! Oh, Women!* (1953), a comedy of the sexes. Jerome was far more successful collaborating with Joseph Fields on many plays, including *My Sister Eileen* (1940), a comedy about

neophytes in Greenwich Village, which ran for over 800 performances. The collaborators in turn adapted the play as the musical *Wonderful Town* (1953), with music by **Leonard Bernstein.** Other Chodorov–Fields successes include the long-running *Junior Miss* (1941), about teen-age vicissitudes, and a sentimental Kitty Carlisle vehicle, *Anniversary Waltz* (1954). RHW

Chong, Ping (1946–) Toronto-born but raised in the Chinatown section of New York. Experimental theatre director, choreographer, performer, and filmmaker who also produces videotapes and site-specific installations. He studied filmmaking at School of Visual Arts (1967–9) and graphic design at Pratt Institute (1964–6). He later joined **Meredith Monk**'s company (1971–8), and continues to collaborate with Monk on video productions and performances, such as their opera/music theatre, *The Games* (1984). He founded his own company, the Fiji Theater Company (1975; since 1988 known as the Ping Chong Company). Beginning with his first theatre piece, *Lazarus* (1972), Chong's multimedia hi-tech and science fiction theatre pieces have explored the alienation of humanoid and android races (*Angels of Swedenborg* [1985], *Kind Ness* [1986], *Elephant Memories* [1990]). His influences by Chinese opera, Brecht, Meyerhold, Kafka, and film producer Robert Bresson represent postmodernist fragmentation. Chong uses futuristic, cinematic, and theatrical stage effects to explore bureaucratic regimentation and the psychological states of the outsider. AF

Chorpenning, Charlotte (1873–1955) One of America's first children's playwrights. A contemporary and associate of **Winifred Ward** at Northwestern University, Chorpenning is best known for her association with the **Goodman Theatre** of Chicago, where many of her plays were given their first production. In 1931, she was made director of children's plays, a position that enabled her to study audience reactions and put these observations to literary use. In addition to creating a large body of literature, she set down guidelines for other playwrights. The American Alliance for Theatre and Education awards the Charlotte Chorpenning Cup annually to an outstanding children's dramatist. NMcC

Chorus Line, A With book by James Kirkwood and Nicholas Dante, music by Marvin Hamlisch (the only surviving member of the team), and lyrics by Edward Kleban, this Pulitzer Prize–winning musical opened at the **New York Shakespeare Festival**'s **Public Theater** on 15 April 1975, then moved to the **Sam S. Shubert Theatre** on 25 July 1975, where it remained for the next 15 years. Its depiction of an audition for Broadway chorus dancers, or "gypsies," was based on 30 hours of taped conversations with 24 dancers, several of whom were also cast in the production. The plot was built on the premise that Zach, a director holding an audition for a Broadway musical, asks the dancers to tell about their own lives so that he can determine if they are suitable for small speaking roles as well as members of the chorus. Director-

choreographer **Michael Bennett** used dance as the major mode of expression in the show, moving the performers from spoken dialogue into dance sequences molded to the characters' anxieties and hopes as they underwent the painful process of self-revelation. The central character of Cassie, a former gypsy trying to return to the chorus after having moved up to featured roles and some television and film work, was played by Donna McKechnie. Closing in April 1990, the show played 6,137 performances and, as of February 1990, had a profit of $50 million. MK

See: K. Mandelbaum, *A Chorus Line and the Musicals of Michael Bennett,* New York, 1989; R. Viagas, B. Lee, and T. Walsh, *The Creation of "A Chorus Line,"* New York, 1990.

Christiansen, Richard (Dean) (1931–) Widely considered to be the most powerful critic in the modern period of Chicago theatre, Christiansen has been a consistent supporter of the Chicago style of naturalistic acting since he began covering amateur theatre for the Chicago *Daily News* in 1963. Noted for his accuracy, fairness, and reportorial style, he was the first major critic to see value in the writing of **David Mamet.** When the *Daily News* folded in 1978, Christiansen moved to the *Tribune,* where he shared reviewing duties with **Linda Winer** until her departure in 1980. Since 1983 he has been both reviewer and entertainment editor at the *Tribune.* SF

Cincinnati Playhouse in the Park Founded in 1960 in a 230-seat Victorian fieldstone structure, once a shelter house, in Eden Park, the Playhouse now serves a three-state region of the Ohio River Valley. The thrust-stage, 632-seat Marx Theatre was built in 1968, and the Vontz Theatre Center – which encompassed theatres, new offices, and an atrium bar and restaurant – was completed in 1980. The Playhouse casts free-lance actors and actresses and employs a resident director and designers in about a dozen professional productions annually. Its broad-spectrum repertory attracts exceptionally strong support from season subscribers. In 1992, Edward Stern became its producing artistic director. WD

Circle in the Square New York's oldest company, founded in 1951 by **José Quintero, Theodore Mann,** Emilie Stevens, and Jason Wingreen. Starting as the Loft Players in 1949 (originally the Villetta Studio Players in Woodstock, NY) and producing in the round (originally on Sheridan Square, whence its name), the company is "artistically committed to the art of acting." Never avant-garde, the company "hold[s] the classics up to our sunshine in the hope of making them glow." Its 1952 revival of *Summer and Smoke* launched Circle's success, Quintero's and **Geraldine Page**'s careers, and **Off-Broadway**'s heyday. In 1961, Circle opened its school, briefly associated with New York University. In 1969–70, Circle produced six shows at Washington's **Ford's Theatre,** and in 1972, maintaining its Greenwich Village house, occupied its Broadway theatre. In 1989, Artistic Director Mann went to Moscow to direct

Night of the Iguana at the Maly Theatre with a Soviet cast.

Under Mann, Circle produced many **O'Neill** works directed by Quintero, contemporary plays, and classics with such stars as **George C. Scott,** Cicely Tyson, **Jason Robards, Jr., James Earl Jones,** Joanne Woodward, **Philip Bosco,** Vanessa Redgrave, and **Dustin Hoffman.** Its productions include Capote's *The Grass Harp* (1953), *The Iceman Cometh* with Robards (1956), Dylan Thomas's *Under Milk Wood* (1961), **Fugard**'s *Boesman and Lena* (1970), *Medea* with Irene Papas (1973), a contemporary adaptation of Molière's *The Cheats of Scapino* (*Scapino!*) with Jim Dale (1974), *The Glass Menagerie* (1975), Ibsen's *The Lady from the Sea* with Redgrave (1976), *Macbeth* directed by Nicol Williamson (1982), *Heartbreak House* with **Rex Harrison** (1983), *Design for Living* directed by Scott (1984), *Arms and the Man* with **Kevin Kline** and **Raul Julia** (1986), Howe's *Coastal Disturbances* (1987), *Sweeney Todd* (1989), and *The Miser* with Bosco (1990). Many later ran on Broadway or television. Circle in the Square's numerous awards include Tonys, Obies, and Drama Desk Awards.

REK

Circle Repertory Company Off-Broadway

theatre, founded in 1969 by **Marshall W. Mason,** Robert Thirkield, Tanya Berezin, and **Lanford Wilson,** dedicated to rediscovering "lyric realism as the native voice of the American theatre." Formed "for the needs of the artists, based on the relation between the actors and the playwright," the group, at Café **La MaMa** and **Caffe Cino** since 1965, founded the American Theatre Project in 1968. Devoted to new American writers, CRC operates a Playwrights' Workshop, Projects-in-Progress Series, and Script Evaluation Service, and launched the Young Playwrights Festival (now at the **New York Shakespeare Festival**). CRC's informal alliance of over 200 artists is committed "to making the action of the play become the experience of the audience." In 1987, founding Artistic Director Mason turned the company over to Berezin.

Many of Wilson's plays moved to Broadway (*The Hot l Baltimore* [1972], *Talley's Folly* [1979], *5th of July* [1977], *Angels Fall* [1983], *Burn This* [1987]); other productions include *When You Comin' Back, Red Ryder?* (1973), *Battle of Angels* (1974), **Jules Feiffer**'s *Knock Knock* (1976), *Gemini* (1977), Marty Martin's *Gertrude Stein, Gertrude Stein, Gertrude Stein* (1979), *Buried Child* (1979), *Fool for Love* (1983), *As Is* (1985), and *Prelude to a Kiss* (1990). In 1985, CRC became the first American company to tour Japan, presenting *Who's Afraid of Virginia Woolf?* and *Fool for Love*. Its many awards include Wilson's Obie for *The Mound Builders* (1975) and a Pulitzer Prize for *Talley's Folly* (1980). CRC received the 1991 Lucille Lortel Award for "Outstanding Body of Work." REK

See: M. Ryzuk, *The Circle Repertory Company: The First Fifteen Years,* Ames, IA, 1989.

Circus in America

Since its founding in the 18th century by the Englishman Philip Astley, the modern circus has been one of the most internationally of entertainments. Its performers have freely

The most famous U.S. one-ring circus, The Big Apple Circus. Courtesy: The Big Apple Circus.

crossed national boundaries, its programs have rarely been tainted with political or social messages, its appeal (music excepted) has traditionally been to the eye rather than dependent on the intricacies of language. In America itself colonialists occasionally had the opportunity to view performances by itinerant trick equestrians, exotic animals taken around the country either singly or in small groups, and exhibitions by individual acrobats and ropedancers. As early as 1785 the American rider Thomas Pool was employing a clown to amuse spectators between his startling feats of horsemanship; consequently, one can argue for his being the first circus manager in America. Pool's career was relatively brief, however, and this distinction is generally accorded the equestrian John Bill Ricketts, who, in the spring of 1793, assisted by several acrobats and a clown, opened what he was pleased to call a "Circus" in **Philadelphia.**

Ricketts later erected circus buildings in New York and other cities while touring with this troupe in the U.S. and eastern Canada. The equestrian, dancer, and clown **John Durang** worked for him and later set down his recollections of their travels. "I rode the foxhunter," he writes of his manifold duties with the show, "leaping over the bar with the mounting and dismounting while in full speed, taking a flying leap on horsback [*sic*] through a paper sun, in character of a drunken man on horsback [*sic*], tied in a sack standing on two horses while I changed to woman's clothes; rode in full speed standing on two horses, Mr. Ricketts at the same time standing on my shoulders, with master Hutchins at the same time standing in the attitude of Mercury on Mr. Ricketts' shoulders forming a pyramid. I performed the drunken soldier on horsback [*sic*], still vaulted, I dancet [*sic*] on the stage, I was the Harlequin in the pantomimes, occasionally [*sic*] I sung a comic song. I tumbled on the slack rope and performed on the slack wire. I introduced mechanical exhibitions in machinery and transparencies. I produced exhibitions of fireworks. In short, I was performer, machinist, painter, designer, music compiler, the bill maker, and treasurer!" As is obvious from Durang's account, early circuses, as in Europe, offered stage exhibitions in addition to performances in the ring.

By the time Ricketts left for the West Indies in 1800, several other managers, often of foreign origin, were touring America with small companies of their own. During the first third of the new century a number of Americans took to the road with large menageries, some of which began merging with circus companies as early as 1823. The first American circus star to achieve international fame, the lion "tamer" **Isaac A. Van Amburgh,** who performed with his big cats at Drury Lane and elsewhere in Europe, began with one such menagerie and eventually ran a large circus of his own. Another important development around this time was the adopting (from menageries) of easily transportable tents, which freed circuses from the necessity of erecting or renting buildings in each locale they visited and allowed them to give single performances in smaller towns.

By the second half of the century some of these "wagon shows" had grown to considerable proportions; gorgeously carved and gilded wagons, initially imported from England, were introduced in what became the traditional street parade; and a few shows were experimenting with new modes of transportation. Beginning in 1852, for example, the circus of Spalding and Rogers plied the Mississippi and Ohio rivers performing on a huge enclosed barge that seated 3,400 spectators [see **showboats**]. The steamboat that towed this *Floating Palace* possessed an auditorium and stage of its own for minstrel and dramatic performances. By the mid-1850s, too, a few managers were taking advantage of the nation's expanding railway system, although the great era of "railroad shows" did not arrive until the 1870s.

The so-called "Golden Age" of the American circus commenced during the decade following the Civil War, by which time managers were almost exclusively American. Various members of the Howes, Nathans, and Sells families; the Chicago-based manager William W. ("Chilly Billy") Cole; and the Philadelphian **Adam Forepaugh** all figured prominently in the development of the circus during this gaudy period. But the one showman whose circus was destined to survive and to epitomize the American circus to the present day was none other than **P. T. Barnum,** who, in time for the 1871 season, teamed up with the young manager William C. Coup to form "P. T. Barnum's Museum, Menagerie & Circus." A year later, by which time the main tent had added a second ring and could seat up to 12,000 spectators, their huge show took to the rails, crisscrossing the country in leaps of up to 100 miles per night, then giving a spectacular parade the next morning and as many as three performances before moving on to another town in time for the following day.

In 1880 Barnum joined with a new partner, James A. Bailey, to create the great concern that came to be known as "Barnum & Bailey." A third ring was added beginning with the 1881 season, and as platforms for acts requiring firm surfaces were set up between the rings, and all these performance areas were in turn encompassed by a great oval "hippodrome track" on which parades and

races were given, spectators were alternately bewildered and delighted by a multiplicity of action. Although Bailey was responsible for daily operations, his veteran partner was indefatigable in thinking up novel ways to publicize the show, and personally negotiated for the acquisition of its most sensational attraction, the mammoth African elephant "Jumbo." The two men ruthlessly set out to crush or absorb all competition, and Barnum himself sometimes dreamed of establishing a monopoly on circus entertainment in America.

Following Barnum's death in 1891, Bailey became sole owner of the "Greatest Show on Earth" and took it to Europe for a five-year tour commencing in 1897. When the show returned to America, it found itself challenged by a powerful new rival, that of the five **Ringling Brothers,** who had begun their circus careers in 1884 with a small wagon show in the Midwest. After Bailey's death in 1906, the Ringlings purchased his circus and continued running it as an independent show until the end of the 1918 season. They then merged it with their own large establishment to create the famous show that has persisted to the present day, "Ringling Bros. and Barnum & Bailey Circus."

By the 1920s many circuses had become motorized or "truck" shows, and today only Ringling Bros. continues to move by rail. The "Big One," as it is known to fans and performers, remains the largest and best known circus in America, although at times it has barely escaped extinction. In 1944 its big top caught **fire** during a performance in Hartford, CT, killing 168 persons and injuring hundreds of others. Several of the show's executives were sent to prison, and, for a while, faced with suits for heavy damages, there was talk of liquidation. In 1956, amid difficulties with labor unions, John Ringling North – nephew of and flamboyant successor to the original Ringling Bros. – announced the show would never again play under canvas, but henceforth only in modern, enclosed civic and sports arenas. To many traditionalists this sounded like a death knell, but the move proved brilliantly successful. Besides cutting down considerably on personnel and expenses, the show was now independent of weather conditions and able to extend its season indefinitely. Spectators themselves, their view no longer obstructed by tent poles, now enjoyed the performance in unprecedented, air-conditioned comfort.

In 1967 the "Greatest Show on Earth" entered upon its latest phase when it was sold to a group of businessmen headed by the rock-music promoter Irvin Feld. The next year Feld opened a "Clown College" at the show's Florida winter quarters, and in 1969 he expanded the circus to two independent units – the "Red" and the "Blue" – each of which changes its program in alternate years and makes a two-year swing through cities in the U.S. and Canada. The "Big One" has always attracted the world's greatest circus artists, and from 1969 until his retirement in 1990 the undisputed star of the Red Unit was the sensational German animal trainer Gunther Gebel-Williams, whose phenomenal command over tigers, elephants, and horses (with leopards, zebras, and even a giraffe thrown in for good measure) earned him a celebrity usually reserved for rock and movie stars. A number of other three-ring circuses continue to tour under canvas. Of these the principal ones, as of 1991, are Carson and Barnes, Circus Vargas, and **Clyde Beatty**–Cole Bros. Circus.

Circus programs can range from the tawdry to the magnificent, and size alone has never been a guarantee of excellence. Some of the best continue to be found in one-ring shows, and among these, since 1977, New York's Big Apple Circus has undoubtedly been the finest and most elegant. Patterned on the European model, with its colorful, modern tent of Italian manufacture and its musicians perched on a small stage above the ring entrance, this show has consistently engaged superb performers drawn from the world over, including the Mexican trapeze troupe of the Flying Gaonas, the Danish equestrienne Katja Schumann, the French high-wire artist Philippe Petit, and the Big Apple's own truly funny clowns, among them Barry Lubin (known to his enthusiastic public as "Grandma"). While touring mainly in the East during the summer months, each winter finds the Big Apple back in New York City, where it erects its heated tent next to the Metropolitan Opera House in keeping with another European tradition, the Christmas season. A school of circus arts is associated with the show, whose influence on other American circuses has been considerable.

In the 1980s a "new wave" type of circus emerged in America, as exemplified by the Pickle Family Circus of San Francisco and above all by the Montréal-based Cirque du Soleil. Typically, their programs entirely dispense with the use of animals, are given on stages rather than in the traditional ring, and emphasize "theatrical" elements: some "story" or plot line that runs throughout the performance; attempts at themes (not always comprehensible) that are social or nobly ecological; dance, mime, and *commedia dell'arte;* together with original music and carefully coordinated costumes, makeup or masks, lighting, and even set design. The story line incorporates and presumably is illustrated by the circus numbers (contortionism, juggling, aerial acts, etc.), and clowns are often the central "characters" in these minidramas. Extravagant claims of "renewing" or "purifying" the circus are made by some of these shows, ticket prices sometimes approach those of a Broadway musical, and fans of more traditional performances have often expressed their outrage at what they see as an attempt to make over the circus into a kind of musical revue.

Interestingly, many of the founders of these "new" circuses began as street performers, both in America and abroad, and have acknowledged their indebtedness to the Big Apple Circus or the "Cirque à l'Ancienne" of Alexis Gruss in France. The latter, which has revived many elegant equestrian and other acts dating back to the 19th century, has itself been a major influence on the Big Apple Circus, whose director and founder, Paul Binder, once performed as a juggler on the streets of Paris. The schools for circus arts that are often attached to these circuses are also largely inspired by French models. Thus things appear to have come full circle, and in this latest attempt to revitalize the circus in America one sees, again, how truly international the entertainment is. (See also **Felix Adler, Otto Griebling, Lou Jacobs, Emmett Kelly, Frank Oakley.**)   AHS

See: J. Culhane, *The American Circus: An Illustrated History,* New York, 1990; J. and A. Durant, *Pictorial History of the American Circus,* New York, 1957; C. P. Fox and T. Parkinson, *The Circus in America,* Waukesha, WI, 1969; L. G. Hoh and W. H. Rough, *Step Right Up! The Adventure of Circus in America,* Crozet, VA, 1990; S. Thayer, *Annals of the American Circus, 1793–1829,* Manchester, MI, 1976, and *Annals of the American Circus, 1830–1847,* Seattle, WA, 1986.

City, The, by **Clyde Fitch.** Subtitled "A Modern Play of American Life in Three Acts," this emotional and violent drama purports to demonstrate how weaker souls can easily be led astray by the temptations and unethical dealings of the big city. Produced posthumously and with great anticipation on 21 December 1909, it created a sensation when Tully Marshall, as the drug-crazed family parasite, uttered "You're a God damn liar!" – using the phrase "God damn" for the first time on the New York stage. It ran for 190 performances in New York before going on a controversial U.S. tour.   MR

City of Angels Two-act musical comedy, music by **Cy Coleman,** lyrics by David Zippel, book by **Larry Gelbart;** opened 11 December 1989 at the **Virginia Theatre,** New York, and closed 19 January 1991 after 912 performances (including 24 previews). An original American musical in an age dominated by British imports, *City of Angels* treats the interplay of the travails in Hollywood of Stine (Gregg Edelman), a movie scriptwriter, and the characters he is creating for the screen, all of them reflections of people in his own life and played by the same actors, with the exception of his own alter-ego, the detective Stone (James Naughton). Gelbart's book cleverly intercuts scenes from the film being written (all in black and white) with scenes from the writer's experience (in color). Coleman's score effectively evokes 1940s popular music, often through the agency of a radio crooner and his back-up group. The show won numerous "best musical" awards, including the Tony.   JD

Ciulei, Liviu (1923–) Romanian-born director, scene designer, actor, filmmaker (with a background in architecture), and seminal figure of the Romanian stage. In the late 1970s he took assignments as guest director in Germany, Canada, Australia, and, finally, the U.S. During 1980–6 he was artistic director at the **Guthrie Theater,** where his eclectic, idiosyncratic, and cerebral productions have included *The Tempest, Eve of Retirement, Peer Gynt, The Threepenny Opera, A Midsummer Night's Dream,* and a stunning *The Bacchae* (1987). Other U.S. credits include *Spring Awakening* and *Hamlet* (1986) at the **New York Shakespeare Festival** (**Public Theater**); *Leonce and Lena* (1977 debut), *Emigrés, Hamlet, Don Juan, The Lower Depths,* and Viktor Slavkin's *Cerceau* (1990) at **Arena Stage;** and *Inspector General* at **Circle in the Square.** In recent years he has directed opera throughout the world, and he is currently on NYU's graduate acting faculty. BM

Civic Repertory Theatre Opened in 1926 by **Eva Le Gallienne** at the **14th Street Theatre** with Benavente's *Saturday Night;* management's progressive ideas for a noncommercial repertory theatre specializing in modern classics and charging low admission was inspired by European subsidized theatres and influenced such American theatres as the **Theatre Guild** and the **Group Theatre.** CRT boasted an all-female professional staff, promoting, for example, the design talents of **Aline Bernstein** and **Irene Sharaff.** Other than modern classics, CRT staged three **Chekhov**s, five **Ibsen**s, and two Rostands; premiered three American plays; and introduced Giraudoux, Goldoni, and **Susan Glaspell**'s *Alison's House* to New York – for a largely neighborhood audience. Throughout 10 seasons and a 37-play repertory, CRT was beset by financial difficulties, forcing Le Gallienne to bend her repertory rule and in 1933 to move her adaptation of *Alice in Wonderland* uptown for a long run. Nevertheless CRT disbanded in 1935, the result of these fiscal problems. EH

Claire, Ina (née Inez Fagan) (1892?–1985) Actress noted for her insouciant charm and high comedic sense and style, specializing – from her first appearance in a straight play (1917) to her final one (*The Confidential Clerk,* 1954) – in what *Time Magazine* called "highly varnished comedies of bad manners and good breeding in which the characters misbehave in venomous, perfectly timed epigrams." **Harold Clurman** considered her "the most brilliant comedienne of our stage" in vehicles such as **S. N. Behrman**'s *Biography* and *End of Summer.* She also had an active career in pre-WW I **vaudeville,** the *Ziegfeld Follies,* silent films, and later the talkies. DBW

Clapp, Henry Austin (1841–1904) Drama critic. Educated at Harvard, Clapp practiced law in Boston, pursuing drama criticism as an avocation. He was music and drama critic of the *Boston Daily Advertiser* from 1868 to 1902, and of the *Boston Herald* during 1902–4. An authority on **Shakespeare,** Clapp was viewed as an erudite, incorruptible, and fair critic. His *Reminiscences of a Drama Critic* (1902) provides an overview of late 19th-century **Boston** theatrical life. TLM

Clark, Bobby (1888–1960) and **Paul McCullough** (1883–1936) A comedy team that perfected its raucous, physical style in the circus and vaudeville, Clark and McCullough made the transition to musical theatre in a London **revue,** *Chuckles of 1922.* Their first Broadway show was *The Music Box* Revue 1922–23, and after other revue appearances they brought their acrobatic antics to a book musical, *Strike Up the Band* (1930). Following McCullough's suicide in 1936, Bobby Clark continued alone, appearing in revues such as *The Ziegfeld Follies* of 1936, musical comedies such as *Mexican Hayride* (1944), revivals of classical comedies such as *Love for Love* (1940), and revivals of operettas such as *Sweethearts* (1947). His last en-

gagement was in the touring company of *Damn Yankees* (1956). The crouching, scampering Clark, with his painted-on eyeglasses, everpresent cigar, and stubby cane, was perfectly matched with the tall, giggling McCullough, the straight man of the act. MK

See: R. L. Taylor, *The Running Pianist,* Garden City, NY, 1950.

Clark, Peggy (1938–) A major figure in the establishment of theatrical lighting design as an independent profession, Clark, born in Baltimore, went to Smith College and Yale (MFA). A costume and scenic designer early in her career, she ultimately concentrated on lighting. In addition to more than 150 productions on Broadway, she has lit for dance (including for choreographer **Agnes de Mille**) and opera. In 1968 she became the first woman to serve as President of the United Scenic Artists, and in 1978 was named a fellow of the U.S. Institute for Theatre Technology. BO

Clarke, John Sleeper (1833–99) Actor and theatre manager who made his professional stage debut in 1851 at Boston's **Howard Athenaeum** as Frank Hardy in *Paul Pry.* A friend of **Edwin Booth** since childhood, Clarke married Booth's sister Asia in 1859. Clarke was a popular, skillful comedian, highly regarded for his portrayal of eccentric characters like Major Wellington De Boots in Joseph S. Coyne's *A Widow Hunt,* Dr. Pangloss and Zekiel Homespun in Colman's *The Heir-at-Law,* and Bob Acres in Sheridan's *The Rivals.* In the 1860s Clarke was associated with Booth in the management of several theatres, including Philadelphia's **Walnut Street Theatre,** the **Boston Theatre,** and the **Winter Garden.** In 1867, Clarke emigrated to England, where he remained for the rest of his life, except for occasional starring tours to America. At various times he successfully managed several English theatres including the Haymarket, the Charing Cross (Toole's), and, for over a decade (1883–99), the Strand. His sons **Creston Clarke** (1865–1910) and **Wilfred Booth Clarke** (1867–1945) also had relatively successful careers in theatre. DJW

Clarke, Martha (1944–) Baltimore-born experimental theatre director and choreographer [see **dance**]. She studied dance as a child and at Juilliard with Louis Horst and choreographers Anthony Tudor and Anna Sokolow, whose company she joined (1965–7). She cofounded Pilobolus (1972–8) and Crowsnest dance companies (1978–). *Nocturne* (1978) and *Portraits* (1979) were early sketches that evolved into large-scale productions, *The Garden of Earthly Delights* (1984, inspired by Hieronymus Bosch's painting), *Vienna Lusthaus* (1986, inspired by Egon Schiele's watercolors of women), and *Endangered Species* (1990, based on Toulouse-Lautrec's circus pastels, the American Civil War, and the Holocaust). Clarke explores the grotesque body, archetypical and psychological preoccupations with forbidden pleasures, and the loss of innocence. Influenced by Martha Graham's modern dance style and 1960s theatre of the body (Grotowski, The **Living Theatre**), her work also shares an affinity with Pina Bausch's Tanztheater and **Robert Wilson**'s Theatre of Images [see **Introduction, §4**].   AF

Classic Stage Company, The see **CSC Repertory, Ltd.**

Claxton, Kate (1850–1924) Actress, sometimes called "the Sarah Bernhardt of America." Born in Somerville, NJ, she first appeared with **Lotta Crabtree** in 1870, then joined the stock companies of **Augustin Daly** and **A. M. Palmer.** Her most successful roles were in *The Two Orphans, Camille,* and *East Lynne.* After touring *The Two Orphans,* she retired in 1911. She was the heroine of a Brooklyn Theatre *fire* in 1876.   SMA

Clayburgh, James (1949–) Designer who joined the **Performance Group** in 1972 after graduating from New York University and designed sets and lights for several of their productions. He was an original member of the **Wooster Group,** which emerged from the Performance Group, and has been their resident designer since its founding in 1980. The Performance Group work was usually environmental whereas that of the Wooster Group is strongly frontal and often designed in collaboration with director **Elizabeth LeCompte.** Typified by simple constructivist components, transformable elements, and unusual spectator–stage spatial relationships, the work contains motifs, patterns, and structures that repeat from one show to the next. Clayburgh has also designed at the **Public Theater,** Second Stage, and elsewhere.   AA

Cleveland Play House East 83–86 Sts. between Euclid and Carnegie Aves., Cleveland [Architects: Philip Small, Charles Rowley, and Francis Draz]. In 1915, Raymond O'Neil, a Cleveland journalist, founded a small amateur theatre group for the production of native plays. Out of it grew the Cleveland Play House, now the oldest producing regional theatre in America. In 1921, Frederic McConnell took over the amateur company and transformed it into a professional organization. Six years later, the company moved into its complex of two theatres, the 500-seat Drury and the 160-seat Brooks, plus offices and workrooms. When McConnell retired in 1958, he was succeeded by K. Elmo Lowe; then, more recently, by Richard Oberlin; and, in 1988, by Josephine Abady. In 1983, the 625-seat Bolton, designed by Philip Johnson, was added to the complex. The theatre maintains its policy of presenting classics, contemporary and new plays, and musicals.   MCH

> See: J. M. Flory, *The Cleveland Play House: How It Began,* Cleveland, 1965.

Clifton (née Miller?), Josephine (1813–47) Actress, popularly styled "The magnificent Josephine" and at one time regarded as rival to **Charlotte Cushman.** She debuted at New York's **Bowery Theatre** in 1831 as Belvidera in *Venice Preserv'd,* one critic comparing her figure to that of Sarah Siddons. That same year she was first seen in Philadelphia, where much of her subsequent career was spent. In 1834 she became the first American actress to star in London, a decade before Cushman crossed the Atlantic. On her return, she created *Bianca Visconti,* written for her by **Nathaniel P. Willis** in 1837. Other roles included Lady Macbeth, Juliet, Mrs. Haller, and Jane Shore. In 1846 she married Robert Place, manager of the **American Theatre** in New Orleans, and died suddenly the next year. A frequent leading lady to **Edwin Forrest,** Clifton, who reputedly had an affair with the actor, figured prominently in his notorious divorce case of 1851.   DBW

Close, Glenn (1947–) Actress who in only a decade established herself as one of the most respected actresses of her generation. Though best known for films such as *The Big Chill, Fatal Attraction,* and *Hamlet,* she is a versatile stage performer as well, noted for her "charged stillness." Her Broadway debut – Angelica in a revival of Congreve's *Love for Love* (1974) – was followed by a series of major roles in regional theatres, **Off-Broadway** appearances (including **Wendy Wasserstein**'s *Uncommon Women and Others* and an Obie Award–winning performance in Simone Benmussa's *The Singular Life of Albert Nobbs* at the **Manhattan Theatre Club**), and various Broadway appearances, including *The Crucifer of Blood* (1978), the musical *Barnum* (1980), and Annie in the American premiere of Stoppard's *The Real Thing* (1984), for which she won the Tony – an honor repeated in the spring of 1992 in **Mike Nichols**'s production of *Death and the Maiden* by Ariel Dorfman.   DBW

Clubs, theatrical By and large a gregarious group, actors in 19th-century America sought to organize themselves into social groups. The first of such clubs was the Actors' Order of Friendship, founded in Philadelphia in 1849. In 1888 a lodge was founded in New York City and almost immediately dominated the organization. Primarily designed to supply relief to indigent members, the organization eventually was replaced by the **Actors' Fund of America.**

The Benevolent and Protective Order of Elks began as a similar charitable organization in New York in 1868. By the turn of this century, however, the organization lost its theatrical nature.

The Lambs Club, primarily social in nature, was founded in 1874 and incorporated in 1877. The Lambs became famous for their Gambols, productions in their private theatre, the receipts from which were donated to charity. This convivial club experienced financial trouble in 1974, but still operates on a modest scale.

Of U.S. theatrical clubs, the most distinguished is the Players at 16 Gramercy Park, NYC. Founded in 1888 by **Edwin Booth,** the club brought together actors and nontheatrical persons; among the charter members were Mark Twain and William Tecumseh Sherman. The clubhouse houses a magnificent collection of theatrical portraits and memorabilia. Booth, who lived in the club for the last five years of his life, donated his personal library to the Players, from which has grown an outstanding American theatre collection. The club for a time gave annual revivals of classic plays, but the practice has been curtailed in recent years. The Players recently voted to accept female members. As of 1992, the club's president is Robert Lansing.

In 1904 theatrical press agents formed the Friars and in 1907 incorporated to promote interaction among agents, managers, and other theatrical men. Like the Players, the Friars recently began to accept women members.

The first actresses' club was the Twelfth Night Club, founded in 1891 in New York to supply aid and social opportunities for actresses. Another organization, the Professional Woman's League, began in 1892 to meet actresses' professional needs.

In 1907 the **Charlotte Cushman** Club offered lodging for actresses in Philadelphia, as it continues to do to this day. A large collection of Cushman papers and memorabilia are housed in the club. SMA

See: B. McArthur, *Actors and American Culture, 1880–1930*, Philadelphia, 1984.

Clurman, Harold (1901–80) Director, critic, author, and teacher who left his mark on the American theatre as founder of the **Group Theatre** (1931–40). In 25 midnight sessions with New York actors and directors he "talked the Group into existence," becoming its inspirational leader and one of its principal directors. He nurtured the talents of **Clifford Odets** and directed five of his plays: *Awake and Sing!* (1935), *Paradise Lost* (1935), *Golden Boy* (1937), *Rocket to the Moon* (1938), and *Night Music* (1940). He also directed **Irwin Shaw**'s *The Gentle People* (1939) and wrote *The Fervent Years* (1945), a history of the Group.

After the Group's demise Clurman continued directing: *The Member of the Wedding* (1950), *The Autumn Garden* (1951), *Bus Stop* (1955), *The Waltz of the Toreadors* (1957), *Incident at Vichy* (1965, in Tokyo), *Long Day's Journey into Night* (1965), and *The Iceman Cometh* (1968).

He was theatre critic for *The New Republic* (1949–52), *The Nation* (1953–80), and the London *Observer* (1955–63). He also assembled three volumes of essays: *Lies Like Truths* (1958), *The Naked Image* (1966), and *The Divine Pastime* (1974), and wrote *On Directing* (1968), *Ibsen* (1977), and *All People Are Famous* (1974), the last in lieu of an autobiography. In addition, he was a professor at Hunter College (1964–80).

Born in New York, he was "reborn in Paris in the 20s" (his words), and became a playreader for the **Theatre Guild** (1929–31). Among his awards, the Donaldson, the **George Jean Nathan,** and four honorary doctorates, he was proudest of La Croix de Chevalier de la Légion d'Honneur. RM

Coates, George (1952–) Philadelphia-born experimental theatre director who studied with directors Antoine Bourseiller (1971–2) and **Gene Frankel** (1972–3), performed **Off-Off Broadway** and with the National Shakespeare Company (1973–4), and worked with Blake Street Hawkeyes and other experimental theatre collectives until he formed his company (1977). Collaborating with scientists and artists, Coates's spectacles include live performers and technology-generated sounds and images. Mixing classical stage traditions with popular culture, he explores the relationship between theatre and science. His work is influenced by 1960s and '70s art and technology collaborations, the symbolist stage, Eisenstein's montage films, Mayakovsky's futurist designs, and Marinetti's mechanized performer. Coates's first production, *2019 Blake* (1977–8), was about nonlinear thinking; *The Architecture of Catastrophic Change* (1990) explored the replacement of body parts; and *Invisible Site* (1991) simulated virtual reality on stage. AF

Cobb, Lee J. (1911–76) Stage, film, and television actor, best remembered for creating the bewildered, dream-chasing Willy Loman in **Arthur Miller**'s *Death of a Salesman.* Born on NYC's Lower East Side, he decided at age 16 to become an actor, ran away from home at 17, and began playing small roles for the **Pasadena Playhouse.** In 1934 he joined the **Group Theatre.** After serving in WW II he returned to Hollywood, but went back to Broadway for *Salesman.* In 1969 he starred in a Broadway production of *King Lear.* SMA

Coburn, Charles Douville (1877–1961) Actor and manager, remembered for his films, who with his wife, Ivah Wills, founded the Coburn Shakespearean Players (1906), touring major Shakespearean plays and other classics. Additional stage appearances included *The Better 'Ole* (1918), *The Yellow Jacket* (1921), *So This Is London* (1922), *The Farmer's Wife* (1924), *Trelawny of the Wells* (1925, all-star revival), *Diplomacy* (1928), and *Three Wise Fools* (1936). The Coburns helped to found the Mohawk Drama Festival (1934) at Union College, Schenectady, NY, performing there in the summers. He retired from the stage in 1937 on his wife's death, returning to play Falstaff in *The Merry Wives of Windsor* for the **Theatre Guild** in 1946, his final appearance on the Broadway stage. DBW

See: B. P. Freeman, Jr., "The Stage Career of Charles Douville Coburn," PhD diss., Tulane U, 1970.

Cocoanuts, The A musical farce by **George S. Kaufman** and (uncredited) **Morrie Ryskind,** music and lyrics by **Irving Berlin;** opened on Broadway 8 December 1925 and ran 218 performances. In this first of Kaufman's two stage vehicles for the **Marx Bros.,** Chico and Harpo visit Florida, hoping to make a killing in the real estate boom, and stay in a hotel run by Groucho, who is speculating in a nearby land development. A society matron (Margaret Dumont) presses her daughter to marry a man who is an unscrupulous fortune hunter; the clowns foil both the matron and the evil suitor, and the lovers happily plan to marry. Groucho and Chico inveigle an exasperated detective into a mock minstrel show, which evolves into a vaudeville routine. Kaufman's script set the pattern for much of the Marx Bros.' subsequent work: a combination of conventional characters (matron, ingenue, juvenile, detective, and villains); an intrigue that threatens a formulaic romance; and a loose situation that gives the clowns the opportunity to wreak mayhem. Paramount released the film version, with Ryskind's screenplay, in 1929.   JDM

Coconut Grove Playhouse The largest regional theatre in Florida opened in 1956 in a lavish old movie palace of the 1920s. Its first production was the American professional premiere of Beckett's *Waiting for Godot.* Over the years the Playhouse has hosted leading writers and directors such as **Tennessee Williams, Edward Albee, Robert Lewis,** and **George Abbott.** The company is committed both to producing plays and musicals of historical significance and to encouraging new works that speak to the multiethnic community it serves. Educational programs such as "Artists of Tomorrow" and the In-School Touring program make theatre more accessible to the people of Miami and southern Florida.   LAB

Cody, William Frederick ("Buffalo Bill") (1846–1917), an Iowa-born western scout who parlayed his notoriety into success as actor and showman. "Buffalo Bill" Cody personified the excitement of the American frontier in the second half of

William "Buffalo Bill" Cody during his career as melodrama actor in the late 1870s. Photo: Gurney & Son, N.Y. Courtesy: Laurence Senelick.

the 19th century. Publicity gilded his accomplishments, but the stories had some factual basis. His nickname came from a job supplying buffalo meat for railroad workers. Cody gained attention after the Civil War as scout for Generals George Custer and Philip Sheridan. Ned Buntline (E. Z. C. Judson) glamorized his exploits in a serial in December 1869, and in November 1872 John B. Studley enacted him in a play in New York. The immense popularity of plays about Buffalo Bill persuaded Cody to take the stage himself in Buntline's *The Scouts of the Prairie,* 18 December 1872, in Chicago. Audiences tolerated the weak play and Cody's amateurish acting to glimpse the hero with the beard, mustache, and flowing hair. For the next 10 years Cody cultivated a striking stage presence as he played himself in action-filled melodramas.

Between seasons Cody scouted for the Army and arranged hunting parties and entertainments for influential businessmen and European aristocrats. In 1883 he and sharpshooter William F. Carver presented an outdoor **Wild West exhibition.** Problems undermined the partnership, and **Nate Salsbury** soon replaced Carver. The Wild West enjoyed phenomenal popularity in America and Europe, but financial setbacks rendered Cody a victim of his success. For 34 years, right up to his death, Buffalo Bill rode out to shoot glass balls and entertain audiences, playing successive farewell tours to pay his bills. Although a 20th-century perspective has altered the perception of Cody's border exploits, his stature as the man who brought the frontier to life for generations of Americans is undeniable.   RAH

> See: D. Russell, *The Lives and Legends of Buffalo Bill,* Norman, OK, 1960; V. Weybright and H. B. Sell, *Buffalo Bill and the Wild West,* London, 1956; N. S. Yost, *Buffalo Bill: His Family, Friends, Fame, Failures, and Fortunes,* Chicago, 1979.

Coe, Richard Livingston (1916–) Drama critic. Born in New York and educated at George Washington University, Coe served as assistant drama and film critic for the *Washington Post* during 1938–42. After military service in the Middle East, he returned to the *Post* in 1946 as its principal critic, a position he held until his semiretirement in 1979. Coe has been regarded as one of the most perceptive, impartial, and supportive critics of the American stage. Joan Fontaine described him (1980) as "the great rarity, a critic who loves actors and loves directors and loves playwrights and even, by God, loves producers." He was named Critic of the Year in 1963 by the Directors' Guild of America.   TLM

Coghlan, Charles (1842–99) British-born actor who, after several successes in London, was brought to New York in 1876 by **Augustin Daly.** At the **Fifth Avenue Theatre** he became a favorite in leading roles such as Alfred Evelyn in Bulwer-Lytton's *Money* and Orlando to **Fanny Davenport**'s Rosalind. Subsequent seasons found him at the **Union Square Theatre, Wallack's,** and in England again. In 1897 he created the part of Alex opposite **Mrs. Fiske**'s Tess. He joined his sister, **Rose,** on several of her tours; together they were outstanding in Sheridan's comedies. Coghlan died in Galveston, TX, on tour in his own play, *The Royal Box.*   DBW

Coghlan, Rose (1850/3?–1932) British-born actress whose debut as a child was as one of the witches in a Scottish production of *Macbeth.* Her first New York appearance was in 1872 at **Wallack's,** where she would reign as leading lady during the 1880s. Her Lady Teazle and Rosalind were declared "unsurpassed" on the American stage. During the 1890s and 1900s she appeared principally in London; after a 1907 U.S. tour in **Shaw's** *Mrs. Warren's Profession,* she divided her time between New York and London. At her retirement in 1921 she had completed a stage career of more than 52 years.   DBW

Cohan, George Michael (né Keohane) (1878–1942) Performer, playwright, director, and producer who was born in Providence, RI, on 3 July while his parents were touring in vaudeville. He first appeared on stage as a child with his family's vaudeville team, the "Four Cohans," and by 15 was writing material for their act. His New York debut came in 1901 with his first full-length play, *The Governor's Son.* In 1904 he formed a producing partnership with **Sam H. Harris,** which lasted until 1920. In 1911 he opened his **George M. Cohan Theatre.** Outstanding among the 50-odd plays and musicals credited to him are *Little Johnny Jones* (1904) – featuring the song that most identifies Cohan ("Yankee Doodle Dandy") – *Forty-five Minutes from Broadway* (1905), *The Talk of New York* (1907), *Get-Rich-Quick Wallingford* (1911), **Seven Keys to Baldpate** (1913), *The Tavern* (1921), and *The Song and Dance Man* (1923). His most famous song, "Over There" (1917), won him a Congressional medal. His most notable performances in plays other than his own were as the father in **O'Neill's** *Ah, Wilderness!* (1933) and as the President in **Kaufman** and **Hart's** *I'd Rather Be Right* (1937).

Although Cohan was always the archetype for the glories of turn-of-the-century show business and the representation of a simplistic patriotism to his audience, he was also a complex and lonely man, rarely popular with critics and something of an outcast to his fellow performers when in 1919 he refused to support the establishment of an actors' **union.** His life story was filmed by Warner Bros. in 1942 (*Yankee Doodle Dandy*); a statue of Cohan was erected in 1959 in Duffy Square, NYC; and a musical based on his career, *George M!,* was produced on Broadway in 1968.   DBW

> See: G. Cohan, *Twenty Years on Broadway and the Years It Took to Get There,* New York, 1924; J. McCabe, *George M. Cohan: The Man Who Owned Broadway,* Garden City, NY, 1973; W. Morehouse, *George M. Cohan: Prince of the American Theatre,* Philadelphia, 1943.

Cohen, Alexander H. (1920–   ) Producer. Born in New York, educated at NYU and Columbia University, Cohen began producing on Broadway in 1941 with *Ghost for Sale* and *Angel Street.* In 1950 his casting of *King Lear* with blacklisted actors established him as a producer of meritorious if not always commercially successful works. In 1959 he began a series called "Nine O'Clock Theatre" and presented *An Evening with Mike Nichols and Elaine May* (1960), *Beyond the Fringe* (1962), and a revival of John Gielgud in *The Ages of Man* (1963). He has presented foreign productions in New York, including the RSC's *The Homecoming* (1967), which won a Tony; David Storey's *Home,* starring Gielgud and Richardson (1970); Ben Kingsley as Edmund Kean (1983); Peter Brook's *La Tragédie de Carmen* (1983); and Dario Fo's *Accidental Death of an Anarchist* (1985). Other productions include **Anna Christie** (1977), **I Remember Mama** (1979), *A Day in Hollywood/A Night in the Ukraine* (1980), and *Brightlights* (1987). Cohen has produced in London and for television, including the Emmy Awards (1978, '85, '86) and the **Antoinette Perry** (Tony) Awards (1967–86). Married to producer **Hildy Parks,** Cohen is a Trustee of the **Actors' Fund of America.**   TLM

Cole, Bob (1869–1912) and **J. Rosamond Johnson** (1873–1954) Lyricist and composer. Pioneers in bringing black musicals to the New York stage [see **musical theatre**], Cole and Johnson were prolific songwriters, librettists, and performers. Cole, in conjunction with Billy Johnson, had written and starred in *A Trip to Coontown* (1898), the first musical entirely created and performed by African Americans. Cole teamed with the classically trained composer J. Rosamond Johnson in 1900. In an era when it was a common practice for songs by several composers to be interpolated into a single musical, Cole and Johnson were in constant demand, providing songs for such shows as *The Belle of Bridgeport* (1900), *Mother Goose* (1903), and *Humpty Dumpty* (1904). Their biggest hit, "Under the Bamboo Tree," was interpolated into *Sally in Our Alley* (1902). Cole and Johnson wrote and appeared in two musicals, *The Shoo Fly Regiment* (1907) and *Mr. Lode of Koal* (1909), but critics of the time were unwilling to accept black performers in musicals that had plots and sympathetic characters. After Cole's death, Johnson continued to write songs and sketches for musicals. Late in his career he appeared in the musicals **Porgy and Bess** (1935) and *Cabin in the Sky* (1940).   MK

Cole, Jack (1914–74) Choreographer and dancer who received his training in modern dance in the Humphrey–Weidman school and as a member of the Denishawn Company, after which he and his own company of dancers appeared in nightclubs. He danced in *Thumbs Up* (1934) and *Keep 'Em Laughing* (1942), and in 1943 was given his first choreographic assignment for *Something for the Boys.* Among the many other shows that he choreographed were *Alive and Kicking* (1950), in which he also appeared; **Kismet** (1953); *Jamaica* (1957); and **Man of La Mancha** (1965). Cole served as both director and choreographer for the short-lived *Donnybrook!* (1961). A student of the Chinese dancer Mei Lanfang, Cole frequently used Oriental movements and gestures in his choreography. He is most noted for creating "jazz dancing," a form characterized by small groupings and angular movements. It became the dominant choreographic style of the 1950s and '60s [see **dance**].   MK

See: G. Loney, *Unsung Genius: The Passion of Dancer-Choreographer Jack Cole,* New York, 1984.

Coleman, Cy (1929–) Composer. A child prodigy, he attended the New York College of Music before playing in nightclubs with a jazz trio. With lyricist Carolyn Leigh he contributed songs to the **revue** *John Murray Anderson's Almanac* (1953), and wrote the scores for the musicals *Wildcat* (1960) and *Little Me* (1962). He then teamed with **Dorothy Fields** for the score of *Sweet Charity* (1966). Among his more successful scores with other lyricists were those for *I Love My Wife* (1977), *On the Twentieth Century* (1978), *Barnum* (1980), *City of Angels* (1989), and *The Will Rogers Follies* (1991). Coleman's early interest in modern jazz influenced the upbeat, rhythmic style of his compositions for the musical stage.   MK

Collective theatre groups During America's burgeoning theatre movement throughout the 1960s, various performance ensembles formed to create an alternative to the prevalent commercial methods of producing. These groups produced such a wide spectrum of work **Off-Off Broadway** that, aesthetically speaking, it is difficult to generalize about the nature of their productions; what they have in common, however, is an organizational structure – or sometimes, simply an organizational point of view – that values each participant in a production as a creative collaborator. Collectives tended – sometimes explicitly, sometimes implicitly – to reject both the commercial aims of Broadway and **Off-Broadway,** as well as their hierarchical and increasingly bureaucratic organization.

Actors especially gravitated to collectives, disenchanted by what they considered the exploitation of their talents in the service of commercial products in the mainstream theatre. Indeed, many collectives, among them the **Open Theatre** and the Talking Band, developed plays out of actors' improvisational exercises.

In many cases "collective" is a misnomer, since some groups have distinct directors whose own style stamps the group's work and who make the final artistic decisions. This is true, for instance, of some of the theatres that emphasized formal experimentation: the **Performance Group,** Manhattan Project (see **Andre Gregory**), **Mabou Mines,** and the **Wooster Group.** Nevertheless, these ensembles, too, involved actors and other company members in a collaborative process of developing plays, not bound by the short rehearsal periods of Broadway.

Perhaps the prototype of the American collective was the **Living Theatre,** founded in 1948 by Julian Beck and Judith Malina. In many cases that followed, the plan to work collectively reflected overt political aims, as in the **Bread and Puppet Theatre,** started by puppeteer Peter Schumann in the early 1960s; the **San Francisco Mime Troupe** founded in 1959 by R. G. Davis, which produced open-air political *commedia*-like plays; **El Teatro Campesino,** a group of Chicano farm workers, founded by **Luis Valdéz** in response to the 1965

California grape strike; and, an outgrowth of the civil rights movement in the American South, the New Orleans–based **Free Southern Theatre.**

According to the same principle, in the 1970s the collective became the principal organizational approach for feminist theatres, among them Minneapolis's **At the Foot of the Mountain** and New York's **Spiderwoman Theatre,** Women's Experimental Theatre, and **Split Britches.** The collective ideal remains a potent precedent for theatres being formed to this day. (See also **alternative theatre.**)   AS

See: T. Shank, *American Alternative Theater,* New York, 1982.

Collins, Pat (1932–) Lighting designer. Though closely associated with the **Hartford Stage,** Collins has worked at many regional theatres and designed over 100 productions for the Washington, Boston, Houston, Netherlands, and English National Opera companies. She has designed several dozen Broadway and **Off-Broadway** shows, including *The **Heidi Chronicles,** Ain't Misbehavin',* and *I'm Not Rappaport* (1985), for which she won a Tony.   AA

Colored Museum, The Using the musical **revue** form and a group of five actors in multiple roles, author **George C. Wolfe** presents a collection of animated museum exhibits that satirize stereotypes and icons from black history and culture. Stingingly lampooned topics range from the harrowing slaveship experience to the prizewinning play, *A **Raisin in the Sun,*** to the show-stopping entertainer **Josephine Baker.** Directed by **Lee Richardson,** the play premiered in 1986 at **Crossroads Theatre** Company in New Brunswick, NJ, moving to **Joseph Papp**'s **Public Theater** and then to the Royal Court Theatre in London. It received the Dramatists Guild Award for 1986.   EGH

Comden, Betty (1915–) and **Adolph Green** (1915–) Librettists, lyricists, and performers. After writing and appearing in a satirical nightclub act, Comden and Green made their Broadway debuts as librettists, lyricists, and featured performers in ***On the Town*** (1944). Their wry wit appeared to best advantage in the librettos and/or lyrics they created for shows with a satirical tinge, such as *Wonderful Town* (1953), *Bells Are Ringing* (1956), and *Say Darling* (1958). When their fast-paced, wise-cracking style of musical comedy declined in popularity in the 1960s, Comden and Green's contributions to the Broadway stage became less frequent. As a taste for satirical books and lyrics returned in the late 1970s and '80s, the partners were again successful with their work for *On the Twentieth Century* (1978) and *Singin' in the Rain* (1985). They began the 1990s with Tony Award–winning lyrics for *The **Will Rogers Follies,*** music by **Cy Coleman.** Comden and Green also wrote the screenplays for several popular musical films of the 1950s. In 1991 they were honored at the **John F. Kennedy Center.**   MK

Come Back, Little Sheba by **William Inge.** Directed for the **Theatre Guild** by **Daniel Mann,**

Inge's first Broadway production opened to mixed reviews on 15 February 1950. *Sheba* featured bravura Tony Award–winning performances by **Shirley Booth** and Sidney Blackmer, and ran for 190 performances after cast and playwright kept it open by taking pay and royalty reductions. Two years later, Booth received an Academy Award for her performance in the popular film version adapted for the screen by Ketti Frings.

Adrift in a sterile marriage, the passions of Doc and Lola boil under the surface as the romance of their young boarder is played out on their front porch. Reflecting contemporaneous trends, the two-act play's realistic surface is imbued with Freudian psychology and symbolism. The titular Sheba was a little puppy, a symbol of happier and livelier times, whose loss is constantly mourned by Lola.
MR

Community theatre/Little Theatre movement
Thespian societies and parlor theatricals were common in America long before the advent of the Little Theatres. In 1901 Jane Addams and Mrs. Laura Dainty Pelham organized the **Hull-House** Players in **Chicago** because they believed that good plays performed by amateurs could have "a salutary influence on the community." The big movement came a decade later with The Players (1909) in Providence, RI, Thomas H. Dickinson's Wisconsin Dramatic Society in Madison and Milwaukee (1911), Mrs. Lyman Gale's Boston Toy Theatre (1912), Alfred Arvold's Little Country Theatre in Fargo, ND (1912), and Maurice Browne's Chicago Little Theatre (1912). The sudden and simultaneous flowering of Little Theatres can be attributed to the following: the visit of Lady Gregory's Irish Players (1911); **Percy MacKaye**'s call for "constructive leisure" in his book **The Civic Theatre** (1912); the founding of The **Drama League** (1909); **George P. Baker**'s "Workshop 47" at Harvard (1912); the numerous articles about the European art theatres; dissatisfaction with the offerings of the commercial theatre; and a passionate belief, if sometimes ill-founded, that the arts and crafts of the theatre could be grasped by enthusiastic and ambitious amateurs eager for "self-expression."

The pioneers were quickly joined by Samuel Eliot's Little Theatre in Indianapolis (1915), **Sam Hume**'s Arts and Crafts Theatre in Detroit (1916), Frederick McConnell's **Cleveland Play House** (1916), Gilmore Brown's **Pasadena Playhouse** (1918), and Oliver Hinsdell's Dallas Little Theatre (1920). By 1920 there were more than 50 groups scattered across the country (e.g., in Cincinnati, Duluth, Galesburg, Rochester, Baltimore, and Ypsilanti) who found further support for their endeavors from Gordon Craig's *Toward a New Theatre* (1913); Hume's exhibition of the New Stagecraft (1914); New York's **Provincetown Players** (1914) and **Washington Square Players** (1915); *Theatre Arts Magazine* (1916, later a monthly); and from **Constance D'Arcy Mackay**'s *The Little Theatre in the United States* (1917).

By WW II, the number of groups had grown to more than 100. They performed in improvised quarters (family mansions, livery stables, churches,

community centers) on temporary platforms framed by proscenium openings of 15 ft or less and with accommodation for fewer than a hundred spectators, most of whom were season subscribers. They specialized in bills of one-act plays, which required minimal scenery and few rehearsals and offered less demanding roles to more members. The more ambitious attempted the plays of **Shaw, Ibsen,** and Strindberg, and at one time or another (in the 1920s) most took a turn at laughing at themselves with **George Kelly**'s *The Torchbearers*. They also sponsored lectures, play readings, and classes in theatre arts and crafts.

Community theatres (now numbering more than 5,000) have become an integral part of the cultural life of their communities, and many have built their own theatre complexes. A 1984 survey by the American Community Theatre Association found nearly 100 that have been in continuous operation for 50 years or more, including The Footlight Club of Jamaica, MA (1877); the Players of Providence, RI (1909); Indianapolis Civic Theatre (1915); Le **Petit Théâtre du Vieux Carré** in New Orleans (1919); Theatre Memphis (1920); and the Omaha Community Playhouse (1925). Some have been transformed into regional professional theatres (e.g., Cleveland, Houston, Washington, Dallas), and even those that have maintained their amateur (or semi-amateur) status can hardly be called "Little"; they operate on budgets approaching a million dollars and present full seasons of major plays, both old and new.

Numerous attempts to organize such theatres into an association include a Little Theatre Conference at the Pasadena Playhouse (1924), the National Theatre Conference (1920s), and the American Educational Theatre Association (AETA, starting in 1936). In 1958 the National Association of Community Theatres joined members of AETA to form ACTA as a division of the American Theatre Association (formerly AETA). The demise of ATA resulted in a new group, The American Association of Community Theatres (1986), which meets annually and sponsors a play festival (ACT-FEST) every other year.   RM

See: S. Cheney, *The Art Theatre*, New York, 1917; A. L. Crowley, *The Neighborhood Playhouse*, New York, 1959; N. Houghton, *Advance from Broadway: 19,000 Miles of American Theatre*, New York, 1941; A. McCleery and C. Glick, *Curtains Going Up*, Chicago, 1939; K. Macgowan, *Footlights Across America*, New York, 1929; P. MacKaye, *The Civic Theatre*, New York, 1912.

Company Two-act musical comedy, music and lyrics by **Stephen Sondheim**, book by George Furth; opened 26 April 1970 at the **Alvin Theatre**, New York, running 705 performances. The first of the innovative series of collaborations between Sondheim and director-producer **Harold Prince** in the 1970s, *Company* is a "concept" musical dealing with the subject of romantic relationships in a contemporary urban setting. Various couples and single women are tied together by their relationship to Robert (Dean Jones; replaced quickly by Larry Kert, the only replacement ever nominated for a Tony), an unmarried man entering middle age.

Rather than advancing the plot, the songs are used (in Sondheim's words) "in a Brechtian way, as comment and counterpoint." Vignettes of Robert and the various characters are used to illustrate various aspects of relationships, and the ending of the show is intentionally vague. The hard-edged urban environment is reflected in Sondheim's relentless music and visually represented by **Boris Aronson**'s metallic, elevator-dominated set. A notable departure from traditional musical-comedy form, *Company* won the Drama Critics' Circle and Tony awards for best musical.   JD

Comstock, F. Ray (1880–1949) Broadway producer renowned for his innovative productions. He managed the **Princess Theatre** when it housed **Holbrook Blinn**'s experimental drama company (1913–15) and when it was home to a series of pace-setting musical comedies (1915–18) by **Jerome Kern, P. G. Wodehouse,** and **Guy Bolton.** With **Morris Gest** he produced Russian variety artist Nikita F. Balieff and members of a semi-independent branch of the **Moscow Art Theatre** called "The Bat" in the ground-breaking cabaret, *Chauve-Souris;* the 1922–3 MAT tour; and **Max Reinhardt**'s *The Miracle* (1924), a prototype of "environmental" theatre.   WD

Conduct of Life, The Spare play by **Maria Irene Fornés** that addresses intersections of power and violence at the sites of gender and the state in 19 enigmatic scenes. First performed at **Theatre for the New City** on 21 February 1985, with Fornés directing, the play has since received attention from feminist and **Hispanic-American** critics and from **alternative theatre** producers. Set in an unnamed Latin American country, *Conduct* explores a domestic situation controlled by an army lieutenant who exercises his political and sexual frustrations on his wife and his very young, unwillingly abducted mistress. Its complex description of victimization and resistance and its pessimism about changing power structures has been both praised and abhorred by contemporary critics.   JDo

Congdon, Constance (1944–) Playwright whose *Tales of the Lost Formicans* premiered at River Arts (1988) before playing **Off-Broadway** (1990). This wry examination of suburban life as seen by aliens won the Oppenheimer Award (1990) and has been performed worldwide. Her other plays include *Native American* (Portland 1983, London 1988), *No Mercy* (cowinner Great American Play Contest, 1985), *The Gilded Age* (Hartford, 1986), a libretto for *The Yellow Wallpaper* (1989), *Casanova* (New York, 1991), and several children's plays.   TH-S

Conkle, E[llsworth] P[routy] (1899–) Playwright, theatre educator, and student of **George Pierce Baker** at Yale (1926–8) who had a half-dozen productions in New York, including the social protest play *200 Were Chosen* (1936, 35 performances), which dealt with Midwest Depression farmers relocated by the government to Alaska. *Prologue to Glory* (1938, 169 NYC performances), on the topic of the young Abraham Lincoln and his romance with Ann Rutledge, received over 20

productions across the country by the **Federal Theatre Project** and was later presented on television (1952). Several collections of plays have been published. During 1939–73 he taught at the Universities of Iowa and Texas.   TP

Conklin, John (1937–) Set and costume designer whose career began in the late 1950s at Yale and the **Williamstown Theatre Festival.** In the 1960s he began an ongoing association with the **Hartford Stage Company.** Most of his work through the 1970s was at these and other regional theatres, but he also began to design for opera and teach at New York University (1980). By the 1990s he was designing regularly for the San Francisco, New York City, Metropolitan, and Chicago Lyric opera companies as well as at opera houses throughout Europe. He worked extensively with directors **Robert Wilson, Mark Lamos,** Jonathan Miller, and **Robert Falls,** among many others, and developed close relationships with such theatres as the **American Repertory Theatre** and the **Goodman** as well as Hartford, where he frequently collaborates with lighting designer **Pat Collins.** These associations and his teaching at NYU have made him one of the most influential designers in the U.S. Working in a largely architectural style, Conklin's work is filled with rich detail, texture, and historical reference. His intelligent use of historical art and culture within his settings was a strong influence on postmodernist tendencies in design.   AA

Connection, The, by Jack Gelber. This play with jazz music by Freddie Redd ran 778 times in the **Living Theatre**'s repertory from 15 July 1959 until 1963. Directed by Judith Malina and designed by Julian Beck, it focused on the lives of heroin-addicted musicians listlessly awaiting their "connection," Cowboy. Critics did not know how to respond (London audiences shouted and booed), but it won three Obie Awards (including best new play) and has been frequently revived, including a 1980 production at New York's Henry Street Settlement directed by the original Cowboy, Carl Lee. The music was recorded in 1960, and a 1962 film of a performance was released despite the New York Board of Regents, which banned it for obscene language.   REK

Connelly, Marc (Marcus Cook) (1890–1980) Playwright, actor, producer, and director who first became known on the Broadway scene as a collaborator of **George S. Kaufman** on such plays as *Dulcy* (1921) and *Beggar on Horseback* (1924), the latter being the most successful of their work together. His greatest contribution as a playwright came with *The Green Pastures* (1930), a Pulitzer Prize–winning adaptation of Roark Bradford's dialect stories. By holding the stage for 640 performances, this funny, touching, and naturally truthful work showed America that a play with an all-black cast could be good box office. Connelly's Broadway acting credits include the Stage Manager in a 1944 production of *Our Town* and Professor Osman in *Tall Story* (1959), a role he repeated for the motion picture. As a producer-director, his

greatest success was *Having Wonderful Time* (1937).
LDC

See: M. Connelly, *Voices Offstage,* New York, 1968.

Conrad, Robert T[aylor] (1810–58) Playwright. Journalist, lawyer, judge, editor, politician, orator, and dilettante in the theatre, Conrad, born to a wealthy Philadelphia family, wrote at least three plays. Neither *Conrad of Naples* (1832), in which **James Wallack** acted the lead part, nor *The Heretic* (n.d.) has survived. Conrad's *Jack Cade* (1835) was not successful until he revised it for **Edwin Forrest,** who produced it first in 1841 and kept it in his repertoire for years. Sometimes called *Aylmere; or, The Kentish Rebellion* or *Aylmere; or, The Bond Man of Kent, Jack Cade* dramatizes the life of a 15th-century villein (partially freed serf still bound to his lord) who incites an insurrection to abolish the institution of villeinage. Its theme of individual freedom was extremely popular in Jacksonian America. Conrad's later years were spent as a judge and the elected mayor of Philadelphia.
WJM

Conried, Heinrich (1848–1909) Theatre manager. Born in Austria, Conried, Mathilde Cottrelly, and **Gustav Amberg** organized the highly successful German-speaking **Thalia Theater** Company in New York in 1879 with the objective of establishing a theatre modeled after repertory theatres in Europe. Conried lured many German actors to America, including Marie Geistinger, Josephine Gallmeyer, Friedrich Mitterwurzer, and Ludwig Barnay in 1883. He became stage manager for **Rudolph Aronson** at the **Casino Theatre** in 1883, managed the Irving Place Theatre from 1892, and became managing director of the Metropolitan Opera House in 1903. He was forced to resign in 1908 after controversy over his staging of *Parsifal* and the U.S. premiere of *Salome.* In 1909 he proposed the building of the **New Theatre** to stage both opera and drama. RE

See: M. J. Moses, *Heinrich Conried,* New York, 1916.

Contemporary Theatre, Inc., A Founded in **Seattle** in 1965 by Gregory Arthur Falls, then Director of the University of Washington School of Drama, the company has kept to its goal of providing regional audiences with a serious alternative to **summer stock** seasons. As its budget has risen from the original $35,000 to an excess of $2 million, the company has increased its commitment to playwrights by commissioning new authors of long-term interest. Also a major regional influence in young people's theatre, the company remains at its original site, a 449-seat thrust theatre, renovated from a business structure for its first season. RW

Contrast, The Perhaps the most popular American play of the 18th century, **Royall Tyler'**s five-act comedy premiered at the **John Street Theatre** on 16 April 1787. Recognized as the first native comedy to be professionally staged, the work resembles Sheridan's comedies of wit, particularly *The School for Scandal,* which Tyler acknowledged as an inspirational source. The play is notable for

Engraving by William Dunlap of the original production of *The Contrast.* Thomas Wignell as Jonathan is pictured at center. Courtesy: Don B. Wilmeth.

its characterization of American types in the wake of the Revolutionary War. Dimple, the snobbish rake who is in line to marry Maria, is exposed as a perfidious fop and hence assumes the vacuous part of the vanquished royalist. Colonel Manly, who eventually wins Maria's hand, embodies the heroic, noble, and victorious American. His servant, Jonathan, the rude country bumpkin (and object of ridicule by Dimple's manservant, Jessamy) is revealed as the folksy and honest **Yankee** character, and would be revived in many manifestations throughout the next century as a fundamental American type. PAD

Conway, H. J. (1800–60) Playwright. Associated with theatres in **Philadelphia, Boston,** and New York, Conway worked as prompter and treasurer and wrote at least 29 plays. Apparently interested in creating a nationalistic drama as well as responding to popular trends, Conway wrote *The Battle of Stillwater* (1840), celebrating the famous Revolutionary War battle of October 1777 with all of the ingredients of successful melodrama, and *Hiram Hireout* (1851), in which he fused patriotism to Yankee humor. WJM

Conway (né Rugg), William Augustus (1789–1828), **Frederick Bartlett** (1819–74), **Sarah Crocker** (1835–75) Anglo–American acting family. William made his London debut 4 October 1813. A leading actor of tragic parts at Covent Garden and Bath, he withdrew because of personal attacks and came to America (1824) where he acted until drowning himself. His son, Frederick, established himself as a leading man in both tragedy and comedy in England before coming to America (1850). In 1852 he married Sarah Crocker, sister of Mrs. D. P. Bowers, and after starring together they leased the Park Theatre, Brooklyn, which Crocker managed (1864–75).   DMcD

Cook, Barbara (1927–) Singer-actress who possesses one of the finest soprano voices ever heard on the American musical stage. She made her Broadway debut in *Flahooley* (1954), and received critical acclaim for her performance as Cunegonde in **Candide** (1956) and a Tony Award for her Marian Paroo in *The Music Man* (1957). Cook appeared in *The Gay Life* (1961), **She Loves Me** (1963), and *The Grass Harp* (1971). She also starred in major revivals of **Oklahoma!, Carousel, The King and I,** and **Show Boat.** In 1965 Cook replaced Sandy Dennis in the comedy **Any Wednesday,** and thereafter appeared in straight plays as well as musicals. She retired from the stage in the early 1970s and has mostly confined her appearances to concert halls and nightclubs, except for a limited Broadway engagement in her **one-person** show, *Barbara Cook: A Concert for the Theatre* (1987). In addition to a singing voice of great range and expressiveness, Cook brought to her roles a winning personality and a deft touch for comedy.   MK

Cook, George Cram (1873–1924) Playwright and director. With his wife **Susan Glaspell,** he founded in Massachusetts the **Provincetown Players** (1915), which opened in 1916 in Greenwich Village, where Cook remained inspirational leader until 1922. Although a minor playwright whose best efforts like *Suppressed Desires* (1915) and *Tickless Time* (1918) were written in collaboration with Glaspell, he was a mentor to **Eugene O'Neill,** for whom he directed *The Emperor Jones* (1920). No art theatre director was more dedicated to promoting serious American playwriting.   RHW

Cook, Joe (né Joseph Lopez) (1890–1959) Comic. **Brooks Atkinson** called him "the greatest man in the world," yet this zany ("a one-man vaudeville show") is virtually forgotten. With his Rube Goldberg contraptions, his "imitation of four Hawaiians" (a convoluted explanation of how he got rich ends with: Why should a wealthy man imitate four Hawaiians?), his landlord gag (attempting to collect rent on a miniature cottage, he finally walks off with it under his arm), and similar absurd novelties, Cook wowed audiences, from his **vaudeville** debut in 1907 to his last appearance in an ice show in 1940. In between, other than vaudeville and **revue** appearances, he was most successful in *Rain or Shine* (1928), *Fine and Dandy* (1930), and *Hold Your Horses* (1933).   DBW

See: S. Green, *The Great Clowns of Broadway,* New York, 1984.

George Frederick Cooke as Richard III: painting by Philadelphia artist Thomas Sully (original at the Pennsylvania Academy of Fine Arts). Courtesy: Don B. Wilmeth.

Cooke, George Frederick (1756–1812) Dublin-born English romantic actor; the first major foreign star on the American stage. Cooke was a traveling actor in the British provinces from at least 1773 until 1800, essaying some 300 roles. After a successful debut at Covent Garden in 1800, he restricted himself to few roles – Richard III, Shylock, Iago, Macbeth, Sir Giles Overreach, and Macklin's Sir Pertinax MacSycophant – those seen most frequently during his American visit (1810–12). Although there was a coarseness in his character and acting, Cooke was often noted for his stately carriage, as well as his broad torso and prominent nose. A chronic alcoholic, Cooke was brought to the U.S. by **Thomas A. Cooper** and **Stephen Price** to appear first at the **Park Theatre** on 11 November. Although his reputation for drunkenness and debauchery preceded him, he was on his best behavior (for the most part) during his 160 performances in New York, **Boston,** Baltimore, **Philadelphia,** and Providence (where he gave his final performance anywhere on 31 July 1812). Cooke intended to take his U.S.-met last wife (of a possible five) back to England, but died of cirrhosis of the liver in New York City in September. Buried in St. Paul's churchyard, his remains were reinterred in 1820 by his admirer Edmund Kean, who erected a monument over them – still a notable theatre shrine refurbished six times (most recently in 1948). DBW

> *See:* A. Hare, *George Frederick Cooke: The Actor and The Man,* London, 1980; D. Wilmeth, *George Frederick Cooke: Machiavel of the Stage,* Westport, CT, 1980.

Cooper, Thomas Abthorpe (1776–1849) British-born actor and manager who became the first star of the American stage and initiated the practice of traveling from one company to another performing only prominent roles. While in his teens Cooper performed in Edinburgh and at various provincial theatres; his London debut was as Hamlet in 1795. In 1796, unhappy with his English acceptance, he went to the **Chestnut Street Theatre** in Philadelphia. After the settlement of an alleged breach of articles with the Philadelphia management, he joined **Dunlap** at the **Park Street** in New York in 1801; during 1806–15 he was in management at the Park. With **Stephen Price** as his partner he played the eastern circuit, excelling in heroic characters in poetic drama, such as Pierre in *Venice Preserv'd.* His popularity continued into the 1820s, but by 1830 it was waning, and by 1835 "he had sadly become the seeker instead of the sought after." DBW

> *See:* J. Ireland, *A Memoir of the Professional Life of Thomas Abthorpe Cooper,* Philadelphia, 1888.

Copperfield (né Kotkin), David (1956–) One of the world's best known stage magicians today [see **magic**], Copperfield has received most attention for spectacular feats designed for television specials – vanishing a Lear jet, the Statue of Liberty, a dining car from the Orient Express. He is best, however, at integrating music, illusion, choreography, and a narrative, so that magical sequences are more like minidramas. His frequent tours are extraordinarily successful class acts. DBW

Copperhead, The A 1918 melodrama by **Augustus Thomas** that featured a virtuoso performance by Lionel Barrymore [see **Drew–Barrymore family**] and established him as a major star. The play opened on 18 February 1918 at the **Sam S. Shubert Theatre** in New York and ran for 120 performances. Adapted from a story by Frederick Landis, Thomas's play about an Illinois farmer who sacrifices his happiness by pretending to be a Confederate sympathizer is split into two "epochs": Acts I and II are set in the 1860s, and Acts III and IV occur 40 years later. Barrymore's triumph was his moving portrayal of Milt Shanks as a young farmer-turned-spy in the first half of the performance and as a dignified, long-suffering old man in the second. Audiences were typically reduced to tears by the play's final scene in which Shanks – his honor at last proven – is restored to the community, proclaiming, "God! It's wonderful . . . to hev friends agin!" MF

Corbin, John R. (1870–1959) Drama critic. Educated at Harvard and Oxford, Corbin brought a well-trained academic mind to drama criticism at *Harper's Weekly* (1897–1900), the *New York Times*

Lionel Barrymore in Augustus Thomas's *The Copperhead.* Courtesy: Becker Theatre Library, Brown University.

(1902–4; 1917–19; 1922–4), and the *New York Sun* (1904–7). Also he was Literary Director of the **New Theatre** (1908–10) and authored 12 books, two on Shakespeare. A conservative critic, Corbin nevertheless supported both realist and American drama but in a style regarded as "learned and plodding." TLM

Cordelia's Aspirations This late installment in **Edward Harrigan**'s "Mulligan Guard" series featured the well-known Dan Mulligan (played by Harrigan) forced by his wife, Cordelia (Annie Yeamans), into leaving his beloved home on NYC's Lower East Side for a more respectable address uptown. Tony Hart performed his blackface character, Rebecca Allup, and Yeamans had a famous drunk scene in this treatment of Irish immigrants who aspire beyond their station. David Braham composed music for the comedy, which opened 5 November 1883 at the Theatre Comique, ran a record-breaking 176 performances, and was frequently revived by Harrigan's company. The *New York Times* called the play (which was never published), "another turn to the kaleidoscope of city life which [Harrigan] has so faithfully constructed." KF

Corio, Ann (née Anna Coria or Coreo) (1907?–) With Georgia Sothern and **Gypsy Rose Lee,** one of the premiere stripteasers of the 1930s, although Corio, "probably the prettiest girl in burlesque," took off few clothes. From a member of the chorus in a **burlesque show** in her hometown of Hartford, CT, Corio rose to soubrette and then headline stripper. Her gimmick became "innocence," dressing as a pretty little girl in a ruffled skirt. "The more innocent I was, the more wicked they [the audience] felt." Under the tutelege of impresario Emmett R. Callahan (who became her husband), she became the star of *Girls in Blue* and other shows. Probably her most important contribution, however, was the revival of old-time burlesque in her *This Was Burlesque* (also the title of a book she cowrote in 1968), which opened in 1962 and featured some of the great top bananas, including Steve Mills and Conny Ryan.   DBW

Cornell, Katharine (1893–1974) Actress. Called "The First Lady of the Theatre" by **Alexander Woollcott,** Cornell, with **Helen Hayes** and **Lynn Fontanne,** was the reigning actress on the Broadway stage during the second quarter of the 20th century. An accomplished interpreter of romantic and character roles, she brought to her characterizations a resonant voice and a remarkably expressive face that captivated audiences; she could create the illusion that a memorable play was being witnessed when in fact the vehicle was weak. Her New York debut was with the **Washington Square Players** (1916); her London debut was as Jo in *Little Women* (1919). Prominence in the American theatre came with *A Bill of Divorcement* (1921). She is best remembered as Elizabeth Barrett in *The Barretts of Wimpole Street* (1931) and as **Shaw**'s *Candida* (1924). Other notable appearances included *Romeo and Juliet* (1934), *The Doctor's Dilemma* (1941), *Antony and Cleopatra* (1947), *The Dark Is Light Enough* (1955), and *Dear Liar* (as Mrs. Patrick Campbell) in 1959. In 1921 she married **Guthrie McClintic,** who was responsible for most of her productions. On his death in 1961 she retired.   DBW

See: K. Cornell, *I Wanted to Be an Actress,* New York, 1938; G. McClintic, *Me and Kit,* Boston, 1955; T. Mosel, w/ G. Macy, *Leading Lady,* Boston, 1978.

Cort Theatre 148 West 48th St., NYC [Architect: Edward B. Corey]. Built and named for John Cort, a West Coast producer [see **Seattle**], the new house was launched in 1912 with a hit production, **Hartley Manners**'s *Peg o' My Heart,* which made a star of **Laurette Taylor.** With about 1,000 seats, it is best suited for comedies and realistic plays and has housed a series of long-running hits. Two Pulitzer Prize–winning plays premiered at the theatre: *The Shrike* (1951) and *The Diary of Anne Frank* (1955). During 1969–72 it operated as a TV studio, but it reverted to legitimate status thereafter. Since 1927, it has been a **Shubert** theatre.   MCH

Costume Although costume design has come into its own as a major design element in 20th-century American theatre, little research has been done on the development of the profession. In the 19th century, designing new costumes for each production was rarely thought necessary. A company of actors who performed a repertory of plays

Chorus men ("Ruby Warrior") design by Alfredo Edel for *Ballet of Jewels,* a 1909 critical disaster at the Hippodrome. Courtesy: Shubert Archive.

could maintain a wardrobe and adequately costume their productions. Established companies amassed large wardrobes, and successful costumes were used repeatedly; but because each actor selected his or her wardrobe, productions rarely possessed visual unity. Some attempt might be made to give period plays a historical look, but this was normally a matter of available garments and conventional taste rather than any overriding concern for consistency.

When actors began to work from production to production instead of remaining with one company for several seasons, wardrobes of costumes could no longer be realistically maintained. Instead, company managers selected costumes, often from rental houses with large inventories [see **support services**], and were more likely to dress a character according to the needs of the role rather than personal preference. If time permitted, a company manager could work toward a unified design of sets, furnishings, and costumes in concert with the intent of the play. Occasionally scenic designers would select or approve costumes, or even design them once the setting was completed. The few individuals who specialized in costumes, including William Henry Matthews, Percy Anderson, and Mrs. John Alexander (who designed for **Maude Adams**), seldom received recognition.

During the early decades of the 20th century, as the number of theatres and plays produced in them multiplied, several developments led to the growing recognition of the contribution that a specialist in the costume area might make to a production. For instance, as it became standard practice for a single designer to control all of the visual elements of a production, including scenery, lights, and costumes, assistants began to take responsibility for following the various elements through the construction process. **Aline Bernstein,** for example, regularly employed Emeline Clarke Roche as her assistant for scenery and **Irene Sharaff** as her assistant for costumes. Over time designers such as Bernstein, **Jo Mielziner,** and **Robert Edmond Jones** admitted the difficulty of maintaining control over this wide range of activities and encouraged their assistants to assume design responsibility. The movement from a single designer for scenery, costumes, and lights to individual ones for each specialty was gradual.

The success of the 1919 actors' strike for better wages and working conditions also aided the trend toward a specialization in costume design. The star system had long been an important aspect of the theatre; performers able to draw large audiences have always had privileged positions – including personal costumes specially designed and constructed by professionals. As a result of this strike, producers were required to provide costumes, wigs, shoes, and stockings for all women in principal roles and in the chorus. Because producers were required to pay for costumes, they increasingly looked to specialists for decisions about costume selections.

Affiliated with the Brotherhood of Painters, Decorators and Paperhangers as Local Union 829 in 1918, the United Scenic Artists Association was known initially as a union for stage painters. In the early 1920s scenic designers began to join, and through **union** activity helped stabilize the role of design in production. By 1936 United Scenic Artists had a special section for costume designers (though not with voting rights until 1966).

The **Federal Theatre Project** also influenced the move toward specialization in costume design. Created during the early days of the Depression, the FTP was founded to provide employment for all varieties of theatre professionals. Having many different individuals doing specialized jobs meant that more individuals were paid – however little – for their work. Once the specializations of costume (and lighting) design were developed, there was little possibility of returning to the old format.

Many talented artists became costume designers as a result of these developments. By the 1930s Irene Sharaff, **Raoul Pène Du Bois,** Charles LeMaire, and **Lucinda Ballard** all designed costumes regularly, principally for the thriving Broadway theatre. By the 1940s, when designers such as Miles White, Freddy Wittop, and Alvin Colt joined the rapidly emerging profession, almost 50% of the playbills for New York productions credited costume designers, compared with 1% at the turn of the century.

Notable theatre artists, such as Patton Campbell, **Ann Roth, Theoni V. Aldredge,** and **Patricia Zipprodt,** began designing costumes in the 1950s, joined in the '60s by **Florence Klotz, Willa Kim,** and **Jane Greenwood,** among others. These costume designers continued to work primarily in the theatre but, like most contemporary theatre artists, also design opera, dance, film, television, industrial promotions, and extravaganzas. More recently, Judith Dolan, Ann Hould-Ward, **William Ivey Long,** Linda Fisher, Martin Pakledinaz, Carol Oditz, Lindsay Davis, and Michael J. Cesario have become familiar names in the New York theatre. As American theatre has become less centralized, many designers, including Robert Morgan, Steven Rubin, **Jeanne Button,** Susan Tsu, and Deborah Dryden, have gained recognition for their quality costume design for regional theatres.

The speciality in costume design has not diminished the need for construction specialists. Many regional theatres maintain their own shops for creating costumes, and costume rental houses throughout the U.S. – including Western Costume Company, Eaves-Brooks, Norcostco, Inc., The Costume Collection, and Stagecraft Studios – are valuable resources.

Today's costume designers come from various backgrounds. Some began as scenic designers, performers, costume construction specialists, or as artists in complementary fields such as sculpture, painting, and fiber arts. Others are fashion designers or employees of costume houses. More often,

Costume design by Freddy Wittop for Ginger Rogers in *Hello, Dolly!* (1966). Courtesy: Freddy Wittop and University of Georgia Library (Hargerett Rare Book and Manuscript Library).

however, many are costume design specialists trained through an apprenticeship with another designer, in a theatre, or in one of the growing number of graduate programs offering a degree in costume design. Frank Poole Bevan at the Yale School of Drama, Paul Reinhardt and **Lucy Barton** at the University of Texas, and Barbara and Cletus Anderson at Carnegie–Mellon have been among those individuals instrumental in training designers and continuing the development of the profession.

Costume designers have gradually gained more recognition for their contribution to theatre as the century has progressed. Presently, it is extremely rare for programs not to acknowledge the costume designers: They are recognized as integral to successful productions not only generally, but individually as well. BO

See: B. and C. Anderson, *Costume Design*, New York, 1964; I. Corey, *The Mask of Reality: An Approach to Design for Theatre*, Anchorage, KY, 1968; B. Owen, *Costume Design on Broadway, Designers and Their Credits: 1915–1985*, Westport, CT, 1987; D. Russell, *Stage Costume Design, Theory, Technique and Style*, Englewood Cliffs, NJ, 1973, 1985.

Couldock, Charles Walter (1815–98) English-born actor, trained as a carpenter, who began acting in the provinces (1836), becoming leading man at Birmingham and Liverpool (1845–9). He made his American debut opposite **Charlotte Cushman** at the **Broadway Theatre**, NYC (October 1849). After traveling as a star in *The Willow Copse*, he became a regular in various New York **stock companies** (1858). His most famous role was Dunstan Kirke in **Steele MacKaye**'s *Hazel Kirke* (1880). Praised for his versatility, he retired in 1896. DMcD

Count of Monte Cristo, The **Lester Wallack** was the first of several U.S. playwrights and actors to adapt Alexandre Dumas's 1844 novel to the stage. **Charles Fechter** prepared versions in 1868 and 1870 and played the starring role of Edmund Dantès until 1877. **James O'Neill**, who first performed Dantès in 1883, bought the rights to Fechter's script in 1885 and toured it until 1916, performing the leading role over 6,000 times to an estimated 15 million spectators. Although O'Neill made further alterations, Fechter's adaptation had already tightened the action of the sprawling novel to emphasize its melodramatic highpoints: Dantès's arrest on the eve of his wedding to Mercedes, his daring escape from prison, his discovery of hidden treasures on the Isle of Monte Cristo, his return to French society as the mysterious count, and his meticulously planned and executed vengeance against the three men who conspired to send him to prison. A pessimistic, postmodern revival of the play, directed by **Peter Sellars** at the **John F. Kennedy Center** (1985), won critical acclaim. BMcC

Country Girl, The A backstage psychological drama by **Clifford Odets** about lies, illusions, and the difficulties of love, this play features an alcoholic actor (modeled, Odets noted, on the life of the actress **Laurette Taylor**) who struggles successfully to return to the stage; a young director

who believes in him yet falls in love with his wife; and the actor's compassionate, maternal wife, who stands by her weak, self-destructive husband, even though he projects his own faults and fears onto her. Lacking a social critique, it still presents Odets's themes of self-deception and the struggle for integrity. He directed the premiere production (1950, 225 performances) starring Paul Kelly, Steven Hill, and **Uta Hagen.** Odets sometimes dismissed the well-received play as a commercial piece, but it has proved to be a durable work, revived notably in 1966 and 1972. Also, in Odets's revised form, it was produced in 1968 as *Winter Journey*. TP

County Chairman, The, by **George Ade,** opened on Broadway 24 November 1903 and ran 222 performances. In a small town in the Mississippi Valley, a local party boss, Hackler, seeks revenge against an old rival in love, Rigby, a man now wealthy and powerful through sometimes scurrilous means. Hackler backs his young law partner, Wheeler, to oppose Rigby in the election for Prosecuting Attorney, even though Wheeler has been courting Rigby's daughter, who objects to her fiancé defaming her father. After a rough but comic campaign, Wheeler wins the election and marries his beloved. JDM

Cowell, Joe Leathley (Joseph Hawkins Witchett) (1792–1863) English-born actor, manager, and scene painter who, after an abortive career in the navy, became an itinerant actor, establishing a reputation as a low comedian. Emigrating to America in 1821, he became a well-known figure in the American theatre, both as an actor and a manager of theatres and **circus**es. His memoirs appeared in 1844. In 1863 he returned to England. Through marriages he was related to the British Siddons and the **Bateman**s. His second son, **Sam**, became a music-hall star. DBW

See: J. Cowell, *Thirty Years Passed among the Players in England and America*, reprint, Hamden, CT, 1979.

Cowell, Sam[uel] Houghton (1820–64) British actor-vocalist, born in the U.S. Most music-hall stars came either from the working class or from a theatrical background. Cowell, one of the earliest recognized music-hall performers and an early star at the Canterbury, was the son of **Joe Cowell**, and began his career in the legitimate theatre, touring the U.S. with his father in the 1830s in Shakespearean productions, billed as "The Young American Roscius." Returning to England at the age of 20, he rapidly converted himself to a comic vocalist – he had already done "coon" songs as entr'actes in America – and burlesque performer. An ugly little man with a lugubrious expression, he specialized at London song and supper rooms in cockney song-and-patter acts. AEG DBW

See: M. W. Willson, ed., *The Cowells in America*, London, 1934.

Cowl, Jane (1884–1950) Boston-born actress, Jane Cowl made her New York stage debut in 1903 in *Sweet Kitty Bellairs*. Her portrayal of the wronged woman, Mary Turner, in *Within the Law*

(1912) established her as a star. Cowl appeared in plays that she wrote or cowrote, including *Lilac Time* (1917), *Daybreak* and *Information Please* (1918), and *Smilin' Through* (1920). In 1923 she offered a "breath-taking" Juliet in a production that ran for 174 consecutive performances. Her successful rendering of Larita in Noël Coward's *Easy Virtue* (1925) was followed by an "appealing" Amytis in *The Road to Rome* (1927) and a "brilliant" Lucy Chase Wayne in *First Lady* (1935). **Brooks Atkinson** praised her "personal beauty, impeccability of manners, humorous vitality, and simple command of the art of acting." The dark-haired, dark-eyed actress was regarded as a distinguished "lady of the theatre" in London as well as New York. TLM

Crabtree, Charlotte (Lotta) (1847–1924) Actress. Born in New York, she and her mother followed her father to the gold-mining town of Grass Valley, CA, in 1853. She soon learned to dance and sing, and became a featured performer in mining camp variety troupes. She conquered **San Francisco** in 1859 and headed east. She achieved widespread popularity when she made the transition to legitimate drama in the dual leading roles of *Little Nell and the Marchioness* (1867), dramatized for her from Dickens's *The Old Curiosity Shop* by **John Brougham.** Though she later had other vehicles, they were only excuses for this tiny, red-haired, black-eyed elf to exhibit her skills at mim-

Lotta Crabtree in *Little Nell and the Marchioness,* John Brougham's adaptation of *The Old Curiosity Shop,* performed frequently during 1867–91. Courtesy: Don B. Wilmeth.

icry, banjo-picking, and clog dancing. She never married, and retired with comfortable wealth in 1891. DMcD

> See: D. Dempsey and R. Baldwin, *The Triumphs and Trials of Lotta Crabtree,* New York, 1968; C. Rourke, *Troupers of the Gold Coast; or, The Rise of Lotta Crabtree,* New York, 1928.

Cradle Will Rock, The, by **Marc Blitzstein** was originally produced by personnel of the **Federal Theatre Project** but premiered outside of WPA supervision at the Venice Theatre on 16 June 1937. In a celebrated bare-stage production directed by **Orson Welles** and featuring **Will Geer** and **Howard Da Silva,** this musical about labor unions in "Steeltown, USA" was performed at the height of battles between "little" steel companies and the CIO and in defiance of a nationwide WPA postponement order. While much of the musical's notoriety concerned the circumstances of its premiere (and cries of government **censorship**), *Cradle* remains a compelling proletarian drama with a vital score by one of America's most prominent composers. Welles and **John Houseman** produced it at their **Mercury Theatre** in 1938; in 1983 Houseman directed a successful revival with **Patti LuPone, Gerald Gutierrez,** and the Julliard **Acting Company** at the **American Place Theatre.** BBW

Craig's Wife A harshly negative character portrait, this **George Kelly** three-act drama depicts the machinations of a woman obsessed with maintaining physical perfection in her beautiful home and controlling her husband's life in order to ensure her own security. The revelation of Harriet Craig's selfishness and dishonesty drives her husband away, along with all other members of their household, leaving her completely alone in the play's final moments. Staged by Kelly and featuring Chrystal Herne and Charles Trowbridge as the unhappy couple, the play opened in New York 12 October 1925 at the **Morosco Theatre,** played for 360 performances, and won the Pulitzer Prize. It was given film and radio treatments before a 1947 Broadway revival, again directed by Kelly, which ran for 69 performances. KF

Crane, William Henry (1845–1928) Actor who, after a long apprenticeship with a small touring opera company, achieved his first major success in *Evangeline* at **Niblo's Garden** in 1873. During 1877–89, Crane and **Stuart Robson** joined together to produce a series of very popular American domestic comedies, such as *Our Boarding House, Our Bachelors,* and *The Henrietta.* Crane was also noted for his Dromio, Falstaff, and Sir Toby Belch. In 1890, he began a successful career as a producer-actor in his own vehicle productions when he appeared as Senator Hannibal Rivers in *The Senator,* with which he was to be associated for the rest of his career. In 1896 he toured in **Joseph Jefferson**'s "All Star" production of Sheridan's *The Rivals* as Anthony Absolute. Crane, a thoughtful artist who contributed a number of essays on acting and the theatre to popular journals of the day, published his autobiography *Footprints and Echoes* in 1927. MR DJW

Craven, Frank (1875?–1945) Actor, playwright, and director, best known for creating the Stage Manager in **Thornton Wilder**'s *Our Town* in 1938. Born in Boston of theatrical parents, Craven was a child actor. At 16 he played in repertory in Philadelphia; his first New York success was in 1910 as James Gilley in *Bought and Paid For*. Craven later wrote several successful scripts for the stage, such as *Too Many Cooks* and *This Way Out*. He played leading roles in several films, adapted some of his scripts to film, and wrote dialogue for Laurel and Hardy. He last appeared on Broadway in 1944. **Brooks Atkinson** called him "the best pipe and pants-pocket actor in the business." SMA

Crawford, Cheryl (1902–86) Producer. As executive assistant to **Theresa Helburn** at the **Theatre Guild** in the late 1920s, as cofounder with **Harold Clurman** and **Lee Strasberg** of the **Group Theatre** (1931), as creator of the **American Repertory Theatre** (1946) with **Eva Le Gallienne** and **Margaret Webster,** and as cofounder with **Elia Kazan** and **Robert Lewis** of the **Actors Studio** (1947), Crawford was at the center of the most vital and idealistic enterprises in the American theatre. A wry, poker-faced midwesterner, she was a remarkably self-effacing impresario. Surrounded by high-strung, visionary colleagues, she always remained level-headed. She kept the peace between Clurman and Strasberg, whom she called Old Testament prophets; she raised money, trimmed budgets, found rehearsal space, arranged theatre rentals, and could always be counted on for a frank opinion of the artistic merit and commercial appeal of both plays and players. For all her commitment to serious theatre, she thought of plays as potential hits or flops, and withdrew from the organizations she helped to foster in order to pursue a career as an independent stage producer with a particular interest in musicals. Her biggest commercial success was *Brigadoon* (1947); other notable Crawford productions include the 1942 revival of *Porgy and Bess;* *One Touch of Venus* (1943); *Paint Your Wagon* (1950); *Mother Courage* (1963); and four plays by **Tennessee Williams** – *The Rose Tattoo* (1951), *Camino Real* (1953), *Sweet Bird of Youth* (1959), and *Period of Adjustment* (1960). FH

See: C. Crawford, *One Naked Individual,* Indianapolis/New York, 1977.

Crews, Laura Hope (1879–1942) Stage and film actress who toured California as a child performer, became in 1898 the ingenue with San Francisco's **Alcazar** Stock Company, then joined New York's Henry V. Donnelly Stock Company, reaching Broadway in 1904. Her work with actor-director **Henry Miller** was especially formative. Notable stage performances included Beatrice opposite **John Drew** in 1913 and the possessive mother in *The Silver Cord* for the **Theatre Guild** in 1926 and for the 1933 film. She went to Hollywood as a diction coach, but made a screen career of fluttery character roles like Aunt Pittypat in *Gone with the Wind* (1939). FHL

Cricket Theatre 1407 Nicollet Avenue South, **Minneapolis;** began producing new American plays in a converted moviehouse under the leadership of William Semans in 1971. Continued success prompted Equity professional status in 1975 and the naming of Lou Salerni as Artistic Director. The Cricket moved to the Hennepin Center for the Arts in 1979 and, after initial growth, became financially overburdened. In 1980 Semans resigned, followed by Salerni in 1985 when the board of directors vacated the theatre space and began reorganization. The Cricket reopened in 1986 in another moviehouse with a new artistic director, William Partlan, and a new mission, defined by Sean Dowse and Marisha Chamberlain: to produce contemporary drama by living playwrights. KN

Crimes of the Heart by **Beth Henley.** Originally produced by **Actors Theatre of Louisville,** where it was cowinner of the Great American Play Contest (1979), the play premiered in New York at **Manhattan Theatre Club** (1980). It moved to the Golden Theatre, opening 4 November 1981 under the direction of Melvin Bernhardt and with a **John Lee Beatty** set. Henley's first full-length play, it won a Pulitzer Prize and New York Drama Critics' Circle Award. Through the reunion of three sisters, this comedy explores female bonding in the face of various repressions. Henley, herself a Southerner, presents a gallery of credible, sympathetic Southern grotesques: a lonely spinster with deformed ovaries, a rebellious artist, and a suicidal, adulterous lawyer's wife support one another while their domineering grandfather is ill and the adulterer is arraigned for shooting her husband. Although the ending is unresolved, the play celebrates a moment of freedom and rebirth. TH-S

Criticism Critics experienced a difficult time establishing themselves as an important force in the American theatre. Since the theatre itself was considered a dangerous public institution in the late 18th century, the role of the critic was seen more in terms of **censorship,** guarding against violations of social and moral laws. The earliest extant review of a play appeared anonymously in the *Maryland Gazette* (1760) at a time when papers usually "noticed" a performance with little or no critical evaluation. The subject prompted **William Dunlap** in his *History of the American Theatre* (1832) to devote a chapter to critics, explaining that in 1796 a group of six "gentlemen" organized themselves into a "band of scalpers and tomahawkers" to write anonymous reviews about New York productions. A few years later, **Washington Irving** wrote the charming and lightly satirical "Letters of Jonathan Oldstyle, Gent." (1802–3), to comment upon the New York stage. Irving also penned reviews for *The Salmagundi* (1807) and *Select Reviews,* later the *Analectic Magazine* (1815). He is regarded as the first American drama critic of importance.

Few daily newspapers published reviews on a regular basis until the 1850s, and even fewer allowed bylines by their critics until the end of the century. Theatre notices and criticism became associated more with short-lived dramatic magazines such as *Theatrical Censor* (1806), *Rambler's Magazine and New York Theatrical Register* (1809), *Mirror of Taste and Dramatic Censor* (1810), and the *Broadway*

Journal and Stranger's Guide (1847), as well as sporting weeklies such as *Spirit of the Times* (1831) and *New York Clipper* (1853). The first important theatrical weekly was the *New York Dramatic Mirror,* founded in 1879. Play reviewing, like the theatre itself, was held in low esteem. It was not uncommon for editors to send untrained reporters to "write up" the opening night of a play; nor was it uncommon for critics to review only productions that advertised in their papers. In 1836, **Edgar Allan Poe** called professional reviewers "illiterate mountebanks." **Walt Whitman,** writing in 1847, blamed the vulgarity and coarseness of the theatre upon the "paid puff" system.

The expansion of the newspaper business in the 1850s prompted separate "amusement" departments and separate dramatic columns of news and reviews. Moralists and puffers tended to dominate the profession, although Henry Clapp, Jr., returned from France in 1855 or 1856 to set up a coterie of critics at Pfaff's Restaurant to rail against tradition and convention. He advocated that the theatre be judged on aesthetic rather than moral grounds, and wrote bright and witty essays for the *Saturday Press* and other weeklies. The Civil War destroyed the movement, however, and what emerged afterward was a highly moralistic and conservative school headed by **William Winter, John Ranken Towse,** and **Henry Austin Clapp.** Winter made his reputation on Horace Greeley's *New York Tribune* from 1865 to 1909. Towse headed the dramatic department of the elitist *New York Evening Post* during 1874–1927. Clapp wrote for the *Boston Daily Advertiser* from 1868 to 1902. These "genteel" critics shared the values of the cultured elite and endured until these values changed.

The popular press, however, demanded bright and clever reviews, not moralistic essays, and the innovations introduced by Henry Clapp, Jr., were carried on in the aggressive and colorful writing of **Andrew C. Wheeler** (alias Nym Crinkle) in the New York *Sun, World,* and "lesser" dramatic and sporting journals. Alfred J. Cohen (alias **Alan Dale**) popularized his "School of the Flippant Remark" from coast to coast for Hearst publications in the late 1890s and early 1900s. Other critics sought reform. **Stephen Ryder Fiske** of Wilkes's *Spirit of the Times* (1879–1902) ridiculed shoddy business practices and productions. He viewed the theatre as a worthwhile place of amusement that should be conducted in a professional manner. **Epes W. Sargent** served vaudeville in a similar way, writing for a number of trade papers including *Variety* in 1905. **Harrison Grey Fiske** of the *New York Dramatic Mirror* (1880–1911) worked to improve business practices and sought a charity (the **Actors' Fund**) to help the profession. He fought to protect the legal rights of playwrights and to bring an end to the blackmailing efforts of the *New York Dramatic News.* Still other critics worked to improve the American drama. **William Dean Howells** in the 1880s sought a realistic native drama from his editor's desk at *Atlantic Monthly,* and encouraged **James A. Herne** and **Bronson Howard.** Edward **Dithmar** of the *New York Times* (1884–1902) encouraged American dramatists and broke with tradition by refusing to judge a play on moral grounds.

Academicians such as **Clayton Hamilton, Walter Prichard Eaton,** and **Brander Matthews** wrote books about the history, practice, and theory of the drama, thus educating the public. An important voice for change, **James G. Huneker,** promoted the new European drama of **Ibsen** and **Shaw,** and insisted (as had Clapp) that art be judged on aesthetic rather than moral grounds. Huneker influenced a generation of writers, including **George Jean Nathan.**

As drama critic of *Smart Set* (1909–23), Nathan attacked the shop-worn dramatic devices of **Belasco,** the pomposity of the cultured elite, and the ignorance of the masses. He used ridicule, sarcasm, and satire to rid the theatre of stultifying tradition and convention. Like Huneker, he championed Ibsen, Shaw, Strindberg, Maeterlinck, and Hauptmann, and unlike Huneker he found value in the new American drama. He discovered **Eugene O'Neill** and published his early work in *Smart Set.* Although he never wielded the power of his New York peers on the daily press, he commanded the respect of the young intellectuals in the 1910s and '20s. His unwillingness to find value in the political theatre of the 1930s eroded his influence as a vital force in the theatre.

The exuberant **Alexander Woollcott** established the power of the *New York Times* in the 1910s with his enthusiastic prose and his battle with the **Shubert**s. **Percy Hammond** moved from the *Chicago Tribune* (1908–21) to the *New York Tribune* (1921–36) and brought his urbane and satirical style to bear upon that theatre's pretensions. He could dismiss a Shakespearean actor with the flick of his pen by noting: "he wore his tights competently." **Burns Mantle** provided good journalistic prose and sound opinions for the *New York Evening Mail* (1911–22) and *Daily News* (1922–43). **Brooks Atkinson** served for 34 years as chief critic of the *New York Times* (1926–60), enhancing the paper's reputation and his own for fairness and accuracy. Unlike Nathan, he encouraged the more revolutionary theatre of the 1930s as did other critics, including **John Anderson** (*Post* and *Journal*), **Gilbert Gabriel** (*Sun* and *American*), **John Mason Brown** (*Post* and *Saturday Review*) and **Richard Watts, Jr.** (*Herald-Tribune* and *Post*). In 1950 **Walter Kerr** began reviewing for *Commonweal,* and a year later for the *Herald-Tribune.* A former drama professor, Kerr brought to his position a historical perspective lacked by most of his colleagues. Upon the retirement of Atkinson in 1960, Kerr was acknowledged as the foremost New York critic, a position he held until his retirement from the *New York Times* in 1983.

Outside New York, the reputation of critics has usually remained local or regional reflecting the institutions they review. Exceptions include **Henry Taylor Parker** of the *Boston Transcript* (1905–35), **Claudia Cassidy** of the *Chicago Tribune* (1942–65), **Elliot Norton** of the *Boston Post* (1934–56) and other papers, and **Richard Coe** of the *Washington Post* (1946–79). These critics gained widespread recognition because their writings had an impact upon the national theatre.

As the number of New York newspapers declined after 1920 (15 in 1920; 7 in 1950; 3 in 1970), magazine critics gained in importance. **Stark Young** appealed to educated tastes in the *New Republic* (1921–47), as did **Joseph Wood Krutch** in the *Nation* (1924–52), and **Kenneth Macgowan, Rosamond Gilder,** and **Edith J. R. Isaacs** in *Theatre Arts Monthly* (1916–64). Discriminating readers also have turned to **Harold Clurman** in the *Nation;* **Eric Bentley, Stanley Kauffmann,** and **Robert Brustein** in *New Republic;* **Henry Hewes** in *Saturday Review;* **Robert Benchley, Wolcott Gibbs, Brendan Gill,** and **Edith Oliver** in *The New Yorker;* and **John Simon** in *New York Magazine.* The general public has depended more on **Louis Kronenberger, T. E. Kalem,** and **William Henry III** in *Time* magazine and **Jack Kroll** in *Newsweek;* members of the theatrical profession have relied on *Billboard* and *Variety. Village Voice* critics **John Lahr, Michael Feingold,** and others have kept its readers abreast of the avant-garde. Television critics have been part of the Broadway scene for over a decade but there is no agreement over their role and influence.

In the 1990s, the *New York Times* remains the most important and powerful newspaper to review the American theatre, and their daily critic, **Frank Rich** (1980–   ), the most powerful individual. However, the nature of this power has changed over the past two decades. In the 1980s and '90s, with decentralization of the American theatre and the demise of major papers nationwide, critics for dominant papers in major markets have gained immense power over theatre in their areas. **Dan Sullivan** and **Sylvie Drake** in Los Angeles, **Richard Christiansen** in Chicago, Kevin Kelly in Boston, and **Bernard Weiner** in San Francisco, for example, have had real power to make reputations and close shows. And with local productions originating with an eye to Broadway, these local critics, indirectly, have gained power over what is seen in New York. The *New York Times*'s critic has immense power in New York but less in the regions, and is no longer as important to theatre in **Los Angeles,** for example, as is Sylvie Drake.   TLM

See: M. E. Comtois & L. F. Miller, *Contemporary American Critics,* Metuchen, NJ, 1977; L. Engel, *The Critics,* New York, 1976; B. Hewitt, *Theatre U.S.A. 1665 to 1957,* New York, 1959; T. L. Miller, *Bohemians and Critics: American Theatre Criticism in the Nineteenth Century,* Metuchen, NJ, 1981; M. J. Montrose and J. M. Brown, eds., *The American Theatre As Seen By Its Critics, 1752–1934,* New York, 1934; J. S. Pratt, "The Vaudeville Criticism of Epes Winthrop Sargent, 1896–1910," PhD diss., U of Nebraska–Lincoln, 1985; A. Van Rensselaer, *American Shakespearean Criticism, 1607–1865,* New York, 1939.

Crocker, Sarah, see **Conway, William A.**

Cronyn, Hume (1911–   ) Actor, director, and writer born in London, Ontario, Canada. Cronyn studied acting at the New York School of the Theatre and the **American Academy of Dramatic Art,** making his professional debut with Cochran's Stock Company in Washington, DC, in 1931. He also worked for the **Barter Theatre** during their second season. His Broadway debut was as the Janitor in *Hipper's Holiday* (1934).

Cronyn soon became a much sought-after char-

acter in Hollywood, where he married **Jessica Tandy** in 1942. While in Los Angeles, Cronyn directed Tandy as Miss Collins in **Tennessee Williams**'s *Portrait of a Madonna* (1946). This exposure led to Tandy's being cast as Blanche DuBois in 1947 on Broadway.

Cronyn and Tandy appeared together for the first time in 1951 in *The Fourposter,* in which they were "compared to the **Lunts,**" in that the team had enough grace, skill, and wit to hold a stage and an audience by themselves." They have since co-starred in *The Physicists* (1964), **Albee**'s *A Delicate Balance* (1966), *The Gin Game* (1977), *Noel Coward in Two Keys* (1974), and *Foxfire* (1982; coauthored by Cronyn). Between these projects, Cronyn and Tandy played several seasons at the **Guthrie Theatre** and at the Stratford Festival in Ontario. In 1964 Cronyn played Polonius to **Richard Burton**'s Hamlet, winning a Tony. Cronyn's memoir, *A Terrible Liar,* was published in 1991.   SMA

Crosman, Henrietta (1861–1944) Stage and film actress. Born in West Virginia, she began acting at 16 with **John Ellsler.** She scored her first success as Celia in *As You Like It* under **Augustin Daly.** After success in *Gloriana* and *Mistress Nell,* she became the outstanding Rosalind of her time, and also scored a hit in *Sweet Kitty Bellairs.* During 1932–6 she appeared in films, retiring in 1939.   SMA

Crossroads Theatre An active and innovative **African-American theatre,** founded in 1978 and located in New Brunswick, NJ. Under the resourceful artistic leadership of Rick Khan, the theatre has attained a distinguished record, presenting an average of six productions each season, often to critical acclaim. It has supported new playwrights, encouraged new forms of staging, presented world premieres, and toured a production annually during Black History Month (February). In 1991 the theatre acquired a new home on Livingston Avenue as part of New Brunswick's Cultural Center complex.   EGH

Crothers, Rachel (c. 1878–1958) Actress, playwright, and director. The "Neil Simon of her day," her many commercially successful plays chronicled the tension in early 20th-century women between their new economic and sexual freedom and their old traditional values. Her first success, *The Three of Us* (1906), was followed by some 30 Broadway plays, most of which she directed and staged herself. Although she wrote some sentimental plays in the teens, her best works were her seriocomic, women-centered plays: *Myself Bettina* (1908), *A Man's World* (1910), *Ourselves* (1913), *Young Wisdom* (1914), *He and She* (1920; first produced 1911), *Expressing Willie* (1924), *Let Us Be Gay* (1929), *As Husbands Go* (1931), *When Ladies Meet* (1932), and *Susan and God* (1937).

Besides her undisputed position as the leading commercial woman playwright and director of her time, Crothers was instrumental in the founding of Stage Women's War Relief Fund (1917), United Theatre Relief Committee (1932), and American Theatre Wing for War Relief (1940; best known for

Long Wharf Theatre 1989–90 production of *The Crucible,* with Maryann Plunkett and Frank Converse. Photo: T. Charles Erickson. Courtesy: Long Wharf Theatre.

the Stage Door Canteen). She received the Chi Omega National Achievement Award for 1938. FB

> See: I. Abrahamson, "The Career of Rachel Crothers in the American Drama," PhD diss., U of Chicago, 1956; L. C. Gottlieb, *Rachel Crothers,* 1979.

Crouse, Russel (1893–1966) Playwright, librettist, and producer who began his stage writing career as librettist for *The Gang's All Here* (1931); but it was only after he teamed with **Howard Lindsay** on *Anything Goes* (1934) that he achieved continued success. Crouse and Lindsay became prolific collaborators. Their first straight play was *Life with Father,* a nostalgic bit of Americana that captured the hearts of the Broadway audience for a contemporary long-run record that held until the 1970s. Working with Lindsay throughout the remainder of his career, Crouse helped write more than 15 plays and librettos, a highly successful example of the latter being *The Sound of Music* (1959). They also teamed to produce many plays in New York, including several of their own and the profitable *Arsenic and Old Lace* (1941). LDC

> See: C. Skinner, *Life with Lindsay & Crouse,* Boston, 1976.

Crucible, The, by **Arthur Miller** opened in New York on 22 January 1953, running for 197 performances. Directed by **Jed Harris,** its cast included **Arthur Kennedy** as John Proctor, Beatrice Straight as Elizabeth Proctor, Madeleine Sherwood as Abigail Williams, and **E. G. Marshall** as the Reverend Hale. Arthur Miller's most-produced play, it ran Off-Broadway for 571 performances in 1957–8,

was first produced in London by Laurence Olivier in 1965 and revived there again in 1990, and served as the inaugural production of Tony Randall's National Actors Theatre (1991). Although the immediate sociopolitical context of this treatment of the 17th-century Salem witch trials was McCarthyism and the actions of the House Un-American Activities Committee in the 1950s, Miller's larger subject is the effect on a community of an oppressive ideology and the fear and mistrust that it breeds. Miller presents the Salem witch trials as a result of repressed feelings of guilt, jealousy, revenge, resentment, and sexual attraction among the Salem people. In the end, John Proctor must decide whether to make a false confession of witchcraft in order to save himself and preserve his farm for his sons or to deny the charge, thus losing his life but maintaining his integrity and his "name" as a legacy of his children.   BCM

Cryer, Gretchen (1935–   ) Playwright, librettist, actor. With Nancy Ford, Cryer writes political rock musicals, including *Now Is the Time for All Good Men* (1967), *The Last Sweet Days of Isaac* (1970, Obie, etc.), *I'm Getting My Act Together and Taking It on the Road* (1978; three years **Off-Broadway**), and *Hang On to the Good Times* (1985). TH-S

CSC Repertory, Ltd. (The Classic Stage Company) Founded in 1967 by Christopher Martin as a workshop of New York University students, it was incorporated as the City Stage Company in 1968. Martin, who led the group until 1984, maintained a resident company that presented an international repertoire of old and modern classics plus a smattering of new plays. Artistic director Carey Perloff (who, in 1992, resigned and was replaced by David Esbjornson) continued in this tradition, but cast each show individually and favored reinterpretations of neglected works, particularly those that combined theatricality and notable language: Typical are recent productions of Tirso de Molina's *Don Juan of Seville* and Pinter's *The Birthday Party*. New translations and adaptations of foreign-language plays are now a house specialty.   CLJ

Cuban–American theatre The origins of Cuban theatre in the U.S. are to be found in the melodramas and Cuban blackface farces that were staged by the Cuban immigrant communities in New York City and Ybor City–Tampa during the final decade of the 19th century. In NYC these were produced by groups made up of professional and amateur players, such as the Club Lírico Dramático, directed by Luis Baralt, a 30-year veteran of the Havana stage; these first productions raised funds to support the war for Cuban independence from Spain.

In the early 20th century, Cuban melodrama and lyric theatre became staples of the commercial stage in the Hispanic community, which supported its own theatre houses and repertory companies, as well as hosting companies on tour from Havana and Tampa. Prior to WW II, one of the most popular theatrical genres in the Hispanic community was the *obra bufa cubana,* or Cuban blackface farce, written and/or improvised by such local playwrights as Alberto O'Farrill and Juan C. Rivera, as well as such masters from Cuba as Arquímides Pous and Armando Bronca (pseud.).

Hispanic theatrical culture developed in Ybor City–Tampa during the late 19th and early 20th centuries on the stages of Cuban and Spanish mutualists societies; these were allied to the tobacco industry that had been transplanted there from Cuba. A mix of amateur and professional players, plus tours by professional companies from abroad, helped to nurture the creation of a full-fledged commercial stage by the 1920s, one that produced talent for the **Hispanic theatre** in New York, Cuba, and Spain. Based on this intense activity, Tampa became the site for the only Hispanic (often called Cuban) **Federal Theatre Project,** which produced 14 shows during 1936–7, including a Spanish-language version of *It Can't Happen Here.*

The Cuban Revolution of 1959 is the most recent event resulting in large-scale theatrical activity in Cuban U.S. communities, principally those in Miami and New York. At first, stages were founded in these two cities to accommodate a primarily political theatre of exile, as well as a vaudevillesque commodity theatre that still relies upon the humor, stereotypes, and music of the *obras bufas cubanas* as entertainment. Among the most active and recognized of the serious exile playwrights are José Cid Pérez, Leopoldo Hernández, Matías Montes Huidobro, Fermín Borges, René Ariza, and José Sánchez Boudy, all of whom primarily write their plays in Spanish and have depended on publication for reaching broader audiences than those attending their limited university-sponsored productions. Of primary concern to these writers has been criticism of Fidel Castro and the communist Revolution, and a nostalgic longing for the land and culture left behind upon taking refuge in the U.S.

Another generation of playwrights has appeared, primarily comprising writers who were educated or began their theatrical careers here in the U.S. The latter are more likely to write their works in English as well as Spanish and to deal with acculturation, bilingualism, culture conflict, the generational gap between immigrant parents and U.S.-raised children, and other themes pertaining to life in the U.S. Included among what can be properly called a generation of Cuban-American playwrights are Iván Acosta, Manuel Martín, Mario Peña, Dolores Prida, and Omar Torres. This generation is characterized by extensive work on the stage as playwrights, actors, and directors in primarily Hispanic nonprofit theatres in New York and Miami, with Acosta and Torres also venturing off to work in the commercial cinema. NK

See: J. A. Escarpanter, *Latin American Theatre Review* (Spring 1986); N. Kanellos, *A History of Hispanic Theatre in the United States, Origins to 1940,* Austin, 1990; M. Watson-Espener in *Hispanic Theatre in the United States,* ed. N. Nanellos, Houston, 1984.

Cullum, John (1930–) Actor-singer. After graduating from the University of Tennessee, he played supporting roles at the **New York Shakespeare Festival.** He had a featured role in *Camelot* (1960), starred in *On a Clear Day You Can See Forever* (1965), and appeared as Edward Rutledge in *1776* (1969). He won Tony Awards for his portrayals of a stalwart Virginia farmer in *Shenandoah* (1975) and a frenetic theatre impresario in *On the Twentieth Century* (1978). Equally at home in drama, he replaced the lead in *Deathtrap* (1979), starred in *The Boys in Autumn* (1986), and in 1990 became a regular on the TV series "Northern Exposure." MK

Cummings (née Halveerstadt), Constance (1910–) American-born actress who, because of her marriage to English playwright Benn W. Levy, has spent most of her career in England. Her first London success, *Sour Grapes,* was followed the same year (1934) by her first important New York appearance (*Accent on Youth*). During her long career she has appeared in modern and classical plays, including *Madame Bovary* (1937); *Goodbye, Mr. Chips* (1938); *Romeo and Juliet* and *Saint Joan* (both 1939, at the Old Vic); *The Petrified Forest* (1942); **MacLeish**'s *J.B.* (1961); *Who's Afraid of Virginia Woolf?* (1964, replacing **Uta Hagen** as Martha in London); Noël Coward's *Fallen Angels* (1967); and *Hamlet* (Gertrude in Tony Richardson's 1969 production). In 1971 she joined the National Theatre of Great Britain, playing Volumnia in *Coriolanus,* Leda in *Amphitryon 38,* Mary Tyrone in *Long Day's Journey into Night,* Mme. Ranevsky in *The Cherry Orchard,* and Agave in *The Bacchae.* She won a Tony Award in **Arthur Kopit**'s *Wings,* first seen in New York (1978) and the following year in London. Since then, she has appeared in *Hay Fever* and *The Golden Age* in London, *The Chalk Garden* in New York, and *Mrs. Warren's Profession* in Vienna. DBW

Curse of the Starving Class by **Sam Shepard.** Although commissioned by **Joseph Papp,** the play premiered at London's Royal Court Theatre (21 April 1977). Even before the American premiere at **New York Shakespeare Festival**'s **Public Theater** (2 March 1978), the play won an unprecedented and controversial Obie Award on the basis of the published text alone. Important revivals include those of **Yale Repertory Theatre** (1980) and **INTAR** (1985). The explosive action focuses on a disintegrating family's craving for food. Father, mother, son, and daughter strain against the blood ties that unite them as the play, according to **Mel Gussow,** "charts the crippling effect of the 'creeping disease' of a consumer society that insists on shortchanging its citizens." FHL

Curtis, Paul J. (1927–) Director, teacher, performer. A student of **Erwin Piscator,** in 1952 he founded The American Mime Theatre in New York City, the first **mime** company and school in the U.S. in this century. He has created 47 mime plays for his company, has taught at major universities, professional performing schools, and art centers, and is author of *American Mime, The Medium* (1963). In 1973 he founded International Mimes and Pantomimists, which produced a directory and a bibliography. TL

Charlotte and Susan Cushman as Romeo and Juliet.
Courtesy: Harvard Theatre Collection.

Cushman, Charlotte Saunders (1816–76) The first native-born actress of the top rank, Cushman, described as commanding rather than handsome, was considered the most powerful actress on the 19th-century stage. Appearing somewhat masculine, with a tall, strong body, unusual voice, and powerful personality, her stage characterizations emerged in heroic outline. Trained as an opera singer, she misused her voice and was forced to alter her career.

Her acting debut was as Lady Macbeth under **James Caldwell** in New Orleans (1836), repeated the same year in New York at the **Bowery.** Her first sensational success was as Nancy Sykes in *Oliver Twist* (1839). A failed manager of Philadelphia's **Walnut Street Theatre,** she appeared opposite W. C. Macready on his American tour in 1843–4 and then went to London, appearing first in 1845 at the Princess's Theatre. After 1844 she performed about 35 roles, with only 10 repeated regularly. By her return to the U.S. in 1849, she was considered by many the greatest living English-speaking actress. During her long career she played over 200 roles, excelling as Meg Merrilies in *Guy Mannering,* Romeo opposite the Juliet of her sister Susan, Lady Macbeth, and Queen Katharine in *Henry VIII.* During 1852–69 she gave a series of farewell appearances, returning permanently to the stage in 1869 to forget the pain she suffered from cancer.

Cushman's style was marked by sweep, power, and majesty, sometimes overly expressive and extravagant. One critic described her movement as "a galvanized distortion of nature," and said her constant activity conveyed the impression she was "suffering under a violent attack of colic." Her definitive biography, *Bright Particular Star* by Joseph Leach, was published (New Haven) in 1970.
DBW

Custis, George Washington Parke (1781–1857) Playwright. Born into a distinguished southern family, Custis expressed nationalistic views in his writing. Of his nine plays, *Pocahontas; or, The Settlers of Virginia* (1830) achieved most success in the theatre. *The Eighth of January* (1828) dramatized his enthusiasm for Andrew Jackson; *The Rail Road* (1828) celebrated the opening of the Baltimore & Ohio; and *Northpoint; or, Baltimore Defended* (1833) honored that famous battle from the war of 1812.
WJM

D

Da Costa (né Tecosky), Morton (1914–89) Highly successful Broadway director during the 1950s. Educated at Temple University, Da Costa cofounded the Civic Repertory Theatre, Dayton, OH (1937) before debuting on Broadway in 1942 as an actor. His New York directing debut was at the City Center with *She Stoops to Conquer* (1949). His first major success was *Plain and Fancy*, followed by *No Time for Sergeants* (both 1955), *Auntie Mame* (1956), and *The **Music Man*** (1957). SMA

Dale, Alan (né Alfred J. Cohen) (1861–1928) English-born critic who came to New York in the early 1880s to write for the *Dramatic Times*. In 1887 Joseph Pulitzer employed him as drama critic for the *World*. Dale switched to Hearst's *Morning Journal* in 1897 and *Cosmopolitan* magazine in 1904. Except for the period 1914–17, he remained a Hearst regular until his death. Dale popularized an aggressive and "smart" style of reviewing. *Who's Who in the Theatre* (1914) concluded that his opinions "probably carry more weight than any others in New York." TLM

Dallas Theater Center 3636 Turtle Creek Blvd., Dallas, TX [Architect: Frank Lloyd Wright]. Founded in 1959 by Baylor University professor **Paul Baker** and a group of Dallas citizens, the Dallas Theater Center sprang into being housed in the only theatre designed by Frank Lloyd Wright that he ever lived to see built. A gift of Dallas businessmen and named after a Texas actress who was killed in a plane crash, the Kalita Humphreys Theatre consists of a geometric poured concrete structure set into a hilly, wooded area a few miles from the center of the city. Its original stage was set at one end of the auditorium and was equipped with a revolve and two side stages. Professor Baker's plan to assemble a permanent acting company to present classics, contemporary plays, and introduce new works in conjunction with a graduate program at Baylor, later at Trinity University, where he transferred his activities, was largely fulfilled but has been discontinued. To the original 516-seat theatre have been added an experimental and flexible stage, *In the Basement*, seating 50–100, and the Arts District Theatre in downtown Dallas (up to 750 seats). Under the leadership of **Adrian Hall** (1983–9), DTC became an Equity company. Hall was replaced by 35-year-old Ken Bryant, who died suddenly in October 1990 following an automobile accident. In December 1991 Richard Hamburger, artistic director of Maine's Portland Stage, was appointed artistic director. MCH

Dalrymple, Jean (1910–) Producer, director, and publicist who began her career as an actress in vaudeville, then became personal representative with **John Golden,** and in 1940 formed her own publicity organization. Her initial venture as producer was in 1945 when she presented *Hope for the Best* by William McCleery. Associated with the New York City Center Light Opera Company and the City Center Drama Company from its inception in 1943, in 1953 she became its general director, a position she held for the next 15 years. This experience was recorded in her book *From the Last Row* (1975). During 1968–70 she was executive director of the **American National Theatre and Academy,** and in 1958 she was coordinator of the performing arts for the U.S. at the Brussels World's Fair. DBW

Daly, [Peter Christopher] Arnold (1875–1927) Producer and actor. Daly should be remembered as **Shaw**'s first truly effective champion in the U.S. Even as he was establishing himself as a player of supporting roles in England and America, he pursued his interest in Shaw by directing and acting in a trial matinee of *Candida*, which opened for a regular run in New York in 1903 and then went on tour with *The Man of Destiny*. After visiting Shaw, Daly returned for the 1904–5 season to produce *How She Lied to Her Husband* (written for Daly), *You Never Can Tell, John Bull's Other Island,* and *Mrs. Warren's Profession*. The first New York performance of this last play was cause for Daly's arrest on moral charges, although he was acquitted. In 1906, Daly added *Arms and the Man* to his repertory and, under the management of the **Shubert**s, conducted a successful national tour. Somewhat dismayed by the vitriolic response of conservative critics, Daly abandoned Shaw for a time to pursue more conventional roles. MR

See: B. Goldsmith, *Arnold Daly*, New York, 1927.

Daly, [John] Augustin (1838–99) Dramatist, managing director, and critic who dominated the theatrical scene in the U.S. during the last half of the 19th century. His plays and especially his productions set a new standard for American theatre and exerted a strong influence in England, beginning with a first European tour in 1884 and culminating with the opening of Daly's own theatre in London in 1893. He began his theatre career as a critic, writing for five newspapers during 1859–67. During this period he also wrote or adapted his first plays, most notably *Leah, the Forsaken* (1862) and the melodrama *Under the Gaslight* (1867). From the inception of his writing career he was assisted at every turn by his brother Joseph, though this collaboration was kept secret. Ultimately, the Dalys had over 90 of their plays or adaptations performed. Of this large number few are significant literary accomplishments, though many show Daly to have been an exceptional contriver of effects and theatrical moments and, during the 1870s and '80s, a writer of melodramas and sentimental comedies superior to most of his contemporaries. Among his more successful productions were *A Flash of Lightning* (1868), *Frou-Frou* (1870), *Horizon* (1871), *Divorce* (1871), *Article 47* (1872), *Needles and Pins* (1880), *Dollars and Sense* (1883), *Love on Crutches* (1884), and *The Lottery of Love* (1888). He also produced adaptations of English classics and **Shakespeare,** one of the most successful of which, *The Taming of the Shrew,* was presented at Stratford-upon-Avon in 1888, supposedly the first performance of the play given there.

Many of his more notable productions featured **Ada Rehan, John Drew, Mrs. G. H. Gilbert,** and **James Lewis,** known as the "Big Four." Daly was usually adept at discerning and developing talent: Over 75 prominent actors owed their success to his training. Daly also managed and built several important theatres, beginning with the rental in 1869 of the **Fifth Avenue Theatre,** and took over briefly the Grand Opera House. In 1879, with these theatres behind him, he took over the old Wood's Museum, which he opened as **Daly's,** remaining there until his death. Constantly striving for an ensemble effect in his productions, Daly was one of the first directors in the modern sense and the first American *régisseur.* [See also **Introduction,** §2.] DBW

See: R. Cullen and D. Wilmeth, eds., *Plays by Augustin Daly,* New York, 1984; J. Daly, *The Life of Augustin Daly,* New York, 1917; M. Felheim, *The Theater of Augustin Daly,* Cambridge, MA, 1956.

Daly's Theatre

1221 Broadway, NYC. Built as a museum in 1867, manager John Banvard used its three-tier, 2,000-seat auditorium for theatrical performances in the afternoons and evenings. A year later, it was taken over by George Wood, who renamed it Wood's Museum and Metropolitan Theatre, in which he presented plays, comic operas, burlesques, and variety for the next few years. In 1876, Banvard reclaimed the lease and renamed it the Broadway Theatre. Its most significant period occurred when **Augustin Daly,** responding to the uptown drift of the theatres, took it over in 1879, renovated it extensively, and transformed it into Daly's Theatre. Here, he and his stock company made their last stand against the new system of booking single plays into a theatre to try for a long run. Even Daly resorted to leasing the theatre to outside producers and summer rentals to keep it afloat, but when he died in 1899, the house passed to a succession of managers, including **Daniel Frohman** and the **Shubert brothers.** It met an inglorious end as a burlesque house when the new theatre district was amalgamating around Times Square. In 1920, it was razed and was replaced by a commercial structure. MCH

Damn Yankees Two-act musical comedy, music and lyrics by **Richard Adler** and **Jerry Ross,** book by **George Abbott** and Douglass Wallop; opened 5 May 1955 at the **46th Street Theatre,** New York, running 1,019 performances. Based on a novel by Wallop, this baseball fantasy treats the struggle of a frustrated baseball fan (Robert Shafer) who sells his soul to the Devil (Ray Walston) and is turned into a star player (Stephen Douglass); trying to abrogate the pact, he has to deal with the Devil's star seductress, Lola (**Gwen Verdon**). Mounted by basically the same production team as Adler and Ross's *Pajama Game* (1954), it was equally successful, contributing two standards ("Heart" and "Whatever Lola Wants, Lola Gets") to popular song literature. After two 1,000-performance successes in two attempts, this was the last Adler–Ross show: Ross died at age 29 six months after it opened. JD

Dance in the American theatre The contrast between the Puritan disapproval of dance in the northern colonies and the leisure social dancing in the wealthier southern colonies created an atmosphere of tension toward the arts in colonial America. Professional performers had difficulties establishing themselves in the northern colonies until the bans against theatrical entertainers began to be relaxed. Initially, American productions were given mainly by amateurs or semiprofessionals, supplemented by professional touring European performers, primarily French and English. Prior to the American Revolution, an assortment of European touring performers (many of a lesser caliber) presented Harlequinades, spectacles, and incidental dances in theatre productions. With the opening of New York's **John Street Theatre** in 1767, visiting artists extended engagements and expanded the range into opera and pantomime. Just when theatrical entertainment had taken hold, the American Revolution prompted legislation to prohibit theatrical performances, which made it impossible for companies to produce plays. **Lewis Hallam,** a refugee from the provincial English theatre, used his fame and popularity to present work under the guise of "lectures." During the first season of "lectures" in Philadelphia, **John Durang** joined Hallam's company as a dancer, and remained with the company when they performed the "lectures" in New York. The Old **American Company** expanded from their evening of Shakespearean excerpts to full-length English pantomimes such as *The Touchstone; or, Harlequin Traveler.* Durang played Scaramouche as well as danced the hornpipe, for which he became most famous later in his career. After the Revolutionary War and the repeal of the antitheatre laws, foreign performers began returning to America. Although theatres were built in many cities by 1800, New York and Philadelphia quickly became centers for drama and dance. The French Revolution inspired new directions for dance, particularly ballet, in Europe, and by the early 1800s the romantic era gave rise to the prominence of the ethereal ballerina image. By the mid-19th century European ballet artists found their way to America and were met with enthusiastic and adoring audiences.

At the same time, the American blackface **minstrel show**s also evolved and became popular. Using bone clappers and jawbones instead of the drum (which was forbidden), the performers combined hand clapping and foot stomping with their songs. By the mid-1800s, Master Juba (William Henry Lane), one of the few blacks in early minstrelsy, became so famous that he toured England and had a profound influence on the British and European theatres. The impact of the blackface minstrel remained in the American theatre through the 20th century, introducing an African American–inspired dance influence.

The first notable production created and produced in America that incorporated extensive use of dance was *The **Black Crook,*** presented at **Niblo's Garden** (New York) in 1866. A musical extravaganza based on a trite melodrama, it featured a French ballet troupe. The show popularized the use of "dancing girls," and was so successful that it toured America for the next 40 years, paving the way for later productions such as the *Follies of 1907* (**Ziegfeld**'s first). As dance became socially acceptable, dancers broke away from theatre companies and appeared in minstrel shows, medicine shows, carnivals, and circuses. These entertainments continued to draw audiences into the early 1900s, when black performers began to "sing the blues," tap dance, and create their own jazz style of music.

On the **burlesque** and **vaudeville** stages, dance was often used with stunts and gimmicks such as "dancing" on a tightrope, whereas the musical **revue** relied on quantities of dancing girls to fill the stage. The quality and type of the dancing, however, was mixed – sometimes elegant, sometimes questionable. Serious dance artists left those forums to explore and eventually to elevate dance as an independent art form – notably Martha Graham, who danced in the *Greenwich Village Follies* (1925) and later developed her own technique and style of modern dance, creating a new spectrum of dance and theatre.

By WW I, the American **musical theatre** was firmly rooted and had developed into an important venue for American dancers. Shows such as *Irene* (1919), *The **Student Prince*** (1924), and *Desert Song* (1926) used period dancing. The influence of the black musical theatre tradition was strong enough for the black musicals to resurface in the 1920s. *Shuffle Along* (1921) set a new standard for dance in musicals and introduced jazz music with jazz dance styles. Although dance artists such as Fred and Adele **Astaire** achieved fame from their successes in musical theatre shows like *Funny Face* (1927), the formula for a musical in the 1920s and '30s made the choreography primarily *divertissements* rather than part of the dramatic action. However, this period was highlighted by the "reuniting" of theatre and dance, as many great dance artists and choreographers collaborated with directors on musicals. Modern dance was emerging in America, but the ballet was still imported from Europe until 1933 when **George Balanchine** came to New York to establish an American ballet company. He went on to become one of the foremost choreographers of the 20th century. In 1936 he choreographed the musical *On Your Toes,* for which he created a ballet within the musical (a story within the story) danced by Russian ballerina Tamara Geva and American **Ray Bolger.** While Hollywood's use of dance in motion pictures enhanced the appeal and appreciation for dance artists, it was not until *Oklahoma!* in 1943 that dance in musical theatre began to change. With the "Dream Ballet" sequence in *Oklahoma!,* **Agnes de Mille,** a highly respected modern dancer and choreographer, retold the plot through dance, thereby enhancing the dramatic value of the dance. *Oklahoma!* was followed by a series of successful shows that incorporated dance as an integral part of the play, including *Carousel* (1945), *South Pacific* (1949), and *The King and I* (1951).

The merger of American musical theatre and black musical theatre styles began to appear in the form of American jazz dance. The vogue for this theatre dance form began with **Michael Kidd**'s choreography in *Guys and Dolls* (1950), and was most dramatic in **Bob Fosse**'s choreography for *Pajama Game* (1954), whose "Steam Heat" was a provocative dance in the new style. However, with *My Fair Lady* (1956), musical theatre choreography returned to the operetta style with period dancing and inserted dance sequences. One year later the choreography by **Jerome Robbins** and **Peter Gennero** in *West Side Story* (1957) captured the dynamic and vibrant style of American jazz/theatre dance. These two different musical styles remained fashionable into the 1960s. The musical *Gypsy* (1959) used dances that reflected the vaudeville and burlesque theatres, whereas the choreography in *Hello, Dolly!* (1961) was another example of American jazz, modified to fit the period with dance numbers in nearly every scene. Later, *Sweet Charity* (1965) gave new importance to the dance and choreography by having a story line in which the dancing was an integral part of and performed by the main character. The social rebellion of the early 1960s was well represented in *Hair* (1968) with rock music, hippie-style costumes, long hair, and the nude scene. Its choreography was based on the free-style social dance of the time and led the way to a new form of collaboration of dance and theatre. The avant-garde movement in dance, which formed in the 1960s and emerged full force in the '70s, had dancers involved with happenings and performance events, with some dancers referred to as **performance art**ists. The avant-garde movement permeated all of the arts in breaking down previous barriers and constraints. Although dance in the American musical theatre continued to dominate the integration of dance and theatre, the artistic movement of the 1970s allowed more freedom for dance in dramatic productions as well as for dance productions to have a drama/theatre focus. The channels for dance on the American stage became more numerous, including modern dance, classical ballet, opera-ballet, jazz dance, tap dance, and musical theatre dance. A few dance artists, such as Fred Astaire and Gene Kelly, created such unique individual dance styles that they defied all the accepted categories.

With a few exceptions, the American musical

theatre struggled for new material during the 1960s, and dancers struggled to maintain significant collaboration with theatre artists. Dance artists moved in individualized directions that ignored the prescribed perimeters that had previously defined dance productions, and incorporated vocalizations, pedestrian movement, and other taboos previously considered appropriate only in dramatic theatre. Yet as these dance artists pursued alternative possibilities for dance, theatre and dance seemed to keep respectable distances other than in musical comedy. Numerous musical revivals during the 1960s aided in the popularity of shows that featured dancing. However, **Patrica Birch** with *A Little Night Music* (1973) redefined the concept of dance in a musical. Far from the splashy extravaganzas of *No, No Nanette* (revival, 1971), *See Saw* (1971), *Pippin* (1971), and *Grease* (1972), *Night Music* was presented with the focus on the story and dramatic action. The music and dance were so cleverly woven into the whole that they were neither distractions nor diversions, but rather an enhancement of the action. This attitude that choreographers no longer considered their work exclusively dance also affected music, which was no longer considered sacred. When Norbert Vesak choreographed and directed **Leonard Bernstein**'s *Mass*, produced in 1974 at Zellerbach Auditorium (Berkeley, CA), it was described as "a theatre piece for dancers." *A Chorus Line* (1975) was written for and about dancers, and again the dance sequences were used as dramatic tools to unfold the story. This work thrust dance to the forefront of the American theatre and established a trend for integrating movement in theatrical productions exemplified by *For Colored Girls Who Have Considered Suicide When the Rainbow Is Enuf* (1977), written by **Ntozake Shange** and choreographed by Paula Moss. In this play, there were no spectacular dance numbers, but all of the actresses presented the emotions and lives of their characters through movement and dance.

Other theatre directors began experimenting with dance movement in both revivals of masterpieces and in new scripts. **Chekhov**'s *The Cherry Orchard*, directed by **Andrei Serban** (1977), used dance movement to express the complexities of the characters, which enhanced and illustrated the underlying meaning. *Fen* (1984) by Caryl Churchill required the actors to switch roles throughout the play, and, in the production directed by Les Walters, the women were specifically choreographed in movements to represent their daily tasks – working in the fields, cooking dinner, and making love. The British musical *Cats* (1983) continued the tradition of the dancing musical, with the focus on the dancing and the music rather than on the book.

By the 1980s, the **Shakespeare**an theatre took on new forms and perspectives with rock-and-roll versions of *Two Gentlemen of Verona* (New York, 1971; 1986), a punk-rock *Hamlet* (Texas, 1986), a Victorian *Winter's Tale* (Texas, 1986), and a roaring-twenties version of *Comedy of Errors* (New York, 1986). The standard Renaissance dances of Shakespeare were replaced with dances appropriate to directors' visions in these renditions. Dance artists such as **Martha Clarke** created theatre/dance works

that could not be singularly categorized, and her *Garden of Earthly Delights* (1987) was praised by drama and dance critics alike. Not simply the use of dance, but the kinds and forms of dance expanded radically in America during the 1970s and '80s. A version of *Medea* (1986), presented by the Japanese Toho Company, Ltd., used traditional Japan theatre (Noh and Kabuki); while traditional opera dance sequences were part of the production of *M. Butterfly* (1989). Yet another innovative concept was explored by Steven Berkoff in his adaptation of Franz Kafka's *The Metamorphosis* produced in 1989. The role of Gregor Samsa who turned into a beetle was played by ballet superstar Mikhail Baryshnikov. The transformation and characterization of Gregor as a beetle was greatly enhanced by the use of dance movement.

The American musical theatre is the most recognized forum for dance in theatre. However, as dance and theatre artists continue to explore new and personal interpretations of their own media, the definition of dance that existed at the turn of the century, which was redefined by modern dance pioneers and continues to be redefined by every generation of dance artists, no longer restricts the use of dance to specific types of productions or limits the kind of movement that can be used.   LF

See: Dance Magazine, January 1960–December 1990; R. Kislan, *Hoofing on Broadway,* New York, 1987; P. Magriel, ed., *Chronicles of American Dance,* New York, 1949, 1970; Curt Sachs, *World History of the Dance,* New York, 1937; M. Stearns and J. Stearns, *Jazz Dance,* New York, 1979; W. Terry, *The Dance in America,* New York, 1956.

Dance Theatre Workshop A leading dance and performance art venue located in the Chelsea district of Manhattan. It was founded in 1965 by a group of neighborhood performers and housed initially in choreographer Jeff Duncan's loft on West 20th Street. In addition to dance, music, and alternative theatrical events, DTW has presented early work by talents such as **New Vaudeville**'s **Bill Irwin,** stand-up comic Whoopi Goldberg, and performance artists John Kelly, **Rachel Rosenthal,** and Laurie Carlos.   CLJ

Daniele, Graciela (1940?–) Argentine-born director-choreographer who came to New York in 1963, where she began her career as a dancer in such productions as *Coco, Follies,* and *Chicago.* Her first effort as choreographer was **Durang**'s *History of the American Film* (1978), followed by **Wilford Leach**'s *Pirates of Penzance, The Rink, The Mystery of Edwin Drood,* and *Alice in Concert* with **Meryl Streep.** In 1990 she moved into direction with the Trinidad-inspired folk-fable musical *Once on This Island;* in 1991 she directed William Finn's *March of the Falsettos* and *Falsettoland* (together) at the **Hartford Stage Company;** these, though performed on Broadway in 1992, were redirected by **James Lapine,** the original director of the individual plays.   DBW

Daniels, William (David) (1927–) Actor. For the cultivated, complacent publisher in *The Zoo Story* (1960), Daniels received **Clarence Der-**

went and Obie awards. A prominent stage actor from 1939 (*Life with Father*) into the 1970s, he is best known as the egotistical surgeon in the TV series "St. Elsewhere" (1982). An **Actors Studio** member, Daniels appeared in over a dozen New York productions, notably as Albert Amundsen in *A Thousand Clowns* (1962) and John Adams in *1776* (1972).   DBW

Danites; or, The Heart of the Sierras, The, credited to **Joaquin Miller;** opened at the **Broadway Theatre** 22 August 1877 and became one of the most popular plays of frontier life. **McKee Rankin** played Sandy McGee, a good-hearted miner who befriended young Billy Piper. Billy, played by **Kitty Blanchard** Rankin, was actually a woman, Nancy Williams, disguised to escape the retribution of the Danites, a band of Mormons sworn to avenge the murder of Joseph Smith. *The Danites,* based on Miller's *The First Fam'lies of the Sierras* (1876), reflected widespread anti-Mormon sentiment. Although originally credited to Miller, who published a version as *The Danites in the Sierras,* lawsuits eventually revealed that the script played by Rankin was composed by P. A. Fitzgerald, an obscure Philadelphia writer.   RAH

Danner, Blythe (1944–   ) Actress, frequently on television (*Eccentricities of a Nightingale,* 1976; *You Can't Take It with You,* 1979), she emphasizes "the individualization of a dilemma or mood . . . that we all recognize." She debuted **Off-Broadway** in *The Infantry* (1966), and on Broadway in Leonard Gershe's *Butterflies Are Free* (Tony, 1969). She often appears regionally and Off-Broadway (e.g., *A Streetcar Named Desire,* **Circle in the Square,** 1988; *Much Ado About Nothing,* **New York Shakespeare Festival,** 1989). Films include *Brighton Beach Memoirs* (1986) and *Another Woman* (1988). Danner received a *Theatre World* Award for *The Miser* (1969) and Tony nomination for *Betrayal* (1980). Her husband is writer-director-producer Bruce Paltrow.   REK

Darkness at Noon Anticommunist melodrama by **Sidney Kingsley.** Commissar Rubashov (Claude Rains) is imprisoned, tried, and executed for "political divergences." Winner of the Drama Critics' Circle Award as the best play of 1951, this adaptation of Arthur Koestler's 1941 novel focuses on Rubashov's purgative remembrances of his shameful excesses as a party official. At the end he heroically apologizes "to his hundred eighty million fellow prisoners," recants his Marxist commitment to History, and acknowledges the failure of the revolution to consider the human soul. Koestler's attack on Stalinism and the 1937 purges seemed, in the cold war milieu in which the **Playwrights' Company** produced the play, a propagandistic repudiation of the Soviet system.   WD

Da Silva (né Silverblatt), Howard (1909–86) Actor, director, and producer. Born in Cleveland, OH, Da Silva studied at the Carnegie Institute of Technology and debuted in **Eva Le Gallienne's Civic Repertory Company** (1929), remaining for five years. His 1936 film debut was in *Once in a Blue Moon.* The same year he directed on radio the Great Classic Series for the **Federal Theatre Project.** He was twice nominated for Academy Awards. Among his outstanding stage roles were Benjamin Franklin in *1776* and Ben Marino in *Fiorello!* Da Silva won an Emmy in 1978 for *Verna – USO Girl.*   SMA

Davenport, Edward Loomis (1815–77) Actor known for his versatility, grace, good taste, musical voice, and gentlemanly manners. **Anna Cora Mowatt** said that he simply looked like a leading man. He began his career in Providence (1835), became Mowatt's leading man (1846), went with her to London, remained there for seven years (often playing in support of W. C. Macready), and returned to acclaim for his "intelligent and impressive" conception of Lanciotto in **Boker's** *Francesca da Rimini* (1885). From then until his final season (1875–6, playing Brutus to **Lawrence Barrett's** Cassius), he became known for his extraordinary versatility. He was equally effective as Bill Sykes, Hamlet, Sir Lucius O'Trigger, and Othello.

He was the father of the actress **Fanny Davenport,** and three of his descendants have been active in recent years: Anne and **William Seymour** as actors, and the late May Davenport Seymour as theatre curator at the Museum of the City of New York.   RM

See: E. Edgett, ed., *Edward Loomis Davenport, A Biography,* New York, 1901.

Davenport, Fanny (1850–98) English-born actress and daughter of actor **E. L. Davenport,** "Miss Fanny" was a popular child actress before her adult debut in 1862 at New York's **Niblo's Garden Theatre.** In 1869 she joined **Augustin Daly's Fifth Avenue Theatre** company and demonstrated remarkable versatility in light comedies, Shakespeare, and finally serious dramatic works like Daly's *Pique* (1876), in which she created Mabel Renfew, one of her most popular roles, along with Nancy Sykes in *Oliver Twist.* A beautiful, "spirited" actress, she formed her own company and gave the American English-language premieres of four Bernhardt vehicles by Sardou: *Fedora* (1883), *La Tosca* (1888), *Cleopatra* (1890), and *Gismonda* (1894).   FHL

Davenport Brothers Ira Erastus Davenport (1839–1911) and **William Henry Harrison Davenport** (1841–77) are credited as the first successful stage mediums. Beginning in their hometown of Buffalo, NY, they first toured the U.S. successfully in the 1860s, producing "inexplicable manifestations" from their mysterious wooden cabinet in which they were securely tied. Denounced as fakes by such prominent British conjurors as John Henry Anderson and John Nevil Maskelyne, they nevertheless toured until William's death, and influenced all subsequent producers of "spirit music."   DBW

Davidge, William Pleater (1814–88) English-born actor who made his U.S. debut at the **Broadway Theatre** in 1850. He reportedly played over

1,100 different roles, but was celebrated for his protrayal of English comic characters like Sir Peter Teazle, Bottom, Toby Belch, and especially Dick Deadeye in *HMS Pinafore*. He was with **Augustin Daly**'s company (1869–77) and the Madison Square company (1885–death). His memoir *Footlight Flashes* (1863), short on biographical insights, occasionally informs about theatrical organization and business. DJW

Davidson, Gordon (1933–) Director. Educated at Cornell (1956) and at Case Western Reserve (1957), Davidson has directed at the Paper Mill Playhouse (NJ), the **Barter Theatre,** and other venues, and stage-managed for Martha Graham. At the **American Shakespeare Festival** he assisted **John Houseman**, who chose him to co-direct *King Lear* with the Theatre Group and serve as Managing Director (1964–6). He is Producing Director of the **Ahmanson (Los Angeles Theatre Center)** and Artistic Director/Producer of the **Mark Taper Forum,** where he directs nearly 20% of the mainstage productions. JDM

Davies, Acton (1870–1916) Drama critic. Born and educated in St. Johns, Quebec, Davies came to New York in 1887. He began contributing to newspapers and became a reporter in 1890. In 1893 he succeeded **Charles B. Dillingham** as drama critic for *The Evening Sun,* remaining until 1914. Davies catered to popular taste in a lively, personal style, and acquired a reputation for having an insider's view of the stage. He wrote extensively for popular magazines and was manager for and literary adviser to the **Shubert**s. TLM

Davis, Henrietta Vinton (1860–1941) **African-American** actress. For 35 years a preeminent actress and solo elocutionist, Baltimore-born Davis was "a singularly beautiful woman . . . with illustriously expressive eyes [and a] rich, flexible and effective voice." She was universally hailed by audiences across America for her powerful and moving interpretations of a range of dramatic heroines that included Juliet, Portia, Ophelia, Rosalind, Lady Anne, Desdemona, Lady Macbeth, and Cleopatra. Excluded by racial prejudice from the established professional stage, Davis gave concert readings and performed dramatic scenes with other black actors. She produced and played leading roles in three plays by African-American dramatists: *Dessalines* (1893) and *Christophe* (1912), both by William Edgar Easton, and *Our Old Kentucky Home* (1898), written for her by the journalist John E. Bruce. During 1919–31 Davis held a major office in the Marcus Garvey movement, working for racial equality and the establishment of a black nation-state in Africa. EGH

Davis, L. Clarke (1835–1904) Editor, lawyer, and drama critic. Born to pioneering stock in Ohio, Davis grew up in Maryland and was educated at the Episcopal Academy in Philadelphia (1855). An early career in law led to editing a legal newspaper, after which he became managing editor of *The Philadelphia Inquirer* (1870). He wrote drama criticism for the *Inquirer* as well as for *Harper's,* the

Atlantic, the *Century, Scribners', Lippincott's,* and *Putnam's.* He ended his career as managing editor (1893) and editor-in-chief of the Philadelphia *Public Ledger.* A perceptive critic of acting, Davis noted the essence of **Joseph Jefferson III**'s *Rip Van Winkle* (1867): "the exquisite beauty and excellence of Mr. Jefferson's acting lie mostly in the fact that he has subdued it to the very complexion of nature." TLM

Davis, Ossie (1917–) African-American actor and playwright who began acting with the Harlem-based **Rose McClendon** Players and made his Broadway debut in the title role of *Jeb* (1946). Davis joined the national tour of *Anna Lucasta* (1947) and played in various New York productions, including *Stevedore* (1949), *The Green Pastures* (1951), and *No Time for Sergeants* (1955), before succeeding Sidney Poitier in *A Raisin in the Sun* (1959). In 1961 Davis assumed the lead role opposite his wife **Ruby Dee** in his hilarious comedy *Purlie Victorious,* which pungently ridiculed racial stereotyping. The film version, *Gone Are the Days* (1963), was unimpressive, but success was renewed with the musical *Purlie* (1970). Davis also wrote *Curtain Call, Mr. Aldridge, Sir* (1963), and has appeared in numerous films and television shows (in the early '90s as a regular on "Evening Shades"), some of which he scripted and directed. Louis D. Mitchell has called him "one of the most gifted men in the modern American theatre." EGH

Davis, Owen (1874–1956) The most successful American writing melodrama at the turn of the 20th century. From *Through the Breakers* (1899) to *The Family Cupboard* (1913), Davis wrote 129 melodramas, such as *Nellie, the Beautiful Cloak Model.* Then he stopped, and in "Why I Quit Writing Melodrama" (*American Magazine,* September 1914) explained his art – for example, the importance of the play title and of the stage carpenter in the third act, on which he later elaborated in *I'd Like to Do It Again* (1931). Abandoning his Harvard-trained writing style, he began to write realistic plays, such as *Detour* (1921), in which he depicted a spiritual barrenness. *Icebound* (1923), concerned with the lost illusions of a New England family, won a Pulitzer Prize. Among later plays, only his adaptation of Edith Wharton's *Ethan Frome* (1936), with his son Donald Davis, was successful. He could not keep pace with the new rank of American dramatists during the 1930s. His autobiography, *My First Fifty Years in the Theatre,* appeared in 1950. WJM

Davis, Richard Harding (1864–1916) Playwright, writer, and journalist (probably the best known of his generation). He romped with the glamorous Barrymores [see **Drew–Barrymore family**], and from the Spanish War in Cuba to WW I reported from the scene. A symbol of the exuberant life-style of his age, he wrote too much, too easily – at least 18 plays, dozens of stories, and nonfiction works – and thought too little about his creativity. John Barrymore had a small role in *The Dictator* (1904), a very successful play. Other plays, showing more theatrical than dramatic power, include *The Taming of Helen* (1903), *The Galloper* (1905), and *The Seventh Daughter* (1910).   WJM

See: G. Lanfford, *The Richard Harding Davis Years,* New York, 1961.

Davy Crockett; or, Be Sure You're Right, Then Go Ahead by **Frank H. Murdoch.** Although not successful when first introduced at the Rochester Opera House on 23 September 1872, *Davy Crockett* emerged as one of the most beloved plays of the 19th century. **Frank Mayo** patiently reworked it and then starred in it for over 20 years. Unlike other frontier plays featuring sensation and gunfire, *Davy Crockett* was romantic and poetic. Davy protected Eleanor Vaughn, his well-educated childhood sweetheart, from a pack of wolves by using his strong right arm to bar the cabin door. Sir Walter Scott's *Lochinvar,* which Davy read aloud, provided the poetic motif as Davy rescued Eleanor from an unwanted marriage and was dramatically transformed from rough-hewn backwoodsman to romantic hero.   RAH

D.C. Black Repertory Theatre Formed by actor **Robert Hooks** in 1970 to bring meaningful black professional theatre to the District of Colum-

bia, the company gave its inaugural production in 1972 and closed in 1976. Funding was a major problem, as were weak administration and an unappealing repertoire that included staged excerpts from the works of black writers. The training school in acting and dance was reorganized in 1977 as The Rep Inc., and continues to present occasional public performances.   EGH

Dead End by **Sidney Kingsley** was a major success in 1935, running on Broadway for 684 performances at the **Belasco Theatre**. It featured **Norman Bel Geddes**'s realistic set of a New York slum complete with a practical East River in the orchestra pit. The play focuses on the brutal city life of a gang of teenagers, and popularized Depression-era notions by linking crime with poverty and class conflict with unequal distribution of wealth. Ironically, after the play was filmed – in 1937 with Humphrey Bogart and six youngsters from the Broadway production – the Dead End "Kids" (Leo Gorcey, Huntz Hall, Gabriel Dell, etc.) went on to considerable material success in a series of films by the same name and ultimately pursued Hollywood careers as *The Bowery Boys.* BBW

Dead End by Sidney Kingsley as designed by Norman Bel Geddes (1935). Photo: White, N.Y. Courtesy: Theatre Collection, Museum of the City of New York.

Dead End Kids: A History of Nuclear Power

This Obie Award–winning play presented by **Mabou Mines** on the promise and perils of nuclear power opened at New York's **Public Theater** on 11 November 1980, conceived and directed by **JoAnne Akalaitis**. A collage of text and images, it presents excerpts from U.S. government films on nuclear research, scientific documents, newspaper reports, scientists' diaries, alchemical recipes, and Faust in a variety of theatrical forms – nightclub acts, lecture demonstrations, magic tricks, and stand-up comedy. In short, the play is a kind of avant-garde **vaudeville,** one of the first American works to explore overt political content through Theatre of Images [see **Introduction,** §4]. More than the "History of Nuclear Power" its subtitle promises, *Dead End Kids* is a surreal history of American hopes and nightmares.   AS

Dean, Julia (1830–68) Actress. Her mother, Julia Drake, was the daughter of pioneer Kentucky manager **Samuel Drake;** her father, Edwin Dean, was a pioneer manager in Buffalo. Making her debut at the age of 11, she was the leading American tragic actress by 1846. Marriage to Samuel Hayne in 1855 was disastrous, so she went west in 1856 and established herself as a star in California and Utah for the rest of her life. She specialized in suffering heroines, such as **Shakespeare**'s Juliet and Bulwer-Lytton's Pauline, in which her height, blonde good looks, and deep voice were assets.   DMcD

Death of a Salesman (1949) by Arthur Miller, with Mildred Dunnock as Linda and Arthur Kennedy as Biff. Courtesy: Belknap Collection for the Performing Arts, University of Florida Libraries.

De Angelis, Jefferson (1859–1933) Comedian-singer and one of the most beloved stars of comic opera, De Angelis performed in vaudeville as a child, and later on tried his hand at dramatic acting. In 1887 he joined the McCaull Opera Company, appearing as a featured performer in comic operas such as *The Lady or the Tiger?* (1888). For several years he was a regular member of the **Casino Theatre** company, along with **Lillian Russell** and **Francis Wilson.** His first solo starring part was in *The Caliph* (1896). De Angelis brought to his comic opera roles both an ability to create consistent and individualized characters and the physical skills of an acrobat. His greatest successes were in *The Jolly Musketeer* (1898), *The Emerald Isle* (1902), *Fantana* (1905), and *The Girl and the Governor* (1907). From 1910 until his death, he performed in revivals of comic operas and in straight plays such as *The Royal Family* (1927). His autobiography (*A Vagabond Trouper*) was published in 1931.   MK

Death of a Salesman by **Arthur Miller.** Elia

Kazan directed the premiere production (1949, 742 performances), starring **Lee J. Cobb** (Willy Loman), **Mildred Dunnock** (Linda), **Arthur Kennedy** (Biff), and Cameron Mitchell (Happy). A masterful blend of realism and expressionism, perfectly captured in **Jo Mielziner**'s evocative design, this award-winning play (Pulitzer, Drama Critics' Circle, Tony) is Miller's masterpiece. The central character, now one of the great roles in modern theatre, is Willy Loman, the self-deceiving but well-intended salesman who dreams of success and fortune for himself and his family but achieves neither. From the point of view of his son Biff, "the man didn't know who he was" – a personal tragedy. But the play also suggests, beyond Biff's summation, that Willy failed to understand the society of success that shaped his dreams; and it is an open question whether Biff, whose role is equally important in the play, achieves sufficient understanding to avoid a similar downward spiral to self-destruction – the tragic pattern (in homecoming drama since the *Oresteia*) of possible, if not inevitable, recapitulation. The play centers on a few days, but it gains part of its complexity through the use of memory scenes that extend the action over a number of years. Despite the amazing theatrical success of *Salesman,* critics have argued for decades that the play is possibly flawed because it fails to clarify whether society or the individual is responsible for human suffering. Other debates have focused on Willy's lack of tragic stature, his failure to achieve a recognition. Ever sensitive, Miller himself has entered into the debate, in essays and many interviews, defending his play as a "tragedy of the common man." The play, performed almost every year around the country by a professional company and often around the world (from London to Beijing), was revived in NY in 1975, with **George C. Scott** (James Farentino as Biff), and again in 1984, starring **Dustin Hoffman** (with **John Malkovich** as Biff).   TP

Deathtrap Two-act drama by **Ira Levin;** opened

26 February 1978 in Broadway's **Music Box The-**

atre and later moved to the **Biltmore Theatre** for a run of 1,809 performances – then the fourth longest running play on Broadway, and the longest running thriller by an American author. Set in Connecticut, this roller-coaster thriller about playwriting juxtaposes murder plots and subplots in a literate script that is chock-full of surprises and twists.   EK

DeBar, Ben (1812–77) Actor-manager. Born in England, he came to America as an equestrian performer in 1837, but soon specialized in low comedy. He was also stage manager for **Noah Ludlow** and **Sol Smith** at the **St. Charles Theatre,** New Orleans; when they retired (1843), he assumed management of their New Orleans and St. Louis theatres. At the outbreak of the Civil War he moved to St. Louis, retaining ownership of the St. Charles until 1876. In St. Louis he moved from the St. Louis Theatre to DeBar's Grand Opera House in 1873. He remained active as a performer, touring the Mississippi River valley as a star every season, and was the most influential manager in the region.   DMcD

Déclassée Three-act drama by **Zoë Akins.** Her first and greatest hit, it opened at the **Empire Theatre** on 6 October 1919 for a run of 257 performances. **Ethel Barrymore** starred as Lady Helen, a woman of somewhat tattered reputation who lives on the fringe of good society. In the midst of a misunderstanding about her future husband, Rudolf Solomon (played by Claude King), she is killed in a tragic but convenient accident.   FB

Dee, Ruby (1923–) African-American actress. Born Ruby Ann Wallace in Cleveland, OH, Dee first acted with the **American Negro Theatre,** and took over the title role for the tour of *Anna Lucasta* (1944). She appeared in various New York productions, attracting attention as Ruth Younger in *A Raisin in the Sun* (1959), after which her reputation advanced. She was acclaimed as Lutiebelle, the innocent pawn in *Purlie Victorious* (1961), and as the long-suffering Lena in *Boesman and Lena* (1970), for which she won the Obie and Drama Desk awards. Her performance in **Alice Childress**'s *Wedding Band* (1973) also earned a Drama Desk Award. In Shakespeare, Dee has played Katharina in *The Taming of the Shrew* (1965), Cordelia to **Morris Carnovsky**'s King Lear (1965), and Gertrude in *Hamlet* (1975). She coauthored the screenplay *Uptight* (1968), in which she starred, and has written plays including *Twin Bit Gardens* (1976), the musical *Take It from the Top* (1979), and the biographical *Zora Is My Name* (1983), about Harlem Renaissance writer and folklorist Zora Neale Hurston. In 1988 she was elected to the Theatre Hall of Fame. Dee possesses an irresistibly enchanting stage personality and is infectiously funny in comedy.   EGH

Deep Are the Roots Melodrama by **Arnaud d'Usseau** and James Gow, produced in 1945 by **Kermit Bloomgarden** and George Heller, directed by **Elia Kazan.** A Negro war hero (Gordon Heath) returns to his small Southern hometown only to be falsely accused of stealing, then beaten and jailed. The play promotes the liberal vision of the deep and tangled roots of white supremacy being eroded by time and the tide of human compassion. Press reports of some audience members' reactionary responses to the romantic tension between the hero and the daughter (**Barbara Bel Geddes**) of a racist U.S. Senator (Charles Waldron) made the production a liberal cause célèbre.   WD

Deering, Nathaniel (1791–1881) Playwright, lawyer, journalist, and poet from Maine. Deering claimed several plays, but the names of only three have survived: In *Carabasset; or, The Last of the Norridgewocks* (1831), Deering defended this Maine Indian leader; *The Clairvoyants* (1844) satirized spiritualism; and *Bozzaris* (1851) celebrated the hero of the Green War of Independence.   WJM

De Foe, Louis V. (1869–1922) Drama critic. After graduating from the University of Michigan, De Foe pursued a career in journalism, first as Sunday editor then as New York correspondent and theatre critic for the *Chicago Tribune* (1891–9). During 1899–1922 he served as drama critic for the New York *World,* and contributed monthly essays to *Red Book Magazine* (1905–13). Conservative and moralistic, De Foe deplored the **Ibsen** drama for its lack of imagination, poetry, and romance.   TLM

De Koven, Reginald (1859–1920) Composer. After an extensive musical education in Europe, De Koven, in partnership with librettist **Harry B. Smith,** set out to prove that Americans could write a comic opera in the European style. Their first show, *The Begum* (1887), while not an unqualified success in New York, drew large audiences in **Chicago,** De Koven's hometown. In 1891 De Koven composed the score of *Robin Hood,* the most popular American comic opera of the era. Carefully mounted by the **Bostonians,** *Robin Hood* was an immediate hit, and the song "O Promise Me" became an enduring American standard. Although he continued to compose comic operas until 1913, De Koven never had another success of the stature of *Robin Hood.* Although his music was largely imitative of European modes, De Koven is remembered for his courage in challenging the supremacy of European comic opera composers on the American stage.   MK

See: Mrs. R. De Koven, *A Musician and His Wife,* New York, 1927.

De Liagre, Alfred, Jr. (1904–87) Yale-educated producer and director who began his professional career in 1930 as stage manager at the Woodstock Playhouse. In 1933 he began producing professionally and worked in both New York and London. De Liagre produced or coproduced more than 30 plays, a number of which he also directed. His more noteworthy credits included *The Voice of the*

Turtle (1943), *The Madwoman of Chaillot* (1948), *Second Threshold* (1950), *The Golden Apple* (1954), *The Girls in 509* (1958), **J.B.** (1959, Pulitzer Prize), *Photo Finish* (1963), *Bubbling Brown Sugar* (1976), **Deathtrap** (1978), and **On Your Toes** (revival, 1983).   TLM

Delicate Balance, A Pulitzer Prize–winning drama by **Edward Albee**; opened at the **Martin Beck Theatre** 22 September 1966, running for 132 performances. **Alan Schneider** directed a cast headed by **Hume Cronyn** and **Jessica Tandy**. The play is an intriguing evocation of modern malaise among materially comfortable people. Critics acknowledged the probity, wit, and truthfulness of the language, but were nonplussed by what **Walter Kerr** saw as an attempt to "get hold of hollowness." The Paris production (26 October 1967) was highly successful. A 1973 American Film Theater version featured **Katharine Hepburn**, Paul Scofield, Lee Remick, **Kate Reid**, and Joseph Cotten. FHL

Dell'Arte Players Company A Blue Lake, CA–based professional touring company of performer-creators working in the *commedia* tradition. Carlo Mazzone-Clementi and Jane Hill co-founded Dell'Arte, Inc. in Berkeley in 1971, and in 1972 taught their first workshop in Blue Lake, where they took up residency in 1973. Co–artistic directors Joan Schirle, Michael Fields, and Donald Forrest became the Dell'Arte Players Co. in 1977. Jael Weisman is Resident Director. The first year of their training program is devoted to physical theatre, the second to ensemble acting, with company members and others as faculty.   TL

de Mille, Agnes (1905–) Choreographer, director, and author. Trained in the techniques of classical ballet, de Mille appeared as a dancer in the *Greenwich Village Follies* (1928). After choreographing two shows in London, she returned to New York to create the dances for *Hooray for What* (1937) and *Swingin' the Dream* (1939). In 1943 **Rodgers** and **Hammerstein** hired her to choreograph *Oklahoma!,* and her use of modern ballet techniques revolutionized musical comedy **dance**. In particular, the success of *Oklahoma!*'s dream ballet made such sequences a common feature of 1940s musicals. She went on to choreograph *One Touch of Venus* (1943), *Bloomer Girl* (1944), **Carousel** (1945), and **Brigadoon** (1947). Her choreography for *Brigadoon* was acclaimed for its dramatic intensity and its use of traditional Scottish dances. Agnes de Mille served as both choreographer and director for *Allegro* (1947) and *Out of This World* (1950). In the 1950s she created the dances for such shows as **Paint Your Wagon** (1951), *The Girl in Pink Tights* (1954), and *Goldilocks* (1958). Less active in the 1960s, de Mille choreographed *Kwamina* (1961), *110 in the Shade* (1963), and *Come Summer* (1969). Best remembered for her pioneering work in musicals of the 1940s, de Mille is credited with demonstrating dance's potential for furthering a musical's dramatic action. Her dozen books include *Dance to the Piper* (1952), *Speak to Me, Dance With Me* (1973), *Reprieve: A Memoir* (1981), *Portrait Gallery* (1990), and *Martha* [Graham] (1991).   MK

DeMille, Henry Churchill (1850–93) Playwright, native of North Carolina, who prepared for his career by securing a position as a play reader at the **Madison Square Theatre** in 1882. His first play, *John Delmer's Daughter* (1883), dealing with family problems resulting from social climbing, failed. His next play, a frontier melodrama, *The Main Line* (1886), written with Charles Bernard, succeeded not only in New York but on tour, in later productions, and even as revised with Rosabel Morrison as *The Danger Signal* (1891). DeMille made his reputation, however, collaborating with **David Belasco**. *The Wife* (1887), which dramatized a husband's resolve to win the love of his wife who had married him out of pique, received 239 performances. They wrote *Lord Chumley* (1888) for **E. H. Sothern**, who made the young English nobleman a memorable theatre experience. *The Charity Ball* (1889) contrasts a strong clergyman with his weak brother in a plot revealing seduction and greed resolved by love. Their last collaboration, **Men and Women** (1890), builds upon banking, speculation, love, and family. Together they produced four of the most popular plays of that period in America.   WJM

See: A. Edwards, *The DeMilles: An American Family*, New York, 1988.

deMille, William C. (1878–1955) Playwright and film director who, following his father's career, made his own contributions to American drama. Although plays written with his brother, Hollywood director Cecil B. DeMille, failed [e.g., *The Genius* (1906)], deMille emphasized powerful confrontations with a socially probing theme in *Strong Heart* (1905), an early treatment of love between a white girl and a Native American. *The Warrens of Virginia* (1907) opposed North and South in a Civil War love story; *The Women* (1911) dramatized political corruption. His daughter is famed choreographer **Agnes de Mille**.   WJM

Denver Center Theatre The $13 million Helen G. Bonfils Theatre Complex opened on New Year's Eve, 1979, as part of the Denver Center for the Performing Arts. The Bonfils complex consists of three separate theatres: the 550-seat thrust; the 450-seat environmental; and a 150-seat theatre laboratory/rehearsal hall for new American works. **Edward Payson Call** served as the first artistic director (1979–83), followed by Donovan Marley (1983–). Maintaining a professional resident company, the Denver Theatre in its inaugural season (December–April) performed five plays: *The Caucasian Chalk Circle*, **Orson Welles**'s *Moby Dick – Rehearsed*, *The Learned Ladies*, *A Midsummer Night's Dream*, and **Steve Tesich**'s *Passing Game*. **Allen Fletcher** was hired in 1984 to head the conservatory training program, now administered by Tony Church (appointed Dean in 1989). The company offers a new play festival (U.S. West) each spring. Notable productions include **Quilters,** which appeared briefly on Broadway in 1984, and *The Immigrant* (1984-5), popular in regional theatres. TLM

Derwent, Clarence (1884–1959) English-born actor-director who fled his London home to become a provincial bit player. By 1910 he appeared back in London; in 1915 he came to the U.S. to appear with **Grace George** in **Shaw**'s *Major Barbara*. He went on to appear in some 500 plays and several movies, and occasionally directed. In 1945 he founded the Clarence Derwent Awards in London and New York for the best performers in supporting roles. Among his many professional offices were two terms as president of **Actors' Equity** and the presidency in 1952 of the **American National Theatre and Academy.** He also chaired the National Center of the International Theatre Institute and was president of the Dramatic Workshop. His autobiography, *The Derwent Story,* appeared in 1954. SMA

Desert Song, The Two-act operetta, music by **Sigmund Romberg,** words by **Otto Harbach, Oscar Hammerstein II,** and Frank Mandel; opened 7 April 1927 at the **Casino Theatre,** New York, running 471 performances. This sweeping romantic saga in the sands of Morocco sees the Frenchwoman Margot (**Vivienne Segal**) carried off by her romantic ideal, the masked leader of the native Riffs (Robert Halliday), only to discover that he is really the shy Frenchman she has disdained. Particularly timely in its day (there really was a Riff rebellion in Morocco, and Valentino's film *The Sheik* was all the rage), the operetta has proved extremely durable. Romberg's soaring melodies are timeless, and his "desert music" was so right that it has been imitated in films ever since. *The Desert Song* was equally popular in London, where it has been revived professionally numerous times over the years. JD

Desire Under the Elms Although this **Eugene O'Neill** play, which opened 11 November 1924, was notorious for years and became the object of a strident **censorship** attack by New York's district attorney and moral crusaders, it proved to be O'Neill's most successful play until *Strange Interlude.* First produced at the Greenwich Village Theatre by Experimental Theatre, Inc., and designed and directed by **Robert Edmond Jones,** this tragedy featured simultaneous staging and removable walls for its lonely, 1850 New England farmhouse. The play, freely adapted from the Hippolytus/Phaedra tragedies of antiquity, is a study in family struggles that erupt in physical combat; cravings for possession of the land; near-incestuous adulteries between wife and stepson (renamed Abbie and Eben, portrayed by **Mary Morris** and Charles Ellis); and misguided, lustful obsessions that culminate in the murder of an infant. Its heavy New England dialects and homiletic, biblical tone provide bitter counterpoint for the seething, reckless sexuality that drives so much of the action. Just as important as the sexual struggle is the oppressive conflict of Eben with his father Ephraim, first played by **Walter Huston.** The uncompromising patriarch drives his young wife and tormented son to subterfuge and their subsequent crimes of passion. RHW

Desmond Players Mae Desmond (née Mary Veronica Callahan) (1887–1982) and her husband, Frank Fielder, formed the Mae Desmond Players, a "popular-priced" **stock company,** in Schenectady, NY, in 1917. After brief stints in Elmira and Schenectady, NY, and Scranton, PA, Desmond and Fielder moved their company to their native **Philadelphia,** where it flourished until 1929. It reached the height of its popular and financial success while occupying the Desmond Theatre in the working-class neighborhood of Kensington, where the management shaped the troupe's repertory to appeal to German and Irish Roman Catholics in the area. Desmond's manifold appeals as a skilled comedienne, as well as a paragon of Irish beauty, Catholic morality, and fashionable correctness, were keys to the company's success. WD

DeSylva, B. G. "Buddy" (né George Gard) (1869–1950), lyricist, librettist; **Lew Brown (né Louis Brownstein)** (1893–1958), librettist, lyricist, director, producer; and **Ray Henderson (né Raymond Brost)** (1896–1970), composer. Although they each worked with others, DeSylva, Brown, and Henderson are best known for the musicals they created together in the 1920s. DeSylva studied at the University of Southern California before writing songs for **Al Jolson**'s shows *Sinbad* (1918) and *Bombo* (1921). With **George Gershwin** he wrote the score of *La, La, Lucille* (1919) and the 1922–4 *George White's Scandals.* Born in Russia, Brown wrote popular songs for the publisher Albert von Tilzer and had some of his songs interpolated into Broadway shows. Henderson received musical training at the Chicago Conservatory of Music before becoming a vaudeville accompanist, music arranger, and song plugger. Together, the three wrote the score for the 1926 and 1928 editions of the revue series *George White's Scandals.* In 1927 they created the book and score of *Good News,* a frothy musical with a college setting that ran for 557 performances. Their subsequent shows included *Hold Everything* (1928), *Follow Thru* (1929), and *Flying High* (1930). DeSylva went to Hollywood to become a film producer in the early 1930s, eventually becoming head of Paramount Studios. He continued to write lyrics and libretti, some in partnership with Brown and Henderson, for such shows as *Take a Chance* (1932), *Strike Me Pink* (1933), **Du Barry Was a Lady** (1939), *Louisiana Purchase* (1940), and *Panama Hattie* (1940). Brown continued to work on Broadway as a librettist, director, and producer, with shows such as *Calling All Stars* (1934) and *Yokel Boy* (1939); he also produced films in Hollywood. Henderson continued to write music for both Broadway shows such as *Say When* (1934) and the **Ziegfeld** *Follies* (1943), as well as for Hollywood films. DeSylva, Brown, and Henderson perfectly captured the lighthearted spirit of the 1920s in songs such as "The Best Things in Life Are Free" and "You're the Cream in My Coffee." MK

Detective Story by **Sidney Kingsley.** Presented by **Crouse** and **Lindsay,** Kingsley directed his play at the Hudson Theatre, with sets by **Boris Aronson,** opening 23 March 1949 (581 performances).

Starring **Ralph Bellamy** as a fanatical Detective McLeod and Meg Mundy as his wife, with strong assists from Lee Grant as a gabby and moronic shoplifter, Horace MacMahon as a tough detective lieutenant, James Westerfield as a slightly boozy compassionate detective, **Joseph Wiseman** and Michael Strong as personifications of evil, and Joan Copeland as a voice for good, it was noted as a rousing, almost-documentary story of good and evil in a New York City police precinct station. Featuring strong characters that could have carried the play in many directions, the ending is powerful, melodramatic, and arbitrary. GSA

Detour Three-act drama by **Owen Davis;** opened 23 August 1921 at the Astor Theatre in New York and ran a brief 48 performances. Davis, credited with writing some 300 plays, was known for his melodramas; *Detour* departed from this style by telling a more realistic story of a New England family seemingly caught in an unending cycle of farm life from one generation to the next. **Effie Shannon** played the role of Helen Hardy, a stalwart farm wife who saves her egg money in hopes of enabling her daughter, Kate (played by Angela McCahill) to escape to the city. Augustin Duncan played the husband, Stephen, and directed the play. Davis credits Duncan in his autobiography (*I'd Like to Do It Again,* 1931) as critical to shaping the play. KN

DeWalden, Thomas Blaydes (1811–73) Playwright and actor, born in London, where he first appeared in the Haymarket in 1834. He came to America in 1844 and became a productive journeyman playwright whose works occasionally reflected American interests. Of such plays, *The Upper Ten and the Lower Twenty* (1854) ridiculed New York society; *Manifest Destiny* (1855) and *Wall Street* (1855) made fun of America's love of independence and speculation; and *British Neutrality* (1869) suggested the author's view of the Civil War. DeWalden created successful vehicles for **F. S. Chanfrau** with *Sam* (1865) – 783 performances – and the pioneer play, *Kit, The Arkansas Traveler* (1870). WJM

Dewhurst, Colleen (1926–91) Canadian-born actress whose robustness qualified her ideally for certain **Eugene O'Neill** heroines, most notably Josie in *A Moon for the Misbegotten,* for which she received a Tony in a 1973 revival directed by **José Quintero.** "I love the O'Neill women," she said. "They move from the groin rather than the brain. To play O'Neill . . . you can't sit and play little moments of sadness or sweetness." Ironically, her professional New York career began as one of the Neighbors in *Desire Under the Elms* in 1952 (in 1963 she played Abbie Putnam at **Circle in the Square**). Other O'Neill productions of note included *More Stately Mansions* (1967), a 1972 revival of *Mourning Becomes Electra,* and 1988 revivals of *Long Day's Journey into Night* and *Ah, Wilderness!* She also appeared in three **Edward Albee** plays, including a 1976 revival of *Who's Afraid of Virginia Woolf?* In 1960 she received her first Tony Award for Mary Follet in *All the Way Home.*

Dewhurst was also praised for her work in the classics, especially Shakespeare, most notably for **Joseph Papp**'s **New York Shakespeare Festival** in the 1950s. In recent years she appeared at Papp's **Public Theater** in several productions, including *O'Neill and Carlotta* (1979). In 1985 she was elected president of **Actors' Equity,** a position she held until shortly before her death. DBW

Dexter, John (1925–90) British director. In addition to successful careers at London's Royal Court Theatre in the mid- and late 1950s and the National Theatre in the mid-1960s, Dexter was well represented on U.S. stages. His production of Wesker's *Chips with Everything* was seen in 1963, followed by a stunning production of Peter Shaffer's *The Royal Hunt of the Sun* (1965). This effort established a reputation for ingenuity, theatricality, and visual impact, noted in later New York productions of Shaffer's *Equus* (1974) and *M. Butterfly* (1988). As the Metropolitan Opera's director of production and later advisor (1974–84), he directed numerous controversial productions, several with David Hockney designs. His final U.S. production was a disastrous revival of *Threepenny Opera* (1989) with Sting. Considered by some "tough, tart, and acerbic" to work for, Dexter, an intuitive rather than intellectual director, also elicited great loyalty from actors willing to adhere to his methodology. DBW

Diary of Anne Frank, The, opened 5 October 1955 at the **Cort Theatre** and ran 717 performances. Adapted by Frances Goodrich (Hackett) and Albert Hackett from *Anne Frank: Diary of a Young Girl,* with Susan Strasberg in the title role, the play dramatizes segments from 13-year-old Anne's diary from July 1942 until her capture in August 1944, and portrays the routine of daily life carried out while the Frank family hid from the Nazis. Anne's persistent attempt to derive joy and a sense of beauty from her rigidly bounded world and the play's poignant optimism are typified in her diary's last line: "In spite of everything I still believe people are really good at heart." The play succeeded internationally, winning the 1956 New York Drama Critics' Circle Award, Tony Award, and Pulitzer Prize. RW

Dietz, Howard (1896–1983) Lyricist, librettist, and director. After serving in the Navy during WW I, he began writing song lyrics, at the same time starting a long career as public relations director for MGM. Teaming with composer **Arthur Schwartz,** he continued to write lyrics for a series of intimate revues, including *The Little Show* (1929), *The Second Little Show* (1930), *Three's a Crowd* (1930), *The Band Wagon* (1931), *Flying Colors* (1932), and *At Home Abroad* (1935). Among later shows were the revue *Inside U.S.A.* (1948) and two book musicals, also with Schwartz: *The Gay Life* (1961) and *Jennie* (1963). His pensive, often ironic lyrics, such as those for "Dancing in the Dark" (the title of his 1974 autobiography), were a distinguishing feature of the 1930s intimate **revue.** MK

Digges, Dudley (1879–1947) Actor and director, born in Dublin and a member of the original

Abbey Players. He made his New York debut in 1904 with **Minnie Maddern Fiske.** In 1919 he appeared in *Bonds of Interest* for the **Theatre Guild,** for whom he eventually played more than 3,500 times (including the role of James Caesar in *John Ferguson*) and staged four plays. Reviewing his final appearance as Harry Hope in **O'Neill**'s *The Iceman Cometh,* Brooks Atkinson remarked that Digges's "command of the actor's art of expressing character and theme is brilliantly alive; it overflows with comic and philosophical expression." Digges also appeared in over 50 films and served as vice-president of **Actors' Equity Association.** SMA

Dillingham, Charles Bancroft (1868–1934) Drama critic for the New York *Evening Post* before becoming a tour manager for **Julia Marlowe** in 1898. He managed several eminent actors and actresses, including **Maxine Elliott, Henry Miller, Fritzi Scheff,** and Irene Castle, and produced over 200 plays, musicals, and spectacles. He was most celebrated for lavish, tasteful musicals scored by **Victor Herbert** or **Jerome Kern,** and for the elaborate spectacles he produced while managing the **Hippodrome** in New York (1914–23). He installed the first moving electric sign in New York for his production of Herbert's *The Red Mill* (1906). He built the Globe Theatre, near Broadway, and managed it from 1910 until losing it in bankruptcy proceedings in 1933. WD

Dining Room, The, by **A. R. Gurney, Jr.,** opened at the Studio Theatre at **Playwrights Horizons** 24 February 1982, running 511 performances. The play uses attitudes of various generations of several nonspecific families toward a formal dining room to represent the passing of WASP tradition and authority. The attitudes of the characters reveal the type and degree of value each generation places on the room and, by inference, the WASP tradition. By means of overlapping scenes, intermixed chronology, and multiple characterizations, the author focuses attention on the room and the tradition it represents, avoiding the appearance of a dynastic chronicle. RW

Dinner at Eight by **George S. Kaufman** and **Edna Ferber,** directed by Kaufman, opened on Broadway 22 October 1932 and ran 232 performances. The plot concerns Millicent Jordan's dinner party for Lord and Lady Ferncliffe, as well as the sordid intrigues of the guests' personal lives, which are revealed as the date approaches. Ultimately, although the guests of honor break their engagement, and the hostess's husband develops a fatal heart condition and loses his business to a takeover artist, they proceed heroically with the party. The original cast included Cesar Romero and **Sam Levene** in secondary roles. MGM released the film version in 1933, starring **Marie Dressler,** Wallace Beery, Jean Harlow, **Billie Burke,** and John and Lionel Barrymore [see **Drew–Barrymore family**]. JDM

Dithmar, Edward A. (1854–1917) Drama critic. Born in New York, Dithmar began his career in 1871 with *The New York Evening Post*. He moved to the *New York Times* in 1877 where he became night editor in 1882 and drama critic in 1884, replacing George Edgar Montgomery. After giving way to **John Corbin** in 1901, he served as the *Times*'s London correspondent (1901–2), editor of its *Saturday Review of Books* (1902–7), and editorial writer (1907–17). He authored *John Drew* (1900) and *Memoirs of Daly's Theatre* (1897), and coedited with **Augustin Daly** *A Portfolio of Players*. His business relationship with Daly may have compromised his reputation. Dithmar is best remembered as an outspoken advocate of American drama. TLM

See: G. W. Loudon, "The Theatre Criticism of Edward A. Dithmar," PhD diss., U of Nebraska–Lincoln, 1981.

Divorce Five-act drama by **Augustin Daly** and, though not the first, the most successful American play of the century on the divorce theme. Opening 5 September 1871, it ran a record 200 continuous performances (236 that season) and had an impressive stage history throughout the 1890s. Daly based the play loosely on Anthony Trollope's novel *He Knew He Was Right,* and added a subplot moving the setting from Europe to the U.S. The threatened divorces of two sisters, Fanny (**Clara Morris**) and Lu (**Fanny Davenport**), are complicated by machinations of the shady divorce lawyer Jitt (**James Lewis**). DBW

See: M. Felheim, *The Theater of Augustin Daly,* Cambridge, MA, 1956.

Dixey, Henry E. (1859–1943) Actor. He began acting at age 9 in a Boston production of ***Under the Gaslight.*** Numerous appearances in musicals and straight plays (mostly comedies) during a 58-year career included a season in **Augustin Daly**'s company and roles in **Gilbert and Sullivan.** His greatest creation, the title role of ***Adonis*** (1884), made him a matinee idol and featured a memorable imitation of Henry Irving. This role was followed in importance by David Garrick in **Stuart Robson**'s *Oliver Goldsmith* (1899), Lieutenant Robert Warburton in *The Man on the Box* (1905), and Peter Swallow (opposite **Mrs. Fiske**) in *Mrs. Bumpstead-Leigh* (1911). DBW

Dockstader, Lew (né George Alfred Clapp) (1856–1925) Comedian who preserved the **minstrel show**'s vitality while injecting it with political satire. He had begun in blackface as a teenager and formed his own company with Charles Dockstader in 1876, retaining the name after his partner retired in 1883. His new partnership with George Primrose created the most popular turn-of-the-century minstrel troupe in the U.S. (1898–1913). Dockstader performed in two-foot-long shoes and a coat with a 30-inch tail; his best song was "Everybody Works but Father." Before he became a solo monologuist on the **Keith** Circuit, he had given a start to **Al Jolson.** LS

Dodson, Owen (1914–83) Poet, novelist, playwright, director, and teacher. A graduate of Bates College and the Yale School of Drama, Dodson became a prominent figure in African-American

The Dolly Sisters, Rosie and Jenny, during an appearance at B. F. Keith's Alhambra Theatre. Courtesy: Laurence Senelick.

academic theatre through his many memorable productions, including Shakespeare. He trained a number of successful actors. Dodson's own plays have been produced in college theatres, including *Divine Comedy,* about the career of the evangelist Father Divine, and *Bayou Legend,* an adaptation of *Peer Gynt* set in Louisiana. EGH

Dolly Sisters (née Deutsch) Hungarian-born twins – **Jenny** (Yansci) (1893–1941) and **Rosie** (Roszika) (1893–1970) – who from their vaudeville debut in 1909 became chic **vaudeville** and **revue** headliners specializing in unvarying dance routines and attempts at singing. The Gabors of their time, they ultimately made their reputation with their wardrobe and costume changes, especially in numerous appearances at the **Palace,** in the *Ziegfeld Follies of 1911,* and in myriad musical comedies. In the 1920s, essentially as part of the art deco movement, they were seen frequently in Paris and London music halls. A 1946 film of their lives starred Betty Grable and June Haver. DBW

Donat, Peter (1929–) Canadian-born actor, nephew of the screen star Robert Donat, who has had success in both regional theatre and films. He trained at the Yale Drama School and spent six seasons at the Stratford, ON, Shakespeare Festival before joining **San Francisco**'s **American Conservatory Theater** in 1968 with his then-wife, actress Michael Learned. With short breaks for meaty TV and movie character roles, Donat has stayed with ACT to appear in many leading roles, including his poignant Cyrano (filmed for PBS), Dysart in *Equus,* and the betrayed Horace Giddens in *The **Little** Foxes.* MB

Donehue, Vincent J. (1920–66) Known as an "unobtrusive though easy and fluent" director, Donehue's Broadway debut was **Foote**'s *The Trip to Bountiful* (1953). He won a Tony for **Schary**'s *Sunrise at Campobello* (1958), and directed *The Sound*

of Music (1959) and the Mary Martin videotape of *Peter Pan* (1960). REK

Douglas (né Hesselberg), Melvyn (1901–81) Actor, director, and producer who first toured in repertory and **stock,** then spent two years with **Jessie Bonstelle**'s company, headed his own company briefly, and debuted on Broadway in 1928. His first hit, *Tonight or Never* (1930), costarred Helen Gahagan, whom he married. From 1931 to 1942 he starred in 45 movies, then returned to the theatre in 1952 with *Time Out for Ginger,* replacing **Paul Muni** as Drummond in *Inherit the Wind* (1955) to critical acclaim. Douglas had begun as a debonair and dapper leading man in romantic comedies, but matured into a forceful character actor of considerable stature. He won the Tony in 1960 for *The Best Man.* SMA

> See: M. Douglas and T. Arthur, *See You at the Movies,* Lanham, MD, 1986.

Douglass, David (?–1786) British-born actor-manager. He became the central figure in the history of the American theatre from his marriage in 1758 to the widow of Lewis **Hallam,** Sr., in Jamaica, to the American Revolution. Douglass returned to New York in 1758 as head of Hallam's Company of Comedians from London (renamed in 1763 The **American Company** of Comedians). For 17 years Douglass's company played up and down the East Coast, erecting temporary theatres in most towns. In 1766 he built the first permanent theatre in the U.S., the **Southwark** in **Philadelphia,** followed in 1767 by the **John Street** Theatre in New York. In April 1767 Douglass announced the first professional production of a play by an American-born writer, a comic opera called *The Disappointment;* this was replaced at the last minute by Thomas Godfrey's *The Prince of Parthia,* the first native tragedy to be presented professionally [see **Introduction,** §1]. Before the outbreak of hostilities, Douglass and his company returned to the West Indies in 1775, where he became a justice, an officer in the militia, and a member of the Council. Douglass was America's first Falstaff and King John; though a poor actor, he was a superb manager. DBW

Peter Donat interprets the title role of *Cyrano de Bergerac* in 1972, the first of *Cyrano*'s three seasons in the ACT repertory. Courtesy: ACT.

Dowling, Eddie (né Joseph Nelson Goucher) (1889–1976) Pulitzer Prize–winning American producer, playwright, songwriter, director, and actor who began his career doing a song-and-dance act in his native state of Rhode Island. His Broadway debut was in **Victor Herbert**'s *The Velvet Lady* in 1919; he appeared in the *Ziegfeld Follies* of 1919, 1920, and 1921. In 1945, after rejecting a sure-fire commercial project, he coproduced and codirected (with **Margo Jones**) **Williams**'s *The Glass Menagerie,* in which he also played Tom. The production made theatrical history and brought Williams out of obscurity. Dowling produced *Richard II* in 1937 with **Maurice Evans,** and during his long career worked with such playwrights as **William Saroyan,** Paul Vincent Carroll, Sean O'Casey, and **Philip Barry.**
DBW

Downing, Robert (1857–1944) Actor. A native of Washington, DC, he began acting there at the **National Theatre** in 1876, eventually succeeding Thomas W. Keene as leading man. Identified with the heroic roles of **Forrest,** he made his New York debut as Spartacus at the **Star Theatre** (December 1886), and toured as a star until 1905, when he opened an acting school in his hometown. In 1908 he became pastor of a church in Portsmouth, RI.
DMcD

Drag shows see **female/male impersonation**

Drake, Alfred (1914–92) Singer and actor. One of the most versatile leading men of the American musical stage, Drake began his musical career in **Gilbert and Sullivan** revivals and made his Broadway debut in the chorus of *White Horse Inn* (1936). After featured roles in such shows as *Babes in Arms* (1937) and *The Straw Hat Revue* (1939), Drake created the role of Curley in **Rodgers** and **Hammerstein**'s *Oklahoma!* (1943). Five years later, he played Fred Graham in *Kiss Me, Kate.* Praised by critics for his romantic, swaggering portrayal of a Shakespearean actor, Drake's comic abilities received a large share of the acclaim. Among his subsequent musical theatre appearances, only his performance as Hajj in *Kismet* (1953) was notable. Drake's career as an actor included performances as Othello and Benedick at the **American Shakespeare Festival Theatre,** and Claudius opposite **Richard Burton** in *Hamlet* (1964). His last major role was in a 1975 revival of *The Skin of Our Teeth.* MK

Drake, Samuel (1769–1854) Actor-manager who, after managing in the English provinces, brought his family to America in 1810. After a few years in Boston, the Drakes joined **John Bernard**'s company in Albany, NY (1813), and in 1815, at the invitation of Luke Usher, Drake took his three sons, two daughters, and five assistants as a company to Frankfort, KY. He extended his influence to Louisville, Lexington, and Cincinnati, a circuit he controlled for many years. While not the leading company in the West at the time, Drake's group improved performance levels in the area and firmly established the frontier theatre. Drake was the grandfather of **Julia Dean.** SMA

> *See:* W. Carson, *The Theatre on the Frontier,* Chicago, 1932; W. Hill, *The Theatre in Early Kentucky,* Lexington, 1971; J. Weisert, *The Curtain Rose,* Louisville, 1958.

Drake, Sylvie (1930–) Drama critic. Born in Alexandria, Egypt, Drake was educated at a British school, where she earned an Oxbridge Higher Certificate with distinctions in French and English literature. She emigrated to the U.S. and entered the **Pasadena Playhouse** in 1949, later working as an actress, director, and television writer. Drake began reviewing theatre in 1969 for the weekly Los Angeles *Canyon Crier* and for the *Los Angeles Times* (on assignment) before joining the *Times* in 1971 as a theatre columnist and critic. In 1991, upon the retirement of **Daniel Sullivan,** she became the *Times*'s leading critic, the most powerful such position in Los Angeles. TLM

Drama League, The The Drama League was founded in 1909 by an Evanston, IL, ladies' literary society, the "Riley Circle." Their first national gathering was held at a church in Evanston (1910), and at their constitutional convention (1910) at the Chicago Art Institute, attended by some 200 delegates representing 63 local centers, Mrs. A. Starr Bast was elected president and proclaimed their goals: "to stimulate interest in the best drama"; "to awaken the public to the importance of the theatre as a social force." The organization expanded rap-

Earle Hyman as Othello, Jacqueline Brooks as Desdemona, and Alfred Drake as Iago in the American Shakespeare Festival *Othello,* directed by John Houseman. Courtesy: Laurence Senelick.

idly: In 1911 they had 12,000 members in 25 states; by the early 1920s, 23,000 members, 100,000 affiliated members, and 114 centers throughout the country. They published *The Drama* (1911), a quarterly "to cultivate a deeper understanding and appreciation for American drama and theatre," with **W. P. Eaton, G. P. Baker, Brander Matthews, Stark Young,** and others as editors; issued 250 bulletins (1910–16) endorsing current productions; sponsored tours of the **Hull-House** Players, the Irish Players, **Mrs. Fiske, George Arliss,** and others; published 20 volumes of "good" plays; conducted summer instructional institutes; and held annual conventions in Chicago, New York, St. Louis, Pittsburgh, and Detroit. After the national organization was disbanded (1931), local centers continued to function, and the New York Drama League was still active in the 1990s. RM

Dramatic theory

19th century Without exception, American men and women who wrote plays before the Civil War were either amateurs, journeymen-playwrights who acted or managed theatres, or literary people who decided to write a play or two. They had objectives – vague or particular, commercial or artistic – and some had read traditional dramatic theory, but they did not contribute to it.

This situation did not, of course, eliminate critics of American drama or stridently voiced observations on particular plays or the directions that American drama should take. Such opinions, generally with a religious or national bias, have always been freely expressed. **James Kirke Paulding** made a somewhat desperate plea for "American Drama" in the *American Quarterly Review* of June 1827. Only occasionally did essayists have a theoretical bent. John Neal wrote five essays on "The Drama" for the *Yankee and Boston Literary Gazette* (August 1829), one concerned with "Strictures of Dramatic Writing, Theatrical Representation and the Laws of Drama." Robert Walsh, editor and journalist, included two essays on "The Stage" and "Tragic Acting" in his collected essays, *Didactics: Social, Literary, and Political* (1836). An abundance of essays, mainly critical, sometimes bordering on the theoretical, appeared through the 19th century: W. A. Jones, "Nationality in Literature," *Democratic Review,* 20 (1847): 264–72; G. H. Calvert, "A National Drama," *Putnam's Monthly Magazine* 9 (February 1857): 148–51; Mary W. Alexander, "Tragedy and Tragedians," *The Ladies Repository* 25 (October 1865): 615–17; Brander Matthews, "The Dramatic Outlook in America," *Harper's New Monthly Magazine* 78 (May 1889): 924–30.

For late-19th-century playwrights, a single outstanding essay should be noted: "American Playwrights on the American Drama," *Harper's Weekly* 33 (2 February 1889): 97–100. In brief space, playwrights **Augustin Daly, Edward Harrigan,** Bronson Howard, **William Gillette,** John Grosvenor Wilson, and **Steele Mackaye** give some ideas about their dramaturgy. It is an uneven but revealing presentation capped by **William Winter**'s summary observation.

Those American playwrights who thought and wrote about their theories of dramaturgy are Dion Boucicault, Bronson Howard, Edward Harrigan, David Belasco, W. D. Howells, and James A. Herne. **Boucicault** expressed his theories most specifically in 13 essays written for the *North American Review* between 1877 and 1889. In "The Art of Dramatic Composition" (*NAR,* January/February, 1878), for example, he defined drama in nearly Aristotelian fashion as "the imitation of a complete action, formed by a sequence of incidents designed to be acted not narrated, by the person or persons whom such incidents befall. Its object is to give pleasure by exciting in the mind of the spectator a sympathy for fellow creatures suffering their fate."

Bronson Howard, a man of definite opinions, presented his theories in a lecture entitled "The Laws of Dramatic Composition" (1886) – published as *The Autobiography of a Play* (1914). This included "Trash on the Stage and the Lost Dramatists of America," in which he emphasized a commonsense approach to character motivations plus those "satisfactory" actions within a well-constructed play that must reach a properly moral and happy conclusion. **Edward Harrigan,** as both comedian and playwright, was caught up in a realistic representation of society in New York City. He wanted to present a "series of photographs of life today," he wrote in the *Harper's Weekly* essay, and believed in "Holding the Mirror up to Nature" (*Pearson's Magazine,* November 1903). This was the major thrust of his dramaturgy.

David Belasco carried his interest in realism to an extreme and constantly wrote about his theories, which he always equated with his life and work: "How I Stage My Plays," *Theater Magazine,* 2 (December 1902): 31–2; "Why I Believe in the Little Things," *Ladies Home Journal,* 28 (September 1911): 15; "Beauty As I See It," *Arts and Decoration,* 19 (July 1923): 9–10; "About Play Production," *Saturday Evening Post,* 10 (January 1920): 17; *The Theatre Seen Through the Stage Door,* 1919. **William Dean Howells,** the father of American realism, looked at drama as a playwright and critic. Most of his theorizing about the drama appears in numerous essays, but *Criticism and Fiction* (1891) contains the essence of his theory of realism as it applied to drama and to fiction. "Prose is now indisputably the dialect of the stage," he stated from "The Easy Chair," in 1902. Dramatists, he noted, are also moralists in both "the larger and lesser sense" – simply propriety or the universal problem of values. Most important, however, the drama must be a truthful and faithful representation of the lives of men and women.

The most significant dramatic theorist of the 19th century was **James A. Herne.** A collaborator with Belasco, influenced by Howells as well as Ibsen, Thomas Hardy, and Emile Zola, Herne created his own theory as "Art for Truth's Sake in the Drama" [*Arena* (February 1897): 361–70]. Truthfulness is the "supreme quality" of all drama, which must "interest" and "instruct." Art for Truth's Sake emphasizes "humanity" and "perpetuates the life of its time." WJM

See: W. J. Meserve, *An Emerging Entertainment: The Drama of the American People to 1828,* Bloomington, IN, 1977; W. J. Meserve, *Herald of Promise: The Drama*

of the American People during the Age of Jackson, 1829–1849, Westport, CT, 1986; A. H. Quinn, *A History of American Drama from the Civil War to the Present Day*, New York, 1936.

20th century At the beginning of the 20th century **Brander Matthews** championed drama as an art separate from literature, emphasizing the importance of action, of appeal to the audience, and of understanding a play in light of its original performance conditions. At the same time Joel Elias Spingarn, a Crocean "new critic," condemned Matthews's interest in drama as a special genre and in its historical surroundings, establishing a debate that echoed in America for several generations between the followers of these influential professors.

The great creative surge in turn-of-the-century European theatre reached America during WW I, its critical voice provided by the journal *Theatre Arts,* founded in 1916 by **Sheldon Cheney.** Major contemporary European theorists were represented here along with their American disciples, led by **Kenneth Macgowan,** who became coeditor in 1919, and **Robert Edmond Jones,** who became editor in 1922. Following theorists like Craig and Symons in England, these called for a reduced emphasis on language in the theatre and a dedication to a total theatre art of light, color, and rhythm. Macgowan and Jones were also codirectors of the **Provincetown Playhouse,** along with **Eugene O'Neill,** whose scattered theoretical comments echo many of their concerns. O'Neill, however, also speculated on the power of tragedy, which he, like many of the German romantics, felt grew out of the very process of human consciousness.

The nature and function of tragedy inspired a major tradition of theoretical writing in America. O'Neill's contemporaries Ludwig Lewisohn, **George Jean Nathan,** and W. M. Dixon disagreed on the audience and precise social function of tragedy, but all felt it an uplifting and powerful force in the modern world. **Joseph Wood Krutch** sharply disagreed in his influential 1929 essay "The Tragic Fallacy," arguing that modern man's loss of faith in himself had made this genre obsolete.

During the 1930s and '40s a number of theorists rejected Krutch's analysis. Kenneth Burke and Francis Fergusson suggested basic rhythms or structures beneath tragedy that were not seriously affected by changing historical beliefs. **Maxwell Anderson** insisted that modern consciousness on such matters was no different from that of the Greeks – an assertion pursued, on more philosophic terms, by Una Ellis-Fermor and James Feibleman. **Eric Bentley,** in his influential *The Playwright as Thinker* (1946), suggested that the serious genre of tragedy in modern times was best combined with a theatre of ideas. Some playwrights also produced theoretical observations on this matter, most notably **Arthur Miller,** who defended the common man as a suitable hero for modern tragedy.

During the 1930s an important part of the American drama and of its theory was concerned with political questions. *New Theatre* was founded by associates of the **Group Theatre** in 1933, specifically to express a more political position than the rather aesthetically oriented *Theatre Arts.* In *New Theatre,* and in the closely related Group Theatre, the work and writings of director **Lee Strasberg,** designer **Mordecai Gorelik,** and playwright **John Howard Lawson** contributed greatly to developing a consciousness of theatre as a social instrument, and to making Russian theatre in general and Stanislavsky in particular a touchstone of excellence in American theatre.

Socially and politically oriented theory almost disappeared in America during the rather apolitical 1950s. Major theatrical theory concerned itself with more formal and aesthetic matters. Susan Langer, in *Feeling and Form* (1953), called moral and social questions in drama like represented subjects in painting – useful but not indispensable, as was the defining form. Northrop Frye's *Anatomy of Criticism* (1957) interpreted drama and all literary expression through an all-encompassing symbolic system of unconscious archetypes. Tragedy continued to inspire major studies – by Herbert Weisinger, D. D. Raphael, and Murray Kreiger – but a kind of watershed was marked by George Steiner's *The Death of Tragedy* (1961), which followed Krutch in finding the mythologies of modernism inadequate to provide a basis for the tragic vision. Although a number of subsequent theorists, most notably Elder Olson, disagreed with this conclusion, major theoretical work on tragedy became much rarer after 1960, to be replaced by an interest in dark, ironic blendings of comedy and tragedy, attracting such theorists as Cyrus Hoy and Karl Guthke.

During the 1960s the *Tulane Drama Review* became, as *Theatre Arts* had been earlier, a major conduit for new directions and new theoretical speculations. Jerzy Grotowski, whose approach to acting became for many in this generation as central as Stanislavsky's had been in the 1930s, was introduced to America by *TDR*. A special issue in 1965, coedited by **Richard Schechner** and **Michael Kirby,** featured John Cage and articles on chance theatre and happenings. Subsequent special issues charted with great accuracy the rapidly changing interests in theory and in performance in America in the late 1960s – politically engaged theatre, **African-American theatre,** and the application of anthropological and sociological theory to theatre. Schechner became particularly interested in this last concern, and his subsequent writings and those of anthropologist Victor Turner resulted in an important convergence of theatrical and anthropological theory in the 1970s.

Also during the 1970s a strong interest in "structuralist" analysis appeared in America, although this had little relationship to European structuralism of the same period. Such theorists as Jackson Barry, Bernard Beckerman, Paul Levitt, Roger Gross, and Richard Hornby were in fact more directly in the tradition of Aristotle and late-19th-century German analysts in their approach to the dynamics of drama as a functioning system. European structuralism proved much more influential in America through the closely related study of semiotics, which approached the theatre as a system of signs produced and presented to be interpreted by an audience. Most of the semiotic theory appearing in America has been European in origin, but a number of American theorists, such as Jean Alter, Marvin Carlson, Martin Esslin, and Michael Isaacharoff, have pursued variations of this approach.

European poststructuralism, challenging the tendency of structuralism and semiotics to assume stable, authenticated systems, had much influence on literary theory in America during the 1980s but relatively little on specifically theatrical theory. An important exception was **Herbert Blau,** who in a series of books beginning with *Take Up the Bodies* (1982), explored relationships between performance and consciousness, of perception utilizing theatre as a means of self-reflection. Another important challenge to semiotically oriented theory came from phenomenological theorists, such as **Richard Foreman** and Bert States, who emphasized the importance of the physical reality of theatre impacting upon consciousness.

A growing interest in the social positioning of the theatre and of the audience's role marked much American theory of the late 1980s and early 1990s. The influence of reception theory, reader–response theory, and the social dynamics of performance are clearly reflected in such semiotic studies as Carlson's *Signs of Life* (1989) or Alter's *A Socio-semiotic Theory of Theatre* (1990). Blau's *The Audience* (1990) positions the concept of the audience at the center not only of theatre and performance, but of cultural expression and psychoanalytic understanding. Other, more directly ideological methodologies also appeared during the 1980s, indeed the new decade was prophetically launched with the publication of Stephen Greenblatt's *Renaissance Self-Fashioning,* a defining work of what its author called new historicism, and with *The Woman's Part,* the first anthology of feminist criticism of Shakespeare.

A common concern with ideology, culture, and the structures of power may suggest a close relationship between the theoretical approaches of new historicism and feminism; however, new historicism has generally differed from feminism in its relative indifference to contemporary sociopolitical concerns. Its focus has been on past practice, especially during the Renaissance, whose theatre is generally seen not as an agent of social change but as a locus of ambiguous flows of energy similar to those poststructuralist that theorists have postulated in the act of performance.

In *The Feminist Spectator as Critic* (1988), Jill Dolan suggested three general orientations in American feminism [see **feminist theatre**]: liberal, cultural or radical, and materialist feminisms. Liberal feminism stresses individuality and "universal human" values and standards. Cultural feminists, fearing that this may simply reinscribe women in the male-dominated patterns of the past, have sought a woman's culture, different and separate from the culture of men. This project was strongly influenced by French poststructuralist psychoanalytic critics as Julia Kristeva and Luce Irigaray.

Materialist feminism has sought to avoid the universalist tendency of liberal feminism and the essentialist of cultural feminism, to study gender not as biological but as culturally constructed and thus related to systems of social relationships and social power formations. Elin Diamond has suggested that Brechtian techniques might be used to reveal this "constructedness," whereas Sue-Ellen Case and others have argued that lesbian performance [see **gay/lesbian theatre**] could offer an alternative representational strategy to disrupt the traditional heterosexual apparatus of drama with the male as the desiring subject.

In the latter part of the 20th century, dramatic theory in America generated for the first time a major part of theatre research, with a rich and diverse field of theoretical approaches being developed. As the 1990s began, social and ideological concerns provided the major new directions, but earlier social, psychoanalytical, linguistic, and philosophical approaches remained important both alone and in combination with the newer strategies. MC

See: M. Carlson, *Theories of the Theatre,* Ithaca, 1984; B. Clark, *European Theories of the Drama, with a Supplement on the American Drama,* New York, 1965; B. Dukore, *Dramatic Theory and Criticism from the Greeks to Grotowski,* New York, 1974.

Dramatists Guild, Inc., The Established in 1920 to protect the rights of dramatic authors for U.S. productions of plays and musicals. Services to more than 7,500 members include the use of **Off-Broadway,** Broadway, and Resident Theatre production contracts that provide "a fair royalty, maintenance of subsidiary rights, artistic control, and ownership of copyright"; subscriptions to the *Dramatists Guild Quarterly* and the *Newsletter;* use of the Guild's headquarters (Sardi Building) for readings and auditions; nationwide symposia by leading professionals; marketing advice; and a member's "Hotline." In 1992 the Dramatists Guild president was **Peter Stone.** TLM

Draper, Ruth (1884–1956) Actress and monologuist who created and performed a repertoire of 54 different characters in some 35 sketches. The range of personalities that she assumed was broad, as was the scope of her travels and reputation. In addition to accolades for her finely wrought characterizations of women of all ages, types, and cultures were plaudits for her ability to evoke throngs of other "unseen" characters. Prior to her professional debut in 1920, at the Aeolian Hall, London, she had been perfecting her craft before family, friends, and charity audiences. In the three and a half decades that followed, she performed almost nonstop, on every continent, and often at the command of royalty. Her letters, edited by Neilla Warren, were published in 1979. DBW

See: M. Zabel, *The Art of Ruth Draper,* Garden City, NY, 1960.

Dressler, Marie (Leila Koerber) (1869–1934) Canadian-born comedienne, daughter of an itinerant musician. At 14 she joined the Nevada Stock Company playing ingenues, but her mastifflike features and stocky build soon relegated her to farcical roles. She entered New York **vaudeville** with "coon" songs and impersonations, and had a real success as the music-hall singer Flo Honeydew

MARIE DRESSLER

IN TILLIE'S NIGHTMARE

An advertising card for Marie Dressler in *Tillie's Nightmare*, on tour in 1910. Courtesy: Laurence Senelick.

in the comic opera *The Lady Slavey* (1896). **Joe Weber** invited her to join his company in *Higgledy-Piggledy* (1904). Her most memorable role was the day-dreaming boarding-house drudge Tillie Blobbs in *Tillie's Nightmare* (Herald Square Theatre, 1910), singing "Heaven Will Protect the Working Girl." This led to a film contract with Mack Sennett for *Tillie's Punctured Romance* (1914), in which she was wooed by Charlie Chaplin; but she never flourished in silent pictures. She was prominent in the Liberty Loan drives of 1917–18 and the Actor's Strike of 1919, but reached such a low ebb in her career by 1927 that she contemplated opening a hotel in Paris. Fortuitously she returned to Hollywood and won a new public with *Anna Christie* (1930), *Dinner at Eight,* and *Tugboat Annie* (both 1933). LS

> See: M. Dressler w/ M. Harrington, *My Own Story,* New York, 1934; R. Raider, "A Descriptive Study of the Acting of Marie Dressler," PhD diss, U. of Michican, 1970.

Drew–Barrymore family The name "Barrymore," with Lionel, Ethel, and John its foremost exponents, stands as a synonym for acting. Franklin Delano Roosevelt was called "a newsreel Barrymore"; Mahatma Gandhi was "the Barrymore of the talking newspapers." *Time* magazine coined

"Barrymorishly" to describe how Ethel held the stage. Thirty years after she, the last of the triumvirate, died in 1959, the Barrymores remain the undisputed royal family of a kingdom called Broadway.

Their theatrical pedigree is genuine, traceable to 1752 and, according to family tradition, to strolling players in Shakespeare's time. Their maternal grandmother, **Mrs. John Drew** (1820–97), was born Louisa Lane in London to Thomas Frederick Lane, an actor of some provincial fame, and Eliza Trenter, a sweet singer of ballads. After her father's early death, the child toured provincial theatres, playing such roles as Prince Agib in *Timour, the Tartar,* before sailing for America with her mother. After playing such roles as the Duke of York to **Junius Brutus Booth**'s Richard III and Albert to **Edwin Forrest**'s William Tell (10 years later, she would graduate to Lady Macbeth opposite Forrest's Thane), she made her debut as a child star in 1828, playing Little Pickle in *The Spoiled Child* and five characters in *Twelve Precisely.*

In 1850, after a distinguished adolescent and adult career, she married her third husband, **John Drew** (1827–62), whose father managed **Niblo's** Theatre in New York. Famous for such popular Irish characters as Dr. O'Toole (*The Irish Tenor*) and Tim O'Brian (*The Irish Immigrant*) and Shakespeare's Andrew Aguecheek and Dromio, Drew briefly managed Philadelphia's National and **Arch Street** theatres. Mrs. Drew undertook the management of the Arch in 1861, one year before her husband's untimely death. During 30 subsequent years at the helm, she essentially contributed to the achievement and acceptance of theatre in America, while continuing to act, by popular demand, in such roles as Mrs. Malaprop and Mistress Quickly.

Two of her children by Drew began illustrious careers at the Arch. **John Drew** (1853–1927) trained under his mother's stern supervision before joining **Augustin Daly**'s **Fifth Avenue Theatre** company in New York (1875). Among his most popular old and new comedy parts were Orlando, Petruchio, and Charles Surface. By the mid-1800s, he and his fellow Fifth Avenue players, **Ada Rehan, James Lewis,** and **Mrs. G. H. Gilbert,** were called "the Big Four." In 1892, Drew agreed to star for manager **Charles Frohman** at the unheard of salary of $500 per week. Following his sensational debut in *The Masked Ball,* his naturalistic acting, elegant bearing, and sartorial correctness won him the uncontested title "First Gentleman of the American Stage" and kept him a reigning star for 35 years.

Georgiana Drew (1856–93), after a strict Arch Street apprenticeship, followed her older brother to the Fifth Avenue in 1876. She made an immediate hit with her breezy manner and unique way of tossing lines like nosegays to an audience – a technique that established her as a popular comedienne in such subsequent hits as *The Senator* (1889) with **William H. Crane** and *Settled Out of Court* (1892) with Frohman's Comedians. Her Fifth Avenue debut, in Daly's popular *Pique,* cast her opposite a young newcomer from England, **Maurice Barrymore** (1847–1905), whom she married in 1876.

Maurice Barrymore and Georgie Drew at Daly's Fifth Avenue Theatre (1876). Courtesy: James Kotsilibas-Davis.

Ethel Barrymore (1879–1959) became the first of the three siblings to achieve stardom. At the age of 21, after six years of apprenticeship with her grandmother, her uncle John Drew, and Sir Henry Irving in England, her name went above the title during the Broadway run of *Captain Jinks of the Horse Marines* in 1901. Under the astute management of Charles Frohman, she became a darling of fin-de-siècle society on two continents. The term "glamour girl" was coined for her, and sons of American millionaires and English peers courted her. Declining Winston Churchill's proposal of marriage, she explained, "I didn't think I could live up to his world. My world was the theatre." Her world remained the theatre as "Ethel Barrymore vehicles," such as *Alice-Sit-By-the-Fire, Cousin Kate, Lady Frederick,* and *Déclassé,* alternated with the stronger stuff of *A Doll's House, The Second Mrs. Tanqueray, The Constant Wife,* Lady Teazle, Camille, Portia, and Juliet. By birth she was queen of the royal family; by achievement, with regal bearing and fluid style, she became the First Lady of the American Theatre – a fact underscored in 1928 when the **Shubert**s opened the **Ethel Barrymore Theatre** with Ethel interpreting three ages of woman in *The Kingdom of God.* After the climax of her stage career in *The Corn Is Green* (1940), she opted for lucrative, less taxing movie work until her death in Hollywood two months before her 80th birthday.

Her older brother, **Lionel Barrymore** (1878–1954), began acting at 15 under the tutelage of his grandmother and his uncle **Sidney Drew** (1868–1919); Sidney was Mrs. Drew's illegitimate son – probably by Robert Craig, an actor in her Arch Street company. Sidney became a noted stage and vaudeville comedian, usually opposite his first wife,

The son of a British district commissioner in India, Barrymore left Oxford, became Amateur Middle-Weight Boxing Champion of England, changed his name from Herbert Blyth to spare his proper family, and tried acting. After his 1872 debut at the Theatre Royal, Windsor, he toured the provincial theatres for three years before sailing for America. His early years there were distinguished by successive inclusion in the companies of America's foremost managers: Augustin Daly, **Lester Wallack,** and **A. M. Palmer.** His striking beauty, sharp wit, and carefree manner made him a popular matinee idol and a sought-after leading man. His most successful characterizations included Orlando (particularly opposite **Helena Modjeska**), and the title roles in *A Man of the World* and *Captain Swift* (1888), which reviewers considered his "Monte Cristo" – a role in which he, like **James O'Neill** as the count, might have toured profitably for years. But Barrymore's volatile temperament and profligate ways precluded such security. Although three of the eight plays he wrote – *Reckless Temple, Roaring Dick & Co,* and *Nadjezda* – also were potentially durable vehicles, the author never exploited them. He died of paresis at the age of 58, deranged and unfulfilled, leaving a legacy of three children by Georgie Drew.

Ethel Barrymore in *Captain Jinks of the Horse Marines* (1901), her debut as a star. Courtesy: James Kotsilibas-Davis.

Gladys Rankin, daughter of actor-manager **Arthur McKee Rankin,** and his actress wife **Kitty Blanchard.** Lionel, in support of his uncle John Drew in *The Mummy and the Humming Bird* (1903), excelled in the small role of an Italian organ grinder without speaking a word of English. His inspired gift for characterization flourished in several subsequent productions – notably as boxer Kid Garvey in *The Other Girl* (1904), written for him by his father's friend **Augustus Thomas.** But in 1906, Lionel retreated to France with his first wife, Doris Rankin (Gladys's sister), to indulge his first love – painting. Three years later they returned to America and what Lionel called "the family curse" – acting. Interspersed with his pioneer acting in the "flickers" from 1912, his foremost stage vehicles – *The Copperhead* (1917), *The Claw* (1921), and *Laugh, Clown, Laugh* (1923) – were eclipsed by two costarring ventures with his brother: *Peter Ibbetson* (1917) and *The Jest* (1919). "To the future of such actors," predicted the *New York Times,* "it is impossible to set any limits." But after the failure of his *Macbeth* in 1921 and a series of mediocre plays, Lionel turned irrevocably to Hollywood. The elder Barrymore became acting's unchallenged Grand Old Man after nearly 200 film roles – the last 40 played in excruciating rheumatic pain, but with no less power, on crutches or in a wheelchair until his death at the age of 76.

His younger brother, **John Barrymore** (1882–1942), was even more resistant to acting. After a brief stint as a newspaper illustrator, he half-heartedly pursued, with the help of family and friends, a career as a stage comedian, while whole-heartedly pursuing debutantes and chorus girls. (Among his conquests in the former category: Katherine Harris, who became his first wife in 1913; in the latter, Evelyn Nesbit and Irene Fenwick, who later became Lionel's second wife.) Then, after a run of light comedy roles like *The Fortune Hunter* (1909), John stunned critics and theatregoers with his expert delineations of tragic roles in *Justice* (1916) and *Redemption* (1918). He followed them with two of the theatre's towering achievements: the **Arthur Hopkins–Robert Edmond Jones** productions of *Richard III* (1920) and *Hamlet* (1922), illuminated by his poetic beauty, vocal grandeur, and subtle strength. "The new prince was entering his kingdom," observed Hopkins. But at the height of his powers, touted as America's greatest actor, the crown prince of the royal family abdicated. He left the stage for films, returning only once after alcohol and self-indulgence had diminished his talents, playing a parody of himself in a travesty of a play (*My Dear Children,* 1939) three years before his death at 60.

Artistry and industry, combined with the color and glamour of their private lives, earned the Barrymores a unique niche in the annals of American theatre. Subsequent Drew–Barrymore generations have pursued theatrical careers with considerably less distinction. Ethel's three children from her marriage to socialite Russell Colt made attempts: two sons, half-heartedly; a daughter, **Ethel Barrymore Colt** (1912–77), with some success, particularly as an opera singer and acting teacher. John's daughter **Diana** (1921–60), by his second

wife, socialite-poetess Michael Strange, had a brief, promising acting career curtailed by excesses similar to those of her father. John's only son (by his third wife, actress Dolores Costello), known as John Barrymore, Jr., or **John Drew Barrymore** (b. 1932), also sacrificed a promising screen and stage career to alcohol, drugs, and self-indulgence. But his daughter, named appropriately **Drew Barrymore** (b. 1975), gained stardom, as her great-great-grandmother Mrs. Drew had, at the age of seven in the film *E.T.* (1982) and, despite a teenage bout with alcohol and drugs, continues in the 1990s to appear in films. JK-D

See: H. Alpert, *The Barrymores,* New York, 1964; E. Barrymore, *Memories,* New York, 1955; L. Barrymore, *We Barrymores,* New York, 1951; E. A. Dithmar, *John Drew,* New York, 1900; J. Drew, *My Years on the Stage,* New York, 1922; L. Drew, *Autobiographical Sketch of Mrs. John Drew,* New York, 1899; G. Fowler, *Good Night, Sweet Prince* [John Barrymore], New York, 1944; J. Kobler, *Damned in Paradise: The Life of John Barrymore,* New York, 1977; J. Kotsilibas-Davis, *The Barrymores: The Royal Family in Hollywood,* New York, 1981; J. Kotsilibas-Davis, *Great Times Good Times: The Odyssey of Maurice Barrymore,* Garden City, NY, 1977; M. Peters, *The House of Barrymore,* New York, 1990.

Drexler, Rosalyn (1926–) Playwright whose **Off-Off Broadway** avant-garde plays satirize sex, violence, and domestic life. Her first play, *Home Movies* (1964), blended Drexler's "camp" style with music by Al Carmines, a partnership that proved successful again with *The Line of Least Existence* (1968). Drexler's anarchic humor, often compared to that of the **Marx Bros.,** shows in *Hot Buttered Roll* (1966) and *The Writer's Opera* (1979), but she also wrote naturalism (*The Investigation,* 1966); a feminist history of Hatshepsut (*She Who Was He,* 1974); and a poignant study of two lesbian wrestlers (*Delicate Feelings,* 1984). She has won three Obies, most recently for *Transients Welcome* (1985), and an Emmy for "The **Lily (Tomlin) Show**" (1974). FB

Dreyfuss, Henry (1904–72) had a brief but notable career as a designer doing about 20 shows on Broadway between 1926 and 1935, including *The Last Mile* (1930) and *The Cat and the Fiddle* (1931). After *Paths of Glory* (1935) he gave up the stage for industrial design, and is remembered for the Perisphere at the 1939 New York World's Fair. AA

Driving Miss Daisy This 1988 Pulitzer Prize-winning drama in one act by Alfred Uhry opened **Off-Broadway** at **Playwrights Horizons** (15 April 1987) before transferring to the **John Houseman** Theatre, running a total of 1,195 performances. Set in and around Atlanta during 1948–73, the play examines the healing, attitudinal changes regarding racism and old age in the relationship between a difficult Southern Jewish widow and her black chauffeur, with extra perspective provided by the widow's son. The show won Obies for actors **Morgan Freeman** and **Dana Ivey;** Drama Desk nominations for author Uhry and director Ron Lagomarsino; the Dramatists' Guild's Morton Award; and the Outer Critics' Circle Award. Rob-

Alliance Theatre of Atlanta's production of *Driving Miss Daisy*, with Mary Nell Santacroce as Daisy and William Hall as Hoke Coleburn. Courtesy: Alliance Theatre.

ert Waldman, Uhry's collaborator on *The Robber Bridegroom,* composed the award-winning incidental music for the production. A film version starred **Jessica Tandy,** Morgan Freeman, and Dan Aykroyd. EK

Drunkard; or, The Fallen Saved, The, by **William H. Smith.** This allegory of moral reform, first performed in 1844 at the **Boston Museum,** where Smith stage-managed (seen first in New York, 1850), was the most popular and enduring of the many temperance melodramas on midcentury American stages. Tracing the decline into dypsomania of Edward Middleton (first played by Smith), the play climaxed in a delirium tremens scene that required the actor to thrash about in agony on the stage. Domestic bliss and social respectability reward Edward's eventual decision to take The Pledge. Antebellum productions at museum theatres in the Northeast spawned several other temperance plays and helped to convince many working- and middle-class theatregoers to conform to the emerging norms of bourgeois society. Performances mocking the values and conventions of the play have been popular since the 1930s, including a Los Angeles production that ran for 16 years. BMcC

Du Barry Historical extravaganza written and staged by **David Belasco** in 1901. This play on the life of a mistress of Louis XV was typical of Belasco's "historical" mode of scenic naturalism: highly sensational plot, lavish and thoroughly researched costumes and set, actual period furniture imported from France, and a cast of nearly 200. The play, featuring **Mrs. Leslie Carter,** opened at the Criterion Theatre on 25 December and had 165 performances. MF

Du Barry Was a Lady Cole Porter musical comedy hit of 1939–40 about a washroom attendant who dreams that he is Louis XV and that the

voluptuous singer he desires is Madame Du Barry. **Bert Lahr** and **Ethel Merman** headed the cast in this energetic romp, first conceived as a film project for **Mae West,** that pressed the limits of sexual and anatomical humor on Broadway. Lahr's madcap performance, along with the release of MGM's *The Wizard of Oz* during the run of the show, affirmed Lahr's reputation as a master of outrageous comedy. Another box-office draw was Betty Grable in her Broadway debut. The show's book was by Herbert Fields and **Buddy DeSylva.** The musical opened at the **46th Street Theatre** on 6 December 1939 and ran for 408 performances. MF

Du Bois, Raoul Pène (1914–85) Staten Island–born scenic and costume designer who, starting with a single costume design for *The Garrick Gaieties* in 1930, went on to a 50-year career designing creative and colorful costumes, imaginative sets, and occasional lighting designs. In addition to notable Broadway credits, including ***Du Barry Was a Lady*** (1939), *Sugar Babies* (1979), and ***No, No, Nanette*** (1971), his costumes and scenery were seen in London and Paris and graced films, ice shows, ballets, nightclubs, aquacades, and commercial illustrations. He received Tony Awards for costumes (*No, No, Nanette,* 1971) and scenery (***Wonderful Town,*** 1953). BO

Duff, Mary Ann (Dyke) (1794–1857) London-born actress, known as "the American Sarah Siddons," after the British actress. She seems to have made her debut in Dublin, but came to America with her husband, John Duff, in 1810 and made her first appearance as Juliet on New Year's Eve that year. Until 1817 she went relatively unnoticed, then suddenly changed her style, showing the "true fire of genius," and emerged as a star. She won fame in Philadelphia and Boston rather than New York as a tragic actress, noted by critics for her "uniformity of excellence." The death of her husband in 1831 left her with seven children; she then married the actor Charles Young, but the marriage was soon annulled. She married again in 1835 and retired in 1838, but returned to the stage sporadically, appearing as late as 1850 in Toronto. Many of the leading actors of the time considered her the greatest actress in America. SMA

See: J. Ireland, *Mrs. Duff,* Boston, 1882.

Dukakis, Olympia (1931–) Actress, teacher, director, and former artistic director of New Jersey's Whole Theatre Company (1976–90), founded with brother Apollo and husband Louis Zorich. Best known for *Moonstruck* (Academy Award, 1987), she won Obies for *A Man's a Man* (1963) and *The Marriage of Bette and Boo* (1985). Cofounding Boston's Charles Street Playhouse (1957–60) and the Edgartown (MA) Summer Theatre (1960), she made her **Off-Broadway** debut in 1960 (Lippa's *The Breaking Wall*) and her Broadway debut in 1962 (*The Aspern Papers*). An associate director at the **Williamstown Theatre Festival,** Dukakis has appeared on TV and in the 1989 films *Steel Magnolias, Look Who's Talking,* and *Dad.* A teacher at New York and Yale universities, she has been a guest artist in the regions (e.g., Amanda in *The Glass Menagerie,* **Trinity Rep,** 1991). In 1991 she was appointed to the board of the New Jersey Performing Arts Center.   REK

Duke, Vernon (né Vladimir Dukelsky) (1903–69) Russian-born composer, educated at the Kiev Conservatory, who composed ballet music for the Ballets Russes, and, after an unsuccessful attempt at an American career, wrote the scores for London operettas and musicals. Returning to America in 1929, he contributed songs to several important **revue**s of the 1930s, such as *Three's a Crowd* (1930) and *Americana* (1932). His first complete score, for the revue *Walk a Little Faster* (1932), included one of his best-known songs, "April in Paris." His most successful score was for *Cabin in the Sky* (1940). In the 1940s and '50s he continued to write musical comedy scores, as well as ballets, symphonies, and concertos, but although individual songs were sometimes memorable, none of his shows was of lasting importance. His autobiography, *Passport to Paris,* was published in 1955 (Boston).   MK

Dukes, David (1945–) San Francisco-born leading man, most recognizable for television appearances (***Strange Interlude*** with Glenda Jackson; "Winds of War"). He debuted on Broadway in *School for Wives* (1971). With over a dozen major New York credits, Dukes has made his principal mark replacing actors in leading roles (*Travesties, Amadeus,* ***M. Butterfly***). He received critical acclaim as Gen. William Tecumseh Sherman in **Thomas Babe**'s *Rebel Woman* (**New York Shakespeare Festival,** 1976) and in the 1979–80 season opposite Richard Gere in Martin Sherman's raw depiction of homosexuality in a Nazi concentration camp, *Bent.*   DBW

Dulcy by **George S. Kaufman** and **Marc Connelly,** directed by **Howard Lindsay,** opened on Broadway 13 August 1921 and ran 246 performances. Based on a character created by humor columnist Franklin P. Adams, Dulcy (**Lynn Fontanne**) is an exaggeration of the "typical" American housewife who invites one of her husband's business associates to a weekend house party, and then sets up the situation to allow her to meddle in everyone else's affairs, happily unaware that anyone might object to the trysts and elopements that she fosters.   JDM

Dunlap, William (1766–1839) Playwright and manager, often termed "the father of American drama." He wrote or translated and adapted more than 50 plays. Half of them were originals; the other half adaptations from the French and German, principally from Kotzebue. He managed the **Park Theatre** (1798–1805), an undertaking that ended disastrously, as he was apparently too good-natured to be hard-headed about financial matters. Still he persisted, managing the Park again (1806–11) for the actor **Thomas A. Cooper.** Even if poor at business, he was the first manager to write and present his own plays, the first to champion native subject matter and dramatists, and the first

to record his experiences and those of others in his *History of the American Theatre* (1832).

Born in Perth Amboy, NJ, Dunlap began his artistic life as a painter, studied with Benjamin West in England (1784–7), became fascinated with the theatre when he saw Sheridan's *The School for Scandal* and *The Critic* with their original casts, and on his return to New York where he saw **Royall Tyler**'s *The* **Contrast.**

Most notable among his original plays: *Darby's Return* (1789); *The Father* (1799); *André* (1798), which he later transformed into a patriotic spectacle for holiday performance as *The Glory of Columbia* (1803), with backdrops and transparencies by Charles Ciceri; *Leicester* (1806); and *A Trip to Niagara; or, Travellers in America* (1828), with a diorama of 18 scenes along the Hudson as a steamboat moves up the river from New York to Catskill landing. His most popular adaptations include (from Kotzebue) *The Stranger* (1798), *False Shame* (1799), and *Pizarro in Peru* (1800), as well as (from the French) *The Wife of Two Husbands* (1804, Pixérécourt) and *Thirty Years; or, the Life of a Gamester* (1828, Goubaux and Ducange).

Besides his work in the theatre, he painted a host of miniatures (one of George Washington), and monumental religious canvases such as *Christ Rejected* (12 × 18 ft). He was director of the American Academy of Fine Arts (1817), a founder of the National Academy of Design (1826), and a professor of historical painting at the National Academy (1830–9). He wrote biographies of the actor **George Frederick Cooke** (1813) and the novelist Charles Brockden Brown (1815), a *History of the Arts of Design* (1834), *Thirty Years Ago; or, Memoirs of a Water Drinker* (1836), and a *History of New York for Schools* (1837).   RM

> See: R. Canary, *William Dunlap,* New York, 1970; O. Coad, *William Dunlap: A Study of His Life and Works and of His Place in Contemporary Culture,* New York, 1917; W. Dunlap, *Diary of William Dunlap, 1766–1839,* New York, 1930.

Dunnock, Mildred (1901–91) Actress and director, remembered by **Arthur Miller** as "a fiercely dedicated artist." She first appeared in New York in 1932, then she played several seasons of stock. After a number of Broadway appearances, she achieved stardom with such roles as Linda Loman in ***Death of a Salesman*** (1949) and Big Mama in ***Cat on a Hot Tin Roof*** (1955). She played a number of seasons with the **American Shakespeare Festival** in both classic and modern roles, and in 1965 directed *Graduation* on Broadway. She usually appeared in major supporting roles (mothers and eccentric ladies), relying on a slight stature and tremendous voice to project an ineffectual gentility.

She made her film debut in *The Corn Is Green* (1945), and later appeared in such successful films as *Death of a Salesman* (1951), *Viva Zapata!* (1952), *The Jazz Singer* (1953), *Baby Doll* (1956), and *Sweet Bird of Youth* (1962). She also appeared on many television series and specials. Her daughter Linda McGuire is an actress, as is her granddaughter Patricia McGuire Dunnock.   SMA

Durang, Christopher (1949–) Playwright and actor, born in Montclair, NJ, and educated at Harvard and Yale. Durang had his first play produced in 1971, emerging as a new breed of American dramatist in the late 1970s and early '80s. His best-known scripts include *A History of the American Film* (1976), *Sister Mary Ignatius Explains It All for You* (1979), *The Actor's Nightmare* (1981), *Beyond Therapy* (1981), *Baby with the Bath Water* (1983), and *The **Marriage of Bette and Boo*** (1973, revised 1985). For *Sister Mary Ignatius* Durang won the Obie Award in 1980. Durang's style, according to **Mel Gussow**, "has the wiggishness of four Marxes and the malice of a Jonathan Swift." His satirical bent, especially when he attacks religion, has provoked considerable controversy and attempted **censorship.** SMA

See: C. Durang, *Christopher Durang Explains It All for You*, New York, 1983.

Durang, John (1768–1822) Actor, clown, equestrian, puppeteer, scene painter, dancer-pantomimist, and manager. Durang spent most of his life in his native Pennsylvania or used it as home base. As a boy he ran away from home to Boston where he made his debut. In 1785 he joined **Hallam** at Philadelphia's **Southwark Theatre** as dancer and pantomimist. With John Bill Ricketts's **circus** in the 1790s, he traveled to Canada as the first-known American-born clown. On his return to Philadelphia he worked as a scene painter and dancer, eventually joining **Thomas Wignell**'s company in the winters while traveling with his own companies in summers (1806–10) into Pennsylvania Dutch country, performing scenes from Shakespeare in German. Durang wrote and illustrated his important memoirs (1785–1816), not published until 1966 (editor, Alan S. Downer) by the University of Pittsburgh Press.

All of Durang's children had theatre careers: **Charles** (1796–1870), actor and dancer-choreographer, wrote *The Philadelphia Stage from the Year 1749 to the Year 1855* (published serially by the Philadelphia *Sunday Dispatch*, 1854–60); **Ferdinand** (1798–1831), an actor-dancer, had a short career primarily in New York; **Augustus** (1800–18?) was a child actor; **Charlotte** (1803–24) was a dancer; and **Juliet** (1805–49) worked (as Mrs. Godey) as a provincial actress in leading roles. DBW

Durante, Jimmy (1893–1980) Comedian, actor, and singer. One of America's most beloved entertainers, Durante began as a saloon pianist on Coney Island and opened his own **nightclub** in 1923 with Eddie Jackson and Lou Clayton. He debuted on Broadway in *Show Girl* in 1929. He later toured England, then appeared on Broadway in such shows as *Jumbo* (1935), *Red, Hot, and Blue!* (1936), and *Stars in Your Eyes* (1939). He made his film debut in *Roadhouse* (1930); among his other films were *Palooka* (1934), *The Man Who Came to* *Dinner* (1941), and *Two Girls and a Sailor* (1944). He starred on radio's "Rexall Show" (1944–50) and later his own TV show, being voted best television performer in 1951. He also received a Citation of Merit from the City of New York in 1956. SMA

See: I. Adler, *I Remember Jimmy*, Westport, CT, 1980; G. Fowler, *Schnozzola*, New York, 1951; J. Robbins, *Inka Dinka Doo*, New York, 1991.

Durham, Jimmie (1940–) Arkansas-born, Wolf Clan Cherokee Indian **performance art**ist, sculptor, and poet. After studying sculpture at L'École des Beaux Arts, University of Geneva (1968–72), he became active in the American Indian Movement (1973–80) and the International Indian Treaty Council (1974–80), and was Representative of the Human Rights Commission to the United Nations (1975). He cofounded Houston's Adept Art Center (1963), and became Executive Director for the New York–based Foundation for the Community of Artists, as well as editor of *Art and Artists* (1982). His first performance, *My Land* (1964), was with boxer Mohammed Ali and Vivian Ayers Allen. In *Thanksgiving* (1982), *Manhattan Giveaway* (1985), and *Savagism & You* (1991), he parodied the "Indian artifact," anthropological constructions of gift-giving ceremonies, and the misinterpretations of indigenous cultures. By representing himself as "savage," and by performing American heroes (George Washington and Davy Crockett) as his counterpersonas, he challenges the political inscription of his identity [see **Native Americans portrayed**]. AF

D'usseau, Arnaud (1916–90) This Los Angeles-born playwright and screenwriter was successful in the theatre only when collaborating with James Gow during WW II. *Tomorrow the World* (1943) is a propagandistic piece attacking Nazi extremism through the reeducation of an indoctrinated German boy. Although homiletic in tone, ***Deep Are the Roots*** (1945) is a moving examination of racial hatred in the deep South, with a black war hero returning only to be punished by intransigent white bigots. RHW

Dutchman Long one-act allegorical drama by **Amiri Baraka** (LeRoi Jones) that heralded the era of black revolutionary drama of the 1960s and early '70s. On a subway train, symbolizing the ship *The Flying Dutchman*, a sexy blond woman teases a black intellectual to an angry outburst, then murders him as other white passengers look on unconcerned. First produced by the Playwrights Unit in New York, the play moved to the Cherry Lane Theatre, where it provoked critical controversy, even though it won an Obie Award as the best **Off-Broadway** play of 1964. It was also produced in Paris, Berlin, and Spoleto, Italy, and was made into a full-length film in 1967. EGH

E

Eagle Theatre Built on the embarcadero in Sacramento at the height of the gold rush, it was the first theatrical facility designed exclusively for that purpose in California, opening 18 October 1849 with a production of *The Bandit Chief; or, The Spectre of the Forest*. It maintained a season until 4 January 1850 but was destroyed in a flood three days later.   PAD

Easiest Way, The The second major success of **Eugene Walter,** it opened at the **Belasco**–Stuyvesant Theatre 19 January 1909 for 157 performances, following its Hartford Opera House preview engagement 31 December 1908. This first **David Belasco**–Walter collaboration yielded near-naturalism, overturning the assumed happy ending and portraying a theatre life that some found too frank. Called grim and immoral, the play drew considerable public notice and was called the hit of its season. Through a series of nearly melodramatic revelations, actress Laura Murdock, producer Willard Brockton's mistress, fails in her attempt to break the mutually exploitative relationship and marry journalist John Madison. Accepting the inevitable, she shocked audiences with the closing line, "I'm going to Rector's to make a hit, and to hell with the rest." Of further note was the scene for which Belasco purchased the contents of a boardinghouse room, steamed the wallpaper, and reapplied it to the stage setting.   RW

East Lynne Domestic melodrama adapted by several playwrights – including **Clifton Tayleure,** Benjamin E. Woolf, **McKee Rankin,** and **Clara Morris** – from Mrs. Henry Wood's novel. The play centers on Lady Isabel's conjugal infidelity, her departure from her home, and her later disguised return, as a governess, to care for her son, who dies. The plot also includes a murder mystery involving Isabel's seducer, and ends with her death. The melodrama evoked tears and self-righteousness from its audience for its scenes of domestic pathos and its lectures on patience and respectability. **Lucille Western** centered her repertory on Lady Isabel, performing Tayleure's 1862 version throughout her career. Other actors, including **Nance O'Neil** and **Blanche Bates,** performed the piece, which was occasionally shortened for vaudeville production after 1895. Several films were made of *East Lynne,* and the **Provincetown Players** burlesqued its embrace of Victorian domesticity in 1926.   BMcC

East West Players The first contemporary **Asian-American theatre** company, founded in Los Angeles in 1965 by seven artists of Asian heritage frustrated by their lack of opportunities in mainstream, white-dominated theatre and film. At first EWP presented Asian-cast versions of Goldoni and Brecht, along with plays set in Asia (such as *Rashomon*). In the mid-1970s, under the management of noted actor-director Mako, the focus changed to nurturing and presenting plays by an exciting new crop of dramatists concerned with modern Asian-American themes: **David Henry Hwang,** Wakako Yamauchi, Valina Houston, and others. Mako left in 1988; actress Nobu McCarthy became artistic director a year later. Under McCarthy, this nonprofit company continues to mount seasons of recent Asian-American works in its small playhouse on Santa Monica Blvd.   MB

Eaton, Walter Prichard (1878–1957) Educator and critic. Born in Malden, MA, and educated at Harvard (1900), Eaton wrote for the *Boston Journal* before moving to the *New York Tribune* in 1902 as an assistant to **William Winter.** In 1907–8 he became drama critic for the *New York Sun,* leaving in 1908 to begin a nine-year association with *American Magazine.* He was Associate editor of *The Drama Magazine* and a free-lance critic during 1919–31. Following the retirement of **George Pierce Baker** in 1933, he became Professor of Playwriting at Yale, a post he held until 1947. Author of six books on the theatre, Eaton opposed Broadway's domination of the American stage, and argued that the greatest sufferer from this system is the intelligent playgoer.   TLM

Ebb, Fred see **Kander, John**

Eckart, Jean (1921–) and **William Eckart** (1920–) This husband and wife design team have done all their work in collaboration with each other. Trained at Yale, they began their Broadway career in 1951 and for the next 15 years were associated with some of the major musicals of the time, including *The Golden Apple, Once Upon a Mattress, **Fiorello!, Damn Yankees,*** and *Mame.* **Off-Broadway** work includes *Oh Dad, Poor Dad* . . . . They have also designed for opera, ballet, television, and industrial shows. Since the 1970s they have done less design work. Mr. Eckart teaches at Southern Methodist University.   AA

Economics The business of American theatre is founded on Puritan principles of commerce and morality dating to the early 18th century. Not only is theatre a vehicle for social intercourse and articulation of moral values, but equally it serves as a traditional commodity, in which its value is only as great as its profit. From the beginning, American theatre has sought to balance these apparently contradictory elements into the Puritans' ideal amalgamation of values: to profit both financially and morally.

The earliest professional players in the New World were mostly English fair performers, seeking new and profitable audiences in a rapidly expanding country. Battling conservative sentiment, hostile merchants, and a deteriorating economy, these performers found security in their traditional touring practices, though they preferred the permanence of a stock company. The first major troupe to arrive was the company of **Murray and Kean.** Beginning in 1749, they toured the principal colonies, performing a typical English repertoire with a general operating mode resembling the itinerant English companies of the same period. They were probably organized as a sharing company, with each member assuming a proportionate risk. Numerous benefit performances helped augment individual performers' incomes, but the extent to which these benefits succeeded is difficult to assess. Thus early performers must have found some consistency in following the annual commodity fairs scattered throughout North America and by accepting remuneration in the form of barter, bills of credit, and exchange.

The **Hallams,** successors to Murray and Kean, clearly fared better, although when they arrived in 1752, they too struggled to find a profitable audience. The outbreak of the French and Indian War in 1754 plunged the region into financial chaos, and the company soon left for Jamaica. Upon their return four years later, the reorganized company, under the direction of **David Douglass,** began one of the most successful eras in theatrical management. For the next 14 years the company regularly toured the colonies and maintained an organization that was financially viable and profitable enough to erect new theatres and replace actors with fresh talent from London. However, rebellious colonists increasingly associated theatre with British goods, and in 1774 when the Continental Congress passed its anti-importation acts to discourage the use and dissemination of British products, theatre was included. Douglass and Company, primarily for financial necessity, left for Jamaica where they remained until war's end.

The professional theatre returned in the early Federalist period to a country ripe for commercial exploitation, though still steeped in the moralist traditions of the past. No longer a threat to midlevel mercantilism nor viewed as a manufacture of British hegemony, theatre prospered in the 1790s after a brief period of difficulty caused by the vestiges of prewar antitheatrical sentiment and a postwar depression. By 1793 **Boston** had suspended its 1750 ban on theatrical amusements, and a new playhouse was opened. Elsewhere the formal opposition to theatre faded and a new confidence, based more on nationalism than economic stability, was reflected in fundamental changes in company

organization. Salaries replaced shares; resident **stock companies** replaced itinerant troupes. These changes begin in earnest in 1789 with the founding of a constitutional government and a federal presidency. But the biggest boost to theatre was the result of the early attempts at creating a regulated national currency.

The founding of the First Bank of the United States in 1791 provided the nation with a modicum of fiscal stability, necessary for rapid expansion and renewed trade. The regulation of state banks and their notes allowed greater financial consistency internally and abroad. Although great disparity still existed among some state's bank notes, the general climate was conducive to commercial growth and international trade. Confidence in the new currency is evident in the sudden rise in the number of theatres built on funds raised by stock and public subscription between 1789 and 1800 (NY's **Park Theatre, Federal Street Theatre** and Haymarket in Boston, as well as theatres in Providence, Charleston, and Washington, DC). Among managers to take advantage of the new financial climate was **Stephen Price,** who revolutionized the American theatre during 1810–40 by importing major English stars, including **George Frederick Cooke, Charles Matthews,** and Edmund Kean [see **international stars**]. Though not a new practice, Price was the first able regularly and successfully to engage individual stars on limited tours, in part because of the relative value and consistency of American currency. As the first American manager who was not also an actor or playwright, he could devote his entire effort to management, leaving the artistry up to his stars. This fundamental shift altered the nature of commercial theatre in America.

Professional managers, stock companies, and the star system expanded during the first half of the 19th century. Most major cities maintained resident stock companies, run by professional managers and supplemented by the occasional star on tour. By 1830 New York had surpassed **Philadelphia** as the nation's theatrical center, with at least five major companies operating; but the demise of the Second Bank of the United States in 1834 and the subsequent overexpansion of credit led to a period of economic stress that culminated in the Panic of 1837. Within a year, the theatrical industry was in serious decline, especially in New York, which saw only the Park survive intact. Theatrical managers sought new forms of theatrical attractions, relying less on imported actors, reluctant to take American dollars. Among the most successful survivors was **William Mitchell** and his Olympic Theatre, which opened in 1839 and continued until 1850. By presenting light comedies (farces, burlesques, and local spectacles) at a reasonable price, Mitchell developed a profitable alternative to the traditional venue, more than covering for the lack of stars. His appeal to the working classes opened up a vast audience base. Along a similar vein, **P. T. Barnum** opened his **Barnum's American Museum** in 1842, with its freakish displays and a theatre that produced popular melodramas. No longer reliant upon touring stars, popular theatres also found support from the growing immigrant class. By exploiting the superficial qualities of melodrama and recent technical innovations, almost any crowd could be attracted.

By midcentury, the business of American theatre had become a multimillion-dollar industry dominated by independent managers and a few leading actors. Touring was limited to occasional stars and western entrepreneurs. Stock companies, on the other hand, controlled the regular seasons in the larger cities. The Civil War changed all that, though the changes were not entirely the direct result of the conflict. Certainly there were managers in New York and elsewhere who exploited the war to stage timely and spectacular representations of Union victories to theatrical audiences starved for frontline "news"; but the real transformation of the industry came about after the war as a result of the economic collapse of 1873. Stock companies not sufficiently protected failed, and managers once again looked to touring as the safest alternative; however, unlike earlier touring troupes, these new "combinations" were cast, rehearsed, and booked well in advance, and sent out on the newly expanded railroad with a minimum of scenery and a limited repertory. Their purpose was to take advantage of remote towns by arranging brief stops along vast circuits throughout the West, generally untouched by the financial panic. Audiences and money were abundant, and the railroads provided an economical means of transportation. By 1880, most of the major stock companies were gone, replaced by combinations.

Success of the combinations created a new theatrical industry – booking **agents.** Within a decade, independent booking agents, located mostly in New York and Philadelphia, controlled much of the national market. In 1895 the six most powerful men controlling the three largest agencies joined forces, effectively monopolizing the American theatre industry overnight. The Theatrical **Syndicate,** as it became known, instantly transformed the business of theatre. Its existence removed the manager as the dominant entrepreneur-artist and placed the ultimate control into the hands of a small group of financiers, whose sole objective was to turn a profit. But despite the Syndicate's inviolable monopoly, it soon fell victim to an even greater organization – the **Shubert brothers.** Utilizing management techniques adapted from other big businesses and the change in corporate financing brought about by the Sherman Anti-Trust Act in 1890, the Shuberts created a modern corporation, fully capitalized and able to outmaneuver the cumbersome structure of the Syndicate. In legal action designed to halt the Syndicate's domination, the Shuberts sued under the Sherman Act, hoping to have the pool declared an illegal monopoly; but the Supreme Court ruling of 1907 absolved the Syndicate by declaring theatrical amusements not subject to the Anti-Trust Act since they are not technically manufactured goods. Initially a setback for the Shuberts, this ruling eventually proved to be a boon: After the collapse of the Syndicate in 1916, the Shuberts found themselves protected as a legal monopoly under the ruling. Not until 1956 would the Supreme Court finally declare them in violation of antitrust laws. Nevertheless, the Shubert brothers' operation served as a corporate model in the entertainment industry, especially for the early film companies.

The abuses of big business in the late 19th century contributed to the rise of labor **unions.** Stagehands organized in 1886, and actors soon followed by forming the Actor's Society of America in 1895, succeeded by **Actors' Equity Association.** Other unions included the United Scenic Artists of America (1912) and **Dramatists Guild** (1919). The Actors' Strike of 1919 solidified the labor movement in theatre, leading to a succession of crucial changes in the rights of theatrical employees; but with these changes came added expense and overhead, reflected in the gradual increase in ticket prices. Additionally, decreases in auditorium size, in part the result of stricter fire codes and changes in aesthetic taste, meant less revenue. By the 1930s, the American theatre industry had lost its financial competitiveness and much of its audience to the more economical business of film. Within 20 years, television would surpass them both.

The arrival of the musical in the early 1940s helped slow theatre's decline, but it was not enough to regain the dominance it once held. Investment in professional theatre became a highly speculative business. In the 1950s, formation of limited partnerships, in which several people shared the financial risks and rewards, replaced corporate financing as the preferred method of capitalization, but the risks were often too great for some, who sought other venues for performance. Alternatives to professional theatre are found as early as the late 19th century. Occasional experiments into nonprofit theatre, like the **Provincetown Players** in 1915, paved the way for the explosion in the 1960s as an alternative to the prohibitive costs of commercial theatre. The establishment of the National Endowment for the Arts in 1966 and changes in the tax law helped expand nonprofit theatre, resulting in the rapid growth of **resident nonprofit professional theatre,** the 20th-century incarnation of the early 19th century stock company.

Today theatre remains a risky investment. Much of professional theatre is still limited to Broadway and though the industry claims its profits continue to grow, its audience has not increased proportionally. Most recent figures indicate that there are fewer people attending the professional theatre in New York now than 30 years ago, and there is no indication that the situation will soon improve: Theatre now plays a distant third to the monolithic industries of television and film. Even though the Puritan profit motive still drives the professional theatre in America, that motive is now better achieved by its competitors. PAD

See: W. J. Baumol and W. G. Bowen, *Performing Arts: The Economic Dilemma,* New York, 1966; H. and W. J. Baumol, eds., *Inflation and the Performing Arts,* New York, 1984; A. L. Bernheim, *The Business of the Theatre* (1932), reprint, New York, 1964; J. Heilbrun and C. M. Gray, *The Economics of Art and Culture,* Cambridge (UK)/New York, 1993; D. Metzer, *The Subsidized Muse,* Cambridge (UK)/New York, 1979; T. G. Moore, *The Economics of the American Theater,* Durham, NC, 1968; J. Poggi, *Theater in America: The Impact of Economic Forces, 1870–1967,* Ithaca, NY,

1968; H. L. Vogel, *Entertainment Industry Economics*, 2d ed., Cambridge (UK)/New York, 1990.

Edmonds, Randolph (1900–83) Considered the dean of African-American academic theatre, Edmonds had an illustrious career as student and educator. He established the first theatre department at a black university (Dillard, 1935) and founded the National Association of Dramatic and Speech Arts to support and enhance drama programs at black institutions. He wrote some 50 plays, the most prominent appearing in collections *Shades and Shadows* (1930), *Six Plays for the Negro Theatre* (1934), and *The Land of Cotton and Other Plays* (1942).   EGH

Edouin, Willie (né William Frederick Bryer) (1845–1908) British-born comedian who began his career in a juvenile company and first appeared in New York in a supporting role in *Ixion* (1870) with **Lydia Thompson**'s troupe. Edouin returned to America in 1877 and remained for several years, appearing in burlesque extravaganzas such as *Hiawatha* (1880). In 1880 he formed his own company, Willie Edouin's Sparks, and offered the popular farce *Dreams; or, Fun in a Photographic Gallery*. He returned to London in 1884, remaining for 16 years before revisiting the U.S. in *Florodora* (1900). As a comedian, Edouin exuded an air of good-tempered perplexity.   MK

Edwards, Ben (1916–) Designer. Edwards began his career at the **Barter Theatre** in Virginia in 1935 and later achieved acclaim with his sets for **Judith Anderson**'s *Medea* (1947). From the 1950s on he designed on Broadway regularly, including *The Waltz of the Toreadors* (1957), **Inge**'s *The Dark at the Top of the Stairs* (1957), *Purlie* (1970), and five **Eugene O'Neill** plays with director **José Quintero.** He has also designed for film and TV and numerous regional theatres. Much of his work since the mid-1960s has been in collaboration with his wife, costume designer **Jane Greenwood.** Though he designs in a variety of styles, Edwards acknowledges an influence from **Robert Edmond Jones,** and his sets are generally suggestive and evocative.   AA

Effect of Gamma Rays on Man-in-the-Moon Marigolds, The Pulitzer Prize–winning drama in two acts by **Paul Zindel,** first produced at the **Alley Theatre** in Houston (1965). On 7 April 1970 it opened **Off-Broadway** at the Mercer–O'Casey Theatre, directed by Melvin Bernhardt and featuring **Sada Thompson.** The play, in the naturalistic tradition, is both comic and serious in tone, dealing with a tyrannical widow and her two daughters. Paralleling the effects of the mother on her offspring, Zindel reveals society's growing concern with exposure to radiation and its possibilities of producing mutations.   ER

Eichelberger, Ethyl (né James Roy Eichelberger) (1945–90) Unique **performance art**ist-writer, a victim of **AIDS** and suicide. **Mel Gussow** described Eichelberger's specialty as "mockery without malice," and called him "the

Varney Knapp in the world premiere of Zindel's *The Effect of Gamma Rays on Man-in-the-Moon Marigolds,* directed by Nina Vance (Alley Theatre, 1965). Photo: Marc St. Gil. Courtesy: Alley Theatre.

ultimate autodidact – actor, clown, playwright, singer, director, composer, accordionist, tumbler and fire-eater." After seven years with the **Trinity Repertory Company,** Eichelberger moved to New York in 1975, began a collaboration with **Charles Ludlum** and the **Ridiculous Theatrical Company,** and established a reputation for outrageous male and female characters (he personally concocted some 30 plays, many challenging sexual barriers), in particular in his deconstructed classics (*Medea, Leer, Ariadne Obnoxious, Hamlette,* and *Jocasta; or, Boy Crazy*). He also appeared at **Lincoln Center** in *Measure for Measure* and *Comedy of Errors,* and in **Dexter**'s 1989 *Threepenny Opera.* [See also **female/male impersonation.**]   DBW

Eigsti, Karl (1938–) Designer and educator. For much of his career Eigsti was associated with the **Arena Stage** in Washington as well as other regional theatres, notably the **Guthrie Theatre, American Shakespeare Festival, Long Wharf Theatre,** and **Cincinnati Playhouse.** Broadway work has been limited, but he has designed numerous shows **Off-Broadway,** including *The House of Blue Leaves* (1971). He has two distinct styles: a simplified realism for much of the commercial work, and a bold symbolism often employed for the arena-style productions. He has taught at New York University and has headed the design program at Brandeis University.   AA

Elder, Eldon (1924–) Designer who studied with **Donald Oenslager** at Yale. Though he designed over 200 productions for Broadway, **Off-Broadway,** opera, and regional theatre, his lasting legacy is as designer of the Delacorte Theater, the

Central Park home of the **New York Shakespeare Festival,** where he was resident designer during 1958–61. He also designed or consulted on several other theatres, including many regional theatres, with over 30 productions at the **St. Louis Municipal** Opera. Elder taught for many years at Brooklyn College.   AA

Elder, Lonnie (1931–) African-American playwright and film/TV scriptwriter, highly regarded for his play *Ceremonies in Dark Old Men* (1969). After the critical acclaim accorded this play, Elder joined the **Negro Ensemble Company** as director of its Playwrights' Unit. He then moved to Hollywood to write scripts for film and television. Among the best known of his screenplays are the award-winning *Sounder* (1972), which shows the effect of the Depression on a black sharecropping family; its sequel *Sounder, Part II* (1976); and *Melinda* (1972), about a black disk jockey's entanglement with a crime syndicate. In 1988 Elder's **one-person** play *Splendid Mummer* opened in NYC: Based on the career of the 19th-century black actor **Ira Aldridge** and featuring Charles Dutton, it failed to win critical approval.   EGH

Eldridge (née McKechnie), Florence (1901–88) Actress whose Broadway debut in 1918 was in the chorus of *Rock-a-Bye Baby*. After several appearances on Broadway, she toured with her husband, **Fredric March**, in the **Theatre Guild**'s productions of such scripts as *Arms and the Man, The Silver Cord,* and *The Guardsman* in 1927–8. She made her film debut in 1929 in *Studio Murder Mystery* with her husband. She frequently appeared with March, as in *The Skin of Our Teeth* (1942) and again in **Ruth Gordon**'s *Years Ago* (1946). One of her greatest successes, again with March, was as Mary Tyrone in *Long Day's Journey into Night* (1956), for which she won the *Variety* New York Drama Critics' Poll.   SMA

Elephant Man, The Play in 21 scenes by Bernard Pomerance, New York–born playwright who lives in England, suggested by the life of Joseph (*not* John) Merrick. This late-19th-century figure suffered from a genetic disorder that made him appear monstrous. Merrick's plight, popularized in a 1971 book by Ashley Montagu, was developed as a play first at London's Hampstead Theatre and then in 73 Off-Broadway performances. Jack Hofsiss directed the **Booth Theatre** production, which began 19 April 1979, ran for 916 performances, and won all major drama awards. Merrick was performed by Philip Anglim, and **Kevin Conway** portrayed Dr. Frederick Treves, the surgeon who rescued Merrick from ignominy and helped him to achieve some degree of human dignity. Although Merrick can never become the ordinary man of his dreams, his dramatized story is one of human courage and spirit. Pomerance has had several plays produced in England, but this is his only U.S. success.   DBW

Eliot, T[homas] S[tearns] (1888–1965) Playwright and poet born in St. Louis, educated at Harvard, the Sorbonne, and Oxford; settled in England in 1915. Eliot's best-known play, *Murder in the Cathedral,* commissioned for the 1935 Canterbury Festival, was seen in the U.S. at Yale that year and was presented by the **Federal Theatre Project** in New York the following year. His other verse plays (*The Family Reunion* [1939], *The Cocktail Party* [1949], *The Confidential Clerk* [1953], and *The Elder Statesman* [1958]) were less successful in the U.S. Only *The Cocktail Party,* in the style of drawing-room comedy, was popular as a play, receiving the 1950 New York Drama Critics' Circle Award as best foreign play. In the 1980s a renewed interest in Eliot resulted from the long-running Andrew Lloyd Webber musical *Cats* – based on Eliot's 1939 poems, *Old Possum's Book of Practical Cats* – which opened at New York's **Winter Garden Theatre** in 1982.   DBW

> See: C. Browne, *The Making of T. S. Eliot's Plays,* London, 1969; R. Malamud, *T. S. Eliot's Drama: A Research and Production Sourcebook,* Westport, CT, 1992; C. Smith, *T. S. Eliot's Dramatic Theory and Practice,* Princeton, NJ, 1963.

Elizabeth the Queen by **Maxwell Anderson**. A **Theatre Guild** production, this three-act verse play opened 3 November 1930 (147 performances). **Alfred Lunt** and **Lynn Fontanne** starred as lovers – the young Earl of Essex and the aging Queen Elizabeth. Arrested for treason, Essex refuses to beg for mercy. As he strides toward his execution, she pleads, "Take my kingdom, it is yours!" Percy Waram played Sir Walter Raleigh, Arthur Hughes Lord Cecil. **Brooks Atkinson** described it as magnificent drama, a searching portrayal of character in dialogue of notable beauty. Anderson's earliest historical drama, one of the few blank verse successes on the American stage, it was revived in 1961 with **Eva Le Gallienne** and in 1966 starring **Judith Anderson**.   GSA

Elliott (née Dermot), Gertrude (1874–1950) Actress; sister to **Maxine Elliott**. After making her New York debut in 1894, she acted with **Marie Wainwright** (1895) and **Nat Goodwin** (1897–9), playing Emily in *In Mizzoura,* Lucy in *The Rivals,* and Angelica Knowlton in *Nathan Hale*. She made her London debut in 1899 as Midge in *The Cowboy and the Lady,* and remained in England to play Ophelia to Forbes-Robertson's Hamlet. After the two were married in 1900, she returned to America several times, playing Maisie in *The Light That Failed* (1903), a character in the mold of Hedda Gabler, and creating the role of Cleopatra in **Shaw**'s *Caesar and Cleopatra* (1906). Critics praised her girlish spirit, playful humor, eloquent speech, and husky beauty. After her husband retired, she managed London's St. James's Theatre (1918).   TLM

Elliott, Maxine (née Jessie Dermot) (1871–1940) Actress and stage beauty; older sister to **Gertrude Elliott**. After making her New York stage debut at **Palmer**'s Theatre in 1890, Maxine Elliott rose rapidly in the theatre, spending a season each with **Rose Coghlan**'s and **Augustin Daly**'s companies (1894, 1895) before her London debut as Sylvia in *Two Gentlemen of Verona* (1895). After an Australia tour with **Nat Goodwin** (1896), she became his leading lady (1897) and his wife (1898). They costarred in numerous successes, including her first big hit as Alice Adams in *Nathan Hale* (1899). They separated in 1902, after which she established herself as a star with Georgiana Carley in *Her Own Way* (1903) written for her by **Clyde Fitch**. Two years later, her Georgiana attracted the attentions of Edward VII in London. She built the Maxine Elliott Theatre in New York (1908) with help from the **Shubert**s, and appeared there in numerous comedies, including *Myself, Settina,* and *The Chaperon.* In 1911 she retired to England, making only occasional stage appearances thereafter. She was praised as a "rare comedienne of the drawing room" during her 1918–19 American tour of *Lord and Lady Algy.* Although she appeared stiff and mechanical to some critics, all praised her dark and lustrous beauty and her statuesque stage presence. She retired to the Riviera after 1920 to live out her life as a "lady of society."   TLM

See: D. Forbes-Robertson, *My Aunt Maxine,* New York, 1964.

Ellsler, Effie (1854–1942) Actress, daughter of **John Ellsler,** she first appeared at her father's theatre where she became the leading lady (1872–6). **Steele MacKaye** brought her to the **Madison Square Theatre,** New York, and wrote the title role of *Hazel Kirke* (1880) for her. Later she starred at the head of her own company. After 1903 she appeared only occasionally, most notably as Cornelia Van Corder in *The Bat* (1920).   DMcD

Ellsler, John (1822–1903) Originally an actor, he assumed management of his own company at Cleveland's Academy of Music in 1855. He opened his lavish **Euclid Avenue Opera House** in 1875, but the Academy of Music remained his center of operation until 1885. His company toured extensively to surrounding towns in the summers, and between 1871 and 1887 he managed at least one theatre a year in Pittsburgh. His theatre was noted as a nursery of talent: **Clara Morris, James O'Neill, James Lewis,** and **Mrs. G. H. Gilbert** apprenticed there. His daughter, **Effie Ellsler,** became a leading lady of the next generation.   DMcD

See: J. Ellsler, *The Stage Memoirs of John A. Ellsler,* ed. E. Weston, Cleveland, 1950.

Elson, Charles (1909–   ) Designer and educator who began his design career in the 1930s. He served as lighting and design assistant to **Donald Oenslager** on several productions in the 1940s, and did his first Broadway show in 1946. Through the 1970s Elson designed sets and lights at the Metropolitan Opera, **American Shakespeare Festival,** and Broadway. During 1948–74 he taught at Hunter College.   AA

El Teatro Campesino (The Farmworkers' Theatre) founded by **Luis Valdéz** in 1965 to support Filipino and Mexican-American strikers against the grape farmers of the San Joaquin Valley in Calfornia. Initially an agitprop group tailoring its *actos* (short plays) to the issues and needs of the moment, in a style at once cartoonlike, comic, and realistic, the company took on a wider political involvement – though still focusing on **Chicano** concerns – during the period of maximum opposition to the Vietnam War. In the 1970s, disillusion with the growing violence of Chicano politics, together with a need to develop artistically, prompted a change of direction. El Centro Campesino Cultural was created on 40 acres of farmland at San Juan Bautista, 97 miles south of San Francisco, for Valdéz and his followers as a research-and-development center, often taking productions premiered in the ETC Playhouse (150 seats) to larger venues (plays such as *Corridos!* and *I Don't Have to Show You No Stinking Badges*). In performance, the early *actos* are often replaced by *mitos* ("myths") such as *El baile de los gigantes* (*The Dance of the Giants,* 1974), though the basic principle of a bilingual theatre using a vivid physical style remains much the same. In the 1990s three to six productions have been presented annually; the company has also returned to the touring practice of the 1970s, when six major tours covered the U.S., Mexico, and Europe.   AEG

Eltinge, Julian (né William Dalton) (1883–1941) **Female impersonator,** first seen professionally in *Mr. Wix of Wixham,* a musical comedy (1904). His biggest hit was *The Fascinating Widow* (1911 and tours), in which he outshone fashion-

JULIAN ELTINGE
IN THE
"FASCINATING
WIDOW"

Julian Eltinge in drag in *The Fascinating Widow.* Courtesy: Michael Gnat.

plate Valeska Surratt. Its success led grateful producer **Al Woods** to build the Eltinge Theatre on 42nd St., New York. "The ambi-sextrous comedian," as **Percy Hammond** called him, chose vehicles that enabled him to shift gender by quick change (one act required 11 separate changes). With his company, the Julian Eltinge Players, he played **vaudeville** (1918–27) and starred in silent films. A large man with a passable baritone voice, he was a favorite primarily with female audiences, not least for the chic of his wardrobe. His last variety appearance – at the White Horse, Los Angeles (1940) – was a fiasco, owing to a police ban on public transvestism.   LS

> *See:* L. Senelick, ed., *Gender in Performance,* Hanover, NH, 1992.

Emery, Gilbert (né Emery Remsley Pottle) (1875–1945)

Dramatist who became an actor after serving in WW I and enjoyed a moderate career writing domestic dramas. *The Hero* (1921), his most highly regarded play, dramatized the effect of an apparently dissolute war hero upon the wife of his brother, who stayed home during the war to care for his family. *Tarnish* (1923), concerned with a naïve young woman's confrontation with a lover's past, was more successful, but *Episode* (1925), dealing with a husband's acceptance and forgiveness of his wife's infidelities in order to maintain his conventional social life, failed. *Love-in-a-Mist* (1926) was written with Amélie Rives. All reflect American society of a particular period.
WJM

Emmet, J[oseph] K[lein] "Fritz" (1841–91)

Variety performer-actor. St. Louis–born Emmet developed a particular German immigrant character ("not very much like any character ever seen in real life"), first on the variety stage and later in a series of "Fritz" plays, beginning with **Charles Gayler**'s *Fritz, Our Cousin German* (1869). His stage actions, including songs ("Emmet's Lullaby") and dances, often seemed unrelated to the plays. In each piece, outfitted in green blouse and cap and wooden shoes, Emmet depicted a slow-witted fellow fond of children. Ultimately, it was his winning personality rather than his talent that pleased the public.   DBW

Emmett, Daniel Decatur (1815–1904)

Ohio-born minstrel who traveled with circuses as a musician from 1835. His popular jig songs, including "Root Hog or Die," achieved folkloric status. He teamed his fiddle with William M. Whitlock on banjo, Dick Pelham (Richard Ward Pell), on tambourine, and Francis Marion Brower on bones, all in blackface, to create The Virginia Minstrels (debut, Bowery Amphitheatre, New York, 6 February 1843). This "jazz band of the nineteenth century" set the format for the **minstrel show** first in the U.S., then in England and Ireland in 1844. After the group dissolved, Emmett opened the first minstrel hall in Chicago (1855). With Bryant's Minstrels, New York, he developed the "walkaround"; an accompanying song, "Dixie's Land" (4 April 1859), became the Confederate anthem.

Late in life he toured with Leavitt's Gigantean Minstrels, recreating his pioneering quartet.   LS

> *See:* H. Nathan, *Dan Emmett and the Rise of Early Negro Minstrelsy,* Norman, OK, 1962.

Emmons, Beverly (1943–)

Lighting designer who, after assisting **Jules Fisher** in the 1960s, became one of the primary lighting designers of the **Off Broadway** and **Off-Off Broadway** movements. She worked on several **Robert Wilson** productions, including *Einstein on the Beach* (1976), as well as works by **Meredith Monk** and **Joseph Chaikin.** Broadway work includes *The Elephant Man* and *Amadeus,* for which she shared a Tony with British designer John Bury. Emmons has also designed extensively for dance, including works by Merce Cunningham, Lar Lubovitch, Trisha Brown, and Lucinda Childs.   AA

Emperor Jones, The, by Eugene O'Neill.

This historically important and still powerful one-act tragedy of a Pullman porter turned small-time West Indies dictator first opened at the Playwright's Theatre of the **Provincetown Players** in New York on 1 November 1920, under the direction of **George Cram Cook** and with **Cleon Throckmorton**'s first theatrical designs. It not only brought popular attention to the Provincetowners, resulting in their first Broadway run, but served as the first important portrayal by a black actor (**Charles Gilpin** as Brutus Jones; later played by **Paul Robeson**) in white-controlled, mainstream American theatre. The semiexpressionistic play explores power hunger and corruption at a crude, visceral level while delving into the myste-

Paul Robeson in the title role of O'Neill's *The Emperor Jones* (1939). Courtesy: New York Public Library for the Performing Arts.

rious world of voodoo, racial memory, and psychological disintegration. A journey play that carries Jones on a dark pilgrimage from sundown to dawn through his memory, fears, guilt, and cultural heritage, it culminates in his destruction by a silver bullet. Interestingly, slowly escalating native drumming underscores nearly all of the play and contributes to, if not causes, the steady breakdown and mounting horror of brutal Brutus Jones.   RHW

Empire Theatre 1430 Broadway, NYC [Architect: J. B. McElfatrick and Co.]. In 1893, when **Charles Frohman** built the gemlike Empire some 25 blocks north of the theatre district at Union Square, the spark was ignited to create a new theatre district uptown. This theatre remained the headquarters of Frohman's activities until he died on the *Lusitania* in 1915. During his lifetime, Frohman was Broadway's principal starmaker, a member of the Theatrical **Syndicate,** and the Napoleon of the American theatre. The roster of the stars who appeared at the Empire is etched into a plaque affixed to the wall of the characterless office building that replaced the theatre after it was torn down in 1953. The theatre was managed by Alf Hayman for the Frohman estate on a run-of-the-play basis, and was later leased to producer **Gilbert Miller** until 1931. With just over 1,000 seats, it was a compact, well-designed playhouse and a favorite among actors and audiences. It enjoyed a latter-day reputation as a house of hits, crowned by the arrival of *Life with Father* in 1939, which did not leave its stage for six years. The theatre changed ownership several times before its demise. At the time it closed, it was presenting *The Time of the Cuckoo* with **Shirley Booth.**   MCH

Empty Space Association, The Founded in 1970 by M[ilton] Burke Walker, Julian Schembri, James Royce, and Charles Younger as a **collective** operating in a 65-seat basement in **Seattle**'s Pike Place Market. The company concentrated on contemporary American and European works, presenting numerous northwestern and world premieres by major playwrights, including Edward Bond, **Lee Breuer,** and **Maria Irene Fornés.** After formalizing cooperative structure in 1974, the original 16-member company disbanded in 1976, Walker remaining as artistic director until 1990, when he became head of the University of Washington's directing program.   RW

Engel, Lehman (1910–82) Conductor, composer, writer, and educator. He attended music schools in Cincinnati before graduating from Juilliard in 1935. Engel worked as a musical director for the **Federal Theatre Project** and then began a 30-year career as a Broadway conductor. He also composed dance music for choreographers such as Martha Graham and Doris Humphrey, and provided background scores for dozens of plays. In 1959 he founded the Lehman Engel Musical Theatre Workshop in conjunction with Broadcast Music, Inc., where he helped to train dozens of young musical theatre talents. He also wrote several highly regarded books about musical theatre, including *This Bright Day,* his 1974 autobiography.   MK

English's Theatre (Indianapolis) Seating nearly 2,000, this theatre opened 27 September 1880 with **Lawrence Barrett** in *Hamlet.* The newest, most lavish theatre in town, it competed with George Dickson's Grand Opera House until 1886, when it was leased by Dickson's partner, Henry Talbott. Under their management it was a member of an Ohio Valley circuit of theatres that eventually became part of the Theatrical **Syndicate.**   DMcD

Enters, Angna (1900?–89) Dancer-**mime,** writer, and artist whose international 40-year solo career began in New York in 1924 with her performance of "stage poems without words." She created the costumes, sets, and often the music for 100 dance episodes, ranging from tragedy to parody and portraying mainly women of many periods and countries. At MGM in Hollywood during the 1940s, she contributed a *commedia dell'arte* sequence for *Scaramouche* and the story line for *Lost Angel.* After her New York art show in 1933, she exhibited annually and also published three books of memoirs, a play, a novel, and *On Mime* (1965) after teaching at Baylor and Wesleyan.   DM

Epstein, Alvin (1925–) Actor and director who studied acting with **Sanford Meisner,** dancing with Martha Graham, and mime with Etienne Decroux (company member, Paris, 1947–51). Joining the Habima Theatre of Tel Aviv, he acted in European, American, and Yiddish plays (1953–5). He made his Broadway debut with Marcel Marceau (1955) and later that year played Lucky in the American premiere of Beckett's *Waiting for Godot.* Notable performances include the Fool in **Orson Welles**'s *Lear* (1956), a controversially comic Trotsky in *The Passion of Josef D.* (1964), and an Obie-winning role in *Dynamite Tonite!* (1968). Many of his best roles have been in absurdist or modern plays (*Henry IV, Endgame, Macbeth*). Epstein, a joyous performer who revels in physical theatricality, has worked extensively in musical theatre, with particular success in **Kurt Weill** vehicles. Cofounder of the Berkshire Theatre Festival (1967), associate director of the **Yale Repertory Theatre** (1973–7), and artistic director of the **Guthrie Theatre** (1977–9), he has been with the **American Repertory Theatre** since 1980.   TC

Erlanger, Abraham Lincoln (1860–1930) Long-time partner (1887–1919) of **Marc Alonzo Klaw** who was introduced to theatre management in Cleveland. In New York in 1880, he was an advance agent for touring productions, then a tour manager. With Klaw, Erlanger was the organizational genius and chief booking agent for the Theatrical **Syndicate,** a trust formed in 1896 to maximize the trustees' profits. Erlanger purchased most of Klaw's interest in the Klaw and Erlanger Exchange in 1919. In 1921, he sold his extensive theatrical real estate but continued to produce plays until his death. To some, Erlanger epitomized the businessman, devoid of aesthetic taste, propelled by ruthless opportunism to a position of suffocating power over theatre artists. To others, Erlanger and his partner are notable for developing a centralized booking system that brought order and increasing profitability to all sectors of the theatrical business world.   WD

Errol, Leon (1881–1951) Australian actor who came to the U.S. only to discover his accent was incomprehensible. He therefore performed as a dancer for two years without speaking, perfecting his panto**mime.** He arrived in New York in 1911, starring in his own show, *The Lillies.* This brought him to the attention of **Ziegfeld,** who featured him in the 1911 *Follies.* Errol was considered the best comedian of the *Follies* prior to WW I. He made a considerable success in *Sally* (1920), later filming the same show. His film roles covered some 20 years, exemplified by Lord Epping in *Mexican Spitfire.*   SMA

Ethel, Agnes (1852–1903) Actress whose brief career ended when she married in 1873. Ethel studied with **Matilda Heron** and made her debut as Camille in Jerome's private theatre in New York. She then joined **Augustin Daly**'s company for additional experience. Her greatest successes were as Gilberte in *Frou-Frou* and the title roles in *Fernande* (1870) and Sardou's *Agnes* (1872). **Olive Logan** praised her fascinating beauty, starry eyes, and red-gold hair, and for a few years Ethel was among the most popular of American actresses.   SMA

Ethel Barrymore Theatre 243 West 47th St., NYC [Architect: Herbert J. Krapp]. **Ethel Barrymore,** the actress, was lured into the management of the **Shubert**s with the promise of Ethel Barrymore, the theatre. Opening late in 1928, it was one of the last playhouses to be built in the theatre district before the Depression. An intimate, well-designed house, it seats just under 1,100 and is well suited to the realistic play and comedy. Although a number of failures have appeared at the Barrymore, it has also housed a fair share of history-making productions, among which have been *The Women* (1936), *Pal Joey* (1940), *A Streetcar Named Desire* (1947), *Look Homeward, Angel* (1957), and *A Raisin in the Sun* (1959). It has remained a Shubert house.   MCH

Ethnic theatre Ethnic theatre in the U.S. is theatre by and for minority communities, whose cultural heritages distinguish them from the Anglo-American mainstream. A pluralistic nation with an indigenous population and immigrants from every corner of the earth, the U.S. has been host to a rich variety of ethnic theatres. Ethnic theatres have helped to meet the intellectual and emotional needs of people separated from the mainstream by language, culture, poverty, and discrimination. They have reinforced indigenous or "old world" languages and traditions, helped immigrants adjust to their new country, provided an arena for talented ethnic actors, directors, and playwrights, and introduced new personalities and techniques to the Anglo-American stage.

Ethnic theatres sprang from a variety of historical conditions. **Native American theatre** is rooted in communal celebrations and ancient rituals reflecting the religious outlook and shared values of the indigenous nations that created it. Conquest by whites destroyed entire "Indian" nations, including, of course, their drama. Moreover, the confinement of Native Americans to reservations and the increasing dominance of Western culture often had a negative influence on the drama of nations that did survive.

White Americans were introduced to black performance as early as 1664 when captive Africans were forced to dance and sing for the crew of the English slaveship *Hannibal.* Autonomous **African-American theatre** began in 1821 in lower Manhattan, where the **African Theatre,** founded by **William Henry Brown,** performed **Shake-spear**an drama for audiences of whites and blacks. In the 19th century whites in "blackface" gave **minstrel shows,** racist parodies of black entertainment; however, independent black theatre persisted, and by the early 20th century, **musicals** written and performed by blacks were appearing on Broadway and in Harlem.

French theatre entered the country in 1803 when the United States purchased Louisiana from France, and Mexican-American (or **Chicano**) theatre entered with the conquest of the Southwest from Mexico in 1848. Immigrants from Europe and Asia established theatres soon after their arrival. German theatres appeared in the rural Midwest in the early 1840s and in New York and New Orleans even earlier. Chinese theatre opened in **San Francisco** in 1852, and Japanese troupes entertained in **Seattle** several decades later. Polish, Yiddish, Italian, and other Southern/Eastern European theatres were active in urban centers by the turn of the century.

Immigrant theatres faced significant problems, including lack of money, quarrels among the actors, directors, and playwrights, and opposition from inside and outside the community. Scandinavian theatre was opposed by the conservative Lutheran clergy, who associated it with drinking; civil authorities closed Chinese theatres for performing on Sunday (when working-class audiences were free to attend); and German theatre was devastated by boycotts during WW I.

Nevertheless, as the number of immigrants rose to a million a year in the decade before WW I, immigrant theatres flourished. Actors trained in their homelands pursued careers in the U.S., joined by enthusiastic amateurs who spent long days in the workplace and then rehearsed far into the night. Audiences with sparse resources saved their pennies for tickets. Large communities supported commercial theatres, and virtually every group enjoyed amateur theatre sponsored by lodges, athletic groups, schools, and cultural, nationalist, and socialist societies. Road companies brought theatre to isolated farm and mining communities.

Moved by the same desire for economic opportunity and personal freedom that brought immigrants from foreign countries to the U.S., native-born blacks migrated from the rural South to the industrial and commercial cities of the North in the opening decades of the 20th century. A burst of African-American theatrical creativity was part of the cultural and intellectual flowering of the 1920s known as the Harlem Renaissance. While black theatre flourished in many cities, its center was Harlem, where race-conscious plays by, for, and about black America were produced in the 1920s and '30s by companies such as the Krigwa Players (founded by W. E. B. Du Bois), the Harlem Experimental Theatre, the New Negro Theatre, and the Harlem Suitcase Theatre (founded by **Langston Hughes**).

An integral part of the life of the immigrant "ghettos" of the early 20th century, ethnic theatres supported the educational, charitable, and political causes important to their communities. Theatre benefits financed Italian parochial schools in St. Louis, social services for Danes and Japanese in Seattle, and orphanages and hospitals in the Ukraine. Their actors having unionized, **Yiddish theatre**s supported the "Uprising of the 20,000," the historic general strike of the largely Jewish shirtwaist makers in New York City in 1909. Thaddeus Dolega-Eminowicz, star and founder of Polish theatres in many American cities, produced and acted in an original play, *With Whom to Side?* in Detroit in 1917 to raise funds for the Polish Legion's participation in WW I.

Immigrant theatres provided a place where the young and old, the educated and the uneducated, the newcomer and the oldtimer, and the poor and the upwardly mobile could gather and share a common experience. To the inhabitants of cramped, dreary tenements, theatres were attractive places to court, gossip, quarrel, eat, joke, and nurture friendships. To actors, directors, and playwrights, the theatre was a self-sufficient social world in which marriages took place and children were reared, sometimes appearing on stage as soon as they could walk and talk. This world was especially important to intellectuals, whose lack of English cut them off from the professions they had pursued in the homeland. It was also important to women, who found in it an alternative to traditional domestic roles and a chance to win money and recognition and adopt unconventional life-styles with relative impunity. African-born Clara Lemberg made her reputation on the Finnish-American stage, Theofilia Samolinska on the Polish, Antonietta Pisanelli Alessandro on the Italian, and **Sara Adler** on the Yiddish. During the Harlem Renaissance (1918–30) 11 black women published 21 plays.

Ethnic theatre made the history and folklore of the homelands accessible to immigrants, many of whom had been deprived of education in the homelands, and introduced American-born children to the heritage of their parents. Based on the complex novel *Romance of the Three Kingdoms,* Chinese opera transmitted traditional Cantonese values of loyalty, self-reliance, and personal integrity. Yiddish plays depicted episodes from centuries of Jewish history. German theatre dramatized the exploits of Frederick the Great. Polish theatres presented so many plays on historical and national themes that a Polish journalist called them "schools of patriotism."

Immigrant theatres introduced dialect-speaking audiences to the "standard" pronunciation and vocabulary of their native languages and, through use of English expressions and performance of American plays, to the language and culture of the U.S. Many also introduced the classics of world theatre.

Shakespeare was performed in Yiddish, German, Swedish, and Italian. Yiddish theatres performed the works of Molière, Schiller, Goethe, Tolstoi, Gorky, Sudermann, Hauptmann, **Ibsen,** Strindberg, Molnár, and **Shaw,** as well as those of Jewish playwrights such as **Jacob Gordin,** Leon Kobrin, and **Sholom Asch.**

Theatre groups of politically progressive Germans, Jews, Swedes, Finns, Hungarians, Latvians, Lithuanians, and others used the works of Shaw, Ibsen, and Strindberg as well as original plays to explore temperance, pacifism, and the problems of workers, women, and the aged. Latvian socialist theatres in New York, Chicago, Cleveland, Detroit, San Francisco, and Boston produced dozens of agitprop-type plays, including original political dramas such as Sīmanis Berǧis's *They Will Overcome,* and Dāvids Bundža's *Celebrating May.* Theatres were prominent features in Finnish "Labor Temples" (socialist community centers) across the nation, where plays, both original and imported from Finland, were used for the political education of children and adults. The first Polish play in Chicago was *The Emancipation of Women* (1873), by feminist actress, writer, and community activist Theofilia Samolinska. Translated or adapted versions of Ibsen's controversial drama *A Doll's House* explored the "woman question" in many immigrant theatres.

Despite the importance of educational and ideological plays, most immigrants attended the theatre for entertainment, glamour, diversion, and emotional release. Folk dramas depicting the regional music, dance, and customs of the homeland were popular in German, Swedish, Danish, Hungarian, and Ukrainian theatres, appealing to nostalgia and the desire to escape urban life. A musical folk play, *The People of Varmland* (text by Fredrik August Dahlgren), was the most popular Swedish play, performed at least 62 times in Chicago alone between 1884 and 1921; 90% of all Danish productions were folk plays or operettas.

"Formula" plays in which wily peasants outwitted landlords, true love triumphed, and villains were punished and heroes rewarded were popular among audiences for whom the problems of life were not so easily resolved. Also popular were vaudeville, comedy, and satire. Comic characters such as Olle i Skratthult (Olle from Laughtersville), created by Hjalmar Peterson, and Farfariello, created by **Eduardo Migliaccio,** satirized the immigrant community itself, especially "green ones" (new immigrants), using wit and irony to help audiences understand, laugh at, and thus transcend their own often painful adjustment to the U.S.

Plays filled with violence, revenge, suicide, and murder were well received, whether classical tragedies or original melodramas. These plays moved audiences because they dealt with familiar problems, though in exaggerated form; Jacob Gordin's *The Jewish King Lear,* for example, about a pious father abused by heartless daughters, brought tears to the eyes of immigrants less than satisfied with the behavior of American-born children. Tragedy, like comedy, provided emotional release, allowing immigrants to express their grief at the absence of loved ones and the frustrations of American life.

European and Asian immigrant theatres active in the early 20th century declined after 1930, undermined by the immigration restriction laws of 1924, the Americanization and geographic dispersion of audiences, and the rise of movies, radio, and television. Federal assistance through the Works Project Administration helped some immigrant and black theatre to survive during the Great Depression of the 1930s; and a few companies with an interest in artistic experimentation, such as the **Folksbiene** (Yiddish) theatre in New York City and the Swedish Folk Theatre in Chicago, continued into midcentury. Meanwhile many actors, directors, and writers from ethnic theatres passed into mainstream American entertainment, bringing elements of their traditions with them.

Ethnic theatre revived after WW II, stimulated by heavy migration of Puerto Ricans to the mainland, and, with liberalized quotas, new immigration from Europe, Latin America, and Asia. The black civil rights movement touched off increased political activism and ethnic awareness not only among African-Americans but also among Hispanics, Native Americans, and Asian Americans, stimulating new "Third World" theatre activity across the nation. Many older European theatres were rejuvenated in the 1960s and '70s, not only by newcomers, but also by the nostalgia of aging immigrants, the desire of acculturated children and grandchildren to explore their roots, and the "new ethnicity," a heightened appreciation of cultural pluralism as an antidote for the anomie and homogenization of modern society.

In the 1960s hundreds of African-American theatres performed throughout the nation. In the late 1960s Miriam Colón's **Puerto Rican Traveling Theatre** brought bilingual productions to the Spanish-speaking neighborhoods of New York City [see also **Nuyorican theatre**], and by the early 1970s provided a laboratory theatre and an actors' training program as well. Original plays about life in contemporary European-American ethnic communities as well as productions of Armenian, Latvian, Lithuanian, Polish, and Yiddish classics (often in English) were mounted by ethnic churches and community centers, universities, and professional companies.

By 1980 almost 9 out of 10 new immigrants were from Asia or Latin America rather than Europe, a shift reflected in increased theatre activity in Asian and Latino communities. In the 1980s at least four **Asian-American theatre** companies performed in New York City. The multiethnic **East West Players** of Los Angeles presented original Asian-American plays and trained actors of Chinese, Japanese, Filipino, Korean, and Pacific Island backgrounds. Korean, Thai, and other recent Pacific-rim immigrants introduced traditional forms of cultural expression that integrated theatre, dance, and music. New Central and South American communities, some of which included foreign-trained actors, playwrights, and directors, produced new Spanish-language theatre in New York, Los Angeles, and other urban centers. **Cuban-American theatre** emerged in southern Florida.

Overshadowed by the mass media (now often available in ethnic languages), theatre in the post-WW II decades was not as central to ethnic community life as it had been half a century earlier; nevertheless, it continued to educate as well as to entertain. In the 1970s **Hanay Geiogamah**'s Native American Theatre Ensemble used "Western"-style drama to transmit Native American traditions, values, and aesthetics. Byelorussians, Hungarians, Latvians, Ukrainians, Slovaks, and others used theatre in schools, summer camps, and youth groups to teach ethnic language and history to a new generation.

Postwar ethnic theatres informed their communities about social and political issues and were more active than their predecessors in reaching out to inform the mainstream community as well. Dramas from the Baltic nations dealt with political oppression and resistance to tyranny in Eastern Europe and, by implication, everywhere. Similar themes were prominent in the theatres of the new Central and South American communities, including NYC's Teatro Cuarto, which followed the Brechtian tradition of political theatre. The Theatre for Asian American Performing Artists in New York City gave a series of skits about anti-Asian discrimination for the United States Commission on Civil Rights, and produced a satirical review based on those skits at Lincoln Center during the 1976 Bicentennial. **Luis Valdéz**'s **El Teatro Campesino** (Farm Workers' Theatre) developed original *actos* to unionize migrant workers in California, and elaborated them into full-length plays that won national and international acclaim. Adopted by cannery workers in San Jose, tomato pickers in South Jersey, hospital workers in Chicago, and dozens of other groups, Valdéz's "Theatre of the People" became a vehicle for labor protest among Hispanics nationwide.

Ethnic theatre allowed Asian-, African-, Mexican-, and Native-American actors, as well as those of other minorities, to move beyond the stereotypical roles usually assigned them in mainstream entertainment. It gave a new generation of playwrights an opportunity to use the language of the ethnic ghetto and to express sensibilities rooted in the unique historic experience of their own communities. "America is illiterate . . . deadset against the Chinese American sensibility," wrote the militant Frank Chin, a seventh-generation Chinese American whose award-winning play *The Chickencoop Chinaman* was produced in New York in 1972; "nothing but racist polemics have been written about us . . . I don't like that . . . All my writing is Chinaman backtalk."

Ethnic theatre offered ethnic and mainstream audiences insights into minority experiences that, despite an increase of ethnic material in mainstream theatre, remained unavailable elsewhere. René Marqués's celebrated play *The Oxcart*, which describes a family's disintegration as it moves from rural Puerto Rico to San Juan to New York City, helped Puerto Rican migrants evaluate their gains and losses. The problems of the black family, the impact of the Vietnam War on the Asian-American soldier, the destruction of ethnic neighborhoods through "urban renewal," Turkish genocide against Armenians in 1915, the impact of the Holocaust on Jewish survivors, the realities of growing up, getting old, or being a woman in ethnic America, discrimination, assimilation, and the survival of ethnic identities – these and similar themes were explored in post–WW II ethnic theatre.

After the revival and expansion of the post–WW II years, ethnic theatres faced serious problems in the closing decades of the century. In the 1980s political and social support for pluralism eroded. Funding provided in the 1960s and '70s by public and private foundations such as the Rockefeller Foundation, the National Endowment for the Arts, and stage and local cultural agencies was curtailed due to budget deficits and changing priorities. Many university and neighborhood programs that had trained ethnic playwrights and actors could no longer afford to do so.

Ethnic theatre had internal as well as external problems. New immigrant populations were sometimes so diverse and transient that neighborhood theatres found it difficult to develop a stable base of support. An unprecedented array of foreign language entertainment – radio, TV, movies, and videos – competed for the immigrant's attention. Well-educated, middle-class immigrants, now a sizable proportion of newcomers, often preferred American theatre or imported classics to the ethnic genres popular with their largely working-class predecessors. The social class and cultural diversity of the new ethnic America was reflected in conflicts about the nature and purpose of ethnic theatre. Should its focus be local or international? Should its methods be traditional or experimental? Should its goal be artistic excellence or social relevance?

Despite the problems, there were reasons for optimism about the future. During the 1980s ethnic theatre gained increased recognition in academic theatre programs, national theatre associations, and scholarly journals, as well as among ethnic and mainstream audiences. Collections of ethnic plays and scholarly works about ethnic theatre were published. Actors, playwrights, and directors experimented with new forms and materials, developed strategies to identify and train new talent, and responded with ingenuity to continuing economic scarcity. In New York City, for example, Italian-American playwrights organized the "Forum" for mutual support, and Spanish-language theatres increased audiences and revenues by offering new ethnic plays in English to "general" audiences. In Los Angeles ethnic theatres formed a consortium with other arts groups for more effective fundraising and marketing. The Black Repertory Company of Winston-Salem, NC, drew financial and moral support from an active, dues-paying auxiliary, the North Carolina Black Theater Guild. Politics reinforced artistic and financial creativity: In 1989 a new law increased legal immigration, ensuring the continued growth of the nation's ethnic populations. These developments suggested that ethnic theatre would continue to survive in the U.S., not as a curiosity or exercise in nostalgia, but as a living force in American culture. MS

See: E. Czerwinski, "Emigrés, Skiers, and Messiahs: Polish Theater in the United States," *Journal of Popular Culture,* Winter 1985; R. J. Garza, ed., *Contemporary Chicano Drama,* South Bend, IN, 1976; H. Geiogamah, *New Native American Drama: Three Plays,* Norman, OK, 1980; N. Gonzales, *Bibliografi de Teatro Puertoiriqueno, Siglos XiX y XX,* San Juan, 1979; Jorge Huerta, *Chicano Theater: Themes and Forms,* Ypsilanti, MI, 1982; L. Walsh Jenkins, "The Performances of Native Americans as American Theatre," PhD diss., U of Minnesota, 1975; N. Kanellos, *Mexican American Theatre,* Pittsburgh, 1987; F. A. H. Leuchs, *The Early German Theater in New York 1840–1870,* New York, 1928; D. Lifson, *The Yiddish Theatre in America,* New York, 1965; R. L. Marquez, "The Puerto Rican Travelling Theater Company: The First Ten Years," PhD diss., Michigan State U, 1977; W. Mattila, ed., *The Theater Finns,* Portland, OR, 1972; H. C. Koren Naeseth, *The Swedish Theater of Chicago 1868–1950,* Rock Island, IL, 1951; M. Schwartz Seller, *Ethnic Theatre in the United States,* Westport, CT, 1983; A. Straumanis, ed., *Baltic Drama: A Handbook and Bibliography,* Prospect Heights, IL, 1981; L. Valdéz, *Actos,* San Juan Bautista, CA, 1971; G. Waldman, "Hispanic Theater in New York," *Journal of Popular Culture,* Winter 1985.

Eugene O'Neill Memorial Theatre Center

In 1964, George C. White, then a 29-year-old TV executive, leased eight and a half acres of the former Hammon Estate – relevant to several plays by **Eugene O'Neill** – from Waterford, CT, White's hometown. Among other goals, White hoped to create a sheltered laboratory for a new generation of American playwrights. Then as now, his vision incorporated three basic elements of professional theatre: playwright, audience, and critics. In 1965, he inaugurated the O'Neill's core program, the **National Playwrights Conference,** with a five-day retreat. After three volatile shakedown seasons, **Lloyd Richards** was appointed the NPC's artistic director; together with White, Richards established structures and methods of play development that would spread throughout the country and guided the O'Neill to international acclaim – as multiple awards, including a 1979 Tony, attest.

Other programs followed, including the **National Theatre of the Deaf** (1966); the National Critics Institute (1967); the National Theatre Institute (1970), an academic program; New Drama for Television (1976); and the National Opera/Music Theatre Conference (1978). The O'Neill also sponsors Creative Arts in Education, which integrates art into the community, trains teachers, and runs a summer arts camp for teenagers. Media Arts explores the impact of technology on the performing arts, and various international programs encourage cultural exchange and subsidize translations. Monte Cristo Cottage – the O'Neill summer house in adjacent New London, featured in *Ah, Wilderness!* and *Long Day's Journey into Night* – houses archives, resident artists, and scholars, and hosts special events. CLJ

Eugene O'Neill Theatre

230 West 49th St., NYC [Architect: Herbert J. Krapp]. In 1925, the **Shubert**s opened another theatre and named it the Forrest in honor of America's first star, **Edwin Forrest.** They sold it in 1945 to City Playhouses, a real estate holding company, which refurbished it and renamed it the Coronet. It was sold again to Lester Osterman, a Broadway producer, who changed its name again to honor America's greatest playwright, **Eugene O'Neill.** Six years later, it

was acquired by **Neil Simon** and David Cogan and served as a showcase for eight of Simon's plays and one of his musicals. As sole owner in 1982, Simon sold it to the **Jujamcyn Organization.** Its early history was inauspicious and contained a long string of flops, but its later history, particularly the Simon era, has included its share of successes.   MCH

Eureka Theatre Company Founded in 1972, this nonprofit theatre has been a vital force in **San Francisco**'s prolific fringe theatre movement and a dynamic producer of politically charged drama (initially under **Robert Woodruff** and Chris Silva). From the mid-1970s to the late '80s, a loose **collective** took over, staging works by Churchill, Dario Fo, **Emily Mann** (her *Execution of Justice* was commissioned by them), and other trenchant, topical authors. ETC lost its first church basement theatre on Market St. to arson in 1981; after several temporary homes, in 1984 it settled into a 250-seat Mission District venue. Regrouping under the new management of Debra Ballinger (1990), ETC has recently offered the premiere of Anthony Clarvoe's computer-industry satire, *Pick Up Axe* (1990), and the debut of Tony Kushner's AIDS saga, *Angels in America* (1991).   MB

Evangeline; or, The Belle of Arcadia Three-act musical burlesque/extravaganza, music by Edward E. Rice, words by J. Cheever Goodwin. Opened 27 July 1874 at **Niblo's Garden,** running 16 performances. This travesty of Longfellow was, despite its brief initial run, one of the most popular and influential of American musicals throughout the late 19th century. Unlike most burlesques of its day, it had an entirely original score and produced several popular tunes. In other ways, it was quite traditional: Straying wildly from its source for scenic effects, which ranged from Arcadia to Africa to Arizona, and loaded with excruciating puns, it featured a woman in tights as the male hero and a man in drag as the heavy elderly woman [see **female/male impersonation**]. Its two most famous gimmicks were a grotesque dancing cow [see **animal impersonation**] and the Lone Fisherman, a mysterious silent character who regularly appeared no matter what the change of setting. *Evangeline* established the careers of both Goodwin, who wrote many more libretti, and Rice, who became a major producer.   JD

Evans, Maurice (Herbert) (1901–89) English-born actor-director-producer who became an American citizen in 1941, following a 15-year acting career in England, most notably as Raleigh in *Journey's End* (1929) and with the Old Vic–Sadler's Wells company in 1934 (including a full-length *Hamlet*). In the U.S. he appeared with **Katharine Cornell** as Romeo (1935) and in 1936 as the Dauphin opposite her Saint Joan. A series of notable **Shakespeare**an performances followed, most directed by **Margaret Webster,** including Richard II (1937), gaining him the reputation as the foremost Shakespearean purveyor on the American stage. During WW II he entertained the troups with his so-called *GI Hamlet.* After the war (during 1947–59) Evans played major roles in four Shavian comedies [see **Shaw**], most notably John Tanner in *Man and Superman.* In 1952 he acted the uncharacteristic role of Tony Wendice in *Dial M for Murder,* in 1960 Rev. Brock in the musical *Tenderloin,* and in 1962 appeared in *The Aspern Papers.* In the 1950s he presented Shakespeare on television and produced several Broadway shows. In the 1970s and '80s he appeared mostly in films and TV, although at the age of 80 he played Norman in *On Golden Pond* in Florida. Shortly before his death he completed his autobiography, *All This . . . and Evans Too!* (Columbia, SC, 1987).   DBW

Experimental Theatre, Inc. Founded in 1940 in New York City to showcase actors and playwrights. Operations halted in 1941, then started again in 1946 with backing from the **American National Theatre and Academy** (ANTA). Craft unions granted concessions, and subscribers supported a five-show season at the **Princess Theatre.** Poor critical response led to reorganization. In 1947–8, the group staged readings of five new plays as well as six productions at **Maxine Elliott**'s Theatre. Though two of these had extended runs, the group lost money. Its 1948–9 season of three staged readings was its last.   WD

Eytinge, Rose (1835–1911) Actress, author, teacher. Her professional debut was in 1852 as Melanie in **Boucicault**'s *The Old Guard* in Syracuse, NY. Considered temperamental and often unmanageable, she acted in England and the U.S., specializing in high comedy and tragedy. She worked under **Lester Wallack, Augustin Daly,** and **A. M. Palmer.** Although she excelled in roles such as Cleopatra (1877), she was best known for her Nancy in *Oliver Twist* (1867) opposite **E. L. Davenport**'s Bill Sykes and the younger **James Wallack**'s Fagin. She dramatized several novels, wrote a play and a novel, and recorded her colorful life in *The Memoirs of Rose Eytinge* (1905).   DBW

F

Faith Healer, The Three-act drama by **William Vaughn Moody** that premiered in St. Louis on 15 March 1909 and in New York at the Savoy on 19 January 1910. The play, though not popular, has remained a critical success to the present day. Focusing on a conflict between science and faith and between love and duty, *The Faith Healer* amply demonstrates the lyrical yet forthright style that is Moody's signature. In refusing to choose among alternatives, proferring instead faith joined to science and love reconciled with responsibility, the play avoids polarizing its characters and their views as good or evil and offers a more liberal view of a classic American subject. RKB

Falls, Robert (1954–) Artistic Director of **Chicago**'s **Wisdom Bridge Theatre** during its most productive period (1977–85), Falls directed more than 30 productions there, many of them marked by energetic staging and ensemble work, most notably an adaptation of Jack Henry Abbott's *In the Belly of the Beast* and premieres of **Keith Reddin**'s *Life and Limb* and John Olive's *Standing on My Knees*. In 1986, he succeeded **Gregory Mosher** as Artistic Director of the **Goodman Theatre,** where he increased subscriptions while deemphasizing new works (an exception being **Steve Tesich**'s *The Speed of Darkness*). He directed Brian Dennehy in *Galileo* and *The Iceman Cometh* at the Goodman. During 1989–91 he was president of the board of the **Theatre Communications Group.** SF

Fantasticks, The Two-act musical comedy, music by Harvey Schmidt, words by Tom Jones; opened 3 May 1960 at the Sullivan Street Playhouse, New York, where, after more than 30 years and over 14,000 performances, it is by far the longest running show in American theatre history. Initially produced on a budget of $16,500, this small show (cast of eight, "orchestra" of piano and harp, and a virtually bare stage) relies on telling a simple romantic story with the charm of simplicity and whimsy. Adapted from Edmond Rostand's *Les Romanesques,* it is the tale of young lovers whose naïve, youthful view of love must be mellowed by temptations and disappointments, engineered by the omniscient narrator-adventurer El Gallo (**Jerry Orbach**), before they are finally ready to enter a mature relationship. The moral suggests that a love without obstacles to overcome is hollow. The score produced a major popular standard, "Try to Remember." JD

See: R. Viagas and D. C. Farber, *The Amazing Story of the Fantasticks: America's Longest Running Play,* New York, 1991.

Fashion; or, Life in New York Five-act comedy written by **Anna Cora Mowatt;** a successful satire of the nouveaux riches and their pretensions. Mrs. Tiffany, a foolish and extravagant woman, almost ruins her husband with her desire for high society and foreign manners; but all is made right through the good sense of the all-American Adam Trueman and his granddaughter, Gertrude. Mowatt wrote the comedy to earn money when her husband's health failed. It opened at the **Park Theatre** on 24 March 1845 and ran for three weeks – a long run in its day. **Edgar Allan Poe,** writing for the *Broadway Journal,* reviewed the play twice. Mowatt later became a successful actress and performed the part of Gertrude in her own play. It has been revived frequently in this century, with a most successful performance in 1924 at the Provincetown Playhouse. FB

Faversham, William (1868–1940) London-born actor who appeared briefly on the stage there before migrating to America in 1887. He was in the companies of both **Daniel Frohman** and **Charles Frohman,** and played opposite **Mrs. Fiske** and **Maude Adams** before becoming a leading man. His physical attractiveness and buoyant personality earned him the label of a "matinee girl's idol." Among his successful Shakespearean roles were Mark Antony in *Julius Caesar* and the title roles in *Romeo and Juliet* and *Othello.* He won his popularity, however, playing vigorous and masculine heroes in such plays as *Lord and Lady Algy, The Squaw Man,* and *The Prince and the Pauper.* His last role came in 1933 when he played Jeeter Lester in the long-running **Tobacco Road.** RAS

Fay, Frank (Francis Anthony) (1897–1961) Actor-vaudevillian, outstanding as the eccentric alcoholic Elwood P. Dodd in the long-running Broadway hit **Harvey** (1944–6), a legitimate-theatre break that came after a long career as headliner in revues and vaudeville (sophisticated satirical humor), and following a series of stage failures written by Fay. Most successful as master of ceremonies at the **Palace** (beginning in 1924), by 1926 he had set a record for number of performances. A volume of reminiscences and humorous stories (*How to Be Poor*) was published in 1945. The latter part of his career was devoted to films, nightclubs, and television.   DBW

Fechter, Charles Albert (1824–79) Actor, born in London to a German father and English mother; educated in France. He made his Comédie-Française debut in 1844 and became a leading melodramatic actor, particularly at the Porte-Saint-Martin. Fechter moved to London in 1860 and performed in English such roles as Othello and Hamlet (the latter played in a controversial flowing blonde wig). G. H. Lewes called him "lymphatic, delicate, handsome"; his iconoclasm was something more than mere display, however. In 1870, he came to the U.S., where he remained, with the exception of a short season in London in 1872, for the rest of his life. He toured for some time, then opened the Globe Theatre in **Boston** as Fechter's Theatre with many innovations, paralleling his earlier managerial experiments at the Lyceum in London, where he had also destroyed many outdated scenic traditions. His managerial ventures in America failed, however, owing to his personal vanity and what his fan and friend Charles Dickens called "a perfect genius for quarrelling." He made his final appearances in 1878 as Monte Cristo, Hamlet, and Ruy Blas at the **Broadway Theatre;** then, due to excessive drinking and a bigamous marriage, he was forced into retirement. He died in Quakerstown, PA, where he had tried to set up a farm.   SMA

See: K. Field, *Charles Albert Fechter,* Boston, 1882.

Feder, Abe (1909–   ) virtually invented the field of **stage lighting** design. One of his earliest projects was *Four Saints in Three Acts* (1934) for director **John Houseman.** He went on to do numerous productions with the **Federal Theatre Project,** including many of the **Living Newspapers** and *The Cradle Will Rock* (1938). He designed the first season of Ballet Theatre (1941) and in the following decades designed extensively for the stage, notably lights for *The Skin of Our Teeth* (1942),

My Fair Lady (1956), and *Camelot* (1960). As an architectural lighting designer, he designed or consulted on lighting for the 1964 New York World's Fair, exterior lighting for many buildings (including Rockefeller Center and the Pan Am Building), and lighting systems and interior lighting for several theatres, including the **John F. Kennedy Center.**   AA

Federal Street Theatre Federal St. at Franklin Pl., **Boston** [Architect: Charles Bulfinch]. When the 1750 law prohibiting playacting was overturned, prominent Bostonians pledged money by shares to erect the city's first theatre. In 1794, a handsome brick building by one of America's first architects opened under the management of **Charles Stuart Powell.** The theatre burned in 1798 [see **fires**] and was rebuilt by Bulfinch the following year. After a succession of managers, the theatre, known as "Old Boston," was supplanted by newer theatres and was not used consistently. It closed in 1852 and was replaced by stores.   MCH

Federal Theatre Project Established under the Works Progress Administration (WPA) in 1935 by an act of the U.S. Congress, this was the first American example of officially sponsored and financed theatre – and therefore the subject of much political controversy. Under the national direction of the indefatigable and intrepid **Hallie Flanagan,** head of the experimental theatre at Vassar, the FTP's objectives were to give meaningful employment to theatrical professionals out of work during the Depression and to provide "free, adult, uncensored theatre" to audiences throughout the country. Indeed, 10,000 people were employed at its peak, with theatres in 40 states. During its almost four years of existence, the FTP launched or established the careers of such notable theatre artists as **Orson Welles, John Houseman,** Joseph Cotten, Arlene Francis, **Will Geer,** John Huston, **Arthur Miller,** Virgil Thomson, **Howard Bay, Paul Green,** Mary Chase, Marc Blitzstein, Canada

Federal Theatre Project's "voodoo" *Macbeth,* directed by Orson Welles (1936). Courtesy: Institute on the Federal Theatre Project, George Mason University.

Lee, and **Elmer Rice.** At low ticket prices, audiences were provided with a large variety of fare, ranging from classics to new plays, **children's theatre,** foreign-language productions, **puppetry,** religious plays, a Negro theatre, musical theatre, a **circus,** and a controversial innovation called the **Living Newspaper,** designed to deal with issues of the day by utilizing documentary sources. In January 1936, with the urging of **Helen Tamiris,** a separate Federal Dance Project was established, although congressional cutbacks forced a merger with the FTP in October 1937.

The FTP played to millions of people throughout the country; it is estimated that over 12 million attended performances in New York alone. Of the hundreds of productions presented by the FTP, those by its Negro theatre [see **African–American theatre**] were among the most innovative and included the "voodoo" *Macbeth* (1936), *Haiti* (1938), and *The Swing Mikado* (1939). In 1936 Sinclair Lewis's *It Can't Happen Here,* written for the FTP, was produced simultaneously in 22 cities. The U.S. premiere of *Murder in the Cathedral,* which had been rejected by the **Theatre Guild,** was successful in 1936 at popular prices. The 1937 premiere of Paul Green's outdoor historical pageant *The Lost Colony* was in a WPA-built outdoor theatre on Roanoke Island, NC, where it has been seen every summer since. The FTP was endlessly willing to take chances in its selection of plays and was, in **Harold Clurman**'s words, "The most truly experimental effort ever undertaken in the American theatre."

Censorship was a problem frequently faced by various units of the FTP; its outspoken criticism, interpreted especially by congressional conservatives as left-wing, ultimately led to a heated debate and the disbanding of the project on 30 June 1939. The epic and convoluted history of the FTP was first recounted by Flanagan in *Arena* (1940). In 1974 the Federal Theatre Project Research Center was established at George Mason University.   DBW

See: T. Buttita and B. Witham, *Uncle Sam Presents,* Philadelphia, 1982; E. Craig, *Black Drama of the Federal Theatre Era,* Amherst, MA, 1980; G. Gill, *White Grease Paint on Black Performers,* New York, 1988; G. Kazacoff, *Dangerous Theatre,* New York, 1989; J. Mathews, *The Federal Theatre, 1935–1939,* Princeton, NJ, 1967; J. O'Connor and L. Brown, eds., *Free, Adult, Uncensored,* Washington, DC, 1978.

Fefu and Her Friends Because of its oblique, poignant discussion of women's oppression, **Maria Irene Fornés**'s *Fefu* is a classic in the **feminist theatre** canon. First performed on 5 May 1977 by the New York Theatre Strategy (directed by Fornés), it was subsequently produced by the **American Place Theatre** on 8 January 1978. Formally, the play challenges the relationship between spectator and performer. The second of its three parts takes place simultaneously in four different locations around a New England country house; the audience moves in four groups to each location, then reconverges for Part III. In evocative monologues and brief, staccato dialogues between characters in its all-female cast, *Fefu* tentatively describes possibilities for strength in women's community.   JDo

Feiffer, Jules (1929–) Playwright and cartoonist. Feiffer studied at NYC's Arts Students' League and Pratt Institute. Since 1956 his cartoons have appeared in the *Village Voice* and have been widely syndicated. His first play, *The Explainers,* a musical review of his cartoons, was presented at the **Second City,** Chicago, in 1961. *Little Murders,* his first full-length script, won honors in London (1967) and an Obie in New York. Other major works include *God Bless* (1968), *Feiffer's People* (1968), *The White House Murder Case* (1970, Obie), *Knock Knock* (1976), *Hold Me!* (1977), *Grownups* (1981), and *Elliot Loves* (1990), which was staged by **Mike Nichols.** His screenplays include *Carnal Knowledge* (1971; staged in play form in 1990), *Little Murders* (1972), *Popeye* (1980), and *I Want to Go Home* (1990), which was directed by Alain Resnais. A satirist with a keen wit, Feiffer depicts the anguish that underlies middle-class American life.   TLM

Feingold, Michael (1945–) Drama critic, translator, and author. Born in Chicago and educated at Columbia and Yale, Feingold has written literate and thought-provoking criticism for the *Village Voice* since 1971. He is a translator of the plays of Brecht, Ibsen, Molière, Wedekind, Diderot, and Thomas Bernhard. He has been literary manager at **Yale Rep** and the **Guthrie Theatre.** TLM

Feist, Gene (1930–) Director and playwright, reared on Coney Island, and founder and artistic leader of **Off-Broadway**'s **Roundabout Theatre,** a revival house. After graduating from Carnegie–Mellon (BFA, 1951) and New York universities (MA, 1952), Feist trained at the **Actors Studio** and the American Theatre Wing, among other places. In 1957 he began five years of directing in regional theatres before making his New York debut with Arrabal's *Picnic on a Battlefield* at the Cherry Lane Theatre in February 1962. With his wife, actress Elizabeth Owen, he launched the Roundabout in 1965 and has continued to direct many of its productions.   CLJ

Female/male impersonation In certain **Native American** tribes, the androgynous *berdache* serves as intermediary with the supernatural – an important function that some scholars think is, in more secular societies, invested in the actor. Europe's saturnalian tradition of men dressing as women on a licensed occasion, to provide a safety valve for gender anxieties, survived in America in several guises: street festivals; all-male college clubs, such as Harvard's Hasty Pudding (founded 1844), Princeton's Triangle Club, and the University of Pennsylvania's Wig & Gown; and small-town "Womanless Weddings" that recruit the whole white male community for its travesties.

Puritans had attacked as "sodomitical" the Elizabethan convention of boys playing girls, and it disappeared with the Restoration; but the accompanying tradition of the "dame" role – an elderly woman impersonated by a male comedian – survived on the American popular stage, carried on

Julian Eltinge in drag in *The Crinoline Girl,* Knicker-bocker Theatre, N.Y. (1914). Photo: White, N.Y. Courtesy: Laurence Senelick.

and a new "drag performer" entered theatrical practice from the homosexual subculture around 1870. Ernest Boulton, who had been unsuccessfully prosecuted in London for solicitation in female garb, introduced to the New York stage (as Ernest Byne) the glamorous impersonator who presented a woman of beauty and chic. At the same time, true male impersonation was introduced by lesbians, the Englishwoman Annie Hindle and her imitator Ella Wesner, in the guise of "fast" young men, swaggering, cigar-smoking, and coarse. These minstrel and music-hall styles lasted longest in African-American **vaudeville,** where the performers' private lives often nourished their characterizations. Female impersonators included Lawrence A. Chenault, known as "Golden Hair Nell," and Andrew Tribble, who created "Ophelia Snow." The best-known male impersonator in Harlem was Gladys Bentley, alleged to have had an affair with Bessie Smith.

Critics objected when glamour drag successfully entered musical comedy with **Julian Eltinge,** who put across the images of an elegant young woman and a clean-cut young man. **Bert Savoy** popularized an outrageous caricature, garish and brassy, gossiping about her absent girlfriend Margie and launching popular catchphrases. Their best-known successors were Francis Renault (Anthony Oriema), "The Slave of Fashion," who sang in a clear soprano; and Karyl Norman (George Podezzi), "The Creole Fashion-Plate," who starred in musical comedy.

The popularity of all-male drag revues in the Armed Forces during WW II persisted into the postwar period. The Jewel Box revue, founded in Miami in 1938, enjoyed an eight-year run after the war and launched a number of talents before it folded in 1973. Similar enterprises include Finocchio's (San Francisco), Club 82 (New York), My-Oh-My (New Orleans), and the Ha Club (Hollywood, FL); but the police in Boston, Los Angeles, and other cities often prevented public cross-dressing. The Gay Liberation Movement of the late 1960s encouraged a resurgence of female impersonation, and lip-synching to tapes became ubiquitous in nightclubs. Many gay bars provided a token stage, and the female impersonator became almost exclusively what Esther Newton calls "performing homosexuals and homosexual performers." However, a successful means of passing with a mixed audience was to present imitators of female superstars: T. C. Jones, a veteran of the Jewel Box, was introduced to the general public in *New Faces of 1956;* Craig Russell, Charles Pierce, and Lynn Carter were the best-known such "impressionists."

Androgyny had infiltrated the rock music scene with Alice Cooper and David Bowie and reached a logical terminus in the asexual Boy George and Michael Jackson (parodied, in turn, by Madonna). The cult following for the British musical *The Rocky Horror Show,* with its transvestite, transsexual hero, showed that teenagers knew their psychopathia sexualis. More anarchic uses of "genderfuck" emerged from the hippie scene on the West Coast: The Cockettes and Angels of Light of San Francisco used campy pastiches of popular culture for radical ends. The Cycle Sluts, hairy bruisers in net

by **Neil Burgess** as the Widow Bedotte, George W. Munroe as various Irish biddies, Gilbert Sarony as the Giddy Gusher, and the Russell Brothers as clumsy Irish maids.

In Victorian staging of Shakespeare, women were traditionally cast as boys or sprites, but many actresses took on male leads. **Charlotte Cushman** played Romeo to her sister's Juliet, and later aspired to Cardinal Wolsey. Other women presented Shylock and Falstaff, but Hamlet proved irresistible: The most memorable was Sarah Bernhardt, who, according to Mounet-Sully, lacked only the buttons on her fly. In our time Dame **Judith Anderson** tried the experiment with dismaying results.

The all-male **minstrel show** featured the "wench," a young man sporting a fashionable female wardrobe and "high-yeller" makeup; he often became the star and manager, as did Francis Leon (Patrick Glassey) and Eugene (D'Ameli). It was also common in the **circus** for boy athletes to be disguised as girls to make the stunts seem more dangerous, as was the case with equestrian Ella Zoyara (Omar Kingsley). Such performers were said to be in "drag," the train on a gown equated with the drag or brake on a coach. Both the word stockings, and the street-theatre group The Sisters of Perpetual Indulgence, parodied traditional drag.

Broad dame comedy persisted in clowns like Pudgy Roberts, the all-male Ballets Trockadero de Monte Carlo (founded 1974), the Trockadero Gloxinia Ballet, and their operatic equivalent, the Grand Scena Opera Co. (founded 1982). Drag has also become a fixture in contemporary **performance art,** as in John (Lypsinka) Epperson's *Ballet of the Dolls* (La MaMa, 1988), a confrontation of pulp fiction with the clichés of ballet, and *I Could Go on Lip-Synching.* This trend is rooted in the "Ridiculous Theatre" movement of 1970s and the Warhol Factory, which fostered Centola, Hot Peaches, and **Charles Ludlam:** Camp was made the cutting edge of the avant-garde. The 300-lb film star Divine (Glen Milstead) was featured in a number of Off-Broadway plays, most memorably as the prison matron in Tom Eyen's *Women Behind Bars.* A leading exponent was **Ethyl (Roy) Eichelberger,** whose one-man *Tempest* and *Jocasta; or, Boy Crazy* are in both the minstrel–vaudeville and avant-garde tradition. Gender confusion is also the main theme of Los Angeles comedian John Fleck. Much of this has percolated into the commercial theatre, as testified by the success of the drag-show musical ***La Cage Aux Folles*** and **David Henry Hwang**'s ***M. Butterfly.***

With the radical changes in dress and manners that followed WW I, the male impersonator became a relic, revived by contemporary **feminist theatre** groups for political reasons, as in Eve Merriam's *The Club* (1976). Current debates over the nature of gender have inspired much experimental performance. At the "dyke noir" WOW Café in the East Village, New York, the **Split Britches Company** parodies traditional "femme" and "butch" roles in the double act of Peggy Shaw and Lois Weaver. The lesbian transsexual Kate Bornstein has created (with Noreen Barnes) shows such as *Hidden: A Gender,* which totally deconstruct traditional gender roles. [See also **gay/lesbian theatre.**] LS

> See: L. Senelick, "Boys and Girls Together: The Subcultural Origins of Glamour Drag and Male Impersonation," in *Crossing the Stage,* ed. L. Ferris, London, 1992; L. Senelick, "Lady and the Tramp: Drag Differentials in the Progressive Era," in *Gender in Performance,* ed. L. Senelick, Hanover, NH, 1992; A. Slide, *Great Pretenders,* Lombard, IL, 1986; E. Carlton Winford, *Femme Mimics,* Dallas, 1954.

Feminist theatre This **alternative theatre** movement began and proliferated in the early 1970s. In tandem with the political movement from which they sprang, activist women's theatres with radical techniques and manifestos organized in major urban centers around the country. The groups were innumerable and local, since the theatre they produced spoke directly to its constituents about women's subordinate position in dominant culture and possibilities for change.

The theatrical and political radicalism of feminist theatre grew from the second wave of U.S. feminism, which followed the civil rights movement and the formation of a vocal, active New Left. From within the political upheaval of the late 1960s,

activists tried to revise interpersonal relationships and cultural value systems according to more egalitarian ideology. However, within the Left's rhetoric of racial and economic liberation, gender politics remained conservative. The contemporary U.S. women's movement rekindled itself partly out of profound disaffection with the misogyny of the male Left. Through a network of ad hoc consciousness-raising groups, white middle-class women with some background in radical politics spoke to each other for what seemed like the first time, without mediation. These groups allowed women to exchange previously unheard details of their personal lives. The apparent commonality of their shared experience provoked a political analysis based on the private sphere their lives seemed to inhabit, and the slogan "the personal is the political" gained currency.

What began in the late 1960s as a grass-roots political movement became, through the 1970s, a political and ideological movement with organized impact and increasingly divergent strains. Networks such as the National Organization for Women (NOW), for example, developed strategies for influencing existing social and political systems around women's issues. The liberal feminist movement that was generated works to reform U.S. systems toward women's equality.

Radical feminism, in contrast to the reformism of liberal feminism, theorized women's oppression as systemic and began to analyze how patriarchal domination relegated women to the private sphere and alienated them from the power men wielded in public life. Radical feminism in the late 1960s and early '70s proposed that gender roles were socially constructed and could be changed only after a revolutionary restructuring of cultural power. This position was claimed in the late '80s by materialist feminist ideology.

Early feminist theatre began as a voice of radical feminism and the first manifestations of what eventually came to be celebrated in women's culture. New York's It's Alright to Be a Woman Theatre, for example, one of the earliest groups, transposed the political movement's consciousness-raising format to performance and used the new public forum to help validate women's personal lives. The troupe used agitprop techniques with a long tradition in political theatre, as well as street theatre and guerilla tactics that they borrowed from the leftist experimental theatres that had multiplied in the U.S. in the late 1960s and early '70s.

Although these experimental theatres addressed in vital ways civil rights issues and the protests against the Vietnam War, they did no more for women than the Left in general. Women such as **Megan Terry** and Roberta Sklar, who had both worked in the shadow of **Joseph Chaikin**'s fame at the **Open Theatre,** left to form specifically women's or feminist theatre groups. At the **Omaha Magic Theatre** (OMT) and the Women's Experimental Theatre (WET), respectively, they brought along many of the experimental theatres' innovations with theatre form, including ritual-based theory and borrowings from Brecht, Artaud, and Grotowski.

The **Living Theatre,** the Open Theatre, and

the **Performance Group,** for example, had broken with the psychological realism that dominated professional U.S. stages. They had formed collectives that disrupted the politically constricting hierarchy of the playwright-actor-director triumvirate and the separation of spectators and performers formalized by the proscenium arch. The text was no longer sacred; "happenings" and rituals became the primary base of theatre work; and social issues and politics explicitly informed every performance choice. Feminist theatre, however, set these theatrical techniques in a political arena where the spectators and performers moved along a revised gender axis.

WET, for example, produced a trilogy of plays called *The Daughters' Cycle,* which recuperated the House of Atreus myth from a female perspective, discussing relationships between mothers and daughters elided in male versions of the story. Their later trilogy focused on women's relationship to food. The OMT, administered by Terry and Jo Ann Schmidman, continues its work in Nebraska; WET's Sklar and her collaborator Sondra Segal, are now on hiatus from production.

While such examples of separatist-inclined women's culture thrived through the 1970s, in the '80s liberal feminism continued to gain viability. Although dogged attempts to pass the Equal Rights Amendment failed, consistent lobbying around women's issues instituted a focus on the "gender gap" in U.S. politics. The situation of urban black women and other minorities received little attention on the liberal feminist agenda, but the movement's focus on political and economic equity for white middle-class women became a force with which the dominant culture had to contend.

Mainstream theatre in the 1980s – no doubt as a result of liberal feminism – began to dole out its major **award**s to women. The visibility of women playwrights, in particular, led to three Pulitzer Prizes for women in that decade: **Beth Henley** for *Crimes of the Heart* (1981), **Marsha Norman** for *'night, Mother* (1983), and **Wendy Wasserstein** for *The Heidi Chronicles* (1989). **Lily Tomlin** and Jane Wagner's *Search for Signs of Intelligent Life in the Universe* (1985) proved a major Broadway success. Women's caucuses in professional theatre organizations and the vitality of Julia Miles's **Women's Project** at the **American Place Theatre** helped women playwrights, directors, producers, designers, and actors seem suddenly to appear where they'd never been before in the ranks of Broadway and regional U.S. theatres.

Mainstream plays by women, however, conformed to more traditional forms and styles, such as psychological realism and social comedy. Feminist theatre troupes in the 1970s and '80s continued to search for a "feminine" or "feminist" aesthetic that would give voice to new contents by developing new theatre forms and modes of production. Because of increasing economic burdens and the fractionalization of radical feminism as a concerted political movement, however, the tradition of flourishing, alternative feminist theatres failed to sustain itself.

Of the numerous radical feminist theatre groups that began in the 1970s, only **Spiderwoman The-** atre, a collective of Native-American women operating in New York, and **At the Foot of the Mountain Theatre** in Minneapolis continued to produce and tour by the early '90s. The multicultural or ethnic focus of these groups indicates the growing awareness in U.S. feminism in the 1990s of difference between and among women. The founding of **Split Britches,** a popular feminist and lesbian troupe that began in the 1980s in the East Village lesbian community in New York City, appropriates popular cultural forms once anathema to feminist theatre to investigate sexuality as well as gender [see **gay/lesbian theatre**].

While alternative feminist theatre practice declined in the 1980s, the decade witnessed the beginning of committed feminist criticism and theory that has become a vital site for activist and intellectual work in the theatre profession and in academia. Such critical feminist writing – sponsored by such organizations as the Women and Theatre Program of the Association for Theatre in Higher Education – holds the potential to revitalize the radical practice of feminist theatre. JDo

See: G. Austin, *Feminist Theories for Drama Criticism,* Ann Arbor, 1990; E. Brater, *Feminine Focus: The New Women Playwrights,* New York, 1989; S. E. Case, *Feminism and Theatre,* New York, 1988; S. E. Case, ed., *Performing Feminisms,* Baltimore, 1990; H. K. Chinoy and L. W. Jenkins, eds., *Women in American Theatre,* New York, 1981 (rev. ed., 1987); J. Dolan, *The Feminist as Critic,* Ann Arbor, 1988, 1991; L. Hart, ed., *Making a Spectacle,* Ann Arbor, 1989; H. Keyssar, *Feminist Theatre,* New York, 1985; E. Natalle, *Feminist Theatre: A Study in Persuasion,* Metuchen, NJ, 1985.

Fences Set in a northern city in the 1950s, this is the second of **August Wilson**'s 20th-century cycle of black experience plays. A 53-year-old garbage hauler and former Negro League baseball star lives with his long-suffering wife and teenage son in a slum neighborhood. Still bitter over his own exclusion from the major leagues, he dissuades his son from accepting a college football scholarship. Unfaithful as a husband, he yet expects his wife to rear the infant child of his latest liaison. The 1983 play, directed by **Lloyd Richards** and featuring **James Earl Jones,** enjoyed pre-Broadway runs at the **Yale Repertory Theatre,** the **Goodman Theatre** in Chicago, and in **San Francisco** before opening at the **46th Street Theatre** in 1987. It established a record for nonmusicals on Broadway by grossing $11 million in its first year, and captured the triple crown: the Pulitzer, the Tony, and the Drama Critics' Circle awards. EGH

Fennell, James (1766–1816) A London-born actor who had a substantial career in America. Fennell first studied law, but made his debut in Edinburgh in 1787 as Othello, which became his most successful role, and soon appeared at Covent Garden with minimal success. **Wignell** brought Fennell to Philadelphia in 1792, where he soon became a star. Well over 6' tall with an expressive, handsome face, Fennell brought considerable dignity to such roles as Othello, Lear, and Jaffier in *Venice Preserv'd;* he was also much admired as Hamlet, Glenalvon in *Douglas,* and Iago. Fennell, however, invested his theatrical income in various unsuccessful money-making schemes (including salt manufacture), was arrested for debt, and spent a time in prison. He retired from the stage in 1810, and in 1814 published his memoirs. In 1815 he attempted Lear, but his memory was gone and the exhibition was one of "pitiable imbecility."   SMA

Ferber, Edna (1885–1968) Playwright. A celebrated author of fiction, Ferber began her theatrical career in 1915 with *Our Mrs. McChesney,* a collaboration with George V. Hobart that starred **Ethel Barrymore.** In 1920 she wrote the unsuccessful *$1200 a Year* with Newman Levy and *The Eldest,* her only solo venture in playwriting, which was composed for the **Provincetown Players.** *Minick* (1924) began a lucrative partnership with **George S. Kaufman,** which also yielded *The Royal Family* (1927), depicting chaotic life in a theatrical dynasty; *Dinner at Eight* (1932), which examined the lives of guests at a fashionable dinner party; and *Stage Door* (1936), which focused on young actresses in a theatrical boardinghouse. Less successful for Ferber and Kaufman were *The Land Is Bright* (1941) and *Bravo!* (1948). Two of Ferber's novels were adapted into the musicals *Show Boat* (1927) and *Saratoga* (1959). Her autobiographies, *A Peculiar Treasure* (1939) and *A Kind of Magic* (1963), contain valuable impressions of the theatrical writing process.   KF

See: J. G. Gilbert, *Ferber,* New York, 1978.

Fernald, John Bailey (1905–1985) Director and teacher. Born in Mill Valley, CA, Fernald was educated at Oxford (1928) and spent most of his professional career directing and teaching in England. He returned to the U.S. in 1966 to establish the John Fernald Company at the Meadow Brook Theatre in Rochester, MN, and to serve as a professor there during 1966–70. In 1970–1 he taught at New York University. He published his memoirs *Sense of Direction* in 1968.   TLM

Ferrer, José (Vicente) (1912–92) Puerto Rican–born actor, director, and producer. His professional debut was in a **showboat** melodrama on Long Island Sound in 1934. He made his Broadway debut in 1935, but his first substantial role came in *Brother Rat* (1936), and he achieved stardom in *Charley's Aunt* (1940). Ferrer employed his rich and powerful voice in two subsequent revivals, as Iago to **Paul Robeson**'s Othello (1943) and in the title role of *Cyrano de Bergerac* (1946). In the latter role, critics praised his "throbbing, vigorous performance." Ferrer directed the New York Theatre Company at the City Center for a time, appearing in several classical revivals.

Two other acting successes were *The Silver Whistle* (1948) and *The Shrike* (1952). Among his directing assignments were *Stalag 17* (1951), *The Fourposter* (1951), *My Three Angels* (1953), and *The Andersonville Trial* (1959). Ferrer appeared often in films, and won an Oscar for his filmed Cyrano; he also appeared in opera and on television. His last stage appearance was in a 1990 musical version of Ionesco's *Rhinoceros* in England. Ferrer was the ninth president of the Players Club.   SMA

Feuer, Cy (1911–) and **Ernest H. Martin** (1919–) Producers. Partners since 1947, Feuer and Martin's Broadway productions include *Where's Charley?* (1948), ***Guys and Dolls*** (1950, Drama Critics' and Tony awards), *The Boy Friend* (1954), ***Silk Stockings*** (1955), *Whoop-up* (1958), ***How to Succeed in Business Without Really Trying*** (1961, Pulitzer Prize; Drama Critics' and Tony awards), *Little Me* (1962), *Skyscraper* (1965), *Walking Happy* (1966), *The Goodbye People* (1968), and *The Act* (1977). They managed (and later owned) the **Lunt–Fontanne Theatre** (1960–5); served as managing directors of the Los Angeles and San Francisco Civic Light Opera Association (1975–80), succeeding **Edwin Lester;** and produced the motion pictures ***Cabaret*** (1972), *Piaf* (1975), and *A Chorus Line* (1985). Feuer has directed or codirected several of their productions, including *Little Me* with **Bob Fosse.**   TLM

Fichandler, Zelda (1924–) Cofounder and from 1951 sole producing director of Washington, DC's **Arena Stage,** the longest artistic tenure in regional theatre annals. From the beginning she was committed to having a resident acting company present the classics, American drama, and recent plays that had failed on Broadway – an artistic mission that continues to this day. Fichandler spent much of the 1950s articulating the promise of the regional theatre movement, and in 1961 built a permanent home for her company; there she continued to nurture her resident ensemble and began to produce new plays, such as *The Great White Hope* (1967), *Indians* (1969), and *Moonchildren* (1971). A tour to the Soviet Union in 1973, the first for an American theatre, fed her interest in Soviet and Eastern European drama and led to productions in the 1970s of works by Frisch, Mrozek, Orkeny, and others, many of which she directed. In 1976 the theatre's successes culminated in a Tony Award for Arena – a first outside of New York City. Continuing a dedication to the development of young actors, Fichandler became chair of the graduate acting program at New York University's Tisch School of the Arts in 1984, and, in 1990, concluded her visionary tenure at Arena to become artistic director of New York's **Acting Company.**   LM

Fiddler on the Roof Based on stories of Sholom Aleichem, with book by Joseph Stein, music by **Jerry Bock,** lyrics by **Sheldon Harnick;** opened at the **Imperial Theatre** on 22 September 1964 and ran for 3,242 performances. Set in a *shtetl* or Jewish village in the czarist Russia of 1905, the musical recounted the struggles of a milkman, Tevye, to survive and keep his family together in the face of government repression and the forces of change that threaten traditional Jewish observance and customs. By turns comic, sentimental, and melodramatic, the plot focused on Tevye's attempts to arrange good marriages for his three oldest daughters, and their insistence on marrying men of their choosing. Warnings that the Jewish settlements are about to be abolished by the government punctuate the plot, until at the end Tevye and the other villagers of Anatevka are forced to gather their possessions and leave on a perilous journey to a new life in America. The score skillfully combined traditional Jewish harmonies with the musical idioms of Broadway. **Jerome Robbins**'s direction and choreography added animation and color to such moments as the wedding of Tevye's oldest daughter. As Tevye, **Zero Mostel** gave an unforgettable performance, whether grappling to comprehend changes taking place in the world or trying to strike a bargain with God in the humorous "If I Were a Rich Man." Maria Karnilova as Tevye's wife Golde and Bea Arthur as Yente the Matchmaker provided strong support.

Fiddler has received a number of major revivals. Mostel returned to Tevye for a limited run at the **Winter Garden** in 1976, and in 1990 Israeli actor Topol appeared in a new staging on Broadway.
MK

Field, Joseph M. (1810–56) Dublin-born playwright and actor. He debuted in Boston in 1827 and moved west, acting in and out of the **Sol Smith–Ludlow** circuit, finally managing Field's Variety Theatre in St. Louis (1852–3). Field also acted and wrote for **Mitchell's Olympic** in New York (1842–3). A man of his time, Field wrote *Oregon; or, The Disputed Territory* (1846), *The Tourist* (1839), and, more seriously, *Job and His Children* (1852), his only extant work.   WJM

Fields, Dorothy (1905–74) Lyricist-librettist. Daughter of comedian-producer Lew Fields [see **Weber and Fields**], she began her career writing songs for shows at the Cotton Club with composer Jimmy McHugh. Together, they wrote songs for *Blackbirds of 1928* and other Broadway **revue**s featuring black performers. She spent most of the 1930s in Hollywood, then returned to Broadway with *Stars in Your Eyes* (1939). In the 1940s she wrote the librettos for such shows as *Mexican Hayride* (1944) and *Annie Get Your Gun* (1946). She wrote lyrics (and, in some cases, librettos) for *A Tree Grows in Brooklyn* (1951), *By the Beautiful Sea* (1954), *Redhead* (1959), and *Sweet Charity* (1966). Her last show was *Seesaw* (1973), and her songs were featured posthumously in *Ain't Misbehavin'* (1978) and *Sugar Babies* (1979).   MK

Fields, Lew see **Weber, Joseph**

Fields, W. C. (né William Claude Dukenfield) (1880–1946) Comedian who ran away from home at the age of 14 and taught himself to juggle. As an eccentric tramp juggler he was the first American headliner at Paris's Folies-Bergère (1902) and a great hit at the London Hippodrome (1904) for his trick pool game and frustrating golf lesson. Taking his cue from Harry Tate's British music-hall persona, the bibulous, bottlenosed Fields developed the character of a grandiloquent but seedy curmudgeon, muttering indignant asides. He starred in the **Ziegfeld** Follies (1915–18, 1920, 1921, 1925), and in *Poppy* (1923) created the type of the moth-eaten but brazen showman he would later repeat on film. His earliest film appearance had been in a short of 1915, and after 1925 he settled in Los Angeles, appearing in a series of comic masterpieces.   LS

See: W. K. Everson, *The Art of W. C. Fields*, New York, 1967; R. Fields, ed., *W. C. Fields by Himself*, New York, 1973.

Fierstein, Harvey (1954–   ) Playwright, actor, producer, and gay activist. Educated at Pratt Institute, Fierstein made his debut as an actor at **La MaMa** in Andy Warhol's *Park* (1971). He garnered sudden fame in 1981 with the success of his *Torch Song Trilogy,* a play presenting various views of male homosexuality [see **gay/lesbian theatre**]. With the commercial success of the musical *La Cage Aux Folles* (1983), for which he wrote the book, Fierstein was considered the most successful Broadway playwright concerned with gay themes in the 1980s, though his efforts since 1983 have been less significant.   TLM

Fifth Avenue Theatre West 24th St. between Broadway and Sixth Ave., NYC. Amos Eno, the owner of the Fifth Avenue Hotel, erected a small structure adjoining it for surreptitious and illegal stock-exchange activities, which he was forced to abandon. In 1865, he decided to convert it into a theatre, and for several years it functioned as a minstrel hall. The railroad magnate James Fisk took it over, gutted the interior, and transformed it into a handsome little theatre, which eventually fell into the hands of **Augustin Daly** for his introduction into theatrical management. During 1869–73, Daly assembled an attractive company, staged comedies and dramas in perfectly tuned productions, and made this theatre the most fashionable and popular playhouse in New York. When it went up in flames in 1873, Daly transferred his company to the New Fifth Avenue Theatre at 728 Broadway. In 1879, **Steele MacKaye** rebuilt the old house, renaming it the **Madison Square.**   MCH

Fifth of July, The, by Lanford Wilson was first presented by the **Circle Repertory Company** in New York on 27 April 1978. Directed by **Marshall**

Lanford Wilson's *Fifth of July* at the New Apollo Theatre (1980), with (left to right) Christopher Reeve, Swoozie Kurtz, Jonathan Hogan, and Joyce Reehling. Photo: © Martha Swope. Courtesy: Martha Swope.

W. Mason, the cast included **William Hurt** as Kenneth Talley, Jr., a paraplegic Vietnam veteran who has returned to his family home in Missouri to resume his teaching career after eight years; Helen Stenborg as his aunt Sally Friedman; Joyce Reehling as his sister June, once politically militant; Amy Wright as June's adolescent daughter Shirley; Nancy Snyder as Gwen Landis, an old friend from Ken's student days at Berkeley who wants to buy the Talley place and turn it into a recording studio; Jonathan Hogan as her husband John; and Jeff Daniels as Ken's lover Jed. The play ran for 168 performances. Often compared to Chekhov, Wilson examines the characters' attempts to free themselves from the effect of the past, particularly the Vietnam War and the events surrounding it. In the course of the play, each finds a way to connect with others and create a new future.   BCM

Finian's Rainbow Two-act musical comedy, music by Burton Lane, words by **E. Y. Harburg** and Fred Saidy; opened 10 January 1947 at the **46th Street Theatre,** running 725 performances. One of the first of a wave of socially conscious postwar musicals, *Finian's Rainbow* tells of an Irishman who, hearing that America's gold is buried in Fort Knox, comes to the Southern state of "Missitucky" to "plant" gold he has stolen from a leprechaun. The pursuing leprechaun (**David Wayne**) creates havoc, notably in turning a racist white politician black, before love turns him human. The show is notable for several reasons beyond its social themes: The central romance ends in separation rather than in union; the cast was thoroughly integrated in an age of mostly all-white or all-black musicals; it marked the Broadway debut as choreographer of **Michael Kidd;** and it featured a mute character who expressed herself solely through dance. However, it is perhaps best remembered for Harburg's satiric jibes at economic, racial, and social policy – and for Lane's score ("Look to the Rainbow," "Old Devil Moon").   JD

Finley, Karen (1956–) Chicago-born visual and performance artist, writer. She studied **performance art** and painting at the Chicago Art Institute (1975–7) and the San Francisco Art Institute (MFA, 1981). She collaborated (1981–4) with Brian Rout (aka Harry Kipper, one of Britain's performance art duo, "The Kipper Kids"), to whom she was briefly married. In her theatre piece *The Theory of Total Blame* (1988) and her solo performances, such as *The Constant State of Desire* (1987) and *We Keep Our Victims Ready* (1989), her subject is the dysfunctional nuclear family and victimizing social conditions. Her strategy of overexposing the body is to deeroticize it.   AF

Fiorello! Two-act musical comedy, music by **Jerry Bock,** lyrics by **Sheldon Harnick,** book by Jerome Weidman and **George Abbott;** opened 23 November 1959 at the **Broadhurst Theatre,** running 795 performances. This musical depiction of the early career of New York mayor Fiorello La-Guardia (Tom Bosley), the first successful Broadway collaboration of Bock and Harnick, won the Pulitzer Prize for drama, as well as the Drama Critics' Circle and (in a tie) Tony awards for best musical. While other recent musicals had featured nonsingers in the leading male role, *Fiorello!* was unusual in that it confined his singing entirely to LaGuardia's campaign speeches. With many musical scenes rather than traditional "numbers," the score produced no standard "hits," but rather helped evoke the historical corruption of the era.   JD

Fires The U.S. has been plagued with devastating performance-venue fires, beginning with Boston's **Federal Theatre** in 1798 and continuing unabated until safer materials and strict laws were introduced early in this century. Prior to 1880, mostly small theatres burned (26 in New York, 21 in San Francisco, 17 in Philadelphia, 11 in Boston, 9 in Cincinnati, 8 in New Orleans, 6 in Baltimore). In one two-year period (1865–7), at least five major New York performance spaces burned (**Barnum's,** "444" Broadway, the Academy of Music, the **Bowery,** and the **Winter Garden**). Some theatres suffered fires frequently (the Bowery, for instance, six times). Most fires occurred when venues were dark, but those with the greatest loss of life struck during performances. In 1811 the Richmond (VA) Theatre fire resulted in 71 deaths; the Brooklyn Theatre fire of 1876 accounted for 295 lives lost; the supposedly fireproof Iroquois Theatre in **Chicago** burned in 1903 during a performance of *Mr. Bluebeard* featuring **Eddie Foy,** with over 600 lives claimed; and in 1908 the Rhoads Theatre in Boyertown, PA, burned with 170 lost. Destruction by fire has not been limited to theatres. Two prime examples were the Cocoanut Grove Nightclub fire in Boston, which in 1942 cost 491 lives, and the **Ringling Bros.** canvas Big Top conflagration in 1944 (in Hartford, CT), with at least 168 deaths – the worst disaster in **circus** history. In many of these, numerous deaths were not from burns, but from asphyxiation or panic-induced crushing and trampling.   DBW

Fisher, Charles (1816–91) English-born actor, son of the theatrical manager Charles Fisher. He came to America in 1852 and for a decade was a member of several New York companies, including **W. E. Burton**'s and **Laura Keene**'s. During 1861–72 he was a principal supporting actor in **Wallack**'s company and then, until 1890, in **Augustin Daly**'s. He appeared in a wide range of classical and contemporary roles during his long career, but was celebrated as a light comedian, particularly for his characterizations of Malvolio, Joseph Surface, Anthony Absolute, Falstaff (*The Merry Wives of Windsor*), and Triplet (*Masks and Faces*).   DJW

Fisher, Clara (1811–98) London-born actress who debuted at Drury Lane at age 6, toured England for a decade, and then came to the U.S. in 1827 for a triumphant debut at the **Park. Ludlow** called her "the finest comedy actress in the United States." Among her more noted roles were Viola, Lady Teazle, Lady Gay Spanker, Pauline, and the Fool in *King Lear*. She retired in 1884, but would occasionally appear in "old-lady parts," and was first

Singing Witch in Macready's *Macbeth* the night of the **Astor Place** riot.   SMA

See: Autobiography of Clara Fisher Maeder, New York, 1897.

Fisher, Jules (1937–   ) Lighting designer, theatre consultant, and producer. Fisher had already designed three **Off-Broadway** shows before graduating from Carnegie Tech in 1960. He has since designed over 100 productions, including *Hair, Pippin, Chicago, Lenny,* and *La Cage Aux Folles.* As a producer his many works include *Beatlemania.* Because of his work as designer and consultant for several rock tours, notably for the Rolling Stones, he has been an innovator in new technology for **stage lighting.**   AA

Fiske, Harrison Grey (1861–1942) Dramatic editor, critic, producer, manager, and playwright. Born of wealthy parents, Fiske served an early apprenticeship on the *Jersey City Argus, New York Star,* and *New York Dramatic Mirror.* He left New York University after his sophomore year (1880) to edit the *Dramatic Mirror* when his father bought him one-third interest in it. He made the paper an important theatrical journal by attacking corruption in the profession and working to raise the tone of the American stage. He led a crusade in 1880 to establish the **Actors' Fund.** In 1890, he married the actress Marie Augusta Davey (**Minnie Maddern Fiske**) and managed her career as well as that of a number of leading actors. For her he wrote or adapted numerous plays, including *Hester Crewe* (1893) and *Marie Deloche* (1895). He leased the Manhattan Theatre in 1901 for Mrs. Fiske, and formed the **Manhattan Theatre Company** to support her. His producing successes included *Kismet* (1911), starring **Otis Skinner.** Financial problems forced him to sell the *Dramatic Mirror* in 1911, and he declared bankruptcy in 1914, although he was discharged the following year. The death of Mrs. Fiske in 1932 effectively ended his career. Fiske fought commercialism in the theatre, and did much to establish **Ibsen on the American stage.**   TLM

Fiske, Minnie Maddern (née Marie Augusta Davey) (1864–1932) Actress and director. From a theatrical family, she began her career at age 3, remaining in steady demand as a child actress. Her adult New York debut was in Charles Callahan's *Fogg's Ferry* (1882). After a brief first marriage, she wed her second husband, **Harrison Grey Fiske,** editor of the *New York Dramatic Mirror,* in 1890, retiring for four years after her marriage. During this interlude she wrote several one-act plays and became interested in the realist movement. After 1893 she focused her energies, despite opposition, on plays of this ilk, and worked toward what she called "natural, true acting" in her productions, especially with her **Manhattan Theatre Company** (1904–8). At the turn of the century she fought the Theatrical **Syndicate,** almost alone, and became a noted humanitarian, fighting against cruelty and abuse to animals. Some of her notable stage appearances were in *Hester*

Crewe (1893), *A Doll's House* (1894), Lorimer Stoddard's dramatization of *Tess of the d'Urbervilles* (1897), **Langdon Mitchell**'s adaptation of *Vanity Fair* (1899), *Becky Sharp* (1899), *Hedda Gabler* (1903), *Leah Kleschna* (1906), *The New York Idea* (1906), *Rosmersholm* (1907), *Salvation Nell* (1908), *The Pillars of Society* (1910), and *Ghosts* (1927). She is considered today one of the most distinguished actresses ever to have performed on the American stage and its chief promoter of **Ibsen.** A contemporary critic noted, "She had a peculiar gift of emotion, uniting tears and smiles in the same breath, which was more pathetic than undiluted grief and more diverting than undiluted laughter."   DBW

See: A. Binns, Mrs. Fiske and the American Theatre, New York, 1955; F. Griffith, Mrs. Fiske, New York, 1912; A. Woollcott, Mrs. Fiske: Her Views on Actors, Acting . . . , New York, 1917 (reprint 1968).

Fiske, Stephen Ryder (1840–1916) Drama critic. Educated at Rutgers, Fiske learned his trade during the Civil War on the staff of the *New York Herald.* He also contributed to the *Leader* and adapted French plays for local managers. After an eight-year hiatus (1866–74) in London as a journalist and theatre manager, he handled **Augustin Daly**'s business affairs, comanaged the **Fifth Avenue Theatre** (1877–9), and cofounded the *New York [Dramatic] Mirror* (1879). His dramatic column for the *Spirit of the Times* (1879–1902) established his reputation. A pragmatic critic, Fiske offered a commonsense view of theatre – not as an art but as a form of mass entertainment.   TLM

Fitch, Clyde (1865–1909) Playwright. Born in Elmira, NY, he graduated from Amherst (1886), where he had been a leader in the dramatic club and frequently played female roles. Fitch was extraordinarily successful and prolific, writing 60 plays from *Beau Brummell* (1890, starring **Richard Mansfield**) to *The City* (1909). In 1901 four of his plays were running simultaneously in New York: *Lover's Lane, Captain Jinks of the Horse Marines* (with **Ethel Barrymore**), *The Climbers,* and *Barbara Frietchie.* Best known among his others: *The Moth and the Flame* (1898), *Nathan Hale* (1898), *The Cowboy and the Lady* (1899), *The Girl with the Green Eyes* (1902), *Her Great Match* (1905), and *The Truth* (1907). Fitch was a master of sprightly dialogue and documentarylike scenes from contemporary life, and as a director he meticulously controlled every detail of the staging. One critic said that his plays gave a better idea of American life than did newspapers and historical records. He died at Châlons-sur-Marne in France.   RM

See: A. Bell, The Clyde Fitch I Knew, New York, 1909; M. Moses and V. Gerson, eds., Clyde Fitch and His Letters, Boston, 1924; J. Murray, "The Contribution of Clyde Fitch to the American Theatre," PhD diss., Boston U, 1942.

Fitzgerald, Geraldine (1914–   ) Actress and director. Born in Dublin and educated at the Dublin Art School, Fitzgerald made her stage debut at the Gate Theatre in Dublin (1932) and her first appearance in New York as Ellie Dunn in **Shaw**'s *Heartbreak House* (1938). While working in both films and the theatre, she has played onstage in the U.S. an impressive array of classical and modern characters: Jennifer Dubedat, *The Doctor's Dilemma* (1955); Goneril, *King Lear* (1956); Gertrude, *Hamlet* (1958); Queen, *The Cave Dwellers* (1961); Mary Tyrone, ***Long Day's Journey into Night*** (1971); Jenny, *The Threepenny Opera* (1972); Juno, *Juno and the Paycock* (1973); Essie Miller, ***Ah, Wilderness!*** (1975); Amanda Wingfield, *The **Glass Menagerie*** (1975); Felicity, *The Shadow Box* (1977); and Nora Melody, *A **Touch of the Poet*** (1978). She has also performed in a **one-person** show, *Songs of the Streets: O'Neill and Carlotta* (1979). One of America's most distinguished character actresses, Fitzgerald has been widely acclaimed for her 1973 portrayal of Juno, of which **Mel Gussow** wrote: "Geraldine Fitzgerald is exactly the actress to play her, managing to be resilient without sacrificing her vulnerability. Informed of her son's death, she marshals her resources, calms her hysterical daughter and then with a spasm of anguish reveals her own personal loss." Fitzgerald has made over 30 films including *Wuthering Heights* (1939), *The Pawnbroker* (1965), *Arthur* (1981), and *The Pope of Greenwich Village* (1984). She is as active today directing as she is acting.   TLM

Flanagan (Davis), Hallie (née Ferguson)

(1890–1969) Playwright, educator, and administrator. Franklin D. Roosevelt called Flanagan the third most powerful woman in America – "after my wife and Frances Perkins" – when she supervised the **Federal Theatre Project.** Born in South Dakota, she graduated from Grinnell College in Iowa, studied with **George Pierce Baker** at Workshop 47, and in 1927 received a Guggenheim Award to study theatre in Europe. On her return she ran a highly successful experimental program at Vassar. In 1935 Harry Hopkins invited her to administer the new theatre program that had been established under WPA supervision to put qualified people back to work. For the next four years she managed the huge national theatre as it struggled with its double charge of art and relief. In spite of government harassment, crippling bureaucratic regulations, and opposition from the professional theatre, the FTP achieved a remarkable record of accomplishments including **Living Newspaper**s, Negro companies, children's theatres, and distinguished alumni. With the demise of the project in 1939 (after a skirmish with HUAC), Flanagan returned to Vassar. There she wrote a memoir (*Arena*, 1940), then moved to Smith College, where she continued to write and direct. She died in 1969 leaving behind several books and a vision of the theatre as a vibrant social institution that must dare to be dangerous.
BBW

See: J. Bentley, *Hallie Flanagan: A Life in the American Theatre,* New York, 1988.

Fletcher, Allen

(1922–85) Director and teacher. Born in San Francisco, Fletcher studied at Stanford and Yale universities, the Bristol Old Vic Theatre School, and LAMDA, on a Fulbright. He made his directing debut in 1948 at the **Oregon Shakespeare Festival** and returned there each year through 1956. Other directing credits include the Antioch

Shakespeare Festival (1957); the **Old Globe** in San Diego (1955–66); and the APA (1960–1). During 1962–5 he served as principal director and head of the professional training program for the **American Shakespeare Festival,** Stratford, CT. In 1966 he took a similar post with the **Seattle Repertory Theatre,** where he modernized the company and ended the rotating repertory. Ousted in 1970, he founded the Actor's Company and became Director of the Conservatory for the **American Conservatory Theatre** (where he had guest-directed since 1965). He left ACT in 1984 for a similar post with the **Denver Center Theatre.** A premiere classical director, Fletcher is remembered for his 1963 *King Lear* with **Morris Carnovsky.**   TLM

Florence, William "Billy" Jermyn (or James) (né Bernard Conlin)

(1831–91) Actor whose professional stage debut occurred in 1849 at the Marshall Theatre in Richmond, VA, as Peter in *The Stranger.* In 1853 he married Malvina Pray, the sister of Maria Pray Mestayer Williams, wife of actor **Barney Williams.** For almost 40 years, the Florences were a successful starring team in both England and America, often in Irish-American roles such as *The Irish Boy and the Yankee Girl.* Florence was a skillful comedian noted for his striking, convincingly human characterizations. After his Irish roles, his outstanding performances were as Bob Brierly in Tom Taylor's *The Ticket-of-Leave Man,* Bardwell Slote in Benjamin Woolf's *The **Mighty Dollar,*** Sir Lucius O'Trigger in *The Rivals,* and Zekiel Homespun in Colman's *The Heir-at-Law.* Florence also presented the first American production of T. W. Robertson's *Caste* in 1867, only four months after its London premiere.   DJW

Florodora

With the exception of **Gilbert and Sullivan,** this musical (score by Leslie Stuart, lyrics by Stuart, Paul Rubens, and Frank Clements) produced at the **Casino Theatre** (opened 12 November 1900) was the most successful British import of its era. With over 500 performances, the New York production exceeded the 1899 London run, reversing the trend of the day. Frequently revived – and highlighted by its sextette of lovely ladies, with six male partners, and their coquettish number "Tell Me, Pretty Maiden" – the show had its last Broadway revival in 1920 for 150 performances. The slight book by Owen Hall concerns an aborted attempt to cheat the heroine out of her inheritance of a famous perfume: Florodora (also the name of the Philippine island where the perfume is manufactured).   DBW

Folk and festival performance

Like folk painting and music, folk performance is nonacademic art based on traditional techniques and content. Both change constantly, however, as the performance is carried from one community to another. Typically, folk performers have considered themselves less creators of an art than "re-creators" of a traditional event of significance. Often that event has its roots in the **ethnic** or immigrant origins of the community – British, Spanish, African American, Native American, or the more recently arrived groups – but adapted to reflect contemporary community needs and interests.

Folk performance is a close cousin to play, games, and sport, on one hand, and to rituals on the other. For example, the line between children's games and fully developed performance is not always clear, but American folk culture contains a rich range of "paraperformance" activities that fall between the two, as in the traditional "play party" activities once common in the rural South.

Performance aspects of a ritual often come to share prominence with its purely functional elements. Examples include the traditional jazz funerals of New Orleans, with their elaborate outdoor processions and marching bands, as well as traditional religious revivals. Many revivalists have become skilled manipulators of the performance element in their religious services, developing complex juxtapositions of song, chant, and exhortation.

Folk plays once existed in abundance throughout the U.S., and may still be found today in some localities. A number originated in mumming or some form of Old World religious drama; many are seasonal and perambulatory in their approach to space, involving movement of performers (and sometimes groups of spectators as well) from one "station" to another, with the presentation of a play at each station. Sometimes these stations are the homes of community members, and the presentations occur during "house visits" in which an ordinary room becomes a temporary performance space. Often improvised outdoor sites are employed.

Between the presentations at various stations there may be a relatively formal procession, as in Hispanic Good Friday commemorations, or a less controlled general movement, sometimes with tricks, jokes, and horseplay in evidence. Often performers are decked out in fantastic masks and costumes, athough there may be little attempt at impersonation, marchers clearly identified first and foremost as community members carrying out a traditional performance in disguise or semidisguise.

The traditional Halloween "trick or treat" or "beggars night," Chinese New Year celebrations in New York, and the Purim masking in Jewish communities represent the idea of the perambulatory performance stripped to its most basic elements, with emphasis on masking and unrestricted wandering between visits. Perambulatory performances with elaborately structured recitations or "plays" have been collected among Spanish communities in the Southwest and among Hungarian-Amerians in Ohio.

Parades and processions, another form of perambulatory performance with little emphasis on the stational, are often presented as part of traditional festivals designed to celebrate, commemorate, reenact, or anticipate events of seasons of significance to the community. New York's St. Patrick's Day parade and Macy's Thanksgiving parade, which initiates the Christmas shopping season in the city, are associated with festival days, but not with specific festival areas beyond those defined by the parades themselves. Many folk festivals, however, are "environmental," transform-

ing an existing space – a street, a square, or a park, for example – into a temporary performance site.

Typically, an environmental festival occurs over too large a space and over too long a period of time to be seen as a literal performance by those involved; but, in effect, it becomes both a performance in the broadest sense and the seedbed for a number of smaller, more easily comprehensible performance events of various types, often including processional performance. The Italian-American street festivals of New York City and Mardi Gras in New Orleans are examples of environmental performances that temporarily transform existing urban spaces, "festivalizing" them for the duration of the event through an elaborate scenography.

The approaches to organization and "staging" used in the creation of American folk and festival performance are, in effect, little different from those found in many other cultures worldwide. Paraperformance, perambulation, and environmental performance all represent time-honored solutions to the practical problem of presenting issues of significance to the community in an effective and memorable way.   BMcN

Folksbiene (People's Stage) Beginning in New York City as one of hundreds of Yiddish amateur theatres, it survived to become the longest continuously performing **Yiddish theatre** in the world, presenting at least one production every winter since 1915. Early on it hired professional directors, such as **Joseph Buloff** and **Jacob Ben-Ami,** and eventually began hiring some professional actors as well. Associated with the Workman's Circle, the group is generally committed to presenting Yiddish plays of literary worth, often classics; but in recent years it has also presented lighter entertainments, such as Yiddish translations of popular Israeli comedies. It is currently housed in the Central Synagogue, 128 East 56th Street.   NS

Follies Intermissionless musical play, music and lyrics by **Stephen Sondheim,** book by James Goldman; opened 4 April 1971 at New York's **Winter Garden Theatre,** running 522 performances. This extravagant and thought-provoking musical probes the various meanings of "follies." Set amid a reunion of former performers in a **Ziegfeld**-like revue the night before their old theatre is torn down, it juxtaposes past and present, memory and reality, dreams and disillusion. Producer-director **Harold Prince** brought back actual celebrities of 50 years before, who performed numbers much like those of yesteryear, but from the perspective of age. He also populated the stage with statuesque showgirls who wandered the stage as ghosts of a bygone splendor, and paired the older actors with younger actors playing their characters' optimistic younger selves. Sondheim's score, combining both a contemporary lyricism and an evocation of older theatre music, has been much admired, while **Boris Aronson**'s set created both the derelict theatre and the sumptuous gingerbread of the dreamlike "Loveland" sequence. *Follies* won the Drama Critics' Circle Award for best musical, but it has rarely been revived because of both expense and casting difficulties.   JD

Fonda (né Jaynes), Henry (1905–82) Nebraska-born actor who made his first stage appearance in 1925 at the Omaha Community Playhouse, and his Broadway debut in 1929. He established himself as a leading actor in *The Farmer Takes a Wife* (1934) before turning almost exclusively to making films. After service in WW II, he played the title role in *Mister Roberts* (1948), which won him a Tony. Working in both Hollywood and New York, Fonda won critical acclaim on Broadway in 1954 with his portrayal of Barney Greenwald in *The Caine Mutiny Court Martial.* He starred with **Ann Bancroft** in *Two for the Seesaw* (1958) and with **Barbara Bel Geddes** in *Silent Night, Lonely Night* (1959). Other important stage appearances include the comedy hit *Generation* (1965) and the **one-person** show, *Clarence Darrow* (1974). Fonda's screen image as the quiet, unassuming man of integrity and strength dominated his appearances on stage. His autobiography (written with Howard Teichman) appeared in 1981. TLM

See: A. Roberts and M. Goldstein, *Henry Fonda: A Biography,* Jefferson, NC, 1984.

Fontanne, Lynn see **Lunt, Alfred**

Fool for Love **Sam Shepard**'s 39th play, the first to feature a fully developed female protagonist. The action of the play is both a love story and a power struggle between a half-brother and -sister. Set in a dingy motel room on the edge of the desert, the play allows several interpretations of the interrelationship of the lovers and an Old Man who seems to exist on another plane of reality. Shepard directed Kathy Baker as May and Ed Harris as Eddie in the original production at San Francisco's **Magic Theatre**, opening 8 February 1983. That production was brought to New York's **Circle Repertory Theatre** on 26 May 1983. A 1985 film directed by Robert Altman starred Shepard along with Kim Basinger, Randy Quaid, and Harry Dean Stanton. FHL

Foote, Horton (1916–) Texas-born playwright and scriptwriter whose best-known work, characterized by a "quietly intense dramatic voice," has been for film (*To Kill a Mockingbird, Tender Mercies, The Trip to Bountiful*) and television. His nine "Orphans Home Cycle" plays set in and around his real hometown of Wharton (called Harrison in his work) and tracing the travails of Horace Robedaux (based on his father) are important evocations of an era in the American Southwest of 1902–28. His cycle began in 1942 with *Texas Town* and has concluded with *Dividing the Estate* (1989) and *Talking Pictures* (1990). Many of his screenplays, such as *The Trip to Bountiful*, began as plays (play, 1953; film, 1985). Most of Foote's plays, drawn from stories handed down from his grandparents' days, are not written out of nostalgia but to help him "separate what is permanent from what is not." DBW

Forbes, James (1871–1938) Playwright. Beginning with domestic farce in *The Chorus Lady* (1906), which developed from a vaudeville sketch, and

plays emphasizing small-town living – *The Travelling Salesman* (1908) and *The Commuters* (1910) – Forbes made his greatest contribution with *The Famous Mrs. Fair* (1919), which explores the problems of a woman, liberated by four years' service in the war, as she returns to a husband and now grown-up family. Consistent with theatre at this time, the traditional domestic pattern is reestablished. Later plays dealt with social situations, such as small-town people trying to gain social status in New York (*The Endless Chain,* 1922) and the problems of youth (*Young Blood,* 1925). WJM

See: C. Grover. "James Forbes: His Works and Career in the American Theatre," PhD diss., U of California at Davis, 1976.

For Colored Girls Who Have Considered Suicide When the Rainbow Is Enuf This choreopoem by **Ntozake Shange,** combining dance, poetry, and music, was developed at the Bacchanal, a bar in Berkeley (1974), and reworked before opening at Studio Rivbea (1975), then **New Federal Theatre,** the **Public Theater,** and finally Broadway's **Booth Theatre** (September 1976), directed by Oz Scott, with Shange as the Lady in Yellow. Seven women, identified by the color of their costumes, explore through passionate, visceral poetry the courageous strength of black women. In Shange's words, the work celebrates "our struggle to become all that is forbidden by our environment, all that is forfeited by our gender, all that we have forgotten." The play won Obie, Outer Critics' Circle, and Audelco awards. TH-S

Ford, John T. (1829–94) Manager. A bookstore owner in Richmond, VA, he became the agent for a variety troupe, and in 1855–6 leased theatres in Richmond, Baltimore, and Washington, DC. The Richmond theatre closed at the beginning of the Civil War. In Washington he built **Ford's Theatre** in 1861; as a result of Lincoln's assassination, it was closed by the army and purchased for offices by the government. He continued to manage one or two theatres in Baltimore, and during 1873–86 he also managed the Grand Opera House in Washington, DC. In the 1880s he became the major producer of combination companies for the entire South. DMcD

Ford, Ruth (1920–) Mississippi-born actress-playwright who began her career as a photographer's model and then burst upon the New York theatrical scene in 1938 as a member of **Orson Welles**'s **Mercury Theatre** Company, appearing in *The Shoemaker's Holiday* and *Danton's Death.* The exotically beautiful actress continued with such diverse plays as *No Exit* and *Requiem for a Nun;* her most recent roles were in *Harold and Maude* (1980 stage version) and *The Visit* (1983). DBW

Ford's Theatre Washington, DC. The site of the assassination of President Abraham Lincoln by **John Wilkes Booth,** 14 April 1865. The building opened in 1834 as the First Baptist Church; in 1861 **John T. Ford** converted it into Ford's Atheneum, which burned down in December 1862. He reopened it on 27 August 1863 and successfully engaged many of America's leading performers, including John Wilkes Booth. After the assassination the government converted the building to an office and storage facility, which collapsed in 1893 during **Edwin Booth**'s funeral in New York. In 1968 the government-restored theatre reopened for public performances. Ford's Theatre also houses a Lincoln Museum.   SMA

See: G. Olszewski, *Restoration of Ford's Theatre,* Washington, DC, 1963.

Foreigner, The Previously produced at the **Milwaukee Repertory Theater** (1983), **Larry Shue**'s farce opened at the Astor Place Theatre on 1 November 1984 for 242 performances. It received the Outer Critics' Circle Award for best play and production **Off-Broadway.** Director **Jerry Zaks** and actor Anthony Heald (as the mysterious visitor who invents his own language) received Obies. Reflecting the majority of critical views, Gerald Weales noted that it was "designed to make a point about the connection between prejudice and ignorance," and that "its success lies in its nonsense language games, its mechanical tricks, above all its speed and timing."   MR

Foreman, Richard (1937–) Director-designer-playwright who began the Ontological-Hysteric Theatre in New York in 1968, where he has presented his own avant-garde works; since 1979 they have been coproduced by the **New York Shakespeare Festival**, the **Music Theatre Group**/Lenox Art Center and the **Wooster Group.**

Until roughly 1975, Foreman was concerned with "putting [an object] on stage and finding different ways of looking at it." In plays like *Total Recall* (1970), Foreman used untrained performers directed not to show emotion; dialogue was disjointed, often recorded, and spoken without inflection. Furniture and props, which were suspended from the ceiling, were accorded as much focus and expressiveness as actors. Foreman ran the show like a conductor. Perched above the stage, he periodically sounded a loud buzzer that separated phrases of the attenuated action. More recently Foreman has created pieces based directly on the ideas and sketches he collects in notebooks, often featuring a recurring character called Rhoda and played by Kate Manheim. With the stop-and-go action, accelerated parade of images, and his recorded comments on the performance in plays like *Pandering to the Masses* (1975), *Le Livre de Splendeurs* (Paris, 1976), *Penguin Touquet* (1981), *Egyptology* (1983), and *Film Is Evil: Radio Is Good* (1987), Foreman seeks to disrupt the audience's logical and teleological thought processes and "force people to another level of consciousness." Foreman has also directed plays by Büchner, Vaclav Havel, **Gertrude Stein,** and Molière for such theatres as the **Hartford Stage Company,** the **New York Shakespeare Festival,** and the **American Repertory Theatre.** In late 1991 he assumed control of the upstairs theatre at St. Mark's Church in NYC ("Ontological at Saint Marks") to showcase his work and that of other companies. Scripts and essays covering his first decade are collected in *Plays and Manifestoes,* edited by Kate Davy (1976),

and in *Reverberation Machines: The Later Plays and Essays* (1985); more recent work appears in *Love & Science* (1991).   AS

See: K. Davy, *Richard Foreman and the Ontological-Hysteric Theatre,* Ann Arbor, 1981; R. Foreman, *Unbalancing Acts: Foundations for a Theater,* New York, 1992.

Forepaugh, Adam (1831–90) **Circus** owner and entrepreneur; a Philadelphia meat and horse dealer who got into the circus when, after selling horses to a circus, he joined the operation to look after his interests. A ruthless businessman, master of deceptive advertising and scams, and a cruel employer, Forepaugh (known everywhere by the symbol "4-Paws") had a circus under his name during 1866–90, ultimately becoming **Barnum** and Bailey's major rival. When Barnum bought a gray albino elephant in 1884 (billed as "Scared White"), Forepaugh countered with a whitewashed elephant and the initiation of the famous "White Elephant Wars." Ironically, in 1886, after a falling out with James A. Bailey, Barnum was forced to align with Forepaugh for a presentation at Madison Square Garden of the largest circus seen to date.   DBW

Forest Rose, The Two-act musical drama by **Samuel Woodworth** with music by John Davies; premiered at the **Chatham Garden Theatre** on 6 October 1825. Combining the romantic and patriotic elements that characterized American native drama during the early Federalist period, it remained a favorite on American and English stages through the 1850s. Principally remembered for its **Yankee** character, Jonathan Ploughboy, it was revived throughout the first half of the 19th century by many of the major Yankee actors, including **G. H. Hill** and Joshua Silsbee, and was one of the most popular American dramas on the London stage despite its unflattering portrayal of the English.   PAD

Fornés, Maria Irene (1930–) **Cuban**-born playwright and director who so exemplifies the concerns and style of **Off-Broadway** theatre that she has won numerous Obies since 1965, including one for sustained achievement (1982). Although her plays and musicals deal with serious individual, national, and global problems – *Tango Palace* (1964), *Promenade* (1965), *The Successful Life of Three* (1965), *Dr. Kheal* (1968), *The Danube* (1984), *The Conduct of Life* (1985), and *Abingdon Square* (1987) – they are most acclaimed for their zany, whimsical humor and the use of innovative, cinematic techniques. Fornés's greatest critical success, *Fefu and Her Friends* (1977), is a feminist perspective on female friendship and women's roles in patriarchal society. In recent years her directorial interests have extended beyond her own plays to include standard works (*Hedda Gabler, Uncle Vanya*) and Latin American plays; other recent work include *Lovers and Keepers* (1986) and *And What of the Night* (1989).   FB

Forrest, Edwin (1806–72) The first American-born star, who dominated the American stage throughout the mid-19th century as Othello, Lear,

Edwin Forrest as Richard III ("A horse, a horse, my kingdom for a horse") in an 1858 engraving. Courtesy: Becker Theatre Library, Brown University.

Richard III, Coriolanus, Hamlet, Macbeth, Shylock, Richelieu, and in his repertoire of American plays: **Stone**'s *Metamora,* **Bird**'s *The Gladiator* and *The Broker of Bogota,* and **Conrad**'s *Jack Cade,* all of which had been winners in his playwriting contests (1829–47). Lear and Metamora were regarded as his best. Forrest's power derived from his commanding physique, penetrating voice, magnetic presence, and strenuous realism in characters whose driving passions paralleled his own. Although only 5′ 10″ in height, on stage his muscular frame seemed to tower like a giant. He was steady and predictable, in top form at every performance.

Born in Philadelphia, Forrest was stage-struck as a youngster, and at 15 studied the playing of **Thomas A. Cooper,** Edmund Kean, and **J. B. Booth.** Six years later, after appearing in Lexington, Louisville, Cincinnati, and New Orleans, he performed with Kean and Cooper, and the next year alternated with Booth as Iago and Othello. He was quickly recognized as a star in the East and South, along the inland waterways, and later in the far West. He appeared in London in 1836 and again in 1845, when he challenged his British rival (W. C. Macready) – a rivalry that precipitated the disastrous **Astor Place Opera House** riot (1849).

A superpatriot, Forrest was a colorful figure offstage and on. The lurid details of his divorce trial (1850) – *Forrest* v. *Catherine Sinclair* (she became a theatre manager in San Francisco) – filled the newspapers. He made a fortune, built Fonthill Castle on the Hudson, and had a spacious home in New York and another in Philadelphia (which was to become the Edwin Forrest Home for "decayed" actors, in existence until the late 1980s). He closed

his career with Shakespearean readings in Philadelphia, New York, and Boston in 1872.   RM

See: L. Barrett, *Edwin Forrest,* Boston, 1881, 1893; G. Harrison, *Edwin Forrest: The Actor and the Man,* Brooklyn, 1889; R. Moody, *Edwin Forrest, First Star of the American Stage,* New York, 1960; M. Moses, *The Fabulous Forrest,* Boston, 1929.

Forty-five Minutes from Broadway A 1905 melodrama with music by **George M. Cohan,** produced by **A. L. Erlanger** and **Marc Klaw;** opened on Broadway 1 January 1906. To accommodate gallery tastes, Cohan made its scenery and costumes calculatedly plain by the era's production standards. Cohan cast vaudevillian **Victor Moore** as Kid Burns, the slangy, Broadway wise guy who finds the missing will and marries the housemaid who is its beneficiary. As the spunky housemaid from New Rochelle, he chose **Fay Templeton,** long-time star of **Weber and Fields** Music Hall. Critics found the music charming but the melodrama trite and the leading male character distastefully brash and violent. It ran 90 performances, then had a long and profitable touring life.   WD

42nd Street A favorite with theatre parties and out-of-town visitors, this musical, with book by **Michael Stewart** and Mark Bramble, music by Harry Warren, and lyrics by Al Dubin, opened at the **Winter Garden** on 25 August 1980 and ran for almost nine years. Based on a 1930s Hollywood film about the auditions, rehearsals, and opening of a Depression-era Broadway musical revue, *42nd Street* made no claims to originality. Its main plot, concerning a chorus girl who becomes an instant star when the leading lady falls ill just before opening night, was familiar to audiences from the original film and many subsequent reworkings; but director-choreographer **Gower Champion** (who died on the show's opening night) infused the well-worn materials with lively production numbers based on the breezy 1930s songs of Warren and Dubin, and stars **Tammy Grimes, Jerry Orbach,** Wanda Richert, and Lee Roy Reams gave agreeable performances as the leading lady, the perfectionist director, the chorus girl, and the juvenile lead. MK

46th Street Theatre see **Richard Rodgers Theatre**

Fosse, Bob (1927–87) Choreographer and director. After beginning in vaudeville and burlesque as a teenager, Fosse appeared as a dancer in touring companies of *Call Me Mister* and *Make Mine Manhattan.* He made his Broadway debut in *Dance Me a Song* (1950). Fosse's first choreography, created for *The* **Pajama Game** (1954), was influenced by **Jack Cole**'s style of jazz dancing [see **dance**]. His success with *The Pajama Game* was followed by choreography for **Damn Yankees** (1955) and *New Girl in Town* (1957). With *Redhead* (1959) Fosse began to direct as well as choreograph. In the 1960s he staged a number of successful musicals, including ***Sweet Charity*** (1966). During the 1970s he created three unusual shows, closer in spirit to the **Sondheim–Prince** concept musicals: *Pippin* (1972),

Chicago (1975), and *Dancin'* (1978). Fosse's frequent use of small groups, jerky, rhythmic steps, and sinuous, slow-motion movement, often coupled with derby hats and white gloves, became his choreographic trademark. He also directed a number of films, including *Cabaret* and the autobiographical *All That Jazz.*   MK

> See: M. Gottfried, *All His Jazz: The Life and Death of Bob Fosse,* New York, 1990; K. Grubb, *Razzle Dazzle: The Life and Work of Bob Fosse,* New York, 1989.

Foster, Gloria (1936–   ) African-American actress noted for playing strong nonblack characters. In her **Off-Broadway** debut in the documentary collage *In White America* (1963), Foster won Obie and Vernon Rice awards. Playing the title role in **Robinson Jeffers**'s *Medea* at the Martinique Theatre (1965–6), she gained the *Theatre World* Award for her outstanding performance. She was Yerma at the **Vivian Beaumont Theatre** in 1966, and has appeared regularly at the **Public Theater** in such roles as Volumnia (*Coriolanus,* 1979), *Mother Courage* (1980), and the mother in *Blood Wedding* (1992). She has also appeared in significant film roles and on television.   EGH

Four Saints in Three Acts Four-act opera, with libretto by **Gertrude Stein** and music by Virgil Thomson; opened in Hartford and then in New York at the 44th Street Theatre on 20 February 1934. Although the story, which actually dealt with over a dozen saints, was almost impenetrable, the opera won critical acclaim. The production was noted for its all African-American cast and its scenery composed entirely of cellophane. Because of her success with this production, Stein became a celebrity and returned to America from France for a lecture tour. Two of Stein's most famous lines occur in the opera: "Pigeons on the grass alas" and "When this you see remember me."   FB

Fourteenth Street Theatre 105–109 West 14th St., NYC [Architect: Alexander Saeltzer]. Although it began as the Théâtre Français for the presentation of French-language drama and opera in New York, the house was known as the Fourteenth St. Theatre for most of its existence. After it opened in 1866, it embarked on an exceedingly rocky course as it changed owners, managers, and policy many times. It became, however, the only 19th-century playhouse to enjoy a renaissance late in its history. After being virtually abandoned in 1911, the actress **Eva Le Gallienne** rediscovered the 1,000-seat house in 1926 and installed the **Civic Repertory Company** in it, presenting well-cast, well-chosen plays in repertory at affordable prices for five years. After her departure, it was used only sporadically, and then razed in 1948.   MCH

> See: M. B. Steinberg, *The History of the Fourteenth Street Theatre,* New York, 1931.

Fox, Frederick (1910–91) Designer. Beginning at the Ivoryton Playhouse in Connecticut in the 1930s, Fox went on to design sets and costumes for over 200 Broadway productions and several at the Metropolitan Opera, including their premiere of

G. L. Fox as Humpty Dumpty. Photo: Gurney and Son, N.Y., 1868. Courtesy: Laurence Senelick.

Tosca (1965). Fox was one of the first stage designers to work in live television in the late 1940s and '50s. In the 1960s he began to work as an airport planning consultant.   AA

Fox, George Washington Lafayette (1825–77) Comedian who, after years of touring with the Fox–Howard clan (see **Howard family**), came into his own during his tenure at New York's National Theatre (1850–8), where his uproarious caricatures made him a favorite. He became influential in management by introducing his family's production of *Uncle Tom's Cabin,* with Fox in the role of Phineas Fletcher. He temporarily managed the Old **Bowery,** the New Bowery, and **Wallack**'s **Fifth Avenue,** losing as lessee what he earned as a comic star. Between 1862–7 he staged pantomimes at the Old Bowery, with himself as Clown and his brother Charles Kemble Fox as Pantaloon. More an expressive **mime** artist than an acrobat, Fox tempered the stage trickery of the **Ravel family** with his own antic drollery to create a purely American brand of pantomime. This culminated in the immensely successful *Humpty Dumpty* (Olympic Theatre, 1868), which ran for more than 1,200 performances. Fox also made a hit in burlesques of *Faust, Macbeth, Richelieu,* and **Edwin Booth**'s *Hamlet.* After recurring fits of insanity, he was forcibly removed from a performance in 1875

Eddie Foy and the Seven Little Foys making an appearance at the B. F. Keith Theatre, N.Y. Photo: White, N.Y. Courtesy: Laurence Senelick.

for committal to an asylum. Fox was reputed to be the funniest performer of his time; he contrived to raise American pantomime to a level of popularity it has never regained.   LS

> See: L. Senelick, *The Age and Stage of George L. Fox, 1825–1877*, Hanover, NH, 1988.

Foy, Eddie (1856–1928) Comedian and singer. Beginning as a child performer in **vaudeville,** Foy brought his acrobatic style of comedy and his amusing delivery of comic songs to musicals produced at the Chicago Opera House in 1889–90. His performance in *Bluebeard, Jr.* (1890) received praise in both **Chicago** and New York. After appearing as a featured performer in several other comic operas, Foy was hired as the principal comedian for *The Strollers* (1901). He starred in a number of musicals in the first decade of the 20th century, including *The Wild Rose* (1902), *Mr. Bluebeard* (1903), *Piff! Paff!! Pouf!!!* (1904), *The Earl and the Girl* (1905), *The Orchid* (1907), *Mr. Hamlet of Broadway* (1908), and *Up and Down Broadway* (1910). Always a popular favorite in vaudeville, Foy spent most of his time on the variety stage after 1910, when he began to include his children, billed as "The Seven Little Foys," in his act. He published his autobiography, *Clowning Through Life,* in 1928.   MK

Francesca da Rimini A five-act romantic tragedy by **George Henry Boker,** widely considered the best of its type by an American, but very nearly marking the end of the romantic tradition in America. Boker's version stresses the tragedy of a lonely and deformed Lanciotto who experiences love before being plunged into despair. E. L. Davenport starred in the 1855 premieres in New York and Philadelphia, but the production ran only briefly. Twenty-seven years later **Lawrence Barrett** staged the script after revising it substantially with **William Winter;** this version won great success in Philadelphia and Chicago before opening on 27 August 1883 in New York, and became a standard for Barrett. In 1901 **Otis Skinner** restaged the script in a production comparable to Barrett's.   SMA

Frankel, Gene (1923–   ) Director. Born in New York and educated at New York University, Frankel made his New York directing debut in 1949 with *They Shall Not Die,* followed closely in 1950 with *Nat Turner.* He received Obies for his direction of *Volpone* (1957) and *Machinal* (1960). Other important New York productions include *The Enemy of the People* (1959), *The Blacks* (1961), *Brecht on Brecht* (1962), *The Firebugs* (1963), *A Cry of Players* (1968), *To Be Young, Gifted and Black* (1969), and *Indians* (1969). Frankel has directed *The Blacks* at the Akademie der Kunst, Berlin, and at the Teatro la Fenice, Venice (1964). His production of *Oh, Dad, Poor Dad . . .* was seen at the Atelje 212 in Belgrade (1965). Other notable productions include *Pueblo* at the **Arena Stage** (1971) and a revival of The **Diary of Anne Frank** at the Hartman Theatre (1979). Founder of the Berkshire Theatre, Frankel is also artistic and executive director of the Gene Frankel Theatre Workshop in New York.   TLM

Franken, Rose (1895?–1988) Playwright and director whose best plays – *Another Language* (1932), *Claudia* (1941), *The Hallams* (1947) – appear to be domestic dramas aimed for the matinee crowd but are actually cold-eyed looks at the American family and the suffocation caused by love. She also wrote *Outrageous Fortune* (1943), which deals with homosexuality and anti-Semitism; *Doctors Disagree* (1943), examining the double standard; and *Soldier's Wife* (1944), about the problems caused when a husband returns from war.   FB

> See: R. Franken, *When All Is Said and Done; An Autobiography,* Garden City, New York, 1963.

Frankie and Johnny in the Clair de Lune by **Terrence McNally** was first produced by **Manhattan Theatre Club** Stage II at City Center in New York on 2 June 1987, with **Kathy Bates** as Frankie and **F. Murray Abraham** as Johnny. The production was transferred to the Westside Arts Theatre later in the year. The play depicts the tentative approach to a romantic relationship by two middle-aged people who have often been disappointed in the past: Frankie, a waitress whose humorously tough manner masks her emotional vulnerability, and Johnny, a cook who seems to have won a battle with alcoholism. During a night in a West Side apartment, Johnny, with the help of Debussy and moonlight, tries to persuade Frankie that good sex can still blossom into love. It was less successful as a 1991 film.   BCM

Frazee, Harry Herbert (1880–1929) Beginning as an usher in Peoria, IL, Frazee became a successful producer in the 1910s and '20s. His hits include *Madame Sherry* (1910); *Ready Money* (1912), with companies in London, Chicago, and New York; *A Pair of Sixes* (1914); *Nothing But the Truth* (1916); *Dulcey* (1921), with **George C. Tyler;** and *No, No, Nanette* (1925), an international success. *Yes, Yes, Yvette* (1927) failed dismally, ending his career. Frazee also owned theatres in Chicago and New York.   TLM

Freedley, Vinton (1891–1969) Producer who entered into management with **Alex A. Aarons** in 1923, together building the **Alvin Theatre,** which they operated until 1932. Their notable productions include the **Gershwin** musicals *Lady, Be Good* (1924), *Tip Toes* (1925), *Oh, Kay!* (1926), *Funny Face* (1927), and *Girl Crazy* (1930). Notable Freedley productions after 1932 include the **Cole Porter** musicals *Anything Goes* (1934), *Red, Hot, and Blue* (1936), and *Leave It to Me* (1938), as well as the unconventional *Cabin in the Sky* (1940). Freedley served as president of the **Actors' Fund of America,** the Episcopal Actors Guild, and the **American National Theatre Academy.** MR

Freedman, Gerald (1927–) Director and producer, born in Ohio and educated at Northwestern University. Freedman began his professional career in 1956 as an assistant for *Bells Are Ringing,* and made his New York directing debut in 1959 with the first revival of *On the Town.* In 1960 he began a long association with the **New York Shakespeare Festival** with an Obie-winning *Macbeth,* and served as artistic director during 1967–71. Other notable productions for the Festival include *Hair,* which opened the Public Theater in 1967, and *Hamlet* in 1972, starring **Stacy Keach, James Earl Jones,** and **Colleen Dewhurst.** He was co-artistic director of the **Acting Company** during 1974–7, with acclaimed productions of Sheridan's *School for Scandal* (1972), and Waldman and Uhry's *The Robber Bridegroom* (1975), which was transferred to Broadway. In 1978–9 Freedman was artistic director for the **American Shakespeare [Theatre]** Festival in Stratford, CT; in 1985 he was appointed artistic director of the Great Lakes Theatre Festival (his production there of *King Lear* with **Hal Holbrook** was at NYC's **Roundabout** in 1990); and in 1991 he also became Dean of the North Carolina School of the Arts. TLM

Freeman, Morgan (1937–) African-American actor first recognized as the Easy Reader character on public television's "Electric Company" (1971–6). He was the wino Zeke in the short-lived *The Mighty Gents* (1978), earning a Drama Desk Award as best newcomer of the Broadway season. He won Obies for his Coriolanus at the Public Theater (1979), for the Messenger in *The Gospel at Colonus* (1984), and for Hoke in the Pulitzer Prize–winning *Driving Miss Daisy* (1987). At the outdoor Delacorte Theater in 1990 he shared honors with Tracey Ullman in **A. J. Antoon**'s Wild West staging of *The Taming of the Shrew.* EGH

Free Southern Theatre Inspired by the goals of the civil rights movement, in 1963 John O'Neal, **Gilbert Moses,** and Doris Derby founded this company, with the support of **Richard Schechner,** to develop a theatre "as unique to the Negro people as . . . blues and jazz." With a home base in New Orleans, the South's first integrated theatre toured poor rural areas, giving free performances and theatre workshops. Although their aim was to promote black theatre for the **African-American** community, productions of *Waiting for Godot* and *Purlie Victorious* appealed more to white than

black audiences. The company was disbanded in 1980. LAB

See: T. Dent, *The Free Southern Theatre,* Indianapolis, 1970.

Friedman, Bruce Jay (1930–) Playwright. Born in the Bronx, educated at the University of Missouri, and primarily known as a writer of novels filled with his own particular brand of black humor, Friedman has ventured his talents into the theatre only twice. His first effort, *Scuba Duba* (1967), won the Obie Award for the outstanding **Off-Broadway** production of the season. Some critics have called this zany, jaundiced look at Jewish intellectual liberalism one of the best comedies of the decade. Friedman's other play, *Steambath* (1970), was an absurd comedy set in a steam room, later identified as Limbo, featuring God, personified by a Puerto Rican steambath attendant. Friedman was also one of the several contributors of sketches for *Oh, Calcutta!* (1969). LDC

Friml, Rudolf (1879–1972) Prague-born composer who studied music under Antonin Dvořák before coming to the U.S. in 1903. His first score for the musical stage was *The Firefly* (1912), which starred opera singer Emma Trentini. Over the next 20 years he composed the scores of numerous operettas and musical comedies, notably *Rose-Marie* (1924), *The Vagabond King* (1925), and *The Three Musketeers* (1928). Although several of his shows were written in collaboration with lyricist **Otto Harbach,** Friml worked with many other lyricists, including **P. G. Wodehouse, Oscar Hammerstein II,** and Brian Hooker. Throughout his long career as a composer for the American musical stage, Friml never abandoned his musical roots; his scores were heavily indebted to the traditions of European operetta. MK

Frohman, Charles (1860–1915) Producer-theatrical manager who, after a decade in theatrical business in various capacities, achieved his first major success as a producer with **Bronson Howard**'s *Shenandoah* (1889). In 1893 Frohman formed the **Empire Theatre** Stock Company, with **John Drew** as his leading actor. Frohman now began to develop and exploit the "star and combination" system: Members of his company would be made "stars" as quickly as possible and sent, with a supporting cast, on national tours after opening in a Frohman theatre in New York. Frohman successfully employed similar methods in London, principally at the Duke of York Theatre after 1898. Stars who benefited from Frohman's patronage included, among many others, **Maude Adams, William Gillette, Arnold Daly, Annie Russell, Margaret Anglin, Julia Marlowe, William H. Crane, Otis Skinner,** and John Drew and Ethel Barrymore [see **Drew–Barrymore family**]. In 1896, in association with Al Hayman, he joined **Mark Klaw** and **Abe Erlanger,** Fred Zimmerman, and Fred Nixon to organize a monopoly known as the Theatrical **Syndicate.** With the security and efficiency afforded by such control, Frohman produced many contemporary playwrights and helped many aspiring actors to achieve stardom, giving him significant influence in matters of taste and method in the commercial theatre. After 1896 he regularly produced over a dozen shows a year, including Wilde's *The Importance of Being Earnest* (1895), Gillette's **Secret Service** (1896, New York; 1897, London; 1900, Paris), Barrie's *The Little Minister* (1896, New York, with Maude Adams), **Fitch**'s *Barbara Frietchie* (1899, with Julia Marlowe), and Barrie's *Peter Pan* (1899, New York, with Maude Adams; 1904, London). Frohman died with the sinking of the *Lusitania* in 1915.   MR   DJW

See: I. Marcosson and D. Frohman, *Charles Frohman: Manager and Man*, New York, 1916.

Frohman, Daniel (1851–1940) Theatre manager. With his brothers, **Charles** and Gustave, Frohman first came to prominence as business manager in 1880 with **Steele MacKaye**'s organization at the **Madison Square Theatre**, where he developed the system of "auxiliary road companies" that toured the country while the original production was playing in New York. Frohman should be noted for his tenure as the producer-manager of the old **Lyceum Theatre** at 4th Avenue and its **stock company** from 1887 to 1902, and in the new Lyceum on 45th Street from 1902 until his retirement in 1909. Enlisting the talents of a fine acting company, from which **E. H. Sothern**'s career was launched and that over the years included **Henry Miller, William Faversham, Effie Shannon, Richard Mansfield, Maude Adams,** and **James H. Hackett,** Frohman presented a fashionable repertory from contemporary authors including **Clyde Fitch,** J. M. Barrie, A. W. Pinero, Henry Arthur Jones, Wilde, and Sardou. Notable productions that featured Sothern included *Lord Chumley* (1888), *The Charity Ball* (1889), and *The Prisoner of Zenda* (1895). The elaborate new Lyceum opened with Barrie's *The Admirable Crichton.* In 1899, Frohman began a four-year term as manager and lessee of **Daly's Theatre,** where he imported many musical comedies from London. Frohman served as president of the **Actors' Fund** from 1903 until his death in 1940. Through his association with the Famous Players–Lasky Film Company after 1912, he brought many theatre stars to the infant film industry.   MR

See: D. Frohman, *Memories of a Manager*, Garden City, NY, 1911; D. Frohman, *Daniel Frohman Presents*, New York, 1935; D. Frohman, *Encore*, New York, 1937.

Frontier theatre Just as the frontier has been described as the single most distinguished feature of American history, it also left a distinguishing mark on American theatre history. Theatre in America began in the early settlements on the eastern seaboard, the frontier of the New World; and after **Philadephia**, New York, and **Boston** became theatrical centers, troupes of actors advanced into the western regions quick on the heels of the pioneers.

The following pattern was repeated several times: A principal city developed as the transportation, supply, and finance center for a series of outlying communities in which the region's raw materials were exploited. If these outlying communities were sufficiently remote, intermediate supply towns developed as well. Theatre responded to this pattern: Permanent companies resided in large city theatres, and a dominant manager sent them on tour to the outlying communities. Intermediate towns were served in the same way, but on a more frequent basis.

The first theatre opened in Williamsburg, VA, in 1718; the second, the Dock Street in Charleston, SC, in 1736. When the Lewis Hallam company arrived from London in 1752, they performed in a new Williamsburg theatre. The **Hallams** and other troupes took to the road, found makeshift halls in such settlements as Annapolis, Norfolk, Newport, and Providence, and set the pattern for the western trek that was soon to follow.

Thespian societies were a part of the cultural life of Lexington (1799), Cincinnati (1801), and St. Louis (1815), even before professional troupes arrived. These troupes began their journey from Albany or Philadelphia to Pittsburgh, thence by flatboat down the Ohio River to Cincinnati and Louisville, and, as the frontier expanded, down the Mississippi to St. Louis, Memphis, Nashville, Montgomery, Mobile, and New Orleans.

The James Douglass troupe arrived in Lexington, Louisville, and Frankfort in 1810, and the **Samuel Drake** company in 1815. Typical of the accommodation they found was Luke Usher's Lexington theatre, a large room (30 × 60 ft) on the second floor of his brewery. Two actors in Drake's company, **Noah Ludlow** and **Sol Smith,** became the leading managers on the frontier, first as competitors and then as partners. Both wrote detailed first-hand accounts of their adventures: Ludlow's *Dramatic Life as I Found It* (1880) and Smith's *The Theatrical Journey* (1854) and *Theatrical Management in the South and West* (1868).

Cramped and improvised quarters were common: a stage 10 ft wide and 8 ft deep, a Memphis theatre where only the women could be seated, and another that had formerly been a livery stable. Even proper theatres like the Columbia Street in Cincinnati (1821), boasting a "spacious gallery," "commodious lobbies," and "two tiers of boxes," squeezed the stage and 800 spectators into a small area (40 × 100 ft). **James H. Caldwell** was the first to provide adequate facilities with his three New Orleans theatres: the **American** or Camp Street (1824), the St. Charles (1835), and a second St. Charles (1843). The Camp seated 1,100 on stuffed seats, had a proscenium opening of 38 ft, and was lighted with gas (Caldwell owned the gas works). The first **St. Charles** (said to be equaled in size and grandeur only by the opera houses in Naples, Milan, and St. Petersburg) seated 4,000 in a pit and had four tiers of boxes. It had a 55-ft proscenium opening and a central chandelier with 23,000 cut-glass drops lighted by 250 gas jets. When the theatre burned down (1842, a common occurrence; see **fires**), Caldwell built the second St. Charles, less ornate and seating 1,500, and turned the management over to Ludlow and Smith.

Frontier theatres were not all land-based. Showboating on the Ohio and Mississippi began early and continued into the 20th century, first with

Ludlow's *Noah's Ark* (1817), then with William Chapman's *Floating Palace* (1831). **Showboats** lured audiences with their calliopes and their picturesque names: *French's New Sensation, Snow Queen, Wonderland, Goldenrod, Cotton Blossom,* and *Majestic.*

Theatres appeared almost immediately after a community was settled; for example, **Chicago** (chartered 1837) got **John B. Rice**'s first theatre (1847), his second (1851), and **McVicker's** (1857).

Development of the trans-Mississippi West was similar to that of the East, but more extreme: Distance was greater, population shift more volatile, and wealth more instantaneous and abundant. While playing conditions were conventional in the cities and towns, they were primitive in the small settlements: Actors arrived by wagon and pack animal, often slept in the open, and performed in stores, houses, and tents. However crude the conditions, though, western audiences were noted for the prodigality of their response.

California was the first region to develop. Its pioneer period began in 1849 and had passed its peak by 1857. The principal city was **San Francisco,** and the outlying communities were the gold mining camps in the Sierra Nevada. In between were the towns of Marysville, Sacramento, and Stockton. During 1850–84 the Napoleon of California managers was **Tom Maguire,** an illiterate cab driver and saloon keeper. With only brief exceptions, he managed one or more theatres in the city, and at least one in each intermediate town, thereby ensuring a smooth flow of attractions to the gold mines during the summer and early fall. During 1859–67 the silver mines of Nevada's Washoe Valley became an extension of the California region, and Maguire used Virginia City as an intermediate town for them.

The West's second mining frontier began in 1857 along the eastern slopes of the Rocky Mountains near the South Platte River, and spread north and east with the gold strikes in Montana during the 1860s and in the Dakotas in the '70s. Denver was the region's city, and it was there that its most important manager, John Langrishe, first struck it rich. An actor seasoned by 15 years of barnstorming in the Mississippi Valley, Langrishe moved with his company in pursuit of bonanza: Denver (1859–67), Helena and Cheyenne (1867–71), and Deadwood (1876–9). The coming of the railroads divided this frontier into separate regions. Denver became the center of the Silver Circuit, which included the mining and resort towns of Colorado and the Mormon communities of Utah; it peaked under the management of Peter McCoart (1885–95). Montana and Wyoming were controlled by John Maguire (no relation to Tom), with its center in Helena (1884–1900), whereas the Dakotas developed their own identity under the management of C. P. "Con" Walker in Fargo after 1892.

Both the Northwest and Southwest waited for eastern rail links in the 1880s. Theatre followed population along the route of the Santa Fe Railroad in the Southwest. **Los Angeles,** where Henry T. Wyatt was the principal manager, became a theatrical center servicing adjacent regions: southern California, the central coast, the central valley, and Arizona–New Mexico. In the Northwest development followed the line of the northern Pacific, which terminated in **Seattle,** where Calvin Heilig and John Cort were the leading managers. A second center was Portland, which was on the way to San Francisco; John Howe was the principal manager there until the coming of the Theatrical **Syndicate.**

Western theatricals had two extensions beyond the continental U.S.: Players had passed through San Francisco to and from the British colonies since 1855, but the management of an American, James Cassius Williamson, in Sydney after 1879 developed the route from Honolulu to Cape Town. The West's final frontier was the Klondike region of Alaska, where there was a gold stampede from 1896 to 1910. Vancouver was the city for this region, and Dawson, Fairbanks, and Nome each had its turn as a principal town.

However unconventional playing conditions and audience behavior in the frontier theatres, productions were otherwise conventional. Each frontier saw the major actors of its day: **J. B. Booth, Edwin Forrest,** William Macready, **Edwin Booth, Anna Cora Mowatt, Joseph Jefferson III, Laura Keene, Tyrone Power, Lotta Crabtree, Adah Isaacs Menken, James Murdoch, George Hill, Dan Marble, John McCullough,** and others. These stars played their standard repertory of Shakespeare, old comedy, contemporary farce, and domestic and sensational melodrama in various permutations to suit the ability of the individual performer and the taste of the audience.   RM   DMcD

See: M. Berson, *The San Francisco Stage: From Gold Rush to Golden Spike, 1849–1869,* San Francisco, 1989; W. G. B. Carson, *The Theatre on the Frontier,* Chicago, 1932; P. Graham, *Showboats,* Austin, 1951; M. Henderson, *History of the Theatre in Salt Lake City,* Salt Lake City, 1941; H. Hoyt, *Town Hall Tonight,* New York, 1955; H. W. Koon, *How Shakespeare Won the West,* Jefferson, NC, 1989; P. C. Lewis, *Trouping,* New York, 1973; D. McDermott, *Theatre Survey* (May 1978); D. McDermott & R. Sarlós, eds., *Theatre West: Image and Impact,* Atlanta, GA, 1990; R. Moody, *America Takes the Stage,* Bloomington, 1955; M. Watson, *Silver Theatre: Amusements of the Mining Frontier in Early Nevada, 1850–1864,* Glendale, CA, 1964.

Front Page, The, by **Ben Hecht** and **Charles MacArthur** is one of America's most endearing comedies and has been revived in numerous productions since its Broadway premiere in 1928. Both authors had experience in the newspaper business, and this melodrama-farce drew liberally on the shenanigans in a big-city press room, where the reporters encounter con men, prostitutes, corrupt politicians, and a runaway convict. Laced with colloquial language and some profanity, the play was lauded for its authenticity in an era in which realism was prominent on the New York stage. The original production was supervised by **Jed Harris** and marked the directorial debut of **George S. Kaufman,** who became one of America's most successful dramatists. Among its featured performers were **Osgood Perkins, Lee Tracy,** and Dorothy Stickney. It ran for 281 performances at the Times Square Theatre. A wonderful revival featuring Robert Ryan, Bert Convy, **Helen Hayes,** and Dody Goodman played at the **Ethel Barry-**

Zakes Mokae, Zeljko Ivanek, and Danny Glover in the world premiere production of Athol Fugard's *Master Harold . . . and the Boys* at the Yale Repertory Theatre, April 1982. Photo: Gerry Goodstein. Courtesy: Yale Repertory Theatre.

more in the 1969–70 Broadway season. It was most recently revived at the **Vivian Beaumont** in 1986 with **Richard Thomas** and John Lithgow, directed by **Jerry Zaks.**   BBW

Front Street Theatre Founded in Memphis, TN, in 1957 by George Touliatos, this pioneer regional company first performed in an empty hotel swimming pool, then moved to a former moviehouse. Offering a wide variety of plays from Shakespeare and Beckett to Broadway musicals, the theatre struggled to find an audience. After Touliatos's departure in 1967, the company moved to Memphis State University, but closed within the year.   LAB

Fugard, Athol (1932–) South African playwright, director, and actor who, with the production of *A Lesson from Aloes* at the **Yale Repertory Theatre,** New Haven (1980), found a gifted and understanding collaborator in **Lloyd Richards,** then artistic director of the theatre. The production moved to Broadway and was followed by three world premieres at the Yale Rep: *Master Harold . . . and the Boys* (1982) also transferred to Broadway and won the Drama Critics' Circle Award; *The Road to Mecca* (1984) reached **Off-Broadway** in 1988; and *A Place with the Pigs* (1987) was produced in 1988 at London's National Theatre. In addition the Yale Rep staged revivals of Fugard's *Boesman and Lena, Hello and Goodbye,* and *The Blood Knot,* thereby ensuring Fugard an honored place on the contemporary American theatre scene. Fugard has acknowledged Richards's contribution in calling him "my artistic leader."   EGH

See: R. Vandenbroucke, *Truths the Hand Can Touch,* New York, 1985.

Fuller, Charles (1939–) African-American playwright. When *A Soldier's Play* (1981), dealing with the murder of an unpopular black army sergeant, received the Pulitzer Prize, Fuller was only the second black playwright to be so honored. Philadelphia-born Fuller had several plays produced **Off-Broadway,** notably by the **Negro En-**

semble Company, which nurtured his talent with productions of *In the Deepest Part of Sleep* (1974), *The Brownsville Raid* (1976), and the Obie Award–winning *Zooman and the Sign* (1980), as well as *A Soldier's Play,* which was turned into an absorbing film (*A Soldier's Story,* 1984). Since then, Negro Ensemble has produced other Fuller plays, including *Sally* and *Prince* (1988–9). Recently he has been working on a series of six plays about the post–Civil War quest for black self-determination; four have been produced at the NEC's Theatre Four to date, but have attracted little serious critical attention.   EGH

Funicello, Ralph (1947–) Designer. Though trained at NYU, since the mid-1970s he has designed primarily on the West Coast, where he has worked extensively with virtually every major theatre and is Director of Design at **American Conservatory Theatre.** Funicello's work is typified by an understated elegance that he brings to plays of diverse styles and periods.   AA

Funny Girl Two-act musical with book by Isobel Lennart, music by **Jule Styne** and lyrics by **Bob Merrill;** opened at the **Winter Garden Theatre** (26 March 1964) for 1,348 performances. Set around WW I, the musical tells the story of **Fanny Brice**'s rise to fame as a **Ziegfeld** star and her disastrous marriage to gambler Nick Arnstein. Songs include "People" and "Don't Rain on My Parade." Directed by **Garson Kanin** and supervised by **Jerome Robbins,** the show featured Kay Medford, **Jean Stapleton,** and Danny Meehan. Critical acclaim went to Barbra Streisand for her comic performance, in which she sang 11 of the show's 16 songs.   EK

Funnyhouse of a Negro **Adrienne Kennedy**'s first successful one-act play opened **Off-Broadway** in 1962 and won a 1964 Obie. *Funnyhouse* incorporates autobiographical elements in a surreal, poetic, and mythical work that portrays a disturbed state of mind rather than a lineal progression. The major character, Sarah, hallucinates and transforms into several alter egos, both male and female, black and white. Central to the play is her racial identity and the struggle inherent in being a black woman in a white world.   FB

Funny Thing Happened on the Way to the Forum, A Two-act musical comedy, music and lyrics by **Stephen Sondheim,** book by Burt Shevelove and **Larry Gelbart;** opened 8 May 1962 at the **Alvin Theatre,** running 964 performances. This bawdy romp patched together from the plays of Plautus, focusing on the efforts of the slave Pseudolus (**Zero Mostel**) to win his freedom, marked Sondheim's Broadway debut as composer as well as lyricist. The songs tend to comment on rather than further the story and sometimes seem ironic "serious relief" from the farcical book scenes. The production was directed by **George Abbott,** although **Jerome Robbins** (uncredited) was brought in to "doctor" the production, to which he added the opening "Comedy Tonight" sequence. The show, Abbott's last Broadway hit, won the Tony for best musical and had a successful

London production (1963) and New York revival with **Phil Silvers** (1972, Tony).   JD

Futz This Obie Award–winning play by **Rochelle Owens** about a man in love with a pig treats society's fickle standards of morality and need for scapegoats. Given one performance 10 October 1965 at the Tyrone Guthrie Workshop, Minnesota Theatre Company, it was then presented 1 March 1967 at the **La MaMa,** New York. **Tom O'Horgan** gave the piece an energetic staging and supplied original music. After raising controversy at the Edinburgh Festival, it reopened in at the Theatre de Lys 13 June 1968. In 1991 La MaMa revived it with O'Horgan once more directing.   KF

Fyles, Franklin (1847–1911) Drama critic and playwright. Born in Troy, NY, Fyles began as a reporter on the *Troy Budget,* moving in the late 1860s to the New York *Sun,* where he became a star reporter (1875) and drama critic (1885–1903). With an eye toward the popular market, he wrote eight melodramas, four in collaboration with others, including *The Girl I Left Behind Me* (1893) with **David Belasco.** Fyles also wrote *The Theatre and Its People* (1900).   TLM

G

Gabriel, Gilbert W. (1890–1952) Drama critic. Born in Brooklyn and educated at Williams College, Gabriel began his career with the *New York Evening Sun* in 1912, serving as music critic during 1917–24. He was theatre critic of the *Telegram-Mail* (1924–5); the *Evening Sun* (1925–9); and the *New York American* (1929–37). After WW II, he served as drama critic of *Theatre Arts* and *Cue* (1949–52). Gabriel's lively prose entertained as well as informed readers. TLM

Gaige, Crosby (né Roscoe Conkling Gaige) (1882–1949) A partner of producers **Edgar and Archibald Selwyn**, Gaige coordinated financing for new Selwyn and Company theatres in New York and Chicago. He produced or coproduced (with the Selwyns and **Jed Harris**) about 150 plays, most notably **George S. Kaufman**'s *The Butter and Egg Man* (1925), Kaufman's only solo full-length play, and the biggest hit of the 1928–9 Broadway season, *Little Accident,* by Floyd Dell and Thomas Mitchell. Gaige retired in 1937, then developed another career in food dehydration and culinary arts. His memoir, *Footlights and Highlights,* was published in 1948. WD

Galati, Frank (1943–) Actor, director, playwright, adapter, and educator. A professor of Performance Studies at Northwestern University, where he earned his PhD in 1971, Galati's professional work bridges the worlds of theatre, opera, literature, and film. Schooled in the theories of Chamber Theatre pioneer Robert Breen, he has continued and extended Breen's work through adaptations of texts by **Gertrude Stein** (in *She Always Said, Pablo*), **John Steinbeck** (*The Grapes of Wrath,* for which he won a Tony), and the novels of Anne Tyler (filmscript for *The Accidental Tourist*). Galati began his professional career as a popular Chicago actor (notably in the **Wisdom Bridge** production of Stoppard's *Travesties*), but in the 1980s turned to directing theatre and opera. In 1986 he joined the **Steppenwolf Theatre Company** and became Associate Director of the **Goodman Theatre.** SF

Gale, Zona (1874–1938) Playwright and regionalist writer whose dramatization of her novel *Miss Lulu Bett* won the Pulitzer Prize in 1921. Gale dramatized her other novels – *Faint Perfume* (1934); *Birth,* produced as *Mr. Pitt* (1924); and *The Neighbors* (1917), a one-act play based on her "Friendship Village" stories – but had no other hits. FB

See: A. Derleth, *Still Small Voice: The Biography of Zona Gale,* New York, 1940; H. Simonson, *Zona Gale,* New York, 1962.

Gallagher, Helen (1926–) Actress, singer, and dancer. Energetic and versatile, Gallagher began in the chorus and rose to lead actress. She made her Broadway debut in *The Seven Lively Arts* (1947), attracted attention in *High Button Shoes* (1947), and received Tonys for *Pal Joey* (1952) and *No, No, Nanette* (1971 revival). She became known for replacing original musical stars, as in *Sweet Charity* (1966), or appearing in revivals. Gallagher developed a cabaret act and performed in straight dramas (*Hothouse,* 1974; *The Gingerbread Lady,* 1977; *Money Talks,* 1990). In the 1970s she joined the television serial "Ryan's Hope" (Emmys – 1976, 1977, 1987). REK

Gallagher and Shean Vaudeville team. Straight man **Ed[ward] Gallagher** (1873?–1929) and comic **Al[bert] Shean (né Schoenberg)** (1868–1949) formed a team in 1910 after years with other partners. For four years they appeared in vaudeville, burlesque, and revues; they then parted, reunited in 1920, and subsequently gained tremendous success, highlighted by 67 weeks in the *Ziegfeld Follies.* An entire routine and career was built around one theme song ("Absolutely, Mr. Gallagher?" "Positively, Mr. Shean"). The team dissolved in 1925, though Shean continued as a character actor on stage and in films. Shean's nephews, the **Marx Bros.,** were given much support by their uncle early in their careers. DBW

Gallo, Paul (1953–) A versatile lighting designer, Gallo has worked on over 200 shows on Broadway, **Off-Broadway,** and at most major regional theatres. He has done several with director **Jerry Zaks,** including revivals of *The House of Blue Leaves* (1986) and *The Front Page* (1986), as well as *Six Degrees of Separation* (1990). He has also collaborated with **Martha Clarke** on most of her works. AA

Garber, Victor (1949–) Canadian-born actor (debut, *Godspell,* Toronto, 1966). A versatile actor "[who] exudes a kind of unassuming self-assurance that commands rather than demands attention," Garber plays classics (*You Never Can Tell* [1986], *Ghosts* [1988, *Theatre World* Award]); contemporary dramas and farces (*Deathtrap* [1978, Tony nomination], Shue's *Wenceslas Square* [1988, Obie], Ludwig's *Lend Me a Tenor* [1989, Tony nomination], Nelson's *Two Shakespearean Actors* [as **Edwin Forrest,** 1991]); and musicals (*Sweeney Todd* [1978]; *Little Me* [1982, Tony nomination]). He also appeared in the film of *Godspell* (1973) and in television specials, including "Valley Forge" (Hallmark Hall of Fame, 1975), **Ah, Wilderness!** (PBS, 1976), and "Liberace: Behind the Music" (title role, 1988). REK

Gardenia (né Scognamiglio), Vincent (1922–92) Italian-born actor who made his professional debut in 1935 and his Broadway debut (*The Visit*) in 1958. Gardenia appeared in *Machinal* (Obie, 1960), *Little Murders* (1969; film, 1971), *The Prisoner of Second Avenue* (Tony, 1971), **Bennett's** *Ballroom* (1978), and *Breaking Legs* (1991). He had acted on television since 1955 and film since 1960 (*Murder, Inc.*); other films included *Little Shop of Horrors* (1986) and *Moonstruck* (1988, Oscar nomination). REK

Gardner, Herb (1934–) Brooklyn-born playwright and author of a successful syndicated cartoon (*The Nebbishes*). In 1962 *A Thousand Clowns* ran for 428 performances at the **Eugene O'Neill Theatre** and was adapted into a successful film, for which Gardner earned an Academy Award nomination. As a New Yorker he considers Broadway his "neighborhood," and his plays are firmly rooted in urban life. *The Goodbye People* (1968) takes place on Coney Island, and *I'm Not Rappaport* (1985) in Central Park. The latter, a poignant and comic study of aging in America, was a success on Broadway and in London, winning the 1986 Tony Award. Gardner's most recent work, *Conversations with My Father* (1991), an autobiographical study exploring ethnic identity in America, premiered at the **Seattle Rep** before moving to New York in 1992. BBW

Garland, Hamlin (1860–1940) An early realist in American fiction who with **William Dean Howells** promoted the "radical" Ibsen drama in the 1890s, and defended **James A. Herne**'s *Margaret Fleming* from charges that it was immoral. Neither his realistic plays about contemporary social problems nor his attempt to establish a Boston independent theatre movement met with success. He remains known for his short stories, *Main-Travelled Roads* (1891), and his autobiography, *A Son of the Middle Border* (1917). TLM

Garrick Theatre 63–67 West 35th St., NYC [Architect: Francis H. Kimball]. In 1890, **Edward Harrigan** built his own theatre just above Herald Square and named it after himself. After five years, he relinquished the house to **Richard Mansfield**, who changed its name to the Garrick by having his signmaker revise the letters at a minimum cost and effort. In 1896, the Garrick changed hands again and was leased to **Charles Frohman** until his death in 1915. When it looked as if the house would be torn down, it was rescued by the millionaire-philanthropist **Otto Kahn,** who installed Jacques Copeau's Théâtre du Vieux Colombier there in 1917. Two years later, he placed it at the disposal of the infant **Theatre Guild,** in whose hands it remained until it built its own theatre in 1925. Within a few years, it descended into cheap burlesque and gradual abandonment as a theatre. In 1932, after extensive fire damage, it was razed for safety purposes. MCH

Gassner, John Waldhorn (1903–67) Anthologist, editor, critic, educator. Born in Hungary and educated at Columbia University (1925), Gassner climaxed a distinguished teaching career at Yale University (1956–67), where he was Sterling Professor of Playwriting and Dramatic Literature; he also served on the Pulitzer Prize drama jury (1957–63). His essays appeared in *New Republic, Atlantic Monthly,* **Theatre Arts,** and other publications; but he established his reputation with more than 20 books, including anthologies of American and world drama, a history of dramatic literature (*Masters of the Drama*, 1940), and works on theory and criticism (*Form and Idea in Modern Theatre,* 1956; *Directions in Modern Theatre and Drama,* 1963). TLM

Gaxton, William (né Arturo Gaxiola) (1893–1963) Broadway and Hollywood musical star remembered today for his stage roles as President John P. Wintergreen in *Of Thee I Sing* (1932) and Billy Crocker in *Anything Goes* (1936). In these and many other musical roles, he was noted for his ability to sell a song. Like **Victor Moore,** with whom he was frequently teamed, he began his career in vaudeville. Notable film musicals featuring Gaxton include *Fifty Million Frenchmen* (1931, adapted from the stage musical in which he had starred in 1929) and the extravagant *Diamond Horseshoe* (1945). MR

Gay and lesbian theatre An offshoot of the Gay Liberation movement that must be distinguished from the mere appearance of homosexuals in drama. Before the 1960s, male "deviants" were depicted as flamboyant effeminates (**Mae West**'s *The Drag,* 1927; *The Pleasure Man,* 1928), destructive decadents (Mordaunt Shairp's *The Green Bay Tree,* 1933), or curable hypersensitives (**Robert Anderson**'s *Tea and Sympathy,* 1953). Lesbians were shown as predatory, doomed, or both, as in Edouard Bourdet's *The Captive* (1926) and **Lillian Hellman**'s *The Children's Hour* (1934).

The proliferation of experimental theatre **Off-Broadway** in the 1950s and the "Sexual Revolution" of the 1960s enabled homosexual playwrights, actors, and directors to address their own problems and constituencies, at a time when more conspicuous fellow-travelers like **Tennessee Williams, William Inge, Carson McCullers,** and **Edward Albee** avoided or downplayed these matters. Foremost was the **Caffe Cino** in Greenwich Village (1960–7), which nurtured such dramatists as Robert Patrick, William Hoffman, and Doric Wilson.

The watershed play, however, was a Broadway offering, *The Boys in the Band* (1968) by Mart Crowley. Although it perpetuated the idea that the "only happy homosexual is a dead homosexual," it was novel in putting him center stage and uncovering subcultural folkways to the general public. Its success prompted a flood of similar confessional dramas, usually about drag queens. Token swishy types appeared in a number of commercial farces, though gay dramatists attempted to infuse the form with insider knowledge (James Kirkwood's *P.S. Your Cat is Dead,* 1975; **Terrence McNally**'s *The Ritz,* 1975). This trend culminated in *Torch Song Trilogy* (1983) by **Harvey Fierstein,** a shrewd blend of soap opera, Simonized sitcom, and drag queen as clown variant. These three plays had evolved **Off-Off Broadway** and then transferred successfully to win a Tony Award.

Even before this profusion, the critical animosity of such widely read pundits as **Stanley Kauffmann** and Howard Taubman had posited a homosexual conspiracy in the theatre that "often poisons what you see and hear." They argued that such playwrights camouflaged their concerns as heterosexual relationships; implicit was a paranoia that show business from costuming to producing was controlled by "perverts." Although LeRoi Jones's (**Amiri Baraka**'s) *The Toilet* (1964) suggested a love-truce between a battered white "queer" and a black youth, the black activist theatre movement of the 1960s was also hostile; typical is the portrayal of the "bull dyke" in **Ed Bullins**'s *Clara's Ole Man* (1965).

The mainstream remained true to form: It welcomed Martin Sherman's *Bent* (1978), a historical play about Nazi persecution, and the glitzy drag musical *La Cage Aux Folles* (1983), but had no time for Alan Bowne's *Forty-Deuce* (1981), an unflinching portrayal of teen-aged hustlers in contemporary Times Square. Still, by the late 1970s, a number of prominent playwrights, themselves gay, could present gay characters as normal features of the American landscape: for example, Robert Patrick in *Kennedy's Children* (1973), **Lanford Wilson** in *The Fifth of July* (1978) and *Burn This* (1987), and **Albert Innaurato** in *Gemini* (1977).

The first gay **revue**s for general consumption were flashy commercial enterprises like *In Gay Company* (1975); more vital was the explosion of transvestite theatre that emerged from urban subculture. Gender-benders like the Cockettes and the Angels of Light in San Francisco and Centola and Hot Peaches in New York combined shock tactics, high camp, glitter rock, and reverse glamour to achieve their effects [see **female/male impersonation**]. Andy Warhol's Factory nurtured drag actor Jackie Curtis and scenarist **Ronald Tavel.** An important hothouse was John Vaccaro's **Theater of the Ridiculous,** which bred one major talent in the person of **Charles Ludlam;** his plays are virtual palimpsests, juxtaposing classical allusions and pilferings from pop art. His influence was strong upon such epigones as Charles Busch, whose plays are less literate, less threatening, and more reliant on pop culture than Ludlam's. There was also a short fad for gay musicals: Al Carmines's *The Faggot* (1973) and *Boy Meets Boy* by Bill Solly and Donald Ward (1975).

Gay producing companies – such as TOSOS (The Other Side of the Stage, 1972–7), founded by Doric Wilson; The Stonewall Theatre; The Glines (1976–82), founded by John Glines; and the Meridian Gay Theatre (1982), founded by Terry Miller and Terry Helbing – were dedicated to promoting plays about the gay experience for gay audiences. The proliferation of similar troupes in other cities (**Theatre Rhinoceros,** San Francisco; Diversity,

Houston; Lionheart, Chicago; Triangle, Boston; Alice B., Seattle) led to the 1978 creation of a network, the Gay Theatre Alliance, which held its first festival in 1980.

Feminist theatre groups inspired a score of lesbian ensembles, among them the Lavender Cellar in Minneapolis (founded 1973), the Red Dyke Theatre in Atlanta (1974), and the Lesbian-Feminist Theater Collective of Pittsburgh (founded 1977). Although producing plays by Pat Surcicle, Joan Schenkar, and Jane Chambers, whose *Last Summer at Bluefish Cove* (1980) became a repertory staple, they emphasized satiric revue. This was especially so in New York's West Village, where the WOW Café , founded by Peggy Shaw and Lois Weaver in 1982, featured Alice Forrester's subversive parody *Heart of the Scorpion* and **Holly Hughes**'s self-regarding satire *The Well of Horniness* (both 1985).

The **AIDS** crisis called forth a number of nonce dramas, modern versions of the problem play, where the message is more important than the medium: Larry Kramer's *The Normal Heart,* William M. Hoffman's *As Is,* Rebecca Ranson's *Warren,* Robert Chesley's *Night Sweat,* Theatre Rhinoceros's *The AIDS Show,* as well as the five-man political revue *The United Fruit Company* (all 1985). AIDS also affected the theatre by decimating its workers, whose deaths reveal how dependent the performing arts are on talented homosexuals.

Currently, the most original and powerful voices can be heard in performance art determined to go "beyond camp." The refusal of the NEA to fund Holly Hughes, Tim Miller, and John Fleck, artists conspicuous for their anarchic irreverence, and the ban on Chesley's radio play *Jerker* indicate that society at large is closing its ears to minority voices. Despite this opposition, the voices have diversified: Evan Smith speaks for Catholic high-school students (*Remedial English,* 1989); Jim Grimsley deals with the pressures of Southern environments (*Mr. Universe,* 1990); Tony Kushner's *Millennium Approaches* (1990) is a Dos Passos–like montage of recent American life; and Janny Becker's *The Story of Bruce* (1991) is aimed at the mental health community. **African-American**s are served by Cheryl West's *Before It Hits Home* (1990) and the satiric trio *Pomo Afro Homos.* The voices are too many and too loud to be easily stilled.   LS

See: S. Brecht, *Queer Theatre,* Frankfurt am Main, 1978; J. Clum, *Acting Gay,* New York, 1992; K. Curtin, *"We Can Always Call Them Bulgarians": The Emergence of Lesbians and Gay Men on the American Stage,* Boston, 1987; N. de Jongh, *Not in Front of the Audience: Homosexuality on Stage,* London/New York, 1992; T. Helbing, *Gay Theater Alliance Directory of Gay Plays,* New York, 1980.

Gayler, Charles (1820–92) Playwright and actor who, after forsaking law to act the title roles of *Hamlet* and *Othello* in Ohio theatres, brought his first play, *The Buckeye Gold Hunters* (1849), to his native New York. Thereafter, he acted, reviewed plays, and wrote, according to contemporary estimates, some 200 tragedies, comedies, melodramas, and operettas. Among his romantic plays were *The Love of a Prince* (1857) and *The Son of Night* (1857). *Bull Run; or, The Sacking of Fairfax Courthouse* was performed in New York on 21 July 1861, less than a month after the event. Further evidence of Gayler's commercial interest in popular subjects is shown in his play titles: *Taking the Chances; or, Our Cousin from the City* (1856), *Our Female American Cousin, Fritz Our German Cousin,* and *Lights and Shadows of New York.* WJM

Geer (né Ghere), Will (1902–78) Actor and director who first acted professionally with **Sothern** and **Marlowe**'s Shakespearean Repertory Company while a student at the University of Chicago (1924). He was active in left-wing theatre in the 1930s, notably with Theatre of Action and the Actors' Repertory Theatre, and he played "Mister Mister" in *The Cradle Will Rock* (1938). Stints with the **American Shakespeare Festival** (Stratford, CT) and the APA (**Association of Producing Artists**) punctuated starring and supporting appearances in theatres on both coasts, in motion pictures and on television. From 1933 he operated the weekends-only Folksay Theater in Los Angeles and taught pre-Shakespearean folklore. He is best known as Grandpa in the long-running television series, "The Waltons." WD

Geiogamah, Hanay (1945?–) Playwright, director, producer. In 1972, Geiogamah founded the first all-Indian repertory company – the American Indian Theatre Ensemble (now the **Native American** Theatre Ensemble). With **Ellen Stewart**'s support, this troupe developed traditional myths and contemporary plays for Indian audiences, working to rekindle ethnic pride. Geiogamah's plays include the nightmarish *Body Indian* (1972) and a musical, *49* (1982). In 1987, he became director of the newly founded American Indian Dance Theatre, which performs an intertribal repertory, both authentic and theatrical. TH-S

Gelbart, Larry (1923–) Chicago-born playwright who has also written for radio, television, and film. He began with comic sketches while still in his teens, and in 1958 won an Emmy for an "Art Carney Special." In 1963 he and Burt Shevelove were awarded a Tony for *A Funny Thing Happened on the Way to the Forum,* and in 1975 he won the distinguished Peabody Award for the television series "M★A★S★H." Gelbart is one of America's most respected comic writers; his theatre credits include *Sly Fox* (1976), *Mastergate* (1989), *Power Failure* (1990), *Feats of Clay* (1991), and the highly praised *City of Angels.* Among his film credits are *Oh, God* (1977) and *Tootsie* (1982), both of which earned him Oscar nominations. BBW

Gemini Set in the backyards of adjoining rowhouses in South Philadelphia, this two-act comedy by **Albert Innaurato** presents the boisterous Italian Geminiani family and their equally colorful Jewish/Irish neighbors. Francis Geminiani, on vacation from Harvard, experiences conflicting feelings about his working-class background, sexual identity, and life in general when two upper-class WASP friends from school arrive unexpectedly on the eve of his 21st birthday. First performed in a workshop production at **Playwrights Horizons** and later at PAF Playhouse, Huntington, NY, *Gemini* was produced at **Circle Repertory Company** (13 March 1977), directed by Peter Mark Schifter, and helped to win Innaurato an Obie Award for distinguished playwriting. It then moved to Broadway's **Little Theatre** (21 May 1977), where it ran until 5 September 1981. KF

Gennero, Peter (1924–) Choreographer for theatre and television. Gennero defined his own style of modern jazz. He was featured in the "Steam Heat" dance from *The Pajama Game* (1954), partnering Carol Haney in **Bob Fosse**'s choreography. Gennero formed the Peter Gennero Dancers, who performed on television variety shows, while Gennero continued to work on Broadway [see **dance**]. He assisted **Jerome Robbins** in *West Side Story* (1957) and choreographed *The Unsinkable Molly Brown* (1960), the revival of *Irene* (1973), and *Annie* (1978). Gennero has also worked at **Radio City Music Hall** as producer and resident choreographer. LF

George (née Doughtery), Grace (1879–1961) Actress, manager, director, translator/adapter. This petite comic actress's greatest success was Cyprienne in Sardou's *Divorçons* (1907). In 1911 she opened The **Playhouse,** built by her husband, producer **William A. Brady.** In 1915–16 she managed a repertory season there that included the U.S. premiere of **Shaw**'s *Major Barbara* (1915, in the title role) and *Captain Brassbound's Conversion* (1916, as Lady Cicely Waynflete). George sometimes appeared in plays she translated or adapted; in 1929 she demonstrated her skill as director (and star) in *The First Mrs. Fraser,* which ran for 352 performances. Her final performance was with **Katharine Cornell** in *The Constant Wife* (1951). DBW

George M. Cohan's Theatre 1482 Broadway, NYC [Architect: George Keister]. Even by Broadway's standards, the active life of George M. Cohan's Theatre was brief. Built in 1911 for the musical comedy star, then at his peak, it was part of the Fitzgerald building, which also housed Gray's Drugstore, for years a gathering place for unemployed actors. **Joe Leblang,** who ran a shoeshine stand at the rear of the drugstore, also dealt quite successfully in cut-rate producers' leftover tickets: He bought the drugstore and, eventually, the building and the theatre. During the Depression the theatre was leased for movies; in 1938, the entire building was razed. MCH

Gerard, Rolf (1909–) Set and costume designer and painter. Born in Berlin, he emigrated to England in 1936 and to the U.S. after WW II. He made his Broadway debut in 1949; his later sets include *Irma La Douce* (1959) and *Tovarich* (1963), but his primary work was for the Metropolitan Opera, where he designed sets and costumes for 18 productions over 30 years. AA

Germania Theatre Company A New York, German-speaking company organized in 1872 by Adolf Neuendorff with the objective of improving ensemble quality and emphasizing classical repertory. The company, comprising many former **Stadt Theater Company** actors, occupied Tammany Hall on 14th Street near Third Avenue until 1881, and the old **Wallack's Theatre** (Broadway and 13th Street) until 1883. Neuendorff introduced German actors to America, including Magda Irschick (1879), **Fanny Janauschek** (1873), Karl Sontag (1881), Friedrich Haase (1882), and **Heinrich Conried.** Contrary to Neuendorff's intent, the repertory offered primarily comedies, folk plays, and operettas. Competition from Conried's **Thalia Theater** forced Neuendorff to close. RE

See: R. Engle in *American Theatre Companies, 1749–1887,* ed. W. Durham, Westport, CT, 1986.

Gershwin, George (1898–1937) and **Ira** (1896–1983) Composer and lyricist. George's first connections with the musical stage were as a song-plugger and rehearsal pianist. In 1918 he teamed up with his brother Ira, who had written prose and verse for various periodicals, to write their first song, "The Real American Folk Song." A year later, George collaborated with lyricist Irving Caesar on one of the most popular songs of the day, "Swanee." For their first ventures in musical theatre, the brothers worked with other collaborators, George contributing songs to *La-La-Lucille!* (1919), ***Morris Gest's** Midnight Whirl* (1919), and the 1920–4 editions of ***George White's** Scandals,* while Ira wrote lyrics for *Two Little Girls in Blue* (1921). George's early show music was steeped in the idioms of jazz, a form he had learned from listening to black musicians. In 1924 the brothers collaborated on *Lady, Be Good,* a musical starring **Fred and Adele Astaire.** Encouraged by the show's success, the Gershwins turned out a number of other popular 1920s musicals, including *Oh, Kay!* (1926), *Funny Face* (1927), and *Rosalie* (1928). Their songs of the 1920s were characterized by George's infectious, driving music and Ira's clever, slangy lyrics.

In the early 1930s, the Gershwins created three satirical musicals, ***Strike Up the Band*** (1930), ***Of Thee I Sing*** (1931), and ***Let 'Em Eat Cake*** (1933). Acclaimed for its trenchant political satire and good-humored score, *Of Thee I Sing* was the first musical to be awarded the Pulitzer Prize for Drama. The brothers did not totally abandon more lighthearted forms of musical comedy, however. *Girl Crazy* (1930) had a frivolous book, but contained some of the Gershwins' best songs, such as "I Got Rhythm" and "Embraceable You."

In 1935 the **Theatre Guild** produced the Gershwins' "American folk opera" ***Porgy and Bess.*** Receiving mixed reviews from both drama and music critics, the original production of *Porgy and Bess* was not a success. Nevertheless, its magnificent score has proven to be the Gershwins' most enduring work.

After George's untimely death in 1937, Ira collaborated with other composers. ***Lady in the Dark*** (1941), which had a score by **Kurt Weill,** was innovative in confining its musical numbers to a few elaborate dream sequences. *The Firebrand of Florence* (1945), which Weill also composed, and *Park Avenue* (1946), with a score by **Arthur Schwartz,** were failures. In addition to composing

for the musical stage, the Gershwins wrote a number of motion picture scores, and George also composed for the concert hall.

As a composer, George Gershwin helped to popularize jazz on the musical stage in the 1920s. His more serious compositions for the concert hall prepared him to write *Porgy and Bess,* one of the most ambitious scores ever created for the American musical theatre. Ira's abilities as a lyricist also grew from the facile rhyming of his 1920s songs to the deeper, more eloquent style of his later work. Together, the Gershwins were major forces in raising the level of musical theatre composition. MK

See: I. Gershwin, *Lyrics on Several Occasions,* New York, 1959; E. Jablonski and L. D. Stewart, *The Gershwin Years,* rev. ed., Garden City, NY, 1973; E. Jablonski, *Gershwin, A Biography,* New York, 1987; A. Kendall, *George Gershwin: A Biography,* London, 1987; R. Kimball and A. Simon, *The Gershwins,* New York, 1973; D. Rosenberg, *Fascinating Rhythm: The Collaboration of George and Ira Gershwin,* New York, 1991.

Gershwin Theatre 1633 Broadway, NYC [Architects: Theatre Planning Associates, **Ralph Alswang**]. Originating as the Uris Theatre, this was the first large Broadway playhouse to be built under relaxed zoning constraints in the building code that permitted theatres to be incorporated within commercial structures. Erected by the Uris Corporation, the 1,900-seat theatre is under long-term lease to the **Nederlander** Organization and Eugene Ostreicher. It opened in 1972 with a spectacular but unsuccessful rock musical; since then, its policy has fluctuated between musical productions and a series of concert appearances of well-known popular performers, dance presentations, and opera productions. In 1979, it received its first critical success with *Sweeney Todd,* the **Stephen Sondheim** musical. In 1983, it was renamed the Gershwin Theatre in honor of **George and Ira Gershwin.** The theatre also encompasses the Theatre Hall of Fame within its spacious public areas. MCH

Gerstein (née Gersten), Bertha (1894–1972) Yiddish actress, born in Cracow and educated in America. She moved when young from vaudeville to drama, playing often with the **Yiddish Art Theatre,** Philadelphia's **Arch Street Theatre,** and on tour, often opposite **Jacob Ben-Ami.** NS

Gest, Morris (1881–1942) Russian-born producer who specialized in promoting foreign talent and in producing opulent spectacles at the Manhattan Opera House (1914–20) and **Century Theatre** (1917–19). Gest and his partner, **F. Ray Comstock,** imported the Ballet Russe from Paris, and the *Chauve-Souris* revue, featuring Nikita Balieff. They produced the 1923–4 tour of the **Moscow Art Theatre,** the 1924 production of **Max Reinhardt**'s *The Miracle,* and the 1925 tour of the Moscow Art Theatre Musical Theatre Studio, under the direction of Vladimir Nemirovitch-Danchenko. After ending his partnership with Comstock in 1928, Gest sponsored the U.S. visit of Aleksandër Moisiu, Reinhardt's leading actor, and he brought the Freiburg Passion Play to the U.S.   WD

Getting Gertie's Garter by **Avery Hopwood** and Wilson Collison. Typical of the sex farces so popular in the late teens and early 1920s, this play, produced by **A. H. Woods,** opened on 1 August 1921. Although not as long-running as Collison and **Otto Harbach**'s *Up in Mabel's Room,* its myriad doors, physical vicissitudes, naughty tone, and traditional morals are emblematic of the type. On her wedding night Gertie is confronted by Ken, an old flame, who is adamant about securing the return of a garter bearing his photograph. The incriminating garter remains upon Gertie's person until she loses it, causing endless difficulties as the item passes from one confused character to another. The most suggestive action transpires in the hayloft, where a shrieking wife loses her clothes.   RHW

Getting Out Marsha Norman's first play premiered at **Actors Theatre of Louisville** (1977), where it was cowinner of the Great American Play Contest. Directed by **Jon Jory** and featuring Susan Kingsley, it opened at the Phoenix Theatre before beginning an eight-month run at Theatre de Lys (1979). The realistic play focuses on the divided character of Arlene (as a child and a young adult). It explores a female criminal's reentry into society, assisted by a former inmate and neighbor, Ruby. Hampered by their "rehabilitation," the two women confront their anger and natural wariness in order to survive their prisonlike existence outside a formal prison. The play won the Oppenheimer Award, John Gassner Playwrighting Medallion, and American Theatre Critics' Association Citation.   TH-S

Gibbs, Wolcott (1902–58) Drama critic. A native New Yorker, Gibbs joined the *New Yorker* in 1927 as copyreader, and became associate editor (1928) and editorial writer (1937) before succeeding **Robert Benchley** as drama critic (1940–58). Gibbs was often criticized by actors and playwrights for his caustic comments, and gained the reputation of leaving the theatre after the first act of plays he disliked. His comedy *Season in the Sun* (1950) ran on Broadway for 367 performances.   TLM

Gibson, William (1914–) Playwright who first made it to Broadway with *Two for the Seesaw* (1958), scoring again in 1959 with a stage adaptation of his television play, *The **Miracle Worker.*** This uncompromising account of Annie Sullivan's struggle to teach the deaf and blind Helen Keller the power of words is now firmly established as a modern American standard. No other Gibson play, including *Miracle Worker*'s sequel, *Monday After the Miracle* (1982), has come close to the success of his first two. He is also the author of *The Seesaw Log: A Chronicle of the Stage Production,* an agonizing account of the compromises necessitated by the collaborative nature of American commercial theatre.   LDC

Gilbert, John (Gibbs) (1810–89) Actor famous for comic roles in classic English comedy. Gilbert,

born in Boston, made his debut there at the **Tremont Theatre** as Jaffier in *Venice Preserv'd* in 1828. He played the frontier theatres until 1834 and made his New York debut in 1839. Although he started as a leading tragedian, his greater successes came in comedy, especially as old men. For a time he managed the **Chestnut Street Theatre.** For 26 years he was with **Wallack**'s company. A very traditional actor, he resisted almost any theatrical change. He died on the road.   SMA

See: W. Winter, *The Life of John Gilbert Together with Extracts from His Letters and Souvenirs of His Career,* New York, 1890.

Gilbert, Mrs. George H. (née Anne Hartley) (1821–1904) British-born actress and dancer who married a dancer-manager in 1846 and moved to America in 1849. Gilbert spent most of her career playing "dear old ladies, foolish virgins and peppery viragos." For 30 years (1869–99) she acted in **Augustin Daly**'s company, inevitably playing opposite the comic **James Lewis** and with **Ada Rehan** and **John Drew** (the "Big Four"). Gilbert, a polished technician, was admired for her cooperative spirit and was venerated by the public. After Daly's death she appeared under **Charles Frohman**'s management until her death.   DBW

See: A. H. Gilbert, *The Stage Reminiscences of Mrs. Gilbert,* New York, 1901.

Gilbert and Sullivan in America Arthur Sullivan (1842–1900), composer, and William

Mrs. G. H. Gilbert and James Lewis in *7-20-8*. Photo: Sarony, N.Y. Courtesy: Laurence Senelick.

Schwenck Gilbert (1836–1911), librettist and lyricist, created the most popular comic operas in the history of the British theatre, most of them in conjunction with London theatre manager and impresario Richard D'Oyly Carte. An initial American production of *Trial by Jury* closed soon after its opening in 1875, but the premiere of *HMS Pinafore* in 1878 took the country by storm. The script and music were quickly pirated by managers, who offered all-black *Pinafores,* children's *Pinafores,* and church-choir *Pinafores.* Concerned about the lack of copyright protection, Gilbert and Sullivan opened *The Pirates of Penzance* in New York in 1879, trusting in British copyright law to protect their interests at home. The team's next few musicals received only lukewarm receptions in America, but the 1885 production of *The Mikado* reestablished their preeminence in the field of comic opera.

The phenomenal success of Gilbert and Sullivan's shows helped comic opera displace French *opéra bouffe* as the dominant form on the American musical stage for the rest of the 19th century, contributed to a sharp increase in the number of musicals offered in American theatres, and inspired American-born composers such as John Philip Sousa and **Reginald De Koven** to adopt the comic opera form for their work. Even after American composers had turned to ragtime and jazz for their musical styles in the 1910s and '20s, producers such as **William A. Brady** and **Winthrop Ames** mounted lavish productions of G&S's work. By the 1930s and '40s the musicals were being adapted to contemporary American tastes: *The Swing Mikado* and *The Hot Mikado* competed for audiences in 1939, and in 1945 *Memphis Bound* and *Hollywood Pinafore* both offered modern versions of *HMS Pinafore.*

After WW II, the D'Oyly Carte Company made regular visits to New York, but audiences for the authentic British stagings and orchestrations dwindled – though amateur G&S societies survive to this day. While purists grumbled, the **New York Shakespeare Festival** had a big success in 1980 with a version of *The Pirates of Penzance* starring rock vocalists Linda Rondstadt and Rex Smith.   MK

See: L. Ayre, *The Gilbert and Sullivan Companion,* New York, 1972; R. Traubner, *Operetta: A Theatrical History,* Garden City, NY, 1983.

Gilder, [Janet] Rosamond (De Kay) (1891–1986) Dramatic editor and critic. The daughter of Helena Gilder and Richard Watson Gilder, Rosamond established her reputation writing for *Theatre Arts Magazine* in the 1920s, later serving as associate editor, drama critic, and editor (1936–48). She headed the **Federal Theatre**'s Bureau of Research and Publication (1935), and helped to found the International Theatre Institute (1947), of which she was president for two terms. As director of the U.S. Center of ITI (later ITI of U.S., Inc.), she promoted the international exchange of theatre artists, companies, and information. Her books include *Enter the Actress* (1931), *A Theatre Library* (1932), and *John Gielgud's Hamlet: A Record of Performance* (1937).   TLM

Gilfert, Charles Antonio (1784–1829) Best known as the first manager of the **Bowery Theatre** in New York, from its opening in 1826 through its burning and reopening in 1828 – until the owners removed him for rent arrears in 1829. Gilfert managed theatres in Charleston, SC, Richmond, VA, and Albany, NY, before securing a theatre lease in his native city, where he was characterized as an able musician but inept businessman and, to some contemporaries, an unprincipled man. Shank suggests Gilfert was an innovative manager, exchanging plays and stars with other theatres; he is credited with introducing press agentry, native plays and players, ballets, and operas. He died 30 July, reputedly deranged by the loss of his theatre.   RKB

See: T. Shank, "The Bowery Theatre, 1826–1836," PhD diss, Stanford U, 1956; N. Stephenson, "The Charleston Theatre Management of Charles Gilfert, 1817 to 1822," PhD diss., U of Nebraska, Lincoln, 1988

Gilford, Jack (1907–90) Actor-comedian who began his career as a comedian, appearing in nightclubs, revues, and vaudeville. His most successful appearances on Broadway include the roles of Bontche Schweig in *The World of Sholom Aleichem* (1953), Mr. Dussell in *The Diary of Anne Frank* (1955), King Sextimus in *Once Upon a Mattress* (1959), Hysterium in *A Funny Thing Happened on the Way to the Forum* (1962), and Herr Schultz in *Cabaret* (1966). His films included *A Funny Thing . . . , Catch-22,* and *Cocoon.* He also starred in televised versions of *Sholom Aleichem* and *Anne Frank.* His last live appearance was in a stand-up comic routine (1988) at New York's The Ballroom, a cabaret.   SMA

See: K. Mostel and M. Gilford, *170 Years of Show Business,* New York, 1978.

Gill, Brendan (1914–) Drama critic and author. After graduating from Yale (1936), Gill began contributing to the *New Yorker,* serving as film critic (1961–7) and drama critic (1968–87). His books include *The Day the Money Stopped* (1957), adapted into a play with **Maxwell Anderson** (1958); biographies *Tallulah* [**Bankhead**] (1972) and *Cole* [**Porter**], with Robert Kimball (1971); and *States of Grace: Eight Plays by* **Philip Barry** (ed., 1975). His informed and intelligent comments about Peter Shaffer's *Equus* seem typical: "Mr. Shaffer offers his big, bow-wow speculations about the nature of contemporary life in the midst of a melodrama continuously thrilling on its own terms."   TLM

Gillette, William (Hooker) (1853–1937) Actor and playwright. Born into a prominent family in Hartford, CT, Gillette left home in 1873 to seek a career on the stage. As an actor he is remembered for his performance in his own *Sherlock Holmes* (1899), which he played over 1,300 times; his most significant achievement as a playwright was his Civil War spy melodrama, *Secret Service* (1895), with its fast-moving action, suspense, and the tension between the demands of love and duty. Gillette was the author of numerous adaptations and dramatizations and several original plays in which he frequently appeared himself, in both the U.S. and England. In addition to Holmes, he played Blane in *Held by the Enemy* (1886), Billings in *Too*

Much Johnson (1894), and Thorne/Dumont in *Secret Service*. His other notable appearances were in Barrie's *The Admirable Crichton* (1903) and *Dear Brutus* (1918). Other Gillette plays include *The Private Secretary* (1884), *All the Comforts of Home* (1890), *Clarice* (1905), and *Electricity* (1910). In 1913 Gillette delivered his influential and subsequently published lecture *The Illusion of the First Time in Acting*, which explains his cool, understated approach to acting – a contrast to the florid and romantic style that dominated the theatre up to his time. DBW

> See: D. Cook, *Sherlock Holmes & Much More*, Hartford, CT, 1970; R. Cullen and D. Wilmeth, eds., *Plays by William Gillette*, New York, 1983.

Gilman, Richard (1925–) Drama critic who championed the European avant-garde of the 1960s in *Commonweal* (1961–4) and *Newsweek* (1964–7), and as literary editor of *New Republic* (1968–70). Gilman has been a professor of drama at Yale since 1967, and is the author of five books, including *Common and Uncommon Masks* (1971), *The Making of Modern Drama* (1974), and *Faith, Sex, Mystery: A Memoir* (1987). He received the **George Jean Nathan** Award for Dramatic Criticism in 1971. TLM

Gilpin, Charles Sidney (1878–1930) **African-American** actor. Introduced at school to amateur theatricals, Gilpin left school at age 14 to become a vagabond vaudevillian, his meager earnings supplemented by sporadic jobs as printer, porter, barber, and elevator boy. In 1907 he joined the all-black Pekin Stock Company of **Chicago,** and later acted at the Lincoln and **Lafayette Theatres** in Harlem. His impressive Broadway performance as the slave Custis in Drinkwater's *Abraham Lincoln* (1919) led to the title role in The *Emperor Jones* (1920), in which he scored a resounding triumph. A victim of sudden fame and racial prejudice, Gilpin took to drink, which cut short his career. The black critic **Theophilus Lewis** lamented: "He rose from obscurity to the peaks, lived his hour of triumph, and returned again to the shadows." EGH

Gilroy, Frank D[aniel] (1925–) Playwright and director who gained attention first with his solid drama, *Who'll Save the Plowboy?* (1962), which won the Obie Award. His next effort was *The Subject Was Roses* (1964), a story of the rivalry of a mother and father for the affection of their son who has just returned from the war. Although thinly funded and with a relatively unknown cast for the time, this play became one of the most honored serious dramas of the past 30 years. Gilroy, also director of five films, continues to write plays, but success has eluded his recent efforts. LDC

Gin Game, The Two-character drama by Texan D. L. Coburn, which opened on 6 October 1977 for 517 performances. Directed by **Mike Nichols,** the play explored the relationship of two lonely residents of a home for the aged, played by **Hume Cronyn** and **Jessica Tandy.** Though it won the Pulitzer Prize, critics were divided on its merits: While it did bring America's aged population into focus, some thought it was a static and predictable drama. MR

Giovanni, Paul (195?–) Actor, director, composer, and playwright who began his career playing the Boy in the original production of *The Fantasticks* Off-Broadway, later joining **Joseph Chaikin's Open Theatre.** Giovanni has been artistic director of the Berkshire Theatre Festival and the Gateway Theatre, and free-lances widely in regional theatres, New York, and London. He made his Broadway directing and playwrighting debuts simultaneously with *The Crucifer of Blood* (1978), starring Paxton Whitehead as Sherlock Holmes. CLJ

Girl of the Golden West, The One of **David Belasco's** western plays and probably the most famous, this three-act melodrama about old California opened in New York on 14 November 1905. The naturalistic *mise-en-scène,* for which Belasco was famous, served this play (with its snowstorm, sunsets, and suspenseful scenes) quite well. Its western dialects and mannerisms drew upon Belasco's familiarity with the region, exemplifying a dramaturgical technique that joined lifelike speech and scenes to exciting melodramatic actions. Puccini utilized this blend of old and new in what is probably the first grand opera on an American theme – his *La Fanciulla del West,* which premiered at the Metropolitian Opera House 10 December 1910, eclipsing the play in revivals and lasting fame. RKB

Gish, Lillian (1893–) and **Dorothy** (1898–1968) Actresses and sisters who, although they worked together in several films, never considered themselves a team. Dorothy made her stage debut in 1907 in **East Lynne.** In 1912 she made her first film with D. W. Griffith, continuing with and without her sister until 1928. Among her films were *Orphans of the Storm, Nell Gwyn,* and *Madame Pompadour.* She then returned to the stage, eventually succeeding Dorothy Stickney in **Life with Father** in 1941. She appeared the next year in *The Great Big Doorstep,* followed by *Magnificent Yankee.*

    Lillian debuted in *In Convict's Stripes* (1902) and first appeared in New York as Margenie in *A Good Little Devil* (1913). She entered films and appeared in such early works as *The Birth of a Nation, Intolerance, Way Down East,* and *The Orphans of the Storm.* She returned to the stage in 1930, starring in such productions as *Camille* (1932), John Gielgud's *Hamlet* (as Ophelia, 1937), *Life with Father* (1940–2), and *The Curious Savage* (1950). During 1969–70 she toured worldwide with a **one-person** concert program. SMA

> See: L. Gish, *The Movies, Mr. Griffith, and Me*, Englewood Cliffs, NJ, 1969, and *Dorothy and Lillian Gish*, New York, 1973.

Glance at New York, A, by **Benjamin A. Baker.** Baker was prompter at **Mitchell's Olympic Theatre** when he wrote a sketch for a benefit performance and asked **Francis (Frank) Chanfrau** to act in it. The first production, 15 February 1848, featured a tough Bowery fireman, Mose the Bowery B'hoy, who generated instantaneous acclaim. Modeled on an actual person, Mose Humphreys, Mose took on epic proportions as a folk hero, a man of the city who could simultaneously fight fires, sing songs, tell jokes, and love women. Chanfrau played the original sketch, rewritten and lengthened, at the Olympic and **Chatham Theatre.** Over the next five years he acted in a dozen different plays featuring Mose.   RAH

Glaspell, Susan (1876–1948) Perhaps best known as one of the founders of the **Provincetown Players** (along with her husband, **George Cram Cook**), Glaspell was also a playwright (contributing 11 plays to the Players), second only to **Eugene O'Neill** in the founding of a modern American drama that combined contemporary American ideas with European expressionistic techniques. Glaspell's early one-act plays satirized contemporary attitudes and interests, such as pop psychology (*Suppressed Desires,* 1915) and ultraidealism (*Tickless Time,* 1918), both written in collaboration with Cook. However, her *Trifles* (1916), one of the most frequently anthologized one-act plays, skillfully portrayed hidden, psychological motivation by using realistic settings and dialogue to reveal women's inner conflicts. This play was also her first to use the device of keeping the central female character offstage, a technique she repeated in *Bernice* (1919). In her most controversial play, *The Verge* (1921), she experimented with symbolism and expressionistic settings to reveal the state of mind of a "new" woman who goes mad striving for both abstract idealism and individual fulfillment.

Throughout her career Glaspell never feared to tackle the new and the immediate. In *The Inheritors* (1921) she contrasted post–WW I narrow Americanism with earlier ideals of individual freedom and tolerance, again creating a female character who sacrifices ease and comfort to remain true to her ideals. In a controversial decision, Glaspell won the 1931 Pulitzer Prize for *Alison's House,* loosely based on the life of Emily Dickinson.

Glaspell's contribution to American drama includes her role in the founding of the Little Theatre movement [see **community theatre**], as well as her creation of modern female characters in search of autonomy, portrayed through new and experimental dramatic techniques. During 1936–8 she headed the Midwest Bureau of the **Federal Theatre Project,** in Chicago.   FB

See: C. W. E. Bigsby, *Plays by Susan Glaspell,* New York, 1987; M. Noe, "A Critical Biography of Susan Glaspell," PhD diss., U of Iowa, 1976; A. Waterman, *Susan Glaspell,* New York, 1966.

Glass, Montague (1877–1934) Playwright who first dramatized (with **Charles Klein**) a number of his stories under the title of *Potash and Perlmutter* (1913). Immediately successful, with 441 performances, the play's Jewish partners – Abe Potash and Mawruss Perlmutter – were transformed into Hebrew comedians, arguing incessantly and wittily, yet sharing joys and sorrows. In America and England the popularity of this play and its sequels – *Abe and Mawruss* (1915, written with **Roi Cooper Megrue** [retitled *Potash and Perlmutter in Society,* 1916]); *Business Before Pleasure* (1917), *His Honor, Abe Potash* (1919), and others written

Williamstown Theatre Festival/Long Wharf Theatre 1986 production of *The Glass Menagerie* with Karen Allen (Laura) and Joanne Woodward (Amanda). Photo: T. Charles Erickson. Courtesy: Long Wharf Theatre.

with **Jules Eckert Goodman** – was intense but brief.   WJM

Glass Menagerie, The Tennessee Williams's first major play opened at Chicago's Civic Theatre on 26 December 1944 and revolutionized the American stage with its expressionistic staging and haunting, lyrical dialogue. **Eddie Dowling** (coproducer, codirecter, star as Tom Wingfield) cast the legendary **Laurette Taylor** (Amanda), **Julie Haydon** (Laura), and Anthony Ross (Jim). On 31 March 1946 *Menagerie* moved to New York's **Playhouse Theatre** for 561 performances (Donaldson Award); that Broadway production never used the slide projections found in the reading text. *Menagerie* has had numerous revivals. Amanda was played in New York by **Helen Hayes** in 1956, **Maureen Stapleton** in 1965 and 1975, and **Jessica Tandy** in 1983. A black cast performed *Menagerie* in 1989 at the **Cleveland Play House.**

The Glass Menagerie was the first Williams play turned into a film (in 1950). In 1987 Paul Newman directed another film version with Joanne Woodward as Amanda, **John Malkovich** as Tom, and James Naughton as the Gentleman Caller. Televised versions include one on CBS (1966) with **Shirley Booth** and **Hal Holbrook,** and on ABC (1973) with **Katharine Hepburn** and **Sam Waterson.** A "memory play," *Menagerie* is translucently autobiographical: The narrator/character Tom Wingfield is Tennessee Williams. Like Williams's mother Edwina, Amanda is a daughter of the Old

South. His sister Rose, like Laura, was sickly and had a glass collection. Laura's only chance for romance is shattered, like the unicorn in her collection, when the gentleman caller announces he is engaged. Though Tom Wingfield tries to escape the domestic and political upheavals of the 1930s, he realizes, as did Williams, that he could never extinguish the light of memory that glows with nostalgia as well as pain. PCK

Gleason, John (1941–) Lighting designer. A graduate of Hunter College, Gleason has designed some 100 Broadway productions and served as resident lighting designer for eight years for the Repertory Theatre of **Lincoln Center.** He teaches at New York University. AA

Glengarry Glen Ross This Pulitzer Prize–winning drama by **David Mamet** is perhaps the most successful example of the playwright's exploration of the deceptive uses of language in power relationships – an exploration begun in *Sexual Perversity in Chicago* and *American Buffalo* and continued in *Speed-the-Plow.* Here we see the battle taken completely out of the personal arena and into the world of fast-talking real estate salesmen, men who make a pretense of camaraderie as they are stealing each other's clients. The focus is on the brutality of human speech. **Jack Kroll** wrote of Mamet's dialogue: "His antiphonal exchanges . . . make him the Aristophanes of the inarticulate." The play premiered in 1983 at the National Theatre of Great Britain; the following year **Gregory Mosher** directed a production at Chicago's **Goodman Theatre** (with **Joe Mantegna**) that transferred to Broadway's **John Golden Theatre,** where it ran for 378 performances. SF

Gods of the Lightning by **Maxwell Anderson** and Harold Hickerson. Although a failure when produced 24 October 1928 at the **Little Theatre,** this moving play was a strong attack on the xeno-phobia that characterized the Sacco and Vanzetti trial of 1921. The playwrights sympathetically explored the corruption behind the anarchists' 1927 execution, renaming the victims Macready (a boisterous union organizer) and Capraro (a pacifist rebel). In a travesty of the judicial system, these two are convicted of robbery and murder. "When you take violence into your hands," Capraro observes, "you lower yourself to the level of government, which is the origin of crime and evil." RHW

Godspell: A Musical Based on the Gospel According to St. Matthew was conceived and directed by John-Michael Tebelak (with music and lyrics by **Stephen Schwartz**), who, along with the cast, had recently graduated college. Previously produced at The Café **La MaMa,** the play opened at the Cherry Lane Theatre on 17 May 1971 and ran 2,124 performances; on Broadway it ran an additional 527 performances. *Godspell* provided a contemporary view of Christianity during a Broadway season that included two other productions of biblical origin: *Two by Two,* the story of Noah, and *Jesus Christ Superstar,* a rock-and-roll spectacular. It was distinctive for portraying Jesus Christ as a clown, and having "flower children" perform other principle roles – a characteristic that supported the popular-style music, most notably "Day by Day," but trivialized heady philosophical issues with a simplistic view of life and peace. KN

Gold Diggers, The This popular **Avery Hopwood** comedy, which inspired three film versions, opened under the aegis of **David Belasco** at the **Lyceum Theatre** on 30 September 1919. A supposed look at the bohemian life and catty humor of chorus girls, all action transpires in a New York apartment where theatrical women, who sometimes dream of becoming real actresses, spend most of their time luring stage-door johnnies, trying to get from men everything they can while returning as little as possible. The leading character of Jerry

Goodman Theatre's 1984 American premiere of David Mamet's *Glengarry Glen Ross* directed by Gregory Mosher with (left to right) Mike Nussbaum and Joe Montegna. Photo: Brigitte Lacombe. Courtesy: Goodman Theatre.

Lamar (played by **Ina Claire**) turns out to be genuinely in love, and in a sentimental ending reveals her gold digging as the means to support her mother and the illegitimate child of a dead chorus girl.   RHW

Golden, John (1874–1955) Producer who championed middle-class values through the production of wholesome family plays. He came from Ohio to New York at age 14 to be an actor, but abandoned this effort at age 21 for a profitable 13-year stint selling chemical products. While in this business he continued to write vaudeville sketches, short plays, and lyrics for show songs. Golden turned his full attention to writing and producing in 1918. His production of *Turn to the Right*, by **Winchell Smith** and John Hazzard – financed by royalties from "Poor Butterfly," written for *The Big Show* (1916) – launched his career as a producer. He produced over 150 plays, more than a dozen of which achieved great popularity. His production of *Lightnin'* (1918), by **Frank Bacon** and Winchell Smith, ran for 1,291 performances, a record that stood for most of the 1920s. He had enduring and productive professional relationships with Smith, actor-author **Frank Craven,** and **Rachel Crothers.** A founder of the American Society of Composers, Authors, and Publishers (ASCAP), he was noted for his gifts of money, personal time, and organizational skill to many civic and cultural groups, including the Stage Relief Fund and the Stage Door Canteen.   WD

Golden Boy by **Clifford Odets.** Produced in 1937 by the **Group Theatre,** directed by **Harold Clurman,** designed by **Mordecai Gorelik** and starring **Luther Adler** (as Joe Bonaparte), **Morris Carnovsky** (his father), and Frances Farmer (Lorna, his girl). The popular play (250 performances), which financially revived the company, tells the story of a young man's struggle to escape the slums by becoming a fighter instead of a violinist. It presents Odets's abiding conflict – in life and art – between idealism and commercialism, integrity and corruption. Odets wrote the play after leaving the Group for Hollywood. The plot is melodramatic, but effectively so. Revived in 1952 and 1975, the play was also filmed in 1939, starring John Garfield (who played Siggie in the original staging). In 1964 it was transformed by Odets and **William Gibson** into a musical starring Sammy Davis, Jr. (lyrics by Lee Adams, music by **Charles Strouse**).   TP

Goldfadn [or Goldfaden], Avrom (né Avraham Goldenfudim) (1840–1908) Playwright and producer, popularly called the "Father of **Yiddish Theatre.**" A Russian intellectual who could not make a living, in 1876 he tried writing sketches to be performed in a wine garden in Jassi, Romania, thereby becoming the first professional Yiddish playwright and producer. Typically, he wrote operettas whose form was European but whose substance was Yiddish folk material and life. Many plays were instant successes – for ex-

ample, *Koldunye; or, The Witch* (1877); *The Fanatic; or, The Two Kuni-Lemls* (1880?); *Bar-Kokhba; or, The Last Days of Jerusalem* (1883); and *Schulamis; or, The Daughter of Jerusalem* (1883?). Some were also performed in other languages. However, Goldfadn spent much of his life wandering between Europe and America, rarely made a living, and fell from fashion entirely in old age. Nevertheless, about 30,000 mourners followed his funeral procession to Washington Cemetery in Brooklyn, for much of his work had already taken on the status of folk culture: for example, the lullaby "Raisins and Almonds," composed for *Shulamis,* and the clownish character types that he named Kuni-Leml and Shmendrik. His plays, in original form or adaptations, have often been revived.   NS

Goldin, Horace (né Hyman Goldstein) (1873–1939) Polish-born magician who emigrated to the U.S. at the age of 16. He started with a comic magic act, but owing to his heavy accent and stammer, converted it to a rapid-fire silent routine, "45 tricks in 17 minutes," baffling audiences with a quick succession of illusions. He appeared in a musical comedy *The Merry Magician* (Theatre Royal, Brighton, 1911) and was the first conjurer to play the **Palace,** New York (1913). His most famous illusion was an improvement on P. T. Selbit's 1879 trick, "Sawing a Lady in Half": Goldin eliminated the box and used a buzz saw, as **Blackstone** did as well.   LS

Goodale, George Pomeroy (1843–1919) Journalist and critic. Born in Orleans, New York, Goodale worked in a printing office and as a newspaper journalist before serving with the Union in the Civil War. He became city and dramatic editor of the Detroit *Free Press* in 1865, and remained at the drama desk until his death. Goodale's criticism was both scholarly and moralistic, not unlike that of his New York compeers **William Winter** and **John Ranken Towse.**   TLM

Good Gracious Annabelle! Clare Kummer's first play and one of her most successful. The three-act comedy, produced by **Arthur Hopkins** at the Republic Theatre, opened on 31 October 1916 and ran for 111 performances. It portrays some agreeably pleasant but insolvent young people who follow the suggestion of Annabelle (played by Lola Fisher) and become servants at a nearby mansion. Annabelle discovers that the wealthy and handsome John Rawson (**Walter Hampden**), who has rented the mansion, is the mysterious man she married as a teenager and who has supported her for years. In 1924 a **Ziegfeld** musical version called *Annie Dear* was a distinct failure.   FB

Goodman, Jules Eckert (1876–1962) Oregon-born playwright, collaborator, and adapter of stories and novels for the stage. Educated at Harvard and Columbia, Goodman followed a short career as a journalist on the *New York Dramatic Mirror* with some recognition in *Mother* (1910), an original play; *The Silent Voice* (1914), an adaptation of a Gouverneur Morris story; *Treasure Island,* based on the Stevenson novel; and *The Man Who Came Back*

(1916), adapted from a John Fleming Wilson novel. A period of successful collaborations followed, including *Business Before Pleasure* (1917), *His Honor, Abe Potash* (1919), *Partners Again* (1922), and *Potash and Perimutter, Detectives* (1926), all cowritten with **Montague Glass.** *Chains* (1923) was a solo effort, followed by a somewhat successful father–son collaboration in *Many Mansions* (1937).   GSA

Goodman Theatre Chicago's Goodman is America's second oldest regional theatre, founded in 1925. Originally funded as a memorial by the parents of playwright Kenneth Sawyer Goodman, the 683-seat theatre, built alongside the Chicago Art Institute, was to house both a resident professional company and a School of Drama; however, the Depression forced the company to disband, whereas the school continued.

In 1969–70 a professional company returned to the Goodman to varying critical and popular reception. In 1978 its leadership was assumed by **Gregory Mosher,** who emphasized new works and classic revivals. Mosher frequently commissioned scripts from leading American playwrights, and in 1985 became codirector of **Lincoln Center** in New York City. He was replaced at the Goodman in 1986 by Robert Falls, under whose leadership classical works have been staged with bold imagination and freshness and new works lavished with unusual care. World and American premieres have included *Glengarry Glen Ross, Hurlyburly,* and Soyinka's *Death and the King's Horseman.*

In 1977 the Goodman Theatre ceased its affiliation with the Chicago Art Institute to become a self-sustaining operation, and in 1978 the School of Drama affiliated with De Paul University.   SMA

Goodspeed Opera House East Haddam, CT [Architect: Jabez Comstock]. Built in 1876 as an indulgence for his taste for theatre by wealthy entrepreneur William R. Goodspeed, the tiny 400-seat theatre on the Connecticut River was often referred to as "Goodspeed's Folly" by the town's citizens. After his death in 1882, the theatre was largely abandoned, becoming offices and storerooms by 1920. In 1958, owned by the state, it was slated for the wrecking ball, but a movement spearheaded by a local citizen, Mrs. Alfred Howe Terry, emerged to save it. Restored to its former Victorian elegance in 1963 through local fund-raising and a contribution from the state, it opened as a year-round theatre with the **Kern–Bolton–Wodehouse** musical, *Oh, Lady! Lady!* Throughout most of its existence, it has been led by Michael P. Price, who established its policy of presenting both old and new musical works, sending more than a dozen productions to Broadway. The Goodspeed has also set up a library-archive of the American musical in a separate building.   MCH

Goodwin, Nathaniel Carl (1857–1919) Actor and manager. Born and educated in Boston, Goodwin began his career as a mimic for drawing-room theatricals. In 1874 he made his professional stage debut at Boston's **Howard Athenaeum,** and in 1875 his first New York appearance at **Tony Pastor**'s Opera House. He enjoyed a major success in 1876 at the New York **Lyceum** in *Off the Stage* by giving imitations of popular actors. While Goodwin excelled as a mimic and eccentric comedian, he also was effective in serious parts, such as Jim Rayburn in *In Mizzoura* (1893) and the title role in *Nathan Hale* (1899). Married five times, he gained notoriety for his offstage antics. With his third wife, **Maxine Elliott,** he starred in numerous plays including *Nathan Hale* and *When We Were Twenty-One* (1900). He was not, however, successful in Shakespearean roles, including Shylock (1901) and Bottom (1903). In his autobiography, *Nat Goodwin's Book* (1914), he took revenge upon his many enemies.   TLM

Gordin, Jacob (1853–1909) Yiddish playwright, driven because of socialist convictions from Russia to New York's Lower East Side, where he became a journalist of enormous personal authority and influence. Although the intelligentsia scorned **Yiddish theatre** as parochial and vulgar, in 1891, trying to feed his nine children, Gordin wrote *Siberia,* and thus initiated the close identification of secular Yiddish literary culture with Yiddish theatre. Characteristic of Gordin's many plays was concern for verisimilitude, despite high-flown language and aphoristic tags. They were most often dark and intense, achieving comic relief through colorful minor characters. Gordin wrote to teach: His plays' themes and subjects included socialism, women's rights, and the broader education of the Yiddish masses. Gordin championed pure and literary Yiddish. He attracted the best Yiddish actors of his time – **Jacob Adler, Keni Liptzin, David Kessler, Bertha Kalich,** Ida Kaminska – and created juicy roles as vehicles for them. His best known dramas include *God, Man and Devil* (1900), based on *Faust; The Jewish King Lear* (1892 [see **ethnic theatre**]); *Mirele Efros* (1898), sometimes called *The Jewish Queen Lear;* and *The Kreutzer Sonata* (1905). The first three were made into films; all remained staples of finer Yiddish intellectual repertory worldwide and are still considered classics.   NS

Gordon, Max (né Mechel Salpeter) (1892–1978) Broadway producer remembered as "a man of wide-ranging tastes, and the possessor of a capacity to gamble." His production of *Born Yesterday* (1945) ran for 1,642 performances. *The Women* (1936), *My Sister Eileen* (1940), *Junior Miss* (1941), and *The Solid Gold Cadillac* (1953) all achieved over 500 performances. His productions of *Roberta, Her Master's Voice, The Shining Hour,* and *Dodsworth* all ran simultaneously in 1934. Gordon came to theatre as a vaudeville advance **agent.** Notable productions presented early in his career in association with **Sam Harris** include *Six-Cylinder Love* (1921) and *The Jazz Singer* (1925). While continuing through the years to work with Harris, he also collaborated on *Missouri Legend* with **Guthrie McClintic** and *Sing Out the News* with **Kaufman** and **Hart** (both 1938). Gordon also produced the film versions of *Abe Lincoln in Illinois* (1940) and

Years Ago (retitled *The Actress*, 1953). He published an autobiography, *Max Gordon Presents*, in 1963.
MR

Gordon (née Jones), Ruth (1896–1985) Actress and playwright whose New York debut in *Peter Pan* (1915) was followed by a succession of relatively insignificant roles. It was a revival in 1936 of Wycherley's *The Country Wife*, in which she was the first American cast in an Old Vic (London) production, that changed the direction of her career: Her Mrs. Pinchwife led to roles that exploited her individualistic technique, whirlwind vivacity, and split-second timing. In 1937 (New York) she played Nora in *A Doll's House*, adapted for her by **Thornton Wilder;** in 1942 she was Natasha in *The Three Sisters*. Her most memorable stage creation was Dolly Levi in *The **Matchmaker*** (1954, London; 1955, New York), a role written for her by Wilder. Her last stage role was Zina in *Dreyfus in Rehearsal* (1974). Gordon was also a successful screen actress, playwright (*Over 21, Years Ago*), and especially screenwriter in collaboration with her second husband, **Garson Kanin.** She was also the author of three lively autobiographies (1971, 1976, 1980). DBW

Gordone, Charles (1925–) **African-American** playwright. With his only successful stage play *No Place to Be Somebody* (1969), Gordone became the first black playwright to win a Pulitzer Prize. A drama major at Los Angeles State College, he came to New York and acted bit parts while working as a bar-room waiter; this experience inspired him to write the play. At a time of militancy in black theatre, Gordone dramatized in a number of highly theatrical scenes the murder of an incorrigible black pimp by his closest friend. The **Negro Ensemble Company** rejected the play, which was eventually staged at **Joseph Papp's Public Theater** in New York. EGH

Gorelik, Mordecai (1899–1990) Director, stage and film designer; born in Russia. Gorelik studied with **Robert Edmond Jones, Norman Bel Geddes,** and **Serge Soudeikine** and began his career with the **Provincetown Players** in 1920. His 1925 design for *Processional* was a rare example of successful expressionism on the American stage. During the 1930s he was the primary designer for the **Group Theatre,** including *Men in White* and *Golden Boy*. He was an organizer of a short-lived leftist group, the Theatre Collective. Gorelik also designed *All My Sons* and *A Hatful of Rain,* among others on Broadway. He was a strong advocate of **Brecht**'s epic theatre, which he emphasizes in his book, *New Theatres for Old* (1940). Much of his design (some 40 productions) can be classified as suggestive realism. AA

Gotanda, Philip Kan (1950–) Leading **Asian-American** playwright, native of Stockton, CA, and third-generation Japanese American. First produced by small Asian-American companies, his work has crossed over to such theatres as the **Mark Taper Forum** and the **Manhattan Theatre Club.**

Though stylistically diverse, all his plays examine the psychosocial dynamics of the Asian-American experience. *The Wash* (1987), about an elderly Japanese-American couple in the throes of a wrenching divorce, and *Song for a Nisei Fisherman* (1980), the story of an immigrant doctor, are lyrical, naturalistic in texture. More satiric, *Yankee Dawg You Die* (1987) is a look at Hollywood stereotyping and the generation gap between two Asian-American actors, while *Fish Head Soup* (1991) is a surreal family drama. His best work conveys the Asian-American milieu with a deftness and compassion that renders it universal. MB

Gottfried, Martin (1933–) Drama critic. Born in New York and educated at Columbia (1955), Gottfried was music critic for the *Village Voice* (1961); drama critic for *Women's Wear Daily* (1962–74); and senior drama critic for the New York *Post* (1974–). Among his books are *A Theater Divided* (1967), which won the **George Jean Nathan** Award for Dramatic Criticism; *Opening Nights* (1969); *Jed Harris: The Curse of Genius* (1984); and *All His Jazz: The Life and Death of Bob Fosse* (1990). Demanding and highly opinionated, Gottfried's personal and aggressive remarks have made him a controversial figure among New York critics. TLM

Gottlieb, Morton (1921–) Producer. An experienced business, company, and general manager when he produced his first ventures (three U.S. tours between 1953 and 1960), Gottlieb's noteworthy productions include *The Killing of Sister George* (1966), *We Bombed in New Haven* (1968), *Sleuth* (1970), and *Veronica's Room* (1973). Playwright **Bernard Slade** has benefited from Gottlieb's expertise with productions of *Same Time, Next Year* (1975), *Tribute* (1978, also U.S. tour 1980), *Romantic Comedy* (1979), and *Special Occasions* (1982). He also produced the film versions of *Sleuth* (1972), *Same Time, Next Year* (1979), and *Romantic Comedy* (1983). Gottlieb was recognized in *Barron's* as a frugal producer whose methods have maximized and speeded returns – when there were any – to investors. To provide a New York tryout with reduced production costs within Equity regulations, he limited the available seating at the Ritz Theatre (now the **Walter Kerr**) to 499 for his production of Bill C. Davis's *Dancing in the End Zone* (1985). MR

Grapes of Wrath, The Adapted and directed by **Frank Galati** for Chicago's **Steppenwolf Theatre Company** in 1988 and subsequently taken to California and London; won Tony Awards for best production and direction when it reached Broadway in 1990. Based on **John Steinbeck**'s 1939 Pulitzer Prize–winning novel about a family of dust-bowl refugees, the production featured Gary Sinise as Tom Joad, Lois Smith as Ma, Robert Breuler as Pa, Nathan Davis as Grampa, and Terry Kinney as Rev. Casey. A string band joined a cast of 41 on spare but evocative sets designed and lit by Kevin Rigdon. The production was created with the permission of Steinbeck's widow, who

John Steinbeck's *The Grapes of Wrath* as adapted and directed by Frank Galati and first seen at Chicago's Steppenwolf Theatre Company. Pictured is the Joad family, with Gary Sinise as Tom Joad at the wheel. Photo: Micha Langer. Courtesy: Steppenwolf Theatre Company.

later praised the company for its faithfulness to her husband's idea of the nobility of the common man.
SF

Grau, Maurice (1849–1907) Austrian-born impresario who came to the U.S. at the age of 5. He worked briefly as a lawyer before beginning his theatrical career as manager for the French opera singer Marie Aimée. In 1879 he founded the Maurice Grau French Opera Company, which helped to popularize *opéra bouffe* in the U.S. In 1883 he began the first of three periods as manager of the Metropolitan Opera House. Grau's productions at the Met were acclaimed for the sumptuousness of the scenery and costumes, and for Grau's innovative use of as many as five stars in a single production. In addition to his operatic activities, Grau managed the American tours of many **international stars,** including Sarah Bernhardt, Tomasso Salvini, Adelaide Ristori, and Constant Coquelin.
MK

Gray, Spalding (1941–) Actor-playwright; product of the avant-garde theatre movement of the 1960s. Gray spent five years as a traditional actor before joining **Richard Schechner** and the **Performance Group** in 1970. With the disbanding of that group in 1980, Gray joined his collaborator and director **Elizabeth LeCompte, James Clayburgh,** Willem Dafoe, Libby Howes, and Ron Vawter to form the **Wooster Group.** Gray's reputation, however, has transcended the Group, primarily because of two bodies of work: *Three Places in Rhode Island (Sakonnet Point,* 1975; *Rumstick Road,* 1977; *Nayatt School,* 1978), a trilogy devised by Gray (who says he is extremely "narcissistic and reflective") and LeCompte from Gray's biography; and a series (1979–91) of 13 monologues ("without peer") drawn from Gray's past, including *Terrors of Pleasure, Sex and Death to the Age of 14, Booze, Cars and College Girls, A Personal History of the American Theatre, India and After, Interviewing the Audience, Swimming to Cambodia,* and *Monster in a Box.* Theodore Shank calls Gray's pieces "the most literally autobiographical work that has been presented in the theatre." In 1988 he scored critical success as the stage manager in **Lincoln Center**'s *Our Town.* DBW

Grease Two-act musical comedy by Jim Jacobs and Warren Casey; opened 14 February 1972 at the **Off-Broadway** Eden Theatre, eventually running (at several Broadway theatres) 3,388 performances. This "New '50s Rock 'n Roll Musical," aping the pop-music idiom and manners of the late 1950s, is a nostalgic look at the "greaser" youth of the bygone era of bouffant hairdos and leather jackets, tracing the transformation of a "nice" girl into one of the gang. Originally written for a **Chicago** community theatre, it benefited from the popularity of such contemporary 1950s nostalgia as the film *American Graffiti* and the TV hit "Happy Days."
JD

Great Divide, The Considered a landmark drama even in its own day, this play by **William Vaughn Moody** was inspired by his travels to Arizona and Colorado. It relates the home invasion of three rape-bound men, two of whom are bought off by the third (Stephen Ghent) when he falls for the intended victim (Ruth Jordan). Marriage, business success, remorse, and a child follow the guilt-stricken heroine to Massachusetts where she is reconciled, across the great divide of conflicting values, with the hero. Its sensational subject matter probably helped the play's triumphal New York opening on 3 October 1906 at the **Princess Theatre** (where it ran through 1907) and the celebrated national and international tours by its stars **Margaret Anglin** and **Henry Miller** (who also produced). Despite continued debate about its premise, the play is still critically praised for its realism,

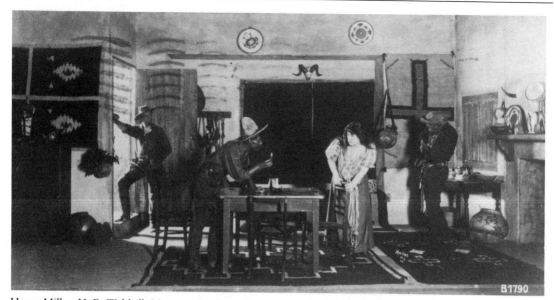

Henry Miller, H. B. Walthall, Margaret Anglin, and Robert Cummings in William Vaughn Moody's *The Great Divide*. Photo: Hallen. Courtesy: Michael Gnat.

suspense, and study of human psychology. It is often called the first modern American drama.
    RKB

Great God Brown, The Perhaps the most mysterious of **Eugene O'Neill**'s plays, this drama nonetheless ran successfully for **Experimental Theatre, Inc.,** opening on 23 January 1926 at the Greenwich Village Theatre. In his most sophisticated experiment with masks, O'Neill with director-designer **Robert Edmond Jones** graphically explored the complexity of human masking and unmasking, split character, personality confusion, and even psychological adoption of the personality of another. All was theatricalized by literal masks that were worn, removed, and even borrowed by four major characters: Dion Anthony (played by Robert Keith), an artist torn between Dionysian pleasures and religious asceticism; Billy Brown (William Harrigan), a successful businessman who jealously "becomes" Dion after the artist expires; Cybel (Anne Shoemaker), a seer prostitute who pronounces the synthesis of Dion and Brown near the play's end; and Margaret (Leona Hogarth), who blindly loves the mask of Dion, be it on the face of either Dion or Brown. Although fascinating in development and spectral in mood, the play is confusing because O'Neill repeatedly alters the mask convention throughout the action.   RHW

Great White Hope, The, by Howard Sackler. Based upon the life of Jack Johnson, this play traces the career of the first black heavyweight boxing champion of the world, whose physical prowess and love affair with a white woman spur a racist society to destroy him. Set in numerous countries, the sprawling three-act drama incorporates direct audience address and dialogue in several foreign languages. **Edwin Sherin** directed the first production, which featured **James Earl Jones** in "a tidal-wave performance" (**Walter Kerr**) and **Jane Alexander** as the ill-fated mistress. Opening at **Arena Stage** in Washington, DC, on 12 December 1967, it moved to Broadway's **Alvin Theatre** on 3 October 1968, where it ran 556 performances and won the Pulitzer and New York Drama Critics' Circle awards.   KF

Green, Adolph see **Comden, Betty**

Green, Paul (1894–1981) Playwright. A student of Frederick Koch at the University of North Carolina, Green was taught that he should write about the life he knew – the South, its people, and its religion. In *The Last of the Lowries* (1920) he recreated the rhythmic language of the Negro and simple Southern folk characteristics. His best play, *In Abraham's Bosom* (1926), portrays the tragedy of a Negro idealist, defeated by his own limitations and by the people he wants to help. In both *The Field God* (1927), showing the spiritual disintegration of a man condemned by the religiosity he rejected, and *Shroud My Body Down* (1934), he dramatized the fascination and violence of religious mania. A liberal and intelligent man of strong opinions, Green broadened his involvement with human protests in *Hymn to the Rising Sun* (1936), a condemnation of the chain-gang system, and *Johnny Johnson* (1936), in which he satirized warmongers through a hero who is confined by society for having "peace monomania." With *The Lost Colony* (1937), a symphonic drama about Sir Walter Raleigh's colony, Green found a new expression. After WW II, he continued to celebrate American history through such pageants as *The Common Glory* (1947), on the efforts of Jefferson during the Revolution; *The Founders* (1957), the story of the Jamestown colony; and *Cross and Sword* (1965). [See also **outdoor drama; pageants.**]   WJM

    See: V. S. Kenny, *Paul Green,* New York, 1971.

Greenberg, Richard (1959–) Playwright, born on Long Island and educated at Princeton and Yale Drama School, initially produced by the Ensemble Studio Theatre and Playwrights Horizons. *Eastern Standard* premiered at the **Seattle Rep** (1988), then transferred to Broadway; *The American Plan* was staged at **Manhattan Theatre Club** (1990); *The Author's Voice* was revived by the Workhouse Theatre in New York (1991); and *The Extra Man* was first produced at the **South Coast Rep** in 1991.
BBW

Greene, Clay Meredith (1850–1933) Successful playwright born and for much of his life based in **San Francisco.** Some of his 80 scripts were written with **David Belasco** or others; most are boilerplate melodramas with strong regional flavor. His first success, *M'liss* (1878), was based on a **Bret Harte** story about a spunky Sierras orphan; *Sharps and Flats* (1880), coauthored by Slauson Thompson, depicted San Francisco's high-stakes financial world. Other popular dramas include *Chispa, His Japanese Wife,* and *The Red Spider.* MB

Green Pastures, The A biblical "fable" by **Marc Connelly** ("inspired by" Roark Bradford's *Ol' Man Adam an' His Chillun*) that was hailed by mainstream critics, awarded the Pulitzer Prize, and counted as one of the most profitable productions of the 1930s. The play opened at the Mansfield Theatre on 26 February 1930 and ran 640 performances. The company then toured continuously for three years, returning to Broadway for 71 more performances in 1935.

Connelly himself directed the large **African-American** cast in this retelling of Bible stories from the creation of the world to the coming to earth of Jesus Christ as the stories might have been imagined by black children in the rural South. The scenes were augmented by "Negro spirituals" performed by Hall Johnson's gospel choir, and were set within an imaginative, cartoonlike setting designed by **Robert Edmond Jones.** Despite the general critical reverence (**Brooks Atkinson** called it "the divine comedy of the modern theatre"), *The Green Pastures* was criticized by African-American intellectuals such as **Langston Hughes** as white America's fantasy of the childlike simplicity of Southern blacks. A controversy arose when the Washington, DC, cast of the play refused to appear before segregated audiences. A film version, codirected by Connelly, was released in 1936; the play was revived briefly on Broadway in 1951.
MF

Green Street Theatre Green St. between Hamilton and Division, Albany, NY. Actor-manager **John Bernard** opened the playhouse on 18 January 1813. Sold to the Baptist Society, it became a church from 1819 to 1852, when it was reconverted into a theatre. It was a concert saloon in 1861 and thereafter passed from theatrical annals. Among the theatre's noteworthy events were **Sol Smith**'s debut at age 14 and **Adah Isaacs Menken**'s appearance for the first time in *Mazeppa.* MCH

Greenwood, Jane (1934–) Costume designer, native of Liverpool, England, who studied at London's Central School of Arts and Crafts and designed for the Oxford Playhouse before emigrating to Canada and subsequently New York City. Her Broadway debut, *The Ballad of the Sad Cafe* (1962), was produced by scenic designer **Ben Edwards,** whom she later married. One of New York's busiest costume designers, her credits include *The Circle, I Hate Hamlet,* and *Othello,* among many others. She also designs costumes for films, operas, and television, and teaches costume design at the Yale School of Drama. BO

[Ben] Greet Players (also Woodland Players) Originating in England in 1886, the Greet Players toured the U.S. beginning in 1902 and continuing (except for 1919, 1920, and 1922–8) until 1931. Philip Ben Greet introduced U.S. audiences to al fresco performances, using little or no scenery, of medieval and Elizabethan drama, mainly the plays of **Shakespeare.** Greet's touring companies also pioneered the "concert booking system," whereby noncommerical producers set admission prices and sold tickets, then kept as profit receipts above the company fee. Greet's companies were especially popular in Boston and Chicago. WD

Gregory, Andre (?–) Director, actor, and producer, identified with the 1960s avant-garde. From producing **Off-Broadway** (1959), Gregory directed at The Writer's Stage (1962), then founded The Manhattan Project, an environmental theatre group that adapted performance spaces to suit each script. He became famous overnight with the success of the company's *Alice in Wonderland* (1970) and *Endgame* (1973). **Joseph Papp** presented the company at the **Public Theater** in [*The*] *Seagull* (1975) and *Jinx Bridge* (1976). Always controversial, The Manhattan Project's six actors performed in an eccentric style with words articulated in a strange and often comic manner, and gestures exaggerated as they played the subtext more often than the text. **Clive Barnes** praised Gregory's work, but **Walter Kerr** dismissed the company as "self-indulgent, slovenly in speech, and childish in antics." Gregory's acting has included *Rumors* on Broadway (1988) and Prospero in *The Tempest* (1989–90) for Shakespeare & Company (Berkshires/Boston). He starred in the film *My Dinner with Andre* (1982), and has appeared in *Protocol* (1984), *The Mosquito Coast* (1986), and *Street Smart* (1987). TLM

Grey (né Katz), Joel (1932–) Cleveland-born actor, singer, and dancer who as a child performed in his father's **nightclub** act. He appeared **Off-Broadway** in *The Littlest Revue* (1956), and had roles in several Broadway plays and musicals before receiving critical acclaim as the decadent Master of Ceremonies in *Cabaret* (1966; film, 1972). Grey's breezy personality and loose-limbed dancing made him a natural choice to portray musical comedy star **George M. Cohan** in *George M!* (1969). His other musical roles, in *Goodtime Charley* (1975) and *The Grand Tour* (1979), met with less success. Grey appeared in a revival of *Cabaret* in 1987. MK

Griebling, Otto (1896–1972) German-born tramp clown who came to the U.S. in 1910; often compared to and sometimes partnered with **Emmett Kelly.** Griebling, as the result of a fall while a bareback rider in 1930, learned to juggle and developed a silent clown act. Unlike the dour-faced Kelly, he was an affectionate plump tramp whose best-known routines centered around a persistent attempt to deliver a package to an audience member or to finesse a kiss from an unsuspecting woman in the crowd. These and other routines were perfected over 20 years. In 1951 he joined **Ringling Brothers,** last appearing with them at Madison Square Garden in 1970.   DBW

Grimes, Tammy (1934–) Actress and expert comedienne, known for her raspy voice; debuted as Cherie in *Bus Stop* (1955), replacing **Kim Stanley.** Her career established with Molly in *The Unsinkable Molly Brown* (1960; Drama Critics' Circle and Tony awards), she then appeared in *Rattle of a Simple Man* (1963) and *High Spirits* (1964) and repeated her earlier awards as Amanda in Coward's *Private Lives* (1969). She starred in New York in *California Suite* (1976), *Tartuffe* (1978), and Simon Gray's *Molly* (1978), and appeared in *Father's Day* (1979), *A Month in the Country* (1979), *42nd Street* (1980), *Over My Dead Body* (1984), and *Paducah* (1985). Her daughter is actress Amanda Plummer. TLM

Grizzard, George (1928–) Actor known for "his ability to become the part." Grizzard made his stage debut in *The Corn Is Green* (1945), then on Broadway in Joseph Hayes's *The Desperate Hours* (1955). He performed for **Arena Stage, Circle Repertory, Circle in the Square, Old Globe, Playwrights Horizons, Hartford Stage Company, Brooklyn Academy of Music,** and **Yale Repertory** in comedies, dramas, farces, and melodramas. Disparaging avant-garde theatre, especially Beckett, Grizzard's work includes classics (*Hamlet,* 1963 [the **Guthrie Theater**'s first production]; *Man and Superman,* 1978); American standards (*The* **Glass Menagerie,** 1965; *The* **Country Girl,** 1972); adaptations (*To Kill a Mockingbird,* 1991); and premieres (*Who's Afraid of Virginia Woolf?,* 1962; **L. Wilson**'s *The Gingham Dog,* 1969; *California Suite,* 1976). Grizzard's recent work includes the films *Seems Like Old Times* (1980) and *Bachelor Party* (1984).   REK

Grosbard, Ulu (1929–) Belgium-born director who emigrated to the U.S. in 1948 and attended the University of Chicago, Yale School of Drama, and **Actors Studio.** He began his directing career in 1957, making his New York debut in 1962 with *The Days and Nights of Beebee Fenstermaker* at the Sheridan Square Playhouse. His notable productions since include *The* **Subject Was Roses** (1964); *A* **View from the Bridge** (1965); *The Investigation* (1966); *The* **Price** (1968); **American Buffalo** (1977); *The Wake of Jamie Foster* (1982); and *Weekends Like Other People* (1982). Since 1961 he has worked also in film and television.   TLM

Group Theatre, The Founded in 1931 by **Harold Clurman, Lee Strasberg,** and **Cheryl Crawford,** the Group was a pioneering attempt to create a theatre **collective,** a company of players trained in a unified style and dedicated to presenting new American plays of social significance. With Stanislavsky's **Moscow Art Theatre** as their model, Group members began a systematic study of an art that had few guidelines and virtually no written record. Prodded by their exacting teacher, Lee Strasberg, and fired by Clurman's messianic fervor, the actors experimented with improvisation, emotional and sensory memories, private moments, and exercises in relaxation and concentration. The inner technique they worked on – which became the basis of the American Method and which Strasberg continued to develop during his 35 years at the **Actors Studio** – resulted in acting that was more natural and earthy, more private, more intense, and more psychologically charged than previous styles. Debates over method erupted in the summer of 1934 when Group member **Stella Adler** returned from her studies with Stanislavsky in Paris to announce that the Master had abandoned his earlier emphasis on inner work in favor of a new external technique, the method of physical actions. Adler and Strasberg squared off in a craft war whose wounds have never healed, Strasberg and his followers continuing to focus on the actor's own emotional resources while Adler and her colleagues have concentrated on the play as opposed to the player.

Among the superb realistic actors the Group helped to develop were John Garfield and **Franchot Tone** (both of whom defected to movies), Margaret Barker, Ruth Nelson, **Morris Carnovsky,** Phoebe Brand, Art Smith, and **Sanford Meisner.** Decades after the Group disbanded in 1941, Strasberg, Adler, Meisner, and Carnovsky continued to be influential teachers, offering their own individual variations of the Method.

Although less successful than its actor-training program, the Group's literary achievement was also substantial. The Group was not a political theatre and, in fact, was strongly criticized by more militant companies; but over a 10-year period it produced 22 new American plays on subjects of contemporary relevance. If only a few of these – **John Howard Lawson**'s *Success Story* (1932) and **Clifford Odets**'s *Awake and Sing!* (1935) and *Paradise Lost* (1935) – have enduring literary value, all of the Group's plays rose above the level of propaganda, and in Odets the company yielded an American original.   FH

See: H. K. Chinoy, ed., *Reunion: A Self-Portrait of the Group Theatre,* New York, 1976; H. Clurman, *The Fervent Years,* New York, 1945; W. Smith, *Real Life: The Group Theatre and America, 1931–1940,* New York, 1990.

Guare, John (1938–) Playwright whose work is characterized by frank theatricality, lyrical quality, autobiographical base, and satiric vivacity. Some critics have found his plays too cerebral or abstract, lacking focus, but few have failed to praise his use of language. Recognized first for his one-act play *Muzeeka* (1968), he received wide acclaim for his first full-length play, *The **House of Blue Leaves*** (1970). Since then his major plays have included the adaptation and lyrics for *Two Gentlemen of Verona* (1971), *Rich and Famous* (1974), *The **Landscape of the Body*** (1977), and *Bosoms and Neglect* (1979). A notable screenplay, *Atlantic City,* written for Louis Malle's 1981 film, was followed by *Lydie Breeze* and *Gardenia* (1982), two parts of a projected tetralogy set in 19th-century New England. *Women and Water,* chronologically first in this series, was seen in various drafts during 1984–5 in **Los Angeles, Chicago,** and Washington, DC. *Moon Over Miami,* originally meant as screenplay for John Belushi, was staged by Yale Rep in 1988. His most successful play to date has been *Six **Degrees of Separation*** (1990), winner of the 1990 Dramatists Guild Hull-Warriner Award (also presented for *Landscape*), which delves into the vulnerability under New York's brittle surface. *Four Baboons Adoring the Sun* was given a 1992 production at Lincoln Center's **Vivian Beaumont Theatre.** DBW

Guernsey, Otis Love, Jr. (1918–) Editor and drama critic. Born in New York and educated at Yale (1940), Guernsey wrote for the *New York Herald Tribune* (1941–60), including service as film and theatre critic. He has been drama critic and senior editor of *Show Magazine* (1963–4), editor of *Dramatists Guild Quarterly* (1964–), and editor of the *Best Plays* series (1965–). Guernsey is author of *Directory of the American Theatre* (1971); *Playwrights, Lyricists, Composers on Theater* (1974); *Broadway Song & Story* (1986); and *Curtain Time* (1987). TLM

Guild Theatre see **Virginia Theatre**

Gunn, Moses (1929–) African-American actor. Gunn's first professional engagement was with the remarkably talented **Off-Broadway** company presenting Genêt's *The Blacks* (1962). Thereafter, he performed five Shakespearean roles at the 1964 Antioch, OH, festival and three additional roles with the **New York Shakespeare Festival,** winning an Obie Award for his portrayal of Aaron the Moor in *Titus Andronicus* (1967). Gunn became a founding member of the **Negro Ensemble Company** and appeared in several productions, gaining a second Obie for his performance in *The First Breeze of Summer* (1975). His "sensual-melodic" Othello for the **American Shakespeare Theatre** in 1970 elicited ecstatic reviews from major New York critics. EGH

Gunter, Archibald Clavering (1847–1907) Playwright and novelist. Born in England and educated as a mining engineer in San Francisco, where he wrote his first play, *Found the True Vein* (1872), he moved to New York in 1879. During the next decade he wrote a number of moderately successful plays showing a broad western influence upon his creativity: *Courage* (1883), with **Effie Ellsler;** *Prince Karl* (1886), **Richard Mansfield**'s first starring role; *Two Nights in Rome* (1886); *The Deacon's Daughter* (1887); and *One Against Many* (1887). In 1888 he dramatized his successful novel, *Mr. Barnes of New York* (1887), the adventures of a

rich, imprudent American, and thereafter mainly wrote fiction. WJM

Gurney, A[lbert] R[amsdell], Jr. (1930–) Playwright. The American theatre's John Cheever, Gurney writes feelingly about what he fears is an endangered species: well-to-do, or at least well-bred, white Anglo-Saxon Protestants. His wry comedies unfold in a nostalgic haze. Typically, his plays are set in a time and place of poignant transition: at the end of summer, of adolescence, of an era. While his characters reluctantly confront the need for making changes, they also lament the passing of an enclosed and carefully regulated way of life. In one of his best plays, *The **Dining Room*** (1981), place is more important than any of the rotating cast of characters who pass through it; his dining room is a cultural artifact threatened with extinction, a metaphor for genteel traditions. In *The Middle Ages* (1983), the library of an exclusive club serves a similar thematic purpose. Other deft Gurney works include *Children* (1976), suggested by a Cheever short story, in which a matron chooses duty over pleasure; *What I Did Last Summer* (1982), about a teenager torn between propriety and bohemianism; *The Perfect Party* (1986); *The Cocktail Party* (1990); *The Snow Ball* (1991); *The Old Boy* (1991); and, arguably his most successful, *Love Letters* (1989), a two-character play that relates a romance from grade school to middle age and has toured worldwide (1990–2). FH

Gussow, Mel (1933–) Drama critic. Born in New York and educated at Middlebury College (1955) and Columbia University (1956), Gussow has served as Associate Editor at *Newsweek* (1959–69) and as drama critic for the *New York Times* (1969–) and the *Times*'s radio station, WQXR. He is author of *Don't Say Yes Until I Finish Talking: A Biography of Darryl F. Zanuck* (2d ed., 1980) and a forthcoming book on **Joseph Papp.** He is also a recipient of the **George Jean Nathan** Award for Dramatic Criticism (1977–8), and an adjunct professor of cinema at NYU. With a penchant for the nontraditional and unusual, Gussow has drawn national attention to the most worthy of **Off-Off** and **Off-Broadway** productions and talent. His intelligent and precise analysis of the stage version of *Carnal Knowledge* (1990) is typical: "In performance, the vignettes in quickly changing settings suffer from the loss of cinematic crosscuts and artful atmospheric selectivity." TLM

Guthrie, Tyrone (1900–71) From the 1930s onward, Irish-born Guthrie was an innovative and popular international director, working extensively in Britain, the U.S., and Canada. His Shakespearean work included Laurence Olivier's *Hamlet* and *Henry V,* and a modern dress *Hamlet* in 1938 with Alec Guinness. He repeated this experiment at the Minneapolis Theatre (later named the **Guthrie Theatre**) in 1963. His other productions included a notable *Peer Gynt* (1944), in which Ralph Richardson starred. He was director (1953–7) of the Stratford Festival Theatre in Ontario, Canada, and there developed (with **Tanya Moiseivitsch**) his

Tyrone Guthrie's 1963 production of *The Three Sisters* at the Guthrie Theatre, Minneapolis. Courtesy: The Guthrie Theatre.

thrust stage theatre form that was later permanently enshrined both there and in **Minneapolis.**

Guthrie's immensely successful operation in Minneapolis, while not the beginning of the regional theatre movement in America, certainly gave it great impetus. A master at directing crowd scenes, Guthrie's successes with classical repertory garnered immense publicity, thus heightening awareness of theatrical potential in other American cities. Guthrie considered Broadway "a murderous, vulgar jungle," but his New York productions included *The Matchmaker, Gideon, Mary Stuart,* and *Candide.* He was knighted in 1961.   SMA

See: J. Forsyth, *Tyrone Guthrie: A Biography,* London, 1976; A. Rossi, ed., *Astonish Us in the Morning,* Detroit, 1980.

Guthrie Theatre 725 Vineland Place, **Minneapolis,** MN [Architect: Ralph Rapson]. Conceiving the idea of founding a theatre away from New York, Oliver Rea and **Peter Zeisler** searched the country for a hospitable city that would support such an enterprise. Enlisting the aid of the director **Tyrone Guthrie,** they eventually chose Minneapolis as their site and brought forth the Tyrone Guthrie Theatre after much effort in 1963. Part of the Walker Art Center, the 1,400-seat Guthrie features a thrust stage, favored by the late director, and in its early seasons presented mainly well-cast productions of classics and significant modern plays. After Guthrie's departure, his place was taken by his assistant Douglas Campbell until 1967, and a few years later by **Michael Langham** (1971–5). In 1981, after years of declining audiences, the direction of the theatre fell to **Liviu Cilieu,** the Romanian-born director, who materially changed its policy: The stage was enlarged, the exterior of the theatre altered, and the production of new American and European plays in addition to the classics in a different mode contributed to a new spirit within the enterprise. In 1986 Cilieu was succeeded by **Garland Wright.**   MCH

Gutierrez, Gerald (1952–) Brooklyn-born and Juilliard-trained director who established his reputation for clear and deliberate productions in the **Off-Broadway** and regional theatre. He has directed for **McCarter Theatre,** including *You Can't Take It with You* (1978); **Playwrights Horizons,** including *She Loves Me* (1980) and *Isn't It Romantic* (1983–4); **Manhattan Theatre Club,** including *Emily* by **Stephen Metcalf** (1988); The **Acting Company,** including *Much Ado About Nothing* (1987); and **Goodspeed,** including *The Most Happy Fellow* (1991; and Broadway, 1992). Other directing credits include *A Life in the Theatre* (1977), *Terra Nova* (1984), and *Fiorello!* (1985–6 revival). Gutierrez has taught at NYC and the

Juilliard School, and has served as an Associate and Artistic Director of The Acting Company (1986–).   TLM

Guys and Dolls Book by Jo Swerling and **Abe Burrows;** music and lyrics by **Frank Loesser.** Based on Damon Runyon's colorful 1930s short stories of Broadway gamblers and their long-suffering girlfriends, this show opened at the **46th Street Theatre** on 24 November 1950 and ran 1,200 performances. It was successfully revived on Broadway in 1976 with an all-black cast, and in 1992 directed by **Jerry Zaks,** with Faith Prince (Adelaide) and Nathan Lane (Nathan Detroit) critically acclaimed. Original choreographer **Michael Kidd** and director **George S. Kaufman** created a fast-moving show about a gambler who loses a bet, and his heart, to an idealistic Salvation Army missionary. The secondary plot, concerning the proprietor of "the oldest established permanent floating crap game in New York" and his cabaret-singer fiancée, allowed Kidd to stage some deliciously second-rate nightclub sequences.

Comedy scenes involving formidable gangster Big Jule, who plays craps from memory with blank dice, and a rousing pseudo-gospel number, "Sit Down, You're Rocking the Boat" (originally sung by Stubby Kaye), at the mission, counterpointed the two romantic entanglements. In the 1950 production, Robert Alda and **Sam Levene** starred as the gamblers, with **Vivian Blaine** as the nightclub singer and Isabel Bigley as the missionary.   MK

Gypsy With book by **Arthur Laurents,** music by **Jule Styne,** and lyrics by **Stephen Sondheim,** *Gypsy* opened at the **Broadway Theatre** on 21 May 1959. Based on the memoirs of stripper **Gypsy Rose Lee,** the show told the story of a grasping stage mother, Mama Rose, who had channeled her own ambitions into an obsession with the vaudeville careers of her two daughters. After her older daughter elopes and the second daughter, Louise, attains success on her own with a striptease act, Rose ruthlessly examines the price she has paid for her ambition in the bitter and wrenching (and show-stopping) soliloquy "Rose's Turn." The role of Rose proved to be the last major triumph of **Ethel Merman**'s career and enabled **Angela Lansbury** and Tyne Daly to win Tony Awards for their performances in the 1974 and 1989 Broadway revivals. Arthur Laurents's book captured the tawdry world of small-time **vaudeville** and **burlesque** in the 1920s, and was perfectly complemented by **Jerome Robbins**'s evocative choreography and Styne and Sondheim's corny vaudeville numbers, raucous stripteases, and artless ballads.   MK

H

Hackett, J[ames] H[enry] (1800–71) Actor, master dialectician, manager, and the first American to appear in London as a star. He first succeeded in New York as Sylvester Daggerwood in *New Hay at the Old Market*. In 1827 he appeared at London's Covent Garden, but failed to win public esteem. Returning to the U.S. he repeated his triumphant Dromio of Ephesus, but audiences preferred his frontier and **Yankee** roles, especially Nimrod Wildfire in *The Lion of the West* and *Rip Van Winkle*. He secured his reputation as the finest Falstaff of his time, first playing the role in 1828. Hackett periodically essayed management, and was manager of the **Astor Place Opera House** at the time of the **Forrest**–Macready riot.

His son **James K[eteltas] Hackett** (1869–1926) was a member of **Frohman**'s **Lyceum** company, starring in such vehicles as *The Prisoner of Zenda*. He married actress Mary Mannering in 1897 and costarred with her in *The Walls of Jericho* (1905). In 1906 he opened **Wallack's Theatre** in New York. In 1914 he and **Joseph Urban** collaborated on a scenically historic production of *Othello*. SMA

See: J. K. Hackett, *Notes & Commentaries upon Certain Plays & Actors of Shakespeare, with Criticism & Correspondence,* New York, 1863; M. Moses, *Famous Actor-Families in America,* New York, 1906.

Hagen, Uta (1919–) Actress and teacher who made her debut in 1938 in the **Lunts**' production of *The Seagull* and has acted only sporadically since then, though almost always in circumstances as notable: in **Maxwell Anderson**'s *Key Largo* (1939); with **Paul Robeson** and **José Ferrer** in *Othello* (1945); opposite Anthony Quinn in *A Streetcar Named Desire* (1950); as the lead in **Odets**'s *Country Girl* (1950); and, most memorably, as tortured, caustic, vulnerable Martha in **Edward Albee**'s *Who's Afraid of Virginia Woolf?* (1962). Known as an actor's actor, Hagen performs in a clean, masterly style; she has an earthy, assertive presence and a deep voice that suggests enormous power in reserve. Although her understatement is ideally suited to film, she has chosen to appear on screen only rarely (notably in *The Other* and *The Boys from Brazil*). Since 1947 she has taught at the HB Studio in New York, begun by her late husband **Herbert Berghof.** Famous for the brevity and incisiveness of her comments, she speaks in technical code words – an actor's shorthand – that her students learn to interpret. Like most American teachers she derives her method from Stanislavsky; unlike **Lee Strasberg,** another Stanislavsky disciple, she is strongly opposed to the use of emotional memory, which she considers both self-indulgent and self-destructive. She has written on acting in *Respect for Acting* (1973; a standard reference for both students and professionals) and *A Challenge for the Actor* (1991). Her memoir, *Sources,* appeared in 1983.   FH

Hailey, Oliver (1932–) Texas-born playwright, trained at Yale (MFA), a working journalist (Dallas *Morning News*) and television writer ("McMillan and Wife"). Hailey's plays have been produced primarily on regional stages and include *For the Use of the Hall* (1974), *Red Rover, Red Rover* (1977), and *Father's Day* (1970). The latter, a provocative and comic study of three divorced couples, is his best known work.   BBW

Hair Two-act musical, music by Galt MacDermot, words by James Rado and Gerome Ragni;

James H. Hackett as Falstaff. Courtesy: Becker Theatre Library, Brown University.

The musical *Hair* (1977 revival). Photo: © Martha Swope. Courtesy: Martha Swope.

first opened at the Off-Broadway **Public Theater** (Anspacher), 29 October 1967, running 94 performances; moved to Broadway's **Biltmore Theatre,** 29 April 1968, running 1,742 performances. This "American Tribal Love-Rock Musical" was a major event in theatre history, as traditional culture met counterculture. *Hair* was a "concept" musical in that it did not attempt to tell a story, but rather to explain a way of life: that of the antiwar dropouts of the East Village who had rejected their parents' values for a life of sex, drugs, and freedom. Seemingly unstructured, with an amplified pop/rock score of atmospheric but essentially undramatic music originally played by a small rock band, it was both a plea for understanding from and an attempt to shock "straight" society. The original production, directed by **Gerald Freedman,** was the inaugural production of **Joseph Papp**'s Public Theater. Papp sold the rights to Michael Butler, who produced a far more lavish revised and reorchestrated version, directed by **Tom O'Horgan,** on Broadway and across the world. Even more popular in London than in New York, it created a rage for rock music (and its attendant amplification) in the theatre, as well as for other essentially nonnarrative musical depictions of minority segments of society. One of its most publicized con-

troversies was the use of **nudity,** unique then in a commercial musical production.   JD

See: L. Davis, *Letting Down My HAIR,* New York, [1973]; B. L. Horn, *The Age of HAIR: Evolution and Impact of Broadway's First Rock Musical,* Westport, CT, 1991.

Hairy Ape, The **Eugene O'Neill**'s final production for the **Provincetown Players** opened 9 March 1922 under the direction of **James Light,** with expressionistic designs by **Robert Edmond Jones** and **Cleon Throckmorton,** and was subsequently moved to Broadway by **Arthur Hopkins.** This journey play functions like a nightmare following the quest of Yank (played by Louis Wolheim), who searches for a place to belong, only to end crushed in the arms of a zoo gorilla. The play's language is brutal throughout, often cast in choric, animal-like chants in the stoker and jail scenes. Although subtitled "A Comedy of Ancient and Modern Life," the play is the tragic destruction of a brutish, suffering, barely articulate stoker. The impetus for Yank's quest is his encounter with a society woman who insults him through her terror of his very appearance. Among the elite on Fifth Avenue, Yank discovers his physical powers drained as he literally bounces off the strolling masked, mechanical socialites – an arresting scene in the first of six O'Neill plays to be produced with masks.   RHW

Hall, Adrian (1928–) Director-playwright. Artistic director of Providence's **Trinity Repertory Company,** 1964–89, Texas-born Hall has had a rocky career as a pioneer leader of the resident theatre movement and an artist with a strong belief in a director's theatre. Controversies have often clouded his mission to create a permanent ensemble company producing innovative and daring theatre (often with designer **Eugene Lee**). At Trinity his fiercely loyal company presented more than 35 American and world premieres, most directed and many adapted from fiction by Hall and his composer-in-residence, Richard Cumming. From 1983 through the '88–9 season he served as artistic director of both Trinity and the **Dallas Theater Center,** a first for an American director. Since then he has free-lanced at such theatres as San Diego's **Old Globe,** the **Mark Taper Forum** (opening the 1990–1 season with *Hope of the Heart*, his adaptation of works by Robert Penn Warren), the **Yale Rep** (premiere of Joshua Sobel's *Underground*), the **American Repertory Theatre** (where he directed **F. Murray Abraham** in *King Lear* [1991], and *Hedda Gabler* [1992]), and the **New York Shakespeare Festival** (*As You Like It,* summer 1992).
    DBW

See: J. M. Woods, "The Theatre of Adrian Hall," PhD diss., City U of New York, 1989.

Hallams, The A family of English actors and the first substantially documented company of professional players to appear on the North American continent. Hallams had apparently been in the English theatre from 1707, one being killed by Charles Macklin in a Green Room brawl at Drury Lane in 1735. By 1750 **William Hallam** (d. 1758) had suffered serious financial reverses while managing Goodman's Fields, but creditors allowed him to try to raise his shortages. He therefore sent an advance agent, Robert Upton, across the Atlantic with considerable money to investigate theatrical conditions and potentials. Hallam never heard again from Upton, who joined the **Murray–Kean** company, took charge of the company, headed an engagement in New York in 1751, and then returned to England. The Murray–Kean company soon afterward disappeared.

In the meantime, William Hallam sent his brother, **Lewis Hallam, Sr.** (1714–55), Lewis's wife, their three children, and an undistinguished company of 10 to America. (One daughter remained in England, later becoming British actress Mrs. George Mattocks.) After a six-week voyage aboard the *Charming Sally,* the Hallam Company opened in Williamsburg, VA, on 15 September 1752 with *The Merchant of Venice* and *The Anatomist.* They remained in Williamsburg for about 11 months, presenting a repertory consisting of **Shakespeare,** Rowe, Lillo, Moore, Farquhar, Addison, Cibber, Vanbrugh, Steele, and Gay. They next played New York, opening 17 September 1753 with *The Conscious Lovers.* Although they faced considerable hostility from local Quakers, the company opened a Philadelphia engagement on 15 April 1754 with

Trinity Repertory Theatre production of *The Tempest,* directed by Adrian Hall and designed by Eugene Lee in 1981–2. Photo: Constance Brown. Courtesy: Trinity Repertory Theatre.

The Fair Penitent and *Miss in Her Teens,* but played only two months. After a three-month engagement in Charleston, the Hallams arrived in Jamaica about January 1755, where they joined forces with a company managed by **David Douglass.** After the elder Hallam's death, Douglass married **Mrs. Hallam** (?–1773) in 1758, also securing **Lewis Hallam, Jr.** (1740–1808) as a leading man.

Mrs. Hallam starred in the **American Company,** as Douglass called his group, being the first actress in New York to play such roles as Juliet, Cordelia, and Jane Shore. Lewis Hallam, Jr., remained on the stage for some 50 years, playing almost every significant role in the repertoire of the time. He appeared in Godfrey's *The Prince of Parthia* (1767), the first script by an American to be given a professional production [see **Introduction,** §1]. After Douglass's death in 1786, the younger Hallam assumed leadership of the American Company with various partners. He retired from management in 1797, but continued to act until his death. His second wife, Miss Tuke, joined the company, but her quarrelsome and intemperate habits caused considerable friction.

Adam Hallam, the younger brother of Lewis Jr., left Jamaica with the company, but his name soon disappeared from the bills. Helen and Nancy Hallam eventually joined the company, as well.   SMA

See: P. Highfill, Jr., K. Burnim, and E. Langhans, *A Biographical Dictionary of Actors, Actresses. . . and Other Stage Personnel in London 1600–1800,* vol. 7, Carbondale, IL, 1982.

Hamblin, Thomas Sowerby (1800–53) Actor-manager who toured the U.S. for five years as an English star before assuming management of New York's **Bowery Theatre** in 1830. He held the lease through the **fires** of 1836, 1838, and 1845, until he died. His controversial private life failed to dim respect for his business ability and charity, and his Bowery in the 1830s and '40s is justly remembered as "the nursery of native talent." Though his own preference was for classics and repertory, they could not survive the popularity of melodrama and stars. His theatre premiered many American character types – stage Negroes, **Yankee**s, and frontiersmen – and lesser forms of popular entertainment. His patrons were increasingly scorned by the *bon ton* as plebeian, and his active management lessened toward the end of his life as theatrical taste moved literally and figuratively uptown.   RKB

Hammerstein, Arthur (1872–1955) Producer, theatre owner, and lyricist who began as an assistant to his father, **Oscar Hammerstein I,** before producing on his own. Starting with *The Firefly* in 1912, he presented a number of successful operettas, including *High Jinks* (1913), *Wildflower* (1923), *Rose-Marie* (1924), *Song of the Flame* (1925), and *Sweet Adeline* (1929). As a producer, he was noted for his lavishness and attention to detail. In 1927 he opened Hammerstein's Theatre, which he was forced to give up after the 1930–1 season. Hammerstein was also a songwriter who contributed lyrics to two songs in *Somebody's Sweetheart* (1918).   MK

Hammerstein, Oscar, I (1847–1919) Impresario, theatre owner, producer. After emigrating to America from Prussia, he worked in a cigar factory. Money from his many patents for improvements in cigar manufacturing enabled him to indulge his passion for opera and theatre. He built a number of playhouses, including the Manhattan Opera House, where his operatic productions were so successful that he was bought out by the Metropolitan Opera, and the **Olympia** Theatre, whose location north of the established theatre district earned him the nickname "The Father of Times Square." In 1899 Hammerstein opened the Victoria Theatre as a legitimate playhouse, but had to switch to **vaudeville** when the Theatrical **Syndicate** lured away legitimate attractions. During 1904–15 Hammerstein's Victoria, under the management of Hammerstein's son Willie, was the top vaudeville house in the country.   MK

See: V. Sheean, *Oscar Hammerstein I: The Life and Exploits of an Impresario,* New York, 1956.

Hammerstein, Oscar, II (1895–1960) Lyricist and librettist. Born into a theatrical family, Oscar Hammerstein II began his career as a lyricist while a student at Columbia University. In the early 1920s he wrote lyrics for four shows with music by Herbert Stothart and two shows composed by **Vincent Youmans.** His first big success came with the lyrics for **Rose-Marie** (1924), an operetta with music by **Rudolf Friml.** Among other shows of the 1920s for which Hammerstein provided lyrics were *Sunny* (1925) and The **Desert Song** (1926). In 1927 Hammerstein wrote both the lyrics and the libretto for the era's most ambitious musical, **Show Boat,** which had a score by **Jerome Kern.** After writing several other musicals with Kern, Hammerstein teamed up with composer **Richard Rodgers** in 1943 to create one of the most influential of all American musicals, **Oklahoma!** This collaboration continued through the 1940s and '50s, resulting in *Carousel* (1945), **South Pacific** (1949), The **King and I** (1951), *Flower Drum Song* (1958), and *The Sound of Music* (1959).

Although Hammerstein's lyrics have sometimes been criticized for their sentimentality, he is generally credited with making major innovations in the form and subject matter of the American musical through his contributions to *Show Boat* and his later musicals with Richard Rodgers.   MK

See: H. Fordin, *Getting to Know Him: A Biography of Oscar Hammerstein II,* New York, 1977; S. Green, *Rodgers and Hammerstein Fact Book,* New York, 1980; O. Hammerstein II, *Lyrics,* Milwaukee, 1985; E. Mordden, *Rodgers and Hammerstein,* New York, 1992.

Hammond, (Hunter) Percy (1873–1936) Drama critic. Born in Cadiz, OH, and educated at Franklin College (1892–6), Hammond began as a reporter and later drama critic for the *Chicago Evening Post* (1898–1908), later serving as theatre critic for the *Chicago Tribune* (1908–21). In 1921 he began a 15-year career as critic for the *New York Tribune,* establishing his reputation as a master of irony and urbane humor. He wrote of the producer **Al Woods:** "The anguish which Mr. Woods experiences when he does a thing like *Gertie's Garter* . . . is assuaged by the knowledge that with its stupendous profits he may speculate in the precarious investments of the worthier drama" (1921).   TLM

See: Franklin P. Adams et al., *Percy Hammond: A Symposium,* Garden City, NY, 1936.

Hampden (Dougherty), Walter (1879–1955) Actor who, though American born, began his career learning the classical repertory and the grand-manner acting style in the British company of F. R. Benson during 1901–4. After playing leading and supporting roles in London and the provinces, he came to the U.S. in 1907 in support of **Alla Nazimova** in her repertory of **Ibsen** and other modern plays. Always more successful in poetic and romantic roles, his desire to act in *Hamlet* and similar plays was not realized until he was able to assume the financial risks for their presentation in 1918. In the 1920s and '30s he brought **Shakespeare**'s plays to appreciative audiences in many American cities. In 1923, he added Rostand's *Cyrano de Bergerac* to his repertory and played the dauntless hero more than 1,000 times in 15 years. From 1925 to 1930 he leased his own theatre, adding the title character from Bulwer-Lytton's *Richelieu* to his repertory in 1929. An active performer for most of his life, Hampden played Cardinal Wolsey in the **American Repertory The-**

Walter Hampden as Shylock in *The Merchant of Venice*, a role he played frequently in the 1920s and '30s. Courtesy: Don B. Wilmeth.

atre production of *Henry VIII* in 1946 and Danforth in **Arthur Miller**'s *Crucible* in 1953.   MR

> *See:* E. Laurent, "Walter Hampden: Actor-Manager," PhD diss., U of Illinois, 1969; G. J. Parola, "Walter Hampden's Career as Actor-Manager," PhD diss., Indiana U, 1970.

Handman, Wynn (1922–) Director and acting teacher, born in New York City and educated at City College, CUNY (BA, 1942), and Columbia University (MA, 1949). He served in the Navy in WW II, then, before entering graduate school, studied at the **Neighborhood Playhouse** under **Sanford Meisner,** who became his mentor. In 1962 he cofounded the not-for-profit **American Place Theatre,** dedicated to new American playwrights. He remains artistic director of the theatre, where in recent years he has developed a personal specialty nurturing solo performers and raconteurs.   CLJ

Hanlon–Lees Six English-born brothers (sons of Manchester, England, Theatre Royal manager Tom Hanlon), aerialists, and knockabout comedians who introduced a new style of stage farce. **Thomas** (1836–68), **George** (1840–1926), **William** (1842–1923), **Alfred** (1844–86), **Edward** (1846–1931), and **Frederick** (adopted; 1848–86) took the name of Lees in honor of their trainer, carpet acrobat John Lees (d. 1856). After touring Europe as children, they created a sensation at **Niblo's Garden** (New York, 1860) with their daring trapeze stunts, and visited both Americas and Europe (1862–6).

Thereafter the troupe split up, forming two troupes, but reconsolidated in 1868. Their *Le Voyage en Suisse* (1879), a farce comedy enlivened with mechanical stunts, played Paris, London, and New York (the Park Theatre, 1881). William and Edward settled in Massachusetts, where, in their studio, they developed and promoted the comic extravaganzas *Fantasma* (1884) and *Superba* (1890), briefly reviving U.S. spectacular pant**o**mime.   LS

Hansberry, Lorraine (1930–65) **African-American** playwright. Born into a comfortable middle-class home but surrounded by poverty in Chicago's South Side, Hansberry early confronted the plight of black families living in ghetto conditions that formed the background for her landmark drama, *A **Raisin in the Sun*** (1959). This first play on Broadway by a black woman had a black director, **Lloyd Richards,** and predominant black financing. It ran for 530 performances and won the New York Drama Critics' Circle Award. Hansberry's next play, *The Sign in Sidney Brustein's Window* (1964), about uncommitted white intellectuals in Greenwich Village, was not successful. After her early death from cancer, her former husband completed and produced two plays from her unfinished manuscripts, *To Be Young, Gifted and Black* (1969) and *Les Blancs* (1970).   EGH

> *See:* S. Carter, *Hansberry's Drama: Commitment Amid Complexity,* Urbana, IL, 1991; A. Cheney, *Lorraine Hansberry,* Boston, 1984.

Hapgood, Norman (1868–1937) Editor and drama critic. Born in Chicago and educated at

Three of the Hanlon-Lees brothers: George (left), Alfred (on the floor), and Thomas, when appearing at Woods Theatre, N.Y., in the 1860s. Photo: C. D. Fredricks, N.Y. Courtesy: Laurence Senelick.

Harvard, Hapgood learned his trade as a reporter and editorial writer before serving as drama critic of the *New York Commercial Advertiser* and *The Bookman* from 1897 to 1902. He left criticism to become editor of *Collier's Weekly* (1903–12), *Harper's Weekly* (1913–16), and *Hearst's International Magazine* 1923–5) before turning to politics. He is author of *The Stage in America* (1901).   TLM

Harbach (né Hauerbach), Otto (1873–1963) Lyricist-librettist, educated at Knox College; taught English and worked as a reporter and copywriter before beginning his Broadway career with the lyrics for *Three Twins* (1908). Over the next 30 years he was one of the most prolific writers for the musical stage, with books and/or lyrics to over 40 musicals. He provided lyrics for several shows with composer **Rudolf Friml,** beginning with *The Firefly* (1912); collaborated with **Oscar Hammerstein II** on lyrics and libretti for 10 shows, notably *Rose-Marie* (1924) and *Sunny* (1925); and contributed to shows ranging from the operetta *Madame Sherry* (1910) to the bouncy 1920s musical *Mary* (1920) and *No, No, Nanette* (1925), to the more innovative **Jerome Kern** musicals *The Cat and the Fiddle* (1931) and *Roberta* (1932).   MK

Harburg, E[dgar] Y. "Yip" (né Isidore Hochberg) (1898–1981) Lyricist, librettist, and composer who attended City College of New York and wrote for newspapers before contributing lyrics to *Earl Carroll's Sketchbook* (1929). During the 1930s he wrote lyrics with several different composers, including Jay Gorney, **Vernon Duke,** and **Harold Arlen;** their songs were used in **revue**s along with the work of other writers. He also coauthored libretti and worked on Hollywood films. In 1944 he wrote the score for *Bloomer Girl* with Arlen, and three years later had his greatest success with *Finian's Rainbow,* for which he also collaborated on the libretto. Among his later musicals were *Jamaica* (1957) and *The Happiest Girl in the World* (1961). Harburg's lyrics often reflected his interest in social issues, as in the 1932 song "Brother, Can You Spare a Dime?".   MK

Harby, Isaac (1788–1828) Playwright. A South Carolinian, Harby became a Jewish leader, a teacher, an editor, and the author of three plays. His first play, *Alexander Severus* (1805) was rejected by the Charleston Theatre. *The Gordian Knot* (1807), set in 16th-century Florence, was not produced until published in 1810. *Alberti* (1819), his best play, followed political intrigues surrounding the Medici. An important early drama critic, Harby's "defense of the drama" is still worth reading.   WJM

Hardwick, Elizabeth (1916–) Literary and drama critic. Born and educated in Kentucky, Hardwick pursued a career in the 1940s as a novelist and literary critic before writing drama criticism, mainly for the *New York Review of Books* (1963–83), of which she was a founder and advisory editor. In 1967 she won the **George Jean Nathan** Award, the first woman so honored. More recently (1974), she reappraised **Ibsen**'s major female characters from a feminist perspective.   TLM

Harned, Virginia (1868–1946) Actress, once married to **E. H. Sothern,** whom she divorced. She debuted in *Our Boarding House* at age 16; her New York debut was in *A Lost Lane*. She attracted considerable attention as Drusilla Ives in *That Dancing Girl* and later created the role of Trilby in *Svengali* (1895) for a long run. For several years she managed her own company.   SMA

Harnick, Sheldon see **Bock, Jerry**

Harper, Joseph (fl. 1790–1800) Comedian with the Old **American Company;** first professional theatre manager in **Boston** by opening his New Exhibition Room 10 August 1792, where initially a variety of paratheatrical amusements were presented, followed soon by plays discreetly advertised as "Moral Lectures." After a performance of *The School for Scandal,* his theatre was closed 5 December 1792; he was arrested, tried for violating the antitheatrical act of 1750, and promptly acquitted. The case, however, led to the eventual rescission of Boston's antitheatre laws. Harper joined **Charles Stuart Powell** in the management of the **Federal Street Theatre** in 1801.   PAD

Harrigan, Edward (1844–1911), playwright-actor, and **Tony Hart (né Anthony J. Cannon)** (1855–91), actor, became the most popular comedy team on the American stage (1871–85). They sang, danced, and played the principal roles (usually Harrigan as the amiable, fun-loving Irish adventurer Dan Mulligan and Hart, in blackface, as the Negro wench Rebecca Allup) in Harrigan's high-spirited "melees": *The Mulligan Guard Picnic* (1878), *The **Mulligan Guard Ball*** (1879), *The Mul-*

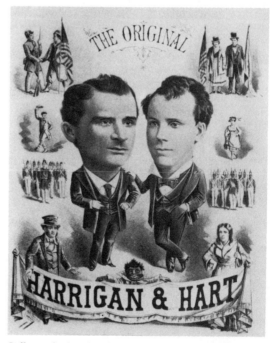

Collage of roles played by Harrigan and Hart. Courtesy: New York Public Library of the Performing Arts.

ligan Guard Chowder (1879), *The Mulligan Guard Christmas* (1879), *The Mulligan Guard Nominee* (1880), *The Mulligan Guard Surprise* (1880), *The Mulligan Guard Silver Wedding* (1881), *Old Lavender* (1877), *The Major* (1881), *Squatter Sovereignty* (1882), *Cordelia's Aspirations* (1883), *Dan's Tribulations* (1884), and *Investigation* (1884). Harrigan's farces were not all "knockdown and slambang"; his documentary explorations of New York's Lower East Side and his striking portraits of the Germans, Italians, Negroes, and particularly the Irish in his 40 plays lead **W. D. Howells** to write, "Here is the spring of a true American comedy, the joyous art of the dramatist who loves the life he observes." Another critic called his plays the "Pickwick Papers of a Bowery Dickens."

Harrigan was born on the NYC's Lower East Side and appeared first as an Irish comic singer in San Francisco (1867). In 1871 he met Hart, a falsetto-voiced singer from Worcester, MA, and wrote "The Little Fraud," which alerted Boston to their extraordinary talents. They turned out 60 more sketches, most notable of which was "The Mulligan Guard," a satire on New York's pseudomilitary companies (with music by David Braham, Harrigan's future father-in-law and thereafter his musical collaborator). Their antics drew boisterous crowds to the Theatre Comique (514 Broadway) and then to Harrigan's Theatre Comique (728 Broadway).

When the second Comique burned down (1884), the partners separated. Hart stumbled in and out of three plays, was committed to an asylum, and died at the age of 35. Harrigan continued writing and acting – *The Leather Patch* (1886), *McNooney's Visit* (1887), and others – and opened a new Harrigan Theatre on Herald Square with *Reilly and the Four Hundred* (1890).

Three of his children – "Eddie," William, and Nedda (Mrs. **Joshua Logan**) – became actors. RM

See: E. J. Kahn, *The Merry Partners: The Age and Stage of Harrigan and Hart,* New York, 1955; R. Moody, *Ned Harrigan: From Corlear's Hook to Herald Square,* Chicago, 1980.

Harris, Jed (1900–79) Producer and director. At the height of the 1920s, Harris presented four plays celebrated for their crisp modern style: *Broadway* (1926), a raucous backstage melodrama overrun with wise-cracking gangsters and gum-chewing chorines; *Coquette* (1927), a tearjerker about the risks of Flaming Youth; *The Royal Family* (1927), a satire about a flamboyant theatrical dynasty modeled on the Barrymores [see **Drew–Barrymore**]; and *The Front Page* (1928), a whirlwind comedy-melodrama set in a newspaper office. Growing quickly bored with his success, Harris was content to rest on his laurels; he worked only sporadically thereafter, most notably on *Uncle Vanya* (1930), a response to critics who complained that he wasted his talents on light entertainment; *The Green Bay Tree* (1933), with Laurence Olivier as a kept homosexual; *Our Town* (1938); and *The Heiress* (1947), based on **Henry James**'s *Washington Square*. After retiring to San Francisco, he broke silence with two books: *Watchman, What of the Night?* (1963), a crusty

and self-justifying account of the backstage warfare on *The Heiress,* and *A Dance on the High Wire* (1979), a curiously muted memoir.

There are two enduring legends about Harris: one, obviously untrue, that he had a golden touch that turned every play he handled into a hit; and the other, which has much greater validity, that he was a monster. Harris directed only a few of his plays (including *Uncle Vanya* and *Our Town*), but all of his productions had superb taste and showmanship, achieved at great cost to his collaborators. **George Abbott** called him "the Little Napoleon of Broadway," and stories of Harris's wild mood swings, withering sarcasm, and cruelty are part of theatrical folklore. FH

See: M. Gottfried, *Jed Harris: The Curse of Genius,* Boston, 1984.

Harris, Julie (1925–) Actress whose Broadway debut was as Atlanta in *It's a Gift* (1945). She rose to stardom with such roles as Frankie Adams in *The Member of the Wedding* (1950); Sally Bowles in *I Am a Camera* (1951), for which in 1952 she won the first of her five best actress Tony Awards (a record); and Joan in *The Lark* (1955, 1956 Tony), performances she later filmed. In 1976 she successfully performed a **one-person** show, *The Belle of Amherst,* subsequently touring the show and playing a season at the Phoenix, London. Critics have been won over by her air of vulnerability and fragility, coupled with remarkable stage techniques. Her Emily Dickinson in *Belle* – one of numerous women she has portrayed culled from history – was called "astonishing in its sagacity and passion . . . shining." She received a Tony in 1969 for *Forty Carats* and in 1972 for *The Last of Mrs. Lincoln.* In 1980 she played the lead in *On Golden Pond* on the West Coast, and in 1989 toured in *Driving Miss Daisy* and in *Lettice & Lovage* in 1992–3. She recently appeared as Isak Dinesen in a one-woman play, *Lucifer's Child* (1991). Harris has also won many awards during her illustrious career in film and television. She is the author of an acclaimed and partially autobiographical text for beginning performers, *Julie Harris Talks to Young Actors* (1972). SMA

Harris, Rosemary (1930–) British-born actress who has appeared in over 140 roles in more than 30 years on the English and American stage, including affiliations with some of the great theatre companies (in England the Bristol Old Vic, Old Vic, the National Theatre, Chichester Festival; in the U.S. the **Association of Producing Artists, Lincoln Center, Brooklyn Academy of Music, American Shakespeare Theatre,** and **Williamstown Theatre Festival**). A versatile actress, who once described herself as "a chameleon on a tartan" and was described in the *New York Times* as "pure presence," she has appeared prominently in *Troilus and Cressida* (**Guthrie**'s 1956 production), *Man and Superman, Much Ado About Nothing, The School for Scandal, The Seagull, Twelfth Night, The Broken Heart* (first Chichester season, 1952), *Hamlet* (Ophelia in National Theatre's inaugural season), *The Lion in Winter* (1966 Tony), *Old Times, Major Barbara, A Streetcar Named Desire* (1973 revival, **Vivian**

Beaumont), *The Royal Family, All My Sons* (1981 London revival), *Pack of Lies,* the Broadway revival of *Hay Fever* (1985–6 season), and as a replacement in *Lost in Yonkers* (1991).   DBW

Harris, Sam H[enry] (1872–1941) Producer who began his theatrical career in 1899 as a stagehand. The following year he became a partner in the firm of Sullivan, Harris, and Woods (1900–4), which produced eight melodramas and burlesques including a hit, *The Fatal Wedding.* He began a 16-year partnership with **George M. Cohan** in 1904, producing more than 50 plays including Cohan's own *Little Johnny Jones, Forty-five Minutes from Broadway,* and *Seven Keys to Baldpate.* After the partnership was dissolved in 1920, Harris independently produced *Rain* (1922), *The Jazz Singer* (1925), *Animal Crackers* (1928), *Dinner at Eight* (1932), *The Man Who Came to Dinner* (1939), and *Lady in the Dark* (1941). His productions of *Icebound* (1923), *Of Thee I Sing* (1932), and *You Can't Take It with You* (1937) won Pulitzer Prizes; and *Of Mice and Men* won the 1938 New York Critics' Circle Award. He preferred comedies and musical comedies to serious drama, and was noted for paying attention to the smallest details of a production.   TLM

Harris, William, Sr. (1844–1916), **Henry B.** (1866–1912), and **William, Jr.** (1884–1946) Producers. William Sr. attained success as a manager and producer in Boston before joining **Marc Klaw, Abe Erlanger, Charles Frohman,** and others in establishing the Theatrical **Syndicate** (1895–6). His older son, Henry, managed the careers of stars including **Amelia Bingham** (1902), became the manager of the Hudson Theatre (1903), and produced such hits as *Soldiers of Fortune* (1901), *The Lion and the Mouse* (1905), *The Chorus Lady* (1906), *The Traveling Salesman* (1908), and *The Third Degree* (1909), before going down with the Titanic. Younger son William Jr. attended Columbia University, then became a successful producer and later a director, presenting *Yellow Jacket* (1912), *Twin Beds* (1914), *The Thirteenth Chair* (1916), *East Is West* (1918), *Abraham Lincoln* (1919), *Outward Bound* (1924), and *The Greeks Had a Word for It* (1930).   TLM

Harrison, Rex (né Reginald Carey) (1908–90) British actor, knighted in 1989, active on both sides of the Atlantic. Underrated, despite considerable interpretative skills, he was described by **Richard Coe** as "Smooth as a pearl, prickly as a porcupine." This debonair star, the quintessential Henry Higgins of *My Fair Lady,* his Tony Award–winning role of 1956 (revived in 1981), appeared frequently in New York during his 66 years on the stage. From his Broadway debut in 1936 to his final role, Lord Porteous in *The Circle* (1989), Harrison appeared most notably as Henry VIII in *Anne of the Thousand Days* (Tony, 1948), Shepherd Henderson in *Bell, Book and Candle* (1950), The Man in *The Love of Four Colonels* (1953), Caesar in **Shaw**'s *Caesar and Cleopatra* (1977), and Shotover in *Heartbreak House* (1983). He wrote two

autobiographies: *Rex* (1974) and *A Damned Serious Business: My Life in Comedy* (1991).   DBW

Harrison, Richard B. (1864–1935) Son of fugitive slaves, Harrison graduated from the Detroit School of Art and began to give public readings throughout the country. He appeared briefly at the **Lafayette Theatre,** where he was spotted for the awesome role of De Lawd in the all-black production of *The Green Pastures* (1930). Harrison was brilliant, and the production ran for five years. He received many honors, including the prestigious Spingarn Medal awarded annually by the NAACP.   EGH

> *See:* W. C. Daniel, *"De Lawd": Richard B. Harrison and The Green Pastures,* Westport, CT, 1986.

Hart, Lorenz (1895–1943) Lyricist and librettist. His first theatrical assignment was as a play translator for the **Shubert**s. In collaboration with **Richard Rodgers,** who was to be his partner for the rest of his career, Hart contributed four songs to the Broadway musical comedy *Poor Little Ritz Girl* (1920). The first complete scores by Rodgers and Hart were for *The Garrick Gaieties* (1925) and *Dearest Enemy* (1925). In the next 18 years they created an almost uninterrupted string of successful shows, including *The Girl Friend* (1926), *A Connecticut Yankee* (1927; revival 1943), *America's Sweetheart* (1931), *On Your Toes* (1936), *Babes in Arms* (1937), *The Boys from Syracuse* (1938), *I Married an Angel* (1938), *Pal Joey* (1940), and *By Jupiter* (1941). Hart's clever, sometimes sardonic lyrics, often employing complicated internal rhyme schemes, are considered among the finest ever written for the musical stage.   MK

> *See:* D. Hart, *Thou Swell, Thou Witty: The Life and Lyrics of Lorenz Hart,* New York, 1976; D. Hart and R. Kimballs, eds., *The Complete Lyrics of Lorenz Hart,* New York, 1986; S. Marx and J. Clayton, *Rodgers and Hart: Bewitched, Bothered, and Bewildered,* New York, 1976.

Hart, Moss (1904–61) Playwright, librettist, and director. Although he had written several unsuccessful plays on his own, it was Hart's teaming up with **George S. Kaufman** during the 1930s that established his career. These two wits delighted American audiences with such hits as *Once in a Lifetime* (1930), *You Can't Take It with You* (1936, Pulitzer Prize), and *The Man Who Came to Dinner* (1939). On his own in the '40s, Hart wrote, among other offerings, the book for the landmark musical about psychoanalysis, *Lady in the Dark* (1941), and the funny theatre in-joke about a play in rehearsal, *Light Up the Sky* (1948). Hart devoted much of the latter decade of his career to directing, winning the Tony Award for his work on *My Fair Lady* (1956). His autobiography, *Act One* (1959), is a classic theatrical memoir.   LDC

Hart, Tony see **Harrigan, Edward**

Harte, Bret (Francis Brett Harte) (1836–1902) Writer. Raised in Brooklyn, he moved to California in 1853 and became famous for stories and poems in *The Overland Monthly* (1868–71). His popularity declined as rapidly as it rose, and after 1878 he lived abroad. His best work combines sentiment and low humor in the manner of Charles Dickens. He wrote *Two Men of Sandy Bar* (1875) for **Stuart Robson,** and collaborated with Mark Twain on *Ah Sin* (1877), a vehicle for Charles Parsloe. Though both failed, they established a genre that **Bartley Campbell** perfected in *My Partner.*   DMcD

> See: T. E. Pemberton, *The Life of Bret Harte,* New York, 1903; G. Stewart, *Bret Harte, Argonaut and Exile,* New York, 1931.

Hartford Stage Company Since founding director Jacques Cartier opened the not-for-profit company in an abandoned supermarket in 1964, the Hartford Stage, located in the capital of Connecticut, has developed into a first-rate regional theatre with a playhouse designed by postmodernist architect Robert Venturi. Cartier was succeeded as artistic director first by Paul Weidner in 1968, then by **Mark Lamos** in 1980. Initially a traditional company mounting old and modern standards, the Hartford now devotes about half of its season to new or recent American plays and dramatizations of nontheatrical works. Lamos has revealed a special gift for large-scale productions of epics, such as Shakespeare's history plays. His costaging with Mary B. Robinson of *The Greeks* (1982), Kenneth Cavender's seven-hour cycle of Greek tragedies, earned the theatre wide acclaim.   CLJ

Hartman Theatre Company Founded (1974) in Stamford, CT, by Margot Hartman Tenney and Del Tenney, who converted a vaudeville house (the Palace Theater) and established a short-lived conservatory in a smaller theatre nearby. An initial focus on new works and the revival of classics changed in two years to more familiar plays. The company, with artistic director **Edwin Sherin,** attracted too few subscribers, even after moving to the more attractive Stamford Theatre, and disbanded in 1987.   WD

Harvey One of the most successful plays in Broadway history. Written by **Mary Coyle Chase,**

it opened at the 48th Street Theatre on 1 November 1944, ran for 1,775 performances, and won the Pulitzer Prize for 1945. **Frank Fay** starred as Elwood P. Dowd, an inebriated, sweet-tempered, but dotty soul, who sees and communicates with an over-6'-tall, invisible rabbit named Harvey. In 1950 Universal Studios released a very successful film version starring James Stewart.   FB

Harwood, John Edmund (1771–1809) British-born comic actor who was brought to the **Chestnut Street Theatre** by **Thomas Wignell** in 1793, remaining in **Philadelphia** until engaged by **William Dunlap** for the **Park** in New York in 1803, where he acted until his death. Among his better roles was Falstaff, which he played first in 1806 opposite the Hotspur of **Thomas A. Cooper.** Dunlap, who called him a man of wit and refinement and highly endowed as an actor, but indolent and careless of study, compared him to the British actor John Bannister. He married a granddaughter of Benjamin Franklin and fathered Admiral Andrew Allen Harwood.   DBW

Hatful of Rain, A Drama by Michael Gazzo on the effects of a young man's drug addiction on his lower-middle-class family. The play opened at the **Lyceum Theatre** on 9 November 1955 and ran for 398 performances. Frank Corsaro directed and the cast featured Ben Gazzara, Shelley Winters, and Anthony Franciosa – all veterans of the **Actors Studio** and acting teacher **Lee Strasberg.** Steve McQueen, also a student of Strasberg's, made his Broadway debut when he replaced Gazzara during the run. The anguished, emotional tone of the play epitomized the "kitchen sink" naturalism that was a characteristic element of American theatre of the 1950s.   MF

Haverly, (Christopher) Col. Jack H. (1837–1901) Variety manager. Apprenticed as a shoemaker, he ran away from his home in rural Pennsylvania to Pittsburgh, where he became associated with theatres as doorkeeper, box office clerk, and treasurer. Organizing his first **minstrel show** company in 1862, he bought his first theatre two

Josephine Hull (left) with Frank Fay in Mary Chase's *Harvey* (1944). Photo: New York *Sun.*

CLEOPATRA   MARY OF SCOTLAND

Helen Hayes as Cleopatra, Mary of Scotland, and (center) Victoria. Courtesy: Don B. Wilmeth.

years later (Toledo, OH). Part owner and manager of Emerson's Minstrels (1875) and Callender's Colored Minstrels (1878), he was identified with Haverly's Mastodon Minstrels (1878–84). He also leased strategically located theatres in **Chicago,** New York, **Philadelphia,** and **San Francisco** for his companies to play in. Business speculation bankrupted him in 1898.   DMcD

Havlin, John see **Stair and Havlin**

Havoc (née Hovick), June (1916–). Actor, director, playwright. Havoc's acting career started at age 2 and continued through **vaudeville** (with sister **Gypsy Rose Lee**), dance marathons, Broadway, Hollywood, major regional theatres, and international tours for over 65 years. Her musical plays are autobiographical: *Marathon 33* (1963), *Love Regatta* (1971), *I Said the Fly* (1973), and *Oh Glorious Tintinnabulation* (1974). She was Artistic Director of New Repertory Theatre in New Orleans (1969–71) and wrote two autobiographies.   TH-S

Haydon, Julie (née Donella Lightfoot Donaldson) (1910–) Actress whose ethereal quality enhanced a handful of outstanding roles: Brigid in *Shadow and Substance* (1938), Kitty Duval in *The Time of Your Life* (1939), and Laura in *The Glass Menagerie* (1944, Chicago; 1945, New York), the latter two roles originated by her. In the 1960s and '70s she performed Amanda in *Glass Menagerie* at various colleges. A champion of her late husband, **George Jean Nathan,** she has presented readings from his works.   DBW

Hayes, Helen (1900–) American actress. With **Katharine Cornell** and **Lynn Fontanne,** Hayes has often been called "the First Lady of the American Theater." Diminutive and homespun, she is distinctly less glamorous than the other Great Ladies; and the qualities of modesty and common sense that she projects help account for her enduring appeal. A stage star for over 50 years (she retired in 1971), she has continued to act occasionally in films and on television, and for a time hosted a radio program addressed to senior citizens.

As a youngster she appeared with **John Drew** and **William Gillette,** and worked for such fabled producers as **Charles Frohman** and **George Tyler.** Opposite **Alfred Lunt** in **Booth Tarkington**'s *Clarence* (1919), she played a saucy flapper, as she did again in the **Theatre Guild**'s *Caesar and Cleopatra* (1925) and *Coquette* (1927). In the 1930s, she had her greatest critical success as the gallant monarchs in *Mary of Scotland* (1933) and *Victoria Regina* (1935). In the 1940s and '50s she starred in showy vehicles like *Harriet* (1943), an episodic biography of Harriet Beecher Stowe; *Happy Birthday* (1946), in which she was a librarian turned siren; and *Mrs. McThing* (1952), in which she was a society matron transformed into a scrubwoman. In her most memorable later work, the Phoenix Theatre 1967 revival of **The Show-Off,** she played **George Kelly**'s no-nonsense mother-in-law with bracing tartness.

Often criticized for her choice of material and for being cloyingly demure, Hayes is more resourceful, modern, and witty than her current reputation allows. She has a remarkably clear, low-pitched, resonant voice, and none of the hamminess that flawed the star acting of the tradition she grew up in. She is the author of several memoirs, most notably *My Life in Three Acts* (1990) with Katherine Hatch. Two NYC playhouses have been named the **Helen Hayes Theatre.**   FH

Hays, David (1930–) Set and lighting designer and producer. Hays is the founder of the **National Theatre of the Deaf** and a cofounder of the **Eugene O'Neill Memorial Theatre Center.** His designs include *The Iceman Cometh* (1956), *Long Day's Journey into Night* (1956), *All the Way Home* (1960), and *No Strings* (1962). He was resident designer for the Repertory Theatre of **Lincoln Center** (1967–8), and created over 30 settings for the New York City Ballet. Many of his earlier sets show the influence of the poetic realism that dominated the 1950s.   AA

Hayward, Leland (1902–71) Producer responsible for two dozen plays and musicals on Broadway between 1941 and his death, two-thirds of which were unqualified successes both critically and financially. Two of his productions (**State of the Union,** 1945; **South Pacific,** 1949) won Pulitzer Prizes. Prior to becoming a producer in 1944 with *A Bell for Adano,* Hayward had established a successful talent agency in Hollywood and New York. Other significant plays produced included **Mister Roberts** (1948), *Anne of the Thousand Days* (1948), **Call Me Madam** (1950), **Gypsy** (1959), *The Sound of Music* (1959), and *The Trial of the Catonsville Nine* (1971). Hayward was also a film and television producer, a pilot and airline executive, and a photographer. In 1936 he married the actress Margaret Sullavan, divorcing in 1948. **Oliver Smith** said that Hayward represented everything that was best in the theatre, being "tenacious and at the same time elegant."   DBW

Hazel Kirke This domestic melodrama by **Steele MacKaye,** one of the first of its kind without a villain, enjoyed enormous popularity throughout the country for 30 years after its premiere. Opening at the **Madison Square Theatre** in 1880, the play by 1882 was being presented by 14 road companies. The melodrama traces the breakdown and eventual replacement of patriarchal family relations with Victorian ones, as a stern Scottish father, Dunstan Kirke, learns to accept the love and independence of his daughter Hazel. At the climax of the play, the blinded father is unable to rescue his daughter from an attempted suicide. **Charles W. Couldock** and **Effie Ellsler** played the father and daughter in MacKaye's original production, and both continued these roles on the road, Ellsler later forming her own company and performing Hazel through 1905. **Georgia Cayvan, Annie Russell,** and Phoebe Davis also played Hazel during their careers.   BMcC

He and She First produced in Boston in 1912 under the title *The Herfords,* this play by **Rachel Crothers** opened on 12 February 1920 at the Little Theatre in New York. Crothers herself played the lead role, Ann Herford, a sculptor who at the end of the play refuses a $100,000 prize she has won in a competition in order to devote herself to her family. Although the play ran for only 28 performances, it was generally praised by critics for dealing forcefully with the issues of a double standard of success and of a woman's role in marriage and in society. **Alexander Woollcott** called it a tragedy, "for something fine and strong dies in the last act."   FB

Hearn, George (1934–) Actor-singer, equally at home in musicals and classical drama. Hearn attended Southwestern University, then worked for several seasons at the **New York Shakespeare Festival.** He had a featured role in *1776* (1969), and appeared in Storey's *The Changing Room* and *An Almost Perfect Person* (1977) before replacing **Len Cariou** in the title role of *Sweeney Todd* (1979). He starred in the musicals *I Remember Mama* (1979) and *A Doll's House* (1982), won a Tony for his portrayal of Albin in **La Cage Aux Folles** (1983), and portrayed the father in *Meet Me in St. Louis* (1989).   MK

Hecht, Ben (1894–1964) Playwright. Although a significant figure in American cinema, Hecht is important theatrically for two popular and frequently revived plays, both collaborations with **Charles MacArthur.** Together the playwrights were viewed as bad boys of Broadway. *The **Front Page,** a frenetic, funny, satirical melodrama on the newspaper business (1928), is based on the playwrights' experiences as reporters in Chicago. *Twentieth Century* (1932), an eccentric comedy depicting a desperate producer trying to make a comeback, inspired a John Barrymore [see **Drew– Barrymore**] film and the musical *On the Twentieth Century.* Hecht wrote other plays and musical librettos as early as 1922 and as late as 1953. His autobiography, *A Child of the Century,* appeared in 1954.   RHW

See: W. MacAdams, *Ben Hecht: The Man Behind the Legend,* New York, 1990.

Heckart, [Anne] Eileen (1919–) Stage, film, and television character actress who made her Broadway debut (as understudy) in the long-running *Voice of the Turtle* (1943). She played many important supporting roles before essaying the title role in *Everbody Loves Opal* (1963). Her performance as Mrs. Baker, the overprotective mother, in *Butterflies Are Free* (1969; film, 1972) garnered a Tony nomination and an Oscar for best supporting actress. She played Eleanor Roosevelt on a tour of U.S. cities in *Eleanor* (1976). Regional performances include Mother Courage at the **McCarter Theatre** (1973), Thelma Cates in *'night Mother* at Westport Country Playhouse (1985), and the title role in *Driving Miss Daisy* at the **Coconut Grove Playhouse** (1991), directed by her son, Luke Yankee.   MR

Hedgerow Theatre Founded in 1923 in Moylan-Rose Valley, PA, by Jasper Deeter, this theatre was for many years the only true U.S. professional repertory theatre, operating year-round with no stars and frequent changes of bill. Although the repertory scheme was dropped in 1956, by 1985 the theatre had amassed a repertory of over 200 plays. Standard plays, with those of **Shaw** most popular, have dominated. Functioning as a cooperative, the theatre operated in a small converted mill with fewer than 170 seats; its future remains precarious since the destruction by fire of its playhouse (late 1985). DBW

Heidi Chronicles, The, by Wendy Wasserstein,

opened **Off-Broadway** at the **Playwrights Horizons** on 18 November 1988 and transferred to Broadway's **Plymouth Theatre** 9 March 1989. Dramatizing key moments in the life of the title character as she searches for self-actualization from the mid-1960s through the late '80s, it is a satirical yet compassionate portrait of an era and of the dreams, frustrations, failures, and triumphs experienced by many middle-class American women of the time. Reproved by some feminist critics as "antifeminist" in its treatment of women and the feminist cause, it was nevertheless a resounding critical and popular success, winning numerous awards, including a Pulitzer Prize. DJW

Heifner, Jack (1946–) Texas-born playwright, educated at Southern Methodist University. His *Vanities* opened in New York in 1976 and ran for 1,785 performances; at its closing in 1980, it was the second longest-running nonmusical in **Off-Broadway** history. Subsequent works include *Patio/Porch* (1978); *Star Treatment* (1980), with songs by Janis Ian; and *Leader of the Pack* (1985), a Broadway musical with Ellie Greenwich. His one-act *Bargains* was published in *The Best Short Plays of 1988*. BBW

Helburn, Theresa (1887–1959) Director and producer. Born in New York, Helburn received her BA from Bryn Mawr in 1908, attended **George Pierce Baker**'s English 47 at Radcliffe, and studied in Paris for a year at the Sorbonne. After a brief career as an actress, she pursued a writing career, becoming drama critic of *The Nation* (1918). Two years later she took over the administration of the struggling **Theatre Guild** with the title of Executive Director. In 1933 she left for a year in Hollywood but returned as administrative director with **Lawrence Langner**. She was responsible for bringing **Alfred Lunt** and **Lynn Fontanne** together for *The Guardsman* in 1924, which established them as the leading dual acting team in America. With Langner she brought *Oklahoma!* to the stage in 1943, and in the same year *Othello* with **Paul Robeson**. A woman of outstanding executive ability, she was described by Langner as possessing nerves "like whipcord" and will power "like steel." Her autobiography, *A Wayward Quest*, was published in 1960. TLM

Held, Anna (1873–1918) Entertainer. Born in Paris of Polish–French parentage, petite Held was discovered in London in 1895 by **Florenz Ziegfeld,** who married her in 1897 (divorced in 1912) and became her producer-publicist, circulating extravagant stories of bizarre behavior. As star of New York musical shows such as *Papa's Wife, The Little Duchess, Mlle. Napoleon,* and *The Parisien Model,* the amply endowed Held, with large, expressive brown eyes and red-brown hair, became synonymous with French sauciness and tease, proffering songs such as "Won't You Come and Play Wiz Me?" and "I Just Can't Make My Eyes Behave." DBW

See: M. Farnsworth, *The Ziegfeld Follies,* London, 1956.

Helen Hayes Theatre Name of two different New York playhouses:
1. 210 West 46th St., NYC [Architects: Herts and Tallant]. Originally conceived as a New York counterpart of the Parisian original, the playhouse was opened in 1911 as the Folies-Bergère, a restaurant-theatre, by producers **Henry B. Harris** and Jesse Lasky. Five months later, recognizing its failure, they rebuilt the interior and, without the restaurant, renamed it the Fulton for the production of legitimate fare. With fewer than 1,000 seats, it became the ideal house for intimate plays. During the depression decade, it changed owners and policy several times, but in 1941 came back as a legitimate house. In 1955, it was renamed the **Helen Hayes** in honor of one of Broadway's first ladies of the stage. In 1982, despite strong protest from the theatrical community, the theatre was torn down to make way for a hotel. Its most famous tenant was the posthumous production of **Eugene O'Neill**'s autobiographical play, *Long Day's Journey into Night* (1956).
2. 238 West 44th St., NYC [Architects: H. C. Ingalls and F. B. Hoffman, Jr.]. In 1912, producer **Winthrop Ames** built a 299-seat house named the Little for the production of unusual plays. Five years later, when it became a strain on his finances, he leased it to a succession of producers. To make it a viable Broadway house, a balcony was added and its seating was almost doubled. In 1931, it was sold to the *New York Times* and thereafter used mainly as a concert-lecture hall and a television studio, but was returned to legitimate production in 1974. In 1983, under different ownership, the theatre was renamed the Helen Hayes during the run of *Torch Song Trilogy.* MCH

Hell-Bent fer Heaven 1924 melodrama by

Hatcher Hughes about a scheming religious fanatic who nearly causes disaster for two Carolina mountain families. Dependent on amazing coincidences and rendered in quaint dialect ("Are you a-stickin' up fer that reptile?"), the play by a Columbia drama professor was a controversial choice for the Pulitzer Prize of 1923–4. Two Pulitzer jurors resigned when they learned that Professor **Brander Matthews** had intervened with the Columbia panel that awarded the prize on behalf of his younger colleague's play. The jury's choice for the prize had been **George Kelly**'s comedy *The Show-Off.* MF

Hellman, Lillian (1906–84) One of America's leading playwrights. Since 1963, when she ceased writing for the theatre, revivals of her plays have been performed regularly throughout the country. She is also known for her controversial books of memoirs: *An Unfinished Woman* (1969), *Pentimento* (1973), and *Scoundrel Time* (1976).

Charles Nelson Reilly and Carol Channing (under central arch) in *Hello, Dolly!* Courtesy: Michael Gnat.

The **Children's Hour** (1934), based on an episode from William Roughead's *Bad Companions,* shocked and fascinated Broadway with the evil machinations of a child who destroys her teachers by whispering about their "unnatural" relationship. Hellman was labeled a "second **Ibsen**," "the American Strindberg," and the play ran for 691 performances. Vigorous and unyielding confrontations became her dramaturgical trademark, both in *Children's Hour* and in *The* **Little Foxes** (1939), **Watch on the Rhine** (1941), *The Searching Wind* (1944), *Another Part of the Forest* (1946), *The* **Autumn Garden** (1951), *The Lark* (1955, adapted from Anouilh's *L'Alouette*), **Candide** (1956, from Voltaire, with music by **Leonard Bernstein**), and **Toys in the Attic** (1960). Her plays were always given high-quality productions, first by **Herman Shumlin** and then by **Kermit Bloomgarden.** Only three plays failed at the box-office: *Days to Come* (1936), *Montserrat* (1949, adapted from Emmanuel Roblés's play), and *My Mother, My Father and Me* (1963, adapted from Burt Blechman's novel, *How Much?*).

Born in New Orleans, she became an editorial assistant to Horace Liveright in New York, a theatre press agent, a play-reader, and (in 1931) a script-reader in Hollywood, where she met detective-story writer Dashiell Hammett, who was to become her constant companion until his death in 1961. She wrote scripts for such films as *Dark Angel* (1935), *These Three* (1936, based on *The Children's Hour*), **Dead End** (1937), and *The North Star* (1943). In 1952 she was called before the House Un-American Activities Committee, and her name was automatically added to Hollywood's blacklist.

RM

See: P. Feibleman, *Lilly: Reminiscences of Lillian Hellman,* New York, 1988; R. Moody, *Lillian Hellman,* New York, 1972; R. Newman, ed., *The Cold War Romance of Lillian Hellman & John Melby,* Chapel Hill, NC, 1989; W. Wright, *Lillian Hellman: The Image, The Woman,* New York, 1986.

Hello, Dolly! Two-act musical comedy, music and lyrics by **Jerry Herman,** book by **Michael Stewart;** opened 16 January 1964 at the **St. James Theatre,** running 2,844 performances. This musical adaptation of **Thornton Wilder**'s *The Matchmaker* chronicles the exploits of Dolly Levi (**Carol Channing**) as she settles people's romantic lives, including her own, in the 1890s. The lavish production, brilliantly staged by director-choreographer **Gower Champion** in the best tradition of old-fashioned glitz and glitter, won the Drama Critics' Circle and Tony awards for best musical and was also a hit in London (with **Mary Martin**). When the New York production began to flag in 1967, producer **David Merrick** gave it fresh life with an all-black cast headed by **Pearl Bailey** (a 1991 black cast in Long Beach, CA, starred Nell Carter). The show was originally written for **Ethel Merman,** who declined to create the role of Dolly, but who was the last Dolly when the show closed in 1970. The rousing title song was the score's biggest hit, although Herman (who had uncredited help from others on the score) settled a plagiarism suit over it out of court.   JD

Hellzapoppin A **vaudeville revue** produced by **Olsen and Johnson,** with songs by Sammy Fain, Charles Tobias, Earl Robinson, Alfred Hayes, Paul Mann, and Stephen Weiss. Staged by Edward Duryea Dowling, *Hellzapoppin* opened on Broadway 22 September 1938 with songs and dances, low-comedy gags, a fiddler, a unicyclist, much noise from gunshots and firecrackers, and some running gimmicks – such as the woman who wandered the audience searching for "Oscar"; the magician who could not escape from his straitjacket; and a man trying to deliver a potted plant, which seemed to grow larger between appearances. At closing on 17 December 1941, its 1,404 performances made it the third longest-running show on Broadway after **Tobacco Road** and **Abie's Irish Rose.**   JDM

Hemsley, Gilbert (1936–83) Lighting designer and production manager who began as **Jean Rosenthal**'s assistant, quickly developing a reputation not only as a lighting designer but as someone who could brilliantly manage the complex tours and load-ins of opera and ballet companies. He designed more than 35 operas for the New York City Opera Company as well as lighting for Martha Graham, American Ballet Theatre, the Bolshoi Ballet, and inaugural celebrations for Presidents Nixon and Carter. He supervised the premiere of **Bernstein**'s *Mass* at the Kennedy Center (1971) and *Einstein on the Beach* (1976) at the Metropolitan Opera. He also taught at the University of Wisconsin at Madison.   AA

Henderson, Ray see **DeSylva, Buddy**

Henley, Beth (1952–) Playwright (and actress) in the Southern Gothic tradition, whose comedies create empathy for bizarre characters who survive their disastrous experiences in outlandish ways. Her first professionally produced play, *Crimes of the Heart,* won the Pulitzer Prize in 1981, the first play to win it prior to a Broadway opening. A family drama gone awry, *Crimes* portrays with absurdist wit and compassion the rallying of three eccentric Mississippi sisters because one of them has shot her husband. Henley's other plays include *The Wake of Jamey Foster* (1982); *Am I Blue?* (1982); *The Miss Firecracker Contest* (1984), another black comedy, about a Mississippi woman's effort to redeem her calamitous life by winning a beauty contest; *The Debutante Ball* (1985); *The Lucky Spot* (1986); and *Abundance* (1990), the exploration of a 25-year friendship of mail-order brides in the Old West. Henley also wrote screenplays for *Crimes* and *Miss Firecracker.*   FB

Henning, Doug (1947–) Canadian-born magician, now semiretired, most responsible for the popularity of **magic in the U.S.** during the 1970s and '80s due to his upbeat, boyish demeanor and polished illusions. In 1973, a show that began in Toronto as *Spellbound* was adapted into the musical *The Magic Show* for Broadway, where it ran four and a half years. For several months in 1982 Henning was back on Broadway in *Merlin.* He now creates illusions for others.   DBW

Henrietta, The **Bronson Howard**'s melodramatic portrayal of Wall Street fascinated audiences for over two decades with its technological accuracy and realistic detail. It opened 26 September 1887 at the **Union Square Theatre.** Despite a fire that precipitated its premature closing, its depiction of high finance and romantic treachery caused quite a stir. The attempts by young Nicholas Van Alstyne, Jr., to manipulate a catastrophic securities collapse for his own gain must have had a chilling effect on a Gilded Age audience swept up in a massive wave of real-life monopolies and robber barons. Although it represented a shift away from his early farces and melodramas into social dramas, Howard's play is remembered as one of his best, ranking among the most important American plays of the 19th century.   PAD

Henry, John (1738–94) Early American actor, born in Ireland and working in London and the West Indies before joining **Douglass**'s **American Company.** Henry made his first American appearance in Philadelphia on 6 October 1767. The matinee idol of his time, Henry was the first actor in America whose lamentable morals were seized on by opponents of the theatre. A chronic sufferer from gout, Henry was also the first American actor to keep a carriage. He first married a Miss Storer; after her death lived with her sister, Ann; and finally married a third Storer sister, Maria.

After the Revolutionary War, Henry comanaged the American Company with **Lewis Hallam, Jr.,** and in 1792 imported **John Hodgkinson,** who shortly forced Henry into retirement. A tall, handsome Irishman, Henry was most successful in comedy, especially Irish characters. **William Dunlap** considered him "one of the best performers in the colonies," but his arrogant manner made him many enemies.   SMA

Henry, William Alfred, III (1950–) New Jersey–born and Yale-educated (1971) drama critic who began a career in journalism on the *Boston Globe* (1971–80). After a short stint on the New York *Daily News* (1980–1), he became an associate editor of *Time* magazine (1981–), press critic (1982–5), and theatre critic (1985–), where with precision and style he sums up the plot, gives credits, and suggests a meaning in limited space.   TLM

Hepburn, Katharine (1907–) Stage and film actress, educated at Bryn Mawr, whose professional debut was in *The Czarina* in Baltimore (1928); her New York debut was in *These Days* (1928). Of her early roles, Tracy Lord in *The Philadelphia Story* (1939) was the most memorable. In 1950 she played Rosalind in *As You Like It* at the **Cort,** then toured. In 1971 she toured in the musical comedy *Coco* after a successful Broadway run. Later stage appearances include *A Matter of Gravity* (1976) and *West Side Waltz* (1981). Her first film role was as Sydney Fairfield in *A Bill of Divorcement* (1932); she has won four Oscars as best actress.

Hepburn has invariably enchanted audiences by appearing in sophisticated comedy, in which her finesse and timing serve her well. In response to *A Matter of Gravity,* critics termed her "radiant . . . enchanting," calling her a "bright, classy, likeably smug, sassy lady." Her autobiography, *Me: Stories of My Life,* was published in 1991.   SMA

See: A. Edwards, *A Remarkable Woman,* New York, 1985.

Herbert, F. Hugh (1897–1958) English-born playwright whose forte was light comedy. *Kiss and Tell* (1943), a play about teenagers, ran for 956 performances, had three road companies, and became a popular radio serial. It was a great escape for a troubled world. In *For Love or Money* (1947) a charming young girl wins the love of an aging leading man. *The Moon Is Blue* (1951) tested moral waters by placing the young heroine in jeopardy. *The Best House in Naples* (1956) was a theatrical failure.   WJM

Herbert, Victor (1859–1924) Irish-born and German-educated composer who came to America at the age of 27 to perform as a cellist with the Metropolitan Opera Orchestra. He became interested in composing for the theatre, and in 1894 his first score, *Prince Ananias,* was heard. The following year, his show *The Wizard of the Nile* had a long run in New York and on tour. After composing the music for several shows for comedian Frank Daniels, Herbert created the score for *The Serenade* (1897), which benefited from an excellent production by the **Bostonians.** In the last years of the 19th century, Herbert served as musical director of the Pittsburgh Symphony Orchestra. Some of his most enduringly popular songs were written for **Babes in Toyland** (1903) and *Mlle. Modiste* (1905), the latter created as a vehicle for opera star **Fritzi Scheff.** Herbert's biggest commercial success came with *The Red Mill* (1906), which was also a big hit when revived on Broadway in 1945. Among Herbert's other popular musicals were **Naughty Marietta** (1910), *Sweethearts* (1913), and *Eileen* (1917). He also contributed songs to the 1921 and 1923 **Ziegfeld** Follies. Herbert was one of the founding members of the American Society of Composers, Authors, and Publishers.

Trained in the conventions and traditions of European operetta, Herbert was adept at composing music that appealed to American audiences. Equally at home writing for comic operas, operettas, and musical comedies, he raised the level of American theatre music through the richness and variety of his scores.   MK

See: E. N. Waters, *Victor Herbert: A Life in Music,* New York, 1955.

Herlihy, James Leo (1927–   ) Playwright who established his career with *Blue Denim* (1958), a play about misunderstood adolescents. Other plays include *Streetlight Sonata* (1950), *Moon in Capricorn* (1953), *Crazy October* (1958), and *Stop, You're Killing Me,* a trilogy of one-acts (1968). *Blue Denim* and his novels *All Fall Down* (1960) and *Midnight Cowboy* (1965) were made into popular films.   TLM

Herman, David (1876–1930) One of the first and most influential of **Jewish Art Theatre** directors, starting with **Hirshbein**'s Troupe in Odessa in 1908, followed by the Arts Corner in Warsaw in 1910, and then the celebrated Vilna Troupe from 1917, where his most memorable of many productions was a stylistic production of *The Dybbuk.* After periods in Warsaw and Vienna, he emigrated to America, exerting a profound influence on the **Yiddish theatre** scene with his inspired direction of the **Folksbiene.**   AB

Herman, Jerry (Gerald) (1932–   ) Composer, lyricist. He attended Miami University, where he wrote and directed a college revue, *I Feel Wonderful,* that impressed audiences and had an **Off-Broadway**

run in 1954. After writing songs for other Off-Broadway **revue**s, he contributed his first Broadway score to *Milk and Honey* (1961). His greatest success was the score for **Hello, Dolly!** (1964). Subsequent shows include *Mame* (1966), *Dear World* (1969), *Mack and Mabel* (1974), *The Grand Tour* (1979), and **La Cage Aux Folles** (1983). *Jerry's Girls* (1985) was a revue that drew upon Herman's catalogue of songs for the stage. Rarely an innovator, Herman is a skillful composer-lyricist of traditional show tunes.   MK

Herne, James A. (1839–1901) Actor, manager, and playwright. Responding to the forces of science and democracy that challenged contemporary society, Herne developed realistic themes and characters in his plays and created a realist creed for drama. Beginning his acting career in 1854, he became a stage manager in **San Francisco,** where he wrote melodramas with **David Belasco** (*Within an Inch of His Life,* 1879; *Hearts of Oak,* 1879). Among his own plays, *The Minute Men of 1774–75* (1886) suggested the New England local color later developed in the temperance play *Drifting Apart* (1888) and **Shore Acres** (1892), in which Uncle Nat Berry, with his language and action, personified the Downeaster and made Herne a millionaire.

With the help of **William Dean Howells** and others who rented Chickering Hall in Boston, Herne staged **Margaret Fleming** (1890–1), his best known work. This insightful play, about a philandering husband whose illegitimate child is accepted by his morally superior and sensitive wife, revealed Herne's interest in realism and social determinism, as well as his playwriting skills; although revised before its New York production, it was still unsuccessful. *The Reverend Griffith Davenport* (1899), based on a novel by Helen Gardner, dramatized the struggle of a slave owner who opposed slavery during the Civil War.

Relating drama to contemporary literature, Herne wrote "Art for Truth's Sake in the Drama" (*Arena* XVII, February 1897) to emphasize the "humanity" and "large truth" in the drama that has a "higher purpose" than to amuse. This was a new concept for commercially minded theatre entrepreneurs of this period. Praised by Howells for his "epoch marking" play *Margaret Fleming,* Herne wrote plays that delineated the beginning of modern drama in America.   WJM

See: H. J. Edwards and J. A. Herne, *James A. Herne: The Rise of Realism in the American Drama,* Orono, ME, 1964; J. Perry, *James A. Herne: The American Ibsen,* Chicago, 1978.

Heron, Matilda (1830–77) Actress who made a life's work of *Camille.* Fascinated by Mme. Doche's playing of Marguerite Gautier in Paris (1854), she made her own adaptation of the play, opening it in New Orleans (1855) and then at **Wallack's** (1857). New Yorkers were captivated by Heron's "elemental power," her "animal vivacity," her uninhibited exploitation of a woman's sexual life, and her lifelike naturalness (even turning her back to the audience); and when Camille coughed her way to the grave, tears flowed throughout the house.

After an initial run of 100 performances, she toured the play for the next 20 years.

Born in Ireland, Heron played Juliet to **Charlotte Cushman**'s Romeo (1852), made her New York debut as Lady Macbeth (1852), and appeared at London's Drury Lane (1854) before she discovered Camille.   RM

> See: A. Humble, "Matilda Heron, American Actress," PhD diss., U of Illinois, 1959.

Herrmann, Alexander (1844–96) German-born **magic**ian whose elder brother by 27 years, Carl, was the first Herrmann to achieve international acclaim, including initial appearances in the U.S. in the 1860s. Alexander, who succeeded Carl, was first seen in New York in 1869 and ultimately settled in the U.S., though he continued touring internationally. Although Alexander was **Harry Kellar**'s major competition in the 1880s – with illusions such as "Cremation," in which a woman was set on fire and then spectral forms were made to rise from her coffin – Herrmann's widow Adelaide and his nephew Leon were unsuccessful in sustaining the popularity of the Herrmann show after his death, and for a time Kellar had little competition. Still, Adelaide performed until 1928, 31 years with her own show, longer than any other Herrmann.   DBW

> See: I. G. Edmonds, *The Magic Brothers*, New York, 1979.

Herrmann, Edward (1943–) Actor. Recognized as FDR from "Eleanor and Franklin" (TV: 1976, 1977; both Emmy nominations), and *Annie* (film, 1982), Herrmann "tends to fade into the people he portrays." He made his debut **Off-Broadway** in *The **Basic Training of Pavlo Hummel*** (1971) and on Broadway in *Moonchildren* (1972). His films include *The Paper Chase* (1973), *Reds* (1981), *The Purple Rose of Cairo* (1985), and *Big Business* (1988). Recently seen in **Richard Nelson**'s "The End of a Sentence" (PBS, "American Playhouse," 1991), he received a Tony for Shaw's *Mrs. Warren's Profession* (1976) and a nomination for Hare's *Plenty* (1983). Herrmann is married to actress-playwright Leigh Curran.   REK

Hewes, Henry (1917–) Drama critic. Born in Boston and educated at Harvard, Carnegie Tech, and Columbia (1948), Hewes worked for the *New York Times* (1949–51) before becoming drama editor (1952–73), drama critic (1954–77), and critic-at-large (1977–) of *Saturday Review*. He was drama critic for *International Theatre Yearbook* (1978–80), and editor of *The Best Play Series* (1961–4) and *Famous American Plays of the 1940s*. A critic of erudition and taste, Hewes writes in a clear and straightforward style.   TLM

Hewlett, James (fl. 1821–31) A tailor by trade, Hewlett became principal actor when in 1821 Mr. Brown formed the **African Theatre** (NYC). He appeared as Richard III, Othello, and as the Carib chieftain King Shotoway in **William Henry Brown**'s drama on the Carib revolt in St. Vincent. When the company folded, Hewlett began to give

one-person performances, in which he imitated leading actors of the day in their celebrated roles. He performed in New York and Pennsylvania and may have appeared at the Coburg Theatre in London. He enlivened his program of recitations by singing songs accompanied by his wife on the piano.   EGH

Heyward, Dorothy (1890–1961) and **[Edwin] DuBose Heyward** (1885–1940) Husband and wife playwriting team, in which he primarily supplied stories from his novels, and she dramatic craftsmanship. Although DuBose wrote one other play and Dorothy had five others produced, their reputation rests on their folk dramas of Negro life – *Porgy* (1927) and *Mamba's Daughters* (1939) – both praised for their realistic depiction of the lives of Southern blacks. *Porgy*, the love story of a crippled black man and an erring woman, became an American legend, particularly after its conversion into a folk opera, *Porgy and Bess* (1935) by DuBose and the **Gershwin**s (a 1977 revival won a Tony Award). The Heywards are credited with providing dramatic opportunities for **African-American** actors: **Ethel Waters**, in *Mamba's Daughters*, was the first black woman to star in a Broadway drama.   FB

> See: F. Durham, *DuBose Heyward, The Man Who Wrote Porgy*, Columbia, SC, 1954; W. Slavick, *DuBose Heyward*, Boston, 1981.

Hickey, William (1928–) Actor, director, and teacher. Best known for the film *Prizzi's Honor* (1985, Oscar nomination), Hickey, an acting teacher at New York's HB Studios since 1953, specializes in bizarre or eccentric characters. Hickey's stage appearances include *St. Joan* (Broadway debut, 1951), *On the Town* (1959), *Happy Birthday, Wanda June* (1970; film, 1971), *Small Craft Warnings* (1972), *Mourning Becomes Electra* (1972), *Thieves* (1974), and *Arsenic and Old Lace* (1986 revival). A regular on television's "Baby Talk" (1991), his films include *The Boston Strangler* (1968), *Little Big Man* (1970), *The Name of the Rose* (1986), and *Bright Lights, Big City* (1988).   REK

Hiken, Gerald (1927–) Wisconsin-born and -educated character actor-director. After six years in regional theatre, Hiken first appeared in New York in 1955 as Trofimov in *The Cherry Orchard*. Although he performed in plays by other dramatists (*Good Woman of Setzuan*, 1956; *The Misanthrope*, 1957; *The Iceman Cometh*, 1957; *Gideon*, 1962; *Golda*, 1977; *Strider*, 1979; etc.), he became something of a **Chekhov** specialist: Telegin in *Uncle Vanya* (1956), Medvedenko in *The Seagull* (1956), Andrei Prozorov in *The Three Sisters* (NY, 1959, 1964; London, 1965), and Gaev in *The Cherry Orchard* (1967). During 1966–8 he served as Artistic Director of the Stanford (California) Repertory Theatre.   DBW

Hill, Arthur (1922–) Canadian-born actor who has had a substantial career in America. His stage debut was in London as Finch in *Home of the Brave*. He played Cornelius Hackl in *The **Matchmaker*** at the Haymarket in 1954, later making his Broadway debut in the same role. In 1962 he starred as George

Mechanical features of the New York Hippodrome. The apron stage in front of the proscenium is shown with two 42-ft circus rings, carried on hydraulic plungers. Below is a tank of water measuring 60 × 100 ft. Original in *Scientific American*. Courtesy: Don B. Wilmeth.

in *Who's Afraid of Virginia Woolf?* (1963 Tony Award), repeating the role in London in 1964. His George was referred to by one critic as "a superbly modulated performance built on restraint." He later appeared as Simon Harford in *More Stately Mansions* (1967). Since then his career has focused on film and television. SMA

Hill, George Handel "Yankee" (1809–49) Actor. In the 1830s and '40s Hill was the leading exponent of the "Yankee" roles in **William Dunlap**'s *Trip to Niagara,* **Samuel Woodworth's** *The Forest Rose,* and **J. S. Jones**'s *The Green Mountain Boy.* Audiences delighted in his plausible cunning, his great industry, and his pliant honesty. One critic said he was "the funniest actor, and cleverest fellow in the Yankee signification of the word – in Christendom." He appeared in London in 1836 and 1838. He first undertook Yankee impersonations with solo recitations of "Jonathan's Visit to Buffalo" and "The Yankee in Trouble; or, Zephaniah in the Pantry." RM

> See: G. Hill, *Scenes from the Life of an Actor,* New York, 1853; W. K. Northall, ed., *Life and Recollections of Yankee Hill,* New York, 1850.

him by e. e. cummings, his only full-length play (21 scenes and 105 characters), published in November 1927. The Experimental Theatre produced *him* with a cast of 30 at the Provincetown Playhouse on 18 April 1928 for 27 performances. William S. Johnstone played the title role, representing various states of consciousness. Erin O'Brien Moore played his romantic interest, Me. A "Warning"

printed in the program instructed playgoers not to wonder what it was "about," admonishing "DON'T TRY TO UNDERSTAND IT, LET IT TRY TO UNDERSTAND YOU." This notice and the production itself unleashed a critical furor. "Precious" and "pretentious" were the adjectives most frequently applied to what the unsigned *New York Times* review called "a facetious cerebration." **Brooks Atkinson** saw it as "a bloodless heart worn on a gawdy sleeve," and noted that as up-to-the-minute aesthetic experimentation, it merely circled "back to the lowly burlesque performance." FHL

Hingle, Pat (1924–) Colorado-born and Texas-educated actor whose professional debut was as Lachie in *Johnny Belinda* in 1950; he made his debut on Broadway as Koble in *End as a Man* in 1953. Among his Broadway hits were the brawling and brusquely considerate Rubin Flood in *Dark at the Top of the Stairs* (1957) and the Job-like, anguished title role of *J. B.* (1958). Later starring roles included the failed brother in *The Price* (1968) and the bewildered Coach in *That Championship Season* (1975). Hingle has appeared in many feature films, as well as numerous television series and programs. SMA

Hippodrama see **animals as performers**

Hippodrome Theatre Sixth Ave between 43rd and 44th Sts., NYC [Architect: J. H. Morgan]. The Hippodrome was conceived and built by Frederic W. Thompson and Elmer S. Dundy, who had created the extravagant Coney Island amusement center Luna Park. Advertised as the world's largest theatre, its auditorium seated 5,000 and its stage was equipped with every device known to create magnificent spectacles. The costs of production and the maintenance of the house overwhelmed even the canniest of producers, including the **Shubert**s and **Charles Dillingham.** In 1923, it was taken over by the **Keith–Albee vaudeville** chain, then leased for popular-priced opera, then as a sports arena. In 1935, **Billy Rose** presented his production of *Jumbo* at the theatre, the last notable event in its history. It was torn down in 1939, but the site was not developed until 1952, when it was covered by a garage and office building.   MCH

See: N. Clarke, *The Mighty Hippodrome,* South Brunswick and New York, 1968.

Hirsch, Judd (1935–) Actor who in over 20 years established a major reputation as a versatile actor in film, television, and on stage, beginning with his Broadway debut in 1966, replacing Herb Edelman as the Telephone Repairman in *Barefoot in the Park.* Unlike many of his successful contemporaries in film or television, Hirsch returns frequently to the New York stage, as the following partial list of credits illustrates: *The Hot l Baltimore* (1973) as Bill, the night manager; **Feiffer**'s *Knock, Knock* (1976); **Neil Simon**'s *Chapter Two* (1977); **Lanford Wilson**'s *Tally's Folly* (1979) as Matt Friedman, an immigrant Jewish accountant; **Circle Repertory Company**'s *The Seagull* (1983) as Trigorin; and **Herb Gardner**'s *I'm Not Rappaport* (1985) at the **American Place Theatre**, which was later transferred to Broadway. He returned to Broadway in 1992 in Gardner's *Conversations with My Father,* for which he won a Tony. According to one interviewer, Hirsch has a rugged "street face, a face of interchangeable ethnicities and professions." His career to date supports such a description.   DBW

Hirsch, Louis A. (1881–1924) Originally aspiring to be a concert pianist and serious composer, Hirsch was drawn to songwriting, contributing songs to such shows as *The Gay White Way* (1907) and *The Girl and the Wizard* (1909). His first full score was for *He Came from Milwaukee* (1910). He continued to write songs for **revue**s, including four editions of the **Ziegfeld** Follies (1915, 1916, 1918, 1922). Among his musical comedy scores were those for *Going Up* (1917), *The Rainbow Girl* (1918), and *Oh, My Dear!* (1918). His most memorable song, "The Love Nest," was written for *Mary* (1920), produced by **George M. Cohan.** Hirsch also wrote the score for Cohan's *The O'Brien Girl* (1921); his last score was for *Betty Lee* (1924). Hirsch was a competent, if not inspired, musical comedy composer.   MK

Hirschfeld, Al(bert) (1903–) Acknowledged today as the dean of American theatrical caricaturists, Al Hirschfeld, a native of St. Louis, studied fine arts in New York and Paris, intending to become a painter or sculptor. Instead, he became fascinated with the manipulation of the thin black line into shapes and attitudes, and hence was drawn into the art of the **caricature.** His early drawings were submitted to several New York newspapers, but since 1925 he has worked almost exclusively for the *New York Times,* flavoring its theatre journalism with drawings of current Broadway personalities and happenings. For many years, Hirschfeld has woven the name of his daughter Nina into the tapestry of his drawings, slipping a small numeral next to his signature to indicate the exact number of times it appears. He is the first American artist to be allowed to sign his name on postage stamp artwork (1991). Among his books are *The American Theatre as Seen by Hirschfeld* (1961), *Hirschfeld by Hirschfeld* (1979), and *Hirschfeld: Art and Recollections from Eight Decades* (1991).   MCH

Hirshbein, Peretz (1880–1948) Playwright who began writing in Hebrew in Russia but in 1906 started writing Yiddish plays, harshly realistic or subtly symbolist. In Odessa he founded the Hirshbein Troupe (1908–10), an acting ensemble dedicated to intellectually ambitious **Yiddish theatre.** After several years of traveling and writing he settled in New York, where his plays *Green Fields, A Secluded Nook, The Blacksmith's Daughters,* and *The Idle Inn* (1912–18), all evocative romances of Russian Jewish rural life, won praise. The film version of *Green Fields* is still screened.   NS

Hispanic theatre Given the substantial and fast-growing Spanish-speaking population within the continental U.S., it is not surprising that a theatre movement reflecting Hispanic language, culture, and values flourishes across the country. This Hispanic population includes immigrants from Spain as well as from every Spanish-speaking country within the Western Hemisphere, but the theatrical impetus derives primarily from three sources: Mexico, Cuba, and Puerto Rico. Although the movement has gained both in strength and popularity within the past 25 years as a result of the widespread civil rights movement, it should be clear that the Spanish-speaking theatre has an extended history, even antedating the first English-speaking theatre. Nicolás Kanellos indicates the first recorded performance took place in a Spanish mission near Miami in 1567, when the Spanish settlers and soldiers utilized the feast day of St. John the Baptist to present a religious play designed to catechize the local Indian population. In the Southwest, Juan de Oñate's band of colonizers was performing religious plays in and around what is today El Paso, TX, before the end of the 16th century. The orientation of these performances reflected the dual mission of the Hispanic conquest, which was not only military but religious, and therefore served well the objective of instructing native populations about Christianity. Interest in the Magi play (*pastorelas*) and other religious performances can still be found in communities throughout the Southwest, especially during Epiphany and Easter.

From its earliest beginnings to the present time, Hispanic theatre has had a checkered and often interrupted history. In many cases documentation is scarce because of its depreciated value in traditional circles. Current scholarship divides the movement into three fairly discrete parts: **Chicano theatre,** primarily in the West and Southwest; **Cuban–American theatre,** mostly in New York and Florida; and the New York theatre, sometimes called **Nuyorican,** which has a heavily Puerto Rican component. None of these classifications is absolute or unilateral. Manifestations of Chicano theatre can be found across the land, from the Northwest to the East, and as the Spanish-speaking population has become more mixed and more integrated, categorization has become more difficult. The theatre is linguistically structured as well: Chicano theatre still tends to rely heavily on a mixture of both languages, combined into "Spanglish." Cuban-American theatre was earlier almost exclusively in Spanish, whereas the younger generation often writes and performs in English. The Nuyorican theatre depends heavily on English, in contrast with the island. [See also **ethnic theatre; folk theatre.**] GW

> See: E. De La Roche, "Hispanic Theatre in New York City," PhD diss., New York U, 1990; N. Kanellos, ed., *Hispanic Theatre in the United States,* Houston, 1984; N. Kanellos, *A History of Hispanic Theatre in the United States: Origins to 1940,* Austin, 1990; Kanellos, *Mexican American Theatre: Then and Now,* Houston, 1983. Additional sources are listed under cross-referenced entries.

Hitchcock, Raymond (1865–1929) Actor. After a debut in 1890, Hitchcock did not have a starring role until 1903. During a 40-year career he starred in two dozen musical comedies and **revue**s, including a series of *Hitchy-Koo* revues (1917–20) – featuring "Hitchy's" whimsicalities and uniquely informal style, and extraordinarily popular until interest suddenly subsided. DBW

Hodgkinson (Meadowcroft), John (1767–1805) British-born actor and manager who, after some provincial experience, accepted an offer in 1792 from **John Henry** to join the **American Company** and spent the rest of his career in the U.S. Although his personal reputation has been much maligned, his private life after his arrival in America seems to have been without blemish. He never became a star, but was a tall, handsome man with an exceptional voice and memory who excelled in high and low comedy, playing at least 379 roles during his 24-year career. During 1794–8 he was joint manager of the **John Street Theatre.** Later he acted in all the principal cities of the Atlantic seaboard until his death from yellow fever. DBW

> See: B. J. Harbin, "The Career of John Hodgkinson in the American Theatre," PhD diss., Indiana U, 1971.

Hoffman, Dustin (1937–) Film and stage actor. Hoffman worked at the Theatre Company of Boston with **David Wheeler** before his 1965 New York debut as Immanuel in *Harry, Noon, and Night.* The next year he played Zoditch in *The Journey of the Fifth Horse.* Also in 1966 he appeared in *Eh?,* winning several awards, as he did in 1968 in the title role of *Jimmy Shine.* After an extraordinarily successful stint in films, he starred in a Broadway revival of *Death of a Salesman*

(1984), acclaimed as a performance of genius and demonic intensity, and in 1989 (after a successful London engagement) appeared on Broadway as Shylock in Peter Hall's production of *The Merchant of Venice.* SMA

> See: R. Bergan, *Dustin Hoffman,* London, 1991.

Hogan's Goat This blank verse tragedy by William Alfred premiered 11 November 1965 at the **American Place Theatre** before moving to East 74 Street Theatre (1966). Directed by Frederick Rolf, with Ralph Waite as Stanton and Faye Dunaway as Kathleen (which earned her the *Theatre World* Award), this melodrama explores the ethical costs of ambition, played out in a political struggle for the mayoralty of Irish Brooklyn in the 1890s. Praised for heightened emotion and historical atmosphere, the play counterpoints Stanton's political battles with the destruction of himself and the two women he loves. Alfred's musical version of the play, *Cry for Us All* (1970), failed. The play won Drama Desk and Vernon Rice awards, as well as the Theatre Club Gold Medal for its author. TH-S

Holbrook, Hal (né Harold Rowe Holbrook) (1925–) Actor and writer who made his debut with a Cleveland **stock company** in 1942 and spent four seasons in stock. With his first wife he toured for six seasons, presenting famous scenes from the classics, from which developed his immensely successful **one-person** show, *Mark Twain Tonight!* He first appeared as Twain in New York in 1955, and has revived the show periodically to immense critical and popular acclaim.

Holbrook spent the 1964 season with the **Lincoln Center** Repertory, alternating Quentin (*After the Fall*) with **Jason Robards, Jr.,** and playing Marco Polo in *Marco Millions.* Recently he has turned to classic roles, appearing at Cleveland's Great Lakes Theatre Festival in 1900 as King Lear (later seen at New York's **Roundabout**) and as Uncle Vanya the following year, as well as Shylock at San Diego's **Old Globe Theatre** (summer 1991). He is married to actress-singer Dixie Carter. SMA

Holiday A finely crafted **Philip Barry** comedy of manners (1928, 230 performances), with **Arthur Hopkins** as producer-director and **Robert Edmond Jones** as designer. Hope Williams starred as Linda Seton, the rich "Barry girl" who resists the conventional values of her father and sister by falling in love with her sister's fiancé, a carefree, charming lawyer who would rather retire, on extended holiday, than chase after money. The theme is sentimental – love and freedom versus staid upper-class values – but the dialogue is witty and supple, and there's a good character role in the alcoholic brother Nick, originally played by Donald Ogden Stewart. The play was revived, less successfully, in 1973 by the New Phoenix Repertory Company, and is also performed occasionally in the regional theatres. The second film version (1938), directed by George Cukor, starred Cary Grant and **Katharine Hepburn** (who had been Hope Williams's untested understudy in 1928). TP

Holland, George (1791–1870) British-born actor called a "comedian of peculiar and irrepressible drollery." After seven years on the London stage, he came to the U.S. in 1827, making his debut at the **Bowery Theatre** in *A Day After the Fair*. For 16 years he toured, gaining immense popularity, especially in the South, where he also entered for a time into management with **Noah Ludlow** and also **Sol Smith**. In New Orleans, where he remained from 1835 until 1843, he worked with **James H. Caldwell**. For the next six years he played in comedies and burlesques at **Mitchell's Olympic**. Beginning in 1855, and for a total of 14 years, he was low comedian with **Wallack**'s company, leaving in 1869 to join **Daly**. Of Holland's six children, four became actors, most notably Edmund Milton and Joseph Jefferson.   DBW

See: Sketch of the Life of George Holland, the Veteran Comedian, etc., New York, 1871.

Holliday, Judy (née Judith Tuvim) (1923–65) Comedienne and singer who appeared, along with **Betty Comden and Adolph Green**, in the **nightclub** act "The Revuers" in 1938 and made her New York theatrical debut in *Kiss Them for Me* (1945). Her wide-eyed, baby-voiced portrayal of Billie Dawn in the comedy **Born Yesterday** (1946) elevated her to stardom. Her first musical role was as meddling telephone operator Ella Peterson in **Bells Are Ringing** (1956), for which she won a Tony Award; she also starred in the short-lived musical *Hot Spot* (1963). Audiences and critics were delighted by her incandescent personality and superb comic timing.   MK

See: W. Holtzman, *Judy Holliday*, New York, 1982.

Holliday Street Theatre Holliday St. between Fayette and Lexington, Baltimore. Built by **Thomas Wignell** and Alexander Reinagle, the theatre was opened on 25 September 1794, intended as a satellite of their **Philadelphia** theatrical operations. Later in its history, it was managed prosperously by **John T. Ford**. It was pulled down in 1813 and a new theatre built on its site; this the city of Baltimore razed in 1917 to construct War Memorial Plaza.   MCH

Holm, Celeste (1919–   ) Film, stage, and television actress whose professional debut was in *The Night of January 16* in a Deer Lake, PA, summer theatre in 1936. Her first New York appearance was as Lady Mary in *Gloriana* in 1938. She created Ado Annie in **Oklahoma!** in 1943. Her first film was *Three Little Girls in Blue* (1946). Most recently (1991) she appeared with Nicol Williamson in Paul Rudnick's *I Hate Hamlet*. Her awards include an Oscar for *Gentlemen's Agreement* (1947) and the Sarah Siddons Award for her performance in the national touring company of *Mame* (1969). In 1979 she was knighted by King Olav of Norway.   SMA

Holm, Hanya (née Johanna Eckert) (c. 1898–92) Modern dancer-choreographer and theatre choreographer who began her training and performance career in her native Germany before arriving in the U.S. to direct the Wigman School in New York (1931). She opened her own school and embarked on a choreographic career that established her as a leading pioneer in American modern dance. Although primarily abstract in form, Holm's choreography was powerful, and critics wrote that she incorporated German constructivism in her work. Not limited to abstract invention, Holm also choreographed using more traditional **dance** movements for musical theatre productions. Among her most notable musical theatre credits are *Kiss Me Kate* (1948), *My Fair Lady* (1956), and *Camelot* (1960).   LF

See: W. Sorell, *Hanya Holm: The Biography of an Artist*, Middletown, CT, 1969.

Holy Ghosts by Romulus Linney. This effective ensemble piece is set in a snake-worshipping religious cult in the present South. Despite a run of three weeks when premiered at New York's **Garrick Theatre** in 1971, it is the most frequently revived of Linney's plays, including New York revivals in 1976 and 1987 (the latter originating at the San Diego Repertory Theatre). Douglas Jacobs, director of the '87 revival, aptly noted that the play "probes the essential need in man to search for a God and spiritual fulfillment." Linney successfully handles his controversial subject with deftness and sympathy – as one critic commented, "neither catering to nor condescending to the sensibilities involved" – and presents in a nonjudgmental manner a group of societal misfits who demonstrate unexpected compassion and humor in the replenishing atmosphere of their community. Published with *The Sorrows of Frederick* in 1977, it was directed by the author at Houston's **Alley** in 1983.   DBW

Home of the Brave by **Arthur Laurents** opened 27 December 1945 at the **Belasco Theatre,** running for 69 performances. This wartime drama stood out from its contemporaries through a frank treatment of anti-Semitism and battle trauma. Using hypnotherapy as a flashback device, the play recounted the anxieties leading to the speech loss of the main character, resulting in his third-act cure. The 1949 United Artists screen version modified the script to feature a black protagonist.   RW

Hooks, Robert (1937–   ) **African-American** actor who, as Bobby Dean Hooks, made his debut in a touring production of *A **Raisin in the Sun*** (1959), then appeared in several plays on and **Off-Broadway** including Genêt's *The Blacks* (1962). The role of Clay in **Dutchman** at the Cherry Lane Theatre (1964) brought him prominence and a name change to Robert Hooks. At the St. Mark's Playhouse he copresented and played in **Douglas Turner Ward**'s double bill *Happy Ending* and *Day of Absence* (1965); this prepared the way for their founding of the **Negro Ensemble Company** (1967). After appearing in the Ensemble Company's early productions, Hooks moved to Washington, DC, where he formed the **D.C. Black Repertory Company.**   EGH

Hooley's Theatre, originally called Hooley's Opera House, was perhaps the most successful theatre in 19th-century **Chicago**. R[ichard] M. "Uncle Dick" Hooley moved to Chicago from Brooklyn in 1870 and opened a new theatre in January 1871, only to see it burn nine months later in the great **fire**. His rebuilt theatre, seating 1,412, became the home of a 30-member **stock company** that included **James O'Neill** as its leading man. The theatre's greatest success began in the late 1870s, when Hooley used the combination system to feature traveling stars. Hooley was replaced after his death in 1893 by longtime employee Harry J. Powers, who refurbished the theatre in 1898 and renamed it Powers' New Theatre.   SF

Hopkins, Arthur (Melancthon) (1878–1950) Producer and director who began his career as a newspaper reporter, then worked as a **vaudeville** press **agent,** and finally booked attractions himself. His first Broadway production was *Poor Little Rich Girl* (1913), which ran for 160 performances. Other early successes include *On Trial* (1914), *Good Gracious Annabelle* (1916), *A Successful Calamity* (1917), *Redemption* (1918) with John Barrymore, and *The Jest* (1919) with John and Lionel Barrymore [see **Drew–Barrymore**]. He featured **Alla Nazimova** in revivals of **Ibsen**'s *Wild Duck, Hedda Gabler,* and *A Doll's House*. In the 1920s, Hopkins directed **O'Neill**'s *Anna Christie* (1921) and *The Hairy Ape* (1922); **Stallings** and **Anderson**'s *What Price Glory* (1924); and **Philip Barry**'s *Paris Bound* (1927) and *Holiday* (1928). His output decreased after 1930, but he staged a successful *The Petrified Forest* in 1935 with Leslie Howard and Humphrey Bogart, and *The Magnificent Yankee* in 1946. His notable productions of **Shakespeare** include John Barrymore in *Richard III* (1920) and in *Hamlet* (1922), and Lionel Barrymore in *Macbeth* (1921). Hopkins discovered **Pauline Lord** and **Katharine Hepburn,** and contributed to the success of **Robert Edmond Jones**. He studied theatrical production in Europe and returned home to develop the revolving stage in America. He placed artistic above commercial merit. While many of his directing methods were modern, his reliance upon pictorial effect made his later productions seem old-fashioned. Hopkins's books included *To a Lonely Boy* (1937) and *Reference Point* (1948), both somewhat autobiographical.   TLM

See: B. Halverson, "Arthur Hopkins: A Theatrical Biography," PhD diss., U of Washington, 1971.

Hopper, De Wolf (1858–1935) Comedian and singer. His abnormally long legs, loose-joined movements, and strong singing voice made Hopper one of the most beloved performers in comic opera. His debut was in *Our Daughters* (1879), after which he appeared in a number of shows under the aegis of the McCaull Opera Company. Hopper left the McCaull company in 1890 and under a new management was given his first starring role in *Castles in the Air* (1890). His two greatest successes, *Wang* (1891) and *Panjandrum* (1893), followed. After forming the De Wolf Hopper Opera Company, he appeared in *Dr. Syntax* (1894), *El Capitan* (1896), and *The Mystical Miss* (1899). Hopper then joined the **Weber and Fields** company for two shows, then starred in *Mr. Pickwick* (1903), *Happyland* (1905),

The Pied Piper (1908), and *A Matinee Idol* (1910). In 1911 Hopper made the first of a number of successful forays into the *Gilbert and Sullivan* repertoire with a revival of *HMS Pinafore*. As the vogue for comic opera waned, Hopper's work was confined to **revue**s, such as *The Passing Show of 1917*, and, on occasion, operettas. His last New York appearance was in *White Lilacs* (1928). Beginning his career at a time when comic opera was at its height, Hopper found ample opportunity to exercise his comic gifts and his forceful singing voice. He was especially noted for his ability to handle long comic speeches and involved patter songs, and for his amusing use of props. Hopper published his autobiography, *Once a Clown*, in 1927.   MK

Hopper, Edna Wallace (1874–1959) Actress and singer who began her stage career at the **Boston Museum** in 1891. As Edna Wallace, she appeared in a number of straight plays produced by **Charles Frohman** before making her comic opera debut as a replacement for Della Fox in *Panjandrum*. Soon after, she married **De Wolf Hopper**, and as Edna Wallace Hopper starred in *Dr. Syntax* (1894), *El Capitan* (1896), *Yankee Doodle Dandy* (1898), and *Chris and the Wonderful Lamp* (1900). She played Lady Holyrood in the American production of *Florodora* (1900). Subsequently, she made the transition from comic opera to musical comedy in such shows as *About Town* (1906), *Fifty Miles from Boston* (1908), and *Jumping Jupiter* (1911). Hopper's popularity in comic opera was generally attributed to her sparkling and vivacious personality rather than to her singing voice, which was too small and delicate. Audiences especially enjoyed her appearances in trousers roles [see **female/male impersonation**].   MK

Hopwood, Avery (1882–1928) A remarkably successful playwright with 18 "hits" in 15 years – four of them running simultaneously in New York theatres in 1920 – Hopwood understood both popular commercial theatre and the slight and ephemeral nature of his artistry. Most of his best works were written in collaboration with others: *Clothes* (1906), his first play, with **Channing Pollock**; four plays, including *The Bat* (1920), with **Mary Roberts Rinehart**; *Getting Gertie's Garter* (1921) with Wilson Collison; and *The Best People* with David Gray. Other play titles suggest the clever, risqué character of his work – *The Gold Diggers* (1919), *Little Miss Bluebeard* (1923), *Naughty Cinderella* (1925) – that almost guaranteed success.   WJM

See: J. F. Sharrar, *Avery Hopwood: His Life and Plays,* Jefferson, NC, 1989.

Horizon by **Augustin Daly** was initially staged by him at the Olympic Theatre, New York, in 1871. The production featured **Agnes Ethel** as the heroine and **George L. Fox** as a comically crooked politician. Influenced by the then-current Indian wars and **Bret Harte**'s fiction, Daly's mix of sensation and local color paints a more realistic picture of frontier life than had been popular in the theatre. His stage Indian, Wannemucka, for example, is cynical, courageous, and lazy, a more complex portrayal than the conventional noble or murdering savage [see **Native Americans portrayed**]. The plot – which includes Indian attacks, lynching committees, corrupt politics, and a last-minute rescue by the army – centers on a romance between a socially prominent officer and a "white flower of the plains." The self-sacrifice of a gambler finally unites the couple in marriage. The popularity of *Horizon* led to the staging of several other frontier dramas at Eastern theatre.   BMcC

Hornblow, Arthur (1865–1942) English-born editor and author who studied in Paris and worked as a correspondent for English and American newspapers before coming to the U.S. in 1889. He pursued a career as a journalist, working first for the *Kansas City Globe* and then the **New York Dramatic Mirror.** He was foreign editor for the *New York Herald* during 1894–9, and copy-editor for the *New York Times* in 1899. During 1910–26 he served as editor of *Theatre Magazine,* frequently reviewing opening nights. Afterward, for two years, he served as Dean of the **John Murray Anderson–** Robert Milton School of Theatre and Dance in New York. Hornblow's greatest financial success came from novelizing popular plays, including *The Lion and the Mouse, The **Easiest Way,*** and *Bought and Paid For.* His two-volume *A History of the Theatre in America* (1919) remains a standard reference work.   TLM

Horner, Harry (1912–) Czechoslovakian-born designer, director, and architect who began as an actor and came to the U.S. as an assistant director to **Max Reinhardt** on *The Eternal Road* (1936). He subsequently developed a career as a designer, receiving his greatest acclaim for **Lady in the Dark** (1941), which employed an elaborate turntable system for scene changes. He began designing for film in the 1940s, and served as production designer or art director on many films, including **Born Yesterday,** *The Hustler, Separate Tables,* and *They Shoot Horses, Don't They?* He has also produced and directed films, and directed television shows, including "Omnibus" and "Gunsmoke."   AA

Horovitz, Israel [Arthur] (1939–) Harvard-educated playwright who spent two years at the London Royal Academy of Dramatic Art (1961–3) and a year as resident playwright with the Royal Shakespeare Company (1965). He attracted critical attention in 1968 with the New York production of two one-acts: *It's Called the Sugar Plum* and *The Indian Wants the Bronx,* plays about urban violence in America. Also in 1968, his one-act *Morning* appeared on Broadway together with short pieces by **Terrence McNally** and Leonard Melfi. Other Horovitz plays include *The Good Parts* (1982); *The Wakefield Plays* (1974–9), which include *The Alfred Trilogy* and *The Quannatowitt Quartet;* and *Park Your Car in Harvard Yard* (1991). In 1979 he founded the Gloucester Stage Company in Massachusetts, where most of his plays have since premiered (e.g., *A Rosen by Any Other Name,* 1987; *The Chopin Playoffs,* 1988). Horovitz deals in a realistic way with the angst of American life.   TLM

Hot l Baltimore **Lanford Wilson**'s three-act comedy-drama is named for its setting, the lobby of a run-down hotel that has lost an "e" from its marquee. The sweetly eccentric characters who interact there and dream of better times were sensitively portrayed by a fine ensemble directed by **Marshall W. Mason.** The Circle Theatre Company (now **Circle Repertory**) opened the play in an **Off-Off Broadway** loft theatre on 27 January 1973. The favorable public and critical response garnered during its 17 performances enabled the production to move **Off-Broadway** to the **Circle in the Square,** where it opened on 22 March 1973 (1,166 performances). It won the Drama Critics' Circle Award for best play and became the basis for an ABC-TV series in 1975.   FHL

Houdini, Harry (né Erik Weisz) (1874–1926) **Magic**ian and escape artist, born the son of a rabbi in Budapest; his stage name was an homage to the 19th-century French conjuror Robert-Houdin. Starting in dime museums and circuses as the self-styled "King of Cards," he gained prominence in 1895 with his escapes from handcuffs and straitjackets. A genius at self-promotion, he was soon challenging police forces throughout the world to keep him pent up, and once escaped from a chained packing crate at the bottom of a river; these escapes were often engineered by concealed keys, one passed in a kiss from his wife. Other tricks involved making an elephant vanish, and swallowing 70 needles and 20 yards of thread and bringing them up threaded. Houdini was also the first to fly an airplane in Australia (1910), enjoyed a career as a silent-film star, and, after his mother's death in 1913, exposed fraudulent mediums. G. B. **Shaw** called him one of the three most famous persons in the world (the other two being Jesus Christ and Sherlock Holmes). *Houdini,* a "circus-opera" by Adrian Mitchell and Peter Schat, was performed in Amsterdam in 1977.   LS

See: M. Christopher, *Houdini: The Untold Story,* New York, 1969; W. B. Gibson, *Houdini's Escapes and Tricks,* repr. ed., New York, 1976.

Houghton, (Charles) Norris (1909–) Indiana-born producer, educator, designer, and writer. A 1931 Princeton graduate, he designed eight Broadway productions and directed four between 1932 and 1957. As founder and comanaging director of the **Off-Broadway** Phoenix Theatre, he helped mount almost 75 productions (1953–64). He has taught at numerous institutions; his last full-time position was at the State University of New York, Purchase (1967–80). A frequent writer and editor, Houghton is the author of six books, including the influential *Moscow Rehearsals* (1936), *Advance from Broadway* (1941), and *Return Engagement* (1962). His superb autobiography, *Entrances and Exits,* was published by Limelight in 1991. Twice a Guggenheim Fellow, in 1962 he became a Fellow of the American Academy of Arts and Sciences.   DBW

Houseman, John (né Jacques Haussman) (1902–88) Bucharest-born director, producer, and actor. Educated in England, Houseman began pro-

John Guare's *House of Blue Leaves* (1971 premiere) with Harold Gould as Artie (at piano), Anne Meara as Bunny (left), and Katherine Helmond as Bananas (behind piano). Photo: © Martha Swope. Courtesy: Martha Swope.

ducing in New York in 1934 and was affiliated for a time with the **Federal Theatre Project.** Some of his finest work was with **Orson Welles** and the **Mercury Theatre,** which he cofounded in 1937 – notably his production of *Julius Caesar* in modern dress. He served as artistic director for such producing agencies as the **American Shakespeare Festival** (1956–9), the professional Theatre Group of the University of California at Los Angeles (1959–64), and the Drama Division of the Juilliard School of the Performing Arts (1968–76). In 1972 Houseman founded the **Acting Company,** originally known as the City Center Acting Company, directing several productions for them.

Houseman won great popular acclaim by playing an acerbic law professor in the television series "Paper Chase." He published three detailed and valuable accounts of his life in the theatre: *Run-Through* (1972), *Front and Center* (1981), and *Final Dress* (1983). The three were conflated into *Unfinished Business* (1989).   SMA

House of Blue Leaves, The, by John Guare was first produced on 10 February 1971 at the Truck and Warehouse Theatre in New York. Its cast, directed by **Mel Shapiro,** included Harold Gould as Artie Shaughnessy, a middle-aged zoo worker who aspires to be a Hollywood songwriter; Katherine Helmond as his wife Bananas, who is most comfortable as a dog; Anne Meara as Bunny Flingus, who will have sex with Artie anytime, but refuses to cook for him until after they are married; Frank Converse as Billy Einhorn, Artie's producer friend, who ends up with Bunny; and William Atherton as Artie's son Ronnie, who blows up Billy's girlfriend with a bomb he had intended for the pope. The play was revived successfully at the **Vivian Beaumont Theatre** at Lincoln Center in 1986 with **Stockard Channing** as Bunny, John Mahoney as Artie, and **Swoosie Kurtz** as Ba-

nanas. The play, set in Queens during Pope Paul VI's visit to New York in 1965, uses absurdist techniques to critique marriage, the American family, the Catholic Church, and contemporary human relationships generally.   BCM

House of Connelly, The, was written by **Paul Green** and produced by the newly formed **Group Theatre** at the **Martin Beck Theatre** on 28 September 1931. It was directed by **Lee Strasberg** and **Cheryl Crawford** and featured prominent members of the Group, including Art Smith, **Morris Carnovsky,** and **Stella Adler.** Set in the American South in 1905, the play dramatized plantation life against a background of family power, class prerogatives, and racial injustice. Widely compared to **Chekhov** and featuring superb ensemble acting, the play received largely positive notices but closed after 72 performances. However, its production was more significant than its dramatic merit: It became the landscape upon which the struggle between the **Theatre Guild** and their "apprentice company" was played out. The Guild optioned the play to the Group, who worked on it almost daily in the summer of 1931 in conjunction with their study of the Stanislavski System. Prior to opening, they squabbled with the Guild Board over the ending, casting, and actor credits. Eventually the Group severed all ties to the Guild and became one of America's most influential companies.   BBW

House of Mirth, The Dramatization with dialogue by Edith Wharton and scenario by **Clyde Fitch** of Wharton's popular novel about Lily Bart, whose true love is thwarted by the viciousness of New York society. Starring Fay Davis, the play opened on 22 October 1906 at the Savoy Theatre for a disappointing 14 performances. Following several dramatizations of novels during 1900–6, the play's failure precipitated media discussion of the difficulty of turning a thoughtful psychological novel into a popular Broadway play.   FB

See: G. Loney, ed., *The House of Mirth: The Play of the Novel*, Rutherford, NJ, 1981.

Howard, Bronson (Crocker) (1842–1908) The first professional American playwright; the first to distinguish the American businessman in his plays and one of the first to define his principles of drama in an essay, "The Laws of Dramatic Composition." Among his businessman plays are *Young Mrs. Winthrop* (1882), a sympathetic treatment of the neglected wife; *The Henrietta* (1887), a satire of life on the stock exchange; and *Aristocracy* (1892), which ridiculed new and old American wealth. Howard's awareness of social class stretched from *Saratoga* (1870), adapted to English circumstance as *Brighton* (1874), and *One of Our Girls* (1885), comparing American and French women. *The Banker's Daughter* (1878), given notoriety by Howard's lecture, "Autobiography of a Play" (1886), and his Civil War melodrama *Shenandoah* (1888) epitomized his popular success. Aided by his association with the Theatrical **Syndicate,** Howard raised the status of the American playwright with his plays and as a founder of the American Dramatists' Club in 1891.   WJM

See: *Bronson Howard: In Memoriam*, New York, 1910.

Howard, Sidney (Coe) (1891–1939) Playwright who, in the 1920s, was a crucial figure in lifting American drama from provincial entertainment to an authentic native literature. In a group of provocative plays – **They Knew What They Wanted** (which won the Pulitzer Prize in 1924), *Lucky Sam McCarver* (1925), *The Silver Cord* (1926), *Ned McCobb's Daughter* (1927), and *Half Gods* (1929) – he looked at such subjects as sex, mother love, psychiatry, and prohibition with a fresh point of view. Like **Eugene O'Neill,** Howard helped to popularize Freudian ideas about family and sexual relationships; but his focus, unlike O'Neill's, was intimate and his tone essentially comic. His best play, *They Knew What They Wanted,* advocates moral and sexual compromise, and in *Ned McCobb's Daughter* he created one of the era's most appealing New Women, a heroine with more sense than any of the men in her life. Because Howard thought of himself as a skilled craftsman rather than as an artist with a distinctive voice, he was a jack of all trades who wrote in a number of genres: spectacle, romance, the war story, and both urban and rural comedy. He frequently collaborated, and he translated and adapted the work of other writers (*The Late Christopher Bean* [1932] and *Dodsworth* [1934] were both acclaimed). He was also an active screenwriter, winning Academy Awards for *Arrowsmith* (1931) and *Gone with the Wind* (1939). His remarkably productive career – 27 plays and 13 screenplays – ended suddenly in 1939 when he had a fatal tractor accident on his Massachusetts farm.   FH

Howard, Willie (1886–1949) and **Eugene** (1880–1965) Comedians. Like many comedians of their day, the Howard brothers developed their comic personae in **vaudeville.** Their first joint appearance on the legitimate musical stage was in *The Passing Show of 1912*. Eugene served as the straight man for the act, while the sad-faced Willie got most of the laughs. Their talents were best displayed in **revues:** In addition to appearing in six of the *Passing Shows,* they starred in six editions of **George White**'s *Scandals*. Willie's abilities as a mimic made him especially valuable in revues that emphasized travesties of the latest performers and shows. In addition to their comic talents, both brothers had fine singing voices, which they often displayed in parodies of grand opera. After Eugene's retirement in 1940, Willie continued as a solo performer, but never again had the success that the brothers had achieved as a team.   MK

See: S. Green, *The Great Clowns of Broadway*, New York, 1984.

Howard Athenaeum Boston theatre that opened in 1845, but burned three months later when a fireball effect during Pizarro went awry [see **fires**]. The second Howard (1846), the first American theatre to have cushioned seats, offered its 2,000 patrons unobstructed views of the stage. **James H. Hackett** was the theatre's first manager, and a **stock company** was maintained there until the late 1860s. Speciality acts and burlesques were initiated by manager **John Stetson** in 1871. By 1953 these had degenerated into poorly performed, if fondly remembered, bump and grind striptease [see **nudity**], and city authorities closed the theatre. The building was razed in 1961.   TC

Howard family Performers. **George Cunnabel Howard** (1820–87), a Canadian-born actor, was engaged at the **Boston Museum,** where he met and married (1844) the actress Caroline Emily Fox (1829–1908). With a **stock company** that included Caroline's mother and three brothers [see **George L. Fox**], they toured New England in abbreviated versions of *The Drunkard* and *The Factory Girl* intermingled with an olio of songs and dances. As a respectable family unit they acclimatized theatre in towns that had hitherto condemned all playacting as damnable. The Howards achieved their most durable success with an adaptation of **Uncle Tom's Cabin** (1852), carpentered by their cousin **George Aiken** and featuring George Howard as St. Clare, Caroline as Topsy, and their daughter Cordelia as Eva; when played in an expanded text at the National Theatre (New York, 1853), it captured the imagination of the times. Cordelia became the star of the family, also creating the title role in *Katy the Hot Corn Girl* and Little Gerty in *The Lamplighter*.   LS

See: L. Senelick, *The Age and Stage of George L. Fox, 1825–1877*, Hanover, NH, 1988.

Howe, Tina (1937–) Playwright whose plays, characterized by a strong central metaphor and contrapuntal, parallel speeches, present the contrast between polished public behavior and quirky private characters. Heavily influenced by the **Marx Bros.,** her early works – *The Nest* (1969), *Birth and After Birth* (publ. 1973, unproduced), *Museum* (1976), and *The Art of Dining* (1979) – are farcical criticisms of pretentiousness. Her later plays, all initially directed by Carole Rothman, are realistic plays filled with fantasy. Her first big success was *Painting Churches* (1983, Outer Critics' Circle Award), an autobiographical play about a painter making peace with her aging parents. *Coastal Disturbances* (1986) and *Approaching Zanzibar* (1989) are comedies concerning love and loss. In 1983, Howe won a collective Obie for "Distinguished Playwriting." TH-S

Howells, William Dean (1837–1920) Novelist, critic, and playwright. "The Father of Realism" in America, Howells not only praised the work of **Edward Harrigan, James Herne,** and **Henrik Ibsen,** but contributed himself to the rise of realism in drama and the development of social comedy. Both *A Counterfeit Presentment* (1877) and *Yorick's Love* (1878) were acted successfully by **Lawrence Barrett.** The author of some 36 plays, Howells wrote 12 one-act farces featuring social events in the lives of two couples (the Robertses and the Campbells), including *The Garroters* (1885), in which Roberts mistakenly garrots a friend; *Five O'Clock Tea* (1887), as Campbell becomes engaged; and *The Unexpected Guest* (1893), when Mr. and Mrs. Campbell entertain. A writer of charming dialogue but incapable of producing the melodramatic confrontations demanded by 19th-century audiences, Howells pictured instead such man–woman struggles as broken engagements (*An Indian Giver*, 1897; *Parting Friends*, 1910). Howells was a gentle satirist of Boston manners who became bitter in later plays (*The Impossible*, 1910; *The Night Before Christmas*, 1910), and his work appealed more to amateur than professional performers. WJM

See: E. H. Cady, *The Realist at War*, Syracuse, NY, 1958; E. H. Cady, *The Road to Realism*, Syracuse, 1956; E. Carter, *Howells and the Age of Realism*, Philadelphia, 1954; M. Howells, *Life in Letters of William Dean Howells*, 2 vols., Garden City, NY, 1928; W. Meserve, ed., *The Complete Plays of William Dean Howells*, New York, 1960.

How to Succeed in Business Without Really Trying Two-act musical comedy, music and lyrics by **Frank Loesser,** book by **Abe Burrows,** Jack Weinstein, and Willie Gilbert; opened 14 October 1961 at the **46th Street Theatre,** running 1,417 performances. Based on Shepherd Mead's book of the same name, this cynical, cartoonlike satire of American big business traces the rise of its charming cad of a hero (**Robert Morse**) from window washer to chairman of the board. Overturning many traditional musical-comedy devices, it downplays any romantic element by making its characters strongly unsympathetic; even the primary love ballad is sung by the character to himself in a mirror. The show won the Pulitzer Prize for drama, as well as the Drama Critics' Circle and Tony awards for best musical. Originally staged by Abe Burrows and choreographed by Hugh Lambert, the production was largely reworked by **Bob Fosse,** who was called in to doctor it and given credit for "musical staging." JD

Hoyle, Geoff (1946–) **New Vaudevillian,** actor. Born in England and trained with Etienne Decroux in Paris, Hoyle has worked in the U.S. since 1975 when he joined the Pickle Family **Circus** in San Francisco. Hoyle toured with them until 1982, when he began a career as a solo performer. He has created and performed three solo shows: *Boomer* (1986), *Feast of Fools* (1988), and *Don Quixote de La Jolla* (1990). TL

Hoyt, Charles (Hale) (1860–1900) A major writer of farce and satire that, in his best plays, showed social themes and realistic characters, Hoyt wrote some 20 plays, drawing his material from his own interests and experiences: small-town life (*A Rag Baby*, 1884), his father's early occupation of hotel management (*A Bunch of Keys*, 1882), superstitions (*The Brass Monkey*, 1888), corrupt politics (*A Texas Steer*, 1890), prohibition (*A Temperance Town*, 1893), the hypocrisy of home guard companies (*A Milk White Flag*, 1893), and baseball (*A Runaway Colt*, 1895). *A Trip to Chinatown* (1891) had the longest run of any play produced in America to that date (650 performances). Theatre was strictly a business with Hoyt, who revised his work with extreme care and made £100,000 (roughly $485,000) in a good year. There was also stress: Committed to the Retreat for the Insane at Hartford, CT (in his native New England) in 1900, he died that year. WJM

See: D. Hunt, *The Life and Work of Charles H. Hoyt*, Birmingham, AL, 1946.

Hsieh, Tehching (Sam Hsieh) (1950–) Conceptual and **performance art**ist, born and raised in rural Noncho, Taiwan; studied painting with Tehgin Shing (1968–9). After being drafted into the Republic of China Army (1970–3), he joined the Merchant Seamen for the Republic of China, jumped ship, and moved to the U.S. (1974). Following his first performance in Taipei (1973), he performed in New York a series of body-art works (1976–7) and a series of one-year-long ordeal performances (1978–84). In his current 13-year-long performance, he privatizes his artwork, neither showing it publicly nor speaking about it (1986–99). His aesthetic is influenced by Asian mysticism and martial arts, the Japanese avant-garde, Christianity, Nietschze and Kafka, European existentialism, and the *Nouveaux Réalistes.* AF

Hudson Guild Theatre Founded in 1896 as part of the settlement house movement, the Hudson Guild was established to keep the poor of NYC's Chelsea neighborhood off the streets by involving them in amateur theatricals. The theatre languished after WW II, but it experienced a renaissance in 1975 when it was taken over by David Heefner and moved into Neighborhood House on West 26th St., amid a multiracial housing project. With professional status, it moved some productions to Broadway. In 1990, the Hudson Guild withdrew its support, and the theatre, newly named the Chelsea Stage Theater, ceased activities. MCH

Hughes, Barnard (1915–) Actor, born in Bedford Hills, NY, and educated at Manhattan College. Hughes made his New York debut in

1934 as the haberdasher in *The Taming of the Shrew*. After minor roles and military service, he developed his range and diversity in major supporting roles: *The Teahouse of the August Moon* (1956), *Enrico IV* (1958), *Advise and Consent* (1960), *A Doll's House* (1963), *Nobody Loves an Albatross* (1963), John Gielgud's *Hamlet* (1964), **Hogan's Goat** (1965), *How Now, Dow Jones* (1967), and *Sheep on the Runway* (1970). Since 1970, Hughes has become one of America's most distinguished character actors, acclaimed for his Dogberry in *Much Ado* (1972), Alexander Serebryakov in *Uncle Vanya* (1973), Falstaff in *The Merry Wives of Windsor* (1974), the title role in *Da* (1978), Father William Doherty in *Angels Fall* (1983), Philip Stone in *End of the World* (1984), Harry Hope in **The Iceman Cometh** (1985), and the father in **Prelude to a Kiss** (1990) by **Craig Lucas**. **Mel Gussow** regarded his award-winning Da as the high point of his career: "he takes a most ordinary man . . . and makes him lovable to his sardonic son and to the audience." **T. E. Kalem** viewed his Da as "an expansive field marshall of lifelong defeat who acts with the authority of an uncaged lion."   TLM

Hughes, Hatcher (1883–1945) This southern playwright and teacher, who specialized in folk drama, produced most of his dramatic work in the 1920s and is primarily remembered for one play: the Pulitzer Prize–winning **Hell-Bent fer Heaven** (1924). Although many claimed the play won by default when the selection committee's choice of *The Show-Off* was overruled, this rustic melodrama of phony religious zealotry and Carolina mountain feuding, with its heavy dialects, moved numerous audiences and was emblematic of a wave of folk dramas appearing on Broadway in that decade. His other plays of note are *Wake Up, Jonathan* (1921), a comic collaboration with **Elmer Rice**; *Ruint* (1925), a comedy of enforced marriage, produced at the Provincetown; and a vehicle for **Minnie Maddern Fiske**, *It's a Grand Life* (1930).   RHW

Hughes, Holly (1951–) Michigan-born poet, playwright, and **performance art**ist who came to New York as a painter and entered the East Village scene of Piezo Electric, Club 57, and the WOW Café. As manager at the WOW Café until 1983, she organized regular "Talking Slide Shows," where artists showed slides and talked about their work. Hughes's first performances were *Shrimp in a Basket* and *The Well of Horniness*. She developed *Dress Suits to Hire* (1987) with Lois Weaver and Peggy Shaw. Her solo performances *World Without End* (1988) and *Dead Meat* (1990) explored the contradictions of multiple pleasures. Hughes's autobiographical style is inspired by 1970s **feminist** insistence on political and sexual autonomy, yet she performs in the stand-up comedic tradition of blasphemy and audience harangues made popular by **Lenny Bruce** in the 1950s.   AF

Hughes, [James Mercer] Langston (1902–67) **African-American** poet, story writer, and playwright. Brought up by his grandmother, whose first husband died in John Brown's raid at Harper's Ferry, he acquired her racial consciousness and a love of literature. He published his first play, *The Gold Piece,* in 1921, and gained his first Broadway success with **Mulatto** (1935), a melodrama on race relations in a Southern town. Hughes achieved substantial New York runs with his folk musical *Simply Heavenly* (1957) and with *Tambourines to Glory* (1963). He received several premieres at the interracial **Karamu** Theatre in Cleveland, where Hughes attended public school. Among these plays are *Little Ham* (1936), *Troubled Island* (1936), *Joy to My Soul* (1937), and *Front Porch* (1938). In addition, Hughes wrote librettos for four produced operas, and the book and lyrics for **Kurt Weill**'s musical version of **Street Scene** (1947). Hughes founded three short-lived theatres: the Harlem Suitcase Theatre, where his polemical *Don't You Want to Be Free?* (1938) ran on weekends for 135 performances; the New Negro Theatre in Los Angeles (1939); and the Skyloft Players in Chicago (1949). In 1991 his previously unproduced play, *Mule Bone* (written with Zora Neale Hurston in 1930) was staged by Lincoln Center at the **Ethel Barrymore Theatre**. Hughes's plays are most appealing when his righteous anger is tempered by gentle satire, humor, and lyricism.   EGH

See: A. Rampersad, *The Life of Langston Hughes: Vol. I: 1902–1941 – I, Too, Sing America,* New York, 1986; *Vol. II: 1941–1967 – I Dream a World,* New York, 1988.

Hull, Josephine (1886–1957) Character actress who specialized in eccentric old lady roles. She began by using her maiden name (Sherwood) as she toured, then retired from the stage when she married Shelley Hull in 1910. Upon Hull's death in 1919 she resumed acting. She attracted attention in 1924 in *Neighbors* and increased her stature with **Craig's Wife** in 1926. Her style, described as "gasping, fluttery, egregiously middle class," established her stardom in **You Can't Take It with You** (1936), **Arsenic and Old Lace** (1941), and **Harvey** (1945), for the film version of which she won an Oscar. Her last starring role was in *The Solid Gold Cadillac,* during which she collapsed in 1954.   SMA

See: W. Carson, *Dear Josephine,* Norman, OK, 1963.

Hull-House Theatre Throughout most of its 90-year history, **Chicago**'s Hull-House offered theatre along with, or as part of, its social work activity. Founders Jane Addams and Ellen Gates Starr felt from the start (1889) that theatre was an apt tool for social rehabilitation, and the efforts that ensued often exceeded that aim to achieve artistic excellence as well.

The Hull-House Players (1897–1941) were a leader in the Little Theatre movement [see **community theatre**]. Edith de Nancrede had long-term (1902–46) success with her children's theatre, and Robert Sickinger's revival of the Hull-House theatre program (1963–9) is often credited with having a seminal effect on the reemergence of theatre in Chicago.

Two theatre structures outlived the social work: The Jane Addams Theater on Broadway once housed the **Steppenwolf** company (among others), and the Parkway Theater on the South Side housed X-BAG (Experimental Black Actors Guild) during the 1970s and the Chicago Theatre Company (and others) thereafter.   SF

Hume, Samuel J. (1885–1962) Set designer and founder of the Detroit Arts and Crafts Theatre. Hume was one of the pioneers of the New Stagecraft [see **scenic design**] and the Little Theatre movement [see **community theatre**]. He studied with Edward Gordon Craig in Florence and subsequently applied Craig's idea of movable screens into "adaptable settings" – unit sets utilizing flats, platforms, draperies, arches, and pylons that could be rearranged, changed, or altered by lighting to fit individual scenes. It was thus a move away from naturalism toward simplification and suggestion, as well as being economical.   AA

Huneker, James G. (1857–1921) Critic who brought serious public attention to continental dramatists in the 1890s and early 1900s. Huneker made his debut as a music critic in 1875 for the *Philadelphia Evening Bulletin*. In 1886, after studying piano in Paris, he moved to New York and a position as music critic for the *Musical Courier*. He began writing drama criticism during his tenure with the *New York Recorder* (1891–5). In 1895 he became music and drama critic for the *Morning Advertiser*, and during 1902–4 held the drama post for the *New York Sun*. He also wrote for *Metropolitan Magazine*, *Puck*, *Smart Set*, and *New York Times*. His 22 books include *Iconoclasts: A Book of Dramatists* (1905) and his autobiography, *Steeplejack* (1920). Huneker opposed the Genteel Tradition and championed the plays of **Ibsen**, Strindberg, **Shaw**, Maeterlinck, and Schnitzler. He brought a lively and impressionistic style to American criticism, and influenced a generation of writers including **George Jean Nathan** and H. L. Mencken.   TLM

Hunt, Linda (1945–) Actress-director, best known as the male Indonesian dwarf in the film *The Year of Living Dangerously* (Academy Award, 1983). Hunt won Obies for **Martha Clarke**'s *A Metamorphosis in Miniature* (1982) and Churchill's *Top Girls* (1983). "Magnetic" with "a kind of wonderful calm and peaceful wisdom," her size (4′ 9′′, 80 lb) became her signature in **Kopit**'s *End of the World* (Tony nomination, 1984); *Mother Courage and Her Children* (Boston, 1984); *Aunt Dan and Lemon* (1985); E. **Mann**'s *Annulla* (New Theatre of Brooklyn, 1988); *The Cherry Orchard* (**Brooklyn Academy of Music**, 1988); and *Three Sisters* (Olga in E. Mann's **McCarter Theatre** production, 1992). Films include *The Bostonians* (1984), *Eleni* (1985), *Waiting for the Moon* (1987), and *If Looks Could Kill* (1991).   REK

Hunter, Kim (née Janet Cole) (1922–) Stage, film, and television actress whose stage debut was in *Penny Wise* (1929); her Broadway debut was as Stella in *A Streetcar Named Desire* (1947), a role she recreated on film in 1951, winning an Oscar for best supporting actress. Hunter has acted for the **Shakespeare Festival Theatre** and various

stock companies in such roles as Catherine Reardon in *And Miss Reardon Drinks a Little*.   SMA

Hurlbut, William J. (1883–?) Playwright who wrote many Broadway shows between 1908 and 1937, but was most successful with melodramas about women. *The Fighting Hope* (1908), presenting a wife attempting to save her imprisoned husband, and *Lilies of the Field* (1921), in which a divorced woman fights to regain her child, are typical. With *Bride of the Lamb* (1926) he turned to the tragedy of a woman caught up in religious revival and blind love, and produced his most arresting work.   RHW

Hurlyburly David Rabe's play about the coke-snorting Hollywood culture of the 1980s. After premiering at Chicago's **Goodman Theatre** in April 1984, *Hurlyburly* opened **Off-Broadway** in June and then transferred to the **Ethel Barrymore** on Broadway for 343 performances. The cast, directed by **Mike Nichols**, included **William Hurt** (Eddie), **Christopher Walken** (Mickey), Sigourney Weaver (Darlene), and Jerry Stiller (Artie). Rabe strongly disapproved of Nichols's satiric interpretation of and cuts in *Hurlyburly*. A 1986 production at **Trinity Rep**, directed by **David Wheeler**, restored Rabe's original script and intent; in 1988 Rabe directed a production at Los Angeles' Westwood Playhouse. Focusing on male bonds and identity, *Hurlyburly* is saturated with violence and self-destruction. Hollywood replaces Vietnam as the new battlefield for Rabe. The play's convoluted semantics, laced with nonsense words, mirror the tumultuous discourse of the times. The title – from *Macbeth*, where it signifies confusion – is a fit description of the physical and psychic disorder Rabe dramatizes.   PCK

Hurt (née Supringer), Mary Beth (1948–) Actress whose "chameleon quality . . . results in a one-woman repertory company," as seen in DeLillo's *The Day Room* (1987), Hare's *The Secret Rapture* (1989), and *Othello* (**New York Shakespeare Festival**, 1991), and the films *Interiors* (1978), *The World According to Garp* (1982), and *Slaves of New York* (1990). She received the 1974–5 Clarence Derwent Award, Tony nominations for *Trelawney of the Wells* (1975) and *Crimes of the Heart* (1981), and Obies for *Crimes* and *Love for Love* (1975). Divorced from **William Hurt**, she is married to screenwriter-director Paul Schrader.   REK

Hurt, William (1950–) An actor of "distilled and concentrated intensity" whose **Off-Broadway** debut was *Henry V* (**New York Shakespeare Festival**, 1977) and Broadway debut was *Hurlyburly* (1984). Active with the **Circle Repertory Company** (1977–82), his recent work includes Pintauro's *Beside Herself* (CRC, 1989) and *Ivanov* (**Yale Repertory Theatre**, 1990), as well as the films *Body Heat* (1981), *The Big Chill* (1983), *Kiss of the Spider Woman* (Academy Award, 1984), *Children of a Lesser God* (1986), *The Accidental Tourist* (1988), and *The Doctor* (1991). Hurt won the Obie and *Theatre World* awards for **Corinne Jacker**'s

My Life (CRC, 1977) and the 1988 Spencer Tracy Award. REK

> *See:* T. Goldstein, *William Hurt: The Man, The Actor,* New York, 1987.

Hurwitz, Moishe (1844–1910) and **Jacob Lateiner** (1853–1935) The two main writers of Shund theatre, characterizing the lowest quality of popular American **Yiddish theatre** (sentimental and melodramatic) during the 1890s. Deliberately writing down to the tastes of the most uneducated and unsophisticated of the "green" immigrants, "Professor" Hurwitz (as he called himself) wrote about 90 plays, and Jacob Lateiner turned out over 150. AB

Huston, Walter (1884–1950) Canadian-born stage and film director, noted for his artistic integrity, lack of affectation, and economic style. He began acting in 1902, returned to school, then reentered the theatre in 1909. For almost 18 years he toured the U.S. and Canada. His New York debut was in 1924 in the title role of *Mr. Pitt,* and in the same year he achieved stardom as Ephraim Cabot in *Desire Under the Elms.* **Stark Young** called Huston's Ephraim "trenchant, gaunt, fervid, harsh," lauding his "ability to convey the harsh, inarticulate life" of the role. Later **Brooks Atkinson** called Huston "the most honest of actors – plain, simple, lucid, magnetic." He was also acclaimed for his title role in Sinclair Lewis's *Dodsworth* and for his work in *Knickerbocker Holiday,* in which he introduced "September Song." In 1948 he won an Academy Award for best supporting actor in *The Treasure of the Sierra Madre,* a film directed by his son, John. His other films included *Dodsworth* and *Duel in the Sun.* SMA

> *See:* L. Bailey, "The Acting Career of Walter Huston," PhD diss., U of Illinois, 1972.

Hutton, Laurence (1843–1904) Author, critic, and editor. Born in New York and educated at private schools, Hutton worked as a journalist for the *New York Mail* during 1867–75, including two years (1872–4) as drama critic; for *Harper's Magazine* during 1886–98, as literary editor; and for the *Mail and Examiner* in 1903–4. A prolific author, Hutton wrote chatty books about literary landmarks, actors, artists, and famous writers, including *Plays and Players* (1875); the *American Actor Series* (1881–2); *Actors and Actresses of Great Britain and the United States,* with Brander Matthews (1886); and *Curiosities of the American Stage* (1891). TLM

Hwang, David Henry (1957–) Born in Los Angeles to immigrant Chinese parents, and educated at Stanford and Yale, Hwang was the first Asian-American playwright to break through to national prominence. He won a Tony (and other prizes) for his 1988 Broadway hit *M. Butterfly,* a dazzling deconstruction of cross-cultural and sexual delusions. Hwang's career took off in 1980 when *F.O.B,* a sly, enigmatic portrait of a young Chinese immigrant who doubles as a mythic Asian folk god, earned raves at the **Public Theater.** In subsequent works – *The Dance and the Railroad, Family Devotions, The Sound of a Voice* – Hwang handily mingled history, fantasy, and naturalism to explore a "fluidity of identity" endemic to the multicultural modern age. Though he links himself to the **Asian-American theatre** movement, he refuses to write only about his own ethnic milieu, as witnessed by *Rich Relations* (1986), a satire of upper-middle-class mores, and *1,000 Airplanes on the Roof* (1988), a science fiction collaboration with composer Philip Glass. MB

Hyman, Earle (1926–) **African-American** actor, renowned in classical and contemporary roles. Hyman began with the American Negro Theatre and at 17 appeared in *Anna Lucasta* (1944) on Broadway and in London's West End. His earliest Shakespearean role was Hamlet (1951) at Howard University, followed by the first of six Othellos played over a 25-year period in Antioch (OH), New York, Connecticut, Norway, and Sweden. Hyman performed 10 other roles with the **American Shakespeare Theatre** (1955–60), received rave notices for his Broadway performance in *Mr. Johnson* (1956), and the State Award in Oslo, Norway, for his portrayal of the title role in *The Emperor Jones* (1965). In 1989 he replaced **Morgan Freeman** as the Chauffeur in *Driving Miss Daisy,* performing the play in Norway and Denmark (in Norwegian and Danish). In 1991 he essayed the role of Pickering in **Roundabout Theatre**'s non-traditionally cast *Pygmalion.* EGH

I

I Am a Camera **John van Druten**'s three-act drama adapted from Christopher Isherwood's *The Berlin Stories;* opened on Broadway at the **Empire Theatre** (28 November 1951) for 214 performances, winning the Drama Critics' Circle Award. Directed by the author, the production was praised for **Julie Harris**'s portrayal of Sally Bowles. Set in prewar Berlin in 1930, the action is seen through the eyes of the sensitive young writer Christopher (Isherwood), who is taking mental photographs of the wild characters and liberal, irreverent attitudes surrounding him. The show was revived **Off-Broadway** in October 1956 at the Actors' Playhouse, Sheridan Square. *Cabaret* (1966), a musical by **Joe Masterhoff** and **Kander and Ebb**, was based on this play. EK

Ibsen on the American stage In 1882 a group of amateurs introduced Ibsen to this country when they presented a version of *A Doll's House* in Milwaukee. A year later, **Helena Modjeska** presented her adaptation of the play in Louisville, KY, but it was withdrawn after one performance. Until the turn of the century Ibsen was considered an iconoclast, and most critics, such as **William Winter**, were hostile, calling his characters dramatic freaks and attacking the plays as overly pessimistic.

Risking their careers, actresses such as Beatrice Cameron, **Blanche Bates, Ethel Barrymore, Nance O'Neil,** and Florence Kahn pioneered. **Minnie Maddern Fiske** revived *A Doll's House* (1894, 1895, 1902) and *Hedda Gabler* (1903), and **Mary Shaw** presented *Ghosts* (1899, 1903) both in New York and on major national tours. In former generations, actresses had turned to Shakespeare's Juliet to exhibit their virtuosity, but now they turned to Ibsen's heroines.

By 1906 opinions had changed. With the growth of the U.S.'s industrial society and the appearance of emancipated women, major literary critics such as **William Dean Howells** and **James Gibbons Huneker** came to Ibsen's defense. Supporting the efforts of Mrs. Fiske were the productions of foreign stars, especially those of the exotic Russian **Alla Nazimova,** who electrified audiences with her sensual performances in *Hedda Gabler* (1906), *A Doll's House* (1907), and *The Master Builder* (1907). A few years later she added *Little Eyolf* (1910), and Mrs. Fiske toured *Pillars of Society* (1910).

Oddly, from 1912 to 1922 there were only four New York seasons that included Ibsen productions. No foreign stars toured his plays to the U.S.; no one took his plays on the road. Besides the occasional revival by Mary Shaw or Nazimova,

Ibsen's name was kept alive only through silent films based on his plays: *Ghosts* and *Peer Gynt* (1915), *Hedda Gabler* (1917), and *A Doll's House* (1917, 1918, 1922). The neglect was due in part to Ibsen's name being linked with the women's movement: As women slowly gained more rights, his pleas for social reform seemed irrelevant. Another reason was the feverish growth of nationalism after WW I. Americans turned inward and rejected their European heritage, including the plays of Ibsen, which seemed unsuitable and remote.

In the atmosphere of reform that spawned the **Off-Broadway** movement, however, important critics such as H. L. Mencken, Edmund Wilson, **Joseph Wood Krutch,** and Herman Weigand turned to Ibsen in the early 1920s and proclaimed his genius. Weigand's *The Modern Ibsen* relied heavily on Freudian psychology, which profoundly influenced future productions. In 1923 the **Theatre Guild** starred **Joseph Schildkraut** in their revival of *Peer Gynt*. That same year Eleanora Duse broke box-office records as she toured America with *The Lady from the Sea* and *Ghosts*. The Actors' Theatre revived *Hedda Gabler* (1924, 1926), *The Wild Duck* (1925), and *Ghosts* (1926). Other revivals included *Rosmersholm* (1925), *Little Eyolf* (1926), *Ghosts* (1927), and *Enemy of the People* (1927). During the 1928–9 season **Blanche Yurka** offered an Ibsen series that included *The Wild Duck, Hedda Gabler,* and *The Lady from the Sea,* and in 1930 she starred in the American premiere of *The Vikings*. **Eva Le Gallienne** established her **Civic Repertory Theatre** with *The Master Builder* and *John Gabriel Borkman* (1925), and later added *Hedda Gabler* (1928). In 1928 Le Gallienne and Yurka appeared in simultaneous productions of *Hedda Gabler* only a few blocks apart; in 1929 there were six Ibsen productions on Broadway.

However, with the trauma of the Great Depression, Americans began to reject foreign classics. The temper of the times was introspective, and theatregoers sought American plays that dealt with the nation's contemporary social and economic problems. Eva Le Gallienne persisted in championing Ibsen with her revivals of *The Master Builder* (1934, 1939), *Hedda Gabler* (1934, 1939, 1948), *A Doll's House* (1934), *Rosmersholm* (1935), *John Gabriel Borkman* (1946), and *Ghosts* (1948), but she was attacked for exhibiting sacred relics that belonged in museums. The real center of Ibsen interest was on university and college campuses: In 1956 an Ibsen play either had been or was being planned for production at two-thirds of all American universities.

When John F. Kennedy won the 1960 election, it inaugurated an atmosphere of change and inspired progress and reform in such areas as civil rights and women's liberation. Predictably, it meant renewed interest in Ibsen. James Walter McFarlane's *Discussions of Henrik Ibsen* (1962) set the tone for new interpretations; Rolf Fjelde and Eva Le Gallienne provided new translations. David Ross began a series of revivals: *Hedda Gabler* (1960), *Ghosts* (1961), and *Rosmersholm* (1962). Le Gallienne directed for the National Repertory Theatre a national tour of *Hedda Gabler* that starred Signe Hasso. Between 1965 and 1975 professional productions were presented at most regional theatres around the country, and Ibsen's plays were finally accepted as popular classics. Washington's **John F. Kennedy Center for the Performing Arts** opened its new Eisenhower Theatre in 1971 with *A Doll's House*.

A new generation of American actresses began their explorations of his heroines: Jane Fonda, Marsha Mason, Carole Shelley, **Jane Alexander, Dianne Wiest, Kim Hunter, Irene Worth,** and **Geraldine Page.** European stars began to import Ibsen: Claire Bloom's *A Doll's House* and *Hedda Gabler* (1971), Liv Ullmann's *A Doll's House* (1975) and *Ghosts* (1982), Glenda Jackson's *Hedda Gabler* (1975), Vanessa Redgrave's *Lady from the Sea* (1976), and Susannah York's *Hedda Gabler* (1981) [see **international stars**].

The Ibsen Society of America (founded in 1979) inspired the establishment in 1982 of the American Ibsen Theater, which lasted three seasons. Ibsen's plays had finally become so absorbed into the fabric of American culture that **Betty Comden** and **Adolph Green** wrote a musical sequel to *A Doll's House* called *A Doll's Life* (1982), and **Charles Ludlam** starred in a transgender interpretation of *Hedda Gabler* (1984). RAS

See: R. Schanke, Ibsen in America: A Century of Change, Methuchen, NJ, 1988; R. Schanke, Shattered Applause: The Lives of Eva Le Gallienne, Carbondale, IL, 1992.

Icebound Pulitzer Prize–winning drama by **Owen Davis,** produced by **Sam Harris;** opened 10 February 1923 at the Sam H. Harris Theatre for 170 performances. Though *Icebound* seemed to confirm Davis's turn from facile melodrama, all of its characters – hardened by greed and a rigorous existence in rural Maine – get their just desserts when the family matriarch dies. The cast featured Robert Ames as the black-sheep son who inherits the estate, and Phyllis Povah as the distant relation. MR

Iceman Cometh, The Although **Eugene O'Neill**'s play premiered 9 October 1946 produced by the **Theatre Guild** at the **Martin Beck Theatre,** ably directed by **Eddie Dowling** and beautifully designed by **Robert Edmond Jones,** it was not regarded as of the first rank until its splendid arena revival of 8 May 1956 at **Circle in the Square,** staged by **José Quintero** with **Jason Robards, Jr.,** in the pivotal role of Hickey. This long, "lower depths" play recaptures many of O'Neill's experiences and friends while habituating cheap West Side gin mills and their back rooms, like Harry Hope's saloon in his alcoholic youth (1912). Into a world of lost dreams and hopeless hopes, where people drink to kill the pain, O'Neill interjects a reformed savior Hickey who attempts to drag his alcoholic friends out of their stupor and pipe dreams to face truth. He convinces some to discard their habitual excuses and actuate their dreams. All fail, of course, and use Hickey's confession of murdering his wife to return to stasis and the oblivion of alcohol. A beautifully written, but depressing study of humankind's inability to act, the play, for O'Neill, after many years of theatrical experiment, marks a return to realism from which he never again diverged. RHW

Idiot's Delight by **Robert E. Sherwood.** Winner of the Pulitzer Prize for 1935–6, this three-act comedy-melodrama with music opened at the **Sam**

Goodman Theatre's 1990 production of O'Neill's *The Iceman Cometh*, directed by Robert Falls with (foreground, left to right) Jerome Kilty (Harry Hope) and Brian Dennehy (Hickey). Photo: Liz Lauren. Courtesy: Goodman Theatre.

S. Shubert Theatre on 24 March 1936 and ran for 299 performances. The elegant **Theatre Guild** production was designed by **Lee Simonson** and featured **Alfred Lunt and Lynn Fontanne** as an American hoofer and phony Russian countess stranded in a resort in the Italian Alps as world war erupts. The unusual tension of the play between its antiwar theme and romantic-comedy framework effectively captured American anxieties about a coming war in Europe. A film version starring Clark Gable and Norma Shearer was released in 1939, and Sherwood's play served as the basis of an unsuccessful 1983 musical by **Alan Jay Lerner** called *Dance a Little Closer*.   MF

Imperial Theatre 249 West 45th St., NYC [Architect: Herbert J. Krapp]. Built by the **Shubert brothers** to house their special brand of musical theatre, the playhouse opened in 1923, and has since booked fewer than 60 productions, giving it a reputation as a "lucky house." Among its most interesting nonmusical tenants have been Leslie Howard's *Hamlet* (1936), Jean Arthur's *Peter Pan* (1950), and John Osborne's *A Patriot for Me* (1969). Leading the list of its extraordinary musical successes have been *Oh, Kay!* (1926), *On Your Toes* (1936), *Annie Get Your Gun* (1946), *Fiddler on the Roof* (1964), *Dreamgirls* (1981), *Jerome Robbins' Broadway* (1989, a pastiche of his past hits), and *Les Misérables* (which transferred from the Broadway in 1990). The 1,500-seat theatre remains a Shubert house.   MCH

In Abraham's Bosom This Pulitzer Prize–winning play by **Paul Green** was originally staged by Jasper Deeter for the **Provincetown Players** in 1926, with designs by **Cleon Throckmorton**. It featured Jules Bledsoe and **Rose McClendon** in leading roles. Though some critics claimed that it was too long and structurally awkward, Green's touching folk play about a Negro man who wants to educate his people eventually won a large following and was transferred uptown to the **Garrick**. McClendon went on to a brief but significant career working with the Negro People's Theatre and starring in *Mullato* before her untimely death.   BBW

Indiana Repertory Theatre Established in Indianapolis, IN, in 1972 by Benjamin Mordecai, Gregory Poggi, and Edward Stern. The group occupied the Atheneum Theater and produced, with a resident company of actors, designers, artisans, and technicians, seasons of up to 10 productions of plays from a broad spectrum of types. In 1980, under the leadership of new artistic director, Tom Haas, it moved to the renovated Indiana Theatre, containing three theatres: a thrust-proscenium facility seating 607, a smaller proscenium theater seating 269, and a cabaret seating 150. After Haas's death in 1991, Libby Appel was appointed artistic director (July 1992).   WD

Indian Princess; or, La Belle Sauvage, The "An Operatic Melo-Drame" by **James Nelson Barker,** with music by English actor John Bray. It was first performed at the **Chestnut Street Theatre** in Philadelphia on 6 April 1808. The libretto offers the earliest surviving treatment of the Pocahontas legend, but focuses less on her rescue of John Smith than on the five pairs of lovers that comprise most of the cast. Bray's music prefigures, by two generations, Sir Arthur Sullivan. The piece was performed at the **Park Theatre** in New York 14 June 1809 and then adapted for its Drury Lane (London) premiere on 15 December 1820 under the title *Pocahontas; or, the Indian Princess*.   JDM

Indians by **Arthur Kopit,** first performed by the Royal Shakespeare Company in London (1968), had its U.S. premiere at Washington, DC's **Arena Stage** (directed by **Gene Frankel**) in May 1969, moving to New York's **Brooks Atkinson Theatre** in October for 96 performances. In a cast of over 50 characters, **Stacy Keach** starred as **"Buffalo Bill" Cody** and Manu Tupou was Sitting Bull. Kopit's epic play, staged on a large, open apron stage in 13 scenes, effectively presented a complex drama concerned with genocide, the myth of the West, and, as Kopit later indicated, an exposure of the madness of our involvement in Vietnam. Though the latter is subtly present, more obvious is the **Wild West exhibition** as symbol for white man's cruelty to, and subjugation of, the Indians [see **Native Americans portrayed**]. In a larger sense, *Indians* deals with the U.S. need to create myths about unpleasant behavior in order to mask historical fact. In demonstrating this theme, Kopit likewise distorts history, but less blatantly than the 1976 film version with screenplay by Robert Altman and Alan Rudolph.   DBW

Indian Wants the Bronx, The A one-act realistic play by **Israel Horovitz** staged by James Hammerstein with Horovitz's *It's Called the Sugar Plum* at the Astor Place Theatre (New York), opening 17 January 1968. In this **Off-Broadway** production, **Al Pacino** appeared as "Murphy," one of two sadistic punks who brutally torment a man from India that they encounter at a street corner in the Bronx. Unable to speak English and apparently separated from his son, the Hindu is subjected to senseless youth violence in a big city.   ER

Industrial drama movement From 1900 into the mid-1920s, American industries subsidized dramatic clubs, staged company shows, and financed community plays and pageants to promote their public image, Americanize immigrant labor, and control their workers' leisure time. Fearful of strikes and radical political action and determined to uphold bourgeois morality, businessmen intended their first company theatricals, such as the "Goodyear Greater Minstrels," to compete with and replace working-class entertainments in dance halls, vaudeville theatres, and saloons. Following WW I, the Playground and Recreation Association of America (founded in 1906), financed by businesses and drawing on its wartime service with the Liberty Theatres, propagated the military-camp theatrical as the model for community drama. By 1921, the Association's activities, plus the onset of Prohibition and the "Red Scare," induced companies in all the industrial cities and over 300 towns to sponsor the production of local theatricals by and for workers. These included a pageant at the Ford Motor Company advocating a "melting pot" for immigrant culture, and a Labor Day celebration glorifying hard work. The concern of industrial psychologists to merge the cultures of work and play shaped later productions, such as the "Hawthorne Follies," sponsored by a subsidiary of AT&T. The industrial drama movement died out during the 1930s, but continued to influence the policies of numerous **community theatre**s.   BMcC

> See: B. A. McConachie and D. Friedman, eds., *Theatre for Working-Class Audiences in the United States, 1830–1980,* Westport, CT, 1985.

I Never Sang for My Father by **Robert Anderson** opened at Broadway's **Longacre Theatre** 25 January 1968 under **Alan Schneider**'s direction for a modest run of 124 performances. The play depicts a man's deep introspection about his inability to develop an open and loving relationship with his father, who is nearing death. Although the playwright was respected for his prior study of sensitivity in relationships (*Tea and Sympathy,* 1953), this work received generally poor notices as indulgent and unrealistic. Critics credited individual performances as its only redemption, especially **Hal Holbrook** as the man, Alan Webb as the father, and **Lillian Gish** as the mother.   KN

Inge, William [Motter] (1913–73) Playwright. On the strength of his first play, *Come Back Little Sheba* (1950), the critics touted Inge as having the promise to join **Arthur Miller** and **Tennessee Williams** in a triumvirate of outstanding American dramatists. Although he never fulfilled that promise, he made considerable impact on American theatre with *Picnic* (1953), *Bus Stop* (1955), and *The Dark at the Top of the Stairs* (1957). Born in Independence, KS, and educated at the University of Kansas, he taught at Stephens College in Columbia, MO, and at Washington University in St. Louis, and he toured for a season under canvas with a **Toby** show; he was thus a product of mid-America, and his works reflected this background. He seemed to cherish his lonely characters: Even as he laid bare their weaknesses, he surrounded them with love and understanding. He also recorded their speech with an accurate, appreciative ear. His later works, such as *A Loss of Roses* (1959), *Natural Affection* (1963), and *Where's Daddy?* (1966), drew neither critical acclaim nor much of an audience. He suffered from depression and alcoholism, and his death was by suicide.   LDC

> See: R. B. Shuman, *William Inge,* New York, 1965; R. Voss, *A Life of William Inge: The Strains of Triumph,* Lawrence, KS, 1989.

Inherit the Wind by **Jerome Lawrence and Robert E. Lee.** Based on the Scopes "Monkey Trial" of 1925, this three-act play dramatizes the furor that erupts when a Tennessee schoolteacher is prosecuted for introducing evolution in the public classroom. The struggle between legislated creationism and freedom of thought is focused in the clash of two powerful men: the persuasive orator Matthew Harrison Brady (based on William Jennings Bryan and first performed in New York by Ed Begley) and the brilliant attorney Henry Drummond (based on Clarence Darrow and performed by **Paul Muni**). The play premiered at Dallas Theatre '55 on 10 January 1955 directed by **Margo Jones,** then opened in New York, directed by **Herman Shumlin,** 21 April 1955 at the National Theatre, where it ran for 806 performances.   KF

In Mizzoura by **Augustus Thomas.** A star vehicle for **Nat C. Goodwin** rather than a high point in Thomas's dramaturgy, this four-act drama opened at New York's **Fifth Avenue Theatre** on 4 September 1893. Its regional sheriff-hero, train-robbing villain, blacksmith father, and three sets of lovers allowed Thomas to tie his characters to both his native state and early career as a railroad employee, and to display the local-color language and mannerisms at which he excelled. Indeed, the dialect is as timely today as when the play was written, despite the melodrama's now shop-worn plot featuring a fair-playing villain, a noble and self-sacrificing hero, a heroine misled by her college education, and a community of poor-but-honest folk of limited social views.   RKB

Innaurato, Albert (1948–) Playwright educated at Temple University and the Yale School of Drama. Drawing on his south Philadelphia background, Innaurato's most successful play, *Gemini,* produced in 1976, deals with an Italian and Catholic family (with the hero, Francis Geminiani, home from Harvard) in this ethnic neighborhood. Other plays include *The Transfiguration of Benno Blimpie* (1973) and *Earth Worms* and *Ulysses in Traction* (New York, 1977). In 1980 a collection of his plays appeared, appropriately titled *Bizarre Behavior.* Efforts since *Gemini* have received scant attention.   DBW

INTAR Hispanic American Arts Center This not-for-profit company's name is an acronym for International Arts Relations, suggesting a portion of its artistic policy. Founded in 1966 by a group including Max Ferra, who remains the artistic director, INTAR develops and presents contemporary Latin and Hispanic plays, native and foreign. Its seasons include at least one musical, a new American play, and a residency by an internationally known artist. While theatre is INTAR's central project, it also houses an art gallery and serves as a social and cultural center for its constituency.   CLJ

Interart Theatre A program of the Women's Interart Center, a not-for-profit, **feminist** arts complex founded in 1971 by Marjorie De Faxio, Alice Rubenstein, Jane Chambers, and Margot Lewitin, who remains artistic director. In addition to theatre, both experimental and more traditional, the Center develops and presents American dance, music, visual art, and video art by or about women, and encourages events that integrate disciplines. Ironically, two of the theatre's most successful productions have been plays by the male German playwright Franz Xaver Kroetz.   CLJ

International stars and companies From its
inception to the present, the American theatre's
artists, institutions, and audiences have been enriched, influenced, stimulated, and entertained by
non-U.S.-born talent. As L. W. Conolly suggests,
the touring and permanent influences of these important individuals and groups "might well be said
to encompass the continent's entire theatrical history." In some areas of popular theatre, the circus
for example, a majority of the stars have been
foreign born. Many artists who began careers abroad
immigrated into the U.S. and established reputations on these shores; others visited often or literally split their professional lives between this country and their native lands; some came only once or
twice. This pattern has changed little up to the
present, although the British invasion has been a
subject of intense controversy during the past decade, reaching a kind of climax in 1990–1 with
Actors' Equity's hesitancy to allow Jonathan Pryce,
the white British star, to play a Eurasian in the
musical *Miss Saigon*.

Initially, the American theatre was essentially a
British institution, so it is not surprising that early
stars were British and that acting styles of the 18th
and early 19th century reflected the grand style of
London's leading actors, the Kembles. Early
American stars such as **John Henry, John Bernard, Mrs. Anne Merry,** and **Thomas A. Cooper**
influenced the American scene with classical British
training. Ironically, however, the first major stars
to appear in the U.S. were of a more romantic
bent. **George Frederick Cooke** in 1810 helped to
place the wedge in the repertory system that led to
the phenomenon of the traveling star, followed by
James W. Wallack in 1818. Edmund Kean, who
appeared in 1821 and 1825–6, though England's
greatest actor at the time, created more controversy
over his refusal to act in Boston than he did in
leaving a lasting influence. Indeed, **Junius Brutus
Booth,** frequently accused of being a copy of
Kean, had a more permanent effect on American
acting.

By the 1830s and for the remainder of the 19th
century, the touring of foreign stars became commonplace, and the age of the international star was
firmly established. A litany of major foreign theatrical names fills the annals of the American stage.
For example, from Britain (with year of first and,
in notable instances, final U.S. appearance) came
Charles Mathews (1822), William Charles Macready (1826; 1849), Charles Kean (1830), Ellen
Tree (1836), Charles Kemble and his daughter **Fanny
Kemble** (1832), **Tyrone Power** (1833), **John M.
Vandenhoff** (1837; 1844), Madame Vestris (1838),
John Baldwin Buckstone (1840), **Charles Fisher**
(1852), **Emma Waller** (1857), **Lydia Thompson**
(1868), Charles Wyndham (1869), **Charles Fech-
ter** (1869), Adelaide Neilson (1872; 1880), Oscar
Wilde (1882, as lecturer), Lillie Langtry (1882),
Henry Irving (1883; 1904), Ellen Terry (1883; 1907),
Johnston Forbes-Robertson (1885; 1915), Wilson
Barrett (1886), Mr. and Mrs. Kendal (1889), Marie
Tempest (1890), Olga Nethersole (1894; 1913), and
Herbert Beerbohm Tree (1895; 1916).

No company (or actor) was more important in the

U.S. during the 19th century than Henry Irving's
Lyceum Theatre company (most often featuring
Ellen Terry). Between 1883 and 1905 Irving toured
eight times, playing most major U.S. cities (the
sixth tour, for example, included 30 cities in six
months) for a total of 209 weeks. Irving illustrated
the quality of his Lyceum productions to American
audiences, demonstrating his careful use of historical accuracy in scenery and costuming, his artistic
use of lighting, and his personal control and coor-
dination of all production elements. In turn, Irving
learned much about American business ethics from
the entrepreneur **Henry E. Abbey.**

Visitors in this century from Britain form a
who's who of the English stage. Since the improvement of transatlantic travel, British actors
have rarely been given international status until an
appearance in New York or on tour. Among the
most notable names (with year of first and, in
certain instances, final U.S. appearance) have been
Robert Loraine (1901), **George Arliss** (1901), Mrs.
Patrick Campbell (1902; 1933), Ben Greet (1902;
1914), **Dudley Digges** (1904), Sybil Thorndike
(1904; 1957), Cathleen Nesbitt (1911; 1981), Leslie
Howard (1920), Basil Rathbone (1922), John Martin-
Harvey (1923), Jack Buchanan (1924; 1948), **Gertrude Lawrence** (1924; 1951), Noël Coward (1925;
1957), John Gielgud (1928; *Hamlet* 1936; 1976),
Laurence Olivier (1929; 1960), **Charles Laughton**
(1931), Edith Evans (1931; 1950), Emlyn Williams
(1932), Ralph Richardson (1935; 1976), **Maurice
Evans** (1935), Gladys Cooper (1936), Cedric
Hardwicke (1936; 1959), Anthony Quayle (1936;
1978), **Rex Harrison** (1936; 1989), Peggy Ashcroft
(1937; 1948), Robert Morley (1938; 1972), Vivien
Leigh (1940; 1966), Flora Robson (1940; 1950),
Margaret Leighton (1946; 1967), Michael Redgrave
(1948; 1965), Alec Guinness (1950; 1964), **Richard
Burton** (1950; 1983), **Rosemary Harris** (1952),
Hermione Gingold (1953), Julie Andrews (1954),
Donald Pleasence (1961), and Paul Scofield (1961).

Of the current mature generation of British ac-
tors, significant U.S. appearances have been made
by such stars as Jim Dale, Albert Finney, Anthony
Hopkins, Alan Howard, Derek Jacobi, Claire
Bloom, Glenda Jackson, Ian McKellen, Jonathan
Pryce, Alec McCowen, Vanessa Redgrave, Diana
Rigg, Maggie Smith, Margaret Tyzack, Paul Rogers, Ian Holm, John Wood, Alan Bates, Roy Do-
trice, Donald Sinden, Jean Marsh, Tom Cour-
tenay, Tom Conti, Joan Plowright, Jane Lapotaire,
Roger Rees, Eileen Atkins, Ben Kingsley, Robert
Lindsay, Nicol Williamson, and Dorothy Tutin,
among many others.

Richard Burton, though his stage career was
disappointing, is typical of British actors who appear in the U.S. as often as they do elsewhere. Of
recent British actor-directors, Sir John Gielgud has
the longest history in this country, having appeared
in 14 productions since his debut and directed half
a dozen productions, including in 1964 the Burton
Hamlet.

The legitimate stage has not been the only recipient of British stars. Variety and music-hall furnished **vaudeville** with such turns as Albert Chevalier, Alice and Marie Lloyd, Ella Shields, Vesta

Tilley, Dan Leno, Vesta Victoria, and the inveterate Scotsman **Harry Lauder** who, between 1907 and 1934, made 25 U.S. tours.

Although the British have dominated among foreign stars on U.S. stages, with several notable periods of influx (most recently the musicals of Andrew Lloyd Webber), the last half of the 19th century and the early 20th century nonetheless saw international stars from many countries: some with their own companies, performing in their native language; others in bilingual productions; and a few acting in English. Foremost among these non–English speaking stars were the Swedish singer Jenny Lind; the French actors Rachel, Sarah Bernhardt, **Mme. Céleste,** Constant-Benoît Coquelin, Jean Mounet-Sully, Gabrielle Réjane, and Yvette Guilbert (singer); and Italian stars Adelaide Ristori, Eleonora Duse, Tommaso Salvini, Ermete Novelli, and Ernesto Rossi. Other European visitors of international renown include Emma Carus (German), **Francesca Janauschek** (Czech), **Helena Modjeska** (or Modrzejewska, Polish), Alexander Moisiu (Albanian), **Alla Nazimova** (Russian), and **Fritzi Scheff** (Austrian singer-actress). Several international stars were especially active in the U.S.: Salvini (a famous Othello), for instance, made five trips to the U.S. (1873–89) and performed opposite **Clara Morris** (who refused to play Desdemona opposite this "Titantic" force) and **Edwin Booth.** Bernhardt, who toured nine times between 1880 and 1918, proved extraordinarily popular, making money even when fighting the Theatrical **Syndicate,** and in 1912 offering (in vaudeville) excerpts from her most famous vehicles.

In this century international stars continued to visit the U.S. in large numbers, including French actor-director Jean-Louis Barrault and his actress wife Madeleine Renaud; French actor-directors Charles Dullin, Marcel Marceau, and Louis Jouvet; the Chinese actor Mei Lanfang, in 1930 the first actor of stature to introduce Chinese theatre to U.S. audiences; Russian actors **Richard Boleslavski** and **Michael Chekhov;** French cabaret artists Maurice Chevalier and Gabys Deslys; and Swedish actress Ingrid Bergman. Nevertheless, notable international companies (especially in the 1920s and '30s) made greater impact than any individual artist, influencing American acting methods, staging techniques, and innovative design concepts (the New Stagecraft). Foremost among these were Israel's Habimah (1926–7 New York season, then headquartered in Moscow); England's D'Oyly Carte (1879, *HMS Pinafore*); the **Moscow Art Theatre** (1922–3); Dublin's Abbey Theatre (1911, 1913, and several visits in the 1930s); **Max Reinhardt** and company (with the Oriental pantomime *Sumurun* [1912], his re-created production of *The Miracle* [1924], and his German troupe [1927]); the Chauve-Souris company (1922–3, Russian vaudeville under Nikita Balieff); and Jacques Copeau and the Vieux-Colombier (in residence at New York's **Garrick Theatre,** 1917–19).

At midcentury there seemed to have been a slacking off of notable foreign visitors. By the 1960s, however, this began to change with visits from such companies as the Moscow Art Theatre, the Royal Shakespeare Company, the D'Oyly Carte, the Comédie-Française, the Piraikon Theatre of Athens, the Schiller Theatre, the Bavarian State Theatre, the Bunraku Puppet Theatre of Japan, the Grand Kabuki, the Jewish Theatre of Poland (with Ida Kaminska), the Vienna Burgtheater, the Compagnie du Théâtre de la Cité de Villeurbanne, and Jerzy Grotowski's Polish Laboratory Theatre. In the past 25 years there has been an explosion of imported foreign plays (especially British), including the introduction of works by such authors as **Athol Fugard** (South Africa); Christopher Hampton, David Storey, Simon Gray, Peter Nichols, Caryl Churchill, Alan Ayckbourn, David Rudkin, David Edgar, Hugh Leonard, Brian Friel, et al. (British Isles); Dario Fo (Italy); Michel Tremblay (Canada); and Franz Xaver Kroetz (Germany). The U.S. has also witnessed notable productions by nonnative directors, including **John Dexter,** Peter Brook, Vittorio Gassman, Anatoly Efros, Grotowski, Jean-Louis Barrault, Franco Zeffirelli, Josef Szajna (Poland), Harold Pinter, Trevor Nunn, Clifford Williams, Ingmar Bergman, Joe Dowling, and Tadeusz Kantor. Foreign companies have continued to travel to the U.S. in sizable numbers, appearing in recent years not only as independent touring companies but as part of major international theatre festivals (e.g., New York International Festival of the Arts, Festival Latino [**New York Shakespeare Festival**], International Theatre Festival at Stony Brook, and the Los Angeles Theatre Festival coordinated by **Peter Sellars.**) Among the most recent companies have been England's Cheek by Jowl, Brazil's Teatro de Ornitorrinco and Grupo de Teatro Macunaíma, Catalan's Muestra Espanola, the State Theatre of Lithuania, the Dublin Gate Theatre, the Royal Dramatic Theatre of Sweden, Yume no Yuminsha from Japan, productions from London's Royal Court Theatre (in exchange with the New York Shakespeare Festival), the Royal Shakespeare Company (notably the 1981–2 production of *The Life and Adventures of Nicholas Nickleby*), the Grand Kabuki from Japan, and Ariane Mnouchkine's Théâtre de Soleil from France.

Since its beginning the American theatre has been, and continues to be, enriched and influenced in every possible way by non-U.S. theatre artists and companies. Although the importation cost of full companies from abroad is often prohibitive, and the number of impresarios and producers able to undertake such projects is limited, the recent festival phenomenon is a hopeful sign that this flow will not be abated. Recent events indicate that U.S. theatrical **unions** and, especially, the U.S. Immigration and Naturalization Service, will make only reasonable restrictions on the importation of individual artists and companies; thus the American theatre should continue to profit from a lively international theatre scene. [See also **ethnic theatre** and the numerous entries on specific nonnatives who made significant contributions to the American stage.]   DBW

See: M. Carlson, *The Italian Shakespearians,* Washington, DC, 1985; L.W. Conolly, ed., *Theatrical Touring and Founding in North America,* Westport, CT, 1982;

O. L. Guernsey, Jr., *Curtain Times: The New York Theater 1965–1987,* New York, 1987; H. Knepler, *The Gilded Stage: The Years of the Great International Actresses,* New York, 1968; L. Senelick, ed., *Wandering Stars: Papers on Russian Emigré Theatre,* Iowa City, 1992.

Into the Woods Two-act musical with book by **James Lapine,** music and lyrics by **Stephen Sondheim;** opened at the **Martin Beck Theatre** on 5 November 1987 (764 performances); it was a critical success in London in the early 1990s. Using the characters and situations of children's fairy tales (primarily the brothers Grimm), including the Baker and his Wife, Cinderella, Jack and the Beanstalk, and Little Red Riding Hood, the musical explored the real human consequences of journeying "into the woods" after one's dreams. As the characters encounter magical and often violent obstacles to getting what they want, they develop more mature perceptions of love, responsibility, and guilt. At the end, those who survive begin to form a new community, assuring one another that "No One Is Alone." Lapine's book and Sondheim's score combined the rollicking adventure of the fairy tale with quiet moments of self-discovery. As the Witch who provokes most of the action, **Bernadette Peters** enchanted the critics, and Joanna Gleason received a Tony Award for her performance as the Baker's Wife. The atmosphere of mystery and wonder was enhanced by **Tony Straiges**'s settings, **Richard Nelson**'s lighting, and Charles Reynolds's special magic effects.   MK

I Remember Mama by **John van Druten** is a two-act drama adapted from Kathryn Forbes's stories, *Mama's Bank Account.* Directed by the author and produced by **Rodgers** and **Hammerstein [II],** the production opened at the **Music Box Theatre** (19 October 1944) for 714 performances, starring Mady Christians and a young **Marlon Brando.** It was later developed into a film (with Irene Dunne) and a television series (with **Peggy Wood**). The play depicts struggling Norwegian immigrants in San Francisco in 1910. Warm, sensible, and devoted Mama is the play's pivotal character who gently and selflessly encourages her family's success. The play served as a nostalgic escape from the war-ridden world of 1944.   EK

Iron Clad Agreement, The Founded in Pittsburgh in 1976, this troupe produced over 30 original pieces there through 1981. Performing mostly at union meetings and in schools, the not-for-profit company dramatized incidents from the American industrial revolution. Well supported by public funding as well as the United Steel Workers, the troupe strove to present nonpolemical history and positive images of industrial workers for its western Pennsylvania audiences. The company moved to New York City in 1981, where it was reorganized to produce films and television documentaries on labor history in addition to live theatre. The company discontinued theatrical productions in the mid-1980s.   BMcC

Irving, Jules (1924–79) New York–born producer and director, educated at New York and Stanford universities. While teaching at San Francisco State College (1949–62), he, together with colleague **Herbert Blau,** founded the San Francisco Actors Workshop (1952–64), which became known for its experimental productions. In 1965 they became codirectors of the Repertory Theatre of **Lincoln Center;** after Blau resigned in 1967, Irving continued as director until 1972. During 1972–9 he worked in Hollywood as producer-director of TV movies. During his controversial tenure at Lincoln Center, Irving became known for his carefully crafted productions of the classics and for innovative presentations of plays by **Brecht,** Beckett, and Pinter. In 1971 he staged the U.S. premiere of Pinter's *Landscape* and *Silence.* His daughter, Amy Irving, acts for films, television, and the theatre.   TLM

Irving, Washington (1783–1859) First important American man of letters, who enjoyed the theatre and wrote occasionally about it. In 1802–3 he published nine letters in the *Morning Chronicle,* under the name of Jonathan Oldstyle, that commented in a lightly satirical style upon the provincial state of New York theatre. Later he collaborated with **John Howard Payne** on *Richelieu; or, The Broken Heart* and *Charles II,* which played in London in 1824. Irving remains best known for *The Sketch Book* (1822), which contains the short stories "The Legend of Sleepy Hollow" and "Rip Van Winkle," the latter adapted into a star vehicle for actor **Joseph Jefferson III** and others.   TLM

See: C. D. Warner, *Washington Irving,* New York, 1981; S. T. Williams, *Life of Washington Irving,* 2 vols., 1935 (repr. New York, 1971).

Irwin, Bill (1950–) Actor, entertainer, and playwright, the best known among disparate practitioners of the so-called **New Vaudeville.** These performers focus on the creation, often in collaboration, of theatre works that draw upon American popular entertainment traditions, from the **circus** to **vaudeville** and experimental theatre techniques. Like others in this group, Irwin attempts to make innovative use of his clown skills to create exciting visual metaphors for the broader actions and emotions of a play. He moved from conventional theatre training at UCLA to experimental theatre training with **Herbert Blau** at Oberlin College, to the Ringling Brothers Clown College, the Pickle Family Circus, and the avant-garde Oberlin Dance Collective before evolving what Ron Jenkins, a former circus clown, calls Irwin's "metaphysical slapstick." Irwin's first major New York vehicle was *The Regard of Flight,* played elsewhere before and after its 1982 performance at the **American Place Theatre.** This production effectively and comedically satirized the so-called new, postmodern theatre. It also established his stage persona of the beleaguered but resilient all-American, a character that he uses often. Other appearances include *The Courtroom; Waiting for Godot* (a memorable Lucky at **Lincoln Center** in 1988); *Accidental Death of an Anarchist;* and his Tony-nominated performance as "Post-Modern Hoofer" in his nonverbal *Largely New York* (1989), which he also directed and choreographed, and for which he received a special citation from the New York Drama Critics' Circle. This effort, which originated at the **Seattle Repertory Theater,** was termed by one writer "a crazy quilt of city denizens." In 1984 he became the first American performing artist to receive the prestigious MacArthur Foundation Fellowship. DBW

See: R. Jenkins, *Acrobats of the Soul,* New York, 1988.

Irwin, May (née Georgia or Ada Campbell) (1862–1938) Canadian-born actress. Dubbed "Secretary of Laughter" in the teens by Woodrow Wilson, she began her career singing duets with her sister Flo at the Adelphi Theatre, Buffalo, NY (1875). By January 1877 they were stock members of **Tony Pastor**'s Music Hall company, remaining six years. In 1883 May joined **Augustin Daly** as a legitimate actress, leaving in 1887 and returning to the legitimate stage only briefly in 1893 under **Charles Frohman.** The balance of her career was devoted to farce comedies with music. She reached star status in *The Widow Jones* (1895), and offered a series of comedies under her own management in the teens. A plump, jolly blonde, known for her rollicking exuberance, she introduced such popular songs as "A Hot Time in the Old Town" and "I'm Looking for de Bully" (in the style later known as Negro ragtime). She retired in 1922. DBW

Isaacs, Edith Juliet Rich (1878–1956) Editor and critic. Born and educated in Milwaukee, Edith began her writing career as a reporter and later literary editor for the Milwaukee *Sentinel* before moving to New York in 1904 to marry and begin a family. She was a drama critic for *Ainslee's Magazine* and a free-lance writer before joining the editorial board of *Theatre Arts* in 1918. During 1922–46 she served as editor (and majority stockholder), moving the magazine from quarterly to monthly (1924) and featuring prominent new artists each month, such as **Eugene O'Neill** and **Robert Edmond Jones.** She was actively involved in establishing the National Theatre Conference (1925), the **American National Theatre and Academy** (1935), and the **Federal Theatre Project** (1935–9) because she believed in a national theatre. TLM

Israel, Robert (1939–) Though a theatre and opera set and costume designer, Israel's background is in fine arts, and his work is more closely related to European theatricalists than to typical American designers. In addition to over 60 opera and ballet productions, including Philip Glass's *Satyagraha* (1981) and *Akhnaten* (1983) and the Seattle Opera's "Ring Cycle" (1985–6), he has worked in collaboration with director **Martha Clarke** on several creations, including *Vienna: Lusthaus* (1986). His postmodernist work is typified by spare though stunning images and intellectual metaphors. AA

It Can't Happen Here occupies a unique position in the American theatre because its production – under the supervision of the **Federal Theatre Project** – allowed for 23 simultaneous openings on the night of 27 October 1936. Adapted by John C. Moffitt and Sinclair Lewis from Lewis's best-selling novel of the same name, the play portrayed the emergence of a fascist dictator in the U.S. and was interpreted by critics as both pro–New Deal and anti-Roosevelt. The circumstances of its production were unusually chaotic because the demand for a nationwide opening raised havoc with individual productions. Rewrites arrived daily in the various theatres; some productions were more advanced than others (but postponements were disallowed); and little provision was made for the variety and richness of individual units (a black company in Seattle; a Yiddish one in New York). Still, the experiment demonstrated the potential for professional theatre outside of NYC and contributed to the political debate that would eventually undermine the WPA theatre. BBW

Ivey, Dana (c. 1945–) Atlanta-born actress and teacher who became a leading actress in Canada before her Broadway debut in *Present Laughter* (**Circle in the Square,** 1982); she returned with *Heartbreak House* (CITS, 1983, Tony nomination; TV, 1984), *Sunday in the Park with George* (1984, Tony nomination; TV, 1985), and Whitemore's *Pack of Lies* (1984). **Off-Broadway,** Ivey did Simon Gray's *Quartermaine's Terms* (**Long Wharf,** 1982; New York, 1983, Drama Desk nomination, Obie), *Driving Miss Daisy* (1987, Obie), *Hamlet* (**New York Shakespeare Festival,** 1990, St. Claire Bayfield Award), *The Subject Was Roses* (**Roundabout Theatre,** 1991), and **Shanley**'s *Beggars in the House of Plenty* (**Manhattan Theatre Club,** 1991). Films include *The Color Purple* (1985) and *Dirty Rotten Scoundrels* (1989). A 1983 Clarence Derwent Award winner, Ivey has taught acting at several schools. REK

Ivey, Judith (1951–) Actress ("A chameleon onstage" able "to be liked in difficult roles") who made her debut in *The Sea* (**Goodman Theatre,** 1974), then on Broadway in Ayckbourn's *Bedroom Farce* (1979). She has performed with such companies as the Evanston (IL) Theatre Company, **Arena Stage, New York Shakespeare Festival,** and **Manhattan Theatre Club.** Recent stage work includes *Piaf* (1981), Nell Dunn's *Steaming* (1983, Tony, Drama Critics' Circle Award), *Hurlyburly* (Goodman, 1983; New York, 1984, Tony, Drama Desk Award), George Furth's *Precious Sons* (1986), *Blithe Spirit* (1987), and **Horovitz**'s *Park Your Car in Harvard Yard* (1991). Films include *Brighton Beach Memoirs* (1986) and *In Country* (1989). In 1990–1 she starred in television's "Down Home." REK

Izenour, George (1912–) Theatre designer, engineering consultant, and inventor of the electronic console for **stage lighting** control, the synchronous winch system, and the steel acoustical shell. He has been a design and engineering consultant for over 100 theatres around the world since the 1950s, and as such is a dominant force in theatre design and technology. Because economics dictates that a single theatre must be employed for many uses (spoken drama, opera, concerts, etc.), he is an advocate of the multiuse and multiform theatre, in which the size and shape and auditorium can be altered for different needs and acoustical requirements. Recipient of the Distinguished Service Award from the American Theater Association, Izenour is the author of two acclaimed books: *Theater Design* (1977) and *Theater Technology* (1988).   AA

J

Jacker (née Litvin), Corinne (1933–)
Writer-playwright who, in addition to science fiction, television miniseries, and science texts, writes plays of evolving self-identity that experiment with form. Her *Bits and Pieces* (1974) and *Harry Outside* (1975) both won Obies. Other plays include *Songs from Distant Lands* (1989), *In Place* (1983), *Domestic Issues* (1981), *After the Season* (1980), *Later* (1978), *My Life* (1977), *Terminal* (1976), and *Other People's Tables* (1975). She has also adapted Ibsen and Chekhov.   TH-S

Jackson, Anne see **Wallach, Eli**

Jacobs, Lou (1904–92) German-born clown and the American **circus**'s best-known *auguste* (slapstick clown who appears stupid and clumsy, appearing in flamboyant costume and makeup). Jacobs, brought to the U.S. in 1923 as a tumbler, was to many the quintessential image of a circus clown, with his enlarged cone-shaped head, distinctive white patches around his eyes, fringed red hair, and red-rubber-ball nose. From 1926 until his retirement in 1988, Jacobs, who was generally recognized as the greatest living circus clown, mesmerized audiences for **Ringling Brothers** by his presence – in particular, with his midget car routine (seen first in 1946) and later his hunting-dog routine, with his mutt Knucklehead.   DBW

James, Henry (1843–1916) Expatriate novelist and critic who found American culture provincial, and its theatre melodramatic and bombastic, lacking subtle character delineation and refinement of style. While spending much of his career in England, he wrote about the theatre in *The Nation, The Atlantic, The Century,* and *The Galaxy* (1875–87), republished in *The Scenic Art* (1948). A failed playwright, James was too dependent on the "well-made" dramas of Scribe and Sardou. Dramatizations of his novels by others have been more successful, including *Berkeley Square* (1928), from *The Sense of the Past; The Heiress* (1947), from *Washington Square; The Innocents* (1950) from *The Turn of the Screw; The Spoils* (1968), from *The Spoils of Poynton;* and *A Boston Story* (1968), from *Watch and Ward.*   TLM

See: L. Edel, *Henry James,* 5 vols., Philadelphia, 1953–72.

Jampolis, Neil Peter (1943–) Designed numerous **Off-Broadway** productions in the 1970s, including *One Flew Over the Cuckoo's Nest* (1971). He won a Tony for lighting design for **Sherlock Holmes** (1974); other Broadway productions include **Lily Tomlin**'s *The Search for Signs of Intelligent Life in the Universe* (1985). Since 1976 Jampolis has designed lights for the Pilobolus Dance Company. He has also designed for the New York City Opera and several international opera productions.   AA

Janauschek, Francesca (Fanny) (1830–1904) Czech-born actress who was an internationally renowned tragedienne before making her 1867 New York debut, performing Medea in German while the rest of the cast acted in English, as did **Edwin Booth** opposite her German Lady Macbeth in 1868. After a year devoted to learning English, she launched her English-speaking career in 1870. With her statuesque figure, emotional power, and vibrant but controlled voice, she excelled in heroic roles. She was also popular in the dual roles of the coquettish French maid and the haughty Lady Dedlock in *Chesney Wold* (based on Dickens's *Bleak House*). She was one of the last great actresses in the "grand style," but ended her career playing melodramas.   FHL

Lou Jacobs, colorful *auguste* clown. Courtesy: Ringling Bros.–Barnum & Bailey Circus.

See: J. Cortez, "Fanny Janauschek: America's Last Queen of Tragedy," PhD diss., U of Illinois, 1973.

Janis (née Bierbower), Elsie (1889–1956) **Vaudeville** entertainer, one of its greatest stars, and considered by many the queen of the form. The product of one of the archetypical stage mothers, from her debut in 1897 to the end of her career in 1932, Janis appeared as a headliner in vaudeville, musical comedy, and **revue.** During WW I she frequently entertained the troops. The society darling of two continents, the attractive, slender Janis specialized in impersonations and comic songs, introducing such popular songs as "Fo' de Lawd's Sake, Play a Waltz" and "Florrie Was a Flapper." On her death, lifelong friend Mary Pickford remarked, "This ends the vaudeville era." Her autobiography, *So Far, So Good!* was published in 1932.
DBW

See: L. A. Morrow, "Elsie Janis: A Compensatory Biography," PhD diss., Northwestern U, 1988.

Jarrett, Henry C (1828–1903) Theatre manager whose career began in 1851 when he purchased the Baltimore Museum. At various times, Jarrett managed several major U.S. theatres, including Washington's **National Theatre,** the **Brooklyn Academy of Music,** and **Niblo's Garden.** When **Edwin Booth** lost his theatre in 1874, Jarrett joined with Henry David Palmer to manage **Booth's Theatre** until 1877. Jarrett and Palmer also produced the popular musical fantasy *The **Black Crook*** at Niblo's Garden in 1866, and in 1875–6 mounted a spectacular production of *Julius Caesar* at Booth's Theatre, with **Lawrence Barrett** as Cassius and **E. L. Davenport** as Brutus. DJW

J. B. by **Archibald MacLeish** won the Tony Award for Best Play (1958) and the Pulitzer Prize (1959). It is based upon the biblical figure Job, and remains one of the few American plays written in verse. Set in a circus environment, it updates the story of his trials. It was first produced at Yale University Theatre (22 April 1958) after Dean F. Curtis Canfield saw excerpts printed in the *Saturday Review of Literature.* **Brooks Atkinson**'s favorable review of that performance led to its New York production (opened 11 December 1958), directed by **Elia Kazan,** which ran 364 performances. KN

Jeffers, [John] Robinson (1887–1962) A Pulitzer Prize–winning poet, Jeffers wrote a modern version of *Medea* that starred **Judith Anderson** on Broadway in 1947. Other plays include *The Tower Beyond Tragedy* (1950), from his own poem of Aeschylus' *Oresteia,* and *The Cretan Woman* (1954) from Euripides' *Hippolytus.* TLM

Jeffersons, The A famous Anglo–American acting family, traced back to **Thomas Jefferson** (1732–1807), an actor with Garrick and an occasional manager of provincial English theatres. One of his children, **Joseph Jefferson I** (1774–1832), came to America in 1795 and remained here. He became a favorite at the **John Street** and **Park** theatres in New York, although somewhat overshadowed by **John Hodgkinson.** In 1803 he moved to the

Pen and ink sketch of Joseph Jefferson III as Bob Acres in *The Rivals.* Courtesy: Don B. Wilmeth.

Chestnut Street Theatre in Philadelphia, remaining until 1830. Most of his children worked in the theatre, including **Joseph Jefferson II** (1804–42), a better scene painter than actor. His marriage to the actress Cornelia Thomas in 1826 made him the step-father of actor Charles Burke.

The greatest of the Jeffersons, however, was **Joseph Jefferson III** (1829–1905), who first appeared on stage at age 4, in support of **T. D. Rice.** Jefferson toured with his family, garnering some fame by the midcentury and visiting Europe in 1856. He then joined **Laura Keene**'s company, winning approval with such roles as Dr. Pangloss in the younger Colman's *The Heir-at-Law.* He spent some time at the **Winter Garden Theatre** in New York, toured Australia for four years, and in London in 1865 first performed the role for which he was most noted, **Rip Van Winkle,** dramatized for him by **Dion Boucicault.** In this role, Jefferson's dignity and sympathetic personality soon won him popular and critical acclaim. Of him, the critic **William Winter** said: "The magical charm of his acting was the deep human sympathy and the liveliness and individuality by which it was irradiated – an exquisite blending of humor, pathos, grace and beauty."

Jefferson also triumphed as Bob Acres in Sheridan's *The Rivals,* Caleb Plummer in *Dot,* and Salem Scudder in *The **Octoroon**; or, Life in Louisiana.* In 1893 he succeeded **Edwin Booth** as President of the Players Club. His autobiography, published in 1890, indicates much of Jefferson's warmth and humanity.

Of his children, four went on the stage, the most distinguished being **Charles Burke Jefferson** (1851–1908), who served for a time as his father's manager. SMA

> See: A. Downer, ed., *The Autobiography of Joseph Jefferson,* Cambridge, MA, 1964; F. Wilson, *Joseph Jefferson: Reminiscences of a Fellow Player,* New York, 1906; W. Winter, *The Jeffersons,* Boston, 1881, and *Life and Art of Joseph Jefferson . . . ,* New York, 1894.

Jenkins, George (1909–) Designer whose theatre career spans the 1940s–70s and includes *I Remember Mama* (1944), *Lost in the Stars* (1949), *Two for the Seesaw* (1958), and *The **Miracle Worker*** (1959). He is best known as a film designer. Since the mid-1940s his film designs include *Klute* (1971), *All the President's Men* (1976), and *Sophie's Choice* (1982). On stage and film Jenkins is admired for precise and detailed settings. AA

Jerome Robbins' Broadway Two-act musical retrospective that opened 26 February 1989 at the **Imperial Theatre,** running 633 performances. Master director-choreographer **Jerome Robbins**'s 23-year absence from Broadway ended not with a new show, but with this compendium of production numbers from his Broadway shows from *On the Town* (1944) to *Fiddler on the Roof* (1967), featuring 50 dancers and 400 costumes. Robbins took scrupulous care in recreating the original choreography, and the large company and long rehearsal process led the producers to charge a then-new high standard ticket price of $60 for the best seats. After debate as to its eligibility, the Tony Awards committee declared it a new musical rather than a revival, and it was awarded the Tony as best original musical. JD

Jessop, George Henry (d. 1915) Irish-born playwright and novelist who began his playwriting career in New York and later went to San Francisco. He returned to Ireland in 1891 when he inherited $100,000. His most popular play, *Sam'l of Posen* (1881), showed a Jewish immigrant store clerk who vowed that he would own the business. With **Brander Matthews,** Jessop wrote *A Gold Mine* (1878) and *On Probation;* with **Augustus Pitou,** *The Irish Artist* and *The Power of the Press.* WJM

Jesurun, John (1951–) Michigan-born playwright, filmmaker, and experimental theatre director who studied sculpture at Philadelphia College of Art (BFA, 1972) and at Yale (MFA, 1974). Producer of several films (1977–89), he became aware of the influence of television on daily life while working for CBS (1976–9) as media analyst and with "The Dick Cavett Show" (1980–2). Jesurun's theatre pieces explore cultural stereotypes and the psychological subtexts of social relationships. His cinematic effects mixed with live action deconstruct and suspend the realities of his characters on stage. His influences are Hitchcock, **Gertrude Stein,** Pirandello, surrealism, Brecht, The **Wooster Group,** and **Richard Foreman.** His first theatre piece, *Chang in a Void Moon* (1982–4), was a serial of half-hour episodes performed weekly at the Pyramid Club in Manhattan. Important recent works are *White Water* (1986) and *Blue Heat* (1991). AF

Jewish Art Theatre, The A company closely modeled on Stanislavsky's **Moscow Art Theatre,** set up by **Jacob Ben-Ami** in 1919 at NYC's Garden Theatre, with Emanuel Reicher, associate of **Reinhardt** and a founder of the German Freie Bühne, as play director. Rave reviews greeted **Peretz Hirshbein**'s *The Haunted Inn* and *Green Fields,* with Ben-Ami scoring a personal triumph in both. In spite of further successes, including **David Pinski**'s *The Dumb Messiah,* Ossip Dimov's *Bronx Express,* and Tolstoi's *The Power of Darkness,* internal dissension brought the venture – which had reached probably the high point of **Yiddish theatre** – to a close after two seasons and 14 productions. AB

Jewish Repertory Theatre Founded in 1974 by Artistic Director Ran Avni. Located in NYC at the 92nd Street YM-YWHA (1395 Lexington Ave.), with production facilities at nearby Playhouse 91, the JRT presents plays in English relating to the Jewish experience. In addition to revivals such as *Awake and Sing!* and *Incident at Vichy,* JRT has rediscovered plays such as *Me and Molly, Success Story,* and *Cafe Crown;* has produced such musicals as *Vagabond Stars* and *Kuni-Leml* (1984), the latter winning four Outer Critics' Circle Awards; and has developed new works in its JRT Writers' Lab. The theatre also stages Jewish-oriented work by such established American writers as **Arthur Miller, Ira Levin,** and **Jerry Herman,** and reinterprets the work of non-American playwrights (Pinter, Sartre, Chekhov, etc.) in the light of Judaism. In 1989 JRT won an Outer Critics' Circle Award for Continued Outstanding Productions. DBW

> See: I. Backalenick, *East Side Story: Ten Years with the Jewish Repertory Theatre,* Lanham, MD, 1988.

Joan of Lorraine by **Maxwell Anderson,** a **Playwrights' Company** production, opened at the **Alvin Theatre** 18 November 1946. Directed by **Margo Jones** with settings, lighting, and costumes by **Lee Simonson,** it starred Ingrid Bergman as Mary Grey (the actress playing Joan), **Sam Wanamaker** as the harrassed director, Romney Brent as an amusingly corrupt Dauphin, and Harry Irvine as the cunning Archbishop. This play about a play marked Bergman's successful return to Broadway after her disappointment in *Liliom* (1940). Described by **Brooks Atkinson** as "an engrossing play that is variously poignant, rhapsodic, and genial," the *New York Post* critic wrote, "*Joan of Lorraine* neither adds to nor decreases the dramatic stature of Maxwell Anderson, but it should make us all appreciate Miss Bergman." GSA

Joe Turner's Come and Gone Another in the black experience cycle of plays written by **August Wilson** (1984) and directed by **Lloyd Richards.** It is set in 1911 in a Pittsburgh boarding house where the tenants, mostly new arrivals from the southland, live aimless lives. They are aroused when Herald Loomis comes in with his young daughter, searching desperately for the wife he left behind when he was impressed for seven years' labor on a plantation owned by Joe Turner, a real-life Mississippi character. Loomis hopes to rebuild his life with his wife and child. Calling this his favorite play, author Wilson claims his work shows how the past must inform the future. The play, like earlier ones, was premiered at the **Yale Repertory Theatre** and presented at several regional venues prior to opening on Broadway in 1988.   EGH

John F. Kennedy Center for the Performing Arts 1701 Pennsylvania Ave., Washington, DC [Architect: Edward Durrell Stone]. A national cultural center had been created by law in 1958 under the presidency of Dwight D. Eisenhower, but did not get started until it was deemed a fitting monument to the assassinated president, John F. Kennedy. It opened in 1971 on the banks of the Potomac and encompassed three theatres: the Eisenhower with 1,140 seats for dramatic presentations, the Concert Hall with 2,670 seats, and the Opera House with 2,200 seats. The Center was guided by **Roger Stevens,** its president during 1961–88; he was succeeded upon his retirement by Ralph Davidson (1989–90) and James Wolfensohn (1990–   ). In 1978 a fourth theatre was added on the roof terrace level: the Studio Playhouse, which seats 500 for films, dance concerts, experimental productions, and **children's theatre.** Some productions originate at the Center, but many others are booked in.   MCH

> See: R. Becker, *Miracle on the Potomac,* Silver Spring, MD, 1989; B. Gill, *John F. Kennedy Center for the Performing Arts,* New York, 1981.

John Golden Theatre 252 West 45th St., NYC [Architect: Herbert J. Krapp]. In 1927, as part of their chain, the Chanin construction interests built the Theatre Masque with only 800 seats, intending it for the presentation of intimate or experimental plays that may not have been able to survive on Broadway at the time. Unfortunately, the playhouse was destined to pass from their control in the early 1930s. In 1934, the **Shubert**s bought it and promptly leased it to producer **John Golden,** who assigned his own name to the theatre. It is considered ideal for **one-person** and small-cast plays, and such performers as Victor Borge, Yves Montand, **Comden and Green, Nichols** and May, Bob and Ray, **Cornelia Otis Skinner,** and Emlyn Williams have presented shows of their own creation on its stage. In 1956, Samuel Beckett's *Waiting for Godot* appeared at the Golden, marking the first (and only) time a Beckett play has appeared on Broadway. Apart from two years when it was leased as a movie theatre, the playhouse has seldom been closed. It remains a Shubert house.   MCH

Johnny Johnson by **Paul Green,** music by **Kurt Weill;** opened on Broadway 19 November 1936 and ran 68 performances. **Lee Strasberg** staged this **Group Theatre** production with scenery by **Donald Oenslager** and a cast including **Sanford Meisner, Lee J. Cobb, Elia Kazan, Luther Adler,** and **Morris Carnovsky** in supporting roles. Against his pacifist principles, Johnny Johnson (Russell Collins) enlists to fight in WW I in order to "end all wars" and prove himself worthy to marry Minny Belle. Overseas, he tries to arrange a cease-fire, but the general staff insist on an offensive. Minny marries a man who avoided enlistment; Johnny spends 10 years in a mental hospital, then hawks toys on the street while everyone in town assembles to celebrate the beginning of the next war.   JDM

Johnson, Albert R. (1910–67) Designer who landed his first Broadway show, *The Criminal Code* (1929), at the age of 19. The next year he did *Three's a Crowd,* which established his reputation as a designer of large musicals. Working frequently with director **Hassard Short,** he became known for his innovative and elaborate use of turntables. Productions included *The Band Wagon* (1931), *As Thousands Cheer* (1933), and *The Great Waltz* (1934), which utilized one of the most elaborate sets in Broadway history. He also designed 30 productions for **Radio City Music Hall** as well as industrials and expositions, including the 1939 New York World's Fair.   AA

Johnson, Gloria Douglas (1886–1966) **African-American** poet and playwright whose Washington, DC, home was for decades a meeting place for black artists, writers, and intellectuals. During the 1920s and '30s, Johnson wrote a number of one-act plays that were published in anthologies and produced by Little Theatre groups [see **community theatre**] such as the Krigwa Players in New York. Two of her plays were cited in the *Opportunity* magazine contest: *Blue Blood,* about a married couple who discover that they have the same white father, received honorable mention in 1926; *White Plumes,* treating the funeral beliefs of poor blacks, won the first prize in 1927.   EGH

Johnson, J. Rosamond see **Cole, Bob**

John Street Theatre 15–21 John St., NYC. The third and most substantial theatre to be built in New York by **David Douglass,** the playhouse in John Street served the city until 1798, when it was replaced by a new theatre afterward known as the **Park.** There were three periods in the John Street's history. The first, prior to the Revolution, consisted of two long seasons beginning in 1767; the second commenced in 1777, when the British troops took it over, renamed it the Theatre Royal, and presented plays as an antidote to tedium in their long occupation; and the last and most important period began in the summer of 1785 with the return of **Lewis Hallam** the younger, who began with "entertainments," which blossomed into full-scale productions. Hallam established a permanent resident company and was joined by actor **John Henry** in its management, but both were replaced

Al Jolson in *Sinbad* at the Winter Garden, N.Y.: one-page fold-out advertising booklet. Courtesy: Laurence Senelick.

by **John Hodgkinson** and **William Dunlap** in its final years.

No iconography exists of the John Street. William Dunlap described it as "principally of wood, an unsightly object, painted red." It contained two tiers of boxes, a pit, and a gallery, with dressing rooms and a greenroom located in a shed nearby. A description of the interior was included in **Royall Tyler**'s *The Contrast* (1787), which premiered at the theatre. When it was closed, it was annexed to a feed-and-grain store next door.   MCH

Johnson, J. Rosamond see Cole, Bob

Jolson, Al (1886–1950) Singer and comedian. After spending his early years in **circus**es, **minstrel shows**, and **vaudeville**, Jolson made his stage debut in *La Belle Paree* (1911). In *The Whirl of Society* (1912), he first played the blackfaced servant Gus, a character he was to impersonate in a series of loosely plotted musicals, including *Robinson Crusoe, Jr.* (1916), *Bombo* (1921), and *Big Boy* (1925).

The use of blackface, a common practice in the minstrel shows where Jolson had received his early training, gave racist overtones to much of the humor in his productions. Most spectators came to Jolson's shows to hear him sing his repertoire of hit songs, and on many occasions he obliged them by stopping the performance, dismissing the other actors, and spending the rest of the evening singing directly to the audience. After his motion picture debut in *The Jazz Singer* (1927), Jolson moved to Hollywood. His only other Broadway appearances were in the revue *The Wonder Bar* (1931) and in the musical comedy *Hold on to Your Hats* (1940). Possessed of a good baritone voice, Jolson was a charismatic performer whose energy, good humor, and emotional singing style made him the most popular musical comedy performer of his day.
MK

> *See:* M. Freedland, *Jolson,* New York, 1972; H. Goldman, *Jolson: The Legend Comes to Life,* New York, 1988.

Jones, James Earl (1931–   ) African-American actor. Son of the actor Robert Earl Jones, James Earl trained at the University of Michigan, the American Theatre Wing, and with **Lee Strasberg** before making his 1958 Broadway debut in *Sunrise at Campobello*. He soon attracted attention, winning several acting awards for performances in **New York Shakespeare Festival** productions (1960–6) as well as in *Moon on a Rainbow Shawl* (1962) and *Baal* (1965) **Off-Broadway.** Jones was unforgettable as the despised prizefighter Jack Jefferson in *The Great White Hope* (1968), a role that earned him a Tony Award. An actor of magnetic physical presence and vocal power, he appears frequently in nonblack roles: He has played King Lear, Macbeth, Coriolanus, Lopahin in *The Cherry Orchard* (1973), Hickey in *The Iceman Cometh* (1973), and Lenny in *Of Mice and Men* (1974). He gave a memorable performance in the monodrama *Paul Robeson* (1978), despite controversy surrounding the production, and he won further acclaim for his Othello to **Christopher Plummer**'s Iago on Broadway in 1982. He has appeared in several of **Athol Fugard**'s South African plays under the direction of **Lloyd Richards**. In 1987 he won the Tony in **August Wilson**'s *Fences*. In the early 1990s he has devoted himself primarily to television.   EGH

Jones, Joseph S[tevens] (1809–77) Actor, manager, and playwright. Beginning with *The Liberty Tree* (1832), he may have written as many as 150 plays (he could never remember). In all, however, he infused his heroes with the qualities of individuality, personal conviction, and freedom of spirit that identified Jacksonian America. For his good friend and **Yankee** actor **George H. Hill,** he wrote *The Green Mountain Boy* (1833) and *The People's Lawyer* (1839), a favorite with several Yankee actors. Melodramas such as *The Surgeon of Paris* (1838) and *The Carpenter of Rouen* (1840) provided the spectacles audiences demanded, but his most lasting play was *The Silver Spoon* (1852), in which **William Warren** acted until 1883. *Zafari the Bohemian* (1856) suggests Jones's greater ambitions as a playwright. Generally associated with **Boston,**

Robert Edmond Jones's design for *The Man Who Married a Dumb Wife* (1915).

where he managed the **Tremont** and National Theatres, Jones was a thoroughly professional man of the theatre who supported copyright protection and adequate recompense for playwrights. A medical doctor (Harvard, 1843), he was advertised in theatres as "the celebrated Dr. Jones." WJM

Jones, Margo (Margaret Virginia) (1913–55)

Director and producer whose major contributions were made in her home state of Texas, where she managed a theatre in Dallas dedicated to the production of new plays. Her New York credits included the codirection, with **Eddie Dowling**, of *The Glass Menagerie* (1945), Maxine Wood's *On Whitman Avenue* (1946), **Anderson**'s *Joan of Lorraine* (1946), *Summer and Smoke* (1948), and Owen Crump's *Southern Exposure* (1950), the latter two first presented in Dallas. The Dallas theatre opened as Theatre '47 (with yearly name changes until Jones's accidental death, when it became the Margo Jones Theatre). During its 12 seasons, 133 plays were presented, 86 of which were new plays, including **Inge**'s *The Dark at the Top of the Stairs,* **Williams**'s *Summer and Smoke,* and **Lawrence and Lee**'s *Inherit the Wind.* Jones's theatre became the most celebrated home of arena staging in the U.S. and a pioneer in the decentralization of the American theatre; others emulated her example in part as a result of her book, *Theatre-in-the-Round* (1951). DBW

> See: H. Sheehy, *Margo: The Life and Theatre of Margo Jones,* Dallas, 1989; D. Wilmeth, "A History of the Margo Jones Theatre," PhD diss., U of Illinois, 1964.

Jones, Robert Edmond (1887–1954)

Set and costume designer whose 1915 design for *The Man Who Married a Dumb Wife,* directed by Harley Granville Barker, is generally considered the beginning of the New Stagecraft in America. Rebelling against the romantic realism of **David Belasco** and other producers of the late 19th century, Jones evolved a style of simplified sets that were suggestive, rather than a reproduction of the real world. Having traveled in Europe and observed **Max Reinhardt** for a year at the Deutsches Theater, Jones returned to the U.S. with an appreciation for the power of symbolic or emblematic elements.

Paraphrasing from *Hamlet,* Jones wrote, "Stage designing should be addressed to [the] eye of the mind." He advocated a style of design that elicited an underlying feeling for the play, not one that eliminated the imagination. For director **Arthur Hopkins,** Jones designed the sets for several **Shakespeare** plays in the early 1920s. The designs employed unit sets – then, virtually unknown – and a strong use of light and shadow in the style of Adolphe Appia. For *Macbeth,* the three witches were portrayed by three large masks hanging over the stage. Jones was also an early member of the **Provincetown Players** and designed most of **Eugene O'Neill**'s plays, including *Anna Christie, The Great God Brown,* and *Mourning Becomes Electra.* From 1923 to 1929 Jones served as a producer, with **Kenneth Macgowan** and O'Neill, of the **Experimental Theatre, Inc.** – the successor to the Provincetown. Perhaps as important as his revolutionary design was his writing – most notably the book, *The Dramatic Imagination* (1941) – in which he expressed the visionary ideas that made him an inspiration to theatre artists in the next generation. AA

> See: R. E. Jones, *Drawings for the Theatre,* 2d ed., New York, 1970; R. Pendleton, ed., *The Theatre of Robert Edmond Jones,* Middletown, CT, 1958; D. Unrah, ed., *Towards a New Theatre: The Lectures of Robert Edmond Jones,* New York, 1992.

Jory, Jon (1938–)

A founder of the **Long Wharf Theatre,** he has been producing director since 1969 of the **Actors Theatre of Louisville,** where (as of 1993) he has directed more than 80 plays and produced over 500. He has also directed at 15 other regional theatres, including **Arena Stage, American Conservatory Theatre,** and the **McCarter.** Committed to regional repertory, the encouragement of new writers, and the production of new American plays, Jory developed the Humana Festival of New American Plays in 1976, the SHORTS Festival (1980–5) for one-act plays, and Classics in Context in 1986. In addition to premiering some 170 works in Louisville, Jory has taken new American plays to 27 cities in 14 foreign countries. A published playwright himself, he has twice received the **Margo Jones** Award for production of new plays, among other awards. He is the son of the late film/stage actor Victor Jory. DBW

Journey of the Fifth Horse by Ronald Ribman.

Presented at the **American Place Theatre** for just 20 days in April 1966 (by subscription, April 11–20; public performances, April 21–30), this Larry Arrick–directed production was widely hailed for Ribman's text and for **Dustin Hoffman**'s performance. Both received Obies, confirming the promise of the year before when Hoffman had appeared in Ribman's American Place Theatre production of *Harry, Noon and Night.* Based on Turgenev's short story *The Diary of a Superfluous Man,* Ribman puts the diary of the gentle Chulkaturin (played by Michael Tolin) into the hands of an invented character, the mean-spirited Zoditch (Hoffman), who cruelly comments on its author. Hoffman displayed the kind of detailed characterization that is now his trademark.   MR

Judah, Samuel Benjamin Helbert (c. 1799–1876) Playwright and lawyer, who, as a young man, had three plays produced at the **Park Theatre** and then disappeared from theatrical circles. His two romantic melodramas with European settings – *The Mountain Torrent* (1820) and *The Rose of Arragon* (1822) – and his nationalistic comedy, *The Battle of Lexington* (1822), depended upon his ability to create spectacular scenes. In addition to two dramatic poems, Judah published a satiric play entitled *Buccaneers, A Romance of Our Own Country* (1827).   WJM

Judson Poets' Theatre (1961–81) A seminal **Off-Off Broadway** venue, located at the Judson Memorial Church on Washington Square South in the heart of Manhattan's Greenwich Village. Starting in 1958, the Rev. Howard Moody opened the 1892 church to local musicians, artists, and poets, among them Allen Ginsberg, **Allan Kaprow,** Claus Oldenberg, and Robert Rauschenberg. In 1961 the new assistant minister, Al Carmines, a gifted composer, founded the JPT, a hub for two decades of **alternative theatre, performance art,** and unfettered social and political dissent. There Nam June Paik sliced his arm with a razor, accompanied by cellist Charlotte Moorman, nude from the waist up; there Carmines and **Maria Irene Fornés** collaborated on *Promenade*, the theatre's greatest hit and – like **Ron Tavel**'s camp classic *Gorilla Queen,* with its Carmines score – among the Judson's transfers to commercial runs.   CLJ

Jujamcyn Theaters A producing company founded in 1956 by 3M Chairman William L. McKnight and named for his grandchildren Judy, James, and Cynthia. The third largest New York theatre owner, its Broadway theatres are the **St. James, Martin Beck, O'Neill, Virginia,** and **Ritz.** It also operates **Boston**'s Colonial and Wilbur, **Philadelphia**'s Shubert, and **Chicago**'s Civic Theatres.

Because president **Rocco Landesman,** producing director Paul Libin, and artistic director Jack Viertel were all associated with resident theatres, Jujamcyn actively develops new works for Broadway. Since 1984 the company has given the Jujamcyn Award to a resident theatre for "contribution to the development of creative talent for the theater." In 1986 Jujamcyn helped launch the American Playwrights Project to commission new plays for commercial production, and, with British producers, the International Theater Development Fund. In 1990 Jujamcyn helped start the short-lived New Musicals at SUNY–Purchase for "the revitalization of the American musical theatre," and in 1991 began similar initiatives in association with Albany's **Capital Repertory Company** (including a revision by **Richard Greenberg** of *Pal Joey*).

Jujamcyn productions include *The **Elephant Man*** (1978), Hauptman and Miller's *Big River* (Tony, 1985), ***Into the Woods*** (1987), **M.** *Butterfly* (1988), ***City of Angels*** (1989), and *The **Piano Lesson.*** REK

Julia, Raul (1940–) Puerto Rican–born film and stage actor whose New York debut was as Astolfo in *Life Is a Dream* in Spanish. Principal stage appearances include classical roles at the Delacorte [see **New York Shakespeare Festival**] and the **Vivian Beaumont** in New York. In 1982 he starred in *Nine* as Guido Contini, in which critics referred to him as "a standout" and "childishly wise, boyishly insincere, and totally right." For *Nine* he was nominated for a Tony Award, as he was for *The Threepenny Opera* (1976), *Where's Charley* (1974), and *Two Gentlemen of Verona* (1971). In 1990 he was largely unsuccessful as Macbeth at the NYSF, where he essayed Othello for the second time the following year (the first was in 1979) opposite the Iago of **Christopher Walken.** He was seen as Don Quixote in a national tour of ***Man of La Mancha*** in 1991 (on Broadway in 1992).   SMA

K

Kahn, Michael (1937–) Director and educator who during his career has staged plays ranging from avant-garde satires to musical comedies. He is known principally, however, as a talented Shakespearean director and as the artistic director of the **American Shakespeare Theatre** (1969–74), the **McCarter Theatre** Company (1974–9), the **Acting Company** (1978–88), and, since 1986, the **Shakespeare Theatre** at the Folger. Drawing eclectically on both traditional and postmodernist directorial approaches, Kahn's Shakespearean stagings are noted for their vigor, clarity, and originality and have contributed significantly to a revival of public interest in **Shakespeare on the American stage** in the 1980s and '90s. In the training of actors, he also has been influential as the Chair of the Acting Department of the Juilliard Drama Division (where he was appointed division head in 1992). DJW

Kahn, Otto H[ermann] (1867–1934) German-born banker who immigrated to New York in 1893 and became the greatest individual patron of the arts the U.S. has yet known. The close personal friend and financial adviser of railroad titan Edward H. Harriman, Kahn was regarded in his time as the most liberal and democratic multimillionaire in the country. He was the chief benefactor of the Metropolitan Opera Company and a founder and backer of the **New Theatre.** His international contacts and his personal wealth facilitated the U.S. tour (1916–17) of Serge Diaghilev's Ballets Russes, a visit that deflected American ballet from an Italian toward a Russian model. He backed the visits of Copeau's Théâtre du Vieux Columbier (1917–19), the **Moscow Art Theatre** (1922–3), and the Théâtre de' l'Odéon (1924–5). He underwrote **Max Reinhardt**'s 1924 production of *The Miracle* in the amount of $600,000. He provided critical support for influential art theatres such as the **Washington Square Players**, the **Provincetown Players**, the New Playwright's Theater, the **Civic Repertory Theatre,** and the **Hedgerow Theatre,** as well as numerous individual writers, actors, and artists. WD

See: M. J. Matz, *The Many Lives of Otto Kahn,* New York, 1963.

Kalem, T[heodore] E[ustace] (1919–85) Drama critic. Born in Massachusetts and educated at Harvard (1942), Kalem served in WW II, after which he began a stock market letter and wrote book reviews for the *Christian Science Monitor* (1948–50). He was book reviewer (1951–61) and an associate editor for *Time* magazine when he replaced **Louis Kronenberger** as drama critic (1961–85). Adapting himself to *Time*'s terse format, Kalem was a master of clever and witty aphorisms. TLM

Kalfin, Robert (1933–) New York–born director and producer educated at Alfred University (BA, 1954) and the Yale School of Drama (MFA, 1957). He made his directorial debut with H. Leivick's *The Golem* at St. Mark's Playhouse in 1959, then free-lanced in regional theatre before founding the influential **Chelsea Theatre Center** in 1965. After the Chelsea closed in 1983, Kalfin spent a season as director of the **Cincinnati Playhouse,** and has subsequently returned to free-lance direction in regional theatre and New York. CLJ

Kalish (Kalich), Bertha (1872?–1939) Polish (Lemberg)-born actress who first performed in Polish opera but shifted to **Yiddish theatre.** In 1896, already successful, she came to America with her husband and children. Her beauty, grace, and dignity won praise as the star of such plays as **Goldfadn**'s *Shulamis* and **Gordin**'s *Sappho* and *The Kreutzer Sonata* (which he supposedly wrote to show off her thrilling voice and beautiful thick hair). In 1905 she contracted with the American producer **Harrison Fiske** to star in productions such as *Fedora* and *Monna Vanna,* as well as English translations of her Yiddish successes, and for the next 20 years she performed at least as much in English as in Yiddish. However, near the end of her life, completely blind, she returned exclusively to the Yiddish stage. NS

Kander, John (1927–) composer, and **Fred Ebb** (1932–) lyricist. After receiving a Master's degree from Columbia University, Kander worked as a rehearsal pianist, conductor, and arranger. His first Broadway score was for *A Family Affair* (1961). Ebb also received a Master's from Columbia; he wrote plays and song lyrics before joining with Kander to write scores for Broadway, notably *Flora, the Red Menace* (1964), ***Cabaret*** (1966), *Zorba* (1968), ***Chicago*** (1975), and *Woman of the Year* (1981). They wrote the songs for two of **Liza Minnelli**'s **one-person** shows, and she appeared in their musicals *Chicago* (as a replacement for **Gwen Verdon**), *The Act* (1977), and *The Rink* (1984). In several of their musicals they proved skillful at duplicating the sounds and idioms of foreign cultures and bygone eras. MK

Kanin, Fay (1916?–) Playwright, producer, film and TV writer. Her most successful play,

Goodbye My Fancy (1948), portrays a postwar professional woman who values her high principles more than marriage. It was produced by her husband, Michael (1910–   ), with whom she collaborated on many plays and screenplays. In the 1970s Kanin turned to TV writing and won several Emmys; in 1978 she and Lillian Gallo formed a production company, which has made several movies for TV dealing with serious, real-life concerns.   FB

Kanin, Garson (1912–   ) Rochester-born actor, director, and author of short stories, novels, documentaries, and stage, screen, and television plays (often with his wife **Ruth Gordon**). Beginning in **vaudeville,** he debuted as Tommy Deal in *Little Ol' Boy* (1933), and appeared in *Spring Song* (1934) and *Ladies' Money* (1934) among others. He directed *Hitch Your Wagon* (1937) and *Too Many Heroes* (1937), and was assistant director to **George Abbott** (1935–7) before moving to Hollywood to direct feature films. With Carol Reed he received an Oscar for Eisenhower's army documentary, *The True Glory* (1945); alone he directed his best-known Broadway work, ***Born Yesterday*** (1946; directed film version in 1956), and his own libretto of *Die Fledermaus* (Metropolitan Opera, 1950). He also directed (among other movies) *The **Diary of Anne Frank*** (1955); wrote the book for and directed *Do Re Mi* (1960); and directed ***Funny Girl*** (New York, 1964) and a revival of ***Idiot's Delight*** (Los Angeles, 1970). Known as a playwright of strong liberal sentiments, he received the American Academy of Dramatic Arts Award of Achievement (1958).   GSA

Kaprow, Allan (1927–   ) New Jersey–born **performance art**ist, art historian, writer. Formerly a painter who had studied with Hans Hoffmann (1947–8) and at New York University (BA, 1949), Kaprow also studied art history at Columbia University (MA, 1952) and music composition with John Cage (1957, 1958). He developed "Happenings" (1959) and other models for merging art with life, such as the "Un-artist" (1971–4) (one who deconstructs art) and the notion of "life-like" art (as opposed to "art-like" art) (1983). Influenced by Marcel Duchamp, Jackson Pollock, Cage, the *Nouveau Réalistes,* Japanese Gutai, and Zen Buddhism, Kaprow's aesthetic of everyday life questions traditional illusionism and theatricality in art. Since the late 1970s Kaprow's performances are meditative and private practices, ethnographic studies, and social interventions, such as *Standards* (1979) and *Digging a Hole* (1980).   AF

Karamu House A private metropolitan center for the arts founded in 1915 by Oberlin College graduates Rowena and Russell Jelliffe and located in Cleveland, OH. The original center burned down in 1939, but a new and expanded facility opened 10 years later, after WW II. The adult theatre group, launched in 1921, was initially called the Gilpin Players, after actor **Charles Gilpin.** It was from the start multiracial, but a demographic change has given it a core constituency of inner-city blacks. The center contains a proscenium and an arena theatre, both nonprofit, in which some 11 productions are mounted each season, including musicals and, in the past, operas. Karamu enjoyed a special relationship with playwright **Langston Hughes** and premiered six of his plays. In 1981 an attempt was made to establish a black Equity unit, but traditional operating procedures thwarted the move and Equity personnel returned to New York. Karamu (Swahili for "a place of enjoyment for all") has celebrated its 75th anniversary and considers its theatre to be the oldest continually active **African-American theatre** in America.   EGH

Kauffmann, Stanley (1916–   ) Drama and film critic. Born in New York and educated at NYU (1935), Kauffmann established his reputation as film (1958–65; 1967–   ) and theatre (1969–79) critic for *New Republic,* and as theatre critic for the *New York Times* (1966) and *Saturday Review* (1979–85). He has held academic appointments at Yale (1967–73; 1977–86), and at CUNY (1977–   ). His books include *Persons of the Drama* (1976), *Theater Criticisms* (1984), and his memoirs, *Albums of Early Life* (1980). Analytical and precise, Kauffmann views contemporary plays and films in a larger cultural and historical context.   TLM

Kaufman, George S[imon] (1889–1961) Playwright and director. A Founding Father of the American popular theatre, Kaufman enjoyed a long and extraordinarily productive Broadway career. On his own he wrote only one full-length play, a satire of the theatre called *The Butter and Egg Man* (1925); in collaboration he wrote 40 plays, more than half of them certified hits. His partners included **Marc Connelly** (*Dulcy* [1921], ***Beggar on Horseback*** [1924]); **Edna Ferber** (*The **Royal Family*** [1927], ***Dinner at Eight*** [1932], *Stage Door* [1936]); **Morrie Ryskind** (*The Cocoanuts* [1925], ***Animal Crackers*** [1928] – two Marx Bros. vehicles – and *Of Thee I Sing* [1931], Pulitzer Prize]); and **Moss Hart** (*Once in a Lifetime* [1930], ***You Can't Take It with You*** [1936, Pulitzer Prize], *The **Man Who Came to Dinner*** [1939]). While his partners were stronger on plot contrivance, Kaufman's speciality was dialogue, which he enlivened with witty, sarcastic rejoinders: the fabled Kaufman wisecrack. He was a born satirist whose targets included not only his own beat, the New York theatre world, but also Hollywood, big business, politics, and provincialism (although Kaufman himself was accused of being parochial in his subject matter). His subjects were drawn from life, but his artificial, well-made plots were manufactured for the theatre. Kaufman's dry wit earned him a seat at the Algonquin Round Table, and his instinctive abhorrence of romance, sentiment, and melodrama provided a counterbalance to his less cynical collaborators. Though his tone was captious and ironic, Kaufman was never so abrasive as to offend the large popular audience his bread and butter depended on; at the finale he tempered his sting with forgiveness.

Kaufman began his directing career in 1928 with a jumpy, frenetic production of *The **Front Page.*** Like a terse Kaufman script, a Kaufman-directed show had remarkable precision. Swift timing was his trademark; he had no patience for analysis or introspection, and when a solemn actor once made the mistake of asking about motivation, Kaufman snapped "Your job." FH

See: M. Goldstein, *George S. Kaufman: His Life, His Theater,* New York, 1979; J. D. Mason, *Wise-Cracks: The Farces of George S. Kaufman,* Ann Arbor, MI, 1988; S. Meredith, *George S. Kaufman and His Friends,* Garden City, NY, 1974; R.-G Pollock, *George S. Kaufman,* Boston, 1988.

Kaye, Judy (1948–   ) Singer-actress who, after attending UCLA, made her Broadway debut as a replacement in *Grease* (1977), then succeeded Madeline Kahn as Lily Garland early in the run of *On the Twentieth Century* (1978). After several years working in **nightclubs,** touring shows, and regional theatre, she received critical kudos for her impressive singing and scene-stealing comedy as opera diva Carlotta Guidicelli in the American production of *Phantom of the Opera* (1988). She subsequently appeared in a New York City Opera revival of *Pajama Game* (1989) and a production of *The Merry Widow* at New Jersey's Paper Mill Playhouse (1991). MK

Kazan, Elia (1909–   ) Director and actor, **Group Theatre** member, and cofounder of the **Actors Studio.** Kazan was long considered America's leading director of actors for both stage and film. His stage productions of *A Streetcar Named Desire* (1947), *Death of a Salesman* (1949), *Cat on a Hot Tin Roof* (1955), and *Sweet Bird of Youth* (1959), and his films *Streetcar . . .* (1951), *On the Waterfront* (1954), and *East of Eden* (1955) have earned him the reputation of preeminent Method director whose overheated, naturalistic style is synonymous with the work of the Actors Studio. A Kazan-directed performance is excitingly high-strung, notable for its depth and intensity of feeling, its verbal stammers and backtracking, its emotional ambivalences, and its sexual vibrancy. Kazan's method, influenced by the ideas of Stanislavsky and **Lee Strasberg,** depends on personal contact with his actors. A shrewd judge of character, he takes actors off to the side, his arm draped casually over their shoulders, to whisper some private confidence or observation. Although he has rarely directed, in films or theatre, since he resigned in 1964 as codirector of the **Vivian Beaumont Theatre,** he remains a revered figure among New York actors. His controversial autobiography was published in 1988. FH

See: M. Ciment, *Kazan on Kazan,* New York, 1974; L. Clark, "The Directing Practices and Principles of Elia Kazan," PhD diss., Kent State U, 1976; L. Michael, *Elia Kazan: A Guide to References and Resources,* Boston, 1985; T. H. Pauly, *An American Odyssey: Elia Kazan and American Culture,* Philadelphia, 1983; S. Vineberg, *Method Actors,* NY, 1991.

Keach, Stacy (1941–   ) Stage, film, and television actor who gained critical attention in the title role of *MacBird!* **Off-Broadway** in 1967, as **"Buffalo Bill" Cody** in Kopit's *Indians* at the **Arena Stage** and on Broadway in 1969, and as Jamie in *Long Day's Journey into Night* (Off-Broadway 1971 revival). He has thrice played

Hamlet, most recently at Los Angeles' **Mark Taper Forum** (1974). In 1990 he appeared as the title character in **Michael Kahn**'s production of *Richard III* at the **Shakespeare Theatre** at the Folger. DBW

Keane, Doris (1881–1945) Actress known for her success in a single role. Educated in Europe, she also studied at the **American Academy of Dramatic Art.** Various roles quickly led to her starring engagement as the opera star and ill-fated lover, Margherita Cavallini, in **Edward Sheldon**'s *Romance* (1913), which she also played to an adoring public in London (1915). She continued to play the role in the U.S. and London until just before her retirement (c. 1930). Critics praised her unfathomable beauty, excellent stage technique, and richly nuanced performance. **Stark Young** attributed her success to a deep spirituality that transcended all of these qualities. MR

Keene, Laura (née Mary Frances Moss) (1826?–73) English-born actress and manager. While facts about her origins, training, and name are disputed, Laura Keene apparently made her London debut in 1851, a year before **James W. Wallack** hired her as leading lady for his company in New York. Her grace and charm as well as her comic ability endeared her with New York audiences in her favorite roles of Lady Teazle, Lady Gay Spanker, and Beatrice in *Much Ado.* After a year with Wallack's company, she spent the next two seasons in Baltimore and **San Francisco** before touring Australia with young **Edwin Booth.** In 1855 she returned to New York and opened her own Laura Keene Varieties Theatre. During 1856–63 she managed and acted in her Laura Keene's New Theatre, which became known for its lavishly mounted comedies. She encouraged the production of new American plays and closely supervised an excellent company that included **E. A. Sothern, Joseph Jefferson III,** Kate Reignolds, **W. J. Florence,** Agnes Robertson, **John T. Raymond,** and **Charles W. Couldock.** She returned to touring in 1863, and was performing in *Our American Cousin* at **Ford's Theatre** in Washington, DC, when President Lincoln was assassinated. During her career, she became closely identified with the emotional drama (e.g., *Camille*). TLM

See: J. Creahan, *The Life of Laura Keene . . . ,* Philadelphia, 1897; H. W. Deutsch, "Laura Keene's Theatre Management," PhD diss., Tufts U, 1992; B. G. Henneke, *Laura Keene: Actress, Innovator and Impresario,* Tulsa, OK, 1990; D. Taylor, "Laura Keene in America, 1852–1873," PhD diss., Tulane U, 1966.

Keith, Benjamin Franklin (1846–1914) **Vaudeville** entrepreneur and theatre proprietor who, with **Edward F. Albee,** created the most extensive vaudeville theatre chain in the U.S. New Hampshire–born Keith grew up on a farm, worked as a mess boy on a coastal freighter, and spent the 1870s working and traveling with **circus**es, where he most likely first met Albee. In 1880 he made and sold brooms in Providence, RI, but by 1883 had moved into the dime museum business with the rental of a vacant store in Boston. After Albee joined him in 1885 and continuous performances had been initiated, he became part owner of the Gaiety Musée; in 1886 he added the adjoining Bijou Theatre. Keith is often credited with the first use of the word "vaudeville" in order to circumvent the stigma attached to "variety" and the earlier concert saloon's sleazy reputation. With the formula of continuous, completely respectable vaudeville, the Keith–Albee circuit (nicknamed "the Sunday School Circuit") grew quickly with the construction or acquisition of vaudeville theatres in many cities, including Boston's Colonial Theatre (1894) and New York's The **Palace** (built by Martin Beck in 1913 but virtually controlled by Keith–Albee) and The **Orpheum** (built in 1899 by **Percy Williams** but bought by Keith in 1912). Despised by many vaudevillians, Keith–Albee sought to monopolize first-class vaudeville through the Vaudeville Managers' Protective Association (1900) and the **United Booking Office** (1906), headed by Keith and his major competitor, **F. F. Proctor.** After Keith's death, Albee ultimately gained control of the operation.   DBW

> *See:* R. Snyder, *The Voice of the City,* New York, 1989.

Kellar, Harry (né Heinrich Keller) (1849–1922) **Magic**ian who acted as assistant to the Fakir of Ava (I. Harris Hughes) and the **Davenport Brothers** before striking out on his own. Kellar tended to appropriate and refashion tricks conceived by others. A master of publicity, he won fame with Buatier de Kolta's "Vanishing Birdcage"; from Maskelyne, he derived the disappearing act "The Witch, the Sailor and the Monkey" and his supreme illusion "The Levitation of the Princess Karnac" (1904). After touring the world in 1880, he resettled in the U.S., where he set a record of 323 consecutive performances at Philadelphia's Egyptian Hall (1884) and 179 at the Comedy Theatre, New York (1886–7). He retired on a well-invested fortune in 1908, naming **Howard Thurston** as his successor.   LS

> *See:* H. Kellar, *A Magician's Tour Up & Down & Around the Earth,* Chicago, 1886.

Kellogg, Marjorie Bradley (1946–   ) Set designer. Strongly in the tradition of American selective realism, Kellogg's sets are meticulously researched, yet moody and evocative. She has worked extensively at regional theatres and has done several shows with the **Circle in the Square.** Broadway credits include *The Best Little Whorehouse in Texas, Da,* and *Steaming.*   AA

Kelly, Emmett (1898–1979) The prototypical tramp clown (as was **Otto Griebling**) and a consummate **mime.** Initially a trapeze artist, Kelly was first seen as the clown "Weary Willie" in 1924, a character he originated as a cartoon. The dirty, unshaven tramp's great popularity began in 1933 during the Depression. The silent, unsmiling clown was – according to Kelly's 1954 autobiography, *Clown* – the hobo who learns that the deck is stacked against him but keeps trying because of that one "spark of hope still glimmering in his

Emmett Kelly, most recognizable of character or tramp clowns, as "Weary Willie." Courtesy: Don B. Wilmeth.

soul." Kelly's most famous routine involved the sweeping of a circle of light from a spotlight. In the 1940s he was the star of **Ringling Bros.** and **Barnum** & Bailey Circus. Sedan, KS, is home to an Emmett Kelly Museum.   DBW

Kelly, George E. (1887–1974) Playwright. A member of the famed Philadelphia Kellys and uncle of Princess Grace, Kelly had three major Broadway successes in the 1920s: *The Torchbearers* (1922), a satire of Little Theatre [see **community theatre**] enthusiasts; *The Show Off* (1924), a comedy of provincial manners about the battle between a commonsensical mother and braggart son-in-law; and *Craig's Wife* (1925, Pulitzer Prize), an exposure of an American ice maiden whose immaculate home is more important to her than her husband. Although he was a practical man of the theatre – he began his career in 1912 as an actor on the **vaudeville** circuit – Kelly did not want to be labeled as a popular entertainer, and he insisted on directing each of his plays to preserve their distinctive rhythms. In later work such as *The Deep Mrs. Sykes* (1945) and *The Fatal Weakness* (1946), he deliberately muted comic elements. Kelly thought of himself as a moralist whose satires were designed to instruct and improve as well as to amuse. His work gains its idiosyncratic stamp from the targets he chose: bossy, smug suburban matrons, untalented would-be actors and playwrights, and freeloaders. Although Kelly worked within a conventional range of modest domestic settings, seemingly dictaphonic dialogue, and characters and situations drawn from middle-class American life, his writing achieves a unique voice: tart, scolding, droll, and delightfully eccentric.   FH

Kelly, Patsy (1910–81) Actress-comedienne who first appeared on the New York stage in *Harry Delmar's Revels* (1927) and was, for the next few years, in the cast of several other **revues**, including the *Earl Carroll's Vanities* (1930), *The Wonder Bar* (1931), and *Flying Colors* (1932). After a stint in **vaudeville** she began a long career in films, usually playing the dumpy, wise-cracking maid or friend of the heroine. She returned to Broadway in the acclaimed revival of *No, No, Nanette* (1970), and received costar billing with Debbie Reynolds for her performance as Mrs. O'Dare in the revival of *Irene* (1973).   MK

Kemble, Fanny (Frances Anne) (1809–93) English actress and author; in 1832 she came with her father, Charles Kemble, for a star tour beginning at New York's **Park Theatre.** Their visit was welcomed by an audience eager to see an element of refinement in the American theatre, though the critic for the New York *Mirror* noted that "many accustomed to a less chaste and more boisterous style" failed to appreciate her. Fanny Kemble pleased her more discerning public with intensely rendered romantic heroines, such as Julia in *The Hunchback* and Shakespeare's Juliet. **Francis C. Wemyss** declared that "she revived the prostrate fortunes of the drama in the United States." Fanny retired in 1834 in order to marry Pierce Butler, a South Carolinian. She was a staunch abolitionist, and the marriage foundered on this issue. For 26 years (1848–74) she gave a well-received series of readings from **Shakespeare** in England and the U.S. Between 1835 and 1890 she published nine volumes of memoirs.   MR

> See: J. C. Furnas, *Fanny Kemble: Leading Lady of the Nineteenth Century Stage,* New York, 1982.

Kennedy, Adrienne (1931–) African-American playwright who blends symbols, historical figures, racial images, and myths to create surreal, highly personalized one-act plays, all of which she claims are autobiographical. *Funnyhouse of a Negro,* which won an Obie in 1964, depicts the final moments before the suicide of Sarah, a mulatto psychically torn by an inability to reconcile herself to her mixed racial heritage. *The Owl Answers* (1969) portrays another mulatto woman caught in a hallucinatory nightmare of confused racial identity in which biographical and historical characters emerge, dissolve, and metamorphose. Kennedy's other plays include *A Rat's Mass* (1966), a fantasy of war and prejudice; *The Lennon Play: In His Own Write* (1967), an adaptation of musician John Lennon's autobiographical writings; *A Movie Star Has to Star in Black and White* (1976); and *A Lancashire Lad* (1980), a **children's theatre** piece based on the early life of Charlie Chaplin.   FB

> See: P. K. Bryant-Jackson and L. M. Overbeck, eds., *Intersecting Boundaries: The Theatre of Adrienne Kennedy,* Minneapolis, 1992; A. Kennedy, *People Who Led to My Plays,* New York, 1987; A. Kennedy, *Deadly Triplets: A Theatre Mystery and Journal,* Minneapolis, 1990.

Kennedy, Arthur (1914–90) Film, stage, and television actor who began acting with the **Group Theatre,** and made his debut on Broadway as Bushy in *Richard II* (1937). Later successes were Chris in *All My Sons* (1947), Biff in *Death of a Salesman* (1949), and John Proctor in *The Crucible* (1953). Awards included a Tony for Biff (1949), the New York Film Critics' Award for *Bright Victory* (1951), and a Golden Globe Award for *Trial* (1955). After his film debut in 1940, Kennedy appeared in over 70 films.   SMA

Kennedy, Charles Rann (1871–1950) Playwright from England who became an American citizen in 1917. An advocate of Christian principles, which he dramatized with more ardor than theatrical effectiveness, Kennedy helped bring the Social Gospel movement to the American stage. In *The Servant in the House* (1907), his best-known play, he presented a Christ figure who reveals the hypocrisy of organized religion. Later plays – many written for his actress wife, Edith Wynne Matthison – include *The Idol Breaker* (1914) and *The Terrible Meek* (1912), a daring antiwar play. Leaving Broadway, the Kennedys became associated with Bennett College, where he continued to write plays and direct Greek plays.   WJM

Kennedy's Children by Robert Patrick, a two-act drama that first appeared (in part) under the title *A Bad Place to Get Your Head* on 14 July 1970 at the Dove Company, New York. In its final form, it opened at Clark Center for the Performing Arts under the auspices of **Playwrights Horizons** (Robert Moss, Exec. Dir.) on 30 May 1973. After establishing itself in London, it reached Broadway directed by Clive Donner, opening 3 November 1975 at the Golden Theatre. A series of unrelated monologues in a downtown New York bar, the play depicts a lost generation of Americans in the aftermath of the Kennedy assassination. Five characters, including a pill-popping Vietnam veteran, a Marilyn Monroe–type blonde, and a young radical, reveal shattered dreams and self-explorations in a painful lament for the 1960s.   ER

Kern, Jerome (1885–1945) Composer who, after studying musical composition, began his theatrical career as a house composer for producer **Charles Frohman** in London. Returning to America, he worked as a song-plugger and rehearsal pianist. Individual songs by Kern were interpolated into several Broadway musicals before he was given his first opportunity to compose a complete score, *The Red Petticoat* (1912). In 1915 Kern was asked by producers **F. Ray Comstock** and **Elisabeth Marbury** to write the score for a modest musical that would be appropriate to the tiny, 299-seat **Princess Theatre.** The result, *Nobody Home,* enchanted critics and audiences with its personable cast, contemporary setting, and lively score. An even greater success was the second Princess Theatre musical, ***Very Good Eddie*** (1915). With librettist **Guy Bolton** and lyricist **P. G. Wodehouse,** Kern created *Have a Heart* (1917), *Oh, Boy* (1917), *Leave It to Jane* (1917), and *Oh, Lady! Lady!* (1918). By replacing the mythical kingdoms and stilted language of European operetta with recognizable characters, believable dramatic situations, and American musical idioms, these shows strongly influenced the direction in which American musical comedy was to evolve in the 1920s.

After writing a number of successful, if conventional, musicals in the first half of the 1920s, Kern again pioneered a new style of musical theatre with his score for *Show Boat* (1927). Conceived as a musical drama, *Show Boat,* with book and lyrics by **Oscar Hammerstein II,** proved that shows with serious librettos and songs that grew naturally out of the dramatic action could be successful. Kern's shows of the 1930s, although containing many fine songs, were more traditional operettas and musical comedies. His last complete score for Broadway was *Very Warm for May* (1939). He is remembered as an innovator whose scores for the Princess Theatre musicals and *Show Boat* were landmarks in the evolution of modern **musical theatre.**   MK

> See: G. Bordman, *Jerome Kern: His Life and Music,* New York, 1980; D. Ewen, *The Story of Jerome Kern,* New York, 1953; M. Freedland, *Jerome Kern: A Biography,* New York, 1981.

Kerr, Jean (1923–   ) Playwright and author who wrote 10 successful plays noted for their light-hearted comedy and witty dialogue, such as *Touch and Go,* with husband **Walter** (1949); *King of Hearts,* with Eleanor Brooke (1954); *Finishing Touches* (1973); and *Lunch Hour* (1980). Her biggest hit was *Mary, Mary* (1961), which ran for 1,572 performances. She is also noted for her humorous writings, particularly *Please Don't Eat the Daisies,* which became both a film and a TV series.   FB

Kerr, Walter (1913–   ) Drama critic, playwright, lecturer, teacher, and director. Kerr was educated at Northwestern University before beginning in 1938 an 11-year career as teacher of drama at Catholic University. There he wrote or cowrote and directed a number of new scripts, four of which reached Broadway. With his wife **Jean,** he collaborated on several shows, including the musical comedy *Goldilocks* (1958). In 1950, Kerr began reviewing for *Commonweal.* The following year, he replaced **Howard Barnes** as drama critic for the *New York Herald Tribune,* a post he held until that paper's demise in 1966. The *New York Times* then hired Kerr as chief critic for the Sunday edition, a position he held until his retirement in 1983. Regarded as the most perceptive critic reviewing the Broadway theatre during the 1960s and '70s, Kerr brought intelligence, insight, knowledge, and a graceful style to his work. He believed that a play's truths must be perceived by an audience intuitively rather than intellectually, and that a play must touch a group consciousness so that there is a "single unified response." His views are expressed in *The Decline of Pleasure* (1962), *The Theatre in Spite of Itself* (1963), *Tragedy and Comedy* (1967), and *Journey to the Center of the Theatre* (1979). He won a Pulitzer Prize for Dramatic Criticism in 1978. The restored Ritz Theatre was renamed the **Walter Kerr Theatre** in his honor (1990).   TLM

Kersands, Billy (c. 1842–1915) African-American minstrel entertainer for over 40 years. Kersands was the leading low comedian of several **minstrel** show companies, including his own. Large of stature, he was nevertheless an excellent dancer, credited with introducing the soft-shoe and buck-and-wing dances. He was also praised for his gymnastic drumming, and his troupe led the Mardi Gras parade in 1886. He caricatured the slow-witted Negro character and used his unusually large mouth to advantage in facial antics. His popularity in the southern states forced theatre owners to suspend segregationist seating to accommodate increased black patronage when he appeared.   EGH

Kerz, Leo (1912–76) Berlin-born theatre and film set designer who studied with Bertolt Brecht and Laszlo Moholy-Nagy, and from 1927 worked as an assistant designer to **Erwin Piscator.** These influences remained with him throughout his career, and his sets tended toward sweeping proportions and emblematic scenic elements. Like Piscator, he also incorporated film and projections into many of his designs. He left Berlin soon after Hitler assumed power, and worked in London, Amsterdam, and Prague before founding the Pioneer Theatre in Johannesburg, South Africa. Kerz came to the U.S. in 1942, assisted **Jo Mielziner, Watson Barrett,** and **Stewart Chaney,** and resumed his work with Piscator. He made his Broadway debut in 1947 with the **Katharine Cornell** production of *Antony and Cleopatra.* He is best known for his opera designs for the Metropolitan and New York City Opera companies, among others, and for his work at the *Arena Stage* during 1969–71. He also designed for television and film, including the controversial *Ecstasy* with Hedy Lamarr (1934).   AA

Kessler, David (1860–1920) Moldavian (Kishenev)-born actor who was 17 when the new invention, **Yiddish theatre,** came to town. Fascinated, he first joined as a stagehand and, by 1886, when he arrived in New York, he had progressed to leading man. Kessler, an emotional actor, was capable both of melodramatic sensationalism, which excited the masses, and sensitive characterizations, which delighted the intelligentsia. His most famous roles were in **Gordin**'s *God, Man, and Devil* (1900) and *Shlomke Charlatan,* and **Pinski**'s *Yankl the Blacksmith* (1906). Much of his career he functioned not only as actor but as star-manager of his own company.   NS

Kidd, Michael (né Milton Gruenwald) (1917–   ) Ballet dancer and choreographer for theatre and film [see **dance**]. Kidd performed with **Balanchine**'s American Ballet, Ballet Caravan, and Ballet Theatre before making his impact in American musical theatre. From his choreographic debut in *Finian's Rainbow* (1947) to the ever-popular barn-raising dance in the film *Seven Brides for Seven Brothers* (MGM, 1954), Kidd has been lauded for his energetic and spirited successes. He had a series of successes – *Guys and Dolls* (1950), *Can-Can* (1953), *Li'l Abner* (1956), and *Destry Rides Again* (1959) – for which he won four successive Tony Awards, becoming the first person ever so honored.   LF

Kiesler, Frederick (1890–1965) Austrian-born architect and designer. Very little of Kiesler's visionary theatre was ever fully realized, yet his plans and projects exerted a strong influence on the development of mid-20th-century theatre architecture and on the emergence of environmental theatre. Most of his projects were variations on the so-called Endless Theatre – a futuristic theatre of ramps and spirals within an ellipsoidal shell. His more practical projects included flexible theatres capable of changing size and configuration, and "space stages," which were essentially nonscenic architectural stages. He came to the U.S. in 1926 with the International Theatre Exhibit – the first look many Americans had at new European design – and stayed, but he never achieved the prominence he had known in Europe. Despite many projects, his only significant theatre fully realized in the U.S. was the Eighth Street Cinema in New York (1930).   AA

Kiley, Richard (1922–) Chicago-born actor-singer who made his acting debut in local radio and, after serving in the Navy, toured as Stanley in *A Streetcar Named Desire.* His Broadway debut was in *Misalliance* (1953), and in the same year he played the juvenile lead in *Kismet.* He received a Tony for his performance opposite **Gwen Verdon** in *Redhead* (1959) and had leading roles in the musicals *No Strings* (1962) and *I Had a Ball* (1964). In 1965 he created the dual role of Cervantes and Don Quixote in the musical *Man of La Mancha,* the show with which he is most closely identified. Possessed of a powerful singing voice, Kiley is also a fine actor with many film and television credits.   MK

Kilty, Jerome (Timothy) (1922–) Actor, playwright, director. Brattle Theatre (Cambridge, MA) cofounder-director (1948–52), Kilty's extensive résumé includes 14 Broadway roles and countless resident theatre assignments (including over a decade at the **American Repertory Theatre**). Author of nine plays, he has directed versions of his best known, *Dear Liar* (1957), in four languages.   DBW

Kim, Willa (1930?–) Costume designer. From the 1950s through the '70s Kim designed costumes for many of the major **Off-Broadway** productions, including *Dynamite Tonight, Scuba Duba, Promenade, Operation Sidewinder,* and Genêt's *The Screens.* She later became associated with large-scale glitzy musicals, such as *Sophisticated Ladies, Dancin', Song and Dance, Legs Diamond,* and *The **Will Rogers Follies*** (1991, Tony). Plays include *Jumpers* and the 1986 revival of *The **Front Page*** at the **Vivian Beaumont.** She first designed for ballet in 1962, and since has designed extensively for the Feld Ballet, the Joffrey, and the San Francisco Ballet, as well as for opera.   AA

Kimball, Moses (1810–95) A merchant and entrepreneur, Kimball opened the **Boston Museum** in 1841 and introduced plays in 1843. Withdrawing from active management in the 1860s to concentrate upon politics, Kimball maintained (until 1893) probably the longest lived repertory company in U.S. theatrical history. The successful formula stressed family entertainment, low prices, prizes for moral dramas (*The **Drunkard*** premiered here in 1844), and quality acting.   RKB

King, Dennis (1897–1971) English-born actor and singer who began his career with the Birmingham Repertory Theatre. After his arrival in New York in the early 1920s, King appeared in the **Theatre Guild** production of Shaw's *Back to Methuselah* and as Mercutio in *Romeo and Juliet.* His fine baritone voice and his training as an actor made King the ideal leading man for operetta. In 1924 he appeared as Jim Kenyon in *Rose-Marie,* and his success in that role was followed by critically acclaimed performances as François Villon in *The Vagabond King* (1925) and as D'Artagnan in *The Three Musketeers* (1928). From the 1920s on, King concentrated on acting in straight plays, returning to the musical stage on rare occasions, most notably to create the role of Willie Palaffi in **Rodgers** and **Hart**'s *I Married an Angel* (1938).   MK

King, Woodie, Jr. (1937–) **African-American** producer and director. King was cofounder and artistic director of Concept East Thatre in Detroit during 1960–3 before moving to New York City. There in 1970 he cofounded and still serves as artistic director of the **New Federal Theatre** at the Henry Street Settlement, where he has produced and directed many plays by budding and significant black playwrights, including **Amiri Baraka, Ed Bullins,** and **Ntozake Shange.** King has written a book of essays entitled *Black Theatre: Present Condition* (1981), coedited *Black Drama Anthology* (1971), and edited *New Plays from the Black Theatre* (1989).   EGH

King and I, The The fifth collaboration between **Richard Rodgers** (music) and **Oscar Hammerstein II** (book and lyrics) opened at the **St. James Theatre** on 29 March 1951 and ran 1,246 performances. Based on Margaret Landon's novel *Anna and the King of Siam,* this musical play recounted the attempts of a widowed Welsh schoolteacher to bring Western values to the court and children of a

Gertrude Lawrence and Yul Brynner in *The King and I* (1951). Courtesy: Belknap Collection for the Performing Arts, University of Florida Libraries.

19th-century Siamese king. The role Anna Leonowens capped **Gertrude Lawrence**'s musical comedy career, while the part of the King would ever after be associated with **Yul Brynner,** who created the part. Rodgers's music cleverly evoked Asian rhythms and sounds while staying within the traditions of the Broadway musical score. Hammerstein's book and lyrics explored the clash between two disparate cultures as exemplified by two hard-headed but likable characters who are attracted to each other despite their philosophical differences. A production highlight was **Jerome Robbins**'s choreography for a Siamese version of *Uncle Tom's Cabin* called "The Small House of Uncle Thomas." Using Thai dance forms, costumes, and masks, Robbins successfully combined the exotic and the familiar in a showstopping production number that also crystallized the central conflict of the story.   MK

Kingsley, Sidney (1906–) Playwright who made his reputation with realistic social melodramas. *Dead End* (1935), concerned with the effect on a group of kids of slum life near New York's East River, is his most memorable success, but *Men in White* (1933), about a young doctor's experiences in a hospital, stabilized the financially troubled **Group Theatre** and won Kingsley a Pulitzer Prize. His antiwar play, *Ten Million Ghosts* (1936), failed, and *The Patriots* (1943), contrasting the political theories of Thomas Jefferson and Alexander Hamilton, was a weak effort. Forsaking propaganda for realistic and vivid melodrama, Kingsley wrote *Detective Story* (1949), featuring a conscientious police detective whose emotional involvement drives him to sadism, and a dramatization of Arthur Koestler's novel *Darkness at Noon* (1951). Later plays include a farce entitled *Lunatics and Lovers* (1954) and *Night Life* (1962), a murder melodrama with overtones of labor and politics. A playwright whose career spans more than half a century, Kingsley remains active in the **Dramatist Guild.**   WJM

Kiralfy (né Königsbaum) family Jewish Hungarian family of dancers and impresarios. After a distinguished European career popularizing Magyar folk dances, the brothers **Imre** (1845–1919), **Arnold** (d. 1908), and **Bolossy** (1848–1932) came to New York with their sisters **Haniola** (1851–89) and **Emilie** (1855–1917) to perform a czardas in **G. L. Fox**'s panto**mime** *Hiccory Diccory Dock* (1869). Imre and Bolossy soon branched out on their own to stage lavish musical spectacles, including a revival of *The **Black Crook*** (1873), *The Deluge* (1874), and three Jules Verne works: ***Around the World in Eighty Days*** (1875), *A Trip to the Moon* (1877), and *Michael Strogoff* (1881), all noted for skillful deployment of throngs of chorines and supernumeraries. They built the Alhambra Palace, Philadelphia (1876), and innovated in ventilation and **stage lighting:** For *Excelsior* (**Niblo's Garden,** 1883) they commissioned Edison to light the whole stage by electricity. In 1886, Imre and Bolossy split over financial differences. Bolossy concentrated his choreographic skills on a series of spectacles staged **outdoor**s or in mammoth exhibition halls, including *King Solomon* (1891), *Constantinople* (London Olympia, 1894), *The Orient* (Berlin, 1896), and *A Carnival in Venice* (Portland, OR, 1905). Imre produced *The Fall of Babylon,* an open-air spectacular with 1,000 participants, and, with **P. T. Barnum,** *Columbus* (1890). He settled in London where his projects during 1892–1912 included a reconstruction of the Earl's Court exhibition hall, the creation of White City, and a number of grandiose expositions.   LS

See: B. M. Barker, ed., *Bolossy Kiralfy, Creator of Great Musical Spectacles: An Autobiography,* Ann Arbor, 1988.

Kirby, Michael (1931–) Educator, editor, playwright, and author, born in California and educated at Princeton, Boston University, and NYU. Kirby has helped define the agenda in **performance art** as editor (1971–85) and contributor to *The Drama Review* and author of *Happenings* (1965), *The Art of Time* (1969), *Futurist Performance* (1971), *The New Theatre* (1974), and *A Formalist Theatre* (1987). Kirby taught in Performance Studies at NYU, and has written and directed performance pieces as well as acted for stage and films.   TLM

Kismet Two-act operetta, music and lyrics by Robert Wright and George Forrest, book by Charles Lederer and Luther Davis; opened 3 December 1953 at the **Ziegfeld Theatre,** running 583 performances. Based on an old **Otis Skinner** vehicle by Edward Knoblock, this "Musical Arabian Night" follows the rise of Hajj (**Alfred Drake**) from beggar to Wazir of Baghdad in a single day. As they had in *The Song of Norway* (1944), Wright and Forrest took their music from the work of a single composer, this time Alexander Borodin; but whereas in *Song of Norway* they had used Edvard Greig's most familiar melodies with lyrics written to them, in *Kismet* they adapted and modified Borodin's music into a novel, romantic, evocatively Oriental score, from which "Stranger in Paradise" and "Baubles, Bangles and Beads" proved the most popular standards. A London production (1955) with many of the leads American proved even more successful. In 1978 an all-black variation, *Timbuktu,* was seen on Broadway, and in 1985 *Kismet* joined the repertory of the New York City Opera.   JD

Kissel, Howard William (1942–) Drama critic, born in Milwaukee and educated in English and comparative literature at Columbia College and in journalism at Northwestern (MS). Kissel served as a reporter for *Daily News Record;* feature writer for *Gentleman's Quarterly;* and Arts editor for *Women's Wear Daily,* reviewing films, books, classical music and the theatre. Since 1986 he has been chief drama critic of the New York *Daily News,* replacing **Douglas Watt.** In straightforward prose, Kissel describes the event, gives credit to the collaborators, and passes judgment on its worthiness.   TLM

Kiss Me, Kate Two-act musical comedy, music and lyrics by **Cole Porter,** book by **Sam and**

Bella Spewack; opened 30 December 1948 at New York's New Century Theatre, running 1,077 performances. This musical, starring **Alfred Drake** and Patricia Morison, about producing a musical version of Shakespeare's *Taming of the Shrew,* stresses the parallels between the relationship of the actors in the play-within-a-play and the Shakespearean characters they play, with the book cleverly weaving sections of Shakespearean dialogue into its scenes. The score (including "So in Love," "Too Darn Hot," and "Always True to You in My Fashion") is perhaps Porter's most dramatic, as the songs are more tightly integrated with the story than usual, and the show was the biggest hit of Porter's career. Winner of the Tony Award for best musical, it is generally listed high among the masterworks of American musical theatre.   JD

Kit, the Arkansas Traveller by Edward Spencer, **Thomas B. DeWalden,** and **Clifton W. Tayleure.** The original *Kit,* written by Edward Spencer, premiered in Buffalo on 20 April 1869. It was revised by DeWalden and then by Tayleure (or Taylor) before its New York success at **Niblo's Garden** theatre in May 1871, which helped to popularize border drama. The play allowed **Francis S. Chanfrau,** already famous for his portrayal of Mose, to create another distinctive characterization with the frontier hero, a role he played over 4,300 times in 15 years. Kit Redding was an Arkansas farmer whose wife and daughter were abducted. Kit tracked the scoundrel for 12 years (15 in one version) until he recovered his daughter and dealt revenge to the villain in a much-imitated Bowie knife fight.   RAH

Klauber, Adolph (1879–1933) Producer and critic. Irregular employment forced Klauber from acting into journalism, first for the New York *Commercial Advertiser,* then for the New York *Tribune,* and finally for the *New York Times,* where he became drama critic during 1906–18. He married actress **Jane Cowl** and was associated with her productions of *Lilac Time* (1917) and *Smilin' Through* (1919), as well as with the **Selwyn**s on *Romeo and Juliet* (1923), *Pelleas and Melisande* (1923), and *Antony and Cleopatra* (1924). Klauber was also coproducer of **Eugene O'Neill**'s *The Emperor Jones* and *Diff'rent* in 1920.   TLM

Klaw, Marc (Alonzo) (1858–1936) Newspaperman and lawyer who formed a partnership in 1887 with **A. L. Erlanger.** The soft-spoken Klaw was the gently persuasive and gracious member of the partnership. Compelled by their business sense to reform a chaotic tour scheduling system, the Klaw and Erlanger Exchange negotiated exclusive contracts with tour managers and theatre managers, thereby imposing needed order and greater profitability but also monopolistic control over nearly 200 theatres, mostly in the South. By 1895 theirs was the second largest booking agency in the U.S. In 1896, Klaw and Erlanger joined with five powerful theatrical entrepreneurs to form the Theatrical **Syndicate,** a trust that monopolized legitimate theatre in the U.S. for 15 years. The Syndicate dissolved in 1916, and Klaw continued his partnership with Erlanger until 1920. He built the Klaw Theatre in New York in 1920 and retired to live in England in 1927.   WD

Klein, Charles (1867–1915) Playwright. Emigrating from London at age 16, Klein had a brief career as a juvenile actor. His first play was *By Proxy* (1891), and he wrote another 15 strong domestic melodramas, the best of which was *The Music Master* (1904), produced by **David Belasco** and starring **David Warfield.** He then wrote six social plays in the muckraking manner of Ida Tarbell and Upton Sinclair. Typical of these were *The Lion and the Mouse* (1905), which exposed legislative corruption at the hands of big business, and *The Third Degree* (1909), which dramatized police brutality.   DMcD

Kline, Kevin (1947–   ) St. Louis–born actor, educated at Indiana University and trained at the Juilliard School, graduating in 1972. As a founding member of the **Acting Company,** he played numerous roles, including Charles Surface in *The School for Scandal,* Vaska Pepel in *The Lower Depths* (1972), Vershinin in *The Three Sisters,* Macheath in *The Beggar's Opera* (1973), and Jamie Lockhart in *The Robber Bridegroom* (1975). Kline won recognition as Bruce Granit in *On the Twentieth Century* (1978) and Paul in *Loose Ends* (1979), followed by critical acclaim as the Pirate King in *The Pirates of Penzance* (1980), which established him as a star, and as Bluntschli in a 1985 revival of *Arms and the Man.* Frank Rich (1981) thought that Kline had "all the ingredients for conventional leading man stardom – big voice, dashing good looks, infinite charm – and . . . the grace and timing of a silent-movie clown." In 1986 Kline first played Hamlet at the **New York Shakespeare Festival,** a role he repeated for that organization in his own production in 1990 (and later televised). Kline's film appearances include *Sophie's Choice* (1982), *The Big Chill* (1983), *A Fish Called Wanda* (1988), and *Grand Canyon* (1991). In 1989 he received the second William Shakespeare Award for Classical Theatre from the **Shakespeare Theatre** at the Folger.   TLM

Klotz, Florence (c. 1920–   ) Costume designer who, by her own admission, became involved in design almost by accident. Through the 1960s she designed several light contemporary comedies. In 1971 she teamed up with director **Harold Prince** to design *Follies,* which had 140 costumes ranging from rags to lavish show costumes spanning half a century. She subsequently designed several Prince–**Stephen Sondheim** musicals, each with a distinctly different style and period. Her costumes manage to combine contemporary sensibilities with period style.   AA

Knickerbocker Holiday (1938) Musical comedy in two acts, book and lyrics by **Maxwell Anderson** and music by **Kurt Weill,** produced by the **Playwrights' Company** on 19 November 1938 (168 performances). Anderson drew upon **Washington Irving**'s *History of New York* (1809) in satirizing the complex mixture of socialism and fascism pervading American politics in the late

1930s, and expressing his concern about the dangers of big government. The hero is a tinker afflicted with a peculiar malady: He can't take orders. The lovably authoritarian Governor Pieter Stuyvesant (**Walter Huston**) sang what became Anderson's most profitable piece, "September Song." Anderson intended his characterization of Stuyvesant to deprecate the incipient despotism of President Franklin D. Roosevelt, but toned down his satire at the urging of associates in the Playwrights' Company. Roosevelt, in a rare visit to the theatre, saw the production in Washington, reportedly enjoyed it, and entertained the cast at the White House.   WD

Komisarjevsky, Theodore (né Fyodor Fyodorovich Komissarzhevsky) (1882–1954) Russian director, designer, teacher, and theorist who, during his international career, searched for an ideal "synthetic theatre" – combining the play's "inner rhythm, spirit and ideology" with the theatre's musical-plastic form – and for the "universal actor" to express it. Despite alienating Stanislavsky by misrepresenting his teachings in a 1916 book, Komisarjevsky became a chief interpreter of Stanislavsky's System in England. His all-star stagings of Chekhov's major plays (1926–7, 1936) fostered a romantic view of the Russian intelligentsia, which suited English classist society. Despite attacking modern-dress Shakespeare in *Myself and the Theatre* (1929), Komisarjevsky's seven productions at Stratford (1932–9) altered the text, tone, and locales of Shakespeare's plays in light of modern history. He directed two productions for the **Theatre Guild** (1923) and in 1939 emigrated to the U.S., where he established the Komisarjevsky Theatre Studio (NYC); taught at Yale University (1940–2); directed three productions for the New York City Opera Company (1948, 1949, 1952), the last two designed by Mstislav Dobujinsky; and staged a famous *Crime and Punishment* (1949), starring John Gielgud. Komisarjevsky also wrote *Theatrical Preludes* (1916), *Costume of the Theatre* (1931), and *The Theatre and a Changing Civilization* (1935).
SG

See: C. J. Johnson, ed., *The Stage Art of Komisarjevsky*, Harvard Theatre Collection, Cambridge, MA, 1991.

Kopit, Arthur (Lee) (1937–) New York–born and Harvard-educated playwright who has had a distinguished place in the American theatre as a serious and inventive writer for more than 25 years, though he has rarely gained popular acceptance. He first received international attention with *Oh Dad, Poor Dad, Mama's Hung You in the Closet and I'm Feelin' So Sad* (1960), a brilliant parody of the Oedipus complex. Since *Oh Dad* he has written a number of plays that experiment with dramatic form, most notably *The Day the Whores Came Out to Play Tennis* (1964), a comic portrayal of social-climbing country-clubbers; *Indians* (1968), a study of genocide of the Indians by white Americans; *Wings* (1978), a portrait of a stroke victim; *The End of the World* (1984), a dark comedy about nuclear proliferation; and *The Road to Nirvana* (1990), a scatological comedy about the business of Hollywood. Kopit also wrote the book for the musical

Nine (1982) and a version of *Phantom of the Opera* (1991).   DBW

Koster and Bial's Music Hall 116–117 West 23rd St., NYC. Built in 1869 as the 23rd Street Opera House, it was leased to **Dan Bryant** and his **minstrel**s the following year. After Bryant's death in 1875, it passed to other managers and eventually to the partnership of John Koster and Albert Bial in 1879. Replacing the stage with a small platform, enlarging the building, and adding outdoor gardens, the partners transformed it into Koster and Bial's Music Hall, a concert saloon that dispensed alcoholic beverages with variety entertainment – skirting existing laws against serving both in the same establishment by using a giant fan as a curtain, which fell apart to reveal the performers. However, when the laws were tightened, they abandoned this enterprise and fell in with **Oscar Hammerstein [I]** to create Koster and Bial's New Music Hall on West 34th Street. The old theatre struggled along for a few more years and was torn down in 1924, but the newer theatre had an even shorter life and was eventually razed to become part of Macy's Department Store in 1901.   MCH

Krasna, Norman (1909–84) Long Island–born playwright, screenwriter, and critic whose early Broadway successes *Louder, Please* (1931), *Small Miracle* (1934), *The Man with Blonde Hair* (directed, 1941), and *Who Was That Lady I Saw You With?* (1958) were followed by the lesser works *Time for Elizabeth* (with Groucho **Marx,** 1948), *Love in E Flat* (1967), and *We Interrupt This Program* (1975). He adapted his *Small Miracle, Dear Ruth, John Loves Mary, Kind Sir,* and *Sunday in New York* to film, and captured screen credits for more than 25 films, including *Princess O'Rourke* (Academy Award, 1943). The plays *Dear Ruth* (1944), a lightweight sex comedy, and *Sunday in New York* (1961) were highlights of a promising Broadway career more attuned to Hollywood.   GSA

Kroll, Jack (19?–) Drama critic for *Newsweek* since the 1960s, Kroll, elusive about his career, has a reputation for fairness and taste in his criticism. An accurate judge of new plays, he writes lucid, knowledgeable, and eloquent opinions in the terse *Newsweek* style for an educated readership. He described **Breuer**'s *The Gospel at Colonus* (1988) as "a triumph of reconciliation, bringing together black and white, Pagan and Christian, ancient and modern in a sunburst of joy that seems to touch the secret heart of civilization itself."   TLM

Kronenberger, Louis (1904–80) Drama critic. Born and educated in Cincinnati, Kronenberger began his career as an editor for Boni and Liveright (1926), Alfred A. Knopf (1933), and *Fortune Magazine* (1935). He was drama critic for *Time* magazine (1938–61) and *PM* (1940–8), gaining a reputation as a demanding but stylish and elegant writer. *Variety* placed him second in toughness among New York critics in 1942–3. He adapted Jean Anouilh's *Mademoiselle Colombe* for Broadway in 1954; edited the *Best Play* Series during 1952–61; and taught at Brandeis University during 1951–70. His books include *The Thread of Laughter* (1952) and his memoirs, *No Whippings, No Gold Watches* (1970).   TLM

> *See:* F. Dyer, "Louis Kronenberger: A Critical Perspective of His Life and Career," PhD diss., U of Nebraska–Lincoln, 1992.

Kruger, Otto (1885–1974) Stage, screen, and television actor who began in **vaudeville** and stock companies. Some note his first appearance in 1900, but Kruger's first professional roles were with a Kansas company during 1906–9. His debut as Jack Bowling in *The Natural Way* (1915) extended to 32 Broadway productions and roles in Chicago, San Francisco, Los Angeles, and touring companies. He succeeded Noël Coward in *Private Lives* (1931), **George M. Cohan** in *The Meanest Man in the World* (1921), and **Paul Muni** in *Counsellor-at-Law* (1931). Between 1923 and 1959, he made 71 films. His television career, begun in 1934, included several 1950s TV playhouses.   RW

Krutch, Joseph Wood (1893–1970) Drama critic. Born in Knoxville, Krutch was educated at the University of Tennessee and Columbia University (MA, PhD) before becoming drama critic for *The Nation* (1924–52); also, he held the **Brander Matthews** Chair of Dramatic Literature at Columbia University during 1943–52. A scholarly critic, Krutch wanted size and style in the American drama but found **Eugene O'Neill** "almost alone among modern dramatic writers" possessing such traits. In the early 1950s, poor health forced him to move to Arizona, where he lived in the desert, writing on natural history. His theatre books include *Comedy and Conscience After the Restoration* (1924) and *The American Drama Since 1918* (1939, rev. 1957).   TLM

Kummer (née Beecher), Clare [Rodman] (1873?–1958) A prolific writer who created a Broadway play almost annually, beginning with her greatest hit, ***Good Gracious Annabelle!*** (1916). In addition to several original plays – such as *Be Calm, Camilla* (1918), *A Successful Calamity* (1917,

written as a vehicle for **William Gillette**), *Rollo's Wild Oat* (1920), *Pomeroy's Past* (1926), and *Her Master's Voice* (1933) – she also successfully adapted foreign plays and wrote a **Florenz Ziegfeld** adaptation of *Annabelle!* called *Annie, Dear*. Although her plays were criticized for their weak plots and contrived situations, audiences enjoyed her humorous dialogue and her pleasant, rather eccentric characters.   FB

Kurtz, Swoosie (1944–) Actress who made her debut at the **Cincinnati Playhouse in the Park** (1966), then **Off-Broadway** in *The Effect of Gamma Rays on Man-in-the-Moon Marigolds* (1970). Portraying "eccentrics with an edge," she received Tony nominations (*Tartuffe,* **Circle in the Square,** 1977), Tonys (***Fifth of July,*** 1981; *The **House of Blue Leaves,*** **Lincoln Center,** 1986), Obies (**Wasserstein**'s *Uncommon Women and Others,* Phoenix Theatre, 1977; *House of Blue Leaves*), and Drama Desk Awards (**Durang**'s *A History of American Film,* 1978; *Fifth of July*). She was recently in **McNally**'s *Lips Together, Teeth Apart* (**Manhattan Theatre Club,** 1991). Her films include *The World According to Garp* (1982) and *Dangerous Liaisons* (1989). Kurtz, in television's "Sisters" (1991–), won Emmys for "Love, Sidney" (1982, 1983).   REK

Kurz Stadt Theater Successful German-language theatre, also known as the German Stock Company, organized by Heinrich Kurz in 1868 in Milwaukee. The company offered 22 seasons, totaling 1,800 productions, until Kurz sold the theatre (217 Third St.) to Frederick Pabst in 1890. Kurz's first business manager, Eduard Härting came from New York's **Stadt Theater Company.** Kurz engaged such German notables as Ludwig Barnay, Franziska Ellmenreich, Friedrich Mitterwurzer, and Ernst von Possart. The company maintained a balanced repertory of popular comedies and German classics. Supported primarily by its box office income, deficits were subsidized by Milwaukee's leading German families.   RE

> *See:* G. W. Gadberry in W. Durham, ed., *American Theatre Companies, 1749–1887,* Westport, CT, 1986.

L

La Cage Aux Folles Two-act musical comedy, music and lyrics by **Jerry Herman,** book by **Harvey Fierstein;** opened 21 August 1983 at the **Palace Theatre,** running 1,716 performances. Based on a French play by Jean Poiret and the subsequent French movie, this was the first large-budget Broadway musical to treat the subject of homosexuality, as two gay men (**George Hearn,** Gene Barry) who own the eponymous transvestite nightclub strive to appear "normal" to impress the family of one of the men's son's fiancée [see **gay/lesbian theatre**]. The extravagant production numbers set in the club (including "The Best of Times Is Now") featured a "female" chorus line with two women among the many men in drag [see **female/male impersonation**], inviting the audience to try to pick out the real women. The show won the Tony Award for best musical. JD

Lackaye, Wilton (1862–1932) Actor who began his professional career in 1883 as Lucentio in **Lawrence Barrett**'s revival of **Boker**'s *Francesca da Rimini.* During a very active career he played hundreds of roles for many managements. In 1886 he supported **Fanny Davenport** at the **Union Square Theatre.** In 1906 he adapted Hugo's *Les Misérables* into the play *Law and the Man,* in which he played Jean Valjean and M. Madeleine. He is remembered, however, as the original Svengali in Du Maurier's *Trilby* (1895), which he revived frequently. A devout Catholic, he founded the Catholic Actors' Guild and assisted with the organization of the **Actors' Equity Association.** DBW

Lacy, Suzanne (1945–) California-born **performance art**ist, writer, and social activist who first studied zoology and psychology, and then social design at California Institute of the Arts (MFA, 1972). Lacy's pageantlike performances are influenced by Judy Chicago's Feminist Art Program (1970–1) and **Allan Kaprow**'s aesthetic of daily life. Her community-building performance strategies include extensive community dialogues that incorporate women's consciousness raising, media analysis, and practices of resistance. In *Three Weeks in May* (1977) Lacy protested violence against women. In *Black Madonna* (1986), performed primarily by women of color as a *tableaux-vivant,* she confronted racism. *Whisper, the Waves, the Wind* (1984) addressed aging and *The Crystal Quilt* (1987) was a dramatic reclamation of social space for women. AF

Lady in the Dark Two-act musical comedy, music by **Kurt Weill,** lyrics by **Ira Gershwin,** book by **Moss Hart;** opened 23 January 1941 at the **Alvin Theatre,** running 467 performances. This inventive musical follows the attempts of magazine editor Liza Elliot (**Gertrude Lawrence**) to resolve the romantic and professional complications of her life through psychoanalysis. Basically a straight play with musical interludes, the music is confined almost entirely to the four elaborate dream sequences she relates in her therapy. The sole exception is "My Ship," a melody that draws her into her dreams and (like the "Mysterious Melody" in *Naughty Marietta*) ultimately provides the key to resolution. The score, an effective amalgam of Weill's European and American styles, was the first to which Ira Gershwin wrote lyrics since his brother George's death. The show also made a star of Danny Kaye, who introduced the tongue-twisting "Tchaikowsky." JD

Lafayette Players (1915–32) An **African-American** stock company organized by actress Anita Bush to provide dramatic entertainment for the Harlem community in place of **vaudeville** and **minstrel shows** that often ridiculed blacks. On a weekly schedule the company presented at the **Lafayette Theatre** abridged versions of popular Broadway comedies and melodramas, hoping to demonstrate that black actors could play dramatic roles as well as song-and-dance clowns. As these productions gained popular support, the Players formed road companies for touring. In 1928 they moved to Los Angeles, where they played successfully to mixed audiences. Overall, they compiled a production record of 250 plays over 17 years before becoming a casualty of the Depression. Among well-recognized former players are **Charles Gilpin,** Clarence Muse, "Dooley" Wilson, Inez Clough, Evelyn Ellis, and Abbie Mitchell. EGH

Lafayette Theatre Located in Harlem at 132nd Street and Seventh Avenue, this theatre had been home to the **Lafayette Players** for 13 years (1915–28) when they moved to Los Angeles. During their Harlem period, the company produced cut versions of standard commercial plays on a weekly basis, sharing the stage with musical **revue**s, **vaudeville** acts, and feature films. During the era of the **Federal Theatre Project** (1935–9), the Lafayette became headquarters for the Negro Theatre Unit in Harlem. It was here that **Orson Welles** produced the well-known "voodoo" *Macbeth* (1936). The theatre's main auditorium was eventually turned into a church. The New Lafayette Theatre established by Robert Macbeth in 1966 used a rehearsal hall in a second-floor wing of the old building; this wing burned down in 1968. EGH

Lahr, Bert (né Irving Lahrheim) (1895–1967) Comic actor. After an apprenticeship in juvenile **vaudeville** acts, Lahr broke into **burlesque** as a Dutch comedian. His first feature part, a punch-drunk fighter in *Hold Everything* (1928), won him critical acclaim and starring roles in musical comedies: *Flying High* (1930), *Hot-Cha!* (1932), and *The Show Is On* (1936). Lahr's stock-in-trade included a grimace like that "of a camel with acute gastric disorder" and a laryngeal bleat "like a love-sick ram." His style was too broad for film, although he is immortalized as the Cowardly Lion in *The Wizard of Oz* (1938). He returned to Broadway in *Du Barry Was a Lady* (1939). Lahr considered the turning point in his career to be Estragon in *Waiting for Godot* (1956), an association with the avant-garde that brought him roles in Shaw, Molière, and Shakespeare (Bottom). He enlivened five roles in **S. J. Perelman**'s *The Beauty Part* (1962). Lahr never retired but died during the shooting of *The Night They Raided* **Minsky**'s. LS

See: J. Lahr, *Notes on a Cowardly Lion*, New York, 1969.

Lahr, John (1941–) Drama critic and author. Born in Los Angeles, Lahr studied at Yale and Oxford University. He worked as a dramaturge for the **Guthrie Theatre** (1968) and for the Repertory Theatre of **Lincoln Center** (1969–71). He has served as contributing editor of *Evergreen Review*, theatre editor of *Grove Press*, and drama critic of the *Village Voice*. Lahr asks that theatre be socially responsible and forge new images to "revitalize the imaginative life of its audience." Such theatre, he feels, must be "shocking, violent, and unpredictable." Lahr is the author of 15 books, including a biography of his father, comedian **Bert Lahr**, and a biography of playwright Joe Orton, *Prick Up Your Ears* (1978). His stage version of *The Manchurian Candidate* (updated to 1996) premiered at London's Lyric Hammersmith Theatre in 1991. TLM

La MaMa Off-Off Broadway theatre founded in 1962 by **Ellen Stewart**, a self-described Cajun who arrived penniless in New York in 1950 and became a successful fashion designer. With her earnings, she began Café La MaMa in a cramped, decrepit Manhattan basement, and moved several times before settling on East 4th Street in 1969, where the theatre now operates two large performance spaces and a cabaret. The Café became La MaMa ETC (Experimental Theatre Club), and Stewart still functions as artistic director, fundraiser, tour manager, and maternal spiritual guardian. Having produced more than 1,000 plays, La MaMa introduced such important American playwrights and directors as **Rochelle Owens, Megan Terry,** Jeff Weiss, **Sam Shepard, Harvey Fierstein,** H. M. Koutoukas, **Lanford Wilson, Julie**

Bovasso, Adrienne Kennedy, and **Tom O'Horgan,** also presenting works by avant-garde directors **Richard Foreman, Meredith Monk, Ping Chong,** and others. In addition, La MaMa has brought to America such artists as Jerzy Grotowski, **Andrei Serban,** Peter Brook, Eugenio Barba, and Tadeusz Kantor. In 1980 La MaMa established the Third World Institute of Theatre Arts and Studies (TWITAS). Through the 1980s and '90s, the La MaMa cabaret has provided a venue for new experimentation in comedy and **performance art.** AS

Lamos, Mark (1946–) Director, actor, and artistic director of **Hartford Stage Company** (1980–). An innovative director of opera and the classics, Lamos specializes in expansive productions emphasizing the spectacular and the fantastic. While remaining faithful to the texts, Lamos alters periods, settings, and moods. His popular *Twelfth Night* (1985) was staged as a late-night party with **Cole Porter** piano background, and his dreamlike *Pericles* (1987) borrowed imagery from both Magritte and the Neo-Expressionists. A *commedia*-inspired *School for Wives* (1988) featured an Arnolphe in the style of Charlie Chaplin. His visually arresting, two-part *Peer Gynt* (1989) starred **Richard Thomas.** The first American to work with a Soviet company, Lamos directed **O'Neill**'s *Desire Under the Elms* at Moscow's Pushkin Theatre (1988). Lamos also develops new plays, notably the work of **Eric Overmyer** and **Constance Congdon;** his production of Timberlake Wertenbaker's *Our Country's Good* (1990) moved from Hartford Stage to Broadway (1991), receiving six Tony nominations. HFP

Landesman, Heidi (1951–) Set and costume designer, producer. One of the more boldly theatrical designers, Landesman often combines semiabstract elements with realistic detail to create striking, dramatic images. On a more intimate scale this has worked well with **Marsha Norman**'s *'night, Mother* (1982) and **Tina Howe**'s *Painting Churches* (1983). For a 1982 *A Midsummer Night's Dream,* she landscaped Central Park's Delacorte Theater with trees, shrubs, and grass. Her large-scale productions include *Big River* (1985) and *The Secret Garden* (1991), the latter using the motif of a child's **toy theatre.** She coproduced and won Tonys for both. AA

Landesman, Rocco (1947–) Producer. A graduate of the Yale School of Drama, where he remained as a faculty member until 1978, Landesman subsequently moved into the stock market and also became the owner of a string of race horses. Coproducing *Big River* (1985; with wife, **Heidi**) and subsequently *Into the Woods* brought him back into the theatre. In 1987 he became president of **Jujamcyn Theaters,** the third largest theatre owner on Broadway, for whom he has overseen a series of successes, including *City of Angels,* a *Gypsy* revival, The *Piano Lesson,* and *Grand Hotel.* DBW

Landscape of the Body by **John Guare** premiered on 12 October 1977 at the **Public Theater**

A scene from the Hartford Stage Company production of Shakespeare's *A Midsummer Night's Dream*, directed by Mark Lamos. Photo: T. Charles Erickson. Courtesy: Hartford Stage.

in New York. John Pasquin directed a cast including Shirley Knight, **F. Murray Abraham,** Peg Murray, and Paul McCrane. In 1984, Gary Sinise directed a successful revival at the Second Stage in New York. An absurdist study of the nature of innocence and experience, the play depicts the journey of Betty Yearn, who comes to Greenwich Village from Bangor, ME, to save her sister Rosalie from a seedy life as a porn actress. In the course of the play, Rosalie is killed, and Betty inhabits her life. She becomes a suspect in the murder of her 14-year-old son Bert, who has been luring gay men to their apartment and robbing them. Betty ends up on the Nantucket ferry with the investigating detective, throwing bottles containing her life's confession into the ocean.   BCM

Langfelder, Dulcena (1955–) Corporeal **mime,** choreographer. After training with Etienne Decroux, Langfelder was a founding member of Omnibus (Jean Asslin and Denise Boulanger, directors) in Montréal (1978–82). Her solo works include *Vicious Circle* (1985), *Lady Next Door* (1988), and *Hockey! O.K.?* (1991).   TL

Langham, Michael (1919–) English director who began his theatre career directing *Twelfth Night* at Coventry's Midland Theatre Company (1946). In the next decade, Langham became a reputable classical director in England and Scotland, but North

American work has comprised most of his career. After productions at Toronto's Crest Theatre (1955), he was appointed **Tyrone Guthrie**'s successor as Artistic Director of the Stratford (Ontario) Festival in 1955. Langham enjoyed great success expanding the Festival to include touring, film, and television projects, a training program, and school performances. Though critically praised, he was criticized often for employing too many Britains. After departing in 1968, Langham directed in English and American venues until 1971, when he was named Artistic Director at the **Guthrie Theatre,** Minneapolis. Again following in his mentor's footsteps, Langham used his Stratford techniques to pull the Guthrie from near financial disaster. In 1979 he left to become Director of Drama at the Juilliard School, where he was responsible for all training and theatrical productions until 1992.   KN

Langner, Lawrence (1890–1962) One of the most enlightened producers in American theatre history, Langner grew up in London and studied to be a patent lawyer. In 1911 he emigrated to New York and established himself in that profession, later heading a large international firm. In 1914 he helped organize the **Washington Square Players** and wrote several one-act plays for the group. After it disbanded because of the war (1917), he brought together members of the group in late 1918 to form the **Theatre Guild.** The most important of these was **Theresa Helburn** who, together with Langner, managed the organization throughout much of its active life. They pursued artistic aims and built a subscription audience of 25,000 by 1925. The success of their second production, *John Ferguson* (1919), established them artistically and commercially. Langner encouraged the production of foreign plays, including works by Toller, Kaiser, Molnár, and Pirandello. He obtained for the Guild **Shaw**'s *Heartbreak House* (1919), *Back to Methuselah* (1921), and *St. Joan* (1923), and he persuaded the Guild to stage **O'Neill**'s *Strange Interlude* (1928). With his wife, Armina Marshall, Langner built the Westport County Playhouse in 1931 and formed an acting company. In the early 1950s he founded the **American Shakespeare Festival** at Stratford, CT. Called by **Brooks Atkinson** "one of the most articulate men alive," Langner brought an able business mind to bear upon the American theatre for almost 50 years. TLM

See: L. Langner, *The Magic Curtain*, New York, 1951.

Langtry, Lillie (née Emily Charlotte le Breton) (1853–1929) English actress and society beauty, born in Jersey, of which her father, the Very Reverend William le Breton, was Dean. She made her London social debut in 1877 and her theatrical debut under the Bancrofts at the Haymarket in 1881. Her notoriety was enhanced by Millais's portrait of her, holding a Jersey lily; and it was as "the Jersey Lily" that she continued to draw audiences in England, South Africa, and, most of all, in the U.S. (where she debuted in 1882 and made numerous visits) until her retirement in 1918. At best a competent actress and a shrewd company manager, she was best known in this country in *Gossip* (1895) and Sydney Grundy's *The Degenerates* (1899), the latter scandalizing her public by offering glimpses of autobiographical sin in high society. The author of an evasive autobiography, *The Days I Knew* (1921), she died in her villa in Monte Carlo. PT DBW

See: N. Gerson, *Because I Loved Him*, New York, 1971; P. Sichel, *The Jersey Lily*, New York, 1958.

Lanier, Sidney (1923–) The cigar-chomping minister of St. Clement's Church on West 46th Street in New York during 1960–5, known to stage liturgical plays instead of delivering sermons. Together with director **Wynn Handman** and actor Michael Tolin, Lanier founded the **American Place Theatre** in 1964. Brooklyn born of Southern parents, he is a distant relative of **Tennessee Williams** and a collateral descendent of poet Sidney Lanier. He now heads the New American Place, a San Francisco center for ethical colloquies. CLJ

Lansbury, Angela (Brigid) (1925–) London-born actress and singer who came to the U.S. for a career in films, under contract to MGM (1943–50), for whom she performed mostly supporting roles. In 1957 she made her Broadway debut in *Hotel Paradiso;* subsequently she appeared as the mother in *A Taste of Honey* (1960). Lansbury made her musical debut as the Mayor in the ill-fated *Anyone*

Can Whistle (1964) before winning the first of her four Tony Awards as the madcap "Auntie Mame" Dennis in *Mame* (1966). Her other Tonys were for performances as the eccentric Countess Aurelia in *Dear World* (1968), the compulsive Mama Rose in a revival of *Gypsy* (1974), and the maniacal Mrs. Lovett in *Sweeney Todd* (1979). She brought a powerful singing voice, a flair for comedy, and a rare depth of characterization to her musical roles. An actress of considerable versatility, she has also appeared with the Royal Shakespeare Company and at the Royal National Theatre of Great Britain. Since the mid-1980s she has starred as a quirky and personable writer and crime buff in the popular TV series "Murder, She Wrote." MK

See: M. Bonanno, *Angela Lansbury: A Biography*, New York, 1987.

Lapine, James Elliott (1949–) Playwright-director. Recognized initially for his plays (*Table Settings*, 1980; *Twelve Dreams*, 1983), Lapine emerged as a resourceful and imaginative director with his staging of William Finn's *March of the Falsettos* (1982). He successfully directed and wrote the books for **Sondheim**'s *Sunday in the Park with George* (1984) and *Into the Woods* (1987). His collaboration with Finn continued in 1990 when he coauthored and directed *Falsettoland*, the third installment of Finn's "Marvin Trilogy" (which had begun in 1979 with *In Trousers*). This **Off-Broadway** hit musical, dealing with AIDS and mortality, was called the first great musical of the 1990s and "a burst of genius" (**William A. Henry III**). Much of its success was due to Lapine's sensitive and intimate direction. Lapine directed and received a Tony as coauthor of the 1992 Broadway musical *Falsettos*, based on parts 2 and 3 of the trilogy. DBW

Larkin, Peter (1926–) Designer. Though not as innovative as his more famous contemporaries, Larkin was one of the major Broadway designers of the 1950s and '60s. His productions include *Dial M for Murder* (1952), *The Teahouse of the August Moon* (1953), the **Mary Martin** *Peter Pan* (1954), *Inherit the Wind* (1955), and *No Time for Sergeants* (1955). His theatre work continued through the 1980s with such productions as *Doonesbury* and *Dancin'*, but he became more active in films such as *Tootsie* and also designed for ballet. He has won four Tonys. AA

Last of the Red Hot Lovers by **Neil Simon;** opened 28 December 1969 at the **Eugene O'Neill Theatre** for 706 performances. This return to Simon's three discrete one-act play form provides stronger thematic integration through main character Barney Cashman (James Coco). The play examines the futility of the sexually promiscuous life-style of the 1960s from Barney's middle-aged viewpoint as he attempts to seduce three separate women in his mother's apartment on three different occasions. More significantly, Barney explicitly voices a notion that runs throughout Simon's work with his third-act realization that life's futility can only be endured by providing aid rather than seeking it. RW

Lateiner, Jacob see **Hurwitz, Moishe**

La Turista by **Sam Shepard**. Originally produced at New York's **American Place Theatre** on 4 March 1967 (29 performances), the play baffled critics and theatregoers alike with its shifting identities and nonlinear structure. Act I is set in a Mexican hotel room, where witch doctors visit a young couple suffering from "la turista." Act II occurs earlier, in an American hotel room; this time the doctors wear Civil War–era costumes. **Charles Marowitz** noted that if one did not already know Shepard's work, "*La Turista* would be a perfect case of the emperor's new clothes. But there is a consistency in Shepard and a richness of texture which encourages one to suspend judgment." FHL

Lauder, Harry (né Hugh MacLennan) (1870–1950) Scottish music-hall performer who became the highest paid British performer of his time. His repertory originally contained a whole gallery of Scottish types, but eventually he settled into a cozy, chuckling caricature of the canny Scot, invariably singing "I Love a Lassie" and "Roamin' in the Gloamin.'" A fixture on U.S. **vaudeville** stages, he made 22 tours of the U.S. between 1909 and 1932. He authored three autobiographies: *A Minstrel in France* (1918), *Between You and Me* (1919), and *Roamin' in the Gloamin'* (1928). LS

See: G. Irving, *Great Scot*, London, 1968.

Laughton, Charles (1899–1962) British-born actor who, with his actress wife Elsa Lanchester, became an American citizen in 1950. His first professional role, in *The Inspector General* (1926), was followed by parts including Hercule Poirot in *Alibi* and William Marble in *Payment Deferred*, the latter also marking his 1931 New York debut. At London's Old Vic (1933–4) he played in seven productions, including leading roles in *The Cherry Orchard*, *The Tempest*, and *Macbeth*. As the first English actor to perform at the Comédie-Française (1936), he appeared in *Le Médecin Malgré Lui*. After a decade of film work, he returned to the stage in 1947 with *Galileo*, adapted with **Brecht** and first performed in Los Angeles. For several years he toured the U.S. reading from the Bible, Shakespeare, and modern classics. As director and the Devil in **Shaw**'s *Don Juan in Hell* (1951), he earned critical acclaim. He played Bottom in *A Midsummer Night's Dream* and King Lear at Stratford-upon-Avon (1959). DBW

See: S. Callow, *Charles Laughton: A Difficult Actor*, New York, 1988; E. Lanchester, *Charles Laughton and I*, New York, 1938, and *Elsa Lanchester, Herself*, New York, 1983.

Laurents, Arthur (1918–) Screenwriter, director, and dramatist. Although not a great success in the theatre, *Home of the Brave* (1945), concerned with a Jewish soldier's wartime problems, won Laurents the interest of critics and a reputation for insight into human nature and an interest in character development and language. In *The Time of the Cuckoo* (1952), *A Clearing in the Woods* (1957), and *Invitation to a March* (1960), he wrote about women whose psychological problems drive them toward disaster. *The Bird Cage* (1950) builds upon the sexual frustrations of a vicious nightclub owner. Laurents is celebrated for writing the book for the musicals *West Side Story* (1957) and *Gypsy* (1959; revivals, 1974, 1989), *Hallelujah, Baby!* (1967), and the ill-fated *Nick and Nora* (1991; also directed). He also wrote the screenplay for *Anna Lucasta* (1949) and *Anastasia* (1956). Laurent's later work – *The Enclave* (1973) and *Heartsong* (1974) – has been less appreciated. WJM

Lavin, Linda (1937–) Maine-born actress who made her New York debut in 1960 with *Oh, Kay!*, establishing her career with such featured roles as Patsy Newquist in *Little Murders* (1969) and Elaine Nevazio in *The Last of the Red Hot Lovers* (1969; Tony nominee). In the 1970s appearances with the **New York Shakespeare Festival, Yale Repertory,** and **American Repertory Theatre** supplemented her work in television, which included Alice Hyatt in the CBS series "Alice" (1976–85). She created the Jewish mother Kate in **Neil Simon**'s *Broadway Bound* (1986), winning a Tony and critical acclaim. **Frank Rich** praised her "meticulously, deeply etched portrait of a woman who is a survivor, not a victim." In 1990 she replaced Tyne Daly as Rose in **Gypsy** on Broadway. TLM

Lawrence, Gertrude (1898–1952) English singer, dancer, and comedy actress. From infancy "Gertie" toured with her actress mother, making her own debut in 1910 as a dancer in *Babes in the Wood*. Her New York debut in *André Charlot's Revue of 1924* launched a brilliant American stage career in which *Lady in the Dark* (1941) and *The King and I* (1951) were high points. Noël Coward wrote *Private Lives* for her (she played Amanda), and they toured together in his *Tonight at 8:30* (1935). During WW II she entertained British and American troops. **John Mason Brown** described her as "a musical comedy performer" who "grew into an admirable actress." Vivacity, warmth, and a sense of fun characterized her remarkable stage presence. Her memoirs were published in 1945. FHL

See: S. Morley, *Gertrude Lawrence: A Biography*, New York, 1981.

Lawrence, Jerome (1915–) and **Robert E[dwin] Lee** (1918–) This pair of Ohio-born dramatists joined in formal partnership in 1942 and have since written dozens of plays, many produced in New York and most extremely popular with regional and amateur groups. Perhaps their best received effort was *Inherit the Wind* (1955), a faithful, flashy, dramatic retelling of the story of the famous Scopes "monkey trial." Also extremely popular was their adaptation of *Auntie Mame* (1956) and the subsequent musical version, *Mame* (1966), for which they wrote the libretto. Their play *The Night Thoreau Spent in Jail* (1970), a standard for several years with amateur groups, was an early offering of the American Playwrights' Theatre. This versatile and prolific team has also been responsible for many one-act operas, screenplays, television plays, and radio programs. A research center/archive at Ohio State University is named for them.   LDC

See: Studies in American Drama, 1945–Present (1992).

Lawson, John Howard (1895–1977) Playwright who, in the theatre of the 1920s, was an anomaly: a dramatist of fiery left-wing convictions. Striking out against the convention-bound commercial theatre on the one hand and the ivory tower art theatre on the other, he attempted to forge a new theatrical style, which he called "political vaudeville." His most successful experiment was *Processional* (1925), a staccato, fragmented series of sketches set in a West Virginia town during a coal strike. In 1926 he was a cofounder of the short-lived, politically radical New Playwrights' Theatre, for which he wrote a strident satire of political campaigning called *Loud Speaker*. Lawson changed his style in the 1930s, replacing extravagance with a richly idiomatic realism that had a strong influence on **Clifford Odets.** The eloquently embittered, working-class antiheroes of his *Success Story* (1932) and *Gentlewoman* (1934) speak a racy urban poetry. An active screenwriter (*Blockade, Action in the North Atlantic*) and a president of the Screen Writer's Guild, Lawson was imprisoned in 1948 for defending the Bill of Rights against the inquisition of the House Un-American Activities Committee. In 1949 he published a now standard work, *Theory and Technique of Playwriting and Screenwriting*.   FH

See: R. Gardner, "International Rag: The Theatrical Career of John Howard Lawson," PhD diss., U of California at Berkeley, 1977.

Layton, Joe (né Joseph Lichtman) (1931–) Theatre and ballet choreographer. As a dancer, Layton made his debut in *Oklahoma!* (1943) and continued dancing in *High Button Shoes* (1947), *Gentlemen Prefer Blondes* (1949), and *Wonderful Town* (1953). Layton's choreographic debut was *Once Upon a Mattress* (1959); in the same year, he choreographed another enormous success, *The Sound of Music.* He worked steadily as a choreographer, making the transition to director in *No Strings* (1962). Layton also revived **George M. Cohan**'s dances for the musical *George M!* (1968). Widely recognized for his work with Hollywood stars on their television specials, Layton has also ventured into ballet, producing works for the Royal Ballet (London) and the Joffrey Ballet.   LF

Leach, Wilford (1929–88) American director, teacher, playwright, and designer. Born in Virginia, Leach attended William and Mary and the University of Illinois (PhD) and then taught at Sarah Lawrence College. During 1970–7 he was artistic director of **La MaMa** ETC. From 1977 he worked mainly for the **New York Shakespeare Festival,** designing as well as directing productions. His major credits included: *Mandragola* (1977); *All's Well* and *The Taming of the Shrew* (1978); *Othello* (1979); *Mother Courage* (1980); *The Pirates*

of Penzance (1980); *The Human Comedy* (1983); *La Bohème* (1984); and *The Mystery of Edwin Drood* (1985). Leach's highly original style drew on **vaudeville,** film, animated cartoon, opera, and **puppet** theatre.   TLM

Leavitt, M[ichael] B[ennett] (1843–1935) Polish-born manager-impresario. A black-face minstrel in the 1850s, Leavitt, after establishing several minstrel troupes under his control, created the first fairly reputable early burlesque show in the U.S. Substituting female performers for male actors, he first feminized a **minstrel show** (Mme. Rentz's Female Minstrels) in 1870, ultimately merging this show, **vaudeville,** and musicalized travesty into what he called **burlesque,** originally in The **Rentz–Santley** Novelty and Burlesque Company (starring Mabel Santley). Leavitt burlesque eschewed the earlier classic, satiric focus for greater suggestiveness and lusty humor. A typical Leavitt afterpiece, *Anthony and Cleopatra,* with Octobus Sweezur, Cheesi Hankipanki, and Hoctasuper, became a favorite of burlesque comics. Leavitt also operated two chains of legitimate theatres. Retiring in 1912, he published that year a sprawling 700-page memoir, *Fifty Years in Theatrical Management.*   DBW

Leblang, Joe (?–1931) Hungarian-born refugee who, beginning in the 1890s, developed by 1913 a thriving cut-rate ticket brokerage in Gray's Drugstore – for years a gathering place for out-of-work actors – where he ran a shoeshine stand. He did so well that, in 1914, he bought the drugstore; eventually, he also bought the building (the Fitzgerald, 43rd St. and Broadway), which included **George M. Cohan's Theatre,** built in 1911 for the musical comedy star and producer. By 1930 Leblang's, New York's leading brokerage, sold over five million tickets annually. After his death, his wife Tillie carried on until shortly after WW II.   DBW

LeCompte, Elizabeth (1944–) American director and playwright and, since 1979, artistic director of the experimental theatre **collective** known as the **Wooster Group.** With **Spalding Gray** and other members of the group, she cowrote and directed *Sakonnet Point* (1975), *Rumstick Road* (1977), and *Nayatt School* (1978), a trilogy called *Three Places in Rhode Island;* in 1979 LeCompte and the Group created an "epilogue" (without dialogue) to this trilogy called *Point Judith.* She was also instrumental in the creation of *Route 1 & 9* (1981) and *L. S. D.* (1984), and participated in the creation of such pieces as *Frank Dell's the Temptation of St. Antony* (1987), *. . . Just the High Points . . .* (1988–9), and *Brace Up!* (1991), the last an epilogue to the company's *The Road to Immortality.* In 1984 she was appointed Associate Director of the short-lived American National Theatre (under **Peter Sellars**) at the **John F. Kennedy Center for the Performing Arts.** In the 1980s and '90s she has been a leader in the nourishing of a sometimes radical avant-garde theatre in New York.   DBW

Lederer, George W. (1861–1938) Producer who originated, with *The Passing Show* (1894), the U.S. version of the musical **revue.** He also pioneered the form and many of the features of American and English musical comedy in producing *The Belle of New York* (1897), *Florodora* (1899), and *Madame Sherry* (1910). Lederer managed vaudeville companies, New York theatres (**Casino, New York Theatre**), was the agent for **Lillian Russell** and other leading players, and produced motion pictures.   WD

Lee, Canada (né Leonard Canegata) (1907–52) African-American actor whose successful boxing career was halted by an eye injury, yet whose fighting spirit was manifested in several memorable roles. He played Blacksnake in the 1934 revival of the antilynching drama *Stevedore,* Banquo in the **Federal Theatre**'s "voodoo" *Macbeth* (dir. **Welles,** 1936), and the emperor Christophe in *Haiti* (1938). His finest performance was as Bigger Thomas in **Richard Wright**'s *Native Son* (1941). Lee played Caliban in **Margaret Webster**'s 1945 production of *The Tempest* and a whiteface Bosola in *The Duchess of Malfi* (1946). He was a powerful actor of animal-like grace who was committed to a theatre of social relevance.   EGH

Lee, Eugene (1939–) Set designer, unique among American designers in both concept and execution. Approaching each production without preconceived ideas, Lee treats the whole space of the theatre – not only the stage – as a place to be designed. From the late 1960s onward (except for 1989–90) he was resident designer for the **Trinity Repertory Company** in Providence, RI, and for seven years head of design at the **Dallas Theater Center.** Together with director **Adrian Hall** he created iconoclastic, often environmental, settings. He brought environmental design to **Off-Broadway** and Broadway with *Slaveship, Alice in Wonderland,* and *Candide.* Even with more conventional productions his sets tend to be large and use moving parts and real materials. Lee has worked with Peter Brook in Shiraz and Paris and with **Harold Prince** on several shows, including *Sweeney Todd.* He also designed television's "Saturday Night Live" from its inception to 1980, and several TV specials as well as concert tours for Paul Simon.   AA

Lee (née Newman), Franne (1941–) Costume designer who began her career at the Theatre of the Living Arts in Philadelphia in 1969, and went on to design costumes for **Andre Gregory**'s *Alice in Wonderland* and Peter Brook's productions of *Orghast* and *Kaspar.* She won Tonys for her costumes for *Candide* and *Sweeney Todd.* Lee was the original costume designer for television's "Saturday Night Live." Film work includes *Dead Ringers* and *One Trick Pony.* Much of her work through the 1970s was done in collaboration with former husband, set designer **Eugene Lee.**   AA

Lee, Gypsy Rose (née Rose Louise Hovick) (1914?–70) **Burlesque** artist and writer. After performing a child-act with her sister **June (Havoc)**

in **vaudeville** (1922–8), she starred in **Minsky**'s Burlesque by the age of 17. Her act comprised more "tease" than "strip," tantalizing with suggestive silk stockings, lace panties, and a rose-garter tossed into the audience as a coda. H. L. Mencken coined the term "ecdysiast" to label her speciality, and her sophisticated pose was parodied in the musical *Pal Joey* (1940). Seen in the *Ziegfeld Follies of 1936,* **nightclubs,** fairs, and carnivals, she was the first celebrity stripper [see **nudity**]. Her writings include a play, *The Naked Genius* (1943); some murder mysteries; and a memoir, *Gypsy* (published 1957), turned into a popular musical comedy (1959). Her final major creative effort was a **one-person** show called *A Curious Evening with Gypsy Rose Lee* (1958), though in the 1960s she appeared frequently on television.   LS

See: J. Havoc, *Early Havoc,* New York, 1959; E. L. Preminger, *Gypsy and Me,* Boston, 1984.

Lee, Ming Cho (1930–) Generally considered the current doyen of American set designers, his style and technique have significantly influenced the look of opera and theatre design since the mid-1960s. Lee was born in Shanghai and studied Chinese watercolor before emigrating to the U.S. in 1949. In 1954 he became an assistant to **Jo Mielziner,** to whose poetic realism Lee's trademark spare, minimalist, emblematic style – best exemplified in the 1964 production of *Electra* at the **New York Shakespeare Festival** – was, in part, a response. Lee is usually associated with pipe-work scaffolding, textured surfaces, and collage; but since the late 1970s, his work has turned to detail and ultra-realism, as in the production of *K2,* for which he created a mountain on the stage. He is constantly working with new materials and new approaches. Despite his importance, he has designed little on Broadway: Much of his work has been with the New York Shakespeare Festival and regional theatres, as well as for opera – most notably, the New York City Opera. Since the mid-1980s Lee, who heads the design program at the Yale School of Drama, has devoted more time to teaching.   AA

Lee, Robert E. see **Lawrence, Jerome**

Leftwich, Alexander (1884–1947) Producer and director. From staging plays for the **Frohman**s and **Shubert**s (c. 1915–26), Leftwich became a leading director of musicals, including *Hit the Deck* (1927), *A Connecticut Yankee* (1927), *Rain or Shine* (1928), *Strike Up the Band* (1930), and *Girl Crazy* (1930). He later produced films in Hollywood.   TLM

Le Gallienne, Eva (1899–1991) Best known as an actress, the London-born Le Gallienne participated in every aspect of American theatre. Her New York debut was in *Mrs. Boltay's Daughter* (1915), but her first big success was as Julie in *Liliom* (1921). For the next 60-plus years Le Gallienne played most of the major female roles in Western drama, receiving critical acclaim for performances in plays by **Ibsen, Chekhov,** and **Shakespeare,** as well as for her Queen Elizabeth both in Schiller's *Mary Stuart* and **Maxwell Anderson's** *Elizabeth the Queen.* She described her acting technique as "getting rid of 'Me' in order to become the part."

Le Gallienne's contribution to American theatre included more than her considerable acting skill. She introduced audiences throughout the country to Ibsen, Chekhov, and French playwrights through her translations and productions of their plays. A lifelong proponent of repertory theatre, Le Gallienne founded the **Civic Repertory Theatre** (1926–33), where she produced, directed, and starred, offering quality theatre at bargain ticket prices. The Civic presented 1,581 performances of over 30 plays, including many of the classics, **Glaspell's** *Alison's House, Peter Pan* (in which Le Gallienne was the first actress to "fly"), and *Alice in Wonderland* (adaptation by Le Gallienne and Florida Friebus). In 1946, Le Gallienne, **Cheryl Crawford,** and **Margaret Webster** founded the **American Repertory Company,** which lasted only one season.

Le Gallienne directed and acted for the National Repertory Theatre (1961–6), and acted in a revival of *The Royal Family* (1976), *To Grandmother's House We Go* (1981), the brief revival of *Alice in Wonderland* (1982; her last stage appearance), and the film *Resurrection* (1980). She also published her translations of **Ibsen** and **Chekhov,** a biography of Eleonora Duse, and two autobiographies – *At 33* (1934) and *With a Quiet Heart* (1953). In addition, she garnered most of the major awards in American performing arts, including Woman of the Year (1947), ANTA (1964, 1977), a special Tony (1964), an Emmy (1978), and the National Medal of Arts (1986). FB

> *See:* R. A. Schanke, *Eva Le Gallienne: A Bio-Bibliography,* Westport, CT, 1989, and *Shattered Applause: The Lives of Eva Le Gallienne,* Carbondale, IL, 1992.

Leiber, Fritz (1883–1949)

Leading actor who began as a member of the Ben **Greet Players** in 1902, playing Shakespearean roles and making his debut in New York in 1905 as Macduff in *Macbeth.* After several silent films and one year with **Julia Marlowe,** he became a leading actor with **Robert Mantell,** playing numerous Shakespearean roles. In 1920 he married Mantell's leading actress, Virginia Bronson, and formed the **Shakespeare** Repertory Company, touring extensively until 1929, when he founded the Chicago Civic Shakespeare Society. Lured to Hollywood in the 1930s with the prospect of playing Shakespearean roles on film, he instead played small character roles (e.g., Franz Liszt in the 1943 *Phantom of the Opera*). The Leiber Collection is at the University of Illinois. RE

> *See:* H. H. Diers, "Fritz Leiber, Actor and Producer of Shakespeare," PhD diss., U of Illinois, 1965.

Lenya, Lotte (née Karoline Blamauer)

(1900–81) Vienna-born actress and singer who went to Germany to begin an acting career. In 1928 she appeared in the Berlin premiere of *The Threepenny Opera.* After immigrating to the U.S. with her husband, composer **Kurt Weill,** she made her Broadway debut in *The Eternal Road* (1937). She appeared in several plays and musicals, but is remembered for the **Off-Broadway** production of *The Threepenny Opera* (1954), the **revue** *Brecht on Brecht* (1961), and the musical *Cabaret* (1966). MK

> *See:* D. Spoto, *Lenya: A Life,* Boston, 1989.

Lerner, Alan Jay (1918–86) and Frederick Loewe (1904–88)

Lyricist and composer. Loewe, a classically trained composer born in Vienna, and Lerner, who had studied at Juilliard and Harvard, collaborated on their first musical score, *What's Up?,* in 1943. Four years later the team had its first major success with *Brigadoon,* a fantasy set in a magical Scottish village. Their next show, *Paint Your Wagon,* achieved a modest run. In 1956, Lerner and Loewe wrote the score for *My Fair Lady,* a musical version of George Bernard **Shaw's** *Pygmalion.* One of the most successful musical comedies ever produced, *My Fair Lady*'s score was a perfect blending of Loewe's operetta music with Lerner's pseudo-Shavian lyrics. Their next show, *Camelot* (1960), was generally conceded to be inferior to its predecessor. Lerner and Loewe collaborated on only one other Broadway musical, a 1973 adaptation of their film *Gigi.* After Loewe's retirement, Lerner worked with other composers on a number of shows.

Loewe's music successfully combined the older operetta tradition with more modern Broadway musical idioms. Lerner's versatility as a lyricist was demonstrated in songs whose styles ranged from the sophisticated verbal trickery of **Lorenz Hart** to the simple treatment of **Oscar Hammerstein II.** MK

> *See:* A. J. Lerner, *The Street Where I Live,* New York, 1978.

Lesbian theatre see Gay and lesbian theatre

Leslie, Amy [Brown; Buck] (née Lillie West)

(1860–1939) Drama critic of the Chicago *Daily News.* An actress early in life, Leslie's reviews and profiles of nearly every famous player of her day were marked by an effusive, star-struck quality. As **Ben Hecht** recalled in *Theatre Arts* magazine (July 1951), "Her prose was ornate and endless . . . No drama critic I have read since, not even **Alexander Woollcott,** could swoon as madly in front of the footlights as our Amy Leslie." She helped make the career of adventurer Frank "Bring 'em Back Alive" Buck, whom she married when she was 35 and he was a 20-year-old bellboy. SF

Lester, Edwin (1895–)

Producer. After establishing himself in the Los Angeles music business (1923–33), Lester organized the Los Angeles Light Opera Festival (1935). He later founded the San Francisco Civic Light Opera Association (1937) and the Los Angeles Civic Light Opera Association (1938), managing both groups until he retired in 1976. His most notable productions include world premieres of *Song of Norway* (1944), *Kismet* (1953), and *Gigi* (1973). TLM

Leve, Samuel (1910–) Russian-born designer who began his career with the **Federal Theatre Project** and the **Mercury Theatre,** where his designs included **Orson Welles**'s *Julius Caesar* (1937). He then worked for **Maurice Schwartz**'s **Yiddish Art Theatre.** On Broadway he designed productions for **Maurice Evans, Katharine Cornell,** and **Judith Anderson.** As a designer for the Metropolitan Opera he created a notable unit set for *The Flying Dutchman;* in the 1950s he designed extensively for television.   AA

Levene (né Levine), Sam[uel] (1905–80) One of the more durable character actors on the New York stage for over 50 years, Levene specialized in roles that capitalized on his dour expression and his prominent New York accent, frequently New York Jewish types. He is best remembered for Patsy in *Three Men on a Horse* (1935), Gordon Miller in *Room Service* (1937), Sidney Black in *Light Up the Sky* (1948), Nathan Detroit in *Guys and Dolls* (1950), Al Lewis in **Neil Simon**'s *The Sunshine Boys* (1972), and Oscar Wolfe in the revival of *The Royal Family* (1975), his last major appearance. Adept in vehicles that ranged from popular farce to the more serious, Levene also appeared notably in *The Last Analysis, The Devil's Advocate, Heartbreak House, Dinner at Eight,* and the London production of *The Matchmaker* with **Ruth Gordon.**   DBW

Levin, Ira (1929–) New York–born playwright and novelist who, in a Broadway presence of three decades, scored major successes with *No Time for Sergeants* (1955, adapted from Mac Hyman's novel), *Critic's Choice* (1960), and *Deathtrap* (1978). Dependent on interesting characters caught in comic situations, his works include *Interlock* (1958), *General Seeger* (1962), *Drat! The Cat!* (1965), *Dr. Cook's Garden* (1967), *Veronica's Room* (1973), *Break a Leg* (1979), *Cantorial* (1989), and successful film adaptations.   GSA

Lewis (né Deming), James (1837?–96) Actor. After a 15-year career as low comedian in various companies throughout the county, Lewis joined **Augustin Daly** in 1869, succeeding notably as Bob Sackett in **Bronson Howard**'s *Saratoga* (1874). In 1880 the short, thin, wiry actor with animated face and eccentric, high voice became part of the "Big Four," performing older, comic foils with **Mrs. G.H. Gilbert** opposite **John Drew** and **Ada Rehan.**   DBW

Lewis, Robert (1909–) Director, producer, and actor, Lewis first appeared with the **Civic Repertory Theatre** during the 1929–30 season. From 1931 to 1941 he worked with the **Group Theatre,** for whom he directed the road company of *Golden Boy* in 1938. He made his first appearance in London in the same year. After the war he directed extensively on Broadway; among his hit productions were *Brigadoon* (1947) and *The Teahouse of the August Moon* (1953). With **Elia Kazan**

and **Cheryl Crawford,** he founded the **Actors Studio** in 1947. Lewis has also appeared in many films, taught acting and theatre at Sarah Lawrence College and Yale, and is the author of *Method – or Madness?* (1958), an explication of the Stanislavsky System of acting. In 1984 he published his autobiography, *Slings and Arrows.* Kent State University, which houses Lewis's papers, initiated the "Robert Lewis Medal for Lifetime Achievement in Theater Research" in 1991.   SMA

Lewis, Theophilus (1891–1974) Leading **African-American** drama critic of the Harlem Renaissance. He wrote for the monthly magazine *The Messenger* during 1923–6, his perceptive notices often censuring the popular vaudeville revues for lack of taste while reserving credit for the talented performer like **Florence Mills.** Lewis believed the serious drama alone could produce a truly racial theatre. He encouraged Little Theatre groups [see **community theatre**] and urged the cultivation of black playwrights and black ownership of theatre buildings.   EGH

Lewisohn, Alice (1883–1972) and **Irene** (1892–1944) Performing artists, directors, producers, and patrons. Orphaned in 1902, the sisters each inherited a fortune along with a commitment to philanthropic service. Their volunteer efforts at the Henry Street Settlement on NYC's Lower East Side soon included organizing amateur dance and drama productions, often reflecting the varied **ethnic** heritages of the "Neighborhood Players" and their audiences, as well as the Asian and Middle Eastern fare that interested the world-traveling sisters. The **Neighborhood Playhouse,** which they built and presented to the settlement, opened in 1915; for 12 years it offered an esoteric repertoire, winning special acclaim for the Hindu *The Little Clay Cart* (1924) and the Yiddish *Dybbuk* (1925). Although the playhouse closed in 1927, the renowned Neighborhood Playhouse School of the Theatre opened in 1928 with Irene as codirector. Alice married Herbert E. Crowley and in 1959 published a memoir, *The Neighborhood Playhouse.*   FHL

Liebler, Theodore A. (1852–1941) Producer of nearly 240 plays in association with **George C. Tyler,** beginning with *The Royal Box* (1897). He also produced the riot-plagued U.S. tour (1911) of Ireland's Abbey Theatre. Many of the greatest hits of Liebler and Company, such as *The Christian* (1898), *Alias Jimmy Valentine* (1910), and *The Garden of Allah* (1911), were adapted from popular fiction. Liebler's greatest hit was **Booth Tarkington**'s chauvinistic *The Man from Home* (1908), which ran 496 performances. He retired when a series of expensive failures after WW I caused the collapse of Liebler and Company.   WD

Lie of the Mind, A, by **Sam Shepard,** who directed the premiere (New York's Promenade Theatre on 5 December 1985) with a cast featuring **Geraldine Page,** Amanda Plummer, Harvey Keitel, and Aidan Quinn, and music by the Red Clay

Howard Lindsay and Dorothy Stickney with their red-headed brood in *Life with Father* (1939). Photo: Vandamm.

Ramblers. A London production opened 14 October 1987 at the Royal Court Theatre. Although episodically structured, the play offers one of Shepard's strongest narratives; it was also his last work for the stage until 1991. It brings together many of Shepard's familiar themes and devices: rival brothers, the disintegrating family, the search for identity, a wounded leg, the road, guns, and a culminating fire. The action, shifting between family homes in California and Montana, proceeds from a head injury inflicted by Jake on his wife Beth. During her slow recovery, she undertakes a bizarre courtship of Jake's brother Frankie. FHL

Life with Father by **Howard Lindsay** and **Russel Crouse** opened on Broadway 8 November 1939. The play was based on the stories of Clarence Day, first published in the *New Yorker, Harper's Magazine,* and the *New Republic* (1920–35), and then collected into novel form (1935). A sentimental and nostalgic domestic comedy set in the late 1880s, the play dramatizes the attempts of Father (Lindsay) to assert his authority and the rather more successful, although affectionate, schemes of his wife (Lindsay's wife, Dorothy Stickney) and their four sons to have their own way in spite of him. At closing on 12 July 1947, it was Broadway's longest-running play, with 3,216 performances. JDM

Light, James (1894–1964) Actor, designer, and director identified with the experimental work of O'Neill and the **Provincetown Players** (and suc-

cessors), with whom he served as a director for 13 years from 1917. A design student at the Carnegie Institute, Light codirected O'Neill's *The Hairy Ape* (1922), and directed *All God's Chillun Got Wings* (1924) and the American premiere of Strindberg's *A Dream Play* (1926). Dean of the theatre faculty at the New School for Social Research (1939–42), he was also codirector of the **Federal Theatre Project** in New York, then its director in Philadelphia. TP DBW

Lightnin' by **Winchell Smith** and **Frank Bacon** opened 26 August 1918 at the Gaiety Theatre, where the humorous rural melodrama recorded a long-run record 1,291 performances. Bacon, who originally conceived and wrote the play, received praise as the slow-talking, slow-moving "Lightnin' " Bill Jones. A boozy prevaricator who claims a variety of previous occupations, Jones conveyed a folk-hero quality, which placed him in the tradition of **Rip Van Winkle** and the stage **Yankee.** Smith collaborated on the script in which Lightnin', who operates a rundown hotel on the California–Nevada border, foils the machinations of land sharks. RAH

Light Up the Sky Comedy by **Moss Hart;** opened on Broadway 18 November 1948 under Hart's direction and ran 216 performances. Its story and the actual circumstances of the production were virtually identical: A play opens in Boston for an out-of-town tryout, the audience and the critics give it a mixed reception, and the playwright retreats to his room in the Ritz-Carlton to revise his creation. JDM

Lillie, Beatrice Gladys (Lady Robert Peel) (1894–1989) Canadian-born comedienne, billed as "the funniest woman in the world," appeared in variety as a child. Her debuts came in London revues *Not Likely* (1914) and *André Charlot's Revue of 1917;* a 1924 edition of the latter brought her to the U.S. Her New York successes include *This Year of Grace* (1929) with Noël Coward; **Shaw's** *Too True to Be Good* (1932); *The Show Is On* (1936) with **Bert Lahr;** *Set to Music* (1939), in which she introduced Coward's "I've Been to a Mahhhvelous Party"; and *Inside USA* (1948). Lillie was the consummate **revue** performer, wielding the slapstick with a raised pinky, puncturing her own poses of sophisticated grandeur with lapses into raucous vulgarity. She performed in the **one-person** show *An Evening with Beatrice Lillie* (1952); a 1957 revival of the **Ziegfeld** *Follies;* as *Auntie Mame* (1958); and in her final New York appearance as the medium Mme. Arcati in *High Spirits* (1964). She also wrote an autobiography, *Every Other Inch a Lady* (1972). LS

See: B. Laffey, *Beatrice Lillie: The Funniest Woman in the World,* New York, 1989.

Lincoln Center, Repertory Theatre of see **Vivian Beaumont and Mitzi E. Newhouse theatres**

Lindsay, Howard (1889–1968) Playwright, director, actor, and producer. Born in Waterford, NY, Lindsay attended Harvard University for one year and the **American Academy of Dramatic Arts** for six months before launching his acting career in 1909. Numerous stage appearances followed in vaudeville and burlesque; on tour with **McKee Rankin;** and as a member of **Margaret Anglin**'s Company (1913–18). After military service in WW I he returned to the stage, and in 1921 directed as well as acted in *Dulcy.* In the 1920s Lindsay established himself on Broadway as both a director and actor. He married actress Dorothy Stickney in 1927, and starred with her in *Life with Father* (1939), a play he cowrote with **Russel Crouse.** Other collaborations with Crouse included the book for *Anything Goes* (1934); *State of the Union* (1945), which won the Pulitzer Prize; the book for *Call Me Madam* (1950); *The Great Sebastians,* which featured **Alfred Lunt and Lynn Fontanne;** and the books for *The Sound of Music* (1959) and *Mr. President* (1962). Lindsay's most popular role, Father in *Life with Father,* drew praise from **Brooks Atkinson** for its "rare taste and solid heartiness." He was a craftsman more than an artist, able to "pull together" stageworthy theatrical pieces with his collaborators.   TLM

See: C. O. Skinner, *Life with Lindsay & Crouse,* Boston, 1976.

Linney, Romulus (1930–) Director and playwright. Trained at the Yale School of Drama, Linney's career has been nurtured primarily by the **resident nonprofit professional theatre** outside New York and by **Off-Broadway,** as well as by repertory theatres of Great Britain, Canada, Germany, and Austria. His critically acclaimed plays include *The Sorrows of Frederick* (1967), *The Love Suicide at Schofield Barracks* (1972), *Holy Ghosts* (1976), *Childe Byron* (1978), *Tennessee* (1979; Obie Award, 1980), *Laughing Stock* (1984), *Woman Without a Name* (1985), *Pops* (1986), *Three Poets* (1989), and *Unchanging Love* (1991). **Martin Gottfried** has called Linney "a playwright of true literacy, a writer in the grand tradition," and **Mel Gussow** terms him "poet of America's heartland." In 1984 he received the Award in Literature from the American Academy and Institute of Arts and Letters. In 1991 he was appointed the first playwright-in-residence at New York's Signature Theatre, which opened its first full season with *The Sorrows of Frederick,* directed by Linney, and devoted the 1991–2 season to his plays (concluding with a new one, *Ambrosio,* in April). In 1992 he was awarded an Obie for sustained excellence in playwriting. His daughter is actress Laura Linney.   DBW

Lion of the West, The, by **J. Kirke Paulding** opened at the **Park Theatre** on 25 April 1831, after winning a $300 prize offered by **James H. Hackett** for a comedy with an American leading character. Paulding's hero was Nimrod Wildfire, a larger-than-life representation, "half horse, half alligator, a touch of the airth-quake," modeled loosely on Davy Crockett and played by Hackett. Hackett's portrayal marked the first appearance of the backwoods character in a drama. Ironically, the play was not set on the frontier but in New York, as Wildfire visited his city relatives. In this satire the city represented greed and corruption while the backwoods stood for strength and honesty. **John Augustus Stone** revised Paulding's work, and in 1833 **William Bayle Bernard** adapted it for production in London, where it was called *The Kentuckian; or, A Trip to New York.* Hackett continued to play Wildfire for over 20 years. [See also *Davy Crockett.*]   RAH

See: J. N. Tidwell, ed., *The Lion of the West,* Stanford, CA, 1954.

Liptzin, Keni (1856–1918) **Yiddish** actress. Survivor of an Eastern European childhood so unhappy that it provided the plot for **Gordin**'s melodrama *Hasye the Little Orphan Girl,* she went on the stage around 1882, performed in London, and arrived in New York in 1887. Although physically tiny, she was known for her commanding presence and intensity. With the help of her husband Michael Mintz, a Yiddish newspaper man and publisher, she consistently chose to produce and star in plays by Gordin and other dramatists of literary worth rather than lighter entertainments. Her most famous role was as Gordin's *Mirele Efros* (*The Jewish Queen Lear*).   NS

Litt, Jacob (1860–1905) Producer who mounted popular melodramas for tours of the midwestern U.S. from his theatres in Milwaukee, WI. He managed midwestern operations for **Charles Frohman** and other Broadway producers, and built theatres in St. Paul and **Minneapolis,** MN. A production of Charles T. Dazey's *In Old Kentucky* (1893) by Litt's **stock company** proved an extraordinary success and propelled Litt to the pinnacle of his career as owner and manager of the **Broadway Theatre,** New York, which he acquired in 1899. Litt also owned **McVicker's Theatre,** Chicago, for a time.   WD

Little Foxes, The Drawing from stories of her mother's Southern family, **Lillian Hellman** created a three-act drama that revealed with devastating directness the ruthless greed of the Hubbard family. The play opened at New York's National Theatre on 15 February 1939, directed by **Herman Shumlin** and starring **Tallulah Bankhead.** It ran for 410 performances, won the Drama Critics' Circle Award, and was praised by critics for its Chekhovian style. The Hubbard brothers, Ben and Oscar, are so driven by ambition and greed that they sacrifice their morals for profit; but they are bested by their sister, Regina, who has married for money and who furthers her own ambition and eventually gains power over her brothers after she coldly refuses to give her husband his heart medicine and lets him die. The play is a classic of American theatre, performed countless times since its premiere. In 1949 it was the basis for an opera, *Regina,* by **Marc Blitzstein.** A Broadway revival in 1981 starred Elizabeth Taylor. Hellman also

Lillian Hellman's *The Little Foxes* (1939) with Tallulah Bankhead (left) at the National Theatre. Photo: Vandamm. Courtesy: Theatre Collection, Museum of the City of New York.

wrote the screenplay for the RKO film in 1941, which starred Bette Davis.   FB

Little Johnny Jones established **George M. Cohan** as playwright and star performer. His fifth full-length play saved him financially, beginning a long-term partnership with producer **Sam Harris.** Supposedly inspired by American jockey Tod Sloan, the play depicts Jones dominating English racing until accused of throwing the Derby, a charge he disproves. Despite melodramatic devices, it was Cohan's most developed plot to date. Critical disfavor contrasted with strong public appeal of the play's chauvinism, typified by the songs "I'm a Yankee Doodle Dandy (The Yankee Doodle Boy)" and "Give My Regards to Broadway." It previewed in Hartford beginning 10 October, played 52 performances from 7 November 1904 at the Liberty Theatre, was revived twice in 1905, and toured successfully. A 1982 revival closed opening night.   RW

Little Mary Sunshine Two-act musical comedy with book, music, and lyrics by Rick Besoyan; opened **Off-Broadway** at the **Orpheum Theatre** (18 November 1959) for a run of 1,143 performances. Critics praised Eileen Brennan (Obie for best actress) in the first Off-Broadway show to feature an "original cast album." Set in the Rocky Mountains at the turn of the century, the musical depicts the antics of resident Indians, Forest Rangers, and young ladies of Eastchester Finishing School in a spoof of the archaic and sentimental operetta form seen in the **Rudolf Friml**–Herbert Stothart 1924 Broadway hit ***Rose-Marie*** and its screen version (1936) starring Jeanette MacDonald and Nelson Eddy. Despite its success, producers refused to move it to Broadway, thus encouraging the development of the Off-Broadway musical.   EK

Little Murders by **Jules Feiffer** was first presented by the Royal Shakespeare Company at the Aldwych Theatre, London, on 3 July 1967. Christopher Morahan directed a cast including Derek Smith as Carol Newquist, Brenda Bruce as his wife Marjorie, John Allison as their budding transvestite son Kenny, Barbara Jefford as their daughter Patsy (who is killed by a stray gunshot on her wedding day), and Derek Godfrey as Alfred Chamberlain, the man she marries. The play failed on Broadway in 1967, but was revived successfully Off-Broadway in 1969 by **Alan Arkin** with a cast including **Linda Lavin** and **Vincent Gardenia.** Set on New York's Upper West Side during the 1960s, the play uses absurdist techniques to depict the grotesque state of urban life in a city overwhelmed by seemingly pointless crime. Feiffer also uses humor to critique marriage, the family, the moral relativism of the '60s, and the legal and law enforcement systems.   BCM

Little Night Music, A Two-act musical comedy, music and lyrics by **Stephen Sondheim,** book by Hugh Wheeler; opened 25 February 1973 at the **Sam S. Shubert Theatre,** running 601 performances. This musical adaptation of Ingmar Bergman's film *Smiles of a Summer Night* was the most conventional of the **Harold Prince**–Sondheim collaborations of the 1970s and the most widely popular. A bittersweet romance set in turn-of-the-century Sweden, it involves a complex game of interchanging romantic partners, all set to music that is mostly in variations on three-four waltz time. One notable aspect of the show was the onstage Leibesleider quintet, which narrates and comments on the action. The show, which won the Drama Critics' Circle and Tony awards for best musical, also introduced Sondheim's only popular "hit" song of the 1970s, the ironic ballad "Send in the Clowns." JD

Little Shop of Horrors, with book, lyrics, and direction by Howard Ashman and music by Alan Menken, was a musical adaptation of the 1960 Roger Corman film. Premiering 6 May 1982 at the WPA Theatre, the play opened 27 July on Broadway produced by David Geffen and Cameron Mackintosh, two powerful entertainment figures of the 1980s. The story, slight but humorous, concerns Seymour, a retiring flower shop clerk whose life changes when a plant responds to the taste of blood, grows to amazing size, and consumes his rivals. The musical is remembered for its pop score and the amazing **puppetry** required to make the plant devour people. KN

Little Theatre movement see **Community theatre/Little Theatre movement**

Living Newspaper
Although antecedents can be identified, this term most frequently is associated with the **Federal Theatre Project.** A documentary methodology was used, defining a problem and then calling for specific action. Bringing together both unemployed newspaper men and theatre personnel, presentations were written on such varied problems as housing, health care, labor unions, public utilities, cooperatives, natural resources, Negroes, and even the motion pictures. Six examples were produced by the New York unit, although the first – *Ethiopia,* on the war in

Living Newspaper: scene from the Federal Theatre Project's *Triple-A Plowed Under.* Courtesy: Institute on the Federal Theatre Project, George Mason University.

Abyssinia – was canceled under pressure from the U.S. State Department. The three most successful attempts were by **Arthur Arent:** *Triple-A-Plowed Under,* on the need for farmers and consumers to unite for improved incomes and cheaper food, which was a great success in 1936; *Power* (1937), a plea for public ownership of utilities; and *One-Third of a Nation* (1938), an exposé of urban housing conditions. Less successful were *1935,* a satire of the public's indifference to social issues, and *Injunction Granted* (1936), an account of labor's treatment in the courts. Units in other cities developed living newspapers on local problems, though few were produced. The techniques have been applied to more contemporary didactic theatre, such as the so-called Theatre of Fact begun in the 1950s. DBW

See: L. Brown, ed., *Liberty Deferred and Other Living Newspapers of the 1930s,* Fairfax, VA, 1989; P. De Rohan, ed., *Federal Theatre Plays,* 2 vols., New York, 1938; C. Highsaw, "A Theatre of Action: The Living Newspapers of the Federal Theatre Project," PhD diss., Princeton U, 1988.

Living picture (*tableau vivant*) see **nudity**

Living Theatre
When Julian Beck and his wife, Judith Malina, founded the Living Theatre in 1948, they inaugurated the experimental **Off-Off Broadway** movement in New York. With one of the most influential and long-lasting avant-garde companies in American history, the Becks became the prophets of the burgeoning theatrical experimentation that was to explode during the 1960s.

From the very beginning, the Living Theatre sought the marriage of a political and aesthetic radicalism. "We insisted," Beck said, "on experimentation that was an image for a changing society. If one can experiment in theatre, one can experiment in life." This principle took a variety of shapes as the LT developed, but the Becks' anarchist-pacifist viewpoint remained a constant.

The Theatre began producing plays by Paul Goodman, **Gertrude Stein,** García Lorca, Pirandello, Cocteau, and **Brecht,** seeking an antirealism that could match the contemporary fervor in the visual arts and music. The group did not find a permanent performance space until 1959, and they lost it four years later when the Internal Revenue Service evicted them for nonpayment of taxes. Early landmark productions before being closed were profoundly influenced by Artaud's *The Theatre and Its Double,* including Jack Gelber's *The Connection* (1959), about heroin addicts awaiting a promised fix; Brecht's *Man Is Man;* and Kenneth Brown's *The Brig* (1963), a detailed documentary of daily brutal routine in a U.S. Marine Corps brig in Japan, which was the company's last New York production. Having defied IRS orders to leave its building, the LT gave its final performance of *The Brig* in a padlocked theatre; the audience had to enter by climbing in the windows.

From September 1964 to August 1968, the LT performed only in Europe, concentrating on works made up of exercises and improvisations, and created collectively. This experimentation culminated in *Paradise Now* (1968), a "spiritual and political voyage for actors and spectators."

A tour to the U.S. in 1968 helped convince the Becks that they no longer wanted to perform for a middle-class audience, but preferred to work in the streets with the people. After a brief return to Europe, the company went to Brazil in 1970 and stayed 13 months experimenting with **collective** creation before returning to the U.S. to work with coal miners and steel mill workers in Pittsburgh. They went back to Europe for further exploration of dramatic form and acting.

In 1984 the LT settled once again in New York. Since Julian Beck's death in 1985, the company has continued under the direction of Judith Malina and Hanon Reznikov. After more than 25 years, the LT once again has a home in Manhattan, a garage-like theatre on East 3rd Street. The company has been presenting plays based on poetry, collaborations with homeless people from the neighborhood, and annual street theatre spectacles.

The Becks' works and ideas are described in Beck's 1972 book, *The Life of the Theatre*, and Malina's *Diaries 1947–57* (1984). AS

See: P. Biner, *The Living Theatre*, New York, 1972.

Lloyd, Norman (1914–) Actor-director, recognized today chiefly for his role of Dr. Auslander on the TV series "St. Elsewhere." During his long, distinguished theatrical career, Lloyd apprenticed with **Eva Le Gallienne**'s **Civic Repertory Theater** (1932), played Japhet in *Noah* on Broadway (1935), appeared in three of the **Federal Theatre Project**'s **Living Newspapers** (1936–7), and became a member of **Orson Welles**'s **Mercury Theatre.** He played Fool in *King Lear* (1950, opposite **Louis Calhern**) and Lucio in *Measure for Measure* (1956, 1957). Though slight in build, Lloyd most often portrayed heavies in his early career, especially on screen. A stage, television, and film director and producer, Lloyd staged or produced numerous serious dramatic works in the 1970s, mostly for PBS ("Hollywood Television Theatre"). His autobiography was published in 1993. DBW

See: F. Parker, *Stages: Norman Lloyd*, Metuchen, NJ, 1990.

Lloyd Webber, Andrew see **Musical theatre**

Lobel, Adrianne (1955–) Having trained with **Ming Cho Lee**, Lobel has become one of the most daring of the postmodern designers and is closely associated with director **Peter Sellars.** Together they have created controversial productions of *Cosí fan tutte* (1986, set in a roadside diner), *Nixon in China* (1987), *The Marriage of Figaro* (1988, set in Trump Tower), and *The Magic Flute* at Glyndebourne (1990, set in Southern California). Her sets are typified by bold uses of line and color to create dominant images with a humorous or ironic sensibility. AA

Lockridge, Richard (1898–1982) Author and critic. Beginning as a journalist, Lockridge wrote dramatic criticism for the *New York Sun* (1928–43). With his first wife, Frances, he created the popular Mr. and Mrs. North detective books, from which a stage success was fashioned in 1941. He also wrote *Darling of Misfortune: Edwin Booth* (1932). A stylist and humorist, Lockridge reviewed *Tobacco Road* (1933) as "a lagging drama which quite frequently achieves the repulsive and seldom falls below the faintly sickening." TLM

Loesser, Frank (1910–69) Composer and lyricist. After contributing songs to *The Illustrators' Show* (1936), Loesser spent 12 years in Hollywood writing the lyrics for numerous motion picture musicals. He returned to Broadway with the score for *Where's Charley?* (1948), a musical version of *Charley's Aunt*. Two years later Loesser wrote his most memorable songs for *Guys and Dolls,* a musical based on Damon Runyan's short stories about tough but soft-hearted New York gamblers and their girlfriends. He then devoted four years to writing the score for *The Most Happy Fella* (1956), an ambitious musical whose 30 songs ranged from operatic arias to typical Broadway speciality numbers. After a failure with *Greenwillow* (1960), Loesser wrote his last Broadway score for *How to Succeed in Business Without Really Trying* (1961), a satire on corporate politics and chicanery. Loesser also operated a musical publishing house, through which he furthered the careers of several young composers. MK

Loew, Marcus (1870–1927) Theatre owner and impresario, dubbed "the Henry Ford of show biz." Considered an honest and generous showman, Loew joined with **David Warfield** and, briefly, Adolph Zukor, in the penny arcade business. In 1904 Loew and Warfield formed their own company, and Loew emerged as a pioneer in the emerging film industry. Subsequently, he added low-price **vaudeville** between pictures. At his death he controlled 300 entertainment venues, headed Metro–Goldwyn–Mayer Pictures, and was president of numerous vaudeville and booking companies. DBW

Loewe, Frederick see **Lerner, Alan Jay**

Logan, Cornelius A[mbrosius] (1806–52) Actor and playwright. A popular comedian, mainly in the West and South, Logan also defended the theatre with a vigor later displayed in the work of his daughter **Olive Logan.** As a playwright, Logan wrote a few successful **Yankee** vehicle plays. He wrote *The Wag of Maine* (1834) for **James Hackett**, revising it as *Yankee Land* (1842) for **Dan Marble**, who portrayed Deuteronomy Dutiful, a talkative country bumpkin, in Logan's *The Vermont Wool Dealer* (1838). Joshua Silsbee acted Lot Sap Sago in Logan's *The Celestial Empire; or, The Yankee in China* (1846). Logan wrote and acted successfully in *Chloroform* (1849), his last play. WJM

Logan, Joshua (1908–88) Director, producer, and playwright associated with many of Broadway's most successful plays and musicals as director, coproducer, or coauthor (frequently all three): *South Pacific* (1949), for which he and coauthor **Oscar Hammerstein II** received the Pulitzer Prize (1950); *The Wisteria Trees* (1950), based on **Chekhov**'s *The Cherry Orchard* and written by Logan; *Wish You Were Here* (1952); and *Fanny* (1954). He was director and coproducer of *John Loves Mary* (1947) and *Picnic* (1953). *Mister Roberts* (1948) was directed by him and written with Thomas Heggen. Other plays and musicals exhibited Logan's skill as an inventive director: *On Borrowed Time* (1938), **Knickerbocker Holiday** (1938), **Morning's at Seven** (1939), *Charley's Aunt* (1940), *By Jupiter* (1942), **Annie Get Your Gun** (1946), and *Happy Birthday* (1946). He also directed the motion pictures **Bus Stop** (1956), *South Pacific* (1958), and **Camelot** (1967).

His apprenticeship began with the Triangle Club at Princeton and continued with the University Players. He married Nedda Harrigan (daughter of **Edward Harrigan**) and wrote two volumes of autobiography: *Josh* (1976) and *Movie Stars, Real People, and Me* (1978). RM

Logan, Olive (1839–1909) Actress, lecturer, playwright. Like her sisters Eliza and Celia, Olive won respect as an actress, but she left the stage in 1866 to concentrate on writing. Having lived in England and France during 1857–63, she drew upon her experiences abroad in novels like *Chateau Frissac* (1862), memoirs like *Photographs of Paris* (1866), and in certain topics during her dozen years on the nationwide lecture circuit. **Augustin Daly** employed her to translate French plays and produced her *Surf* (1870) and *Newport* (1879). In lectures, articles, and pamphlets she called for equal rights for women while deploring "the leg business," which put scantily clad women on stage. Her major books were *Apropos of Women and Theatre* (1869), *Before the Footlights and Behind the Scenes* (1870), and *The Mimic World* (1871). FHL

Long, William Ivey (1947–) Pennsylvania-born costume designer, educated at the College of William and Mary, Yale, and the University of North Carolina, known for his wide range of activities. He received the 1982 Tony, Maharam, and Drama Desk awards for his costume designs for *Nine,* the 1991 Obie for sustained excellence, and the 1992 Tony for *Crazy for You.* Long's designs are seen in the theatre (**Six Degrees of Separation,** *The Homecoming, Private Lives, Lend Me a Tenor,* **True West**), opera (*A Quiet Place, Trouble in Tahiti*), rock concerts (The Pointer Sisters, The Rolling Stones), and dance (Twyla Tharp, Paul Taylor, Peter Martens). BO

Longacre Theatre 220 West 48th St., NYC [Architect: Henry B. Herts]. Built by H. H. Frazee, a baseball magnate who liked to dabble in play production, the compact Longacre is ideally suited for small musicals and intimate comedies and dramas, which indeed have been its regular fare. Seating just over 1,000, it was leased to the **Shubert**s during the Depression and has since passed to their ownership. During 1944–53 it was used as a radio and television playhouse, but was returned to play production and has remained a legitimate house since. Among its noteworthy tenants have been *Paradise Lost* (1935), *On Borrowed Time* (1938), *Rhinoceros* (1961), *Ain't Misbehavin'* (1978), and *Children of a Lesser God* (1980). MCH

Long Day's Journey into Night by **Eugene O'Neill** was first produced at the Royal Theatre, Stockholm. Its American premiere opened 7 November 1956, 16 years after the play's completion. Directed by **José Quintero** and starring **Fredric**

José Quintero's production of O'Neill's *Long Day's Journey into Night* with Florence Eldridge and Fredric March. Courtesy: Louis Sheaffer.

March as James Tyrone, **Florence Eldridge** as his wife Mary, **Jason Robards, Jr.,** as their son Jamie, and Bradford Dillman as their son Edmund, it ran for 390 performances and won O'Neill his fourth Pulitzer Prize. Actors such as Laurence Olivier, Timothy West, **Colleen Dewhurst,** and **Geraldine Fitzgerald** have appeared in the play's many revivals since. Generally considered O'Neill's finest play, it is an autobiographical account of the tragic family life of the four haunted Tyrones and their struggle to escape the effects of lost dreams and illusions through alcohol and morphine. Unable to confront the fact that her son Edmund has consumption, Mary resumes taking morphine after a temporary "cure" when the play begins. The play depicts the harrowing events of the next 16 hours, as each family member simultaneously drifts further into drug-induced oblivion and reveals his personal suffering to the audience. BCM

Long Time Since Yesterday by P. J. Gibson, produced by **Woodie King, Jr.,** directed by Bette Howard, and featuring Denise Nicholas, Loretta Devine, and Ellen Holly; premiered 10 October 1985 at the **New Federal Theatre.** Set in the past and present, the play concerns female friends from college who meet at the funeral of a mutual friend who has committed suicide. The women explore the changes in their lives and the events leading to the suicide. KME

Long Wharf Theatre (New Haven, CT) Founded in 1965 by **Jon Jory** and Harlan Kleiman, this nonprofit resident theatre, playing to more than 160,000 patrons annually, is now under the leadership of artistic director **Arvin Brown** (since 1967) and M. Edgar Rosenblum. Known as an actor's theatre, Long Wharf, with two intimate performance spaces (484 and 199 capacities) in the New Haven Meat and Produce Terminal, emphasizes the production of new and established, homegrown and foreign works that explore human relationships (25 world and 36 U.S. premieres among its 211 productions during its first 25 years). Although transference to New York is not a priority at LWT, many important productions have made the move virtually intact, including *Shadow Box, Streamers, The Changing Room, Sizwe Banzi Is Dead, The Gin Game, Quartermaine's Terms,* and revivals of *Ah, Wilderness!, All My Sons, A View From the Bridge* (1982), and *American Buffalo* (1984). LWT has won praise and numerous awards, including the **Margo Jones** Award for production of new works, a special citation from the Outer Critics' Circle, the **Jujamcyn Theaters** Award (1986), and a special Tony Award (1978) for the quality of its productions as well as the stability of its organizational structure.   DBW

Look Homeward, Angel by Ketti Frings. Based on the novel by Thomas Wolfe, this emotional family drama set in 1916 focuses on 17-year-old Eugene, whose artistic temperament and thirst for knowledge lead him to break free of the stifling atmosphere of his mother's boardinghouse. For the first production, director George Roy Hill set a style of speaking and movement that was "wild and frenetic without seeming to be uncontrolled" (**Brooks Atkinson**). Anthony **Perkins** created the role of Eugene, Jo Van Fleet his shrewd, domineering mother, **Arthur Hill** his doomed older brother, and Hugh Griffith his once-titanic father. Designed by **Jo Mielziner**, the play opened at the **Ethel Barrymore Theatre** 28 November 1957, ran for 564 performances, and won the Pulitzer and New York Drama Critics' Circle awards.   KF

Loos, Anita (1893?–1981) Actress, screenwriter, and playwright noted for her satiric comedies. Loos, who wrote some 200 scripts for both silent and sound movies, created the art of writing film captions, beginning with D. W. Griffith's silent films, such as *Intolerance* (1916). In 1926 she and her husband, John Emerson, dramatized her successful novel, *Gentlemen Prefer Blondes*. Noted for Lorelei Lee, the stereotypical "dumb blonde," the play was made into a musical in 1949 by Loos and Joseph Fields. Throughout her career Loos wrote plays (*Happy Birthday*, 1946) and screenplays (*San Francisco*, 1936; *The Women*, 1939); adapted French plays into hit American shows (*Gigi*, 1951); and wrote witty, gossipy memoirs of her career in Hollywood (*A Girl Like I*, 1966; *Kiss Hollywood Goodbye*, 1974; *Cast of Thousands*, 1977).   FB

See: G. Carey, *Anita Loos*, New York, 1988.

Loose Ends Written by **Michael Weller** and directed by **Alan Schneider;** premiered at the **Arena Stage** and subsequently (6 June 1979) transferred to the **Circle in the Square** in New York, where it ran for 284 performances. Seen by some critics as a continuation of ideas in Weller's earlier *Moonchildren* (1972), *Loose Ends* chronicles the relationship of a young couple who have experimented

with an alternative life-style and are now confronted with the demands of career, family, and social responsibility in the 1970s. The production featured excellent performances by **Kevin Kline** (Paul, a thoughtful drifter who ultimately longs for a family) and Roxanne Hart (Susan, a successful photographer who enjoys her professional and material success), as well as some of Weller's best writing.   KF   BBW

Loquasto, Santo (1944–) Set and costume designer; master of both realistic detail and conceptual and theatricalist productions. Early Broadway and regional successes, such as *That Championship Season* and *American Buffalo* and later work including *Cafe Crown* are almost photorealist in their painstaking detail. His work in the 1970s with the **New York Shakespeare Festival,** especially at the outdoor Delacorte Theater, and his extensive work for dance, notably with Twyla Tharp and Mikhail Baryshnikov, emphasized sculptural and emblematic design and often included angular, large-scale, constructivistlike designs. Many of these tendencies came together in Broadway's *Grand Hotel: The Musical,* which won him a 1990 Tony. His costumes possess the same detail, sense of color, and texture as his sets, and for dance he often designs costumes alone. Loquasto has worked frequently on films, notably with **Woody Allen.**   AA

Lord, Pauline (1890–1950) Actress who at 13 made her professional debut playing the maid in *Are You a Mason?* at the **Alcazar Theatre** in San Francisco, her hometown. After years of touring engagements, she achieved New York success in *The Talker* (1912). Among her great roles were the downtrodden Sadie in *The Deluge* (1917), Anna in *Anna Christie* (1921), Amy in *They Knew What They Wanted* (1924), and Nina in the touring production of *Strange Interlude* (1928–9). Often compared to Duse, she conveyed – according to **Stark Young** – "a subtle variety and gradation and shy power that are indescribable."   FHL

Lortel, Lucille (1902–) Producer. Born in New York, Lortel attended the American Academy of Dramatic Arts (1920) before studying in Germany with Arnold Korff and **Max Reinhardt.** After a year in stock (1924), she made her Broadway debut in a minor role. Upon her marriage in 1931, she gave up the stage until 1947, when she offered her Westport, CT, barn for a dramatic reading. After two seasons of readings, she remodeled the White Barn Theatre into a functioning theatre that served as a showcase for new talent and continues summer seasons. Lortel acquired New York's Theatre de Lys in 1955 as a transfer venue for worthy White Barn productions. Her first Theatre de Lys production, *The Threepenny Opera,* ran for seven years. In 1956 she began offering a Matinee Series, which continued for 20 years. At both theatres she has presented lesser known plays by **Brecht,** Ionesco, Genêt, Mario Fratti, and **Athol Fugard.** The more successful presentations at the Theatre de Lys include *Dames at Sea, A Life in the Theatre, Buried Child, Getting*

Out, Cloud Nine, and *Woza Albert*. In 1981 the theatre was rechristened the Lucille Lortel Theatre in her honor. She is a cofounder of the **American Shakespeare Festival** and a recipient of the **Margo Jones** Award for her dedication to new plays. She is the subject of a documentary film, *The Queen of Off-Broadway*.   TLM

Los Angeles The city's first English-language theatrical performances were given in 1848 by the Seventh New York Volunteers in Don Antonio Coronel's 300-seat, open-air theatre. Stearns' Hall was the area's first commercial theatre (1859), and on 28 October 1860 the Stark Company from San Francisco gave the first performance by a professional troupe, appearing in John Temple's remodeled hall in an upper story of the City Market. The three major houses of the late nineteenth century were the Merced Theatre (1870); the 1500-seat Grand Opera House (1884) built by Ozro Childs for over $100,000 (where **Edwin Booth** grossed $14,046 in five performances during March 1888); and the New Los Angeles Theatre (1888), which served as the city's principal roadhouse during 1894–1903.

In the early 1890s, David S. Burbank, a dentist, built the Burbank Theatre and established a resident **stock company; Oliver Morosco** took control (1899) and combined the roles of business manager with producing artistic director, during 1905–22 presenting not only **Ibsen** but 84 premieres, including *Peg o' My Heart* and *Abie's Irish Rose*. **Pageant** plays became popular with John Steven McGroarty's *The Mission Play,* produced 1912–29 at the Mission San Gabriel Arcangel. Other pageants included *The Pilgrimage Play* (1920), an "authentic" life of Christ composed of dialogue from the New Testament, and *Ramona* (1923–80s), performed at the foot of the San Jacinto Mountains with a cast of 250.

Theatre prospered in the 1920s and led to the construction of the Biltmore, the El Capitan, the Belasco, the Vine Street Theatre (later renamed the Mirror, then the Huntington Hartford), the Hollywood Playhouse, and the Figueroa Playhouse.

In the 1930s, activity subsided due to the Depression and the advent of talkies, but there were exceptions: The Theatre Mart production of *The Drunkard* opened on 6 July 1933 and played 9,477 performances, closing on 17 October 1959; also, **Max Reinhardt**'s Hollywood Bowl production of *A Midsummer Night's Dream* (1934), which included the Los Angeles Philharmonic playing the complete score by Mendelssohn, drew 150,000 people to seven performances.

During the 1940s, the Actors' Lab produced plays in a building behind Schwab's Drugstore before falling victim to the Tenney and House Un-American Activities committees; in 1947, **John Houseman** directed **Charles Laughton** in **Brecht**'s *Galileo* at the new Coronet Theatre. 1960s debuts included Actors Studio West (1965), a branch of New York's **Actors Studio**; the **East West Players** (1965), a prominent Asian-American troupe; the Globe Playhouse (1967), home of the Shakespeare Society of America; and Ron Sossi's Odyssey Theatre (1968). **Actors' Equity** instituted the

Workshop Code (no advertising, no charge for admission, at least nine performances), but the actors rebelled and in 1972 Equity established the Waiver, which allowed theatres seating up to 99 to charge admission for open-ended runs and hire Equity actors on nonunion contracts. This was revised in 1988 as the more heavily regulated "99-seat plan."

The 1970s saw the opening of the 1,824-seat **Shubert** Theatre (1972), a major roadhouse, as well as the creation of Teatro Intimo (1974), a Spanish-language company. Theatre in Los Angeles has for decades lived in the shadow of the film and television industries; commercial producers frequently engage the services of a prominent film star in order to market a production to the Los Angeles audience. Because many actors are reluctant to make long-term stage commitments that would preclude more lucrative work in front of a camera, resident theatres tend to cast each production separately rather than try to maintain a core company for even one season. Offerings in the 1980s and early 1990s included large touring musicals from New York, diverse subscription seasons by the large nonprofit companies, more daring fare from smaller troupes, plays presented by and for the city's larger ethnic minorities (basically **Hispanic, African-American,** and various **Asian-American** groups), and a wide variety of academic and amateur theatre.   JDM

See: D. Alexander, *Playhouse,* Los Angeles, 1984; E. Kaufman, "Theatre in Los Angeles – The Early Years," in program for *The Crucible* at the Ahmanson Theatre (1972); H. W. Koon, *How Shakespeare Won the West,* Jefferson, NC, 1989; G. R. MacMinn, *The Theater of the Golden Era in California,* Caldwell, ID, 1941; M. Mann and R. Tatar, eds., *The Los Angeles Theatre Book,* Los Angeles, 1978; A. Woods, "Popular Theatre in Los Angeles at the Turn of the Century," *Players* (April–May 1973).

Los Angeles Theatre Center began as the Los Angeles Actors' Theatre (1975) under Ralph Waite and Diane White, modeled after New York's **Public Theater.** In 10 years, the company presented over 200 world, American, and West Coast premieres. In 1985 it moved to Spring Street in downtown Los Angeles to take over a remodeled bank building, where it adopted its ultimate name under Artistic Director Bill Bushnell, who ran the group from 1978. Performance spaces included a 99-seat black box, a 296-seat proscenium house, a 323-seat thrust stage, and a 503-seat open stage. The typical season involved 14 plays, over half being world premieres, including works by **Luis Valdéz, David Henry Hwang, Adele Edling Shank,** and Anna Deavere Smith. In 1989, the operating budget was $7.4 million. Special projects, which reflected the company's multicultural urban mission, included the Latino Theatre Lab, the Black Theatre Artists Workshop, the Asian American Theatre Project, the Women's Project, and the Young Conservatory. In late 1991 its doors closed, and as of this writing its future is unknown.   JDM

Lost in the Stars by **Maxwell Anderson** and **Kurt Weill;** opened 30 October 1949 at the **Music**

Box Theatre for 273 performances. The successful adaptation of Alan S. Paton's *Cry, the Beloved Country* achieved operatic unity of action and music in a serious American drama. The play suggests hope amid the tragic irony and despair of apartheid when a black minister and a white landowner are united following the execution of the minister's promising son for killing the liberal son of the landowner. The 39-performance 1972 **Imperial Theatre** revival drew Tonys for best actor and supporting actor in a musical. RW

Lost in Yonkers by **Neil Simon**, his 27th effort, a two-act comedy set in Yonkers in 1942; opened in February 1991 at the **Richard Rodgers Theater.** After two failures (*Rumors*, 1988; *Jake's Women*, 1990 San Diego production), *Lost in Yonkers* was not only a critical success, despite a somewhat formulaic Simon ending, but garnered the award that had always eluded the playwright – the Pulitzer Prize (plus the Tony for best play and the Drama Desk Award). Unlike Simon's previous autobiographical plays, this darkest and most complex of his comedies pulls "the family itself out of shape" and turns "it into a grotesque version of itself" (in critic David Richards's words). The characters here are deeply disturbed, dominated by a tyrannical German-Jewish grandmother (**Irene Worth**) who is given the responsibility of superintending two grandsons while their father goes South to sell scrap iron. Directed by **Gene Saks** (his sixth Simon stage production) and designed by **Santo Loquasto,** the production also starred Mercedes Ruehl and Kevin Spacey as two of the old lady's children. Ruehl won the Tony for leading actress in a play, while Worth and Spacey garnered Tonys for featured roles. DBW

Lotito, Louis A. (1900–80) Theatre manager and one of the most powerful theatre executives in New York. Lotito managed the Center Theatre in Rockefeller Center (1934), followed by the **Martin Beck Theatre** (1938), and during 1943–67 served as President of City Playhouse, Inc., owners of Broadway theatres including the ANTA, **Helen Hayes, Martin Beck,** and **Morosco,** as well as the **National Theatre** in Washington, DC. He also served as president of the **Actors' Fund of America** (1969–80). TLM

Lowell, Robert (né Traill Spence, Jr.) (1917–77) Pulitzer Prize–winning poet and playwright, considered by many the best English-language poet of his generation. He is best known for the trilogy of plays adapted from Nathaniel Hawthorne and Herman Melville, titled *The Old Glory* (*Benito Cereno; My Kinsman, Major Molineux;* and *Endecott of the Red Cross*), which was first performed at the **American Place Theatre** in 1964. *Benito Cereno,* the most successful of the trilogy, was seen in 1967 at London's Mermaid. Lowell also adapted Racine's *Phèdre* (publ. 1960) and Aeschylus' *Prometheus Bound* (1966), the latter seen at the Mermaid in 1971. DBW

Lucas, Craig (1951–) Playwright. Born in Atlanta and educated at Boston University, Lucas

was one of the most produced American dramatists during the 1980s. *Reckless* (1983) and *Blue Window* (1984) both premiered at The Production Company, and *Three Postcards* (1986) and ***Prelude to a Kiss*** (1987) at the **South Coast Repertory.** Each has had subsequent professional productions, including a Broadway run for *Prelude.* Lucas has won numerous prizes, including Guggenheim and Rockefeller grants and the GLAAD Award for his screenplay *Longtime Companion* (1990). BBW

Lucas, Sam (1848–1916) Son of former slaves, Lucas rose from farmhand to become "dean of black theatricals." He came to New York City with the Original Georgia Minstrels in 1874 (see **minstrel show**) and appeared in the Hyers Sisters' musical comedy *Out of Bondage.* He was the first authentic black in the title role of **Uncle Tom's Cabin** (1878) and headed up *The Creole Show* (1890) organized by Sam T. Jack. Lucas appeared in **Cole and Johnson**'s three musical comedies from 1897 to 1909. In the movie version of *Uncle Tom's Cabin* he allegedly was required as Uncle Tom to leap into a partially frozen river to save little Eva, catching the pneumonia that led to his death. EGH

Luce, Clare Boothe see **Boothe, Clare**

Ludlam, Charles (1943–87) Actor, director, playwright and an early member of **John Vaccaro**'s Play-House of the Ridiculous, an **Off-Off Broadway** theatre that presented his *Big Hotel* (1967) and *Conquest of the Universe* (1967). Splitting with Vaccaro in 1967, Ludlam started his own theatre, The **Ridiculous Theatrical Company,** where his plays included *Bluebeard* (1970), *Camille* (1973; revived 1990), *Stageblood* (1975), *Professor Bedlam's Punch and Judy Show* (1975), *Der Ring Gott Farblonjet* (1977), *Le Bourgeois Avant-Garde* (1982), and *The Mystery of Irma Vep* (1984). These plays combined popular and high art forms, mixing colorful staging, scatological humor, and **female impersonation** with plots and styles drawn from dramatic and operatic literature. Ludlam's treatments of *Hamlet,* Wagner's *Ring,* and *Camille* went beyond mere spoofing; his depth of involvement, he explained, gave rise to independent works that transcend parody. The Ridiculous Theatrical Company, one of the first New York theatres to deal explicitly with homosexual themes, often featured Ludlam in female roles – which he didn't necessarily play campily. In 1984 Pittsburgh's American Ibsen Theatre invited Ludlam to play Hedda Gabler. *The Complete Plays of Charles Ludlam* was published after his death from **AIDS** in 1987. AS

See: S. Samuels, ed., *Ridiculous Theatre: Scourge of Human Folly – The Essays and Opinions of Charles Ludlam,* New York, 1992.

Ludlow, Noah Miller (1795–1886) Actor-manager who, with **Solomon Franklin Smith,** brought the legitimate theatre to the Ohio and Mississippi valleys. First employed by **Samuel Drake** in 1815 to barnstorm in Kentucky, Ludlow formed his own company, playing New Orleans and remote corners of the South and West. In 1828 he joined **T. A. Cooper** as manager of the **Chatham Theatre** in New York, but failed financially. With Smith, Ludlow formed the American Theatrical Commonwealth Company (1835–53), building and operating theatres in Mobile, New Orleans, St. Louis, and other cities, engaging many of the leading stars of the day. The partnership dissolved in hostility: Smith's journals never mention his partner. Ludlow's autobiography, *Dramatic Life as I Found It* (1880), although bitter in condemnation of Smith, offers an unequaled factual account of the **frontier theatre** in America. SMA

Lunt, Alfred (1892–1977) and **Lynn Fontanne (Lillie Louise)** (1887–1983) Actors. Alfred Lunt became a star as the oafish lead in **Booth Tarkington**'s *Clarence* in 1919. Lynn Fontanne's first major role was as a dizzy matron addicted to clichés in **Kaufman** and **Connelly**'s 1921 satire, *Dulcy.* It wasn't until they appeared together, two years after their marriage, in the **Theatre Guild**'s sparkling 1924 production of *The Guardsman,* Molnár's droll comedy of sexual intrigue, that their reputations and the future course of their career were ensured. From then on they were known as the Lunts and, until their farewell in *The Visit* in 1958, had what was probably the most successful acting partnership of the 20th century. Audiences, critics, and fellow actors were delighted by the charged intimacy of their dual performances; their good friend Noël Coward quipped that they were really one person. Though every gesture and fraction of a pause was scrupulously intentioned, the Lunts created the illusion of spontaneity. To later generations they came to represent an outmoded stylized tradition, overdeliberate and genteel, but in their heyday they were thought to have introduced a new American style. They broke with old-fashioned Broadway acting techniques by playing comedy in a conversational way, their love scenes were startlingly physical, and their overlapping method of speaking their lines – at times they seemed to be talking simultaneously – surprised audiences of the 1920s.

Individually, each had a few notable achievements in dramas: Fontanne was the original Nina Leeds in *Strange Interlude* (1928), a role she professed not to understand, and Lunt was memorable when cast against type as a tough-talking bootlegger in **Sidney Howard**'s *Ned McCobb's Daughter* (1926); but it was in a high comedy that they excelled. Their favorite playwrights, **Robert E. Sherwood** and **S. N. Behrman,** provided them with vehicles in which the war between the sexes is a duel of wit and sly, charming manipulation. Highlights of their career include Behrman's *The Second Man* (1927), *Amphitryon 38* (1937), and *I Know My Love* (1949); Sherwood's *Reunion in Vienna* (1931), *Idiot's Delight* (1936), and *There Shall Be No Night* (1940); Sil-Vara's *Caprice* (1928); a rollicking *Taming of the Shrew* (1935), noted more for its vaudevillian spirits than for its poetry; *The Seagull* (1938); and Coward's *Design for Living* (1933). They became so closely identified with cosmopolitan comedy that producers as well as audiences were reluctant to let them try anything else; at the end of their career the Lunts expressed regret that they hadn't been asked to do such plays as *Death of a Salesman* and *Long Day's Journey into Night.*

The Lunts were renowned among actors for their dedication (holding rehearsals for minor adjustments on the last day of a run) and for their career-long devotion to "the road" (playing more one-night stands in remote towns than any other stars). They were also remarkable for their lack of greed: Unlike other stage stars, they resisted Hollywood except for one unhappy venture in 1931, when they made a film of *The Guardsman;* and when they could have commanded higher salaries from independent producers, they maintained their loyalty to the Theatre Guild. FH

See: J. Brown, *The Fabulous Lunts,* New York, 1986; P. Runkel, *Alfred Lunt and Lynn Fontanne: A Bibliography,* Waukesha, WI, 1978; M. Zolotow, *Stagestruck: The Romance of Alfred Lunt and Lynn Fontanne,* New York, 1965.

Lunt–Fontanne Theatre 205 West 46th St., NYC [Architects: Carrere and Hastings]. Producer **Charles Dillingham** achieved the hallmark of success when he was able to build a theatre for his own productions in 1910. Originally known as the Globe, the Renaissance-style structure also housed his offices and apartments where he could entertain his stars and backers. In 1931, Dillingham lost his theatre, which was bought by a movie chain. It was reclaimed in 1958 by new owners, who completely renovated it and renamed it the Lunt–Fontanne for the famous husband and wife acting team. The entrance, which was originally on Broadway, was diverted to West 46th Street. The first production in the restored house was the American premiere of Friedrich Dürrenmatt's *The Visit,* starring the Lunts. The theatre is now owned by the **Nederlander** Organization. MCH

LuPone, Patti (1949–) Actress. Born in Northport, NY, LuPone studied acting at the Juilliard School, graduating in 1972. A founding member of the **Acting Company,** she demonstrated her versatility in a variety of roles: Lady Teazle in *The School for Scandal,* Kathleen in *The Hostage* (1972); Irina in *The Three Sisters,* Lucy Lockit in *The Beggar's Opera* (1973); and Rosamund in *The Robber Bridegroom,* Kitty in *The Time of Your Life* (1975). LuPone's portrayal of the title character in *Evita* (1979) won her a Tony Award and praise from **Walter Kerr** for "rattlesnake vitality." Her last major stage role was Reno Sweeney in the 1987 revival of *Anything Goes!* In recent years she has largely devoted her time to television. TLM

Luv by **Murray Schisgal,** starring **Anne Jackson, Eli Wallach,** and **Alan Arkin,** opened at New York's **Booth Theatre** on 12 November 1964 under the direction of **Mike Nichols.** This two-act comedy combines a number of styles, including farce, comedy of manners, vaudeville, and low comedy, as it hints at absurdist drama as well. As marriages are made and unmade between two men and a woman, each ends up with greater misunderstandings and problems, and the play ends in an apparent circular pattern just as nonsensical as it had begun. In 1984 it was adapted into the musical *What About Luv?*, revived at the York Theatre in 1991.   ER

Lyceum Theatre Theatre at 149 West 45th Street, NYC; designed by the architectural firm of Herts and Tallant for manager **Daniel Frohman.** Originally known as the New Lyceum to distinguish it from Frohman's earlier playhouse on Fourth Avenue and 23rd Street, the theatre opened on 2 November 1903 with a performance of *The Proud Prince,* starring **E. H. Sothern.** Under Frohman's management, the Lyceum was the home of first-class productions; it suffered a serious decline during the Depression, however, and was in danger of being torn down in 1939 when it was purchased by a group of investors that included playwrights **George S. Kaufman** and **Moss Hart** and producer **Max Gordon.** The investors sold the Lyceum in 1945, and it is presently owned by the **Shubert Organization.** During the late 1960s it was leased to the APA–Phoenix Repertory Company (see **Association of Producing Artists**).

The Lyceum seats approximately 900 and contains the most extensive complex of scene shops of any Broadway theatre, as well as an elaborate penthouse apartment. The penthouse is currently the home of the Shubert Archive, a collection of materials related to the history of the Shubert Organization. The Lyceum, which is the oldest Broadway theatre still in operation, was declared a landmark in 1975.   BMcN

Lyceum Theatre, NYC, designed by Herts and Tallant (1903) and typical of turn-of-the-century Broadway houses. Courtesy: Shubert Archive.

M

Mabou Mines A collaborative, experimental theatre company, founded formally in 1970 after years of collaborative work among founding members **JoAnne Akalaitis, Lee Breuer,** and **Ruth Maleczech** in San Francisco, and later in Europe with Philip Glass and **David Warrilow.** The company has developed a formal performance style that synthesizes traditional motivational acting, narrative techniques, and mixed media – revealing the influence of the group's regular collaboration with painters, sculptors, video artists, filmmakers, and composers. Though this distinctive acting style is always evident in Mabou productions, the group's directors leave their own particular stamps. Breuer's *The Red Horse Animation* (1970), *The B. Beaver Animation* (1974), and *The Shaggy Dog Animation* (1978) are theatrically clever and inventive, funny, and self-reflexive; as opposed, for instance, to Akalaitis's ironically romping *Dead End Kids* (1982) or her hyperreal production of Kroetz's *Through the Leaves* (1984). In addition to creating original works, Mabou is considered one of the foremost interpreters of Samuel Beckett: Its influential productions of *The Lost Ones, Play, Come and Go, Cascando,* and *Company* combine narration and elaborate visual spectacle. More recent productions include Linda Hartinian's *Flow My Tears, the Policeman Said* (1988) and a gender-reversed *King Lear* (1990). In residence for three years at **La MaMa,** Mabou has performed at the **New York Shakespeare Festival** and elsewhere since 1975. In 1986 they received an Obie for sustained achievement. AS

See: B. Marranca, ed., *Animations: A Trilogy for Mabou Mines,* New York, 1979.

McAnuff, Des (1952–) Artistic Director of the La Jolla (CA) Playhouse. A playwright, composer, and director in Toronto in the early 1970s, McAnuff moved to New York (1976) to become Associate Director and Literary Manager of the **Chelsea Theater Center.** He cofounded the Dodger Theatre at the **Brooklyn Academy of Music** (1978) and joined the faculty of the Juilliard School (1979). Artistically, he directed a new version of his own *Leave it to Beaver Is Dead* for the **New York Shakespeare Festival**'s **Public Theater,** staged *Henry IV, Part 1* in the Festival's Delacorte Theater in August 1981, and became artist-in-residence at the Festival for the 1981–2 season. The La Jolla Playhouse had been a summer theatre for film actors (1947–64), and in 1978 its Board of Trustees contributed $3.25 million to the University of California, San Diego, for the purpose of reviving the company. Under McAnuff, the Playhouse offered 47 productions during 1983–91, including 10 world premieres and six West Coast premieres, and featuring such artists as **Peter Sellars, Robert Woodruff, Geoff Hoyle, Bill Irwin, Lee Blessing,** and Lynn Redgrave. JDM

MacArthur, Charles (1895–1966) Playwright. A Chicago newspaperman who collaborated with **Ben Hecht,** another Chicago newspaperman, on their most famous play, *The Front Page* (1928), a farcical caricature of newspaper life. Before this, he had collaborated with **Edward Sheldon** on *Lulu Belle* (1926), about a black courtesan, and with **Sidney Howard** on *Salvation* (1928), about a woman evangelist; both are weak melodramas. The partnership with Hecht also produced *Twentieth Century* (1932), a broad comedy on theatre people; *Jumbo* (1935), a circus musical; *Ladies and Gentlemen* (1939), a murder mystery that served as a vehicle for his wife, **Helen Hayes;** and *Swan Song* (1946), a suspense melodrama. Alone, he wrote *Johnny on a Spot* (1942), a political satire. He also did some screenwriting. TP

See: B. Hecht, *The Improbable Life and Times of Charles MacArthur,* New York, 1957.

Macauley, Barney (1837–86) Actor and manager. Beginning his career as an actor in Buffalo, NY (1853), he became a leading actor in the Ohio

Frederick Neumann and Ruth Maleczech in the Mabou Mines production of *Through the Leaves* by Franz Xaver Kroetz, directed by JoAnne Akalaitis. Photo: Joseph Schuyler. Courtesy: Mabou Mines.

Valley in 1861, and made his New York debut opposite **Matilda Heron** during 1864–5. He entered management in partnership with John Miles of Cincinnati (1868–72), and in 1872 assumed solo management in Louisville, where he had always been popular. He built his **Macauley's Theatre** there in 1873; in 1878 he turned the management over to his brother, John, spending the rest of his career as the star of his own combination playing a rural melodrama, *The Messenger from Jarvis Section.*
DMcD

Macauley's Theatre (Louisville) Seating 1,800, it was the leading theatre in town when it opened in 1873. Its **stock company** was disbanded in 1878, and it became a combination house under **Barney Macauley**'s brother, John. After 1880 it was part of the circuit organized by George Dickson, though John Macauley bought it from his brother's creditors in 1881. The last live performance staged there was in 1925. DMcD

MacBird! by Barbara Garson. The Obie-winning satire opened 22 February 1967 and, despite negative reviews, ran 386 performances at New York's Village Gate, **Circle in the Square,** and **Garrick Theatre.** Directed by Roy Levine, replaced a few weeks before opening by **Gerald Freedman,** the play uses Shakespeare's *Macbeth* to blame Lyndon Johnson for President Kennedy's death. The cast included **Stacy Keach** (Macbird), Rue McClanahan (Lady Macbird), William Devane (Robert Ken O'Dunc), and Paul Hecht (John Ken O'Dunc). REK

McCann, Elizabeth (Ireland) (1931–) and **Nellie Nugent** (1939–) Producers who met while working for **James Nederlander.** McCann came to Nederlander in 1967 with a law degree and experience with other producers; Nugent came in 1971 after a decade of stage managing. In 1976, they formed McCann and Nugent Productions, one of the most successful firms in New York until its dissolution in 1987. By 1985, when Nugent went to California to produce film and television, the team had earned 58 Tony nominations and 20 awards for their 22 Broadway productions. Their most successful shows include *Dracula* (1978 revival), *The **Elephant Man*** (1979), *Amadeus* (1980), *Morning's at Seven* (1980 revival), *Mass Appeal* (1981), *Nicholas Nickleby* (1981), *The Dresser* (1981), *Crimes of the Heart* (1982), and **Howe**'s *Painting Churches* (1983). In 1978, they became general managers of the **Vivian Beaumont Theatre.** Working together harmoniously, McCann handled the overview (contracts, marketing) and Nugent the details (designers, crews). They were closely involved in all their projects, and worked effectively with the feuding Nederlander and **Shubert organization**s. As women lacking established financial backers, their success was unusual. Nugent is now managing and general partner of Foxboro Entertainment in California, and McCann produces theatre in New York. TH-S

McCarter Theatre Center for the Performing Arts Located on the campus of Prince-ton University (NJ) and built originally in 1929 as home for Princeton's Triangle Club, the theatre, with over 1,000 seats, became a favorite in the 1930s and '40s for pre-Broadway tryouts and post-Broadway tours. (*Our Town* and *Bus Stop* premiered there.) In 1973 the Center became a nonprofit corporation presenting a resident theatre company presenting a core of five productions annually (with over 400 presentations at the center each year). New play development and international exchange have been key ingredients in McCarter programming. In 1990 playwright-director **Emily Mann** succeeded Nagle Jackson as artistic director, offering as her inaugural production (January 1991) *The Glass Menagerie* with Shirley Knight. DBW

McCaull, John A. (c. 1845–94) Scottish-born impresario of American comic opera in the 1880s. From soldiering for the South during the Civil War, McCaull turned to theatre as a promoter and producer. **Francis Wilson** suggests that "he had been trained to the law" and, after "defending some theatrical suit," found a career in the theatre. He established the McCaull Opera Comique Company, with branches in Philadelphia, Washington, DC, and New York. He produced the operettas of American composers, including John Philip Sousa and the team of **Harry B. Smith** and **Reginald De Koven,** and presented imported European *opéra bouffe.* Comic opera stars Marion Manola, Lilly Post, **Francis Wilson,** and **Jefferson De Angelis** worked with McCaull in their early days. TLM

McClendon, Rose (1884–1936) African-American actress who became totally committed to theatre after winning a scholarship to the **American Academy of Dramatic Art.** Playing her first professional role in Galsworthy's *Justice* (1919), she advanced steadily to the top of the profession, holding lead roles in **Paul Green**'s 1926 Pulitzer Prize play *In Abraham's Bosom* and in **Dorothy and DuBose Heyward**'s melodrama *Porgy* (see *Porgy and Bess*), in which she was called "the perfect aristocrat of Catfish Row." Known on Broadway as the "Negro race's first lady," she used her influence with the union to promote the needs of fellow black actors. In 1935 she appeared as Cora in **Langston Hughes**'s long-running melodrama *Mulatto,* from which she withdrew in ill health and died the following year. EGH

McClintic, Guthrie (1893–1961) Actor, director, and producer. Born in Seattle, McClintic studied acting at the **American Academy of Dramatic Arts** before making his first stage appearance in 1913, and his New York debut a year later. During the 1915–16 season, he appeared in numerous roles with **Grace George**'s Company at the **Playhouse Theatre,** followed by a 10-year association with producer **Winthrop Ames.** McClintic began his career as a director and producer in 1921 by presenting A. A. Milne's *The Dover Road.* In the same year he married actress **Katharine Cornell** and began a long professional association with her as the director of her major successes. Recognized as one of the most distinguished directors in the American theatre, McClintic staged more than

90 productions, including the Pulitzer Prize–winning *The Old Maid* (1935) and **Winterset** (1935), which won the New York Drama Critics' Circle Award. His other major credits include *The Barretts of Wimpole Street* (1931); *Yellow Jack* (1934); *Ethan Frome* and *The Wingless Victory* (1936); *High Tor* and *Candida* (1937); **No Time for Comedy** and *Key Largo* (1939); *The Doctor's Dilemma* (1941); *You Touched Me* (1945); *The Playboy of the Western World* (1946); *Antony and Cleopatra* (1947); *Life with Mother* (1948); *Medea* (1949); *The Constant Wife* (1951); and *Bernadine* (1952). He was known for casting his shows wisely and knowing how to get the most out of his actors. **Brooks Atkinson** called McClintic "one of our most accomplished directors, especially for plays that depend on taste and elegance." TLM

See: J. Tillinghast, "Guthrie McClintic, Director," PhD diss., Indiana U, 1964.

McCloskey, James J. (1825–1913) Actor, playwright, manager. For some time the manager of the Park Theatre in Brooklyn, the Canadian-born McCloskey was best known as a playwright. His action-packed melodramas, such as **Across the Continent** (1870), which starred Oliver Doud Byron, and *Jesse James, The Bandit King* (1881), which he wrote for James H. Wallick, often drew on his California mining experiences. It was said that five of McCloskey's dramas once played in five New York theatres at the same time. In addition to his theatrical activities, McCloskey served for 35 years as clerk of the City Court of New York. RAH

McCree, Junie (né Gonzalvo Macrillo) (1866–1918) Vaudevillian and writer. As a member of the Bella Union **stock company** in **San Francisco**, McCree worked out the "dope fiend" character he played with great success on the variety stage in the sketch "Sappho in Chinatown." He was elected Big Chief of the early **vaudeville** union The White Rats, directing its strike in 1916. After opening an agency in New York, McCree became the most sought-after writer in vaudeville and **burlesque**, supplying sketches and patter for hundreds of acts. His material, including such standards as "Roxie" and "The Travelling Salesman," launched slang and catchphrases (e.g., "coffin nails" for cigarettes) that became part of the American vernacular, but lexicographers have never given him the credit he deserves. LS

McCullers, (Lula) Carson (1917–67) Novelist and playwright whose 1950 dramatization of her novel **The Member of the Wedding** was acclaimed and later successfully filmed and televised. With Mary Rodgers, McCullers also wrote a musical version called *F. Jasmine Addams* (1971). Although other playwrights dramatized her novels, McCullers's only other play was *The Square Root of Wonderful* (1957). FB

See: V. Carr, *The Lonely Hunter: A Biography of Carson McCullers,* Garden City, NY, 1975; M. McDowell, *Carson McCullers,* Boston, 1980.

McCullough, John (1832–85) Irish-born actor who made his stage debut at the **Arch Street Theatre** in Philadelphia in 1857 in *The Belle's Stratagem.* He subsequently toured with **E. L. Davenport** (1860–1) and **Edwin Forrest** (1861–5). A tall, classically handsome man in the heroic mold, McCullough's volatile, physically robust acting style resembled Forrest's. After the latter's death in 1872, he assumed several of Forrest's major roles, including Spartacus in *The Gladiator,* Virginius, and Jack Cade. He also excelled as Othello, King Lear, Coriolanus, and Mark Antony. During 1866–77 he managed the **California Theatre** in **San Francisco,** for the first four years in association with **Lawrence Barrett.** A heavy financial loss forced his retirement from management, and he spent the rest of his career as a successful touring star. In 1881 he made a brief starring engagement at London's Drury Lane, appearing as Virginius and Othello. In 1883, his health declined; in the summer of 1885, he was placed in a mental institution. DJW

See: W. Winter, ed., *In Memory of John McCullough,* New York, 1889.

McCullough, Paul see **Clark, Bobby**

MacDonald, Christie (1875–1962) Singer and actress who began her career in a summer theatre in Boston, and by 1892 was singing supporting roles in the **Francis Wilson** Opera Company. Her first starring role was in *Princess Chic* (1900), after which she appeared in a succession of comic operas, including *The Toreador* (1902), *The Sho-Gun* (1904), *The Belle of Mayfair* (1906), *Miss Hook of Holland* (1907), and *The Prince of Bohemia* (1910). MacDonald made her greatest success in *The Spring Maid* (1910). In 1913 she starred as Sylvia in the operetta *Sweethearts,* which **Victor Herbert** had composed with her in mind. She was also seen in a revival of *Florodora* (1920). Possessed of a sweet, delicate, slightly weak singing voice of impressive range, MacDonald captivated audiences with her vivacious, unaffected personality and her nimble dancing. MK

Macgowan, Kenneth (1888–1963) Producer and critic. For years Macgowan wrote reviews chiefly for the *New York Globe* and *Theatre Arts,* sometimes whimsically reviewing plays he produced for **Experimental Theatre, Inc.,** which he founded with **Robert Edmond Jones** and **Eugene O'Neill** (1924). There he produced six of O'Neill's plays, including **All God's Chillun Got Wings** (1924), **Desire Under the Elms** (1924), and *The **Great God Brown*** (1926), as well as the first New York production of Strindberg's *Ghost Sonata* (1924) and a popular revival of **Mowatt's** *Fashion* (1924). Although he produced into the 1930s, perhaps his greatest contributions were his books on masks and modern theatrical practice. The most influential of these were *The Theatre of Tomorrow* (1921), *Footlights Across America* (1929), *Continental Stagecraft* (1922) with Robert Edmond Jones, and *Masks and Demons* (1923) with **Herman Rosse.** RHW

Machado, Eduardo (1953–) **Cuban**-born playwright who grew up and performed as an actor in California before working with **Maria Irene**

Fornés in the Padua Hills Playwrights' Festival (1978) and in the first **INTAR** playwriting workshop in New York. The author of more than 20 plays, Machado has been produced at major theatres in New York, San Francisco, Los Angeles, London, and Santa Fe. He has written four plays based on the tribulations of his family in Cuba, including *Broken Eggs,* first produced by New York's Ensemble Studio Theatre and part of **Theatre Communications Group**'s *Plays in Process* series in 1984, and *In the Eye of the Hurricane,* produced by the **Actors Theatre of Louisville** Humana Festival (1991).   ER

Machinal Sophie Treadwell loosely based her innovative drama on the sensational Ruth Snyder–Judd Gray murder trial. Produced by **Arthur Hopkins,** with sets by **Robert Edmond Jones,** it opened on 7 September 1928 at New York's **Plymouth Theatre** for 91 performances. Starring Zita Johann as the "young woman" and a little known actor, Clark Gable, as her lover, the play depicted a woman victimized and dehumanized by all around her. Nine short episodes deal with various stages of her numbed life. Only briefly, with her lover, is she freed from her stupor – enough so that she kills her husband and is sentenced to the electric chair. The play, which **John Gassner** called "one of the most unusual plays of the 20s," was praised for its expressionistic style and staccato dialogue, which so aptly matched the theme. In 1933 it was performed successfully in Moscow, and it has had several revivals in the U.S., most recently a critically acclaimed one by the **New York Shakespeare Festival** (1990).   FB

McIlrath, Patricia [Anne] (1917–   ) Director and educator. She left her theatre faculty position at the University of Illinois (Urbana) to chair the University of Kansas City (now UMKC) theatre department. An **Off-Broadway** directing job in 1959 demonstrated to her the failure of academic programs to prepare students for professional theatre, so she made it her mission to provide that experience, founding the **Missouri Repertory Theatre** in 1964 and serving until 1985 as its artistic director while continuing to chair the department. She personally directed over 100 productions. Recipient of many national honors, "Dr. Mac" is a radiant spirit.   FHL

McIntyre, James (1857–1937) and **Thomas Heath** (1852–1938) Two-man blackface act, the longest lasting (1874–1924) of all major **minstrel–vaudeville** duos. Though born elsewhere, both grew up in the South, where they learned to mimic blacks. McIntyre, a former clog dancer and small-time actor, was the comic; Heath, the straight man, was an ideal feeder for his partner, leading him into preposterous predicaments in sketches such as "The Georgia Minstrels," "The Man from Montana," "Chickens" (with McIntyre in drag), and "The Ham Tree" (the last becoming a full-length piece presented by **Klaw** and **Erlanger,** first in 1905). In 1916 the *New York Dramatic Mirror* carped that 90% of their act was tedium, 10% laughs; yet they persisted for almost a decade longer. Rumor that

they did not speak for 25 years was vehemently denied.   DBW

Mack, Charles see **Moran, George**

Mackay, Constance D'Arcy (1887–1966) Pioneer in **children's theatre,** community drama, and **pageantry.** A prolific writer, she published her first collection of children's plays in 1909 and her first pageant in 1911; her last play was published in 1952. Her book *The Little Theatre in the United States* (1917) was an early effort to proselytize for **community theatre.** During 1918–19 she was Director of Pageantry and Drama for the War Camp Community Service. Her plays and pageants were imaginative and well crafted, drawn from folk and historical sources.   NP

MacKaye, Percy (1875–1956) Playwright whose grand dramatic visions resembled those of his father, **Steele MacKaye.** He wrote *St. Louis Masque* (1914), celebrating the 150th anniversary of the city's founding; *Caliban by the Yellow Sands* (1916, in Central Park), to commemorate the tercentenary of Shakespeare's death; and his tetralogy, *The Mystery of Hamlet* (1949), which explored 30 years of the Hamlet saga prior to Shakespeare's play.

His best known plays were *The Scarecrow* (1909), adapted from Hawthorne's *Feathertop,* and *Jeanne D'Arc* (1906). He crusaded for "a theatre for the people" in *The Playhouse and the Play* (1909), *The Civic Theatre* (1912), and *Community Drama* (1917), wrote 13 other plays and seven masques, six volumes of stories and poems, and an opera, *Rip Van Winkle* (1919, music by **Reginald De Koven**). [See also **pageants/pageantry.**]   RM

MacKaye, [James Morrison] Steele (1842–94) Actor, playwright, teacher, architect, and inventor. A brilliant, if erratic, dreamer, MacKaye's innovations in stage mechanics and his crusade for realism in acting and "true-to-life" dialogue marked him as "the most unsuccessful successful figure in the American theatre."

His early dreams of becoming an actor and artist, supported by unrestricted family funds, permitted him to study painting with George Inness and acting with François Delsarte (in Paris, 1869), and to found a "school of expression" in New York (1871) for propagating the Delsartian system. He made his professional debut as actor, playwright, and manager with *Monaldi* (New York, 1872), played Hamlet in London (Crystal Palace, 1873), and then achieved success as a playwright with *Rose Michel* (1875) and *Won at Last* (1877). Of his 30 plays, *Hazel Kirke* (1880), presented in his **Madison Square Theatre,** was the best: It ran for over a year and was repeatedly revived during the next two decades; but MacKaye had unwittingly contracted to assign the profits to his financial backers, the Mallory brothers.

The Madison Square Theatre, MacKaye's first venture into architecture, had an elevator stage that changed scenes in two minutes, a lighting system devised by Edison, folding seats, and an ingenious ventilating system. His second theatre, to be combined with a hotel, never progressed beyond the blueprint stage. His third, the **Lyceum** (1885), incorporated new stage machinery, fire-fighting equipment, an orchestra pit on an elevator, and quarters for America's first dramatic school.

His ultimate theatrical dream, a Spectatorium (480 ft long, 380 ft wide, and 270 ft high) for the Chicago World's Fair (1893) to house his chronicle of Columbus's adventures, *The World Finder,* was disrupted by the national financial panic and was reduced to a scaled-down Scenitorium.

A detailed account of his life and work has been written by his son, playwright **Percy MacKaye** (*Epoch,* 1927).   RM

MacLeish, Archibald (1892–1982) Poet and playwright whose dramatic reputation rests chiefly on the success of one script, *J. B.* Educated at Harvard and Yale, MacLeish had twice won the Pulitzer Prize for Poetry (1932, 1953) and had written a few unsuccessful scripts before the 1958 production of *J. B.,* a 20th-century version of the Book of Job. Besides the Pulitzer Prize for Drama in 1959, *J. B.* won the Tony Award for the same year. **Brooks Atkinson** said, "it portrays in vibrant verse the spiritual dilemma of the twentieth century"; other critics were mixed in their reactions. MacLeish's other verse dramas did not succeed, nor did *Scratch* (1971), based on Benét's story "The Devil and Daniel Webster."   SMA

> *See:* E. Mullaly, *Archibald MacLeish: A Checklist,* Amherst, 1986.

McMartin, John (1932–   ) Actor and singer. McMartin first appeared Off-Broadway in *Little Mary Sunshine* (*Theatre World* Award, 1959), and subsequently in *Sweet Charity* (Tony nomination, 1966; film, 1969), *The Great God Brown* (Drama Desk Award, 1973), *Don Juan* (Tony nomination and Drama Desk Award, 1973), *Julius Caesar* (1988), and Stoppard's *Artist Descending a Staircase* (1989). He is often on television, and his films include *All the President's Men* (1976), *Pennies from Heaven* (1981), and "Separate but Equal" (TV, 1991).   REK

McNally, Terrence (1939–   ) Playwright whose first produced script was *And Things That Go Bump in the Night* at the **Guthrie Theatre** in 1964 and on Broadway the following year. *Bad Habits,* a double-bill of *Ravenswood* and *Dunelawn,* was produced Off-Broadway and moved to Broadway in 1974. Other Broadway productions include *The Ritz* in 1975 and *Broadway* in 1979. McNally has also written drama for television and radio. Other plays include *Where Has Tommy Flowers Gone?,* (1971, New York's Eastside Playhouse), *It's Only a Play* (1982, 1986 at **Manhattan Theatre Club**), *Frankie and Johnny in the Clair de Lune* (1987, Off-Broadway and subsequently a popular regional play; 1988 Hill–Warriner Award), *The Lisbon Traviata* (1985, 1989 at MTC), and *Lips Together, Teeth Apart* (1991, MTC). His initial plays involved the major concerns of the late 1960s and early '70s – assassination, the Vietnam War, rebellion, and the sexual revolution. Although he began as an angry and outraged playwright, his more recent work is in contrast more lyrical and positive, offering unsen-timental hope for intimacy at a time when fear and death rule.   SMA

McNeil, Claudia (1917–   ) **African-American** actress best known for her role as Lena Younger in *A* **Raisin in the Sun** (1959), which ran on Broadway for three years. McNeil was a nightclub singer before her **Off-Broadway** debut as Mamie in **Langston Hughes**'s *Simply Heavenly* (1957). She was next seen as Tituba in *The* **Crucible** (1958), played a Jewish mother in *Something Different* (1967), and was Ftatateeta in *Her First Roman* (1968). Appearing in London as Sister Margaret in **James Baldwin**'s *The* **Amen Corner** (1965), she was voted best actress of the year by the critics. She had a variety of film and television appearances and returned to cabaret in 1978. McNeil was hospitalized for surgery in 1982 and later admitted to Inglemore Nursing Home in New Jersey.   EGH

McRae, Bruce (1867–1927) India-born actor of British parents. As support to such stars as Marie Burroughs, **Olga Nethersole, William Gillette** (the original Watson to his Holmes in 1899), **Julia Marlowe, Ethel Barrymore** (for seven years), and **Mrs. Fiske** (John Rosmer in *Rosmersholm*), McRae developed into a solid craftsman and leading man but never reached true stardom.   DBW

McVicker, James Hubert (1822–96) Actor and theatre manager who first achieved national recognition as an actor of "**Yankee**" characters in the 1850s. In 1857 he settled in **Chicago** and built his **McVicker's Theatre,** which he managed successfully until his death. Although the theatre was destroyed in the great Chicago fire of 1871 and burned again in 1890, it was rebuilt on both occasions in less than a year. McVicker was a highly regarded manager, noted for the quality of his stock company and for his carefully mounted revivals of *The School for Scandal, A Midsummer Night's Dream,* and *The Tempest.* His adopted daughter Mary Runnion McVicker married **Edwin Booth** in 1869, and McVicker managed one of Booth's starring tours, including an engagement at the **Lyceum Theatre** in New York in 1876.   DJW

McVicker's Theatre Madison Street, Chicago [Architect: Otis Wheelock]. Built in 1857 by actor-manager **James H. McVicker,** the theatre was a commodious clapboard version of an Italianate palazzo and the best theatre in the West. Although he maintained a **stock company,** McVicker presented a succession of stars, from Sarah Bernhardt to **Eddie Foy.** At his death in 1896, the house passed to **Jacob Litt,** who tried to retain first-rate legitimate fare in the face of competition from vaudeville and the movies; in 1913, the house was surrendered to first one, then the other. During its history, it was rebuilt four times. In 1871, after a remodeling, the theatre was consumed by the Chicago fire and was rebuilt. In 1885, McVicker engaged Adler and Sullivan to remodel it and, in 1890, after it burned for a second time, it was again resurrected. In 1922, it was razed and a new house for movies was erected on the site; it, too, was demolished in 1984.   MCH

Madison Square Theatre. Courtesy: Becker Theatre Library, Brown University.

Madame Butterfly Conceived as a curtain-raiser to a full-length farce, this one-act by **David Belasco** provided the basis for Giacomo Puccini's famous opera. Belasco adapted the play from a short story by John Luther Long and produced it with **Blanche Bates** at the Herald Square Theatre in 1900. His lighting effects – especially one 14-minute scene of lighting changes without dialogue – plus Bates's innocence and motherly passion helped to ensure the production's success. Billed as a "tragedy of Japanese life," the play represents Cho-Cho-San as a typical and trusting Japanese woman who, believing she is married to an American naval officer named Pinkerton, awaits his return with the child of their love. When Pinkerton finally arrives with his American wife, Cho-Cho-San kills herself. Belasco's production toured widely in the U.S. and to London, where Puccini saw it in 1900. In his *M. Butterfly* (1988), playwright **David Henry Hwang** attacked the gendered ethnocentrism of Puccini's opera and, implicitly, Belasco's play. The opera also served as inspiration for the musical *Miss Saigon*.   BMcC

Madison Square Theatre West 24th St., between Broadway and Sixth Avenue, NYC. When the **Fifth Avenue Theatre** burned and its manager **Augustin Daly** moved to another theatre, the house was not immediately rebuilt. Four years later, in 1877, it was resurrected to become Minnie Commings's Drawing Room with an open stage. In 1879, backed by the Mallory brothers, **Steele MacKaye** gutted and redesigned the house, installing his famous double stage, experimenting with atmospheric lighting, relocating the orchestra above the stage, and improving the comfort of his patrons with his invention of the folding chair. The theatre

was renamed the Madison Square. In 1880, he had his greatest triumph with *Hazel Kirke;* the play brought about a falling-out with the Mallorys, and MacKaye left the playhouse. In 1884, **A. M. Palmer** was asked to take over, and his businesslike methods and his policy of presenting stars in imported and stageworthy plays brought great prosperity to the house. In 1891, **Charles H. Hoyt** secured the lease to showcase his own plays and eventually changed the name to Hoyt's Theatre. On his death, it was rented on a run-of-the-play basis; but in 1908, obsolete and too far downtown, it was razed to make way for an office building.
    MCH

Magic in the United States Outlawed from performance by strict New England Puritans in the 17th century, by the mid-1700s itinerant conjurors cut a path through burgeoning American communities with their trunks full of wonder. Performing in taverns and assembly rooms, a handful of performers, skillful and audacious, earned a reputation and a living.

Native Americans created fascinating magic as part Shamanistic rites and ritual performances; but the first American magician to gain fame, Jacob Meyer, born in 1734, was ironically never acknowledged in his homeland. Adopting the name of his native city, **Jacob Philadelphia** became one of the most famous performers of Europe. His show was a combination of mechanical and sleight-of-hand illusions and ghostly projections of eerie figures produced by a hidden magic lantern, called "Phantasmogoria."

At the beginning of the 19th century **Richard Potter** became the first indigenous magician to gain prominence in the U.S. Potter, a mulatto, performed successfully, also exhibiting ventriloquism and fire resistance, and was able to retire with a small fortune.

By the middle of the 19th century, magicians were performing in legitimate theatres and presenting full-evening shows. Native-born stars like Jonathan Harrington and John Wyman enjoyed great popularity. Wyman was an early proponent of gift shows, promising the members of his audience prizes of a variety of items, such as glassware, comestibles, and livestock, in a minilottery designed to boost attendance.

The relationship of magic to religion was responsible for a distinctly American branch of performance that began with the birth of spritiualism in 1848. In that year, Margaret and Kate Fox, young daughters of a modest farmer on the outskirts of Rochester, NY, produced strange rapping noises that were interpreted to be communications from the spirit world. Although the Fox sisters later confessed they were able to make these mystical sounds by imperceptibly cracking the knuckles of their toes, millions of people embraced spiritualism, and entertainers began to exploit the phenomenon by staging shows that apparently utilized psychic agency.

A host of performers, like the **Davenport Brothers** from Buffalo, NY, learned methods to extricate themselves from restraints, produce phenomena, and then cleverly rebind themselves. These performers led the way to stage mind-readers, another American innovation, which began with the performances of J. Randall Brown and Washington Irving Bishop. Bishop, in a spectacular test, would ask for a pin to be hidden anywhere within a five-mile radius. Blindfolded and placed in a horse-drawn carriage, he madly led his team through the streets of New York; stopping suddenly in front of a particular building, he would rush into the lobby and retrieve the hidden object.

By the 1870s, American magic had its first superstar in **Alexander Herrmann,** whose father and elder brother were also conjurers of note. Alexander captured the imagination of the American public with his skill, personality, and appearance (his formally dressed, lean and goateed look set the standard for magicians for decades to come). At his death in 1896 he was one of the country's most beloved theatrical figures, much lauded and lamented. His wife Adelaide, a former trick cyclist and long-time assistant, continued with the show, becoming the country's most famous woman magician during a 40-year career.

Harry Kellar, an Ohio-born conjurer, ascended to the position of America's most prominent and beloved magician. Heavily influenced by England's great magicians, Maskelyn and Devant, Kellar imported mysteries and stamped them as his own. His exquisite levitation of a sleeping lady was a sensation.

In 1907 Kellar toured with **Howard Thurston,** to whom he awarded his mantle of magic upon retirement. The youngster greatly enlarged the Master's show and presented the biggest illusion spectacle ever seen. Traveling with tons of equipment, Thurston became the premier prestidigitator in America with his massive and intriguing illusions.

Only one performer rivaled him: **Harry Houdini,** the legendary perplexer whose name became synonymous with magic itself. Born in Budapest in 1874, Houdini claimed to have come from Appleton, WI, where his family emigrated. He built his act on a unique principle – the challenge – daring his audience to find a restraint from which he could not escape. He extricated himself from straitjackets, tanks of water, prison cells, giant footballs, and even the belly of a sea-serpent. An unrelenting publicist, he continually dreamed up stunts to keep his name in front of the public. Recognizing the importance of the nascent cinema industry, he appeared in films and even started his own movie company. Ironically, he never succeeded with a large-scale magic show.

When Houdini died in 1926 magic was enjoying enormous popularity. The big illusion show of Thurston, as well as those of Carter, Nicola, Raymond, **Blackstone,** and Dante, entertained thousands both in the U.S. and abroad.

Surprisingly, a much more modest show by an American emigrant from Austria-Hungary, Max Malini, generated the headlines the big illusionists greatly coveted. A combination of startling impromptu sleight-of-hand, unlimited chutzpah, and a distinctive personality ensured Malini's success.

He pioneered the lucrative field of private entertainments in the homes of America's most prominent and wealthy families, often entertaining presidents and foreign royalty.

The **vaudeville** era brought specialty to magic. Houdini with his escapes, "King of Koins" T. Nelson Downs, Nate Leipzig the elegant card worker, and others who performed exclusively with objects such as watches, billiard balls, or silk handkerchiefs out-lived vaudeville itself.

The **Chautauqua and Lyceum** circuits provided a home for magicians specializing in family entertainment. The **nightclub** era introduced great acts like Cardini, with his impeccable production of lit cigarettes, and Channing Pollock, who elegantly produced live doves. These two influential stage magicians spawned more imitators than can be imagined, as a consequence of both live and televised appearances in the 1950s.

American magicians have excelled in the presentation of impromptu or close-up magic using sleight-of-hand. A Canadian performer transplanted to California set the standard for all such artists in the 20th century: **Dai Vernon** revolutionized this branch of the conjurer's art with his approach to naturalness, his technical innovations, and his dignified presentations.

Television created both opportunities and problems for magicians who suddenly found a single audience numbering more people than would witness an entire career of live theatrical performances. In spite of the credibility gap created by magic on television, the medium has proven most viable for modern performers. **Doug Henning, Siegfried and Roy, Penn and Teller,** and **David Copperfield** utilized television appearances to attract large audiences to their live shows, attesting to the continuing popularity of magic as a theatrical entertainment.   RJ

See: M. Christopher, *The Illustrated History of Magic,* New York, 1973; S. Clarke, *The Annals of Conjuring,* New York, 1983; E. J. Coleman, *Magic: A Reference Guide,* Westport, CT, 1987; E. Dawes, *The Great Illusionists,* Secaucus, NJ, 1979; R. Jay, *Learned Pigs and Fireproof Women,* New York, 1987; C. Pecor, *The Magician on the American Stage, 1752–1874,* Washington, DC, 1977; T. A. Waters, *Encyclopedia of Magic and Magicians,* New York, 1988.

Magic Theatre, The Though it has premiered works of numerous modern playwrights, this **San Francisco** company is best known for unveiling major plays by **Sam Shepard:** *Buried Child* (1978), *True West* (1979), and *Fool for Love* (1983). Founded in a Berkeley bar in 1967 by director John Lion, an admirer of European absurdism, the Magic soon turned to new American plays and **performance art,** forming alliances with Shepard, Michael McClure (whose *The Beard* catalyzed a **censorship** battle in 1974), **Adele Edling Shank,** and others. In 1977 the Magic settled into two small theatres in Fort Mason Center, naming critic-scholar Martin Esslin dramaturge. New, nonnaturalistic plays were emphasized until the late 1980s, when mainstream Off-Broadway hits (and even an **O'Neill** drama) crept onto the schedule. In 1990 Lion resigned, replaced by Harvey Seifter. Though more eclectic, the Magic still premieres new plays, for which in 1986 it received the **Margo Jones** Award.   MB

Maguire, Thomas (1820?–96) Dominant gold rush theatre producer, dubbed the "Napoleon of the San Francisco stage." Born in New York of poor Irish immigrants parents, he worked as a hackney driver and bartender before moving west in 1849. In **San Francisco** he first managed a gambling saloon, then opened three different theatres called the Jenny Lind. (The first two burned down; the last became the town's first City Hall.) He later operated Maguire's Opera House, Alhambra Theatre, Baldwin Theatre, and other key venues. A flamboyant risk-taker with a keen eye for talent, he lured stars like **Ada Isaacs Menken** and **Clara Morris** to California, formed the San Francisco Minstrels (1853), set up an early western touring circuit, and gave breaks to young **David Belasco** and **Lotta Crabtree**. In 1882, after financial ruination at the Baldwin, Maguire returned to New York and died there in obscure poverty.   MB

Maher, Joseph (1933–) Irish-born actor, director, and playwright. Maher plays farce (*Entertaining Mr. Sloan*, 1981; *Loot*, 1986; *What the Butler Saw*, 1989 [each by Joe Orton]), drama (Roose-Evans's *84 Charing Cross Road*, 1982–3), and "horrendous villains" (*The Evil That Men Do* [film, 1984]). He debuted in *The Taming of the Shrew* (Toronto, 1959), Off-Broadway in *The Hostage* (1962), and on Broadway in Bagnold's *The Chinese Prime Minister* (1964). Maher won an Obie for Hampton's *Savages* (1978) and Tony nominations for Parker and Kennedy's *Spokesong* (1979), Stoppard's *Night and Day* (1980), and *Loot*. Also a playwright-director, he wrote *Dance for Me, Simeon* (George Street Playhouse, 1979). He frequently acts in film and on television.   REK

Majestic Theatre 245 West 44th St., NYC [Architect: Herbert J. Krapp]. The Majestic was the last of the Chanin-built houses in the theatre district and, like the **46th Street Theatre,** it was designed with a rising orchestra floor somewhat like an amphitheatre. Intended for operetta and musical comedy, it had an original seating capacity of 1,700, later increased to make it one of the largest of the Broadway theatres. In 1934, it was taken over by the **Shubert brothers,** and has remained a Shubert house ever since. During most of its early history, it presented a less-than-notable series of musicals and operettas, except for its **Gilbert and Sullivan** revivals; but during its later history, it could boast of four **Rodgers** and **Hammerstein** musicals, beginning with *Carousel* (1945) and continuing with *Allegro* (1947), **South Pacific** (1949), and *Me and Juliet* (1953). In 1957, The **Music Man** took its stage, only to give it up to *Camelot* in 1960. The long-running *Phantom of the Opera* opened there in 1988. Because of its large seating capacity, musicals that become hits at other theatres are frequently moved to the Majestic to take advantage of the extra seats. A case in point is the musical *42nd Street,* which originated at the **Winter Garden** and continued its run at the Majestic.   MCH

Major, Clare Tree (1880–1954) Founder and director of the company that bore her name; an English actress who came to the U.S. in 1916. She was first associated with the **Washington Square Players,** but her interest in entertainment for young people led her to establish a professional company that toured nationally from 1923 to 1954. By 1940 the company had tripled, with a repertory of six plays for sponsors booking a series.

With a school in Pleasantville, she trained her own performers and worked with the New York Board of Education to present plays of literary quality and appropriate content for elementary and high school students [see **children's theatre**]. Mrs. Major stressed the use of international material to promote appreciation of different cultures. Her scripts were generally her own dramatizations of folk and fairy tales and children's classics. Many actors in adult theatre today got their start in Clare Tree Major's Company.   NMcC

Male Animal, The Comedy by James Thurber and **Elliott Nugent,** more closely associated with Thurber due to his established reputation as a cartoonist and writer for *New Yorker* magazine. The play follows a professor facing accusations of Communist sympathies by college regents while his wife is wooed by a former football star. It is a situational comedy similar to Thurber's stories and cartoons – an ordinary man dealing with extraordinary circumstances – yet offers poignant commentary on pre-WW II ideals regarding personal freedom and gender-related expectations. *Male Animal* opened at the **Cort Theatre** 9 January 1940 to run 243 performances. It was produced and staged by **Herman Shumlin** and starred the coauthor, Nugent, as Professor Tommy Turner, Ruth Matteson as his wife, and, in a smaller role, Gene Tierney.   KN

Maleczech, Ruth (1939–) **Mabou Mines** cofounder, actor, and director. Maleczech worked with the Actors Workshop and the **San Francisco Mime Troupe** in the 1960s, then studied in Europe with Grotowski and the Berliner Ensemble before returning to New York in 1970 to form the experimental **collective** Mabou Mines with **Lee Breuer, David Warrilow, JoAnne Akalaitis,** and Philip Glass. Her acting – direct, distanced, economical – has earned acclaim (and several Obie Awards) in Mabou Mines productions such as *The Shaggy Dog Animation* (1978), *Hajj* (1983), and *Through the Leaves* (1984). In 1990 she played the title role in Mabou's gender-reversed production of *Lear*. As a writer-director, Maleczech has collaborated on the music-theatre works *Suenos* (1988), about dictatorship, and *Fire Work*s (1987), about **censorship.**   AS

Male impersonation see **female/male impersonation**

Malina, Judith see **Living Theatre**

Malkovich, John (1953–) Actor and director, who as a member of **Chicago's** **Steppenwolf Theatre Company** since its founding in 1976 became both its most famous actor and the one whose physically engaging approach best typified the company's appeal to audiences locally and abroad. Malkovich's extraordinary ability to generate a menacing physical presence was evident when he played the violent brother in **Sam Shepard's** *True West,* a performance that won him a Joseph Jefferson Award (Chicago, 1982) and Clarence Derwent and Obie awards (1983). At the opposite end of the emotional spectrum, his tearful vulnerability in a flashback scene as Biff (opposite **Dustin Hoffman**) in *Death of a Salesman* helped earn him a Drama Desk Award (1984) and an Emmy (1986). Malkovich's work as a director includes dynamic revivals of **Lanford Wilson's** *Balm in Gilead,* for which he won Jefferson (1981), Obie (1985), and Drama Desk (1985) awards. Beginning in the mid-1980s, he appeared in a series of films, including *Places in the Heart, Making Mr. Right,* and *Dangerous Liaisons.* In 1991 he appeared in Wilson's *Burn This* in London and in a new Shepard play in New York. SF

Malpede, Karen (1945–) Writer. Malpede writes theatre history (*People's Theatre in Amerika,* 1972; *Three Works by the Open Theatre,* 1974; *Women in Theatre,* 1983) and plays combining myth, movement, and poetry to reexamine history as a **feminist** and pacifist. Many of her works appeared at New Cycle Theatre (Brooklyn), which she founded with Burl Hash in 1977. Influenced by Malina, Beck [see **Living Theatre**], and **Chaikin,** she focuses on birth and nonviolent change in *Lament for Three Women* (1974), *Rebeccah* (1976), *The End of War* (1977), *Making Peace* (1979), *A Monster Has Stolen the Sun* (1981), *Sappho and Aphrodite* (1983), and *Us* (1988). TH-S

Mamet, David (1947–) One of the most important and highly regarded dramatists to emerge from the 1970s, Mamet first attracted attention with such one-acts as *Sexual Perversity in Chicago* and *Duck Variations.* The 1977 production of *American Buffalo,* which marked his Broadway debut, offers a minimal plot; subtle character development emerges in its place. A similarly minimal script, *A Life in the Theatre* (1977), presents an elderly and a youthful actor, both on- and backstage, contrasting their different attitudes toward their work. While many traditionalists have been hostile toward or bewildered by Mamet's work, or offended by his liberal use of profanity and sexual language, the 1983–4 London and New York productions of *Glengarry Glen Ross* led to a Pulitzer Prize for Mamet. His most recent success was the **Lincoln Center** production of *Speed-the-Plow* (1988). Much of Mamet's attention since the late 1980s has been devoted to filmwriting, directing, **Chekhov** adaptations, and nonfiction efforts such as *Writing in Restaurants* (1986). In 1992 a new play, *Oleanna,* served as the first production of **Boston's** Back Bay Theater Company, which he founded with producer Patricia Wolff. SMA

See: C. Bigsby, *David Mamet,* New York, 1985; A. Dean, *David Mamet: Language as Dramatic Action,* Rutherford, NJ, 1990.

Mamoulian, Rouben (1897–1987) Russian-born director. While preparing for a law career at the University of Moscow, Mamoulian attended Vakhtangov's Studio Theatre. After graduation he went to London, and in 1922 successfully staged *The Beating on the Door* at the St. James's Theatre. In 1923 he was invited to Rochester, NY, by George Eastman, and for the next three years headed the Eastman Theatre. In 1926 he became a teacher at the **Theatre Guild** in New York, and a year later made his Broadway directing debut with *Porgy,* gaining a reputation for integrating music, drama, and dance into a rhythmic whole. He staged six plays in 1928, including **O'Neill's** *Marco Millions;* two plays in 1929, including Karel Capek's *R.U.R.;* and four in 1930, including *A Month in the Country.* Dividing his time between Hollywood and New York during the 1930s, his theatrical output declined. His other outstanding stage credits include *Porgy and Bess* (1935); *Oklahoma!* (1943); *Carousel* (1945), which won him a Donaldson Award for best director; and *Lost in the Stars* (1949). His 16 films include *Applause* (1929), *Dr. Jekyll and Mr. Hyde* (1932), *Golden Boy* (1939), *Blood and Sand* (1941), and *Silk Stockings* (1957). TLM

See: T. Miln, *Rouben Mamoulian,* Bloomington, IN, 1969; M. Spergel, "Rouben Mamoulian: Reinventing Reality – His Art and His Life," PhD diss., City U of New York, 1990.

Manhattan Punch Line New York comedy theatre, founded in 1979 by Mitch McGuire, Faith Caitlan, and Steve Kaplan, who remains artistic director. Devoted to comedy in theory and practice, MPL maintains a Comedy Institute as well as developing and producing comedic plays and revues, including a Festival of One-Act Comedies. CLJ

Manhattan Theatre Club Off-Broadway company founded by Philip Barber (first artistic director), **Gene Frankel, William Gibson,** Barbara Hirschl, A. E. Jeffcoat, Peregrine Whittlesley, Margaret Kennedy, George Tabori, Girard L. Spencer, and Joseph Tandet in 1970 to develop new work. Under Artistic Director (since 1972) **Lynne Meadow,** MTC's goal is "to present well-crafted, bold, challenging plays by major writers from America and around the world"; but, according to Meadow, "we don't do non-linear plays."

MTC's productions include **McNally's** *Bad Habits* (1973–4); **Jacker's** *Bits & Pieces;* **Fugard's** *The Blood Knot* (Obie, 1976); David Rudkin's *Ashes* (Obie, 1976; with **New York Shakespeare Festival**); *Ain't Misbehavin'* (Tony, 1978); Beckett's *Play, That Time,* and *Footfalls* (1978); Bill C. Davis's *Mass Appeal* (1980); **Henley's** *Crimes of the Heart* (Pulitzer Prize), 1981) and *The Miss Firecracker Contest* (1984); **van Itallie's** new translations of **Chekhov's** *The Seagull* (directed by **Joseph Chaikin,** 1975) and *The Three Sisters* (1982); *Loot* (1985); *Frankie and Johnny in the Clair de Lune* (1987); *Hunting Cockroaches* (1987); **Richard Greenberg's** *Eastern Standard* (1988); McNally's *The Lisbon Traviata* (Lucille Lortel Award, Directing, 1989); Friel's *Aristocrats* (Lucille Lortel Award, 1989); **Wilson's** *The Piano Lesson* (1990, with **Yale Rep** and **Center Theatre Group**); Ayckbourn's *A Small Family Business* (1991–2); and the operas *Little Mahagonny* (1973) and *The Breasts of Tiresias* (1974). MTC received a 1977 Obie for "Sustained Excellence" and a 1989 Drama Desk Award for "setting high standards, encouraging new playwrights and importing unusual plays from abroad."   REK

Manhattan Theatre Company Harrison Grey Fiske established this company at the Manhattan Theatre (formerly the Standard Theater) in 1901 to produce plays starring his wife, popular actress **Minnie Maddern Fiske.** H. G. Fiske, editor of the *New York Dramatic Mirror* and arch opponent of the Theatrical **Syndicate,** employed a small nucleus of continuing performers and many new players for each production. The group produced from two to nine plays each season. From 1906, when Fiske abandoned the Manhattan Theater, to 1914, the Manhattan Company was on tour in support of Mrs. Fiske. Fiske was noted for his tasteful direction, his exciting crowd scenes, and his attention to detail in acting, scenery, and costumes. He recruited fine performers and molded them into an expressive ensemble.   WD

Mann, Daniel (Chugerman) (1912–91) Director. Starting at the Canadian Drama Festival (Toronto, 1939), Mann made his mark with *Come Back, Little Sheba* on Broadway (1950), followed by the film version (1952). He also directed *The Rose Tattoo* (stage, 1951; film, 1955), *Paint Your Wagon* (1951), and *A Loss of Roses* (1959). His major directing assignments from the late 1950s to 1980 were film and television projects, including "Playing for Time" (TV, 1980).   REK

Mann, Emily (1952–) Director and playwright. Currently the **McCarter Theatre** Company's artistic director, Mann has directed at the **Guthrie Theater, Brooklyn Academy of Music, American Place Theatre,** and **Actors Theatre of Louisville.** *Execution of Justice* (1986) marked her Broadway directing and playwriting debut. Mann describes her plays – *Executive, Annulla: An Autobiography* (1977), *Still Life* (1980), *Betsey Brown* (1985, with **Ntozake Shange**), and the screenplay *Winnie: The Winnie Mandela Story* – as "theatre of testimony."

Productions of *Execution of Justice* won regional awards and a 1986 Drama Desk Award; *Still Life* won 1981 Obies for Distinguished Playwriting and Direction.   REK

> See: K. Betsko and R. Koening, *Interviews with Contemporary Women Playwrights,* New York, 1987; D. Savran, *In Their Own Words,* New York, 1988.

Mann (né Goldman), Theodore (1924–) Producer and director. Mann cofounded **Circle in the Square** Theatre (with **José Quintero,** 1951), and, as artistic director, directed Circle's Broadway premiere, *Mourning Becomes Electra* (1972); other plays include *A Moon for the Misbegotten* (1969), *Ah, Wilderness!* (1969, **Ford's Theatre,** Washington, DC), *The Iceman Cometh* (1973), *The Glass Menagerie* (1975), *Pal Joey* (1976), and *The Boys in Autumn* (1985); he has also directed various operas and teleplays. Mann cofounded Circle's school (1961), and initiated an exchange with Moscow's

Maly Theatre (1989). He received 1956 Tony and Drama Critics' awards for *Long Day's Journey into Night* and a special 1976 Tony.   REK

Manners, J. Hartley (1870–1928) Playwright and director. Although he was London-born, his career after 1902 transpired in New York. Many of his plays were written as vehicles for his wife, **Laurette Taylor,** especially *Peg O' My Heart* (1912), a sentimental comedy of the poor outsider who reforms her rich relatives. This play, which ran for over 600 performances, proved one of the most popular comedies of the American theatre. Manners was also successful with *The Harp of Life* (1916) and *Happiness* (1917).   RHW

Man of La Mancha Intermissionless musical play, music by Mitch Leigh, lyrics by Joe Darion, book by Dale Wasserman; opened at the ANTA Washington Square Theatre 22 November 1965, running 2,328 performances. This musical version of the Don Quixote story adds the further dimension of Cervantes, arrested for heresy, telling his story in prison as it is acted out by the prisoners. The ultimate lesson of Cervantes/Quixote (**Richard Kiley**) is that it is the dream, not the truth, that keeps humankind going. The show was produced, on Broadway contracts, in a large temporary theatre in Greenwich Village, where the lack of an orchestra pit led to placing the orchestra (featuring acoustic guitars) upstage and split on either side of the action – a practice continued after the show transferred to a traditional Broadway house. Leigh's score, vaguely reminiscent of Spanish music, produced one huge hit, "The Impossible Dream." The show was originally produced at the **Goodspeed Opera House** before coming to New York, where it won the Drama Critics' Circle and Tony awards for best musical. For its 25th anniversary production (1991–2), **Raul Julia** took the title role in a touring production that opened on Broadway in March 1992.   JD

Man of the Hour, The Political melodrama by **George H. Broadhurst** that premiered 4 December 1906 at the Savoy Theater, New York, and ran 479 performances. Set in "any large city in America," it concerns the efforts of an unscrupulous financier and a corrupt alderman to obtain a perpetual franchise for a streetcar line. Needing the mayor as an ally, they back the wealthy and popular but naïve Alwyn Bennett (Frederick Perry) for the office. Alwyn loves the financier's niece, Dallas Wainwright (Lillian Kemble), who stirs Bennett to resist the blandishments and slanderous allegations of the corrupters, although her trust is invested in the streetcar line. A tough, honest alderman sides with him; in addition the financier's secretary (played by Douglas Fairbanks), secretly avenging the financier's ruination of his father, provides helpful information. Critics approved Broadhurst's adept plotting, his natural dialogue, and the forceful characterizations.   WD

Mansfield, Richard (1854–1907) Actor-producer. Hailed by many as America's answer to Henry Irving after the death of **Edwin Booth,** this strong personality generated critical controversy whenever he performed. He played his first important role of Baron Chevrial in *A Parisian Romance* in 1883 after a series of minor roles in England and the U.S. In 1886 he launched a production with himself as the star in the title role of *Prince Karl;* with this role, he began his successful career as a star and producer. Each year, Mansfield would arrange to occupy theatres in New York and on the road to present a repertory consisting of one or two new characters and revivals of his more successful previous vehicles. A compelling, intense actor and skillful producer, his notable roles and productions included the dual role *Dr. Jekyll and Mr. Hyde* (1887); *Richard III* and *Henry V;* Clyde Fitch's *Beau Brummell* (1890); Bluntschli in *Arms and the Man* (1894, the first production of **Shaw** in the U.S.); the title role in *Napoleon Bonaparte* (1894); Dick Dudgeon in Shaw's *The Devil's Disciple* (1897); *Cyrano de Bergerac* (1889); **Booth Tarkington**'s *Beaucaire* (1901); and **Ibsen**'s *Peer Gynt* (1907). Mansfield also produced, but did not play in, *A Doll's House* in London (1888) and in New York (1889), with Beatrice Cameron (whom he was to marry in 1892) as Nora. His productions were characterized by lavish spectacle and a meticulous attention to realistic detail. Mansfield was a forceful transitional figure on the American stage at the turn of the century, representing the waning traditions of the old era and the emerging tendencies of the new century.   MR   DJW

> *See:* P. Wilstach, *Richard Mansfield: The Man and the Actor,* New York, 1908; W. Winter, *Life and Art of Richard Mansfield,* 2 vols., New York, 1910.

Man's World, A One of **Rachel Crothers**'s earliest plays, it remains one of her most provocative as well. In a serious study of the effects of the double standard, Crothers tells the story of Frankie Ware, a successful feminist writer who rejects marriage with the man she loves, Malcolm Gaskell, when she learns he is the father of the waif she has adopted and when he insists that men can live a different kind of morality from women. Called by Arthur Hobson Quinn "one of the most significant dramas of the decade," it opened 8 February 1910 at the Comedy Theater and ran for 71 performances. The play elicited much debate in the press as well as a parody a year later by **Augustus Thomas,** called *As a Man Thinks,* which defended the double standard that Crothers attacked.   FB

Mantegna, Joe (1948–) Chicago-born actor whose work has been closely identified with plays and films of **David Mamet,** a long-time friend and associate. He appeared in premieres at the **Goodman Theatre** of Mamet's *A Life in the Theatre, The Disappearance of the Jews,* and ***Glengarry Glen Ross*** (the role of Richard Roman), winning a Tony on Broadway for the latter in 1984. He also appeared in Mamet's *Speed-the-Plow* (1988) and his films *House of Games* (1987), *Things Change* (1988), and *Homicide* (1991). *Jack Kroll* described Mantegna in 1988 as "gloriously Mametic" (with actor **Ron Silver**). Active early with Chicago's **Organic Theatre Company,** Mantegna's career has fo-

Richard Mansfield as Beau Brummel, performed first in 1890. Courtesy: Don B. Wilmeth.

cused more on films than stage work in recent years.   DBW

Mantell, Robert Bruce (1854–1928) Scottish-born actor who trained in England under some of the leading late 19th-century practitioners of "classical" acting, such as Barry Sullivan and Samuel Phelps. He came to America in 1878 as a member of **Helena Modjeska**'s touring company. He returned to England, but came back to play in support of **Fanny Davenport** in *Fedora* in 1883. In 1886 he made his first star appearance in *Tangled Lives,* a modern domestic melodrama. A series of starring tours in modern heroic melodramas outside of New York were only limited successes until he began to incorporate the tragedies of **Shakespeare** and the "classical" romances of Bulwer-Lytton into his repertory in the 1890s. In 1904 he made a triumphant return to New York and established himself as the last remaining representative of a robust, passionate "old school" of tragic acting in America, generating much discussion over the merits of this system. Among his more celebrated roles were Othello, Shylock, King John, King Lear, Macbeth, Richard III, Richelieu, and Louis XI.   MR   DJW

> *See:* A. Favorini, "The Last Tragedian: Robert Bruce Mantell and the American Theatre," PhD diss., Yale U, 1969.

Mantle, (Robert) Burns (1873–1948) Drama critic and annalist. Trained as a printer, Mantle turned to dramatic criticism in 1898 for the *Denver Times,* moved to the *Denver Republican* in 1901, and during the same year left for Chicago and a six-year stint as critic for the *Inter-Ocean* (1901–7). In 1907 he spent a year as reviewer for the *Chicago Tribune* before becoming that paper's Sunday editor. In 1911 he accepted the dramatic post for the *New York Evening Mail,* and changed jobs one last time in 1922 when he moved to the *Daily News* (1922–43). A strong supporter of the American drama, Mantle wrote in a bright and newsy style. His *Best Play* series, which he edited from 1919 until 1947–8, remains his most enduring contribution to the American stage.   TLM

Man Who Came to Dinner, The by George S. Kaufman and Moss Hart,

directed by Kaufman with scenic design by **Donald Oenslager;** opened on Broadway 16 October 1939 and ran 739 performances. The authors intended to create a vehicle for their friend **Alexander Woollcott,** the theatre critic and raconteur, and so modeled the leading role after him. Other principal roles were travesties of **Gertrude Lawrence,** Noël Coward, and Harpo **Marx.** Woollcott decided against playing himself on Broadway (although he did assay the role in California in 1940), so Monty Woolley created Sheridan Whiteside. The gimmick of the farce is that Whiteside slips on the ice outside the Ohio home he has just visited, is compelled to remain for some weeks while his broken leg knits, and takes over the household. Other cast members included Mary Wickes as Miss Preen, the nurse, and Edith Atwater as Maggie Cutler, Whiteside's confidential secretary. Warner Bros. released the film version in 1942, featuring Woolley, Wickes, Bette Davis, and **Jimmy Durante.**   JDM

Ma Rainey's Black Bottom

First (1982) of **August Wilson**'s 20th-century cycle of plays (one for each decade) on the black experience to reach Broadway. The action takes place in 1927 Chicago, where the relationships between black musicians and white managers in the confined space of a recording studio symbolize the oppressive nature of the larger society outside. Gertrude "Ma" Rainey, reigning queen of the blues, insists on maintaining the integrity of her music while an ambitious and volatile trumpeter in her band turns to violence out of frustration. The play was first produced at the **Yale Repertory Theatre** by artistic director **Lloyd Richards** before moving to the **Cort Theatre** on Broadway and winning the Drama Critics' Circle Award. The cordial and productive relationship between playwright and director has served Wilson well in his later plays.   EGH

Marble, Danforth

(1810–49) Actor who began a successful career in 1832 telling Yankee stories. In competition with **George H. Hill** and **James H. Hackett,** Marble developed a distinctive **Yankee** character with broad American idiosyncrasies. His vehicles included *The **Forest Rose,** The Vermont Wool Dealer, Yankee Land,* and *The Backwoodsman; or, The Gamecock of the Wilderness,* but his particular success was as *Sam Patch; or, The Daring Yankee* (1836). The real Sam Patch made a career

of jumping from high places: His last jump was from the top of the Genesee Falls in 1829, a distance of 125 feet. Marble made his jumps in theatres as spectacular as possible. A consummate teller of tales and strikingly costumed, he enjoyed a successful visit to England in 1844, playing before the king and queen; he sponsored a playwriting contest for new material in 1845 and toured America extensively. He died of cholera on the night of his benefit – the play, *A Cure for the Cholera.*   WJM

See: J. Kelly, *Dan Marble: A Biographical Sketch,* New York, 1851.

Marbury, Elisabeth

(1856–1933) Agent, producer, playwright. First dramatist's **agent** in the U.S., Marbury developed an international clientele of writers and performers, including **Frances Burnett,** Shaw, Wilde, Barrie, Sardou, Feydeau, **Fitch, Crothers,** the Castles, and Rostand. An astute socialite and businesswoman, she convinced international authors to negotiate royalties rather than one-time fees. She sometimes influenced casting and script development, and lobbied for improved conditions for actors. With John W. Rumsey, she founded the American Play Company in 1914, a worldwide agency. She produced the **Princess** musicals (beginning 1915), developing the story-focused musical. Decorated for war services, she was politically active.   TH-S

See: R. Strum, "Elisabeth Marbury, 1856–1933: Her Life and Work," PhD diss., New York U, 1989.

Theresa Merritt as the blues singer Ma Rainey in August Wilson's *Ma Rainey's Black Bottom*. The play transferred to Broadway from Yale Repertory Theatre in New Haven. Photo: George G. Slade. Courtesy: Yale Repertory Theatre.

March, Fredric (né Frederick McIntyre Bickel) (1897–1975) Actor. Educated at the University of Wisconsin, March made his theatrical debut (under his real name) in 1920 in Sacha Guitry's *Deburau,* and followed it closely in **George Ade**'s *County Chairman* (1921). His first major role was in **William A. Brady**'s production of *The Law Breaker* (1922). After an assortment of juvenile leads, he performed in Molnár's *The Swan* in Denver with actress **Florence Eldridge** (1926). They were married a year later and worked together for the rest of their careers. After spending most of the 1930s in Hollywood, March returned to the stage in 1938, costarring with his wife in *Ye Obedient Husband.* Working in both media, he created for the stage the roles of Mr. Antrobus in *The Skin of Our Teeth* (1942); Major Victor Joppolo in *A Bell for Adano* (1944); Nicholas Denery in *The Autumn Garden* (1951); and James Tyrone in *Long Day's Journey into Night* (1956), which won him a Tony. He appeared in 69 films, including starring roles in *Dr. Jekyll and Mr. Hyde* (1935), which won him an Oscar; *Les Misérables* (1935); *A Star Is Born* (1937); *The Best Years of Our Lives* (1946), which won him an Oscar; *Inherit the Wind* (1960); and *The Iceman Cometh* (1973). March considered the role of James Tyrone his finest work. **Brooks Atkinson** wrote: "As the aging actor who stands at the head of the family, Fredric March gives a masterly performance that will stand as a milestone in the acting of an **O'Neill** play." TLM

See: M. Burrows, *Charles Laughton and Fredric March,* St. Austell, 1969.

Margaret Fleming Domestic drama (1890) in four acts by **James A. Herne. William Dean Howells** hailed its production at **Boston**'s Chickering Hall on 4 May 1891 as "epoch-making" (or "marking") in the rise of realism in American fiction and drama. **Hamlin Garland,** Herne's friend and promoter among Boston's radical intelligentsia, proclaimed it "one of the most radical plays from a native author ever performed in America." Margaret's husband fathers a child with a mill worker in his hire. Early versions of the play end with Margaret spurning her husband's efforts at reconciliation. In the revised version, Philip is permitted to return, and emphasis shifts to a critique of the double standard of sexual morality: defamation and death for the woman offender; forgiveness and acceptance for the man. Critics who rejected the play were especially offended by the spectacle of Margaret breast-feeding her husband's starving bastard. Nevertheless, Katharine Corcoran Herne, the author's wife and a major collaborator in writing and revising the play, won nearly universal acclaim for her acting in the title role. WD

Margolis, Kari (1955–) and **Tony Brown** (1951–) Co–artistic directors of Margolis/Brown Adaptors, a multimedia movement theatre in New York City. Students of Etienne Decroux during 1975–8, they were founding members of Omnibus (Montréal), directed by Jean Asslin and Denise Boulanger, from 1978 to 1982. Group works they have created with students trained in their school

are *Autobahn* (1984); *Deco Dance* (1986); *Bed Experiment One* (1987); *Deco Danz: The Dilemma of Desmodus and Dyphilla* (1991), a duet for Margolis and Brown; and *Koppelvision and Other Digital Deities* (1991), a work for 18 actors. TL

Mark Hellinger Theatre 237 West 51st St., NYC [Architect: Thomas W. Lamb]. In the early years of the Depression, many theatres that became unprofitable for their owners were turned into moviehouses, but the Hollywood Theatre, built by Warner Bros. to showcase their most important movies, appeared to have reversed the trend. Opening in 1930, it switched to legitimate fare in 1934, but from then until 1949, when the film company disposed of it, it changed name and policy frequently. Even the entrance was diverted from Broadway to West 51st Street in 1936. In 1949, its name became the Mark Hellinger in honor of the Broadway columnist, and so it has remained. In 1956, the theatre received its most illustrious tenant in its lackluster history when *My Fair Lady* opened and held its stage until 1962. Since then, with the exception of the rock musical *Jesus Christ Superstar* (1971) and *Sugar Babies* (1979), which introduced Mickey Rooney to Broadway, there have been few outstanding productions at the theatre. Until late 1991 part of the **Nederlander** chain, it was closed in 1989, leased to a church organization for five years, and then sold to them. MCH

Mark Taper Forum Theatre 135 North Grand Ave., **Los Angeles** [Architect: Welton Beckett]. Rising from the center of a cultural mall in downtown Los Angeles is the giant, concrete, mushroom-shaped Mark Taper Forum, the home of **Gordon Davidson**'s **Center Theatre Group,** which grew out of a professional company attached to the University of California at Los Angeles. Opening in 1967, the theatre and its company are dedicated to producing new and old musicals and dramas, and to introducing new works with a West Coast flavor. The playhouse is named after a Los Angeles financier-philanthropist who was instrumental in planning and building the Los Angeles Music Center, of which the 740-seat Mark Taper Forum is part. Davidson operates two other theatres in Hol-

Mark Taper Forum, Los Angeles, designed by Welton Beckett (1964). Courtesy: Mark Taper Forum.

Falk photo (1892) of Julia Marlowe. Courtesy: Don B. Wilmeth.

lywood, from which he sometimes transfers productions into the Mark Taper.   MCH

Marks, Josephine Preston Peabody (1874–1922) Playwright-poet with a dominating interest in historical or literary material. She wrote *Marlowe* (1901), an idealized view of the poet-dramatist as revealed through his "passionate shepherd" poem, and in *The Wolf of Gubbio* (1913) dramatized the influence of St. Francis of Assisi in a man's struggle between love and greed. *Portrait of Miss W* (1922) was based on the love of Mary Wollstonecraft and William Godwin. None of these was produced. Marks's best work, *The Piper* (1910), impressed **Otis Skinner** and won the Stratford Competition. Her piper was a "fanatical idealist" in whom the forces of love, greed, and the supernatural present a universal human struggle as cynical bitterness wars with self-denying love. Marks's plays are more appreciated in the library than in the theatre.   WJM

Marlowe, Julia (1866–1950) Actress. From 1904, when **E. H. Sothern** and Julia Marlowe first appeared together, until her retirement in 1924, American theatregoers identified **Shakespeare** with Sothern and Marlowe. They were an established team even before their marriage in 1911. The roles of Rosalind, Viola, Juliet, Ophelia, and Portia became her property, and she captured the critics who praised her feminine loveliness, magnetic warmth, and admirable grace. When they appeared in England in 1907, Arthur Symons wrote: "No

actors on the British stage could speak English verse so beautifully."

Marlowe had a long and steady apprenticeship. Her family emigrated from England when she was five and settled in Cincinnati, where she appeared with a juvenile company and was tutored in the "classic" repertoire by Ada Dow, a retired actress. In 1884 Miss Dow brought her to New York, securing touring engagements for her in roles such as Lady Teazle and Miss Hardcastle, and (in 1886) as Lydia Languish with **Joseph Jefferson**'s touring company. Her first New York triumph came in 1899 in the title role in **Clyde Fitch**'s *Barbara Frietchie*.   RM

See: C. Russell, *Julia Marlowe: Her Life and Art,* New York, 1926; E. H. Sothern, *Julia Marlowe's Story,* New York, 1954.

Marowitz, Charles (1934–   ) Director and critic. American-born and English-educated, Marowitz remained in England during 1958–81 as Director, In-Stage Experimental Theatre (1958); as an associate of Peter Brook's on *King Lear* (1962) and a "Theatre of Cruelty" season (1964), which was reflected in his "collage" versions of *Hamlet* (1966), *Macbeth* (1969), *Othello* (1972), *The Taming of the Shrew* (1974), and *Measure for Measure* (1975); as Assistant Director, RSC (1963–5); Artistic Director, Traverse Theatre (1963–4); and founder of the Open Space Company (1968–81), which introduced the American avant-garde to English audiences. Returning to the U.S., Marowitz founded the Open Theatre of Los Angeles (1982) before becoming Associate Director, **Los Angeles Theatre Center** (1984–9). He has written for *Encore Magazine* (1956–63), *Plays and Players* (1968–75), the *Village Voice* (1955–   ), the *New York Times* (1966–   ), and *TheatreWeek*. His books include *The Method as Means* (1960), *Confessions of a Counterfeit Critic* (1973), *The Marowitz Shakespeare* (1978), *Recycling Shakespeare* (1990), and his memoirs, *Burnt Bridges* (1990).   TLM

Marquis Theatre 1535 Broadway, NYC [Architect: John C. Portman, Jr., with **Roger Morgan**]. The newest Broadway playhouse and the first theatre built as an integral part of a hotel, the Marriott Marquis, it is under lease to the **Nederlander** Organization for 35 years. The theatre is on the third floor, with the box office at street level. It boasts many innovations, notably concealed lighting and sound equipment in the ceiling, a steeply raked orchestra floor, and complete accessibility for handicapped persons. With a seating capacity of 1,600, it is best suited for musicals, which have been its fare since opening with *Me and My Girl* in 1986, a show that ran for nearly three and a half years.   MCH

Marriage of Bette and Boo, The, by **Christopher Durang.** After productions of a shorter version at the Yale School of Drama and the **Williamstown Theatre,** the full play was presented by **Joseph Papp**'s **New York Shakespeare Festival** on 16 May 1985, directed by **Jerry Zaks,** with a cast including Christopher Durang as the narrator Matt, whose memory play this is; Joan

Allen as his mother Bette; Graham Beckel as his father Boo; and **Olympia Dukakis** as his grandmother Soot. Using Thomas Hardy's naturalistic novels as a literary context, Durang's black comedy depicts the effects of alcohol, emotional instability, and the Catholic Church on a contemporary American family's inability to function. Attempting to understand his own life by analyzing it as if it were a literary work, narrator Matt guides the audience through the series of hilariously tragic events that he feels have determined his character and defined his life.   BCM

Marshall, E[dda] G[unnar] (1910–) Stage, film, and television actor. A distinguished veteran performer who has taken on a wide range of character types, Marshall came to Broadway in the 1930s. Notable early roles included Willie Oban in *The Iceman Cometh* (1946), Rev. John Hale and John Proctor in *The Crucible* (1953), and Vladimir in the famous production of Beckett's *Waiting for Godot* with costar **Bert Lahr** (1956). More recently he has appeared in such revivals as *John Gabriel Borkman* (1980) and *She Stoops to Conquer* (1984). Four years on the television series "The Defenders" (1961–5) earned him two Emmy Awards (1962, 1963).   MR

Marshall, Ethelbert A. (d. 1881) Manager, credited as the first businessman to dominate the American theatre. After an apprenticeship as a printer, Marshall turned to theatrical management about 1838, beginning his empire in 1840 with the **Walnut Street Theatre** (Philadelphia). By the mid-1940s, with the additional control of theatres in Baltimore and Washington, DC, he turned to starring vehicles with actors such as **Forrest, Booth, Wallack,** and **Cushman.** In 1848 he moved into New York, controlling the 4,500-seat **Broadway Theatre.** By 1850 he was the acknowledged starmaker of the American stage. Despite alliances with theatre owners in Cincinnati, Louisville, St. Louis, and New Orleans, by the mid-1850s his operation began to decline. He sold the Broadway in 1858 and spent the balance of his career as manager of the Philadelphia Academy of Music.   DBW

Martin, Ernest H. see **Feuer, Cy**

Martin, Mary (1913–90) Singer and actress who made her Broadway debut in *Leave It to Me* (1938), in which she stopped the show with her teasing rendition of "My Heart Belongs to Daddy." Her first starring role was as a statue come to life in *One Touch of Venus* (1943). Three years later, she played the faithful wife in *Lute Song,* a musical version of a traditional Chinese play. In 1947 she headed the national company of *Annie Get Your Gun.* Martin had the greatest success of her career as Nellie Forbush, a native nurse from Little Rock, AR, in **Rodgers** and **Hammerstein's** *South Pacific* (1949). Among the songs she introduced in the show were "A Cockeyed Optimist," "I'm Gonna Wash That Man Right Outa My Hair," and "I'm in Love with a Wonderful Guy." The role was ideally suited to her sunny temperament and

buoyant singing style, and also gave her an opportunity to demonstrate her skill as an actress during the show's more serious scenes. In 1954 she appeared in a musical version of James M. Barrie's *Peter Pan,* a role she repeated in two television versions of the show. Although rather mature for the part of a young novice, Martin's performance in *The Sound of Music* (1959) was a favorite with audiences. Her next show, *Jennie* (1963), was a failure. Martin starred in the London company of **Hello, Dolly!** before appearing with **Robert Preston** in *I Do! I Do!* (1966), a two-character musical that followed a couple through 50 years of married life. In most of her musical theatre roles Martin portrayed a warm-hearted idealist who ultimately triumphs over the problems she faces. Her clear singing voice, winning personality, and high spirits contributed greatly to the success of the shows in which she appeared. Her final stage role was in *Legends* in 1986 with **Carol Channing.** Her autobiography (*My Heart Belongs*) was published in 1976; a museum devoted to her career was established in her hometown of Weatherford, TX.   MK

Martin Beck Theatre 302 West 45th St., NYC [Architect: G. Albert Lansburgh]. Built in 1924 as a monument to its owner, the 1,300-seat playhouse was named after Martin Beck, a leading **vaudeville** producer of the era. Located west of 8th Avenue on the edge of the theatre district, the theatre was thought to be too far away to attract productions and audiences, but the skeptics were confounded. Opening with an operetta, it has subsequently housed a mixture of large and small productions, musical (recently *Grand Hotel*) and nonmusical, and did not endure long periods of inactivity. Its most noteworthy tenants have included productions by the **Theatre Guild,** the Irish Abbey Players, and the D'Oyly Carte Company, and plays by **Eugene O'Neill, Robert E. Sherwood, Lillian Hellman, Maxwell Anderson, Philip Barry, Edward Albee,** and **Tennessee Williams.** The theatre was a special favorite of **Katharine Cornell** and **Guthrie McClintic,** who booked the house for their repertory. Two Pulitzer Prize–winners opened at the Martin Beck: *The Teahouse of the August Moon* (1953) and *A Delicate Balance* (1966). When Martin Beck died in 1940, his widow continued to operate the theatre, but in 1966 she sold it to the **Jujamcyn** Organization.   MCH

Marx Bros. (their preferred billing) Comedy team. The first to perform were **Gummo** (Milton, 1897–1977) and **Groucho** (Julius, 1895–1977), with material written by their uncle Al Shean of **Gallagher & Shean; Chico** (Leonard, 1891–1961) and **Harpo** (Adolph, 1893–1964) joined later. Shean wrote their act "Fun in Hi Skool" (1912), with Groucho as a Dutch-accented schoolmaster, and "Home Again" (1914), directed by their formidable mother Minnie Palmer. When Gummo was drafted into war service, **Zeppo** (Herbert, 1901–79) stepped in. By the time they topped the bill at the **Palace** in 1920, they were commanding $10,000 a week for their hilarious mayhem. By then, their distinctive characteristics were in place: Zeppo, the handsome, bemused straight man; Harpo, the uninhibited curly-headed mute, honking his horn, goosing showgirls, and taking every metaphor literally; Chico, the saturnine Neapolitan, interrupting his con games only to crack bad puns and play ragtime piano; and Groucho, with his greasepaint moustache and eyeglasses, stooping lope, and unflagging cigar, confuting reason on every plane. They played London in 1922, but tiring of **vaudeville** moved to **revue** in *I'll Say She Is* (**Casino,** 1924), with its famous Napoleon scene in which Groucho ordered the band to strike up "The Mayonnaise." Their next shows, *The Cocoanuts* (Lyric, 1926) and *Animal Crackers* (44th St., 1928), were cowritten by **George S. Kaufman,** who, with **S. J. Perelman,** was largely responsible for perfecting their verbal style. With the filming of these productions, the brothers moved successfully to Hollywood, although they continued to make stage appearances during their MGM period to try out the comic scenes in their screenplays. Not so much satirists as anarchists, they flouted normality whenever they confronted it. Their film career petered out in the 1940s; Groucho became the star of a television quiz show and played a **one-person** show at Carnegie Hall. LS

See: J. Adamson, *Groucho, Harpo, Chico – and Sometimes Zeppo,* New York, 1973; R. J. Anobile, *The Marx Brothers Scrapbook,* New York, 1973.

Mary, Mary Three-act comedy by **Jean Kerr,** opened at the **Helen Hayes Theatre** 8 March 1961 for 1,572 performances; then Broadway's ninth longest-run production and fifth longest-run play. Starring **Barbara Bel Geddes** (for whom Kerr wrote the role) and **Barry Nelson,** the play comments on the attractions and distractions of marriage, divorce, and reconciliation. Critics praised Kerr, an established writer with popular books *Please Don't Eat the Daisies* and *The Snake Has All the Lines,* for her charming, articulate script liberally laced with witticisms and wisecracks. A film version starring Debbie Reynolds was made early in the run, but the play long outran the film's run. EK

Mason, Marshall W. (1940–) Director and a cofounder and artistic director of the **Circle Repertory Company** in New York. Trained at the **Actors Studio,** Mason specializes in the production of new American plays, especially those of **Lanford Wilson** (most notably *The Hot l Baltimore,* 1973; *Fifth of July,* 1978; *Talley's Folly,* 1979; *Angels Fall,* 1983; and *Burn This,* 1987). In 1985 his award-winning Circle Rep production of William M. Hoffman's *As Is,* one of the first American plays to deal with the disease **AIDS,** was transferred to Broadway. He is the recipient of an Obie Award for Sustained Achievement. In 1986 Mason resigned from Circle Rep, replaced in 1987 by Tanya Berezin. Although Mason continues to direct at Circle Rep, in recent years he also has worked at such theatres as **Steppenwolf** and **South Coast Repertory.** DBW

Massey, Raymond Hart (1896–1983) Canadian-born actor and director who became a U.S. citizen in 1944. From 1922, when he made his debut in London as Jack in **O'Neill**'s *In the Zone* at the Everyman Theatre, until 1931, when he made his Broadway debut in **Norman Bel Geddes**'s unorthodox production of *Hamlet,* he acted in England in several dozen plays and directed numerous others. Subsequently his career, largely limited to the U.S., ranged from **Shakespeare,** Strindberg, **Shaw,** O'Casey, and O'Neill in the theatre, to a wide range of villains and heroes in films (over 70), and the role of Dr. Gillespie in the television series "Dr. Kildare." His most memorable role was Lincoln in **Robert Sherwood**'s *Abe Lincoln in Illinois* (1938), which suited his imposing presence, craggy handsomeness, and vibrant voice. Other notable roles included Ethan Frome in an adaptation of the novel (1936), Harry Van in *Idiot's Delight* (1938), Sir Colenso Ridgeon in *The Doctor's Dilemma* (1941), James Morell in *Candida* (1942), Higgins in *Pygmalion* (1945), Mr. Zuss in *J. B.* (1958), and Tom Garrison in *I Never Sang for My Father* (his return to the London stage in 1970). Massey was the author of two autobiographies, *When I Was Young* (1976) and *A Hundred Different Lives* (1979). His children Daniel and Anna, born in England, have had successful careers in the theatre. DBW

Masteroff, Joe (Joseph) (1919–) Philadelphia-born librettist educated at Temple University. His first success came with the libretto for *She Loves Me* (1963), the musical adaptation of the film *The Shop Around the Corner.* In 1966 working in collaboration with producer-director **Harold Prince,** he wrote the book for *Cabaret,* a musical based on **John van Druten**'s play *I Am a Camera* and Christopher Isherwood's *Berlin Stories.* With Prince, he invented the character of the decadent Master of Ceremonies, whose musical sequences punctuate and comment upon the action. He worked with others on the libretto of *70, Girls, 70* (1971) and the **Off-Broadway** *Jane White, Who* (1980). He also wrote the libretto for the opera *Desire Under the Elms* (1989). MK

Mastrosimone, William (1947–) New Jersey-born playwright, educated at Tulane, Rider College (BA, 1974), and Rutgers (MFA, 1977). His controversial *Extremities* (1983), which dealt with attempted rape and its subsequent violence, won an Outer Critics' Circle Award and was adapted as a film with Farrah Fawcett. Like many talented writers of his generation, his work has been produced in the regional theatres rather than on Broadway. *Cat's Paw* (1986) and *The Understanding* (1987) both premiered at the **Seattle Repertory,** and *Sunshine* (1989) at the **Circle Repertory.** Among his awards are an LA Critics' "Best" for *The Woolgatherer* (1982) and a Warner Communication citation for *Shivaree* (1984). His play about the Russian invasion of Afghanistan, *Nanawatai* (1984), was released by Columbia Pictures in 1988 as *The Beast.* BBW

Matalon, Vivian (1929–) Director who studied at the **Neighborhood Playhouse** and made his professional debut as Urban in *The Caine Mutiny Court Martial* (1956) in London. He joined the LAMDA staff in 1959 and directed his first professional show, *The Admiration of Life,* in 1960. Later in London he directed *The **Glass Menagarie*** (1965), *I **Never Sang for My Father*** (1970), and **Neil Simon**'s *The Gingerbread Lady* (1974). In New York Matalon has directed *First Day of New Season* (1967); *P.S. Your Cat Is Dead* (1975); and ***Morning's at Seven*** (1980). During 1970–3 he served as Artistic Director at London's Hampstead Theatre Club, and in 1979 was appointed Artistic Director of the Academy Festival Theatre, Lake Forest, IL. Since 1960 he has also directed on television. SMA

Matchmaker, The* Thornton Wilder** play, a revision of his 1938 comedy *The Merchant of Yonkers,* which had been a disappointment in a New York production directed by **Max Reinhardt.** Wilder reshaped the comedy by focusing more on the character of Dolly Levi and the talent of **Ruth Gordon,** who recreated her earlier performance with a new director, **Tyrone Guthrie.** After an English tryout, *The Matchmaker* opened at the **Royale Theatre** in 1954 and was an immediate hit, running for 486 performances. Its cast – which included **Sam Levene** and Eileen Herlie – delighted the critics. The play has had a number of professional and amateur revivals (most recently at New York's **Roundabout Theatre** in a 1991 production featuring Dorothy Loudon), but it's probably most famous as the inspiration for ***Hello, Dolly! (1964). BBW

Mathews, Charles (1776–1835) English actor who owed most of his contemporary fame to his gift for mimicry and was a major influence in the U.S. During 1813–17, he reshaped an earlier vehicle, *Mail Coach Adventure* (1808), for himself alone. This evolved into a famous series under the title *Mr. Mathews at Home,* an annual feature of his career from 1818 until its end. A combination of mimicry, storytelling, quick-change artistry, comic songs, and improvisation, this series was equally popular in England and the U.S., which Mathews toured in 1822–3 and 1834. On his first trip he became the first performer to exploit the stage Yankee, and provided a strong influence on the subsequent development of **Yankee theatre.** His son, **Charles James Mathews** (1803–78), became an actor after his father's death, touring the U.S. in 1839 (with his wife, the manager-actress Madame Vestris) and in 1857–8, immediately after his first wife's death and a second term of imprisonment for bankruptcy (both the result of theatre mismanagement). PT DBW

See: R. L. Klepac, *Mr. Mathews at Home,* London, 1979; A. Mathews, *Memoirs of Charles Mathews, Comedian,* 4 vols., London, 1857.

Mathews, Cornelius (1817–89) Playwright remembered by the ***New York Clipper*** in its obituary as the "Father of American Drama," and called by historian George Seilhammer "the most prom-

Actor-playwright Charles Mathews in an 1824 engraving of the many characters he played in *Trip to America,* an important stimulus for Yankee plays and characters. Courtesy: Don B. Wilmeth.

ising and successful American dramatist of the last generation" (1881). Mathews's first effort, *The Politicians* (1840), a satire on elections, was not performed. *Witchcraft; or, The Martyrs of Salem* (1846) dramatizes the tragedy of Gideon Bodish, whose mother is accused of witchcraft. A poetic sensitivity and craftsmanship place this work among the first rank of plays written before the Civil War. Mathews also wrote *Jacob Leisler, The Patriot Hero* (1848), *Broadway and the Bowery* (1856), and *False Pretenses* (1858). WJM

Matthews, (James) Brander (1852–1929) Educator, scholar, critic, and playwright. Born in New Orleans to wealthy parents, Matthews grew up in New York and was educated at Columbia University. He entered law school in 1871, but became more interested in French drama and in writing novels and plays. From 1875 to 1895 he wrote for the *Nation;* in 1878 he penned his first original play, *Margery's Lovers;* and from 1891 until his retirement in 1924 he taught drama at Columbia. In 1902 he was given the title of Professor of Dramatic Literature, the first such post in American universities. His wide knowledge of French, English, and American theatre is reflected in his 24 books; the best known are *The French Dramatists of the Nineteenth Century* (1882); *Development of the Drama* (1903); and *Principles of Playmaking* (1919). He also wrote two volumes of memoirs: *These Many Years* (1917) and *Rip Van Winkle Goes to the Play* (1926). His position that a play is intended primarily to be performed rather than read brought credibility to theatre as an academic subject. TLM

Mayer, Edwin Justus (1896–1960) This playwright's interest in historical events and novels resulted in occasional works for the theatre. Most notably, the popular *The Firebrand* (1924), which followed the comic adventures of Benvenuto Cellini in the Renaissance, was considered risqué at the time. The both cynical and sentimental *Children of Darkness* (1930), based on an 18th-century Fielding novel, was revived very successfully by **Circle in the Square** in 1958 with **George C. Scott** and **Colleen Dewhurst.** RHW

Mayo, Frank (1839–96) Actor and manager. Born and educated in Boston, Mayo made his stage debut in 1856 at the **American Theatre** in **San Francisco;** served as leading man at **Maguire's** Opera House during 1863–5; and took a similar position at the **Boston Theatre** during 1865–6. He was competent in roles such as Hamlet, Iago, Othello, and Jack Cade, but garnered critical and popular acclaim for his Badger in *The Streets of New York.* Making his New York debut in 1869, Mayo remained an outsider, touring as a star in his own company. In 1872 he first acted the frontiersman in the play *Davy Crockett,* a part he would perform over 2,000 times. He wrote several plays in the 1880s but none was successful. In 1895 he adapted Mark Twain's *Pudd'nhead Wilson* for the stage and played the title role to popular acclaim until his death the following year. In his day he was thought a "natural" actor because he under-

Frank Mayo as Davy Crockett. Photo: Mora, N.Y. Courtesy: Laurence Senelick.

played the emotional scenes. While a versatile actor, Mayo found success only in roles that promoted **Yankee** individualism or the myth of the American frontier. TLM

See: D. Fike, "Frank Mayo: Actor, Playwright, and Manager," PhD diss., U of Nebraska, 1980.

Mayrhauser, Jennifer von (1948–) Costume designer most closely identified with the **Circle Repertory Company,** where she has designed several dozen shows. Broadway credits include *Da, Talley's Folly,* and *Steaming.* She has also designed for television. Though associated with modern-dress productions, she is equally adept at period costumes. AA

M. Butterfly The first play by an **Asian American** to win a Tony Award, this enigmatic two-act drama by **David Henry Hwang** debuted at the **Eugene O'Neill Theatre** 20 March 1988 and ran 777 performances. **John Dexter** directed; John Lithgow and **B. D. Wong** starred. It also won the Drama Desk, **John Gassner,** and Outer Critics' Circle awards, and toured nationally. Set in Bejing from the 1960s to the '80s, and loosely based on a true incident, the plot is a sly reversal of the

Madame Butterfly story. It tracks the cross-culture love affair between René Gallimard, an insecure French diplomat, and Liling Song, a Chinese Opera "actress" – really a Maoist male spy posing as a woman. A series of impressionistic flashbacks reveal how Gallimard is duped by his own chauvinistic assumptions. Asian theatrical sensibilities and Western dramaturgy are fused into an intricate meditation on the tensions between the sexes, East and West, truth and fantasy, art and authenticity. Hwang has called the play "an extreme example of the self-delusion any of us go through when we fall in love."   MB

Meadow, Lynne (Carolyn) (1946–) Director who has served as artistic director of the **Manhattan Theatre Club** since 1972. Her recent directorial work includes David Rudkin's *Ashes* (Obie, 1976), David Edgar's *The Jail Diary of Albie Sachs* (1979), Simon Gray's *Close of Play* (1981), Ayckbourn's *Woman in Mind* (1988), **Lee Blessing**'s *Eleemosynary* (1989), and Ayckbourn's *A Small Family Business* (1992). Her style is described as "smooth and unobtrusive," aimed at getting "something reduced to its essence." A Yale School of Drama graduate, Meadow received 1981's **Margo Jones** Award, 1989's Drama Desk Award for Outstanding Achievement and Torch of Hope Award, and 1990's Distinguished Woman's Award from the Northwood Institute. She has served on advisory panels of the National Endowment for the Arts, New York State Council on the Arts, and Fund for New American Plays, and taught in the **Circle in the Square** Theatre School, Yale University, New York University, and SUNY–Stony Brook.   REK

Medicine shows The North American descendants of the mountebanks of Renaissance Europe, these itinerant peddlers of patent medicines, working from caravan wagons, enlivened their sales pitch with variety acts, ranging from simple card tricks and banjo solos to the elaborate powwows and war dances of the turn-of-the-century Kickapoo shows. To meet competition from **vaudeville,** the medicine show began to offer an idiosyncratic form of variety only occasionally broken by a commercial message. The performances, often changed nightly, were dominated by a blackface comedian generically called Sambo or Jake, a hybrid of **minstrel** endman and hobo clown. The shows themselves, a mixture of ventriloquism, chalk talks, burlesque comedy, prestidigitation, and banjo picking, usually lasted two hours, the 8 or 10 numbers interrupted by a few lectures with their medicine "pitches." The afterpiece, an audience favorite, was a chaotic farce involving a sheeted ghost. Certain medicine men like Fred Foster Bloodgood and Tommy Scott continued to play their routes well into the late 20th century, and in 1983 *The Vi-Ton-Ka Medicine Show,* a reconstruction with original performers, was staged at the **American Place Theatre,** New York.   LS

See: M. Calhoun, *Medicine Show,* New York, 1976; B. McNamara, *Step Right Up,* Garden City, NY, 1976; V. McNeal, *Four White Horses and A Brass Band,* Garden City, NY, 1947.

Medina, Louisa (c. 1813–38) Unique in her day as a successful woman dramatist, Medina is credited with 34 plays between 1833 and 1838; however, only 11 have been documented and only three are extant. All of her plays were written for **Thomas S. Hamblin,** manager of the **Bowery Theatre** and possibly her husband, and probably all were dramatizations of historical and adventure novels. Medina's talent for increasing the dramatic and spectacular elements of the novels made her plays successful and profitable melodramas, the staple of the Bowery. Her dramatization of Bulwer-Lytton's *Last Days of Pompeii* had 29 performances in 1835 – the longest run on a New York stage to that date; and her dramatization of **Robert Montgomery Bird**'s *Nick of the Woods* (1838) remained a consistent draw for most of the century. Other successes include *Rienzi, Norman Leslie,* and *Ernest Maltravers.*   FB

Mednick, Murray (1939–) Brooklyn-born playwright, one of several **Off-Off Broadway** writers who thrived in the late 1960s as advocates of the counterculture and opponents of the Vietnam War. Mednick's most widely produced play, *Sand* (1967), was a devastating attack on American values and published in *The New Underground Theatre* (New York, 1968). For several years he was associated with Theatre Genesis before moving to Los Angeles, where he directed the Padua Hills Playwrights Festival and developed *The Coyote Cycle* (1978–80).   BBW

Medoff, Mark (1940–) Playwright, director, educator, and actor. Medoff first won success **Off-Broadway** with ***When You Comin' Back, Red Ryder?*** (1973) and *The Wager* (1974). ***Children of a Lesser God*** ran 887 performances in 1980–1, winning Medoff a Tony Award for best script. *Children* concerns an instructor for the deaf who marries a deaf student; fear of having a deaf child contributes to the marriage's destruction. After *Children* Medoff worked primarily in film and television, but in 1985 the **American Conservatory Theatre** staged his *The Majestic Kid* and in 1989 a sequel to *Red Ryder, The Heart Outright,* was presented at New York's **Theatre for the New City.** Since 1966 he has taught at New Mexico State University.   SMA

Megrue, Roi Cooper (1883–1927) Playwright, director, and producer who frequently directed his own scripts. He was associated with **Elisabeth Marbury,** and with the **Selwyn**s, who produced several of his plays. His *Under Cover* (1914), *Under Fire* (1915, codirector), and *Under Sentence* (1916, coauthor-director) are effective thrillers. *It Pays to Advertise* (1914, coauthor), *Potash and Perlmutter in Society* (1915, coauthor-director), *Seven Chances* (1916), and *Tea for Three* (1918, also director) are contemporary farces. He directed and coproduced the Pulitzer Prize–winning ***Why Marry?*** in 1917. His career was cut short by an untimely death due to illness.   MR

Meisner, Sanford (1905–) Actor, teacher, director. As an original member of the **Group The-**

atre, Meisner appeared in most of their productions throughout the 1930s. He codirected, with **Odets, *Waiting for Lefty*** (1935), and had roles in all the other Odets plays, from *Awake and Sing!* (1935) to *Night Music* (1940). Before joining the Group, he acted in several productions at the **Theatre Guild**. In 1935 he began teaching the Group's "Method" acting at the **Neighborhood Playhouse** School of Theatre, and became head of the school the following year. He continued in this position until 1959, then taught in Los Angeles for two years at Twentieth Century–Fox before returning to NYC and his headship position in 1964. During the 1940s and '50s he directed several plays, including a revival of The *Time of Your Life* (1955). He continued to act occasionally.   TP

> See: S. Meisner and D. Longwell, *Sanford Meisner on Acting,* New York, 1987.

Melmoth, Mrs. [Courtney] Charlotte (Mrs. Samuel Jackson Pratt) (1749–1823) British actress who debuted in the U.S. in March 1793 (recitations in NYC), joining the **John Street Theatre** company eight months later, remaining until 1798, then moving to the new **Park**. She continued to act in NY and Philadelphia until 1812. **Dunlap** in 1793 claimed she was the "best tragic actress" New York had ever seen. After retirement she taught elocution and did some dairy farming.   DBW

Member of the Wedding, The, by **Carson McCullers**. Adapted from the author's novel, this sensitive character study focuses upon Frankie, a gangling, imaginative girl on the brink of adolescence, and Berenice, her father's housekeeper and Frankie's only maternal influence. McCullers weaves an impressionistic portrait of life in a small Southern town of 1945, touching upon race relations, changing personal relationships, and deep feelings of loss. Directed by **Harold Clurman,** the play opened in New York 5 January 1950 at the **Empire Theatre** and featured **Julie Harris** and **Ethel Waters**. Critics doubted that a piece with little overt dramatic action would attract a wide public, but they were impressed by stunning performances. Defying predictions, the play ran for 501 performances, won the New York Drama Critics' Circle Award, and became a successful motion picture in 1952.   KF

Men and Women This fourth collaborative effort by **Henry C. DeMille** and **David Belasco** for producer **Charles Frohman** opened in 1890 with William Morris and Frank Mordaunt in leading roles and **Maude Adams** in a minor part. The plot hinges on a bank robbery, based on a contemporary scandal, and involves four pairs of lovers. At its climax, William Prescott seizes the handcuffs meant for his friend, a clerk accused through circumstantial evidence, and confesses the crime. After running the play for over 200 performances in New York, Frohman toured it intermittantly through 1906, when the William Morris Stock Company bought the rights to the play and continued its touring.   BMcC

Men in White by **Sidney Kingsley** was the first major success of the **Group Theatre,** opening 26 September 1933 and running for 351 performances. The cast, directed by **Lee Strasberg** in a truly ensemble performance, included **Luther Adler,** J. Edward Bromberg, Alexander Kirkland, **Sanford Meisner, Robert Lewis, Morris Carnovsky,** Art Smith, and Ruth Nelson. The production's precision and finish, particularly in the operating room scene, which achieved an almost balletic quality, helped establish the reputation of the Group Theatre and Strasberg's Method. The play, a reverent treatment of the medical profession, depicts the conflicts of a young doctor who wants to dedicate his life to scientific research, but must resist the pressure from his fiancée and her family to pursue a lucrative practice instead.   BCM

Menken, Adah Isaacs (née Ada C. McCord or Adèle Theodore) (1835?–68) Actress and poet, born near New Orleans or in Memphis (her mythmaking hopelessly obscures her early years). Legally separated from the musical conductor Alexander Isaacs Menken, she embarked on an acting career, making her debut in Shreveport as Pauline in *The Lady of Lyons* (1857); her dark good

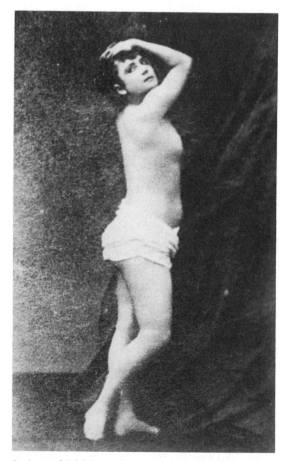

A pinup of Adah Isaacs Menken in her naked lady guise. Courtesy: Laurence Senelick.

looks and splendid figure compensated for her mediocre talent. When a bigamous marriage to the pugilist John Heenan (1859) ended in scandal, she exploited it by appearing in flesh-colored tights bound to a "wild horse of Tartary" in Milner's melodrama *Mazeppa* (**Green St. Theatre**, Albany, NY, 1861). This role, played throughout the U.S. North and West, brought her notoriety and stardom as the "Naked Lady." Marriage to humorist Orpheus C. Kerr (R. H. Newell) made her popular with the literati of New York and San Francisco. At Astley's Amphitheatre, London (1864), she played Mazeppa and Don Leon in *The Child of the Sun* for £500 a performance, the highest salary yet earned by an actress. After a fourth marriage, the last phase of her career unfolded in Paris, in a silent equestrian role in *The Pirates of t'e Savannah* (Gaîté, 1867). Her last performance was at **Sadler's Wells** (1868), before sudden death from peritonitis. LS

See: W. Mankowitz, *Mazeppa: The Lives, Loves, and Legends of Adah Isaacs Menken*, New York, 1982.

Mercury Theatre, The A repertory company established in New York in 1937 by **Orson Welles** and **John Houseman.** The brief but historically significant two-year history – from the Welles–Houseman withdrawal from the **Federal Theatre Project** over the denial by Washington bureaucrats to produce **Marc Blitzstein**'s proletarian drama with music *The **Cradle Will Rock,*** to the final production of *Danton's Death* (1938) – is told vividly in Houseman's *Run-Through* (1972). Other imaginative productions were *The Shoemaker's Holiday, Heartbreak House,* and a modern-dress *Julius Caesar* intended as an anti-Fascist tract – though, in fact, Welles's cutting of the text led to confusion. The ensemble included **Norman Lloyd,** Joseph Cotten, Martin Gabel, Vincent Price, **Ruth Ford,** Hiram Sherman, and **Geraldine Fitzgerald.** The Mercury Theatre of the Air was responsible for the infamous broadcast of "The War of the Worlds" (1938), and many of the company members appeared in Welles's film *Citizen Kane* (1940). DBW

Meredith, (Oliver) Burgess (1907–) Actor-director. Identified today as the crusty trainer in the *Rocky* films, the diminutive actor with the crumbled look had established himself by the 1940s as an actor variously described as impressive, brilliant, heartbreaking, sinewy, and sensitive. From his apprenticeship with the **Civic Repertory Theatre** (1929–33) to his outings as an innovative director (*Ulysses in Nighttown*, 1958; *A Thurber Carnival,* 1960; *Blues for Mr. Charlie,* 1964, etc.), Meredith appeared in a long series of productions, including *She Loves Me Not* (Buzz Jones, 1933), *Winterset* (Mio, a part written for him), *Liliom* (title role, 1940), *Candida* (Marchbanks, 1942), *The Remarkable Mr. Pennypacker* (Pa, 1953), and *Major Barbara* (Cusins, 1956). In the late 1930s he held various offices in **Actors' Equity.** DBW

Merman, Ethel (1909–84) Singer and actress who made an auspicious stage debut in *Girl Crazy* (1930), where her renditions of two **Gershwin** songs, "I Got Rhythm" and "Sam and Delilah," stopped the show nightly. She was soon typecast as a brassy, big-hearted nightclub singer, a role she played, with slight variations, in *Take a Chance* (1932), *Anything Goes* (1934), and *Red, Hot and Blue* (1936). Although she appeared in secondary roles in these shows, Merman was often given the best songs to sing because of her powerful voice and exemplary diction. She received her first solo star billing for *Panama Hattie* (1940), in which she again portrayed a nightclub singer. After a change-of-pace role as a defense worker in *Something for the Boys* (1943), Merman appeared in **Irving Berlin**'s *Annie Get Your Gun* (1946). The part of western sharpshooter **Annie Oakley** gave Merman a rare opportunity to portray a character that differed significantly from her own personality. Four years later Merman was back in another Berlin show, *Call Me Madam,* in which she portrayed a Washington hostess appointed ambassador to a tiny European kingdom. Her next musical, *Happy Hunting* (1956), gave her a similar role as a Philadelphia socialite seeking a husband for her daughter. In 1959 Merman capped her career with her performance as Rose, the quintessential stage mother, in *Gypsy.* Both her singing and her acting received superlative reviews from the critics. A decade later Merman made her last Broadway appearance when she took over the title role in *Hello, Dolly!*

Although most of the shows in which she appeared were haphazard assemblages of stale musical comedy formulas, their major appeal lay in Merman's electrifying interpretations of songs by such important musical comedy composers as the Gershwins, **Cole Porter,** and Irving Berlin. She published autobiographies in 1955 and 1978 (with George Eells). MK

Merrick, David (1912–) Producer. Beginning with his first success, *Fanny,* in 1954, Merrick produced or coproduced over 70 plays, including many imported foreign hits. Some of his more successful have included *The Entertainer* (1958), *Gypsy* (1959), *Becket* (1960), *Stop the World – I Want to Get Off* (1962), *Luther* and *One Flew Over the Cuckoo's Nest* (1963), *Oh What a Lovely War!* and *Hello, Dolly!* (1964), *Marat/Sade* (1965), *I Do! I Do!* (1966), *Rosencrantz and Guildenstern Are Dead* (1967), *Play It Again Sam* (1969), *Travesties* (1975), and *42nd Street* (1981).

Merrick's publicity stunts for his shows are legendary on Broadway. To publicize *Fanny,* he commissioned a nude statue of Nejla Ates, the show's belly dancer, and had it placed in Central Park, opposite a bust of Shakespeare; *Life* covered the story, and *Fanny* ran for 888 performances. Of such stunts, Merrick said, "Other things being equal, using promotion stunts would allow me to get ahead of my competitors. I'd say that's been a big factor in my success."

In 1983 Merrick suffered a stroke that rendered him incapable of administering his $50–70 million estate; but in 1985 the New York Supreme Court ruled him sufficiently recovered to manage his affairs. His first production since recovery (his 88th overall) was an unsuccessful all-black revival in

1990 of the musical *Oh, Kay!*, which had originated in 1989 at the **Goodspeed Opera House.** SMA

Merrill, Bob (né Henry Robert Merrill Lavan) (1921–) Composer-lyricist. After serving in WW II, Merrill was an actor, radio writer, casting director, nightclub singer, and writer of a number of popular songs (such as "How Much Is That Doggie in the Window?") before turning to Broadway. His first score was *New Girl in Town* (1957), followed by *Take Me Along* (1959) and *Carnival* (1961), and the lyrics for *Funny Girl* (1964) and *Sugar* (1972). His few attempts at writing scores in the 1970s and '80s were failures. Merrill's most successful scores captured the mood and musical idioms of the first decades of the 20th century. MK

Merry (née Brunton), Anne (1769–1808) British-born actress and manager noted for appearances on the American stage, where, according to her biographer Gresdna Doty, she was the artistic pacesetter. Daughter of John Brunton, provincial English actor-manager, she followed her successful debut at Bath in 1785 with an engagement at London's Covent Garden for the next season, remaining there until her retirement in 1792 after her marriage to minor poet Robert Merry. Soon Merry lost his money, and Anne accepted an offer in 1796 from **Thomas Wignell** to join the **Chestnut Street Theatre** company in Philadelphia. Widowed four years, she married Wignell in 1803. When he died seven weeks later, she comanaged the Chestnut Street. In 1806 she married **William Warren;** two years later she died in childbirth at 39. As an actress she was known for her excellence in tragic roles and especially for the sweetness of her voice, her gentleness, simplicity, and grace on stage. Her brother John and sister Louisa were also actors.
DBW

See: G. Doty, *The Career of Mrs. Anne Brunton Merry in the American Theatre,* Baton Rouge, LA, 1971.

Merry Widow, The Two-act operetta, music by Franz Lehár, words by Victor Leon and Leo Stein. First produced in Vienna in 1905, *Der lustige Witwe* was soon seen throughout the German-speaking world. The sentimental yet light-hearted story, set to Lehár's enduring melodies (the most famous: the waltz "I Love You So") tells of a rich Eastern European widow in Paris pursued by legions but won by the seemingly indifferent embassy secretary. In 1907, George Edwardes produced a version by Adrian Ross and Edward Morton, which changed place and character names, in London, where it ran 778 performances. This adaptation opened 21 October 1907 at New York's **New Amsterdam Theatre,** running 416 performances and becoming the rage of its day, generating an entire industry of "Merry Widow" fashions, hairstyles, and even cocktails. It has since never left the international stage and remains a staple of the light opera repertoire. JD

Metamora; or, The Last of the Wampanoags by **John Augustus Stone,** selected by **Edwin Forrest** as the first winner of a contest for an aboriginal drama by an American; premiered 15 December 1829 at New York's **Park Theatre** and remained in Forrest's repertoire for 40 years. Based loosely on King Philip's War (1675–6), it gained the greatest popularity of all Indian plays produced during the Jacksonian period, due partially to Forrest's protean performance. The drama illustrated the incompatibility of the two races and suggested the impossibility of reconciliation. The title character incorporates traits of both the noble savage and its antithesis, the red devil, often rising above both stereotypes [see **Native Americans portrayed**]. Metamora justifies his actions with a coherent moral code until he sees no options, becomes single-minded in his attack, and then is considered by his enemies part of a "savage race, hated of all men – unblessed of heaven." Numerous Indian plays followed Stone's, including a **John Brougham** burlesque treatment of it and Forrest: *Metamora; or, The Last of the Pollywogs,* 1847. DBW

See: R. Moody, *Dramas from the American Theatre, 1762–1909,* Cleveland, 1966.

Metcalfe, James Stetson (1858–1927) Drama critic. Born in Buffalo, NY, and educated at Yale, Metcalfe made his reputation writing for *Life* magazine (1888–1920). Afterward he wrote for *Judge* (1920–1) before becoming the first drama critic of the *Wall Street Journal* (1922–7). His satirical style often offended: The Theatrical **Syndicate** barred him from their theatres and accused him of being anti-Semitic. Although conservative and reactionary, he exposed corruption in the commercial theatre. TLM

See: R. L. Doxtator, "James Stetson Metcalfe's Signed Criticism of the Legitimate Theatre in NYC: 1888–1927," PhD diss., U of Nebraska–Lincoln, 1985.

Metcalfe, Stephen (1953–) Playwright. Produced mainly by the **Manhattan Theatre Club** and at San Diego's **Old Globe,** he is author of some 10 plays, including *Vikings* (1980), concerning three generations of Danish-American men; *Strange Snow* (1982), about Vietnam veterans; and *Emily* (1988), about a woman obsessed with material success. TLM

Method acting see **Actors Studio**

Mexican-American theatre see **Chicano theatre**

Middle Ages, The, by **A. R. Gurney, Jr.,** opened at the The Theatre at St. Peter's Church (23 March 1983) for 110 performances; this followed productions at the **Mark Taper Forum** Lab in January 1977, a three-week run at the **Hartman Theatre** in Connecticut beginning in January 1978, and a showcase production at New York's **Ark Theatre** in March 1982. Using the trophy room of a men's club as an emblem of the East Coast establishment, Gurney shows protagonist Barney on the day of his father's funeral recalling incidents from the mid-1940s to the late '70s in which he systematically demolishes every standard of the upper class.

Jo Mielziner's design for *Death of a Salesman*. Courtesy: National Museum of American Art, Smithsonian Institute.

Barney's final acceptance by childhood girlfriend Eleanor and ownership of the club both confirms his persistent romanticism and the emergence of a new social order. The New York run coincided with that of *The Dining Room,* producing a double success.   RW

Mielziner, Jo (1901–76) The most dominant figure in American set and lighting design from the mid-1920s until his death, Mielziner created the sets for virtually every major American drama and musical in the 1930s, '40s, and '50s, exerting a great influence not only on the field of design but on the plays themselves. Dramas such as *A Streetcar Named Desire* and **Death of a Salesman** were in part shaped by his designs, and their success was to some degree dependent upon them. His use of scrims and a painterly style created a visual counterpart to the poetic realism of the plays of the period, notably the works of **Tennessee Williams.** The scrims, together with fragmented scenic units, allowed a cinematic transformation from one scene to the next through the manipulation of light rather than the shifting of scenery; this was in keeping with the trend in playwriting toward a cinematic structure. He was equally capable of realism, as demonstrated by his set for *Street Scene* (1929), in which he recreated the façade of a tenement and a New York City street. His designs for musicals such as *Carousel, Annie Get Your Gun,* and *Guys and Dolls* captured the vibrancy of the American musical at its peak. The power of Mielziner's designs is demonstrated by the fact that some of his designs have outlasted the plays or are integrally entwined with them: His design for **Maxwell Anderson**'s *Winterset* – a soaring panorama of the Brooklyn Bridge receding into the fog – is better

remembered than the play itself; and designers today trying to recreate *Death of a Salesman* must compete with the ghost of Mielziner's set. Mielziner also lit most of his own plays in order to control light, mood, and color. Working together with Edward F. Kook, he was responsible for many improvements in lighting instruments. Mielziner also worked as a theatre designer and consultant on many theatres, including the somewhat controversial **Vivian Beaumont Theatre** in New York.   AA

See: J. Mielziner, *Designing for the Theatre: A Memoir and a Portfolio,* New York, 1965. Mary C. Henderson is writing an authorized biography of Mielziner.

Mighty Dollar, The A four-act comedy by Benjamin E. Woolfe produced at the **Park Theatre** (NYC), 6 September 1875. Billed as "an American comedy," this play is set in a Washington, DC, salon (Grabmoor) where "polished and unpolished scoundrels . . . congregate." Starring **W. J. Florence** as a Congressman, the Hon. Bradwell Slote, and Mrs. Florence as Mrs. General Gilflory, the play lampooned Washington politicians but made little sense to critics. Nevertheless, it ran 104 performances and established Slote as an American type.   TLM

Migliaccio, Eduardo (Edoardo; Edward) (1882–1946) Actor-impressionist. Born in Cava dsei Terreni, near Naples, Migliaccio came to America in 1897. In Little Italy's *caffé-concerto,* restaurants offering entertainments, Migliaccio created *machietti coloniali,* character sketches combining verse, prose, and song, satirizing the immigrant experience. Around 1900, he created Farfariello, the greenhorn who "turned the tables on the **ethnic**

stereotype," as whom he became nationally known. Using dialect and immigrant types, Migliaccio, some of whose songs were recorded by RCA Victor, became one of the most popular figures in Italian-American theatre.   REK

See: E. F. Aleandri, "A History of Italian-American Theatre: 1900–1905," PhD diss., City University of New York, 1984.

Miles, George H[enry] (1824–71) Playwright and poet. When **Edwin Forrest** commended Miles's tragedy, *Michael DiLando, Gonfalonies of Florence* in 1847, Miles immediately submitted *Mohammed, the Arabian Prophet,* for which Forrest awarded $1,000 as the "best original tragedy," though he never produced it. Miles's *DeSoto* (1852), produced by **James Murdoch,** was popular for a decade. *Blight and Bloom* (1854), *Mary's Birthday* (1857), and *Senor Valente* (1858) are comedies. Among his other plays are *Oliver Cromwell, The Parish Clerk Emily Chester,* and *Thiodolf the Icelander.*   WJM

Millay, Edna St. Vincent (1892–1950) Actress, poet, playwright, and director. In 1917 Millay began her acting career with the **Province-town Players,** where she performed in productions of her own plays, such as *The Princess Marries the Page* (1918) and *Aria da Capo* (1919). She also wrote *The Lamp and the Bell* (1921) and the libretto for Deems Taylor's opera *The Kings' Henchmen* (1927).   FB

See: N. Brittin, *Edna St. Vincent Millay,* New York, 1967, rev ed., Boston, 1982; M. Gurko, *Restless Spirit: The Life of Edna St. Vincent Millay,* New York, 1962.

Miller, Arthur (1915–) Playwright and director. Following the death of **Tennessee Williams** in 1983, and in spite of the paucity of his own recent output, Arthur Miller remains relatively unchallenged as America's greatest living playwright. His first play, *The Man Who Had All the Luck* (1944), was a consummate failure, but *All My Sons* (1947) proved that Miller could create powerful scenes and believable characters. His next play, *Death of a Salesman* (1949), won him both the Pulitzer Prize and the Drama Critics' Circle Award. Shifting neatly between realism and expressionism, this piercing study of an aging drummer (commercial traveler) elicited highly praised, prize-winning efforts from the entire original production company and has subsequently been performed all over the world. His adaptation of Ibsen's *An Enemy of the People* (1950) was a thematic prelude to *The Crucible* (1953), a drama of the Salem witchcraft trials written in passionate response to Senator Joseph McCarthy's investigations of accused subversives. This spellbinding drama of real conflict and impassioned action, revived on Broadway in 1991, has outlived the immediacy of its inception and may yet prove to be Miller's finest work. *A View from the Bridge* (1955), which played in New York the same year Miller married Marilyn Monroe, continued his exploration of the tragedy of the common man. This time his hero is a hard-working Sicilian longshoreman who is killed because he breaks the community's law of silence about some

illegal immigrants. Miller's stage voice was silent for the next eight years, during which time he divorced Marilyn Monroe (1961) and married photographer Ingeborg Morath (1962). He returned to the stage in 1964 with *After the Fall,* apparently a highly personal play based on his life with beautiful film star Monroe. *Incident at Vichy,* an examination of the Nazi–Jewish conflict during WW II, followed in the same year. *The Price* (1968), a heart-wrenching confrontation between two brothers, became the last Miller play to achieve anything like a popular success. *The Creation of the World and Other Business* (1972) and *The American Clock* (1980) failed and were hastily withdrawn. In recent years Miller's plays have been given significant revivals or premieres in England, where he seems more popular today than in the U.S. (In 1989 the University of East Anglia opened the Arthur Miller Centre for American Studies.) In 1987 two new one-acts were presented at **Lincoln Center** as *Danger: Memory!,* though the bill was more successful in London. *The Archbishop's Ceiling* was staged by the Royal Shakespeare Company in 1986 and has yet to be seen in the U.S.; Miller's most recent play, *The Ride Down Mount Morgan,* opened in London in 1991. Throughout his career Miller produced a rich collection of essays about the craft of playwriting, especially the nature of modern tragedy. These pieces, published as *The Theatre Essays of Arthur Miller* (ed. Robert A. Martin, 1971), remain the closest thing to a complete "poetics" yet written by an American playwright.   LDC DBW

See: A. Miller, *Timebends,* New York, 1987; C. Bigsby, ed., *Arthur Miller and Company,* London, 1990; L. Moss, *Arthur Miller,* rev. ed., Boston, 1980; J. Schlueter and J. Flanagan, *Arthur Miller,* New York, 1987; D. Welland, *Arthur Miller: The Playwright,* London, 1983.

Miller, Gilbert Heron (1884–1969) Producer, director, theatre manager; son of actor **Henry Miller** and actress Bijou (Heron). Miller produced a half-century career. He was known for his elegant staging of high comedy by such writers as **Philip Barry,** Somerset Maugham, and other masters of literate dialogue. He introduced to the American stage such British actors as **Charles Laughton,** Alec Guinness, and Leslie Howard. From 1918 until its demolition in 1958 he owned the St. James's Theatre, London; from 1929 until his death, the Lyric Theatre, London; and during 1926–68 the Henry Miller Theatre in New York. His greatest success was *Victoria Regina* (1936) with **Helen Hayes.** Other significant productions included Maugham's *The Constant Wife* (1927), Sherriff's *Journey's End* (1928), **Eliot**'s *The Cocktail Party* (1950), and Thomas's *Under Milkwood* (1957).   DBW

Miller, Henry (1859–1925) London-born actor and manager who emigrated with his parents to Canada, where he made his debut in 1876. He quickly became a juvenile leading man in America opposite a variety of young actresses, including Bijou Heron, whom he married in 1883. In 1893 he became leading man of **Charles Frohman**'s new **Empire Theatre** Stock Company. During

1905–8 he and **Margaret Anglin** starred under their own management, notably in *The Great Divide* by **William Vaughn Moody.** Though he continued to act until after WW I, Miller's principal occupation after 1908 was as a producer for others. He launched the career of **Alla Nazimova,** and became manager and producer for **Walter Hampden, Laura Hope Crewes,** and Ruth Chatterton, among others. As an actor, Miller personified the American ideal of honest, sympathetic, taciturn masculinity.   DMcD

> *See:* F. Morse, *Backstage with Henry Miller,* New York, 1938.

Miller, Joaquin (né Cincinnatus Hiner Miller) (1839–1913) Writer.

His early life among the miners and Indians of California and Oregon is confused by his autobiographical embroidery. In 1863 he settled as a newspaper editor in Oregon. When his early poems and stories were favorably received, he moved to San Francisco (1870), but his Byronic appearance, behavior, and writing were most popular in England. His best works were the books *Songs of the Sierras* (1871) and *Life Among the Modocs* (1873). He also wrote four plays, and *The Danites in the Sierras* was performed in a heavily revised version by **McKee Rankin** (1877–81).
> DMcD

> *See:* O. Frost, *Joaquin Miller,* New York, 1967; H. Wagner, *Joaquin Miller and His Other Self,* San Francisco, 1929.

Miller, Marilyn (Marilynn; née Mary Ellen Reynolds) (1898–1936) Dancer and singer.

As a child she appeared in **vaudeville,** and was dancing in a London club when she was discovered by Lee **Shubert.** She made her Broadway debut in *The Passing Show of 1914.* Miller was a featured performer in two editions of the *Ziegfeld* Follies (1918, 1919). In *Sally* (1920), she was given her first starring role, as a poor dishwasher who becomes a star of those same *Follies.* Critics found her performance enchanting, complimenting her on her graceful dancing, her delicate beauty, and her buoyant personality. After a long run and national tour in *Sally,* Miller returned to Broadway in *Sunny* (1925), where her weekly salary was reported to be $3,000, making her the highest-paid musical comedy performer of the 1920s. Her next shows, *Rosalie* (1928) and *Smiles* (1930), were not as successful as the previous two. In 1933 she made her final Broadway appearance in *As Thousands Cheer,* a **revue** with a score by **Irving Berlin.** Although her singing voice was so weak as to be inaudible at times, Miller's radiant beauty and elegant dancing made her the reigning queen of musical comedy in the 1920s.   MK

> *See:* W. Harris, *The Other Marilyn,* New York, 1985.

Miller, May (1899–) African-American poet and playwright.

Active in plays at school and college, Miller trained with Montgomery Gregory at Howard University and Frederick Koch at Columbia University. She entered *Opportunity* magazine playwriting contests, gaining third prize and a citation, and was a member of the Washington, DC, branch of the Krigwa Players. She has written some 14 plays, a number of which have been published in early anthologies of black plays.   EGH

Mills, Florence (1895–1927) African-American comedienne, singer, and dancer

who became the idol of Harlem. At age 5 she appeared in Williams & Walker's musical comedy *Sons of Ham* [see **Bert Williams**], and at 15 joined her two sisters in a musical trio, *The Mills Sisters,* that toured the country in **vaudeville** shows. Her first major billing came when she replaced Gertrude Sanders as leading lady in the hit musical *Shuffle Along* (1921) at NYC's 63rd Street Theatre. The next year Mills was on Broadway in *Plantation Revue,* which extended her fame internationally. Performances followed in Paris and London in *From Dover to Dixie* (1923–4) and as the star of *From Dixie to Broadway* (1924) back in the U.S. In Lew Leslie's *Blackbirds* (1926), written specially for her, she again toured Paris and London, leaving the show because of ill health. She died in 1927. A pixie of a woman, small, delicate, and stunningly attractive on stage, she was beloved by the 150,000 people who followed her funeral procession in Harlem.   EGH

Milner, Ron (1938–) African-American playwright

whose first major play, *Who's Got His Own* – underscoring the plight of black manhood in a racist society – was produced at the **American Place Theatre** in 1966 and toured New York state colleges. Milner's other plays have premiered in Chicago, Detroit, Los Angeles, and in New Brunswick, NJ, where *Roads of the Mountaintop,* a portrait of Dr. Martin Luther King, Jr., was commissioned by the **Crossroads Theatre Company** and presented in 1986.   EGH

Milwaukee Repertory Theater Organized in 1954 as the Fred Miller Theater Company,

a professional stock company, in Milwaukee, WI. After seven years in the Miller Theater (a converted moviehouse) and the production of 71 plays with well-known guest stars, the governing board employed a resident ensemble, turning first to the **Association of Producing Artists,** then to the **American Conservatory Theatre** for brief seasons. The organization became the Milwaukee Repertory Theater in 1964, and has since featured its resident professional acting company. Three artistic directors have been standouts: Tunc Yalman (1966–71), who managed the company's move to the Todd Wehr Theater in Milwaukee's Performing Arts Center and the growth of the group's subscription base to 16,000; Nagle Jackson (1971–7), added productions at the Court Street Theater in 1974 and at the historic Pabst Theater; and John Dillon (1977–93), who included resident playwrights in the company, conducted international tours with the group, and, in 1987, moved it to a new three-theater facility on the east bank of the Milwaukee River. Typical of Dillon's productions was a nontraditionally cast *Our Town* (1991).   WD

> *See:* S. O'Connor and S. Myers, *Working Space: The Milwaukee Repertory Theatre Builds a Home,* New York, 1992.

Mime and pantomime

Beginnings through the 19th century Mime and pantomime first came to these shores in the guise of "night scenes," the simplified *commedia dell'arte* sketches performed by French actors in early 18th-century London. The tricks of Harlequin and Scaramouche were performed at Henry Holt's Long Room in New York in 1738–9. These were supplanted by bipartite English pantomime, with its opening drawn from classical mythology or traditional folktale and its transformation of characters into Harlequin, Pantaloon, and Columbine for the knockabout comedy of the harlequinade. Some were adapted to American material, such as *Harlequin Traveller and the Temple of the Sun* (1800) and *Harlequin Panattahah; or, The Genii of the Algonquins* (1810).

Although the innovations of Regency pantomime and Grimaldi's Clown were brought to New York in 1831 by Charles Parsloe, they did not catch on. The first truly popular exponents of mime were the **Ravel family,** who interspersed the French ballet-pantomime with elaborate acrobatic feats, elegant staging, and magic trickery. The silence and spectacle were more appealing to naïve audiences than were the pun-filled scripts of the English panto. The Ravels were imitated by the great clown **George L. Fox,** who featured pantomime at the **Bowery Theatre** in the 1850s, Americanizing the locales and emphasizing violent slapstick comedy at the expense of acrobatics and grace. The longest-running show of its time, Fox's *Humpty Dumpty* (1868), the first American panto in two acts and the first to play Broadway, was widely imitated. The word "pantomime" became generic for any entertainment that mingled variety acts, ballets, and harlequinade characters. Such shows toured the country well into the 1880s, although their popularity was superceded in larger cities by that of the extravaganza and the musical comedy.

Exuberant acrobatic comedy was returned to the form by the **Hanlon–Lees** in *Le Voyage en Suisse* (1881) and The Byrne Brothers in *Eight Bells;* as impresarios the Hanlons also toured the spectacular fairy pantomimes *Fantasma* (1884) and *Superba* (1890), which mingled horseplay with sumptuous scenic effects. However, silent comedy quickly became the province of the cinema, and many of its stage exponents, including the Hanlons and Buster Keaton, gravitated to it.

A more recherché form of pantomime was imported from France in the shape of *L'Enfant Prodigue* (1890) by Michel Carré: This delicate *divertissement* featured a Pierrot (played by an actress) who leaves home for modern urban fleshpots but soon sees the error of his ways. Fashionable among theatrical sophisticates, it promulgated the fin de siècle of the lovelorn Pierrot, which would crop up in such precious pieces as Edna St. Vincent Millay's ***Aria da Capo*** (1921) and the more chichi **revue**s of the 1920s. LS

20th century Distinguishing a stage tradition as wholly distinct from film and television is impossible in 20th-century America, as most performers work wherever they can. However, American vaudeville performers (later **New Vaudevillians** and **performance art**ists) and film (and later TV) actors were the natural heritors of the traditions of the Greek mime and the *commedia dell'arte.*

Historically, mime and pantomime have been silent for few brief periods, and then usually because of governmental restriction. Technological limitation, however, caused the muteness of American silent-film actors of the early years of this century, who in the verve and clarity of their physical acting have influenced generations of performers. The Keystone Cops, Chaplin, and Keaton, the first great American mimes, were influenced by the English music-hall tradition and were a part of American vaudeville. When sound was added successfully to film, the **Marx Bros.** continued in the line of the *commedia dell'arte* with brilliantly improvised physical, musical, and verbal comedy.

In 1952 **Paul Curtis** founded the American Mime Theatre in New York, a school and performing organization that continues today; it has defined a form of silent acting outside the charming, white-faced image popularized in the U.S. as of 1955 by Marcel Marceau through television performances that made his name a household word and ensured months of sold-out performances. In 1957 Etienne Decroux, innovator of corporeal mime or modern mime, began five years of teaching and performing in the U.S.

The **San Francisco Mime Troupe,** founded in 1959 by R. G. Davis, quickly found its voice and joined the thousand-year-old mainstream of mime performance: mime as an actor's theatre of voice, movement, poetry, and music, a politically engaged *commedia dell'arte.*

Those who think that mime is a charming interlude performed by lithe whitefaced mutes will find little of it currently in America outside shopping malls. However, the incisive energy, the zany, manic, ribald, ironic, and dangerous wit mime has always manifested as marginalized, unofficial, actor's theatre – these qualities are found among American performance artists who are testing limits politically, socially, and theatrically in lofts and storefront theatres of metropolitan and university centers. Many of them don't know the performance tradition of which they are a part; they think they made it up, and would cringe at the word "mime," yet mimes they are, in the fullest and most historically accurate sense of the word. Others, students of Decroux and Jacques Lecoq who have innovated U.S. postmodern mime, know that speech is as much a part of mime as is movement. TL

See: T. Leabhart, *Modern and Post-Modern Mime,* New York, 1989.

Miner, Henry Clay (1842–1900) Theatre businessman. Son of an engineer, he served in the Civil War and attended the American Institute of Physicians and Surgeons; this was the basis on which he entered the drug business, manufacturing and retailing cosmetics, including those for theatrical use. After 1875 he began to build and lease theatres, owning five in the NYC area. He also served as an agent for traveling theatrical companies, and published a theatrical directory in 1885. He served in the Fifty-fourth Congress (1895–7).   DMcD

Minneapolis–St. Paul

Also known as the Twin Cities, they rest along the shores of the Mississippi River in east central Minnesota and have the largest population (2,413,873 in 1990) of metropolitan areas in the upper Midwest. Since the mid-1970s, the cities have been credited with the greatest number (per capita) of performing arts groups outside New York, including a multitude of educational, community, and professional profit and nonprofit theatres. The history of Twin Cities theatre activity began before statehood (1858), and may be generalized into four developmental periods: touring troupes (1850–1900), stock companies and roadhouses (1900–30), amateur groups and early professional groups (1930–60), and the post-1960s expansion.

The first troupe that visited Minnesota was the New Orleans–based Placide's Varieties, which performed in St. Paul's Mazourka Hall in August 1851. Such touring performances would comprise the majority of theatre activity in St. Paul for 30 years, though there were attempts at establishing resident companies, notably Henry Van Liew's People's Theatre (1857) and various German-language presentations at the Athenaeum Theatre during 1857–86.

After the Civil War, Minneapolis would join St. Paul in hosting touring troupes as theatres were constructed in both cities. In February 1867 the Opera House opened in St. Paul, and in June of the same year the Pence Opera House opened in Minneapolis. Though the permanent theatres fostered competition between these cities for better entertainment, often the same company would perform in both places, such as the A. McFarland Company (1864) or the Mrs. James A. Oates Burlesque Opera Company (1869).

After 1878 **stock companies** began developing in addition to roadhouses. The Murray–Cartland Company (also known as The Great Metropolitan Theatre Company), formally a touring group, returned to St. Paul's Pence Opera House in September 1878 and began residency there as a stock company.

After 1900 two stock companies, the Ferris Stock Company and the Bainbridge Players, became the models for others to follow. Dick Ferris began his company with his actress wife, Grace Hayward, in 1902 at Minneapolis's Lyceum. Known for producing melodramas, Ferris acted as manager, director, and star in many of the productions. The Company lasted three years. The Bainbridge Players, led by Buzz Bainbridge, was formed in Minneapolis (1911) and developed a credible reputation by performing plays by Shakespeare, Ibsen, and O'Neill, as well as more popular fare. Bainbridge was quite popular in Minneapolis and was elected Mayor in 1933, two years following the Players' demise.

The development of a road organization with national touring connections can be linked to Louis Napoleon (L. N.) Scott, who began his career as St. Paul's Grand Opera House manager in 1883. He moved to St. Paul's Metropolitan Opera House in 1890 and acquired controlling interest in the Metropolitan, Duluth's Lyceum, the Grand in Superior, WI, and, in 1895, the new Minneapolis Metropolitan Opera House. He initiated contact in 1888 with **Marc Klaw** and **Abe Erlanger,** who subsequently purchased the local Taylor Talent Agency and furthered their development of the Theatrical **Syndicate.**

Another important manager between 1900 and 1930 was Theodore Hayes, who managed the People's Theatre (later the Bijou) in Minneapolis and the **Jacob Litt** Grand Opera House in St. Paul during 1886–1917. His importance lies less in managing theatre than for organizing the Twin City Scenic Studio in 1895: He employed Peter Gui Clausen, a popular scenic artist, and began to produce scenery for opera houses, theatres, schools, and Scottish Rite temples throughout the upper Midwest. Twin City Studio cornered this market until the last studio closed in Detroit in 1937.

After the Great Depression, professional theatre productions declined significantly. Many theatres were converted to moviehouses or were simply destroyed. Activity continued during 1930–60 but in other venues, and principally by amateur groups.

St. Paul enjoyed the Edyth Bush Theatre between 1940 and 1965. Started by its namesake, whose husband helped found the Minnesota Mining and Manufacturing Company (3M), Mrs. Bush personally ran the theatre until illness prevented her continuance.

Eleven years later (1951) the Theatre in the Round Players began performing in Minneapolis. The group offered a diverse playbill from Shaw and Shakespeare to **Mamet** and **Shepard,** and included original plays.

Educational groups offered plays as well. Principal among these **academic theatres** was that of the University of Minnesota, which produced plays from 1930 onward. Under the leadership of Frank M. Whiting during 1943–73, the theatre began offering a recurring **children's theatre** program, produced plays on a converted riverboat, contributed to the formation of the American Educational Theatre Association, hosted Arthur Ballet's Office of Advanced Drama Research, and helped attract the **Guthrie Theatre** to Minneapolis.

Two smaller professional organizations started in this period. Don Stolz opened his Old Log Theatre outside Minneapolis in 1940; it offers a popular bill of comedies and farces. Dudley Riggs, a former circus performer, opened his Brave New Workshop in 1958 and has continually offered topical plays built upon improvisation.

The year 1961 marked the beginning of a great expansion in theatre, as Beth Linnerson started the Moppet Players for children. Three years later John Clark Donahue split from the Players and formed the **Children's Theatre Company** at the Minneapolis Society of Fine Arts; it quickly became distinguished for dazzling productions of classic and contemporary children's stories. In 1974 the Children's Theatre moved into a newly constructed facility adjacent to the Minneapolis Institute of Arts, and thereafter gained international acclaim for its productions of works by Theodore Geisel, Tomie dePaola, and Maurice Sendak, among others. The Children's Theatre received great favor until 1984, when Donahue was convicted of sexual misconduct with adolescents. The Theatre's Board of Directors rallied to save the organization, hired Jon Cranney as artistic director, and entered a successful period of reorganization.

One year prior to the beginning of the Children's Theatre (1960), **Tyrone Guthrie,** Oliver Rea, and **Peter Zeisler** chose Minneapolis as the home for their new professional theatre operation, the Minnesota Theatre Company (renamed the **Guthrie Theatre** following Guthrie's death in 1971). Three years later, on May 7, 1963, *Hamlet* was offered as its first production in a new Ralph Rapson–designed theatre. Conceived as a professional resident acting company performing classic plays, the Guthrie Theatre has been termed the "flagship" of regional professional theatres, distinguishing itself with productions such as *The Caucasian Chalk Circle* (1965), *The House of Atreus* (1967), *Oedipus the King* (1972), *The Tempest* (1980), *Peer Gynt* (1983), *The Misanthrope* (1986), and, in the same season, *Richard II, Henry IV (1 & 2),* and *Henry V* (1990). Following Tyrone Guthrie's initial leadership (1963–6), the theatre has been shaped mainly by three artistic directors: **Michael Langham** (1971–7), **Liviu Ciulei** (1981–6), and **Garland Wright** (1986–).

The success of the Children's Theatre Company and the Guthrie Theatre in particular coincided with growth in the Twin Cities' young, educated, and affluent population and the continued rise in white-collar employment, all enabling great growth in theatre. Between 1971 and 1983 a number of groups began offering specialized repertories: The **Cricket Theatre** (1971) offered new American works; the Playwright's Center (1971) nurtured new playwrights; the Heart of the Beast Theatre (1973) featured **puppets** of all shapes and sizes to inner-city audiences; the Illusion Theatre (1974) pioneered socially conscious productions with its sexual awareness program; **At the Foot of the Mountain** (1974) was a pioneering theatre for and by women; Mixed Blood Theatre (1976) instituted color-blind casting; Penumbra Theatre (1977) became Minnesota's first **African-American** professional theatre; Actor's Theatre of St. Paul (1977–90) emphasized intimate actor vehicles; the Great North American History Theatre (1978) produced original plays about Minnesota history; Brass Tacks Theatre (1979) offered new alternative plays; Theatre de la Jeune Lune (1979) performed half a year in Minneapolis and half in Paris; and Red Eye Collaboration (1983) began producing new works, including those of **Lee Breuer.** Touring theatre activity expanded as well as at such venues as Northrop Auditorium, the Orpheum Theatre, and the Walker Art Center in Minneapolis, and at Ordway Music Theatre in St. Paul.

Few theatres begun since 1970 were closed in 1991, though many had changed structures. Even in the current economic recession – which began in 1990 and threatened attendance and charitable contributions – new theatres have continued to open, giving the impression that theatre would remain healthy in Minneapolis–St. Paul.   KN

See: C. Bellville, *Theatre Magic: Behind the Scenes at a Children's Theatre,* Minneapolis, 1986; T. Blegan, *Minnesota: A History of the State,* Minneapolis, 1975;

C. L. Brockman, *Twin City Scenic Collection: Popular Entertainment, 1895–1929,* Minneapolis, 1987; T. Guthrie, *A New Theatre,* New York, 1964; B. Morison and K. Fliehr, *In Search of an Audience,* New York, 1968; W. O'Connor, *A History of the Arts in Minnesota,* Minneapolis, 1958; F. Whiting, *Minnesota Theatre: From Old Fort Snelling to the Guthrie,* St. Paul, 1988.

Minnelli, Liza (1946–) Actress–singer, daughter of Hollywood luminaries Judy Garland and **Vincente Minnelli.** She made her New York debut in an **Off-Broadway** revival of *Best Foot Forward* (1963). Two years later critics applauded her oversized singing voice and gamine personality in *Flora, the Red Menace,* but expressed reservations about *The Act* (1977), although it won her a Tony, and *The Rink* (1984). She has been more successful with her **one-person** Broadway **revue** *Liza* (1974), and in concerts and film, especially as Sally Bowles in the film version of *Cabaret* (1972).   MK

See: J. Spada, *Judy and Liza,* Garden City, NY, 1983.

Minnelli, Vincente (1910–86) Director and designer who began his theatrical career at the age of 3 with the family **tent show.** In his teens in Chicago he designed sets for the stage shows that accompanied movies. In 1930 he moved to New York to design stage shows at the Paramount theatre. He subsequently designed for *Earl Carrol's Vanities* (1931) and several Broadway musicals, and served as art director at **Radio City Music Hall** during 1933–5, designing sets and lights for all the weekly shows, as well as directing some. Moving to Hollywood, his film directorial credits include *Cabin in the Sky* (1943), *Meet Me in St. Louis* (1944), *An American in Paris* (1951), and *Gigi* (1958), for which he won an Oscar.   AA

Minskoff Theatre 1515 Broadway, NYC [Architect: Robert Allan Jacobs]. Like the **Gershwin Theatre** to the north, the Minskoff resides within the lower floors of a commercial office building and is reached by banks of escalators. The building stands on the site where the Hotel Astor formerly stood, and the playhouse is named after its original owners and builders. A large house seating more than 1,600, it is best suited for musicals and opened with a successful revival of *Irene* (1973). Since then, its fare has been a succession of original musicals and revivals, the most notable being the **New York Shakespeare Festival** Company's adaptation of **Gilbert and Sullivan**'s *The Pirates of Penzance* (1981) and a revival of the musical *Sweet Charity* (1986). The **Nederlander** Organization shares the management of the theatre with Jerome Minskoff.   MCH

Minsky Brothers Synonymous with post-1920s stock **burlesque** in New York, in particular the popularization of the striptease [see **nudity**]. **Billy (Michael William)** (1887?–1932), the showman of the family, was soon joined by **Abe (Abraham)** (1881–1949), **Herbert Kay** (1892?–1959), and, by the early 1920s, **Morton** (1902–87) in running their father Louis's National Theatre and Winter Garden (1912). The theatre ran the gamut of entertainment ventures until 1923–4, when it emerged as the

Boston Minstrels, illustrating two stereotypes: "dandy-ism" of the North and "Ethiopians of the Southern States." An Endicott lithograph sheet music cover for "Cudjo's Wild Hunt" by Anthony Winnemore (playing banjo, second from left in both rows), 1843. Courtesy: Special Collections, Brown University.

National Winter Garden, a paradigm for all burlesque theatres in the country, including a dozen subsequent Minsky houses (in particular, The Republic, 1931). Innovations included illuminated runways; slim, attractive, and scantily clad Minsky girls, such as **Gypsy Rose Lee** and Margie Hart; and good comics (such as Steve Mills and **Phil Silvers**). Some feel the Minskys caused burlesque's downfall, for as they developed dirty, escapist shows that attracted sizable patronage, censors also took notice. Mayor Fiorello LaGuardia helped effect the closing of their operation in 1937, although a legal ban did not exist until 1942. DBW

See: M. Minsky and M. Machlin, *Minsky's Burlesque,* New York, 1986.

Minstrel show An American medley of sentimental ballads, comic dialogue, and **dance** interludes, ostensibly founded on Negro life in the South. Its origin is attributed to **T. D. Rice,** who copied the eccentric mannerisms of an elderly black in Baltimore in 1828 and adopted blackface and banjo to produce the wildly popular "Jim Crow." At first a solo act, minstrelsy grew to four performers of violin, banjo, bones (a rhythm instrument), and tambourine with the Virginia Minstrels, founded by **Dan Emmett** (1842–3); despite the burnt cork, their repertoire drew heavily on traditional English choral singing and lugubrious parlor ballads. The same held true of the troupe of

E. P. Christy, who invented whitefaced master-of-ceremonies Mr. Interlocutor and the semicircular arrangement of performers; his troupe had 30 members and gave 2,500 performances in New York in a single year. By the early 1850s Christy had evolved what was to be the standard tripartite program: In the first part, the performers would enter in the "walkround" until told, "Gentlemen, be seated." Vocal numbers, both lively and sentimental would be sung, interspersed with comic chat from the "endmen" (in England, "cornermen"), Mr. Tambo and Mr. Bones. Part Two, the olio, was a fantasia of speciality acts before the drop curtain; these included the stump speech, perfected by James Unsworth, and the wench impersonation, originated by George N. Christy (Harington). Part Three comprised a sketch, either a plantation scene with dancing "darkies" or burlesques of **Shakespeare**an plays and melodramas. Originally most of the performers and composers were white Northerners who, like Stephen Foster, had little firsthand acquaintance with Southern life; consequently the blacks they portrayed (like Zip Coon, the urban dandy) were extravagant fictions, and blackface comprised a theatrical mask not unlike Harlequin's.

After the Civil War, competition from other popular forms, especially variety and musical comedy, compelled the minstrel show to expand and change its homely character. In 1878 **J. H. Haverly** combined four troupes in his United Mastodon Minstrels with his slogan, "Forty – Count 'Em – Forty." Sumptuous costumes and lavish scenery became the rule. Primrose and West even omitted the blackface and dressed their minstrels in 18th-century court dress. From 1880 the traditionalists complained loudly about such changes.

A more significant factor was the presence in troupes of **African-American**s themselves. As early as the 1850s, black troupes, such as the Luca Family, toured the Eastern states, often performing for abolitionist societies. These black-owned companies were popular throughout the Civil War years, but in the 1870s were taken over by white managers. Thus, Callender's Georgia Minstrels, featuring the great comic **Billy Kersands**, was sold to Haverly, who then claimed falsely to have launched "colored minstrels." A major component of black shows, whatever the race of the management, was female performers: Sam T. Jack's Creoles even had an all-black female first part. By adopting such stereotypes as the loyal uncle, warm-hearted mammy, and shifty lazybones, black performers perpetuated the notion that these caricatures were true to life. Nevertheless, the minstrel show provided a valuable training ground for such talents as **Sam Lucas,** Billy McLain, and composer James Bland.

The minstrel show was one of the few truly indigenous American entertainments, and made a profound impression worldwide. Its influence can be traced in much American popular music and theatre, and many outstanding performers, including **Eddie Cantor, Al Jolson,** and **Bert Williams,** owed a great deal to its traditions. Great Britain took rapidly to minstrelsy, sending its own troupes as far afield as India and Australia. Anglo-

Saxon blackface artists were well entrenched throughout the British Empire long before the first minstrels arrived in strength in the 1870s; as a result, the ingrained stereotypes were even more remote from African-American reality than in the U.S. LS

See: J. Boskin, *Sambo: The Rise & Decline of an American Jester,* New York, 1986; H. Nathan, *Dan Emmett and the Rise of Early Negro Minstrelsy,* Norman, OK, 1962; E. L. Rice, *Monarchs of Minstrelsy,* New York, 1911; P. Sampson, *Blacks in Blackface,* Metuchen, NJ, 1980; R. Toll, *Blacking Up: The Minstrel Show in Nineteenth Century America,* London, 1974; C. Wittke, *Tambo and Bones,* Durham, NC, 1930.

Miracle Worker, The **William Gibson**'s play dramatically condenses the true story of Annie Sullivan's early attempts to teach the deaf and blind Helen Keller. Cutting across time and place, the three-act play suggests strong motivation in Sullivan's wretched childhood, but concentrates more specifically on the struggle of wills between a stubborn young woman and bright but virtually untamed child. The first production, staged by **Arthur Penn,** opened 19 October 1959 at The **Playhouse,** New York, and fascinated audiences with its highly physical confrontations of the principals, **Anne Bancroft** and Patty Duke. Although criticized for its loose construction, the play was praised for the power of its emotional moments, particularly Keller's miraculous awakening to the concept of language. It ran until 1 July 1961. KF

Miss Lulu Bett **Zona Gale**'s dramatization of her novel premiered at Sing Sing prison to inaugurate a portable stage given by **David Belasco,** but it opened the next night, 27 December 1920, at the Belmont Theatre (NYC) for a successful run. The play tells the story of a spinster who is economically dependent on her sister's husband, the unctuous Dwight Deacon, and exploited by her relatives to be little better than a servant. It won an even greater following when Gale changed the ending. In the original, Lulu becomes a more liberated woman, but with a tenuous future; in the changed version, she is happily married. The play was awarded the Pulitzer Prize for 1921. FB

Missouri Repertory Theatre Begun in 1964 as a two-play summer repertory theatre, the company had expanded by 1977 to an eight-play, year-round rotating repertory season. Founder **Patricia McIlrath** served as its artistic director until her retirement in 1985, when she was succeeded by George Keathley. In 1979 The Rep moved into the 733-seat Helen F. Spencer Theatre and became a nonprofit corporation separate from its host institution, the University of Missouri–Kansas City; however, the University's professional theatre training program ensures an ongoing organic relationship with the company. The Rep currently boasts the longest continuing annual professional tour in the U.S. FHL

Mister Roberts Comedy by Thomas Heggen and **Joshua Logan** from Heggen's collection of stories with the same title. Directed by Logan, it opened on 18 February 1948 at the **Alvin Theatre** for 1,157 performances, with **Henry Fonda** as the irrepressible Lieutenant and **David Wayne** as his debonair sidekick, Ensign Pulver. Three separate road companies played between 1949 and 1951; productions in London and Paris were also well received. The film version (1955) was successful and led to a spin-off movie featuring the ensign (1964), and to a later television series (1966). A superb ensemble supporting Fonda's performance, broad humor, and patriotic sentiment were the key ingredients to the success of this tale about an assortment of sailors sailing around the Pacific on the periphery of WW II. America loved Mister Roberts, a positive vision of the quintessential American who had just won the war: He was fun-loving, humble, heroic, loyal, self-sacrificing, and warm. MR

Mitchell, David (1932–) Set designer whose early work (late 1960s, early '70s) was split among realistically oriented frontal and symmetrical designs for shows like *The Basic Training of Pavlo Hummel* (1971) and *Short Eyes* (1974); a variety of works for the **New York Shakespeare Festival,** many influenced by **Ming Cho Lee;** and opera. With *Annie* (1977), however, he became associated with large-scale musicals and fluid, cinematic sets, as in *La Cage Aux Folles* (1983) and *Brighton Beach Memoirs* (1983), a nonmusical but cinematic play. He has also designed many classical ballets, including the New York City Ballet's *Sleeping Beauty* (1991). AA

Mitchell, Julian (1854–1926) Director. After an early career as a performer, Mitchell served as assistant director on several of **Charles Hoyt**'s farce comedies. He directed a number of burlesques for **Weber and Fields,** after which he turned to the staging of elaborate comic operas such as *The Wizard of Oz* (1903) and *Babes in Toyland* (1903). During 1907–14 he directed the *Ziegfeld Follies,* and is credited with creating the chorus of beautiful, lively, and individualized girls that became the hallmark of those shows. He continued to be in demand as a director of musicals up to the time of his death. MK

Mitchell, Langdon Elwyn (1862–1935) Playwright. Son of the eminent physician and novelist Silas Weir Mitchell, he is principally known for one play, *The New York Idea* (1906). This witty satire on easy divorce and easy marriage, defined as "three parts love and seven parts forgiveness of sin," prompted critics to call him "the American **Shaw.**" "What I wanted to satirize," Mitchell once wrote, "was the extreme frivolity of our American life." Written for **Minnie Maddern Fiske,** it was revived by **Grace George** (1915), and was produced by **Max Reinhardt** in Berlin (1916).

Mitchell also wrote *In the Season* (1893); *Becky Sharp* (1899), an adaptation of *Vanity Fair* and a vehicle for Mrs. Fiske; *The Kreutzer Sonata* (1906), an adaptation from the Yiddish of **Jacob Gordin;** *The New Marriage* (1911); and *Major Pendennis* (1916), adapted from Thackeray's novel.

He was educated at St. Paul's, studied in Dresden

and Paris, attended law school at Harvard and Columbia, was admitted to the New York bar in 1886, and in 1892 married English actress Marion Lea, who appeared in *The New York Idea*. RM

Mitchell, Loften (1919–) **African-American** playwright, teacher, and theatre historian who studied playwriting with **John Gassner** and had three of his early plays produced in Harlem before gaining recognition with *A Land Beyond the River* (1957), a drama based on the life of the Rev. Dr. Joseph DeLaine, who fought to end discrimination in public schools. Mitchell cowrote the book for *Ballad for Bimshire* (1963) and the freedom pageant *Ballad for the Winter Soldiers* (1964). Alone, he wrote the television documentary "Tell Pharaoh" (1963), dramatized the **Bert Williams** story in *Star of the Morning* (published 1971), and also wrote the successful *Bubbling Brown Sugar* (1976). His informal history *Black Drama* (1967) and *Voices of the Black Theatre* (1975) chronicle the experiences of African Americans in the American theatre. EGH

Mitchell, Margaret (Maggie) (1832–1918) A tiny, boyish ingenue, she followed two half-sisters on stage, making her debut in June 1851 at **Burton's Theatre,** NYC. Often playing breeches parts, she achieved her first starring success in Cleveland (1853). She became identified with the title role of *Fanchon, The Cricket,* which she first played at the **St. Charles Theatre,** New Orleans (January 1861). It became her starring vehicle, and into it she interpolated an extensive repertory of songs, dances, and impersonations of other performers. She retired in 1892. DMcD

Mitchell, William "Billy" (1798–1856) English-born actor, playwright, and theatre manager. A distinguished comedian from London and English provincial theatres since 1831, Mitchell appeared first at the National Theatre in New York in 1836. His particular achievement was his management of **Mitchell's Olympic** in New York from 9 December 1839 to 9 March 1850, the year of his retirement. Advertising the production of "Vaudevilles, Burlesques, Extravaganzas, Farces, Etc.," Mitchell made the Olympic a popular success when other theatres were failing. As an actor Mitchell was a favorite as Vincent Crummles in a farce created from Dickens's *Nicholas Nickleby* entitled *The Savage and the Maiden*. A staff of actor-playwrights – Henry Horncastle, **Charles Walcot,** Alexander Allen, and **Benjamin A. Baker** – provided him with novelties. *1940; or, Crummles in Search of Novelty* was repeated as *1941 . . .* and *1942. . . .* Catching the topic of the day was the clue to Mitchell's success. When **Boucicault's** *London Assurance* came to New York, Mitchell responded with *Olympic Insurance;* he burlesqued Dickens's visit in *Boz* and the **Edwin Forrest**–William Macready feud in three sketches; he starred in and wrote *Billy Taylor,* a local extravaganza. The greatest event at Mitchell's Olympic, however, was Baker's *A Glance at New York,* 1848, with Mose the fire b'hoy. WJM

Mitchell's Olympic 442–4 Broadway, NYC [Architect: Calvin Pollard]. In 1837, Willard and Blake opened the Olympic, patterned after Madame Vestris's famous London Olympic both in physical structure and policy. They presented comedies, farces, vaudevilles, and musical pieces and, since the city was surfeited with theatres and entertainment, quickly lost their theatre. In 1839, despite hard times, **William "Billy" Mitchell** revived the fortunes of the house with a combination of his own talents and managerial prowess. His reduced prices and his diet of light comic entertainment and burlesques made it the most popular theatre in town. When he retired in 1850, the playhouse passed to other managements and was used briefly as a minstrel hall and a German-language theatre. In 1852, it was converted to business uses and two years later, the structure burned to the ground. MCH

See: D. Rinear, *The Temple of Momus: Mitchell's Olympic Theatre,* Metuchen, NJ, 1987.

Mitzi E. Newhouse Theatre see **Vivian Beaumont and Mitzi E. Newhouse theatres**

Modjeska (Modrzejewska), Helena (née Jadwiga Benda/Jadwiga Opid) (1840–1909) Polish-born actress, daughter of the widowed Madame Benda, she used the name of the family guardian Michal Opid until she married Gustave Sinnmayer Modrzejewski in 1856 and made her stage debut as Helena Modrzejewska in 1861. Managed by her second husband Count Bozenta, she became an **international star** before emigrating to the U.S. in 1876. She learned English and made her American debut in 1877 in Scribe's *Adrienne Lecouvreur,* one of her great roles, along with Camille and Shakespeare's Rosalind, Viola, Beatrice, and Portia. The tall, comely actress was noted for her charm, naturalness, and, in **William Winter**'s words, "exquisite refinement and grace." Her memoirs were published in 1910. FHL

See: M. M. Coleman, *Fair Rosalind: The American Career of Helena Modjeska,* Cheshire, CT, 1969.

Moeller, Philip (1880–1958) Director, producer, and playwright. Born in New York, Moeller graduated from Columbia University and joined the **Washington Square Players** in the winter of 1914. His one-act plays, *Two Blind Beggars and One Less Blind* and *Helena's Husband* were produced by the group and attracted critical attention; but Moeller made his reputation as a director, and was regarded by **Lawrence Langner** as one of the most brilliant directors of comedy in this country. A founder and director of the **Theatre Guild,** he staged their first production, *Bonds of Interest,* in 1919. He was especially adept in directing the plays of **Eugene O'Neill.** His Guild credits include *Strange Interlude* (1928), *Dynamo* (1929), *Mourning Becomes Electra* (1931), and *Ah, Wilderness!* (1933). **Brooks Atkinson** called his direction of *Strange Interlude* a "tremendous achievement" because he found a way to distinguish between the speeches and the asides. Atkinson also praised Moeller for finding the "exact tempo and style" in *Mourning Becomes Electra*. Moeller thought of himself as an inspirational director. After directing films for RKO Radio in the early 1930s, he went into virtual retirement. TLM

See: D. Wiley, "Philip Moeller of the Theatre Guild: An Historical and Critical Study," PhD diss., Indiana U, 1973.

Moffat, Donald (1930–) British-born actor and director who made his debut in *The Admirable Crichton* (revival, 1947) and on Broadway in *Under Milkwood* (1957), then did *The Bald Soprano* (1958), Hailey's *Father's Day* (1970), Howe's *Painting Churches* (1983), *The Iceman Cometh* (revival, 1985), and Jeremy Lawrence's *Uncommon Ground* (1991, Evanston, IL). He has acted at the Ohio and Akron Shakespeare Festivals and regional companies like the **McCarter Theatre,** and directed at the Great Lakes Shakespeare Festival, **Association of Producing Artists** (APA)–Phoenix, and Los Angeles Actors Theatre. After Moffat's first film, *Pursuit of the Graf Spee* (1957), he appeared in *Rachel, Rachel* (1968), *The Right Stuff* (1983), *The Unbearable Lightness of Being* (1988), and *The Bonfire of the Vanities* (1990), as well as a number of TV performances, including "Tartuffe" (1979). Moffat received 1967 Tony nominations for *The Wild Duck* and *Right You Are*.   REK

Mogulesko, Sigmund (1858–1914) Born in Bessarabia (Moldavia), this Yiddish actor and composer began performing in childhood as a choirboy and joined **Goldfadn,** the "Father of **Yiddish Theatre,**" in his early efforts. He acted – in women's roles, for there were no Yiddish actresses as yet – and also composed. When he arrived in America in 1886, his fame preceded him, and he continued for the rest of his life to be the public's darling for his mischievous charm, especially in character roles, and his sweet voice. He continued to perform and compose with great success despite a period of difficulties with his voice.   NS

Moiseiwitsch, Tanya (1914–) British-born set and costume designer noted for her collaborations with director **Tyrone Guthrie** and the bold thrust stage and innovative auditorium she designed for the Shakespeare Festival Theatre in Stratford, ON (1957) and the similar **Guthrie Theatre** in Minneapolis (1963). Moiseiwitsch began her career in London in 1934. The following year she went to the Abbey Theatre in Dublin, where she designed over 50 productions through 1939. She subsequently designed for the London's Old Vic beginning in 1944 and at the Shakespeare Memorial Theatre in Stratford-upon-Avon from 1949, as well as commercial theatre in London and theatres in Italy, the U.S., and Australia. She is most closely associated with the plays of Shakespeare, but notable productions include *Oedipus Rex* at Ontario (1954; film 1957) and *The House of Atreus* in Minneapolis (1968), both of which contain what is perhaps the most successful use of masks in the 20th century. Beginning with her work at the Abbey, Moiseiwitsch's designs have been typified by simple, direct, presentational sets that embodied the visual metaphor of the play. Since she generally designed costumes as well there was a strong visual unity to her productions. With the polygonal, stepped stages at Ontario and Minneapolis that jutted into the steeply banked auditoriums, Moiseiwitsch was able to eliminate most scenery and provide a space in which her highly textured costumes could be sculpted by light.   AA

Monk, Meredith (1942–) Choreographer, composer, director, **performance art**ist, and leading innovator in the so-called Next Wave since the mid-1960s and her association with the Judson Dance Theatre (NYC). Her dances have evolved into multimedia, nonverbal theatre pieces, such as *Vessel* (1971–2) and *Quarry* (1975–6), both termed "opera epics." In the early and mid-1970s she also created several chamber theatre works: the "travelogue" series (*Paris, Chacon, Venice/Milan*) in collaboration with **Ping Chong,** and the "archaeology" pieces (*Small Scroll, Anthology, The Plateau Series, Recent Ruins*). In the late 1970s she began to concentrate on musical composition and performance, having begun to "distrust the theatre a little bit," although by the early 1980s two multimedia theatre pieces had been added to her canon: *Specimen Days* (1981) and *The Games* (1983), the latter commissioned by Peter Stein's Schaubühne repertory theatre in West Berlin, with its U.S. premiere at the **Brooklyn Academy of Music**'s Next Wave Festival the following year. In the early 1990s she devoted attention to her unique form of opera, such as *Atlas* (1991), most notably with commissions from the Houston Opera.   DBW

Monodrama see **one-person performances**

Montague (né Mann), Henry James (or John) (1843–78) English-born actor whose American debut in 1874 (Tom Gilroy in *Partners for Life*) at **Wallack's Theatre** followed a successful London career. Handsome and gentlemanly, he became a popular leading man in New York and later on tour in such roles as Captain Molyneux (*The Shaughraun*), Captain D'Alroy (*Caste*), and Tom Dexter (*The Overland Route*). He died suddenly while playing an engagement at San Francisco's **California Theatre.**   DJW

Montanaro, Tony (1927–) Illusionistic **mime** and storyteller, teacher. A student of Louise Gifford at Columbia University, and (to a lesser extent) of Etienne Decroux, Montanaro was most strongly marked by his studies with Marcel Marceau in Paris. Montanaro lived and worked in New York City until the early 1970s, when he founded the Celebration Barn Theater in Maine. An influential teacher, he has inspired generations of performers and created a video book entitled *Mime Spoken Here* (1991).   TL

Montano, Linda (1942–) Conceptual and **performance art**ist-writer. A native of Saugerties, NY, Montano attended Catholic schools, joined the missionary order of Maryknoll Sister (1960–2), studied art at the College of New Rochelle (BA, 1965) and sculpture at the Villa Schiffanois, Italy (MA, 1966) and the University of Wisconsin, Madison (MFA, 1969). Montano's performances draw on spiritual traditions and practices (Catholicism, Buddhism, Zen, Hinduism) and are based on an aesthetic of everyday life developed by Marcel

Duchamp, Claes Oldenburg, John Cage, and **Allan Kaprow**. For her early performances (1969–72), she developed the "Chicken" persona. Other important performances were *Handcuffed for Three Days to Tom Marioni* (1973), *Mitchell's Death* (1978), *Art/Life, One Year Performance* (1983–4) with **Tehching Hsieh,** and *Seven Years of Living Art* (1984–91). AF

Montez, Lola (née Maria Dolores Eliza Rosanna Gilbert) (1818–61) Irish-born adventuress, who, when her first marriage failed, went on stage as a dancer (London, 1843), performing in Europe, America, and Australia. Her beauty and charm compensated for her lack of talent and musical sense. Her liaison with Ludwig I of Bavaria (1847–8) culminated in his forced abdication, and she came to the U.S., making her New York debut (1851) in *Betley the Tyrolean;* a biographical play, *Lola Montes* [sic] *in Bavaria,* by C. P. T. Ware (1852), capitalized on her sensational past. She toured to the gold rush country, performing a spider dance that shocked **San Francisco** audiences, and took child actress **Lotta Crabtree** under her tutelage. After 1856, she appeared as a spiritualist and lecturer, speaking on fashion, gallantry, and Roman Catholicism. She underwent a religious conversion and became a recluse after 1859. LS

See: *Lectures of Lola Montez, including her autobiography,* New York, 1859; H. Holdredge, *Lola Montez,* London, 1957; H. Wyndham, *The Magnificent Montez,* New York, 1935.

Montgomery, Dave (David Craig) (1870–1917) and **Fred [Val] (Andrew) Stone** (1873–1959) Comedy team (1894–1917) prominent in **vaudeville** and musical comedy. Initially a black-face act, they soon became headliners, appearing at London's Palace as early as 1900. Their greatest successes came in *The Wizard of Oz* (1902) and **Victor Herbert**'s *The Red Mill* (1906). In the former Stone played the Scarecrow and Montgomery the Tin Woodsman; in the latter Stone, who began a long association with **Charles Dillingham,** was a hit as Con Kidder. Montgomery and Stone were also two of the seven founders of the White Rats (1900), a fraternal order for vaudevillians. After Montgomery's death, Stone, an unusually versatile performer, appeared in films and on stage, his last major appearance being Grandpa Vanderhof in *You Can't Take It with You* (City Center, New York, 1945). Stone's daughters (Paula, Dorothy, and Carol) were in show business. His autobiography, *Rolling Stones,* was published in 1945. DBW

Montresor, Beni (1926–) Italian-born designer who has designed extensively for opera companies in New York, San Francisco, London, Paris, and Munich, as well as for La Scala. Frequently identified with fairy-tale operas, he has a lush painterly style. Before coming to the U.S. in 1960, Montresor designed over 30 films with Fellini, Rosselini, and de Sica, as well as writing and directing his own films. He also writes and illustrates children's books. He has done little theatre but has designed at the **Guthrie** and **American**

Repertory Theatre, as well as *Do I Hear a Waltz?* on Broadway. AA

Moody, William Vaughn (1869–1910) Indiana-born dramatist who took a degree in English at Harvard (1893) and taught there and at the University of Chicago (1895–1902). He cowrote a standard history of English literature, and was widely regarded as the best lyric poet of his generation. With Harriet Brainard, whom he married (1909), he was active in Donald Robertson's New Theatre. He experimented with two verse plays, but turned to prose when he dramatized a story about a woman kidnapped by a band of drunken cowboys. *The Great Divide* was premiered by **Henry Miller** and **Margaret Anglin** at a matinee in Chicago (April 1906). It was easily the finest American play of its time, successfully blending realistic motivation with poetic treatment of the national myth. His last play, *The Faith Healer* (1909), was a failure in performance, and Moody died of a brain tumor soon after. DMcD

See: M. Brown, *Estranging Dawn,* Carbondale, IL, 1973; M. Halpern, *William Vaughn Moody,* New York, 1964.

Moonchildren by **Michael Weller** was first produced as *Cancer* at the Royal Court Theatre in London, 14 September 1970, directed by Roger Hendricks Simon and Peter Gill. As *Moonchildren,* it was first produced at Washington, DC's **Arena Stage** in 1972, with **Alan Schneider** directing a cast including James Woods, Jill Eikenberry, **Robert Prosky,** and Cara Duff-MacCormick. When **David Merrick** moved the production to Broadway, 21 February 1972, it closed after 16 performances; but it ran for a year at the Theatre de Lys, and has had over 1,000 productions worldwide. Set in a college apartment shared by five men and two women in the mid-1960s, the play is a microcosm of a college generation whose every action was taken in reference to the Vietnam War. Through a thin layer of dark and evasive humor, Weller depicts the hopelessness of a generation for whom life decisions and permanent commitments are impossible. BCM

Moon for the Misbegotten, A by **Eugene O'Neill.** Four-act drama written in 1943 that failed to reach New York in its original 1947 **Theatre Guild** production, and ran but 68 performances a decade later on Broadway (2 May 1957) starring Wendy Hiller, **Franchot Tone,** and Cyril Cusack. The play gained stature with the 1968 revival at the **Circle in the Square** Theatre, and was acclaimed a masterpiece with the 1973 revival on Broadway directed by **José Quintero** and starring **Colleen Dewhurst,** Ed Flanders, and **Jason Robards, Jr.**

The play is autobiographical, an attempt by O'Neill to understand and forgive his brother Jamie's actions before and after the death of their mother in Los Angeles and the subsequent return of her body by train to New York. In terms of the theatre, however, the play concerns the ill-fated mating of the guilt-ridden and alcoholic Jamie with Josie, a large, shy woman who pretends to be a wanton to hide her shyness and real feelings for

Jamie. Although O'Neill paints life in harsh colors and depicts his characters as having little control over it, Jamie does find a measure of forgiveness and redemption through Josie's love.   TLM

Moore, Victor (1876–1962) Broadway actor described in the *New York Times* as "the chubby little comedian with the teetering walk and the quavering voice." His first of many Broadway roles was Kid Burns in *Forty-five Minutes from Broadway* (1906). His best-known roles were those of vice-president Alexander Throttlebottom in *Of Thee I Sing* (1932) and Reverend Dr. Moon (Public Enemy #13) in *Anything Goes* (1934). He was frequently cast as a foil to **William Gaxton**'s leading man. He received the New York Drama Critics' Circle Award for Gramps in the 1952 revival of *On Borrowed Time*. He appeared in many films, including *The Seven Year Itch* (1955).   MR

Moorehead, Agnes (1906–74) Stage, film, and television actress. She appeared in **summer stock** aged 10 and spent four years with the St. Louis Municipal Opera. Moorehead earned a doctorate in literature at Bradley University, taught dramatics at the Dalton School, and began to appear on Broadway in such shows as *Marco Millions*. During the Depression, she turned to radio, appearing on "The March of Time" and in the suspense classic "Sorry, Wrong Number." She was a charter member of the **Mercury Theatre,** and made her movie debut in *Citizen Kane* with **Orson Welles**. In 1951 Moorehead appeared with the highly acclaimed First Drama Quartet. She made about 100 films, winning five Academy Award nominations, but was best known to modern audiences as Endora in the television comedy "Bewitched."   SMA

See: W. Sherk, *Agnes Moorehead: A Very Private Person*, Philadelphia, 1976.

Moran, George (1882–1949) and **Charles Mack** (1888–1934) Blackface comedy team ("The Two Black Crows") in the tradition of **McIntyre and Heath.** Never consciously racist in their routine, the team garnered black as well as white fans. Partnered first in the late teens, they became stars in 1927 after recording "The Early Bird Catches the Worm," featuring Mack as a shuffling, lazy black. Though they each began as singles in **vaudeville,** as a team they were most successful in 1920s **revue**s. When Mack – who wrote most of the material and owned the Moran and Mack name as a trademark – refused Moran equal pay, Moran left the act briefly in 1930 (returning a few months later), and was replaced by Bert Swor (still billed as Moran and Mack).   DBW

Morehouse, Ward (1899–1966) Theatre journalist and critic. A native of Georgia, Morehouse was best known for his "Broadway After Dark" column and for vivid and racy theatrical interviews with stars. His writings appeared in the New York Sun (1926–48), the *New York World-Telegram and the Sun* (1950–6), and from 1956 until his death with S. I. Newhouse Newspapers. His books include *Forty-five Minutes Past Eight* (1939), *Matinee*

Tomorrow (1949), and *George M. Cohan, Prince of the American Theatre* (1943).   TLM

Moreno, Rita (1931–) Puerto Rican–born actress who initially worked as a Spanish dancer and **nightclub** entertainer. She appeared in *The Sign in Sidney Brustein's Window* (1964) and several other plays before winning a Tony Award for her supporting role in *The Ritz* (1975). In 1985 she toured in a female version of *The Odd Couple*. Moreno is the only performer to have won an Academy Award, an Emmy, a Tony, and a Grammy.   MK

Morgan, Roger (1938–) Lighting designer and theatre consultant who designed lights for many of the significant **Off-Broadway** and **Off-Off Broadway** productions in the late 1960s and '70s, as well as productions for the **New York Shakespeare Festival, American Place Theatre,** and the **Circle in the Square.** Broadway credits include *Dracula, Agnes of God,* and *Me and My Girl.* Since the 1980s Morgan has been active as a consultant to numerous new theatres and renovations, including the **Marquis Theatre** in New York, the **Denver Center** Theatre complex, and the Playhouse Square project in Cleveland.   AA

Morning's at Seven by **Paul Osborn** premiered in 1939 at the **Longacre Theatre** in a production directed by **Joshua Logan** and designed by **Jo Mielziner.** This gentle comedy about the lives of four sisters in a Midwestern community evoked Chekhov and **Wilder** but generated little enthusiasm and totaled only 44 performances. In 1980, however, a splendid revival directed by **Vivian Matalon** at the **Lyceum** featured Nancy Marchand, Teresa Wright, Maureen O'Sullivan, and **Elizabeth Wilson** as the Gibbs sisters, with strong supporting work by Gary Merrill and David Rounds. It ran 564 performances and won Tonys for best revival, direction, and featured actor (Rounds).   BBW

Morosco, Oliver (Mitchell) (1876–1945) Utah-born manager and producer who moved to San Francisco at an early age and appeared as an acrobat in the troupe of Walter Morosco. After adopting his mentor's name, he managed several theatres in the Bay area, later acquiring on his own at least six theatres in **Los Angeles.** He began producing in 1909, and later offered in New York *The Bird of Paradise* (1912) and *Peg O' My Heart* (1912), both starring **Laurette Taylor;** and in 1915, *The Unchastened Woman* with **Emily Stevens.** The **Shubert**s built the **Morosco Theatre** for him in New York (1917), which he opened with his own play, *Canary Island.* The author of numerous plays, all undistinguished, Morosco went bankrupt in 1926 in a scheme to build a motion picture settlement in California.   TLM

See: H. Morosco and L. Dugger, *Life of Oliver Morosco, the Oracle of Broadway*, Caldwell, ID, 1944.

Morosco Theatre 217 West 45th St., NYC [Architect: Herbert J. Krapp]. The Morosco was

Clara Morris in the late 1870s. Courtesy: Don B. Wilmeth.

the first of many theatres to be designed for the **Shubert**s by Herbert J. Krapp, a talented young architect who had served his apprenticeship with Henry B. Herts, an earlier favored Shubert architect. Built in 1917, it was intended as a showcase for the productions of **Oliver Morosco**. An intimate, 1,000-seat, one-balcony house, it was well suited to realistic dramas and intimate musicals. On its stage was launched the Broadway career of **Eugene O'Neill**, whose first full-length play, *Beyond the Horizon* (1920), was presented at a matinee performance. The same year the long-running *The Bat* opened there. In 1936, the Shuberts were forced to relinquish the theatre, which changed hands several times before it was razed in 1982 to make way for a new hotel. In addition to O'Neill, its stage had proved kind to such American playwrights as **Thornton Wilder, Tennessee Williams, Arthur Miller, Robert Anderson,** and **Arthur Kopit.** MCH

Morris (née Morrison), Clara (1846/8–1925) Actress, possibly born in Canada of a bigamous union, who received her early training in **John A. Ellsler**'s **stock company** in Cleveland (1861–9). For years she sustained a reputation as one of America's greatest emotionalistic actresses, although her career is one of incongruities. In the 1870s she was praised as realistic, though by the '80s she was denounced by many as the queen of spasms and the mistress of the tricks of the acting trade. In 1870 she began her New York career as a member of **Augustin Daly**'s company, excelling in plays like *Man and Wife, Divorce,* and especially Daly's *Article 47,* in which she played Cora the Creole. She left Daly in 1873 and spent most of her remaining career as a traveling star, appearing in popular roles such as Camille and Miss Moulton (in a version of *East Lynne*). Although she attempted classical roles, she was always more successful when playing pathetic girls in melodrama, which allowed her to use her "tearful" voice and to loose a veritable flood of emotion on her audience. She appeared in **vaudeville** in the 1900s and made her last appearance in Washington, DC, in 1906. She wrote three unreliable autobiographies (1901–6). DBW

See: M. Howard, "The Acting of Clara Morris," PhD diss., U of Illinois, 1957.

Morris, Mary (1895–1970) Actress. At Radcliffe College Morris performed in **George Pierce Baker**'s Workshop 47, but left to gain practical theatre experience. After a year as an unsalaried prompter, she made her professional debut in *The Clod* with the **Washington Square Players** in 1916. In 1918 she toured *Alexander Hamilton* with **George Arliss,** whom she credited with teaching her the most about acting. For two years (1924–6) she played Abbie in *Desire Under the Elms.* She appeared with numerous stock companies, on Broadway, and in two films. In 1937 she made her London debut. She taught and directed at Carnegie Institute of Technology (1939–60) and at the **American Shakespeare Festival** and Academy (1961–2). FHL

Morse, Robert (1931–) Actor and singer first seen on Broadway in *The Matchmaker* (1955); his musical debut was in *Say Darling* (1959). He charmed critics and audiences as the boyish but determined J. Pierpont Finch in *How to Succeed in Business Without Really Trying* (1961) and starred in the long-running musical *Sugar* (1972) and the less successful *So Long, 174th Street* (1976). After a long absence, he returned to Broadway in the acclaimed, Tony Award–winning **one-person** show *Tru* (1989) as Truman Capote. MK

Mortimer, Lillian (c. 1880–1946) Actor, author, and manager who produced her own and other plays on the **Stair and Havlin** 10-20-30 circuit (1903–9). Declining receipts led her to disband her company and headline as a comedienne on the Keith circuit from 1909 until about 1930, when she retired. RKB

Morton, Martha (1865?–1925) "The dean of America's women playwrights," Morton, also a director, was the first to crack the gender barrier on Broadway, with her many commercial, if not critical, successes. In 1891 she wrote *The Merchant,* followed by *Geoffrey Middleton* (1892), *A Fool of Fortune* (1896), *A Bachelor's Romance* (1896), *The Triumph of Love* (1904), and others. In 1907 she organized the Society of Dramatic Authors because the American Dramatists Club refused to accept women. FB

Moschen, Michael (1955–) **New Vaudeville** and **performance art**ist who is to juggling what **Fred Astaire** was to tap dancing. He has performed with **circus**es (Big Apple Circus, Lotte Goslar's Pantomime Circus), **Bill Irwin**, and with Fred Garbo and Bob Berky. He created a solo show, *Moschen in Motion* (1988) for the **Brooklyn Academy of Music**'s "Next Wave Festival." Sculptor John Kahn has inspired and been a collaborator in much of Moschen's work, which uses beautifully designed objects manipulated daringly and poetically in ways that fully engage the imagination and attention. Moschen has received, among other prestigious awards, a five-year MacArthur Foundation Fellowship.   TL

Moscow Art Theatre (MAT) MAT's five-nation European and American tours (1922–3) were undertaken for several purposes: to regain internal stability and financial solvency for a company denied government subsidies and attacked for being bourgeois elitist under the new Soviet regime; to demonstrate the new centralized Soviet theatre's good health; and to introduce American audiences to ensemble, as opposed to "star" acting. Producer **Morris Gest** widely and unrealistically promoted MAT as an ideal acting ensemble, prior to the American tour, which originated in New York City (**Jolson**'s 59th Street Theatre, 8 January–31 March 1923). Stanislavsky was struck by theatre's devaluation in such an advanced society, while the American press accused MAT of being a communist propaganda tool. MAT performed (in Russian) A. N. Tolstoi's *Tsar Fyodor Ioannovich*, Gorky's *The Lower Depths*, Chekhov's *Three Sisters, Uncle Vanya,* and *The Cherry Orchard* (despite Stanislavsky's questioning of Chekhov's continued relevance in Soviet society), and Turgenev's *A Provincial Lady*. The tour was a popular and artistic success (especially the Chekhov) but a financial failure for the company. Praised for its new style of play, MAT performed only its accessible, realistic repertory staples, not the symbolist and new Soviet plays and stylized stagings of the classics it offered in Russia. MAT's visits inspired the American studio theatre movement's continued growth, the dissemination of early and false versions of the Stanislavsky system, and Stanislavsky's hasty publication of his autobiography *My Life in Art* – a valuable but patchwork and awkwardly translated reminiscence that the author edited and improved for its Russian publication. To erase a $25,000 debt incurred on a second European tour, MAT again toured the U.S., November 1923–May 1924. The company added *An Enemy of the People, The Mistress of the Inn,* Nemirovich-Danchenko's adaptation of *The Brothers Karamazov,* A. N. Ostrovsky's *Too Clever by Half,* and Chekhov's *Ivanov* to its touring repertory and eight cities to its touring circuit. MAT actors Maria Ouspenskaya, Leo and Barbara Bulgakov, Akim Tamirov, and Vera Soloviova remained in the U.S. permanently.   SG

See: J. Benedetti, *Stanislavski: A Biography,* New York, 1988; C. Edwards, *The Stanislavsky Heritage: Its Contribution to the Russian and American Theatre,* New York, 1965; O. Korneva, *Konstantin Stanislavsky: Selected Works,* Moscow, 1984; V. Nemirovich-

Danchenko, *My Life in the Russian Theatre,* London, 1937.

Moses, Gilbert, III (1942–) Director. Born in Cleveland and educated at Oberlin College, Sorbonne, and NYU, Moses edited the *Free Press,* Jackson, MS, before cofounding with John O'Neal the **Free Southern Theatre** (1963) in Jackson and later New Orleans. Important to the Black Theatre movement [see **African-American theatre**], Moses directed LeRoi Jones's (**Amiri Baraka**'s) *Slaveship* (1969), which won an Obie (1970); *The Taking of Miss Janie* (1975), which won both Obie and Drama Desk awards (1977); and *Ain't Supposed to Die a Natural Death* (1971), a Drama Desk winner and Tony nominee (1973). Television credits include segments of "Roots," episodes of "Call to Glory," and "The Ossie's Ruby Series" (1988), of which he was producer.   TLM

Moses, Montrose Jonas (1878–1934) Scholar and critic. Born in New York City, Moses began his career with the *Literary Digest* (1900–2), becoming dramatic editor of the *Reader's Magazine* (1903–7) and drama critic of the *Independent* (1908–18), the *Book News Monthly* (1908–18), and the *Bellman* (1910–19). His books include *Famous Actor Families in America* (1906), *Henrik Ibsen, The Man and His Plays* (1908), *The American Dramatist* (1911, 1917), and *The Fabulous Forrest* (1929). His edited collections include *Representative Plays by American Dramatists* (3 vols., 1918) and *The American Theatre as Seen by Its Critics, 1752 to 1934* (with **John Mason Brown**).   TLM

Mosher, Gregory (Dean) (1949–) Best known as the first director of works by **David Mamet,** Mosher was also the first artistic administrator to have popular success with the theatre program at New York's **Lincoln Center.** Having studied theatre at Oberlin, Ithaca, and Juilliard, Mosher went to Chicago's **Goodman Theatre** in 1974 to direct its Stage 2 program. As Goodman artistic director (1978–85), he concentrated on new works by such authors as Mamet, **John Guare, David Rabe, Michael Weller,** Wole Soyinka, **Tennessee Williams,** and **Edward Albee,** a policy that met with some resistance from subscribers. Ironically, Mosher's tenure at Lincoln Center (1985–91) was criticized for being *too* popular, for blurring the line between nonprofit and commercial production. Mosher left Lincoln Center in 1991 to pursue independent film and theatre work, including a 1992 revival of *Streetcar Named Desire.*   SF

Mostel, Zero (Samuel Joel) (1915–77) Trained as an artist, Mostel became an immensely talented comic actor, noted for his sagging jowls and large paunch but dancer's grace, acrobat's control, and enormously expressive face. After appearing in sketches at a Greenwich Village **nightclub** in 1942, he made his Broadway debut the same year in *Keep 'Em Laughing.* Subsequent roles of note included Shu Fu in *The Good Person of Setzuan* (1956), Leopold Bloom in *Ulysses in Nighttown* (1958, 1974), Jean in *Rhinoceros* (1961), Pseudolus in the musical *A Funny Thing Happened on the Way to the*

Alice Brady in *Mourning Becomes Electra*. Courtesy: New York Public Library of the Performing Arts.

Forum (1962), and his greatest popular triumph, Tevye in *Fiddler on the Roof* (1964, 1976). He died in Philadelphia rehearsing Shylock in Arnold Wesker's *The Merchant*. His son **Josh** is also an actor (Milo Crawford in *Texas Trilogy,* 1976; Norman in *The Boys Next Door,* 1987).   DBW

> See: J. Brown, *Zero Mostel: A Biography,* New York, 1989; K. Mostel, M. Gilford, J. Gilford, and Z. Mostel, *One Hundred Seventy Years of Show Business,* New York, 1978.

Most Happy Fella, The Three-act musical comedy by **Frank Loesser,** opened 3 May 1956 at the **Imperial Theatre,** running 676 performances. Frank Loesser's masterwork, for which he wrote all music and words, is almost entirely sung. Based on **Sidney Howard**'s *They Knew What They Wanted,* it tells of a hardbitten waitress (Jo Sullivan) who goes to California's wine country as a mail-order bride and finds herself torn between a younger and an older man. Skillfully through-composed in virtually operatic dimensions, it required far above-average voices, notably Metropolitan Opera baritone Robert Weede, who played the title role. The score's greatest popular hits, however, came from the comic subplot: "Standing on the Corner (Watching All the Girls Go By)" and "Big D." The original production won the Drama Critics' Circle Award for best musical, and a production starring Giorgio Tozzi played New York in 1979. The show is now in the repertoire of the New York City Opera, and in 1991 was revived by the **Goodspeed Opera House,** a production brought to Broadway in early 1992.   JD

Mourning Becomes Electra This dark, brooding, majestic adaptation by **Eugene O'Neill** of *The Oresteia* opened 26 October 1931 at the Guild Theatre. Under the direction of **Philip Moeller,** and graced by impressive Greek-revival designs by **Robert Edmond Jones,** the tragic trilogy, like *Strange Interlude,* was produced with a dinner intermission and required over five hours of performance time. Featuring characters with masklike faces, the play capitalizes on formality, frustration, and hidden passion. The House of Atreus at the close of the Trojan War becomes the powerful New England Mannon family at the end of the American Civil War. Clytemnestra is Christine (played with sinister charm by **Alla Nazimova**), and Electra becomes calculating Lavinia (played as stoically merciless by **Alice Brady**), who takes the focus Aeschylus awarded Orestes, renamed Orin (played by Earl Larimore). Orin's furies are not personified but haunt the young matricide and drive him to madness and suicide. Lavinia, who experiences incestuous and protective feelings for the men in her family, dominates all but her father, Ezra Mannon, and is the chief instrument for revenging Christine's murder of Ezra before sentencing herself to imprisonment within the unpeopled Mannon mansion, haunted by the ghosts of her family's cruel history.   RHW

Mowatt (Ritchie), Anna Cora Ogden (1819–70) Playwright and actress. Although now best known for *Fashion* (1845), a satire on the nouveaux riches who make themselves ridiculous by aping foreign manners, in her own time she was also known as a public reader and actress. Encouraged by Longfellow, she began her readings in Boston (1841) and the following year in New York. After the success of *Fashion,* she toured for 200 nights as Lady Teazle, Juliet, and Pauline in Bulwer-Lytton's *The Lady of Lyons;* she toured again in 1852, and performed in England (1847, 1851). As an actress she was admired for her grace, radiant smile, and naturalness, which **Edgar Allan**

Poe found "so pleasantly removed from the customary rant and cant."

Her second play, *Armand* (1847), was also well received, and she wrote two vivid accounts of theatrical life: *Autobiography of an Actress* (1854) and *Mimic Life; or, Before and Behind the Curtain* (1856).

She had read all of Shakespeare by age 10; at 14 translated, staged, and acted in Voltaire's *Alzire* in the family parlor; wrote her first play, *Pelayo*, when she was 17; and became a regular contributor to *Graham's Magazine* and the *Columbian*. She married James Mowatt when she was 15, and after his death (1851) married William F. Ritchie.   RM

> *See:* E. Barnes, *The Lady of Fashion: The Life and Theatre of Anna Cora Mowatt,* New York, 1955.

Mulatto Play by **Langston Hughes** on miscegenation and filial rejection; intended as a tragedy but altered by producer Martin Jones into a melodrama. However, the 1935 production was saved by scenes of strong racial antagonisms and by the performance of **Rose McClendon** as Cora, Colonel Norwood's black mistress and the grieving mother of a rebellious son who was lynched. The production ran for 373 performances on Broadway, then toured the country for eight months. The play is based on Hughes's short story "Father and Son," and was later turned into an opera titled *The Barrier* (1950). The author's original version is published in *Five Plays by Langston Hughes,* 1963.   EGH

Mulligan Guard Ball, The **Edward Harrigan**'s first highly successful play in his Mulligan series, this was a comic depiction of immigrant life in NYC's Lower East Side. Regarded by contemporaries as a realistic chronicle of the city, the piece focuses on rivalries between various ethnic groups, while the elopement of a young couple furnishes a pretext for the action. It opened 13 January 1879 at the Theatre Comique with Harrigan as Dan Mulligan, ringleader of the Irish; his long-time partner, Tony Hart, as his son Tommy; and Annie Yeamans as his wife, Cordelia. With music by David Braham, the popular mixture of song, dance, broad physical action, and scenic display ran 153 performances and then became a staple in the Comique repertory.   KF

Mummers Theatre Founded in Oklahoma City in 1949 as a summer tent theatre. Mack Scism soon emerged as leader of the group, which grew to professional status in 1964. A grant of $1,250,000 facilitated the construction of a new theatre, completed in 1970. The group mounted 150 plays from its founding until its demise in 1972, including a few heretofore unproduced. Revivals of Broadway comedies and of *Hamlet* and *Macbeth* were most popular.   WD

Munford, Robert (c. 1737–83) Playwright and politician. An influential member of Virginia's elected representatives, both before and after the Revolution, Munford wrote two plays that are outstanding examples of America's early comic drama and its interest in satire. *The Candidates; or, The Humours of a Virginia Election* (1770) satirizes the methods by which politicians win elections.

The Patriots (1779) attacks half-hearted and hypocritical patriots as well as Tory and Whig politics. Not interested in a playwriting career, Munford wrote mainly to air his views, showing some skill in contriving plots and creating amusing scenes with stereotypical characters. Both plays were published in 1798.   WJM

> *See:* R. M. Baine, *Robert Munford: America's First Comic Dramatist,* Athens, GA, 1967.

Muni, Paul (né Muni Weisenfreund) (1897?–1967) Actor who emigrated with his parents, trouping Yiddish actors, from Lemberg to Cleveland in 1902. By 1913 he was actively touring, often in female or greybeard roles. He became a leading man in the **Yiddish Art Theatre** in 1920 in such plays as Sholom Aleichem's *Hard to Be a Jew*. In 1927 he moved to Broadway, and a year later to Hollywood, where he starred in such films as *The Life of Emile Zola* and *The Last Angry Man*. Broadway stardom came with his Jewish lawyer (George Simon) in *Counsellor-at-Law* (1931). His final major stage appearance was as Henry Drummond (Clarence Darrow) in *Inherit the Wind* (1955).   NS

> *See:* J. Lawrence, *Actor: The Life and Times of Paul Muni,* New York, 1974.

Murder in the Cathedral A 1935 Canterbury Festival verse play by **T. S. Eliot** about the martyrdom of Archbishop Thomas à Becket in December 1170. Following its American premiere at Yale in 1935, it has become a modern classic. Set as a medieval morality play, with four Tempters personifying Becket's thoughts, and supported by a Greek chorus of Canterbury women who have a premonition of doom, it objectifies the preparation of Becket's soul for the final ordeal: "Unbar the door!" declares a resolved Archbishop, "It is out of time that my decision is taken . . . To which my whole being gives entire consent." The drunken knights enter and Becket is martyred. The play ends with a chorus of *Te Deum;* the priests celebrate the church's new saint.   GSA

Murdoch, Frank Hitchcock (1843–72) Actor and playwright. An actor of comedy roles who borrowed last name from his uncle, **James E. Murdoch**, Murdoch spent his entire career with **Louisa Drew**'s **Arch Street Theatre** Company in **Philadelphia**. Murdoch wrote *Davy Crockett* (1872) for **Frank Mayo,** who, after its early discouraging reception, helped create the popular version that emphasized the gentle side of the Westerner in scenes of spectacle and romance. His other plays include *Light House Cliffs* (1870?); *Bohemia; or, The Lottery of Art* (1872), a satire on critics; and *Only a Jew* (1873).   WJM

Murdoch, James Edward (1811–93) Actor whose debut was in 1829 at the **Arch Street Theatre** in **Philadelphia** as Frederick in Kotzebue's *Lover's Vows.* In 1833, he supported **Fanny Kemble** during her appearance at the **Chestnut Street Theatre.** For the next decade, he appeared in various theatres in New Orleans, Mobile, Pittsburgh, Philadelphia, New York, and Boston. For two years, he retired from the stage and lectured on

Shakespearean characters and "The Uses and Abuses of the Stage," and gave elocution lessons. He returned to the stage in 1845, and for the next 15 years established a reputation as both a tragedian and a light comedian. In 1856, he appeared at London's Haymarket Theatre for 110 nights and was also engaged briefly in Liverpool. He retired again in 1861 and 1879, but appeared intermittently until 1889. Among his more acclaimed roles were Hamlet, Charles Surface in Sheridan's *The School for Scandal,* Benedick, Orlando, and Mercutio. His reminiscences, *The Stage; or, Recollections of Actors and Acting from an Experience of Fifty Years,* were published in 1880.   DJW

Murray, Walter and **Thomas Kean** led one of the first professional groups of touring players in colonial America (1749–52). Often following a crude circuit of commodity and racing fairs, they performed a typical English repertoire. After opening in **Philadelphia** with a production of *Cato,* the company performed two seasons in New York before moving to Williamsburg (fall 1751). In 1752 they briefly toured Maryland and Virginia, then disappeared. Murray surfaced in 1760 as a member of **David Douglass**'s company performing in Maryland.   PAD

Murray Hill Theatre 162 East 42nd Street, NYC. The first playhouse to be opened on what was then the Upper East Side, the Murray Hill was built on property owned by the Goelet family and began performances on 19 October 1896, under manager Frank B. Murtha; but it was leased to the Henry V. Donnelly and W. T. Keogh **stock companies** for the next decade and to **vaudeville** thereafter. In 1917, it began to present movies as Loew's 42nd Street. It was demolished in 1951.   MCH

Musical theatre The first musical performances on the American stage occurred during the colonial period, when ballad operas were presented by touring companies of English actors. After the Revolution (1776–83), resident composers and writers created the first American comic operas. Notable among these was *The Archers,* with book and lyrics by **William Dunlap** and music by Benjamin Carr.

By the 1840s several types of European entertainments were contributing to the growth of American musical theatre. Burlesque reached the United States in the 1830s, and by the 1850s there were numerous American burlesques on native subjects, such as **John Brougham**'s *Po-ca-hontas; or, The Gentle Savage* (1855). Another imported form that proved popular with American audiences was the spectacle, which made use of lavish scenery and special effects as well as music and dance to tell its story. Meanwhile, the **minstrel show** brought a uniquely American form of musical entertainment to its audience.

Theatre activity in the United States was retarded by the Civil War. After the war, pantomime reached the height of its appeal in America with *Humpty Dumpty* (1868) starring **George L. Fox,** while **burlesque** received a boost from periodic visits by the English star **Lydia Thompson**

and her troupe of "British Blondes." Minstrelsy continued to be popular, with several companies establishing permanent theatres in the larger cities in addition to taking advantage of the expanding railroad lines to tour across the country.

Despite the existence of this lively and diverse assortment of musical forms, the event most often singled out as the starting point of American musical theatre is the production of *The **Black Crook*** in 1866. This show, created when a melodrama on Faustian lines was augmented with dances by a French ballet company stranded in New York, is viewed as a primitive example of musical comedy because of its use of music, dance, and spectacle, as well as scantily clad chorus girls, in the telling of its story. *The Black Crook* was successfully revived a number of times during the 19th century, and spawned a host of imitators. Other spectacles combined elaborate settings with a burlesque of some classical or current literary work in a form called "extravaganza." *Evangeline,* the most popular show of this type, opened in 1874 and toured the country in various revivals for the rest of the century

Opéra bouffe, particularly the works of Jacques Offenbach, had a vogue on the American stage in the 1870s and '80s, when noted French singers were imported to the U.S. by impresario **Maurice Grau.** Also available to audiences were native entertainments such as the Mulligan Guard series of musical plays, created and performed by **Edward Harrigan and Tony Hart,** depicting life among New York's Irish, Germans, and blacks.

The triumphant American premiere of **Gilbert and Sullivan**'s *HMS Pinafore* in 1879 made British comic opera the dominant musical form for the rest of the century. Most distinguished of the American composers of comic opera was **Reginald De Koven,** whose *Robin Hood* (1891) was frequently revived. Since comic opera plots typically combined high-flown romantic fantasy with comic horseplay, star billing often went to comedians such as **Jefferson De Angelis, De Wolf Hopper, Francis Wilson,** and **Eddie Foy.**

Most musical theatre librettos in this period were constructed in such a way as to allow for interpolations of unrelated songs and dances by members of the company. This taste for unrelated specialities – also found in the "olio" portion of the minstrel show and the second act of farce comedies such as *The Brook* (1879) – led to the development of the **revue,** a form of musical theatre in which songs, dances, comedy sketches, and elaborate production numbers were loosely connected by a plot or recurring theme, such as a "review" of the year's events. The first American revue was *The Passing Show* (1894).

In the last decade of the 19th century, comic opera and *opéra bouffe* declined, while burlesque was given a temporary reprieve in the shows of **Weber and Fields,** many of which featured comic opera soprano **Lillian Russell.** As the 1890s progressed, signs of change began to appear in the musical stage. In 1894, the **Bostonians** presented the comic opera *Prince Ananias,* which contained the first full score by **Victor Herbert,** destined to be one of the most important composers of operettas for the American stage. Also appearing in

Alfred Drake and Joan Roberts in *Oklahoma!* (1943). Photo: Vandamm.

1894 was *A Gaiety Girl,* a British musical that abandoned the exotic locales and stilted language of comic opera in favor of a contemporary setting and more topical humor. In 1898 two musicals written and performed by **African-Americans** made their appearance: **Bob Cole** and Billy Johnson's *A Trip to Coontown,* and Paul Laurence Dunbar and **Will Marion Cook**'s *The Origin of the Cakewalk; or, Clorindy.* Despite the warm reception these two shows received, few black artists were seen on the Broadway stage before the 1920s.

Comic opera, operetta, musical comedy, and revue were the dominant forms on the American musical stage at the dawn of the new century. While New York was now the theatre capital of the country, the vast national system of railroads made possible extensive tours for shows that had been a success on Broadway. The most successful show of the decade was *Florodora* (1900), a British comic opera. Victor Herbert continued to compose operettas such as *Babes in Toyland* (1903), *Mlle. Modiste* (1905), *The Red Mill* (1906), and *Naughty Marietta* (1910). The increasing prestige of American operetta lured European opera stars such as **Fritzi Scheff** onto the musical stage.

With the arrival of Franz Lehár's *The Merry Widow* in New York in 1907, a vogue for Viennese operetta was launched that lasted until the advent of WW I. In the same year, **Florenz Ziegfeld** produced the *Follies of 1907,* the first in a series of annual revues that diverged from the traditional topical humor toward a greater emphasis on elaborate scenery, beautifully costumed chorus girls, and star comedians and singers such as **Fanny Brice, Bert Williams,** and **Will Rogers.** The native comic tradition of Harrigan and Hart was continued by **George M. Cohan** in a series of musical comedies, such as *Little Johnny Jones*

(1904), that emphasized contemporary characters and settings, wise-cracking humor, and a generous dose of patriotic sentiment.

Some significant innovations took place in the American musical stage during WW I. Several of the shows written during that era rejected European styles in favor of American musical idioms, most notably ragtime. Developed by black musicians, ragtime was first heard on the musical stage in the form of individual songs interpolated into shows. In 1914 **Irving Berlin** composed a ragtime score for the revue *Watch Your Step.* Although it has been argued that many of Berlin's songs were not true ragtime, the success of his work brought ragtime to the forefront of musical styles for the legitimate stage.

Meanwhile, composer **Jerome Kern** and librettist **Guy Bolton** (later joined by lyricist **P. G. Wodehouse**) were experimenting with small casts, simple settings, and recognizable characters and situations in their **Princess Theatre** shows, such as *Very Good Eddie* (1915) and *Oh, Boy!* (1917). In the years immediately following the war, such musicals as *Irene* (1919) and Kern's own *Sally* (1920), which starred **Marilyn Miller,** demonstrated that contemporary American plots and settings and fresh musical styles could be effectively employed in more elaborate shows.

Despite the changes being wrought in American musical comedy, the demand for operetta did not abate. A new generation of European-trained composers, most notably **Rudolf Friml** and **Sigmund Romberg,** joined Victor Herbert in the creation of operetta for the American stage. Friml's scores during the 1920s included *Rose-Marie* (1924), *The Vagabond King* (1925), and *The Three Musketeers* (1928). Among Romberg's best works were *Maytime* (1918), *The Student Prince* (1924), *The*

Desert Song (1926), and *The New Moon* (1928). American singers such as **Vivienne Segal** and Robert Halliday starred in many of these new operettas.

In the early postwar years a number of new revue series appeared, including the *Greenwich Village Follies*, **George White**'s *Scandals*, the *Music Box Revues*, the *Grand Street Follies*, and **Earl Carroll**'s *Vanities*. The early 1920s also marked the reappearance of the black musical on the American stage: Although there had been a few isolated efforts since the turn of the century, including *In Dahomey* (1903), *Abyssinia* (1906), and *The Shoo Fly Regiment* (1907), African-Americans had their greatest impact on the Broadway musical stage in the 1920s. Beginning with **Sissle and Blake**'s *Shuffle Along* (1921), a succession of black book musicals and revues popularized a form of jazz that replaced ragtime as the dominant musical comedy style, and also introduced many new **dance** steps, such as the Charleston, to the musical stage. In addition, a number of black performers, including **Bill Robinson**, Adelaide Hall, and **Florence Mills,** were featured in shows created by whites.

During the 1920s a new generation of composers began to make their mark on the Broadway stage. Writing in the jazz-influenced style that had evolved in the years following the Princess Theatre shows, **George and Ira Gershwin** had a series of successes with *Lady, Be Good!* (1924), *Tip-Toes* (1925), *Oh, Kay!* (1926), and *Funny Face* (1927). The Gershwins' tricky rhythms and sophisticated lyrics ideally suited the talents of **Gertrude Lawrence** and dancers **Fred and Adele Astaire**. As the 1930s dawned, the Gershwins moved into political satire with *Strike Up the Band* (1930) and the Pulitzer Prize–winning *Of Thee I Sing* (1931). Matching the Gershwins in sophistication were the new songwriting team of **Richard Rodgers** and **Lorenz Hart**, whose successes in the 1920s included *The Garrick Gaieties* (1925), *Dearest Enemy* (1925), *A Connecticut Yankee* (1927), and *Present Arms* (1928). Other composers writing musical comedies in the 1920s included **Vincent Youmans** and **DeSylva, Brown, and Henderson.**

Jerome Kern, who had pioneered the style of contemporary musical comedy so popular in the 1920s, took musical theatre in another direction when he composed *Show Boat* (1927), an operetta that used both traditional and contemporary musical idioms in depicting the lives of a family of showboat performers from the 1880s to the 1920s. With lyrics by **Oscar Hammerstein II,** *Show Boat* pointed the way to the serious musical plays of the 1940s and '50s.

The 1927–8 season, with some 250 shows, was a quantitative high point in the history of the Broadway stage. Events outside of the theatre, including the advent of sound films and the stock market crash of 1929, would prevent it from ever again reaching that level of production. By the 1930–1 season there was a marked decline in the number of shows produced on Broadway, and those that did appear were usually presented on a more modest scale. Although Florenz Ziegfeld, George White, and Earl Carroll were able to mount a few more spectacular editions of their trademark shows, most revues now emphasized singing, dancing, and satiric comedy rather than expensive sets and costumes.

The musical theatre was invigorated at the end of the 1920s by the appearance of some new composers and lyricists. **Cole Porter** wrote insinuating melodies and clever lyrics for a number of frothy musical comedies, including *Fifty Million Frenchmen* (1929), *The New Yorkers* (1930), and *Anything Goes* (1934), while the songwriting team of **Arthur Schwartz** and **Howard Dietz** brought a new, more subdued and melodic sound to their scores for the revues *The Little Show* (1929), *Three's a Crowd* (1930), and *The Band Wagon* (1931).

Despite the appearance of these new contributors to the musical theatre, two of the more impressive musicals of the 1930s were created by composers, lyricists, and librettists who had begun their careers in the previous decade: *Porgy and Bess* (1935) by the Gershwins (with **DuBose Heyward**), and *On Your Toes* (1936) by Rodgers and Hart (with choreography by **George Balanchine**).

As the Depression worsened, musicals began to reflect the country's growing unrest. In 1936 the **Group Theatre** produced *Johnny Johnson,* a musical with an antiwar message; the following year the International Ladies' Garment Workers' Union presented a "socially significant" revue called *Pins and Needles,* with songs by **Harold Rome**; and in 1938 the **Mercury Theatre** offered Marc Blitzstein's controversial capitalist vs. labor parable, *The Cradle Will Rock.* This interest in the issues of the day was short-lived, however, for with the advent of WW II the musical theatre once again turned its back on political and social commentary in favor of escapist shows with flimsy plots. Nevertheless, a few musicals of the early 1940s demonstrated that the seriousness of the '30s had not entirely dissipated. Rodgers and Hart's *Pal Joey* (1940) had an amoral gigolo, played by Gene Kelly, for its hero, while the **Kurt Weill**–Ira Gershwin musical *Lady in the Dark* (1941) dealt with a mentally disturbed magazine editor (**Gertrude Lawrence**) whose problems were solved through psychoanalysis.

Musical theatre experienced another change in direction in 1943 as a result of the unprecedented popularity of *Oklahoma!,* the first musical by the new partnership of Richard Rodgers and Oscar Hammerstein II. *Oklahoma!*'s affirmation of the simple values of an earlier America gave it a broad and lasting appeal. Although it adhered in many ways to the traditions of operetta, its departures from standard musical theatre practice – such as allowing a murder to take place on stage and using a "dream ballet" to amplify the dramatic action – made *Oklahoma!* the most influential and widely imitated musical of its day. Among the subsequent "musical plays" created by Rodgers and Hammerstein were *Carousel* (1945), *South Pacific* (1949), *The King and I* (1951), *Flower Drum Song* (1958), and *The Sound of Music* (1959). **Mary Martin,** whose winsome personality and good humor made her an ideal Rodgers and Hammerstein heroine, starred in both *South Pacific* and *The Sound of Music*.

Despite the pervasive influence of Rodgers and Hammerstein, the formulaic musical comedy continued to flourish in the 1940s and early '50s. *Annie Get Your Gun,* with a score by Irving Berlin and a bravura performance by **Ethel Merman** as backwoods sharpshooter **Annie Oakley,** opened to critical acclaim in 1946. **Frank Loesser** received enthusiastic notices for *Guys and Dolls* (1950), a musical about Broadway gamblers and their perennial girlfriends. *Wonderful Town* (1953), by the team of **Leonard Bernstein** and **Comden and Green,** dealt with life in New York's Greenwich Village in the 1930s. *Pajama Game,* a musical about management–labor strife in a pajama factory, introduced the songwriting team of **Richard Adler and Jerry Ross** to Broadway in 1954. A year later *Damn Yankees,* also by Adler and Ross, combined the Faust legend with baseball, and elevated dancer **Gwen Verdon** to stardom.

In 1956, **Alan Jay Lerner and Frederick Loewe** adapted **Bernard Shaw**'s comedy *Pygmalion* into the musical *My Fair Lady.* Like *Show Boat* and *Oklahoma!* before it, *My Fair Lady* changed the course of musical theatre: Its opulent **Oliver Smith** setting and **Cecil Beaton** period costumes inspired a vogue for operettas set in bygone eras; the matchless performance of **Rex Harrison** as Henry Higgins inaugurated a trend toward hiring actors rather than singers for important musical theatre roles; and the skill with which Lerner converted the Shaw play into a musical led other librettists to concentrate on adapting already successful plays, films, and novels rather than creating original librettos.

Although they had changed greatly in the past two decades, the two basic threads of musical theatre, operetta and musical comedy, continued to flourish from the mid-1950s through the mid-1960s. As usual, the operettas tended to be the more elaborate and ambitious works. Leonard Bernstein, **Arthur Laurents,** Stephen Sondheim, and **Jerome Robbins** based *West Side Story* (1957) on the Romeo and Juliet legend. The songwriting team of **Jerry Bock** and **Sheldon Harnick** caught the flavor of European operetta with *She Loves Me* (1963), and in the following year created one of the most popular of all American musicals, *Fiddler on the Roof. Man of La Mancha,* based on Cervantes's *Don Quixote,* received excellent reviews when it opened in 1965.

The creators of musical comedy tried to vary the traditional formulas by exploring new settings and subjects. *Gypsy* (1959) was based on the life of stripper **Gypsy Rose Lee.** *Fiorello!* (1959) followed the career of New York mayor Fiorello La Guardia. *How to Succeed in Business Without Really Trying* (1961) satirized corporate backstabbing and in-fighting. *Hello, Dolly!,* while blazing no new trails in subject matter, made more extensive use of dance than was the custom in musical comedy. *Cabaret* (1966) was set in the decadent Berlin of the 1930s. *Hair* (1968) brought a more authentic rock sound and **nudity** to the Broadway musical stage.

Music, particularly rock, was an integral part of many **alternative theatre** pieces of the 1950s and '60s, such as **Megan Terry**'s *Viet Rock* (1966). Traditional notions of musical theatre were challenged by a number of **Off-Broadway** and **Off-Off Broadway** artists, notably composer-lyricist-librettist Al Carmines, who created several experimental musicals, including *Peace* (1968) and *Promenade* (1969), the latter with book and lyrics by **Maria Irene Fornés.** Several more traditional shows produced Off-Broadway, such as *The Fantasticks* (1960) and *Dames at Sea* (1968), demonstrated anew that elaborate spectacle was not a necessary component of the musical stage; and several modest shows produced in **nightclub**s and Off-Broadway theatres by Ben Bagley and Julius Monk continued the revue custom of emphasizing satire and topical humor.

By the beginning of the 1970s, however, it had become clear that the musical theatre was failing to develop new artists and audiences. The Off-Off Broadway revolution was fading away, having contributed relatively few new performers, composers, or choreographers to the mainstream theatre. On Broadway an increasing number of revivals of older shows, coupled with revues created out of the songs of veteran composers, held the stage. The only new composer-lyricist to contribute importantly to the musical theatre in the 1970s was **Stephen Sondheim.** His brilliant but often controversial shows of the 1970s and '80s included *Company* (1970), *Follies* (1971), *A Little Night Music* (1973), *Pacific Overtures* (1976), *Sweeney Todd* (1979), *Merrily We Roll Along* (1981), *Sunday in the Park with George* (1984), and *Into the Woods* (1987). Aided by orchestrator **Jonathan Tunick,** Sondheim created a unique sound using electronic instruments and tempered rock rhythms. His lyrics were often cerebral, unflinching, and cynical.

The Sondheim shows produced and directed by **Harold Prince** popularized the "concept musical," a show in which the director and designers, instead of attempting to translate a preexisting libretto and score into theatrical terms during rehearsals, collaborate with the composer, lyricist, and librettist during the creation of the show, so that every element is conceived in terms of production. Because of the emergence of the concept musical – and because so few new composers, lyricists, and librettists of stature appeared during the period – the musical theatre of the 1970s and '80s was dominated by the choreographer-director. Such shows as **Bob Fosse**'s *Pippin* (1972), *Chicago* (1975), and *Dancin'* (1978), **Michael Bennett**'s *A Chorus Line* (1975) and *Dreamgirls* (1981), and **Tommy Tune**'s *Nine* (1982) and *The Will Rogers Follies* (1991) benefited immeasurably from the imaginative and energetic staging that their director-choreographers created for them. The concept musical went out of fashion in the 1980s as its most talented practitioners died or retired; by the end of the decade only Tommy Tune was still actively creating shows for the Broadway stage. Producers turned instead to shows with librettos based on vintage Hollywood films, such as *Grand Hotel* (1989), *City of Angels* (1989), and *Nick and Nora* (1991), the last a disappointing $4.3 million failure that had been under development for several years.

The period of the 1970s and '80s was a time of reassessment of the musical theatre in the light of rising production costs and prohibitive ticket prices.

Many artists and producers preferred to work in the more relaxed surroundings of Off or Off-Off Broadway, some of their more successful creations eventually finding their way to the Broadway theatre. Also contributing shows to Broadway were regional theatres, notably the **Goodspeed Opera House** in East Haddam, CT, where *Annie* premiered. Since relatively few American musicals were produced each year, writers, directors, and performers often worked more frequently in film and television than in live theatre. The current generation of musical theatre stars, such as **Mandy Patinkin** and **Bernadette Peters,** appeared only sporadically on the Broadway stage. The dearth of American musicals led producers to look to Europe and Great Britain for new shows: *Les Misérables* and *Miss Saigon* were created by a French songwriting team, while Andrew Lloyd Webber brought New York a number of his London successes such as *Cats* and *Phantom of the Opera.*

Sometimes called the only uniquely American contribution to world theatre, the Broadway musical faces some severe economic and artistic tests in the years to come. MK

See: G. Bordman, *American Musical Theatre: A Chronicle,* 2d ed., New York, 1992; D. Ewen, *New Complete Book of the American Musical Theatre,* New York, 1970; M. Gottfried, *Broadway Musicals,* New York, 1979; M. Gottfried, *More Broadway Musicals,* New York, 1991; S. Green, *Encyclopedia of the Musical Theatre,* New York, 1976; S. Green, *Broadway Musicals: Show by Show,* Milwaukee, 1985; A. J. Lerner, *The Musical Theatre,* New York, 1978; G. Mast, *Can't Help Singin',* Woodstock, NY, 1987; J. Mates, *The American Musical Stage Before 1800,* New York, 1962; J. Mates, *America's Musical Stage: Two Hundred Years of Musical Theatre,* Westport, CT, 1985; T. L. Riis, *Just Before Jazz: Black Musical Theater in New York, 1890 to 1915,* Washington, DC, 1989; C. Smith and G. Litton, *Musical Comedy in America,* New York, 1981; J. P. Swain, *The Broadway Musical: A Critical and Musical Survey,* New York, 1990; A. Woll, *Black Musical Theatre From Coontown to Dreamgirls,* Baton Rouge, LA, 1989.

Music Box Theatre 239 West 45th St., NYC [Architect: C. Howard Crane]. The Music Box was named by **Irving Berlin,** one of its three original owners, who also lent the name to a series of **revue**s that opened the house in 1921 and continued annually until 1925. With a seating capacity of 1,000, its presentations have alternated between musicals and plays, but more recently it has housed nonmusical productions or intimate, small-cast musicals. Till his death, Berlin was half-owner of the theatre with the **Shubert Organization.** During the Depression years, one of its tenants, *Of Thee I Sing* (1931), not only became the first musical to win the Pulitzer Prize but also helped to save the theatre for its owners. During its history, not quite a dozen of the **George S. Kaufman** collaborations appeared on its stage. MCH

Music Man, The Two-act musical comedy by **Meredith Willson,** opened 19 December 1957 at the **Majestic Theatre,** running 1,375 performances. This nostalgic story of con man Harold Hill (**Robert Preston**) selling dreams in 1912 Iowa marked the Broadway debut, at age 54, of Willson,

a bandleader and occasional pop composer. It became the hit of the season, winning both the Drama Critics' Circle and Tony awards for best musical, over *West Side Story.*

The show evokes the heartwarming exuberance of period Middle America, and the inventively rhythmic score draws on popular musical forms from barbershop to polka to sentimental ballad ("Till There Was You"). A particularly effective musical device is having the heroine's wistful ballad ("Goodnight, My Someone") and the hero's central march ("Seventy-Six Trombones") built on the same melody, thus prefiguring their ultimate union. JD

See: M. Willson, *But He Doesn't Know the Territory,* New York, 1957.

Music-Theatre Group Founded in 1971 by director Lyn Austin, former associate of **Roger Stevens,** this innovative nonprofit organization is dedicated to the development of works in which theatre, music, dance, and the visual arts are combined to create new forms. Originally called the Lenox Arts Center, MTG produces **Off-Broadway** (often in Stockbridge, MA, summers) and on tour, utilizing artists as diverse as **Martha Clarke, Anne Bogart, Tommy Tune, Richard Foreman, Bill Irwin,** and **Elizabeth Swados.** Recepient of numerous awards, including 30 Obies (one for sustained achievement), MTG has developed such productions as *The Garden of Earthly Delights, Vienna: Lusthaus, The Mother of Us All,* and *Endangered Species.* DBW

Musser, Tharon (1925–) Lighting designer who began her career as designer and stage manager for the José Limon Dance Company and made her Broadway debut with the premiere production of ***Long Day's Journey into Night.*** By the late 1960s she was probably the dominant lighting designer on Broadway. Her versatility is apparent from her credits, which include several seasons with the **American Shakespeare Festival,** all of **Neil Simon**'s plays since *Prisoner of Second Avenue* (1971), and musicals such as *Mame.* From 1975 she teamed up with designers **Robin Wagner** and **Theoni Aldredge** and the late director **Michael Bennett** to design *A Chorus Line, Dreamgirls,* and several others. Her style ranges from flashy production numbers to painstakingly researched recreations of specific light qualities and moods (such as *A **Little Night Music,*** 1973). AA

My Fair Lady by **Alan Jay Lerner and Frederick Loewe** (book/lyrics and music, respectively); opened on 15 March 1956, running for a then–record-breaking 2,717 performances. A musical adaptation of Bernard **Shaw**'s comedy *Pygmalion,* the musical related the transformation of a Cockney flower girl into a stately lady by a phonetics expert who bets that improving the girl's speech will convince everyone she is a duchess. **Rex Harrison,** a perfect choice for phonetician Henry Higgins, was given a number of witty patter songs that made the most of his limited singing range while remaining faithful to Shaw's irascible character. Julie Andrews brought a freshness and vitality to Eliza Doolittle, the Cockney flower girl. *My Fair Lady* was a fine example of the "integrated musical," in which the songs and dances helped to further the plot rather than existing for thier own sake. Thus, in the "Ascot Gavotte" sequence, **Cecil Beaton**'s black-and-white costumes, Lerner and Loewe's comically understated recitative, and the severely repressed dance movements created by choreographer **Hanya Holm** vividly illustrated the world of upper-class decorum that Eliza was about to shatter. Notable revivals were staged in 1976 and 1981, the latter with Harrison, who also recreated his role in the 1964 film version.   MK

My Heart's in the Highlands **William Saroyan**'s play was produced **Off-Broadway** by the **Group Theatre** before opening at the **Guild Theatre** in New York on 13 April 1939 for 44 performances. **Robert Lewis** directed this major artistic success for the Group, its cast including Philip Loeb as the penniless poet Ben Alexander, Sidney Lumet as his young son Johnny, Art Smith as the old violinist Jasper MacGregor, and William Hansen as Mr. Kosak the grocer. It was revived Off-Broadway in 1949. The play is a fantasy about the importance of art to ordinary people and the devaluation of artistic creativity by the American socioeconomic system. While the people of a poor neighborhood welcome the musician and support the poet with gifts of food, neither artist can survive for long.   BCM

My Partner **Bartley Campbell**'s play, produced by **A. M. Palmer** at the **Union Square Theatre** on 16 September 1879, was one of the most suc-

cessful plays of the 1880s, extending the popularity of **frontier** drama. The gold-mining partners of the title were the dapper but shallow Ned Singleton and the plain, good-hearted Joe Saunders. Ned's dalliance with Mary Brandon, Joe's secret love, led Josiah Scraggs to kill Ned and frame Joe. To shield Mary from disgrace, Joe claimed to be her husband. Eventually Wing Lee, a Chinese servant, revealed evidence that convicted Scraggs and freed Joe to wed Mary.

My Partner starred Louis Aldrich (Joe) and Charles T. Parsloe (Wing Lee), the latter a specialist in comic Chinese caricatures (also in Mark Twain's *Ah Sin,* Twain and **Bret Harte**'s *Two Men of Sandy Bar,* and *The Danites*). Aldrich gained prominence as the Parson in *The Danites* before starring as the quiet mining hero of *My Partner*. Aldrich retired from the stage in the late 1890s to devote full time to the presidency of the **Actors' Fund of America.**   RAH

My Sister Eileen Three-act comedy by Joseph Fields and **Jerome Chodorov,** adapted from the stories by Ruth McKenney; opened at the **Biltmore Theatre** (26 December 1940) for 864 performances. Directed by **George S. Kaufman** and featuring **Shirley Booth,** this light-hearted comedy, set in Greenwich Village, relates the wild antics of two sisters who have moved to New York from Columbus, OH, in search of fame and fortune as writer and actress. A film version starring Rosalind Russell appeared in 1942. The authors later collaborated with **Leonard Bernstein** and **Betty Comden and Adolph Green** on *Wonderful Town,* a 1953 musical adaptation of the play.   EK

N

Nathan, George Jean (1882–1958) Critic. Born of wealthy parents in Fort Wayne, IN, Nathan graduated from Cornell University in 1904 and studied abroad for a year at the University of Bologna (1905). In 1906 he worked as a reporter for the *New York Herald,* after which he reviewed plays for *Outing* and *The Bohemian.* He became drama critic of *Smart Set,* in 1909 joining H. L. Mencken, who had been hired in 1908 to review books. The two served as coeditors during 1914–24 and made *Smart Set* a cult publication among young intellectuals. Their irreverence and iconoclasm seemed to epitomize a generation attempting to rid itself of the Genteel Tradition. They founded the *American Mercury* in 1923 but quarreled in 1924, with Nathan continuing only as drama critic until 1932. He founded and edited the *American Spectator* (1932–5), then reviewed for numerous publications including *Newsweek, **Theatre Arts**, Saturday Review,* and *Esquire.* Influenced by **James Huneker** and George Bernard **Shaw,** Nathan wrote in a lively, impressionistic style and fought for a drama of ideas. He became a champion of **Eugene O'Neill,** publishing his early plays in *Smart Set,* and arranging for professional productions of his work. He reviewed musical **revue**s, noting that "Good drama is anything that interests an intelligently emotional group of persons assembled together in an illuminated hall." His reputation declined after his death in 1958 because his "hot" impressionistic style cooled with age, and many of his opinions after 1930 proved to be erroneous. Nathan reworked his criticism into books, which appeared almost every year during 1915–53. From 1943 to 1951 he published an annual *Theatre Book of the Year.* In 1955 he married actress **Julie Haydon,** and in his will left a provision for the George Jean Nathan Award for Dramatic Criticism to be given annually.　TLM

See: C. Angoff, ed., *The World of George Jean Nathan,* New York, 1952; T. F. Connolly, "George Jean Nathan and the Emergence of Modern American Criticism," PhD diss., Tufts U, 1991; T. Q. Curtiss, ed., *The Magic Mirror,* New York, 1960.

National Alliance of Theatrical and Stage Employees Stagehands began organizing a union locally in the late 1880s, and on 17 July 1893 representatives from New York, Brooklyn, Chicago, Pittsburgh, Cincinnati, St. Louis, Denver, Philadelphia, Syracuse, Buffalo, and Boston agreed to form a national union. In 1898 they became affiliated with their Canadian counterpart, and in 1902 changed their name to the International Alliance (IATSE).　DMcD

See: G. Quinn, *Fifty Years Backstage,* Minneapolis, 1926.

National Black Theatre Founded by actress and play director Barbara Ann Teer in 1968 as a temple of liberation, this **African-American theatre** group first met in a ramshackle building in central Harlem "to educate and spiritually enlighten the people it serves." Initial performances took the form of rituals based on the black experience and developed in training workshops. By 1978 standard plays such as *Wine in the Wilderness* by **Alice Childress** were being produced. When the building burned in 1983, activities continued in an adjacent space while funds were sought for rebuilding. In 1990 a new $10 million home was opened containing a 288-seat theatre.　EGH

National Playwrights Conference Established in 1965 by George C. White and directed since 1968 by **Lloyd Richards,** the NPC is the most prestigious program of the **Eugene O'Neill Memorial Theatre Center** in Waterford, CT. The granddaddy of American play development workshops, the NPC's philosophies and methods dominate developmental perspectives in the U.S. and have spread internationally.

The month-long summer workshop focuses on a dozen stage plays and two television scripts each year. Dramaturgs, directors, and professional actors concentrate on each play for four or five days, then present two staged readings – a format that tends to favor realistic theatre. Stressing process not results, actors work with book in hand, production is minimal, and reviews and bids from producers are forbidden.

An important crucible of new American plays, NPC's alumni include such well-known playwrights as **John Guare, Wendy Wasserstein, Arthur Kopit,** and **August Wilson.**　CLJ

National Theatre 1321 Pennsylvania Avenue North, Washington, DC [Architect: McElfatrick, 1885]. In 1834, the first National Theatre opened its doors through the financial support of six Washington businessmen, who decided that the city needed a new place of entertainment. **Fires** destroyed the house in 1845, 1857, 1873, and 1885, and all but obliterated the early features in the rebuilt versions. In 1885, the theatre was completely redesigned, and is the structure that still stands. The fortunes of the National followed the pattern typical of the 19th-century playhouse, beginning with a resident **stock company** and ended as a theatre for booked-in performances. During long periods in the 20th century the house was not used. Owned and renovated in 1984 by the Pennsylvania Avenue Development Corp., it is leased to the **Shubert Organization,** which manages the theatre and books its touring Broadway attractions.

MCH

See: D. B. Lee, R. Meersman, and D. B. Murphy, *Stage for a Nation: The National Theatre, 150 Years,* Lanham, MD, 1985.

National Theatre of the Deaf

In 1967, Broadway set designer **David Hays** gathered the nucleus of a company from actors at Gallaudet, the renowned college for deaf students, to found the National Theatre of the Deaf, which remained a project of the **Eugene O'Neill Memorial Theatre Center** until 1983. Under Hays's direction the NTD established a training institute, a core professional troupe, and the Little Theatre of the Deaf, which tours story theatre to young audiences.

NTD has peformed on Broadway, throughout the U.S., and worldwide, appeared in films and on television, and has collaborated with director Peter Brook at his International Center of Theatre Research in Paris. Ten years of acclaim were marked in 1977 with a special Tony Award for "Theatrical Excellence."

NTD's repertory ranges from classics such as *Iphegenia in Aulis* or *Volpone* to avant-garde works like **Gertrude Stein**'s *Four Saints in Three Acts* and to group-created collages – all performed in a theatricalized sign language that has helped to remove long-standing prejudice against signing by elevating it to an art. As deaf players pantomime the action, hearing actors in the background speak the lines, a convention familiar in such Japanese theatre forms as Kabuki and Bunraku.

The NTD has inspired the formation of other companies of deaf actors and has helped stimulate signed performances everywhere from classrooms to the Academy Awards broadcasts. In its wake, some commercial roles have opened to deaf actors. NTD's Linda Bove has been a regular on TV's "Sesame Street," and in 1980 founding NTD member Phyllis Frelich won a Tony for her performance in **Mark Medoff**'s *Children of a Lesser God.* CLJ

See: S. Baldwin, "A History of the National Theatre of the Deaf from 1959 to 1989," PhD diss., U of Texas at Austin, 1989; B. Bragg (as signed to E. Bergman), *Lessons in Laughter: The Autobiography of a Deaf Actor,* Washington, DC, 1989.

Native-American ritual/theatre

Native American theatre is rooted in communal celebrations and ancient rituals reflecting the religious outlook and shared values of the indigenous nations that created it. Unlike Western drama, it is charged with cosmic significance that sets it apart from events in the ordinary world, and the "audience" are participants rather than passive spectators. Because the native population contains many distinct nations, Native-American drama is diverse, ranging from the polished one-person dramas of storytellers and the improvisations of the shamans to the Navajo chantways: 100-hour-long celebrations involving the entire community in which no costume, word, gesture, movement, or song is left to chance.

Native American theatre encountered enormous difficulties. Conquest by whites destroyed entire nations, including, of course, their drama. The confinement of native peoples to reservations and the increasing dominance of Western culture often had a negative influence on the drama of nations that survived. The potlatch drama of the coastal Northwest, for example, in which the wealthy distributed gifts, degenerated from a mechanism for cementing the interrelationships of family and village into ostentatious displays of hierarchy and privilege. Nevertheless, many dramas, such as the Plains Sun Dances, the Cheyenne Sacred Arrow Ceremony, the Iroquois False Face Drama, and the Navajo chantways, survived into the 20th century and continued their time-honored functions of uniting their communities and reinforcing traditional beliefs. In the 1970s **Hanay Geiogamah**'s Native American Theatre Ensemble used "Western"-style drama to transmit Native American traditions, values, and aesthetics. Despite isolated attempts to encourage Native American theatre and drama, there is only a small body of contemporary literary plays written by Native Americans, and performances by Native Americans about themselves and their native culture are infrequent. Annual powwows and ritualistic enactments continue, however. [See also **Jimmie Durham; female/male impersonation; Rollie Lynn Riggs; Spiderwoman Theatre.**] MS

See: H. Geiogamah, *New Native American Drama: Three Plays,* Norman, OK, 1980; G. P. Horse Capture, *Powwow,* Seattle, 1992; L. Walsh Jenkins, "The Performances of Native Americans as American Theatre," PhD diss., U of Minnesota, 1975.

Native Americans portrayed on stage

One of a number of native types depicted on the American stage, the stage "Indian" – represented in over 600 plays from 1606 to the present (both South and North American aborigines) – has inevitably been stereotyped, ranging from the noble savage to ruthless, varmint redskins or lazy, drunken, dissipated rascals, and from the Indian princess to the squaw on the fringe of white society.

Plays featuring American Indians can rarely be defined by geography; most have focused on forest, northwestern, or East Coast Indians; surprisingly few take place on the geographical plains, in the Indian Territory, or in the far West. The frontier inhabited by the stage Indian is more commonly a mythic area. The earliest plays with Indians were seen on the London stage; the first seen in North America were French, performed in Nova Scotia (1606) and possibly as early as 1753 in New Orleans. Most early Indian plays, including the influential *Columbus; or, A World Discovered* (1792) by Thomas Morton, the first of many Columbus plays, view the Indian in European terms, in keeping with Rousseau's noble savage.

Indians were promising material for drama from the beginning, combining the strange and the familiar, though the genus never became a major one. The earliest extant plays, however, had little influence (Robert Rogers's *Ponteach,* 1766); Joseph Croswell's *A New World Planted,* 1802; **James Nelson Barker**'s *The Indian Princess,* 1808, the first Pocahontas play). From the turn of the century to about 1825 (and excluding Peruvian Indian plays), more than 25 such plays were written (most notably Anne Kemble Hatton's *America Discovered; or, Tammany, the Indian Chief,* 1794; **Mordecai Noah**'s *She Would Be a Soldier,* 1819; Henry J. Finn's *Montgomery,* 1825; **G. W. Parke Custis**'s *The Indian Prophecy,* 1827). This spurt of activity parallels a period of great stress and clash between Indians and white settlers. During this influential period, and even later, few real Native Americans participated in theatrical performances; those who did were given minor roles or simply demonstrated theatrical elements of their special culture.

The play that gained the greatest popularity and had the largest impact during this early era was **John Augustus Stone**'s *Metamora,* chosen in 1829 as a vehicle for **Edwin Forrest** and based in part on King Philip's War. A rush of plays followed *Metamora*'s enormous success, some based on specific Indians (**Richard Penn Smith**'s *William Penn,* 1829; **Nathaniel Deering**'s *Carabasset,* 1830; R. M. Bird's *Oralloossa,* 1832; Richard Emmons's *Tecumseh,* 1836; Alexander Macomb's *Pontiac,* 1836; **Nathaniel Bannister**'s *Putnam,* 1844; **Louisa H. Medina**'s *Nick of the Woods,* 1838; and three new Pocahontas plays by Custis, Robert Dale Owen, and Charlotte Barnes).

Following the Indian play's apogee in the 1830s – and as the Indian problem became severe in the '60s – the subject's popularity declined and the Indian figure became a more villainous and dangerous antagonist or a burlesqued figure, as in the plays of **John Brougham** at midcentury. However, after the Civil War, a desire for western spectacle, customs, and characters led to a new rage for Indian melodramas (**James McCloskey**'s *Across the Continent,* 1870; **Augustin Daly**'s *Horizon,* 1871; and especially melodramas with or about **William F. Cody** [and, in the '80s, his **Wild West exhibition**]). Through the 1890s real Indians were seen in variety and the **circus,** and were parodied in **minstrel shows.** Somewhat serious efforts at the turn of the century by writers such as **Herne, Belasco, William C. deMille,** Edwin Milton Royle, and Mary Austin (*The **Arrow Maker***) did little to change the distorted image of the Indian, though verisimilitude seemed greater. New venues for Indian characters included **pageants,** operettas, and operas.

Some interest in Indian plays existed in the 1920s and '30s, paralleling new Indian reform movements, though most Indians (especially of the red varmint variety) transferred to the movies. Over the past half-century Indian characters have appeared from time to time, most notably in historical outdoor dramas and in plays such as **Kopit**'s *Indians* (1968) and the early work of **Sam Shepard.**

Only a few Native American writers, such as **Rollie Lynn Riggs, Hanay Geiogamah,** and

Pulitzer Prize–winning novelist N. Scott Momaday, have written Native American plays; fewer have lived up to their early promise [see **Native-American ritual/theatre**]. Most Indian drama has depicted Indians conceived by white writers for predominantly white audiences, contributing little to the understanding of the problems and frustrations of Native Americans. DBW

> *See:* E. Jones, *Native Americans as Shown on the Stage, 1753–1916,* Metuchen, NJ, 1988; D. Wilmeth, "Noble or Ruthless Savage?", *Journal of American Drama and Theatre* (Spring 1989).

Native Son by **Richard Wright** and **Paul Green.** Adapted from Wright's powerful novel depicting the corrosive effects of racism, this drama in 10 scenes follows Bigger Thomas, a young black man whose hatred and fear lead him to murder a young white woman accidentally. **Orson Welles** directed a stunningly theatrical production starring **Canada Lee,** which opened 24 March 1941 at NYC's **St. James Theatre.** After playing three months, it toured major U.S. cities and reopened on Broadway in a "popular-priced revival," 23 October 1942, for 84 performances. KF

Naughty Marietta Two-act operetta, music by **Victor Herbert,** words by Rida Johnson Young; opened 7 November 1910 at the New York Theatre, running 136 performances. Set in 18th-century New Orleans, this romance tells of a vivacious "casquette girl" (Emma Trentini) and the dashing Captain (Orville Harrold) who proves himself her true love when he knows her haunting "mysterious melody" ("Ah, Sweet Mystery of Life"). Commissioned by **Oscar Hammerstein I** for his leading opera singers, this quintessential American operetta gave Herbert scope to write soaring melodies for highly trained voices. Standards from the score include the march "Tramp, Tramp, Tramp" and the coloratura showpiece "The Italian Street Song." JD

Nazimova, Alla (1879–1945) Russian-born actress who studied with Vladimir Nemirovich-Danchenko, acted with the **Moscow Art Theatre,** and became leading lady of a St. Petersburg theatre. She toured Europe and America in 1905. In New York in 1906 she presented, in English, matinee performances of **Ibsen**'s *Hedda Gabler, A Doll's House,* and *The Master Builder.* She appeared different from the popular personality actresses of the day, since she could transform herself externally into different characters. She remained in America, but by 1918 her fame had faded, and she was considered another personality actress capitalizing on her sensuous exoticism. After 10 years starring in Hollywood films such as *Camille* and *Salome,* she performed with the **Civic Repertory Theatre** and the **Theatre Guild.** In 1935 she directed and starred in her own version of *Ghosts,* after which she returned to filmmaking. RAS

Nederlander, James (1922–) Scion of a family prominent for three generations in producing and the operation of theatres. Born in Detroit,

Nederlander was a member of the Air Force staff, producing *Winged Victory* in New York in 1943. One of the major forces in the Broadway theatre, the Nederlander Organization owns or operates 10 Broadway theatres and runs a large chain of legitimate theatres, including some in Detroit, Chicago, San Francisco, San Diego, Los Angeles, and London. Among Nederlander's successful productions are *On a Clear Day You Can See Forever* (1967), *Applause* (1970), *Abelard and Heloise,* and *The Effect of Gamma Rays on Man-in-the-Moon Marigolds* (1971). Most recent Broadway productions include *Nicholas Nickleby, Whose Life Is It Anyway?, Orpheus Descending, Me and My Girl, Shadowlands,* and revivals of *Peter Pan* (two), *Sweet Charity, Hello, Dolly!,* and *Porgy and Bess.* Robert E. Nederlander (1933–), one of five brothers, serves as president of the organization, but is less involved in legitimate theatre activities than James.   SMA

Nederlander Theatre 208 West 41st St., NYC [Architect: William Neil Smith]. Built as the National in 1921 by Walter C. Jordan, a leading theatrical **agent,** it stands today as the only commerical Broadway theatre below 42nd Street. With about 1,200 seats, it can be used both for musicals and dramas. In 1927, the **Shubert**s added it to their chain, then sold it in 1934, bought it back in 1944, only to be forced to relinquish it again in 1956 to satisfy a court-mandated consent decree. In 1958, it was acquired by **Billy Rose,** who reopened it after extensive renovation under his own name the following year. In 1979, it was bought from his estate by the Nederlander Organization, which renamed it briefly the Trafalgar, then the David Nederlander after the founder of the theatrical dynasty, who died in 1967. Among its noteworthy tenants have been **Ethel Barrymore** in *The Corn Is Green* (1940); **Katharine Cornell** in *Dear Liar* (1960), which ended her long career; and Lena Horne in a **one-person** show in 1981. In 1991 it housed the first critically successful venture of the **Broadway Alliance** (Wertenbaker's *Our Country's Good*).   MCH

Negro Actors Guild An organization formed in 1937 to provide financial assistance and comfort to indigent theatre people and to uphold the highest standards of the stage. An internal struggle for control of the guild led to its demise circa 1982. In 1986 the Afro-American Guild of Performing Artists was established in its place.   EGH

Negro Ensemble Company (1967–) Established in racially troubled times with a generous Ford Foundation grant, the predominantly **African-American** company inhabited the **Off-Broadway** St. Mark's Theatre. Under **Douglas Turner Ward**'s inspired leadership, it began an ambitious program of training young theatre aspirants and producing plays relevant to black Americans. The company was initially criticized for locating outside the black community and producing foreign plays, but its successful nurturing of black writers, performers, directors, and technicians, and the sustained excellence of its productions have brought it national

and international renown. In over 25 successive seasons, through good times and lean, it has presented over 50 major productions of new plays, with twice that number of workshop presentations and staged readings. It has undertaken national tours and performed abroad in London, Rome, Bermuda, Munich, and on tour in Australia. Among its many awards are the 1982 Pulitzer Prize for *A Soldier's Play,* Tony Awards both for "special achievement" and for *The River Niger* (1973), and 13 Obie Awards for outstanding new plays, performances, and productions such as *Dream on Monkey Mountain* (1971), *The First Breeze of Summer* (1975), and *Eden* (1976). In 1980 the company relocated its offices in NYC's theatre district and its productions to Theatre Four (West 55th St.); but as of 1988 it has been renting various Off-Broadway theatres while searching for a more permanent home.   EGH

Neighborhood Playhouse, The Like the **Provincetown Players** and the **Washington Square Players,** the Neighborhood Playhouse (1915–27) was a pioneering **Off-Broadway** theatre. Remote both geographically and temperamentally from the commercial theatre, the Playhouse, located on NYC's Lower East Side, was an experimental outpost connected with the Henry Street Settlement House, a social agency for the area's immigrant population. The Playhouse's major interest was in exploring through **folk** drama the theatre's ritual, lyric, mystical roots. Among its celebrated offerings were an ancient Hindu comedy entitled *The Little Clay Cart* (1924), *The Dybbuk* (1926), a 14th-century French mystery, a Japanese *Nō* drama, a dance drama based on Celtic legend, a Norse fairy tale, and a medieval interlude, as well as such more conventional fare as Galsworthy's *The Mob* (1920), **O'Neill**'s *The First Man* (1922), James Joyce's *Exiles* (1924), and five editions of a musical **revue** called *The Grand Street Follies.*

Organized as an educational and philanthropic enterprise, the Playhouse achieved a renown its amateur patrons **Alice and Irene Lewisohn** had never envisaged. Ellen Terry, Yvette Guilbert, **Ethel Barrymore,** and **Richard Boleslavski,** among others, offered their services. The theatre provided an important impetus to Martha Graham and to scene designers **Aline Bernstein** and **Donald Oenslager,** and generated both the Neighborhood Playhouse School of the Theatre, begun in 1928 and still flourishing (for over 50 years under the direction of **Sanford Meisner**), and the Costume Institute of the Metropolitan Museum, founded in 1937. In 1959 Alice Lewisohn Crowley published *The Neighborhood Playhouse: Leaves from a Theater Scrapbook,* a modest and charming memoir.   FH

Neil Simon Theatre 250 West 52nd St., NYC [Architect: Herbert J. Krapp]. As the Alvin Theatre, the 1,400-seat playhouse on the outer fringe of the theatre district had enjoyed a spectacularly successful history under the management of its two founders, **Alex Aarons** and **Vinton Freedley,** who combined the first syllables of their names to give it its name. They opened it in 1927 to house

the highest forms of musical comedy; and until 1932, when they lost control of the house, they fulfilled their promise by presenting works by the **Gershwin**s, **Rodgers and Hart,** and **Jerome Kern.** In 1934, a young **Ethel Merman** debuted there, and in 1964 the veteran **Beatrice Lillie** bade her farewell from its stage. Under a succession of owners, the Alvin presented nonmusical fare as well – *Mister Roberts* (1948), *The **Great White Hope*** (1968), and *No Time for Sergeants* (1957) – but nothing to equal its musical triumphs, which continued with *Lady in the Dark* (1941), *A **Funny Thing Happened on the Way to the Forum*** (1962), *Company* (1970), and *Annie* (1977). The one musical production presented on its stage that should have been successful but was not at its introduction was *Porgy and Bess* (1935). In 1983 **Neil Simon**'s *Brighton Beach Memoirs* opened to hold its stage for two years; perhaps in gratitude, the **Nederlander**s renamed the theatre for him the same year.
MCH

Nelson, Barry (né Robert Nielson) (1925–) Popular leading man of the 1950s and '60s. Nelson specialized, as **Brooks Atkinson** noted in his 1951 review of *The Moon Is Blue,* in playing "the perfect comic counterpoint," a role he played successfully in such vehicles as *Mary, Mary* (1961) and *The Cactus Flower* (1965). DBW

Nelson, Richard (1938–) Lighting designer whose career includes modern dance, avant-garde theatre, and Broadway. Much of his early work was with choreographers Merce Cunningham, Louis Falco, Alvin Ailey, and Laura Dean, among others. He stage managed or designed lights for three early works for **Robert Wilson,** including *The King of Spain* (1969) and *Deafman Glance* (1970). His Broadway credits include *Sunday in the Park with George* (for which he won a Tony), *Into the Woods,* *Tap Dance Kid,* and Tony Randall's National Actors' Theatre (1991–2). AA

Nelson, Richard (1950–) Playwright and dramaturge born in Chicago and educated at Hamilton College (BA, 1972); America's most prolific dramatist during the decade of the 1980s, with such productions as *Rip Van Winkle or "The Works"* (1981), *The Return of Pinnochio* (1983), *Between East and West* (1984), and *Principia Scriptoriae* (1986). He won Obies for *Vienna Notes* (1978) and for his "innovative programming" while Literary Manager at the **Brooklyn Academy of Music.** He has adapted a number of classics, such as *The Suicide* (1980), *The Marriage of Figaro* (1982), and *The Three Sisters* (1984); was dramaturge for the **Guthrie Theatre;** and wrote the book for the musical *Chess* (1988). His plays have a wide following in England, where he has written radio dramas for the BBC; both *Americans Abroad* (1989) and *Two Shakespearean Actors* (1990) debuted at the Royal Shakespeare Company prior to **Lincoln Center** productions. BBW

New Amsterdam Theatre 214 West 42nd St., NYC [Architects: Herts and Tallant]. When built in 1903 by **Klaw and Erlanger,** this was intended to be their premier theatre for musical productions and spectacles. Between 1913 and 1937, 12 editions of the *Ziegfeld Follies* were presented on its stage; but in 1937 it was sold to motion picture interests and became one of the "grind" (continuous-show) moviehouses lining 42nd Street. In 1982, as part of the reclamation program of 42nd Street, NYC's Industrial Development Agency took title to the theatre and leased it to the **Nederlander** Organization to return it to legitimate fare. Work began on the building, but unforeseen structural faults halted the project and the theatre was boarded up. Extensive renovations have been postponed until the city agencies coordinate efforts for the greater 42nd Street project. Almost as famous as the ornate 1,700-seat auditorium is the Roof Garden above the theatre, which dispensed light entertainment and refreshment to after-theatre crowds for many years. In 1930, it was rented first as a radio studio, then as a television studio; in recent times, it has served as a rehearsal hall. It is in the process of reconstruction as a small theatre. MCH

New Dramatists (1949–) Service organization for playwrights. Founded in New York by Micaela O'Harra with assistance from **Robert Anderson, Richard Rodgers,** and **Howard Lindsay,** New Dramatists exists to "encourage and develop playwriting in America." After a screening process, accepted members are provided a cast and director for readings of their plays. A critique session with other playwrights and professionals gives the writer a frank evaluation and suggestions for rewriting. Members also may be assigned to review a Broadway production from beginning rehearsal to opening. New Dramatists informs members about current writing opportunities; provides classes on the craft of writing; solicits tickets to current theatre productions; maintains a library of current theatre periodicals and trade journals; and provides loans for members with plays in production. Successful alumni include **John Guare, Lanford Wilson, William Inge, Ed Bullins, Megan Terry, Maria Irene Fornés, Paddy Chayefsky, Horton Foote, Eric Overmyer,** and **August Wilson.**
TLM

New Federal Theatre Stimulated by a NYSCA initiative in ghetto arts, in 1970 director and producer **Woodie King, Jr.,** founded the not-for-profit theatre, which he named for the Depression-era **Federal Theatre Project.** NFT is located at the Henry Street Settlement's Arts for Living Center at 466 Grand Street on Manhattan's Lower East Side. Reflecting the ethnic composition of the district, the theatre usually produces new work by minority dramatists, and has played a role in bringing minority theatre to national attention. Funded by the philanthropic **Lewisohn** sisters in 1915, the main auditorium, now renamed the Henry DeJur Playhouse, was originally the **Neighborhood Playhouse,** a crucible of the Stanislavsky System in America. CLJ

New Moon, The Two-act operetta, music by **Sigmund Romberg,** words by **Oscar Hammerstein II,** Frank Mandel, and Laurence Schwab;

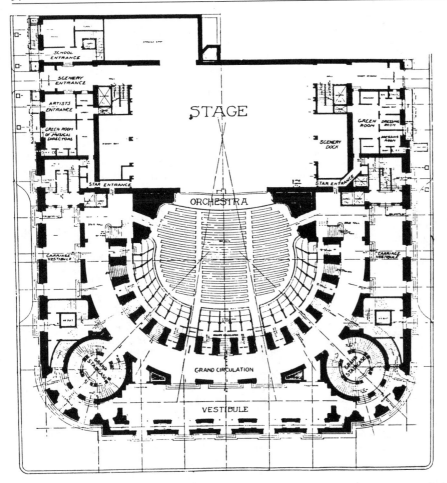

Ground plan for the New Theatre (1909), considered at the time an advanced and innovative theatre plant. Courtesy: Don B. Wilmeth.

opened 19 September 1928 at the **Imperial Theatre,** running 509 performances. This soaring romance, set in 18th-century New Orleans, tells of the French bond servant Robert Mission (Robert Halliday) who, with his love, the noble Marianne (Evelyn Herbert), establishes a free government on a Caribbean island. The score is often characteristic of traditional operetta (the march "Stouthearted Men" and several romantic waltzes), but it also shows Romberg's capacity for adapting less traditional forms to operetta, notably the lyric tango "Softly, as in a Morning Sunrise" and the rhythmic ballad "Lover, Come Back to Me." The last of Romberg's great 1920s operettas, it has consistently held the stage and is currently in the New York City Opera's repertoire.   JD

New Theatre New York's first major art theatre, at Central Park West and 62nd Street – a stone's throw from the present **Lincoln Center** complex – had an auspicious dedication ceremony (6 November 1909) with speeches by J. Pierpont Morgan, Woodrow Wilson, **George Pierce Baker, W. D. Howells,** Thomas A. Edison, and William Archer, preceding the performance of *Antony and Cleopatra* with **E. H. Sothern** and **Julia Marlowe.**
The idea for the New Theatre originated with **Heinrich Conried,** director of the Metropolitan Opera. Funds were subscribed by 30 wealthy opera patrons to build an elegant Italian Renaissance structure with magnificent staircases and lobbies, a roof garden, a spacious orchestra pit, and the latest stage equipment, including the first electrically operated revolving stage. **Winthrop Ames** from Boston's Castle Square Theatre was appointed director.
The New got off to a poor start. The production was not ready, the house (seating 2,500) was too large, and the acoustics were abominable. Clearly, the plan to stage operas and plays in the same theatre had been a mistake. In two seasons only Galsworthy's *Strife,* **Edward Sheldon**'s *The Nigger,* and Mary Austin's *The Arrow Maker* could properly be called "new." The lessons from its brief life (1909–11) were clear: An art theatre could not be bought with dollars. The new theatre movement demanded intimate quarters.
The **Shubert brothers** acquired the building and renamed it. As the Century (1911–30), it housed an assortment of musicals by **Victor Herbert,** Offenbach, **Romberg,** and Oskar Straus; **Morris Gest**'s production of **Reinhardt**'s *The Miracle* (1924), for which **Norman Bel Geddes** transformed the theatre into a massive Gothic cathedral; and, that same season, Eleonora Duse in 11 matinees of five plays, including *Lady from the Sea* and

Ghosts. It was demolished in 1930 and replaced with the Century Apartments.   RM

New Vaudeville Sprawling category of performers who harness traditional popular entertainment skills and a carnival spirit to a postmodern aesthetic. The versatility of such actor-athletes as clown, mime, and eccentric dancer **Bill Irwin** (McArthur Award, 1984), dancer and master juggler **Michael Moschen** (McArthur, 1990), or musician and puppeteer Bruce D. Schwartz is a hallmark. Unlike the players of old-time variety shows, New Vaudevillians are mostly college-educated children of the middle class. While acknowledging forebears from *commedia dell'arte* to the Three Stooges, these are the thinking man's clowns, whose physical talents serve thematic and stylistic agendas with roots in the antiestablishment theatres of the 1960s (themselves in debt to such diverse influence as **Brecht,** Meyerhold, dada, and Bunraku).

Before enrolling in **Ringling Brothers** Clown College, Irwin studied with **Herbert Blau**'s experimental theatre company, KRAKEN. Autobiographical monologist **Spalding Gray** was a member of **Richard Schechner**'s environmental **Performance Group** and its spin-off, the **Wooster Group.** Table-top puppeteer and political satirist Paul Zaloom apprenticed with the pacifist **Bread and Puppet Theatre.** The founders of two **circus**es, the Pickle Family and the Big Apple, met in the radical **San Francisco Mime Troupe.**

While each is unique, New Vaudevillians share a number of traits. Most reject the conventions of realistic theatre, substituting physical virtuosity and violating the fourth wall with direct address and audience interaction: Slack-wire acrobat and silent clown Avner "the Eccentric" Eisenberg brings audience members on stage; crackerjack banjo player and storyteller Stephen Wade pitches ballpoint pens to the house; and during Bill Irwin's *In Regard of Flight,* the quintessential New Vaudeville show, players invade the auditorium.

Despite their avant-garde affinities, New Vaudevillians forsake elitist aspects of experimental theatre for populist perspectives, and expose the mysteries of their entertainment specialities. Irwin explains the special "lean shoes" that allow him to cantilever his body at impossible angles; disillusionistic magicians **Penn and Teller** unmask their own tricks; the Flying Karamazov Brothers, a five-man juggling team, maintain an ironic, midact commentary on their craft. Together with their self-reliance, such egalitarian attitudes constitute a reaction against the modern, technological world, demonstrating, as Ron Jenkins puts it, "an affirmation of what a human being can accomplish without the aid of machines."

Although New Vaudevillians originally congregated in fringe venues like **Dance Theatre Workshop,** the Serious Fun Festival at **Lincoln Center,** and the New Wave Festival at the **Brooklyn Academy of Music,** a number have now appeared in their own shows in regional theatre, on and **Off-Broadway,** in television specials, films, and in legitimate productions of Brecht, Dario Fo, and even Shakespeare. Such mainstream popularity suggests the appeal and staying power of the fresh theatrical visions that New Vaudevillians have created using familiar means.   CLJ

See: R. Jenkins, *Acrobats of the Soul,* New York, 1988.

New York City theatres From its inception, New York – or, more specifically, the island of Manhattan – was blessed with an air of cosmopolitanism. Settled by the Dutch at the toe of the island early in the 17th century, its population grew to include English, French, Irish, German, and Jewish inhabitants plus Negro slaves. If, when the English took over the settlement later in the century, the Anglican church dominated its religious life, the tone had been set by the fundamentalism of the Dutch Reformed church. The arrival of the Presbyterians and Methodists served to strengthen the conservatism of the early population, which found its entertainment within the family and home and in simple outdoor pursuits and sports.

The creation of a miniature English court at the beginning of the 18th century, plus the growing prosperity of the colonials, brought people out of their homes and into society. Early records suggest amateur theatrical entertainment in and around the colonial court and, perhaps, itinerant performers in the early taverns. Then, in 1732, a newspaper advertisement referred to a theatre owned by "the honourable Rip Van Dam"; later a map (1735) showed a playhouse close to the English fort, the site of the governor's residence. Both theatres were probably rudimentary and makeshift, but they point to a greater interest in theatrical activity among the colonial population.

By the mid-18th century, two theatrical companies visited New York, the second of which was composed of professional actors from London. They settled in a theatre on Nassau Street, which may well have been the Rip Van Dam warehouse theatre used by the amateurs some 20 years before. Although it still encountered religious opposition, a company assembled by **David Douglass** in Jamaica from the remnants of the old **Hallam** company returned to New York in 1758, and was emboldened by a palpable interest in theatrical entertainment to build three theatres in the next nine years. One of them, the Theatre in **John Street** built in 1767, was to serve Douglass until his withdrawal from the mainland before the Revolution, and was later used by the occupying English troops during the war. When Lewis Hallam the younger returned to New York in 1785, he reopened the theatre and used it until 1798.

The first substantial playhouse to be built in New York was subscribed by the city's important and wealthy citizens and located in a site destined to become an early municipal center: at a place where Broadway was to merge with the Bowery, the main road to Boston from the city. Here, in 1798, theatre was established as a necessary concomitant of urban living. Designed by French architect Joseph Mangin, the playhouse, which came to be known as the **Park Theatre,** had an ugly exterior but provided reasonable comfort for its patrons in the auditorium; it represented a distinct improvement over the old unattractive and uncomfortable wooden John Street house.

While the Park dominated theatrical activity

through the early years of the 19th century, it provided the spur for the building of other theatres in the burgeoning city. To the east and north of it, a more elegant theatre was built on the **Bowery,** but quickly fell out of favor with the fashionable class and survived into the 20th century as a "neighborhood house," catering for the tastes of its shifting and immigrant population. For the sixth and last time, it was destroyed by **fire** in 1929.

By 1825, New York had emerged as the premier theatre city of America. Theatres dotted the urban landscape, but they never strayed too far from Broadway, the principal thoroughfare of the city. Stars from England and Europe generally made New York the first stop on their lucrative tours. When the fortunes of the Park waned, other theatres arose to take its place. Comedian **William "Billy" Mitchell** made **Mitchell's Olympic Theatre** the most popular theatre on Broadway in the late 1830s and early '40s. Another comedian, **William E. Burton,** turned a little opera house into **Burton's Chambers St. Theatre,** dispensing his merry entertainment to enthusiastic audiences. Theatres tended to get bigger and more comfortable, culminating in the 4,500-seat **Broadway Theatre,** modeled on London's Haymarket.

As the city pushed northward, so did the theatres. By midcentury, Broadway was no longer residential, but mixed factories, office buildings, shops, and department stores together with theatres along its way. Playhouses purveyed everything from **minstrel shows** to opera to urbane English comedy, and became more attractive architecturally as they reflected the trends from Europe. **Niblo's Garden** had a grand foyer for its patrons, and most theatres included refreshment stands. Seats were upholstered in the National Theatre [NW corner of Leonard and Church Sts.], and the pit was rendered into the orchestra and made respectable, as the gallery became the family circle to combat the rowdyism of its early denizens. The familiar tiers of boxes atrophied into ceremonial sidewall appendages, as the stage was pulled closer to the curtain line.

In the last decades of the 19th century, following the process of urbanization, a theatre district began to form around Union Square, at the junction of Broadway and Fourth Avenue at 14th Street. The Academy of Music, **Wallack's Theatre,** the **Union Square,** and **Tony Pastor**'s all offering different entertainment, forming a core around which a small support industry of agents, costumers, photographers, managers, restaurants, theatrical boardinghouses, and hotels sprang up. More theatres were built above Union Square, reaching to Herald Square and beyond, to satisfy an entertainment-hungry population. In 1869, **Edwin Booth** built his elegant **Booth's Theatre** at the corner of Sixth Avenue and 23rd Street and provided a new look in theatres: Gone was the raked stage and, with it, the wing-and-drop setting; in their place, illusory walls of canvas and lath were fastened to the stage floor to create rooms and scenes of extraordinary realistic detail.

In 1893, **Charles Frohman** built his **Empire Theatre** on Broadway at 40th Street, and **Oscar Hammerstein [I]** crossed 42nd Street to build his

Olympia at 44th Street just two years later. Both structures signaled the development of a new theatre district around Longacre (later Times) Square. During 1900–28, an unprecedented boom in theatre building ensued, providing New York's population with more playhouses than it could support. The new theatres reflected the change in theatrical production. The 19th-century **stock company** resident in its own theatre was supplanted by the "combination system," the assembling of a cast for the presentation of a single play to be produced at a rented theatre. Consisting of a stage, dressing rooms, a box office, an auditorium, and a small lobby, 20th-century playhouses served the new system; with fewer than 2,000 seats, they were well-suited to the plays and musicals presented their stages.

Some 80 theatres were built during this era and filled Broadway from 39th Street to 54th Street and its side streets. Some were erected on odd-shaped parcels of land; others had proper façades designed in a variety of styles from Egyptian to Georgian; all were proscenium theatres. They were largely the architectural work of J. B. McElfatrick and Company and Herbert J. Krapp. Beginning with the Depression and extending into the years beyond WW II, more than half of them fell victim to the competitive effects of movies and television and the rise of New York's **alternative theatre, Off-Broadway** and **Off-Off Broadway.** Some were torn down, others were converted to moviehouses (those lining 42nd Street), and a few were rebuilt to serve other purposes.

With the recognition that New York's theatres were rapidly becoming an endangered species, a succession of the city's mayors began to take steps to protect the standing playhouses while stimulating the erection of others. Zoning laws were changed to permit the incorporation of theatres within tall office buildings, which resulted in the **Gershwin** and **Minskoff** theatres and two smaller playhouses in the early 1970s. Only a few have been protected by the landmark law, and the fate of the others depends heavily on the availability of plays and musicals suitable for production and the willingness of investors to wager ever greater sums of money to mount them. In 1982, an advisory panel was appointed by then-Mayor Edward I. Koch to study the situation and to make recommendations for the preservation of the remaining theatres; but as of the early 1990s, the project is at a standstill.

MCH

See: K. Bloom, *Broadway,* New York, 1991; L. Botto, *At This Theatre: An Informal History of New York's Legitimate Theatres,* New York, 1984; J. Frick, *New York's First Theatrical Center,* Ann Arbor, 1985; M. Henderson, *The City & the Theatre,* Clifton, NJ, 1973; *Places, Please: Broadway's Historic Theatres,* New York, 1984; N. Van Hoogstraten, *Lost Broadway Theatres,* Princeton, NJ, 1991.

New York Clipper Founded in 1853 by Frank Queen as a sporting and theatrical paper, the *Clipper* published news about music halls, minstrel shows, circuses, fairs, concerts, plays, and operas under the heading of "Amusements." Dramatic editors **T. Allston Brown** (1860s), Henry Ashley

(1870s), and J. Austin Fynes (1880s) developed theatrical coverage. With much of the profession "on the road," the *Clipper* provided routes, playing dates, and mail information. It maintained a circulation of around 20,000 until first challenged by (1905) and then incorporated into *Variety* (1924).   TLM

New York Idea, The This social satire by **Langdon Mitchell** opened at New York's Lyric Theatre 19 November 1906, after out-of-town tryouts in Chicago and St. Louis, and ran for 66 performances. The all-star cast included **Minnie Maddern Fiske, George Arliss,** and **Dudley Digges.** Long a staple of American **stock companies** and critically well-regarded for its witty language, the play satirizes ideas about marriage and divorce among the well-to-do, eventuating in the separation of one couple and the reuniting of another. Though its views of marriage now seem dated and the invalid divorce decree a stock device for reuniting a loving couple, the play exemplifies quite well Mitchell's skill as a social analyst of contemporaneous American life. In 1977 British director Frank Dunlop successfully revived the play as high comedy at the **Brooklyn Academy of Music** with a cast headed by **Blythe Danner, Rosemary Harris,** and Stephen Collins.   RKB

New York Mirror (later *Dramatic Mirror*) Founded in 1879 by **Stephen Ryder Fiske** and Ernest Havier to combat the blackmailing practices of the *New York Dramatic News,* the *Mirror* became an important theatrical journal under the editorship of **Harrison Grey Fiske** from 1879 to 1911. Fiske worked to eliminate corrupt practices and to raise standards of production, while fighting the Theatrical **Syndicate** and promoting the career of his wife, **Minnie Maddern Fiske.** In decline after his departure, the *Mirror* incorporated *The Theatre World* (1920) and ceased publication in 1922.   TLM

New York Public Theater see **Public Theater**

New York Shakespeare Festival New York's busiest company, founded in 1954 by **Joseph Papp** "to encourage and cultivate interest in poetic drama with emphasis on . . . **Shakespeare** . . . and to establish an annual summer Shakespeare Festival." Forming the Shakespeare Theatre Workshop on the Lower East Side, Papp believed "theatre with the highest professional standards can and should reach a broadly based public." Every summer, NYSF performs free productions in Central Park's Delacorte Theater, built for it in 1957. Bernard Gersten became Associate Producer in 1960 (until 1978). In 1967, NYSF established the **Public Theater** in the East Village. During 1973–7, Papp directed Lincoln Center's **Vivian Beaumont and Mitzi E. Newhouse theatres.** In 1982, NYSF started the Festival Latino de Nueva York, and in 1983 adopted the Young Playwrights Festival (until 1985) and established an exchange with London's Royal Court Theatre. In 1986, NYSF launched a short-lived project, directed by actress **Estelle Parsons,** to present Shakespeare on Broadway for

schoolchildren, and in 1987 inaugurated a six-year plan to produce all of Shakespeare's plays. (By the end of the 1990–1 season, they had produced 18 of them.) In 1990, Papp appointed **JoAnne Akalaitis** artistic associate and **George C. Wolfe,** David Greenspan, and Michael Greif Festival directors. Akalaitis had assumed the day-to-day control of the NYSF by August 1991, with Papp retaining the title "producer" until his death in late October 1991.

NYSF has also staged new American plays, including *Hair* (1967), *No Place to Be Somebody* (Pulitzer Prize for **Off-Broadway,** 1969), Galt MacDermot's musical *Two Gentlemen of Verona* (Tony, 1971), *Sticks and Bones* (Tony, 1971), *That Championship Season* (Tony and Pulitzer, 1972), *A Chorus Line* (Tony, 1975, and Broadway's longest-running show), *For Colored Girls Who Have Considered Suicide When the Rainbow Is Enuf* (1976), **Elizabeth Swados**'s *The Haggadah* (1982), *The Marriage of Bette and Boo* (1985), Larry Kramer's *The Normal Heart* (1985), Rupert Holmes's *The Mystery of Edwin Drood* (1985), **Shawn**'s *Aunt Dan & Lemon* (1986), **Shue**'s *Wenceslas Square* (1987), **George C. Wolfe**'s *The Colored Museum* (1986), and Harry Kondoleon's *Zero Positive* (1988).

NYSF also hosts visiting companies and artists, such as **Mabou Mines, Meredith Monk, Richard Foreman, Joseph Chaikin,** and **Andrei Serban,** and produces American premieres of foreign works, including Václav Havel's *The Memorandum* (1968) and *Largo Desolato* (1986), Roberto Athaye's *Miss Margarida's Way* (1977), David Hare's *Plenty* (1983), Caryl Churchill's *Top Girls* (1983), *Fen* (1984), and *Serious Money* (1987), and Louise Page's *Salonika* (1985). Over the years NYSF productions have won over 150 awards, including Tonys, Obies, Pulitzers, Drama Desk, and New York Drama Critics' awards. As of the end of 1991, 17 shows had been transferred to Broadway.   REK

See: C. King and B. Coven, eds., *Joseph Papp and the New York Shakespeare Festival: An Annotated Bibliography,* New York, 1988.

Niblo, William (1789–1878) Victualler and businessman, Niblo opened the Sans Souci Park in 1828, a restaurant garden containing a 1,200-seat concert hall. Under various managers (including **Gilfert,** Joseph Sefton, and **J. W. Wallack**) it became home to **vaudeville** and light entertainment. **Niblo's Garden** expanded in 1839 to include a conventional theatre catering to musical events and standard fare. In 1848, after the complex burned, Niblo took the lease of the **Astor Place Opera House,** which he held during the riot that year. The Garden's theatres reopened in 1849 and continued to feature stars of music, comedy, dance, panto**mime,** and extravaganza. Niblo retired from management in 1861.   RKB

Niblo's Garden Northeast corner of Broadway and Prince St., NYC. A tavern keeper, **William Niblo,** leased the Columbian Gardens from the Van Rennselaer family and turned it into a summer retreat for New Yorkers. In 1828, he converted a stable into a summer theatre named the Sans Souci.

Interior view of Niblo's [Garden] Theatre, NYC, during a performance of Auber's opera *Masaniello*. From *Ballou's Pictorial*, 24 Feb. 1855. Courtesy: Laurence Senelick.

He later added a proper theatre as a year-long enterprise and presented regular dramatic fare. From then on, it simply became known as "Niblo's Garden." When the complex was leveled by **fire** in 1846, Niblo retreated to his country estate a millionaire; however, he was induced to rebuild it a few years later. The Van Rennselaers built the Metropolitan Hotel on part of the same site, and the theatre was entered through the hotel lobby. During its long history, every kind of entertainment and most of the reigning stars appeared on its stage, but none more popular than the **Ravel** family of comedians, who appeared here for 30 years, and *The Black Crook,* which opened in 1866 and ran for 16 months. Another fire in 1872 destroyed the theatre, but it was rebuilt and survived until 1892, when both the hotel and the theatre were razed.   MCH

Nichols, Anne see *Abie's Irish Rose*

Nichols, Mike (né Michael Igor Peschkowsky) (1931–) Actor, director, and producer. Born in Berlin, Nichols fled to New York with his parents to escape the Nazis. He attended the University of Chicago for two years, after which he studied with **Lee Strasberg** at the **Actors Studio.** He began his professional career in Chicago performing with a comedy group that included Elaine May. In 1957 Nichols and May developed their own act, which comprised regular satirical sketches and improvisations. They gave two New York concerts in 1959, followed by *An Evening with Mike Nichols and Elaine May* on Broadway in 1960, establishing both performers as major stars. Nichols turned to directing in 1963 with **Neil Simon**'s *Barefoot in the Park,* followed by *The Knack* (1964), *Luv* (1964), *The Odd Couple* (1965), *The Apple Tree* (1966), *Plaza Suite* (1968), and *The Prisoner of Second Avenue* (1971). His comic inventiveness made him one of the most sought after directors in New York. Beginning in the 1970s Nichols turned to more serious fare, including *Streamers* (1976), *Comedians* (1976), *The Gin Game* (1977), *The Real Thing* (1983), *Hurlyburly* (1984), *Waiting for Godot* (1989), *Elliot's Loves* (1990), and *Death and the Maiden* (1992), demonstrating skill and vitality in shaping complex dramatic works. Richard Schickel (*Time*) praised his "uncanny sense of modern body language" in communicating the shapeless lives in **David Rabe**'s *Hurlyburly*. Nichols produced the musical *Annie* (1977) and *The Gin Game*. His major films include *Who's Afraid of Virginia Woolf?* (1965), *The Graduate* (1968), *Catch-22* (1970), *Carnal Knowledge* (1971), and *Silkwood* (1983). Winner of five Tonys and one Oscar, Nichols remains one of the most successful American directors of the contemporary theatre.   TLM

Nick of the Woods Adapted from the 1837 novel of the same name by **Robert Montgomery Bird, Louisa Medina**'s dramatization – one of several by her on a frontier subject – opened 5 February 1839 at the **Bowery Theatre** for a week's uninterrupted run (then quite a success). With its Kentucky setting, fiendish Indians [see **Native Americans portrayed**], "ring-tailed roarer" brag speech, and the Jibbinainosay (Nick – or Satan – of the Woods), Bird's novel provided ample opportunity for spectacular raging cataracts, canoes of fire precipitated over waterfalls, rescues from bridges dangling over rocky passes, and songs. The melodrama served Joseph Proctor as a starring vehicle for years, remained in the Bowery repertory for decades, and was the abiding dramatization of the novel, still played in 1921.   RKB

Nigger, The Edward Sheldon's controversial play was produced by **Winthrop Ames** and opened 4 December 1909 as part of the initial season at the **New Theatre.** The play, which received conflicting critical notices, concerns Philip Morrow, the governor of a Southern state who discovers on the eve of his marriage that his grandmother was a Negro. Rather than allow his enemies to destroy him, he resigns his office and engagement to work for his "new" race. Originally titled *Philip Morrow,* Sheldon changed the name to reflect what he perceived as the attitude of white people toward blacks in the play. Fox Films produced a cinema version in 1915, but it was withdrawn and retitled *The New Governor* after protests in a number of cities.   BBW

Nightclubs, where the consumption of food and drink is interspersed with entertainment, may have originated in concert saloons like the Melodeon (New York, 1859), dance cellars, beer gardens, or Bowery joints like Harry Hill's. The earliest distinct avatars are cabarets, restaurants in New York, Saratoga, Boston, and New Orleans that offered variety acts between the courses. With the Folies-Bergère of 1911, rathskellers took on the name "cabaret" to acquire chic, and by WW I had become major tourist attractions. Reisenweber's in Columbus Circle (NYC), was a pioneer in dinner entertainment, popularizing the floor show, a Dixieland Jazz Band, Hawaiian music, and the *thé dansant.* New York roof garden theatre presentations, such as **Ziegfeld**'s *Midnight Frolics* on the **New Amsterdam** roof and **Morris Gest**'s *Midnight Whirl* on the **Century** roof, offered attractive **revue**s in a relaxed atmosphere.

Although hotels benefited from not having to observe a 3 A.M. curfew, wartime censorship caused many cabarets to turn into dance palaces, and Prohibition sounded their deathknell. They were replaced by nightclubs (the first so-called was the Club Deauville, which had no closing time) and speakeasies; there were 5,000 in Manhattan by 1922. Critical to a club's popularity was often the master or mistress of ceremonies: Texas Guinan with her cynical greeting "Hello, Sucker" was the most celebrated. Nightclubs were valuable showcases for such talent as Clayton, Jackson, and **Durante, Sophie Tucker,** Helen Morgan, **Harry Richman,** and the bands of Rudy Vallee and Paul Whiteman; but the link with bootlegging made for the entrance of organized crime into show biz, particularly in Chicago, where comedian Joe E. Lewis was brutalized for his recalcitrance. Harlem's Cotton Club was also run by the mob; it and such other uptown New York "niteries" as Connie's

Place presented all-black entertainment to all-white thrill-seekers. "Clip joints," where customers were wildly overcharged, became common.

Prohibition's repeal and the New Deal led to a proliferation and aggrandizement of the nightclub: Many of them offered seminude shows [see **nudity**] and did away with the exorbitant cover charge. **Billy Rose** set the pace with the Casino de Paree; other prominent New York night spots included the glass-walled Rainbow Room, El Morocco, and Leon & Eddie's. The exclusive Stork Club maintained a color bar well in the 1950s. These "supper clubs," often staffed by debutantes, boasted a kind of pseudosophistication, heavy on "French-style" *diseuses* like Hildegarde and intimate songs with suggestive lyrics. During WW II, a federal amusement tax temporarily curbed profits, but by 1945 such clubs as the Copacabana, the Latin Quarter, and the Diamond Horseshoe were high-profit business enterprises.

With the advent of television, Americans, even outside New York, could stay at home and watch the Stork Club on its own program. By the late 1950s, younger audiences were bypassing the old-style metropolitan nitery to attend folk-song clubs and improvisational comedy **revue**s: Chicago made the breakthrough with the Gate of Horn and **Second City.** However, in resorts like Las Vegas and Miami, the floor show was pumped up into a hyperbolic extravaganza, a backdrop for star singers, comedians, and even animal trainers, playing to what Noël Coward called "Nescafé society." The nightclub's more intimate attractions bifurcated into the piano bar and the comedy club, a forcing-house for standup comics, where entertainment and food vie in monotony.   LS

See: J. Durante and J. Kofoed, *Night Clubs,* New York, 1931; L. A. Ehrenberg, *Steppin' Out. New York Nightlife and the Transformation of American Culture 1890–1930,* Westport, CT, 1981; J. Gavin, *Intimate Nights: The Golden Age of New York Cabaret,* New York, 1991; A. Green and J. Laurie, Jr., *Show Biz from Vaude to Video,* New York, 1951; S. Johnson, *The Roof Gardens of Broadway Theatres 1883–1942,* Ann Arbor, 1985.

'night, Mother by **Marsha Norman.** This intermissionless, 90-minute two-act character drama was given a staged reading at **Circle Repertory Theatre** (November 1981) prior to its January 1983 premiere production at **American Repertory Theatre,** which subsequently moved to Broadway (**John Golden Theatre,** 31 March 1983). It won both the Pulitzer and the Susan Smith Blackburn prizes. **Kathy Bates** played Jessie, an overweight divorcée who can find nothing of value in her very ordinary existence. The uncompromising action – a last evening with her mother before committing suicide – is structured in classic sonata form. Although it "looks like simplicity itself," noted **Frank Rich,** it is "a shattering evening." Many regional productions followed, as well as a 1986 film with **Anne Bancroft** and Sissy Spacek.   FHL

Night of the Iguana, The by **Tennessee Williams** premiered 26 December 1961, directed by Frank Corsaro at New York's **Royale Theatre,** with Patrick O'Neal (Shannon), Bette Davis (Max-

ine), and Margaret Leighton (Hannah). Running for 316 performances, it won the New York Drama Critics' Circle Award. A 1976 revival starred Richard Chamberlain, Dorothy McGuire (Hannah), and Sylvia Miles (Maxine). A 1963 screenplay by Tony Veiller, directed by John Huston, featured **Richard Burton,** Ava Gardner (Maxine), and Deborah Kerr (Hannah). T. Lawrence Shannon, a defrocked priest turned tour conductor, guides women from a Baptist female college to Hotel Costa Verde in Mexico. Shannon is caught between two women who represent different yet (for Williams) typical poles – Maxine, the sensualist, and Hannah, the spinster/Madonna. Earlier, Williams had combined these types in Blanche DuBois. The iguana symbolizes animal passion and the characters' common humanity, chained and then liberated in the play.
PCK

Nina Vance Alley Theatre see **Alley Theatre**

Noah, Mordecai M[anuel] (1785–1851) Playwright. Noah was an active Zionist who sought his livelihood in politics (surveyor of the Port of New York, judge of the Court of Sessions) and journalism (New York *Enquirer, The Commercial Advertiser, The Times and Messenger*) and his diversion in the theatre. He was an inveterate theatregoer, an intimate of the managers (**Price, Simpson, Dunlap,** and **Sol Smith**), and an occasional playwright. His ardent patriotism was reflected in his documentarylike plays: *She Would Be a Soldier* (1819), based on the Battle of Chippewa (1814) and written for Catherine Leesugg; *The Siege of Tripoli* (1820), the piratical menace with which Noah had had firsthand experience as Consul to Tunis; *Marion; or, The Hero of Lake George* (1821), based on the Battle of Saratoga; *The Grecian Captive* (1822), on the Greek Revolution; and *The Siege of Yorktown* (1824), set in the Revolutionary War. *She Would Be a Soldier* became a popular patriotic piece for national holidays for over 40 years.
RM

See: I. Goldberg, *Major [Mordecai M.] Noah: American-Jewish Pioneer,* Philadelphia, 1936; J. D. Sarna, *Jacksonian Jew: The Two Worlds of Mordecai Noah,* New York, 1981.

Noguchi, Isamu (1904–88) Los Angeles–born sculptor and designer who moved to Japan with his Japanese mother at age 2, returning to the U.S. in 1917. Although he designed almost solely for dance, his abstract design, use of objects, and ability to focus the cubic volume of the stage space had a significant effect on mid-20th-century design. In 1926 he went to Paris as assistant to the sculptor Brancusi, and also that year designed masks for actress Ito Michio in Yeats's *At the Hawk's Well,* his first theatre work. In 1935 choreographer Martha Graham asked him to design a set for *Frontier;* it was the first set she had ever used, and it began a collaboration that lasted until 1966 and included *Appalachian Spring* (1944) and *Seraphic Dialogue* (1955). Drawing on the tradition of *Nō* and the vocabulary of his own sculptures, his designs were simple distillations of images creating psychological rather than literal space. He has also designed for **George Balanchine,** Erick Hawkins, Merce

Cunningham, and the Royal Shakespeare Company (*King Lear, 1955*).
AA

No, No, Nanette Three-act musical comedy, music by **Vincent Youmans,** words by Irving Caesar, **Otto Harbach,** and Frank Mandel; opened 11 March 1925 in London, running 665 performances, and 16 September 1925 at the Globe Theatre, New York, running 321 performances. The most successful musical comedy of the 1920s, it does not have the longest New York run; but by its New York opening it had played a year in Chicago and had numerous American road tours, in addition to beginning its smash-hit London engagement. This youth-oriented flapper comedy, stressing the conflict between open-minded modernity and repressive conservatism, follows the complex romantic misunderstandings surrounding a big-hearted Bible salesman (Charles Winninger) and his flapper ward Nanette (Louise Groody). Hip, flip, and up-to-the-minute, it introduced two enduring standards: "I Want to Be Happy" and "Tea for Two." A thoroughly revised version, broadly adapted by Burt Shevelove, appeared on Broadway in 1971, running 861 performances and setting off a series of Broadway "revivals" (actually adaptations) of 50-year-old musicals.
JD

Noonan, John Ford (1943–) Award-winning playwright and actor. From his first full-length play, *The Year Boston Won the Pennant* (1969), Noonan has revealed in a dozen produced full-length plays a unique, caustic comic turn, most fully realized in *A Coupla White Chicks Sitting Around Talking* (1980). In 1990 he appeared in his 1987 play *Talking Things Over with Chekhov* at NY's Actors' Playhouse.
DBW

No Place to Be Somebody First Pulitzer Prize-winning play (1967) by an **African-American, Charles Gordone.** A bar owned by small-time hustler Johnny is inhabited by a motley group of black and white social outcasts. Johnny's plans to swindle the Mafia come to nought, but the lives of his companions are sympathetically revealed. The play was first presented at the Sheridan Square Playhouse in New York and later at the **Public Theater.** Gordone is also an actor and director. In 1964 he won an Obie for his role as George in the all-black production of ***Of Mice and Men.***
EGH

Norman, Marsha (1947–) Playwright whose realistic characters confront some devastation in their past to determine whether and how to survive. *Getting Out* (1978) reveals the internal conflict of a woman parolee in her choice for a new beginning – dramatized by two actresses who simultaneously portray her violent, younger self and her present, numbed self. In 1983 Norman won the Pulitzer Prize for *'night, Mother,* a wrenching enactment of the last night in the life of a hopeless young woman as she prepares herself and her mother for her suicide, and of the mother's desperate attempts to prevent it. Other works include *Third and Oak: The Laundromat (and) The Pool Hall* (1978), *The Holdup* (1983), *Traveler in the Dark* (1984), *Winter Shakers* (1987), *Sarah and Abraham* (1988, a

musical with Norman L. Berman), several tele-
vision plays, and the screenplay for *'night, Mother.*
An eight-year absence from Broadway ended with
The Secret Garden (1991), a musical based on **Frances
Hodgson Burnett**'s classic novel, with book (Tony
Award) and lyrics by Norman (as part of an all-
female creative team).   FB

Norton, (William) Elliot (1903–   ) **Boston**-
born critic who attended Harvard University, where
he studied with George Lyman Kittredge and
George Pierce Baker. After graduation in 1926,
he worked as a reporter for the *Boston Post,* taking
over as drama critic when Edward Harold Crosby
retired in 1934. With the demise of the *Post* in 1956,
he switched to Hearst's *Record American,* retiring in
1982. Norton acquired the reputation of being
honest and reliable about new shows that were
Broadway-bound. **Mike Nichols** and **Joshua Logan** thought that he had a "smell for the public"
and for "what the public is feeling." He was not a
great stylist, nor did his reviews break new critical
ground; but New York producers respected his
opinion and made changes in their shows based
upon his reviews. He received the first **George
Jean Nathan** Award for Dramatic Criticism in
1964, and a special Tony in 1971.   TLM

No Time for Comedy Three-act comedy by **S.
N. Behrman** featuring **Katharine Cornell** and
Laurence Olivier; opened at the **Ethel Barrymore
Theatre** on 17 April 1939 and ran for 185 performances. Chronicling Behrman's own doubts about
writing comedy in a time of economic disaster and
impending war, the play shows a popular comic
playwright who attempts to write a "serious" play
to please a pretentious dilletante. Cornell's re-
strained performance as the witty actress-wife who
restores her husband's belief in the value of laughter
was a fine match to Behrman's intelligent comedy.
A specific and personal response to its cultural
moment, the play has seldom been revived.   MF

Nudity A loosely interpreted phenomenon in the
theatre. Most of what passed for flesh on stage was
cunningly dyed fabric; often it was the contour of
breast and leg, uncamouflaged by current fashion,
that was read as nakedness. The chorines in *The
Black Crook* (1866) scandalized with shocking pink
tights, and **Adah Isaacs Menken** won her
billing of "The Naked Lady" while wearing fleshings and a gauze drapery.

The display of the relatively undraped human
form on stage was chiefly confined to static configurations. *Tableaux vivants* or living pictures were
introduced into New York in 1831 by Ada Adams
Barrymore illustrating the painting *The Soldier's
Widow.* This respectable exercise of *tableaux vivants,* a flesh-and-blood imitation of a famous work
of art, was returned to the legitimate stage by
Laura Keene in 1856, and it has persisted to our
day in musical comedy, with the reproduction of
Copley's *Signing of the Declaration of Independence* in
1776 (1976) and of Seurat's *Sunday on the Isle of La
Grande Jatte* in **Sunday in the Park with George**
(1983).

Canny entrepreneurs, such as Dr. Collyer with

Scene from *Oh! Calcutta!* (1969). Photo: Friedman–
Abeles.

his Living Models (1847), found that by exhibiting
facsimiles of classical sculpture they could venture
barer skin and sharper outlines than the dramatic
stage allowed. The female form was incarnated in
artist's models and prostitutes, while prizefighters
and strong men exhibited male musculature. Such
poses plastiques, despite their alleged biblical or Grecian inspiration, were usually staged in night cellars
and dime museums, subject to police raids and
harassment by moralists and reformers. This type
of exhibition was given a high-culture gloss by the
Hungarian Eduard Kilyanyi starting with *1492*
(1894); and a relaxation in American mores permitted **Florenz Ziegfeld, Earl Carroll,** and **George
White** in their **revue**s to mass bevies of scantily
clad beauties in slowly moving pageants.

Stage nudity was pictured in the early 20th century less as the high-minded, undraped dance innovations of Isadora Duncan and Ted Shawn than
as the **burlesque show.** The striptease, a ritual
wherein various garments are serially discarded
leaving the performer more or less undressed,
evolved in France. Legend has it introduced to the
U.S. by the trapeze artist Charmian, who accidentally lost her tights during her act; but it more
likely made its entrance with Omeena's cooch dance
at the St. Louis World's Fair (1896). By 1920 it had
become a burlesque attraction offered by Millie de
Leon, and was later perfected as a dance number
by **Gypsy Rose Lee** and **Ann Corio.** The pasties
that covered the nipples might be flung to the
audience, but the *cache-sexe* or G-string usually
stayed in place, and a blackout or fall of curtain
would supervene. **Sally Rand**'s fan dance, first

seen at the Chicago Exposition in 1933, became a byword for teasing nonrevelation. By the 1960s performers left nothing to the imagination, but a 1991 Supreme Court decision permits communities to ban nude dancing for reasons of "public morality."

The alternative theatre of the 1960s employed nudity as a tactical weapon, a direct assault on middle-class sensibilities and an alignment with "Nature," though it was usually seen in semiprivate Happenings. Its *annus mirabilis* was 1968, when the rock musical *Hair* displayed its unclad cast frontally; the **Living Theatre**'s players were arrested in San Francisco for disrobing ("We can't take off our clothes in public" became one of their opening plaints), and Sally Kirkland was the first New York actress to appear nude throughout an entire play, **Terrence McNally**'s *Sweet Eros*. The commercial theatre was quick to adopt this licence in *Oh! Calcutta!* whose company, male and female, shed its bathrobes in the first moments. Nudity soon turned into a token of stage realism (David Storey's *The Changing Room*, 1971) and a touchstone of gender identification (**David Henry Hwang**'s *M. Butterfly*, 1989). **Performance art**ists like **Karen Finley** exaggerate and abuse the naked body for shock effect, to make political points about sexual exploitation; but the resurgence of **censorship** and recent court decisions create a chilling climate that compels actors to put their clothes back on. LS

See: J. W. McCullough, *Living Pictures on the New York Stage,* Ann Arbor, 1983.

Nugent, Elliott (1896–1980) Playwright, actor, producer, and director. Nugent performed with his parents (J. C. and Grace Nugent) and on the Keith–Orpheum **vaudeville** circuit before making his Broadway debut as Tom Sterrett in *Dulcey* (1921). *Kempy* (1922), which he wrote and produced with his father, was his first successful play. He is best remembered for *The Male Animal* (1940), which he wrote with James Thurber; for acting Bill Page in *The Voice of the Turtle* (1943); for directing *Tomorrow the World* (1943); and for coproducing *The Seven Year Itch* (1952). TLM

Nugent, Nellie see **McCann, Elizabeth**

Nuyorican theatre The term "Nuyorican" refers to Puerto Rican culture in New York, which typically is bilingual, bicultural, and working class in socioeconomic orientation. Moreover, "Nuyorican" or "Rican" is used by the children of working-class Puerto Rican migrants to the city. During the ethnic revivalist and civil rights movements of the 1960s, young Puerto Rican writers and intellectuals began using the term as a point of departure in affirming their own cultural existence and history as diverging from that of the island of Puerto Rico and that of mainstream America. A literary and artistic flowering in the New York Puerto Rican community ensued in the late 1960s and early '70s as a result of greater access to education for Puerto Ricans raised in the U.S. and as a result of the ethnic consciousness movement. Nuyorican Theatre has included such diverse theatrical manifesta-

tions as street theatre, as collectively created and performed by Teatro Orilla, Nuevo Teatro Pobre de América, Teatro Jurutungo, Teatro Guazabara, and Teatro Cuatro; but it is also exemplified by a wide range of works by individual playwrights produced in prisons, at small nonprofit **Hispanic theatre**s, such as Teatro Repertorio Español and the **Puerto Rican Traveling Theatre,** at the Henry Street Settlement's **New Federal Theatre** and **Joseph Papp**'s **New York Shakespeare Festival,** and even at large commerical houses on Broadway.

Although the term was first applied to literature and theatre by playwright-novelist Jaime Carrero in the late 1960s, and finds some stylistic and thematic development in his plays *Noo Jall* (a play on the Spanish pronunciation of New York and the word "jail") and *Pipo Subway No Sabe Reír,* it was a group of playwright-poets associated with the Nuyorican Poets' Cafe and Joseph Papp that first defined and came to exemplify Nuyorican Theatre. Included in the group were Miguel Algarín, Lucky Cienfuegos, Tato Laviera, and **Miguel Piñero**, all of whom focused their bilingual works on the life and culture of working-class Puerto Ricans in New York. Two members of the group, Cienfuegos and Piñero, were ex-convicts who had begun their writing careers while incarcerated, and they chose to develop their dramatic material from prison, street, and underclass culture. Algarín, a university professor and proprietor of the Nuyorican Poets' Cafe, created a more avant-garde aura for the collective, while the virtuoso bilingual poet Tato Laviera contributed a lyricism and a folk- and popular-culture base. It was Piñero's work (and life), however, that became most celebrated, his prison drama *Short Eyes* having won an Obie and the New York Drama Critics' Award for best American play in the 1973–4 season. His success – coupled with that of fellow Nuyorican writer and ex-convict Piri Thomas, and that of Pedro Pietri who developed the persona of a street urchin – often resulted in Nuyorican literature and theatre becoming associated with a Jean Genêt–type naturalism and the themes of crime, drugs, abnormal sexuality, and generally aberrant behavior, thus leading to a reaction against the term by many writers who were, in fact, affirming Puerto Rican working-class culture in New York.

Today there is a new generation of New York Puerto Rican playwrights who were nurtured on the theatre of Piñero and the Nuyoricans, and who have also experienced greater support and opportunities for developing their work. They quite often repeat and reevaluate many of the concerns and the style and language of the earlier group, but with a sophistication and polish that has come from drama workshops, playwright residencies, and university education. Among these are Juan Shamsul Alam, Edward Gallardo, Federico Fraguada, Richard Irizarry, Yvette Ramírez, and Cándido Tirado. NK

See: J. Antush, *Recent Puerto Rican Theatre: Five Plays from New York,* Houston, 1991; N. Kanellos, ed., *Biographical Dictionary of Hispanic Literature in the United States,* Westport, CT, 1989; J. Miller in *Hispanic Theatre in the United States,* ed. N. Kanellos, Houston, 1984.

O

Oakley, Annie (née Phoebe Anne Oakley Mozee) (1860–1926) Sharpshooter, born in Ohio, where she developed her shooting skills hunting game. When almost 16 she competed with vaudevillian Frank Butler, defeating him by one point. Subsequently they married and she became the star of their act; he acted as assistant and business manager. In 1885 Oakley joined **Buffalo Bill Cody**'s **Wild West exhibition,** and for 17 years, with one brief interruption, she remained a chief attraction. Despite a paralyzing injury in a 1901 railroad wreck, she performed for two more decades. A legendary shot with shoulder and hand arms, her friend Sitting Bull dubbed her "little sureshot." Her career was inspiration for the musical *Annie Get Your Gun.*   DBW

> See: W. Havighurst, *Annie Oakley of the Wild West,* New York, 1954; I. Sayers, *Annie Oakley and Buffalo Bill's Wild West,* New York, 1981.

Oakley, Frank "Slivers" (?–1915) **Circus** clown, considered during the first decade of this century the greatest of the solo pantomime jesters. For five minutes Oakley held **Barnum** & **Bailey** audiences spellbound with his one-man pantomime baseball game, portraying 18 players, climaxed with a heated argument with an umpire, with Slivers in both roles. In 1905 he compared his circus outing to a "scrimmage against Yale." As circuses became larger and clowning more flamboyant, solo clowns became passé. Oakley's act was cut and his salary reduced from $750 weekly to $50. He quit in disgust and in 1915 committed suicide.   DBW

O'Brien, Jack (1939–) Artistic Director of the **Old Globe Theatre.** O'Brien taught at Hunter College before joining the **Association of Producing Artists** (APA) as **Ellis Rabb**'s assistant (1964–9). After several years of free-lance work, he became associate director of **John Houseman**'s The **Acting Company** at the Juilliard School (1974–5). Directing credits include the Houston Grand Opera production of *Porgy and Bess* (1976), *The Magic Flute* for the San Francisco Opera, *Street Scene* for the New York City Opera, *Mary Stuart* and *A Man for All Seasons* at the **Ahmanson Theatre,** and several productions at the **American Conservatory Theatre.** Television directing credits include the PBS production of "The Good Doctor" and five productions for "American Playhouse." O'Brien made his directing debut at the Old Globe with *The Comedy of Errors* (1969), and directed 37 productions through 1991, including the world premiere of **A. R. Gurney**'s *The Cocktail Hour* (1988).   JDM

Octoroon, The; or, Life in Louisiana A sensation melodrama by **Dion Boucicault** first performed at the **Winter Garden Theatre** in 1859 as a vehicle for him and his wife, Agnes Robertson. This adaptation of the novel *The Quadroon* centers on the sale of Zoe, a freed, "one-eighth" African-American woman, back into slavery to pay the debts of respectable plantation owners in Louisiana. Although noncommittal on the divisive issue of the expansion of slavery, the play confirmed the racism of most of its northern audiences in its assumption that the "taint" of Negro blood rendered Zoe helpless and pitiable. Contributing to the play's success were a bowie-knife fight, the use of a camera on stage, **minstrel**-like scenes involving loyal "darkies," and the explosion of a steamboat, the sensational climax of the play. The initial production also featured **Joseph Jefferson III** as a sympathetic **Yankee** who unmasks the villain. *The Octoroon* remained popular on nothern and western stages into the 1890s.   BAMcC

Odd Couple, The, by **Neil Simon** opened 10 March 1965 at the **Plymouth Theatre,** running 964 performances. The play followed *Barefoot in the Park* both chronologically and thematically. Newly separated, obsessively tidy Felix Ungar (Art Carney) and his slovenly poker friend Oscar Madison (Walter Matthau) become roommates and illustrate the impossibility of coexistence without compromise, carrying on Simon's concern for moderation. More significantly, Simon attempts to avoid confining the theme to domestic behavior stereotypes by playing the theme out through two male characters. Even so, the characters still embody supposedly gendered traits, rather than a combination; Felix exhibits assumed feminine behavior, while Oscar caricatures the masculine. The characters' incompatibility is intended to be in terms of their inability to modify their habitual behavior, rather than in terms of gender conflict. A 1985 reprise of the play with a female cast ran 295 performances, suggesting the attempt to transcend gender roles was only partly successful.   RW

Odets, Clifford (1906–63) In the entire sweep of American theatre history, Odets is the one true company playwright. In the early days of the **Group Theatre,** as he listened to **Harold Clurman**'s orations and followed **Lee Strasberg**'s formulations of the basic principles of Method acting,

Odets was absorbing the elements of a theatrical style that erupted on 14 January 1935, when the Group presented **Waiting for Lefty,** his incendiary play about taxi drivers driven to call a strike. In a series of short, jabbing scenes and in language alive with the rhythms and inflections of urban folk idiom, Odets expressed the fury and passion and sorrow of the dispossessed working class. With this play the Group discovered its voice: *Lefty* released the full potential of the new realistic acting style that its members had been investigating for four years.

Later in the same year the Group produced two other Odets plays, **Awake and Sing!** and **Paradise Lost,** family dramas whose contemporary but archetypal Jewish sufferers speak in a language of their own, a dense idiom of metaphor and incantatory repetition that alternates irony with exultation and brief, stabbing sentences with longer speeches of operatic intensity. When Odets left for Hollywood at the end of his triumphant year, his Group colleagues felt betrayed. As if in compensation, Odets presented them with a new play, *Golden Boy* (1937). In it, his hero's hard choice between being a violinist and a prizefighter expresses Odets's own conflict about whether to serve art or commerce. Though this central premise is spurious, the play proved to be the Group's biggest moneymaker. Odets's final works for the Group, **Rocket to the Moon** (1938) and *Night Music* (1940), are diminished in their thematic scope and vitality. By 1940, when the Group itself had lost its focus, Odets had also apparently reached a creative impasse. Despite their ripe language and strong conflict, Odets's four remaining dramas – *Clash by Night* (1941), *The Big Knife* (1949), *The* **Country Girl** (1950), and *The Flowering Peach* (1954) – don't have the same sense of occasion as even the least of the Group efforts. To accomplish his most vibrant work Odets seemed to require a Depression background; he is now regarded as the quintessential 1930s playwright, who transmuted working-class pressures into timeless theatrical eloquence.   FH

See: W. W. Demastes, *Clifford Odets: A Research and Production Sourcebook,* Westport, CT, 1991; M. Brenman-Gibson, *Clifford Odets: American Playwright, The Years from 1906 to 1940,* New York, 1981; G. Miller, *Clifford Odets,* New York, 1989; G. Weales, *Odets, The Playwright,* London and New York, 1985.

Oenslager, Donald (1902–75) Set designer and educator. His influences include **George Pierce Baker;** the work of Appia and Craig, which he saw in Europe in 1921; and **Robert Edmond Jones,** whom he assisted in the early 1920s. Oenslager designed some 250 productions, including **Anything Goes, You Can't Take It with You,** and *The Man Who Came to Dinner.* Although he emphasized the need to find the proper style for each play, his designs were frequently decorative and elegant. His greatest influence, however, was as a teacher: He was a professor of design at Yale University for nearly 50 years (1925–71), and many of the major figures in American design were trained by him. He is author of *Scenery Then and Now* (1936) and *Stage Design: Four Centuries of Scenic*

Invention (1975), the latter illustrated with drawings from his extensive private collection.   AA

See: D. M. Oenslager, *The Theatre of Donald Oenslager,* Middletown, CT, 1978.

Off-Broadway The term, coined in the 1950s, both for NYC productions or theatres outside the so-called Broadway area surrounding Times Square – including several houses along **Theatre Row** – and for an **Actors' Equity Association** contract for theatres with 100–299 seats. (Other unions adopted Equity's designation.) Critic Stuart Little notes, however, that "Off-Broadway is a state of mind, . . . a way of looking at theater at every point at odds with Broadway's patterns."

Off-Broadway began in the early 1900s as the "Little Theatre movement" [see **community theatre**]. Offering artistically significant plays in an inexpensive, noncommercial atmosphere, groups such as the **Washington Square Players** and the **Provincetown Players** staged, in small, out-of-the-way theatres, plays Broadway ignored. Other companies included the **Neighborhood Playhouse,** Cherry Lane Theatre, **Civic Repertory Company,** and **Group Theatre.** Many were not only experimental but amateur as well, lasting only a few years before falling victim to their own success as artists parlayed triumphs into jobs in commercial theatre and, later, Hollywood. After WW II, however, Off-Broadway attracted critical attention. Several successes transferred to Broadway, beginning with New Stages' production of Sartre's *The Respectful Prostitute* (1948).

In the 1950s and early '60s, several companies had an impact on American theatre. With untried, noncommercial, or experimental plays or productions, using then-unknown talent and shoestring budgets, Off-Broadway became an artistic magnet. Serious attention started with the 1952 revival of **Tennessee Williams**'s **Summer and Smoke,** launching the careers of **José Quintero** and **Geraldine Page.** Such companies as the **Living Theatre,** Phoenix Theatre [see **Association of Producing Artists**], **New York Shakespeare Festival, American Place Theatre, Negro Ensemble Company, Roundabout Theatre Company, Chelsea Theatre Center, Circle Repertory,** and **Manhattan Theatre Club** presented failed commercial or neglected plays. Over the years, a split developed between commerical Off-Broadway houses such as the Astor Place, **Lucille Lortel, Orpheum,** Westside Arts, Perry Street, Promenade, Minetta Lane, and Criterion Center – represented by the League of Off-Broadway Theatres and Producers – and nonprofit companies like the WPA, **Jewish Repertory, Pan Asian Repertory Theatre, Brooklyn Academy of Music, Ridiculous Theatrical Company, Hudson Guild, Lincoln Center** Theatre Company, Second Stage, and **Negro Ensemble Company** that still foster new works and U.S. productions of European plays. Mostly, however, real experimental and avant-garde theatre has moved to **Off-Off Broadway.**

Off-Broadway theatres have presented such works as Beckett's *Endgame,* **Albee's** *The* **Zoo Story,**

Gelber's *The Connection,* Jones and Schmidt's *The Fantasticks* (America's longest-running play, opening in 1960), Genêt's *The Blacks,* Orton's *What the Butler Saw,* Pomerance's *The Elephant Man,* Fuller's *A Soldier's Play,* Churchill's *Cloud 9,* Ngema's *Sarafina!,* Uhry's *Driving Miss Daisy,* Bennett's *A Chorus Line,* Brook's *Mahabharata,* Fugard's *The Road to Mecca,* Harling's *Steel Magnolias,* Henley's *Crimes of the Heart,* Shue's *The Foreigner,* Fierstein's *Torch Song Trilogy,* and Ashman and Menken's *Little Shop of Horrors.* Other writers have included **Kopit, Schisgal, Baraka, van Itallie, Lanford Wilson, Guare, Bullins,** Vonnegut, **Rabe, Mamet, Zindel, Innaurato, Bogosian, Durang, Fornés, Gurney, Hwang,** Larry Kramer, **Shepard, Wasserstein,** and **Robert Wilson.**

The talent in these productions included directors **Anne Bogart, Quintero, Schneider,** Grotowski, **O'Horgan, Serban, Zaks,** and **Grosbard,** and actors **Jason Robards, Jr., Colleen Dewhurst, George C. Scott, James Earl Jones, Julie Harris, Dustin Hoffman, Meryl Streep, Kevin Kline, Stacy Keach, Ruby Dee,** Claire Bloom, **Kathy Bates,** Adolph Caesar, **Morgan Freeman,** Paul Hecht, **Edward Herrmann, Swoosie Kurtz, John Malkovich, Bernadette Peters, Christopher Reeve,** Danitra Vance, and **Al Pacino.** Off-Broadway is also a place for established actors to try unfamiliar roles, including that of director. Recent productions have been directed by actors **Geraldine Fitzgerald** (*Mass Appeal* and an all-black *Long Day's Journey into Night*), **George C. Scott** (*Present Laughter* and *Design for Living*), and Kevin Kline (*Hamlet*). Off-Broadway stages have also lured film and television actors such as Demi Moore, **Richard Thomas,** Malcolm-Jamal Warner, Molly Ringwald, and Robert De Niro, and singers such as Linda Ronstadt and Rex Smith. In 1955, the *Village Voice* established the Obie Awards to recognize accomplishments in this arena. The Lucille Lortel Awards are also given for excellence Off-Broadway. REK

See: H. Greenberger, *The Off-Broadway Experience,* New York, 1971; S. Little, *Off-Broadway: The Prophetic Theatre,* New York, 1972; J. Price, *The Off-Broadway Theatre,* New York, 1962.

Off-Off Broadway The term coined in the early 1960s to distinguish professional, commercial theatre (Broadway and **Off-Broadway**) from noncommercial theatre presented in coffeehouses, churches, lofts, and storefronts in New York's Greenwich Village and Lower East Side. Technically, the term also refers to productions that fall under **Actors' Equity** Tiered Non-Profit Theatre Code for performances with limited runs that feature unsalaried union actors in noncontractual theatres of not more than 100 seats.

Often perceived as a movement, Off-Off Broadway encompasses a wide spectrum of theatrical activity so diverse in impulse, conception, method, and intent that no common objective characterizes it. Off-Off Broadway has spawned works of numerous types and terms to go with them: experimental, **collective, alternative,** environmental,

radical, guerilla, and Theatre of Images [see **Introduction, §4**].

Off-Off Broadway is usually considered an alternative theatre grounded in exploration and experimentation, and questioning the limits of performance. The initial impulse was to generate new approaches and methods in a climate free from the demands of popular taste that inform commercial theatre artistically and economically. Frequently, though, Off-Off Broadway productions mirror commercial theatre values and standards.

Caffe Cino became the first Off-Off Broadway theatre when Joe Cino began to present plays in his one-room coffeehouse in 1959. By 1965 there were several small producing organizations; the major ones include **Judson Poet's Theatre,** formed in 1961 by Al Carmines; Café **La MaMa,** founded by **Ellen Stewart** in 1962; and Theatre Genesis, founded in 1964 by Ralph Cook. Devoted primarily to producing work of new American playwrights, these houses mounted plays by writers like **Julie Bovasso, Ed Bullins, Rosalyn Drexler,** Tom Eyen, **Maria Irene Fornés,** Paul Foster, **Israel Horowitz, Adrienne Kennedy,** H. M. Koutoukas, Ruth Krauss, **Charles Ludlam, Terrence McNally,** Leonard Melfi, **Rochelle Owens, Sam Shepard, Ronald Tavel, Megan Terry,** John Vaccaro, **Jean-Claude van Itallie,** Jeff Weiss, and **Lanford Wilson.**

The term quickly expanded to include a new breed of theatrical work as Off-Off spawned a visually oriented, nonlinear, nonnarrative – some might even say, nondramatic – type of performance by such companies as the **Wooster Group,** Manhattan Project [see **Gregory**], **Mabou Mines, Ridiculous Theatrical Company,** and **Split Britches,** and by individual artists who mount their own productions, like **Meredith Monk, Richard Foreman, Robert Wilson,** and Stuart Sherman.

In the 1980s and '90s, as theatrical techniques once associated with Off-Off Broadway have become commonplace in commercial Broadway venues (e.g., the autobiographical and spare nature of *A Chorus Line,* the cross-dressing theme in **David Henry Hwang**'s *M. Butterfly,* or the postmodern mixing of stage and filmic perspectives in the musical *City of Angels*), the boundaries among Broadway, Off-Broadway, and Off-Off Broadway have become more and more slippery.

Off-Off still, however, evokes experimental or alternative theatre. That rubric has expanded to include not only the collectives and performance spectacles that developed in the 1970s, but also the explosion in the late '80s of **performance art** – small-scale pieces, often combining abstract movement or visual elements with nonlinear, often autobiographical text, usually performed by its author (e.g., **Spalding Gray, Holly Hughes, Eric Bogosian, Karen Finley,** and Robbie McCauley). AS

Of Mice and Men by **John Steinbeck** opened 23 November 1937 in New York, running for 207 performances. The cast included Broderick Crawford as Lennie, a mentally retarded man of tremendous physical strength; Wallace Ford as George, who travels with him and looks out for him; Sam Byrd as Curley, the mean-spirited son of the owner of the ranch where they find work; Claire Luce as Curley's wife, whom Lennie kills in a moment of panic; and **Will Geer,** John F. Hamilton, Charles Slattery, Walter Baldwin, and Leigh Whipper as the other cowboys. An adaptation of Steinbeck's novella, the play depicts the relationship between Lennie and George, which is based on a human need for companionship. Their dream of a ranch of their own sustains them until the reality of sex intrudes on their private world in the person of Candy's wife and Lennie destroys her, leaving George no choice but to destroy Lennie.   BCM

Of Thee I Sing Musical comedy by **George S. Kaufman** and **Morrie Ryskind,** with lyrics by **Ira Gershwin** and music by **George Gershwin;** directed by Kaufman, it opened on Broadway 26 December 1931 and ran 331 performances. Awarded the Pulitzer Prize for Drama in 1932 (the first musical so honored), *Of Thee I Sing* was the first American musical to be published (Knopf, 1932). In this political burlesque, John P. Wintergreen (**William Gaxton**) runs for president on a platform of love, first vowing to woo the winner of a beauty contest, but instead falling for Mary, an "ordinary" girl who bakes corn muffins without corn (pun and absurdity intended). The beauty queen, who is of French extraction, enlists the advocacy of the French ambassador, and Wintergreen escapes impeachment only because Mary gives birth to twins. **Victor Moore** played the vice-president, Alexander Throttlebottom, whose presence and name is virtually unknown.   JDM

Oh! Calcutta! A musical **revue** of erotica (skits, song, dance) devised by **Kenneth Tynan,** and conceived and directed by Jacques Levy, with contributions by Samuel Beckett, **Jules Feiffer,** John Lennon, Leonard Melfi, and **Sam Shepard,** among others. It opened **Off-Broadway** at the Eden Theatre (17 June 1969), running for 704 performances before transferring to Broadway's **Belasco Theatre** (26 February 1971) for 610 performances. Due to its extensive **nudity** and blatant sexual content, the show achieved notoriety, prompting nationwide debates about the issue of **censorship.** Musical numbers include "Was It Good for You Too?" and "Coming Together, Going Together." Revived on 24 September 1976 at the Edison Theatre for 5,959 performances, *Oh! Calcutta!* closed on 6 August 1989, the second longest running musical in Broadway's history.   EK

Oh Dad, Poor Dad, Mamma's Hung You in the Closet and I'm Feelin' So Sad by **Arthur Kopit** opened at the Phoenix Theatre in New York on 26 February 1962, running for 454 performances. The cast included Jo Van Fleet as Madame Rosepettle, **Austin Pendleton** as her son Jonathan, and Barbara Harris as Rosalie. The play opened on Broadway on 27 August 1963, running for 47 performances. An absurdist treatment of the destructive effect of the castrating woman and domineering mother, the play depicts Madame Rosepettle's bullying of her son Jonathan, whose dead father she has had stuffed and takes with her on her travels.   BCM

O'Hearn, Robert (1921–) After designing 60 productions at the Brattle Theatre in Cambridge, MA, O'Hearn came to New York, where he achieved recognition for **Cyril Ritchard**'s production of *The Relapse* (1950), though he had only moderate success for the next decade. In 1960 he became a primary designer for the Metropolitan Opera, and he has designed dozens of operas around the world.   AA

O'Horgan, Tom (Thomas Foster) (1924/27?–) Avant-garde composer and director who describes his work as "theatrical disobedience." O'Horgan is most famous for *Hair,* a **New York Shakespeare Festival** workshop that moved to Broadway in 1968. He also staged **Rochelle Owens**'s *Futz* (Obie, 1967; film, 1969; revival, 1991), Foster's *Tom Paine* (Obie, 1968), Julian Barry's *Lenny* (Drama Desk Award, 1971), *Jesus Christ Superstar* (1971), and Arrabal's *The Architect and the Emperor of Assyria* (1976). He directed the film *Rhinoceros* (1974), and "The Eighth Wonder," the Brooklyn Bridge centenary sound-and-light show. His productions favor contact and confrontation with the audience, and "emphasized the physical . . . side of performance."   REK

Oklahoma! The first Broadway collaboration between **Richard Rodgers** (music) and **Oscar Hammerstein II** (book and lyrics), based on **Lynn Riggs**'s play *Green Grow the Lilacs;* opened 31 March 1943 (2,212 performances). The musical's nostalgic story of farmers and cowmen in the 1907 Oklahoma Territory, acclaimed for its innovations, touched wartime theatregoers. Its main plot – a rather melodramatic love story in which the romance of a cowboy, Curly, and a farm girl, Laurey, is threatened by the machinations of a villainous farmhand, Jud – was brightened by a cast filled with talented newcomers, such as **Alfred Drake** (Curly), Joan Roberts (Laurey), and **Celeste Holm** (the man-crazy Ado Annie of the subplot). Rodgers and Hammerstein's rich score was filled with charming love songs and playful comic numbers. *Oklahoma!*, with its onstage death (Curly kills Jud in self defense), brought a new seriousness to the musical stage, but its major innovation lay in the extent to which dance was employed to advance the plot and express latent emotion. **Agnes de Mille**'s choreography – particularly in the "Dream Ballet" in which Laurey's repressed fears of Jud were given colorful and menacing life on stage – established dance, and particularly the idiom of modern dance, as an important feature of musical comedy. A road company toured for over a decade; revivals were staged in 1969 and 1979, following the 1955 film.   MK

Olcott, Chauncey (né Chancellor John) (1860–1932) Singer-actor who, after beginning in **minstrel shows,** appeared in comic operas with **Lillian Russell.** Following the death of W. J. Scanlan, American-born Olcott was the most pop-

Scene from a turn-of-the-century production of *The Old Homestead*. Courtesy: Michael Gnat.

ular "Irish" tenor on the musical stage. For decades he starred in idealized musicals of Irish life, such as *The Irish Artist* (1894) and *A Romance of Athlone* (1899). Olcott introduced a number of his songs, notably "When Irish Eyes Are Smiling."   MK

See: R. Olcott, *Song in His Heart,* New York, 1939.

Old Globe Theatre opened 29 May 1935 in San Diego as a temporary replica of the original Globe and one of the attractions at the 1935–6 California Pacific International Exposition. A group of citizens raised $10,000 to remodel the theatre in order to prevent its postexposition demolition, and the San Diego Community Theatre was chartered 3 February 1937; in 1958, the name was changed to the Old Globe to conform to popular usage. Craig Noel, who had acted and directed with the company since 1937, became artistic director in 1947. The company joined with San Diego State College to present summer productions of Shakespeare (1949–52), then took the name of the San Diego National Shakespeare Festival (1954) and began hiring Equity actors (1959). Noel began producing plays at the Falstaff Tavern (1963), and the space was remodeled to become the 225-seat Cassius Carter Centre Stage (1969). An arsonist's **fire** destroyed the Old Globe on 8 March 1978; the board raised $6.5 million in 20 months to rebuild it. In January 1981, Noel became executive producer and **Jack O'Brien** was named artistic director. The rebuilt 581-seat Old Globe Theatre opened on 14 January 1982, part of a three-theatre complex named the Simon Edison Centre for the Performing Arts. The company received a special Tony Award for regional theatre (1984). Another arsonist's fire destroyed the Festival Stage (29 October 1984); in its place the 612-seat outdoor Lowell Davies Festival Theatre opened on 7 June 1985. A typical season includes 12 productions ranging from Shakespeare to world premieres; as of 1991 the annual operating budget was $7.5 million.   JDM

Old Homestead, The Denman Thompson's sentimental tribute to rural American values opened

5 April 1886 at the **Boston Museum.** It was the singular creation of Thompson, who conceived, wrote, and acted it. Thompson first performed a shorter version in 1875, which he extended in 1877 and then, with George Ryer, revised again for the 1886 production. He enacted the central role of Yankee farmer Joshua through 1910. With his homespun philosophy and local color jokes, Joshua represented a late 19th-century updating of the traditional **Yankee** character. In the play, Joshua journeys to New York to find his son, Reuben, who fled after being accused of a crime. The action provides ample opportunity for humorous comments on New England speech and customs as well as contrasts between city and country living.   RAH

Old Maid, The Dramatization by **Zoë Akins** of Edith Wharton's novel, opened at the **Empire Theatre** on 7 January 1935 for a run of 305 performances. Although critics considered it too sentimental, audiences, particularly the women in the matinee crowd, loved its theme of the maternal instinct. The story tells of the sacrifice made by two cousins for the sake of respectability: Delia (**Judith Anderson**) by marrying a properly rich man, and Charlotte (Helen Menken) by denying her illegitimate daughter and allowing Delia to adopt her. When the play was awarded the 1935 Pulitzer Prize, the critics were so enraged at the exclusion of other superior plays – particularly **Lillian Hellman**'s *The Children's Hour* – that they formed their own group to award the Drama Critics' Circle Award.   FB

Oldmixon, Mrs. John (née Georgina George) (?–1835) Recruited by **Thomas Wignell** in 1793 for Philadelphia's **Chestnut Street Theatre** company, this British-born actress-singer made her U.S. debut on 14 May 1794 as Clorinda in *Robin Hood.* In 1798 she joined **Dunlap**'s company in New York. She continued to perform intermittently until 1813, giving occasional concerts in Philadelphia after that date. Although never a major star in England, she was considered the most accomplished early vocalist in America, and excelled as a comic actress.   DBW

Oliver, Edith (1913–) Drama critic who, after attending Smith College (1931–3) and studying acting privately, pursued a career in radio (1937–52), acting on programs like "True Detective" and "Philip Morris Playhouse," and writing and producing quiz shows such as "The 64 Dollar Question." In 1948 she joined the staff of the *New Yorker* and became **Off-Broadway** reviewer (1961–) and senior critic (1986–). Attuned to the American avant-garde, she has discovered and introduced important young talent to a national audience.   TLM

Olsen, (John Siguard) "Ole" (1892–1963) and **(Harold Ogden) "Chick" Johnson** (1891–1962) Comedy team. Infamous for "gonk" ("hokum with raisins," their unique blend of slapstick), Olsen and Johnson, each with a zany character, played **vaudeville** in the U.S., England, and Australia beginning in 1915; by the 1930s they were well known on stage and in forgettable films. In 1938 they brought their mayhem to the critically damned but enormously popular and ultimate-in-comic-vaudeville-style **revue**, *Hellzapoppin*. The balance of their career was spent trying, with limited success, to recycle this hit in four subsequent revues and a 1941 film version of *Hellzapoppin*.   DBW

Olympia, The (music hall and theatre) Broadway between 44th and 45th Sts., NYC [Architect: J. B. McElfatrick and Co.]. **Oscar Hammerstein [I]** officially launched the new theatre district at Longacre (Times) Square with the opening of the Olympia in 1895, an entertainment center that was to include three theatres, a roof garden, billiard rooms, a bowling alley, a turkish bath, and restaurants for one admission. He completed only two theatres, which he lost to creditors within three years. His Music Hall became the New York Theatre for **vaudeville,** and **Charles Frohman** changed the Lyric to the Criterion for legitimate fare. Under **Klaw** and **Erlanger,** the roof garden became the Jardin de Paris, where the prototype of **Florenz Ziegfeld**'s *Follies* was presented in 1907. The theatres quickly succumbed to films and were razed in 1935.   MCH

Omaha Magic Theatre Founded in 1968 by Jo Ann Schmidman, the OMT has created and presented over 100 new American music theatre plays and **performance art** events in its storefront theatres in downtown Omaha. Its mission has been to "push the boundaries of what has previously been recognized as theatre to new limits . . . to present the freshest text, directorial performer, and visual art images and clearest musical voice in an integrated performance form." A founding member of **Joseph Chaikin**'s **Open Theatre, Megan Terry** joined OMT as resident playwright in 1974 and, together with Schmidman, has brought national recognition and major grants to this Midwest theatre. The company tours both in Nebraska and nationally. A recent work, *Body Leaks* (1990–1), is

a collaborative performance art piece about self-**censorship.**   TLM

See: J. A. Schmidman, S. Kimberlain, and M. Terry, eds., *Right Brain Vacation Photos: New Plays and Production Photographs from the Omaha Magic Theatre, 1972–1992*, Omaha, 1992.

Once in a Lifetime Comedy by **Moss Hart** and **George S. Kaufman;** directed by Kaufman, opened on Broadway 24 September 1930 and ran 406 performances. Hart wrote the first version, then Kaufman agreed to collaborate on the revision. The play concerns three young vaudevillians who hear that "talkies" are changing Hollywood and head West in search of fame and fortune. The only one to succeed is George, an ingenuous innocent whose blunders become master strokes through sheer luck and the inexplicable lunacy of the film industry. Kaufman played the role of Larry Vail, a New York playwright, who comes to Hollywood as a screenwriter, suffers from the studio's neglect, and finally breaks down from underwork; Hart took over the role 4 May 1931.   JDM

O'Neal, Frederick (1905–92) African-American actor and theatre administrator. O'Neal performed in St. Louis and organized the **Ira Aldridge** Players before moving to New York City, where he attended the New Theatre School in 1936–40. With Abram Hill he founded the **American Negro Theatre** (1940–50), and in 1944 he appeared as Frank in its Broadway production of *Anna Lucasta* (Drama Critics' and **Clarence Derwent** awards). Subsequently he played a variety of roles on and **Off-Broadway** (*Lost in the Stars,* 1949; *Take a Giant Step,* 1953), on television, and in films. O'Neal held several important positions, such as President of the **Negro Actors Guild** (1961–4) and of **Actors' Equity Association** (1964–73). His many awards testify to his achievements as actor and leader in the theatrical profession.   EGH

O'Neil, Nance (1874–1965) Actress who joined the **Arthur McKee Rankin** company in San Francisco in 1893. Rankin soon built her into a star, booking her into several national tours, and in 1900 sponsored her world tour of *Magda, Fedora, La Tosca,* and *Camille.* In 1903 she added **Ibsen**'s *Lady Inger of Ostrat* to her repertoire and played it in San Francisco and Boston. Two years later she began performing *Hedda Gabler* and eventually took it to New York. Billed as the great tragedienne, she was usually considered to stand in the shadow of other great emotional actresses.   RAS

O'Neill, Eugene (Gladstone) (1888–1953) The first U.S. playwright of major talent, the only one ever to win the Nobel Prize for Literature (in 1936), and still universally regarded as America's finest. Also, having written his autobiography not only in *Long Day's Journey into Night* but also piecemeal, under less or greater disguise, in most of his works, he is among the most subjective of dramatists. Probably only August Strindberg, whom he called his mentor, was as obsessed with his own life and family history. The son of actor **James O'Neill,** Eugene used to deride the sentimental and melo-

The O'Neill family (left to right, Eugene, Jamie, and James, Sr.) at their New London, CT, home (c. 1900). Courtesy: Louis Sheaffer.

dramatic theatre of his father's day, yet he stood on his father's shoulders in attaining his preeminent position. Immersed in a theatrical milieu from birth, he unconsciously absorbed, as though by osmosis, the basics of stagecraft and playwriting. In youth and early manhood, however, there was virtually no indication that he would ever, in any field, amount to much: It appeared, rather, that he, like his self-destructive older brother, Jamie, would become a hard-drinking wastrel.

Perhaps the key to understanding him is that he suffered from lifelong feelings of guilt, born apparently of the fact that his mother, a shy, devout Catholic, innocently became a drug addict as a result of his birth. Recalling how wretched he felt on learning of her morphinism and of his role in her downfall, he says through his counterpart in *Long Day's Journey:* "God, it made everything in life seem rotten!" Turning against his ancestral faith, the apostate began to question all orthodoxies, all authority. Despite his familiarity with the ancient Greeks and Shakespeare, his sense of tragedy grew from his own life, not from the classics. He was an emotional hemophiliac whose family-inflicted wounds never healed. Here, then, we find the original of his somber outlook on life, the major source of the power and anguish pounding throughout his writings.

After an unimpressive record at Catholic and secular schools, he sought the lower depths, intent on experiencing "real life." He went to sea, drifted on the waterfronts of Buenos Aires and New York, and once became so depressed that he attempted suicide. O'Neill often said that he never thought of being a writer till his health broke down, in his midtwenties, confining him to a TB sanatorium for months. While recuperating, he "really thought" about his life for the first time and resolved to become a playwright. After his recovery in 1913, plays began to pour out of him, most of them tales of the sea and of the underside of life; what, in other words, had seemed misspent years, proved to be a major part of his working capital as a writer.

In a move beneficial to both parties, Eugene in 1916 joined a group of amateur playmakers on Cape Cod, who became known as the **Provincetown Players** on moving to Greenwich Village,

with O'Neill as their most imaginative and gifted writer. When he made his Broadway debut in 1920 with **Beyond the Horizon** (written in 1918), a story of defeat on a farm with the sea beckoning in the background, most of the critics, though faced with something novel in their experience – an American tragedy – were enthusiastic; but several complained that the play was too long, while another criticized its many changes of scene. The harsher critics failed to realize that the author, who eventually would ignore most stage conventions, was determined to hack out his own course. The play enjoyed a good run for so somber a work and won for O'Neill the first of his four Pulitzer Prizes. The others were for **Anna Christie** (written in 1920), **Strange Interlude** (1926–7), and *Long Day's Journey into Night* (1939–41).

A veritable Proteus of the drama, O'Neill kept changing his style. Starting as a realist, with occasional returns to the genre, he also wrote expressionistic works (*The **Emperor Jones,** 1920*, and *The* **Hairy Ape,** 1921), costume drama (*The Fountain,* 1921–2, and *Marco Millions,* 1923–5), Strindbergian views of marriage (*Welded,* 1922–3), biblical fables (*Lazarus Laughed,* 1925–6), and even a comedy (**Ah, Wilderness!,** 1932). As though set on avenging his father's bondage to plays pandering to popular taste, he made demands on his audiences with extra-long works, namely *Strange Interlude,* nine acts; **Mourning Becomes Electra** (1929–31), a trilogy in 13 acts; and *The Iceman Cometh* (1939), twice the standard length. He also, testing what the public would accept, wrote *The **Great God Brown** (1925), a bewildering work in which the characters constantly mask and unmask; **All God's Chillun Got Wings** (1923), a poignant story ahead of its day about a white girl married to a black; and **Desire Under the Elms** (1924), a drama of greed, incest, and infanticide. In writing some 30 long works and nearly a score of short ones in so many different styles, O'Neill almost exhausted the stage's nonverbal resources through his use of song, pantomime, dance, masks, imaginative scenic devices, and novel sound effects. In the end, though, after all his imaginative flights, realism proved his forte, as was demonstrated by *The Iceman Cometh* and *Long Day's Journey into Night,* his masterpieces.

In the 1930s he worked for years on his most ambitious project, a cycle entitled "A Tale of Possessors Self-Possessed" that would span a large part of the American past in dramatizing highlights in the history, generation after generation, of a "far from model" family. In the work, first envisioned as five plays (then 7, next 9, and, for a time, 11), O'Neill aimed to show that materialism and greed had corrupted America. Unfortunately, a number of factors, particularly ill health and his despair as WW II loomed, prevented him from achieving his goal. After he had destroyed most of his cycle writings, all that survived was one finished play, *A **Touch of the Poet** (1935–42), and, by chance, a rough draft of another, *More Stately Mansions* (1935–40), which was staged posthumously in truncated form.   LSh

See: T. Bogard, *Contour in Time: The Plays of Eugene O'Neill,* New York, 1972; T. Bogard and J. Bryer, eds., *Selected Letters of Eugene O'Neill,* New Haven, CT, 1988; V. Floyd, ed., *Eugene O'Neill at Work,*

James O'Neill as Edmond Dante in *Monte Cristo,* at the moment when, having escaped from the Chateau d'If, he is about to proclaim, "The world is mine!" Photo: Marc Gambier, N.Y. Courtesy: Laurence Senelick.

New York, 1981; M. L. Ranald, *The Eugene O'Neill Companion,* Westport, CT, 1984; L. Sheaffer, *O'Neill: Son and Artist,* Boston, 1973, and *O'Neill: Son and Playwright,* Boston, 1968; R. Wainscott, *Staging O'Neill: The Experimental Years, 1920–1934,* New Haven, CT, 1988.

O'Neill, James (1846–1920)

O'Neill, James (1846–1920) Irish-born actor. Despite his great popularity in the late 19th century, he is primarily remembered today as the father of **Eugene O'Neill.** For a time, appearing opposite such stars as **Charlotte Cushman,** Adelaide Neilson, and **Edwin Booth,** it appeared that he would attain similar stature, that he would become Booth's successor. His promise faded, however, particularly after he had, as his son said, "the good bad luck" to find a gold mine in **Charles Fechter**'s dramatization of Dumas's *The Count of Monte Cristo.* Initially O'Neill, who had suffered a hungry childhood, rejoiced in his prosperity as the Dumas hero, but as the decades piled up and the audiences flocked to see him only when he played Edmond Dantès, the role became a straitjacket that gradually diminished his talent. Fragments of his history are woven into his son's devastating family portrait, *Long Day's Journey into Night.* LSh

> *See:* L. F. Fisher, "A Descriptive Study of the Acting Career of James O'Neill," PhD diss., U of Michigan, 1969.

One-person performance

One-person performance Though the phenomenon of one-person telling or acting out a story to a group is obviously spread widely through space and time, and despite the fact that certain 18th-century British satirical performers are immediate predecessors of solo artists in the U.S., the form, with its emphasis on the self-sufficient individual, seems especially suited to the American psyche. One-person performance has flourished in this country since the mid-19th century, and is much in vogue today.

Well into the 20th century much of the popularity of solo performance in America resulted from the theatre's disrepute, grounded in puritan prejudice. Many too proper to attend the theatre turned out for "platform performances" by a renowned actor or writer. Charles Dickens put on the 19th century's most successful one-man shows; those of Mark Twain were also popular throughout the English-speaking world. The appeal of these events derived from the celebrity of the performers, which in turn came from the power of their prose. When in the 1950s the contemporary renaissance of one-person performance was launched by **Hal Holbrook** as Twain and Emlyn Williams as Dickens, the drawing power of this well-loved material was again confirmed.

The tradition of leading actors (John Gielgud, Ian McKellan, **Brian Bedford**) performing solo recitals of Shakespeare also shows the pull of great literary content. Biographical shows, rather frequent in the American theatre since the 1950s, are often about writers whose work as well as lives can be used, and they frequently base their hopes for success on the double celebrity of subject and star performer – **Julie Harris** as Emily Dickinson, James Whitmore as **Will Rogers, Zoë Caldwell** as **Lillian Hellman.** Nonliterary biographical shows have included **Henry Fonda** as Clarence Darrow and **James Earl Jones** as **Paul Robeson.**

Other solo performers create their own material – and their own renown. Among these artists **Ruth Draper** is preeminent, captivating audiences and fellow actors from early appearances in the 1920s until her death in 1956. Through their platform performances of Shakespeare and other literature, the courageous 19th-century artists **Anna Cora Mowatt, Fanny Kemble,** and **Charlotte Cushman** had established the propriety one-woman shows. Draper composed playlets that featured impersonations of a wide range of characters, making her the godmother of such current performers as **Lily Tomlin** and Whoopi Goldberg (also heirs of the stand-up comedy tradition, they do not necessarily write their own monologues). Men like **Eric Bogosian** and John Leguizamo, whose characters are drawn from contemporary urban life, can also be considered Draper descendants. Ron Vawter joined the tradition in 1992 with a solo performance that examined homosexual identity in America [see **gay/lesbian theatre**].

Solo performance is an extreme of theatre, the opposite of epic extravaganza. As such, it has interested any number of playwrights, notably the subversive minimalist Samuel Beckett. Well-known American playwrights **Lanford Wilson, Christopher Durang, Emily Mann,** and **David Mamet** have written monologues for actors to perform. This sort of one-person performance is simply a part of contemporary playwriting, a way to test supposed requirements of the art form (*is* conflict the essence of drama?); and the one-character play is more likely to be produced, in an era when most theatres are short of funds, than a large-scaled experiment.

The 1980s saw the rise of the autobiographical monologue, its leading practitioner **Spalding Gray,** the WASP from Rhode Island who portrays himself as an innocent abroad in a crazy contemporary world. Storytellers who enact their narratives with vigorous physicality include John O'Keefe, who recreates the hardships of his Iowa childhood and

San Francisco young manhood with exuberant intensity, and Kevin Kling, whose depictions of his Minnesota-based life are both comic and touching. Others, like Gray and Mike Feder, who grew up in Queens and began telling his life on New York radio, pride themselves on their theatrical minimalism, and simply sit and talk. Audiences come to autobiography for direct connection and great stories, both sometimes hard to find in today's theatre.

Heading into the '90s, women **performance artists** have come to the fore, their daring and imaginative pieces often semiautobiographical but also given to flights of poetry or political outrage. Two of the best are over 65: Beatrice Roth, who recollects her Jewish upbringing in a mostly Protestant Pennsylvania town, and **Rachel Rosenthal,** born abroad, whose concerns encompass the earth and its nonhuman inhabitants. **Holly Hughes** is wittily, outrageously, eloquently lesbian; the shamanistic **Karen Finley** breaks sexual taboo. Anna Deavere Smith presents a series of monologues based on personal interviews to explore through impersonation urban racial and class conflict. Laurie Carlos, Robbie McCauley, and Jessica Hagedorn, two black women and a Filipino, find individual ways, even when working together, to convey their particular experience of late 20th-century America. MEO

See: J. S. Gentile, Cast of One: One-Person Shows from the Chautauqua Platform to the Broadway Stage, Urbana and Chicago, 1989; J. R. Young, Acting Solo: The Art of One-Man Shows, Beverly Hills, 1989.

One-Third of a Nation A **Living Newspaper** produced by the **Federal Theatre Project** in 1938. Although it was performed by 10 other units, the New York production was the most famous and was a highlight of the short-lived WPA theatre. Written by **Arthur Arent** and his Living Newspaper staff, the play depicted New York City slums and the poverty and greed that created them. Inspired by Roosevelt's second inaugural address, the production provoked a controversy because it quoted actual politicians and congressional bills. It also featured an imposing 70-ft-tall tenement set designed by **Howard Bay,** which added realistic detail to the plight of the poor and was used dramatically in the first scene to suggest a slum fire. BBW

On the Town Musical comedy with books and lyrics by **Betty Comden and Adolph Green,** and music by **Leonard Bernstein,** based on an idea by **Jerome Robbins;** opened at the Adelphi Theatre on 28 December 1944. Staged by **George Abbott** with choreography by Jerome Robbins, it ran for 463 performances, featuring Sono Osato, Betty Comden, Adolph Green, and Nancy Walker. In two acts and 17 scenes, New York is viewed through three sailors on shore leave. When sailor Gabey sees a picture in the subway of "Miss Turnstiles," he falls in love with her. His two buddies help him search for her in Central Park, Carnegie Hall, and Coney Island. *On the Town*'s themes of patriotism and nationalism proved extremely popular on the American stage in the midst of WW II. A film version (1949) starred Gene Kelly and Frank Sinatra. Comden and Green went on to write many film musicals, including *Singin' in the Rain*. ER

On the Verge; or, The Geography of Learning The premiere production of **Eric Overmyer**'s play (8 January 1985) at Baltimore's **Center Stage** was directed by Jackson Phippin with set design by **Tony Straiges,** costumes by Del Risberg, and music by Paul Sullivan. Stan Wojewodski, former artistic director of Center Stage, chose *Verge* as his opening production as head of the **Yale Repertory** (1991) after stagings in regional theatres throughout the U.S. in the 1980s. In a linguistically rich, magical tour of the comic imagination, three time-traveling Victorian women venture "forward, into the future," assisted by will, intelligence, passion, confidence, courage, and "plot thickener" from 1888 to 1955, when they reach the pinnacle of the future, "Paradise 55." GSA

On Your Toes Two-act musical comedy, music by **Richard Rodgers,** lyrics by **Lorenz Hart,** book by Rodgers, Hart, and **George Abbott;** opened 29 November 1936 at the **Imperial Theatre,** running 315 performances. The chronicle of a former **vaudeville** hoofer (**Ray Bolger**), now a WPA music teacher, who convinces a Russian ballet company to produce his "jazz ballet," it was a milestone in music theatre history for its integration of dance into musical comedy. Choreographer **George Balanchine,** in his first Broadway "book musical," staged two lengthy ballet sequences, both vitally integral to the story. The first-act "Princess Zenobia" was a burlesque of classical ballet, but the jazzy second-act "Slaughter on Tenth Avenue" served as the climactic moment of the plot and has had continued life as a concert piece. The rest of the score provided several standards, notably "There's a Small Hotel." The show has been revived on Broadway twice, most recently in a 1983 production supervised by Abbott and Balanchine, which ran 505 performances and won a Tony Award. JD

Opatoshu (né Opatovsky), David (1918–) Actor and writer who made his debut in *Golden Boy* (Newark, 1938) and on Broadway in *Night Music* (1940). Working in **Yiddish theatre,** Opatoshu also appeared in *Silk Stockings* (1955), *Does a Tiger Wear a Necktie?* (1969), and *The Big Winner* (1974), which he wrote and directed, as well as in regional and Off-Broadway theatres. He wrote the film *Romance of a Horsethief* (1971), and acted in *The Naked City* (1948), *The Brothers Karamazov* (1958), *Exodus* (1960), *Torn Curtain* (1966), and *Who'll Stop the Rain* (1978), and in many television shows. REK

Open Theatre An experimental **Off-Off Broadway** acting company during 1963–73. **Joseph Chaikin** left the **Living Theatre** after playing Galy Gay in Brecht's *Man Is Man* to establish a study group for exploring new styles of acting. This collection of actors, writers, and dramaturges came to be known as the Open Theatre. Chaikin believed that the creative intervention of the performer could lead to a new dramatic expression, and he developed a technique based on the ideas of *presence* (focusing on the performer, not the character) and *transformation* (the actor changing from one role to another before the audience's eyes). This approach is described in Chaikin's book, *The Presence of the Actor*. Open Theatre workshops combined vigorous physical, vocal, breathing, and improvisational exercises with discussions led by critics Gordon Rogoff and **Richard Gilman.** Gradually the group began to work on ensemble creations shaped by a single writer, resulting in *Viet Rock* by **Megan Terry** (1966), *The Serpent* by **Jean-Claude van Itallie** (1968), and *Terminal* by **Susan Yankowitz** (1969). The Open Theatre gave these works full productions and then created some chamber works, including *The Mutation Show* (1971) and *Nightwalk* (1973); but as it edged away from being an acting workshop toward becoming a producing company, it decided to close – in Rogoff's words, it was "doomed to succeed." AS

> See: E. Blumenthal, *Joseph Chaikin,* New York, 1984; R. Pasolli, *A Book on the Open Theatre,* New York, 1970.

Oppenheimer, George (1900–77) Drama critic. After graduating from Williams College (1920), Oppenheimer worked for Alfred A. Knopf (1921), and cofounded Viking Press (1925) before becoming a screenwriter for MGM (1933–49). Beginning in 1955 he wrote the column "Onstage" for *Newsday,* becoming daily critic in 1963 and Sunday critic in 1972. A master of the clever one-liner, Oppenheimer thought much of the 1960s avant-garde theatre formless and obscure. His books include *The Passionate Playgoer* (1958) and his memoirs, *View from the Sixties* (1965). TLM

Orbach, Jerry (1935–) Actor-singer who, after attending the University of Illinois, went to New York to study acting. He appeared in the **Off-Broadway** revival of *The Threepenny Opera* in 1955 and created the role of the Narrator in *The Fantasticks* (1960). A year later he played the embittered puppeteer in *Carnival.* After starring in a number of revivals and straight plays, including the controversial *Scuba Duba* (1967), he returned to the musical stage in *Promises, Promises* (1968), for which he won a Tony. He abandoned his "nice guy" image to star as the shyster lawyer in *Chicago* (1975) and as the perfectionist director in *42nd Street* (1980). MK

Oregon Shakespeare Festival (1935–) The Festival was founded by Angus L. Bowmer in Ashland, OR, to produce Shakespeare's plays in an Elizabethan-style setting. Beginning on a rough, wooden platform, the Festival built the present stage in 1959, modeled largely after John Cranford Adams's reconstruction, with a seating capacity of 1,173 and standing room for 115. In 1970 the Festival opened the new 601-seat indoor Angus Bowmer Theatre to house modern works; and in 1977 the 138-seat Black Swan for more experimental productions. Today, in addition to an eight-month season (10–11 plays) at Ashland, there is also a five-play, six-month season in Portland. Noted for a house style that emphasizes the clarity

Oregon Shakespeare Festival (Ashland). Elizabethan stagehouse designed by Richard L. Hay with dimensions based on the contract of the Fortune Theatre (1599). Photo: Hank Kranzler. Courtesy: Oregon Shakespeare Festival.

and beauty of the text, the Festival has completed the Shakespeare canon twice: for the first time in 1958 with *Troilus and Cressida;* and for the second time in 1978 with *Timon of Athens.* The 1990–1 budget of over $10.6 million supported 16 productions in the three theatres before an audience of more than 420,000. Artistic Directors have included Angus L. Bowmer (1935–71), Jerry Turner (1971–91), and Henry Woronicz (1991–). TLM

Organic Theater Company Nonprofit operation founded in 1969 by Stuart Gordon and fellow University of Wisconsin students. Not long after the forced closing of its partly nude [see **nudity**] production of *Peter Pan,* the company moved to Chicago, where it found temporary quarters at the **Body Politic** before establishing its own spaces on the north side. Populist, often ribald, comedic fantasy typified much of the company's work under Gordon's direction (1969–85). Notable productions include *WARP* (which had a short Broadway run in 1973), **David Mamet**'s *Sexual Perversity in Chicago,* Ray Bradbury's *The Wonderful Ice Cream Suit,* and the collaborative *Bleacher Bums* and *E/R.* SF

Orpheum Theatre 126 Second Avenue, NYC. Opening in 1905 as the Orpheum Concert Gardens, the small theatre quickly switched to movies in 1911 as the Orpheum Moving Pictures Theatre. During the 1920s and '30s, it became renowned for its accompanying **Yiddish** variety shows. For many years, it remained a neighborhood moviehouse. In 1958, it was legitimatized into an **Off-Broadway** theatre and housed several hits under a succession of managements: *Little Mary Sunshine* (1959), a revival of *Anything Goes* (1962), capped by a 5-year run of *Little Shop of Horrors* (1982). MCH

Orpheum theatre circuit Established in 1899 by Morris Meyerfield, owner of **San Francisco**'s Orpheum Theatre, and Martin Lehman, owner of a **vaudeville** theatre in **Los Angeles.** The pair acquired other theatres in West Coast cities, then established a **Chicago** booking office, with Martin Beck in charge. By 1923 Beck booked a circuit of more than 250 theatres in the West from offices in New York. In 1928, the Orpheum circuit merged with the **Keith-Albee** vaudeville theatre chain, dominant in the East, and in 1930, as motion pictures displaced vaudeville, the whole merged with the Radio Corporation of America to form RKO. WD

Osborn, Paul (1901–88) Playwright. Educated at the University of Michigan and Yale, Osborn's best remembered plays are *On Borrowed Time* (1938; revived in 1991 with **George C. Scott**) and *Morning's at Seven* (1939). The former was a touching study of an old man's attempt to cheat death. The latter, although praised by some critics after its brief original production and kept alive in anthologies, had to wait until a 1980 revival to achieve wide acclaim. It took a nostalgic and sometimes bittersweet look at the life of four sisters in an American small town. Most of Osborn's works to reach Broadway were adaptations of novels, such as *A Bell for Adano* (1944), *Point of No Return* (1951), and *The World of Suzie Wong* (1958). His plays provide a *mélange* of characters drawn with skill and affection. LDC

> *See:* E. Lammel, "Paul Osborn: A Professional Biography," PhD diss., Ohio State U, 1973.

Ostrow, Stuart (1932–) Producer, born in New York and educated in music at NYU, who began his career with a failure, *We Take the Town,* which closed during its pre-Broadway tryout. He then produced *Here's Love* (1963), which he also directed; *The Apple Tree* (1966); *1776* (1969), which won the Drama Critics' and Tony awards; *Scratch* (1971); *Pippin* (1972); *Stages* (1978), of which he was also author; *Swing* (1980), of which he was also director; *The Moony Shapiro Songbook* (1981); *American Passion* (1983); **M. Butterfly** (1988); and *La Bête* (1991). Ostrow heads the Stuart Ostrow Foundation for the advancement of musical theatre. TLM

Our American Cousin Englishman Tom Taylor wrote this farce in 1851 as a vehicle for Joshua Silsbee, then performing in England, but it remained unproduced until 1858 when **Laura Keene** staged it in New York. She cast **Joseph Jefferson III** as Asa Trenchard, the aggressive but sympathetic **Yankee** hero, and convinced **Edward A. Sothern** to perform the minor comic role of Lord Dundreary by telling him to "gag" it as he wished. Sothern's Dundreary became the hit – a lisping, hopping, fatuous English lordling, played in a foppish costume, drooping whiskers, and a monicle. The farce concerns the misadventures of Asa in England, where he has arrived to claim Trenchard Manor as an inheritance. Its slight plot has Asa foil the greed of the family's financial agent

E. A. Sothern as Lord Dundreary in *Our American Cousin.* Photo: Heath & Box, London. Courtesy: Laurence Senelick.

and win the heart of a rustic maid. The popular farce gained further notoriety as the play President Lincoln was watching at **Ford's Theatre** when he was assassinated. BMcC

> *See:* R. L. Ray, "A Stage History of Tom Taylor's 'Our American Cousin,'" PhD diss., New York U, 1985.

Our Town by **Thornton Wilder,** produced in 1938 at the **Henry Miller** Theatre in New York, is one of the most famous and most produced plays in the history of American drama. Wilder dispensed with realistic stage conventions and created "Grovers Corners, N.H." with some furniture, ladders, and the narration of a Stage Manager who addresses the audience directly. The play chronicles the daily lives of the residents of a rural community in the years prior to WW I, and its simplicity created a vivid impression on both audiences and critics. It ran for 336 performances and won the Pulitzer Prize. In 1940 a film version with Martha Scott as Emily and music by Aaron Copland further enhanced its popularity. In subsequent years *Our Town* has been revived in thousands of professional and amateur productions. It was performed by American soldiers in Italy during WW

Thornton Wilder's *Our Town* (Morosco Theatre, 1938). Photo: Vandamm. Courtesy: Theatre Collection, Museum of the City of New York.

II, by countless high schools and **community theatre**s, and in a television musical adaptation with Frank Sinatra. Significant New York revivals include a 1959 production at **Circle in the Square** directed by **José Quintero** (385 performances), an "all-star" version at the **American National Theatre and Academy** (ANTA) in 1969 with **Henry Fonda** as the Stage Manager, and a 1988 **Lincoln Center** production directed by **Gregory Mosher** with **Spalding Gray** as the Stage Manager. BBW

Outdoor drama This phenomenon could be considered a late phase of the American civic **pageantry** movement, gaining impetus in 1937 with **Paul Green**'s *The Lost Colony,* a retelling of the story of the first English colonization effort by Walter Raleigh on Roanoke Island, staged in Manteo, NC. These works, many written by Green, Kermit Hunter, William Hardy, or Allan Eckert, are sometimes called "symphonic dramas" and usually recount some notable historical event of a specific region or locale, combining drama, dance, music, and spectacle. More than half of these productions pay, in full or part, staff and cast members (some with **Actors' Equity** contracts). The dramas are staged during the summer months and have annual repeats (often for many years). In recent years as many as 70 outdoor dramas (including religious pageants, outdoor Shakespearean productions, etc.) have been presented, a number celebrating runs of nearly 50 years (the total number of historical/symphonic dramas is closer to 26 in 13 states). Among the most celebrated examples of the latter variety (with the year and location of their inaugural season) are (in addition to *The Lost Colony*): *The Common Glory* (1947, Williamsburg, VA), *Faith of Our Fathers* (1950, Washington, DC),

Unto These Hills (1950, Cherokee, NC), *Wilderness Road* (1955, Berea, KY), *The Stephen Foster Story* (1959, Bardstown, KY), *Texas* (1966, Canyon, TX), *The Trail of Tears* (1969, Tahlequah, OK), and *Trumpet in the Land* (1970, Dover, OH).

Much of the impetus for the outdoor drama movement came from the Department of Dramatic Art at the University of North Carolina, Chapel Hill, where Frederick Koch founded the Carolina Playmakers, originally dedicated to instructing students in the techniques of writing and producing plays focused on regional sections of the South. Green participated in theatre activities under Koch in the 1920s and helped perpetuate the interest in outdoor drama after he became a philosophy professor at North Carolina in the 1930s. In 1963, when it became burdensome for the Department of Dramatic Art to serve as a conduit for information on outdoor drama, the Institute for Outdoor Drama was established. The Institute (University of North Carolina at Chapel Hill, CB# 3240, NCNB Plaza, Chapel Hill, NC 27599) continues to serve as a source of stimulation, advice, and information. DBW

See: G. McCalmon and C. Moe, *Creating Historical Drama,* Carbondale, IL, 1965; W. Spearman, *The Carolina Playmakers,* Chapel Hill, NC, 1970; M. Summer, *A Selected Bibliography on Outdoor Drama,* Chapel Hill, NC, 1979.

Overmyer, Eric (1951–) Colorado-born playwright who served as Literary Manager of **Playwrights Horizons** (1983–4) and Associate Artist at Baltimore's **Center Stage** (1983–91). Fascinated with language, he was a favorite playwright of 1980s regional theatres. His plays include *Native Speech* (1983), **On the Verge; or, The Geography**

of Learning (1986), *In a Pig's Valise* (1986), *In Perpetuity Throughout the Universe* (1988), *Don Quixote de La Jolla* (1990), *The Heliotrope Bouquet by Scott Joplin & Louis Chauvin* (1991), and *Dark Rapture* (1992). His work has won him grants from the McKnight, LeComte Du Nuoy, and Rockefeller Foundations, and The New York Foundation for the Arts. GSA

Owens, John Edmond (1823–86) Liverpool (England)-born actor and manager who came to Philadelphia in 1828, began as a supernumerary at **Burton**'s National Theatre (1841), quickly graduated to speaking roles, and then played in all the principal American cities and in London (1865). He bought and managed the Baltimore Museum (1849–52), made his New York debut (1851) as Uriah Heep in **John Brougham**'s adaptation of *David Copperfield,* and in 1864 appeared as the "**Yankee**" Solon Shingle in **Joseph Jones**'s *The People's Lawyer* – the role for which he became best known and which prompted the critics to speak of his "merry temperament, his exuberant and incessant glee."
RM
See: M. Owens, *Memories of the Professional and Social Life of John E. Owens,* Baltimore, 1892.

Owens, Rochelle (1936–) Playwright and triple Obie winner who creates her own cultural anthropology complete with myths, ritual, chants, and symbols in her experimental, **Off-Off Broadway** plays. Her highly controversial play *Futz* (1967, Obie; revived in 1991 at **La MaMa**) is a tragicomedy relating the sexual love of a man and his pig and the violent, demented response of his repressed neighbors to his sodomy. Owens continued to explore perversity, violence, and sexuality as responses to the conflict of individual primal impulse with a self-righteous society in such plays as *Beclch* (1967) – an example of Theatre of Cruelty with its depiction of savagery and depravity; *Istan-*

John E. Owens as Solon Shingle in *The People's Lawyer.* Photo: J. Gurney & Son, N.Y. Courtesy: Laurence Senelick.

boul (1965); *Kontraption* (1970); *He Wants Shih* (1975); *Chucky's Hunch* (1981); and two surreal historical biographies – *The Karl Marx Play* (1973) and *Emma Instigated Me* (1977). FB

Pacific Overtures Two-act musical play, music and lyrics by **Stephen Sondheim,** book by John Weidman; opened 11 January 1976 at the **Winter Garden Theatre,** running 193 performances. Perhaps the most daring of the 1970s **Harold Prince**–Stephen Sondheim collaborations, *Pacific Overtures* traces the opening of Japan to the West from the Japanese point of view, focusing on the tension between tradition and modernization as represented by Manjiro (Sab Shimono) and Kayama (Isao Sato). Performed by an all-Asian (and, until the final scene, all-male) cast, Prince's production was highly stylized and used a wide range of Japanese staging devices, particularly Kabuki, brilliantly melded in **Boris Aronson**'s spectacular scene design. Similarly, Sondheim's score drew on a wide range of Japanese theatre-music styles, enhanced by Japanese instruments, which became progressively more "westernized" as the play progressed. The show, which won the Drama Critics' Circle Award for best musical, was revived Off-Broadway in 1984 and by the English National Opera in 1988.   JD

Pacino, Al (1940–) Actor who studied with **Lee Strasberg** and is a member of the **Actors Studio.** Pacino made a strong impression on stage in the late 1960s playing jittery, violent low-life New Yorkers, **Off-Broadway** in *The **Indian Wants the Bronx*** (1968), and in his Broadway debut as a drug addict in *Does a Tiger Wear a Necktie?* (1969). His naturalistic style proved ideal for film (*The Godfather, Serpico, Scarface*). In his periodic returns to the stage, Pacino has tried with limited success to overcome the typecasting of his films. His *Richard III* (1973) was brave though unavoidably contemporary. He was more comfortable as **Tennessee Williams**'s Everyman in the 1970 **Lincoln Center** revival of ***Camino Real;*** as the nonentity swept up by the Vietnam War in the 1977 revival of The ***Basic Training of Pavlo Hummel*** (Tony); and as a wheezing, shuffling, pinch-voiced crook with a battery of tics in a revival of **David Mamet**'s ***American Buffalo*** (1982). In summer 1992 he appeared in two plays in repertory at **Circle in the Square:** Wilde's *Salomé* and Ira Lewis's *Chinese Coffee.*   FH

See: A. Yule, *Life on the Wire,* New York, 1991.

Page, Geraldine (1924–87) Missouri-born actress who attended the **Goodman Theatre** Dramatic School (1942–5) in Chicago before making her New York debut in the Blackfriar's Guild production of *Seven Mirrors* (1945). **José Quintero** cast her as Alma in the **Off-Broadway** production of ***Summer and Smoke*** at the **Circle in the Square** (1951–2) to rave reviews, establishing her career. Her Broadway debut as Lily in *Midsummer* (1953) again received critical acclaim; **Wolcott Gibbs** in the *New Yorker* praised her "charm and pathos and almost matchless technique." Her later work included Lizzie in *The **Rainmaker*** (1954); Alexandra del Lago in ***Sweet Bird of Youth*** (1959); Olga in *The Three Sisters* (1964); Baroness Lemberg in *White Lies* and Clea in *Black Comedy* (1967); Marion in *Absurd Person Singular* (1974); and Mother Miriam Ruth in *Agnes of God* (1982). From 1983 she was a member of the Mirror Theatre Company. Her husband was actor **Rip Torn.**

While Page appeared too often in neurotic roles, she was a versatile actress capable of a wide emotional range. Her Alexandra del Lago provoked **Brooks Atkinson** to eloquence: "Loose-jointed, gangling, raucous of voice, crumpled, shrewd, abandoned yet sensitive about some things that live in the heart, Miss Page is at the peak of form in this raffish characterization." Her numerous film appearances included *Summer and Smoke* (1961) and **Woody Allen**'s *Interiors* (1978). In 1986 she won an Academy Award for her portrayal of Carrie Watts in *The Trip to Bountiful* (her eighth Oscar nomination).   TLM

Pageants/pageantry Refers to a widespread phenomenon from 1908 through the 1920s of secular scripted spectacles for seated audiences, instrumental in development of regional theatres, university-based performing arts programs, utilization of American thematic material, and new techniques of creative expression in music, theatre, and dance. Initiated by a community to celebrate an important historical event or person, they differed from conventional plays in comprising three to seven self-contained episodes covering 200–2,000 years. Introduced by a spoken prologue, they concluded with a colorful "march past," integrating vocal and orchestral music, expressive and symbolic movement, group panto**mime,** poetry, and dialogue throughout. Performances usually took place **outdoor**s on a site symbolic of the event or person, though armories and schools were also used. Audiences numbered 2,000–80,000; participants included as many as 5,000 on stage and no fewer than 200 in preparation and production.

Community committees were established for funding, publicity, costuming, stage design, and historical research. The pageant master was hired

Women's Suffrage Allegory, written and staged by Hazel Mackaye on the steps of the Treasury Building, Washington, DC, 3 March 1913. Courtesy: Brown University Library.

months in advance. Budgets were in the range of $10,000–100,000; pageant master salaries were $1,000–2,000, dance directors $500, and music commission or performance $2,000–6,000. Wealthy community members were asked to guarantee backing if the pageant was not self-sustaining, and sometimes boards of trade or state, city, or local agencies supplied seed funding. Productions were often repeated several times within a period of a few weeks related to specific historic celebrations, but were not designed for commercial gain or further performance. Tickets were usually 25¢–$2, with free tickets often available.

Written and organized by Progressive era reformers (settlement workers, civic leaders, playground organizers, suffrage activists, and innovators in education and the arts), pageants were designed to entertain and educate, and reflected multiple forces in early 20th-century America, including urbanization, escalated immigration, and corporate control in economic and political spheres. Pageantry's legacy comes to us through the work of several individuals who saw the form in the broad context of society's needs.

George Pierce Baker, Frederick Henry Koch, and Thomas Wood Stevens developed **academic theatre** programs at Harvard and Yale (Baker), the Universities of North Dakota and North Carolina (Koch), and Carnegie Institute of Technology (Stevens) while actively writing and directing pageants. They passed on to their students the belief in theatre as a creative and moral force in daily life and the need for American playwrights to develop indigenous thematic material. They also utilized their pageant work to explore the integration of music, poetry, dance, and new lighting and staging techniques. Among their students were **Eugene O'Neill, Sidney Howard,** Agnes Morgan, **Paul Green,** Munroe Pevear, **Theresa Helburn, Robert Edmond Jones,** John Reed, **Heywood Broun,** Thomas Wolfe, **Hallie Flanagan,** and Frederick McConnell.

Percy MacKaye lectured and wrote extensively on pageantry as an essential component of democracy through the educated participation of individuals in the life of the community, creating "art of the people, by the people, for the people." His major ideas are encompassed in three books: *The Playhouse and the Play* (1909), *The Civic Theatre* (1912), and *A Substitute for War* (1915). His sister Hazel was active in pageantry and made pageants a powerful tool for women's suffrage. William Chauncy Langdon, who published many articles on pageantry in popular magazines during the time he was a professional pageant master, was instrumental in spreading the idea of theatre as an essential component of community life and instrument for social change.

Pageantry was seen as a respectable form of theatre, and women assumed significant roles as writers and directors. Mary Porter Beegle not only created several acclaimed pageants but also was instrumental in making expressive dance an integral part of the university curriculum, as part of pageantry courses and as a separate entity. With Jack Randall Crawford she coauthored *Community Drama and Pageantry* (1916), which has extensive pioneering material analyzing dance as a creative form. Other women active as pageant masters were Lotta Clark, Gertude Colby, Margaret McLaren Eager, **Constance D'Arcy Mackay,** Mary Wood Hinman, and Virginia Tanner.

The American Pageant Association was created in 1913, and through 1921 issued bulletins and organized meetings focused on various aspects of pageants and masques. By the late 1920s pageants became standardized and scripts had very little artistic merit; the image of America as land of the free, home of the brave espoused by many of the writers was an image tarnished when juxtaposed with existing conditions. NP

See: D. Glassberg, *American Historical Pageantry*, Chapel Hill, NC, 1990; N. Prevots, *American Pageantry*, Ann Arbor, 1990.

Paid in Full Eugene **Walter**'s first major success opened at the Astor Theatre 25 February 1908 for 167 performances. One of the earliest dramas to tour for revision, the play drew great attention in spite or because of its controversial portrayal of a young wife nearly coerced into prostituting herself to advance her ruthless young husband's business career. Criticized as melodramatic and seamy, the play avoids several melodramatic devices when the wife saves herself from degradation, recognizes her husband's ruthlessness, and chooses to leave him. She then emerges as the strongest character in the work. The play produced a strong effect, though actually antimelodramatic. The impact of the play attracted the attention of **David Belasco,** resulting in his later collaboration with Walter on *The Easiest Way.*   RW

Paint Your Wagon Two-act musical comedy, words and music by **Alan Jay Lerner and Frederick Loewe** (respectively); opened 12 November 1951 at the **Sam S. Shubert Theatre,** running 289 performances. Lerner and Loewe's excursion into period Americana tells of a widowed prospector (**James Barton**) whose land, when gold is discovered, becomes a boomtown until the gold runs out. The gold-rush setting provides an occasion for hoedown production numbers, and a touching sentimentalism is added by the prospector's habit of talking to his dead wife and by his ultimate death. The score occasionally descends into bathos ("I Still See Elisa"), but also evokes both Western optimism (the rousing title number) and emptiness (the haunting "They Call the Wind Maria").   JD

Pajama Game, The Two-act musical comedy, music and lyrics by **Richard Adler and Jerry Ross,** book by **George Abbott** and Richard Bissell; opened 13 May 1954 at the **St. James Theatre,** running 1,063 performances. Based on Bissell's novel *7 1/2 Cents,* the story tells of the romance between a management superintendent (**John Raitt**) and an activist worker (Janis Paige) amid a threatened strike in a pajama factory. Director George Abbott wanted **Jerome Robbins** to choreograph, but Robbins wanted to direct and assigned the choreography to **Bob Fosse,** who made his Broadway choreographic debut on this show. Fosse's most notable contribution was the staging of "Steam Heat," which became his seminal signature piece. Other notable hits from the show include "Hey, There" and "Hernando's Hideaway." It won the Tony Award for best musical and had a successful London production. The 1957 film version, with many of the stage cast, reproduced much of the original staging.   JD

Palace Theatre   The legendary mecca for **vaudeville** performers, this New York theatre was built by Martin Beck, who then had to turn over 75% of the stock to **Edward F. Albee** for permission to use **Keith** Circuit acts; Albee in turn paid **Oscar Hammerstein [I]** $225,000 for the rights to offer Keith acts in that neighborhood. Located at Broadway and 47th St., the theatre, which seated 1,800, opened on 25 March 1913 and, after a slow start, gained popularity with the booking of Sarah Bernhardt. "Playing the Palace" was the ambition of every American variety act, although names did not go up in lights until 1928. The record bill was for a nine-week teaming of **Eddie Cantor** and George Jessel in 1931. On 7 May 1932, the Palace

became a four-a-day theatre – the live performance mingled with newsreels and cartoons – and on 16 November turned into a five-a-day cinema; this date marks the official death of vaudeville as a dominant entertainment form. After a period as a **burlesque** house and a brief revival of vaudeville in 1950, the Palace was converted into a theatre for musical comedy in 1965; in 1987 it closed for extensive renovations, reopening in April 1991 with the musical *The **Will Rogers** Follies.*   LS

See: M. Spitzer, *The Palace,* New York, 1969.

Pal Joey Two-act musical play, music by **Richard Rodgers,** lyrics by **Lorenz Hart,** book by John O'Hara; opened 25 December 1940 at the **Ethel Barrymore Theatre,** running 374 performances. A musical of major historical import, *Pal Joey* follows the adventures of Joey Evans (Gene Kelly), an unscrupulous womanizing nightclub singer in Chicago who dumps his good-hearted girlfriend (Leila Ernst) for Vera (**Vivienne Segal**), a wealthy older married woman. After she tires of him, the curtain falls on Joey, unrepentant, pursuing another fresh young thing. The show was recognized as an important departure, but its immoral, self-serving central characters were very controversial. Not until a 1952 Broadway revival, which ran 542 performances and won the Drama Critics' Circle Award for best musical, was *Pal Joey* fully appreciated. Beyond the many intentionally tacky **nightclub** numbers, the score produced two enduring standards: Joey's insincere song of seduction "I Could Write a Book" and Vera's contemplative "Bewitched, Bothered, and Bewildered." It also included, well before *Oklahoma!,* a dream ballet, choreographed by Robert Alton, at the end of Act I.   JD

Palmer, A[lbert] M[arshman] (1838–1905) Theatrical manager who first entered the business in 1872 as comanager of the **Union Square Theatre** with Sheridan Shook. Although trained as a lawyer and without theatrical background or experience, he established a reputation as one of the leading managers of his time, with a keen business sense and cultivated theatrical tastes. During his 10-year tenure at the Union Square, he improved both the quality of the acting company and production standards. He also fostered the production of contemporary (particularly American) drama, often commissioning new plays, translations, and adaptations. In 1883, following a dispute with Shook, he left the Union Square; however, he subsequently managed the **Madison Square Theatre** during 1884–91. In 1888, he secured control of **Wallack's Theatre,** renaming it Palmer's, and in 1891 he moved his famous Madison Square **stock company** to this theatre.

Unlike **Daly** and **Frohman,** Palmer was not a "star maker," but he did promote the careers of numerous actors and actresses, including **Agnes Booth, Richard Mansfield, W. H. Crane,** Maurice Barrymore [see **Drew–Barrymore**], **Clara Morris,** and **James O'Neill.** Among his more notable productions of American plays were **Bronson Howard's** *The **Banker's** Daughter* (1878),

Bartley Campbell's *My Partner* (1879), **Clyde Fitch**'s *Beau Brummel* (1890), **James A. Herne**'s *Margaret Fleming* (1891), and **Augustus Thomas**'s *Alabama* (1891). He also produced plays by Henry Arthur Jones, Oscar Wilde, W. S. Gilbert [see **Gilbert and Sullivan**], and a popular dramatization of Du Maurier's *Trilby* (1895). Palmer was also among the first American managers to pay foreign authors royalties for the performance of their plays, and he was a major force in the founding in 1882 of the **Actors' Fund of America**. [See also **Introduction**, §2.] DJW

> *See:* P. Ryan, Jr., "Albert M. Palmer, Producer," PhD diss., Yale U, 1959.

Palmo's Opera House see **Burton's Chambers Street Theatre**

Pan Asian Repertory Theatre Founded in 1977 by artistic director **Tisa Chang**, this **Off-Off Broadway** group is the vital New York link in the **Asian-American theatre** network. Intended as a major showcase for the talents of professional Asian-American artists, it is committed to producing contemporary Asian-American authors, translated Asian masterworks, and multicultural adaptations of Western classics. This eclectic mandate has yielded such noteworthy productions as *Teahouse,* Lao She's drama about 50 years of modern Chinese history; R. A. Shiomi's *Yellow Fever,* a wry twist on the hard-boiled detective genre; *Shogun Macbeth,* a Japanese reworking of the classic tragedy; plus works by **David Henry Hwang**, Momoko Iko, **Philip Gotanda**, and a collaboration with experimental director **Ping Chong**. Though much of the work has had an East Asian slant, in the 1990s it broadened to include plays with South Asian and Southeast Asian themes (*Gandhi, Cambodia Agonistes*). MB

Pantomime see **mime and pantomime**

Paper Bag Players, The Founded in 1958 by Judith Martin, this is one of America's best known and most imaginative children's theatre companies. Its format of short skits has influenced other companies to experiment with subject matter, style, and form. The "Bags" deliberately eschewed elaborate costumes and sets in favor of uniform garments, adding accessories as needed. Props are moved on- and offstage by the four actors. The composer-accompanist works with the group to develop original scripts. NMcC

Paper Dolls by Elaine Jackson. This drama was first produced January 1983 by the Richard Allen Center for Culture and Art in New York. Part **minstrel show** and part **vaudeville**, it is a searing look at how society has framed the standard of beauty for black women. Two aging beauty queens rewrite their history, targeting painters, the film industry, and beauty pageants, to change the perceptions of black woman. KME

Papp (né Papirofsky), Joseph (1921–91) Director and producer; founder of the **New York Shakespeare Festival** in 1954. Starting as a Broadway and CBS-TV stage manager (1952–60), Papp began the Shakespeare Theatre Workshop on NYC's Lower East Side in 1953. After *Cymbeline* (1954) and *The Changeling* (1956), Papp continued to direct occasionally for NYSF: *Twelfth Night* (1958, 1963, 1969), *Hamlet* (1964, 1967, 1968, 1983), **Rabe**'s *In the Boom Boom Room* (1973), **Babe**'s *Buried Inside Extra* (1983), and *Measure for Measure* (1985). For television, he directed *The Merchant of Venice* (1962), *Antony and Cleopatra* (1963), and *Hamlet* (1964). During 1973–7, Papp ran Lincoln Center's **Vivian Beaumont and Mitzi E. Newhouse Theatres.** In 1990 he appointed **JoAnne Akalaitis** his artistic associate and hired three young staff directors, easing away from the Festival's daily operation. By mid-1991 he had retained the title "producer" but was no longer involved with the actual running of the NYSF, having appointed Akalaitis artistic director several months before his death in October 1991.

In 1958, Papp, "driven . . . to create theater without regard for . . . cost or human interference," received a Tony for Distinguished Service to Theatre. That year, he refused to identify left-wing artists for the House Committee for Un-American Activities, causing problems later when he proposed taking productions into city schools. Frequently taking chances, Papp advocated creative freedom, saying, "If this theatre isn't being criticized for being too extreme, there's something wrong." In 1990 he rejected $748,000 from the National Endowment for the Arts because of its restrictive antiobscenity pledge. In 1988 he became the first recipient of the William Shakespeare Award for Classical Theatre from the **Shakespeare Theatre** at the Folger. He also received Equity's 1987 **Paul Robeson** Award. REK

> *See:* C. King and B. Coven, eds., *Joseph Papp and the New York Shakespeare Festival: An Annotated Bibliography,* New York, 1988; S. W. Little, *Enter Joseph Papp: In Search of a New American Theater,* New York, 1974. A book by Mel Gussow on Papp and the NYSF is forthcoming.

Paradise Lost by **Clifford Odets**. Produced in 1935 by the **Group Theatre**, it ran for only 73 performances and disappointed most critics, who compared it unfavorably to *Awake and Sing!* **Harold Clurman** was director, **Boris Aronson** designer. A rambling story of family life and work in the Depression, it provided a variety of interesting character roles for the company actors, thus illustrating the ensemble approach that was forging together. Though realistic in its social setting and characters, it has qualities that tend toward symbolic typology and rhetorical flourish. Occasionally revived by companies around the country (such as Baltimore's **Center Stage** in 1987–8), it reveals that the initial response was perhaps too harsh. TP

Parichy, Dennis (1938–) Lighting designer associated with the new poetic realism of writers like **Tina Howe** and **Lanford Wilson**, he is considered one of the best creators of mood, time, and place through light in the contemporary theatre. He has done over 50 productions with the **Circle**

Repertory Theatre and numerous shows with **Manhattan Theatre Club** and the **New York Shakespeare Festival,** as well as on Broadway. Productions include *Burn This, Talley's Folly, Crimes of the Heart, Coastal Disturbances,* and *As Is.*   AA

Paris Bound This comedy of manners by **Philip Barry** captured popular audiences with its glib style and serious subject, marital infidelity. Opening at the **Music Box Theatre** on 27 December 1927, produced and directed by **Arthur Hopkins** and designed by **Robert Edmond Jones,** this play presents a wealthy six-year marriage that theoretically claims openness and trust, though an apparent affair nearly wrecks the family. Interestingly, both marriage partners, Mary and Jim Hutton (played by Madge Kennedy and Donn Cook), suffer at the thought of a spouse involved with another, yet both avoid confrontation and all ends happily without the expected showdown. In Barry's greatest success until *Holiday,* he demonstrated some of his most scintillating dialogue, especially among partying supporting characters, which enthralled his critics and audiences.   RHW

Parker, Dorothy (Rothschild) (1893–1967) Author and critic who, after writing for *Vogue* and *Vanity Fair* in the 1910s, began her long association with Harold Ross's the *New Yorker* in 1925, contributing sharp and witty dramatic reviews for the rest of her career. She founded the Round Table at the Algonquin Hotel, which brought together in the 1920s New York's sharpest wits, including **Robert Benchley,** Ross, **George S. Kaufman,** and James Thurber. While the author of more than 20 screenplays, eight plays or revues, four books of poetry, and three collections of short stories, she is best remembered for her witty one-liners.   TLM

See: M. Meade, *Dorothy Parker,* New York, 1987.

Parker, H[enry] T[aylor] (1867–1934) Drama critic. Born in Boston and educated at Harvard, H. T. (as he was called) served as the New York correspondent for the *Boston Transcript* (1892–8, 1901–3), and later covered London for the *Transcript* and *New York Commercial Advertiser* (1898–1900). He became dramatic and music critic for the *New York Globe* (1903–5) and for the *Transcript* (1905–34), establishing his reputation as one of the most perceptive and influential critics of his generation. Parker had no equal in capturing the essence of a production in a few well-turned phrases.   TLM

Parks, Hildy (De Forrest) (1926–) Producer, writer, actor. A stage and television actor (1945–58), Parks, with her third husband, **Alexander Cohen,** resuscitated the **Antoinette Perry** (Tony) Awards ceremonies by producing them as television extravaganzas (1967–86) written by Parks, with annual themes that sell Broadway – like her "Welcome Home" show (1974) featuring television stars who began on Broadway. They have also produced shows in New York and London, including *Baker Street* (1965), *Anna Christie* (1977), and *I Remember Mama* (1980). Parks has written and produced other celebratory shows for television, and won Emmys for the "Tonys" (1980) and "Night of 100 Stars" (1982).   TH-S

Parks, Suzan-Lori (1963–) African-American playwright. A graduate of Mount Holyoke College, Parks was named in 1989 "the year's most promising new playwright" by **Mel Gussow** in the *New York Times.* She won an Obie for her play *Imperceptible Mutabilities in the Third Kingdom* – a dreamlike exploration of the black experience – produced at BACA Downtown, Brooklyn. In 1990 BACA also produced *The Death of the Last Black Man in the Whole Entire World,* which Parks calls "a requiem mass in the jazz aesthetic." Her one-act *Betting on the Dust Commander* (1991) was presented at the Working Theatre on **Theatre Row,** Manhattan.   EGH

Park Theatre 21–25 Park Row, NYC [Architect: Joseph Mangin]. In 1795, tired of the deteriorating and déclassé **John Street Theatre,** a group of prominent New Yorkers subscribed money to erect a new theatre in an area that promised to become the heart of the early 19th-century city. Three years later, it opened as the New Theatre in an unfinished state. The unattractive exterior belied a comfortable and handsome interior, which was designed continental-style with three tiers of boxes overhanging a U-shaped pit, and a gallery above the highest tier. The first managers were actors **John Hodgkinson** and **Lewis Hallam,** who moved their John Street company into the new house.

Painting of Park Theatre interior by John Searle (November 1822). Courtesy: New-York Historical Society, NYC.

William Dunlap was added to the management, and he succeeded them as sole manager for several years until forced into bankruptcy in 1805. The house, by then known as the Park, was bought by John Jacob Astor and John Beekman, who eventually leased it in 1808 to **Stephen Price.** Credited with introducing the "star system" to American theatre practice, Price bolstered flagging box office receipts by importing English stars and managing their tours. In 1810, he brought over **George Frederick Cooke,** and in 1820 lured Edmund Kean to America. Because he spent so much time in England, Price left actor **Edmund Simpson** in charge of the theatre during his absences. In 1820, the Park burned to its exterior walls, but was rebuilt the following year. For more than a decade, the Park established itself as the first theatre in the land with an outstanding resident company. In addition to English stars, it helped to create such American stars as **Edwin Forrest** and **Charlotte Cushman.** In its last decades, the high status of the Park was eclipsed, and Simpson was forced to place meretricious fare on its stage. In 1848, **fire** again consumed the house, and the Astor heirs replaced it with commercial buildings.   MCH

Parsons, Estelle (1927–) Actress, best known for her brash Academy Award–winning performance in *Bonnie and Clyde* (1967) and her recent TV appearances as the mother of "Roseanne." Parsons prefers theatre, which she considers an actor's medium, to film, which she feels belongs to directors and editors. With her sharp nasal voice and lived-in face, Parsons sounds and looks refreshingly real; and though she was trained in **Lee Strasberg**'s method of psychological realism she has eagerly sought work in other styles, from Shakespeare to musical theatre. Her richest parts on Broadway have been as **Tennessee Williams**'s dotty, good-natured stripper in *The Seven Descents of Myrtle* (1968); as the alcoholic title character in ***And Miss Reardon Drinks a Little*** (1971, revived 1990); in the **Public Theater**'s *Pirates of Penzance* (1981); and as the caustic, deranged, dictatorial schoolteacher in Roberto Athayde's *Miss Margarida's Way* (1977), a virtuoso **one-person** show in which she fenced improvisationally with the audience. Her experiments Off-Broadway and regionally include **Brecht**'s *Mahagonny* (1970), **June Havoc**'s *Tintinnabulation of the Bells* at the **Actors Studio** (1975), Lady Macbeth at the University of Hawaii (1980), and another one-woman extravaganza, Dario Fo's *Orgasmo Adulto Escapes from the Zoo* (1983).   FH

Participatory theatre Environmental theatre of the 1960s and early '70s – concerned with social and political issues and sexual repression, often urging audience involvement, and invariably taking itself very seriously – has given way in the 1980s and '90s to a new, less intimidating, escapist form of participatory theatre. From mystery trains in the Midwest and New England, to mystery weekends, Renaissance fairs, and role-playing events such as *Dungeons and Dragons* or *Assassin,* to satiric cabarets in New York and Los Angeles, this phenomenon has spread throughout the U.S. Prime examples include *Shear Madness,* a mystery comedy with audience members as questioners, which ran in Boston 11 years and had long runs in Chicago and Washington, DC; *Forbidden Broadway* in several editions in Boston and New York since 1982; *Tony n' Tina's Wedding* (1987, New York; restaged in five other cities), where the audience travels from the marriage ceremony to a restaurant reception; *Tamara,* a Canadian import that leads patrons through a villa in dramatizing its story of sex and intrigue (seven years in Los Angeles as of 1991; two and one-half in NYC); *Song of Singapore* (1991), a lavish entertainment (with slim plot) designed by **John Lee Beatty** that evolved over eight years; *Forever Plaid* in New York (1990) and Boston; and *Pageant,* a 1991 **Off-Broadway** offering in which audience members judge six beauty contestants (played by men) in an effective commentary on the packaging of women and coopting of their images by society.   DBW

Pasadena Playhouse Founded in 1917 by Gilmor Brown and incorporated in 1918, the Pasadena Playhouse grew into an important theatre institution. Brown depended upon amateur talent and volunteer help. He built a new theatre in 1925, adding a school for training actors in 1928 and an intimate Playbox Theatre in 1929. Premieres of new works, including **O'Neill**'s *Lazarus Laughed* (1928), and revivals of seldom-produced classics made the Playhouse famous. Beginning in 1935 it offered a series of Midsummer Drama Festivals that attracted wide attention. The theatre gained a reputation as a showcase for aspiring film actors, with Randolph Scott, **Tyrone Power,** and Robert Young among the stars discovered. Brown served 31 years as President and retired as director of the Playhouse in 1959. After it closed in 1970, the Playhouse was designated a historical landmark, renovated, and reopened in 1985, with Paul Lazarus III as artistic director since 1990. The facility was heavily damaged by a 1991 earthquake.   TLM

Pastor, Tony (Antonio) (1837–1908) Variety performer and manager, called "The Father of Vaudeville." The son of a theatre violinist, he made his professional debut in 1846 as an infant prodigy at **Barnum's American Museum.** He later traveled as a **circus** clown, **minstrel,** and ballad singer, with a repertory of some 1,500 songs, arranging concerts in small towns. He first booked variety into the rowdy American Theatre, at 444 Broadway, New York (1861), and, determined to attract a respectable audience, took over the Volksgarten at 201 Bowery in 1865. Renaming it the Opera House, Pastor advertised it as "The Great Family Resort" and invited women and children to special matinees; but even door prizes of turkeys, hams, and barrels of flour were insufficient to attract a God-fearing public. The fat man with the waxed mustache and mincing step moved his clean bill of variety to 585 Broadway in 1875, where he introduced the theatre checkroom, and then to 14th Street in 1881. There he finally succeeded in promoting clean **vaudeville** to a family audience, paving the way for **Keith** and **Albee;** performers he sponsored include **Nat Goodwin, Lillian Rus-**

sell, and **Weber and Fields.** A devout Catholic who kept a shrine backstage, he continued to pay low salaries, lost his stars to sharper managers, and died a relatively poor man.   LS

See: P. Zellers, *Tony Pastor: Dean of the Vaudeville Stage,* Ypsilanti, MI, 1971.

Patinkin, Mandy (1952–   ) Actor-singer who attended Juilliard and then spent several years playing supporting roles for the **New York Shakespeare Festival.** Possessed of a fine tenor voice, he received a Tony Award for his performance as Ché Guevara in **Evita** (1980). He created the role of Georges Seurat in **Sondheim**'s musical *Sunday in the Park with George* (1984), appeared in the British musical *The Knife* at the **Public Theater** (1987), and played Archibald Craven in *The Secret Garden* (1991). He has also appeared on Broadway in the **one-person** show *Mandy Patinkin in Concert: Dress Casual* (1989).   MK

Patrick, John (1905–   ) Prolific playwright who has been a favorite among American regional theatres, dinner theatres, and amateur groups. His two best remembered Broadway successes both grew out of WW II: *The Hasty Heart* (1945) told the touching story of an obstreperous Scottish soldier dying in a field hospital filled with a comic group of recuperating soldiers, representing most of the Allied armies, tended by a sympathetic nurse. *The Teahouse of the August Moon* (1953) pictured the foibles of an attempt to Americanize an Okinawan village. Regional and amateur groups also continue to revive *The Curious Savage* (1950) and *Everybody Loves Opal* (1961). Patrick lives in the Virgin Islands, where he writes two or three plays a year for companies seeking light, entertaining comedies.   LDC

Paulding, James Kirke (1778–1860) is significant in American theatre for two reasons. Writing about "American Drama" for the *American Quarterly Review* (1827), he urged a carefully supported "National Drama." His play, *The Lion of the West* (1830), won a prize from **James H. Hackett.** From its conventional plot involving lost relations and international characters, as revised by **John Augustus Stone,** Hackett created a substantial vehicle with Colonel Nimrod Wildfire, a humorous imitation of Davy Crockett. As *A Kentuckian Trip to New York in 1815,* the play was adapted by **William Bayle Bernard** for English audiences in 1833. Paulding also wrote *The Bucktails; or, American in England* (publ. 1847).   WJM

See: A. Herold, *James Kirk Paulding: Versatile American,* New York, 1926.

Pawley, Thomas D., III (1917–   ) African-American educator, play director, and playwright. After completing doctoral studies at the University of Iowa, Pawley embarked on an outstanding career as a professor of theatre at traditionally black colleges. Since 1940 he has been on the faculty of Lincoln University, Jefferson City, MO. He has written 11 plays, the most outstanding being *The Tumult and the Shouting* (1969), about a dedicated

teacher rejected by the system toward the end of his career. Pawley has served on numerous regional and national professional organizations and is coauthor with William Reardon of *The Black Teacher and the Dramatic Arts,* 1970.   EGH

Payne, Ben Iden (1881–1976) British director, educator, and actor. A full career in the British theatre (actor with Frank Benson, director of the Abbey Theatre, Manchester's Gaiety Theatre, the Shakespeare Memorial Theatre, etc.) was balanced with over 50 years in the U.S. During 1913–34 he directed such prominent actors as **John Drew** and **Helen Hayes,** acted, and began teaching. During 1919–34 he taught at Carnegie Institute, returning there in 1943 after a decade in England to head Drama and develop his "modified Elizabethan staging"; subsequently he worked at many universities, most notably the University of Texas (1946–73), which named its main theatre after him in 1976. During 1949–61 he directed at the **Old Globe** (San Diego) and the **Oregon Shakespeare Festival.** His autobiography, *A Life in a Wooden O,* was published in 1977.   DBW

Payne, John Howard (1791–1852) Actor and playwright. Now remembered for the lyrics to "Home, Sweet Home!" (music by H. R. Bishop) in his *Clari, the Maid of Milan* (London's Covent Garden, 1823), he wrote or translated and adapted from the French some 60 plays. Among the best known are *Brutus; or, The Fall of Tarquin* (with Edmund Kean, London's Drury Lane, 1818; with **Edwin Forrest** in New York, 1829); *Thérèse; or, The Orphan of Geneva* (Drury Lane, 1821; with Forrest in New York, 1829); *Clari;* and two collaborations with **Washington Irving** – *Charles II; or, The Merry Monarch* (Covent Garden, 1824); and *Richelieu* (Covent Garden, 1826). In spite of close friendships with Irving, Coleridge, Lamb, and (in Paris) Talma, who encouraged him to translate French melodramas – and in spite of his occasional appearances as an actor and one season as manager of London's Sadler's Wells (1820) – Payne's years abroad (1813–32) were marked by financial distress: Twice he was confined to debtor's prison.

Payne made his acting debut as Young Norval in Home's *Douglas* (New York's **Park Theatre,** 1809), appeared as Hamlet and Romeo, quickly became known as "Master Payne, the American Roscius," and was favorably compared with "Master Betty."

His writing debut had come earlier with little magazines: *The Fly* (coedited with **Samuel Woodworth,** 1804); *Thespian Mirror* (1805); and his first play *Julia; or, The Wanderer* (1806).

In 1842 President Tyler appointed Payne Consul at Tunis (a reward for his crusade on behalf of the Cherokee Indians), where he served until 1845 and again from 1851 until his death.   RM

See: G. Overmyer, *America's First Hamlet,* New York, 1957.

Peabody, Josephine Preston (Marks) (1874–1922) Poet and playwright who wrote historical

Peg O' My Heart with Laurette Taylor (second from left), 1912. Photo: White, N.Y. Courtesy: Theatre Collection, Museum of the City of New York.

plays in verse, beginning with *Fortune and Men's Eyes* (1900) and *Marlowe* (1901). In 1910 she won the $1,500 Stratford-on-Avon Memorial Prize for *The Piper,* based on the story of the Pied Piper of Hamelin. Her later plays were *The Wolf of Gubbio* (1913) and *Portrait of Mrs. W* (1922). Although her plays were not commercial successes, they were important for continuing the tradition of verse drama. FB

> *See:* C. Baker, ed., *The Diary and Letters of Josephine Preston Peabody,* New York, 1925.

Peg o' My Heart Tested out of town, **J. Hartley Manners**'s blockbuster hit for his actress-wife **Laurette Taylor** opened at New York's **Cort Theatre** 20 December 1912 and ran for 604 performances. It played for a year in London, had eight companies simultaneously on tour during the 1914–15 season, and logged nearly 6,000 performances by 1918. Taylor's Peg was much celebrated, and she performed it over 1,000 times, trapped in the role of the Irish waif (she escaped 32 years later with Amanda in **Glass Menagerie**). Manners is remembered for little else than this sentimental comedy–drama of a half-orphaned heiress who, initially spurned by her aristocratic relations, wins their approval, the hero's heart, and the fortune by play's end. RKB

Pemberton, Brock (1885–1950) Born and raised in Kansas, Pemberton was first a journalist who gravitated to New York to work as a drama critic, eventually for the *Times* (1911). He resigned in 1917 to assist director **Arthur Hopkins,** becoming a full-time producer with *Enter, Madame.* He next produced **Miss Lulu Bett,** which won the Pulitzer Prize in 1920. Another major success was Pirandello's *Six Characters in Search of an Author* in 1923. Other shows included Sturges's *Strictly Dishonorable* (1929); **Clare Boothe [Luce]'s** *Kiss the Boys*

Goodbye (a 1938 hit); and his biggest success, **Harvey,** the 1944 Pulitzer Prize winner.

In addition to numerous articles, Pemberton wrote summaries of Broadway seasons for the *Times.* President of the League of New York Theatres (among many other leadership positions), he had a generous nature and outspoken manner (he was an early opponent of the **Federal Theatre Project**) and won respect in all branches of the profession. SMA

Pendleton, Austin (1940–) Ohio-born actor, director, and teacher, educated at Yale University (BA, 1961), who made his New York debut as the henpecked Jonathan in **Kopit**'s absurdist farce **Oh Dad, Poor Dad . . .** (1962). His slight build and buck-toothed profile have ensured many related roles on and **Off-Broadway:** the tailor, Motel, in **Fiddler on the Roof** (1964), Irwin in *Hail, Scrawdyke* (1966), Leo in *The* **Little Foxes** (1967), and Isaac in *The Last Sweet Days of Issac* (1970), earning him Obie, Drama Desk, and **Clarence Derwent** awards. Both as an actor and a director, Pendleton also works at prominent regional theatres, such as **Williamstown,** the **Long Wharf,** and the **Tyrone Guthrie.** Among his directorial achievements is his 1974 staging for the **Manhattan Theatre Club** of Milan Stitt's *The Runner Stumbles,* which transferred to Broadway. CLJ

Penn, Arthur (1922–) Director who began his career as an actor, studying with **Michael Chekhov** and debuting in New York in 1940. In 1958 he directed his first Broadway show, **William Gibson**'s *Two for the Seesaw,* which he also directed in London the same year. Among his other directing credits are *The Miracle Worker* (1959), **Toys in the Attic** and Tad Mosel's *All the Way Home* (1960), **Golden Boy** (1964), and *Wait Until Dark* (1966). Other credits include *Felix* (1972), *Sly Fox* (1976), and *Golda* (1977). Penn has also directed many films, including *The Left-Handed Gun* (1957), *The Miracle Worker* (1962), *Bonnie and Clyde* (1968), and *Little Big Man* with **Dustin Hoffman** (1970). SMA

Penn (Jillette) (1955–) and **Teller** (1947?–) **Performance art**ists and magicians who first teamed in 1975 as part of an act called "Asparagus Valley Cultural Society," which ran for two and a half years in **San Francisco.** They appeared **Off-Broadway** in 1985 and then received rave reviews on Broadway in 1987. Their 1991 "Refrigerator Tour" culminated in their "Rot in Hell" show at the **John Houseman** Theatre. Called by one critic "hilarious hustlers," Penn (6′ 6″ and very talkative) and Teller (5′ 9″ and mute) are known for their idiosyncratic approach to magic, replete with plenty of madness, mayhem, and bizarre humor. Their apparent exposure of magical effects has gained resentment from some in the magic community, yet they have enlivened the stage **magic** show for a new generation.   DBW

See: C. Trillin, *American Stories,* New York, 1991.

Perelman, S[idney] J[oseph] (1904–71) Humorist, occasional playwright, and one of the U.S.'s greatest erudite wits. After two **Marx Bros.** screenplays in the 1930s, he collaborated with Ogden Nash on the book for **Weill**'s *One Touch of Venus* (1943) and wrote his only well-known Broadway play, *The Beauty Part* (1962).   DBW

Performance art Combines elements from the visual, verbal, and performing arts, popular culture, and daily life to introduce the artist's body as a formal art medium, an ideological construction, and a political agent. While performance artists are often trained in one or several artistic traditions, and may use video and slides or film projections, performance art is at its roots antiart. A performance art work can occur anywhere and be of any duration. It can also be entirely conceptual and exist only in the mind. Central to the history of performance art are the emergence of artistic practices that both deconstruct the "body" as a political sign and as object, and antiaesthetic and critical positions toward material culture and institutions. Wearing the body as a mask, or using it to resist institutional control and market consumption, performance artists become sites for visual self-representation and reflection, conceptual figuration, political agency, and narration.

The inception of American performance art in the 1960s was in part a response to global shifts of power due to U.S. foreign policy, and an outgrowth of public protests surrounding U.S. involvements abroad. It also coincided with a destabilization of prevailing modernist assumptions that had the individual firmly positioned within time and space. Since the 1960s, domestic racial struggles, the rise of the women's movement, gay liberation, and **AIDS** activism, however, have called these assumptions into question.

Intending social change and attempting to revise 18th-century standards of excellence in art that continued to shape modernist aesthetics, performance artists problematized a Kantian-derived formalism and the modernist primacy of vision. Deploying the theatricality of daily life – resistance, confrontation, and disruption – they challenged their political reality. Sit-ins, peace marches, and riots served as structural and ideological models for the arts activism and interventionist practices of performance artists.

As a revisionary art form and political art movement, performance art is conceptually and strategically linked to Platonic antitheatrical prejudices against representation and illusion; the history of revolutionary social movements; the subtext of social realism basic to historical avant-garde art movements; and to the anarchy in Japanese Butoh and the naturalism in Gutai. From the 1940s to the '60s, Marcel Duchamp, John Cage, Jackson Pollock, **Allan Kaprow,** and Claes Oldenburg linked the international avant-garde with American idioms, such as Abstract Expressionism, Minimalism, Pop Art, and Conceptual Art, finally to create a distinct, yet evolving, American performance art practice and aesthetic.

Duchamp and Oldenburg represented the commodity value of the body and the art object. Cage's and Kaprow's performances promoted a Zen-inspired art practice of relaxed "attention." These approaches advocated the dissolution of linear time, the rupture of traditional narrative structures, the use of nontraditional theatre and art spaces, the merging of art with life, decentering the position of the artist as director, and dissolving oppositional relations between performers and spectators.

Some women artists in the late 1960s and early '70s confronted issues of sexual discrimination in art and in their lives. To free themselves from oppression and define a place of their own, they used their bodies and the structures of their daily lives as tools with which to politicize and *de*-naturalize women's bodies in the private and public spheres.

Carolee Schneemann's early **feminist** performance, *Naked Action Lecture* (1968), where she continuously undressed and dressed while she showed and discussed slides of her visual art work, reframed the political and art historical debates about voyeurism and male fantasies raised in *Site* (1964), an early minimalist performance by Robert Morris, in which Schneemann had been posed as the artist's model, finally revealing her reclining center stage like Manet's *Olympia,* nude except for a black choker. In *Naked Action Lecture,* Schneemann repositioned herself against the spectator and the nature of voyeuristic pleasure.

Site shared the problem of representing male–female relationships with Yoko Ono and John Lennon's "Bed-Ins" (1969), **Linda Montano**'s *Three Days Handcuffed with Tom Marioni* (1973), and **Tehching Hsieh**'s *Art/Life One Year Performance* with Montano (1983–4). These partnering performances insisted on the political dimension of space and body – the core issue of 1970s and '80s feminist performance art, and one also addressed in performances by men.

Ablutions (1972), a collaborative project about rape by Judy Chicago, **Suzanne Lacy,** Aviva Rahmani, and Sandra Orgel, based on oral histories collected by Lacy and Chicago, represented metaphors of violence against women, aimed so as to effect women's reempowerment. In this work, cathartic autobiography and self-scrutiny was developed as an important survival tool and community-building strategy.

Ablutions set the stage for later pageantlike women's performances – Chicago's *Dinner Party* (1973–9), Lacy's *Crystal Quilt* (1987) – and anticipated the collaboration of groups such as the Waitresses, the Guerilla Girls, and the V-Girls. It prefigured such autobiographical performances as Lynn Hershman living as Roberta Breitmore (1973–8); or Robbie McCauley's *Sally's Rape* (1989–90), the story of McCauley's great-great-grandmother's struggle to survive as Thomas Jefferson's slave and mistress; and **Adrian Piper**'s ongoing performance of *My Calling Card (to be handed out at cocktail parties)* (1986–present), which directs a cool but pointed rage against racism.

During the 1970s male artists began to identify with the victimization usually attached to female roles, and produced performances such as **Chris Burden**'s *Shoot* (1971), **Vito Acconci**'s *Conversions* (1971), Tom McCarthy's *Sailor Meat* (1974), and Tehching Hsieh's "Cage" performance (1978–9). Such work foregrounded the artist's often conflicted position toward formations of power, among other issues. While these artists explored the margins of their sexuality, the relationship between aggression and their fear of death, they also confronted their bodies as objects – probing their humanity and their objecthood.

In *Trappings* (1971), Acconci staged an "occasion for self-sufficiency by dividing [himself] in two." He cradled his penis like a baby, spoke to it as a playmate, and covered it with cloth. In *Seedbed* (1972), he hid from spectators and while sexually arousing himself amplified his (orgasmic) voice into the gallery space, forcing spectators to participate vicariously in his autoerotism. Through an inversion of voyeurism, *Seedbed* addressed processes of seduction, dispersal, the exhaustion of the body, and self-empowerment.

By the 1980s performances like *Naked Action Lecture, Seedbed,* and *Ablutions* had raised issues about the body and representation that would become the focus of major postmodernist theoretical and artistic debates. One of the most prominent participators in this debate, **Laurie Anderson,** projected her media-consumed body onto the proscenium stage. Speaking at times in a "masculine" and "authoritarian" voice, other times as if a girls choir, Anderson sent her "O Superman" (1980s) voice through electronic filters and loops, and played with a dimpled smile for *and* against technology's seduction, "Hold me mom, in your long arms, in your automatic arms, your electronic arms . . ."

Unlike 1960s and '70s performances that explored the liminal space between art and life, emerging 1980s cabaret art genres were cross-overs from mainstream entertainment. They replaced both art and life with serial and digitized encounters from MTV, phone sex, and the 11 o'clock news. Remakes of popular culture, vaudeville, B-movies, and soaps were reedited into "queer theater" and "talent shows," or recycled into "living film

serials" (e.g., **John Jesurun**'s *Chang in a Void Moon,* 1982–8), or "dyke noir" plays (e.g., **Holly Hughes**'s bawdy solo performances and her scripts for *Well of Horniness* and *Dress Suits for Hire*).

Mixing essentialist identities with difference, urban environments, and border cultures generated styles of "third world" trash and chic. Club performers like Carmelita Tropicana, the Alien Comic, Michael Smith, John Kelly, and **Ethyl Eichelberger** took their cues from film and television stock characters and melodramas. Others, like **Eric Bogosian** and John Cale, were indebted to theatrical traditions and to classical **nightclub** entertainers, such as stand-up comics **Lenny Bruce** or Karl Valentin.

The success of early 1980s performances at NYC's East Village clubs was limited by the required profit margins of club managers, the clipped attention span of audiences raised on 24-hour TV, and white middle-American family values. Appropriating both censorship and apathy through a dialectic of rage and redemption, performance artists, such as **Karen Finley** (as "Ass Man," 1985) or Martha Wilson (as "Nancy Reagan," 1984–8), parodied the Pollyannish rhetoric of the American Way. Wilson/Reagan for example, advocated anorexia as a cure for world hunger and blamed "Ronny's" presidential failures on his "bad scripts."

By the end of the 1980s, Reaganomics and gentrification had closed cabaret doors. Performance artists were turning to mainstream stages, or, like Laurie Anderson, being absorbed by popular culture. The California-based performance group, Survival Research Lab, replaced the human body with a self-destructing scrap metal machine. James Luna re-presented his **Native American** body at San Diego's Museum of Man (1986) and at the Studio Museum in Harlem (1990) as an "Artifact" and as a site for political agency.

Art activist performers (e.g., Guillermo Gómez-Peña and **Jimmie Durham,** and activist **collectives** (e.g., The Border Arts Workshop, the Los Angeles Poverty Department [LAPD], and AIDS ACT UP) have survived Reagan's years by holding on to the "body" with a vengeance. Senator Jesse Helms's 1990–1 **censorship** campaign and the performance artists who explicitly address the endless range of human bodies in their work have raised the "body" to national discussion. Current trends in performance art are covered in *The Drama Review* and *High Performance* (a quarterly). AF

See: A. Bronson and P. Gale, *Performance by Artists,* Toronto, 1979; L. Champagne, *Out from Under: Texts by Women Performance Artists,* New York, 1990; R. Goldberg, *Performance Art,* New York, 1988; M. Tucker, *Choices: Making an Art of Everyday Life,* New York, 1986; R. Moira, ed., *The Amazing Decade: Women and Performance Art in America,* Los Angeles, 1983.

Performance Group, The One of the most controversial and visible of the environmental theatre groups of the 1960s and '70s; formed in New York City in 1967 by **Richard Schechner,** critic, director, and editor of *The Drama Review.* Although in practice the work of the Group often seemed amateurish and self-indulgent, Schechner

broke through traditional barriers of a text- and stage-bound theatre with productions such as *Dionysus in 69* (1968), *Makbeth* (1969), *Commune* (1970), and Genêt's *The Balcony* (1979). Schechner's ideas were codified somewhat in his book on *Environmental Theatre* (1973). Though only partially successful, Schechner's group, performing in the Performing Garage in Wooster Street, was notable for its risk-taking, its concern with social issues, and (with some direct influence from Grotowski) its investigation into ritual and the use of other cultures in the development of a new performance art. Schechner left the Garage in 1980, and the Group, renamed the **Wooster Group,** has continued under the nominal leadership of **Elizabeth LeCompte.**
DBW

Periodicals/serials Between 700 and 800 periodicals or magazines devoted to the American theatre have come and gone since 1798; a definitive number is difficult to ascertain because many disappeared after a few issues, some after one. General magazines have been part of the French and English worlds of letters since the 17th century, and many contained news of the stage; but the first successful American example did not take hold until Benjamin Franklin's weekly *General Magazine* (founded in 1741), which did *not* report theatrical news.

In 1798, the *Thespian Oracle; or, Monthly Mirror, Consisting of Original Pieces and Selections from Performances of Merit, Relating Chiefly to the Most Admired Dramatic Compositions and Interspersed with Theatrical Anecdotes* appeared in **Philadelphia,** but did not survive its first issue. Theatrical news was reported sparingly in the principal newspapers of **Boston,** New York, and Philadelphia, but lingering prejudices against the theatre and the turbulence of the times politically (both in the late colonial and early republic periods) precluded anything more than announcements of performances, sometimes paid for by the trouping companies themselves.

In 1831, the weekly *Spirit of the Times,* part newspaper and part magazine, was founded in New York, combining theatrical and sporting news; it endured until 1902. In 1853, another weekly, the ***New York Clipper*** became the *Spirit*'s principal rival, and it, too, included news of the playing fields. It supplemented its weekly editions with a sporting and theatrical annual, which recorded **Charlotte Cushman**'s stage triumphs with records of aquatic, track and field, and horse-racing feats. In 1924, the *Clipper* was absorbed by *Variety,* sans its sports pages.

The last important 19th-century theatrical weekly was the ***New York Dramatic Mirror,*** which began publication in 1879 and survived until 1922 without the customary sports coverage. In 1881, the *Mirror* was acquired by the 20-year old theatre-fixated **Harrison Grey Fiske.** Under his aegis the magazine found a *cause célèbre* in the emergence of the Theatrical **Syndicate,** and from 1896 until 1911, when he left the weekly, Fiske crucified the trust and its evil geniuses in every issue.

The *Spirit,* the *Clipper,* and the *Mirror* carried play reviews, commentaries, biographies, personal notices, obituaries, advertisements, feature articles,

and editorials on the theatre and performers. They also included illustrations – usually drawings of performers and buildings – and, occasionally, cartoons. Although quartered in New York, they were national publications, which was reflected in their coast-to-coast coverage.

The phenomenon of theatrical publishing remains *Variety,* a weekly that was founded in 1905 by Sime Silverman to report news of the **vaudeville** world. Silverman expanded its coverage to include "legit," and his successors have kept the publication alive by focusing on the dominant entertainment medium at any given moment. Silverman created for it a special journalistic argot full of ellipses, abbreviations, and Broadway colloquialisms, which has become its trademark. Although *Variety* devotes a few pages to theatre both in New York and around the country, its emphasis today is on movies and television.

Theatre, the magazine of record for the peak years of the American stage, appeared in 1900, and was edited throughout most of its existence by **Arthur Hornblow.** Changed to *Theatre Magazine* in 1917, it was a monthly magazine dedicated to the stage and stage folk and profusely illustrated. Chromolithographs of stage stars adorned the covers of its first issues, which were followed later by color photographs once it became possible to transfer them to the printing process. Eventually news of the movie world usurped an increasing number of pages, and when it ceased publication in 1931 it was more a casualty of a diminished theatre, shrinking audiences, and changing tastes than a victim of the Depression.

Two magazines, **Theatre Arts** and *The Stage,* grew out of the art theatre movement. Founded by **Sheldon Cheney,** *Theatre Arts* was launched as a quarterly sponsored by the Detroit Society of Arts and Crafts in 1916. It moved to New York and, under the leadership of **Edith Isaacs,** went monthly in 1923, changing its focus in the 1930s to the commercial theatre. In 1923, the still-experimental **Theatre Guild** brought out an occasional publication, *Theatre Arts Bulletin,* which gradually appeared quarterly and then monthly. In 1932, it was enlarged both physically and editorially as *Stage* and was liberally illustrated. In 1939, with both magazines near bankruptcy, they were merged as *Theatre Arts Magazine,* which continued publication until 1964.

Theatre Arts represents the last of the significant broad-based theatre magazines. Current survivors target specific audiences: *Theatre Crafts,* founded in 1967, covers technical aspects of professional and university theatre; *American Theatre,* a creation of **Theatre Communications Group** in 1984, reflects events of regional theatres throughout the country; *Playbill Magazine,* a monthly version of the Broadway theatre program, simply omits show credits; *Theater Week,* published since 1987 as a tabloid, aims mainly at the New York audience; and a variety of other publications are issued by learned societies (see Bibliography at the end of the Guide). MCH

See: M. C. Henderson, *Broadway Ballyhoo,* New York, 1989; C. Stratman, *American Theatrical Periodicals,* Durham, NC, 1970.

Perkins, Osgood (1892–1937) Stage and film actor noted for his versatility and polish. Perkins graduated from Harvard in 1914 after having participated in some of the **George Pierce Baker** plays. After serving in WW I, he formed the Film Guild, a cinematic production company, and appeared in several of its productions. **Winthrop Ames** then cast him as Homer Cady in *Beggar on Horseback,* his Broadway debut; **Jed Harris** next hired him for *Weak Sister.* Perkins later starred as Walter Burns in *The Front Page* (1928) and played Astrov in *Uncle Vanya* (1930). He also appeared in films such as *Scarface* and *Madame Du Barry.* He was described as "wiry, nervous, [and] unerring in his attack." Perkins's son, **Anthony (Tony) Perkins,** of *Psycho* fame, enjoyed a highly successful stage and film acting career, including stage appearances in *Look Homeward, Angel, Greenwillow, The Star-Spangled Girl, Equus,* and *Romantic Comedy.* SMA

Perry, Antoinette (1888–1946) Actress, producer, director, and activist. Following her 1905 Chicago debut, she acted in New York until her 1909 marriage to socially prominent businessman Frank Frueaff. After his death, she returned to the stage in 1924, acting under **Brock Pemberton,** then assisting him, and finally directing such successes as *Harvey* (1944). As chair of the American Theatre Council's Apprentice Theatre (1937–9), she inaugurated and conducted 5,000 auditions to encourage young talent. In 1941 she was president of the Experimental Theatre. She held leadership positions with the Stage Relief Fund, the Actors Thrift Shop, and the American Theatre Wing and its Stage Door Canteen. The annual Antoinette Perry (Tony) Awards, named for her, commemorate her extraordinary service to the theatre. FHL

Peters (née Lazzara), Bernadette (1948–) Singer, dancer, and actress. After singing and dancing for several years in Broadway choruses, beginning with the 1959 revival of *The Most Happy Fella,* she achieved critical recognition in the 1930s spoof *Dames at Sea* (1968). She appeared in *George M.* (1968) and the revival of *On the Town* (1971), then starred as silent-movie comedienne Mabel Normand in *Mack and Mabel* (1974). She played in *Sunday in the Park with George* (1984), won a Tony Award for her performance in *Song and Dance* (1985), and created the role of the witch in *Into the Woods* (1987). MK

Peters, (Charles) Rollo (1892–1967) Designer and actor. From the 1920s through the '40s Peters was known as a romantic actor, frequently playing opposite **Jane Cowl.** He was also one of the important figures of the New Stagecraft movement and a founder of the **Theatre Guild.** He began acting with the **Washington Square Players** and designed all their early sets. With the Theatre Guild he designed and acted in *Bonds of Interest* and *John Ferguson,* among others. One of his most notable settings was for **Minnie Maddern Fiske**'s production of *Madame Sand* (1917). AA

Petit Théâtre de Vieux Carré, Le New Orleans's oldest performing arts organization was founded in 1916 as one of America's earliest "Little Theatres." It soon purchased its present property, a Spanish colonial structure built in 1797 in the French Quarter; later renovations added a 450-seat auditorium and a smaller children's theatre. The theatre currently produces six main-stage plays and musicals each season, plus two children's series, and is home to the **Tennessee Williams**/New Orleans Literary Festival. LAB

Petrified Forest, The by **Robert Sherwood.** In a superb production directed by **Arthur Hopkins,** this play opened at the **Broadhurst Theatre** on 7 January 1935. Capturing the spirit of the 1930s, with arguments over Marxist ideology and the down-and-out, the play combined the excitement of American gunfights with the uplift of newfound purpose – even if that resolve results in assisted suicide to effect the dreams of a young, spirited woman, Gabby (Peggy Conklin). In an isolated gas station/diner in the wilds of Arizona, Alan Squier, a wandering failed writer (Leslie Howard), finds an unlikely kindred spirit in a fugitive killer, Duke Mantee (Humphrey Bogart). Appropriately, Squier, if killed, requests burial in the Petrified Forest – a symbol both of lost souls like Alan and of the useless wishes of Gabby's father, who perpetuates outworn images of what it means to be American. RHW

Philadelphia Colonial Philadelphia's theatre history was marked by conflict between Quaker-led religious opposition and the more liberal viewpoint represented by the British crown. Strolling players were noted in 1724, and the next year comedians performed at the "new Booth in Society Hill." In 1749 actors led by **Walter Murray and Thomas Kean** rented a warehouse owned by a former Quaker, William Plumstead. The only play known to have been performed was Addison's *Cato.* The Common Council voted to suppress this "disorder" in January 1750, so Murray and Kean moved on to New York.

Plumstead's Warehouse (center), Philadelphia, 1749. Courtesy: Hoblitzelle Theatre Collection, University of Texas at Austin.

Lewis Hallam's company arrived in 1754. Despite opposition, Plumstead's building on the waterfront at Pine Street again served as a playhouse. Under special license from the royal governor, the company successfully gave 30 performances before heading for Charleston. **David Douglass** brought Hallam's company back to Philadelphia in 1759. A new governor gave him a permit to construct a simple theatre on Society Hill, just outside the city's jurisdiction. The company played for six months, beginning with *Tamerlane* on 25 June. This was the longest, most brilliant season thus far in America.

In 1766 Douglass built the **Southwark,** at South and Apollo Streets, considered the first permanent theatre in America. Again located just beyond the city limits, it opened 12 November 1766. Here Douglass was successful enough to return nearly every winter until 1773. The first American tragedy, *The Prince of Parthia* [see **Introduction, §1**] by Thomas Godfrey, Jr., was presented at the Southwark on 24 April 1767.

During the Revolution the Continental Congress banned plays and other entertainments; the occupying British Army, however, mounted plays at the Southwark in 1777–8. Restrictions against plays were still in force when Douglass's stepson Lewis **Hallam,** Jr., came to the theatre in 1785 with lectures, music, and songs. Finally in 1789 prominent citizens successfully petitioned the Pennsylvania Legislature to repeal these laws. Hallam's Old **American Company** responded by offering 15 legal play performances before continuing its tour.

Two years later Alexander Reinagle and **Thomas Wignell** began to raise money from the city's leading citizens to build a new theatre in the center of town. The **Chestnut Street Theatre** (1794) was considered the most handsome playhouse in the country, with the finest **stock company.** Recruited mainly in England, the company also toured to Baltimore, Washington, DC, and Alexandria.

On 9 April 1793 equestrian John Bill Ricketts opened America's first **circus,** along with a riding academy. The circular wooden building, with its single dirt ring, stood near the State House and across the street from the Chestnut Street Theatre; it burned in 1799. A new circus building was begun in 1808 at 9th and Walnut Streets, opening as the New Circus on 2 February 1809. Variety acts were part of its program, and by 1812 a stage was added for a new acting company. The circus became first the Olympic and finally the **Walnut Street Theatre.**

The Chestnut Street Theatre, under the able management of **William Warren the elder** and **William Wood,** withstood the competition. It burned in 1820 [see **fires**], but was rebuilt and active when the **Arch Street Theatre** opened in 1828. Rivalry among the three theatres almost proved fatal, but they reorganized and survived. Although subsequent changes in management and policies eventually helped diminish Philadelphia's status as the country's premier theatrical city, the theatres were able to maintain solid stock companies, occasionally augmented by guest stars.

Philadelphia remained a vital theatrical and cultural center. A group of mid-19th-century playwrights, known as the "Philadelphia School," included **Robert Montgomery Bird** and **Richard Penn Smith.** A century later would come Pulitzer Prize winners **George Kelly** and **Charles Fuller.** America's most important early stage stars built careers in or came from Philadelphia: **Edwin Forrest, Charlotte Cushman,** and **Joseph Jefferson.** Among later stars were the **Drew–Barrymores:** not only actor sibs Lionel, Ethel, and John Barrymore, but their grandmother, Mrs. John Drew, who managed the Arch Street Theatre during 1861–92.

In 1876 Mrs. Drew's theatre was one of the first in the city to drop the stock company in favor of a combination house that booked individual productions. During her era at the Arch, Philadelphia's theatrical scene had expanded and diversified. By 1880 there were nine legitimate theatres, five variety houses, two minstrel halls, and a theatre for German plays.

Philadelphia became a leading **minstrel** center. In 1853 Sam Sanford gave the city its first all-minstrel theatre; but the most important was the 11th Street Opera House, opened by Sanford in 1855. He was succeeded there by the Carncross and Dixey Minstrels, and then by Frank Dumont's Minstrels in 1895. The final show there, 13 May 1911, ended its 56-year record as a minstrel house. Although popular for another decade, minstrels had to compete with **vaudeville,** especially the family shows at **B. F. Keith**'s Theatre (1902).

By the 1920s Philadelphia had become an important tryout town: A convenient 90 miles from Times Square, it had several large downtown playhouses attracting a sophisticated and discriminating audience. The theory was that if a show could survive in Philadelphia, it would have a long run on Broadway. This theory often proved correct, and the city took pride in its favored position.

Over a 50-year period, circumstances of geography and tradition created a dependence on the vitality of the Broadway stage. When times were hard in New York, there were fewer tryouts and road shows coming through Philadelphia. Also, the city was unable to maintain a significant professional showcase for Shakespeare, the classics, and contemporary drama. These factors contributed to the early rise and continued popularity of Little Theatre [see **community theatre**] groups. Plays and Players (1911) is one of the country's oldest theatre **clubs,** and still operates its own playhouse on Delancey Street. The Society Hill Playhouse has been producing since 1959. By 1960 there were 100 amateur community and college companies in the city and surrounding area producing over 400 plays per season.

Inspired by Jasper Deeter's **Hedgerow Theatre,** the Theatre of the Living Arts (1965–9) made a noteworthy but short-lived attempt at professional resident repertory. During the 1970s, with dwindling competition from Broadway shows, amateur theatres had the opportunity to develop into professional resident companies. The Philadelphia Drama Guild (1959) turned professional in 1971, and 20 years later maintains a subscription audience of over 19,000. The Philadelphia Theatre Company

(1974) gained full Equity status in 1981. The more avant-garde Wilma Theatre (1973) became professional in 1983 and is planning a new playhouse.

Having survived several restorations, the Walnut Street Theatre was made a National Landmark in 1968 and its interior modernized. It is considered the "oldest theatre in continuous use in the English-speaking world." A resident company was formed there in 1982; with 33,033 subscribers in 1990, it had the largest mainstage subscription base of any resident theatre in America.

As of 1990 Philadelphia's thriving theatre scene included 24 **resident nonprofit professional theatre** companies, plus many amateur and youth groups. Although only four large downtown theatres remain, the University of Pennsylvania's Annenberg Center (1971) also provides space for a variety of performances, including those of the Philadelphia Festival Theatre for New Plays (1981).
GD

See: I. R. Glazer, *Philadelphia Theatres, A–Z,* New York, 1986; R. D. James, *Old Drury of Philadelphia* [1800–35], Philadelphia, 1932, and *Cradle of Culture, 1800–1810,* Philadelphia, 1957; T. C. Pollack, *The Philadelphia Theatre in the Eighteenth Century,* Philadelphia, 1933; *Theatre Arts* 44(2) (1960); A. H. Wilson, *A History of the Philadelphia Theatre, 1835 to 1855,* Philadelphia, 1935.

Philadelphia, Jacob (né Jacob Meyer) (1721–c. 1800) Conjuror, the son of Polish Jews, and the first American-born **magic**ian to gain international acclaim. He acted as a scientific jester for William Augustus, Duke of Cumberland, performing mathematical and physical experiments. After the Duke's death in 1765, he went public, traveling through Europe billed as "An Artist of Mathematics." He gained the reputation of a true sorcerer who could pass through doors, grow a second head, and read minds.   LS

Philadelphia Story, The Following seven unsuccessful years, this play confirmed **Philip Barry**'s reputation as master of polite comedy, lasting 417 performances from its 28 March 1939 opening at the **Sam S. Shubert Theatre.** The play details the romantic awakening of spoiled, aristocratic Tracy Lord, who achieves emotional security and returns to her former husband following a harmless interlude with a reporter assigned to cover her second wedding. The lack of complication was offset by sophisticated innuendo, such as an implicit nude swim, and, more important, by dialogue that retains its cleverness. By design, the comedy showcased **Katharine Hepburn,** who shared a 75% investment with Barry and Howard Hughes. The play's complete triumph also resolved one of several financial crises for the **Theatre Guild,** which had supplied the remaining backing.   RW

Photographers Although photography in the form of daguerrotypy had been introduced in America shortly after being officially recognized as Louis Daguerre's invention in France in 1839, the value of the photograph to the theatre was not fully comprehended until the arrival of Jenny Lind in America in 1850. Wherever she traveled on her tour, Madame Lind posed for local photographers, and the resulting daguerrotypes were collected avidly by her admirers. By the time the daguerrotype was supplanted by the paper photograph, collecting likenesses became a national mania.

Performers, recognizing the publicity value of portrait photographs, became eager to comply with a request for a picture. Two sizes of photographs were particularly favored: Both the small *carte-de-visite* and the larger cabinet photograph were hawked by street peddlers, stocked in bins at photography shops, inserted as advertisements in candy, cigarette, soap, and corset boxes, and sold through mail-order catalogs.

The first photographer to make a specialty of taking celebrity pictures was Napoleon Sarony. Operating in a 19th-century studio crammed with curios located in his heyday in the Union Square theatrical district, he photographed hundreds of show people, posing them with a special flair against exotic backgrounds. Sarony had imitators in New York and throughout America as the specialty grew. One of his competitors, Benjamin Falk, claimed to have taken the first onstage dramatic scene in America in 1883 at the **Madison Square Theatre.**

After Sarony, photographic studios took over theatrical photography. With improved techniques for indoor photography, the Byron Studio, founded in 1888, began to record productions regularly for producers, who, by this time, knew the value of the scene still. Byron was followed by the White Studio, which, in turn, was succeeded by the Vandamm Studio. The Vandamms held sway over Broadway theatrical photography for more than 30 years. Eventually, the Vandamms' perfectly composed shot was supplanted by the freer candid or instant photography practiced by Eileen Darby and the Friedman–Abeles Studio and, more recently, by Martha Swope, whose camera continues to dominate the field. From Sarony to Swope, the New York theatre has been blessed with an unparalleled and unbroken iconographic record.
MCH

See: S. Appelbaum, ed., *The New York Stage: Famous Productions in Photographs,* New York, 1976; B. L. Bassham, *The Theatrical Photographs of Napoleon Sarony,* Kent, OH, 1978; M. Henderson, *Broadway Ballyhoo,* New York, 1989.

Piano Lesson, The by **August Wilson.** This Pulitzer Prize–winning drama on black life in America opened at the **Walter Kerr** Theatre 16 April 1990 after beginning at **Yale Repertory Theatre** and touring several regional theatres. Directed by **Lloyd Richards** and featuring Charles S. Dutton and S. Epatha Merkerson, the play is set in Pittsburgh during the 1930s, and tells the story of a young man's attempt to sell a family piano to buy land on which his ancestors were slaves. The piano has great meaning, however, for his sister, and in the argument that follows, Wilson makes a

August Wilson's *The Piano Lesson* at the Walter Kerr Theatre, directed by Lloyd Richards, with Charles S. Dutton and Rocky Carroll. Photo: Gerry Goodstein. Courtesy: Jujamycyn Theaters.

point about African Americans finding a connection with their past. TLM

Picnic by **William Inge** opened on 19 February 1953, produced by the **Theatre Guild** and director **Joshua Logan.** Inge's second Broadway production, this Pulitzer Prize–winning play solidified his reputation and generated a storm of controversy. Spanning two seasons for 477 performances, it featured a bare-chested Ralph Meeker as the virile Hal Carter – a Midwestern Dionysus – who wanders into the otherwise sterile lives of four women in a sleepy rural town. With a realistic surface, it is a psychological and ritualistic play in which the longings and fears of each of these women are brought to the surface through their contact with Hal. Still frequently staged by amateur and professional groups, *Picnic* was also successful as a 1956 film and garnered four Academy Award nominations. Logan directed and William Holden was Hal in this version, adapted by Logan and screenwriter Daniel Taradash. A reworked version of *Picnic*, called *Summer Brave*, was first staged in 1973. MR

Picon, Molly (1898–1992) Entertainer who began performing as a child in Philadelphia, where her mother sewed costumes for Yiddish actresses. After a stint in **vaudeville**, she starred internationally in **Yiddish theatre**, cabaret, and films with husband Jacob Kalich as producer, writer, or co-performer. Known for her saucy but innocent gamine charm, through much of her life she has been associated with the roles of very young women and even mischievous schoolboys. She also starred in English-language plays and films, such as *Milk and Honey, A Majority of One*, and *Come Blow Your Horn*, and on television and radio. Her autobiography, *So Laugh a Little*, appeared in 1962. Active well into her eighties, in 1979 she wrote and performed in the **revue** *Those Were the Days*. NS

Pilgrim, James (1825–79) English-born playwright and actor who came to the U.S. in 1849, acted first in his own play, *The Limerick Boy*, in

Philadelphia, eventually managed theatres in Boston, Philadelphia, and New York, and wrote more than 200 entertainments and plays, some for particular actors – Mr. and Mrs. **Barney Williams, Maggie Mitchell,** Mary Devlin, and **F. S. Chanfrau.** Among his popular plays are *Irish Assurance and Yankee Modesty, Shandy MaGuire,* and *Paddy the Piper.* WJM

Piñero, Miguel (1947–88) Puerto Rican playwright, author of **Short Eyes** (1974), *The Sun Always Shines for the Cool* (1984), *Outrageous: One Act Plays* (1986), and other plays. A former inmate of Sing-Sing, Piñero was a member of "The Family," a theatrical troupe of former prisoners. He is considered a major influence on young Puerto Rican writers of his generation. ER

See: N. Kanellos and J. Huerta, *Nuevos Pasos: Chicano & Puerto Rican Drama*, Houston, 1989.

Pins and Needles Satirical musical **revue** originally produced in 1936 under the auspices of the ILGWU (International Ladies' Garment Workers' Union) to spoof labor and other "leftish" topics. The first edition at the Labor Stage featured the work of **Harold Rome** and Earl Robinson and was enormously popular. After considerable revision it was produced again in 1937 and was a box-office success. **Arthur Arent** and **Marc Blitzstein** contributed delightful satire, and Eleanor Roosevelt invited the company to give a "command performance" at the White House. There were several subsequent editions featuring amateur actors from the union and material that satirized **Bertolt Brecht** and **Hallie Flanagan,** as well as more visible right-wing targets like Father Coughlin. The last edition – *New Pins and Needles* – was produced on 26 November 1939 at the Windsor Theatre, and included a spoof of **Clifford Odets** called "Paradise Mislaid." BBW

Pinski, David (1872–1959) **Yiddish** playwright who, like many of his contemporaries, began writing in Eastern Europe (Warsaw) and died in Israel. In 1899 he arrived in America, where he wrote most of his 38 plays, as well as novels, short stories, and articles. *Isaac Sheftl* (1896) is a naturalistic tragedy. *The Tsvi Family* (1904) and *The Eternal Jew* (1906) are serious symbolic dramatizations of Jewish history, past and contemporaneous. *Yankl the Smith* (1906), eventually filmed, is a domestic drama about love and jealousy. *The Treasure* – staged first in German by **Reinhardt** in 1910, then in Yiddish, and then in English by the **Theatre Guild** – is a comedy about poverty and human greed.   NS

Pioneer Playhouse of Kentucky Located on 200 acres in Danville, Pioneer Playhouse boasts being the oldest outdoor repertory dinner theatre in the state. Founded in 1950 by Eben Henson, the Playhouse offers an accredited drama school that has trained over 3,000 young actors. The grounds include both an outdoor and indoor theatre, a sound stage, campgrounds, and a 19th-century Main Street with train station, general store, and ice cream parlor, used as the setting for several films. Henson also helped start the Kentucky Council of Performing Arts.   LAB

Piper, Adrian (1948–) New York–born conceptual and **performance art**ist whose art practices cross many media: visual art, video installation, film, artists' books, and choreography. A student of sculpture at the New York School of Visual Arts, and of philosophy at City College of New York (BA, 1977) and Harvard University (PhD, 1981), her performances are influenced by conceptual art, popular culture, and Kantian and analytic philosophy. In her performances, she identifies racial and gender discrimination embedded in the visual pathology of white America. She began performing with *Meat into Meat* (1968); this was followed by *Catalysis Series* (1970–1) and *Being Mythic on the Street* (1973), both street performances. *My Calling (Card)*, ongoing since 1986, is a reactive guerrilla performance against racism.   AF

Piscator, Erwin (1893–1966) German director who developed agitprop staging techniques with film, projected scenery, and many ingenius mechanical devices to promote and support the political context of his productions. Dismissed in 1927 for promoting political ideas at the Volksbühne in Berlin, in protest he established his own theatre (Piscator Bühne) and wrote *The Political Theatre* (1929), which documented his work and ideas. In 1929 he produced **Maxwell Anderson** and **Stallings**'s antiwar play *What Price Glory,* adapted by Zuckmayer (*Rivalen*) in Berlin, using elaborate back projections and a treadmill with soldiers marching toward the audience. His documentary approach influenced the **Living Newspaper** of the **Federal Theatre Project** and provided a model for **Bertolt Brecht**'s ideas on epic theatre. He came to New York in 1939 and headed the Dramatic Workshop in the New School of Social Research, staging over 100 experimental works, including his adaptation of *War and Peace* (1942). He was also active in the President and Roof-Top Theatres. In 1951 he returned to Germany, and in 1962 became director of the new Freie Volksbühne, where he staged Hochhuth's *The Deputy* (1963) and Weiss's *The Investigation* (1965).   RE

> See: M. Ley-Piscator, *The Piscator Experiment*, New York, 1967; G. F. Probst, *Erwin Piscator and the American Theatre*, New York/Bern, 1991.

Pitou, Augustus (1843–1915) Manager and producer. Beginning as a supporting actor in **Edwin Booth**'s company (1867), Pitou turned to management, handling **Booth's Theatre** and the **Fifth Avenue** for **John Stetson,** and later managing the **Fourteenth Street Theatre** and the Grand Opera House. He managed the careers of stars including W. J. Scanlan, **Robert B. Mantell, Chauncey Olcott,** and **Rose Coghlan**. He wrote and produced romantic plays about Irish life for Olcott and others, as well as a book of memoirs, *Masters of the Show* (1914).   TLM

Pitt, Leonard (1941–) Performer, teacher, and co–artistic director of Life on the Water, a **San Francisco** theatre. As author and performer of *2019 Blake, Meantime,* and *Not for Real,* he has drawn upon abilities (developed with Etienne Decroux and in visits to Bali) in **mime** and masks.   TL

Pittsburgh Playhouse A **community theatre** established in 1933 that presented its first productions at the Frick Training School for Teachers. It occupied the Hamlet Street Theatre (formerly a speakeasy) in 1935 and attempted professionalization. The community withdrew its support, but returned it under the general management (1937–63) of Frederick Burleigh. The Playhouse acquired the Craft Street Theatre in 1952 and edged again toward greater professionalization. Concerted efforts during 1963–8 to establish a **resident nonprofit professional** company brought the organization to the brink of collapse. Point Park College assumed operational control in 1968, making the Playhouse and its personnel its performing arts department and continuing to offer a professional main-stage season.   WD

Pixley (née Shea), Annie (1858–93) Popular "soubrette" in a string of forgotten comedies (often with songs and dances), although she always longed to perform comic operas. (Her Eastern debut in Philadelphia was as Josephine in *HMS Pinafore*.) Born in Brooklyn but reared in San Francisco, where she supported **Joseph Jefferson III** (as Gretchen in *Rip Van Winkle*) and McKee Rankin (in *The Danites*) in the late 1870s, she soon came east, where *M'liss, the Child of Sorrow* (**Niblo's Garden,** 1878) made her a star. Late in her career she was successful in *The Deacon's Daughter* (1887). It was said she combined "a most piquant and agreeable brusquerie" with "all the bewitching softness and charm of an Irish girl."   DBW

Placide family A famous family of actors, less known but equal in American theatrical importance to the **Booths** or **Jeffersons**. The U.S. Placides begin with **Alexander Placide** (?–1812), a French rope dancer and pantomimist [see **mime**] of some distinction, who fled from France during the Revolution. He emigrated to the U.S., and first appeared in America at the **John Street Theatre** in 1792. He married a Miss Wighten, the daughter of a celebrated London actress. For a time, Placide managed theatres in Charleston and Richmond, and was scheduled for a benefit on 26 December 1811, the day of a disastrous Richmond theatre **fire.**

Of Placide's many children, the best known was **Henry Placide** (1799–1870), considered one of the finest character actors of the American stage. After appearing as a child actor in 1814, he made his adult debut in 1823 at the **Park Theatre** as Zekiel Homespun. He remained at the Park for 20 years, acting more than 500 roles, 200 of which he created. He attempted one London engagement, unsuccessfully. American audiences considered him best in traditional English comedy, Sir Peter Teazle being among his most successful parts.

Henry Placide's older sister **Caroline** (1789–1881) married **William Rufus Blake,** and his siblings **Eliza** (?–1874) and **Thomas** (1808–77) both had theatrical careers, Thomas managing the Park Theatre for some years. **Jane** (1804–35), another sister, made her debut in Norfolk, VA, in 1820, and in 1823 she appeared in New Orleans, playing there almost exclusively for a decade. At that time she appeared as a singer, as well as a dramatic and comic actress. She was said to be the most polished actress in the South in her time, and was referred to as the "Queen of the Drama in New Orleans," her Lady Macbeth and Cordelia being especially admired. She appeared at London's Covent Garden in 1834 and died shortly after her return to the U.S. SMA

See: J. Kaough, Jr., "Henry Placide, American Comedian," PhD diss., U of Kansas, 1970.

Platt, Livingston (1885–1968) Designer. As artistic director of the Toy Theatre of Boston, Platt pioneered the New Stagecraft in America, though his contributions are often overlooked. He went on to a successful Broadway career that included *Rain* (1922), *Grand Hotel* (1930), and ***Dinner at Eight*** (1933). AA

Playbill/program By the time professional actors appeared in the American colonies in the mid-18th century, the playbill, handbill, or program, as it has been variously known, was an established institution in English and continental theatre. The American playbills of this period look very much like provincial English playbills, most giving the name of the play, the cast, time and date, the theatre, and price of admission. The early playbills – usually about 9″ × 7″ in size and printed on the same stock used for newspapers – often doubled as posters, and were frequently hand-distributed by company members to the homes of citizens.

As advancing technology in printing in the 19th century led to the increase in size and variety of typefaces for printed matter, more information could be included in the larger playbill. Managers used it as an advertisement to extol themselves, their stars, the scenery, and costumes, and additionally to provide a brief synopsis of the play along with previews of coming attractions. The introduction of lithography made it possible to print line drawings of the stars or scenes by mid-century.

The customary long, narrow playbills were supplanted by small, folded programs in the late 19th century. By the 1870s, theatres either published their own or were provided with copies of pamphletlike programs that owed their existence to a multitude of large and small advertisements (secured by the publisher as revenue) that effectively smothered the information about the play and the cast. When the long-running show became established, managers seized the opportunity for more self-promotion by issuing souvenir programs, often printed on silk or satin, to commemorate landmark performances of 100 or more.

In New York, a young Ohioan, Frank V. Strauss, secured the right in 1884 to gather advertisements for **Madison Square Theatre** programs and later to print programs for it and other theatres. Thus was launched the company that hereafter set the standard for American theatre programs. Strauss standardized playbills by printing them on a better quality paper, giving them attractive covers, making the size uniform for all theatres, providing feature articles about the theatre, personalities, fashion, local events, and so on, and in other ways transforming them into compact and informative magazines distributed for free. The name *Playbill*® was eventually copyrighted by a subsequent owner, and that publication dominates the field in New York, although facsimiles of its format abound in professional, regional, and amateur theatres across America. MCH

Playhouse Theatre 137 West 48th St., NYC [Architect: Charles A. Rich]. In 1911, Broadway producer **William A. Brady** built the small Playhouse for his own productions, which often starred his wife **Grace George.** With an auditorium seating fewer than 1,000, the theatre also contained his own offices and those of other producers, press agents, and the League of New York Theatres and Producers (see **Producing Managers' Association**). At the age of 81, Brady sold his theatre, which eventually passed to Rockefeller real estate interests in 1967; a year later, it was demolished. Its most notable tenants included the first Broadway production of **Shaw**'s *Major Barbara* (1915), the Pulitzer Prize–winning *Street Scene,* and *The Miracle Worker* (1959). On its stage, **Laurette Taylor** played her last and greatest role, Amanda Wingfield, in *The* **Glass Menagerie.** MCH

Playwrights' (Producing) Company Founded in 1938 by **Maxwell Anderson, S. N. Behrman, Sidney Howard, Elmer Rice,** and **Robert E. Sherwood** to present their own best efforts, the Playwrights' Company became a major production force in the American theatre for several decades. **Kurt Weill** and **Robert Anderson** were invited to join as partners, as were attorney John Wharton and producer **Roger L. Stevens.** Although dedicated to its own scripts, the Playwrights' Company also coproduced presentations by nonmembers. Their first venture, ***Abe Lincoln in Illinois*** (1938), was followed by such landmarks as *Knickerbocker Holiday* (1938), *Key Largo* (1939), *Dream Girl* (1945), the musical ***Street Scene*** (1947),

Lost in the Stars(1949), *Tea and Sympathy* (1953), and *Cat on a Hot Tin Roof* (1955). The death of its key partners forced the dissolution of the company in 1960 after the production of **Vidal**'s *The Best Man*.   MCH

See: J. F. Wharton, *Life Among the Playwrights*, New York, 1974.

Playwrights Horizons (1971–   ) Writer's theatre founded in New York by Robert Moss to develop and produce new scripts. Working in two small theatres on **Theatre Row,** the organization – through readings, workshops, and full-scale productions – has presented more than 250 new plays, including *Kennedy's Children, Gemini,* Sister Mary Ignatius Explains It All for You, The **Dining Room, Sunday in the Park with George, Driving Miss Daisy,** The **Heidi Chronicles,** and *March of the Falsettos*. André Bishop (artistic director, 1981–91) and Paul S. Daniels (managing director) worked with a stable group of resident playwrights that included **Christopher Durang, A. R. Gurney, Jr., Albert Innaurato, Ted Tally,** and **Wendy Wasserstein.** Bishop was succeeded in 1992 by Don Scardino, director of the 1990 Broadway success *A Few Good Men*.   TLM

Plaza Suite The first of **Neil Simon**'s combinations of three one-act plays opened 14 February 1968 at the **Plymouth Theatre** and ran for 1,097 performances. Although the plays are apparently linked only by their occurring in Suite 719 of New York's Plaza Hotel, each act suggests thematic connections with the others. The room's occupants for the successive acts are a financially secure middle-aged couple on a doomed second honeymoon, a young Hollywood producer and his former high-school girlfriend in an unsatisfying seduction, and successful middle-class parents on their reluctant daughter's wedding day. As each couple meets its respective crisis, the apparently different circumstances emphasize the similarity of the dissatisfactions they each face. The characters struggle to cope with lives that are lacking fulfillment and essentially empty, despite material stability; the only ones who seem to communicate are the third-act bride and groom, suggesting both the problem and its solution.   RW

Plummer, (Arthur) Christopher (Orme) (1929–   ) Toronto-born actor who, after playing nearly 100 roles with the Canadian Repertory Theatre, beginning in 1950, made his New York debut in 1954. In the 1950s and '60s his speciality was **Shakespeare,** appearing at the **American Shakespeare Theatre** (1955), the Stratford Ontario Shakespeare Festival (1956, 1957, 1960, 1962), and with the Royal Shakespeare Company (1961). Roles included Mark Antony, Henry V, Hamlet, Sir Andrew Aguecheek, Benedick, Leontes, Mercutio, and Richard III. In 1981 he returned to the American Shakespeare Theatre as Iago and in the title role and as Chorus in *Henry V*. He was Nickles in **MacLeish**'s *J. B.* (1958), Pizarro in *The Royal Hunt of the Sun* (1965), won the Tony Award as best actor in a musical version of *Cyrano de Bergerac* in 1973, and played Chekhov in **Neil Simon**'s *The Good Doctor* (1973). In London he played King

Henry in *Becket* (1961) and joined the National Theatre at the New Theatre in 1971. In 1990 he received the third William Shakespeare Award for Classical Theatre from the **Shakespeare Theatre** at the Folger.

His daughter, by actress **Tammy Grimes,** is actress **Amanda Plummer** (*Agnes of God,* 1982, Tony), who has appeared on the New York stage some nine times during 1979–91, recently as Bess Johnson in **Beth Henley**'s *Abundance* (1990).   DBW

Plymouth Theatre 236 West 45th St., NYC [Architect: Herbert J. Krapp]. In 1917, backed by the ubiquitous **Shubert**s, producer-director **Arthur Hopkins** built the Plymouth as the theatrical home for himself and his productions. A man of quiet daring, Hopkins tended to produce the unusual play during his lifetime. At his theatre, he staged *The Jest* (1919, adapted by **Edward Sheldon**) with John and Lionel Barrymore [see **Drew–Barrymore**]; the antiwar *What Price Glory* (1924); and **Sophie Treadwell**'s *Machinal* (1927). Unfortunately, the Depression years tempered his activities, and he was forced to relinquish his 1,000-seat, one-balcony house to the Shuberts after 1935. In its history, the Plymouth has had many notable tenants, none more extraordinary than the Royal Shakespeare Company's production of *Nicholas Nickleby* (1981), which ran for eight hours with a dinner intermission and a ticket price of $100. The theatre has remained a Shubert house.   MCH

Po-ca-hon-tas; or, The Gentle Savage A two-act musical burlesque by **John Brougham** with music adapted by James G. Maeder. Arguably the best of Indian burlesques [see **Native Americans portrayed**], Brougham's second such effort opened at Wallack's Lyceum [see **Wallack's Theatre**] 24 December 1855, and remained a standard burlesque afterpiece until at least 1884. With **Charles M. Walcot** as Capt. John Smith, Georgina Hodson in the title role, Brougham as her father (King H. J. Pow-ha-tan I), and Charles Peters as a Dutchman (Mynheer Rolff) promised Pocahontas's hand, Brougham turned the popular story inside out (Smith wins Pocahontas via a card game). With corny but clever puns and rhymed-couplet doggerel, it provided music, a libretto, and subjects all relevant to New York life and the country as a whole in the 1850s.   DBW

See: R. Moody, *Dramas from the American Theatre 1762–1909,* Cleveland/New York, 1966.

Poe, Edgar Allan (1809–49) Short-story writer, poet, and critic. The author of "The Raven" and "Annabel Lee" was knowledgeable about the drama, writing occasional essays for *Southern Literary Messenger* (1835–7), *Burton's Gentleman's Magazine* (1839–40), *Graham's Magazine* (1841–2), and the *New York Mirror* (1845). When he became editor of *Broadway Journal* (1845–6), he reviewed live theatre, including Mrs. **Mowatt**'s *Fashion.* Poe advocated a more realistic aesthetic and criticized such conventions as soliloquies, asides, and the reading aloud of private letters. He insisted that American drama must reflect American life, and that native dramatic criticism be rescued from corrupt journalistic practices.   TLM

See: N. Bryllion Fagin, *The Histrionic Mr. Poe*, Baltimore, 1949; K. Silverman, *Edgar A. Poe*, New York, 1991.

Polakov, Lester (1916–) Designer and teacher, perhaps best known as the founder (1958) of the Polakov Studio and Forum of Stage Design, the most significant nonuniversity training program in the country. He began designing in 1940 and designed on and **Off-Broadway** and for opera, film, and industrial shows. AA

Pollock, Channing (1880–1946) Playwright and critic who wrote dramatic criticism for the *Washington Post* and *Washington Times* before becoming press representative for **William A. Brady** (1899–1903) and for the **Shubert**s (1903–6) while establishing himself as a playwright. His more than 30 plays include the potboilers *The Sign on the Door* (1919), *The Fool* (1922), and *The Enemy* (1925). Pollock wrote on theatre for magazines including *Ainslee's*, *Munsey's*, and *The Smart Set*. TLM

See: C. Pollock, *Harvest of My Years*, Indianapolis, 1943.

Ponisi, Madame (née Elizabeth Hanson) (1818–99) English-born actress who came to the U.S. in 1848 and established herself as a popular romantic actress in the 1850s, playing opposite **Edwin Forrest** in several roles. She created the title role of *Francesca da Rimini*, **George Henry Boker**'s poetic tragedy (1855). In the 1870s and '80s, she played "first old woman" roles in the **stock company** at **Wallack's Theatre,** and was long remembered for the "vigor and drollery" of those interpretations. FHL

Poole, John F. (1835–93) Dublin-born playwright and actor who came to America in 1847 and by 1852 was house dramatist at the Old **Bowery Theatre.** Among his numerous plays are *The Massacre of Wyoming* (1859), *Cudjo's Cave* (1864), and *Di-vorce* (1872). He managed several theatres and owned Poole's Theatre in Astor Place. WJM

Poor of New York, The Dion Boucicault's popular adaptation of *Les Pauvres de Paris* (by Brisbarre and Nus) opened at **Wallack's Theatre** in 1857. This "sensation melodrama" drew praise for its depiction of local New York scenes – including the slums of Five Points and the Academy of Music opera house – and for its thrilling plot. The play begins with a banker stealing money during the Panic of 1837, and then jumps to the Panic of 1857 to examine the consequences of this theft on a business–class family. The "real" poor of New York in the melodrama are the respectable bourgeoisie struggling to hide their poverty – not the unemployed and "the beggar at home whose mattress is lined with gold." Altering the local references to suit the city, Boucicault pieced out new scripts with the same plot entitled *The Streets of Philadelphia* and *The Rich and Poor of Boston*. Later, he adapted his adaptation as *The Poor of Liverpool, The Streets of London,* and even *The Streets of New York,* the title used when the play was further transformed into a melodramatic musical. BMcC

Porgy and Bess Based on the play *Porgy* by **Dorothy and Du Bose Heyward** (produced by the **Theatre Guild** in 1927), with book by Du Bose Heyward and music and lyrics by **George and Ira Gershwin** (respectively), *Porgy and Bess* opened at the **Alvin Theatre** on 10 October 1935. Billed as "an American folk opera," it is about the black inhabitants of Catfish Row, a slum neighborhood in Charleston, SC. Drawing on black musical idioms, including blues and spirituals, George Gershwin used recitative, arias, and production numbers to tell the story of the crippled Porgy and Bess, the troubled woman he loves. Although its sordid story of gambling, drugs, and violence did little to shatter the stereotypical portrayal of black characters on the musical stage, it did provide unprecedented opportunities for black singers with trained voices. At its 1935 opening, *Porgy and Bess* received negative reviews from music critics and had a short run. A 1942 revival that cut much of the recitative and several of the musical sequences was a greater success. A return to the full score and libretto by the Houston Opera Company in 1976 demonstrated anew the show's power. In 1985 it entered the repertory of the Metropolitan Opera. MK

See: H. Alpert, *The Life and Times of Porgy and Bess,* New York, 1990.

Pornographic theatre For the Puritans, all theatre was pornographic: It inflamed illicit passions. Even when the offerings were unobjectionable, moralists complained of the playhouse's third tier, where prostitutes congregated and trawled for trade. They, with the lobby bar, were often the real economic pillars of the theatre.

Truly pornographic theatre connotes the graphic enactment of sexual acts intended to bring spectators to a state of sexual arousal. Such spectacles, usually staged in brothels, were rare in the U.S. It was not until the so-called Sexual Revolution of the 1960s that these representations became programmatically exploited, less for erotic effect than as statements of liberation. Michael McClure's play *The Beard* (1967), which climaxes in Billy the Kid performing cunnilingus on Jean Harlow, was merely a tame prelude to Lennox Raphael's *Che!* (1969), featuring a nude Uncle Sam whose participation in oral sex and sodomy caused the cast to be arrested by the New York police. This blatancy was done often in the name of theatrical experimentation and dadaism, and often as political protest (Tuli Kupferberg's *Fuck Nam*), but much was purely commercial. **Kenneth Tynan**'s revue *Oh! Calcutta!* celebrated randiness with full **nudity** and sketches by Samuel Beckett, **Gore Vidal,** and **Jules Feiffer;** imitations like *Let My People Come* had less pretence to wit.

Throughout the 1980s, actual rather than simulated copulation took place in porno palaces such as Show World in Times Square; the rationale of the mildly comic revue sketches was invariably a sex act. Sadomasochistic demonstrations were offered by The Project and Belle de Jour [*sic*] at private clubs, which encouraged audience participation. **Feminist** attitudes were split between condemnation of pornography as a degradation of

Porgy and Bess (1935), designed by Cleon Throckmorton for the Theatre Guild. Courtesy: New York Public Library for the Performing Arts.

women and promotion of it as a life-enhancing liberation. The latter attitude prevails in the performance art of **Karen Finley,** Annie Sprinkle, and others who parody standard responses by grotesque caricature. This approach has been widely misconstrued by conservatives who take the parody to be the real thing, and the recent revival of puritanical **censorship** even proscribes radio simulations of masturbation.   LS

> *See:* A. M. Rabenalt, *Theater ohne Tabu,* Emsdetten (Germany), 1970; *The Drama Review,* March 1981 and Spring 1989.

Porter, Cole (1891–1964) Composer and lyricist. Born into a wealthy midwestern family, Porter abandoned his plans for a legal career to study at the Harvard University School of Music. He contributed songs to the Broadway musical *See America First* in 1916. After a stint with the French Foreign Legion, Porter lived in Europe for most of the 1920s. At the end of the decade he wrote songs for two Broadway shows with French settings: *Paris* (1928) and *Fifty Million Frenchmen* (1929). In the 1930s Porter wrote the scores for a series of frothy musical comedies, including *The Gay Divorce* (1932), **Anything Goes** (1934), *Red, Hot and Blue!* (1936), *Leave It to Me!* (1938), and **Du Barry Was a Lady** (1939). His songs for these shows, generally characterized by ingenious lyrics and unusual rhythms, placed him in the forefront of musical comedy composers.

After his legs were crushed in a riding accident in 1937, Porter's creativity seemed to wane. His shows of the early 1940s were financially successful but artistically undistinguished. However, in 1948 he created what many consider to be his most theatrically effective and versatile score: **Kiss Me, Kate,** a musical version of Shakespeare's *The Taming of the Shrew*. During the 1950s Porter wrote his last two hit shows: **Can-Can** (1953) and **Silk Stockings** (1955).

For most of his career Porter was content with providing sophisticated songs for shows with trivial librettos. As a consequence, although his songs still remain popular, few of his shows are revived in their entirety.   MK

> *See:* R. Kimball, ed., *Cole,* New York, 1971, and *The Complete Lyrics of Cole Porter,* New York, 1983; C. Schwartz, *Cole Porter,* New York, 1977.

Porter, Stephen A director who trained at the Yale School of the Drama, Porter taught in Canada for a time, then directed his first play, *The Misanthrope,* at the Theatre East, New York (1956). Among the companies for whom he has directed are Theatre of the Living Arts, **American Shake-**

speare Festival, Guthrie Theatre, Mark Taper Forum, Old Globe (San Diego), Circle in the Square, American Conservatory Theatre, Cincinnati Playhouse in the Park, Milwaukee Repertory Theatre, and the Studio Arena (Buffalo). During 1972–5 he served as the Artistic Director of the New Phoenix Repertory Company, New York.

Something of a Shaw and Molière specialist, Porter's recent productions have included *The Devil's Disciple* (1988) and *The Miser* (1990, starring **Philip Bosco**), both at **Circle in the Square**. In 1971 he was nominated for a Tony for his direction of *School for Wives*.   SMA

Potter, Richard (1783–1835) The first successful American conjuror; son of a British tax collector for the port of Boston and a black slave. Potter first joined a British circus and then became assistant to conjuror John Rannie, a Scot who first appeared in the U.S. in 1801 (in Boston). Rannie retired in 1811, leaving the field open to Potter, who toured the U.S. and eastern Canada for 20 years with his "Evening's Brush to Sweep Away Care; or, a Medley to Please." His son, Richard Potter, Jr., was also a **magic**ian and ventriloquist.   DBW

Potts, Nancy (1940–) Tennessee-born costume designer. Educated at Washington University (BA), Potts designed contemporary clothing before turning to costume design. Her New York debut, *Right You Are If You Think You Are* for the **Association of Producing Artists**–Phoenix Company (1964) led to numerous additional credits with that company and its artistic director, **Ellis Rabb**. She has also designed numerous plays for other **Off-Broadway** companies, regional theatres, and on Broadway, including *Hair* in 1968. Potts received a Maharam Award for *The Cherry Orchard, Exit the King,* and *Pantagleize* at APA–Phoenix in 1968.   BO

Powell, Charles Stuart (1748–1811) Welsh-born actor-manager who came to America after little success on the London stage, first offering one-man entertainments in **Boston** (1792) before joining **Joseph Harper**'s Boston troupe at the New Exhibition Room and then becoming manager of the **Federal Street Theatre**. Dismissed after its second season (1795), he opened the Haymarket Theatre in December 1796, but was bankrupt by June. After acting in Boston and Hartford for two years, Powell went to Halifax, Nova Scotia, where he ran a theatre for 12 years (with a brief engagement in Boston in 1806–7). Powell's wife, Mary Ann, and two daughters acted, as did his younger brother, Snelling, who had success in the U.S. during 1794–1821.   DBW

Powell, Frederick Eugene (1856–1938) Originally a civil engineering teacher, Philadelphia-born Powell became a master of large illusion shows [see **magic**] and toured the U.S., West Indies, and South America. Known late in his career as the "Dean of American Magicians," after **Kellar**'s death, Powell's show – which was twice destroyed (by

fire in 1915 and flood in 1921) – featured such spectacles as "She," his version of a "Cremation" illusion.   DBW

Powers, The A family of actors, originally from Ireland, most of whom spent large portions of their careers in the U.S. The first, **Tyrone Power** (1795–1841), successfully played stage Irishmen in London and wrote a number of comedies before coming to the U.S. in 1840. A great success here, he returned often and was drowned at sea on a transatlantic trip. His 1836 *Impressions of America* offers a sympathetic and detailed view of the American theatre at the time. Power's son **Maurice** (?–1849) was also an actor. Another son, Harold, sired **[Frederick] Tyrone [Edmond] Power** (1869–1931), a leading man and member of **Daly**'s company, with whom he appeared in London. Frederick first appeared successfully with Madame **Janauschek**, and for a time acted with **Minnie Maddern Fiske,** his Lord Steyne in *Becky Sharp* being especially well received. In later life, he appeared almost exclusively as major support in Shakespearean revivals.

In turn, his son **Tyrone Power** (1914–58) was for some time on the stage, but won his most substantial reputation as a film actor. He made his debut as Benvolio in **Katharine Cornell**'s production of *Romeo and Juliet*. After his film career began he appeared in *John Brown's Body* and *The Dark Is Light Enough*. In the 1980s his son, **Tyrone, Jr.,** also became an actor.   SMA

See: H. Arce, *The Secret Life of Tyrone Power,* New York, 1979; W. Winter, *Life of Tyrone Power,* New York, 1913.

Powers, James T. (1862–1943) Actor who began as a song and dance man (1878). His first musical was a revival of *Evangeline* (1882) with **Willie Edouin;** they then starred together in New York and London in **Charles Hoyt**'s *A Bunch of Keys* (1883). A founding member of the company at New York's **Casino Theatre** (1887), he replaced **James Lewis** in **Augustin Daly**'s company (1893–9). From then until 1915 he toured as a star in a new musical each season. He last appeared in a revival of *Seven Keys to Baldpate* (1935). Short, red-haired, and acrobatic, he was described as having "rubber heels."   DMcD

See: J. T. Powers, *Twinkle Little Star,* New York, 1929.

Prelude to a Kiss by **Craig Lucas** premiered at **South Coast Repertory Theatre** in January 1988 and was subsequently produced in March 1990 at New York's **Circle Rep.** This comic fantasy about the transfer of "souls" between an aging man and a new bride delighted **Off-Broadway** audiences. In May 1990 it reopened at the **Helen Hayes Theatre** on Broadway, with Timothy Hutton replacing Alec Baldwin as the puzzled bridegroom, and Mary-Louise Parker (winner of a *Theatre World* Award) and **Barnard Hughes** recreating their roles (and winning applause) as the time travelers. A film version with Baldwin was released in 1992.   BBW

Preston (Meservey), Robert (1918–87) Actor and singer, who, after studying at the **Pasadena Playhouse,** worked for several years in film and then first appeared on Broadway as a replacement for **José Ferrer** in *Twentieth Century* (1950 revival). He was in several plays before making a triumphant musical comedy debut as fast-talking salesman Harold Hill in *The Music Man* (1957). He played in the all-star revival of Shaw's *Too True to Be Good* (1963) and in *Nobody Loves an Albatross* (1963) before returning to musicals with *Ben Franklin in Paris* (1964). He created the role of Henry II in *The Lion in Winter* (1966) and starred opposite **Mary Martin** in the two-character musical *I Do! I Do!* (1966). He was also seen as silent-movie director Mack Sennett opposite **Bernadette Peters** in *Mack and Mabel* (1974).   MK

Price, Stephen (1783–1840) The first successful American theatre manager who was neither a playwright nor an actor. Price began gaining control of the **Park Theatre** in New York in 1808, and in 1810 started importing English stars; this practice gradually destroyed the resident repertory tradition in America. Price, with **Simpson,** managed to keep the Park open during the War of 1812, and after the war went frequently to London to recruit new talent. In 1816 he imported Mrs. John Barnes from Drury Lane, beginning an especially prosperous period for the Park. From 1826 to 1830 Price managed the Drury Lane Theatre in London, gaining a monopoly over English stars, forcing other American managers to deal with him for their services. This power caused **Washington Irving** to refer to Price as "King Stephen." Price drained the London stage of its talent to supply visiting stars for the Park; other managers were forced to employ his visiting stars on Price's terms in order to compete. Price was shrewd, even unscrupulous in his dealings, but he read audiences' tastes and preferences accurately on both sides of the Atlantic.   SMA

See: J. Donohue, ed., *The Theatrical Manager in England and America,* Princeton, NJ, 1971.

Price, The, by **Arthur Miller** opened 7 February 1968 in New York and ran for 429 performances. **Ulu Grosbard** directed **Pat Hingle** as Victor Franz, the middle-aged policeman who gave up his dream of doing scientific research in order to support his father, a businessman who was ruined in the Depression; **Kate Reid** as Esther, Victor's long-suffering wife; **Arthur Kennedy** as Walter Franz, Victor's brother, who has become a successful surgeon after leaving the family behind to pursue his medical career; and Harold Gary as Gregory Solomon, the octogenarian who wants to revive his used-furniture business by buying the Franz's family furniture – a remnant of the Depression that Victor wants to sell in order to finance his education after his retirement from the police force. The furniture provides the occasion for the brothers to confront their feelings about each other, their father, the family, and their own lives. Through Solomon's agency, Victor and Esther come to an understanding about their personal values and an acceptance of the life they have chosen. Revived in

1992 at the **Roundabout,** it was directed by **John Tillinger** and starred **Eli Wallach.**   BCM

Prince, Harold (1928–) Producer and director. Launching his career as a producer in partnership with Robert E. Griffith and **Frederic Brisson,** Prince had immediate success with *The Pajama Game* (1954) and *Damn Yankees* (1955). With Griffith he produced *West Side Story* (1957) and *Fiorello!* (1961), and on his own he produced *Fiddler on the Roof* (1964). Beginning with *She Loves Me* (1963), he served as both producer and director of a number of successful musicals. Prince's most notable contribution to the musical stage was the series of "concept musicals" he produced and directed in conjunction with composer-lyricist **Stephen Sondheim:** *Company* (1970), *Follies* (1971), *A Little Night Music* (1973), *Pacific Overtures* (1976), *Sweeney Todd* (1979), and *Merrily We Roll Along* (1981). In recent years he has devoted considerable attention to the direction of opera, in the U.S. and abroad; his most successful musical theatre production of the past few years has been the spectacular Lloyd Webber *Phantom of the Opera* (London, 1986; New York, 1988). Current projects include the adaptation of O'Casey's autobiographies; a new production of *Show Boat* (to open in Toronto in 1993); and the further development of *Kiss of the Spider Woman* (begun in 1990). Winner of seven Tony Awards for direction of a musical, in 1991 Prince received the Richard Rodgers Award for excellence in musical theatre (which had only been given previously to **Mary Martin** [1988] and Julie Andrews [1989]).

Hirsch believes Prince and his collaborators "have altered the popular idea of what a musical can be," and Ilson concludes that as a risk-taker Prince's greatest contribution has been "his unwillingness to repeat himself." His autobiography, *Contradictions,* was published in 1974.   MK

See: F. Hirsch, *Harold Prince and the American Musical Theatre,* New York, 1989; C. Ilson, *Harold Prince: From Pajama Game to Phantom of the Opera,* Ann Arbor, MI, 1989; G. Perry, *The Complete Phantom of the Opera,* New York, 1988.

Prince Karl Comedy by **A. C. Gunter,** first performed at the **Boston Museum** 5 April 1886, with **Richard Mansfield** in the title role. Its presentation at the **Madison Square Theatre** on 3 May 1886 was the occasion of Mansfield's first starring appearance in New York. Prince Karl von Ahrmien, a penniless, young nobleman, escapes an unwanted marriage by feigning suicide. He reappears as a commoner employed in the entourage of his true love. In the end, Karl gains an inheritance, resumes his titled identity, and wins his beloved. Mansfield persistently revised Gunter's play, purging the melodrama and emphasizing the romance and farce. Though it was a staple of Mansfield's repertory until 1899, permitting him to display his manifold talents as a comic actor, pianist, and vocal parodist, he thought it "trash" and "stupid."   WD

Princess Theatre 104 West 39th Street, NYC [Architect: William A. Swasey]. **F. Ray Com-**

stock, who built the tiny playhouse in 1914, was the unwitting godfather of the intimate musical. After trying experimental drama, he hired **Jerome Kern, Guy Bolton,** and **P. G. Wodehouse** to put together shows that would be long on imagination but short on cast, scenery, and orchestra. The results were the Princess musicals – notably *Very Good Eddie* (1915), *Leave It to Jane* (1917), and *Oh Lady! Lady!* (1918) – that launched the careers of all three. Except for one period when, as Labor Stage, it housed *Pins and Needles* (1937) for 1,108 performances, the theatre showed films since 1933. It was razed in 1955.   MCH

Prisoner of Second Avenue, The Neil Simon's comedy opened at the **Eugene O'Neill Theatre** 11 November 1971 for 780 performances. Main character Mel Edison (Peter Falk) progressively disintegrates under the pressures of the deteriorating society around him. Though a comedy, the play paints a pessimistic picture of the future as Mel suffers a mental breakdown in the face of seeming futility. In the second act, however, Simon returns to his emphasis of individual interdependence. When Mel's brother offers financial help, he declines. In the final scene, he has recovered enough to help wife Edna, whose life is unraveling. Implicit in Mel's seemingly self-generated recovery is Simon's belief in the effectiveness of collaboration as an antidote to life's futility. Here Simon transfers the notion to society's challenges.   RW

Processional A "jazz symphony of American life" by **John Howard Lawson,** first produced by the **Theatre Guild** in 1925 and revived by the **Federal Theatre Project** in a revised version of 1937. Lawson's play was ground-breaking as a piece of antirealistic political theatre on a Broadway stage. Conceived as a bitter and ironic vaudeville loosely centered around the events of a West Virginia coalminers' striker, *Processional* ridiculed racial stereotyping, small-town businessmen, corporate leaders, the government, and the Klan. The work proved to be Lawson's most enduring, far surpassing the dramatic effectiveness of the Socialist Realism he turned to in the 1930s at the behest of communist cultural theorists.   MF

Proctor, F[rederick] F[rancis or Freeman?] (1851–1929) **Vaudeville** manager ("dean of vaudeville") and theatre owner. Maine-born Proctor began his career touring the U.S. and Europe as Fred Levantine, an equilibrist. In 1886 he bought an interest in an Albany theatre; in 1889 he opened the 23rd Street Theatre, a legitimate house, in NYC. By the 1890s his focus was clean, continuous vaudeville, first at New York's Proctor Pleasure Palace (1894), then with the first vaudeville circuit, and ultimately controlling a group of 25 eastern theatres. Proctor joined his rival **B. F. Keith** in 1906 as head of the **United Booking Office;** his theatrical holdings were taken over by the Radio–Keith–Orpheum circuit in 1929.   DBW

See: W. Marston and J. Feller, *F. F. Proctor: Vaudeville Pioneer,* New York, 1943.

Producing Managers' Association (PMA) Apparently the brainchild of producer **John Golden** (and headed by **Sam H. Harris**), this organization was formed in 1918 as a result of the growing struggle with **Actors' Equity** and ultimately as a replacement for the disintegrating United Managers' Protective Association (which included theatre owners and bookers). An unwillingness on the part of PMA to negotiate with Equity precipitated the actors' strike of 1919 and the establishment of PMA's unsuccessful rival company union, Actors' Fidelity League. Ultimately, PMA was forced to sign the first American labor-management contract. In 1924 a group of disgruntled producers withdrew from PMA and formed the Managers' Protective Association, which evolved in 1930 into the League of New York Theatres and Producers. (Its named was changed in 1985 to League of American Theatres and Producers [LATP; see **Societies and associations**].)   DBW

See: A. Harding, *The Revolt of the Actors,* New York, 1929; B. McArthur, *Actors and American Culture, 1880–1920,* Philadelphia, 1984.

Prolet-Buehne A New York worker's theatre group formed in 1925 by immigrant German workers. Led by John E. Bonn in 1928–9, they introduced agitprop techniques into their performances by 1929 to promote socialist and workers' class consciousness and political activism similar to groups in Berlin [see **Piscator**] and Moscow. They influenced the performance style of the Workers' Laboratory Theatre, and eventually the **Living Newspaper.** The group disbanded in 1934, and Bonn was later appointed to the German section of the **Federal Theatre Project.**   RE

See: D. Friedman and D. McDermott in B. McConachie and Friedman, eds., *Theatre for Working-Class Audiences in the United States, 1830–1980,* Westport, CT, 1985.

Prosky, Robert (1930–) Actor, most closely associated with Washington, DC's **Arena Stage,** where from 1958 he performed over 130 roles spanning 24 seasons. As the company's leading actor, he lent his particularly American blend of gravity and warmth to the Stage Manager in *Our Town* (1972, 1976, 1990) and played such roles as Mr. Willis in *Moonchildren* (1972), Willy Loman in *Death of a Salesman* (1975), Azdak in *The Caucasian Chalk Circle* (1977), and Grandpa in *You Can't Take It with You* (1979). After leaving Arena in 1982, he appeared on Broadway as Alfieri in *A View from the Bridge* (1983), Levine in *Glengarry Glen Ross* (1984), and Botvinnik in *A Walk in the Woods* (1988 and a subsequent Soviet tour).   LM

Provincetown Players Led by George Cram Cook, an enthusiastic visionary from Iowa who revered the ancient Greek drama. In the summer of 1915 a band of amateurs staged several of their own plays in Provincetown, MA. The following year, after **Eugene O'Neill** joined the group and contributed the outstanding work *Bound East for Cardiff,* Cook – backed by O'Neill and journalist John Reed, among others – decided to move their playmaking to Greenwich Village, NYC. Launched in a brownstone at 139 Macdougal Street on 3 November 1916, the Provincetown Players initially featured short works, with O'Neill and **Susan Glaspell** as their leading writers. After two years, the Players moved into larger quarters at 133 Macdougal Street. Though Cook gave unstintingly of himself for O'Neill's writings, most notably for The **Emperor Jones** (1920), he himself had literary ambitions and envied the other's growing fame. In 1922 he and his wife Susan Glaspell sailed for Greece, where he died two years later. After a hiatus (1922–3), the Players were headed by a triumvirate of O'Neill, **Kenneth Macgowan,** and **Robert Edmond Jones,** who in turn were succeeded by **James Light** as director. A casualty of the stock market crash and the Depression, the Players folded in 1929.   LSh

See: H. Deutsch and S. Hanau, The Provincetown, A Story of the Theatre, New York, 1931; R. Sarlós, Jig Cook and the Provincetown Players, Amherst, MA, 1982.

Public Theater In 1966, **Joseph Papp,** founder of the **New York Shakespeare Festival,** acquired a large Italianate building at 425 Lafayette Street in New York for its permanent home. The building dates to 1854, when the Astor family dedicated it as a library for New Yorkers. After two additions, it was completed in 1881, becoming part of the city's public library system until 1911. In 1920, the building was sold to the Hebrew Immigrant Aid Society, which had intended to sell to a developer until the Landmarks Preservation Commission designated it a landmark in 1960. Papp originally assigned Giorgio Cavaglieri and **Ming Cho Lee** to convert it into theatres. Struggling to keep as much of the original building intact, the designers during the next few years created the Newman Theater (proscenium, 299 seats), Martinson Hall (flexible, 190 seats), LuEsther Hall (flexible, 150 seats), Susan Stein Shiva Theater (flexible, 100 seats), and Anspacher Theater (3/4 arena, 275 seats). In 1992 (on April 23, Shakespeare's birthday), the building's name was officially changed to the Joseph Papp Public Theater.   MCH

Puerto Rican Traveling Theatre In 1966, stage, film, and television actress Miriam Colón, a student of **Erwin Piscator** and the first Puerto Rican member of the **Actors Studio,** joined a group of bilingual actors to play storefronts, jails, parks, and street corners. Building on this experience, Colón founded the bilingual PRTT. Under her direction, the theatre has become a hospitable venue for contemporary Hispanic drama, native and foreign, as well as a center for Hispanic cultural activity in New York City – a role that includes free training units for young people and playwrights. Although the PRTT still travels locally and abroad, its home is now a former firehouse on West 47th Street, renovated in 1974 to provide rehearsal and production facilities.   CLJ

Puppetry in the United States A puppet, any object animated by human control, has three requirements: an object to be animated, a person to do the animating, and a method of controlling the object by using all or part of the puppeteer's body (or an extension of it through rods, strings, wires, magnets, poles, cables, or any combination of these). Variations include hand puppets, finger puppets, rod puppets (Sicilian style rods are operated from above; Asian and European style rods are operated from below), shadow puppets, mouth puppets, costume/body puppets, and string puppets (marionettes). In the 1930s "puppet" superseded "marionette" as the generic term for the worldwide family of fantasy figures. Jim Henson coined the term "Muppet" (marionette + puppet) to describe the unique characters he created for television and films, and pioneered in the use of "Waldos" (electronic, remote movement-sensing puppets).

At the beginning of this century, traditional performers were secretive of their work, sometimes masking the back of their setups to keep stagehands from seeing them in action. A new generation turned things around by writing the histories and "how-to's" explaining everything. Performers who published included Tony Sarg, Helen Haiman Joseph, Edith Flack Ackley, Remo Bufano, Paul McPharlin, and Marjorie Batchelder.

Sarg was especially instrumental as a pioneer with marionettes, first performing at his studio (1915–16). His company toured The Rose and the Ring, Don Quixote, **Rip Van Winkle,** and others to eager audiences. Tony Sarg and "marionette" became synonymous. An artist-illustrator of note, Sarg also invented the inflatable figures for the Macy's Parade. His advertising shows at the Chicago World's Fair added to his fame and reputation. Other touring companies included Rufus and Margo Rose, Bil Baird, Remo Bufano, Martin & Olga Stevens, The Tatterman Marionettes, Ralph Chessé, Sue Hastings Marionettes, Kingslands Marionettes, the Yale Puppeteers, Leselli Marionettes, Proctor Puppets (on strings), Basil Milovsoroff (rods), and Pauline Benton (shadows). Marionette companies dominated the scene during the pretelevision era.

Touring was a way of life for most puppeteers. Their portable puppet stages were designed to set up easily in any space that could draw an audience. Department stores hired puppeteers for holiday engagements (a practice today of theme and amusement parks for seasonal engagements).

"Permanent" puppet theatres have been difficult to sustain. In 1941 the Yale Puppeteers opened The Turnabout Theatre in Los Angeles, and it ran for 13 years. The 1942 Kungsholm Restaurant in Chicago offered dinner patrons a lavish opera theatre in miniature. Partially destroyed by fire, it was rebuilt and stayed open until 1966. The Bil Baird Theatre on Barry Street (NYC) opened in 1967; productions played there and on tour for 11 years.

The Center for Puppetry Arts in Atlanta has pioneered the concept of a multilayered program of community service beyond performance – maintaining a resident company, a touring company, a puppet museum with an extensive collection on permanent display, and theme exhibits that tour. In addition, various on-site educational programs are offered (for adults and children), plus an experimental project and a summer series featuring the best American companies performing for family audiences.

Broadway has beckoned a few – Bil and Cora Baird played Radio City Music Hall, the *Ziegfeld Follies,* and *Flahooley,* a musical about life in a toy factory. The marionettes of Walton and O'Rourke were featured in *Sons o' Fun* (1941), and in 1951 this West Coast team created the memorable hand puppets for MGM's technicolor film *Lili,* starring Leslie Caron. Ten years later **David Merrick** produced *Carnival,* a grittier version of the story set to music with **Jerry Orbach** as the puppeteer; Tom Tichenor of Nashville actually designed and performed the puppets. For the **Off-Broadway** musical *Little Shop of Horrors,* Martin P. Robinson created Audrey II, a plant that grew to gargantuan proportions by feeding on humans.

Such bizarre imagery is the province of puppetry. Puppets and actors who perform together blend the best of both worlds and bridge the distance between the real and the possible. In the 1930s, ventriloquist Edgar Bergen and his sassy sidekick Charlie McCarthy won a national audience on radio: The illusion was so powerful they did not have to be seen to be believed. In 1947 Burr Tillstrom began a daily show on Chicago television called "Kukla, Fran and Ollie" (which continued as a network show until 1957). The Kuklapolitans performed on a puppet stage built to their scale, while Fran Allison, their special friend, stood out front to chat and sing with them. Daily episodes were improvised from a bare outline.

Jim Henson built a global audience for his Muppet characters, but his performances were confined to the camera. A master of camera technique, Henson was an avid experimenter with the technology of computer-generated "images" and remote controls. In a curious reversal, his characters moved off the screen to appear on arena-type stages in touring productions for family audiences. For these "personal appearance" shows ("Sesame Street Live," "The Muppet Show on Tour") the scale was enlarged by using costume/body puppet versions of Kermit, Miss Piggy, and cast. With prerecorded authentic voices, dancers and skaters in mask/body costumes matched lip sync and movement, creating the pace and energy of a dry ice show. In 1980 The Henson Foundation was established to assist American puppeteers in the creation of new works for adult audiences.

Modern puppetry is a mix and match of the traditional and the unexpected. The solo performer (long a staple of the field for economic or artistic reasons) is moving toward collaboration with peers. Some puppeteers have moved out from behind the masking to work in the actor's stage space in full view of the audience (Japanese style). The options for variety seem endless because puppet actors can be formed in any size, shape, and substance the designer chooses. Figures can be articulated or rigid, three-dimensional or flat, representational or abstract, smaller-than-human or larger-than-life. Peter Schumann's **Bread and Puppet Theatre,** for example, uses stilt walking and pole puppets for his annual August outdoor Domestic Resurrection Circus. Small side shows are preliminaries to the main event, which is staged on a hillside of his farm in Glover, VT. The heroic scale gives a primitive power to the evocative images he uses to dramatize social and political issues. Paul Zaloom, a solo performer, uses puppets, objects, and wild, satiric humor to alert his audiences to the hazards of our day. **Julie Taymor**'s *Juan Darién, A Carnival Mass* changed image size in a cinematic approach to live performance.

Although the public perception that puppetry is primarily an entertainment for children is slow to change, today puppeteers who speak to adults are developing their own material and their own unique imagery. The puppet theatre appears to be on the brink of another giant surge forward, as was dramatically illustrated in September 1992 with the presentation of the first International Festival of Puppet Theatre, featuring 17 of the world's best and most innovative companies at the Joseph Papp **Public Theater.**

Contemporary puppeteers are served by The Puppeteers of America and its publication, *The Puppetry Journal.*   GL

> See: P. Arnott, *Plays Without People,* Bloomington, IN, 1964; B. Baird, *The Art of the Puppet,* New York, 1965; M. Batchelder, *The Puppet Theatre Handbook,* New York, 1947; F. Brown, *Small Wonder,* Metuchen, NJ, 1980; P. McPharlin, *The Puppet Theatre in America: A History 1524 to 1948* (supplement since 1948 by M. B. McPharlin), Boston, 1969; A. R. Philpott, *Dictionary of Puppetry,* Boston, 1969.

Purdy, Alexander H. (c. 1815–62) Little known except as manager of New York's National Theatre during 1850–9, Purdy here introduced **George L. Fox** (1850–8); presented the **Howard family** in *Uncle Tom's Cabin* for 325 consecutive performances (1852); premiered *Ten Nights in a Bar Room* (1858); introduced holiday morning and afternoon matinees; created segregated seating for African Americans; and featured such stars as **Chanfrau** as Mose, **T. D. Rice** as Jim Crow, G. E. Locke in **Yankee** roles, as well as **J. B. Booth** and the **Wallacks.** Repeated remodeling eventually led Purdy to bankruptcy and prefigured the theatre's razing in 1862.   RKB

Purdy, James (1923–) Distinguished novelist and poet and author of such plays as *Cracks* (1963), *Wedding Finger* (1974), *Two Plays (A Day at the Fair* and *True,* 1979), *Scrap of Paper* and *The Berrypicker* (1981), and *Proud Flesh* (four short plays, 1980). His novel *Malcolm* (1959) was adapted into a play by **Edward Albee.**   TLM

Purlie Victorious At a time when African Americans were angry at the slow pace of desegregation, **Ossie Davis** wrote and, with his wife **Ruby Dee,** starred in this outrageous satire on race relations in the deep South. The play was a relief from serious race drama, treating stereotyped characters, black and white, with equal absurdity. The play ran for 261 performances on Broadway in 1961, enjoyed limited success as the movie *Gone Are the Days* (1963), and in 1970 was converted to the hit musical *Purlie,* which played for 688 performances.   EGH

Q

Quilters by Molly Newman and Barbara Damashek, with music and lyrics by Damashek, is based on *The Quilters: Women and Domestic Art* by Patricia Cooper and Norma Bradley Allen. A celebration of feminine strength and creativity, this episodic piece pulls together both horrifying and joyous stories of pioneer life on the prairie through monologue, song, mime, and multiple role-playing. *Quilters* was originally developed and produced at the **Denver Center Theatre** and proved popular in regional theatres throughout the country, despite a New York run of only 24 performances beginning 25 September 1984 at the Jack Lawrence Theater. KF

Quintero, José (1924–) Panamanian-born American director specializing in the plays of **O'Neill.** Having begun directing in 1949, Quintero helped launch **Circle in the Square** in 1951. Attracted by theatre's passion, he firmly believes "the collective product more important than any individual contribution." His O'Neill productions include the definitive *The Iceman Cometh* with **Jason Robards, Jr.** (1956; Vernon Rice Award), *Long Day's Journey into Night* (1956; Tony), *A Moon for the Misbegotten* (Broadway, 1973; Tony and Drama Desk awards), *Strange Interlude* (**Actors Studio,** 1963), and *A Touch of the Poet* (Broadway, 1977). Awarded the 1981 O'Neill Birthday Medal, Quintero, a member of the Theatre Hall of Fame, toured a 1985 revival of *Iceman* with Robards, which won the **Helen Hayes,** Los Angeles Drama Critics' Circle, and O'Neill Gold Medal awards.

Other Quintero productions include the revival of **Tennessee Williams**'s *Summer and Smoke* (1952), Behan's *The Hostage* (1954) and *The Quare Fellow* (1958), **Jules Feiffer**'s *Knock Knock* (1976), and Cocteau's *The Human Voice* (1978, Melbourne, Australia; 1979, Broadway). After the Broadway failure of Tennessee Williams's *Clothes for a Summer Hotel* (1980), Quintero left New York. He won the 1986–7 Drama League Award for "bringing to renewed life the plays of O'Neill." His autobiography, *If You Don't Dance, They Beat You,* was published in 1974. REK

See: E. McDonough, *Quintero Directs O'Neill,* Chicago, 1991.

R

Rabb, Ellis (1930–) Actor, director, and producer; founder (1960) and artistic director of the **Association of Producing Artists** (APA), which in 1964 joined with the Phoenix Theatre to become APA at the Phoenix. Until its dissolution in 1970, Rabb directed most of this company's productions and acted in many as well. Prior to the APA he was with the Antioch Arena Theatre, Yellow Springs, OH (1952–7) and spent a season at the **American Shakespeare Festival** (1958). Since 1963 he has also directed at the **American Shakespeare Theatre,** the **Old Globe** in San Diego, and the Kansas City Opera. Of his New York productions, most notable have been *Twelfth Night* at **Lincoln Center** (1972), *The **Royal Family*** (1975), *Caesar and Cleopatra* (1977), and *Anatol* at **Circle in the Square** in 1985. A flamboyant and stylish actor and director, Rabb has made significant contributions to the American theatre in both areas and been recognized with numerous awards, including the Obie and Vernon Rice awards for his Off-Broadway season with the APA (1962–3) and the Tony for direction in 1976. To Rabb's credit he has worked diligently throughout his career to bring true repertory to the American stage.   DBW

Rabe, David (1940–) Iowa-born playwright and screenwriter known for his work about the Vietnam War. Rabe, a Loras College graduate (1962), also attended Villanova University, where a number of his early plays were performed. Drafted in 1965, he was then sent to Vietnam. Rabe's big break came when, discovered by **Joseph Papp,** five of his early plays were staged by the **New York Shakespeare Festival.** In 1971 *The **Basic Training of Pavlo Hummel*** and *Sticks and Bones* ran simultaneously, *Pavlo* at the **Public Theater** and *Sticks* (Tony Award) on Broadway. Far less successful were *In the Boom Boom Room* (1973–4), about the victimization of a Philadelphia go-go dancer, and *The Orphan* (1974), Rabe's adaptation of the *Oresteia*. *Streamers,* the third play in Rabe's Vietnam Trilogy (*Pavlo* and *Sticks* being the others), was staged in 1976. Rabe, however, is more than a Vietnam War playwright: *Goose and Tomtom* (1982, 1986) is an existential comedy about a bizarre robbery; *Hurlyburly* (1984) is about Hollywood image making and failed dreams. A prequel to *Hurlyburly,* entitled *These the River Keeps,* premiered in 1991. Rabe's screenplays include *I'm Dancing As Fast As I Can* (1981) and *Casualties of War* (1990). Rabe's plays, filled with violence, racism, betrayals, foolish heroism, and male tribal customs, combine grotesque comedy, surrealistic fantasy, and bitter satire.   PCK

See: P. Kolin, *David Rabe: A Stage History and a Primary and Secondary Bibliography,* New York, 1988.

Rachel by Angelina Weld Grimke, presented as one of the first productions by the NAACP Drama Committee (March 2 and 4, 1916), was an effort to enlighten the American people by using the stage for race propaganda. Reactions were mixed. The play in three acts focuses on the effects of race prejudice on a family, the central conflict born by Rachel, the daughter, who comes to grips with the struggle between the races. Her brother can find no work because of his color; her father and an older brother were lynched when she was a child. Throughout the play, the audience is made aware of how the innocence of young children will be destroyed by the prejudice and hatred of others.   KME

Radio City Music Hall West 50th Street and Avenue of the Americas, NYC [Architects: Feinhard and Hofmeister, Hood and Foulihoux, and Corbett, Harison and MacMurray]. Built in 1932 by S. L. "Roxy" Rothafel with Rockefeller money, the 6,200-seat, art deco theatre was originally intended to present popular-priced **vaudeville,** but policy and leadership changed quickly: The new formula of showing a movie in combination with a stage show highlighted by the Rockettes, a precision tap-dancing chorus, endured for many years. When the supply of "family-type" films fell off and the attraction of the stage show wore thin, the theatre seemed doomed; but it was declared a landmark in 1979, and was thoroughly renovated to reopen as a showplace for large spectacles and star appearances. In 1985 it earned its first profit since 1955.   MCH

See: C. Francisco, *The Radio City Music Hall: An Affectionate History of the World's Greatest Theater,* New York, 1979.

Rahman, Aishah (1936–) African-American playwright whose play ***Unfinished Women Cry in No Man's Land While a Bird Dies in a Gilded Cage*** (1977) focuses on teenage pregnancy and absentee lovers. The play toured NYC's five boroughs with the **New York Shakespeare Festival** Mobile Theatre. Among Rahman's other produced plays are the musical *Lady Day* (1972) on the life of Billie Holiday, *The Mojo and the Sayso* (1989), and the opera *Marie Laveaux* (1989).   EGH

Rainmaker, The This only successful drama by N. Richard Nash premiered at the **Cort Theatre** 28 October 1954, running 125 performances. The play focuses on Lizzie Curry, a repressed 27-year-old woman whose infatuation with Bill Starbuck, a roguish, wandering rainmaker, gives her the self-esteem necessary to propel her into maturity. By nearly every definition a romance, the play avoids the traditional romantic conclusion when Lizzie declines to run away with Starbuck, realizing the merit of her own appreciation of herself over the opinions of others. In 1963, Nash wrote the book for the musical adaptation, *110 in the Shade*.   RW

Raisin in the Sun, A Warm-spirited drama of black family life by **Lorraine Hansberry** that opened at the **Ethel Barrymore Theatre** on 11 March 1959, won the Drama Critics' Circle best play award, and ran 530 performances. Directed by **Lloyd Richards,** it starred **Claudia McNeil** as the widowed Mama who wants to use her insurance money to move out of the family's poverty-stricken southside Chicago neighborhood, and Sidney Poitier as her son Walter, who loses the nest egg in a futile effort to open a liquor store. Also in the superb cast were **Ruby Dee,** Diana Sands, Louis Gossett, **Lonne Elder II,** Ivan Dixon, and **Douglas Turner Ward.** The play was hailed for the honesty of its portrayal of a family that struggles to maintain its dignity despite the injustices of the larger world. A musical version, *Raisin,* won accolades in 1973. New York revivals of the original play were presented at the **New Federal Theatre** in 1979 and at the **Roundabout** in 1983.   FHL

Raitt, John (1917–) Singer-actor who, after starting out in opera, played Curly in the national tour of *Oklahoma!* (1944). He created the role of Billy Bigelow in *Carousel* (1945), and starred in *Three Wishes for Jamie* (1952), *Carnival in Flanders* (1953), and *The Pajama Game* (1954). He lent his fine baritone voice to Broadway revivals, **summer stock,** and **nightclubs** from the 1960s to the 1990s. His most recent Broadway appearance was in *A Musical Jubilee* (1975).   MK

Ramicova, Dunya (1950–) Czechoslovakian-born costume designer who has designed at most regional theatres, working extensively at the **Hartford Stage, Arena Theatre, Guthrie Theatre, American Repertory Theatre,** and the **Yale Repertory Theatre.** She has also designed at European and American opera houses. Working frequently with directors **Andrei Serban, Liviu Ciulei,** and **Mark Lamos,** Ramicova is most closely associated with director **Peter Sellars,** for whom she has designed *Nixon in China* (1987), the Mozart–Da Ponte cycle at Pepsico Summerfare (1989), and *The Magic Flute* at Glyndebourne, England (1990), among others, as well as the Sellars film *The Cabinet of Dr. Ramirez.* She is equally at home with meticulously researched period pieces and postmodern opera.   AA

Ramsay, [Gustavus] Remak (1937–) Actor who often plays stuffy Englishmen. He made his debut **Off-Broadway** in a **revue,** *Hang Down Your Head and Die* (1964) and on Broadway in *Half a Sixpence* (1965). He frequently appears Off-Broadway and regionally, recently in *The Winslow Boy* (**Roundabout Theatre,** 1981; Drama Desk Award), Simon Gray's *Quartermaine's Terms* (**Long Wharf,** 1982; Off-Broadway, 1983; Obie and Drama Desk awards), Ayckbourn's *Woman in Mind* (**Manhattan Theatre Club,** 1988). His films include *The House on Carroll Street* (1988) and *The Money Juggler* (1989).   REK

Rand, Sally (née Hazel Gould Beck) (1904–79) Dancer who scandalized America in 1933 by performing a fan dance at the Chicago World's Fair. Born Helen Beck in Hickory County, MO, she worked as an acrobat in circuses and carnivals, then went to Hollywood in the mid-1920s to appear in such silent films as *King of Kings* and *Getting Gertie's Garter.* After the Depression she changed her name and began working Chicago speakeasies. She then toured the vaudeville circuit, headlining at the **Palace** in 1928, there reviewed as "indifferently pleasant." After breaking in the fan dance in 1932 in a Chicago **nightclub,** her World's Fair appearance made her a star, and she worked steadily almost till her death. Rand also appeared nude as Lady Godiva – she called it her form of social protest during the Depression – and also developed a bubble dance. Critics called her "saucy, piquant . . . a cute, lithesome charmer . . . radiates personality."   SMA

Rankin, Arthur McKee (1841–1914) A dashing actor-manager, Canadian-born Rankin was a theatrical gambler whose charm usually kept him one step ahead of disaster. Acting with his wife, **Kitty Blanchard,** Rankin achieved his greatest success as the stalwart miner Sandy McGee in *The Danites* (1877), a tale of Mormon revenge in a gold-mining town. Other roles included another miner, "'49," in a play of that title (1881) and a Canadian hero in *The Canuck* (1891). In 1883–4 Rankin managed the Third Avenue Theatre, and in the 1890s he coached actress **Nance O'Neil,** who would not perform without his assistance. Rankin's legal and marital problems are legend; in 1904 he declared bankruptcy. His oldest daughter, Gladys, married Sidney Drew and another daughter, Doris, married Lionel Barrymore [see **Drew–Barrymore**].   RAH

Ravel family French **mime**s and dancers, arguably the most popular and influential performers in early 19th-century America. The Ravels included **Gabriel** (1810–82), an excellent pantomimist and acrobat, the troupe's businessman; **Jérôme** (1814–90), author of such durable scenarios as *The Green Monster, Mazulme or The Night Owl,* and *Pongo the Intelligent Ape;* and **Angélique** (1813–95), **Antoine** (1812–82), and **François** (1823–81). They brought their skillful acrobatics, graceful dance, and advanced trickwork to the **Park Theatre,** 1836–7, and then became a fixture at **Niblo's Garden** (1842–6, 1849–50, 1857–60), where they were much admired by the boy Henry James and inspired rival clown **G. L. Fox.** In 1850 the troupe split, with Jérôme and Antoine touring the U.S. and François and Gabriel playing Europe. After the elder Ravels retired to France in 1866, Angélique's children Marietta and Charles Winter Ravel perpetuated the family traditions, while the **Kiralfy family** revived their pantomimes in spectacular versions. LS

> See: M. G. Swift, *Belles and Beaux on Their Toes: Dancing Stars in Young America,* Washington, DC, 1980.

Raymond (né O'Brien), John T. (1836–87)

A low comedian, Raymond made his debut at Rochester, NY (27 June 1853). After supporting such actresses as **Julia Dean** and **Anna Cora Mowatt,** he succeeded **Joseph Jefferson III** as Asa Trenchard in *Our American Cousin* with **Laura Keene.** As a member of the **stock company** at the **California Theatre,** San Francisco, he created the role of Colonel Mulberry Sellers in an adaptation of Mark Twain's *The Gilded Age* (1873), which sustained the rest of his career. Noted for his extravagant gestures and his poker face, his comic invention often ignored the dramatic situation. DMcD

Reddin, Keith (1956–)

Playwright. Educated at Northwestern and the Yale Drama School, Reddin won the Charles McArthur Award after *Life and Limb* (1984) premiered at **South Coast Repertory.** *Rum and Coke* (1984) was produced at Yale and the **Public Theater,** *Big Time* (1988) at the **American Repertory Theatre,** and *The Innocents' Crusade* (1991) at the **Long Wharf.** Reddin has twice won the San Diego Critics' Circle Award, and *Big Time* was filmed by PBS for "American Playhouse." BBW

Red Horse Animation, The

One of three "animations" – along with *The B. Beaver* (1974) and *The Shaggy Dog* (1978) – that **Lee Breuer** wrote and directed for the experimental **collective** he cofounded, **Mabou Mines.** *The Red Horse* (1970) – combining autobiography, a fragmented, nonlinear structure, and an enormous dose of irony – is regarded as one of the prototypical American avant-garde plays of the 1970s. Using a broken cartoon-like, fabulistic narrative, it examines the flow of consciousness, the process of making art, and what it means to be male. A stage prose poem filled with verbal and visual puns, it is by turns romantic and arch, elegiac, and formalistic. *Red Horse* premiered at NYC's Guggenheim Museum, performed by **JoAnne Akalaitis, Ruth Maleczech,** and **David Warrilow.** AS

Rees, James (1802–85)

Playwright and critic, best known as author of *The Dramatic Authors of America* (1845), a valuable resource for historians; he had only moderate success as a playwright. Like most of the actor-playwrights, Rees adapted popular fiction (J. F. Cooper's *The Headsman,* 1834), wrote many national plays (*Washington at Valley Forge,* 1832; *Lafitte, the Pirate of the Gulf,* 1837; *Mad Anthony Wayne,* 1845), and capitalized on current events (*Patrick Lyons; or, The Locksmith of Philadel-* phia, 1843, a man victimized and jailed by bankers). Rees's other plays include *The Miniature* (1834), *The Squatter* (1839), and *Mike Fink, the Last Boatman of the Mississippi* (n.d.). WJM

Reeve, Christopher (1952–)

Actor, identified with Superman from four films (1978, 1981, 1983, 1987), who began acting as a teenager at the **Williamstown Theatre Festival,** where he still performs frequently. His Broadway debut was in Bagnold's *A Matter of Gravity* (1976). Reeve has performed for the **Circle Repertory Company** (*Fifth of July,* 1980), **Circle in the Square** (*The Marriage of Figaro,* 1985), and **New York Shakespeare Festival** (*The Winter's Tale,* 1989). Films include *Deathtrap* (1982), *The Bostonians* (1984), and *Switching Channels* (1988). Reeve won a special 1988 Obie recognizing his work for Chilean artists. REK

Regional theatre movement see **resident nonprofit professional theatre**

Rehan, Ada (1860–1916)

Actress whose family migrated to Brooklyn from Ireland when she was 5. She made her debut at age 13, and at 15 became a member of Mrs. **Drew's Arch Street Theatre** company in Philadelphia. In 1877 **Augustin Daly** spotted her in Albany and engaged her to appear in New York in his own play *Pique* (1878). He was so impressed with her talents that he persuaded her to join him permanently, and from then until his death (1899) she was his leading lady.

During her 31 years on stage in the U.S. and in England, Rehan played over 200 roles, ranging from the title role in Daly's *Odette* (1882), to Lady Teazle in *The School for Scandal* (1894), and a host of Shakespearean roles: Katherina, Rosalind, Viola, Beatrice, Miranda, and Portia. She appeared in London at Toole's Theatre (1884), played Katherina at the Shakespeare Memorial Theatre (1888), opened Daly's Theatre (just off Leicester Square) as Viola (1893), made a cross-country tour of the U.S. (1896), and finally after Daly's death toured again with **Otis Skinner** in *The Taming of the Shrew* (1904–5).

Critics called her "sweetly reckless," "ardently impetuous," and "piquantly alluring." Ellen Terry described her as "the most lovely, humorous darling I have ever seen on the stage." RM

> See: A. Hendricks-Wenck, "Ada Rehan: American Actress," PhD diss., Louisiana State U, 1988; M. MacGhee, *The Acting of Ada Rehan,* Canton, MO, 1927; W. Winter, *Ada Rehan: A Study,* rev. ed., New York, 1898.

Reid, Kate (1930–)

Canadian actress of international stature noted for her work in roles demanding intense emotional energy. Her London (England) debut was in the title role of *The Stepmother* (1958). She returned to Canada to appear at the **Stratford Festival** (1959–62). In 1962 she went to New York to play Martha in the matinee cast of **Edward Albee's** *Who's Afraid of Virginia Woolf?* (1962), and in 1964 was nominated for a Tony for her performance opposite Sir Alec Guinness in *Dylan.* She costarred in **Tennessee Williams's**

Slapstick Tragedy (1966) and spent almost two years in **Arthur Miller**'s *The Price* in New York and London. For the **American Shakespeare Festival** she played Gertrude in *Hamlet* in 1969 and, in 1974, the Nurse in *Romeo and Juliet* and Big Mama in *Cat on a Hot Tin Roof*. In 1985 she played opposite **Dustin Hoffman** in a major revival of *Death of a Salesman*. She appeared as the Countess in **Mark Lamos**'s production of *All's Well That Ends Well* at the **Hartford Stage Company** in 1991. She has also had a successful film and television career.   JA DBW

Reilly, Charles Nelson (1931–) Actor, teacher, and director. A native New Yorker, Reilly appeared on Broadway in *How to Succeed in Business Without Really Trying,* winning a Tony for his Bud Frump (1960); in *Bye Bye Birdie* (1960); in *Hello, Dolly!,* winning the Drama Critics' Circle Award for his Cornelius Hackl (1964); in *Skyscraper* (1965), *God's Favorite* (1974), and *Charlotte* (1980). He directed *The Belle of Amherst* with **Julie Harris** (1979). His recent work has been in films, TV, and the direction of opera. He is also a respected acting teacher.   TLM

Reinhardt, Max (1873–1943) Austrian *régisseur* who gained a reputation throughout Europe as an innovative director, utilizing new stage and lighting techniques in theatre spaces both large and intimate, but primarily in vast spectacles with huge casts and, later, outdoor stagings. Reinhardt's New York production of *Sumurun* (1912) introduced audiences to the New Stagecraft inspired by Appia and Craig. **Norman Bel Geddes**'s lavish design for Reinhardt's *The Miracle* (1924) transformed New York's Century Theatre [the renamed **New Theatre**] into a cathedral. Reinhardt's ensemble toured the U.S. in 1927–8 with *A Midsummer Night's Dream* and *Danton's Death,* among others. Reinhardt became interested in Hollywood and the prospects of filming Shakespeare. He directed his twelfth *Midsummer* in the Hollywood Bowl, and directed the film version in 1935. He staged Franz Werfel's pageant of Jewish history, *The Eternal Road,* in a spectacular production (Bel Geddes design, 1937) at the Manhattan Opera House in New York, and settled permanently in the U.S. in 1938. He popularized **Thornton Wilder**'s *The Merchant of Yonkers* (**Boris Aronson** design, 1938) on Broadway. His son Gottfried directed his successful 1929 Berlin version of Strauss's *Die Fledermaus* (retitled *Rosalinda*, 1942) on Broadway. His final production was **Irwin Shaw**'s *Sons and Soldiers* (1943).   RE

> See: G. Reinhardt, *The Genius: A Memoir of Max Reinhardt,* New York, 1979; J. L. Styan, *Max Reinhardt,* Cambridge (UK)/New York, 1982.

Rentz–Santley Novelty and Burlesque Company Credited as the first American **burlesque show,** created by **Michael B. Leavitt** in 1870. Leavitt first feminized the traditional **minstrel show** (as Madame Rentz's Female Minstrels, a name suggested by a European circus), then added variety acts (the traditional olio) and, as the third act of his show, a musicalized travesty (after-

piece), adapting the tripartite minstrel format. One of the first stars, Mabel Santley, helped establish the model for most reputable burlesque of the 1880s and '90s (editions of the show appeared annually). Rival burlesque companies soon followed, with Sam T. Jack (former Rentz–Santley manager) the most notorious competitor.   DBW

Repertorio Español Award-winning (Obies, 1981 and 1989) nonprofit, Spanish-language repertory company founded in 1968 by Gilberto Zaldívar and René Buch to produce the best of Latin American, Spanish, and **Hispanic**-American theatre. Headquartered at New York's Gramercy Arts Theatre (since 1972), the company offers 300 performances annually of 16 dramatic, musical (especially popular are its Spanish zarzuelas), and dance productions in rotating repertory and on tour. With its infrared simultaneous translation for English-speaking audiences, the company has served as a catalyst for cultural interaction.   DBW

Repertory Theatre of St. Louis Founded in 1966 as the Repertory Theatre at Loretto–Hilton Center, then operating as the Loretto–Hilton Repertory Theatre during 1973–81, this regional nonprofit theatre was conceived by Marita Woodruff and Wayne Loui on the Webster University campus. The Sisters of Loretto administer the University, and Conrad Hilton, a former student, contributed $1.5 million to the project. The Repertory Theatre presents a substantial series of productions in a main-stage facility seating 733, a studio seating about 125, and the Imaginary Theatre Company, the last being the chief organ of the company's outreach program.   SMA

Resident nonprofit professional theatre This movement, which gained its greatest momentum in the 1960s, has variously been called the regional, repertory, or resident theatre movement. Although its initial impetus was the creation of an alternative, decentralized U.S. theatre network outside of New York, the movement's most current nomenclature is "resident," so as not to exclude NYC not-for-profit theatres. Its nonprofit status is significant in that box-office income is not of prime concern; rather the focus is on the art of the theatre, the development of theatre artists, craftsmen, and administrators dedicated to establishing a new American theatre, the production of classical and innovative contemporary drama, and often community service. Most resident theatres have a set season with subscribers and are established in their own building. From a handful of theatres three decades ago, today there are more than 200 theatres playing to over 15 million people annually, forming a complex network and comprising the nearest thing in the U.S. to a national theatre institution. Today these theatres – which by 1966 employed more actors than Broadway and the road combined – are the chief originators and producers of significant theatre in America. According to a 1989–90 **Theatre Communications Group** survey of 185 theatres, more than 23,700 artists, administrators, and technical and production personnel are currently employed by these theatres. Surviving on the basis of both public and private subsidy, these theatres have been in jeopardy since the mid-1980s due to the erratic pattern of contributed support that has failed to close the growing gap between income and expenses, intensified by the recession of recent years. Since 1980 almost 40 theatres, including at least two that have existed for more than 30 years, have ceased operation. (One was New York's Chelsea Stage, which as the **Hudson Guild** dated back to 1896.) Nonetheless, as a result of this movement, most major American cities, such as **Chicago, Los Angeles, San Francisco,** and **Seattle,** today are important centers of theatre activity.

Claiming as antecedents the amateur **community theatre/Little Theatre movement** of the 1920s, the **Group Theatre** of the 1930s, and the **Federal Theatre Project** of the Depression, the movement most frequently marks its beginning with the founding of the **Cleveland Play House** in 1915 (still in existence), although its impetus and inspiration is credited to **Margo Jones,** who in the 1940s devised the prototype for the regional theatre with her Theatre '47 in Dallas, TX. In her book on arena staging (1951), which was the manifesto for the movement for many years, she proposed a network of regional theatres. Following Jones's lead, Nina Vance founded Houston's **Alley Theatre** in 1947 and **Zelda Fichandler** cofounded the **Arena Stage** in an old Washington, DC, moviehouse in 1950. With Jones and Vance deceased, Fichandler, who has left Arena, is now considered the prime representative of the movement's beginnings and still a visionary voice for its future, though the earlier cohesiveness of the movement has dissipated.

From these beginnings other theatres followed in quick succession: the **Milwaukee Repertory Theatre** and the **New York Shakespeare Festival** (1954); the **Dallas Theater Center** (1959); Baltimore's **Center Stage,** the **Seattle Repertory Theatre,** and the **Guthrie Theatre** (founded by **Tyrone Guthrie,** Olivier Rea, and **Peter Zeisler**) in Minneapolis (all 1963); in 1964, the **Actors Theatre of Louisville,** NYC's **American Place Theatre,** the **Hartford Stage Company** and **Eugene O'Neill Theatre Center** (both in CT), **South Coast Repertory** (Costa Mesa, CA) and **Trinity Repertory Company** (Providence, RI); San Francisco's **American Conservatory Theatre** and New Haven, CT's **Long Wharf Theatre** (1965); New Haven's **Yale Repertory Theatre** and the Arizona Theatre Company (1966); Los Angeles's **Mark Taper Forum** and San Francisco's **Magic Theatre** (1967); and Atlanta, GA's **Alliance Theatre** and NYC's **Circle Repertory Company** in 1969. During the 1970s the number of theatres established increased appreciably, only to ebb during the '80s and early '90s. The movement was helped extensively early in its history by the Ford Foundation (under the dynamic leadership of W. McNeil Lowry) and Rockefeller Foundation, and later by the National Endowment for the Arts – though under recent administrations this source of support failed to increase as it had during the 1960s and '70s – and state arts agencies.

As theatres associated with specific communities, these institutions have attempted to serve their specific areas in terms of individual needs and profiles. In addition to preserving the classics as exciting living theatre for their patrons, these theatres have the potential to achieve the ensemble acting possible only in companies that work together in numerous productions over many years (though, in practice, only a few companies have been somewhat successful in this regard). They can also be educational resources for their communities, create professional theatre training programs, and – perhaps their major mission – develop new texts without restrictions on theme and content, as is often not true of the commercial theatre. However, regional audiences are often more conservative than those in New York, and as more varied philosophies and programs develop, some companies are, in fact, less concerned with new plays or traditional classics.

Still, the number of playwrights who owe allegiance to the resident theatre is impressive, though not as extensive as it might be. For example, Chicago's **Goodman Theatre** (founded in 1925) devoted much of its energy to the development of early plays by **David Mamet** (who had previously worked extensively at Chicago's now defunct St. Nicholas Theatre) and **John Guare. Jon Jory**'s Actors Theatre of Louisville has demonstrated an intense interest in new plays with an annual new play festival; playwrights such as **Marsha Norman** and **Beth Henley** have emerged from this program. Writers as diverse as **Sam Shepard, Lanford Wilson,** and **Charles Fuller** have been nurtured by the nonprofit theatre. It is significant that nine consecutive Pulitzer Prizes (1976–84) premiered in nonprofit theatres before being transferred to commercial theatres on Broadway, although such a trend predates 1976 (one of the first was Arena Stage's 1968 production of Howard Sackler's *The Great White Hope*) and continues today. Indeed, the nonprofit theatre has been accused of becoming nothing more than a tryout institution for the commercial theatre, a charge that ignores the natural desire to prolong the life of and give greater visibility to significant plays. It is, therefore, noteworthy that David Mamet's *Glengarry Glen Ross* (1984 Pulitzer) began at the Goodman, that Marsha Norman's *'night, Mother* (1983 winner) came to New York from the **American Repertory Theatre,** that a play like **Mark Medoff**'s *Children of a Lesser God* originated at the Mark Taper Forum, and that **August Wilson**'s plays to date were developed at Yale Repertory Theatre. Other examples of plays first presented regionally include **Fugard**'s *A Lesson from Aloes* and *Master Harold and the Boys* (Yale), **David Rabe**'s *Hurlyburly* (Goodman), **Herb Gardner**'s *I'm Not Rappaport* (Seattle Rep), and the **Steinbeck–Galati** *Grapes of Wrath* (Chicago's **Steppenwolf Theatre**). In 1990 *A Chorus Line,* produced by the nonprofit New York Shakespeare Festival, closed after a significant 15-year Broadway run; this and other transfers, and the considerable profits accrued as a result, allowed **Joseph Papp** to produce dozens of less profitable or more risky plays and musicals.

Unquestionably, in today's nonprofit resident

theatre there is a true danger of allowing artistic product to take second place to an institution, of creating a regional theatre that moves away from indigenous needs to a more traditionally commercial, conservative, and safe product that appeals to a mass audience and guarantees the box office needed to supplement other sources of income for survival. It is certainly a fact, with notable exceptions, that little avant-garde or true experimentation has taken place in the regions. Since the mid-1970s, in fact, the lines between commercial and noncommercial theatre have blurred. However, as long as the American resident theatres allow strong personalities to operate these theatres with vision and sensitivity, they will remain more individual than similar. In this regard, however, it is significant that a true network is beginning to emerge that perhaps stresses important similarities of goals and aspirations. For example, one of the most popular resident theatre plays of the 1980s, Sam Shepard's **Fool for Love,** originated at San Francisco's Magic Theatre before it played at New York's Circle Repertory Company – both nonprofit theatres. Michael Cristofer's *The Shadow Box* (1977) went from the Mark Taper to New Haven's Long Wharf to Broadway. **Christopher Durang**'s *A History of the American Film* was staged in different productions at the Hartford Stage Company, the Arena Stage, and the Mark Taper Forum before it was presented in New York. **Emily Mann**'s *Execution of Justice* (about political assassination) was seen at the Arena Stage in 1985 after an earlier production at the Actors Theatre. Such a pattern of movement within the regional network is becoming more commonplace, as are coproductions with two or more theatres sharing production costs and extending the life of productions.

The U.S. nonprofit theatre network is served by dozens of organizations, although two are of special importance. Theatre Communications Group, founded in 1961, serves as a communications network for its institutional members and individual artists. Among their goals is "to foster cross-fertilization and interaction among different types of organizations and individuals that comprise the profession." One of TCG's services is the annual publication of *Theatre Facts,* which provides a statistical guide to the finances [see **economics**] and productivity of the nonprofit professional theatre in America. Recent reports underscore the increasing number of large deficits of major institutions since 1980, and the ominous news that "the costs of doing business have grown faster than available income" and that long-range planning efforts "are increasingly hampered by the shifting philanthropic terrain." In 1991 half of the nation's nonprofit theatres ended the year with deficits brought on by the recession; during this same year attendance declined for the first time since 1973. The second vital organization, the League of Resident Theatres (LORT), represents about 80 nonprofit professional theatres, is active in labor relations, and concerns itself with the artistic and management needs of its members.

What seems clear from all available evidence is that the nonprofit professional theatre is being forced to reexamine its structure and product in order to

Fanny Brice and Bobby Clark in *The Music Box Revue of 1924.* Courtesy: New York Public Library of the Performing Arts.

ensure stability throughout the 1990s. Thus far action has included reducing the number of plays produced in a season, making administrative cuts and changes, and frequently seeking a balanced season that both restricts the size and scope of productions while minimizing changes in artistic integrity and vision. The future of small to midsize theatres is especially in jeopardy as support continues to decline. Although the future for the nonprofit theatre sector is uncertain, it is clear that it has entered a new phase requiring creative and imaginative adjustments.   DBW

See: G. M. Berkowitz, *New Broadways: Theatre Across America 1950–1980,* Totowa, NJ, 1982; M. Jones, *Theatre-in-the-Round,* New York, 1951; J. Novick, *Beyond Broadway: The Quest for Permanent Theatres,* New York, 1968; L. Ross et al., eds., *Theatre Profiles,* New York, published annually by TCG; J. W. Zeigler, *Regional Theatre: The Revolutionary Stage,* Minneapolis, 1973.

Revue A form of musical entertainment that includes songs, dances, and sketch or stand-up comedy, usually tied together by a theme or narration rather than a story. Among the forerunners of the revue in the American theatre were the olio segments of the **minstrel show,** the literary travesties of **John Brougham** and others, the topical humor of the comic opera, the variety programs of concert saloons and **vaudeville** houses, and the elaborate spectacle of the extravaganza. The French form of the spectacular revue, seen at such theatres as the

Folies-Bergère, did not exert a major influence on the American stage until after the turn of the century.

The Passing Show (1894), produced by **George Lederer,** is generally considered the first successful American "review" (the English spelling was employed at first). It combined topical humor, a chorus of beautiful girls posing as "living pictures" [see **nudity**], and an elaborate ballet. Because of its popularity, subsequent revues on the American stage represented variations on its formula: Some were conceived on a modest scale, with sophisticated topical humor and a small but ingratiating cast as their main assets; others emphasized spectacle, ever-growing numbers of scantily clad chorus girls, and the greatest singers, dancers, and comedians of the day.

Producer **Florenz Ziegfeld** applied his unique brand of showmanship to the revue when he presented the *Follies of 1907,* the first edition of what would be an annual series of "revues" (now using the French spelling) lasting until Ziegfeld's death in 1932. In the early editions, Ziegfeld followed the prevalent revue style by including a good deal of topical humor in his shows. Nevertheless, his revues were most noted for the beauty of the chorus girls, led at first by Ziegfeld's wife, **Anna Held.** By "glorifying the American girl," Ziegfeld found a successful formula that spawned a host of imitators, including the **Shubert brothers'** two series, *The Passing Show* (1912–19, 1921–4) and *Artists and Models* (1923–5, 1927, 1930, 1943); *George White's Scandals* (1919–31, 1935, 1939); the **Earl Carroll Vanities** (1924–8, 1930–2, 1940); and many other individual revues.

Topical humor was still the main attraction in three revues put together by **George M. Cohan:** *Hello Broadway* (1914) and two editions of *The Cohan Revue* (1916, 1918). Satire on the people and events of the day was also prevalent in several revue series that appeared in the early 1920s: *The Greenwich Village Follies* (1919–25, 1928), the *Grand Street Follies* (1922, 1924–9), and the *Garrick Gaieties* (1925, 1926, 1930). Much of the humor in these shows involved imitations of celebrities and parodies of the season's most notable shows and movies; they thus appealed to a more sophisticated audience than did the "girlie shows." **Irving Berlin**'s series of *Music Box* Revues (1921–4) benefited from some of his most popular and enduring songs, as well as from a skillful blend of lavish decor and topical humor. In addition to Berlin, many of Broadway's greatest composers and lyricists, including **George and Ira Gershwin, Richard Rodgers** and **Lorenz Hart,** and the team of **DeSylva, Brown, and Henderson,** wrote for the revues of the 1920s. The decade also saw the first all-black revues on Broadway, including *The Plantation Revue* (1922), *Africana* (1927), *Blackbirds of 1928,* and *Hot Chocolates* (1929) [see **African-American theatre**].

The period 1900–30 saw the production of some 228 revues on Broadway. Although the 1929 stock market crash and resulting Depression caused a severe curtailment in the number of shows produced on Broadway each season, the revue, with its flexible framework, survived and even flourished in a modest way during the 1930s. A more intimate style of revue – relying on a small, versatile cast, scores by a new generation of composers (including **Arthur Schwartz** and **Vernon Duke**), and comedy sketches poking fun at such topics as the Depression and international politics – emerged as the old series of lavish revues died out. Among the most notable of this new style were *The Little Show* (1929), *Three's a Crowd* (1930), and *The Band Wagon* (1931). One of the longest running revues of the 1930s, **Pins and Needles** (1937), began as an amateur show put together by the International Ladies' Garment Workers' Union as an entertainment for the union's members; but it received such critical acclaim that it ran (with changes and updates) for almost three seaons. *New Faces,* a revue series featuring Broadway newcomers, debuted in 1934 and continued to appear sporadically through 1968.

The revue stagnated in the late 1930s, but producers began offering them in greater numbers with the advent of WW II, since the form's flexibility made it possible to piece together a show out of the talent remaining after the incursions of the draft and the USO. Shows such as *Priorities of '42* and *Bright Lights of 1944* amused war-weary audiences without moving the revue in new artistic directions. Among the most popular revues of the war years were the all-military shows, made up of songs, dance, and comedy by members of the armed services under the guiding hand of professional theatre artists. Thus, Irving Berlin wrote the score for *This Is the Army* (1942), a revised version of his WW I show, *Yip, Yip Yaphank* (1918). Also available to audiences were the dance revues of Katherine Dunham, notably *A Tropical Revue* (1943) and *Bal Negre* (1946), as well as several ice shows.

After the war, topical satire once again flourished in such revues as *Call Me Mister* (1946), *Make Mine Manhattan* (1948), and *Inside U.S.A.* (1948). Ironically, some of the people associated with these revues, including Sid Caesar and Carl Reiner, would contribute indirectly to the demise of the topical revue on Broadway when they brought their satires and imitations to live television, which would achieve a topicality impossible in the Broadway theatre.

Though few revues made it to Broadway in the 1950s, intimate revues became a staple of **Off-Broadway** and **nightclubs.** Beginning in 1955 Ben Bagley produced a series called the *Shoestring Revue,* while the Phoenix Theatre offered *Phoenix '55.* Julius Monk produced a sporadic series of revues at his nightclub, Upstairs at the Downstairs. Most of these shows featured young performers and heavy doses of satire.

The 1960s saw a resurgence of topical humor in the revues that opened on Broadway, including *A Thurber Carnival* (1960), *From the Second City* (1961), and *The Mad Show* (1965). An even sharper type of satire was seen in two British imports, *Beyond the Fringe* (1962) and *Oh, What a Lovely War!* (1964). This vogue for ruthless satire and parody was relatively short-lived, and by the 1970s the revue had taken a turn toward nostalgia with several shows built around the work of noted composers, such as *Ain't Misbehavin'* (1978), which featured the songs of Fats Waller; the Duke Ellington–inspired

Sophisticated Ladies (1981); and *Side by Side by **Sondheim*** (1977). Once again, topical humor moved Off-Broadway, with the opening in 1982 of the satirical revue series *Forbidden Broadway*, built around constantly updated parodies of Broadway shows and performers. Meanwhile, the few revues to be seen on Broadway in the late 1980s and early '90s, such as ***Jerome Robbins' Broadway*** (1989), tended to emphasize spectacle and nostalgia rather than satire and innovation. Ironically, a book musical, *The **Will Rogers Follies*** (1991), achieved success primarily through director **Tommy Tune**'s imaginative recreations of 1920s *Ziegfeld Follies* production numbers.

While the form no longer dominates the musical stage, audiences still seem to enjoy the topical humor, captivating stars, and spectacular chorus numbers that have characterized so many of America's best revues.   MK

See: R. Baral, *Revue: The Great Broadway Period*, New York and London, 1962; G. Bordman, *American Musical Revue: From The Passing Show to Sugar Babies*, New York, 1985; M. Farnsworth, *The Ziegfeld Follies*, London, 1956.

Reynolds, James (1891–1957) Designer. Reynolds's *Tents of the Arabs* (1919) was one of the outstanding examples of the New Stagecraft, but he established himself as a designer of lavish and sophisticated **revue**s, including several of the *Ziegfeld Follies* and *Greenwich Village Follies*. Broadway credits include *Fifty Million Frenchmen* (1929) and *Jumbo* (1935).   AA

Ribman, Ronald (1932–   ) Playwright, born in New York and educated at the University of Pittsburgh, who attracted critical attention in 1965 with his *Harry, Noon and Night* at the **American Place Theatre.** During the following year, his *The Journey of the Fifth Horse* won an Obie. Other major dramatic works by Ribman include *The Ceremony of Innocence* (1965), *Passing Through from Exotic Places* (1969), *Fingernails Blue as Flowers* (1971), *A Break in the Skin* (1972), *The Poison Tree* (1973), *Cold Storage* (1977, Dramatists Guild Award–winning comedy about the function of death), *Buck* (1983), and *Sweet Table at the Richelieu* (1987). More respected than loved, Ribman's plays deal with man's entrapment by a universe he cannot change.   TLM

See: P. Egan, "Ronald Ribman: A Classified Bibliography," *Studies in American Drama, 1945–Present* (1987).

Rice (né McLaren), Dan (1823–1900) Clown, son of a New York provisioner. He led a checkered career as a jockey, strong man, blackface **minstrel**, and (he alleged) agent for the Mormon leader Joseph Smith, before setting up his own show in 1841 with Lord Byron, "the most sapient of pigs." His debut as clown was ostensibly made in Galena, IL, in 1844, and he was soon a favorite for his native American humor with its heavyhanded mockery of local politicians. His red-and-white striped costume, top hat, and chin-whiskers later became attributes of Uncle Sam. Rice popularized the term "one-horse show," originally an insult flung at him by a competitor; and, as the "Great Shakespearian clown," rival to the English jester William Wallett, he bandied mangled quotations with his audience. He was half-seriously proposed for president in 1868; alcoholism undermined his abilities before he made a comeback as a temperance lecturer in the 1870s and '80s (evil tongues claimed that the water pitcher on the podium contained gin). His final **circus** appearances were made in and around New York City in 1891–2. Feisty and quarrelsome, alternately populist and genteel, Rice neatly suited the tastes of an adolescent nation.   LS

See: M. Brown, *The Life of Dan Rice*, Long Branch, NJ, 1901; J. Kunzog, *The One-Horse Show*, Jamestown, NY, 1962.

Rice (né Reizenstein), Elmer (1892–1967) Playwright whose career started in 1914 with *On Trial*, an experimental play that used flashbacks to reveal aspects of the crime being tried. A New Yorker who graduated from law school before becoming a playwright, Rice used his legal knowledge in several plays, in various disputes with theatres, and in the causes he served – from Marxism in the 1930s to the American Civil Liberties Union. A wise and fearless man, Rice wrote with considerable skill on subjects both popular and unpopular. When his efforts with the **Federal Theatre Project** were threatened with government **censorship,** he was outraged and resigned his administrative post. Responding to the high-handed methods of the **Theatre Guild,** he and four other playwrights – **Robert Sherwood, S. N. Behrman, Sidney Howard,** and **Maxwell Anderson** – founded the **Playwrights' Company** in 1938. He later vigorously opposed Senator Joseph McCarthy's attacks on theatre artists.

Rice's plays reflect his various interest in theatrical experiments, realistic scenes, and protest drama. His best work, *The **Adding Machine*** (1923), an expressionistic play about the dehumanization of humankind, was followed by further experiments – *The Subway* (1929) and *Dream Girl* (1945). Man's social condition both fascinated and angered Rice, who exclaimed through a character in ***Street Scene*** (1929): "Everywhere you look, oppression and cruelty!" *We, the People* (1933), a bitter attack on Depression times, ended in an agitprop call for democratic ideals. In *Judgment Day* (1934) Rice scourged Nazi fascism, and in *Between Two Worlds* (1934) he contrasted the political systems of Russia and America. Finally, in *American Landscape* (1938), Rice maintained his support for American idealism but, disillusioned with both Marxism and American commercial theatre, threatened to stop writing plays. Post–WW II theatre brought him little satisfaction. *The Grand Tour,* a romance in Europe (1951), *Winners,* a crime melodrama (1954), and *Cue for Passion,* a weak story of a California Hamlet (1958) did little for his reputation. He recounted his experiences in *The Living Theatre* (1959) and *Minority Report* (1963), where, always a liberal idealist, he preached individual freedom from all tyranny.   WJM

Rice, J[ohn] B. (1809–74) Actor, manager, theater owner, and politician. Discovered at 27 singing as he worked in a shoemaking shop in Baltimore, Rice later left the chorus of Philadelphia's **Walnut Street Theatre** (1837) for a series of theatre managing jobs in Albany, Buffalo, Milwaukee, and **Chicago** – where, in 1847, he erected that city's first theatre building to coincide with a convention of canal builders. In subsequent years, Rice and his wife performed there, as did such prominent players as **Edwin Forrest, Junius Brutus Booth,** and **James H. McVicker.** The theatre burned in 1850, was rebuilt the following year, and closed in 1861, having been eclipsed in 1857 by the construction of **McVicker's Theatre.** Rice, who amassed a small fortune in real estate, subsequently served two terms as a popular Republican Mayor of Chicago (1865–9), and was at the end of his first term in Congress when he died.   SF

Rice, Thomas Dartmouth "Daddy" (1806–60) Blackface performer ("Ethiopian delineator") considered the "father of American **minstrel**sy." Between 1828 and 1831 Rice, according to tradition, observed a crippled Negro stableman (possibly in Louisville, KY) sing a refrain and dance with a jerky jump – thus "Jump Jim Crow," after the slave's name. From this single song and dance Rice developed full-length entertainments called "Ethiopian operas." He toured the British Isles in 1836, 1838, and 1843, leaving his stamp on the English stage. In 1858, he played the title role at the **Bowery Theatre** in *Uncle Tom's Cabin* (1850), though

T. D. Rice as the original Jim Crow (c. 1830). Courtesy: Laurence Senelick.

generally Rice remained a solo entertainer throughout his career.   DBW

Rich, Frank (1949–) Drama critic. Born in Washington, DC, and educated at Harvard in American history and literature (1971), Rich was cofounder, reporter, and editor of the *Richmond [VA] Mercury* (1972–3); the senior editor and film critic of *New Times Magazine* (NYC, 1973–5); film critic of the *New York Post* (1975–7); film and television critic of *Time* magazine (1977–80); and chief drama critic of the *New York Times* (1980–). He is author of *The Theatre Art of* **Boris Aronson** (cowritten with Lisa Aronson, 1987). As daily critic of the *New York Times,* Rich is arguably the most powerful drama critic in the U.S. Intelligent, demanding, and generally knowledgeable about theatre and popular culture, Rich writes for the literate reader with style and authority but with a hard intellectual edge and – in the estimation of the New York theatre community – little sympathy or affection for the theatre. "*Lettice and Lovage,*" he wrote, "is a high camp, female version of the archetypal [Peter] Shaffer play, most recently exemplified by *Equus* and *Amadeus* in which two men, one representing creativity and ecstatic passion and the other mediocrity and sterility, battle for dominance" (1990).   TLM

Richard Rodgers Theatre 226 West 46th St., NYC [Architect: Herbert J. Krapp]. Renamed in 1990 in honor of America's foremost theatre music composer, what was formerly known as the 46th St. Theatre was built in 1924 by the Chanin Brothers as part of their chain of Broadway playhouses [cf. **Royale Theatre**]. For several years, it was a theatre in search of a hit; but in 1939, **Ethel Merman** took its stage as a full-fledged star in *Du Barry Was a Lady,* returning the following year in *Panama Hattie.* Thereafter, the theatre housed successful musicals, beginning with *Finian's Rainbow* (1947) and continuing more recently with *Nine* (1982). Among its more successful nonmusical tenants have been *The Merchant of Venice* (1989) with **Dustin Hoffman** and **Neil Simon**'s Pulitzer Prize–winning *Lost in Yonkers* (1991). When the Chanins lost their theatres to creditors in the early depression, the lease was acquired by the **Shubert**s, who ran it until 1945, when it became part of City Playhouses. It is now part of the **Nederlander** chain.   MCH

Richards, Beah (19?–) **African-American** actress who trained under **Randolph Edmonds** at Dillard University, New Orleans, and at the San Diego Community Theatre. Her principal roles on Broadway were Viney in *The* **Miracle Worker** (1959), Idella in **Purlie Victorious** (1961), and Sister Margaret in *The* **Amen Corner** (1965), which brought her a *Theatre World* Award. For many years she has taught acting at the Inner City Cultural Center, Los Angeles, where her play *One Is a Crowd* (1971) and poetic monologue *A Black Woman Speaks* (1974) were produced. Her work in films has earned her an Academy Award nomination for best supporting actress in *Guess Who's Coming to*

Dinner? and induction into the Black Filmmakers Hall of Fame. EGH

Richards, David Bryant (1942–) Drama critic who established his reputation in Washington, DC, with radio station WGMS (1969–71), the *Star* (1971–81), and the *Post* (1981–90) before becoming chief Sunday critic for the *New York Times* (1990–). A native of Concord, MA, Richards was educated in French at Occidental (1964) and Middlebury (1965) colleges, and in speech/drama at Catholic University (1969). He has taught French at Howard University, acted for the National Players, and served as producer for "Voice of America." A witty and graceful stylist, Richards demands vitality and imagination in the theatre, and deplores conventional and academically "correct" productions. He is author of *Played Out: The Jean Seberg Story* (1981) and a contributor to the **Burns Mantle** *Best Plays* series. TLM

Richards, Lloyd (1923–) **African-American** actor, director, and educator, Richards began his professional career as an actor **Off-Broadway** and as resident director at regional theatres. His major directorial opportunity came with *A Raisin in the Sun* (1959), whose success is legendary. Richards then turned his attention to directing and teaching, accepting assignments at colleges and opening the Lloyd Richards Studio (1962–72). In 1968 he was named artistic director of the **National Playwrights' Conference** at the **Eugene O'Neill Theatre Center** in Waterford, CT, for the development of new plays. Appointed dean of the Yale Drama School and artistic director of the **Yale Repertory Theatre** in 1979, he used his strategic positions of leadership to promote the work of contemporary playwrights, the most prominent being **August Wilson** and the South African **Athol Fugard.** He has produced seven of Fugard plays and, so far, directed all five of Wilson's, working collaboratively with the author. He has won a Pulitzer Prize and a Tony Award as best director for Wilson's *Fences* (1987). In 1990 Richards was elected to the Theatre Hall of Fame. His term at Yale expired in 1991. EGH

Richardson, Leander (1856–1918) Theatre journalist whose aggressive and personal style helped establish the tone of theatrical weeklies. Richardson began with the *New York Dramatic News* (1879), which he edited during 1888–96. He wrote for the *Morning Telegraph* (1896–1903) and edited the *New York Enquirer* (1903) before becoming a press **agent** for **William A. Brady.** TLM

Richardson, Lee (1926–) Actor known originally as Lee Richard and considered a leading classical repertory actor. He was in the 1952 **Circle in the Square** revival of *Summer and Smoke,* making his Broadway debut in *The Legend of Lizzie* (1959). He acted in many classical plays at the **New York Shakespeare Festival, Hartman Theatre, American Shakespeare Festival,** and **Yale Repertory,** and was a founding member of the **Guthrie Theatre,** appearing there during 1963–70. He also performed in such plays as **Albee**'s *The Death*

of Bessie Smith (1961), Bolt's *Vivat! Vivat Regina!* (1972), A *Texas Trilogy* (1976), **Hailey**'s *Father's Day* (1979), and Gray's *Quartermaine's Terms* (1983), as well as in *Ivanov* (1990) and *Getting Married* (1991). Appearing frequently on television, his film work includes the narrator of *Network* (1976) and roles in *Prizzi's Honor* (1985) and *The Fly II.* Richardson was nominated for a Tony for *Vivat!* and has been a faculty member at the Yale School of Drama. REK

Richardson, Willis (1889–1977) **African-American** playwright whose one-act play *The Chip Woman's Fortune* (1923), produced by the Ethiopian Art Theatre of Chicago, made history as the first known drama by a black author to be shown on Broadway. A clerk in the U.S. Department of Engraving and Printing, Richardson was inspired to write plays by *Crisis* magazine's contests, of which he was twice winner (1925, 1926). He wrote some 30 one-act and five full-length plays, mostly about rural folk and black historical figures. He is also noted for editing two collections of black plays for adults and a third for children. He was a founder of the Washington, DC, branch of the Krigwa Players. EGH

Richman (né Reichman), Harry (1895–1972) Song-and-dance man and composer. Suave, debonair ("Beau Broadway"), and loaded with personality, Richman headlined **vaudeville,** *George White*'s *Scandals* (1926, 1928), and served as master of ceremonies for *The Ziegfeld Follies* of 1931. With his top hat and tails (or strawhat and blazer) and cane, he established his reputation with such songs as "On the Sunny Side of the Street," "Walking My Baby Back Home" (which he wrote), and "Puttin' on the Ritz." His Club Richman on Park Avenue was a top **nightclub** in the 1920s. In the 1940s his voice and career deteriorated. His autobiography appeared (written with Richard Gehman) in 1966; titled *A Hell of a Life,* it was a fitting epitaph for his colorful and amorous life. DBW

Ridiculous Theatrical Company Off-Off **Broadway** theatre founded by the late actor, director, and playwright **Charles Ludlam** after he split off from **John Vaccaro**'s Play-House of the Ridiculous [see **Theatre of the Ridiculous**] in 1967. The Ridiculous was one of the first American theatres to deal explicitly with homosexual themes. Known for their flamboyant style, high camp, and combinations of the lofty and the lowly, plays at the Ridiculous are often based on classical dramatic and operatic texts, which are then both spoofed and celebrated with cross-dressing, scatalogical humor, sight gags, and puns. Ludlam starred in many of his own plays, among them *Bluebeard* (1970), *Camille* (1973, revived 1990), *Der Ring Gott Farblonjet* (1977), and *The Mystery of Irma Vep* (1984). Since Ludlam's death from **AIDS** in 1987, the Ridiculous has continued under the directorship of Ludlam's life-partner Everett Quinton, a long-time actor and designer with the theatre. The company has been reviving Ludlam works as well as developing new pieces, such as Quinton's giddy adap-

Everett Quinton in the Ridiculous Theatrical Company's *Dr. Jekyll and Mr. Hyde*. Photo: Anita and Steve Shevett. Courtesy: Ridiculous Theatrical Company.

tation of *A Tale of Two Cities* (1988) and Georg Osterman's *Dr. Jekyll and Mr. Hyde* (1989). AS

Riggs, (Rollie) Lynn (1899–1954) Oklahoma-born playwright of Cherokee descent whose only successful play was **Green Grow the Lilacs** (1931), later transformed into the musical **Oklahoma!** Riggs's central concern was cowboy culture of the Indian Territory, although he wrote two plays with Native Americans as major characters – *The Cherokee Night* (written 1930) and *Cream in the Well* (1941). These, along with plays such as *Roadside* (1930), considered too obscure or nontraditional, were commercial failures. DBW

Rinehart, Mary Roberts (1876–1958) Journalist, novelist, and playwright who dramatized her novels, which were a cross between comedies and detective stories. Her best plays were written with **Avery Hopwood,** the most successful being *The Bat* (1920), an adaptation of her 1908 novel *The Circular Staircase*. Other hits written with Hopwood include *Seven Days* (1909) and *Spanish Love* (1920). She also wrote two less successful plays by herself: *Cheer Up* (1912) and *The Breaking Point* (1923). Her autobiography was published in 1948.
FB

> *See:* J. Cohn, *Improbable Fiction: The Life of Mary Roberts Rinehart,* Pittsburgh, 1980.

Ring, Blanche (1876–1961) Boston-born singer-actress, a great **vaudeville** star, master of the sing-along (which she probably introduced into vaudeville), and an accomplished monologuist of Irish characters. No single act topped hers for over two decades, beginning 10 years after her debut in a small role opposite **Richard Mansfield** in *The Defender* (1902), in which she introduced "In the Good Old Summertime." In 1909 she first sang what became her theme song, "I've Got Rings on My Fingers," in *The Midnight Sons*. When she introduced "Yip-I-Addy-I-Ay" to a vaudeville audience in 1913, she was encouraged to repeat it five times. She debuted her most famous role, *The Yankee Girl,* in 1909 (filmed 1915; she appeared in

two additional films [1926, 1940] and made a number of early recordings). Other hit musicals included *The Jersey Lily* (1903), *About Town* (1906), *The Wall Street Girl* (1911), and *The Passing Show of 1919*. DBW

Ringling (né Rungeling) Brothers Baraboo, WI, brothers who entered the American **circus** just prior to its golden age and, in the words of John Culhane, "outperformed, outmaneuvered, outacquired [and] just plain outlasted all their competition." In 1882 Brothers **Al[bert]** (1852–1916), **Otto** (1858–1911), **Alf[red] T.** (1861–1919), **Charles** (1863–1926), and **John** (1866–1936) formed a variety show, "Classic Comic and Concert Company." In 1884, in partnership with ailing circus pioneer Yankee Robinson, who later died that summer, they staged their first circus in Baraboo. Within six years their circus was traveling on rails; by 1895 they opened each spring in Chicago. Gaining momentum during a five-year European tour by their major rival, **Barnum** & Bailey, they arranged in 1905 to buy a half interest in one of James A. Bailey's properties (**Forepaugh**–Sells Bros. cir-

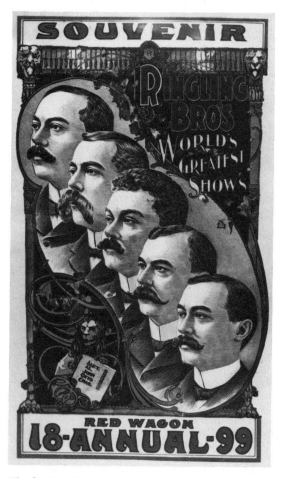

The five Ringling Brothers pictured on a souvenir route book. Courtesy: Ringling Bros.–Barnum & Bailey Circus.

cus); in 1907, after Bailey's death, they purchased all of his interest and the Barnum & Bailey title from his estate. Brother **Henry** (1869–1918) joined the fold, and in 1919 their two properties were combined into Ringling Bros. and Barnum & Bailey. The only member of the family to head Ringling Bros. after the brothers' deaths was their nephew, John Ringling North. In 1967 Ringling Bros. was sold to showmen Irwin and Israel Feld.   DBW

See: E. Albrecht, *A Ringling by Any Other Name,* Metuchen, NJ, 1989; D. L. Hammarstrom, *Big Top Boss: John Ringling North and the Circus,* Urbana/Chicago, 1992; G. Plowden, *Those Amazing Ringlings and Their Circus,* New York, 1967.

Rip Van Winkle by **Joseph Jefferson III** and **Dion Boucicault** opened at the Adelphi Theatre in London on 5 September 1865 and ran for 170 nights; the next fall it played New York. Thus began for thousands of Americans from coast to coast and for the next 40 years a habit of enjoying Joseph Jefferson as Rip Van Winkle.

Rip Van Winkle as a play, however, did not happen instantaneously. Prior to 1865 there were at least four dramatizations of **Washington Irving**'s story: an anonymous adaptation in Albany, NY (1828); a second by John Kerr (1829); a third by Charles Burke, Jefferson's half-brother (1850); followed by a fourth, Thomas Lacy's British version. Jefferson performed his own creation in Washington, DC, in the fall of 1859 and occasionally on a later tour to Australia. Returning to America through London, he commissioned Boucicault to do a rewrite. Although it is impossible

Joseph Jefferson III as the aged Rip and Miss Godsall as his grown daughter Meenie in a London production of *Rip Van Winkle*. Photo: W. Walker & Sons, London. Courtesy: Laurence Senelick.

to determine the individual work of either author, their intent was to increase the tension and attract more attention to the title role. As a happy-go-lucky ne'er-do-well, Rip/Jefferson dramatically mingled the comic and the pathetic. Jefferson's sympathetic personality, personal charm, and natural style of acting contributed to the play's tremendous success, but there was also plenty of spectacle and, for many, a delightful wish-fulfillment.   WJM

See: J. Jefferson, *Rip Van Winkle as Played by Joseph Jefferson,* New York, 1902; S. Johnson, "Joseph Jefferson's *Rip Van Winkle* (1865)," *The Drama Review* 26 (Spring 1982).

Ritchard, Cyril (1897?–1977) Actor and director, born in Sydney, Australia. He made his debut as a chorus boy in a Sydney musical in 1917 and came to America in 1924 to appear in New York in *Puzzles of 1925.* He is best remembered for Captain Hook in the musical *Peter Pan* (1954) and leading roles in *Visit to a Small Planet* (1957) and *The Roar of the Greasepaint, the Smell of the Crowd* (1965). Ritchard directed both for the theatre and opera and appeared in films. His awards included a Tony for Captain Hook and two Donaldson Awards for Hook on television in 1955.   SMA

Ritman, William (1928?–84) began his design career in television for the "Steve Allen Show" and "Kukla, Fran and Ollie" (among others) before becoming involved with the **Off-Broadway** theatre. He designed many of the Cherry Lane Theatre productions in the early 1960s, including all of **Edward Albee**'s work – an association that continued to Broadway with *Who's Afraid of Virginia Woolf?* (1962), *Tiny Alice* (1964), and most of Albee's subsequent plays. He also designed many of the American productions of the plays of Harold Pinter and Joe Orton, as well as numerous more commercial works, such as *6 Rms Riv Vu* (1972) and *Same Time, Next Year* (1975).   AA

Ritz Theatre see **Walter Kerr Theatre**

Rivera, Chita (née Dolores Conchita Figueroa del Rivero) (1933–) Dancer, singer, actress; attended the American School of Ballet before beginning her career as a Broadway dancer in *Guys and Dolls* (1950). Praised by critics for her performance as Anita in *West Side Story* (1957), she brought impressive dancing talent and a lively personality to starring roles in such musicals as *Bye Bye Birdie* (1960), *Bajour* (1964), *Chicago* (1975), *The Rink* (1984), and *Jerry's Girls* (1985).   MK

Rivera, José (1955–) Playwright. Born in Puerto Rico, Rivera's family moved to Long Island (NY) at age 4. Upon graduating from Denison University, he returned to New York, joining Theatre Matrix in the Bronx. In 1983, his *The House of Ramon Iglesias,* selected by Ensemble Studio Theatre as winner of the FDG/CBS New Play Awards, was produced under the direction of Jack Gelber, with the teleplay airing nationally as part of the "American Playhouse" series in 1986. *The Promise* (1988) premiered at the **Los Angeles Theatre**

Center, and *Each Day Dies With Sleep* premiered at **Berkeley Repertory Theatre** in 1990 before its **Off-Broadway** premiere at **Circle Repertory Theatre** in 1990. Rivera's plays revolve around Puerto Rican traditions and culture [see **Nuyorican theatre**], with an increasing interest in magical realism. ER

Road Company, The Grassroots ensemble based in Johnson City, TN, that creates original shows reflecting the culture and concerns of the upper Tennessee Valley. Artistic director Bob Leonard and several actors formed the group in 1975. Their first piece, *The Momentary Art of State-Making* (1977), was a *commedia dell'arte*–style look at Tennessee history. Later shows have used a **Chautauqua** format, Greek legends, mountain ballads, and multimedia techniques to tackle environmental and community issues. *Daytrips,* by company member Jo Carson, earned the Kesselring Prize for 1989. In addition to extensive regional touring, the company performs annual home seasons. MB

See: C. Lutenbacher, "The Road Company of Johnson City, Tennessee," PhD diss., Northwestern U, 1989.

Road to Rome, The **Robert Sherwood**'s play was a mild sensation in 1927 because of its sexual innuendos about the Carthaginian conqueror Hannibal and Amytis, wife of the Roman dictator Fabius Maximus. Sherwood, whose conversion from pacificist to "hawk" (*There Shall Be No Night,* 1940) reflected an intense American debate about war, argues in this play that human love can overcome the desire of countries to slaughter one another. **William A. Brady** produced it at the **Playhouse Theatre,** where it ran for 392 performances and won a "Best Play" accolade. It was designed by **Lee Simonson** and featured **Jane Cowl** and Philip Merivale as the articulate lovers. BBW

Robards, Jason, Jr. (1922–) Actor, praised for his rich voice and intense characterizations, who made his debut as Nick in the **American Academy of Dramatic Art**'s production of *Holiday* (1946). His Broadway debut was in D'Oyly Carte's *Mikado* (1947), after which he stage-managed for a time. He attracted considerable attention as Hickey in a now-legendary production of *The Iceman Cometh* (1956) at the **Circle in the Square.** Robards secured his stardom as James Tyrone in *Long Day's Journey into Night* (1956), in which he was noted as "an actor of tremendous dynamic skill." Another triumph was as Quentin in **Arthur Miller**'s *After the Fall,* for which critics lauded him as "brilliant," "magnificent," and "beyond praise." In 1988 he appeared with **Colleen Dewhurst** in revivals (in repertory) of *Long Day's Journey* and *Ah, Wilderness!* His most recent New York stage appearance was **Horovitz**'s *Park Your Car in Harvard Yard* (1991–2). His distinguished film and television career includes *Long Day's Journey* and *A Thousand Clowns,* as well as film scripts in which he has played various curmudgeons and outcasts. SMA

Robbins, Carrie (1943–) Costume designer who began her professional career in the late 1960s and has become one of the busiest in the theatre. Although she has done contemporary costumes, her best work is in detailed yet theatrical period costumes, such as the 1971 *Beggar's Opera,* or lavish operatic ones, such as for the San Francisco Opera's *Samson et Dalila,* which combined a 19th-century sensibility with a biblical epic style. Her work is typified by rich textures and bold lines, and her sketches are detailed and almost frenetic, creating a sense of energy and movement. She has frequently collaborated with set designer **Douglas Schmidt,** notably on **Grease** and *Frankenstein.* AA

Robbins, Jerome (1918–) Choreographer and director. Trained in the techniques of classical ballet, Robbins joined the American Ballet Theatre in 1940 and danced in several of its programs. In 1944 he choreographed *Fancy Free,* a ballet with music by **Leonard Bernstein.** Later the same year Robbins repeated his role as choreographer when *Fancy Free* was transformed into the Broadway musical **On the Town.** For *High Button Shoes* (1947), Robbins created a hilarious Keystone Kops ballet that remains one of the few masterpieces of comic choreography in the American musical theatre. Among his other memorable **dance**s of the period was the "Small House of Uncle Thomas" ballet for *The King and I* (1951). For the teenage gang members of *West Side Story* (1957), Robbins created a restless, explosive, yet balletic style of movement. He directed and choreographed two other acclaimed musicals: *Gypsy* (1959) and *Fiddler on the Roof* (1964). In 1989 Robbins recreated his most successful numbers in the retrospective *Jerome Robbins' Broadway* (Tony for best musical). He was given the Common Wealth Award of Distinguished Service in Dramatic Arts in 1990. MK

See: C. Schlundt, *Dance in the Musical Theatre: Jerome Robbins and His Peers,* New York, 1989.

Robertson, Agnes see **Boucicault, Dion**

Robertson, Peter (1847–1911) Critic and playwright; many years the theatre reviewer for the *San Francisco Chronicle,* known for his deft wit and penchant for writing some of his reviews in dialogue form. He also coauthored the play *Curse of Cain* with **David Belasco** (1882), and as an avid early member of the Bohemian Club, he penned at least one of their ritualistic Grove Plays. MB

Robeson, Paul (1898–1976) **African-American** actor. A Columbia Law School graduate, Robeson opted for a stage career and gained prominence in 1924–5 when he appeared in the **Provincetown Players**' revival of *The Emperor Jones* (1925) and as Jim Harris, the black lawyer who marries white in **O'Neill**'s controversial play, *All God's Chillun Got Wings* (1924). Robeson took the lead in *Black Boy* (1926), played Crown in *Porgy and Bess* (1927), and was Joe in the London performance of *Show Boat* (1928), in which he sang "Ol' Man River," the song he refashioned into a lifelong protest against oppression. With a commanding physique, deep, resonant voice, and humane spirit, Robeson was a magnificent Othello, a role he played three times: in London (1930), in New York for a record-breaking run (1943), and at Stratford-upon-Avon (1959). He was also renowned as a concert artist and film actor. Robeson's outspoken opposition to racial discrimination, his embrace of leftist causes worldwide, and his communist sympathies led to professional ostracism at home and the withdrawal of his passport. In failing health, he retired from public life in the 1960s. His life was dramatized in Philip Hayes Dean's 1978 monodrama *Paul Robeson,* which starred **James Earl Jones.** EGH

> *See:* M. B. Duberman, *Paul Robeson,* New York, 1988.

Robin Hood Comic opera with libretto by **Harry B. Smith** and music by **Reginald De Koven;** opened at New York's Standard Theatre on 28 September 1891. This production by The Bostonians (see **Boston Ideal Opera Company**) featured an excellent ensemble and memorable songs. Challenging the craze for imported light opera, after 40 performances it was moved and played continuously in various theatres. It was successfully revived for almost 50 years. Music theatre historian Gerald Bordman notes that *Robin Hood* bestowed "a certain theatrical immortality" on Jessie Bartlett Davis who, in the trouser role of Alan-a-Dale, sang "Oh, Promise Me" over 5,000 times in 2,000 performances of the initial production. Bordman notes that this early all-native effort was earthier, plainer, and more realistic than its European counterparts. MR

Robins, Elizabeth (1862–1952) Kentucky-born actress and author who made her acting debut with the **Boston Museum** Stock Company in 1885 and subsequently toured with **Edwin Booth, Lawrence Barrett,** and **James O'Neill.** She visited London in 1889, remaining there rather than return to New York. Soon she was playing Martha Bernick in *Pillars of Society* (1889); two years later in a revival of *A Doll's House* she played Mrs. Linde. Ultimately, Robins became identified with the introduction of Ibsen to the English stage, appearing as Hedda (1891), Hilda in *The Master Builder* (1893), Rebecca West in *Rosmersholm* (1893), Agnes in *Brand* (1893), Astra in *Little Eyolf* (1896), and Ella in *John Gabriel Borkman* (1897), and holding the stage rights to many of these plays. With the exception of starring in the short-lived U.S. premiere of **Ibsen**'s *Hedda Gabler* (1898), she never performed again in her native land. She retired from the stage in 1902 and devoted herself to writing. Using the nom de plume "C. E. Raemond," she published several novels as well as the suffragist play *Votes for Women* (1907). In later years she wrote *Ibsen and the Actress* (1928), *Theatre and Friendship* (1932), and *Both Sides of the Curtain* (1940). RAS

> *See:* M. G. Cima, "Elizabeth Robins: Ibsen Actress-Manageress," PhD diss., Cornell U, 1978.

Robinson, Bill (1878–1949) Dancer and singer who, after many years as a star of **vaudeville,** made his musical theatre debut in *Blackbirds of 1928,*

where his seemingly effortless tap dancing helped the show become a hit. Robinson was next seen in *Brown Buddies* (1930), *Blackbirds of 1933,* and *The Hot Mikado* (1939), a jazz version of the **Gilbert and Sullivan** classic. Unlike the 1920s, when a number of black musicals had been successful on Broadway, the shows of the 1930s were unable to garner long runs, even when featuring popular stars like Bill Robinson. In the 1940s he appeared in two other failures, *All in Fun* (1940) and *Memphis Bound!* (1945), the last a jazz adaptation of Gilbert and Sullivan's *HMS Pinafore.* Although few of Robinson's shows were big successes, his performances were uniformly praised for the matchless ease and grace of his tap dancing. MK

> *See:* J. Haskins and N. R. Mitgang, *Mr. Bojangles: The Biography of Bill Robinson,* New York, 1988.

Robson, Stuart (né Henry Robson Stuart) (1836–1903) Actor who made his stage debut as Horace Courtney in *Uncle Tom's Cabin as It Is,* a dramatic retort to **Uncle Tom's Cabin,** at the Baltimore Museum in 1852. Subsequently he appeared with numerous **stock companies,** including those of **Laura Keene**'s Theatre in New York, **Mrs. John Drew**'s Theatre in Philadelphia, and the Globe Theatre in Boston. From 1877 to 1889, he teamed with **W. H. Crane,** starring in such farces as *Our Bachelors* and *Our Boarding House,* but also in *A Comedy of Errors* as the two Dromios, and *The Merry Wives of Windsor* as Falstaff (Crane) and Slender (Robson). **Bronson Howard**'s *The Henrietta* was especially written for them. After 1890, Robson starred on his own, most notably as Tony Lumpkin in *She Stoops to Conquer.* DJW

Rocket to the Moon by **Clifford Odets.** A **Group Theatre** production, it opened at the **Belasco Theatre** 24 November 1938 (131 performances). Directed by **Harold Clurman** and designed by **Mordecai Gorelik,** it starred **Morris Carnovsky** (dentist Ben Stark), Ruth Nelson (his wife Belle), **Luther Adler** (Belle's father), and Eleanor Lynn as Cleo Singer, Ben's secretary and the object of his affections in this triangle play. The Depression is the backdrop for the plot; the focus, however, is not its economic effects but the personal plights of a collection of troubled souls, with the social situation less crucial than in many Odets plays. Mixed reception led to text alterations, but its run remained modest and, despite some brilliant writing and lively characters, it has little stage history. DBW

Rodgers, Richard (1902–79) Composer. After studying music and writing scores for amateur musicals, Rodgers teamed up with lyricist **Lorenz Hart** in 1919. Their songs were heard in *A Lonely Romeo* (1920) and *Poor Little Ritz Girl* (1920). After their first successful score for *The Garrick Gaieties* (1925), they created an almost unbroken stream of hit musicals, including *Dearest Enemy* (1925), *The Girl Friend* (1926), *Peggy-Ann* (1926), and *A Connecticut Yankee* (1927). In the early 1930s Rodgers and Hart wrote the songs for several Hollywood musical films, then returned to Broadway to create some of the most popular scores of the late 1930s and early '40s, including *Jumbo* (1935), **On Your Toes** (1936), **Babes in Arms** (1937), *I'd Rather Be Right* (1937), *I Married an Angel* (1938), *The Boys from Syracuse* (1938), *Too Many Girls* (1939), and *By Jupiter* (1942). **Pal Joey** (1940), a musical chronicling the adventures of an amoral nightclub owner, was initially unpopular with critics and audiences, but more successful in its 1952 revival.

In 1943 Rodgers initiated his partnership with lyricist-librettist **Oscar Hammerstein II.** Their first show was **Oklahoma!,** one of the most popular and influential of all American musicals. The Rodgers–Hammerstein partnership was responsible for some of the longest running shows of the 1940s and '50s, including *Flower Drum Song* (1958) and *The Sound of Music* (1959). Their shows were noted for the care with which music and dance were integrated with the libretto.

After Hammerstein's death in 1960, Rodgers served as his own lyricist for *No Strings* (1962), then collaborated with other lyricists on *Do I Hear a Waltz?* (1965), *Two by Two* (1970), *Rex* (1976), and *I Remember Mama* (1979). His autobiography, *Musical Stages,* was published in 1975.

Early in his career Rodgers composed bouncy, jazz-influenced music that complemented the clever lyrics of Lorenz Hart. After demonstrating that he could compose on a grander, more sweeping scale with the "Slaughter on Tenth Avenue" ballet for *On Your Toes,* Rodgers wrote dramatic, emotionally expansive scores for his "musical plays" of the 1940s and '50s. MK

See: S. Green, ed., *The Rodgers and Hammerstein Fact Book,* New York, 1980.

Roger Bloomer by **John Howard Lawson.** This early foray with expressionism was first produced by the Equity Players on 1 March 1923, starring Henry Hull and designed by **Woodman Thompson.** The action centers on a confused young loner who flees the Midwest to "chase rainbows" in New York, where he falls into dissipation. Roger is bombarded by commercialism and greed, finally losing his love Louise to suicide after stealing money. In jail, suspected of killing Louise, Roger has a long expressionistic nightmare, which seems to exorcise many of the demons of commercialism and sexual confusion that plague Roger throughout the action. RHW

Rogers, Will (William Penn Adair Rogers) (1879–1935) This warm, gum-chewing American folk hero began in **Wild West** shows, billed as "The Cherokee Kid, the wonderful Lasso-Artist," making $20 a week. At the St. Louis World's Fair in 1904 he dazzled audiences by circling a horse and rider with a lasso in each hand. He made his first appearance in New York in 1905 with a trick roping and riding company (Madison Square Garden) and gradually evolved his technique of commenting drolly on current events in his Oklahoma drawl while playing with his lariat. His stage personality, which used no makeup or comic properties, was basically an extension of his own, winning the audience's trust and affection. Rogers appeared in musicals, the **Ziegfeld** *Follies*

(1916, 1917, 1918, 1922, 1924), on the **vaudeville** stage, and in 24 films. In 1934, he played the father in **O'Neill's** *Ah, Wilderness!,* and the next year was lost flying over Alaska with aviator Wiley Post. He has been portrayed by James Whitmore in Paul Shyre's **one-person** show *Will Rogers' USA* (1972), and in 1991 his persona was used as the central character (originated by Keith Carradine) in the musical *The* **Will Rogers Follies.** LS

See: E. Alworth, *Will Rogers,* New York, 1974; D. Day, ed., *The Autobiography of Will Rogers,* New York, 1949; R. Ketchum, *Will Rogers: His Life and Times,* New York, 1973.

Romberg, Sigmund (1887–1951) Hungarian-born musician who came to the U.S. as a young man and became one of the prolific composers of operetta and musical comedy scores. In 1914 he began a long association with the **Shubert brothers** when he wrote the score for *The Whirl of the World.* As the Shuberts' staff composer, he wrote songs for their **revue** series *The Passing Show,* and also turned out scores for dozens of commonplace musicals. In 1921 he adapted Franz Schubert's melodies for the musical biography **Blossom Time,** whose phenomenal success gave him greater freedom in choosing projects. As the 1920s progressed, he wrote the operettas by which he is most remembered: *The* **Student Prince** (1924), *The* **Desert Song** (1926), and *The* **New Moon** (1928). He continued to write operettas and musicals up to his death, though with less success. MK

Rome, Harold (1908–) Composer, lyricist. After receiving a degree in architecture from Yale, Rome studied piano in New York. His first score was for the **revue** *Pins and Needles* (1937), sponsored by the International Ladies' Garment Workers' Union. He contributed songs to other revues, including *Sing Out the News* (1938), *Star and Garter* (1942), the **Ziegfeld** *Follies* (1943), and *Call Me Mister* (1946). In the 1950s he wrote the scores to several successful book musicals, including *Wish You Were Here* (1952), *Fanny* (1954), and *Destry Rides Again* (1959). Barbra Streisand catapulted to fame singing Rome's "Miss Marmelstein" in *I Can Get It for You Wholesale* (1962). In the early 1970s Rome wrote the score for *Scarlett,* an ill-fated musical version of *Gone With the Wind* that played in Tokyo, London, and Los Angeles. MK

Room Service Three-act farce by John Murray and Allen Boretz; opened on Broadway at the **Cort Theatre** (19 May 1937) and ran 500 performances. Originally directed and produced by **George Abbot,** the play has been revived once on Broadway (The **Playhouse,** 6 April 1953 for 16 performances, in which Jack Lemmon made his New York debut) and twice **Off-Broadway** (Edison Theatre, 12 May 1970 for 71 performances, directed by Harold Stone; **Roundabout Theatre,** 29 January 1986 for 64 performances, directed by **Alan Arkin**). Praised for its physical comedy and uninhibited lunacy and gusto in portraying the dodges and makeshifts of show business, the play appealed to the escapist demands of its post-Depression audience. *Room Service* inspired two film versions, one a 1938 **Marx Bros.** vehicle.   MK

Rooney, Pat[rick James], Jr. (1880–1962)
Performer, songwriter. The diminutive, perennially young song-and-dance man is remembered as master of the waltz clog to the tune of "The Daughter of Rosie O'Grady," the song he introduced at The **Palace** in 1919. (In 1925 he starred in a musical built around the song and dance.) The son of performers, Rooney was best known on the **vaudeville** stage (1904–32 with his wife Marion Bent; afterward with Herman Timberg in a Jewish–Irish twosome), although as Arvide Abernathy singing "More I Cannot Wish You" in *Guys and Dolls* (1950) he created a memorable moment in musical theatre annals. His son, Pat III, was also an entertainer. "As long as I can move my feet, I'm gonna keep working," Rooney once said, which he did right up to his death. In popularity, the Rooneys ranked with the **Cohan**s and the **Foy**s.
   DBW

Roosters This two-act drama by Milcha Sanchez-Scott was developed at **INTAR**'s Hispanic Playwrights-in-Residence Laboratory (1984) under the direction of **Maria Irene Fornés**, and at Sundance Institute Playwrights Laboratory (1986). First published in *American Theatre, Roosters* was co-produced by the **New York Shakespeare Festival**, premiering at INTAR in 1987 under the direction of Jackson Phippin. Set in the Southwest, the play depicts a harsh reality involving a **Chicano** family in crisis as a young daughter strives for identity within the family while the father and son compete for dominance. The poetic style in the vein of Latin American magical realism mixes naturalism with the surreal. Through numerous plays, Sanchez-Scott is recognized as a spokesperson for **Hispanic** American issues.   ER

Rose, Billy (né Samuel Wolf Rosenberg)
(1899–1966) Flamboyant showman ("I sell bally-hoo, not genius") and lyricist ("Barney Google," "Without a Song," "Me and My Shadow," etc.). His ventures ranged from **nightclubs** and theatre-restaurants (Back Stage Club, Casino de Paree, the Billy Rose Music Hall in New York during the 1920s and '30s; Casa Mañana in Ft. Worth in the 1930s; New York's Diamond Horseshoe, 1939–52) to epic spectacles such as *Jumbo* (1945) and the aquacades at the 1939–40 New York World's Fair and the San Francisco Golden Gate Exposition (1940), as well as 11 legitimate Broadway productions, including *Carmen Jones* (1943) and *The Immoralist* (1954). In the 1950s and '60s he owned two New York theatres. Among Rose's five marriages was one to **Fanny Brice** (1929). The Billy Rose Theatre Collection of the New York Public Library was funded by his foundation (organized in 1958).
   DBW

> See: E. Conrad, *Billy Rose: Manhattan Primitive,* New York, 1968; S. Nelson, *"Only a Paper Moon": The Theatre of Billy Rose,* Ann Arbor, MI, 1987.

Rose, George (Walter) (1920–88) English-born
actor. Although to many Rose was the archetype

of the British character actor, he lived in New York City from 1961, the year he played The Common Man in *A Man for All Seasons,* until his untimely death. Trained at the Central School of Speech and Drama, Rose joined the Old Vic Company in 1945. In the 1950s he moved between parts in contemporary plays in London's West End and roles in classical repertory at the Shakespeare Memorial Theatre. His Dogberry in Gielgud's 1959 production of *Much Ado About Nothing* established him as a first-rate Shakespearean clown. After settling in New York City, he appeared prominently in *The Royal Hunt of the Sun* (1965), *My Fair Lady* (Doolittle in 1968 and 1976 revivals), the musical *Coco* (1969), *My Fat Friend* (1974), *The Kingfisher* (1978), the musical *Peter Pan* (Captain Hook and Mr. Darling in a 1979 revival), *The Pirates of Penzance* (Major General Stanley in **New York Shakespeare Festival**'s 1980 revival), the 1983 revival of *You Can't Take It with You,* and *The Mystery of Edwin Drood* (1985).   DBW

Rose-Marie Book and lyrics by **Otto Harbach** and **Oscar Hammerstein II**, music by **Rudolf Friml**, additional songs by Herbert Stothart. One of the great musical hits of the 1920s, it opened at the **Imperial Theatre** on 2 September 1924 and ran for 557 performances. Eschewing the European settings of most operettas, Hammerstein and Harbach employed the Canadian Rockies as a backdrop for their tale of singer Rose-Marie LeFlamme (played by opera star Mary Ellis) and her romance with Canadian Mountie Jim Kenyon (played by British singer-actor **Dennis King**). Although the creators of *Rose-Marie* believed the musical sequences were so integral to the plot that they refused to list them separately in the program, the operetta is remembered today for its songs, particularly "Indian Love Call" and the title song, rather than for its story. Long a favorite of warm-weather audiences, *Rose-Marie* has frequently been revived by **summer stock** and tent theatres.   MK

Rosenthal, Jean (1912–69) Theatre, architec-
tural, and industrial lighting designer who virtually invented the field of lighting design. When she began working with **Orson Welles** and **John Houseman** in the **Federal Theatre Project** there were no lighting designers; the job was done by the set designer or electrician. In 1938 she began working for Martha Graham as lighting and production supervisor (and continued until her death). Because dance is so dependent on light, Rosenthal was able to develop the new art of lighting design. A common element in all her designs is an evocative sense of mood. Critics and directors commented on her apparent ability to work magic with her effects. Rosenthal's hundreds of theatre designs include *West Side Story* and *The Sound of Music.* She also designed the architectural lighting for theatres and projects ranging from airline terminals to hotels. Her ideas and techniques are presented in her book *The Magic of Light* (1972, with Lael Wertenbaker).   AA

Rosenthal, Rachel (1926–) **Performance**
artist. Born in Paris of Russian emigré parents, she

studied ballet as a child. Fleeing Nazism, she moved first to Brazil (1940) and then to New York, where she attended school and trained as an actress and visual artist (Jean-Louis Barrault School of Theater, 1947–8; graphic art with William Hayter and painting with Hans Hoffman, 1946–8; acting with **Herbert Berghoff**, 1954). She assisted **Erwin Piscator** (1949–50) and set designer Heinz Condell, befriended John Cage, and danced with the Merce Cunningham Dance Company. She founded Instant Theater (1956–66) and Espace DBD (1980–3), and cofounded and cochaired Womanspace (1971–4) in Los Angeles. In the mid-1970s she began working with autobiographical material and social and environmental issues. She incorporates into her performances meditation, martial arts, Asian and Euro-American radical dramatic traditions. Important performances include *The Death Show* (1978), *Gaia, Mon Amour* (1983), and *Pagaean Dreams: A Shamanic Journey* (1990).   AF

Ross, Jerry (Jerold) see **Adler, Richard**

Rosse, Herman (1887–1965) Theatre/film designer and architect. Born in The Hague, Rosse came to the U.S. in 1908, though he returned to the Netherlands for 1933–47. He was head of the School of Design of the Art Institute of Chicago (1919–23). His more than 200 settings for stage and film were typified by a strong modernist style and range from several of the *Ziegfeld* Follies to *Ulysses in Nighttown* (1958), including 10 years as resident designer for the Papermill Playhouse (1950–60) in New Jersey. His films include *Frankenstein, Murders in the Rue Morgue,* and *The Emperor Jones.* Rosse also designed the medallions used for the **Antoinette Perry** (Tony) Awards.   AA

Roth, Ann (1931–) Since designing costumes for *Maybe Tuesday* on Broadway in 1958, Roth has amassed credits for over 100 Broadway productions, including *Purlie* (1970; 1972 revival), *The Royal Family* (1975), and *The Crucifer of Blood* (1978). She began her long-term association with **Mike Nichols** and **Neil Simon** with *The Odd Couple* in 1964, and is also known for her collaborations with John Schlesinger. Her film credits include costumes for *Midnight Cowboy* (1969), *Hair* (1979), *Regarding Henry* (1991), and *The Mambo Kings* (1991). A major in scene design at Carnegie Institute of Technology (1953), she began her career assisting **Irene Sharaff** on films, including *The King and I* (1956).   BO

Roth, Wolfgang (1910–88) Designer who joined the Piscator-Buehne in 1928 as assistant to Traugott Müller. Over the next five years he worked with **Piscator** and **Brecht** and was an assistant to Caspar Neher on *Die Dreigroschen Oper.* He then worked in Zurich and Vienna before coming to the U.S. in 1938. He designed for Broadway, **Off-Broadway,** and the Metropolitan and New York City Operas as well as for several regional theatres. His designs for the 1952 revival of *Porgy and Bess* are considered among his best. He was also an artist with many gallery shows.   AA

Roundabout Theatre Company Off-**Broadway** theatre founded in 1965 by **Gene Feist,** who remains artistic director. The Roundabout, a not-for-profit organization, specializes in faithful revivals of modern repertory standards using name performers, a policy that has earned it a large and loyal subscription audience. Its Second Stage series addresses smaller-scale or more offbeat plays. At the start of the 1991–2 season, the Roundabout moved to a Broadway house, the 499-seat Criterion Center Theatre at 1514 Broadway, opening in October with Pinter's *The Homecoming.*   CLJ

Rowson, Susanna Haswell (1762–1824) English-born playwright, actress, and novelist who came to the U.S. for the second time in 1793 as part of **Thomas Wignell**'s company and acted in Philadelphia and Boston before retiring in 1796 to open a girl's school. Of her plays, *Slaves in Algiers; or, A Struggle for Freedom* (1794), which savaged tyranny, was her best. Other titles include *The Female Patriot* (1795); *The Volunteers* (1795), her reaction to the Whisky Rebellion; and *Americans in England* (1797).   WJM

See: P. Parker, *Susanna Rowson,* Boston, 1986.

Royale Theatre 242 West 46th St., NYC [Architect: Herbert J. Krapp]. Built as one of a chain of six theatres by the Chanin brothers [cf. **Richard Rodgers Theatre**], the Royale opened early in 1927. The Chanin control did not survive the Depression, and all of their theatres passed to other interests. The **Shubert**s became part owner of the house but did not directly control it until 1940. With 1,100 seats, the playhouse has presented both musical and nonmusical fare. When leased by **John Golden** (1934–6), it was briefly named after him and served for his own productions. It was also used (1937–40) as a CBS radio studio during this era. It has housed two Pulitzer Prize winners: *Both Your Houses* (1932) and *The Subject Was Roses* (1964). Other memorable productions on its stage have included *Diamond Lil* (1928), *The Boy Friend* (1954), *The Matchmaker* (1955), *Grease* (1972), *A Day in Hollywood, A Night in the Ukraine* (1981), and *Speed-the-Plow* (1988). It remains a Shubert theatre.   MCH

Royal Family, The This **George S. Kaufman** and **Edna Ferber** romantic comedy, produced by **Jed Harris,** opened on Broadway 23 October 1928 and ran 345 performances. The play is about the escapades of an extended family of actors modeled after the **Drew–Barrymore** clan. Paramount released the film version in 1930, starring **Fredric March.** The American Bicentennial Theatre's revival opened on Broadway 30 December 1975 under **Ellis Rabb**'s direction. The cast included **Eva Le Gallienne** as Fanny, **Sam Levene** as Wolfe, **Rosemary Harris** as Julie, and **George Grizzard** as Tony.   JDM

Russell, Annie (1864–1936) English-born actress who, two years after her New York stage debut in 1879, established her career with a brilliant portrayal of the title character in *Esmeralda.* Ill

Annie Russell as Esmeralda, a role she first played in 1881. Courtesy: Don B. Wilmeth.

health forced her from the stage for three seasons (1891–4), but she returned to regain her popularity and invite comparison with Eleonora Duse for her simplicity and naturalism. She was effective especially in emotional and comic roles. In 1905 she created **Shaw**'s heroine in *Major Barbara,* and gave memorable performances as Puck in *A Midsummer Night's Dream* (1906), Viola in *Twelfth Night* (1909), Beatrice in *Much Ado* (1912), and Lady Teazle in Sheridan's *The School for Scandal* (1914). Her charming stage presence made her the ideal ingenue. She retired from the stage in 1918 to head the dramatic program at Rollins College, Winter Park, FL.   TLM

Russell, Henry (1812–1900) English entertainer and songwriter of Jewish descent; after studying music with Rossini and Bellini, he descended to being an organist and choral director in Rochester, NY. In 1837, he made a debut as a ballad singer at the Brooklyn Lyceum; in a short time he became a hugely popular performer, offering the first solo vocal programs in America, aimed at the common man. He not only sang in a pleasant baritone and accompanied himself on the piano, but composed his entire repertory. This included such warhorses-to-be as "Cheer, Boys, Cheer!," "Woodman! Spare That Tree," "A Life on the Ocean Wave," and "The Old Armchair," as well as temperance, anti-slavery, and humanitarian ballads. He repeated his triumphs in England, and his entertainment "The Far West; or, The Emigrant's Progress from the Old World to the New" inspired British immigra-

tion to the American frontier. He retired about 1865.   LS

See: H. Russell, *Cheer, Boys, Cheer,* London, 1895.

Russell, Lillian (née Helen Louise Leonard) (1861–1922) Singer and actress whose name is synonymous with one of her show titles, *An American Beauty.* Rising from obscurity in Clinton, IA, she became a much sought after star in comic opera, **burlesque, vaudeville,** and drama. **Tony Pastor** billed her as "The English Ballad Singer" at his Broadway variety theatre in 1880. Cross-country tours and engagements in New York and England followed. She was applauded for her physical and vocal charms in such vehicles as *The Pie Rats of Penn Yan* (Pastor's burlesque of *The Pirates of Penzance*), *The Snake Charmer, The Sorcerer, The Princess of Trebizonde, Iolanthe,* and *The Princess Nicotine.* She enjoyed five seasons (1899–1904) with **Weber and Fields**'s celebrated troupes. Roles in *Lady Teazle* (musical version of Sheridan's *The School for Scandal*), *The Butterfly,* and *Wildfire* furthered her already flourishing reputation. She died in Pittsburgh, survived by her fourth husband and a daughter.   DBW

See: J. Burke, *Duet in Diamonds: The Saga of Diamond Jim Brady and Lillian Russell,* New York, 1972; P. Morell, *Lillian Russell: The Era of Plush,* New York, 1940.

Russell, Sol Smith (1848–1902) Actor born in Maine and raised in St. Louis, where he became a drummer boy during the Civil War. His first regular engagement was at Deagle's in St. Louis; he

Sarony photo (1894) of Lillian Russell as the Duchess in Offenbach's *The Grand Duchess,* in which she first appeared in 1889. Courtesy: Don B. Wilmeth.

later accepted a position with **Ben DeBar**'s **stock company** there. In 1868 he joined the Berger family of bell ringers, giving character impersonations and songs. He first starred in 1880 in *Edgewood Folks,* in which he appeared 1,500 times. Although Russell never succeeded in New York, he was extremely popular in the rest of the nation in such shows as *The Country Editor, Pa, Bewitched,* and especially *The Poor Relation,* his greatest success. His best roles were uncouth country types whose alert minds and large ambitions won the day. Russell left an estate of over two million dollars. SMA

See: C. Bazaldua, Jr., " 'Going to the People': The Career of Sol Smith Russell," PhD diss., U of Missouri, 1975.

Ryskind, Morrie (1895–1985) Librettist and lyricist who, after working as a newspaperman and Broadway press **agent,** contributed sketches and lyrics to the revue *The 49ers* (1922). He wrote librettos for two **Marx Bros.** shows, *The Cocoanuts* (1925) and *Animal Crackers* (1928), then collaborated with **George and Ira Gershwin** on three musicals offering trenchant satire of American politics and mores: ***Strike Up the Band*** (1930), the Pulitzer Prize–winning ***Of Thee I Sing*** (1931), and *Let 'Em Eat Cake* (1933). From the mid-1930s on he spent most of his time working on Hollywood films as writer, producer, and director. Adopting a conservative political stance, in 1960 he became a columnist for the Los Angeles Times Syndicate and later for the Los Angeles *Herald Examiner.* MK

S

Saddler, Donald (1920–) Ballet dancer and theatre choreographer who, before joining the company of *High Button Shoes* (1947), was a soloist with Ballet Theatre (1940–3, 1946–7). He was a featured dancer along with **Bob Fosse** and Joan McCracken in *Dance Me a Song* (1950). Saddler's choreographic career began with **Wonderful Town** (1953) and **John Murray Anderson's** *Almanac* (1953). From the unsuccessful *Shangri-La* (1956), Saddler went on to choreograph *Milk and Honey* (1961), *Tricks* (1973), and **No, No, Nanette** (1971 Broadway revival), for which he received critical and popular acclaim: Capturing the spirit of the show, Saddler had his dancers performing on beach balls [see **dance**]. Saddler was also recognized for his work in industrial shows as a producer and choreographer. LF

Sag Harbor Domestic comedy by **James A. Herne** that premiered at the Park Theatre, Boston, 24 October 1899, and ran a record 107 performances. Herne's last play is a revision of his *Hearts of Oak* (1879), written in collaboration with **David Belasco.** Kindly and wise Captain Dan Marble (played by Herne himself) teaches a man in love with his brother's wife to accept his situation with equanimity. After an eight-week tour, a brief run in Chicago, and a summer layoff, *Sag Harbor* opened the new Republic Theatre in New York on 27 September 1900. Its reputation is based on its realistically detailed dinner-party scene, its expert character drawing, and the scenic realism of its rustic shipyard setting. WD

St. Charles Theatre St. Charles Street between Poydras and Gravier, New Orleans [Architect: An-

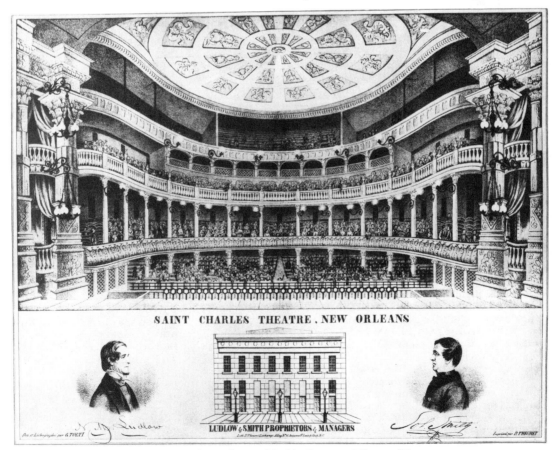

Saint Charles Theatre, New Orleans, under Ludlow and Smith. Courtesy: Library of Congress.

toine Mondelli]. Built by **James H. Caldwell** in 1835, the St. Charles was the largest, handsomest, and probably the most expensive theatre built in America to that date. The original **stock company** included **Charlotte Cushman** and **James E. Murdoch**. In 1842, it burned to the ground and was replaced by a lesser structure, which eventually passed to the management of Caldwell's rivals, **Noah Ludlow** and **Sol Smith**. During its high-water years, most American and English stars played at the theatre, and the last known performance of **J. B. Booth** occurred on its stage. In 1899, it burned again [see **fires**] and was rebuilt in 1901 as a **vaudeville** house, which changed to films in the movie era. For a number of years, it served as a rehearsal hall for the New Orleans Symphony Orchestra because of its excellent acoustics, but was torn down in 1966.   MCH

See: J. Kendall, *The Golden Age of the New Orleans Theater,* Baton Rouge, 1952.

Saint-Denis, Michel (1897–1971) French director, nephew of Jacques Copeau, whose first directing work was with La Compagnie des Quinze, a group of Copeau's former pupils. In 1935 he left France to direct Gielgud in an English version of the Quinze's success: *Noah* by Obey. He stayed on in London to found the London Theatre Studio, a theatre school modeled on Copeau's ideas, but the venture failed. He helped to revive the Old Vic and establish its theatre school but left in 1951. In 1957 he came to the U.S. to advise on theatres and theatre training, later becoming codirector of the Juilliard School at **Lincoln Center**. He also served as artistic adviser to the Royal Shakespeare Company and to the Canadian National Theatre School. In 1960 he published *Theatre: a Rediscovery of Style,* in which methods and approaches derived from Copeau are set out.   DB   DBW

St. Emanuel Street Theatre Theatre in Mobile, AL, associated with **Noah Ludlow** and **Sol Smith** during their five-year dominance of the St. Louis and Mobile stages in the 1830s. Ludlow managed Mobile's first theatre (1824–8), then joined with Smith to open the St. Emanuel Street Theatre in 1835. The playhouse's burning in 1838 ended the Ludlow–Smith domination of Mobile theatre.   DBW

St. James Theatre 246 West 44th St., NYC [Architects: Warren and Wetmore]. Intended to be a personal monument to its builder, **Abraham Erlanger,** a partner in the infamous Theatrical **Syndicate,** the theatre was named the Erlanger for the first five years of its existence. Opening in 1927 with a lesser **George M. Cohan** musical, the theatre reverted to the Astor estate in the early Depression. It was then leased to a succession of producers until it was bought by the **Shubert**s, who were later forced to relinquish it to comply with the terms of a consent decree limiting the number of theatres in their control in 1957. It was bought by and has remained a property of the **Jujamcyn Organization.** Built as a musical house with more than 1,600 seats, Broadway history has been made on its stage. Starting in 1943, the **Rodgers** and

Hammerstein musical *Oklahoma!* held its stage for five years. *The **King and I,*** another Rodgers and Hammerstein production, opened in 1951, and did not close for three years. Their *Flower Drum Song* followed in 1958. Other notable musicals have included ***Hello, Dolly!*** (1964), *Barnum* (1980), *My One and Only* (1983), and *The Secret Garden* (1991).   MCH

St. Louis Municipal Outdoor Theatre (MUNY) In 1919 an outdoor theatre with a massive stage and seating 9,500 opened in St. Louis's Forest Park. After a few seasons of presenting comic opera and operetta with local performers, the MUNY changed to a policy of importing Broadway and Hollywood stars to augment their casts. After the 1950s, full touring productions and concerts by individual performers were being added to the MUNY's nationally acclaimed musical comedy seasons.   MK

See: M. Kimbrough, *The MUNY: St. Louis' Outdoor Theatre,* St. Louis, 1978.

St. Philip Street Theatre The second theatre built in New Orleans, this 700-seat auditorium was constructed in 1808 for the performance of French plays and operas, but soon became the first theatre in the city to house a permanent English-speaking theatrical company. After years of success as home to the companies of **Noah Ludlow** and **James H. Caldwell,** the theatre closed in 1832 and soon after was demolished.   LAB

See: J. Kendall, *The Golden Age of the New Orleans Theater,* Baton Rouge, 1952.

Saint-Subber, Arnold (1918–) Producer. Born in Washington, DC, and educated at New York University, Saint-Subber began his theatrical career in 1938 as assistant stage manager for ***Hellzapoppin.*** He then served as assistant to **John Murray Anderson** for numerous productions, including the *Ziegfeld Follies* of 1943. His close association with playwright **Neil Simon** established him as an important name on Broadway in the 1960s. Of the more than 25 shows he has produced or coproduced, the more notable are ***Kiss Me, Kate*** (1948), *The Grass Harp* (1952), *My Three Angels* (1953), *The Dark at the Top of the Stairs* (1957), *The Tenth Man* (1959), ***Barefoot in the Park*** (1963), *The Odd Couple* (1965), ***Plaza Suite*** (1968), ***Last of the Red Hot Lovers*** (1969), *The **Prisoner of Second Avenue*** (1971), *Gigi* (1973), and *1600 Pennsylvania Avenue* (1978).   TLM

Saks, Gene (1921–) Director and actor. Born in New York City and educated at Cornell University (1939–43), Saks studied acting at **The Actors Studio** and Dramatic Workshop. He made his New York debut in 1947 as Joxer in O'Casey's *Juno and the Paycock.* During the next decade he appeared mainly in supporting roles before attracting critical attention in 1962 as Leo Herman in *A Thousand Clowns.* He turned to directing in 1963, establishing himself as one of Broadway's premier directors of comedy, known for his inventiveness and attention to detail. His major directing credits include *Nobody Loves an Albatross* (1963), *Generation* (1965), *Mame* (1966), *Sheep on the Runway* (1970),

How the Other Half Loves (1971), *Same Time, Next Year* (1975), *I Love My Wife* (1977), *Supporting Cast* (1981), *Special Occasions* (1982), **Brighton Beach Memoirs** (1983), **Biloxi Blues** (1984, Tony), and **Lost in Yonkers** (1991). He is married to actress Beatrice Arthur. Numerous films include **Barefoot in the Park,** *The* **Odd Couple,** *Last of the Red Hot Lovers,* and *Mame.*   TLM

Sally Musical by **Guy Bolton** (book), Clifford Grey (lyrics), with music by **Jerome Kern** and **Victor Herbert;** represented prevalent performance styles when it opened 21 December 1920. Like Kern's *Irene* (1919) and *Sunny* (1925), *Sally* combined wonderful melodies with Cinderella plots. **Florenz Ziegfeld** produced *Sally* with popular stars – **Marilyn Miller, Leon Errol,** and Walter Catlett – and lavish sets and costumes by **Joseph Urban.** Sally is a talented dancer who coincidentally meets an exiled European Duke and is given a break at stardom when a Russian ballerina fails to make a performance. Such contrivances were willingly accepted in 1920, when the musical ran 570 performances, but dulled the popularity of the play's 1948 revival (which closed after 36 performances).   KN

Salsbury, Nathan (Nate) (1846–1902) Actor, playwright, and manager; best known for contributing superb organizational skills to **William F. (''Buffalo Bill'') Cody**'s **Wild West exhibition,** for which he was vice-president and general manager from the show's second season in 1883 until his death. Prior to that partnership, Salsbury had organized Salsbury's Troubadours, a popular five-member comic troupe, in 1875. Salsbury wrote the group's first plays (loosely knit concoctions of songs, stories, and dances); *The Brook* (1875) influenced early musical comedy by precipitating a fad for spirited, small-scale pieces. In the 1880s the Troubadours adapted a more structured farce format. Although Salsbury left to devote his time to the Wild West, the Troubadours continued under the leadership of comedienne Nellie McHenry. In

1895 Salsbury produced *Black America,* an entertainment with 300 **African-American** performers intended to display black culture, but it lasted only one season.   RAH

Salt Lake Theatre This elegant 1,500-seat theatre, modeled after London's Drury Lane, opened 1862 under Brigham Young's ownership to provide entertainment for the Mormon community. In 1865, actors earned \$12–65 per week. Through the 1870s, the theatre boasted such actors as **J. A. Herne, E. L. Davenport, John McCullough, Dion Boucicault, Tony Pastor,** and **Harrigan and Hart.** Young incurred large debts to the Mormon church, which after his death (1877) took control of the theatre and ran it until it was razed in 1928.   JDM

See: M. Henderson, *History of the Theatre in Salt Lake City,* Salt Lake City, 1941.

Salvation Nell Local-color melodrama by **Edward Sheldon;** opened 17 November 1908 for 71 performances. Yet another serious work produced and directed by **Harrison Grey Fiske** to showcase the considerable abilities of **Minnie Maddern Fiske** as Nell, it marked the appearance of Sheldon, just graduated from **George Pierce Baker**'s Workshop 47 at Harvard, as a promising playwright. *Salvation Nell* depicted the attraction between a God-fearing, selfless Salvation Army officer (Fiske) and a violent, drunken, tough (**Holbrook Blinn**), surrounded by a careful re-creation of the Army's work in the midst of inner-city squalor. A triumph of realistic staging and dialect acting, the vivid depiction of New York's squalid, vulgar, mostly immigrant underclass was a sensation. Mrs. Fiske's portrayal of Nell's unshakable faith and love in the face of such violent conditions generated much pathos, and provided the idealistic ending that made the production palatable.   MR

Sam'l of Posen A starring vehicle by **George H. Jessop** for M. B. Curtis, this popular farce capital-

Holbrook Blinn and Mrs. Fiske (center) in the Act I barroom scene of Sheldon's *Salvation Nell.* Photo: Byron. Courtesy: Culver Service Collection.

izes on stereotyped Jewish behavior. Copyrighted by Jessop in 1880, the play was bought by Curtis (little is known of either), and played on regional circuits for years after a successful opening at **Haverly's Fourteenth Street Theatre,** New York, in 1881. With its ethnic types, imperiled hero, loathsome villain, and urban setting, this comedy (of the **Harrigan** variety) may be considered typical of the "play factory" fare of the commerical New York–based touring theatre of the late 19th century.   RKB

Sam S. Shubert Theatre 225 West 44th St., NYC [Architect: Henry B. Herts]. In 1913, Lee and J. J. **Shubert,** their position as producers and theatre owners ensured, bought a site that ran through the block from West 44th to West 45th Street behind the Hotel Astor. There they built two theatres, one of which they named after their brother Sam S. Shubert, who had been killed in a railroad accident in 1905. It was to become the flagship of the Shubert enterprises and their headquarters, which it has remained. Ultimately, with the **Booth Theatre,** it formed the western wall of Shubert Alley. For most of its history, the Shuberts have presented their own brand of musical drama and comedies. In 1975, **Joseph Papp** moved *A Chorus Line* to the Shubert, where it broke all standing records as the longest running production (6,137 performances) on a Broadway stage.   MCH

Sandbox, The, by **Edward Albee** was first produced on 15 April 1960 at The Jazz Gallery in New York. An **Off-Broadway** revival in 1968 ran for 55 performances. The play places the image of the sandbox at the center of an absurdist critique of America's treatment of the elderly as well as of the contemporary American family. Two characters called Mommy and Daddy deposit Grandma in a sandbox and wait for her to die. She sits and complains about the treatment she has received from her overbearing daughter, gradually covering herself with sand, until a young man announces that he is the Angel of Death, come to take her. The play ends as Grandma congratulates the young man on his reading of his line.   BCM

Sanderson (née Sackett), Julia (1887–1975) Actress-singer who made her Broadway chorus debut in 1902 and the next year was promoted from the chorus to the title role in *Winsome Winnie.* She remained a musical theatre leading lady into the 1920s, after which she became a radio singer. Tiny and wide-eyed, she introduced, with Donald Brian, **Jerome Kern**'s first hit song, "They Didn't Believe Me," in *The Girl from Utah* (1914).   JD

Sandow, Eugen (né Ernst Friedrich Möller) (1867–1925) German-born strongman, the first to parlay his physique into a commercial property. Having developed a body-building system based on individual muscle groups, he made his New York debut at the **Casino Theatre,** June 1893. His refusal to meet a challenge from Canadian champion Louis Cyr altered his reputation from strongman to showman of the physique. At the Chicago Columbian Exposition of 1893, **Florenz Ziegfeld**

Eugen Sandow in a typical pose, which led contemporaries to debate how the fig leaf was kept on. Photo: Giesen Bros., Berlin. Courtesy: Laurence Senelick.

glorified him with spectacular publicity and abbreviated costumes. Settling in England, Sandow promoted corsets, health oils, and physical culture magazines until 1907; he died of pneumonia a few weeks after lifting a car out of a ditch.   LS

See: G. Nisivocchia, *Sandow the Mighty Monarch of Muscle,* Newark, 1947; C. Trevor, *Sandow the Magnificent,* London, 1946.

San Francisco From its gold rush past to its cosmopolitan present, San Francisco has nurtured a freewheeling theatre culture marked by diversity and adventurousness.

Drama took root in the city in 1849, when California's legendary gold rush swelled the remote coastal outpost with fortune seekers from around the world. That year the city saw its first play: Sheridan Knowles's *The Wife,* enacted by members of Sacramento's **Eagle Theatre** at Washington Hall. Soon astute impresarios realized SF's droves of new settlers, most of them male and single, comprised an eager audience for theatre. From 1850–9 over 50 theatres were built (many soon lost to **fires**), and 1,100 performances of classical dramas, operas, **minstrel show**s, and melodramas given. Though SF was still remote and rustic, artistic standards were surprisingly high; respected acting clans (the Chapmans of **showboat** fame, the Starks) took up residence, and plucky stars (**Lola**

Montez, Charles Kean) appeared. Top venues included the American Theatre (erected in 1851), the Metropolitan (managed 1853–9 by Catherine Sinclair, ex-wife of **Edwin Forrest**), and Maguire's Opera House (built in 1857 by **Thomas Maguire,** SF's leading producer). Chinese opera houses, **circus** structures, playhouses for French, Italian, and German drama, and Barbary Coast melodeons (cabarets) added to the entertainment mix. Mark Twain penned an occasional drama review, and young **Edwin Booth, Lotta Crabtree,** and **David Belasco** honed their crafts.

The colorful, chaotic pioneer phase of SF theatre ended with the 1869 completion of the transcontinental railroad. More accessible now, SF by the mid-1870s was one of the largest, wealthiest, most culturally sophisticated U.S. cities. A short but lavish California silver boom yielded three important new theatres: the **California** (1869), managed by **John McCullough** and **Laurence Barrett,** with a superior **stock company** backing guest stars (Salvini, **Modjeska,** Booth); the **Baldwin** (1876), run by Maguire and David Belasco, with **James O'Neill** as leading man; and the Grand (originally Wade's) Opera House (1876), soon a major opera/drama touring arena for Sarah Bernhardt, Enrico Caruso, and other titans.

Toward the century's end, stock drama gave way to touring "combinations" and the populist allure of variety and melodrama. The Bush Street Theatre was a linchpin of **Michael Leavitt**'s early **vaudeville** circuit; Gustave Walter's huge Orpheum Theatre became a major vaudeville house in Morris Meyerfield's **Orpheum theatre circuit.** "Sensation" melodrama thrived at the Grand Opera House during Walter Morosco's 1890s reign. By 1900 only one decent stock company was left (the **Alcazar**), and the top drama venue was a **Syndicate**-controlled touring house, the Columbia.

In 1906 a ferocious earthquake destroyed much of the city, including more than a dozen theatres; only one minor facility, the Chutes, survived. Recovery was speedy, however: Within a year several houses had been rebuilt (the Orpheum, the New Columbia) and new ones added (the Colonial, the Davis), with more soon following. After 1910, half the theatres featured vaudeville; but in the next decade many vaudeville palaces would start showing movies, and "legit" drama outlets dwindled to a few – by 1919, principally the Columbia (later renamed the Geary), Cort, Alcazar, and Shubert (later the Curran).

From 1920 to 1950 SF remained a major tour stop for Broadway plays and visiting companies (e.g., the **Moscow Art Theatre** Players, 1924), and in 1943 the SF Civic Light Opera formed to produce big musicals with star leads; but during this era literary drama was kept alive mainly by the semiprofessional Little Theatres [see **community theatre**]. The Players Club (1912), founded by Reginald Travers, introduced new **Shaw** and **O'Neill** plays to SF. In the 1930s the Theatre Union mounted topical dramas, the Wayfarers did the classics, and **Federal Theatre Project** units produced plays, **puppet** shows, and a hefty research study of SF theatre history. Later, the Inter-

players (1946–68) showcased important new plays and classics.

A new dramatic chapter began in 1952 when SF State College professors **Herbert Blau** and **Jules Irving** founded the Actor's Workshop. This iconoclastic troupe was the most daring American regional theatre of its era, pursuing vigorous artistic goals in bold versions of innovative European plays. The company worked first in loft spaces and later at the downtown Marines Memorial Theatre; its stagings of *Blood Wedding, Caucasian Chalk Circle,* and *The Balcony* were especially praised. Despite great reviews and foreign touring, not enough subscribers or financial support were generated – due partly to the directors' unwillingness to curry favor with the rich. In 1965 they left to manage a new theatre at **Lincoln Center,** and the Workshop soon disbanded.

The seeds had been sown for more resident drama, however. In 1959 R. G. Davis started the influential **San Francisco Mime Troupe,** a radical ensemble employed *commedia dell'arte* tactics in political satires like the Obie-winning *L'Amant Militaire.* Then, in 1966, flamboyant director **William Ball** and his two-year-old **American Conservatory Theatre** relocated from Pittsburgh to SF's Geary Theatre. ACT's splashy stagings of modern masterworks (Pirandello's *Six Characters in Search of an Author*) and classics (Rostand's *Cyrano de Bergerac*), excellent rep company (**Peter Donat,** Marsha Mason), and top-notch acting school attracted the support that eluded the Workshop; it became the city's flagship regional theatre.

From the mid-1960s to the '80s, social-artistic ferment and increased public arts funding catalyzed an explosion of nonprofit drama in SF. Several new resident Equity companies sprang up in satellite cities: the **Berkeley Repertory Theatre** (1968), Berkeley (now California) Shakespeare Festival (1974), and San Jose Repertory (1980). In SF a multiethnic plethora of "fringe" groups emerged, among them the Julian Theatre (1965); the playwright-centered **Magic** (1965), which debuted major works by **Sam Shepard;** the **Eureka** (1972); the Asian American Theatre Workshop (1973); and the gay-oriented **Theatre Rhinoceros** (1977). All began as "Equity Waiver" theatres, allowed to cast union actors without pay in houses with less than 100 seats. (In 1984, the union restricted this practice, resulting in many new Equity minicontracts.) Experimental theatre flourished, spurred on by **George Coates,** Chris Hardman, Soon 3, the Blake Street Hawkeyes, and other artists, and innovative venues including Intersection, Life on the Water, and Theatre Artaud.

The early 1980s also brought a resurgence of downtown commercial theatre. Carol Shorenstein Hays and her ex-partner **James Nederlander** revamped the venerable Orpheum, Golden Gate, and Curran theatres for the "Best of Broadway" series of touring musicals and plays. The Marines Memorial Theatre, Mason Street Playhouse, and Theatre on the Square also became active again.

Although a severe 1989 earthquake damaged ACT's Geary Theatre home and (along with economic recession) hurt other theatres as well, the service organization Theatre Bay Area counted over

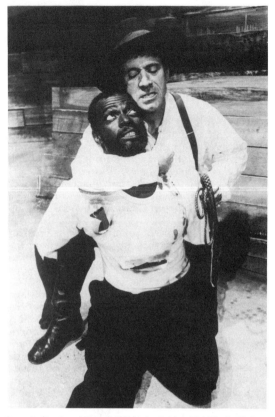

Lonnie Ford and Jim Griffiths in *I Ain't Yo' Uncle*, Robert Alexander's adaptation of *Uncle Tom's Cabin*. Originally produced by the San Francisco Mime Troupe and the Lorraine Hansberry Theatre. Photo: Adrian Ordenana. Courtesy: San Francisco Mime Troupe.

100 drama groups in the SF region in 1991, with new ensembles constantly cropping up. Given diminishing arts funding, the impaired economy, and the loss of some key artistic personnel, SF theatre faces a challenging time. However, throughout its volatile history the city has displayed a flair for live drama and continually attracted the creative artists to deliver it.   MB

> See: M. Berson, *The San Francisco Stage, 1849–1869,* San Francisco, 1990; Berson, *The San Francisco Stage, 1869–1906,* San Francisco, 1992; H. Blau, *The Impossible Theatre,* New York, 1964; L. Estevan, ed., *History of the San Francisco Stage,* vols. 1–21, San Francisco, 1938–42; L. M. Foster, *Annals of the San Francisco Stage,* San Francisco, 1937; E. Gagey, *The San Francisco Stage,* New York, 1950; D. Goodman, *San Francisco Stages,* San Francisco, 1986; G. McMinn, *The Theatre of the Golden Era in California,* Caldwell, ID, 1941.

San Francisco Mime Troupe, The, had existed in embryonic form since 1955, but was founded in 1962 by R. G. Davis, who moved to **San Francisco** in 1958 after several years of **mime** study in Paris. Over the years it moved from silent mime to avant-garde happenings to outdoor *commedia dell'arte*–styled performance and on to radical politics. This theatre **collective,** an expression of the members' social and political concerns, is based on the highly physical expression of *commedia dell'-arte* and R. G. Davis's dance and mime training. This amplified aesthetic perfectly suits the outdoor venues in which the troupe performs for part of every year. Davis left the troupe in 1970; Joan Holden has been the chief resident playwright since 1967. In recent years the troupe has undertaken extensive touring in the U.S. as well as in Europe and in Central America, including the successful *I Ain't Yo' Uncle,* an African-American deconstruction of **Uncle Tom's Cabin.**   TL

> See: R. G. Davis, *San Francisco Mime Troupe: The First Ten Years,* Palo Alto, 1975.

Santley, Mabel see **Rentz–Santley Novelty and Burlesque Company**

Sargent, Epes (1813–80) Author of four plays who also made an impression as a critic. *The Bride of Genoa* (1837), an imitative verse tragedy, was written for **Josephine Clifton.** *Velasco,* based on *Le Cid,* was well received in America and later in London, where it opened the 1849–50 season at the Marylebone Theatre. Critics praised Sargent's theatrical effectiveness and his use of poetic language. With *Changes Makes Change* (1845) Sargent attempted to capitalize on the Downeast **Yankee,** one Nathaniel Bunker. His five-act blank verse version of Bellini's *Norma,* entitled *The Priestess* (1855), was ambitious but not successful on stage. Two "Dramatic Pieces," as he called them – *The Candid Critic* and *The Lampoon* – reveal a dramatist's view of theatre and theatre reviewers.   WJM

Sargent, Epes Winthrop (1872–1938) **Vaudeville** critic. Born in Nassau and educated in Troy, NY, Sargent worked for the *Musical Courier* (1891–4) before joining **Leander Richardson**'s *Dramatic News* as vaudeville critic (1895–6). He wrote for *Metropolitan Magazine* (1896), switching to the *Morning Telegraph* in 1897 under the pen name Chicot. He changed jobs frequently: Pulitzer's *Evening World* (1903); **Variety** (1905–6); *Chicot's Vaudeville Weekly* (three issues); and the *New York Review* (1909). He spent much of the 1910s and '20s writing movie articles and some 350 screenplays before resuming his Chicot column in *Variety* from 1931 until his death. An astute observer of popular entertainment, Sargent was the first significant critic of vaudeville in America.   TLM

> See: J. S. Pratt, "The Vaudeville Criticism of Epes Winthrop Sargeant, 1896–1910," PhD diss., U of Nebraska–Lincoln, 1985.

Saroyan, William (1908–81) This Californian Armenian made his debut as a playwright with **My Heart's in the Highlands** (1939). Both the **Group Theatre** and the **Theatre Guild** had a hand in its production, and although most playgoers were baffled by its loose allegorical form, the play received enough critical acclaim to establish Saroyan as the leading avant-garde playwright of the day. His next play, *The* **Time of Your Life** (1939), solidified his critical reputation by winning the Pulitzer Prize and the Drama Critics' Circle Award (the first time the two groups ever agreed on a choice). Saroyan rejected the Pulitzer Prize on the grounds that material awards were debilitating to the recipient. Now a modern American classic, *The Time of Your Life* not only is revived periodically in New York but also has appeared on the bill of almost every professional regional theatre, pleasing audiences with its originality, imagination, wit, humanity, and local San Francisco color. Continuing to write for the stage through the late 1950s, Saroyan never again achieved the success of his first two plays, although amateur groups everywhere have produced his uncharacteristically conventional one-act play, *Hello Out There* (1942). *The Beautiful People* (1941), directed by the playwright, and *The Cave Dwellers* (1957) found a brief audience and are occasionally revived, but his other works including *Love's Old Sweet Song* (1940) and *Get Away Old Man* (1943) were quick failures. Much of Saroyan's later years were spent writing novels and autobiographical remembrances.   LDC

See: H. Foan, *William Saroyan*, New York, 1966; L. Lee and B. Gifford, *Saroyan: A Biography*, New York, 1984.

Savoy, Bert (né Everett McKenzie) (c. 1888–1923) **Female impersonator.** "Chair dancer" in a Boston dime museum, chorus boy, and passing as a female singer from Montana to Alaska, Savoy wound up in New York where he teamed up with Jay Brennan (c. 1913). In their doubles-act Brennan played a fey "feed" to Savoy's flamboyant red-haired tart, always talking about her girlfriend Margie. Savoy's brassy style and catchphrases – "You musssst come up," "You slay me," "You haven't heard the half of it, dearie," and "I'm glad you ast me" – may have inspired **Mae West.** The act, an eruption of homosexual subculture into the mainstream, earned $1,500 a week in vaudeville and revue: *The Passing Show of 1915*, *The Ziegfeld Follies of 1918*, and *The Greenwich Village Follies* (1920–3). After Savoy was killed by a lightning bolt on Long Island Beach, Brennan continued the act with other partners.   LS

See: L. Senelick, ed., *Gender in Performance*, Hanover, NH, 1992.

Satz, Ludwig (1895–1944) Much-loved leading "star" comedian of the American **Yiddish theatre** from 1918 until his death. Billed as "the man who makes you laugh with tears and cry with a smile," he was a master of characterization, improvisation, and makeup.   AB

Scarecrow; or, The Glass of Truth, The A "tragedy of the ludicrous" by **Percy MacKaye.** Published in 1908, it was first produced in 1910 at the Middlesex Theatre in Connecticut, and then on Broadway at the **Garrick Theatre** in 1911, where it ran for 23 performances. Staged by **Edgar Selwyn,** players included Alice Fisher, Edmund Breese, Fola La Follette, Earle Browne, Brigham Royce, and Frank Reicher. It is considered the best of the early plays written by MacKaye. Set in late 17th-century Massachusetts, this symbolic drama in four acts carries the message of love as a redemptive force that triumphs over evil and deception.   NP

Scenic design There is almost no documentation regarding the earliest efforts at scenic design in North America. Generally working in makeshift spaces, early theatrical ventures no doubt used some sort of improvised scenery, perhaps pressing easel painters into service to provide a backcloth or a curtain and wings. The few records that make any mention of scenery neither mention artists' names nor describe the decor. The first professional scenery in the colonies arrived with Lewis **Hallam, Sr.**'s London Company of Comedians in Virginia in 1752; though the decor was advertised as newly built, it is generally believed that it came from their defunct London theatre. After a period in Jamaica, the troupe returned to the colonies in 1758 under the management of **David Douglass** and apparently without its scenic stock. In 1759 they opened the Society Hill Theatre in **Philadelphia** with a new stock of scenes created by easel painter William Williams. The next scene painter known by name is Jacob Snyder, who most likely joined Douglass's company in 1762. Descriptions of scenes by these painters mention "views" (most likely painted backdrops) and "transparent scenes." In 1765 and later, Douglass imported new scenery from England, including work by Nicholas Thomas Dall and John Inigo Richards, suggesting that the work of his American painters was inadequate.

Having spent part of the Revolution in Jamaica, Douglass's company, now known as the **American Company** and headed by Lewis Hallam, Jr., returned to the States in 1784 with a French scene painter, Charles Busselotte, who was apparently skilled at stage machinery and shadow **puppets.** Of the artists who came to America after the Revolution the two most notable were Luke Robbins and M. C. Milbourne. The former worked with the Old American Company and later as house artist for the **Park Theatre** in New York. **Thomas Wignell** imported Milbourne, resident designer for Philadelphia's **Chestnut Street Theatre** (1793–6). He introduced topographical scenes to the American theatre and was one of the strongest influences on the development of American scenography. Milbourne, like many of the English emigrés, had worked at Covent Garden. A third major artist of the postcolonial period was the Italian-born Charles Ciceri, who came to the U.S. in 1793 and worked primarily at the Park Theatre. John Joseph Holland, master scene painter at the Chestnut Street Theatre from 1796, developed a major reputation and trained most of the significant American scenic artists of the first half of the 19th century.

The scenery of this period included topographical views, transparent scenes, and spectacular effects as described in a production of *The Tempest* in Richmond in 1791: "a troubled Horizon and Tempestuous Sea where the Usurper's Vessel is tossed a considerable time in sight . . . amidst repeated claps of Thunder, Lightning, Hail, Rain &c and being dashed on a Chain of Rocks. . . ." Stock scenery of this sort continued to travel with companies through the first half of the 19th century. The most significant development, however, was the introduction of gaslight [see **stage lighting**]. First used for auditorium lighting at the Chestnut

Jo Mielziner's design for the poker scene in *A Streetcar Named Desire*. Courtesy: National Museum of American Art, Smithsonian Institute.

Street Theatre in 1816, gas lighting became increasingly common onstage in the next decade. Its increased brightness and evenness, as well as the ability to control its intensity, altered the entire approach to scene painting. Colors had to be subdued and the increasingly visible details made more realistic. The first use of overhead border lights may have occurred at the **Chatham Theatre** in New York in 1827; their introduction allowed the light ladders in the wings to be abolished and opened the wings further, providing the scenic artist greater possibilities.

Melodrama's popularity early in the 19th century necessitated scenery that would suggest exotic locales and allow for special effects. The increasingly cavernous theatres, especially in New York and Philadelphia, required large and grandiose scenery and depended upon spectacular effects such as fires, waterfalls, and earthquakes. While stock scenery sufficed at first, managers and audiences began to demand new scenery, leading to the emergence of the scenic artist as a dominant figure in American theatre.

Early in the 19th century a few scenic artists began to establish reputations and became attached to specific actor-managers or to specific theatres. Harry Isherwood, for example, worked with the company of **Joseph Jefferson [I]** during 1830–45, and Russell Smith was chief scenic artist for the Academy of Music in Philadelphia in midcentury. The most notable scenic artist of the 19th century, however, was **Charles W. Witham,** who began painting scenes for **Edwin Forrest** in **Boston** in 1863 but was soon hired as **Edwin Booth**'s primary painter. He is virtually the only artist of the latter half of the 19th century to receive notice from the critics; the evolution of his art suggests the course of American design of the period. Beginning with architectural settings for Booth, he evolved a more romantic style by the 1880s, and his last work showed the influence of realism.

Although a few dozen scenic artists are known by name, there is little detailed knowledge about their work or lives. In part this is due to the emergence in the last third of the 19th century of scenic studios [see **support services**]; these created scenery and decor for productions, generally without credit to individual artists. Also, it was not unusual for different scenes within a production to be designed by different artists, or for productions to mix stock and newly built decor.

As in Europe, the influence of antiquarianism upon the stage was great, and increasingly realistic and historically accurate details began to appear in the decor. The real impetus for antiquarianism came with the visit of Charles Kean for the 1845–6 season: Although his "illustrated Shakespeare" productions were still several years off, early attempts in that direction were visible here. A new mounting of *Richard III* stunned and delighted audiences with its magnificent scenery. Kean's crusade was taken up by American actor-manager **William Evans Burton,** who began mounting full stagings of Shakespeare in the 1850s, culminating in a historically accurate production of *A Midsummer Night's Dream* in 1854, for which scholarly citations were published in the program to legitimize his scenic decisions.

With the advent of gentlemanly melodrama, box sets and interiors came to dominate the legitimate stage. The wing and groove system for changing scenes became obsolete. At first, much of the detail for interiors was painted two-dimensionally on flats, but starting in the 1880s, notably in the productions of **Augustin Daly,** three-dimensional scenic pieces and architectural elements became more prominent. This trend reached its apex with the work of **David Belasco** at the turn of the century. Belasco's attention to the minutiae of decor, insistence on absolute accuracy, and innovations in lighting combined to create the most thorough illusionism seen in America, and possibly the world, to that time. So dominant was his influence that the style became known as "Belasco realism." Belasco, however, was the producer and director (and sometimes writer), not the designer. Although he worked with several artists, his most successful collaborations were with the now virtually forgotten Ernest Gros and electrician Louis Hartmann. Among Belasco's memorable productions were *The Governor's Lady* (1908), in which Child's Restaurant was completely reproduced on the stage, and *The **Easiest Way*** (1909), for which he purchased the actual furnishings of a cheap boardinghouse. This style of photographic realism could be found through the rest of the 20th century in productions such as **Elmer Rice**'s *Street Scene* designed by **Jo Mielziner** or the **Group Theatre**'s production of **Clifford Odets**'s *Awake and Sing!*, though rarely with Belasco's fervor. There was even a self-consciously ironic resurgence of photographic realism in the 1970s inspired by a movement of the same name in the art world. The **Performance Group**'s production of *Cops* designed by **James Clayburgh** and **Santo Loquasto**'s setting for **David Mamet**'s *American Buffalo* are notable examples.

The reaction to Belasco-style realism was the New Stagecraft, arguably the most significant development in 20th-century American theatre. Inspired principally by the work and writings of Edward Gordon Craig and Adolphe Appia – but also by the work of **Max Reinhardt**, Oskar Strnad, and Georg Fuchs in Europe, as well as the work of Viennese emigré **Joseph Urban**'s at the Boston Opera beginning in 1911 – it led American designers to abandon detailed realism for simplified realism, suggestion, and abstraction. Scenery evolved from background and decoration to become an integral part of the production, often encapsulating the themes of the play in a metaphorical image. In addition to Craig's *The Art of the Theatre* (1905) and his monthly journal, *The Mask,* Americans were introduced to the new developments in European staging through Hiram Moderwell's 1914 book, *The Theatre of Today.* That same year, designer **Sam Hume** put together an exhibition of new designs from Europe that was seen in Cambridge and New York. Furthermore, the work of the Ballets Russes was becoming known, though the troupe would not visit for several more years. The first examples of the New Stagecraft were seen at Boston's Toy Theatre, founded in 1911 as one of the first of the U.S. Little Theatres [see **community theatre**], in the designs of **Livingston Platt,** and at Maurice Browne's Little Theatre founded in Chicago in 1912.

However, the production generally acknowledged to mark the arrival of the New Stagecraft in America was *The Man Who Married a Dumb Wife* (1915), directed by British director Harley Granville-Barker and designed by **Robert Edmond Jones.** Unlike the dominant Belasco realism commonly found on Broadway, Jones's set was monochromatic and done in the style of a Japanese woodcut. The medieval costumes were in flat primary and secondary colors. Though this was a radical break with accepted practice, it did not create an immediate revolution in scenography. The true impact of the New Stagecraft began to be felt later that year when Jones teamed up with director **Arthur Hopkins** on *The Devil's Garden* and the effectiveness of simplified realism became evident. Jones also began to work with the **Provincetown Players.** Related to the idea of simplification was the concept of the unit set, which Jones helped popularize. Jones's association with Hopkins over the succeeding decade, especially on the Shakespeare plays with John Barrymore [see **Drew–Barrymore**], and his designs for most of the major **Eugene O'Neill** plays established an ineluctable connection between the emergent American drama and production and the New Stagecraft. The simplicity of much of this style of stage decor also had economic benefits, and the New Stagecraft flourished in the burgeoning Little Theatre movement.

A second pillar of the New Stagecraft movement was **Lee Simonson,** who began designing with the **Washington Square Players** and then with their successor, the **Theatre Guild.** As designer of some half the productions of the Guild through the 1920s, Simonson was to be, through sheer volume alone, the most influential of the new designers. He championed the unit set and the "island" stage, in which a scenic unit sat in the midst of the stage surrounded by space; this was often accompanied by projected scenery on a cyclorama. The third pillar of the movement was **Norman Bel Geddes,** whose collaboration with **Max Reinhardt** on *The Miracle* and his several unrealized projects (for which plans and models were nonetheless constructed and well known) created a bold, theatrical, and uniquely American abstract style. Ironically, Bel Geddes's most successful Broadway design was in a photorealist style for *Dead End* (1935). Other significant designers of the New Stagecraft included **Hermann Rosse, Claude Bragdon, Cleon Throckmorton, Rollo Peters, Woodman Thompson,** Irving Pichel, and Robert R. Sharpe. The next generation of American designers began to emerge during the 1920s, including **Aline Bernstein, Donald Oenslager,** Jo Mielziner, **Watson Barratt,** and **Mordecai Gorelik.**

Though dozens of significant artists can be added to this list, the period of roughly 1920–60 is really dominated by five men: Jones, Simonson, Oenslager, Mielziner, and (from the mid-1940s onward) **Oliver Smith. Boris Aronson** is a presence from the late 1920s, but while he was eventually acknowledged as the most significant artist and greatest innovator of the American stage by peers, colleagues, and critics alike, his greatest commercial successes did not come until the 1960s, when he began to collaborate on a series of musicals with **Harold Prince.**

While the simplified realism of Jones and Simonson continued through the 1930s, as did naturalism and expressionism and a host of variations on these genres, a more lyrical and elegant style of design began to emerge in the 1930s, largely influenced by Oenslager. The style, best known as poetic or lyric realism, ultimately became associated most closely with Mielziner. Painted scenery resurfaced, often incorporating fanciful and fantastic images, decorative flourishes, and curved lines. In the 1940s, as symbolism and expressionism melded with American psychological realism in the plays of **Tennessee Williams** and in **Arthur Miller**'s *Death of a Salesman,* Mielziner found the perfect scenic solution to the flow of internal and external reality with the use of the scrim. This device also gave a soft and dreamlike feel to many scenes that emphasized mood over harsh reality. These same characteristics were picked up by Smith, though not always with the use of scrim, in such productions as *My Fair Lady* and *West Side Story.* The painterly, atmospheric setting was the dominant style in the post–WW II era. While the Oenslager–Mielziner approach was largely superseded in the 1960s, its essence reemerged in the 1970s – albeit with a different vocabulary – in the work of **John Lee Beatty.**

Although the Berliner Ensemble never visited the U.S., its work and that of several other German designers exerted a profound influence on a new generation of American directors and designers. Most notable among the designers was **Ming Cho Lee,** who shaped a whole generation of American design in theatre and opera: His 1964 *Electra* for the **New York Shakespeare Festival** is generally considered a turning point in postwar American scenography. The shift in design aesthetics was also shaped by the work of **Rouben Ter-Arutunian** and Boris Aronson, who was finally getting his long-deserved recognition. The work of Lee and Ter-Arutunian in particular moved design from a moody, painterly style to a strongly sculptural, textured, and emblematic approach. Largely influenced by Aronson, constructivist elements, the symbolic use of color, and the introduction of new materials and technologies began to dominate the theatre. Through the 1980s, in the designs of Lee and Aronson as well as of Santo Loquasto, **Douglas Schmidt, Marjorie Kellogg, David Mitchell, Robin Wagner, John Conklin,** and others, sets were typified by the use of metal and wood scaffolding, wooden-plank flooring, erosion cloth, collage, mylar mirrors, emblematic scenic pieces, and, above all, a highly sculptural use of space. Significantly, as the quantity and, arguably, the quality, of traditional American playwriting diminished, most of these designers worked in opera and dance as much as in theatre. As a result, American design evolved as a vital force in the theatre of the time.

The renascent avant-garde theatre of the period also inspired design. One popular approach was environmental theatre, which sought to destroy the frontal and separate relationship of performer and spectator. Though with roots going back to the turn of the century, and with precedents in the Middle Ages and various forms of ritual theatre, the modern environment movement in America is associated with director **Richard Schechner** and The **Performance Group.** His production of *Dionysus in 69* placed the audience on scaffolds shared with the performers, who also involved the audience in parts of the performance. **Eugene Lee**'s designs with **Andre Gregory** and later with **Adrian Hall** encompassed the audience in various environments and scattered the performance throughout the auditorium or performance space. The introduction of environmental staging on Broadway in the early 1970s, especially in the Hal Prince production of *Candide,* seemed to signal the end of the proscenium era, but it proved short-lived, though it did reemerge in the 1980s as a popular gimmick for certain instances of **participatory theatre.**

Two avant-garde theatre artists had a profound effect upon many designers: **Robert Wilson** and **Richard Foreman.** The former produced "operas" with large-scale and spectacular scenery in a symbolist–surrealist vein. While Wilson designed most of his early work himself, his more recent work is often done in collaboration with designers like John Conklin and lighting designer **Jennifer Tipton,** thus creating a direct link with much contemporary theatre, opera, and dance production. Foreman also does much of his own design, though he has also worked in collaboration with Nancy Winter. His idiosyncratic work, which consciously refers back to Renaissance design, often manipulates perspective, alters spatial relationships, calls attention to the process of viewing, and juxtaposes objects and images from a wide range of sources simultaneously. This latter characteristic, together with the "ugliness" and homemade quality of much of his work, was a forerunner of postmodernism in American design.

This last movement, whose practitioners include **Adrianne Lobel, Michael Yeargan, Robert Israel, George Tsypin,** John Conklin, and the work of the **Wooster Group** and **James Clayburgh,** is typified by a strong frontality, juxtaposition of dissociated images, quotations from historical productions and imagery, a visual irony, and a self-conscious opposition to "prettiness" among other things. Though this style has been used in certain dramatic productions, notably at regional theatres such as the **Hartford Stage, American Repertory Theatre,** and the La Jolla Playhouse, it is most common in opera production.

While certain trends or design styles – whether lyric realism or postmodernism – may become the dominant forces in a particular period, certain tendencies continue. The bulk of mainstream American drama remains realistically based, and the selective realism first seen in the New Stagecraft remains, in one form or another, appropriate today. Moreover, despite a brief trend toward more minimal musicals, audiences still seem enthralled by glamor and spectacle; thus **Tony Walton**'s version of spectacle, though it may be grounded in a late-20th-century sensibility, is directly connected to the glamor and spectacle of the early part of the century.   AA

See: S. Appelbaum, ed., *The New York Stage: Famous Productions in Photographs,* New York, 1976; A. Aronson, *American Set Design,* New York, 1985; S. Cheney, *The Art Theatre,* New York, 1925; B. Owen, *Scenic Design on Broadway,* Westport, CT, 1991; O. K. Larson, *Scene Design in the American Theatre from 1915 to 1960,* Fayetteville, AR, 1989; R. Smith, *American Set Design 2,* New York, 1991; *The Twin City Scenic Collection* (catalogue), Minneapolis, 1987; J. R. Wolcott in *Theatre Survey* (May 1977).

Schary, Dore (1905–80) Playwright and producer. From stage actor to production head at Metro–Goldwyn–Mayer (1948), Schary became one of the most powerful men in Hollywood. After dismissal by MGM in 1956, he wrote and coproduced *Sunrise at Campobello,* which won five Tony Awards for the 1957–8 season. Three other plays by Schary were unsuccessful. He also coproduced and directed *The Unsinkable Molly Brown* (1960). TLM

Schechner, Richard (1934–) Director, author, and educator who, as editor of *Tulane Drama Review* [now *The Drama Review*] (1962–9) and founder of the **Performance Group** (1967–80), established himself as a leader of the new environmental theatre based on the ideas of Artaud and Grotowski. With the Performance Group he explored the nature of **collective** creation, audience participation, and theatrical language in *Dionysus in 69, Makbeth* (1969), and *Commune* (1970). Later he turned to primitive ritual and shamanism. Schechner has been a Professor of Performance Studies at NYU since 1967. Among his books are *Public Domain* (1968), *Environmental Theatre* (1973), and *Between Theatre and Anthropology* (1985). He is again editor of *TDR*.   TLM

Scheff, Fritzi (née Friedrike Jaeger) (1879–
1954) Vienna-born lyric soprano and actress, Scheff made her Metropolitan Opera debut in 1901, where she was known as the "Little Devil of the Opera" because of her diminutive size, red hair, and fiery temper. On Broadway she starred in four **Victor Herbert** operettas: *Babette* (1903), *Mlle. Modiste* (1905), *The Prima Donna* (1908), and *The Duchess* (1911), as well as several other comic operas and *opéras bouffes*. She appeared in **vaudeville** in the early 1920s, and later in the decade starred in several straight plays. In 1929 she received critical praise in a revival of *Mlle. Modiste*. She had a radio show for several years in the 1930s; her last Broadway appearance was in the **revue** *The ANTA Album* (1950).   MK

Schenck, Joe see Van, Gus

Schildkraut, Rudolph (1862–1930) and Joseph Schildkraut (1896–1964).
Father and son actors. Rudolph, born in Constantinople, won fame playing such powerful roles as Lear in German, notably with **Max Reinhardt;** he also made German films. While appearing in New York and the then–German-language Irving Place Theatre (1910), he first guest starred in **Yiddish theatre** as Shylock. He probably began on the Yiddish stage by speaking his lines in German, but eventually performed altogether in Yiddish, culminating in his best known Yiddish role, **Sholom Asch**'s *God of Vengeance,* which he later played in English on Broadway (1924).

Joseph performed in Yiddish with his father in his youth in New York. He studied theatre in Germany and performed with Reinhardt, but had his first starring role for the **Theatre Guild.** Thereafter he alternated between Broadway (*Liliom,* 1921; *The Firebrand,* 1924; *Uncle Harry,* 1942; *The Diary of Anne Frank,* 1955) and Hollywood (winning two Academy Awards), as well as television. He was also a member of **Eva Le Gallienne**'s **Civic Repertory Theatre** in the early 1930s. His autobiography, *My Father and I,* appeared in 1959.   NS

Schisgal, Murray (1926–)
This Brooklyn-born playwright had an auspicious start in British theatre – *The Typists, The Postman,* and *A Simple Kind of Love Story* (1960); however, **Luv** (1963) failed in London before becoming a Broadway hit. Selected works produced in New York were primarily one-acters with clever dialogue: *Fragments* (1967), *Jimmy Shine* (1968), *Dr. Fish* (1970), and *Men Dangling* (1988). His awards include the **Off-**Broadway Vernon Rice Award and the Outer Critics' Circle Award (both 1963).   GSA

Schmidt, Douglas (1942–)
Set and costume designer, most closely associated with large-scale, kinetic, multiscene musicals and operas that evoke an almost 19th-century sensibility. Schmidt is also capable of sculptural scenery and realistic detail. After graduating from Boston University he assisted **Ming Cho Lee** and also designed at **Cincinnati Playhouse in the Park.** Lee's influence is very clear in his early work. He was resident designer for the Repertory Theatre at **Lincoln Center** during 1960–73. Schmidt has collaborated frequently with directors **Richard Foreman, Des McAnuff,** Tom Moore, and **Jack O'Brien.** His productions include *Grease* and *Over Here!,* as well as several productions with the San Francisco Opera and other opera companies.   AA

Schneemann, Carolee (1939–)
Performance artist, painter, filmmaker, writer. A native of rural Pennsylvania and Vermont, Schneemann studied painting and sculpture at Columbia University (1958), the New School for Social Research, Bard College (BA, 1959), and the University of Illinois (MFA, 1961). She cofounded Judson Dance Theatre and participated in Happenings, Fluxus events, and environmental and kinetic theatre pieces. Her ritual-like group performances, such as *Meat Joy* (1964), were influenced by Artaud, the Nouveaux Réalistes, abstract expressionism, Simone De Beauvois, John Cage, and Wilhelm Reich. Her early erotic film, *Autobiographical Trilogy: Fuses, Plumb Line, and Kitsch's Last Meal* (1964–8), and such performances as *Up to and Including Her Limits* (1973–6) and *Interior Scroll* (1975) – including her kinetic sculpture/installation, *Cycladic Imprints* (1990) – are **feminist** statements against the **censorship** of women's self-representation.   AF

Schneider, Alan (Abram Leopoldovich Schneider) (1917–84)
Russian-born director, known as Beckett's American interpreter. Schneider worked at Washington's **Arena Stage** (Artistic Director, 1952–3; Acting Producer, 1973–4), New York's **Neighborhood Playhouse,** and elsewhere across the U.S. Director of the Juilliard Theater Center (1976–9) and, at his death, a co-artistic director of the **Acting Company,** Schneider headed the graduate directing program at the University of California at San Diego and was president of the **Theatre Communications Group,** which initiated the annual Alan Schneider Director Award in 1986.

Schneider, who believed his main function was "to serve as the intermediary between the playwright and the actual stage production," directed premieres of Beckett's *Waiting for Godot* (1956), *Endgame* (1958), *Happy Days* (1961), *Play* (1964), and the movie *Film,* starring Buster Keaton (1964). He received an Obie for *The Pinter Plays* (*The Collection* and *The Dumbwaiter,* 1963), a Tony for **Albee**'s *Who's Afraid of Virginia Woolf?* (1963), and a Drama Desk Award for his direction of Preston Jones's *Texas Trilogy* (1976); he was nominated for Tonys for Albee's *Tiny Alice* (1965) and

A Delicate Balance (1967) and **Robert Anderson's**
You Know I Can't Hear You When the Water's Running (1968). Schneider, killed in a traffic accident in
London, left an autobiography, *Entrances: An
American Director's Journal,* published in 1986.   REK

Schwartz, Arthur (1900–84) Composer, producer, and librettist, trained as a lawyer; his first
songs were written for **vaudeville.** He contributed
songs to several shows before teaming with lyricist
Howard Dietz on a series of sophisticated **revue**s:
The Little Show (1929), *The Second Little Show*
(1930), *Three's a Crowd* (1930), *The Band Wagon*
(1931), *Flying Colors* (1932), *Revenge with Music*
(1934), and *At Home Abroad* (1935). Schwartz collaborated with lyricist **Dorothy Fields** on *Stars in
Your Eyes* (1939), *A Tree Grows in Brooklyn* (1951),
and *By the Beautiful Sea* (1954), and reunited with
Dietz on the revue *Inside U.S.A.* (1948) and the
musicals *The Gay Life* (1961) and *Jenny* (1963).
During 1939–46 he composed 46 film scores.
Schwartz was particularly adept at writing pensive,
pulsating ballads, such as "You and the Night and
the Music."   MK

Schwartz, Maurice (1890?–1960) Yiddish actor, producer, and director. At age 1, en route
from the Ukraine to America, he was separated
from his family and remained in London; there he
supported himself and attended the new **Yiddish
theatre.** In America he became an amateur actor
and then a professional, soon making a name for
his fire and panache. In 1919 in New York he
organized the **Yiddish Art Theatre** and managed
to keep it going, most seasons, until 1950. Among
its most successful productions were *The Brothers
Ashkenazi* and *Yoshe Kalb* (1932), both by I. J.
Singer, and *Shylock's Daughter* (by Zahav), as well
as Yiddish classics and translations of classics from
other cultures. Not only was Schwartz personally
famous as an actor – in Sholom Aleichem's *Tevye
the Dairyman,* for example, onstage and in film –
he was also an institution through his Yiddish Art
Theatre, which, whether on Second Avenue, on
tour, or in temporary disarray, seemed the last
bastion of Yiddish theatre's energy, color, and
sustained intellectual aspirations. Schwartz was still
touring till the year he died.   NS

Schwartz, Stephen (1948–) Composer-
lyricist. After studying at Juilliard and Carnegie
Institute of Technology, Schwartz wrote the title
song for the play *Butterflies Are Free* (1969). While
still at Carnegie Tech he had written the score for
Godspell, a musical based on St. Matthew's Gospel, which opened **Off-Broadway** in 1971 and ran
for five years before moving to Broadway. Among
Schwartz's other scores were those for *Pippin* (1972),
The Magic Show (1974), *Working* (1978), and the
ill-fated *The Baker's Wife* (1976) and *Rags* (1986).
He also wrote the lyrics for **Leonard Bernstein's**
Mass (1971). Schwartz's shows are notable for their
unusual subject matter and the contemporary rock
style of his scores.   MK

Scott, George C. (1927–) Film and stage
actor and director, noted for a strong artistic integrity and intense acting style. His first stage appearance was at the University of Missouri after WW
II. After playing some 150 roles in stock companies, Scott made his New York debut as Richard
III in the **New York Shakespeare Festival** (1957).
He received excellent response to *Children of Darkness* (1958). Alternating stage work with an outstanding film career, he appeared as Ephraim Cabot
in *Desire Under the Elms* (1963). More recent
successes on Broadway include *Sly Fox* (1976),
based on Ben Jonson's *Volpone.* Although noted
for his dramatic intensity, Scott directed and starred
in Noël Coward's *Present Laughter* in 1982, directed
Design for Living in 1984, and directed and starred
in **Osborn's** *On Borrowed Time* in 1991, all at
Circle in the Square. He refused in 1971 to accept
the Academy Award for best actor in the title role
of *Patton.* Scott has also appeared with the NYSF
playing Antony and Shylock. Campbell Scott, the
son of Scott and the late **Colleen Dewhurst,** is
also an actor (Pericles, 1991, at the **Public Theater**).   SMA

Seattle Also known as The Emerald City, Seattle
lies on the eastern shore of Puget Sound in northwestern Washington State. Settled in 1851, it is the
region's largest metropolitan area (2,500,000) and
claims one of the most active theatre communities
west of the Mississippi. Seattle's theatre history
roughly defines three periods: the stock and vaudeville era; an academic and resident company era of
mingled artistic, political, and entertainment impulses; and the 1960s renaissance. Affiliation between academic and professional theatre developed
during the last two periods, evolving into a supportive cross fertilization.

Formal entertainment spaces coincided with Seattle's industrial beginning, when Henry Yesler,
later mayor, built Yesler Hall (1861), replacing the
makeshift space in his sawmill's dining hall (1852).
Official recognition followed in an 1865 ordinance
taxing "theatrical exhibitions." Entertainment halls
such as Yesler's Pavilion (1865) and Plummer's
Hall (1859) multiplied, primarily offering **minstrel
show**s, ventriloquists, and "variety acts."

The year 1870 brought traveling companies, the
first major group, Fanny Morgan Phelps's troupe,
visiting in 1875. "Opera houses," **stock company**
venues, appeared relatively late in Seattle, as in
much of the West Coast, but by 1880 Squire's
Opera House (1879) and others regularly housed
touring shows.

On 6 June 1889, a 25-block fire left only the 600-
seat Turner Hall (1886), once considered the finest
on the West Coast, and Armory Hall (1888), never
a full-time theatre. Owners rebuilt within months,
the Standard (1888) reopening in November after
five months' tent operation.

The 1898 Klondike gold rush and resulting boom
prompted a surge in entertainment houses but left
theatre behind: During 1899–1901 no stock companies booked into Seattle. In 1902 the Seattle
Theatre (1892) and the Third Avenue Theatre (1896),
amid 10 **vaudeville** houses, began an upswing that
peaked in 1909.

Road show and vaudeville energy increased, as
syndication made Seattle the base for three national

figures. John Cort arrived in 1887 from Illinois and built the first electrically lighted theatre, the second Standard, a year later; this postfire Standard introduced matinees. In 1898 he formed The Fraternal Order of Eagles as an association of theatre managers. By 1890 he held theatre leases in every major town along the Northern Pacific Railroad, effectively shutting out the **Klaw-Erlanger** trust. In 1910, he formed the National Theatre Owners' Association with 1,200 theatres and effectively excluded both Klaw–Erlanger and the **Shubert**s from the West Coast.

John Considine came to Seattle from Chicago in 1889 and built People's Theatre (1891). Forming a partnership with Timothy Sullivan in New York, he opened the Coliseum (1907), the largest theatre west of the Mississippi. Seattle quickly became the main office of Sullivan–Considine, the first popularly priced transcontinental vaudeville circuit.

Alexander Pantages arrived from Alaska in 1902 and opened the Crystal (1902), also a vaudeville house. Through keen audience assessment and a strategy that included duplicating his competitors' billings at half admission, Pantages controlled theatres through half the country by 1911 and was able to offer a 50–60-week tour.

La Petite (1902), Seattle's first moviehouse, signaled the end of the era, however. The Odeon chain appeared in 1907, and by 1915 lower overhead and admission had nearly finished the stock and vaudeville houses. By then Considine was ruined. Cort had left for New York, and Pantages operated from Los Angeles.

In 1914, Nellie C(entennial) Cornish founded The Cornish School, the transition from road and vaudeville dominance to the resident companies of the second period. Cornish promoted the arts vigorously and precipitated the enduring connection between **academic theatre** and professional theatre. With faculty including Martha Graham, John Cage, Alexander Koiransky, Ellen Van Volkenburg, and Maurice Browne, she attempted to bring an "Eastern" notion of the arts to Seattle, producing such figures as Merce Cunningham and Elena Miramova. The school remains a successful performing arts conservatory.

In 1922, Cornish hired Florence and Burton James to expand her school's theatre program. The Jameses enhanced its already strong reception, producing both classic and contemporary American and European works. After a 1928 **censorship** dispute, the Jameses resigned to form the Seattle Repertory Playhouse (SRP). On the model of New York's **Theatre Guild,** SRP subsidized its first and later seasons through subscription sales. After renting for two years, they built a 342-seat structure in 1929. For 23 seasons, SRP produced classical and contemporary European plays and American plays from the works of **O'Neill** and **Odets** to contemporary hits and original scripts. They built the first revolve in the Northwest for **Ibsen**'s *Peer Gynt,* only the play's fifth presentation nationally.

In 1935, with **Federal Theatre Project** subsidy, SRP sponsored the Negro Repertory Company (NRC), the nation's second most productive black troupe. NRC emphasized script creation and adaptation by its members, resulting in productions

of *Lysistrata* and an original **revue,** *Swing, Gates, Swing.*

SRP's success coincided with increased community impact by the University of Washington School of Drama, chaired from 1930 by Glenn Hughes, who featured popular Broadway material. With WPA subsidy, Hughes built the Penthouse Theatre (1940), the nation's first permanent arena theatre. Originally designed by John Ashby Conway and Hughes to be movable, the 172-seat structure was relocated in 1991 after 51 years' continuous use. Although Hughes intended the theatre as a laboratory for film acting, **Brooks Atkinson** called it ". . . the finest arena theatre in America."

Commitment to working-class theatre and productions of George Sklar's *Stevedore,* O'Neill's *The Hairy Ape,* and Odets's *Waiting for Lefty* brought SRP conservative attack in 1947. The James's contempt convictions by a state un-American activities committee brought financial collapse in 1951. Glenn Hughes immediately acquired the building for his department, and it is presently named for him.

Growing movie popularity during the 1930s completed the 15-year vaudeville and road-house decline. The Cornish School, the Seattle Repertory Playhouse, and Hughes's School of Drama, however, sustained and stimulated an active Seattle theatre environment through the Depression.

The 1962 Seattle World's Fair furnished the **Seattle Repertory Theatre** Company (1963) a site and marked Seattle's theatrical rebirth. The Rep's 1990 Tony for outstanding regional theatre acknowledged its aggressive development of new works by major playwrights. The energy of the period persists in such groups as A **Contemporary Theatre, Inc.** (1965); The Bathhouse Theatre (1970), an ensemble group; The **Empty Space** (1970); Intiman Theatre (1972), a classics-based organization; Seattle Children's Theatre (1975), the nation's second largest **children's theatre** company; and The Annex Theatre (1978), which supports new actors, directors, and playwrights.

Interest-specific companies have also excelled, whether reliant on restricted or broad-based audiences. Northwest Asian American Theatre (1972) remains the most significant such company nationally; On The Boards (1979) supports regional and national **performance art;** Seattle Group Theatre (1978) retains its multiethnic emphasis; New City/Theatre Zero (1982) has presented more than 100 world or regional avant-garde premieres; and Alice B. Theatre (1984) provides a **gay/lesbian** voice.

Local economic vitality allowed Seattle's theatre community to ride out the recession of the late 1980s. The growth of software- and technology-based industries also provided a middle-class audience willing to support the arts through regional economic reverses in the 1970s. Patrons of Northwest Civic, Cultural and Charitable Organizations (PONCHO, 1963) has generated millions of dollars, the vast majority supporting performing arts. Other groups have followed suit, and a corporate 1% arts subsidy has lent further stability. Seattle's unique combination of public and private support has been called the future of the arts as federal funds dwindle.

Seattle's historic theatre buildings disappeared at

an increasing rate as victims of development in the early 1990s, but companies remained intact. A thriving fringe community of more than 30 companies suggests a continued healthy theatre climate in Seattle.   RW

See: M. D. Bennett, "The Glenn Hughes Years, 1927–1961," PhD diss., U of Washington, 1982; E. C. Elliott, *A History of Variety–Vaudeville in Seattle,* Seattle, 1944; A. Ernst, *Trouping in the Oregon Country,* Portland, OR, 1961; H. F. Grant, *The Story of Seattle's Early Theatres,* Seattle, 1934; E. A. Johnson, "A Production History of the Seattle Federal Theatre Project Negro Repertory Company, 1935–1939," PhD diss., U of Washington, 1981; M. K. Rohrer, *The History of Seattle Stock Companies,* Seattle, 1945.

Seattle Repertory Theatre Founded in **Seattle** in 1963 by **Stuart Vaughan** in a building erected for the 1963 World's Fair, the company met financial difficulties in its early days; by 1969–70 their deficit was over a quarter of a million dollars. W. Duncan Ross was appointed managing director at that time; six years later the company had 22,000 season subscriptions.

In 1974 SRT leased a second building, called Stage 2, to house a second season of five plays. In 1979 Ross accepted a position elsewhere and was replaced by **Daniel Sullivan;** two years later Sullivan became artistic director. Sullivan continued previous policy, but added a New Plays workshop (four scripts each spring) and began to employ more local actors.

In 1983 the company opened the 850-seat Bagley Wright Theatre at the Seattle Center, which also contains a 140-seat PONCHO Forum for new works. The Wright Theatre annually presents a six-play season, balancing classics, contemporary works, and premieres of new plays; Stage 2 offers three productions.   SMA

Second City Over the years, the work of this **Chicago** comedy institution has had an incalculable effect on the nature of satire in American theatre, radio, television, and film. At the very least, it has trained dozens of our most successful performers, such as Alan Alda, **Alan Arkin,** Ed Asner, Dan Aykroyd, John Belushi, Shelley Berman, Peter Boyle, John Candy, Valerie Harper, Robert Klein, **Linda Lavin,** Shelley Long, Elaine May, Paul Mazursky, Ann Meara, Bill Murray, **Mike Nichols,** Gilda Radner, Joan Rivers, Paul Sand, Avery Schreiber, Martin Short, David Steinberg, Jerry Stiller, George Wendt, and Fred Willard. More significantly, the company's approach to character, scene, and performance has arguably become the dominant mode of American comic acting.

Ironically, this theatre, known for spontaneity and ensemble, traces its beginnings to the theories of a single person. Viola Spolin, author of the popular *Improvisation for the Theater* (revised 1983) and other texts, got started as a recreational director inventing games for inner-city Chicago children in the 1920s and '30s. Spolin's methods for eliciting spontaneous behavior – based in part on the theories of Stanislavsky – were passed on to her son, **Paul Sills.** The idea for the first improvisational

theatre came from David Shepherd, Sills's classmate at the University of Chicago. The two had directed a progressive repertory company called Playwrights Theatre Club, with which Shepherd quickly grew dissatisfied, wanting instead to create a theatre in the spirit of both *commedia dell'arte* and German cabaret. With a company developed and selected through theatre game workshops led by Spolin, Sills, and Shepherd opened the Compass Players in 1955. Four years later, Sills joined forces with Bernard Sahlins and Howard Alk to found the Second City, which met with immediate success.

In subsequent years, Second City toured, opened new companies in Toronto (which launched the popular "SCTV" series) and other cities, and was copied everywhere (most notably on NBC's "Saturday Night Live"). The basic format has remained the same: half a dozen actors on a mostly bare stage perform a series of skits satirizing the city's politics and cultural life. A piano player (for many years Fred Kaz) accompanies an occasional comic ditty, and provides mood and interlude music. For the main show, the skits are predominantly set routines, but they are derived from improvisations worked up from audience suggestions at late-night sessions. The program changes two or three times each year.

From its beginnings, the question has always been this: Is Second City successful because of the inborn talent of its improvisers, or are the individuals successful because the system works? Spolin and Sills would explain that the system depends on inborn talent, which the system unlocks.   SF

See: J. Coleman, *The Compass,* New York, 1990; D. McCrohan, *The Second City,* New York, 1987; J. Sweet, *Something Wonderful Right Away,* New York, 1978.

Secret Service A four-act Civil War melodrama by **William Gillette,** first seen on 13 May 1895 in Philadelphia with Maurice Barrymore [see **Drew-Barrymore**] in the central role of the Union spy. After radical revision, the play opened in New York on 5 October 1896 with Gillette as Captain Thorne/Lewis Dumont, a part Gillette played 1,791 times. Gillette's best play, it focuses on the rival claims of patriotism and love. The high point is a suspenseful scene in a telegraph office, full of superficial realism, in which the spy is in constant danger of exposure. In 1976 the play was revived by the Phoenix Theatre Company in New York and was later televised.   DBW

See: R. Cullen and D. Wilmeth, eds., *Plays by William Hooker Gillette,* Cambridge (UK)/New York, 1983.

Segal, Vivienne (1897–92) Actress-singer. Originally trained in opera, Segal became, after her Broadway debut in 1915, a leading musical-theatre performer, appearing as the ingenue in such musical comedies as *Oh, Lady! Lady!* (1918) and as the coloratura heroine of romantic operettas, notably *The* **Desert Song** (1926). Ten years later, she turned to playing sultry older women, most memorably Vera in *Pal Joey* (1940, 1952) and Morgan Le Fay in the 1943 revival of *A Connecticut Yankee.* JD

Seldes, Gilbert (1893–1970) Critic of popular culture, Seldes worked as a journalist, editor, and drama critic before writing *The 7 Lively Arts* (1924), a defense of popular over highbrow culture in America. His *The Great Audience* (1950) and *The Public Arts* (1956) discussed the impact of popular culture upon society. Seldes headed television programming for CBS during 1937–45, and was Dean of the University of Pennsylvania's Annenberg School of Communications during 1959–63. TLM

Seldes, Marian (1928–) Actress, director, and teacher; daughter of critic **Gilbert Seldes.** A member of the theatre and dance faculties at the Juilliard School since 1969, Seldes, an award-winning actress trained in her teens at the **Neighborhood Playhouse,** appeared in the complete Broadway runs of *Equus* and **Deathtrap.** Originally a dancer, the tall, regal, articulate Seldes is considered an actor's actor. Most recently starring in **Howe**'s *Painting Churches* (1983–4) and Win Wells's *Gertrude Stein and a Companion* (1985–6), she is the author of an unusual theatre memoir, *The Bright Lights* (1978; revised 1984), a superb analysis of the chemistry of acting. In 1990 she married actor-playwright **Garson Kanin.** DBW

Self Satire on New York society, produced by **William Burton** at **Burton's Chambers Street Theatre;** ran for 18 performances, beginning 27 October 1856. Burton also played the part of John Unit, a **Yankee** character whose homespun good sense rights the wrongs caused by the extravagant Apex family and proves the honesty of his niece, Mary. Owing much to **Mowatt**'s *Fashion, Self* was written by Sidney Frances Cowell **Bateman,** an actress who married into a theatrical family. She assumed management of the Lyceum Theatre in London when her husband died, and continued as manager of Sadler's Wells until her death in 1881. FB

Sellars, Peter (1957–) Controversial director who had staged over 100 productions by the age of 27 and first came to prominence as a Harvard undergraduate when he directed *The Inspector General* for the **American Repertory Theatre** (1980–1). After one year as artistic director of the Boston Shakespeare Company (1983–4), Sellars became head of the American National Theatre (ANT) Company at the **Kennedy Center** in Washington, DC, a post which he left in 1986, becoming head of the Los Angeles Festival and serving as artistic advisor of the Boston Opera Theater, both in 1990. Among Sellars's ambitious and controversial productions have been Handel's *Orlando* (1982), **Brecht**'s *The Visions of Simone Marchard* (1983), a Gorky–**Gershwin** mélange at the **Guthrie** called *Hang On to Me* (1984), *The* **Count of Monte Cristo** (1985) for the ANT in Washington, and Sophocles' *Ajax* (1986), featuring a Rambo-type Vietnam general gone cuckoo. After being fired as the original director of Broadway's *My One and Only* in 1983, he received the same week an unsolicited grant for $136,000 from the MacArthur Foundation. Since the late 1980s he has concentrated on opera, on both sides of the Atlantic, including premiere productions of the contemporary operas *Nixon in China* and *The Death of Klinghoffer;* an iconoclastic 1989 Mozart trilogy (*Don Giovanni* set in a crime-ridden ghetto, *Figaro* in the Trump Tower, and *Cosi fan tutte* in Despina's Cape Cod diner); and a *Tannhäuser* in Chicago staged as the sexual scandal of a television evangelist. DBW

Selwyn, Archibald (1877?–1959) and **Edgar Selwyn** (1875–1944) Producers. After an early career as actor and playwright (1896–1911), Edgar, with his brother Arch, organized a play brokerage business, which merged with that of **Elisabeth Marbury** and John Ramsey to form the American Play Company. After successfully producing *Within the Law* (1912), starring **Jane Cowl,** they formed Selwyn and Company (1914) and produced such hits as *Fair and Warmer* (1915), **Why Marry?** (1917), *Smilin' Through* (1920), *The Circle* (1921), and *Romeo and Juliet* (1923). They dissolved the company in 1924 but continued to produce independently. Arch brought Noël Coward, **Gertrude Lawrence,** Diana Wynyard, **Beatrice Lillie,** and others to Broadway. Edgar was successful with *Gentlemen Prefer Blondes* (1926) and **Strike Up the Band** (1930). They built three theatres in New York (the Selwyn, the **Apollo,** and the Times Square) and two in Chicago (the Selwyn and the Harris). In 1916, together with Samuel Goldwyn, they organized Goldwyn Pictures Corporation (later MGM), where Edgar wrote and directed films. The Selwyns – not innovators but astute judges of public taste – gave the public what it wanted. TLM

Serban, Andrei (1943–) Romanian-born director. Immigrating in 1969, he staged *Arden of Faversham* at **La MaMa** ETC (1970) and, after a year with Peter Brook, *Medea* (Drama Desk Award), *The Trojan Women,* and *Electra* (1974), using music by **Elizabeth Swados** and obscure languages. He received an Obie for the trilogy, reviving it in Iran (1975), outdoors in France (1976), and again at La MaMa (1987). He soon became one of the prominent figures in contemporary American theatre, with productions of *The Good Woman of Setzuan* (La MaMa, 1975); a controversial comic interpretation of **Chekhov**'s *The Cherry Orchard* in an all-white setting (**New York Shakespeare Festival,** 1976); *The Ghost Sonata* (**Yale Repertory Theatre,** where he worked during 1977–8); *Agamemnon* (**Lincoln Center,** 1977); *Happy Days* and *The Umbrellas of Cherbourg* (NYSF, 1979); *The Seagull* (NYSF, 1980); *The Marriage of Figaro* (**Guthrie Theatre,** 1982); and *Uncle Vanya* (La MaMa, 1983, with **Joseph Chaikin**). He has worked frequently at the **American Repertory Theatre:** Gozzi's *The King Stag* and *The Love for Three Oranges* (1984); Philip Glass and Robert Moran's *The Juniper Tree* (1985); **Ribman**'s *Sweet Table at the Richelieu* and Bulgakov's *The Master and Margarita* (1986); and *The Serpent Woman* (1989). He has also staged operas for the Juilliard American Opera Center and the New York City Opera. His productions are noted for "their minimalism and simplicity of detail" and transform "the spoken word into . . . emotive music," treating "speech as sound rather than as language." While continuing to direct in the West, in 1990 he was appointed head of Romania's National Theatre; in 1992 he was also appointed director of the **Oscar Hammerstein II** Center for Theatre Studies at Columbia University. BM REK

Servant in the House, The **Charles Rann Kennedy**'s five-act play opened 23 March 1908 with **Walter Hampden** and Tyrone **Power** and ran 80 performances. A messianic, mystic bishop mysteriously returns incognito from his episcopate in Benares to help his two brothers, a vicar and a "drain man" (laborer) to face the truth about themselves and become reconciled. The play seems to be an unsuccessful attempt to follow the example **Bernard Shaw** set in *Candida* and *Major Barbara*. JDM

Set design see scenic design

Seven Keys to Baldpate A 1913 melodramatic farce in two acts and an epilogue, adapted from Earl Derr Biggers's novel of the same name, reputedly **George M. Cohan**'s best play. Billy Magee, a writer of popular mysteries, comes to deserted Baldpate Inn, where he tries, on a bet, to write a novel in just 24 hours. Strangers seeking access to cash in the inn's safe and using six duplicates of Billy's key are actors, parties to a stunt pulled by Billy's betting friend. The epilogue reveals that the play has been an enactment of Billy's novel. Cohan produced and staged this play-within-a-play-within-a-novel, which thrilled Broadway audiences during a year-long run on Broadway. WD

Sexual Perversity in Chicago The first critical and popular success by **David Mamet** received Chicago's **Joseph Jefferson** Award for best new play following its premiere by the **Organic Theater Company** in 1974, and an Obie following productions at St. Clements and Cherry Lane in New York in 1975. The comedy consists of 30 short scenes written in the style of **Second City,** where Mamet once bused tables. The initially hopeful romance of Danny Shapiro and Deborah Soloman is fatally infected by the sexually hostile language of their best friends, misogynist Bernie Litko and cynic Joan Webber. As in subsequent Mamet works, abusive speech generates, rather than reflects, abusive thought. The film version, *About Last Night,* was released in 1985. SF

Seymour, William (1855–1933) Actor, director, stage manager. A child actor in New Orleans until 1865, when he went to New York, Seymour served as a callboy at **Booth's Theatre** and performed with **Edwin Booth, Joseph Jefferson III, Charlotte Cushman,** and **Edwin Forrest.** Among Seymour's many management positions were the **Union Square Theatre,** the **Madison Square Theatre,** the Metropolitan Opera House, and **Charles Frohman's Empire Theatre** in New York, and a decade (1879–88) at the **Boston Museum.** In 1882 he married May Davenport, daughter of **E. L. Davenport** and younger sister of **Fanny Davenport.** His theatrical memorabilia and personal library form the nucleus of the extensive Princeton University Library theatre collection (integrated, sans curator, into other Princeton holdings in 1992). FHL DJW

See: R. Miller, "William Seymour, American Director," PhD diss., Wayne State U, 1973.

Shakespearean festivals In the U.S., the modern idea of a "festival" of Shakespearean plays seems to have been initiated by Angus L. Bowmer, who founded the **Oregon Shakespeare Festival** in 1935, still the oldest surviving American Shakespearean festival. The San Diego National Shakespeare Festival can also trace its origins back to 1935, although it did not offer a summer festival of plays until 1949. In the 1950s and '60s several other important festivals were founded, including the **American Shakespeare Theatre** Festival (Stratford, CT) in 1955, the **New York Shakespeare Festival** (as the Shakespeare Theatre Workshop) in 1954, and the Great Lakes Shakespeare Festival in 1961. Although initially confined to summer seasons, most of the major festival theatres have gradually extended their seasons and expanded their operations. The Oregon Shakespeare Festival, for example, went from a two-month summer season to a virtual year-round operation. In 1970 the modern, indoor Angus Bowmer Theatre was built adjacent to the outdoor Elizabethan Theatre modeled after John Cranford Adams's Globe reconstruction. The present Elizabethan Theatre opened in 1959, replacing two earlier outdoor theatres. Typically, the Oregon festival also operates a small "studio" theatre named the Black Swan. In the late 1960s and '70s, the San Diego and New York festivals also expanded into additional theatres and longer seasons. In 1984, the Alabama Shakespeare Festival moved into a new two-theatre, multimillion-dollar complex in Montgomery. With such expansion, these major festival theatres have also stretched their repertoires well beyond Shakespeare's plays. A typical season will now include not only two or three Shakespearean plays, but also revivals of international classics and productions of contemporary comedies, dramas, and musicals. As an indication of its less restricted repertoire, the Great Lakes festival has recently dropped "Shakespeare" from its name.

Although Shakespeare's plays present producers with formidable artistic and financial challenges, a Shakespearean festival remains an attractive concept, particularly for theatres operating mainly in the summer. Almost every American region has at least one summer Shakespearean festival; in fact, in 1991 there were over 80 Shakespeare festival theatres operating in the U.S. Among the principal ones, in addition to those noted above, are California Shakespeare Festival in Orinda, Shakespeare at Santa Cruz, The Utah Shakespeare Festival, The New Jersey Shakespeare Festival, Shakespeare & Company at Lenox (MA), the Shakespeare Festival of Dallas, the Three Rivers Shakespeare Festival in Pittsburgh, The Colorado Shakespeare Festival, and The North Carolina Shakespeare Festival. The quality of presentation can vary widely from festival to festival and season to season, but the various festivals do offer thousands of theatregoers the

Katharine Hepburn as Portia, Morris Carnovsky as Shylock, Richard Waring as Antonio, Donald Harron as Bassanio, Lois Nettleton as Nerrissa, and John Colicos as Gratiano in the American Shakespeare Festival *Merchant of Venice*. Directed by Jack Landau. Courtesy: Laurence Senelick.

opportunity to experience **Shakespeare on the American stage.** Moreover, they also provide Shakespearean performance and production opportunities for numerous aspiring and accomplished American actors, directors, and designers. Many festival productions are usually reviewed on an annual basis in issues of *Shakespeare Quarterly* or *Shakespeare Bulletin.* Glen Loney and Patricia MacKay's *The Shakespeare Complex* (New York, 1975) provides an excellent if somewhat out-of-date overview of both year-round and summer festivals. An international guide to Shakespeare festivals (and companies) is in progress (edited by R. Engle, F. Londré, and D. J. Watermeier) and promises a more comprehensive survey. In 1991, the Shakespeare Theatre Association of America was founded to facilitate communication among the various Shakespearean producing organizations. DJW

Shakespeare on the American stage Professionally staged Shakespeare in America can be traced back to at least 1750, when the **Walter Murray and Thomas Kean** company presented *Richard III* in New York and then toured this and other plays to towns in Maryland and Virginia. Since Murray and Kean seem to have been little more than amateurs, usually the first *professional* production of Shakespeare in America is taken to be *The Merchant of Venice* staged by **Lewis Hallam**'s Company of Comedians from London at a theatre in Williamsburg, VA, on 15 September 1752. Until the Continental Congress, preparing for Revolution, prohibited all theatrical activity in 1774, the Hallam company and its successor, the **American Company,** were the principal presenters of Shakespeare in the colonies.

Despite antitheatrical laws and attitudes, eco-nomic depression, and outbreaks of yellow fever, theatre in America gradually expanded in the decades after the Peace of 1782. With this expansion, staged Shakespeare increased in quantity and quality, mainly through the presence of British actors recruited by enterprising American managers. Among the more important early actors were **Anne Brunton Merry** and **Thomas Abthorpe Cooper,** both of whom were recruited by Philadelphia manager **Thomas Wignell** in 1796. Merry was America's leading actress for over a decade, excelling especially as Juliet, and Cooper eventually became America's foremost tragedian, with a repertoire that included most of Shakespeare's major roles. As comanager of the **Park Theatre,** Cooper in 1810 helped recruit London star **George Frederick Cooke** for an American tour. Cooke excited admiration with his fiery interpretations of Richard III, Shylock, Lear, and Macbeth, and, despite his reputation for drunkenness, remained largely on his best behavior before he died anticipating his return to England. He was but the first of many English Shakespeareans who crossed the Atlantic to enhance their fame and fortune as "visiting stars" [see **international stars**]. The great Edmund Kean, for example, came in 1820 and 1825; William Charles Macready appeared in 1826, 1843, and 1848. Many, like **James William Wallack** and **Junius Brutus Booth** came and stayed, founding dynasties of actors and managers who would significantly influence the development of American Shakespeare throughout the 19th century.

By the 1820s there began to emerge native-born actors whose talents and skills rivaled their British counterparts. **James Henry Hackett,** although renowned mainly for his creation of distinctive "Yankee" characters, was for many American

Tommaso Salvini as Othello. Courtesy: Becker Theatre Library, Brown University.

theatregoers the definitive Falstaff for over 40 years. **Charlotte Cushman,** generally regarded as the greatest American actress of the 19th century, won plaudits on both sides of the Atlantic for her forceful, domineering Lady Macbeth and, in later years, her majestic Queen Katherine. **Edwin Forrest** was acclaimed for his physically compelling portraits of Macbeth, Othello, Coriolanus, and Lear. A belligerent chauvinist opposed especially to visiting British stars, Forrest's bitter quarrel with Macready led to the bloody **Astor Place** Riot of 1849.

Segregated from white mainstream theatre, **African American**s developed their own theatrical tradition, including productions of Shakespeare. From **William Henry Brown**'s **African Theatre** (1820s) came America's first black Shakespearean actor, **James Hewlett; Ira Aldridge,** during a career spent mainly abroad, was celebrated for his naturalistic performances of Othello, Lear, and Aaron the Moor (*Titus Andronicus*).

As American theatre expanded during the 1830s – and despite Forrest's opposition – a new generation of visiting British actors introduced a more refined style of acting to American audiences. In 1832–3, for example, Charles and **Fanny Kemble** (his daughter) charmed the increasingly sophisticated middle-class audiences of New York, Boston, and Philadelphia with their interpretations of Hamlet and Ophelia, Romeo (or sometimes Mercutio) and Juliet, Beatrice and Benedick. Ellen Tree spent three seasons (1836–9) in America, gaining

recognition for her decorous, ladylike Rosalind, Viola, and Beatrice. In 1844 she married Charles Kean, and the following year the Keans began a two-season American tour marked especially by their "historically accurate" productions of *Richard III* and *King John*. In so doing, they set a standard for American Shakespearean production throughout the century. In the early 1850s, for example, actor-manager **William Burton** followed Kean's lead with his own full productions of *The Merry Wives of Windsor, A Midsummer Night's Dream,* and *The Winter's Tale.* A generation later, America's principal *régisseur,* **Augustin Daly,** won praise in both New York and London for his carefully prepared, visually lavish productions of Shakespeare's comedies.

The last third of the 19th century was in many respects a "golden age" for Shakespeare on the American stage. The ties to the British theatre remained close, but American performers and producers achieved an identity of their own. **Edwin Booth,** a key figure in this period, served his apprenticeship in the frontier theatres of **San Francisco** and Sacramento. Returning East in the late 1850s as a touring star, he gradually built a reputation, sustained for over 30 years, as the finest Shakespearean tragedian of his era, acclaimed not only in the U.S., but also in England and Germany – where he toured in the 1880s – for his masterful Iago, Lear, Shylock, and especially Hamlet. Numerous lesser lights illuminated Shakespeare's plays during this period, among them **E. L. Davenport, Emma Waller, John McCullough,** and **Laurence Barrett.** An expanding rail system brought these traveling stars to the developing towns and cities of America's heartland and far West. In the late 1880s, Booth and Barrett, complete with their own company and stock of "historically accurate" costumes and scenery, embarked on a series of highly successful, nationwide "joint-starring" tours. African-American tragedian **J. A. Arneaux** won acclaim for his portrayals of Iago, Macbeth, and Richard III, touring the black communities of New York, Philadelphia, and Providence (RI).

During the "Gilded Age" improved transatlantic travel and a vast theatre market, including many European immigrants, attracted numerous distinguished Shakespeareans from England, Germany, Italy, Poland, and France. Booth's British counterpart, Henry Irving, paid eight visits to the U.S. between 1883 and 1904, bringing his costar Ellen Terry and his entire Lyceum Theatre company and *mise-en-scènes* on each occasion. Tommaso Salvini visited five times between 1873 and 1889, riveting American audiences with his Macbeth, Lear, and especially his passionate, intensely realistic Othello – even though he played exclusively in Italian. In 1886 he played Othello and the Ghost to Booth's Iago and Hamlet. Such polyglot Shakespearean performances became almost commonplace at the time. Booth, for example, at various times in his career teamed with Bogumil Dawison, Adelaide Ristori, **Helena Modjeska,** and **Fanny Janauschek.** In 1900, the "divine" Sarah Bernhardt, on one of her numerous American tours, titillated audiences with her Frenchified and feminized portrait of Hamlet. Many of America's new emigrés could also attend performances of Shakespeare completely in their native languages. Antonio Maiori, for example, toured his Italianized adaptations of *Hamlet* and *Othello* to Italian-American communities. The well-organized German-language stock companies of New York, Milwaukee, Baltimore, and Chicago regularly mounted high-quality productions of Shakespeare, frequently featuring leading guest artists from Germany or Austria, such as Ludwig Barnay, Adolph Sonnenthal, and Ernst Possart.

At the turn of the century, the American approach to acting and staging Shakespeare established by Booth and Barrett, Daly, and contemporaries, began to wane. It was maintained to some extent by **Richard Mansfield, Robert Mantell,** and especially by the team of **Julia Marlowe** and **E. H. Sothern.** By the second decade of the 20th century, however, this old way – and indeed even Shakespeare – was being replaced by a growing taste for modern drama and theatrical entertainment, for movies, and for modern methods of stage production and acting. Certainly one tendency of the modern way with Shakespeare was demonstrated by English director Harley Granville-Barker, who brought his original, audacious production of *A Midsummer Night's Dream* to New York in 1916. Influenced by Barker and the New Stagecraft movement, director **Arthur Hopkins** teamed with designer **Robert Edmond Jones** and John Barrymore [see **Drew–Barrymore**] for striking modernist productions of *Richard III* (1920) and *Hamlet* (1922). Barrymore's Hamlet was widely regarded as the finest since Booth's, but he left the stage for a more lucrative but less significant career in film. It was a route followed by many potentially great American Shakespearean actors in succeeding decades.

In the 1930s and '40s Shakespeare's flame flickered only faintly in the American theatre, although there were several singular productions and performances. In 1936 **Orson Welles** mounted a controversial "voodoo" version of *Macbeth* with an all-black cast, and a year later presented a provocative modern-dress version of *Julius Caesar* that ominously suggested parallels to Fascist Italy. **Katharine Cornell** and her husband, director **Guthrie McClintock,** successfully toured more traditional productions of *Romeo and Juliet* (1933–4) and *Antony and Cleopatra* (1947). In 1937 British-born director **Margaret Webster** moved to the U.S. to stage with her former colleague, actor **Maurice Evans,** a series of very successful Shakespearean revivals, including *Richard II* (1937), *Hamlet* (1938), *1 Henry IV* (1939), *Twelfth Night* (1940), and *Macbeth* (1941) with **Judith Anderson** as Lady Macbeth. In 1942 Webster staged an outstanding *Othello* on Broadway with actor-singer **Paul Robeson** in the title role, **Uta Hagen** as Desdemona, and **José Ferrer** as Iago. Robeson's example was followed by several distinguished African-American Othellos, including **Earle Hyman** and **James Earl Jones.** (It also contributed significantly to the integration generally of black actors into mainstream American Shakespearean productions.) After WW II Webster organized the Margaret Webster Shakespeare Company, and for two years toured all over the U.S. and Canada, often to audiences who had little or no exposure to "live" Shakespeare. Indeed, with a decline of interest in classical theatre generally in the U.S., there were relatively few opportunities even for theatregoers in major cities to see productions of Shakespeare.

In the 1950s, however, this situation changed with the emergence of American **Shakespearean festivals.** In 1955, for instance, the **American Shakespeare Festival** opened in Stratford, CT; two years later, the **New York Shakespeare Festival** inaugurated its summer series of free Shakespearean productions in Central Park's outdoor Delacorte Theater. (Though founded in 1935, neither the **Oregon Shakespeare Festival** nor the one in San Diego became fully professional until the 1950s.) The success of these pioneering festivals inspired a Shakespeare renaissance in the American theatre. In the 1970s and '80s numerous festivals were founded all across the U.S. In addition, many of America's regional theatres regularly included a production of Shakespeare in their annual seasons. With increasing frequency, American Shakespearean perspectives also were enriched by visiting productions from various foreign lands, including England, Japan, Sweden, Italy, Romania, Brazil, and Venezuela. By the early 1990s, American theatregoers very likely had greater access to more productions of Shakespeare than any other theatre audience in the world.   DJW

See: E. C. Dunn, *Shakespeare in America,* New York, 1939; E. G. Hill, *Shakespeare in Sable,* Amherst, MA, 1984; L. W. Levine, *Highbrow Lowbrow,* Cambridge, MA, 1988; C. H. Shattuck, *Shakespeare on the American Stage* (2 vols.), Washington, DC, 1976 and 1987.

Shakespeare Theatre, The When the Folger Shakespeare Library building (301 East Capitol Street, SE, Washington, DC) was completed in 1932, it included a small auditorium (243 seats) designed to suggest, on a reduced scale, a model Elizabethan theatre. Originally intended for lectures and musical and dramatic recitals, it was converted to theatrical use in 1970 with the founding of the Folger Theatre Group (FTG). In the 1970s the FTG gained national recognition for its fresh, youthful interpretations of Shakespeare and presentations of new, often provocative American and foreign plays. Financial difficulties almost closed the FTG in 1985. With a successful campaign to save the theatre, a new name, and the artistic directorship of **Michael Kahn,** the Shakespeare Theatre at the Folger rebounded in the late 1980s to become a small but distinguished theatre concentrating on the classics. In early 1992 it dropped "at the Folger" from its name and moved to Washington's 7th Street Arts District (Lansbrugh Bldg.). DJW

Shange, Ntozake (née Paulette Williams) (1948–) African-American playwright. Born in Trenton, NJ, Barnard College–graduate Shange's first play, ***For Colored Girls Who Have Considered Suicide When the Rainbow is Enuf*** (1976), brought immediate acclaim to an exciting and innovative playwright. The play called for seven women in individual recitations to recount life experiences.

More conventional was *A Photograph: A Study in Cruelty* (1977), followed by *Spell #7* (1978), an extended choreopoem of character revelations using poetry, song, dance, and masks; *Boogie Woogie Landscapes* (1980); a revisionist adaptation of Brecht's *Mother Courage* (1980); and, with **Emily Mann** and Baikida Carroll, a rhythm-and-blues musical, *Betsey Brown* (1991), based on her 1985 novel. Scheduled for **Crossroads Theatre Company** in 1992 is *The Love Space Demands*. Shange's free-form theatre pieces give her a distinctive voice on the contemporary stage.   EGH

Shank, Adele Edling (1940–) Minnesota-born playwright and academic, educated at the University of California, Davis (BA, 1963; MA, 1966). She is best known for her California Series (1979–85), an interlocking, six-play cycle of hyper-real plays that explores an unraveling American dream and draws on photo-real painting for its style and methodology.   CLJ

Shanley, John Patrick (1950–) Playwright, director, and screenwriter. A native New Yorker, educated at New York University, Shanley is best known for his Oscar-winning screenplay *Moonstruck* (MGM, 1987). Author of some 10 plays, including *Danny and the Deep Blue Sea* (1984), *Savage in Limbo* (1985), *Italian-American Reconciliation* (1988), and *Beggars in the House of Plenty* (1991), Shanley writes powerful domestic comedy about romantic misadventures and familial misdeeds in a style comparable to **John Guare** and **Christopher Durang.**   TLM

Shannon, Effie (1867–1954) Actress who, billed as La Petite Shannon, played Eva in *Uncle Tom's Cabin* in Boston at age 7 and grew up to stardom on Broadway. She joined **David Belasco**'s Lyceum Stock Company in 1889, and soon married leading man Herbert Kelcey. Outstanding among her hundreds of roles were the leads in *The Moth and the Flame* (1891), *Years of Discretion* (1912), *She Stoops to Conquer* and plays by **Bernard Shaw.** Her popularity continued when she moved into character roles, culminating in a two-year stint as Martha Brewster in *Arsenic and Old Lace* (1942).   FHL

Shapiro, Mel (1939?–) Director, playwright, and educator who took his MFA at Carnegie Institute of Technology in 1961. He was Resident Director of **Arena Stage** (1963–5), Producing Director of the **Guthrie Theatre** (1968–70), and Resident Director of **New York Shakespeare Festival** (1971–7). During 1971 he had two plays by **John Guare** running simultaneously: the **Off-Broadway** premiere of *The House of Blue Leaves* and an irreverent musical adaptation of Shakespeare's *Two Gentlemen of Verona* (which he cowrote) for the NYSF. The latter transferred to Broadway and London and won Shapiro Tony, Obie, and Drama Desk awards for direction. Shapiro's teaching posts have included New York University and Carnegie-Mellon University, where he headed the Drama Department (1980–7).   CLJ

Sharaff, Irene (1910–) Theatre and film costume designer who began as an assistant to **Aline Bernstein** and by the early 1930s was designing major Broadway plays and (primarily) musicals such as *As Thousands Cheer* and *On Your Toes*. Through the 1960s she designed many significant musicals, including *The King and I* and *West Side Story*. Her Hollywood career began in 1944 with *Meet Me in St. Louis* and later included *An American in Paris, Cleopatra,* and *Who's Afraid of Virginia Woolf?* Although this last film demonstrated her ability to create pedestrian costumes, she is best known for stylish design and her use of color. She also had the unusual ability to translate stage productions into film.   AA

See: I. Sharaff, *Broadway & Hollywood: Costumes Designed by Irene Sharaff,* New York, 1976.

Shaw and the American theatre Success in New York with the lightly cynical *Arms and the Man* (Herald Square Theatre, 1894) and again with the satirical melodrama *The Devil's Disciple* (5th Avenue Theatre, 1897) secured for Bernard Shaw a reputation abroad and the financial independence that made possible his relinquishing drama criticism to focus on playwriting. The genie who extracted Shaw's audacious stage genius from the bottle of rejection in England was actor-manager **Richard Mansfield.** The Shaw boom continued when a young actor, **Arnold Daly,** secured *Candida,* which had already received two nonprofessional productions (Chicago, 1899; Philadelphia, 1903). Daly managed a New York opening (Prince's Theatre, 8 December 1903) and added *The Man of Destiny* (Vaudeville, 11 February 1904), following that with *You Never Can Tell* and *John Bull's Other Island,* both at the Garrick (1905). He boasted thereafter that he had made Shaw's fortune, and indeed most of his plays were seen in New York soon after their openings across the Atlantic. *Major Barbara,* the major exception, had to wait 10 years (Playhouse, 1915), until a war made its themes timely.

While Shaw's American theatrical reputation burgeoned, his popular image remained vague until the notorious reception of *Mrs. Warren's Profession* in New Haven and then in New York (Garrick, 30 October 1905), when, abetted by Anthony Comstock's puritanical Society for the Suppression of Vice, the press attacked the play as obscene. The cast went briefly to jail, but thereafter the play drew large audiences, and Shaw became a household word.

Appropriately, given Shaw's launching as a playwright in America, what may be his greatest dramas received their world premieres in the New World: *Heartbreak House* (Garrick, 1920) and *Saint Joan* (Garrick, 1923), both produced by the fledgling **Theatre Guild,** which would present the American premieres of seven Shaw plays, including the first performance anywhere of *Back to Methuselah* (Garrick, 27 February 1922) and *The Simpleton of the Unexpected Isles* (Guild, 18 February 1935). *Back to Methuselah,* impracticable when performed over three nights, was expected to lose at least $30,000; when losses proved to be only $20,000,

Poster postcard for the NYC company of Shaw's *Fanny's First Play* (c. 1911). Courtesy: Michael Gnat.

Shaw quipped that the Guild had saved $10,000 because of the clout of his name.

Shaw's impact had long been felt by American playwrights. **Clyde Fitch,** in plays like *The Girl with the Green Eyes* (1902) and *The City* (1909), already had suggested Shaw, and like **Langdon Mitchell,** whose *New York Idea* (1906) resonated with what might be perceived as Shavian satire, Fitch had experienced Shaw plays in their home settings in London. Of the same generation, **Edward Sheldon,** who remained in New York and could not have seen *Major Barbara* before he wrote *Salvation Nell* (1908), nevertheless may have been inspired by reading Shaw's Salvation Army play. Of Sheldon's time, the most obviously Shavian playwright was **Rachel Crothers,** whose serio-comic *He and She* (1911) was seen as influenced by Shaw and "the drama of discussion." Many of her works, whether social satires or ironic feminist dramas, continued to evidence Shavian traits, even as late as her last major play, *Susan and God* (1937).

Eugene O'Neill claimed Shaw as one of his formative influences, in particular Shaw's *The Quintessence of Ibsenism* (1891), which O'Neill read in prep school. Shaw is also in the bookcase in the Tyrone's summer home in *Long Day's Journey into Night.* The elongated, multipart concept of *Strange Interlude* may take its inspiration from Shaw's *Back to Methusaleh;* and the broad historical satire of *Marco Millions* may be inspired by Shaw's extravagances in *Caesar and Cleopatra* (1899), produced in New York in 1906 – the year in which *Ah, Wilderness!* is set – when O'Neill was nearby at school.

The most Shavian of later American dramatists was **Robert E. Sherwood,** whose earliest produced play, *The Road to Rome* (1927) – combining elements of *The Man of Destiny* with *Caesar and Cleopatra* – had been rejected by impresario **Gilbert Miller** with the sneer, "I don't like even first-rate Shaw!" The play – gibed at as "Shaw in short pants" – established Sherwood in the theatre. His *The Petrified Forest* (1935) has been called an "Arizona *Heartbreak House*" and *Idiot's Delight* (1936) a "cosmopolitan *Heartbreak House,*" whereas his last play, *Small War on Murray Hill* (1957), echoes *The Devil's Disciple.*

In the same generation, the social satires of **Philip Barry** and **S. N. Behrman** suggest Shaw, Behrman even announcing his admiration in the preface to his *Rain from Heaven* (1934). Behrman not only wrote about Shaw and acknowledged taking Shaw's playwriting advice, but, beginning with *The Second Man* (1927), developed a Shavian drama of ideas adapted to American conventions of high comedy.

With Shaw's reputation in America still strong in the 1930s, the hit **Federal Theatre** all-black production of *Androcles and the Lion* (1938) re-opened at the 1939 World's Fair in New York. Also in that year, Shaw received Hollywood's Academy Award for best screenplay (of 1938) for his adaptation of his own *Pygmalion.* The 1939–45 war, however, would be a watershed, as by its end he was 90, and a new generation of playwrights had begun to displace him.

Although the major American play of the WW II years – **Thornton Wilder**'s *The Skin of Our Teeth* (1942) – has been linked to James Joyce's *Finnegans Wake* as a burlesque history of humankind, a case can also be made for a Shavian dimension. In Wilder's philosophical farce audiences discovered – as in *Back to Methuselah,* a history of the world from the Garden of Eden to the indefinable future – a Lilith (Sabina in *Skin of Our Teeth*) and a Cain (Henry in Wilder's play) who weave through time, as well as other elements suggesting that the playwright knew his Shaw. The elder dramatist had been attempting to find meaning during one world war; the younger writer was seeking understanding during the next.

Postwar American dramatists largely turned elsewhere, although **Tennessee Williams,** at college in the 1930s, wrote a term paper on *Candida.* In the early play he wrote with Donald Windham, *You Touched Me!* (1942), he borrowed from *Heartbreak House.* That Williams kept reading Shaw is clear from his afterword to *Camino Real.*

An exception to the decline in Shavian influence was the musical theatre, where *My Fair Lady* (1956), a close adaptation of *Pygmalion,* inaugurated a new era in the musical play, in which song and dance and lyrics arose out of situation and character. In *My Fair Lady* many of the lyrics and much of the dialogue came not only directly from *Pygmalion* but also from Shaw's preface.

Among postwar indebtedness was **Gore Vidal**'s historical satire *Romulus* (1962), with its open thefts from Shaw ("Thank heaven," says one character. "No, don't thank heaven, dear, thank me," quips Romulus, in a steal from Undershaft in *Major Barbara*.) Although **Edward Albee**'s *Who's Afraid of Virginia Woolf?* (1963) has been equated with *Heartbreak House* as an unmasking game, with some lines uncannily parallel, little else in Albee suggests Shaw. Later playwrights have also gone elsewhere for inspiration, although plays in which wit coruscates and paradox abounds are still often labeled Shavian. Today, although the major festival devoted to Shaw is in Canada, an annual Shaw festival has been held at Milwaukee's Chamber Theatre since 1982.   SW

See: R. Mander & J. Mitchenson, *Theatrical Companion to Shaw,* New York, 1955; S. A. Sabah, "Bernard Shaw in America," PhD diss., Southern Illinois U, 1989; R. Weintraub, ed., *Shaw Abroad,* University Park, PA, 1985.

Shaw, Irwin (1913–84) Writer best known for his popular fiction and short stories, though his career began in the 1930s as a left-wing playwright with his antiwar one-act *Bury the Dead* (1936), followed by the more popularly successful melodramatic comedy, *The Gentle People* (1939).   DBW

See: M. Shnayerson, *Irwin Shaw: A Biography,* New York, 1989.

Shaw, Mary (1854–1929) Actress and feminist who debuted with the **Boston Museum** Stock Company in 1878. She championed **Ibsen**'s plays, especially *Ghosts,* which she toured around the country for five months in 1903 and often revived. She played *Hedda Gabler* in Chicago (1904) and starred in the sensational premiere of *Mrs. Warren's Profession* (1905) as well as other controversial plays: *Votes for Women* (1909), *Divorce* (1909), and *Polygamy* (1914). She was a charter member of the Professional Women's League, founder of the Gamut Club, and represented American theatre at the International Congress of Women held in London in 1899.   RAS

See: J. Irving, *Mary Shaw: Actress, Suffragist, Activist,* New York, 1982.

Shawn, Wallace (1943–) Actor (study with **Herbert Berghof** has led to over 30 stage and film roles) and playwright: *The Mandrake; Marie and Bruce; A Thought in Three Parts; My Dinner with Andre* (coscripted film version); *Our Late Night* (1975, Obie Award); *Aunt Dan and Lemon; The Hotel Play; Ode to Napoleon Bonaparte; The Fever* (1991, Obie). TV and stage appearances include "Taxi"; *Aunt Dan and Lemon; The Mandrake; Carmilla; The Master and Margarita; The Hotel Play; Chinchilla; Gallery;* and *A Doll's House.* In their treatment of sex, violence, and cruelty, his plays shock, confuse, and sometimes bore audiences.   GSA

Shean, Al see **Gallagher and Shean**

Sheldon, Edward (Brewster) (1886–1946) Playwright. A graduate of **George Pierce Baker**'s Workshop 47 at Harvard College, Sheldon was an early proponent of social realism in America with *Salvation Nell* (1908), in which a girl avoids a repulsive "profession" by joining the Salvation Army; *The Nigger* (1909), concerned with the struggle of a southern governor who discovers that his grandmother was an octoroon slave; and *The Boss* (1911), a drama of labor-management conflicts. However, his romantic conclusions in these plays (with the exception of *The Nigger*) suggest his true interests, as revealed in *The High Road* (1912), a search for beauty, and *Romance* (1913), as an American clergyman explains his love for an Italian diva. When poor health apparently incapacitated Sheldon, he collaborated with such dramatists as **Sidney Howard** (*Bewitched,* 1924) and **Charles MacArthur** (*Lulu Belle,* 1926). Although none of his later works was outstanding, Sheldon remained a source of inspiration and help on dramaturgical problems for a number of prominent dramatists.   WJM

See: E. W. Barnes, *The Man Who Lived Twice,* New York, 1956.

She Loves Me Musical written by the same creative team that produced *Fiorello!* (1959) and *Fiddler on the Roof* (1963): **Joe Masteroff** (book), **Jerry Bock** (music), and **Sheldon Harnick** (lyrics). It was an adaptation of the Miklos Laszlo play *Parfumerie.* Set in a middle European city during the mid-1930s, the play is a love story of employees at a cosmetic shop. They fight while working but, after hours, carry on a love affair by writing letters to "Dear Friend," completely oblivious to the other's identity until the play's conclusion. *She Loves Me* was produced and directed by **Harold Prince,** and included Jack Cassidy and **Barbara Cook** in the cast when it opened 23 April 1963 at the **Eugene O'Neill Theatre** for a run of 360 performances.   KN

Shenandoah One of **Bronson Howard**'s most popular dramas; a romantic and sweeping epic of the Civil War. Opening in Boston, November 1888, the play was declared an immediate failure. After some revision, it reopened the next year at New York's **Star Theatre** where it ran for 250 performances. Its complex plot, multiple characters, grand spectacle, and patriotic sentiment made it a durable hit and may have presaged the film epic. The theme and action are typical of the age and reflect a long-standing tradition in American playwriting; but it was Howard's attempts to introduce social drama and a modicum of realism to the commercial stage that makes this play an important milestone.   PAD

Shepard, Sam (né Samuel Shepard Rogers) (1943–) Playwright who, though lacking a major commercial Broadway success, is arguably the most critically acclaimed, if the most obscure and undisciplined U.S. dramatist of the past 20 years. *New York Magazine* called him "the most inventive in language and revolutionary in craft," as well as the "writer whose work most accurately maps the interior and exterior landscapes of his society." Uniquely American and contemporary in his subject matter, ranging from myths of the American West, American stereotypes, the death or betrayal of the American dream, the travail of the family, to the search for roots, Shepard defies easy classification. Influenced by rock and roll, the pop and countercultures beginning in the 1950s, the graphic arts and dance, the West of Hollywood, hallucinatory experiences, and a dozen other eclectic forces, his path as a writer is hard to plot. Richard Gilman suggests that it is best to accept the volatility and interdependence of Shepard's plays – "they constitute a series of facets of a single continuing act of imagination." Of his more than 40 plays, 11 of which have received Obie Awards (beginning with the Theatre Genesis [NYC] productions of *Cowboy* and *The Rock Garden* in 1964), the following are major works: *La Turista* (1966); *The Tooth of Crime* (1972), a rock-drama written during a four-year period in London; *Curse of the Starving Class,* written in 1976 and produced first in 1978 at the **New York Shakespeare Festival** with a successful New York revival in 1985; *Buried Child* (1978), for which he won the 1979 Pulitzer Prize; *True West* (1980) and *Fool for Love* (1979), both originally staged at the **Magic Theatre** in San Francisco, where he was playwright-in-residence for several years; and *A Lie of the Mind* (1985). In 1991, *The States of Shock,* Shepard's first drama in six years and his ambiguous look at post-Vietnam America, played a brief season at the **American Place Theater.** Shepard has also coauthored three pieces with **Joseph Chaikin** – one, *The War in Heaven* (1985), was also revived in 1991 at the American Place.

A film actor and screenwriter as well, Shepard has appeared in several successful films, including his own *Fool for Love.* For his screenplay *Paris, Texas* he won the Golden Palm Award at the 1985 Cannes Film Festival. DBW

See: L. Hart, *Sam Shepard's Metaphorical Stages,* Westport, CT, 1987; K. King, "Sam Shepard: A Casebook," New York, 1989; R. Mottram, *Inner Landscapes: The Theatre of Sam Shepard,* Columbia, MO, 1984; D. Shewey, *Sam Shepard,* New York, 1985.

Sherin, Edwin (1930–) Director-actor. After a modest acting career in the 1950s, Sherin established a reputation as a director while Associate Producing Director at Washington's **Arena Stage** (1964–8), peaking with his direction of Howard Sackler's *The Great White Hope* (1968), seen that year on Broadway. A handful of Broadway productions followed, including *6 Rms Riv Vu* (1973) and *Eccentricities of a Nightingale* (1976). In 1973 he directed a successful revival of *Streetcar Named Desire* with Claire Bloom in London. During 1980–5 he was director at the **Hartman Theatre,** Stamford, CT. He is married to actress **Jane Alexander,** whom he directed in *The Visit* (1992). DBW

Sherlock Holmes by **William Gillette.** Four-act play loosely based on three Conan Doyle stories. After a Buffalo (NY) tryout, it opened at NYC's **Garrick Theatre** on 6 November 1899 with Gillette as Holmes – his greatest histrionic creation – **Bruce McRae** as Dr. Watson, and George Wessels as Holmes's nemesis Professor Moriarty, and ran for an initial 236 performances. Through 1932 Gillette appeared in the role more than 1,300 times in numerous revivals. The play concerned Holmes's efforts to acquire a packet of incriminating letters for a royal client, and, in the process, capture criminal mastermind Moriarty. It succeeded, despite negative criticism, due to Gillette's superb performance, the play's suspenseful action, and Gillette's innovative technical elements. Over the years, Gillette revised it often: As he grew older,

William Gillette as Holmes and Bruce McRae as Dr. Watson in Gillette's *Sherlock Holmes,* 1902. Photo: Byron. Courtesy: The Byron Collection, Museum of the City of New York.

for instance, the romantic element was altered for the sake of verisimilitude. Successfully revived by the Royal Shakespeare Company, it played Broadway in 1974.   DBW

> See: R. Cullen and D. Wilmeth, eds., *Plays by William Hooker Gillette*, Cambridge(UK)/New York, 1983.

Sherwood, Robert E[mmet] (1896–1955) Playwright, screenwriter, essayist, historian, and propagandist; a man of strong emotions and good will who preached simplistic solutions to complicated problems. His career started with *The Road to Rome* (1927) and continued with *Waterloo Bridge* (1930) and *Reunion in Vienna* (1931), sentimental and frivolous comedies about emotional problems. With *The Petrified Forest* (1935), a story of frustrated idealism, *Idiot's Delight* (1936), an antiwar play, and *Abe Lincoln in Illinois* (1938) Sherwood won three Pulitzer Prizes. During the 1930s he also wrote screenplays, served as president of the **Dramatists Guild,** and helped found the **Playwrights' Company** (1938).

With the advent of war in Europe, Sherwood dramatically changed his thinking about conflict and the purpose of drama. Having complained that his plays started with a message and ended only as good entertainment, he wrote *There Shall Be No Night* (1940), a militant condemnation of American isolationism, trumpeted across the land by actors **Lunt and Fontanne.** Having shown his ability to write brilliant propaganda, and his hatred of Hitler, he became a speechwriter for President Roosevelt, who appointed him director of the Overseas Branch of the Office of War Information. Sherwood's postwar plays – *The Rugged Path* (1945) and *Small War on Murray Hill* (1957) – were failures. Only in his history of *Roosevelt and Hopkins* (1948) did he again show his considerable writing skills.   WJM

> See: J. M. Brown, *Mirror to His Times: The Worlds of Robert E. Sherwood*, New York, 1965; W. J. Meserve, *Robert Sherwood: Reluctant Moralist*, Indianapolis, 1970; R. B. Schuman, *Robert Emmet Sherwood*, New York, 1964.

She Would Be a Soldier Best known of **M. M. Noah**'s seven plays, its comic/romantic portrayal of a young woman who disguises herself to join her fiancé at camp during the Battle of Chippewa remained a favorite on the American stage until the 1840s. The play, written specifically for the leading actress, Catherine Leesugg, was first performed at the **Park Theatre** in 1819. Using a historical event as background, as in all of Noah's works, the play, a blatant appeal to American nationalism, portrayed a magnanimous American army defeating the effete Europeans. The "noble savage" is portrayed by the Indian Chief who ultimately converts to the American side [see **Native Americans portrayed**].   PAD

Shore Acres A domestic comedy written by **James A. Herne,** with the collaboration of Katharine Corcoran Herne, which premiered at **McVicker's Theatre,** Chicago, 17 May 1892. It dramatizes the near destruction of the harmony of a coastal Maine family by its greedy, domineering father. Uncle Nat, played with great distinction by Herne, helps his niece run away with the man she loves and saves the family farm when his brother mortgages it in a speculative scheme. Its long run contributed to the demise of the **Boston Museum** stock company in 1893. It ran a full season (1893–4) in New York and on the road for five years, earning Herne over a million dollars and restoring his fortune, which had been decimated by his efforts to produce *Margaret Fleming.*   WD

Short, Hassard (1877–1956) Director. Initially associated with lavish **revue**s, Short became during the 1920s–40s the director to call upon for stylish opulence. He frequently served as codirector responsible for staging production numbers rather than book scenes. Revues he staged included such landmarks as the **Music Box** *Revues* (1921–3), *The Bandwagon* (1931) and *As Thousands Cheer* (1933); book shows included *Roberta* (1933) and *Lady in the Dark* (1941). A sometime designer as well as a director, he frequently worked for such showy producers as **Max Gordon** and **Michael Todd.**   JD

Short Eyes A two-act drama by **Miguel Piñero** first produced by the Theatre of the Riverside Church. **Joseph Papp** imported the play to the **Public Theater** (Anspacher), and, after a two-week run at the Zellerbach Theatre in Pennsylvania, to the **Vivian Beaumont Theatre** at Lincoln Center, where it opened as part of the **New York Shakespeare Festival** on 9 May 1974. Directed by Marvin Felix Camillo and acted mostly by former prisoners at Bedford Hills (NY) Correctional Facility called "The Family," the play was performed internationally, receiving the New York Drama Critics' Circle Award and two Obies. Through vivid character portrayals instead of stereotypes, *Short Eyes* provides a realistic view of prison life both comic and tragic in tone. The title is prison vernacular for men convicted of child-rape; through his play, Piñero reveals a crime that outrages even the most hardened criminals.   ER

Show Boat Based on **Edna Ferber**'s novel, with book and lyrics by **Oscar Hammerstein II**, additional lyrics by **P. G. Wodehouse,** and music by **Jerome Kern,** *Show Boat* opened 27 December 1927, sumptuously produced by **Florenz Ziegfeld** at his **Ziegfeld Theatre.** One of the landmarks of the musical stage, it had a complex plot that traced the lives of a family of showboat performers over four decades, focusing particularly on the love story of Magnolia Hawks, daughter of a **showboat** captain, and gambler Gaylord Ravenal. The sprawling plot inspired Kern and Hammerstein to write a brilliant score that employed leitmotifs and reprises (notably the haunting "Ol' Man River") to frame and contextualize the action. Although the musical sequences were not as fully integrated into the plot as in later musicals such as *Oklahoma!,* the combination of serious plot and ambitious score made *Show Boat* far superior to the typical musical fare of the 1920s. Kern and Hammerstein produced a successful Broadway revival in 1946, and it has received a number of other full-

Spalding and Rogers's Floating Circus Palace. Courtesy: Library of Congress.

Showboats From the early 19th century, flatboats, then steamers and paddlewheelers, plied the Mississippi and Ohio rivers, offering entertainment to the residents along the banks. Although **Noah Ludlow, Joseph Jefferson II,** and **Sol Smith** dabbled in such amusements, the first intentionally designed showboat was that of William Chapman, Sr., launched at Pittsburgh in 1831. The Chapman family in their *Floating Theatre,* a rude shed set on a barge and poled downriver, soon became a familiar sight, making annual tours of the major waterways with a repertory of Kotzebue, **Shakespeare,** and musical farces. Before Chapman's widow sold out in 1847, they had set the style for similar enterprises, although imitators tended to song-and-dance and lecture entertainments and sometimes lacked the respectable domestic veneer of the Chapmans. The crafts ranged from ramshackle scows to grandiose arks. **Circus** boats, led by Spalding and Rogers's *Floating Circus Palace* (1851), were capable of seating up to 3,400 spectators and offered **minstrel show**s and a museum of curiosities in addition to sawdust acts.

After the disastrous hiatus of the Civil War, a new period of prosperity came to the showboat. The leading entrepreneur was Augustus Byron French, a riparian **Barnum** who operated five boats from 1878 to 1901; he pioneered the use of marching bands on shore to advertise his lavish variety bills, and launched both the apt term and the luxurious vessel, the "floating palace." His double-decker *Sensation No. 2* seated 759, but the only full-length drama ever offered was *Uncle Tom's Cabin.* French's main rival was E. A. Price, whose press agent Ralph Emerson came up with sensational innovations in publicity, using calliopes, billboards, and postcards to herald the boat's arrival.

The reliance on variety was challenged by the Eisenbarth–Henderson *Temple of Amusement,* which

purveyed drama exclusively; these "moral amusements," which included *Faust,* were lit by electricity. As *The Cotton Blossom* under Emerson's management, it featured Broadway hits and spectacular melodramas until 1931. Drama was also the fare provided by Norman Thom, "the **John Drew** of the Rivers," the first actor since Chapman to own a boat; for *The Princess,* he shrewdly chose plays of regional interest. The Bryants specialized in lurid melodrama, offered in direct competition to the rival silent pictures.

During its history, more than 76 verifiable showboats (as they had come to be known) have existed. There were 26 active in 1910, 14 in 1928, and 5 in 1938. (The last recorded by Philip Graham was *The Goldenrod,* tied up in St. Louis in 1943 [recently refurbished and moved to St. Charles, MO], although the *Majestic,* built in 1923, operates May–September on the Cincinnati city landing.) The decline can be attributed to the closure of the frontier: Unable to compete with the urban entertainments that sprang up in the wake of civilization, the owners suffered greatly from the depression of 1929. Behind the fashion even in their heyday, the boats became a nostalgic artifact, and imitations were much in use by society promoters in the 1930s. It was **Jerome Kern** and **Oscar Hammerstein II**'s musical adaptation of *Show Boat* (1927), a novel by **Edna Ferber,** that simultaneously immortalized the phenomenon and encased it in an aura of quaintness. Once a unique product of westward expansion, showboats are now adjuncts of tourism and municipal festivals. LS

> See: B. Bryant, *Children of Ol' Man River,* New York, 1936; C. R. Gillespie, *The James Adams Floating Theatre,* Centreville, MD, 1991; P. Graham, *Showboats: The History of an American Institution,* Austin & London, 1951; D. McDaniel, ed., *Showboat Centennials Reference,* Worthington, OH 43085 (76 Glen Drive), 1991.

Show-off, The, by **George Kelly** is a three-act, realistic comedy set in the living room of a Philadelphia family. The Fishers are dismayed when young Amy is smitten with the vain and boastful Aubrey Piper, whom sister Clara rightly predicts will end up ensconced in their house. In Aubrey, Kelly creates an exasperating yet likable antihero, thrown into relief by the sometimes bittersweet lives of the people who surround him. Premiering 4 February 1924 at the **Playhouse Theatre,** NYC, the play ran for 571 performances, was revived in New York in 1932, in 1950 as the first use of arena staging on Broadway, and in 1967 by the **Association of Producing Artists**–Phoenix Repertory Company, with **Helen Hayes** as the irascible Mrs. Fisher. KF

Shubert brothers Theatre owners and producers. The family business was founded by three brothers – **Sam S.** (1877?–1905), **Lee** (1875?–1953), and **Jacob J.** (1879?–1963) Shubert – who began their careers in Syracuse, NY, in the late 19th century. The brothers moved to NYC in 1900 and began producing and acquiring theatres, including the Herald Square and the **Casino.** Among the stars who worked in Shubert shows during the

scale productions in both theatres and opera houses around the world, as well as three film versions. In 1988 John McGlinn supervised a restored score for EMI Records Limited. MK

> See: M. Krueger, *Show Boat: The Story of a Classic American Musical,* New York, 1977

early years were **Richard Mansfield,** Sarah Bernhardt, and **Lillian Russell.** Sam Shubert died in a train crash in 1905, but his brothers continued to operate the business on an increasingly lavish scale, often coming into conflict with the Theatrical **Syndicate,** a rival group of theatre owners and managers that dominated American theatrical activity in the early 20th century. By 1916, however, the Shuberts had broken the Syndicate monopoly and had themselves become the nation's most important and powerful theatre owners and managers. During the 1910s and '20s, the Shubert brothers built many of Broadway's theatres, including the **Winter Garden,** the **Sam S. Shubert,** and the **Imperial.** In addition, they came to own or operate more than 100 theatres across the country and to book more than 1,000 others. Among their major stars of the period were **Al Jolson** and **Eddie Cantor,** both of whom were great successes at the Winter Garden. The Shuberts were especially well known for their productions of operettas by **Sigmund Romberg,** among them *Maytime* (1917), *Blossom Time* (1921), and *The Student Prince* (1924). They were also known for their popular annual **revue**s – *The Passing Show,* which appeared regularly during 1912–24, and *Artists and Models,* produced in a number of editions from 1923 to 1943. Although the Shuberts' business was badly hurt by the Depression, they continued to produce throughout the 1930s and '40s, presenting a number of well-known musicals and revues, including the later editions of the *Ziegfeld Follies,* **Cole Porter**'s *You Never Know* (1938), and **Olsen and Johnson**'s *Hellzapoppin'* (1938), as well as such popular straight plays as *Ten Little Indians* (1944) and *Dark of the Moon* (1945). During the 1950s the U.S. government brought an antitrust suit against the Shuberts, who were forced to divest themselves of a number of their theatres in 1956. During the 1950s and early '60s the company was run by J. J. Shubert's son **John** (1909–62), and after his death by a great-nephew of the founders, **Lawrence Shubert Lawrence, Jr.** (1916–92).   BMcN

> *See:* B. McNamara, *The Shuberts of Broadway,* New York, 1990; J. Stagg, *The Brothers Shubert,* New York, 1968.

Shubert Organization Theatrical real estate and producing company founded in the late 19th century by the **Shubert** family. Since 1972 its chief operating officers have been two former Shubert lawyers, Gerald Schoenfeld and Bernard B. Jacobs. Jacobs serves as President of the Shubert Organization and Schoenfeld as Chairman of the Board. In addition, they are respectively President and Chairman of the Shubert Foundation, a related philanthropic institution that provides support to many nonprofit theatre and dance producing groups. The Shubert Organization currently owns and manages 16 of the operating Broadway theatres, including the **Ambassador, Ethel Barrymore, Belasco, Booth, Broadhurst, Broadway, Cort, John Golden, Imperial, Longacre, Lyceum, Majestic, Plymouth, Royale, Sam S. Shubert,** and the **Winter Garden.** In addition, the company has a half interest in the **Music Box Theatre.** Outside NYC, the Shubert Organization owns and operates the Shubert and Blackstone in **Chicago,** the Forrest in **Philadelphia,** and the Shubert in **Boston.** It leases and manages two other theatres, the Shubert in **Los Angeles** and the **National** in Washington, DC. Although the company was not active in theatrical production during the 1950s and '60s, in recent years it has once again become involved in Broadway producing. Some of its recent productions have included *Sly Fox* (1976), **Gin Game** (1977), *Ain't Misbehavin'* (1978), *Dancin'* (1978), *Amadeus* (1980), **Children of a Lesser God** (1980), *Dreamgirls* (1981), *Nicholas Nickleby* (1981), *Cats* (1982), **Glengarry Glen Ross** (1984), and **Sunday in the Park with George** (1984). The Shubert Organization has also produced a highly successful **Off-Broadway** show, **Little Shop of Horrors** (1982). The company has been influential in the revitalization of the Times Square theatrical district and has pioneered a number of innovative theatre business practices, among them the introduction of telephone and charge ticket sales and a computerized ticketing system.   BMcN

Shue, Larry (1946–85) Playwright-actor born in New Orleans and educated at Illinois Wesleyan (1968). After graduation he acted in dinner theatres, eventually becoming a member of the **Milwaukee Repertory.** There his writing flourished with premieres of *The Nerd* (1981) and *The* **Foreigner** (1982). Both became hits in the regional theatres, and in 1984 *The Nerd* had a successful run in London's West End and *The Foreigner* at the Astor Place Theatre in New York. Shue was writing a screenplay for *The Foreigner* – and had just appeared in *The Mystery of Edwin Drood* at the **New York Shakespeare Festival** – when he was killed in a plane crash in Virginia.   BBW

Shuffle Along A 1921 black musical comedy that swept New York when it opened at the 63rd Street Theatre and played for 504 performances. **Vaudeville** duo Flournoy Miller and Aubrey Lyles teamed with lyricist Noble Sissle and composer Eubie Blake (see **Sissle and Blake**) to produce what the *New York American* called "an infection of amusement." With a simple story line, catchy lyrics, an unforgettable score, and a talented and energetic cast, the show was irresistible. Two disreputable characters, Sam and Steve, played by Miller and Lyles, contest a mayoralty race in Jimtown on the understanding that the winner will name the other as his chief of police. With the election over, the former buddies quarrel over the spoils of office. Eventually they are run out of town by reform candidate Harry Walton, who wins the next election with his popular song: "I'm Just Wild About Harry." The show's success spawned a rash of new black musicals and established the genre on Broadway.   EGH

> *See:* R. Kimball and W. Bolcom, *Reminiscing with Sissle and Blake,* New York, 1973.

Shumlin, Herman (1898–1979) Director and producer who established himself as **Lillian Hellman**'s champion with productions of *The Children's Hour* (1934), *Days to Come* (1936), *The* **Little Foxes** (1939), **Watch on the Rhine** (1941), *The*

Searching Wind (1944), and a revival of *Regina* (1953). Other noteworthy productions include *The Last Mile* (1930), *The Merchant of Yonkers* (1938), *The Male Animal* (1940), *The Corn Is Green* (1940), *Inherit The Wind* (1955, on which he collaborated with **Margo Jones**), and Hochhuth's *The Deputy* (1964). A film director in the 1940s, he made the film version of *Watch on the Rhine* (1943). Producer of serious and worthy drama, called a "crusty perfectionist," his liberal political philosophy was reflected in the plays he chose to present.   MR

Shyre, Paul (1929–89) Playwright, actor, director, and educator who died of septicemia, infections linked to **AIDS.** He is best known for his adaptations (in which he also performed) – *Pictures in the Hallway* (1956) and *I Knock at the Door* (1957), based on O'Casey's autobiographies; and *U.S.A.,* based on John Dos Passos's work (NYC, 1959; his first production at the Westport Country Playhouse, CT, 1953) – and for those of his plays he also directed – *Drums Under the Windows* (1960), also drawn from O'Casey; *A Whitman Portrait* (1966); *Will Rogers' USA* (1972); *Blasts and Bravos: An Evening with H. L. Mencken* (1975), in which he also played Mencken; and *Paris Was Yesterday* (1980), from Janet Flanner. Shyre was the recipient of Tony, Obie, Drama Desk, and Emmy awards.   DBW

Siegfried [Fischbaker] (1939–) and **Roy [Horn]** (1944–) German-born illusionists who are the current masters of the spectacular stage **magic** show and considered by some the most successful magicians in history – certainly their million-dollar Las Vegas contract makes them the best paid. Together since 1960, they limit their work to Las Vegas and are known primarily for their "Beyond Belief" show at the Frontier Hotel (beginning 1981) and in the 1990s at the Mirage, featuring tigers, elephants, lasers, fire, fog, and slick high-tech illusions.   DBW

Sign in Sidney Brustein's Window, The Lorraine Hansberry's final work was first presented at New York's **Longacre Theatre** 15 October 1964, directed by Peter Kass and featuring Gabriel Dell, **Rita Moreno,** and Frank Schofield (with a Tony for supporting actress for Alice Ghostley). It ran 101 performances despite lukewarm reviews. This small mixed-cast play, set in Greenwich Village, explores the lives of a group of artists and rebels as they struggle with their disillusionments. It mixes styles as it challenges the apathy of American intellectuals.   KME

Silk Stockings Two-act musical comedy suggested by Melchior Lengyel's screenplay *Ninotchka,* with music and lyrics by **Cole Porter** and book by **George S. Kaufman,** Leueen MacGrath, and **Abe Burrows;** opened on Broadway (24 February 1955) at the **Imperial Theatre** for 478 performances. Critics hailed the performances of Don Ameche, Hildegarde Neff, and especially Gretchen Wyler, whose comic timing stole the show. Due to the notorious scare about communism at this time, audiences were interested in a musical about

U.S.–Soviet relations. Set in Paris and Moscow, the musical focuses on the budding romance between a Russian commissar and an American agent, with subplots about the film and entertainment industry. Songs include "All of You," "Stereophonic Sound," and "Silk Stockings."   EK

Sills, Paul (1930?–) Director. The son of Viola Spolin, author of *Improvisation for the Theater,* Sills has spent most of his life finding practical applications for his mother's theories. He cofounded The Compass Players (1955) and **Second City** (1959), helped found the **Body Politic Theatre** (1966), developed an audience participation experiment called Game Theater (1967), and developed an adaptive form called Story Theater, one version of which he took to Broadway in 1970. He currently directs an actor-training school in NYC with **Mike Nichols** and George Morrison.   SF

Silver (né Zimelman), Ron (1946–) NYC-born actor, educated at the University of Buffalo and St. John's University in Chinese studies, with subsequent acting training at the **Actors Studio** and **Berghof's** HB Studios. He made his stage debut in *Kaspar* and *Public Insult* (1971). His major appearances have been in **Rabe's** *Hurlyburly,* Andrew Bergman's *Social Security* (both directed by **Mike Nichols**), and **Mamet's** *Speed-the-Plow,* the last winning him Tony and Drama Desk awards. He has appeared frequently in television and film, notably as the attorney in *Reversal of Fortune* (1990).   DBW

Silver Cord, The **Sidney Howard's** three-act play, produced by the **Theatre Guild,** opened on Broadway at the **John Golden Theatre** 20 December 1926 and ran 112 performances. Mrs. Phelps (**Laura Hope Crews**) smothers both of her grown sons with love. The elder breaks free and saves his marriage, but the younger is "engulfed," and his fiancée (Margalo Gillmore) breaks their engagement. Critics compared Howard's effort to **George Kelly's** earlier *Craig's Wife,* though the latter was far more popular.   JDM

Silvers, Phil (né Philip) (1912–85) Brooklyn-born comic actor who began his career at 13 as a singer with Gus Edwards's **vaudeville** troupe. In 1935 he joined **Minsky's burlesque** as a comic, advancing to the Broadway stage by 1939. Although Silvers won Tonys for *Top Banana* (1951) and *A Funny Thing Happened on the Way to the Forum* (1972 revival), the bald, bespectacled funnyman is best remembered for his numerous films and his television creation of the scheming con man Sergeant Ernie Bilko (1955–9).   DBW

Simon, John (1925–) Yugoslavian-born drama and film critic. Educated at Harvard (PhD, 1959), Simon has been regarded as a brilliant stylist who demands that the theatre be intelligent and articulate. He wrote about the drama for *Hudson Review* (1960–81); about films and drama for *New York Magazine* since 1969; and about films for the *New Leader* since 1962. He is author of at least eight books, including *Singularities: Essays on the Theatre,*

1964–73 (1976). Simon believes that the critic is responsible first to himself then to his audience, and that a piece of criticism should be both pleasurable to read and philosophical in nature. A penchant for invective and harsh personal comments, however, has put him at odds with the theatre community and his colleagues.   TLM

Simon, (Marvin) Neil (1927–) Playwright.
Critical acclaim has come slowly for Simon, who has had more smash hits than any other American playwright. Even with almost a hit a year since 1961, he fights a reputation of being a gag writer who caters to the moral hangups and material greed of middle-class America; however, his most recent hit, **Lost in Yonkers** (1991), won both the Tony for best play and the Pulitzer Prize.

Born in New York. Simon learned his craft by writing comic material for radio and television personalities. With his brother Danny, he wrote sketches for Broadway shows, *Catch a Star* (1955) and *New Faces of 1956.* His first full-length comedy, *Come Blow Your Horn* (1961), was a hit, followed closely by the musical farce *Little Me* (1962, with **Cy Coleman** and Carolyn Leigh). After **Barefoot in the Park** (1963), he penned one of the funniest and wisest plays in 1965, The **Odd Couple;** and a year later added both *The Star-Spangled Girl* and the musical **Sweet Charity.** With four shows running simultaneously on Broadway, Simon was the most successful playwright of the 1960s. He added **Plaza Suite** to his list of smash hits in 1968 together with the musical *Promises, Promises* (with Burt Bacharach and Hal David). After **Last of the Red Hot Lovers** (1969), Simon wrote *The Gingerbread Lady* (1970), which attempted to deal honestly with alcoholism. While audiences rejected it, the playwright seemed more willing to attempt serious themes, and two bittersweet comedies followed: *The* **Prisoner of Second Avenue** and *The* **Sunshine Boys** (both 1972).

Following the death of his wife in 1973, Simon reached a low point in his career with two failures: *The Good Doctor* (1973), adapted from short stories by **Anton Chekhov;** and *God's Favorite,* adapted from the Bible (1976). However, a move to California resulted in another hit, *California Suite* (1976), a Beverly Hills version of *Plaza Suite.* His marriage to actress Marsha Mason resulted in *Chapter Two* (1977), regarded by some critics as his finest play to that point in his career. His fourth musical, *They're Playing Our Song,* proved popular in 1979, but his next three efforts were not successful: *I Ought to Be in Pictures* (1980), *Fools* (1981), and a revised version of *Little Me* (1982). Simon then returned to his own past for a charming **Brighton Beach Memoirs** (1983) and the Tony Award–winning **Biloxi Blues** (1984); and by recasting the two major roles in *The Odd Couple* for women, Simon found himself with three hits in 1985, and new respect from the critics. The following year, **Broadway Bound** proved to be another popular success, followed by two failures (*Rumors* [1988], and *Jake's Women* [1990], the latter initially seen only in San Diego but revised for Broadway [1992] with Alan Alda). *Lost in Yonkers* (1991) has proven

to be his most critically acclaimed play to date. TLM

See: R. Johnson, *Neil Simon,* Boston, 1983; E. McGovern, *Neil Simon: A Critical Study,* New York, 1979.

Simonson, Lee (1888–1967) Set designer; a
founding member and director of the **Theatre Guild.** Simonson studied for three years in Paris and, like **Robert Edmond Jones,** returned to the U.S. with great excitement about the New Stagecraft. He advocated simplified realism: While creating sets that were based in realism, he stripped away all scenic elements that were unnecessary for mood or information. As resident designer for the Theatre Guild he designed over half their productions, including *Heartbreak House, Liliom,* and *Green Grow the Lilacs.* His designs for *The* **Adding Machine** were among the most successful examples of expressionism on the American stage. He authored several important books, including *The Stage Is Set* (1932) and *Part of a Lifetime: Drawings and Designs, 1919-1940* (1943).   AA

Simpson, Edmund Shaw (1784–1848) Manager. From stage manager in 1810 to acting manager in 1821, Simpson became sole lessee of the **Park Theatre** in 1840 upon the death of **Stephen Price.** Shrewd manipulators of public taste, Simpson and Price early managed to associate the Park with fashion, despite a commonplace repertory. Extravaganzas and stars like Macready and the **Kemble**s, **Charlotte Cushman,** and **William Wheatley** failed to breast economic reversals or the deterioration of the building. Characterized as industrious but unremarkable as a manager, Simpson sold out to **Thomas S. Hamblin** in 1848, the year the Park burned [see **fires**].   RKB

Sissle, Noble (1889–1975) and Eubie Blake
(1883–1983) lyricist and composer. Pianist and composer Eubie Blake met singer-lyricist Noble Sissle in 1915. For several years they performed in **vaudeville** in an act featuring their own songs. In 1921 they joined with the vaudeville comedy team of Flournoy Miller and Aubrey Lyles to create the first black musical to play a major Broadway theatre during the regular theatrical season: **Shuffle Along.** With a book by Miller and Lyles, who also starred in it, *Shuffle Along* was a big hit both in New York and on tour. Critics and audiences delighted in the vitality of the score and the lively dancing of the chorus.

Sissle and Blake went on to write the scores for several other musicals, including *The Chocolate Dandies* (1924) and *Shuffle Along of 1932,* but without the success that had been achieved by *Shuffle Along.* On his own, Blake wrote the music for several other shows. A revival of *Shuffle Along* in 1952 was a failure, but with the rediscovery of ragtime in the 1960s and '70s Sissle and Blake songs were again heard on Broadway in *Doctor Jazz* (1975), *Bubbling Brown Sugar* (1976), and *Eubie* (1978).   MK

See: R. Kimball and W. Bolcom, *Reminiscing with Sissle and Blake,* New York, 1973; A. Rose, *Eubie Blake,* New York, 1979.

Six Degrees of Separation by **John Guare** ran **Off-Broadway** at the Mitzi E. Newhouse Theatre 19 May–28 October 1990, and was moved to the **Vivian Beaumont Theatre** on 8 November. Directed by **Jerry Zaks,** its 17-member cast included **Stockard Channing** as Ouisa Kittredge, John Cunningham as her husband Flan, and James McDaniel as Paul Poitier, as well as Sam Stoneburner, Stephen Pearlman, and Kelly Bishop. London's Royal Court staged the play with Channing during the summer of 1992. The play is based on an incident in 1983, when a young man posing as the son of Sidney Poitier worked his way into the lives of some wealthy New Yorkers and robbed them. Its theme is implied in its title, which refers to a statistical theory that everyone on earth is connected to everyone else by a trail of only six people. Guare uses the incident to satirize liberal guilt, the isolationism of modern urban life, and the generational hostility in the contemporary American family. At the same time he celebrates the creativity of the young con artist who takes advantage of the lack of imagination in his victims.   BCM

Skelton, Thomas (1927–) One of the more influential of the "second generation" of lighting designers following **Jean Rosenthal** and **Abe Feder,** Skelton has designed extensively for dance and is closely associated with the Paul Taylor and José Limon companies, the Ballet Folklorico de Mexico, and the Joffrey Ballet, where his work included a startling set and lighting design for the rock ballet *Astarte.* He has designed **circus** and ice shows as well. Theatre designs include *Purlie, Gigi,* **Oh Dad, Poor Dad . . . ,** and *Coco,* as well as several notable revivals.   AA

Skinner, Cornelia Otis (1901–79) Actress, monologuist, humorist, and author; daughter of actor **Otis Skinner,** with whom she made her professional debut in 1921 in *Blood and Sand.* She established her reputation as a fine actress beginning in the 1920s touring the U.S. and Britain in monodramas [see **one-person performances**] she wrote and staged herself. These included *The Wives of Henry VIII* (1931), *The Empress Eugenie* (1932), *The Loves of Charles II* (1933), and *Paris '90* (1952). In more traditional theatre she appeared in *Candida* (1939), *Theatre* (1941), *Lady Windermere's Fan* (1946), and *The Pleasure of His Company* (1958), the last coauthored with **Samuel Taylor.** She also wrote memoirs, light verse, essays, and three critically acclaimed theatrical biographies: *Family Circle* (1948), the story of her famous family; *Madame Sarah,* a life of Sarah Bernhardt (1967); and *Life with Lindsay and Crouse* (1976). She is probably most remembered for the 1942 travelogue she cowrote with Emily Kimbrough, titled *Our Hearts Were Young and Gay.*   DBW

Skinner, Otis (1858–1942) One of America's most versatile actors who, by his own account,

played over 140 roles during 1877–9 with the resident companies of the Philadelphia Museum and the **Walnut Street Theatre.** Between 1879 and 1892, Skinner played in the companies of **Edwin Booth, Lawrence Barrett, Augustin Daly, Helena Modjeska,** and **Joseph Jefferson III,** and occasionally starred as romantic hero, classical tragedian, comedian, and character actor. From 1892, Skinner was a confirmed and popular star who continued to play a varied repertory. In his own time and for later generations, he was best remembered for the role of Hajj, the beggar, in *Kismet,* which he created in 1911, played exclusively for three years, and preserved in two film versions. Skinner, and his actress daughter, **Cornelia Otis Skinner,** were both prolific writers, the former author of *Footlights and Spotlights* (1924), *The Last Tragedian* (1939, on Edwin Booth), and *One Man in His Time: The Adventures of Harry Watkins, Strolling Player, 1845–1863* (1938, with his wife, Maud).   MR

Skin of Our Teeth, The, by **Thornton Wilder** premiered in 1942 in a stormy production featuring **Frederic March, Florence Eldridge,** Montgomery Clift, and **Tallulah Bankhead,** directed by **Elia Kazan.** Wilder's daring, nonnaturalistic allegory of the human race, which included episodes from the ice age to a seven-year war, puzzled many of its cast members, who were already reeling from Tallulah's flamboyant rehearsal behavior. The opening was a success, however, and eventually led to 355 performances and a Pulitzer Prize. Still, controversy stalked the production when two scholars charged in the *Saturday Review* that Wilder had plagiarized some of the play's ideas from Joyce's *Finnegan's Wake.* The accusations – and their subsequent discussions – were overblown, but did contribute to a squabble among the critics, who denied the play their prestigious Circle Award. Time and numerous revivals have vindicated Wilder's imaginative vision, and the play has been directed and performed by dozens of theatrical luminaries, including Laurence Olivier, **John Houseman, George Abbott, Helen Hayes,** and Vivien Leigh.   BBW

Slade, Bernard (1930–) Playwright. Born in Toronto and educated in England, Slade was a successful television writer before his comedy *Same Time, Next Year* was a Broadway hit in 1975. His other plays include *Tribute* (1978, starring Jack Lemmon), *Romantic Comedy* (1979), *Special Occasions* (1982), *Fatal Attraction* (1984), *Return Engagements* (1986), *Sweet William* (1987), and *An Act of the Imagination* (1987).   TLM

Slave Ship Historical pageant by LeRoi Jones (**Amiri Baraka**) that traces the journey of African slaves to America and their experiences on arrival. The 1967 play consists of pantomimed actions that portray the revolting conditions below deck accompanied by cries and moans in the Yoruba language; then the slave market, aborted uprisings, and the symbolic destruction of white America. Directed by **Gilbert Mose** at the **Chelsea Theatre**

in Brooklyn, to music by Archie Shepp, the production was accounted to be devastating.   EGH

Slow Dance on the Killing Ground Three-act drama by William Hanley; opened on Broadway at the **Plymouth Theatre** (11 November 1964) for 88 performances. It was revived **Off-Broadway** at Sheridan Square Playhouse (13 May 1970) for 36 performances. Although realistic, it is laden with symbolism, as three lost souls late one night in a New York City candy store confess their innermost secrets to each other regarding racism, murder, family loyalty, and personal worth.   EK

Smith, Harry B[ache] (1860–1936) Librettist and lyricist. Smith's first connection with the theatre was as a dramatic and musical editor for a Chicago newspaper. For composer **Reginald De Koven** he created the libretto and most of the lyrics for the most beloved American comic opera of the late 19th century, **Robin Hood** (1891). Although much of his writing was mediocre by modern standards, Smith's ability to adapt to changing styles and tastes in musical theatre ensured him a long and prolific career, in the course of which he was reported to have written some 300 librettos and 6,000 lyrics. His autobiography appeared in 1931.   MK

> See: R. Friedman, "The Contributions of Harry Bache Smith to the American Musical Theatre," PhD diss., New York U, 1976.

Smith, Joe (né Joe Sultzer) (1884–1981) and **Charlie Dale (né Charles Marks)** (1881–1971) Comic **vaudeville** team (for 73 years); inspiration for **Neil Simon's** The **Sunshine Boys.** Smith and Dale began in 1898 as a blackface act, singing and dancing in Bowery saloons while working as hash-slingers at Childs' Restaurant. New names were adopted when calling cards for another team, who chose to change their name (to **Moran and Mack**), were used by a theatre owner to advertise them. In 1901 they joined the Imperial Vaudeville and Comedy Company. When the company folded they stayed with two other members (Will Lester and Jack Coleman) to form the Avon Comedy Four, developing such classic sketches as "Hungarian Rhapsody," "Dr. Kronkhite," "The New School Teacher," and "Venetian Knights." Numerous comics served with the Avon troupe before "Smith and Dale" became headliners in the 1920s, featuring their "Dr. Kronkhite" sketch (Smith the patient, Dale the doctor), thereafter inseparably associated with them. In their sketches Smith, lanky with a pencil mustache, received the punch lines while Dale, smaller and deadpan, was his foil. **Brooks Atkinson** characterized them as "professional performers, acting two low-comedy parts with style, authority and abandon."   DBW

> See: M. Matlaw, ed., American Popular Entertainment, Westport, CT, 1979.

Smith, Oliver (1918–   ) Set designer and theatrical producer who has designed some 400 theatre, dance, opera, and film productions since 1941, and also served as codirector of American Ballet Theatre (1945–81). He began his career designing for dance, notably Rodeo and Fall River Legend for **Agnes de Mille,** and Fancy Free for **Jerome Robbins.** Starting with the 1944 production of **On the Town** (which he also coproduced), Smith designed a steady stream of long-running musicals, including **My Fair Lady, West Side Story,** and **Hello Dolly!** Smith believes that scenery for musicals should be bright, entertaining, and change quickly and unobtrusively. He has talked about scenery in terms of choreography: In Fall River Legend, the scenery is, in fact, an integral part of the choreography. In terms of style he frequently mixes painterly backgrounds with sculptural scenic elements. He also has an almost formulaic approach to the arrangement of scenic elements and space, which meshed well with the musicals of the 1940s and '50s and contributed to his prodigious output.   AA

Smith, Richard Penn (1799–1854) One of many American intellectuals who wrote fiction and poetry and edited journals, Smith created some 20 plays, five of them staged in 1829. Of these, The Eighth of January celebrated Andrew Jackson's victory, while William Penn reveals Smith's talent for comedy. Caius Marius (1831), a tragedy based on this Roman's love of country, was selected as a Prize Play by **Edwin Forrest,** who performed the title role only a few times. Although Smith enjoyed some success, his interest in the theatre was momentary.   WJM

> See: B. McCullough, The Life and Writings of Richard Penn Smith, Menasha, WI, 1917.

Smith, Solomon Franklin (1801–69) Theatre manager and actor, especially noted for his pioneering work on the **frontier.** He began his theatrical career in Vincennes, IN, in 1819, and by 1823 had organized his own company, which he managed for four years. He then toured the Mississippi Valley with **J. H. Caldwell,** and in 1835 entered into a partnership with **Noah Ludlow.** They dominated the frontier theatre of their time, but ended the partnership in 1853.

As an actor, Smith, affectionately known as "Old Sol," was particularly effective as a low comedian in such roles as Mawworm in The Hypocrite. He eventually went into law and became a Missouri state senator. His three autobiographical volumes, Theatrical Apprenticeship (1845), The Theatrical Journey-work and Anecdotal Recollections of Sol. Smith (1854), and Theatrical Management in the West and South for Thirty Years (1868), are flawed but valuable insights into theatrical conditions of the time.   SMA

Smith, William Henry Sedley (1806–72) Playwright, actor, and stage manager. Born in Wales, Smith began acting with the Theatre Royal, Lancaster (1822), joined Philadelphia's **Walnut Street** company (1827), the **Tremont Theatre** in Boston (1828), and the **Boston Museum** (1843) as stage manager and actor. Smith's The **Drunkard;**

or, The Fallen Saved (1844) was the first successful temperance drama and the most enduring. After the initial 100-performance runs in Boston and New York, the play blanketed the country. His later career was spent in San Francisco as manager of the **California Theatre.**   RM

Smith, Winchell (1872–1933) Playwright who, starting as an actor, learned how to pick collaborators and to please the public with farce and comic caricature. With Byron Ongley, he wrote *Brewster's Millions* (1906), in which a young man must spend a million dollars. This play marked the first appearance of the theatre's favorite fictional performer, George Spelvin, whom Smith would use many times. *Via Wireless* (1908) written with Paul Armstrong failed, but *The Fortune Hunters* (1909) proved a successful vehicle for John Barrymore [see **Drew–Barrymore**]. *The Boomerang* (1915), with Victor Mapes, was a successful play about a man consumed with jealousy. Equally popular with audiences was *Turn to the Right!* (1916), about two convicts who reform and marry into respectable families. Smith's greatest success came with *Lightnin'* (1918), written with **Frank Bacon,** who acted the lovable ne'er-do-well hero. With 1,291 performances, *Lightnin'* broke the old record held by **Charles Hoyt**'s *A Trip to Chinatown.*   WJM

Societies and associations, theatrical The *Encyclopedia of Associations* (Detroit, 1991) lists well over 130 theatrical societies and associations in the United States. Among the better known are the following:

1. American Association of Community Theatre (AACT): L. Ross Rowland, 8209 N. Costa Mesa Dr., Muncie, IN 47303. Founded in 1986, membership 500. Promotes **community theatre** and sponsors the Community Theatre Foundation; has a placement service; publishes *AACT Directory of Community Theatre in the United States* and newsletters.

2. American Society for Theatre Research (ASTR): Theatre Department, University of Rhode Island, Kingston, RI 02881. Founded 1956, membership 750. ASTR is an organization for theatre scholars to promote knowledge of theatre history. It is affiliated with the International Federation for Theatre Research, and publishes *Theatre Survey* and a newsletter. Annual meeting.

3. American Theatre Critics Association (ATCA): Clara Hieronymus, The Tennessean, 1100 Broadway, Nashville, TN 37203. Founded 1974, membership 350. ATCA seeks to foster communication among American theatre critics, encourages freedom of expression in the theatre and theatre **criticism,** and advances theatrical standards. Publishes *Critics Quarterly* and a newsletter. Annual convention.

4. Association for Theatre in Higher Education (ATHE): Theatre Service, P.O. Box 15282, Evansville, IN 47716. Founded in 1986 after the collapse of the American Theatre Association (founded 1936), membership 1,750. ATHE promotes the exchange of information among individuals engaged in theatre study and research, performance, and crafts. It

operates a placement service, and publishes *Theatre Journal, Theatre Topics,* and newsletters.

5. Catholic Actors Guild of America (CAG): 1501 Broadway, Suite 518, New York, NY 10036. Founded 1914, membership 1,200. CAG was founded for the spiritual and temporal welfare of theatre people. Publishes (monthly) *Call Board.*

6. International Theatre Institute of the United States (ITI/U.S.): 220 W. 42nd St.., Suite 1710, New York, NY 10036. Founded 1948. The ITI/U.S. was established by UNESCO to serve as an international theatre organization and clearinghouse for information and services. ITI/U.S. maintains a library of international theatre covering 142 countries. Biennial congress.

7. League of Historic American Theatres: 1511 K Street, NW, Suite 923, Washington, DC 20005. Founded 1977, membership 175. The League is primarily concerned with the restoration of important historic theatres, and maintains the Chesley Collection on American historic theatres. Publishes (monthly) *LHAT Bulletin; National Directory of Historic American Theatre;* others. Annual meeting.

8. League of American Theatres and Producers (LATP): 226 W 47th St., New York, NY 10036. Founded 1930, membership 250. This organization negotiates labor contracts and government relations, and conducts and sponsors theatrical research concerning the commercial theatre. Presents the **Antoinette Perry** (Tony) Awards, compiles statistics, and has audience development, research, and educational programs. Formerly League of New York Theatres (name changed 1985).

9. League of Off-Broadway Theatres and Producers (LOBTP): George Elmer Productions, Ltd., 130 W. 42nd St., Suite 1300, New York, NY 10036. Founded 1957, membership 50. LOBTP seeks to advance the **Off-Broadway** theatre in New York.

10. League of Resident Theatres (LORT): c/o Tom Hall, Old Globe Theatre, Box 2171, San Diego, CA 92112–2171. Founded 1965, membership 64. LORT seeks to advance the U.S. **resident nonprofit professional theatre** (regional theatre). Semiannual convention.

11. Literary Managers and Dramaturgs of America (LMDA): CASTA, Room 1206A, CUNY Graduate Center, 33 W. 42nd St., New York, NY 10036. Founded in 1985. LMDA holds national and regional conferences, publishes a newsletter, and conducts programs for new dramaturgs.

12. National Theatre Conference (NTC): c/o Prof. Barry B. Witham, School of Drama DX–20, Seattle WA 98195. Founded 1925, membership 120. NTC membership is limited to 120 leaders of the noncommercial **academic** and nonacademic theatre, NTC seeks to collaborate on matters of policy and action with other major theatre organizations.

13. New York Drama Critics' Circle (NYDCC): c/o Michael Kuchwara, Associated Press, 50 Rockefeller Plz., New York, NY 10019. Founded 1935, membership 23. NYDCC seeks to uphold the standards of dramatic **criticism** in NYC. Semiannual meetings.

14. **Theatre Communications Group** (TCG): 355 Lexington Ave., New York, NY 10017.

Founded 1961, membership 304. TCG is a service organization for **resident nonprofit professional theatre**s and performers, fostering interaction among members.

15. Theatre Historical Society (THS): Archive Center, 2215 W. North Ave., Chicago, IL 60647. Founded 1969, membership 900. THS seeks to preserve and disseminate the history of the popular theatre in the U.S., especially the cinema. Publishes annual and directory, and *Marquee* (quarterly). Annual convention.

16. Theatre Library Association (TLA): 111 Amsterdam Ave., Rm. 513, New York, NY 10023. Founded 1937, membership 500. TLA furthers the interests of gathering, preserving, and making available any records of theatre in all its forms. Its membership is composed of curators, librarians, and theatre scholars. Publishes *Broadside* and *Performing Arts Resources*.

17. United States Institute for Theatre Technology (USITT): Richard Devin, School of Drama, DX-20, University of Washington, Seattle, WA 98195. Founded 1960, membership 3,000. USITT seeks to serve those interested in the advancement of theatre techniques and technology. Publishes (quarterly) *Theatre Design and Technology,* newsletter, directories.

Other theatrically oriented U.S. organizations include the American Theatre and Drama Society; Association for Asian Performance; Council of Resident Summer Theatres; Drama Desk; **Dramatists Guild;** Episcopal Actor's Guild of America; **Ford's Theatre** Society; Institute for Advanced Studies in the Theatre; Institute of **Outdoor Drama;** National Costumers Association; **National Playwrights Conference; National Theatre of the Deaf; New Dramatists;** Outer Critics Circle; Society for the Preservation of Variety Arts; **Alliance of Resident Theatre/NY;** Society of Stage Directors and Choreographers; Theatre Development Fund; and the **Yiddish Theatre** Alliance. SMA

Society of American Dramatists and Composers

Playwrights' union founded by **Bronson Howard** and **Augustus Thomas** (1891). It was absorbed into the **Dramatists Guild** of America (1919), which achieved the first standard playwright's contract shortly after the successful strike by **Actors' Equity Association.** DMcD

Soldier's Play, A Pulitzer Prize–winning play written by **Charles Fuller** and staged in 1981 by the **Negro Ensemble Company** at Theatre Four, NYC. The play focuses on the search for the killer of an unpopular black sergeant in a segregated army camp in Louisiana during WW II. Possible suspects include members of the sergeant's own company, a white officer, and rednecks from the nearby town. The investigation, carried out by a black captain from Washington, DC, probes the characters of the men involved. Although the play received fine ensemble acting and a strongly favorable press, black opinion was reserved, holding that the play's resolution was cleverly contrived to appease white sensitivities. EGH

Sommer, (Maximilian) Josef (1934–) German-born actor who, after debuting at the University of North Carolina at 7, went on to specialize in "hard-boiled, avuncular roles" in "emotionally deep . . . performances." After his New York debut in *Othello* (1970), he appeared with **Lincoln Center Repertory, American Shakespeare Festival, American Conservatory Theatre, Circle in the Square, Seattle Repertory, Hartford Stage, Mark Taper Forum,** and **Long Wharf.** His stage performances include *The Trial of the Catonsville Nine* (1971), *The Shadow Box* (1977), *The 1940's Radio Hour* (1979), *Whose Life Is It Anyway?* (1980), *Lydie Breeze* (Obie, 1982), *Largo Desolato* (1986), *A Walk in the Woods* (1988), and *The Visit* (1991, **Goodman Theatre**). Sommer's films include *Dirty Harry* (1971), *The Front* (1976), *Reds* (1981), and *Silkwood* (1983); he also narrated *Sophie's Choice* (1982). Sommer's TV work includes "The Scarlet Letter," "The Adams Chronicles," and a televised *Mourning Becomes Electra.* He was the recipient of a Fulbright Grant to study theatre in Germany. REK

Sondheim, Stephen (1930–) Lyricist and composer. After an apprenticeship with **Oscar Hammerstein II** and some early writing for television, Sondheim created the lyrics for *West Side Story* (1957) and *Gypsy* (1959). In 1962 he received his first opportunity to write both music and lyrics for *A Funny Thing Happened on the Way to the Forum.* After a failure with *Anyone Can Whistle* (1970), Sondheim startled the **musical theatre** world with the scores for a series of highly experimental shows. *Company* (1970) was a collage of musical vignettes about married life in contemporary New York. *Follies* (1971) used a reunion of musical comedy performers to examine the effects of middle age on love and marriage. *A Little Night Music* (1973) had a score written entirely in three-four time. *Pacific Overtures* (1976) employed the conventions of Japanese Kabuki theatre and an all-Asian cast to tell of the opening of Japan to the West. *Sweeney Todd* (1979) adapted Victorian melodrama to modern sensibilities by suggesting the tormented soul behind the "demon barber of Fleet Street." *Merrily We Roll Along* (1981) examined the myth of the American success story by tracing the lives of its central characters backward from middle age to youth. *Sunday in the Park with George* (1984) explored the process of artistic creation by bringing to life the work of French painter Georges Seurat. *Into the Woods* (1987) explored the darker Freudian aspects of classic fairy tales. Sondheim's scores for each of these shows were characterized by brilliant, often cerebral lyrics and driving, unsentimental music. Of his recent work, only *Assassins* (1991), which probed the minds of those who had attempted to assassinate U.S. presidents, has failed to succeed. He is generally considered to have been the most distinguished composer-lyricist in the musical theatre since the 1970s. In the late 1980s and early '90s several major revivals of Sondheim shows demonstrated anew his brilliance as lyricist and composer. MK

See: J. Gordon, *Art Isn't Easy,* Carbondale, IL, 1990; Craig Zadan, *Sondheim & Co,* 2d ed., New York,

E. H. Sothern and Julia Marlowe in *Hamlet*. Photo: Hall. Courtesy: Michael Gnat.

1986. A biography by Martin Gottfried is to be published in 1993.

Sothern, E[dward] A[skew] (1826–81) and **E[dward] H[ugh] Sothern** (1859–1933) Actors. Beginning his career as an eccentric comedian on English stages, the elder Sothern made his American debut as Dr. Pangloss in *The Heir-at-Law* in 1852. He achieved sudden star status with **Laura Keene**'s company when he assumed the role of Lord Dundreary in Tom Taylor's *Our American Cousin* in 1858 for an uninterrupted run of five months. In 1861, after 400 consecutive performances, Londoners indulged in frequent "Dundrearyisms," and his distinctive sidewhiskers, known as "Dundrearies," became popular. Other Sothern roles included Dundreary's Brother Sam in the play of that name (1862), and the title roles in T. W. Robertson's *David Garrick* (1864) and H. J. Byron's *The Crushed Tragedian* (1878). Excelling in original comic business, the British-born actor remained popular on both sides of the Atlantic and died in London. In 1879, Sothern provided the opportunity for his American-born son, E. H. Sothern, to make his debut in New York in a small role in *Brother Sam*. Playing in England and America, the younger Sothern gained experience in the companies of **John Mc-Cullough,** Helen Dauvray, and others. In 1887 **Daniel Frohman** engaged Sothern for the newly formed company at the **Lyceum Theatre.** Sothern quickly established himself as a dashing romantic hero in such roles as Prince Rudolph in *The Prisoner of Zenda* (1895). Still under Frohman's manage-

ment, Sothern broadened his range to poetic drama in 1900 as the hero in Hauptmann's *The Sunken Bell* and as Hamlet. Under the management of **Charles Frohman,** Sothern first appeared with **Julia Marlowe** (whom he married in 1911) in *Romeo and Juliet* in 1904. Together, until Marlowe's retirement, they reigned for a decade as America's foremost Shakespearean players. Sothern retired in 1927.   MR

See: T. E. Pemberton, *Lord Dundreary: A Memoir of Edward Askew Sothern, with a Brief Sketch of the Career of E. H. Sothern,* New York, 1908; E. A. Sothern, *The Melancholy Tale of "Me,"* New York, 1916.

Soudeikine, Sergei (1882–1946) Russian-born designer and painter who studied art in Moscow and designed in Moscow and St. Petersburg for Meyerhold and Tairov, among others. In 1920 he emigrated to Paris and then to the U.S. in 1922 with Balieff's Chauve-Souris cabaret, for which he continued to design over the years. He designed extensively for the Metropolitan Opera and at **Radio City Music Hall** (1934–9). He also designed *Porgy and Bess* (1935).   AA

Sound American theatre inherited a tradition of property sound effects from European theatre. That craft of devising mechanical tricks to simulate the auditory quality of a particular noise is the discipline to which the traditional term "sound effects" legitimately belongs. The craft of property sound remained vital until the new theatres and changing aesthetics of the 20th century rendered it obsolete.

20th-century American theatre, in response to aesthetics based on cinematic realism, developed a new, visual stagecraft based on novel advances in technology. Prior to 1950, however, neither general understanding of auditory perception nor technical resources in audio electronics were sufficiently mature to permit sound to keep pace with the new stagecraft.

The seminal figure in the development of sound in American theatre was Harold Burris-Meyer. Active in theatre during the 1930s, Burris-Meyer's work occurred at a time of significant advances in the science of human perception; he applied the gain in scientific knowledge toward the development of an art of sound in theatre. With Vincent Mallory, Burris-Meyer built a specialized audio system for theatrical production and devised experiments in acoustical reinforcement and use of psychoacoustics to enhance dramatic impact. Both men were associated with a number of theatre productions in New York, as sound designers as well as consultants. They were directly involved in the **Federal Theatre Project,** and designed the first application of acoustical reinforcement to opera at the Metropolitan Opera House. Burris-Meyer's active work in theatre sound ended when he and Mallory were drafted into wartime research.

Although Burris-Meyer initiated an expanded use of audio for theatre, his primary interest was the potential of sound to serve as a controllable psychological tool for the enhancement of dramatic impact. During the period 1940–60, however, most theatre people were simply concerned with understanding and applying the craft of audio. Audio gave promise of enabling a more flexible and extensive use of sound than the property tradition had been able to offer. Midcentury amplifier technology was adequate for almost any theatrical requirement, but early sound capture and storage systems were difficult and inflexible. The two main needs were (1) a facile, editable method of sound storage and retrieval, and (2) a microphone to pick up actors' voices clearly without imposing an unsightly and bulky device into the view of the audience.

The advent of tape recording provided a satisfactory storage and retrieval system, enabling theatre to make adequate use of facsimiles of real sounds instead of simulated effects. Audiotape provided a medium that almost anyone could use, and one that could be edited easily to rearrange the extent and sequence of sounds.

Acoustical reinforcement prior to 1960 was not easily applied to theatre, because reinforcement at that time required a relatively fixed usage of a facility. Development of the wireless (radio) microphone encouraged significant use of acoustical reinforcement, especially in musical theatre. Greater audibility implied the possibility of serving larger audiences, hence larger box-office revenues. Reinforcement techniques for concert performance of popular music were translated to theatre with rock musicals of the 1960s and '70s. Modified concert reinforcement methods have now become a permanent part of American musical theatre.

As of 1992, American theatre sound falls into two major categories: acoustical reinforcement and sound scoring. The former, dominantly a technical craft, is the more marketable trade and is served by professionals who work mostly in New York and other major theatre centers. Reinforcement has also generated a growing rental and supply industry to serve the needs of the major designers.

"Sound scoring" (the term, promulgated by the Sound Design Commission of the U.S. Institute for Theatre Technology, for auditory enhancement of the dramatic environment) is the lesser art, at least for the time being. Environmental sound has always been important to aesthetic impact in drama, but property sound simulators were extremely limited, and extended effects could easily become distracting. By the 1980s, audio offered control technology sensitive enough to underscore live drama, but the artists capable of creating extended environments were few. Extended sound scoring first began during the late 1960s in university and experimental theatres. By 1980, sound scoring was used in regional professional theatre companies. By 1990 the number of sound artists working in theatre had shown a remarkable increase. Many regional theatre companies now retain both composers and sound designers as part of their permanent staff. As of the early 1990s, sound scoring has not become a common aspect of Broadway professional theatre, however. JLB

See: D. Kaye and J. LeBrecht, *Sound Design for the Theater*, New York, 1992; G. D. White, *The Audio Dictionary*, 2d ed., Seattle, 1991.

Sound of Music, The

Sound of Music, The The last, and one of the most successful, of the **Richard Rodgers–Oscar Hammerstein II** collaborations (with book by **Howard Lindsay** and **Russel Crouse**), it opened at the **Lunt–Fontanne Theatre** on 16 November 1959 and ran 1,443 performances. Based on the life of Maria Von Trapp – a former religious postulant who became governess to the seven children of an Austrian naval captain, married the captain, and fled with him and the children when the Nazis took over Austria – the show gave Rodgers the opportunity to write music ranging from a Gregorian chant to typical Broadway "charm" numbers. Hammerstein's lyrics moved from the unabashed sentiment of "Edelweiss" and the title song to the ironic wit of "No Way to Stop It" and "How Can Love Survive?" **Mary Martin** gave a winning performance as Maria and **Theodore Bikel** was suitably dignified as the Captain. While some critics were less than enthusiastic about the show's sentiment and idealism, audiences kept it running for over three years, followed by a successful 1965 film with Julie Andrews and **Christopher Plummer.** MK

South Coast Repertory

South Coast Repertory Founded in 1964 as a summer company by David Emmes and Martin Benson, who opened a year-round operation in a rented 60-seat space in Newport Beach, CA, presenting *Tartuffe* on 12 November 1964. Their first permanent home, a marine hardware store that they converted to a 75-seat theatre, opened on 12 March 1965 with *Waiting for Godot*. They moved into a larger space in Costa Mesa (1967), and in 1972 organized their first board of directors as a nonprofit theatre and established both the Summer Conservatory (for aspiring professionals) and the Young Conservatory. They hired their first Equity artist in 1974, and in 1976 initiated a $3.5 million fund-raising campaign to build a 507-seat Main Stage (1978) and 161-seat flexible Second Stage (1979) in a new complex in Costa Mesa. A typical season includes one or two classics but five to eight local or world premieres; the company maintains a separate endowment expressly for the purpose of developing new plays. In spite of this challenging repertory, they have built a large and faithful subscription audience among the highly conservative and conventional Orange County community. JDM

South Pacific

South Pacific Based on James A. Michener's novel *Tales of the South Pacific,* with book by **Oscar Hammerstein II** and **Joshua Logan,** music by **Richard Rodgers,** and lyrics by Hammerstein, this Pulitzer Prize–winning musical opened at the **Majestic Theatre** on 7 April 1949 and ran 1,925 performances. Set on a small island in the early days of WW II, it tells of two sets of lovers, French exile planter Émile de Becque and Navy nurse Nellie Forbush, and Navy Lieutenant Joe Cable and the Tonkinese girl Liat. Racial prejudice figures in both plots: Nellie is finally able to overcome her aversion to de Becque's two children by a native woman, but Cable cannot bring himself to marry the Asian girl he loves. These two stories unfold against the backdrop of American sailors trying to cope with the exotic island world into which they have been plunged. As Nellie, **Mary Martin** gave a buoyant performance, and Metropolitan Opera star Ezio Pinza brought stature to the role of Emile. Logan, who had served in the Navy, staged the show adeptly, particularly the sailors' chorus number, "There Is Nothing Like a Dame." MK

Southwark Theatre South St. between 4th and 5th Sts., **Philadelphia.** In 1766, **David Douglass** erected America's first substantial theatre just outside Philadelphia's city limits to avert official interference; it was to remain active for 51 years. On its stage, Douglass presented the first play by a American-born playwright, Thomas Godfrey's *The Prince of Parthia* (1767) [see **Introduction,** §1]. Closed by the Continental Congress in 1774, it was used briefly as a hospital, then reopened by British occupation troops for entertainments to benefit widows and orphans. A drop curtain attributed to Major John André continued to be used until the theatre closed. The playhouse was two and a half stories high, painted red, brick in its lower story, and surmounted by a cupola. In 1784, **Lewis Hallam, Jr.,** reoccupied the theatre, skirting the laws against play-acting by presenting "moral lectures." In 1789, the ban was lifted, and the Southwark was in full operation. Outmoded as newer theatres were built and better companies assembled, the playhouse closed its doors in 1817. When the structure was damaged by **fire** a few years later, a brewery was built on its foundations and survived until 1912. MCH

Sovey, Raymond (1897–1966) This designer's prodigious output through four decades included such classics as *The* **Front Page** (1928), **Animal Crackers** (1928), *Green Grow the Lilacs* (1931), *The* **Petrified Forest** (1935), **Our Town** (1938), **Arsenic and Old Lace** (1941), and *The Cocktail Party* (1951). He was noted for his ingenious solutions to design problems and his ability to capture the essence of a scene or play with deftly selected images. AA

Spewack, Sam (1899–1971) and **Bella (Cohen) Spewack** (1899–1990) One of the most successful husband-and-wife writing teams, the Spewacks collaborated on 12 plays and 20 screenplays. Married in 1922 when both were journalists, they created such classical, madcap comedies and social satires as *Clear All Wires* (1932), *Boy Meets Girl* (1935, Megrue Prize), **Kiss Me, Kate** (1948, Tony and Page One awards; film 1953), and *My Three Angels* (1953). Before their theatre work, Bella wrote primarily fiction; Sam was a foreign correspondent, the basis for the four plays (including *Two Blind Mice,* 1949) and three novels that he authored alone. TH-S

Spiderwoman Theatre One of the oldest producing U.S. **feminist theatre** groups. The core members of the troupe, founded in 1975, are three Cuna/Rappahannock American Indian sisters – Lisa Mayo and Gloria and Muriel Miguel. They borrow their name from the Hopi goddess of creation, who first created designs and taught her people to weave. Spiderwoman's storyweaving technique – spun with words and movement – result in loosely structured

pieces that include *Lysistrata Numbah, Sun, Moon, and Feather,* and *Winnetou's Snake-Oil Show from Wigwam City.* A mix of media and an interweaving of various narrative threads characterizes Spiderwoman's productions, which are aggressively nonlinear and improvisatory. They borrow freely from **Native American ritual** traditions and myths and from slapstick comedy. JDo

See: R. Schneider in *Acting Out: Essays on Feminist Performance,* L. Hart, M. Phelan, eds., Ann Arbor, 1992.

Split Britches Feminist and lesbian theatre troupe (see **gay/lesbian theatre**) founded in 1981 by Lois Weaver, Peggy Shaw, and Deborah Margolin as an offshoot of **Spiderwoman Theatre.** First presented at NYC's WOW Café, Split Britches' productions – *Split Britches* (1981), *Beauty and the Beast* (1982), *Upwardly Mobile Home* (1984), *Little Women* (1988) – include eclectic combinations of realistic detail with flights of surrealistic fancy. They employ Brechtian techniques and appropriate popular culture genres to critique strict gender roles and compulsory heterosexuality. Their nonlinear political comedies entertain but confront dominant values. JDo

See: S. Case in *Feminine Focus,* E. Brater, ed., New York, 1989.

Spoleto Festival, USA Founded in 1977 in Charleston, SC, by composer Gian Carlo Menotti as a counterpart to his "The Festival of Two Worlds" (1958, Spoleto, Italy), this annual May–June festival brings together established performers and talented young artists from all over the world to exchange ideas and share their appreciations for the arts. In recent years the theatrical fare has become more experimental, with offerings such as Philip Glass and Allen Ginsberg's *The Hydrogen Jukebox* and *Pioneer* by the Paul Dresher Ensemble. With attendance at all events over 75,000, all available venues are used, including Gaillard Auditorium, the Dock Street Theatre, and the Garden, a converted moviehouse. Running concurrently is Piccolo Spoleto, a fringe festival celebrating local and regional artists. DBW

Spooner Stock Companies Mary Gibbs Spooner (1853–1940) established the first Spooner resident **stock company** at the Park Theatre, Brooklyn, in 1901 to support her daughters **Edna May** (1875–1953) and **Cecil** (1888–1953). The group charged low admission prices to productions of familiar plays and catered to the interests of middle-class women, especially homemakers. It moved to the **Fifth Avenue Theatre** in Manhattan in 1907. After 1908, Mrs. Spooner and Charles E. Blaney founded companies in several U.S. cities. Cecil headed troupes residing in New York City until 1918. WD

See: W. Durham, ed., *American Theatre Companies, 1888–1930,* Westport, CT, 1987.

Stadt Theater Company A German-speaking **stock company** organized in 1854 by Otto Hoym in New York (old Amphitheatre, 37–39 Bowery).

Joined by Eduard Hamann in 1855, the Stadt Theater produced a variety of German comedies, operettas, and classics. In 1864 the company became the Neues Stadt Theater and moved to 45–47 Bowery, where Hoym and Hamann engaged German notables Bogumil Dawison (1866–7) and Friedrich Haase (1868–9). Following Hoym's retirement in 1867, novelty acts and opera became increasingly popular. Hamann went bankrupt in 1872, and many company members joined Adolf Neuendorff's **Germania Theater Company.**   RE

Stage lighting The history of stage lighting, dating back several centuries, forms a continuum with that of candles, oil lamps, and gas as general illuminants. Candles were the principal source of illumination until gas illumination, first installed in the **Chestnut Street Theatre** in **Philadelphia** in 1816, enabled control from a single "gas table" and the simultaneous dimming or brightening of large groups of lights. During the last half of the 19th century, use was also made of limelight or calcium light, requiring a mixture of oxygen and hydrogen gases to heat a block of lime to incandescence. Limelight, first used in the theatre in 1837 (first used extensively in the U.S. for the extravaganza *The **Black Crook*** in 1866), made possible special lighting effects such as sunlight and moonlight, as well as projections (fire, rainbows, clouds, rain, snow), which depended upon a relatively intense source of light; nearly 20 times brighter than acetylene gas and 750 times brighter than a candle, limelight could be used to advantage. Methods to produce special effects became very highly developed. Hand-painted mica slides were placed within manually operated cam, tilt, and rotating devices designed to create the appropriate motion – altered in our own times mainly by the imposition of photographic methods and electronic controls.

A rapid transition from gas to electric sources in the theatre followed the introduction of Edison carbon filament lamps in 1879, producing three times the light of the acetylene gas jets and considerable improvement in safety. The transformation from gas to electric lamps was almost completed by the turn of the century. In the remodeling of New York's Metropolitan Opera House, following the destruction of its interior by fire in 1892, the new borderlights and footlights combined both traditional gas jets and new electric lamps. (It is not clear whether the gas connections were maintained until the complete renovation of all stage equipment in 1903, but at this time all lighting throughout the building was converted to electric lamps, over 15,000 of them.) As late as 1906, 8 families out of 10 in the U.S. were still using candle and gas flame sources at home.

Although electric borderlights and footlights, similar strips called winglights (mounted vertically and placed at the sides of the stage), and special effects machines comprised the main sources of illumination, theatres also used spotlights with simple lenses to concentrate the light ("lens boxes") or as follow spotlights ("chasers"). Open-box floodlights ("Olivettes" and later "bunch lights") could be colored with dyed, translucent silk screens. Carbon-arc light sources (first used in the theatre

in 1846), became more prevalent, replacing the limelight source in spotlights and box floodlights. Though safer than calcium lights, carbon-arc sources were sometimes not fully enclosed; sparks from the exposed arc presented a great danger of **fire,** particularly due to close proximity with the cloth and wooden scenery. The Iroquois Theatre fire in 1903, which originated from a spark from an open-box carbon-arc source falling on the scenery, hastened the adoption of more stringent fire regulations throughout the U.S. Carbon-arc sources could be thereafter used only in enclosed or screened housings, and the theatre became a much safer place for patron and actor alike.

Each successive new development resulted in higher brightness levels; each such increase in brightness revealed rather disturbingly the painted nature and cloth construction of the wing and border settings. This potential of higher and higher brightness levels was to continue throughout the 20th century, and ultimately forced a change in the design of the settings themselves. Control over the intensity of stage lights in the gas era had been achieved by means of stopcock valves on the "gas table," whereas the operation of each limelight or carbon-arc source required the presence of a nearby operator. The introduction of the electric lamp and three or four alternating sequential colors of lamps in footlights and borderlights multiplied the need for controlling an increasing number of individual lights and groups of colored lights. In the U.S. early liquid or water-barrel dimmers were soon superseded by variable-resistance wire dimmers, made available in plate form as early as 1892 to allow closer stacking and to regulate voltage going to the lamps and, therefore, their brightness. Over the next three decades a number of mechanical systems were designed to facilitate operation of the increasing number of dimmers. The end of this period saw switchboards, sometimes 30–40 ft long in larger installations, with dimmers rising upward in three or more tiers, and capable of being locked or unlocked to master color shafts which, in turn, were actuated by a grand master lever or slow-motion wheel.

David Belasco and his electrician, Louis Hartmann, worked together during 1900–30, attempting to make lighting in the theatre more realistic. Belasco's production of ***Madame Butterfly*** (1900) was acclaimed for its subtle naturalistic color effects, in which silk color rolls achieved a slow fade from day to night behind the translucent screens of the setting. Belasco had an affection for the early low-wattage spotlights, and used small "baby lenses" in the production of ***Du Barry*** in 1901 for the specific purpose of throwing a special hue of light on the star, the red-headed **Mrs. Leslie Carter.** Only 10,000–15,000 watts of lighting were sufficient for most Belasco productions. In 1915, during the remodeling of the **Belasco Theatre,** Belasco installed permanent "front-lighting" on the audience side of the proscenium arch, utilizing four sections of "X-ray" (silvered-glass) reflectors, each with only four 100-watt lamps. At the same time footlights were discarded.

The introduction of ductile-tungsten filament lamps in 1910 to replace carbon-filament lamps

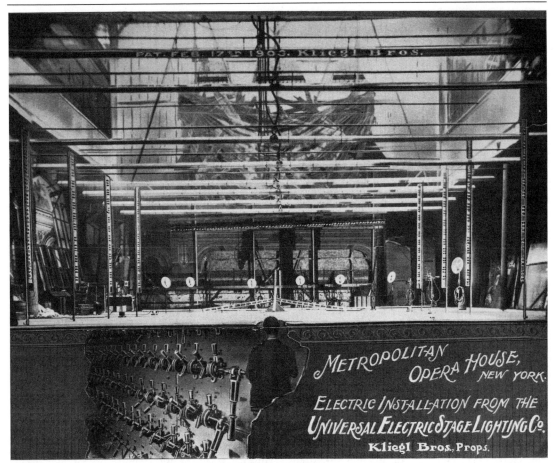

Electrical installation in the Metropolitan Opera House (1903). First published in Kliegl Bros. catalog for 1906. Original in the collection of Joel E. Rubin.

doubled the efficiency of light sources. Within five years greater efficiency was provided by adding a gas-fill to tungsten lamps (first nitrogen and then, in 1919, argon), enabling lamp efficiency nearly two-thirds of that in today's tungsten lamps. Although these new efficient sources were eagerly adopted by the theatre, soon a reaction set in decrying the new higher brightness levels and "over-illuminating" of the scene.

Maude Adams, Winthrop Ames, Joseph Urban, Robert Edmond Jones, and S. L. ("Roxy") Rothafel are among those credited with the early use of spotlights in the period 1915–20. In 1922, **Lee Simonson** used over 60 spotlights for *The Insect Comedy,* and in 1925 he and **Norman Bel Geddes** installed over 100 permanent spotlights in the Guild Theatre in New York (now the **Virginia**). Stage lighting in America had entered the "spotlight era."

The new era was heralded in the early 1920s by "bridge" and "C-clamps," suspension devices that easily repositioned lighting units as appropriate rather than depending on permanent mounts. Monroe Pevear in **Boston** introduced ground glass slides to soften the hard beam edges of planoconvex lens spotlights; within a few years a spotlight of greater intensity but with the same soft beam edge was produced by the use of square prismatic lenses. By the early 1930s these took the form of the round "Fresnel" lens, still in use today. Simultaneously, studies were undertaken by "lighting consultant" (an early use of the term) Stanley R. McCandless while planning for theatres in Radio City (Rockefeller Center) in New York. McCandless, his associate Edward B. Kirk, and Richard Engelken (then on the staff of Kliegl Bros. Lighting) designed an ellipsoidal reflector unit for general illumination of the auditorium in the RKO Roxy Theatre (1932; later the Center Theatre). This concentrated beam downlight was forerunner to the ellipsoidal-reflector spotlights, demonstrated by the Kliegl firm in the spring of 1933.

McCandless, trained as an architect, introduced the first academic stage lighting coursework in the U.S. at Yale University in 1926; his first "syllabus" was published in 1927, and a definitive work, still popular, *A Method of Lighting the Stage,* was published in 1932. McCandless students in turn became prominent teachers of stage lighting. Theodore Fuchs, an "illuminating engineer," whose book *Stage Lighting* was published in 1929, undertook teaching stage lighting at Northwestern University in the early 1930s. Two McCandless students, **Jean Rosenthal** and **Peggy Clark** were the first to be titled "lighting designers" in the Broadway theatre, along with **Abe Feder,** who was trained at Carnegie Institute of Technology.

By the mid-1930s stage lighting instrumentation now still in use was in place. Skilled specialists, "lighting designers," were being increasingly used to perform work that had been largely performed by stage electricians. The most predominant dimmer in the 1930s was still the resistance plate, largely unchanged in spite of slow improvement over 30 years. The number of stage circuits and instruments continued to escalate, however, rising to 300–400 for the average Broadway production by 1950. The Broadway theatre had traditionally used all portable equipment, bringing in lighting instruments, electric cables, and "road board" dimmer controls anew for each production. A number of non-Broadway theatres and auditoriums, however, were built with permanent equipment. During 1920–30 over two dozen installations were made of reactance dimmers, including the Public Auditorium in Cleveland, the Convention Hall in Atlantic City, the Civic Opera House in Chicago, and the **Earl Carroll** and RKO Roxy Theatres in New York. The resistance dimmer rows banked offstage became the "pilot" controls for the reactance dimmers, which controlled the heavy lighting loads. Not much seemed to have changed; but the next step was not long in coming.

Beginning with Severance Hall in Cleveland (1931) and **Radio City Music Hall** (1932), the Westinghouse Electric Company and the General Electric Company competed with established manufacturers of dimming controls, such as Ward–Leonard and Cutler–Hammer, in developing "remote-control" consoles with miniature "potentiometers" to control remote banks of thyratron tubes, which in turn regulated the reactance dimmers. "Presets" – that is, systems in which a row of potentiometers could be set in advance while an additional row was in actual use – could now be developed. Three-scene preset controls were installed in Radio City Music Hall and the Metropolitan Opera House (1933). The Severance Hall console, designed by McCandless and built by Westinghouse, had a particularly sympathetic layout: By grouping controls it could accommodate eight presets of lighting.

George C. Izenour, who began in 1939 to develop a theatre lighting control system at Yale, resumed work postwar and in April of 1947 demonstrated a system employing pilot controllers to modulate the output of a pair of back-to-back vacuum tubes, which in turn controlled a pair of back-to-back thyratron tubes. Izenour's design of the main lighting console and an associated preset panel with 10 full presets provided control by only one or, at most, two electricians. Because of its relatively small size it could be placed in the auditorium, where the stage could be seen clearly. The Izenour system, in commercial production by 1951, was eventually installed in hundreds of theatres, along with similar controls developed by others.

In 1959–60 the silicon-controlled rectifier was introduced, soon replacing the thyratron tube as the power element in the control system. This made possible the first major downgrading in size of the dimmer bank, and, since designs could now be made modular, more dimmers would fit into the same allotted space. The mid-1960s witnessed the first electronic computers; developments in stage lighting utilized each new computer device and data storage system as it was introduced. Punch cards, staple cards, magnetic storage drums, and ferrite core memories were employed first – more frequently as learning devices for manufacturers than as reliable lighting tools in the theatre. By the early 1970s systems became more reliable. A major breakthrough was accomplished when *A Chorus Line* (1975) used the first lighting "memory" system on Broadway. Large numbers of dimmers and controls through memory computers and miniature consoles was complete by the early 1980s. Lights on the Broadway stage leaped from 300–400 in 1950 to frequently well over 1,000 as the U.S. entered the 1990s.

Like their counterparts in television, concert music spectaculars, and **nightclubs,** theatrical lighting designers now literally paint with light. Exacting intensity control over an almost unlimited number of lighting units is possible. Increasingly, technologies are being brought to the movement and composition of the light beam itself. Moving lights, long postulated for the theatre and now made economically feasible by the spectacular concert stage, in turn find use in the theatre. Color scrollers (reminiscent of Belasco's moving silk color rolls for *Madame Butterfly* in 1900) also find important use. All of these devices and instruments, along with the more traditional "effect machines," may be controlled from the same miniature lighting console, operated by a single master electrician. Composition, direction, movement, color, and intensity of light are now precisely controlled to bring mood and atmosphere to the theatrical scene, to reveal or obscure, to highlight or unify the actor and the stage environment, to produce effects of sheer spectacle, or to offer what appears to be verisimilitude with the effects of nature. Stage lighting has increasingly through this century become the arbiter of the total stage picture as it is revealed in any given moment of the theatrical production to the audience.   JER

See: G. M. Bergman, *Lighting in the Theatre,* Totowa, NJ, 1977; L. Hartmann, *Theatre Lighting: A Manual of the Stage Switchboard,* New York, 1930; S. R. McCandless & J. E. Rubin, in *Illuminating Engineering: Significant Developments for the Past Fifty Years,* New York, 1956; B. Owen, *Lighting Design on Broadway,* Westport, CT, 1991; R. Pilbrow, *Stage Lighting,* London, 1979; T. Rees, *Theatre Lighting in the Age of Gas,* London, 1978; H. D. Sellman & M. Lessley, *Essentials of Stage Lighting,* Englewood Cliffs, NJ, 1982; L. Watson, *Lighting Design Handbook,* New York, 1990.

Stair and Havlin Theatrical Management Syndicate

John H. Havlin (1847?–1924) was business manager for **Barney Macauley** and built his own theatre and hotel in Cincinnati (1883). Financing the first Hagenbeck Circus, he later built several theatres in St. Louis. In 1900 he formed a partnership with Edward D. Stair (1859–1951), who owned the *Detroit Free Press* and had acquired

Michigan theatres that could not pay their advertising bills in the depression of 1893. Until the dissolution of the firm (1915), Stair and Havlin controlled more than 150 theatres and monopolized the production and booking of popular-priced melodrama.   DMcD

Stallings, Laurence Tucker (1894–1968) Playwright, journalist, and screenwriter. After losing a leg in WW I, Stallings collaborated with **Maxwell Anderson** to write *What Price Glory* (1924), the first realistic treatment of war in the American drama. Two other collaborations with Anderson failed, and Stallings turned to screenwriting and journalism.   TLM

Stanley, Kim (née Patricia Kimberly Reid) (1925–) Actress who studied at the **Pasadena Playhouse** (1945–6), performed with stock companies in Louisville and New Jersey, and made her Broadway debut in 1949 as **Julie Harris**'s replacement in *Montserrat*. Further training at The **Actors Studio** (under **Strasberg** and **Kazan**) influenced her psychoanalytic approach to characterization. Her career peaked in the 1950s with such award-winning performances as Millie in *Picnic* (1953) and Cherie in *Bus Stop* (1955), and with her acclaimed London debut performance as Maggie in *Cat on a Hot Tin Roof* (1958). In the 1960s she turned to teaching, with occasional stints in film and television.   FHL

Stapleton, Jean (1923–) New York–born and Hunter College–educated actress-singer who began her career with the Robert Shaw Chorale and graduated to stock in 1941. She made it to Broadway in the mid-1950s, appearing in such musicals as *Damn Yankees* and *Bells Are Ringing.* Identified inevitably with Edith Bunker on the 1970s TV series "All in the Family," Stapleton continues her stage career, most frequently in **summer stock** and national tours (for example, as Princess Puffer in *Drood!* in 1988).   DBW

Stapleton, Maureen (1925–) Actress who made her New York debut as Sara Tansey in *Playboy of the Western World* (1946). Among her outstanding roles has been Serafina in **Williams**'s *The Rose Tattoo* (1951, Tony as best supporting actress), Flora in *27 Wagons Full of Cotton* (1955), Lady Torrance in *Orpheus Descending* (1957), and Carrie in *Toys in the Attic* (1960). For Eva, the alcoholic performer in **Neil Simon**'s *The Gingerbread Lady* (1970), she won the Tony as best actress with a performance described as "remorselessly honest." Stapleton has appeared in a number of feature films and many television programs. As Carrie, critics described Stapleton as "comic, discerning, awkward and pathetic" and "splendid . . . gabby, open-hearted." In 1981 she appeared as Birdie in a major revival of *The Little Foxes* with Elizabeth Taylor. In 1969 the actress received a National Institute of Arts and Letters Award.   SMA

Starr (né Grant), Frances (1886–1973) Actress who made her debut in her hometown **stock company** (Albany, NY, 1901), and for the next four years worked in similar companies in San Francisco, Boston, and NYC. **Belasco** hired her as a replacement for the ingenue during the run of *The Music Master,* and then starred her as Juanita in *The Rose of the Rancho* (1906) and as Laura Murdock in *The Easiest Way* by **Eugene Walter** (1909). In the latter role she personified the dilemma of the modern woman, morally liberated but economically enslaved. She continued to act until 1940.   DMcD

Star Theatre Corner Broadway and 13th Street, NYC. As **Wallack's,** the theatre became New York's most celebrated playhouse. Opening in 1861 under the management of **James W. Wallack** and later his son Lester, it was the home of "genteel comedy" gracefully presented by a seasoned company in a comfortable, well-appointed house. When Lester joined the uptown movement in 1881, new managements changed its name to the Star and produced German-language drama and opera followed by a return to English drama. Eventually, it was leased as a "combination" house before being demolished in 1901.   MCH

State of the Union Pulitzer Prize–winning (1946) satire by **Howard Lindsay** and **Russel Crouse;** played 765 performances following its 14 November 1945 Hudson Theatre opening. This three-act play was the ninth in their 12-year collaboration and their eighth success, following *Life with Father.* A gibe at politics in general, the comedy recounted fictitious Republican efforts to run a successful presidential candidate, however dishonestly. Using the unexpectedly honest candidate Grant Matthews's disapproval, the playwrights targeted the manipulation of group interests, tempering their caricature with domestic comedy. To maintain timeliness, the authors supplied the touring company with current headlines for use during performances. The role of Matthews's wife, written for **Helen Hayes,** marked Ruth Hussey's Broadway debut after Hayes, **Katharine Hepburn,** and Margaret Sullavan declined the part.   RW

Stavis, Barrie (1906–) Playwright. Though infrequently produced in the U.S., Stavis's plays are mainstays in Europe (produced in over 20 languages), where his voice seems prototypically American. Concerned with people who take action against manifest evils, his major works form a tetralogy: *Lamp at Midnight* (1947), Galileo and truth; *The Man Who Never Died* (1954), Joe Hill and human dignity; *Coat of Many Colors* (1966), Joseph of Egypt and power; and *Harper's Ferry* (1967), John Brown and freedom. He is currently writing another tetralogy on war, revolution, and peace.   DBW

See: *Cardozo Studies in Law and Literature,* vol. II (1990); *Studies in American Drama, 1945–Present,* vol. 6 (1991).

Stein, Daniel (1952–) Corporeal **mime,** teacher, and director. Stein's early studies with Jewel Walker at Carnegie Mellon University were followed by apprenticeship with Etienne Decroux in Paris. He has performed creations *Timepiece* (1978), *Scenes Apparant* (1981), *Inclined to Agree* (1984), and *Windowspeak* (1990) at international festivals, as well as roles in traditional plays written and directed by others. In 1991 he created *Going Forward Backward* with the **Milwaukee Repertory Theatre.** A recipient of grants from the National Endowment for the Arts and the Guggenheim Foundation, Stein makes his home in Paris. TL

Stein, Douglas (1948–) Set designer who has worked frequently with director **JoAnne Akalaitis.** Several of his early productions were done at the **American Repertory Theatre,** including a controversial production of Beckett's *Endgame* set in a New York City subway station. Other designs include the Akalaitis-directed *Through the Leaves,* for which he won an Obie, *Falsettoland,* and the **Lincoln Center** revival of *Our Town.* AA

Stein, Gertrude (1874–1946) Playwright, poet, and American icon, Stein wrote over 75 plays published in three collections: *Geography and Plays* (1922), *Operas and Plays* (1932), and *Last Operas and Plays* (1949). Most were never produced because of the obscurity of the writing, which represented in words the surrealistic techniques of modern art. *Yes Is for a Very Young Man* (1944), *The Mother of Us All* (1945), and *Four Saints in Three Acts* (1934), the last two with music by Virgil Thomson, are sometimes produced. FB

> See: G. Stein, *Autobiography of Alice B. Toklas,* New York, 1933, and *Everybody's Autobiography,* New York, 1937.

Steinbeck, John (Ernest) (1902–68) Nobel Prize–winning (1962) novelist who wrote 24 works of fiction but only three plays, each adapted from a novel. The first, *Of Mice and Men* (1937), a tragic fable of the strong and the weak, was dramatized with **George S. Kaufman** (a musical version was produced in 1958). *The Moon Is Down* (1942), an anti-Nazi play, followed, and *Burning Bright* was adapted in 1950. Others have also adapted Steinbeck's works to the stage: *Tortilla Flat,* about California Mexican-American peasants, was dramatized by Jack Kirkland in 1938; in 1955 **Oscar Hammerstein II** adapted Steinbeck's novel about Cannery Row, *Sweet Thursday* (1954), into the musical *Pipe Dream* (music by **Richard Rodgers**); and in 1988 *The Grapes of Wrath* was adapted by **Frank Galati** for the **Steppenwolf Theatre,** whose production, after a season in London, moved to Broadway and won the 1990 Tony for best play. DBW

Steppenwolf Theatre Company is the most celebrated group to emerge during **Chicago's** period of theatrical growth in the 1970s and '80s. Begun in 1976 in the basement of a suburban parochial school, Steppenwolf rapidly became the foremost exemplar of a highly physical, naturalistic approach to acting often referred to as the "Chicago Style." By subordinating repertory to the needs of the actors, this company of recent college graduates (predominantly from Illinois State) developed both a strong sense of ensemble and a number of powerful individual actors, many of whom found success beyond the company, including **John Malkovich,** Terry Kinney, Laurie Metcalf, Gary Sinise, Joan Allen, Glenne Headly, and John Mahoney. Since the mid-1980s, Steppenwolf has regularly toured successful productions to Broadway and other venues. Notable productions include *True West, Balm in Gilead, And a Nightingale Sang, Orphans, Coyote Ugly, Burn This,* and company member **Frank Galati**'s adaptation of *The Grapes of Wrath.* In 1991 it moved into its fourth home, a newly built $8 million facility including 500- and 100-seat houses.

The history of Chicago theatre is dotted with the corpses of companies that tried to increase revenue by moving into larger venues. As Steppenwolf settled into its new home, it faced both a national recession and the continual struggle of maintaining a cohesive ensemble combining new members with those who have increased commitments to other theatres and media. If past success is any indication, however, Steppenwolf's future looks bright. Among Steppenwolf's many awards are four Tonys, including the 1985 award for regional theatre excellence. SF

Sternhagen, Frances (Hussey) (1930–) Actress. After a Vassar education (BA, 1951) and a year of advanced study at Catholic University, she studied acting with **Sanford Meisner** and made her professional debut in 1948 as Laura in *The Glass Menagerie* and Mrs. Manningham in *Angel Street* at Bryn Mawr Summer Theatre. Her New York debut was at the Cherry Lane Theatre (1955). Obie Awards followed for performances as Lydia Carew in *The Admirable Bashville* (1956), Margary Pinchwife in *The Country Wife,* and roles in *The New Pinter Plays* (1965). For her several roles in **Neil Simon**'s *The Good Doctor,* she received a Tony Award. Three other Tony nominations have complemented frequent critical recognition of her work, especially in *Equus* and Thompson's *On Golden Pond.* An actor's actor, she was called by **Clive Barnes** one of "the great players of Broadway." FHL

Stetson, John (1836–96) Financially successful and innovative manager-impresario who managed theatres in **Boston** and New York. In 1871 at Boston's **Howard Athenaeum** he presented **Harrigan and Hart** for the first time, and in 1881 conceived the novel notion of presenting the Italian star Tommaso Salvini in bilingual performances. He also managed tours for **Lillie Langtry, Helena Modjeska,** and **James O'Neill,** and presented some of the early imported productions of **Gilbert and Sullivan.** A Massachusetts native, he began his career as a paid athlete and then publisher of a Boston periodical. DBW

Stevedore Left-wing melodrama by Paul Peters and George Sklar produced by the **Theatre Guild** at the **Civic Repertory Theatre** for 174 performances in 1934. This highly effective production (it left **Joseph Wood Krutch** ready "to crack someone over the head") presented the story of a black dock worker (played by Jack Carter) who succeeds in uniting the black community of New

Orleans with sympathetic white union members who rally to fight off a lynch mob. *Stevedore* was the first commercial production in America to feature an integrated cast, in which black and white members were treated on equal terms, and to be played before an integrated audience. The play was also successfully staged by the "Negro Unit" of the **Federal Theatre Project** of Seattle in 1936–7.   MF

Stevens, Ashton (1872–1951) Chicago drama critic. A former banjo teacher who parlayed a chance meeting on a ferry with William Randolph Hearst into a long career on various Hearst papers, Stevens became known as the dean of American theatre critics. Although his reviews were usually quite sunny, the tact of his negative notices earned him a reputation as "the mercy killer."   SF

Stevens, Emily (1882–1928) Actress whose stage debut was with her cousin **Minnie Maddern Fiske** in *Becky Sharp* (1900). After her vampire role in *The Unchastened Woman* (1915), she built a career playing charming, predatory, and sexually restless women. After two years in films, she returned to Broadway in *The Madonna of the Future* (1918), the **Theatre Guild**'s *Fata Morgana* (1924), and the Actors' Theatre *Hedda Gabler* (1926), and replaced **Lynn Fontanne** in *The Second Man* (1927) before dying from a drug overdose.   RAS

Stevens, Roger Lacey (1910–   ) Detroit-born producer who, since producing *Twelfth Night* on Broadway in 1949, has worked steadily with great distinction in the American theatre and has been associated with many of the leading theatrical groups of the U.S.: the Producers Theatre, Phoenix Theatre, **American National Theatre and Academy**, Metropolitan Opera Company, **Actors Studio Theatre, American Shakespeare Festival** and Academy, New Dramatists Committee, and **John F. Kennedy Center for the Performing Arts.** Stevens chaired the National Council on the Arts during 1964–9.

While Stevens was a member of the **Playwrights' Company** (1951–60), that organization produced or coproduced 38 Broadway plays, including *The Fourposter* (1951), *Tea and Sympathy* (1953), *Ondine* and *The Bad Seed* (1954), and *Cat on a Hot Tin Roof* (1955).

As head of the Kennedy Center, Stevens produced over 30 productions that went on to other theatres. In 1957 he received the Sam H. **Shubert** Foundation Award for the outstanding producer on Broadway; in 1971 was given a special **Antoinette Perry** (Tony) Award; and in 1988 received the Kennedy Center Honor and the President's Medal of Freedom. His productions have won numerous New York Drama Critics', Tony, and Outer Critics' Circle awards. In 1988 he retired from the Kennedy Center to pursue his dream of a national theatre, undeterred by the failure of a similar effort in 1984, and to serve as president of ANTA.   SMA

Stewart, Ellen (1920?–   ) Director, manager, and one of the most influential producers in the annals of the contemporary theatre; founder of **La MaMa** ETC (Experimental Theatre Club), she is **Off-Broadway**'s first lady. Stewart, noncommittal about her early life, came to New York from her native Louisiana in the early 1950s, worked as an elevator operator, and then became a fashion designer, opening in 1961 a combination boutique-theatre in a tenement basement on NYC's East 9th Street. By 1968 La MaMa, as it became, settled in its fourth and permanent home on East 4th Street. Stewart, inspirational leader of La MaMa and a nurturer of a generation of young theatre talent numbering in the hundreds, has always focused on new plays, for which she was awarded the **Margo Jones** Award in 1979. An abiding interest in "internationalism" has driven Stewart to take La MaMa to over 20 countries, exerting considerable influence abroad, and to encourage affiliated groups in a dozen major cities in other countries. She has also brought the very best European and Third World theatre to American audiences at affordable prices and in intimate venues. In 1985 she received a MacArthur "genius" fellowship.   DBW

Stewart, Michael (1929–87) Librettist who received an MA from Yale in 1953, then wrote sketches for **Off-Broadway revue**s and television. He had his first Broadway success with the book for *Bye Bye Birdie* (1960), for which he won a Tony Award. Notable among his other librettos were *Carnival* (1961), **Hello, Dolly!** (1964), *George M!* (1968), *Seesaw* (1973), *I Love My Wife* (1977), *Barnum* (1980), and *42nd Street* (1980). Stewart proved equally adept at writing original scripts and adapting plays and films to the musical stage.   MK

Sticks and Bones Second play in **David Rabe**'s Vietnam Trilogy. Premiered at Villanova University in 1969 (as *Bones*), the play opened at New York's **Public Theater** November 1971, and in March 1972 moved to the **John Golden Theater** (Rabe's first Broadway production; Tony for best play, 1971–2). The same month CBS canceled a televised version for fear of offending returning Vietnam vets; after lengthy wrangling, the teleplay was aired in August. A pirated version of *Sticks,* denounced by Rabe, was staged in Moscow in 1972 under the title *Brat Bratu* (*As Brother Is to Brother*). A satire of the complacent American family (the Nelsons: Ozzie, Harriet, Ricky) and their crass materialism, *Sticks* dramatizes the homecoming of blind son David, whose lyrical outrage contrasts with the Nelsons' cliched and bigoted thinking. Ironically, he sees moral evils they do not.   PCK

Still Life by **Emily Mann** premiered at the **Goodman** Studio Theatre (1980) and opened in New York at the **American Place Theatre** (1981), directed by the author. Despite critical attacks on the play's politics and form, it garnered Obies for playwriting, directing, production, and all three performers. This documentary drama drawn from interviews with three people in Minnesota – a Vietnam veteran who learned to love killing, his battered, pregnant wife, and his mistress – explores the domestic and international legacy of violence from Vietnam. As the three characters speak directly to the audience and show slides of war and family life, the widespread emotional trauma of Vietnam becomes painfully clear. The play transcends the topic of Vietnam by exploring chains of violence in human relations. It has been produced at many regional theatres and internationally, winning the Fringe First Award at the Edinburgh Theatre Festival.   TH-S

Stock companies 19th-century play production in England and America was typified by the independent stock company of a permanent troupe of actors headed by an actor-manager and performing a number of different works in repertory rotation, either in a permanent house or on tour. Actors were cast according to type or "line," which usually resulted in "stock" characterizations, and productions were mounted from the company's meager collection or "stock" of scenery and props (actors furnished costumes).

Economically undermined by the advent of expensive, visiting **international stars** (mainly from England), American stock companies were further diminished by the 1880s when rail travel facilitated the growth of "combination companies," which traveled complete with star, full cast, scenery, and costumes. By century's end most professional theatre production was centralized in New York City and most of the nation's theatres were controlled by the Theatrical **Syndicate,** an infamous booking outfit. During the first decade of this century, the **Shubert brothers** gained control of legitimate theatre activity, while **Keith–Albee** monopolized vaudeville production and booking. Although a few stock companies persisted into the new century, they mostly employed decidedly young and second-rate actors and produced plays with recently completed engagements at first-class theatres. It was during this period that "stock theatre" assumed an inferior connotation (reinforced later by the term "strawhat theatre" to refer to **summer stock**).   SL

See: S. Langley, *Theatre and Management & Production in America,* rev. ed., New York, 1990.

Stoddart, James Henry (1827–1907) English-born actor; U.S. debut, **Wallack's Theatre** (1854) in the small role of Mr. Sowerberry in the farce *A Phenomenon in a Smock Frock.* During his long career, he was associated with most major New York companies, including those managed by **Lester Wallack, Laura Keene, A. M. Palmer,** and **Charles Frohman.** Although a versatile actor, he was chiefly known for masterly portrayals of eccentric old men, such as Moneypenny (**Boucicault**'s *The Long Strike*), Pierre Michel (**Daly's** *Rose Michel*), Jacob Fletcher (H. A. Jones's *Saints and Sinners*), and the old trainer in *The Sporting Duchess.* His autobiography, *Recollections of a Player* (1902), is an important theatrical resource.   DJW

Stone, Fred see **Montgomery, Dave**

Stone, John Augustus (1800–34) Playwright and actor whose *Metamora; or, the Last of Wampanoags* (1829) was the winner over 13 other entries in **Edwin Forrest**'s first playwriting contest (judged by W. C. Bryant, William Leggett, Prosper Wetmore, et al.). The play became Forrest's property and his "war-horse" piece with over 200 performances. The Stone–Forrest Indian chief epitomized the natural goodness of the "noble savage" [see **Native Americans portrayed**]. Stone's acting debut was as Old Norval in **Douglas** (1820), and through most of his career he played eccentric comics or "rough and bluff" old men. He wrote nine other unsuccessful plays, among them *The Demoniac* (1831), *The Ancient Briton* (1833), and *The Knight of the Golden Fleece* (1834).   RM

Stone, Peter (1930–) Los Angeles–born librettist, a Yale MA (1953), whose first Broadway libretto was for *Kean* (1961), a musical adaptation of a Jean-Paul Sartre play. He wrote the scripts for numerous Hollywood films and television shows and continued his libretto writing with *Skyscraper* (1965), an adaptation of **Elmer Rice**'s play *Dream Girl.* Stone's most successful libretto was for *1776* (1969), an original musical about the signing of the Declaration of Independence. Subsequent shows included *Two by Two* (1970), *Sugar* (1972), *Woman of the Year* (1981), *My One and Only* (1983), and *The Will Rogers Follies* (1991). Aside from *1776*, most of Stone's librettos were skillful adaptations of already successful plays and films.   MK

Straiges, Tony (1942–) Set and costume designer best known for his sets for *Sunday in the Park with George* (1984), for which he won a Tony, and for *Into the Woods* (1987). Straiges has designed extensively at the **Arena Stage, Yale Repertory,** and several other regional theatres, as well as for **Off-Broadway** companies. His sets often have a sparse elegance or sense of fantasy about them.   AA

Strange Interlude Eugene O'Neill's most successful production in his lifetime opened for the **Theatre Guild** on 30 January 1928 at the **John Golden Theatre** and subsequently won O'Neill his third Pulitzer Prize. Under **Philip Moeller**'s direction, this nine-act experiment with interior monologue (extended asides) commenced at 5:15 P.M. and took some four and a half hours to perform, interrupted by a dinner break. Although the story of the play is not unusual in its tale of desire, adultery, and power, the production was intriguing as it revealed fully not only the characters' speech but also their thoughts. The audience was able to eavesdrop on the subtext and articulated motivation as the physical action of all but the speaker was arrested for each interior monologue; the subtext proved much more telling than the dialogue. Albeit set realistically by **Jo Mielziner,** the play seemed mysterious, even eerily otherworldly as Nina Leeds (played by **Lynn Fontanne**) cast her erotic, spiritual, and sometimes evil spell over her three men, and ultimately over the audience as well.   RHW

Strasberg, Lee (1901–82) Director and acting teacher who studied at the **American Laboratory**

Theatre, acted with the **Theatre Guild,** and in 1931 helped found and directed for the **Group Theatre,** espousing the work of the Russian director, Konstantin Stanislavsky. Among his directorial successes were *The House of Connelly, Night Over Taos, Men in White,* and *Clash by Night.*

In 1950 Strasberg became a director for the **Actors Studio** and emerged as the leading exponent of the Method, based on the Stanislavsky System. In 1965 he directed a highly controversial *The Three Sisters,* which played at the Aldwych Theatre in London during the World Theatre Season. A great many of America's leading film and stage actors studied with Strasberg, either privately or at the Studio, among them **Marlon Brando,** whose internal style as Stanley in *A Streetcar Named Desire* became popularly associated with Method acting. Among Strasberg's more famous students were Montgomery Clift, **Ann Bancroft,** Shelley Winters, Paul Newman, and Joanne Woodward.

Although his methods and results excited great controversy, little doubt remains that Strasberg had a major effect on modern acting. His thoughts on the "Method" (*A Dream of Passion*) were published posthumously in 1987. SMA

See: C. Adams, *Lee Strasberg: The Imperfect Genius of the Actors Studio,* New York, 1980; D. Garfield, *The Actors Studio,* New York, 1980; R. Hethmon, *Strasberg at the Actors Studio,* New York, 1965.

Strawhat theatre see summer stock

Streamers The last play in **David Rabe**'s Vietnam Trilogy premiered in January 1976 in New Haven; in April it moved to **Lincoln Center** and ran for 400 performances. Directed by **Mike Nichols,** it starred Kenneth McMillan as Sgt. Rooney, Dolph Sweet as Sgt. Cokes, and Dorian Harewood as the menacing Carlyle. Robert Altman directed the film version (1983). *Streamers* is about sexual and psychic violence (with an onstage rape and stabbing) in a stateside barracks, where five young soldiers on their way to Vietnam confront the two old sergeants. The title refers to a parachute that fails to open, symbolizing the madness and treachery of Rabe's domestic America. PCK

Streep, Meryl (1949–) Film and stage actress, trained at the Yale School of Drama, who made her New York debut as Imogen in *Trelawny of the Wells* (1975). For the Phoenix she next played Flora in *27 Wagons Full of Cotton* and Patricia in *A Memory of Two Mondays* in 1976, also appearing in *Secret Service.* Over the next two years she played Katharine in *Henry V,* Isabella in *Measure for Measure,* Dunyasha in *The Cherry Orchard,* Lillian in *Happy End* (Broadway), and Katharina in *The Taming of the Shrew.* Streep soon after began a brilliant film career, during which she has won two Academy Awards. Equally at ease in drama or farce, Streep is noted for meticulous preparation, a wide-ranging intellect, and intense truthfulness in her acting. Since the 1980s she has concentrated on her film career. SMA

Streetcar Named Desire, A Tennessee Williams's masterpiece opened on Broadway 3 De-

Marlon Brando and Jessica Tandy in *A Streetcar Named Desire* (1947). Courtesy: Theatre Collection, Museum of the City of New York.

cember 1947 and ran for 855 performances, winning every major honor, including the Pulitzer Prize, the Donaldson, and the New York Drama Critics' awards. Directed by **Elia Kazan** and produced by Irene Selznick, *Streetcar* starred **Jessica Tandy** (Blanche), **Marlon Brando** (Stanley), **Kim Hunter** (Stella), and Karl Malden (Mitch). **Uta Hagen** replaced Tandy and Anthony Quinn, Brando, at the end of the run. A whirlwind of European premieres followed in 1948–9, including Rome (sets by Franco Zefferelli), Manchester (Olivier directing Vivien Leigh), and Paris (Jean Cocteau's adaptation with Arletty). Other national premieres include Tokyo (1953), Torun and Wroclaw, Poland (1957), and Tianjin in 1988. The first of many revivals began in 1956 with **Tallulah Bankhead.** On the play's 25th anniversary, *Streetcar* was done in Los Angeles (Faye Dunaway and Jon Voigt) and in New York (**Rosemary Harris** and James Farentino). A 1974 British revival starred Claire Bloom. Jack Gelber directed the play in 1976 (with **Geraldine Page** and **Rip Torn**); **Blythe Danner** and Aidan Quinn starred in 1988; and a revival directed by **Gregory Mosher** (with Jessica Lange and Alec Baldwin) opened in April 1992.

Kazan's acclaimed film version in 1951 featured the original Broadway cast except for Leigh replacing Tandy. In 1952 Valerie Bettis choreographed a ballet *Streetcar* (revitalized by the Harlem Dance Theatre in 1982). In 1984 John Erman directed a graphically sexual television adaptation (Ann-Margret and Treat Williams).

Set in New Orleans, *Streetcar* chronicles Blanche DuBois's search for protection and her eventual destruction at the hands of her brutish brother-in-law Stanley Kowalski. It is filled with competing mythologies and representations, including two recurring character types – the faded Southern belle, both madonna and sensualist, and the seed-bearing male. Blanche's "tender feelings" compete with Stanley's "brutal desire" as these two struggle for control of Stella and Mitch. Written in Williams's lyrically Southern idiom, *Streetcar* has made indelible contributions to our national mythology. PCK

Street Scene Largely realistic 1929 three-act drama by **Elmer Rice** depicting the life of some 50 lower-middle-class characters living in a New York brownstone tenement, trapped in a seemingly hopeless environment. Its purpose, writes C. W. E. Bigsby, is "to recreate the social texture of the world of the tenement and partly to suggest the degree to which that variousness was homogenised by context." With two plot lines, one melodramatic and one romantic comedy, Rice illustrates various strains of life intermingled with commonplace incidents, though both the melodrama and romantic intensity are effectively deflated at the end of Acts I and II.

Although a Pulitzer Prize winner, the play had trouble finding a producer, Rice eventually directing it himself with a setting by **Jo Mielziner**. It opened 10 January and ran 601 performances, garnering considerable critical success. Adapted into an opera in 1947 with music by **Kurt Weill** and lyrics by **Langston Hughes,** this musical version was revived successfully by New York City Opera in 1959, 1979, and 1990. Since the mid-1930s, Rice's play has often been compared to **Sidney Kingsley**'s *Dead End.* DBW

Striptease see **burlesque**

Strike Up the Band Slight musical comedy in three acts written by some of the most influential music and theatre people of the early 20th century: **Morrie Ryskind** and **George S. Kaufman** (book), and **George and Ira Gershwin** (music and lyrics, respectively). Originally produced in 1927, it was recalled for rewrites after tryout performances and opened on Broadway at the Times Square Theatre, 14 January 1930, to run 191 performances. The play satirizes war in a story about a rich chocolate maker who instigates war on Switzerland in order to corner the sweet chocolate market. The production featured two popular comedians, **Bobby Clark and Paul McCullough,** and the tunes "Strike Up the Band" and "I've Got a Crush on You." KN

Stritch, Elaine (1925–) Actress and singer who studied at the Drama Workshop at the New School for Social Research before making her Broadway debut in *Loco* (1946). She stopped the show with her rendition of "Zip" in the revival of *Pal Joey* (1952), appeared in the revival of *On Your Toes* (1954), and played Grace in *Bus Stop* (1955). She starred in the musicals *Goldilocks* (1958) and *Sail Away* (1961), and played Martha in matinees of *Who's Afraid of Virginia Woolf?* (1963). Her gravelly voice and acid delivery perfectly suited

the role of Joanne in **Stephen Sondheim**'s musical *Company* (1970). MK

Strouse, Charles (1928–) Composer. After studying at the Eastman School of Music, Strouse worked as a rehearsal pianist. He wrote songs for *The Littlest Revue* (1956), then teamed in 1960 with lyricist Lee Adams on *Bye Bye Birdie,* a show that poked fun at rock singing idols. With Adams he wrote *All American* (1962), the musical version of *Golden Boy* (1964), *It's a Bird, It's a Plane, It's Superman* (1966), and *Applause* (1970). With lyricist **Martin Charnin** he wrote the songs for the long-run hit **Annie** (1977). His later musicals, such as *Bring Back Birdie* (1981), *Dance a Little Closer* (1983), and *Rags* (1986) were failures. Strouse's bubbly, vibrant music complemented the contemporary settings of his shows. MK

Student Prince, The Four-act operetta, music by **Sigmund Romberg,** words by Dorothy Donnelly; opened 2 December 1924 at the **Jolson** Theatre, New York, running 608 performances. Originally produced as *The Student Prince in Heidelberg* and given a sumptuous production by the **Shubert**s, this was the longest-running musical of the 1920s and is considered by many the masterpiece of American operetta. The story tells of Karl Franz (Howard Marsh), crown prince of Karlsberg, who as a student in Heidelberg falls deeply in love with Kathie (Ilse Marvenga), a waitress at the local tavern. Their dreams are shattered when he is called home to become king, and when he returns to Heidelberg, he finds that the "golden days" of youth cannot be recaptured. Romberg's score, filled with marches and drinking songs as well as such indelible melodies as the "Serenade," is lushly romantic and dramatically served by his skillful use of leitmotifs; a particularly effective device is having each act end with the same song ("Deep in My Heart"), the effect of which alters from romantic hope to heartbreak. Challenging even to highly trained singers, it has remained a staple of the light opera repertoire, receiving frequent major revivals throughout the world. JD

Studio Arena Theatre Not-for-profit regional (LORT) theatre, founded in 1965 by Neal Du-Brock as a professional extension of the 1927 Studio Theatre School of Buffalo, NY (a city with a rich theatrical past, and presently also home to the African-American Cultural Center/**Paul Robeson** Theater, Alleyway Theater, Buffalo Ensemble Theater, and the Theater of Youth). The Studio Arena operates a 637-seat, thrust-design main stage, has had a budget of almost $3 million, and produces seven productions during September–July. Initially, the theatre imported name actors to supplement a resident company, but in recent years it has usually hired pickup casts of local performers for an eclectic, main-stage repertory of old and modern standards plus light, commercial entertainments, and a second-stage program of riskier works. In 1991 artistic director David Frank resigned after 11 seasons due to budget cuts; he was replaced by Gavin Cameron-Webb. CLJ DBW

Styne, Jule (né Julius Kerwin Stein) (1905–) Composer and producer. Styne attended the Chicago College of Music, then organized a dance band on the West Coast in the 1930s. He wrote his first Broadway scores for *High Button Shoes* (1947) and *Gentlemen Prefer Blondes* (1949). *Two on the Aisle* (1951) marked the beginning of a partnership with librettists-lyricists **Betty Comden and Adolph Green** that included *Bells Are Ringing* (1956), *Say Darling* (1958), *Do Re Mi* (1960), *Subways Are for Sleeping* (1961), and *Hallelujah, Baby* (1967). Other notable Styne shows were *Gypsy* (1959) with lyricist **Stephen Sondheim** and *Sugar* (1972) with **Bob Merrill**. He also produced several plays and musicals, including *Mr. Wonderful* (1956) and *Will Success Spoil Rock Hunter?* (1955). Styne's music had a traditional Broadway sound but skillfully underscored the show's characters and situations.   MK

See: T. Taylor, *Jule: The Story of Composer Jule Styne,* New York, 1979.

Subject Was Roses, The Three-character drama by **Frank D. Gilroy.** Directed by **Ulu Grosbard,** it opened on 25 May 1964 for 832 performances and received the Pulitzer Prize, Drama Critics' Award, and Tony. **Jack Albertson,** Irene Dailey, and Martin Sheen were featured in this delicate and moving tale of a son, newly matured after serving in the armed forces, who returns to his estranged parents. This cast worked with great subtlety to portray the evolving relationships of this psychological exploration of an American postwar family. Dailey was replaced by Patricia Neal for the 1968 film, which was a critical, but not a popular, success. A 1991 **Roundabout Theatre** revival with John Mahoney, **Dana Ivey,** and Patrick Dempsey suggested that the play had lost much of its initial impact.   MR

Sullivan, Arthur see **Gilbert and Sullivan in America**

Sullivan, Daniel (1935–) Drama critic. Born in Worcester, MA, and educated there at Holy Cross College (1957), Sullivan served as drama and music critic of the *Minneapolis Tribune* (1962–4) and music writer (1965–6) and assistant drama critic (1966–8) for the *New York Times* before becoming drama critic of the *Los Angeles Times* from 1969 until his retirement in 1991. Erudite and analytical, Sullivan provided a context for a performance that enlarged the experience for his readers.   TLM

Summer and Smoke Lyrical play by **Tennessee Williams,** revised as *Eccentricities of a Nightingale.* Premiering in Dallas July 1947, it was directed by **Margo Jones** and starred Katherine Balfour (Alma) and Tod Andrews. The play opened at the **Music Box Theatre** October 1948 and ran for 100 performances, again directed by Jones with Andrews as John, but Margaret Phillips as Alma. **José Quintero**'s **Off-Broadway** production in 1952 starred **Geraldine Page** and **Lee Richardson.** Page recreated Alma in the 1961 film version with Laurence Harvey and **Rita Moreno** (Rosa). In 1971, *Summer* was made into an opera (music by Lee Hoiby, libretto by **Lanford Wilson**). Lee Remick starred in a BBC production (January 1972).

Set in Glorious Hill, MS, the play tells of Miss Alma's love for her childhood sweetheart Dr. John Buchanan. At first, Alma is all spirit and soul while John is a creature of the flesh and pleasure. At play's end, "the tables have turned with a vengeance." In suffering the "affliction of love," Alma has a spiritual kinship with Blanche DuBois. The play is almost perfectly balanced between the flesh and the spirit, the worldly and the sensitive that haunted Williams.   PCK

Summer stock As traditional, ongoing stock disappeared, a number of seasonal theatres, descendants of the 19th-century **stock company,** began to operate in city parks and popular resorts, where people went in the summer to cool off and relax. Elitch's Gardens Theatre in Denver (1890) and Lakewood Playhouse in Showhegan, ME (1901), were prototypical: Operation was seasonal, there was a resident company of actors, and productions were presented only for a week or two of consecutive performances, often in a converted barn or similarly rustic structure.

Notable among early summer stock theatres are the Provincetown Playhouse (1916), which produced **Eugene O'Neill**'s *Bound East for Cardiff* during its first season on Cape Cod and subsequently opened a winter theatre in New York's Greenwich Village (thereby, arguably, becoming the first **Off-Broadway** theatre company); the **Hedgerow Theatre** (1932), Moylan, PA, which upheld the repertory tradition and produced serious works; the University Players (1928) on Cape Cod, which was organized by two Princeton students, **Bretaigne Windust** and **Norris Houghton,** and provided early training for such talents as **Joshua Logan,** Mildred Natwick, James Stewart, and Margaret Sullavan; and the Westport Country Playhouse (1931), founded by **Lawrence Langner** as an informal laboratory for the **Theatre Guild.**

It appears the first "star" hired in this century to perform with a resident stock company was **Jane Cowl,** who was paid $1,000 in 1935 for a week's engagement at the Cape Playhouse in Dennis, MA. The idea caught on and soon the shaded townships of America's resort communities were brightened by seasonal visitations of such luminaries as **Billie Burke, Bea Lillie, Helen Hayes, Lillian Gish,** and the perennial **Tallulah Bankhead. Gertrude Lawrence** often appeared in productions on Cape Cod where her husband, **Richard Aldrich,** was the founding producer for Falmouth Playhouse (1949) and the Cape Cod Melody Tent (1950), along with the Cape Playhouse (1926), where Bette Davis and **Henry Fonda** gained early experience. By the mid-1950s, stars began traveling from theatre to theatre along with their supporting cast and costumes, all assembled and usually rehearsed in NYC. Thus the "package" system was born – nearly identical to the combination system of the previous century, except each theatre built its own season. As a result of packages, the number of professional (unionized) resident stock companies diminished, and producer–theatre owners essentially became presenters who booked productions that had been assembled by a "packager" in NYC. Nonetheless, producers still assumed full liability for all royalties and Equity contracts – except in the rare case of a "unit package" for which the packager assumed all such obligations in exchange for a flat fee from each theatre that booked the show.

When the Stock Managers' Association negotiated its first contract with **Actors' Equity** in the early 1930s, only about a dozen summer theatres had been under union jurisdiction; by 1950 that number had increased to about 130. To negotiate with Actors' Equity on the one hand and packagers on the other, package theatres with less than 1,000 seats that performed indoors formed the Council of Stock Theatres (COST). The vast majority of these (including the aforementioned) were located in the Northeast, although there were also a few well-known "winter stock" operations, such as the Royal Poinciana and the **Coconut Grove** Playhouses in Florida.

Larger seasonal theatres that often performed under canvas, presenting book musicals as well as variety shows featuring headliners, formed the Musical Theatre Association (MTA). The prototype was the Music Circus in Lambertville, NJ, founded by St. John Terrell in the 1940s. In 1954 John Lamar Price, Jr., founded Musicarnival, Inc., which controlled a summer theatre in Cleveland and a winter one in Palm Beach. Messrs. Guber, Cross, and Ford operated five tent theatres just south of New York; others included the North Short Music Circus in Beverly, MA, the Warwick Music Tent in Rhode Island, and Westbury Music Fair in New York.

Those theatres that continued to maintain a resident company of Equity actors (at least five principle actors and one stage manager under contract) formed the Council of Resident Stock Theatres (CORST), and included at one time the **Williamstown Theatre Festival** (MA), Hampton Playhouse (NH), and Totem Pole Playhouse (PA).

During the 1960s and '70s there was also an Association of Civic Musical Theatres to negotiate Equity agreements for such outdoor operations as the **St. Louis Municipal** Opera, Jones Beach Marine Theatre (Long Island), and the Starlight Theatre (Kansas City). Finally, there have been throughout the 20th century numerous amateur (nonunion) stock theatres operated on a commercial basis by a college, community, or private group on a nonprofit basis. A number of these groups perform annual **pageants** and historical drama, in addition to professional **outdoor drama** companies.

From the 1930s into the '70s summer stock theatres provided more workweeks and more productions than any other single branch of the professional theatre industry, while also serving as training ground for aspiring actors, craftspeople, and managers (and once considered important credits). Stock also provided tryout opportunities for many new plays, some becoming commercial hits (e.g., *Life with Father, The Fourposter, A View from the Bridge, Barefoot in the Park, Butterflies Are Free*). By the 1980s, however, as resort areas increasingly resembled urban centers and life-styles increasingly revolved around electronic arts and media outlets, professional stock almost disappeared, though amateur groups still function, if sporadically. Fortunately, **resident nonprofit professional theatre** (which owes a nod to its stock predecessors) grew proportionate to the decline of professional stock during the 1960s and '70s. More recently, summer theatre has returned to the nation's cities within the format of arts festivals, such as those held periodically in New York, Chicago, Los Angeles, and Charleston. SL

See: S. Langley, *Theatre and Management & Production in America,* rev. ed., New York, 1990.

Stephen Sondheim and James Lapine's *Sunday in the Park with George* (1984, Booth Theatre). Scenic design by Tony Straiges and costumes by Patricia Zipprodt and Ann Hould-Ward. Photo: © Martha Swope. Courtesy: Martha Swope.

Sunday in the Park with George Two-act musical play, music and lyrics by **Stephen Sondheim,** book by **James Lapine;** opened 2 May 1984 at the **Booth Theatre,** running 604 performances. This musical, originally developed at **Off-Broadway**'s **Playwrights Horizons,** deals with the nature of artistic creation and revolves around a famous Georges Seurat painting. The first act, set in the 1880s, shows Seurat (**Mandy Patinkin**) creating the painting and dealing with his model-mistress Dot (**Bernadette Peters**). The second act shows their descendants (played by the same actors) dealing with the contemporary art world. Virtually without dance, yet highly inventive visually through Lapine's staging and **Tony Straiges**'s scenery, the show won the Pulitzer Prize for drama and the Drama Critics' Circle Award for best musical.   JD

Sunshine Boys, The, opened on 20 December 1972 and ran for 538 performances at the **Broadhurst Theatre,** marking **Neil Simon**'s return to a nongendered depiction of the destructive effect of extreme behavior. Main characters Willie Clark (**Jack Albertson**) and Al Lewis (**Sam Levene**) allow Simon to present his theme outside of his customary upper-middle-class setting. The two retired **vaudeville** performers (based, in part, on **Smith and Dale**) address the relative helplessness of the elderly in society as they continue their long-standing feud over apparent trivialities. Their dialogue sharply outlines the actual basis for the conflict. The characters carry on their battle almost entirely in terms of running gags and one-liners because such choices are much a part of their lives as is their self-destructive behavior; their implicit recognition of both implies they may be able to work within that which they cannot change. The characters' advancing age underscores Simon's suggestion that a refusal to reconcile differences can only result in isolation. It was turned into a successful film with Walter Matthau and **George Burns** in 1975.   RW

Sun-up, written by **Lula Vollmer,** opened on 24 May 1923 at the Provincetown Playhouse and was immediately hailed for its portrayal of North Carolina mountain life. The Widow Cagle (Lucille La Verne) struggles against laws she cannot understand that tragically intrude on her simple mountain life. Still suffering from the death of her moonshiner husband, she resists the Great War, which takes her son away from her. The play ran for two years in New York after moving to the **Princess Theatre,** and was also performed in several foreign countries. Vollmer donated all royalties from the play for the education of the mountaineers.   FB

Support services, theatrical Developments in the American theatre in the late 19th century hastened the industrialization of production practices. Prior to the Civil War, most theatres carried their own personnel for all backstage work, which embraced building and painting scenery, making stage properties, and sewing costumes. With the expansion of theatrical activity and the building of thousands of theatres after the war, managers resorted to outside sources to obtain scenery and costumes; by the end of the century, and for the first time in history, the theatre building was erected without the customary workrooms and paint frames. When the **stock company** ceased to be a production entity, specialty houses dealing in scenery, costumes, and (later) lighting equipment sprang up to supply the needs of independent producers and managers. The expansion of the railroad from coast to coast made it possible to ship even bulky pieces great distances via railway express. New York emerged as the center of most of the support services.

Scenery In 1894, Richard Marston, one of New York's leading and busiest scene painters, decried the "scenery factories" that turned out theatrical settings imitating the work of recognized scene painters but using cheap materials and paints. Although there were indeed scenery studios that fit Marston's descriptions, many produced high-quality work to meet an ever-expanding market. In 1875, Mathias Armbruster, a young German scene painter, settled in Columbus, OH; there he set up the Armbruster Scenic Studios, which became one of the largest manufacturers of stock scenery [see **scenic design**] in the country. Like other studios, Armbruster could supply Victorian interiors, tropical exteriors, Atlantic City seascapes, Japanese gardens, and deserts in the Holy Land – at a price. By using aniline dyes, backgrounds painted on canvas could be folded or rolled; but pieces painted with distemper had to be shipped flat. In addition to specialty scenes, most studios could supply stock interiors and exteriors that would serve for a variety of scenes within most plays.

The studio that advertised itself as the world's largest came into existence in 1891. A young painter, Lee Lash, working on an olio curtain in San Francisco, conceived the idea of incorporating the names of advertisers in natural places within a street scene (rather than the customary practice of painting the names in patchwork style). His idea worked so well that he founded the Lee Lash Studios, which expanded its operations to serve the country. The studio moved to Philadelphia in 1893 and to New York in 1898, selling its scenery to the major producers in New York for the next 30 years and to smaller enterprizes throughout the country. Like other studios, it distributed a stock book with illustrations (many in color) of its scenes and curtains. All could be ordered by submitting measurements and diagrams as required.

With the demise of the stock company, the gradual devolution of vaudeville, and the road to movies and radio after WW I, most of the studios went out of business or reduced their operations to serve their immediate areas. The remaining studios were centered in New York, but no longer producing stock scenes: Each stage set was (and continues to be) customized according to specifications submitted by the designer assigned to the production. In the years immediately following the war, **Joseph Urban** established a scenic studio that introduced continental stagecraft techniques to America and later (as Triangle Scenic Studios) became the most active on Broadway. Several studios limited their function either to the building or the painting of scenery, whereas others did both. The lifespan of a studio proved to be short, and Triangle was succeeded by a number of others, the most durable of which is the Nolan Scenery Studios, which was founded at about the same time as Triangle. Although it provided both the building and painting of sets at its inception, it exists today as a painting studio. With ever greater demands imposed by producers for spectacular effects, particularly in musical theatre, small but highly specialized companies, among which is Feller Precision, have arisen to provide the technology for such effects.

Costumes Until the last half of the 19th century, one of the enduring conventions of theatre in the Western world was the costuming of actors in contemporaneous clothing, with such occasional concessions to period or exotic background or status of the character as turbans for Arabs, feather headdresses for Indians, crowns and ermine for kings, togas over kneebreeches for Greeks, and so on. Although the great patent theatres of England had accumulated extensive wardrobes from which actors could be fitted, the small provincial companies, on which the American system was patterned, depended on actors to costume themselves, which often resulted in a hodgepodge of styles and periods within one production [see **costume**].

As the 19th century wore on, however, and the costume practices of William Charles Macready and Charles Kean were introduced in America, managers were disposed to add to theatrical spectacle authentic-looking costumes for period plays. Prosperous American theatres established their own costume collections and installed resident costumers in their own workrooms; small, shoestring companies relied on costume supply houses, which began to spring up at midcentury in most cities with theatres. The earliest was Dazian's, founded in 1842 by Wolf Dazian, a Bavarian immigrant, who started with a dry-goods store in lower Manhattan, supplying such as **P. T. Barnum** with stage fabrics. He later expanded into costume making shortly after the invention of the industrial sewing machine at midcentury. Dazian's followed the uptown movement of the theatre district, coming to rest just off Times Square. In 1919, under different management, Dazian's abandoned its costume-making business, and it remains in existence today as a fabric-supply house.

Most costume houses did a thriving rental business, supplying the needs of amateur and collegiate as well as professional theatres. The founders of the Van Horn Costume Company in Philadelphia and Eaves Costume Company in New York began as actors with a talent for the needle: Albert Van Horn established his business in 1852, and Albert Eaves, in 1867; both prospered in the late 19th century. In 1902 Ely Stroock bought out Brooks Costume Company, a small uniform supply house; in 1919 he bought out producer **Charles Frohman**'s costume warehouses, adding a custom costume shop that dominated Broadway for many years. When the activity on Broadway diminished, so did the costume business, and in 1981, Eaves,

Brooks, and Van Horn merged under Eaves's administrative umbrella.

The theatre has also been served by small costume companies, the favorites of leading designers and managers. **Robert Edmond Jones** patronized Mme. Elise Freisinger's costume house. Helene Pons made the costumes for the Chauve-Souris company during the 1920s and for the **Playwrights' Company** for many years. Decreasing production on Broadway has reduced further the number of active costumers, whose existence continues to be precarious. Today, Barbara Matera Ltd., Parsons-Meares Ltd., and the Grace Costume Company supplement theatrical work with costuming for ballet and opera companies. Specialty costuming and armor by the Martin Izquierdo Studios are fabricated frequently in conjunction with regular costume companies.

As a service for regional and collegiate theatre, the Theatre Development Fund established the Costume Collection, which rents costumes (most donated by producers of Broadway shows) at nominal rates, shipping them throughout the country.

Stage lighting In the era of gaslight, which embraced most of the 19th century, the equipment necessary to light a production was installed as part of the theatre's permanent equipment [see **stage lighting**]. With the introduction of electricity into the theatre building, all that was really necessary was to have a power source to which controls and conducting cables could eventually be attached; the rest of the equipment could be brought into the theatre to serve each production. This concept coincided in time almost exactly with the industrialization of theatrical production at the close of the 19th century, and was responsible for the creation of another support service: the theatrical electrical supply house.

In 1896, two immigrant Austrians founded Kliegl Brothers, a firm that designed and manufactured special housings for incandescent lamps used in theatres throughout the country. They also developed the Kliegl light, whose name became eponymous for any intense, bright white spotlight. Other companies followed in its wake, and the principle of renting equipment to independent producers, rather than selling it outright, had become established; this proved to be both lucrative to the lighting supply companies and a godsend to the producers, who could avoid buying equipment and storing it in a warehouse. One of the most prosperous suppliers, the Century Lighting Company, founded in 1929 by Joseph Levy and Edward Kook, combined rentals and fabrication of specialized lighting instruments, the most successful of which was the Lekolite, named by assembling the first two letters of their last names; the "Leko," a compact ellipsoidal spotlight equipped with shutters and lenses to direct lighting on specific areas, has become the workhorse of stage lighting. Kliegl and Century, like many of their competitors, leased (and sold) equipment throughout the country and established branch offices outside of New York.

After WW II, other theatrical lighting supply houses arose to challenge the domination of Century and Kliegl, both of which are no longer in business. Leading the field today is Four Star Stage Lighting and, to a lesser degree, Bash Theatrical Lighting Company and Vanco Stage Lighting. Because of the ever-diminishing number of New York productions both on and **Off-Broadway** and on the road, the solvency of these suppliers depends on their serving regional theatres, industrial shows, college and university theatres, touring companies, popular music concerts, and amusement and theme parks.   MCH

Suppressed Desires Written by **Susan Glaspell** in collaboration with **George Cram Cook,** this one-act satire on fashionable psychoanalysis played an important part in the founding of the Little Theatre movement [see **community theatre**] in the U.S. After being rejected by the **Washington Square Players,** it was produced on the opening bill of the **Provincetown Players,** first in the home of two members of the group and later at their Wharf Theatre in the summer of 1915. Glaspell performed the role of Henrietta Brewster, a disciple of Freudian psychology who repudiates its benefits when her husband Stephen (performed by Cook) and sister Mabel are found to have "suppressed desires" that will destroy her marriage. The easy comic treatment of the newly converted has kept the play popular.   KF

Susan and God by **Rachel Crothers** marked the author's return to the theatre after five years of writing in Hollywood and was her last produced play. **Jo Mielziner** designed the sets for the first production, directed by Crothers, which opened at the **Plymouth Theatre** 7 October 1937 and ran for 288 performances. Susan Trexel returns from England with a newfound religious fervor and a desire to reform the lives of her upper-class friends, but finds herself cornered into making a new start with her estranged husband and awkward teenage daughter. **Gertrude Lawrence** gave a virtuoso performance of the vain yet charismatic Susan. Crothers's sharp dialogue and sensitively drawn characters allow her to explore the theatrics of fashionable conversion and its effects upon delicately balanced relationships.   KF

Swados, Elizabeth (1951–) Composer, writer, and director. After graduating from Bennington College in 1972, Swados became a composer and musical director for renowned director Peter Brook. Beginning in 1977 she was composer-in-residence for several years at **La MaMa** ETC. For the **New York Shakespeare Festival** she developed the score of *Runaways* (1978), a musical about troubled children. Among her other scores are *Nightclub Cantata* (1977), *Dispatches* (1979), and *Alice in Concert* (1980). She worked with Garry Trudeau on the musical *Doonesbury* (1983); composed the score for **Ellen Stewart**'s production of *Mythos Oedipus* (1985) and **Andrei Serban**'s *Fragments of a Greek Trilogy* (1986); developed *Job: A Circus* (1992) with a group of professional clowns and actors; and wrote, composed, and directed *The New Americans* (also 1992). She also wrote the music for *Rap Master Ronnie* (1986). Although only *Runaways* has been popular with general audiences, her compositions for **Off-Off Broadway** plays and musicals have won her consistent critical praise. In 1991 she published a moving, nontheatrical family memoir, *The Four of Us.*   MK

Sweeney Todd, the Demon Barber of Fleet Street Two-act musical play, music and lyrics by **Stephen Sondheim,** book by Hugh Wheeler; opened 1 March 1979 at the Uris Theatre, New York, running 558 performances. Based on a Victorian thriller, this tale of a demented barber (**Len Cariou**) slaughtering Londoners as he pursues the judge who ruined his life, and forming a partnership with a woman (**Angela Lansbury**) who makes meat pies from his victims, was an unlikely basis for a musical. Director **Harold Prince** turned it into a parable of the dehumanization of the Industrial Revolution, a Grand Guignol in which Dickens met Brecht, with a dissonant chorus wryly narrating the action amid an iron-foundry superstructure so heavy that it necessitated shoring up the theatre's stage. The show is almost entirely sung, and Sondheim's score frequently sets gruesome events and imagery against ironic lyricism, undercut by a dissonant accompaniment. It won Drama Critics' Circle and Tony awards for best musical, and has subsequently entered the opera repertoire.   JD

Sweet Bird of Youth **Tennessee Williams**'s play about the "enemy, time, in us all." A one-act work-in-progress version at the Studio M. Playhouse in Miami in 1956 was subsequently revised and expanded to premiere in New York in March 1959 (383 performances). **Elia Kazan** directed **Geraldine Page** (as aging Hollywood actress Alexandra Del Lago), Paul Newman (as wanderer Chance Wayne), and Sidney Blackmer (Boss Finley). The 1962 film adaptation by Richard Brooks also starred Newman and Page, but Ed Begley played Boss. A 1975 revival starred **Irene Worth** and **Christopher Walken.** A 1989 NBC television production starred Elizabeth Taylor, Mark Harmon, and **Rip Torn.** The Princess (Alexandra) and Chance futilely attempt to regain their youth amid drugs, alcohol, physical and sexual violence, and grotesqueries associated with Williams's mythological South.   PCK

Sweet Charity A two-act musical comedy conceived, directed, and choreographed by **Bob Fosse,** with book by **Neil Simon,** music by **Cy Coleman,** and lyrics by **Dorothy Fields.** Based on the screenplay *Nights of Cabiria* by Federico Fellini, Tullio Pinelli, and Ennio Flaiano, *Sweet Charity* starred **Gwen Verdon** and featured the choreography of Fosse (Tony Award) when it opened 29 January 1966, running for 608 performances. A film version starring Shirley MacLaine was released in 1968. It was revived on Broadway (27 April 1986) starring Debbie Allen. Set in New York City, *Sweet Charity* follows the romantic aspirations and desperation of a warm-hearted dance-hall hostess. Songs include "If My Friends Could See Me Now" and "Big Spender."   EK

Syndicate, Theatrical The origins of the Syndicate lay in the combination system of producing. The expansion of railroads after the Civil War made it possible to tour a production anywhere in America. This proved more profitable than the previous system of resident companies hosting visiting stars. Consequently, by 1885 nearly all the first-class **stock companies** had been replaced by combinations from New York City, and both producers and regional theatre owners had opened booking offices there to arrange these tours. In 1896 producer **Charles Frohman** joined the booking agency of **Marc Klaw** and **Abraham Erlanger** in a partnership with Alfred Hayman, who leased the most important theatres in the west, and with Fred Nixon and Fred Zimmerman, who controlled Philadelphia and the mid-Atlantic region. This arrangement was called the Theatrical Syndicate, and by 1903 it governed first-class theatrical production in America. The source of its power was its insistence upon exclusive representation: Its clients had to agree to do business only with it, taking the attractions, routes, and dates it specified, and playing the fees it levied.

Its monopoly was broken not by rebellious clients, but by even more ruthless monopolists. The **Shubert brothers,** Sam, Lee, and Jacob, were regular clients of the Syndicate, operating some 30 theatres in the Northeast. In 1905, concerned about potential rivalry, the Syndicate ordered them to stop acquiring theatres; instead, the Shuberts secured bank financing and declared war, and by 1913 controlled twice as many theatres as the Syndicate. The last Syndicate agreement expired in 1916; the Shuberts retained a national monopoly on theatres until 1930, and a Broadway one until 1950.

The Syndicate was a means of maximizing profit, not a vehicle for artistic innovation or social welfare; consequently, it was ruthless in its methods and rapacious in its charges. However, monopoly was the accepted way of doing business in the 19th century, and the Syndicate was only doing in theatre what Standard Oil, United States Steel, and American Telephone and Telegraph were doing in their industries. Furthermore, the Syndicate was only one theatrical monopoly: The so-called popular price theatres were monopolized during 1900–11 by the **Stair and Havlin Theatrical Management Syndicate.** In 1900 **B. F. Keith** and **Edward F. Albee** organized their **United Booking Office,** which monopolized all of **vaudeville;** and Samuel Scribner's Columbia Amusement Exchange virtually monopolized **burlesque** after 1905.
DMcD

See: A. L. Bernheim, *The Business of The Theatre* (1932), reprint, New York, 1964.

T

Tableau vivant see **nudity**

Take a Giant Step by Louis Peterson. Opening at New York's **Lyceum Theatre** 24 September 1953 (also on Broadway in 1956–7), it was directed by John Stix and featured Louis Gossett, Jr., Frank Wilson, and **Frederick O'Neal.** The seventh work by an African-American playwright to reach Broadway, the play explores the struggles of a young, middle-class, black youth growing up in a predominantly white neighborhood; it also includes generational and racial conflicts. KME

Talley, Ted (1952–) North Carolina–born playwright, educated at Yale. His first success, *Hooters* (1978), was followed by *Terra Nova* (1979), which has been produced by more than 20 major American theatres as well as by companies in England, Japan, and Sweden. This dramatization of the race to reach the South Pole won two Drama-Logue Awards and was made into a BBC television play in 1984. *Coming Attractions* (1981) was produced by **Playwrights Horizons** and won an Outer Critics' Circle Award. Tally has also written screenplays for *The Father Clements Story* (1987) and *The Silence of the Lambs* (1991, Academy Award). BBW

Talley's Folly A long one-act (90-minute) play by **Lanford Wilson** that won him the Pulitzer Prize and Drama Critics' Circle Award in 1980. Directed by **Marshall Mason,** designed by **John Lee Beatty,** and starring **Judd Hirsch** and Trish Hawkins, this second of Wilson's trilogy about the Talley family opened **Off-Broadway** in 1979 at the **Circle Repertory** for a limited run before transferring to Broadway's **Brooks Atkinson Theatre** (1980) for 277 performances. Set in 1944, the play tells the story of WASPish Sally Talley's wooing by Matt Friedman, a Jewish immigrant accountant, at a decayed boathouse on the Talley farm in Lebanon, MO. *Talley's Folly* drew wide critical praise; **Walter Kerr** called it "a charmer, filled to the brim with hope, humor and chutzpah." TLM

Tamiris [Becker], Helen (1905–66) Modern dancer-choreographer and theatre choreographer. After establishing herself in modern dance primarily as a solo artist, she continued her concert work while choreographing for Broadway musicals. Initially, Tamiris worked with experimental theatre groups, including the **Provincetown Players** and the **Group Theatre.** Her first musical theatre pro-

ductions were ***Annie Get Your Gun*** (1946) and *Park Avenue* (1947). She directed *The Great Campaign* (1947) and choreographed the Jules Munshin–**Pearl Bailey** political **revue,** *Bless You All* (1950). Tamiris was highly regarded by her modern dance contemporaries, many of whom danced in the musicals she choreographed. Using trained dancers raised the standard of **dance** in musical theatre and made Tamiris's productions tremendously popular. LF

Tandy, Jessica (1909–) British-born actress who in 1954 became a naturalized American citizen. Trained in drama school (1924–7), she made her London debut in *The Rumour* (1929) and before she was 25 had become a star. She made her debut on Broadway as Toni Rakonitz in 1930 in *The Matriarch.* Among her later outstanding roles were Ophelia to John Gielgud's *Hamlet* (1934) and Blanche DuBois (Tony Award) in *A **Streetcar Named Desire*** (1947). As Blanche she won rave reviews and achieved Broadway stardom; a critic called the role "deeply moving . . . acted gloriously . . . one of the most arresting and moving performances you are likely to thrill to in many a semester."

Having divorced actor Jack Hawkins in 1940 after eight years of marriage, in 1942 Tandy married **Hume Cronyn,** with whom she has since appeared in six Broadway productions: *The Fourposter* (1951), *The Physicists* (1964), *A **Delicate Balance*** (1966), *Noël Coward in Two Keys* (1974), *The Gin Game* (1977), and *Foxfire* (1982). She won Tony Awards for the latter two.

Tandy and Cronyn have appeared regularly in American regional theatres, chief among them the **Guthrie Theatre,** which they admired for its adequate rehearsal periods and superior facilities compared to most Broadway theatres. At the Guthrie, Tandy played such roles as Linda in ***Death of a Salesman,*** Gertrude in *Hamlet,* and Madam Ranevskaya in *The Cherry Orchard.*

Tandy, one of the great ladies of the American stage, has also appeared in numerous British and American television programs, first appearing on British television in 1939. In recent years she has devoted more time to film acting, winning an Academy Award for ***Driving Miss Daisy,*** her first major film role, at age 80. SMA

See: M. S. Barranger, *Jessica Tandy: A Bio-Bibliography,* Westport, CT, 1991.

Tanguay, Eva (1878–1947) Canadian-born singer, the "oomph" girl of **vaudeville**'s heyday, epitomized by her best known song, "I Don't Care," first sung in *The Chaperones* (1903). Beginning in variety in 1886, she toured for five years with the Redding Company as a child actress, graduating to musical comedy roles (*The Merry World, My Lady, The Sambo Girl,* etc.). After *A Good Fellow* (1906), she entered vaudeville, becoming its leading star and leaving it infrequently over the next 25 years. Described by one critic as "not beautiful, witty or graceful," her appeal defies explanation; she claimed it was in the force of her personality. Flamboyant, a bit risqué in costumes (she said her 1908 Salomé costume consisted of two pearls) and songs (e.g., "I Want Someone to Go Wild with Me"), and tempestuous on- and offstage, she seemed to her audiences perennially young. Financial reverses and poor health forced an early retirement.   DBW

Tarkington, Booth (1869–1946) Novelist and playwright. Better known as a novelist, Tarkington was the author of 21 produced plays. Whether taking his theme from history or a contemporary event, Tarkington was a romanticist who enjoyed writing for actors: *Monsieur Beaucaire* (1900) for **Richard Mansfield,** *Master Antonio* (1916) for **Otis Skinner,** *Poldekin* (1920) for **George Arliss.** When the success of *The Man from Home* (1907), written with **Harry Leon Wilson,** was followed by failures, Tarkington stopped writing plays for four years. Later, his most successful play, *Clarence* (1919), written for **Alfred Lunt** and **Helen Hayes,** showed the disruption caused in a normal household by a handsome, bumbling hero. Never feeling that he was taken seriously as a playwright, Tarkington distrusted the theatre as a place for serious art. A collection of his letters (*On Plays, Playwrights, and Playgoers*) was published in 1959.   WJM

See: J. Woodress, *Booth Tarkington: Gentleman from Indiana,* Philadelphia, 1955.

Tavel, Ronald (1941–) A cofounder of **Theatre of the Ridiculous** (1965), Tavel helped popularize a trashy satirical style termed "camp" as an American theatrical language. His satires on American culture include *The Life of Juanita Castro* (1965), *Gorilla Queen* (1967), *Bigfoot* (1970), *The Ovens of Anita Orangejuice* (1978), and *Notorious Harik Will Kill the Pope* (1986).   TLM

Tavern, The Play in two acts by **George M. Cohan** that burlesques the conventions of theatrical romanticism, as well as the intellectual pretensions of G. B. **Shaw** and the sentimental wistfulness of James M. Barrie. All characters were costumed in a pastiche of period styles. In the 1920 premiere **Arnold Daly** played the nameless "Vagabond," seen in 18th-century wig and boots and 19th-century hat, cloak, and coat. It was revived by the **Association of Producing Artists** (APA) in 1962.   WD

Tayleure, Clifton (1830–91) Playwright. Born in South Carolina and associated with Baltimore theatres, Tayleure combined careers in theatre and journalism. His version of **Uncle Tom's Cabin** (1852) reflected Southern political sympathies. Other plays include an adaptation of *Horseshoe Robinson*

(1856), *The Man of Destiny* (1856), *The Boy Martyrs of September 12, 1814* (1859). He is best known for his dramatization of **East Lynne** (1863).   WJM

Taylor, Bayard (1825–78) A popular writer of travel literature before the Civil War, Taylor is one of a number of literary-minded people who attempted to write verse drama. Never considered for production, his plays – *The Masque of Gods* (1872), *The Prophet* (1873), *Prince Deukalion* (1878) – explore the human interest in religion.   WJM

Taylor, Charles Western (1785-1874) English-born playwright and actor who in 1819 came to America and became a character actor and journeyman playwright, mainly for New York's National Theatre. Like many others, he dramatized current fiction (J. F. Cooper's *The Water Witch,* 1831; Mrs. Stowe's *Dred,* 1856). He also adapted **Uncle Tom's Cabin** (opened 23 August 1852), providing a happy ending with Tom's homecoming; wrote *The Drunkard's Warning* (1856); and always emphasized spectacle, as in *The Orange Girl in Venice* (1856).   WJM

Taylor, Laurette (Cooney) (1884–1946) Actress who debuted as a child in Gloucester, MA, then went in 1903 to the Boston Athenaeum. She first appeared in New York the same year in *From Rags to Riches.* Her first substantial success came in 1910 in *Alias Jimmy Valentine,* but she achieved stardom in the title role of **Peg O'My Heart** in 1912, a script by **J. Hartley Manners,** who married Taylor in 1911.

Later roles included Nell Gwyn in *Sweet Nell of Old Drury* and Rose Trelawny in *Trelawny of the Wells.* After her husband's death in 1928, Taylor retired from the stage, but she returned as Mrs. Midgit in the 1938 revival of *Outward Bound.* She costarred in *The* **Glass Menagerie** (1945), a smash hit that made her once more the toast of Broadway.   SMA

See: M. Courtney, *Laurette,* New York, 1955.

Taylor, Samuel (1912–) Chicago-born playwright and librettist who gained his first Broadway experience as a play reader and play doctor. He coauthored *Stop-Over,* which had a brief run in 1938, and then wrote or adapted scripts for *The Happy Time* (1950), *Sabrina Fair* (1953), *The Pleasure of His Company* (1958), *First Love* (1961), and *Avanti '68.* The librettist for **Richard Rodgers's** musical *No Strings,* Taylor also wrote extensively for radio and television.   MK

Taymor, Julie (1952–) Massachusetts-born designer, director, puppeteer, playwright, and actress; educated at Oberlin College (BA, 1974). Taymor is one of the foremost contemporary American theatre artists who exploit time-honored strategies of popular entertainment for innovative ends, favoring theatricality over realism, visual imagery over language, and populist perspectives over elitist ones.

Trained with **mime** Jacques Le Coq, the **Bread and Puppet Theatre,** Herbert Blau's experimen-

The Stag King (American Repertory Theatre, 1984), directed by Andrei Serban, sets by Michael Yeargan with costumes, masks, and puppets by Julie Taymor. Photo: Richard Feldman. Courtesy: ART.

tal **collective** Kraken, and with Asian dance, **puppetry,** and wood-carving masters, Taymor evolved an eclectic aesthetic. During a four-year residency in Bali (1974–8), she organized Teatr Loh, a multinational company that cross-pollinated Asian and Western approaches. The 1980–1 New York premieres of their complex, imagistic works, *Way of Snow* and *Tirai,* together with her acclaimed set and puppet designs for **Elizabeth Swados**'s *Haggadah* (**Public Theater,** 1980) launched a career that would bring Taymor an Obie Award for "Visual Magic" (1985) and a so-called genius award from the McArthur Foundation (1991). Her "Fool's Fire," based on a **Poe** short story, aired on "American Playhouse" in March 1992.

Her master work to date is *Juan Darién,* a dramatization of a Uruguayan short story, adapted by Taymor and composer Elliott Goldenthal, her collaborator since 1980. Typically epic in scale and cinematic in structure, this magical carnival mass for people and puppets addresses a favorite Taymor theme: physical and spiritual transformation.   CLJ

Tea and Sympathy is the drama by **Robert Anderson** that catapulted him onto the national theatre scene when it opened at the **Ethel Barrymore Theatre** in New York (30 September 1953) under **Elia Kazan**'s direction; it ran 712 performances. Set in a New England boy's school, the play is the story of a sensitive young man subjected to group harassment by the machinations of a homophobic housemaster. The strong cast featured Deborah Kerr as the housemaster's wife, John Kerr (no relation) as the young man, and Leif Erickson as the housemaster. Deborah Kerr's character is remembered for boldly rejecting her husband's behavior and gently introducing the boy to his sexuality.   KN

Teal, Ben (1857?–1917) California-born director who, other than coauthoring a few plays (notably *The Great Metropolis* with **George H. Jessop,** 1889), devoted a 34-year career to direction, including over 80 productions in New York alone. Possibly the first successful free-lance director in the American theatre, Teal, who began his New York career in 1883, peaked as a director (with **Klaw and Erlanger,** 1899–1903) of spectacular melodramas with *Ben-Hur* (1899); subsequently he specialized in staging musical comedy, though after 1900 such directors as **David Belasco,** Herbert Gresham, **Julian Mitchell,** and **Ned Wayburn** were considered superior to Teal.   DBW

Teatro Campesino, El see **El Teatro Campesino**

Templeton, Fay (1865–1939) Favorite actress of the musical comedy stage at the turn of the 20th century. Born in Little Rock, AR, on Christmas Day, she appeared on stage as a child. She toured extensively with her parents, then joined **Weber and Fields** for four seasons, making a hit of the song, "Rosey, You Are My Posey." In 1905 she appeared in **Cohan**'s *Forty-five Minutes from Broadway* as Mary, singing "Mary Is a Grand Old Name," a huge success. She later appeared in **Gilbert and Sullivan,** retiring from the stage in 1931 after appearing in *HMS Pinafore.* Templeton lived for a time in the **Actors' Fund** Home in Englewood, NJ, and died in San Francisco.   SMA

Ten Nights in a Bar-Room Initially produced at New York's National Theatre in 1858, this adaptation by William W. Pratt of T. S. Arthur's 1854 novel became one of the most popular temperance melodramas in the nation. Its allegorical plot traces the drunkenness and sudden reformation of Joe Morgan after his "angel child" daughter sings "Father, Dear Father, Come Home with Me Now" (added to the play in 1864) and dies when struck on the head by a rum glass. Morgan's eventual success is contrasted to the drunken decline of Frank Slade, who finally kills his father, a bartender. The play was second only to **Uncle Tom's Cabin** on the country circuits of the late 19th century, and endured frequent burlesque revivals in the 20th.   BMcC

Tent show A style of theatrical presentation in which plays or variety shows are trouped from community to community and staged under canvas. One of the earliest entrepreneurs was Fayette Lodowick "Yankee" Robinson, whose touring company performed in the river towns of Iowa and Illinois in 1851; prosperity led him to switch from drama to **circus.** By the late 19th century, traveling troupes with repertories extensive enough to provide a week's worth of entertainment had become popular in the summer, when local opera houses were too poorly ventilated to attract the public. The influence of the **Chautauqua** circuit, with its portable theatres lit by naphtha lamps, was strong after 1904; its tents were brown to distinguish its education purpose from the white tops of the circus. In France, Firmin Gémier had commissioned an elaborate canvas structure to house the tours of the Théâtre Antoine in 1911; the average American show tent, however, was limited to a width of 50 or 60 ft, with bare benches or bleachers and a platform stage designed for portability.

The earliest repertories were imitations, often pirated, of standard dramatic fare, primarily melodrama; but as these grew stale and copyright laws stricter, tent showmen composed their own plays, carpentered to a limited company and the familiar themes of rural life. The standbys of this repertory include Charles Harrison's *Saintly Hypocrites and Honest Sinners* (1915) and W. C. Herman's *Call of the Woods,* which pitted homespun virtue against urban corruption. The comic character **Toby,** developed c. 1911, became the popular hero of these works, often partnered with the tomboy Susie and the eccentric known as the G-string character, a sage descendant of the stage **Yankee.**

After WW I, motor vehicles replaced rail transport and tent shows proliferated, doubling their rate to $1 admissions. Some 400 shows were traveling through the U.S. by 1927, playing to an estimated audience of 78 million; but the catastrophic effect of the Depression and dust storms on the agricultural population led to a decline in these "rag opries." Price cutting and unionization, the competition from local cinemas, and inability to organize were also contributory factors to the closure of hundreds of long-standing companies in the 1930s. The **Federal Theatre Project** absorbed many of these entertainers, and in the 1950s only some dozen troupes survived. In 1976 a revival of the Harley Sadler Show, one of the most prosperous in its time, was staged at Texas Tech University, which houses a Tent Show Collection. Another relevant archive is the Museum of Repertoire Americana in Mount Pleasant, IA.   LS

See: C. Ashby and S. D. May, *Trouping Through Texas: Harley Sadler and His Tent Show,* Bowling Green, OH, 1982; J. Martin, *Henry L. Brunk and Brunk's Comedians,* Bowling Green, OH, 1984; J. C. Mickel, *Footlights on the Prairie,* St. Cloud, MN, 1974; N. Schaffner (w/ V. Johnson), *The Fabulous Toby & Me,* Englewood Cliffs, NJ, 1968; W. L. Slout, *Theatre in a Tent: The Development of a Provincial Entertainment,* Bowling Green, OH, 1972.

Ter-Arutunian, Rouben (1920–92) Armenian-American set and costume designer; born in Russia, educated in Berlin 1927–43, emigrated to the U.S. in 1951. Broadway credits include *New Girl in Town* (1957), *Redhead* (1959; Tony for best costumes), *Advise and Consent* (1960), *The Milk Train Doesn't Stop Here Anymore* (1964), *Eh?* (1966), *Exit the King* (1968), *All Over* (1971), and *The Lady from Dubuque* (1980). In addition to theatre and opera, Ter-Arutunian designed for television in the 1950s (*Twelfth Night,* 1957, Emmy). His work fell primarily into two categories: "decorative" (or painterly), such as his famous *Nutcracker* for the New York City Ballet; and sculptural, such as *Riceracare* for American Ballet Theatre. Ter-Arutunian preferred the latter style, which allowed him to create space around a minimal amount of scenery. He said that he designed "visual counterpart to drama, poetry, music and movement, . . . with simplicity, clarity, and a certain element of mystery."   AA

Terry, Megan (1932–) One of the most important playwrights of the avant-garde, **Off-Off Broadway** theatre of the 1960s, Terry wrote plays reflecting important political, social, and sexual issues. In her association with the **Open Theatre** (1963–8), she helped develop many techniques introduced by that group, such as audience contact, experimental staging, and "transformation," whereby characters, place, time, and action change rapidly and actors switch roles, often regardless of gender. Terry achieved international acclaim with *Viet Rock* (1966), a collaborative effort that was the first rock musical and the first protest play about the Vietnam War. Other plays by Terry include *Calm Down Mother* and *Keep Tightly Closed in a Cool Dry Place* (1965), *The People vs. Ranchman* (1967), *Hothouse* (1974), and *Approaching Simone* (1970) – an Obie-winning chronicle of the brief, heroic life of Simone Weil. Since 1974, Terry has written more than 60 plays as playwright-in-residence and literary manager at the **Omaha Magic Theatre,** including *Babes in the Bighouse* (1979), her first full-length play after the appointment. A recent project, *Walking Through Walls* (1987), was a collaborative theatre piece on autonomy and the unification of self and planet.   FB

See: J. Larson, "Public Dreams: A Critical Investigation of the Plays of Megan Terry," PhD diss., U of Kansas, 1986.

Tesich, Steve (né Titovo Utice) (1942–) Playwright, born in Yugoslavia and educated at Indiana University and Columbia; also a successful screenwriter (*Breaking Away,* 1979; *Four Friends,* 1981; *The World According to Garp,* 1982). His play *Baba Goya* (1972) won the Drama Desk Award;

Division Street (1980) played on Broadway with John Lithgow and Christine Lahti; and both *Commencement Exercises* (1991) and *On the Open Road* (1992) premiered at the **Goodman Theatre.**   BBW

Texas Steer, A, by **Charles Hale Hoyt,** author of plays on contemporaneous subjects. Hoyt's four-act farce premiered 8 January 1894 at his **Madison Square Theatre.** Focused on American politics, a subject Hoyt observed as a New Hampshire legislator, Congressman Maverick Brander and his family exploit Hoyt's experience as a western stock raiser to display culture shock, political naïveté, frontier slang, and Texas gaucherie transplanted to Washington, DC. Discounted as of no literary merit, Hoyt's play stands with **Harrigan**'s as topical ethnic and racist urban farces, influencing variety and other forms popular at the turn of the 19th century.
RKB

Texas Trilogy, A, by Preston Jones includes *The Last Meeting of the Knights of the White Magnolia, Lu Ann Hampton Laverty Oberlander,* and *The Oldest Living Graduate.* The three plays were produced in repertory at the **Dallas Theater Center** (1973–4) under the direction of **Paul Baker.** The trilogy was presented in repertory at the **John F. Kennedy Center for the Performing Arts** for a 10-week season starting on 29 April 1976 under the direction of **Alan Schneider;** it was brought back to the Kennedy Center on 5 August 1976 for a five-week run prior to its New York opening on 21 September 1976 at the **Broadhurst Theatre.** Set in a mythical West Texas town, the play reflected local color and humor, with attitudes and language that significantly defined regional drama on Broadway.
ER

Thalia Theatre 46–48 Bowery, NYC [Architect: Ithiel Town]. Built by the city's wealthiest citizens with high hopes of its becoming New York's premier theatre, the New York Theatre (later to be rechristened the **Bowery** and, later, the Thalia) opened in 1826 and survived five **fires** (1828, 1836, 1838, 1845, and 1923), but did not survive a final fire in 1929. Considered the handsomest playhouse of its time, it was abandoned by its society patrons as its environs deteriorated. It became a house of melodrama and popular entertainments, reflecting the tastes of its audiences; at its demise, it was presenting Chinese vaudeville.
MCH

That Championship Season Two-act drama by Jason Miller that opened to critical acclaim 2 May 1972 in the Estelle Newman Theatre of the New York **Public Theater.** Transferred to Broadway's **Booth Theatre** (14 September), it ran 988 performances and won the Drama Critics' Circle Award for best play (1972) and the Tony Award (1972–3). The drama reunites four members of a championship high school basketball team with their coach; their memories, contrasted with their adult lives, offers insightful commentary on American values. The cast included Walter McGinn, Charles Durning, Paul Sorvino, and Richard Dysart as Coach; **A. J. Antoon** directed. Playwright Miller, who

was an outstanding high school athlete, became a respectable stage and film actor and was nominated for an Oscar in 1974 for his role in *The Exorcist.*
KN

Theatre Arts Monthly Theatre journal established as a quarterly by **Sheldon Cheney** in 1916, and published in Detroit by the Arts and Crafts Society. *Theatre Arts* proclaimed its intention to "develop the creative impulse in the American Theatre" and to eliminate the speculator. Cheney moved the magazine to New York in 1917 when a photograph of a German theatre upset war-sensitive Detroit. **Edith J. R. Isaacs, Kenneth Macgowan,** and Marion Tucker joined Cheney in 1919, with Isaacs assuming the editorship in 1922. As publisher and editor, she expanded *Theatre Arts* into a monthly in 1924, and hired **Rosamond Gilder** as associate editor. Gilder served with distinction until 1948, the last two years as editor. As the magazine became more international in scope, Ashley Dukes became English editor. Essays on Adolphe Appia, Gordon Craig, the **Federal Theatre, Eugene O'Neill,** and other topics of current interest raised the intellectual tone, especially when compared with the gossipy quality of its competitors. Contributors included **Robert E. Sherwood,** Louis Jouvet, **Hallie Flanagan, Robert Edmond Jones, Ray Bolger, Thornton Wilder,** and John Gielgud. Both visionary and practical, *Theatre Arts* transmitted new ideas about theatrical art to a new generation of artists and audience. In 1948 it combined with *The Stage,* ending, for all practical purposes, the original publication. It ceased publication in 1964.   TLM

Theatre Communications Group (TCG)
Founded in 1961 (office in NYC), and under the leadership of long-time director **Peter Zeisler** and 23 elected board members (plus four officers) from the theatrical professions, TCG serves as the national organization for **resident nonprofit professional theatre,** providing a support system that "addresses the artistic and management concerns of theatres, as well as institutionally based and freelance artists nationwide." Its constituency of 329 theatre institutions (as of late 1991) across the country are served in numerous ways, including a communications network highlighted by the magazine *American Theatre,* its annual *Theatre Profiles* and *Theatre Directory, Plays in Progress,* and *Art-SEARCH* (for job placement). TCG has also been an effective lobbying force.   DBW

Theatre for the New City
Not-for-profit **Off-Off Broadway** theatre founded (in the spirit of the **Judson Poets' Theatre**) in 1970 by Lawrence Kornfeld, Theo Barnes, George Bartenieff, and Crystal Field to produce and present untraditional theatre and **performance art,** mostly by American playwrights. Bartenieff and Field, a husband-and-wife team, remain the artistic directors. TNC provided an early home for such innovative groups as **Richard Foreman**'s *Ontological-Hysteric Theatre* and the **Mabou Mines.** By 1990, it had produced over 600 original American plays, among them work by adventurous writers such as **Rosalyn Drexler,**

Sam Shepard, Rochelle Owens, Harvey Fierstein, and **Maria Irene Fornés.** TNC also mounts free summer street theatre tours to all five NYC boroughs, and its annual Halloween festivities, initiated in 1973, have become a Greenwich Village institution.   CLJ

Theatre Guild, The In 1915, a group of young actors and writers dissatisfied with the conventions of the commercial theatre organized the **Washington Square Players.** For three seasons they presented a series of one-act plays distinctly modern in both content and form. After the war, in 1919, a patent lawyer and sometime playwright named **Lawrence Langner** restructured the Players as the Theatre Guild. Langner and his board – which included **Philip Moeller** (who was to become the Guild's leading director), **Theresa Helburn** (a play reader soon to be made Executive Director), actress Helen Westley, banker Maurice Wertheim, and scene designer **Lee Simonson** – were determined to shed their amateur downtown status and present challenging full-length plays on Broadway. In its first few years the Guild's notable achievements were with European expressionism (Kaiser's *Man and the Masses,* 1924) and with the world premieres of several plays by **Shaw** (*Heartbreak House,* 1920; *Back to Methuselah,* 1922; *Saint Joan,* 1923; and *Caesar and Cleopatra,* 1925). Although the Guild was criticized for neglecting American writers, two American plays that it presented early in its history – **Elmer Rice**'s The **Adding Machine** (1923) and **John Howard Lawson**'s *Processional* (1925) – testify to the influence its productions of European plays had on native experiment. Later in the 1920s, and for the following three decades, the Guild produced the work of major American dramatists, including **Sidney Howard** (*They Knew What They Wanted,* 1924; *The Silver Cord,* 1926); **S. N. Behrman** (*The Second Man,* 1927; *Biography,* 1932); **Robert E. Sherwood** (*Reunion in Vienna,* 1931; *Idiot's Delight,* 1936); and **Maxwell Anderson** (*Elizabeth the Queen,* 1930; *Mary of Scotland,* 1933). In 1928, with *Strange Interlude* and Marco Millions, the Guild began regularly to produce the plays of **Eugene O'Neill.**

If in the 1920s the Guild had the luster of an experiment conducted by idealistic upstarts, by the early 1930s it had begun to acquire the reputation of a theatrical dowager. In 1931 some of its younger members defected to form the **Group Theatre,** whose agenda of knitting systematically trained actors into a true ensemble and encouraging the development of socially relevant plays highlighted two areas where the Guild had failed. Throughout the 1930s and '40s, as it produced popular shows like *Philadelphia Story* (1939) and musicals like *Oklahoma!* (1943) and *Carousel* (1945) – and depended over and over again on its in-house stars, the **Lunt**s, to rescue it from a financial abyss (thereby violating its original policy of starring the play rather than the player) – the Guild became little different from a commercial producer. Despite its lack of success in maintaining a repertory setup or in developing a company of actors – and despite its concessions to popularity and its literary shortcomings (its predilection for airy comedies and stodgy historical romances) – the Guild's record is unique in the history of the American theatre. Through its subscription policy and its extensive national tours the Guild brought more worthwhile, well-produced plays to a greater number of people, and over a longer period of time, than any other theatrical organization.   FH

See: W. P. Eaton, *The Theatre Guild: The First Ten Years,* New York, 1929; R. Waldau, *Vintage Years of the Theatre Guild 1928–1939,* Cleveland, 1972.

Theatre of the Ridiculous In 1967 the Play-House of the Ridiculous opened on **Off-Off Broadway** with *The Life of Lady Godiva,* written by **Ronald Tavel,** directed by **John Vaccaro,** and featuring **Charles Ludlam** as actor. Though these three men did not stay together long, they independently continued their "ridiculous" work – a self-consciously wild dramaturgy full of witty wordplay, sexual double entendre, theatrical flamboyance, sexual ambiguity, and bad taste. Tavel left the Play-House within a year to pursue a writing career, and in 1967 Vaccaro directed two Ludlam works, *Big Hotel* and *Conquest of the Universe,* before Ludlam left to become actor-manager of his own company. Vaccaro toured Europe with the Play-House and then operated it out of **La MaMa** until 1972, when he closed his theatre. At the **Ridiculous Theatrical Company,** Ludlam went on to write, direct, and perform in plays such as *Turds in Hell* (1968), *Camille* (1973), and *Der Ring Gott Farblonjet* (1977).   AS

Theatre Owners' Booking Association A chain of theatres formed to provide year-round work for black entertainers. The principal instigator was S. H. Dudley, a variety showman who had appeared in the Smart Set productions. He began in 1912 with the Dudley Circuit, which rose to 28 black theatres by the end of 1916. In 1919 white-managed theatres were admitted to the circuit, and in 1921 the expanded association came into being. Its abbreviation, TOBA, was often sarcastically interpreted as "tough on black actors" because of the allegedly small salaries paid except to headliners; in some circles the TOBA was called the Chitlin Circuit. The association declined and was disbanded during the Depression. [See also **African-American theatre.**]   EGH

Theatre Rhinoceros Founded in **San Francisco** in 1977 by Allan Estes and others, it is one of the oldest resident theatres specializing in **gay and lesbian theatre.** Works by noted homosexual authors (**Harvey Fierstein,** Jane Chambers, Robert Chesley) have been produced under an artistic policy that embraces sex farces and musical **revues** as well as serious dramas. One of the most meaningful productions was *The AIDS Show* (1984), an amalgam of comic and tragic skits exploring the **AIDS** epidemic in its nascent stage. Three of the company's artistic directors, including Estes, eventually perished from the disease.   MB

Theatre Row West 42nd St. between 9th and 10th Aves., NYC. In 1975, when Robert Moss, director of the **Off-Off Broadway** group **Playwrights Horizons,** found himself without a theatre, he rented a building on West 42nd Street – amid a neighborhood of pornographic shops, burlesque houses, and massage parlors – and transformed it quickly and cheaply into a performing space. His success signaled the development of an alternative theatre district a few blocks west of Broadway for Off-Off Broadway companies. A quasi-governmental agency, the 42nd Street Redevelopment Corporation, was persuaded to buy the block from 9th to Dyer Avenues to begin Phase I of the transformation; the created spaces were then rented out to companies, which accepted the responsibility to rebuild them into theatres and offices. In 1978, amid much official fanfare, Theatre Row was opened and comprised 10 working companies, all to be operated on a nonprofit basis and representing diverse artistic goals as well as ethnic backgrounds. Phase II, which encompasses the block between Dyer and 10th Avenues, has added four other members and one west of 10th Avenue. Most companies have been upgraded to **Off-Broadway** theatres.

In 1982, with most of the original companies struggling to survive under the weight of mortgages and escalating operating expenses, they decided collectively to rent out their theatres when they were not being used by themselves. This formula has worked for most of the theatres. Through a fortunate and generous donation, **Playwrights Horizons** has acquired its theatres outright.

The theatres and companies utilize a collective box office, Ticket Central, to serve their patrons and offer a variety of entertainment at relatively low cost. Theatre Row provides a testing ground for actors, directors, playwrights, and designers, many of whom move their activities to Broadway, Off-Broadway, and regional theatre. The presence of restaurants, shops, and Manhattan Plaza, a subsidized housing complex for performing artists, has stabilized and revitalized the surrounding area.

The theatres and companies comprising Theatre Row are the Samuel Beckett, the **Harold Clurman,** the **Judith Anderson,** Playwrights Horizons (main stage and studio theatres), Theatre Row Theatre, **INTAR** Hispanic American Arts Center, The **Acting Company,** Alice's Fourth Floor, Theatre Arielle, the Douglas Fairbanks, Nat Horne Musical Theatre, the **George S. Kaufman,** and the **John Houseman** Center. MCH

Theatre Union, The Though short-lived (1933–7), this was the most professional of the various nonprofit 1930s groups dedicated to the presentation in theatrical terms of problems central to the working class (unemployment, racial discrimination, political corruption, and other social, political, and economic injustices). With a board representing the full spectrum of radical opinion, The Theatre Union offered, at popular prices, eight largely left-wing dramas by writers such as George Sklar, Albert Maltz, Paul Peters, and **John How-**ard Lawson,** author of its last play, *Marching Song.* DBW

> *See:* M. W. Weisstuch, "The Theatre Union, 1933–1937: A History," PhD diss., City U of New York, 1982.

Theatre X Founded in 1969 by Conrad Bishop, Linda Bishop, and Ron Gural, this Milwaukee-based, nonprofit, avant-garde company made a name for itself by touring *X Communication* (written by the company) and **Brecht**'s *The Measure's Taken.* Since the mid-1970s, while maintaining a company orientation, Theatre X has gained its greatest renown with pieces written by John Schneider (*Razor Blades, A Fierce Longing* [winner of an Obie], *My Werewolf*) and collaborative pieces such as *A History of Sexuality,* a response to the language theories of Michel Foucault. SF

They Knew What They Wanted by **Sidney Howard** earned the Pulitzer Prize in drama for the 1924–5 season, edging out *What Price Glory* and *Desire Under the Elms.* Featuring strong performances by **Richard Bennett** and **Pauline Lord** – who had played Anna Christie three years earlier – Howard's play was a touching retelling of the Tristram and Yseult [Isolde] story transferred to a contemporary California vineyard. Lord's performance as the waitress who commits adultery but is given a second chance was in keeping with the "new realism" of the period but raised the ire of conventional groups, such as the Play Jury, which found the drama offensive. In 1956 the play became the libretto for **Frank Loesser**'s soaring musical *The Most Happy Fella.* BBW

Thomas, Albert Ellsworth (1872–1947) The author, alone or with collaborators, of 20 plays, Thomas was not able to achieve distinction in spite of his recognized talent in comedies dealing with marriage problems. His first play, *Her Husband's Wife* (1910), builds upon the idea of a supposedly dying woman attempting to select her husband's next wife. *The Rainbow* (1912) shows the daughter of separated parents stimulating their reunion. His final play, *No More Ladies* (1933), also dealt with marriage. WJM

Thomas, Augustus (1857–1934) Playwright who always dealt with well-documented American scenes in such plays as *Alabama* (1891), *In Mizzoura* (1893), and *Arizona* (1899). *The Copperhead* (1918), which made Lionel Barrymore [see **Drew-Barrymore**] a star, details the story of an Illinois farmer who, at the request of President Lincoln, pretends to be a sympathizer with the Confederacy. Many plays explored contemporary issues: capital and labor in *New Blood* (1894); politics in *The Capitol* (1895); hypnotism in *The Witching Hour* (1907); and mental healing in *As a Man Thinks* (1911). Even his farces, *The Earl of Pawtucket* (1903) and *Mrs. Leffingwell's Boots* (1905), had a distinctively American flavor. The prefaces to many of his more than 60 plays provide a lively and intimate account of the dramatist at work. Thomas's autobiography, *The Print of My Remembrance,* was published in 1922.   RM

Thomas, Richard (1951–) Actor whose Broadway debut was in *Sunrise at Campobello* (1958) and who as a child performed with such companies as the **American Shakespeare Theatre** and **New York Shakespeare** festivals. Recent plays include *Fifth of July* (1981), *Citizen Tom Paine* (**John F. Kennedy Center,** 1986), *The Front Page* (**Vivian Beaumont,** 1986), *Hamlet* (**Hartford Stage,** 1987), **Gurney**'s *Love Letters* (1989), **Tesich**'s *Square One* (1990), and **McNally**'s *The Lisbon Traviata* (1991). After the film *Last Summer* (1969), Thomas became known as John Boy on television's "The Waltons" (1972–7; Emmy, 1973). Other screen appearances include *Red Sky at Morning* (1971), "Roots: The Next Generation" (TV, 1979) and "Andre's Mother" (PBS, 1990). *Poems by Richard Thomas* was published in 1974.   REK

Thomashefsky (Tomashevsky), Boris (1868–1939) **Yiddish** actor. In 1882, newly arrived from Russia and still a 13-year-old soprano, he appeared in the first professional Yiddish production in America (**Goldfadn**'s *The Witch,* on the Lower East Side). His mellifluous tenor voice and florid good looks were especially suited to the costume operettas popular through the first half of his career, and his reputation as an irresistible ladies' man enhanced his romantic onstage image. He often produced and costarred with his wife Bessie in New York (especially at the National and People's Theatres) or on tour. He also contributed to the writing of some musicals, the best known of which was Moshe Zeifert's *Dos Pintele Yid* (*The Little Spark of Jewishness,* 1909), and appeared in several Yiddish films. Late in life he ventured, mostly unsuccessfully, onto Broadway and into some nontheatrical enterprises.   NS

Thompson, Denman (1833–1911) New England actor-playwright who became a specialist in ethnic and eccentric comedy. He first played his sketch featuring Uncle Josh Whitcomb in 1875; by 1877 it had become a three-act play, and in 1886, with George Ryer, he completely revised it as *The Old Homestead,* which he played until 1910. A derivation of temperance melodrama, *The Old Homestead* was the epitome of sentimental rural Americana.   DMcD

See: J. J. Brady, *Life of Denman Thompson (Joshua Whitcomb),* New York, 1888.

Thompson, Lydia (1836–1908) British-born actress. Fair-haired and sprightly, she had already made a name for herself as a dancer and comedienne in London, the English provinces, and Germany when she brought her troupe of British Blondes to New York (1868). Heralded by a barrage of publicity, her production of *Ixion; or, The Man at the Wheel,* the first modern burlesque in more than one act, did not so much introduce **burlesque** to America as combine it with pulchritude in tights to create the "leg show." A strict taskmistress to her underlings and a shrewd busi-

Lydia Thompson as Robinson Crusoe in H. B. Farnie's burlesque of that name (1877). Photo: Mora, N.Y. Courtesy: Laurence Senelick.

nesswoman, Thompson was the first actress to horsewhip a libellous newspaper editor. Teamed with **Willie Edouin** for a while, she toured the U.S. several times (1868–71, 1877–8, 1886, 1888–9, 1891), retaining her popularity on both sides of the Atlantic. Her last appearance was with Mrs. Patrick Campbell in *A Queen's Romance* (Imperial Theatre, London, 1904).   LS

See: M. Moses, "Lydia Thompson and the 'British Blondes' in the United States," PhD diss., U of Oregon, 1978.

Thompson, Sada (1929–) Actress, trained at the Carnegie Institute of Technology, who made her professional debut in *The Beautiful People* in 1947 and first appeared in New York in a reading of *Under Milkwood* in 1953. Among her best received efforts have been *The Misanthrope* (1956), Valerie Barton in *The River Line* (1957), Dorine in *Tartuffe* (1964–5), Beatrice in *The **Effects of Gamma Rays on Man-in-the-Moon Marigolds*** (1970), and Ma in *Twigs* (1971), for which she received a Tony. Of her work in George Furth's *Twigs,* it was said that Thompson "has long since demonstrated a depth of acting technique and a variety of performing outputs while working the range of dramatic literature." Most recent work has been on television, although in 1987 she performed in Chicago the title role in ***Driving Miss Daisy.***   SMA

Thompson, Woodman (1889–1955) Set and costume designer who taught set and costume design at the newly established program at Carnegie Tech (1915–21) and was probably the first design teacher in the country. He had a notable career in the 1920s and '30s with productions such as *Beggar on Horseback* (1924), *What Price Glory* (1924), and *The Cocoanuts* (1925).   AA

See: P. Leitner, "The Scene Designs of J. Woodman Thompson," PhD diss., U of Nebraska–Lincoln, 1990.

Three Men on a Horse by John Cecil Holm and **George Abbott.** One of the most popular farces between the wars, this play opened at the **Playhouse** in New York under Abbott's direction on 30 January 1935. Capitalizing on Depression economics and popular fascination with gangsters, the playwrights created a host of good-hearted, goofball characters. The most memorable were Erwin, greeting-card poet and theoretical racehorse speculator, played by William Lynn; and an ex-Follies girl (**Shirley Booth**) whose fascination with the versifier causes trouble with her gambling boyfriend, who exploits Erwin's uncanny talent for picking winning horses. Through much misunderstanding, Erwin wanders from his tract house in Ozone Heights to a New York gambling den and finds confidence in himself along the way.   RHW

Throckmorton, Cleon (1897–1965) Set designer who began his career with the **Provincetown Players** and designed many of **Eugene O'Neill**'s early plays, including *The Emperor Jones* and *The Hairy Ape.* In the same way that O'Neill was experimenting with expressionism, Throckmorton employed stylized settings in the manner of various European movements. He designed several plays for the **Theatre Guild,** including *Porgy* (see *Porgy and Bess*).   AA

Thurston, Howard Franklin (1869–1936) **Magic**ian. The son of a carriage maker, he began as a card manipulator, playing at **Tony Pastor**'s 14th St. Theatre, New York, but developed into a specialist in spectacular illusions. In his acts, he would make vanish an Arabian horse, a girl playing a piano, a Whippet automobile; in "The Triple Mystery" he made a girl materialize in a nested box, suspended her in a mummy case above the stage, and then caused her to appear in a roped trunk above the spectators' heads. He was held over at the London Palace for six months in 1900, purchased **Harry Kellar**'s show in 1907, and introduced his version of the Indian Rope Trick in 1926. Having lost millions, he toured a ghost play *The Demon* (1929), finally retiring in 1935. His autobiography, *My Life of Magic,* was published in 1929 (reprinted as *Our Life of Magic* in 1989 with augmentations, including a section by his step-daughter Jane).   LS

Tillinger, John [Joachim] (1939–   ) English-born, Bristol Old Vic–trained director, actor, and playwright who worked as an actor in London and New York before establishing his reputation as a director at the **Long Wharf Theatre** and Off-

Tour poster for magician Howard Thurston and his step-daughter Jane who first appeared with the act in 1928. Courtesy: Don B. Wilmeth.

Broadway (with transfers to Broadway). Credits include *Entertaining Mr. Sloan* (1981), *Serenading Louie* (1984), *The Lisbon Traviata* (1985), *Loot* (1986), *Sweet Sue* (1986), *Corpse!* (1986; premiered on Broadway), *The Perfect Party* (1986), *Another Antigone* (1987), *Love Letters* (1989), *What the Butler Saw* (1989), *Prin* (1990), and *Lips Together, Teeth Apart* (1991). Of Tillinger, critic **Frank Rich** wrote: He "has a keen way with comedies that have a sharp, idiosyncratic edge."   TLM

Time of the Cuckoo **Arthur Laurents**'s greatest commercial success ran 263 performances from its 15 October 1952, **Empire Theatre** premiere. The play deals with a vacationing American woman in her thirties desperately seeking romance, but finding inhibition and disillusionment in an affair with an Italian businessman. The play revived for 105 performances in 1958, at the Sheridan Square Theatre. Laurents, **Richard Rodgers,** and **Stephen Sondheim** collaborated on its musical adaptation, *Do I Hear a Waltz?,* opening 18 March 1965 at the **46th Street Theatre** for 220 performances, the shortest run for a Rodgers-scored work. The 1955 film version of the play starred **Katharine Hepburn.**   RW

Time of Your Life, The by **William Saroyan**

was produced by the **Group Theatre,** opening in New York on 25 October 1939 and running for 185 performances. Its cast included **Eddie Dowling** as Joe, who is seeking the way to a civilized life; Edward Andrews as Tom, his helper; **Julie Haydon** as Kitty Duval, the prostitute who dreams of a home; Grover Burgess as Blick, the sadistic cop; and a large ensemble cast including Gene Kelly, William Bendix, and **Celeste Holm.** It was revived in 1940, 1946, and 1955. An example of Saroyan's romance of the commonplace, the play pits the wholesome American values embodied in the mythic figure of Kit Carson against the evil of an oppressive social system embodied in Blick. Good wins out when Kit kills Blick and Tom marries Kitty.   BCM

Time Out for Ginger by Ronald Alexander was

first produced by the **Alley Theatre** and opened on Broadway 26 November 1952. Starring **Melvyn Douglas** as the beleaguered father, this family situation comedy reinforced middle-class values and proved popular enough to run 248 performances. Ginger, the 14-year-old heroine, creates social havoc when she joins the high school football team, but chooses traditional feminine behavior in the end. Alexander followed this play with three other works for the stage (produced 1955–63) and one screenplay (1961). His acting credits include eight roles on Broadway between 1943 and 1948.   KF

Tiny Alice by **Edward Albee.** A baffling "alle-

gory about the passion of . . . Christ himself" (Howard Taubman) that opened to mixed reviews on 19 December 1964 at the **Billy Rose** Theatre, directed by **Alan Schneider,** with **Irene Worth** and John Gielgud in lead roles. **Brustein** complained of Albee's "huge joke on the American public"; **Clurman** sniffed, "the play was the sort of thing a highly endowed college student might write"; whereas **Henry Hewes** suggested the play "established Albee as the most distinguished American playwright to date." **Bill Ball**'s 1969 **American Conservatory Theatre** revival drew consistently positive response.   GSA

Tipton, Jennifer (1937–) Lighting designer,

director, and teacher whose early interest in dance led to an appreciation of the potential of light and its uses and impact on performance. She studied with lighting designer **Tom Skelton,** began her career designing for choreographer Paul Taylor, and since 1965 has designed every production by choreographer Twyla Tharp as well as productions for Mikhail Baryshnikov and Robert Joffrey. In theatre she has designed frequently for the **New York Shakespeare Festival,** the **Goodman Theatre,** and many regional theatres. Broadway credits include *La Bête* and *Jerome Robbins' Broadway*. Her preference for more "abstract" theatre has led to collaboration with **Mabou Mines, Robert Wilson, Andrei Serban,** and the **Wooster Group.** In 1991 she directed *The Tempest* at the **Guthrie Theatre.** Tipton's work is typified by a sense of sculptured and textured space.   AA

Tobacco Road Three-act drama-folkplay by Jack

Kirkland, from the novel by Erskine Caldwell; opened at the 48th Street Theatre 4 December 1933 and ran for 3,182 performances, the longest-running Broadway show at the time. The play is set on the tenant farm of Jeeter Lester in the back country of Georgia, and depicts poverty, ignorance, and degradation in the rural South. Its Rabelaisian qualities – obscene language and unconventional sexual behavior – helped give the production "scandal value," which **Brooks Atkinson** credits for its immediate success. Henry Hull created the role of the patriarch Jeeter; Sam Byrd the youngest son Dude; Ruth Hunter the harelipped Ellie May; Dean Jagger the son-in-law Lov Bensey; and **Margaret Wycherly** the mother of the clan, Ada. Few critics liked the play. **Edith Isaacs** called it "one of the bitterest plays ever produced in New York, but one of the most compelling."   TLM

Jack Kirkland's *Tobacco Road* directed by Arvin Brown and designed by Michael Yeargan at the Long Wharf, 1984, with Tom Aldredge as Jeeter Lester, Pamela Payton-Wright as his wife Ada, and Lucinda Jenney as their daughter Pearl. Photo: T. Charles Erickson. Courtesy: Long Wharf Theatre.

Frederick R. Wilson, the creator of "Toby," as he appeared in costume in 1912. Courtesy: Don B. Wilmeth.

Toby The principal character of the North American **tent show** – a redhaired, freckle-faced farmboy. He appears to derive from the rustic low comedians of 18th-century farce; accepted tradition is that Fred Wilson of Horace Murphy's Comedians combined all his "silly kid" roles under the blanket name Toby around 1909. His dramatic function resembles that of the "comic man" in melodrama, providing laughs while contributing to the happy ending. Wilson's Toby was still recognizable as a farmhand in his checked shirt and boots, but the character grew more grotesque. Harley Sadler turned him into a Texas cowpoke in woolly chaps and a phallic pistol, and Neil Schaffner into an awkward dude, whose large freckles and blacked-out front teeth constituted a kind of *commedia* mask. The female equivalent was Sis Hopkins, created by Rose Melville c. 1898, an "Indiana jay" in pigtails and a pinafore; the type became known as Susie. The growing predominance of Toby and his antics, to the detriment of the dramas in which he appeared, has been cited as a factor in the declining popularity of the tent show. LS

Todd, Michael (né Avrom Hirsch Goldbogen) (1907–58) A flamboyant producer and showman, Todd believed in giving his customers "high dames and low comedy." His 21 Broadway shows include *The Hot Mikado* (1939), a jazz version of **Gilbert and Sullivan,** starring **Bill Rob-**inson; *Star and Garter* (1942); *The Naked Genius* (1943); *Mexican Hayride* (1944); *Up in Central Park* (1945); *As Girls Go* (1948); and *Michael Todd's Peepshow* (1950). His film **Around the World in 80 Days** (1956) won an Oscar for best picture. TLM

See: M. Todd, Jr., *A Valuable Property: The Life Story of Michael Todd,* New York, 1983.

Toilet, The First produced in 1964 at the St. Mark's Playhouse, in New York's East Village, this one-act play by Le Roi Jones (**Amiri Baraka**) depicts the severe beating of a Puerto Rican youth by a gang of high school blacks for writing a love letter to their leader. The incident takes place in the school's toilet. The play's indecent language overshadowed its message against stereotyped behavior and prompted a request to the New York District Attorney for obscenity charges to be brought against the work. Los Angeles newspapers refused to advertise a local production, bringing protests of prior **censorship** from the Authors' League of America. EGH

Tomlin, Lily (Mary Jean) (1939–   ) Inventive Detroit-born comic performer whose break came in TV's "Laugh-In" (1969), especially with her portrayal of her creation Ernestine, the nasal-voiced, feisty telephone switchboard operator. (She later declined a half-million-dollar phone commercial offer.) Master of the live concert stage, Tomlin received Broadway acclaim for two **one-person** shows developed with longtime partner Jane Wagner: *Appearing Nitely* (1977, special Tony Award) and *The Search for Signs of Intelligent Life in the Universe* (1985, Tony for best actress; 398 performances). Often compared to **Ruth Draper,** Tomlin created more than a dozen characters of different ages, race, sexes, and classes in her shows. DBW

Tone, [Stanislas Pascal] Franchot (1905–68) Actor. Although an original member of the **Group Theatre,** he only remained in the company until 1932, when he went to Hollywood and developed a successful film career. Before joining the Group, he had already established himself on Broadway, acting in several **Theatre Guild** productions, including the role of Tom Ames in **Philip Barry**'s *Hotel Universe* (1930) and Curly McClain in **Lynn Riggs**'s *Green Grow the Lilacs* (1931). Tone returned for a Group Theatre production of **Irwin Shaw**'s *The Gentle People* (1939), and during the next two decades continued to act in New York, appearing in revivals of works by **Behrman, Saroyan, Chekhov,** and **O'Neill.** He maintained his career in film and also acted often on television (with over 50 credits). TP

Tooth of Crime, The The action of this two-act **Sam Shepard** play with music builds to a duel of language and style between two pop stars, Hoss and Crow: Hoss's "true style" loses to the brash newcomer Crow's heartless, manipulative use of shock techniques. The original production, which opened 17 July 1972 at London's Open Space Theatre (directed by **Charles Marowitz**) struck British critics as "an intensely American play." The

American premiere at the **McCarter Theatre** (NJ) on 11 November 1972 featured Frank Langella as Hoss. A 1973 revival by The **Performance Group** (at New York's Performing Garage), directed by **Richard Schechner,** was filmed for the Whitney Museum. For **Walter Kerr,** the play evoked "modern man as killer, as faith-merchandiser, as machine." According to **Clive Barnes,** "the language, hip, original, unexpected and rhythmic, flows in and out of the music, which Mr. Shepard himself composed and which is an integral part of the play's design." FHL

Torch Song Trilogy by **Harvey Fierstein** consists of three one-act plays that opened separately at New York's **La MaMa:** *The International Stud* (1978); *Fugue in a Nursery* (1979); and *Widows and Children First!* (1979). As *Torch Song Trilogy,* they opened at the Richard Allen Center (1981); transferred to the **Off-Broadway** Actors Playhouse (1982); and opened on Broadway 10 June 1982 at the Little Theatre – now the **Helen Hayes** – running for 1,222 performances and winning a Tony (1983) for best play.

The central character throughout is Arnold Beckoff, a Jewish homosexual drag queen, played originally by Fierstein. In *The International Stud,* Arnold meets the bisexual Ed at a gay bar and, amid 1920s "torchsongs," begins a romance; Ed later rejects Arnold for a heterosexual relationship with Laurel. In the second play, Ed and Laurel invite Arnold and his new love (Alan) to their country house, where Ed is again confused over his sexual preferences. Five years later in *Widows and Children First!,* Ed has left Laurel; Alan is dead from a "fag bash"; and Arnold is planning to adopt David, a gay teenager. In a scene of great hilarity, Arnold's mother arrives to sort things out. **Jack Kroll** calls *Torch Song Trilogy* Beckoff's "odyssey from self-centered promiscuous drag queen to the oddest solid citizen in the republic." [See **gay/ lesbian theatre.**] TLM

Torn, Rip (né Elmore Rual Torn) (1931–) Texas-born actor-director, a vivid presence in film since *Baby Doll* (1956) but also a successful actor on Broadway, Off-Broadway, in regional theatre, and on television. Student of **Sanford Meisner** and **Lee Strasberg,** Torn assumed the role of Brick in *Cat on a Hot Tin Roof* (1956) and subsequently appeared in several **Williams** plays (*Orpheus Descending,* 1958; ***Sweet Bird of Youth,*** 1960, first as Tom Junior and then as Chance Wayne, succeeding Paul Newman; *The **Glass Menagerie,*** 1975; *A **Streetcar Named Desire,*** 1977). An Obie winner for his role in Norman Mailer's *The Deer Park* (1967) and for direction of McClure's *The Beard* (1968), other significant acting roles include Eban in *Desire Under the Elms* (1963), Bernie Dodd in *The **Country Girl*** (1966), Edgar in *The Dance of Death* (1970), Richard Nixon in *Expletive Deleted* (1974), Captain in *The Father* (1975), and the Howard Hughes role in *Seduced* (1979). He was married to actress **Geraldine Page.** TP DBW

Tortesa, the Usurer Five-act romantic comedy written in blank verse; one of **N. P. Willis**'s most popular plays. The story concerns a moneylender (Tortesa) who agrees to cover the debts of Count Falcone in exchange for the count's daughter (Isabella). Isabella, of course, loves the young painter Angelo, and, after much romantic maneuvering, all is resolved happily, with the young lovers reunited and Tortesa content with Zippa, the glover's daughter. The play, first performed on 8 April 1839 at the NYC's National Theatre, starred **James Wallack,** for whom the play was written, as Tortesa. Despite its many faults, the work was sufficiently admired to be revived many times over the next decade. PAD

Touch of the Poet, A by **Eugene O'Neill** opened in New York on 2 October 1958, running for 284 performances. **Harold Clurman** directed a cast including **Helen Hayes, Kim Stanley,** and Eric Portman. The play was revived in New York 1967, and in 1988 a successful production with Vanessa Redgrave and Timothy Dalton was produced by London's Young Vic. The only surviving complete play from O'Neill's projected nine-play cycle, *A Tale of Possessors Self-Dispossessed,* it is set in a Massachusetts tavern in 1828. It centers on Irish-American innkeeper Con Melody's pretensions to being an aristocratic Byronic hero and his daughter Sara's desire to marry Simon Harford, the son of a wealthy Yankee family. Both have their pretensions and their pride deflated in the course of the play, as Simon tries to challenge the elder Harford to a duel over an imagined insult but is forcibly ejected from his house and carted off to the police station, and Sara stoops to entrapping Simon through sex. In the end, both accept the social identities that the culture dictates for them. BCM

Towse, John Ranken (1845–1933) Drama critic. Born in England and educated at Cambridge, Towse came to New York in 1869 as a reporter for the *Evening Post.* In 1874 he was given the drama desk, a position he held until his retirement in 1927. Regarded as a scholarly and trustworthy critic, Towse fought to maintain Victorian tastes in drama and 19th-century standards in the theatre. Like his contemporaries, **William Winter** and **Henry Austin Clapp,** he could not accept realism, especially the plays of **Ibsen.** His book *Sixty Years of the Theatre* (1916) provides a detailed account and analysis of 19th-century actors. TLM

See: T. L. Miller, "The Theatre Criticism of John Ranken Towse," PhD diss., U of Illinois, 1968.

Toys in the Attic This last major play by **Lillian Hellman** opened at Broadway's Hudson Theatre on 25 February 1960 and ran for 556 performances. Hellman focused on a decaying Southern culture to show the claustrophobic, almost incestuous relationship of two spinster sisters, Carrie (**Maureen Stapleton**) and Annie (Anne Revere), and their wastrel brother, Julian (**Jason Robards, Jr.**). When Julian marries and brings his wife to live with his sisters, the family is torn apart by jealousy, repressed longings, and the sisters' fear that Julian might break away from his dependence upon them. The play won the New York Drama Critics' Circle Award in 1960. FB

Toy theatre/juvenile drama originated in Regency London as "penny plain, tuppence-coloured" sheets of characters and scenery from popular dramas, to be cut out and staged in miniature playhouses; such sheets were sold from Elton's Theatrical Print Warehouse, New York, but no American work was reproduced. Scott & Co. issued "Seltz's American Boys' Theatre" (1866–74), renamed versions of plays in *The Boys of England* series, which differed only in the occasional inclusion of an American locale: an Indian encampment or Niagara Falls. From 1894 to c.1923, many newspaper supplements and magazines included mechanically colored sheets, often of popular fairy tales and generic plays such as *Rip Van Winkle* and *Uncle Tom's Cabin.* More anachronistically, c.1950 a pink plastic **showboat** was sold for the staging of *Pinocchio, Heidi,* and *The Wizard of Oz.* However, in the U.S. the toy theatre was never used to commemorate contemporary productions. LS

Tracy, Lee (1898–1968) A commercially successful actor for over 50 years, Tracy, noted for his exuberance and excitement on stage, is best remembered for his Roy Lane, the hoofer in *Broadway* (1926), and Hildy Johnson, the newspaperman, in *The Front Page* (1928). From his New York debut in *The Show-Off* to his last major role as the ex-President in *The Best Man* (1960), he appeared in a steady stream of forgettable plays, although his London debut as Harry Van in *Idiot's Delight* (1938) and his Australian debut as Queeg in *The Caine Mutiny Court Martial* (1955) are noteworthy. DBW

Training, theatrical Till the late 19th century most actors learned their craft as apprentices, usually in resident **stock companies.** Edwin Forrest, for example, studied elocution, took part in amateur theatricals, then began his professional career in small roles, touring the frontier from company to company. **Edwin Booth** and **Joseph Jefferson III** learned the theatrical profession by touring with their fathers. **Charlotte Cushman** trained as an opera singer, ruined her voice by straining it, then converted to tragedienne. Talent and industry could help an actor progress beyond small parts and eventually lead one to the top of the profession. Most actors had similar beginnings.

Professional theatre schools did not emerge until the late 19th century, when the combination company replaced the resident stock company. **Augustin Daly** personally instructed his apprentice actors, but this was the exception rather than the rule. **Steele MacKaye**, an innovator in several areas of the theatre, heavily influenced the beginnings of professional actor training. MacKaye, a student of François Delsarte in Paris, imported the Frenchman's theories to America. Drawing upon his experiences, MacKaye founded the Lyceum Theatre School (later the **American Academy of Dramatic Art**) with Franklin Sargent. Although this was the first formal school, others attempted to offer training, including the Lawrence School of Acting in New York, the James E. Frobisher College of Oratory and Acting, and the School of Elocution and Dramatic Art and a Delsarte School of Oratory and Dramatic Art, both in Boston.

The success of the Lyceum School, however, stimulated the growth of dramatic schools toward the end of the century. Performers such as **Rose Eytinge**, E. J. Henley, and **McKee Rankin** lent their names to schools; others sprang up in Chicago, Philadelphia, Boston, St. Louis, and Cincinnati. MacKaye's influence spread Delsartism far and wide, although such professionals as **David Belasco** opposed the system. Some schools spent most of their instructional time in rehearsal; others felt the essentials must be taught off the stage.

Several private teachers also began to give lessons. The best known, Alfred Ayres, author of *Actors and Acting* and *The Essentials of Elocution,* actually castigated dramatic schools, calling half of them confidence schemes. Others felt a year in a dramatic school was the equivalent of 10 years of the slipshod training found in stock companies.

At the turn of the century, the proliferation of schools continued until they appeared in most of the major American cities. The American Academy of Dramatic Art grew in prestige by gathering support from professional leaders, including the **Frohman**s, David Belasco, **John Drew,** and **William Gillette.**

Other notable institutions included the Alvienne Academy in New York, founded by Claude M. Alvienne in 1894; the National Dramatic Conservatory begun by F. F. Mackay in 1898; the Stanhope–Wheatcroft Dramatic School in 1900; and the American School of Playwriting, led by William T. Price. Several schools were operated in conjunction with producing theatre companies, such as the Henry Jewett School of Acting at the Boston Repertory Theatre. A theatrical training school was associated with the Detroit Civic Theatre, managed by **Jesse Bonstelle.** Mae Desmond founded a School of Theatre in Philadelphia; even the **Washington Square Players** and the **Theatre Guild** operated training programs for a time. **James E. Murdoch,** who had entertained troops during the Civil War, carried on the scientific methods of James Rush; others such as S. S. Curry, Charles Wesley Emerson, and Leland Powers offered a more holistic approach to the actor's problems.

An important influence on the evolution of American acting arrived in 1922–3 in the form of the **Moscow Art Theatre.** By the next year **Richard Boleslavski,** trained at the MAT, opened the **American Laboratory Theatre** School in New York, using students in productions in their own theatre. Stanislavsky's System dominated the work of the **Group Theatre** and later the **Actors Studio,** especially as advocated by **Lee Strasberg.**

At present, apprenticeship remains a viable entry to professional acting. Positions are available from LORT (League of Resident Theatres) or from **summer stock** theatres, some associated with URTA (University/Resident Theatre Association), which holds annual auditions for non-Equity actors. Regional theatre conferences hold auditions as well for summer work.

Commercial or professional training offers another avenue into the profession. Dozens of commercial programs are available, mostly located in

New York (with over 40 such programs) and Los Angeles (with about 24). Among the most respected in New York are the **Neighborhood Playhouse** School of the Theatre, the HB [**Herbert Berghof**] Studio, The **Stella Adler** Conservatory of Acting, The Drama Tree, and The Actors Institute; in Los Angeles the Film Actors' Workshop is notable. The Actors Studio conducts classes in both cities. Many theatre companies have training programs, workshops, or conservatories, such as **Circle in the Square** (NYC), **American Conservatory Theater** (SF), and the **Denver Center** for the Performing Arts.

The vast majority of American actors, however, receive their first training in colleges and universities [see **academic theatre**]. A typical pattern might be for a student to pursue a Bachelor of Arts degree in theatre, possibly followed by a Master of Fine Arts, then move to a metropolitan area to continue study with a commercial school or teacher. In some cases, apprenticeships and academic credit may be combined. In the past few decades regional theatres and universities have sought to combine forces, offering the student the best of both worlds: The **Tyrone Guthrie Theatre** in Minneapolis and the University of Minnesota, Florida State University and the **Asolo Theatre** of Sarasota, Harvard University and the **American Repertory Theatre,** the University of San Diego and the **Old Globe Theatre,** the University of Utah and Pioneer Theatre Company, and others have offered joint programs. Other outstanding performance-oriented programs can be found at the Yale School of Drama, Rutgers, California Institute of the Arts, NYU's Tisch School of the Arts, North Carolina School of the Arts, the Juilliard School, and at other quality institutions.

Some American students seek the more classic training of the Royal Academy of Dramatic Art or the London Academy of Music and Dramatic Art, both of which hold annual U.S. auditions. SMA

See: C. Lawless, *The New York Theatre Sourcebook,* New York, 1990; E. Mekler, *The New Generation of Acting Teachers,* New York, 1987.

Treadwell, Sophie (1885–1970) California-born playwright and journalist (war correspondent, 1916–18). Although other plays of hers were produced – *Gringo* (1922), *Plumes in the Dust* (1936), and *Hope for a Harvest* (1941) – Treadwell's reputation rests predominantly on her innovative *Machinal* (1928). In nine expressionistic scenes, the play perfectly combined form and content, as it told the story of a woman who is robotized by life. FB

See: N. Wynn, *Sophie Treadwell: The Career of a Twentieth Century American Feminist,* Ann Arbor, 1982.

Tremont Theatre 76 Tremont St., Boston [Architect: Isaiah Rogers]. In 1827, although they were hardly able to support the **Federal Street Theatre,** Bostonians were presented with a second theatre, a handsome and elegant edifice built through the largesse of a group of wealthy and prominent citizens. For the next 16 years, the house struggled to survive as stars were lured to its stage and an excellent **stock company** was assembled. It was never able to pay for itself, and its managers resorted to a succession of novelties to keep it afloat. In 1835, **Charlotte Cushman** there made her first appearance onstage as a singer in *The Marriage of Figaro*. In 1843, the theatre was sold to the Baptist church and transformed into the Tremont Temple; nine years later, it burned down [see **fires**] and was rebuilt as a church. MCH

Trifles by **Susan Glaspell** is a tightly constructed, realistic one-act in which the major character never appears. Set in an isolated farmhouse, the play creates suspense and a sense of quiet revelation as two women piece together bits of domestic evidence to prove their absent peer murdered her husband. First produced 8 August 1916 by the **Provincetown Players** at their Wharf Theatre, *Trifles* is generally considered one of the best works to be mounted by this group and was widely translated, studied, and performed. It has more recently been examined as an early treatment of gender issues: The male authority figures, charged with solving the crime, miss essential clues because of their scorn for household matters and their inability to read emotional signs. As the women slowly make discoveries, they increasingly identify with their oppressed counterpart, find justification for her actions, and ultimately decide to conceal their knowledge. KF

Trinity Repertory Company Founded in 1964 in Providence, RI, by a group of local citizens, this ensemble became one of the more adventurous of the regional theatres in the U.S. (with over 25 world premieres). During 1965–89 its artistic director was **Adrian Hall.** Before moving in 1973 into their present complex (the Lederer Theatre, a converted vaudeville/cinema house), the company performed primarily in a converted church. A federal grant in 1966 (Project Discovery) covered many of the theatre's expenses for three years, allowing it to reach true professional stature. A major grant from the National Endowment for the Arts allowed financial security for its theatre artists beginning with the 1985–6 season. A varied bill of approximately 10–12 productions is staged annually in two theatres. In 1978 a **training** program for actors, directors, and playwrights was initiated, and in 1986 "Square" was removed from the theatre's original name. **Anne Bogart** presented a controversial season (1989–90) after Hall's departure, and was succeeded by a long-time company actor-director, Richard Jenkins. DBW

Trip to Chinatown, A by **Charles Hale Hoyt.** Opening at Hoyt's New York **Madison Square Theatre** on 9 November 1891, this "musical trifle" is thought to hold the consecutive long-run record (657 performances) for the 19th century. It also toured every region of the country. Enormously successful at writing comic farces – here in the more modern vein – for which he authored popular songs ("The Bowery," "Reuben, Reuben"), Hoyt would typically revise his plays over months on the road before bringing them to New York. The lively characters (Welland Strong, Rashleigh Gay, Wilder Daly, et al.), songs, dances, breeches and

Peter Barnes's *Red Noses*, Adrian Hall's final production and the end of the 25th anniversary of Trinity Repertory Theatre. Designed by Eugene Lee. Photo: Mark Morelli. Courtesy: Trinity Repertory Theatre.

gymsuit soubrette parts, and the stylish settings of *Chinatown* capture Hoyt's typically light and chaste, nationalized social satire, here set against a masquerade ball and a fraudulent trip to San Francisco's Chinatown.   RKB

Trouble in Mind by **Alice Childress** opened at **Off-Broadway**'s Greenwich Mews Theatre 4 November 1955 and ran 91 performances. This first major production for this nascent playwright won an Obie for new play. The play is an analysis of black and white relations, shown against the backdrop of rehearsals for a mixed-cast play set during slavery to explore the tensions between the races in the 1950s. Its central character is a black actress who must decide whether to continue playing traditional stereotyped roles or to stand up for her beliefs.   KME

True West This **Sam Shepard** play premiered at **San Francisco**'s **Magic Theatre,** directed by **Robert Woodruff,** with Peter Coyote as Austin. Although credited also as director when the play opened at New York's **Public Theater** on 23 December 1980 for a 24-performance run, Woodruff disowned the production, as did Shepard. **Frank Rich** called it "little more than stand-up run-through of a text that remains to be explored." The Cherry Lane Theater's "act of theatrical restitution and restoration" (**Mel Gussow**) opened 18 October 1982 to the relief and acclaim of critics who had come to expect such theatrical excitement of Shepard. **John Malkovich** and Gary Sinise made their New York debuts as Lee and Austin, the shiftless drifter and the Hollywood screenwriter whose sibling rivalry carries them into a virtual exchange of identities while evoking the decay of what the West once signified. It remains one of Shepard's most produced plays.   FHL

Jim Haynie as Lee in Magic Theatre's highly acclaimed 1981 production of *True West* by Sam Shepard. Ebbe Roe Smith as Austin. Photo: Allen Nomura. Courtesy: Magic Theatre.

Truth, The Social comedy by **Clyde Fitch** that opened 1 January 1907 and ran only 34 performances, though the play was regarded as Fitch's best. **Clara Bloodgood** starred as Becky Warder, a congenital liar who creates such a web of deceit that she destroys her husband's confidence in her. In many ways, the characters and action of this play parallel those in Ibsen's *A Doll House,* though the resolution here is a happy one. The failure of the play was devastating to Bloodgood, all the more so because the London production featuring Marie Tempest received unqualified accolades. Feminist scholar Kimberley Marra suggests that Bloodgood's sensational suicide on 5 December 1907 was consequential to a vision of feminine perfection that dominated American culture and that was promulgated in Fitch's plays.   MR

Tsypin, George (1954–) Soviet-born designer who studied at the Institute of Architecture in Moscow before coming in 1979 to the U.S., where he studied stage design at New York University with **John Conklin.** Tsypin is the foremost practitioner of the postmodern school of design. Working frequently with directors **Peter Sellars** and **JoAnne Akalaitis,** he has designed startling settings for classic and new plays and operas such as *The Death of Klinghoffer* (1991). The sets show a strong constructivist influence and often utilize metal, moving parts, and an overlay of projected images; images from contemporary culture mingle with references to classical architecture and theatre. In addition to work at the **New York Shakespeare Festival, Guthrie Theatre, Goodman Theatre,** and other regional theatres, Tsypin has had a gallery show of his sculptures and did the art direction for Peter Sellars's film *The Cabinet of Dr. Ramirez* (1991).   AA

Tucker, Sophie (née Sophia Kalish) (1884–1966) **Vaudeville** singer, born in Russia; known as "The Last of the Red-Hot Mammas." She made her professional debut at the 116th St. Music Hall, New York, in 1906 in blackface, and won a reputation as a "Coon Shouter," singing ragtime melodies. A brief moment in **Ziegfeld**'s *Follies of 1909* (from which she was ejected when **Nora Bayes** found the competition too daunting) was followed by stardom in vaudeville, where she capitalized on her girth and her innuendo in such songs as "He Hasn't Up to Yesterday, but I Guess He Will Tonight." In 1911 she introduced "Some of These Days," which became her theme song. She moved easily from ragtime to jazz, made a huge success in England beginning in 1922, appeared in the musicals *Leave It to Me* (1938) and *High Kickers* (1941), and helped in organizing vaudevillians into the short-lived American Federation of Actors, of which she served as President in 1938.   LS

> See: S. Tucker with D. Giles, *Some of These Days,* New York, 1945.

Tune, Tommy (Thomas James) (1939–) Dancer, actor, and choreographer who made his Broadway debut in the chorus of *Baker Street* (1965), followed by **Michael Bennett**'s *A Joyful Noise*

(1966). Fabulous tap dancing in the film version of *The Boyfriend* was followed by his Broadway show-stopping clog dance in *Seesaw* (1973), co-choreographed with Bennett: The lanky, 6' 6'' Texan tap-danced in clogs, traveling down a staircase onto a stage covered with balloons.

Tune's choreography of **dance** sequences has been enormously popular: the locker room dance in *Best Little Whorehouse in Texas* (1978); the "dance of the feet" in *A Day in Hollywood/A Night in the Ukraine* (1980); the flirtatious water tap dance in *My One and Only* (1988); and Klingelein's ecstatic Charleston in *Grand Hotel: The Musical* (1989). Tune is the only person to receive Tony Awards in four different categories: featured actor (*Seesaw*); choreography (*Hollywood/Ukraine*); director (*Nine,* 1980); and leading actor, *My One and Only* (also winning in choreography with Thommie Walsh). He is also the first to win Tony Awards in choreography and direction of a musical for two consecutive years with *Grand Hotel* and the spectacular extravaganza *The* **Will Rogers Follies** (1991). In 1991 he toured in *Bye Bye Birdie*.   LF

Tunick, Jonathan (1938–) After receiving a Master's degree from Juilliard in 1960, Tunick began writing songs for **revues** done **Off-Broadway.** In 1968 he orchestrated the musical *Promises, Promises* using electronic music and a rock beat. With *Company* (1970), Tunick began his long association with composer-lyricist **Stephen Sondheim.** In orchestrating for him, Tunick preserved the texture and emotion of the music while allowing the complex lyrics to be heard clearly. In addition to orchestrating many other hit shows of the 1970s and '80s, such as *A* **Chorus Line** and *Nine,* Tunick has arranged and conducted the scores of several films.   MK

Turner, Darwin (1931–91) **African-American** educator and anthologist. Having earned a bachelor's degree at age 16 and a master's at 18 from the University of Cincinnati, Turner began a distinguished teaching career at traditionally black colleges, gaining a doctorate from the University of Chicago when he was 25. He became professor of English and chairman of Afro-American studies at the University of Iowa in 1972. Turner was a member of several organizations devoted to the study of African-American history, literature, and culture, and edited *Black American Literature* (1970) and *Black Drama in America* (1971).   EGH

Tyler, George Crouse (1867–1946) Ohio-born manager and producer who managed his first theatre in Chillicothe at the age of 20. Afterward, he moved to New York and worked as a dramatic reporter, advance agent, and producer. In 1897, he joined forces with **Theodore A. Liebler** to found Liebler and Company, which for the next 17 years produced some 300 plays, brought to America Mrs. Patrick Campbell, Eleonora Duse, Madam Réjane, and the Abbey Theatre, and managed such stars as **Arnold Daly, James O'Neill,** and **Gertrude Elliott.** After the firm failed in 1915, Tyler was associated with **Klaw** and **Erlanger** until he became an independent producer in 1918. His best known presentations include **Booth Tarkington**'s *Clarence* (1919), **Eugene O'Neill**'s *Anna Christie* (1921), **Kaufman** and **Connelly**'s *Dulcy* (1921), and O'Casey's *The Plough and the Stars* (1927). His revival of *Macbeth* in 1928 was designed by Gordon Craig. Tyler is noted for bringing European talent to the U.S., and for preferring new works to revivals. His memoirs (with J. C. Furnas), *Whatever Goes Up,* were published in 1934.   TLM

Tyler, Royall (1758–1826) Playwright, author of *The* **Contrast** (1787), the first script by an American to receive a successful professional production. Born in Boston and educated at Harvard, Tyler showed some early literary talent and wrote *The Contrast* in three weeks after seeing his first stage production, a New York production of Sheridan's *The School for Scandal*. The script contrasts the effete world of fashion and the more manly types of Americans, and introduced the **Yankee** character to the American stage. Tyler also wrote a farce, *May Day in Town; or, New-York in an Uproar* (**John Street Theatre,** 1787) and the comedy *A*

Georgia Spec; or, Land in the Moon (Boston and New York, 1797), as well as four other plays, probably never performed.   SMA

See: A. and H. Carson, *Royall Tyler,* New York, 1979; G. T. Tanselle, *Royall Tyler,* Cambridge, MA, 1967.

Tynan, Kenneth (Peacock) (1927–80) British drama critic whose acerbic and erudite writings in the London *Observer* (1954–8; 1960–3) and in the *New Yorker* (1958–60; 1976–80) made him influential on both sides of the Atlantic. He championed the new realism of John Osborne and Arnold Wesker, calling Osborne's *Look Back in Anger* (1956) "the best young play of its decade." He promoted Brecht and other socially conscious playwrights. He was the first Literary Manager of Britain's National Theatre (1963–9). His "elegant erotica," **Oh! Calcutta!** (1969), challenged standards of morality. Tynan's most memorable line may be his characterization of *Flower Drum Song* as "the world of woozy song."   TLM

See: K. Tynan, *The Life of Kenneth Tynan,* New York, 1987.

U

Ulric (née Ulrich), Lenore (1892–1970) Actress who, like **Blanche Bates, David Warfield,** and **Mrs. Leslie Carter,** was a **David Belasco** creation. From her debut in 1916 as an Indian maiden in *The Heart of Wetona* [see **Native Americans portrayed**], Belasco cast her as a temptress in a series of exotic potboilers. In *The Son-Daughter* (1919) she was a Chinese siren, in *Kiki* (1921) a Parisian chorus girl, in *Lulu Belle* (1925) a Harlem whore, and in *Mima* (1928) a slinky mannikin. Raven-haired, with large dark eyes in an oval face, Ulric made a beguiling 1920s vamp, sultry and sharp-tongued, voluptuous and swivel-hipped. She received good notices even when the primitive, scenically spectacular Belasco vehicles she starred in were critical howlers.   FH

Uncle Tom's Cabin No other American play has had such a remarkable stage history. Mrs. Stowe's novel, published March 1852 (after its serialization), was first dramatized and performed in Baltimore (January 1852); another version played in New York in August, and a third, by **George L. Aiken** (now the accepted version), with the **Howard family** in Troy, NY, in September. The Howards made a life's work of "Tomming," as did a host of American actors. In the 1850s productions were seen also in London, Berlin, and Paris.

"Tom" shows were on the road by 1854; by 1893 a national exchange for "Tom" actors opened in Chicago, and in the '90s some 400 troupes were barnstorming across the country. Every season companies in the major cities called in the hounds to pursue Eliza across the Ohio River, a spectacle not included in the novel. Theatrical novelty became the "Tommer's" stock-in-trade: Bloodhounds, "Jubilee Singers," and dioramas became featured attractions; some troupes carried as few as three actors. In 1901 **William Brady**'s production dwarfed its predecessors with 200 buck-and-wing dancers and singers plus a transformation sequence of 21 scenes. A dozen companies were still on the road in 1927; in 1933 a Players Club revival featured **Otis Skinner** and **Fay Bainter.**

Gossett notes how strongly the play has affected American and international thinking on the character of African Americans, the nature of life in the old South, and the struggle between good and evil. Though not essentially antislavery, it served as propaganda for abolition. In this century the popular belief, as expressed by **James Baldwin,** has been that *UTC* spread the lie that "black equates with evil and white with grace." Few revivals have been seen since the 1930s; however, in 1978 **Trin-** ity Repertory Company offered a version with some success. Moreover, as recently as 1990–1 three adaptations were developed: a melodramatic version by the **San Francisco Mime Troupe** and the **Loraine Hansberry** Theatre; an epic dance-theatre piece by the dancer-choreographer Bill T. Jones (*Last Supper at Uncle Tom's Cabin/The Promised Land*); and *Unkle Tomm's Kabin: A Deconstruction of the Novel by Harriet Beecher Stowe* by Seattle's **Empty Space** Theatre. Apparently, with racial tensions resurfacing in our society, *UTC* has once more emerged as one vehicle for investigating collective racial images and attitudes, as Misha Berson has suggested in *American Theatre* (May 1991).
   RM   DBW

See: H. Birdoff, *The World's Greatest Hit: Uncle Tom's Cabin,* New York, 1947; T. F. Gossett, *Uncle Tom's Cabin and American Culture,* Dallas, 1985.

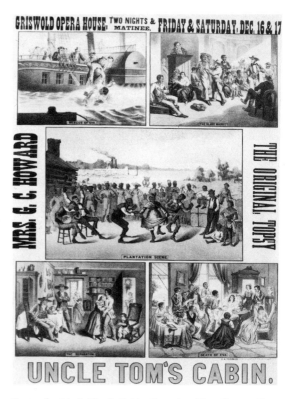

Poster for *Uncle Tom's Cabin,* featuring Mrs. George C. Howard as Topsy and a series of plantation scenes. Courtesy: Harvard Theatre Collection.

Advertising woodcut for climactic final scene of Act IV of Augustin Daly's *Under the Gaslight:* Laura rescues Snorkey from the oncoming train. Courtesy: Don B. Wilmeth.

Under the Gaslight; or, Life and Love in These Times by **Augustin Daly.**

Five-act sensational melodrama produced 12 August 1867 at the New York Theatre, with over 100 performances during the season. Daly's first original play led to two similarly constructed plays the next season, *A Flash of Lightning* and *The Red Scarf.* Each has one consummate climactic moment, which, though superficially realistic, was sheer spectacle. In *Gaslight* it was a railroad scene in the final scene of Act IV in which Snorkey (J. K. Mortimer), a thoroughly likable character who suffers without self-pity, is tied to railway tracks. Laura (**Rose Eytinge**), the heroine, is nearby in a shed, locked up intentionally for her safety while she waits for the 10:30 P.M. train. Frantically she attempts to escape in order to free Snorkey while the sounds of the train get progressively closer. Despite its improbable and overly complicated plot, *Gaslight* is one of the best American plays of the 1860s, demonstrating Daly's belief that a new American society should be based on industry rather than inherited wealth and family.　DBW

Unfinished Women Cry in No Man's Land While Bird Dies in a Gilded Cage by **Aishah Rahman** was first produced by the **New York Shakespeare Festival** in June 1977. Directed by Bill Duke with Kirk Kirksey, LaTanya Richardson, and Rosana Carter, this abstract play juxtaposes the death of a jazz musician (Charlie Parker) with the decision of a group of unwed mothers to give up their children for adoption.　KME

Unions, theatrical

Although performers had organized themselves for social and beneficial purposes since the middle of the 19th century, the stagehands were the first to achieve collective bargaining. The **National Alliance of Theatrical and Stage Employees** was formed in 1893 and became the International Alliance through affiliation with its Canadian counterpart (1898).

Though some performers resisted organization because work was abundant and salaries reasonable, working conditions at the end of the 19th century were intolerable. Actors were required to rehearse without pay for as long as necessary. There was no limit to the number of performances they were required to give during a week, but any cancellation meant a salary reduction. Moreover, actors furnished their own costumes in modern and standard period plays, paid their own way to where a tour started, and paid their own way home; yet they played at the pleasure of the management. Disputes over wages and working conditions were settled by the management, and dismissal required neither notice nor reason.

The first performers to achieve collective bargaining were those in the **Yiddish theatre.** The Hebrew Actors' Union was founded in 1899 and recognized in 1902. English-language players had formed the Actors' Society in 1896, but it failed to achieve a standard contract. Its last act was to authorize a study group, which then organized itself as **Actors' Equity Association** (1913). Their affiliation with the American Federation of Labor was delayed because the AFL had issued a charter for all performers to The White Rats **vaudeville** union in 1910: Formed in 1900, it was crushed in a lockout (1916–17) and surrendered its charter in 1919; with AFL support, Equity then struck in the fall. Ultimately, their membership swelled from 2,700 to 14,000, and the producers capitulated in a month. Subsequently, Equity won a closed shop (1924), and producer contributions to pension and welfare funds (1960).

New unions were created in response to new media. The Screen Actors Guild (SAG) was formed in 1933. The American Federation of Radio Artists was born in 1937, and was expanded to include television (AFTRA) in 1952. The American Guild of Musical Artists was founded in 1936, and the American Guild of Variety Artists (AGVA) in 1939.

Organization of nonperformers also emerged in the 20th century. The **Dramatists Guild** of America became a separate branch of the Authors' League of America (founded in 1912) in 1920. In the same year the Screen Writers Guild was formed. Designers affiliated in the United Scenic Artists (1918), the Association of Theatrical Press Agents and Managers was formed in 1928, and the Society of Stage Directors and Choreographers (SSDC) in 1959.　DMcD

Union Square Theatre

Union Square South, between Broadway and Fourth Ave., NYC. Sheridan Shook, the owner of the Union Place (later the Morton House) Hotel, installed a theatre within the hotel and opened it in 1871 as the Union Square Theatre. A year later, he entrusted it to **A. M. Palmer.** With no experience in theatrical management but with a passion for the theatre, Palmer succeeded in finding the right actors and in producing a succession of successful romantic melodramas to become a competitor of the nearby **Wallack's.** After he left the theatre in 1883, it passed to the management of J. M. Hill prior to its destruction by **fire** in 1888. When it was rebuilt, it was taken over by the **Keith-Albee** chain for continuous **vaudeville** in 1893. During 1908–36 it served mainly as a moviehouse. When it was finally closed, the section of the theatre fronting 14th Street was rebuilt into shops; the rear section, however, was walled up and still stands.　MCH

United Booking Office With the Vaudeville Managers' Protective Association and the National Vaudeville Artists, the dominant business force in big-time **vaudeville.** Founded by **B. F. Keith** and **E. F. Albee** in 1906 as a kind of clearinghouse that matched managers and performers and ultimately determined what acts could play the major circuits, the UBO created a virtual monopoly of first-class vaudeville. Despite opposition from numerous vaudevillians (and the White Rats, their fraternal organization [see **unions**]), attacks in the press, and even a Federal Trade Commission investigation for blacklisting, the UBO survived until the demise of vaudeville itself.   DBW

Urban, Joseph (1871–1933) Austrian-American set designer. Many of the approaches and techniques adopted by **Robert Edmond Jones, Lee Simonson,** and others were first introduced in America by Urban. In the 1890s in Vienna he designed palaces, exposition pavilions, and a bridge. In 1904 he began to work with the Vienna Burgtheater and spent the next years designing operas throughout Europe. He came to the U.S. in 1912 to design for the Boston Opera. He was discovered by showman **Florenz Ziegfeld,** who persuaded him to design for the *Follies*. Urban's designs were simple in terms of line, but vibrant color created a sense of lushness and complexity. He achieved this by applying pointillist techniques – the juxtaposition of dots of color – to scene painting. This not only added new dimensions to painted scenery, but also allowed parts of the image to appear or disappear under different colored lights. He was also one of the first to use platforms and portals – arched scenic units at the side of the stage, connected at the top. This framed and focused the stage while providing continuous elements for unit sets.   AA

Uris Theatre see **Gershwin Theatre**

V

Vaccaro, John (19?–) Actor, director, and producer of campy underground **performance art** in the 1960s and '70s, Vaccaro is noted for his bawdy, violent, orgiastic, and strongly visual directing style for the Play-House of the Ridiculous [see **Theatre of the Ridiculous**], which he co-founded (1966) with Harvey and **Ron Tavel,** Bill Walters, **Charles Ludlam,** and others. TLM

Vagabond King, The Four-act operetta, music by **Rudolph Friml,** words by Russell Janney and Brian Hooker; opened 21 September 1925 at the **Casino Theatre,** running 511 performances. Set in 15th-century France, this is the tale of vagabond poet François Villon (**Dennis King**), who, made king of France for a day, saves king and country from Burgundy and wins the heart of the noble Katherine (Carolyn Thomson). Second in popularity among Friml's works only to *Rose-Marie* (1924), it is quintessential old-fashioned, romantic operetta, brimming with stirring melodies that include rousing anthems, drinking songs, and waltzes (notably "Only a Rose"). A London production (1927) was equally popular. JD

Valdéz, Luis (1940–) Chicano director and playwright responsible for the **Chicano theatre** revolution. University trained and a student activist at San José State, he visited Cuba before joining the **San Francisco Mime Troupe** in 1964. Knowledgeable about *commedia dell'arte,* Brecht, and panto**mime,** he used bilingual theatre to help César Chávez organize the migrant workers around Delano, CA, in 1965. His efforts led to the creation of the *actos,* one-act revolutionary pieces, and the creation of **El Teatro Campesino** (Farmworkers' Theatre), which in turn inspired the formation of other Chicano theatre groups. His early titles include *Las dos caras del patronicito* (*The Boss's Two Faces*), *Quinta temporada* (*Fifth Season*), *No saco nada de la escuela* (*I Don't Get Anything out of School*), *Vietnam campesino* (*Vietnam Farmer*), *Soldado razo* (*Buck Private*), and *Huelguistas* (*Strikers*). **Zoot Suit** (1978), based on the Sleepy Lagoon murder trial during WW II, dramatized the stereotypical *pachuco* in a successful run in Los Angeles, but failed on Broadway. Teatro Campesino became professional and later moved into new facilities in San Juan Bautista. Valdéz's folk musical *Corridos,* based on popular Mexican folk ballad traditions, opened in 1983. Each season the El Teatro Campesino stages plays by Valdéz, including the annual *La Pastorela,* his adaptation from Mexican folklore of the journey of the shep-

herds to the manger. Valdéz also created the film *La Bamba.* GW

Vampire Lesbians of Sodom A campy comedy by Charles Busch satirizing Hollywood of the 1920s and contemporary Las Vegas, first produced at the Limbo Lounge in the East Village (NYC) before opening **Off-Broadway** at the Provincetown Playhouse (19 June 1985) as part of a double bill with Busch's *Sleeping Beauty or Coma.* A female impersonator, Busch appeared in both plays, which ran together for 2,024 performances (until 27 May 1990), attracting a cult following and making Busch a star. TLM

Van, Gus (né August Van Glone) (1888–1968) and **Joe (Joseph T.) Schenck** (1892?–1930) **Vaudeville** singing team; boyhood chums in Brooklyn (where they both worked as trolley car operators) and professional partners ("The Pennant Winning Battery of Songland") from 1910 when they entered vaudeville. Van, a baritone, specialized in dialect songs in Italian or Yiddish; Schenck played the piano and harmonized in his tenor voice. In addition to vaudeville, they appeared in *The Century Girl* (1916), *Ziegfeld* Follies (1919–21), and **nightclubs.** Their most famous song, **Irving Berlin**'s "Mandy," was introduced in the 1919 *Follies.* After Schenck's death, Van continued as a successful solo act into the 1940s. DBW

Van Amburgh, Isaac A. (1811–65) "The Lion King" (also "Monarch of the Forest") and, though not the first American **circus** performer to enter a cage of big cats, considered the first modern wild animal trainer – and, according to Joys, the first legendary performer in circus history (his name was used as a circus title as late as 1922). Van Amburgh, born in Fishkill, NY, began as an animal caretaker (cage boy), and in 1833 first appeared in a cage with wild animals. To counter religious prejudice against circuses, he quoted the Bible to justify his traveling menagerie. As a trainer, he reportedly combined cruelty with mesmerizing control (his eyes were apparently extraordinary). Between circus seasons he took theatrical roles, such as Constantius the Greek in *The Lion Lord,* and the Arab who rescues a princess thrown to his cats in *The Daughter of the Emir.* DBW

See: J. Joys, *The Wild Animal Trainer in America,* Boulder, CO, 1983.

Vandenhoff, George (1813–85) British-born actor and lawyer, son of the actor John Vandenhoff. After a debut at Covent Garden in 1839, George began his American career at the **Park Theatre** in 1842 as Hamlet. As an actor he was noted for his correctness, but he lacked power and apparently never liked the stage. After returning to England in 1853, where he and his new wife acted in the provinces, he retired from the stage in the mid-1850s. Although admitted to the New York Bar in 1858, he spent much of his time teaching elocution and giving public readings. In 1860 he published his reminiscences, *Leaves from an Actor's Notebook.*   DBW

Van Druten, John (1901–57) Playwright whose dramatic career began in London, though in New York he created his most successful work, which is characterized as witty, domestic comedy that usually reflects contemporary middle-class society. *The Voice of the Turtle* (1943), a romantic three-character, wartime comedy, ran for over 1,500 performances. Nostalgic *I Remember Mama* (1944) was adapted from a novel; the adaptation *I Am a Camera* (1951), which is more cynical in its portrait of Berlin, inspired *Cabaret. Bell, Book and Candle* (1950) is a clever play about a beautiful witch who must abjure her craft to secure the man she loves. An autobiography, *This Way to the Present,* was published in 1938.   RHW

Van Itallie, Jean-Claude (1936–) Playwright, director, producer, and teacher. Born in Brussels, Belgium, Van Itallie became a naturalized American citizen in 1952. After studying at Harvard and the **Neighborhood Playhouse,** Van Itallie made his debut as a writer in 1963 with *War.* His *Motel* and *Pavanne* were produced at the Café **La MaMa** in 1965, attracting considerable attention to him as a new talent. *America Hurrah* appeared at the Pocket Theatre, NYC, in 1966; *The Serpent* premiered in Rome in 1968 and was produced by the **Open Theatre,** NYC, in 1969. Other scripts include *King of the U.S.* (1972), *Mystery Play* (1973), and his own version of *The Seagull* in 1973. Van Itallie has adapted two other **Chekhov** scripts, *The Cherry Orchard* (1977) and *The Three Sisters* (1979). His 1991 play about the effects of **AIDS,** *Ancient Boys* (La MaMa), failed to receive critical acceptance.

Van Itallie's affiliation with the Open Theatre and **Joseph Chaikin** placed him at the forefront of experimental dramaturgy in the 1960s and '70s. Especially with the Open Theatre, Van Itallie merged European traditions with a poetic vision of American experience.   SMA

Varieties (Gaiety) Theatre (New Orleans) The first Varieties Theater, built in 1849 and leased to **Thomas Placide,** burned in 1854. The second structure, built in 1855 on the site of the first, was called the Gaiety. **Stock companies** managed by **Dion Boucicault,** William Crisp, Thomas Placide (when the building was renamed the Varieties), and **John Owens** occupied the theatre until the Civil War closed it in 1861. Reopened in 1863, it burned in 1870. The Third Varieties, built in 1871 and renamed the Grand Opera House in 1881, featured touring attractions; it was razed in 1906.   WD

Variety Theatrical trade paper founded by Sime Silverman in 1905 as a weekly to cover all phases of show business. *Variety* has been characterized by its jargon (e.g., show biz, Hollywood pix, Broadway legit) and its financial assessment of the entertainment business. It incorporated *The **New York Clipper*** (1924), added a daily *Variety* published in Hollywood (1933), and expanded international coverage. Reviews, weekly grosses, attendance figures, and end-of-the-year statistics provide an accurate record of legitimate productions.   TLM

Vaudeville This essentially American form of variety has nothing to do with the French *vaudeville,* a farce studded with songs set to popular tunes; rather, the term attempted to lend a veneer of elegance to what was originally rough-and-ready entertainment. A so-called vaudeville house had been opened by William Valentine in 1840, and H. J. Sargent's Great Vaudeville Co. was playing in Louisville in 1871, but the term did not catch on till later.

The usual venue for variety performances in the late 1860s was the concert saloon, its waitresses and dancing girls closely allied to the prostitutes that preyed on the all-male audience. **Minstrels** and chorines, unemployed after the decline of the leg show, drifted into these "olio entertainments," as did newly formed doubles acts. Unlike European variety, where song was the standard unit, broad comedy and exuberant dance predominated here. This "honky tonk" style permutated into **burlesque,** while respectable variety gained greater professionalism and urbanity during 1876–93 to become vaudeville.

Tony Pastor, hoping to lure a family audience with giveaways and promises of clean amusement, was instrumental in this development, and the traditional, if debatable, date given for the birth of vaudeville is the opening of his 14th St. Theatre, New York, on 24 October 1881. The innovation was enlarged and expanded by **Benjamin Franklin Keith** and his associate **Edward F. Albee.** Keith began with a "store-show," the Gaiety Museum, **Boston,** and had Albee transform it in 1885 into a Japanese tea garden offering a tabloid opera. So great was their success that they soon owned several theatres, and in 1894 opened the first exclusively vaudeville house, the Boston Colonial, typical of the opulent palaces designed to lure the middle-class spectator into a fairy-tale world of luxury. Keith and Albee eliminated offensive material, fined offenders, and introduced the continuous show, so that one could enter the theatre at any time between 9:30 A.M. and 10:30 P.M. and see a performance. The invention of "continuous vaudeville," well ensconced by 1896, is also attributed to **F. F. Proctor,** a sometime partner, who claimed "to give the masses what they want," but forbade smoking and drinking in the auditorium.

Competing with these robber barons were Martin Beck, credited with establishing the touring vaudeville company, who backed "class acts" to educate the public; **Oscar Hammerstein I,** who aimed his Roof at an elitist and his Olympic at a more popular public; William Morris, J. J. Murdoch, and Sylvester Poli. The Keith–Albee circuit dominated the eastern U.S. through its many theatres (over 400 by 1920) and booking offices; Beck's **Orpheum theatre circuit** played the West, though he also built the New York **Palace,** which soon was regarded as vaudeville's Valhalla. In addition, there were thousands of small houses scattered throughout the nation, enabling performers to play one-night stands during the season. Vaudevillians became a nomadic race, living much of the year on railway carriages and platforms and in dreary boardinghouses.

By 1900 the typical "polite vaudeville" bill had grown formulaic, and was divided into two parts by an intermission. The first part would open with a "dumb act," animals or acrobats, whose effect would not be damaged by a noisy entering audience. The number three slot was intended to wake up the house, the number four to deliver the first solid punch, and the last before the interval a knockout that would bring them back wanting more. The prime position was "next to closing," where the "headliner" or star of stars appeared. The concluding act was meant as a "chaser," often a cinematic offering, like a newsreel. Turns or "numbers" seldom lasted more than 10–20 minutes, although some popular egoists like the Scot **Harry Lauder** and **Al Jolson** might usurp a whole hour. According to **George Burns,** a performer needed only 17 good minutes, which he could play year in, year out across the country, until the act became too pirated or shopworn for use. The diversity of performance was considerable: In addition to the song-and-dance and comedy acts, there were **mime**s, ventriloquists, eccentrics, musical virtuosi, acrobats and jugglers, **female and male impersonators,** miniature musicals, monologuists, trained animals, conjurers, demonstrations of new inventions, and even famous criminals discoursing on their lurid past.

Much of the comedy in vaudeville dealt in racial stereotypes, with the Dutch, Irish, Jewish, blackface, Swedish, and Italian comics the most familiar, reflecting the melting-pot nature of urban American society; by 1910 many of the older types, including the hick and Bowery tough, were *passé.* Low comedy was categorized as "jazz," a fast routine to speed up an act, or "hokum," crude fun verging on vulgarity. Despite the efforts of the managers, innuendo was often resorted to, particularly in the 1920s, when more sophisticated audiences expected it.

Dance tended to be acrobatic until WW I, when adagio and exhibition ballroom dancing and even imitations of the Ballets Russes arrived. Singers were either sentimental or strenuous, but American audiences – unless exhorted by such devices as "following the bouncing ball" on a projected songsheet – seldom joined in the chorus, another token of the heterogeneity of the public. Among the leading performers spawned by vaudeville or trained in its excellent school were **Eva Tanguay,** the "I Don't Care" Girl; **Elsie Janis; Nora Bayes; W. C. Fields** who moved from juggling to comic skits;

Eddie Cantor and **Al Jolson,** who retained the corked face of minstrelsy, as did black comedian **Bert Williams; George M. Cohan,** whose family had been variety pioneers; **Will Rogers,** with his low-keyed commentary; and **George Burns and Gracie Allen,** whose doubles act refined the Dumb Dora creation of Ryan and Lee. As vaudeville increased in respectability and popularity, stars of the "legit," like **Lillie Langtry,** Ethel Barrymore [see **Drew–Barrymore**], and **Alla Nazimova,** played "tab" (shortened) versions of their dramatic hits on the circuits.

The American language was enriched by vaudeville slang: a success was a "wow," a "panic," or a "riot"; a failure a "flop," "all wet," or "all washed up." Duffey and Sweeney originated the phrase, "We died in . . ." to indicate an utter fiasco. The minstrel Billy Emerson's "hoofer" for dancer became popular, along with the injunction "Strut your stuff" and the exit "Shuffle off to Buffalo." Some terms were too technical to become widespread, such as "grouch bag" for a purse pinned to the underwear for safety's sake, "feeder" for straight man, "split time" for three days' work in any theatre, or "death trail" for a circuit of small towns; but "coffin nails" for cigarettes, which came from **Junie McCree**'s act, and "belly laughs," coined by Jack Conway, did enter the language.

Vaudeville was the dominant form of American entertainment by 1890, and grew exponentially: In 1896 New York had seven vaudeville theatres; by 1910, 22. It came to be clearly differentiated into the Big Time, with its two-a-day offerings of an eight- or nine-act bill, and the Small Time, with fewer acts and a film played continuously. The empire building of the leading managements created booking agencies that could blacklist performers who did not conform to the rules or who failed to kick-back percentages of their salaries (often levies were imposed by the house manager before the salary was paid). Keith–Albee created the **United Booking Office** (UBO) in 1906, whose impositions were so outrageous that the performers banded into a protective society, the White Rats, which failed to sustain its strike in 1900 [see **unions**]. Astutely, Albee backed a new organization, the National Vaudeville Artists (NVA), in 1916, which ameliorated some of the abuses without seriously harming the managers' interests.

African-American performers were exploited in vaudeville by the **Theatre Owner's Booking Association** or Chitlin Circuit – a busy group of segregated theatres stretching from New York to Florida, Chicago to New Orleans, but primarily centered in the South – offered black vaudevillians low pay and little future.

The decline of vaudeville is attributable to a number of factors. Between 1905 and 1912, the Big Time had grown in sophistication, putting its emphasis on glamour, novelty, and lavish wardrobes; the influence of the musical comedy and **revue** could be felt. Before 1925, it reached its period of greatest growth, but the cinema proved a powerful rival for lower-class audiences made uncomfortable by vaudeville's aspirations to gentility and its increased admission prices (the Palace went as high as $2). The automobile, put within everyone's financial reach by Henry Ford, enabled city dwellers to escape to the country. During Prohibition, the proliferation of **nightclubs** offered a sophisticated and alcoholic alternative to those bored by vaudeville's stale material. By the mid-1920s many vaudeville houses were converted to cinemas, and the succumbing of the Palace in 1932, its *coup de grâce* delivered by the Depression, is considered the symbolic terminus of the form. Some managers like **Marcus Loew** persisted in alternating films with live performance at their houses, but gradually vaudeville came to be regarded as the seedbed for mass media: Many of the most popular comedians, singers, and dancers in the movies, on the radio and, later, television had honed their skills in vaudeville.   LS

> See: C. Caffin, *Vaudeville*, New York, 1914; J. E. DiMeglio, *Vaudeville USA*, Bowling Green, OH, 1973; D. Gilbert, *American Vaudeville*, New York, 1940, 1963; J. Laurie, Jr., *Vaudeville: From the Honky-tonks to the Palace*, New York, 1953; A. F. McLean, *American Vaudeville as Ritual*, Louisville, KY, 1965; B. Page, *Writing for Vaudeville*, Springfield, MA, 1915; F. Renton, *The Vaudeville Theatre: Building, Operation, Management*, New York, 1918; A. Slide, *The Vaudevillians*, Westport, CT, 1981; B. Smith, *The Vaudevillians*, New York, 1976; R. W. Snyder, *The Voice of the City: Vaudeville & Popular Culture in New York*, New York, 1989; S. Staples, *Male–Female Comedy Teams in American Vaudeville 1865–1932*, Ann Arbor, 1984; C. W. Stein, ed., *American Vaudeville As Seen by Its Contemporaries*, New York, 1984.

Vaughan, Stuart (1925–) Director, actor, and playwright. Indiana-born and educated at Indiana University, Vaughan created lucid productions of the classics in nonprofit regional and New York theatres from the early 1950s until late '80s. He served as artistic director of the **New York Shakespeare Festival** (1956–8), Phoenix Theatre (1958–63) [see **Association of Producing Artists**], and **Seattle Repertory Theatre** (1963–6). He was founder and producer-director of the Repertory Theatre of New Orleans (1966–9), followed by visiting professorships and free-lance directing assignments. In the 1987–8 season, his *Two Gentlemen of Verona* for the NYSF was praised for being sexy and funny, but his *Julius Caesar* and *King John* were condemned as pedantic and conventional. Vaughan adapted *Henry VI, Parts 1–3* and *Richard III* as *The War of the Roses* for the NYSF (1969); he has also written several original plays, and is the author of *A Possible Theatre* (1969), a record of his regional theatre experiences.   TLM

Vernon, Dai (né David Frederick Wingfield Verner) (1894–) Termed by conjuror-magic historian Ricky Jay "the most influential, compelling, and venerable figure" in the art of sleight-of-hand and a "magician's magican," Canadian-born Vernon, known throughout the world as "The Professor," is arguably the greatest card expert who ever lived, an unrivaled close-up performer (though he began as a stage magician), and the most influential individual in modern **magic.** His numerous books (several with Lewis Ganson) are among the best in the field, especially for card manipulation.   DBW

Verdon, Gwen (1926–) American dancer, singer, and actress. Considered to be the finest musical comedy dancer of the 1950s, Verdon studied with choreographer **Jack Cole** and assisted him with the choreography for *Magdalena* (1948) and *Alive and Kicking* (1950), making her Broadway debut as a dancer in the latter. Given a supporting role in **Can-Can** (1953), Verdon stole the show with her exuberant dancing and her impish clowning. Following her success as the seductive Lola in **Damn Yankees** (1955), Verdon surprised critics and audiences with her poignant acting in *New Girl in Town* (1957), a musical version of **Eugene O'Neill**'s **Anna Christie.** She next appeared in *Redhead,* a vehicle written especially for her. In 1966 she created the role of Charity Hope Valentine in **Sweet Charity,** which was choreographed and directed by her then-husband, **Bob Fosse.** Despite reservations about the show's libretto, critics praised Verdon's performance for its innocence and vulnerability. Verdon's only musical of the 1970s was the tawdry, flamboyant **Chicago** (1975), in which she was again directed by Fosse. In all of her musicals, Verdon's sinuous, energetic style of dance ideally suited the jazz choreography created for her by Cole and Fosse.   MK

Very Good Eddie Two-act musical comedy, music by **Jerome Kern,** lyrics by Schuyler Green, book by **Guy Bolton;** opened 23 December 1915 at the **Princess Theatre,** running 341 performances. The second of the innovative "Princess Musicals" of Kern, Bolton, and (later) **P. G. Wodehouse,** this tale of embarrassingly mismatched couples on a Hudson River cruise was the first big hit of the series. Small in scope, simple in story, and substituting charm for gaudiness, it became a standard for its diminutive successors. A 1975 "revival" at the **Goodspeed Opera House,** revised with numerous songs from other early Kern musicals added, moved to Broadway on 21 December 1975, running 304 performances.   JD

Victory Gardens Theater Theatre founded by a group of eight **Chicago** theatre artists in 1974 that has been led by Dennis Zacek and Marcelle McVay for virtually all of its existence. Unlike more famous Chicago theatres, Victory Gardens has not sent many productions on to commercial success. However, it has excelled as a creative center for playwrights and actors of various ethnic backgrounds: The Latino Chicago company began as a Victory Gardens project. Among the playwrights who have worked there are Jeffrey Sweet, Alan Gross, Charles Smith, Rick Cleveland, Claudia Allen, Darrah Cloud, Steve Carter, Dean Corrin, Nicholas Patricca, and Lonnie Carter.   SF

Vidal, Gore (1925–) The prolific author of novels *Myra Breckinridge* (1968), *Burr* (1974), and *Lincoln* (1984) has been successful in the theatre with *Visit to a Small Planet* (1957), a comedy about an invasion from outer space, and *The Best Man* (1960), a drama about political infighting over the nomination for president. Other plays include *On the March to the Sea* (1961), *Weekend* (1968), and *An Evening with Richard Nixon and . . .* (1972).   TLM

View from the Bridge, A, by **Arthur Miller** opened, in its original one-act form, in New York on 29 September 1955, running for 149 performances. Martin Ritt directed a cast including Van Heflin, J. Carrol Naish, **Eileen Heckart,** and Gloria Marlowe. A more successful two-act version opened in London in 1956, and an **Off-Broadway** revival in 1965 with Robert Duvall ran for 780 performances. Michael Gambon's Eddie won accolades in a 1987 London revival. Set on the Brooklyn waterfront, the play depicts longshoreman Eddie Carbone's too intense love for his niece Catherine, which causes him to violate the code of the Sicilian community by informing on the illegal immigrant she wants to marry. As narrator Alfieri points out, the play has the primal elements of classical tragedy in the seemingly inevitable course of events that leads to Eddie's destruction. BCM

Virginia Theatre 245 West 52nd St., NYC [Architect: C. Howard Crane]. In 1925, with a good deal of ceremony, the **Theatre Guild** opened its new house, the Guild, which was intended for its own productions. For a number of reasons relating to the design of the theatre and the paucity of seats (under 1,000), it proved to be unpopular with actors and audiences; the Theatre Guild turned to other theatres for its most significant productions while leasing the Guild to other producers. During 1943–50 it was rented as a radio playhouse, then sold to the **American National Theatre and Academy** to be operated by its board as a not-for-profit "home for the living arts." After extensive renovation, the newly named ANTA Playhouse was only intermittently used for ANTA-sponsored productions and more often leased to commercial producers. In 1981, the **Jujamcyn** Organization bought it from the ANTA board, renovated it, increased its seating, and renamed it the Virginia after the wife of the owner, James Binger. MCH

Vivian Beaumont and Mitzi E. Newhouse Theatres Lincoln Center, NYC [Architects: Eero Saarinen with **Jo Mielziner**]. Part of the Lincoln Center for the Performing Arts, this repertory theatre and its experimental appendage began under the aegis of **Elia Kazan** and **Robert Whitehead,** who spent two years planning it. Named after Mrs. Vivian Beaumont Allen, its benefactress, the larger theatre opened in 1965. The playhouse was designed with 11,000 sq ft of stage space (compared to the 3,000 of the **Martin Beck Theatre** on Broadway) and was intended to shift from a proscenium to a thrust stage and to be able to store scenery for the repertory. All of the mechanical and electrical elements are concealed, and the auditorium, with a flexible 1,090–1,140 seats, is gently amphitheatrical. The smaller stage (originally the Forum), with its 299 seats, was designed with all of the structural, mechanical, and electrical equipment exposed and was intended for experimental productions. Kazan and Whitehead resigned and were replaced by **Herbert Blau** and **Jules Irving** in the first year, then by Irving alone in 1967. He was succeeded by **Joseph Papp** (1973–7), who obtained operating funds from Mrs. Mitzi E. Newhouse, after whom he renamed the Forum. Since Papp's departure, the theatres were reopened only intermittently, as the Lincoln Center management struggled to find both a purpose for them and new creative leaders; finally, in 1985, **Gregory Mosher** of the Chicago **Goodman Theatre** and Bernard Gersten, a Broadway and **Off-Broadway** producer, began their leadership – though in 1992 Mosher was succeeded by André Bishop, artistic director for a decade of **Playwrights Horizons.** MCH

See: E. B. Young, *Lincoln Center: The Building of an Institution,* New York, 1980.

Voelpel, Fred (1927?–) Illinois-born costume and scenic designer, a Yale MFA, who has been designing costumes and sets professionally since 1956 for television and theatre. Nominated for numerous awards, he received a New York Critics' Award, a *Variety* Poll Award, and an Obie for scenic design for **The Effect of Gamma Rays on Man-in-the-Moon Marigolds** (1970) and a Critics' Award for *No Strings* (costumes). He has been a master teacher of design at New York University since 1964, and has been associated with the **National Theatre for the Deaf,** the **National Playwrights' Conference,** and the National Theatre Institute (since 1975). BO

Vollmer, Lula (or Lulu) (1895–1955) Folk dramatist who portrayed strong, righteous North Carolina mountain women. *Sun-up* (1923) ran for two years and received praise for its presentation of the Widow Cagle, caught between the law and her own beliefs. Vollmer followed *Sun-up* with lesser hits such as *The Shame Woman* (1923) and *The Dunce Boy* (1925). FB

W

Wagenhals, Lincoln A. (1869–1931) and **Colin Kemper** (1870–1955) Producers and managers. Beginning their partnership in 1893 as managers of Stone Opera House in Binghamton, NY, Wagenhals and Kemper had arrived on Broadway by 1906 when they leased the new Astor Theatre. They established themselves as producers with the success of **Eugene Walter**'s *Paid in Full* (1908). Other hits include **Mary Roberts Rinehart** and **Avery Hopgood**'s *Seven Days* (1909) and *The Bat* (1920), the latter running 867 performances. They managed the careers of major stars, including **Frederick Warde, Modjeska, Henry Miller,** Blanche Walsh, and **Annie Russell.** Their last production was *The Joker* (1925). TLM

Wagner, Robin (1933–   ) Set designer who has been associated with some of the most successful musicals of the post-1960 period, including *Hair, A Chorus Line,* and *Dreamgirls.* He began his career in **San Francisco** and worked with the Actor's Workshop, where he was greatly influenced by director **Herbert Blau** and Brechtian aesthetics. His work at the **Arena Stage** in the mid-1960s led to explorations of stage space and moving scenery. Wagner is generally associated with spectacular sets, moving scenery, and stylish decor, but by and large his sets are minimal; it is the way in which the sets move and are integrated into the production that gives the illusion of a great deal of scenery. His best set (and best known) was for *A Chorus Line:* For most of the show it consisted only of a white line on the floor; in the final scene the upstage wall revealed mylar mirrors. This seemingly simple set was the result of over a year of stripping away excess and unnecessary scenic elements to arrive at a design that simply and boldly expressed the essence of the play. Wagner has never followed tradition or conventions; he has always explored new ideas, new materials, and new configurations of space. In addition to Broadway he has also designed for opera, dance, and rock concerts. AA

Wainright, Marie (1853–1923) Philadelphia-born actress, daughter of a commodore; educated abroad, including three years of dramatic arts studies in Paris. She made her 1877 debut at **Booth's Theatre** as one of five Juliets appearing in a benefit for George Rignold. She was the first American to play Josephine in **Gilbert and Sullivan**'s *HMS Pinafore.* After touring for five years with **Lawrence Barrett,** with London performances in 1884, she formed her own company. Other highlights of a career that ranged from vaudeville to Shakespeare

were her 1886 tour as leading lady in the **Edwin Booth**–Salvini company and performances opposite **William Gillette.** FHL

Waiting for Lefty Developed by **Clifford Odets** and others in the **Group Theatre** (yet finished by Odets alone), this one-act play presents, in a series of vignettes, the events leading up to a taxi strike. Codirected by Odets and **Sanford Meisner,** it was first performed at the **Civic Repertory** Theatre on 6 January 1935 as part of a Sunday benefit organized by the League of Workers Theatres for the *New Theatre Magazine.* Immediately it became the historical highlight of the 1930s theatre, the quintessential piece of proletarian drama and agitprop theatre. The audience, in response to calls for action from the stage, erupted with chants of "Strike! Strike!" The Group Theatre soon moved it to Broadway, where it ran for almost 200 performances. In that same year, dozens of productions were mounted across the country. The play launched Odets as a playwright and was decisive in convincing the Group Theatre to produce another of Odets's plays, *Awake and Sing!* (which actually had been drafted before *Lefty*). Though clearly of its era, the play has been revived occasionally, including a **Roundabout Theatre** production in 1967. TP

Walcot, Charles Melton, Sr. (1815–68) Actor and playwright. Coming to America in 1839, Walcot became associated with William **Mitchell's Olympic** in New York as a superb comic actor and prolific playwright (*Fried Shots* [1843, a burlesque of Weber's opera *Der Freischütz*]; *Brittania and Hibernia* [1849]). In **John Brougham**'s *Po-ca-hon-tas* (1855) – he as Captain John Smith, Brougham as Powhatan – these two "brainy men" brought new heights to burlesque acting. At **Wallack's Theatre** (1853–61) Walcot also did some of his best writing with *Hiawatha; or, Ardent Spirits and Laughing Water* (1855), a burlesque loaded with local allusions, that appeared soon after the publication of Longfellow's poem. WJM

Walken, Christopher (1943–) New York–born actor who alternates his career among stage, film, and television. Since his Broadway debut at 16 in *J. B.,* he has appeared in more than 100 stage productions (in 1991 as Iago in *Othello* for the **New York Shakespeare Festival**) and over 20 films (including a 1979 best supporting actor Oscar as a suicidal soldier in *The Deer Hunter*). Known as a sensitive, often understated actor, Walken won an Obie in *Kid Champion* (1975) and a Theatre World

Award for his role of Jack Hunter in the City Center revival of *Rose Tattoo* (1966).   DBW

Walker, George see **Williams, Bert**

Wallach, Eli (1915–) and **Anne Jackson** (1926–) Brooklyn-born Wallach made his New York debut as the crew chief in *Skydrift* (1945). He won stardom as Alvaro Mangiacavallo, a sexually driven truck driver in **Tennessee Williams**'s *The Rose Tattoo* (1951). Both Wallach and his wife, Anne Jackson, had substantial successes before their marriage in 1948, but were acclaimed as an acting duo in *The Typists* and *The Tiger* in 1963. Jackson made her professional debut in a touring production of *The Cherry Orchard,* later appearing with **Eva Le Gallienne**'s **American Repertory Theatre** in 1946. Jackson and Wallach appeared together in *Luv* (1964), a revival of *The Waltz of the Toreadors* (1973), and *Twice Around the Park* (1982). Both Jackson and Wallach have appeared in numerous films and television programs, though Wallach has been more prolific as a film actor, beginning with *Baby Doll* in 1956.

Both members of the team use an internal intensity (both studied at the **Actors Studio**) suitable for drama or comedy. Of them in *Luv*, critics said "Miss Jackson can play comedy as straight-faced and doggedly as if she were mining coal, but she turns up diamonds," and "Mr. Wallach has a flair for enduring indignities, whether of poverty or affluence, marriage or divorce."   SMA

Wallack family A dynasty of actor-managers, of English origin, in the American theatre, inseparably linked with the history of the New York stage for over 50 years. **Henry John Wallack** (1790–1870) – the eldest son of William H. Wallack (1760–1850) and Elizabeth Field (Granger) (d. 1850), popular performers at London's Astley's Amphitheatre and later at the Surrey – came to the U.S. in 1819 with his first wife, dancer Fanny Jones. After lengthy stays in Baltimore, Philadelphia, and Washington, DC, Wallack made his NYC debut at the Anthony Street Theatre in 1821; in 1824 he became leading man at the **Chatham Theatre**. During 1828–32, 1834–6, and during the summer of 1840 and for some time afterward, he was back in England, acting sporadically. In 1837 he was stage manager, under his brother, at the National Theatre. He gained considerable acclaim for his Sir Peter Teazle in 1847 at New York's **Broadway Theatre**. One of his last roles was Falstaff in 1858.

Though a versatile and accomplished actor, Henry did not win the fame of other family members in the U.S. Two of his sisters were actors – Mary (Mrs. Stanley) and Elizabeth (Mrs. Pincott), mother of the actress Leonora, later known as Mrs. Alfred Wigan – as was his brother **James William Wallack** (1795?–1864), known as the elder to distinguish him from his nephew. This Wallack, also born in England, appeared first in the U.S. at the **Park Theatre** as Macbeth in 1818. For the next 35 years he shuttled between the U.S. and England, though he was best known on the American stage. The most distinguished member of this notable family, he was admired for roles in tragedy and

Sarony photo (1870s) of Lester Wallack in *Rosedale,* first performed in 1863. Courtesy: Don B. Wilmeth.

comedy, especially the latter. Although most historians categorize him as a member of the Kemble school, **James E. Murdoch** called him "the first romantic actor of America." An exceedingly handsome actor, his Shylock and Jaques in *As You Like It* were considered innovative. During 1837–9 he managed the National Theatre; after its destruction by **fire,** he managed **Niblo's Garden** for a time. In 1851 he settled permanently in New York City, assuming control the following year of **Brougham**'s Broadway Lyceum, as **Wallack's;** for nine years this theatre prospered. For almost 35 years his company was the leading American ensemble, first under his leadership and later under his son Lester. In 1861 he built the second Wallack's on Broadway at 13th Street.

James's nephew, **James William Wallack, Jr.** (1818–73), son of Henry and born in London, became a credible actor in tragedy. More than any other member of the family, he spent most of his career away from New York, spreading the Wallack name to all the major American theatrical centers, retiring in 1872.

Next to James the elder, **Lester Wallack** (John Johnstone) (1820–88), his nephew, made the greatest contribution to the American stage. The only major member of the family born in the U.S., he nonetheless served his apprenticeship in England and Ireland, making his American debut in 1847 at the **Broadway Theatre** as Sir Charles Coldstream in *Used Up*. During his career with the Wallack company he played nearly 300 roles, excelling as Benedick, Charles Surface, Sir Andrew Ague-cheek, and Sir Elliott Grey in his own adaptation of *Rosedale* (1863). Lester stage-managed for his father at Wallack's Lyceum, and became the manager of the second Wallack's until 1882, when he opened a new Wallack's, where he remained until 1887. Although Lester did little to encourage American works, depending heavily on an English repertoire, he was a highly honored member of the profession until his death. His important memoirs were published posthumously in 1889.   DBW

> See: *A Sketch of the Life of James William Wallack, Late Actor and Manager,* New York, 1865.

Wallack's Theatre Broadway and 13th St., NYC [Architect: John M. Trimble]. Although the playhouse on 13th Street was the most famous of the theatres bearing the name of Wallack, there were actually three theatres associated with the Wallack family. The first was built by **John Brougham** in 1850 at 485 Broadway, but passed to **James W. Wallack** two years later and was operated by him as Wallack's Lyceum for nine years. In 1861, a new Wallack's went up in the theatre district forming around Union Square and was managed by **Lester Wallack,** who was its principal star for many years. For nearly 20 years, it dispensed impeccably cast English plays with a company of mainly English actors to an elitist audience. Following a trend, Wallack relocated his company to a third theatre at the northeast corner of Broadway and 30th Street, but fortune did not follow him. In ill health and faced with an indifferent theatrical public, he retired in 1887. A year later, Wallack died and the house was leased to **A. M. Palmer,** who changed the name to Palmer's; it reverted to its original name in 1896. All three theatres were torn down: the first in 1869; the second, which was renamed the **Star Theatre** and continued to be leased to producers, in 1901; and the third in 1915. MCH

> See: C. D. Jones, "The Policies and Practices in Wallack's Theatre, 1852–1888," PhD diss., U of Illinois, 1958.

Waller, Emma (1820–99) British-born actress who married American actor Daniel Wilmarth Waller in 1849 and came with him to the U.S. in 1851. Her earliest known performance was in 1855 on tour in Australia, followed by a London debut in 1856. For her American debut in 1857 at the **Walnut Street Theatre** in Philadelphia, she appeared on successive nights as Ophelia to Mr. Waller's Hamlet, Pauline in *The Lady of Lyons,* and Lady Macbeth, the latter performed with an "almost painful" intensity of passion. Fullness of characterization and a stately presence were her strengths in roles like Queen Margaret and Queen Katharine and Meg Merrilies in *Guy Mannering.* She also achieved *succès d'estime* as Iago in the 1860s and '70s. She and her husband often performed together from her 1858 New York debut as Marina in *The Duchess of Malfi* (R. H. Horne's adaptation) until her retirement in 1878.   FHL   DJW

Walnut Street Theatre 9th and Walnut, **Philadelphia.** Miraculously eluding the American penchant for tearing down the old and building up the new, the Walnut Street survives today as the oldest functioning playhouse in America. It was opened in 1809 as a domed arena for the Pepin and Breschard **circus,** but in 1811 came the first of a string of renovations to transform it into a workable theatre. It was enlarged, fitted with a stage and orchestra pit, and renamed the Olympic. In 1820, the dome was removed and the name changed to the Walnut Street, and it briefly housed a company that rivaled the **Chestnut Street.** In 1828, John Haviland designed a new Greek-revival façade for it. Eventually, it passed to the ownership of **John Sleeper Clarke, Edwin Booth**'s brother-in-law, and remained in his estate until 1919. Intending to raze it and replace it with a new theatre, the new owner discovered that the building code restricted him to a smaller theatre, and decided to rebuild the old house. In 1968, it was declared a National Landmark, and money was raised to restore it to Haviland's 1828 version, although the interior was thoroughly modernized.   MCH

Walter, Eugene (1874–1941) Playwright and film writer. Associated in business management with numerous theatrical enterprises – **minstrel show**s, circuses, symphony orchestras – Walter contributed most importantly to American theatre with a score of successful, social realistic melodramas. Essentially, he emphasized the victims of overwhelming social and personal forces: a man caught in the political machine of New York City (*The Undertow,* 1906); a weak husband pushed to immoral limits by the power of business (***Paid in Full,*** 1908); a man corrupted by money and brought to ruin and death (*Fine Feathers,* 1913). Walter's best play, *The **Easiest Way*** (1908), remembered for its realistic stage setting by **David Belasco,** featured a weak woman who understands and accepts her frailty. Other plays include *The Wolf* (1908), *A Plain Woman* (1912), and *The Knife* (1917). Walter's skills were easily adapted to films. In 1925 he published a series of lectures entitled *How to Write a Play.*   WJM

Walter Kerr Theatre 219 West 48th St., NYC [Architect: Herbert J. Krapp]. Built by the **Shubert**s in 1921 as the Ritz, the theatre was rushed to completion in 66 days. With slightly under 1,000 seats, it was a frequently booked house during the 1920s and '30s and was leased by the **Federal Theatre Project** for 1936–9. During 1939–64, it was used as a studio for radio and then television. Thereafter, it entered a rocky period when it served as a theatre, a pornographic moviehouse, and massage parlor, and briefly as the Robert F. Kennedy Children's Theatre. In 1983, after a complete renovation, it returned as a legitimate playhouse owned by the **Jujamcyn** Organization. A second renovation and a name change to the **Walter Kerr** occurred in 1990.   MCH

Walton, Tony (1934–) British-born set and costume designer for theatre, film, television, opera, and ballet. Walton studied at the Slade School of Fine Arts in London and began work at the Wimbledon Theatre; his first New York production was in 1957. He soon became associated with a range of witty and elegant musicals, including *A Funny Thing Happened on the Way to the Forum, Pippin, Grand Hotel: The Musical, The Will Rogers Follies,* and the 1992 revival of **Guys and Dolls.** However, like his idol **Boris Aronson,** his style is mutable. Dramas include *The Real Thing,* **Hurlyburly,** the **Lincoln Center** revivals of *The House of Blue Leaves* and **Anything Goes, Six Degrees of Separation,** and the **Dustin Hoffman** revival of *Death of a Salesman* on Broadway and television. Film work includes *Mary Poppins* and *All That Jazz.* He has received Tony, Oscar, and Emmy awards and many more nominations.   AA

Wanamaker, Sam (1919–) Born in Chicago, Wanamaker studied for the stage at the **Goodman Theatre.** He debuted on Broadway in 1942, then made his first London appearance in 1952 in *Winter Journey,* which he also directed. Remaining in England he became artistic director of the New Shakespeare Theatre, Liverpool, in 1957, and joined the Shakespeare Memorial Theatre Company in Stratford in 1959. Although still seen frequently in films and on television, since 1970 he has served as executive director of the Globe Playhouse Trust and World Centre for Shakespeare Studies, Southwark, London, where he has campaigned tirelessly for the erection of a replica Globe Theatre.   SMA

Ward, Douglas Turner (1930–) **African-American** actor, director, and playwright. Born in Louisiana but educated in the North, Ward trained at the Paul Mann Theatre Workshop in New York. He acted in **Off-Broadway** plays before accepting a minor role on Broadway in *A Raisin in the Sun* (1959). Working with **Robert Hooks** in 1965, Ward produced his two one-act satiric comedies, *Happy Ending* and *Day of Absence,* for a 14-month Off-Broadway run. In 1968 Ward, Hooks, and Gerald Krone founded the **Negro Ensemble Company,** where Ward continues as artistic director. He has directed and played leading roles in the company's productions, notably **Ceremonies in Dark Old Men** (1969) and *The River Niger* (1972), for which he won an Obie. He directed the 1982 Pulitzer Prize–winning *A Soldier's Play* and has also written *The Reckoning* (1969) and *Brotherhood* (1970).   EGH

Ward, Winifred (1884–1975) Pioneer in child drama [see **children's theatre**]. In articulating the principles and demonstrating the effectiveness of creative drama versus formal theatre for children, she changed the direction of drama education in the U.S. She authored four texts: *Creative Dramatics, Playmaking with Children, Stories to Dramatize,* and *Theatre for Children.* Her philosophy, developed during her early years as a classroom teacher, culminated in university courses at Northwestern University and the establishment of the Evanston Children's Theatre. Her most lasting accomplishment was the founding of a professional organization in 1950, now called the American Alliance for Theatre and Education.   NMcC

David Warfield in the title role of Belasco's *The Return of Peter Grimm* (1911). Courtesy: Harvard Theatre Collection.

Warde, Frederick (1851–1935) A successful English provincial actor, he made his American debut (1874) as a supporting player, and found success as a regional star after 1880. Like his contemporaries Thomas Keene, Louis James, Charles Hanford, Joseph Grismer, Phoebe Davis, Kathryn Kidder, and **Marie Wainwright,** who had similar careers, he played an older repertory in an elevated, declamatory style that was innocent of realism. Warde specialized in serious, older men. He continued on the stage and the lecture platform until 1915, and made films of *Richard III* and *King Lear* (1916). His memoirs, *Fifty Years of Make-Believe* appeared in 1920 (New York).   DMcD

Warfield, David (1866–1951) **Belasco**'s one great male star was a native of San Francisco, who began acting with a traveling **stock company** in Napa, CA (1888). He played a variety of parts in New York City and on tour until he became a member of the company at the **Casino Theatre** in 1893. He quickly became a specialist in musical parody, which led to an engagement as an eccentric ethnic comic with **Weber and Fields** (1899–1901). Belasco coached him in a series of pathetic older parts, in which he was always the gentle, slightly humorous, forgiving victim. His first vehicle was *The Auctioneer* (1901), followed by *The Music Master* (1904), *The Return of Peter Grimm* (1911), and culminating in an unsuccessful production of *The Merchant of Venice* (1924), after which he retired.   DMcD

Warren, Mercy Otis (1728–1814) Patriot and political satirist, the best representative of "The War of Belles Lettres" during the Revolutionary War. Her propaganda plays – really dialogues without plot, character development, or women – satirized British officials and American Loyalists and were published anonymously in Massachusetts periodicals and as political pamphlets. Several plays have been falsely attributed to Warren; she acknowledged authorship of only *The Group* (1775). Other plays identified as her work include *The Adulateur: A Tragedy: As It Is Now Acted in Upper Servia* (1772), which refers to the Boston Massacre and attacks Governor Thomas Hutchison; *The Defeat* (1773); and two blank-verse historical tragedies, *The Ladies of Castille* and *The Sack of Rome*, both published in *Poems, Dramatic and Miscellaneous* (1790), her first signed work. FB

See: K. Anthony, *First Lady of the Revolution: The Life of Mercy Otis Warren*, Garden City, NY, 1958; J. Fritz, *Cast for a Revolution*, Boston, 1972.

Warren, William, the elder (1767–1832) British-born actor and manager whose 1784 debut was as Young Norval in *Douglas*. When engaged by Tate Wilkinson for his provincial company in 1788, Warren acted in support of Sarah Siddons. In 1796 he joined **Thomas Wignell**'s company. At the **Chestnut Street Theatre** he first appeared as Friar Lawrence in *Romeo and Juliet* and Bundle in *The Waterman*. Other than infrequent appearances in New York, the remainder of Warren's career, both as actor and manager, was associated with the theatres in Baltimore and **Philadelphia**. In 1806 he married the second of his three wives, actress **Mrs. Merry**. In partnership with **William B. Wood**, Warren's management in Philadelphia and Baltimore prospered until late in his career; in 1829 he retired from management. As an actor, Warren was especially adept at old men in comedy, but he was also capable in tragedy. He was noted especially for his performances as Old Dornton, Sir Robert Bramble, Falstaff, and Sir Toby Belch. He had six children with his third wife, Esther Fortune [sister-in-law of **Joseph Jefferson**], all of whom were associated with the stage.

Warren, William, the younger (1812–88) The son of **William Warren the elder,** his acting career is almost totally associated with the **Boston Museum,** the **stock company** he joined in 1847. During his 50-year career, until his retirement in 1883, he is reported to have given 13,345 performances and to have portrayed 577 characters. No actor of his period was identified so thoroughly with a single theatre, and none received more respect and affection from the public. His versatility in comic roles was practically limitless, although his special talent was with eccentric types. His most famous roles included Dogberry, Polonius, Bob Acres, Sir Peter Teazle, Micawber, Touchstone, and Launcelot Gobbo, although he also appeared in leading roles in numerous forgettable contemporary plays. DBW

See: W. T. Ball, *Life and Memoirs of William Warren, Boston's Favorite Comedian*, Boston, 1888; M. E. McConnell, "William Warren II, the Boston Comedian," PhD diss., Indiana U, 1963.

Warrilow, David (1934–) British-born actor and cofounder of **Mabou Mines.** Warrilow was working as a magazine editor in Paris when **Jo-Anne Akalaitis, Lee Breuer, Ruth Maleczech,** and Philip Glass invited him to work with them on a production of Samuel Beckett's *Play* (1965). He came to New York with them and helped found the experimental collective Mabou Mines in 1970. Warrilow performed in Breuer's *The **Red Horse Animation*** (1970) and *The B. Beaver Animation* (1974), and, to great acclaim, in an adaptation of Beckett's *The Lost Ones* (1972). Lanky and langorous, and with a deep, sonorous voice, Warrilow has often been called the "consummate" or "quintessential" Beckett actor. Warrilow left Mabou Mines in 1978 and the next year toured in *A Piece of Monologue*, a play Beckett wrote specifically for him; in 1984 he performed in the premieres of Beckett's *Ohio Impromptu, Catastrophe,* and *What Where*, directed by **Alan Schneider.** AS

Washington Square Players A pre–WW I producing agency, founded in 1915 by amateurs (Edward Goodman, **Lawrence Langner,** et al.) to improve the level of drama in New York City. Their first three one-acts were produced at a cost of $35 in a theatre seating 40 persons. They received favorable reviews and continued producing one-acts by **Chekhov,** Musset, **Akins, Moeller,** and other then-little-known playwrights. After a disastrous production of *The Seagull,* they moved to the Comedy Theatre, just off Broadway, seating 600. There they presented the first Broadway production of **Eugene O'Neill**'s *In the Zone.* Several important American actors began or worked with the Washington Square Players: Roland Young, **Rollo Peters,** Frank Conroy, Helen Westley, and **Katharine Cornell.** In 1918 the group disbanded, but restructured in 1919 as the **Theatre Guild,** New York's most influential producing organization. SMA

See: O. M. Sayler, *Our American Theatre*, New York, 1923.

Wasserstein, Wendy (1950–) Playwright who portrays with wit and understanding the plight of the modern woman caught between feminism and traditionalism. Obie-winning *Uncommon Women and Others* (1977) depicts the reunion of five women graduates of Mt. Holyoke and their hilarious reflections on their past college days. *Isn't It Romantic* (1983) follows two such women as they confront their parents, their lovers, and their own unclear futures. *The **Heidi Chronicles,*** which traces the history of the women's movement through the life of one woman and her friends, won a Pulitzer Prize and a Tony Award in 1989. FB

Watch on the Rhine Lillian Hellman's fourth play contrasted the comfortable life in the U.S. of 1941 with the dangerous world of Europe, where moral choice led inevitably to perilous action. Paul Lukas created the role of the German Kurt Müller, a quietly heroic anti-Fascist, who briefly returns with his American wife to the safety of her upper-class home. Directed by **Herman Shumlin** with set design by **Jo Mielziner**, the first production opened on Broadway 1 April 1941 at the **Martin Beck Theatre**. Immediately recognized as "a compassionate drama of men, women and children" (**Brooks Atkinson**), the play won the New York Drama Critics' Circle Award and was directed in London the following year by Emlyn Williams.   KF

Waters, Ethel (1896–1977) African-American singer and actress. Born into poverty, Waters started at age 17 as a vaudeville singer in Baltimore for nine dollars a week. In 1933, she was featured in **Irving Berlin**'s revue *As Thousands Cheer.* Moving from honky-tonks to cellar cafés to New York socialite clubs, Waters attained a glowing reputation as comedienne and singer of such songs as "St. Louis Blues," "Dinah," and "Stormy Weather." Waters emerged as a superb dramatic actress of warmth and sensitivity in stage or film productions of *Mamba's Daughters* (1939), *Cabin in the Sky* (1940), *Pinky* (1949), and *The Member of the Wedding* (1950). Earl Dancer termed her "the greatest artist of her generation." Her autobiography (with Charles Samuels) appeared in 1951 (*His Eye Is on the Sparrow*).   EGH

See: T. Knaack, *Ethel Waters: I Touched a Sparrow,* Waco, TX, 1978.

Waterston, Sam[uel Atkinson] (1940–) Actor. Born in Cambridge, MA, and educated at Yale and the Sorbonne, he made his New York debut in 1962 as Jonathan in *Oh Dad, Poor Dad.* For the **New York Shakespeare Festival** he has portrayed Silvius in *As You Like It* (1963), Prince Hal in *Henry IV, Parts 1 and 2* (1968), Cloten in *Cymbeline* (1971), Benedick in *Much Ado* (1972, Obie and Drama Desk awards), Prospero in *The Tempest* (1974), and the title role in *Hamlet* (1975). **Mel Gussow** praised his Benedick as "boyish but not immature" while **Julius Novick** found his Hamlet "easy to like" but not intellectually satisfying. Other appearances on Broadway include *Half-Way Up the Tree* (1967), **Indians** (1969), *The Trial of the Catonville Nine* (1971), *A Doll's House* (1975), *Benefactors* (1986), and *A Walk in the Woods* (1988). **Off-Broadway** credits include *Muzeeka* (1968), *Waiting for Godot* (1978), *Chez Nous* (1979), and *The Three Sisters* (1982). Waterston has appeared in numerous films, including *The Great Gatsby* and *The Killing Fields* (Academy Award nominee, 1985); "Oppenheimer" for public television; and as a southern lawyer in the NBC series "I'll Fly Away" (1991–2).   TLM

Watson, Billy "Beef Trust" (né Isaac Levie) (1866–1945) New York–born "Dutch" comedian-singer and producer, known as "King of Burlesque." His debut, as Billy Buttons, occurred at the Chatham Square Museum (1881). Success as a comedian in vaudeville and **burlesque** led to ownership of a Brooklyn theatre, Watson's Cozy Corner (1905). Although Watson first gained prominence in the 1890s as producer-star of *Krausmeyer's*

Promotional postcard for Billy Watson's "Beef Trust" (1911). Courtesy: Michael Gnat.

Alley (in which he played a German clarinetist opposite Billy Spencer's Irish sausagemaker), with a theme similar to Nichols's *Abie's Irish Rose,* he is remembered as producer of *Watson's Beef Trust* (named after the Chicago stockyard trust): a comic burlesque show, often censored, featuring 190-pound chorus girls made to appear even larger with striped tights. Watson's chorines actually were quite decorous, appearing in one skit as Salvation Army lassies led by Capt. Billy Watson with a big brass drum. Prior to retirement in 1925, Watson, calling himself "Original," was challenged by comic "Sliding" Billy Watson.   DBW

Watt, Douglas (1914–) Drama critic. Born in New York and educated at Cornell (1934), Watt began his long career with the *New York News* in 1936. He served as dramatic reporter (1940–71), senior drama critic (1971–87), and critic-at-large (1987–). He also has written for the *New Yorker* since 1946. A simple elegance characterizes his style. **David Rabe**'s *Sticks and Bones* (1971) he described as a "beautifully controlled and even poetic work of the imagination that becomes unbearably moving as it unfolds."   TLM

Watts, Richard, Jr. (1898–1981) Drama critic. Born in West Virginia and educated at Columbia University, Watts began his career as a reporter for the old Brooklyn *Times* in 1922. He became film critic for the *New York Herald* in 1924, a position he held until 1936, when he succeeded **Percy Hammond** as drama critic (1936–42). He spent the war years in the Far East (1942–6) to return as drama critic for the *New York Post* (1946–74). Succeeded by **Martin Gottfried** in 1974, Watts wrote a weekly column until his retirement in 1976. An early champion of Tom Stoppard, Harold Pinter, and **Edward Albee,** Watts has been characterized as a gentle, judicious, and civilized critic of taste who loved the theatre.   TLM

Wayburn, Ned (né Edward Claudius Weyburn) (1874–1942) Director and choreographer who, after starting out as a singer and dancer in vaudeville, made his theatrical debut in *The Swell Miss Fitwell* (1897). He served as assistant director of *The Governor's Son* (1901), and was soon in demand as a producer, director, and choreographer of musical comedies and **revue**s. Among the shows he staged in New York were two editions of *The Passing Show* (1912, 1913), and six of *The Ziegfeld Follies* (1916–19, 1922, 1923). In addition to producing and staging hundreds of musicals, Wayburn operated dance studios that trained many of the musical theatre's finest dancers.   MK

Way Down East by Lottie Blair Parker (alterations by Joseph R. Grismer) is a four-act "rural" melodrama that opened at the Manhattan Theatre, 7 February 1898, ran for 152 performances, and was revived over the next 20 years. Reminiscent of the popular melodramas *The Old Homestead, Shore Acres* and *Hazel Kirke,* the play impressed the *New York Times* reviewer as less crude and uncouth than the usual "rustic" fair, with simple and effective dialogue, acting, and scenery. Lottie Blair Parker also wrote *White Roses* (1897), *Under Southern Skies* (1901), *The Light of Home* (1903), and *The Redemption of David Corson* (1906).   TLM

Weaver, Fritz (1926–) Actor who made his professional debut with the **Barter Theatre** and his New York debut as Fainall in *The Way of the World*. After 1955, Weaver appeared frequently with the **American Shakespeare Festival.** He has also appeared in several films and numerous television network films and series. Among his awards are the **Clarence Derwent** Award for Flamineo in *The White Devil* (1955) and a Theatre World Award for Maitland in *The Chalk Garden* (1956). For *Child's Play* (1970), Weaver received the *Variety* Critics Poll, the Outer Critics' Circle, the Drama Desk, and a Tony award. In 1991 he portrayed King Lear at the **Shakespeare Theatre** [at the Folger] and appeared with Tony Randall's National Actors Theatre in NYC, playing Danforth in its inaugural production of *The Crucible.*   SMA

Weber, Joseph (1867–1942) and **Lew Fields** (1867–1941) Comedians. After learning their craft as child performers in museums, circuses, and variety houses, Weber and Fields evolved a knockabout "Dutch comic" act in which the short, rotund, innocent Weber was the foil for the tall, skinny, bullying Fields. They toured for many years in **vaudeville** before playing their first legitimate theatre engagements at the Harlem Opera House and **Hammerstein**'s **Olympia Theatre** in 1894. Two years later they opened the Weber and Fields Music Hall, where they offered hilarious burlesques of current Broadway successes. The Weber and Fields company, which at various times included such stars as **Lillian Russell,** Peter F. Dailey, **Sam Bernard, De Wolf Hopper, David Warfield, Fay Templeton,** and Bessie McCoy, was also noted for the beauty and animation of its female chorus. Weber and Fields chose many talented writers, designers, and directors to assist them in mounting their shows.

In 1904 the partners separated, with Weber continuing at the Music Hall and Fields producing and starring in musical comedies. In 1912 they reunited for a "jubilee" production at a new Music Hall, after which they toured with the show. Following some vaudeville appearances the partners again split up and concentrated on their producing careers.

The rough, acrobatic comic style of Weber and Fields, coupled with the fractured English they spoke in their "Dutch" personas, made them favorites of audiences in New York and across the country in both legitimate theatres and vaudeville houses.   MK

See: F. Isman, *Weber and Fields,* New York, 1924.

Webster, Margaret (1905–72) Actress and director. The daughter of Benjamin Webster III and Dame May Whitty, she was the last member of a 150-year-old English theatrical dynasty. Her professional career began in *The Trojan Women* with Sybil Thorndike (1924), followed the next year with a small role in John Barrymore's [see **Drew–Barrymore**] *Hamlet.* After several years of **stock** experience she joined the Old Vic in 1929, returning to play Lady Macbeth in 1932–3. In 1934 she began to direct, and this became her chief endeavor, mostly in America. Notable U.S. productions under her direction included *Richard II* with **Maurice Evans** (1937), *Hamlet* (1938), *Twelfth Night* (1940), *Othello* with **Paul Robeson** (1943), *The Cherry Orchard* (1944), and *The Tempest* with **Canada Lee** as Caliban (1945). She founded with **Eva Le Gallienne** and **Cheryl Crawford** the **American Repertory Theatre** (1946–8). In 1950 she began directing operas, becoming the first woman to direct at the New York Metropolitan Opera. She was the author of important books on theatre, including *The Same Only Different* (1969) and *Don't Put Your Daughter on the Stage* (1972).   DBW

Wedding Band by **Alice Childress.** Subtitled "A Love/Hate Story in Black and White," this two-act drama examines the effects of racism through the doomed love affair of a black woman and white man. Julia and Herman are otherwise ordinary working-class people, but their commitment to a 10-year relationship makes them outlaws in the South Carolina of 1918, and Herman's sudden illness brings his scandalized family into direct contact with the multifaceted black community. First produced at the University of Michigan in 1966, *Wedding Band* opened in New York at the **Public Theater** 26 October 1972 directed by Childress and **Joseph Papp,** with **Ruby Dee** and James Broderick in the major roles. In 1973 the honest treatment of interracial love still raised controversy when the play was nationally televised by ABC.   KF

Weill, Kurt (1900–50) Composer, born in Dessau, Germany; studied music and directed a small opera company before collaborating with Bertolt **Brecht** on such works as *The Threepenny Opera* and *The Rise and Fall of the City of Mahagonny.* With his wife, actress **Lotte Lenya,** he came to America in 1935. He composed scores for *Johnny Johnson* (1936), *Knickerbocker Holiday* (1938), *Lady in the Dark* (1941), *One Touch of Venus* (1943), the opera *Street Scene* (1947), and *Lost in the Stars* (1949). His Berlin shows have also been frequently revived in America. Although Weill's compositions for the American stage were more lyrical and optimistic than his Berlin scores, he worked with such noted writers as **Paul Green, Maxwell Anderson,** and **Langston Hughes** in creating shows that tackled serious issues in an uncompromising way.   MK

> *See:* R. Sanders, *The Days Grow Short,* New York, 1980.

Weiner, Bernard (1941–   ) Born in Pittsburgh and educated at the University of Miami and Claremont Graduate School, Weiner was chief drama critic for the *San Francisco Chronicle* (1971–91). During his tenure he encouraged an explosion of new fringe theatre activity and championed the work of such visually based experimental artists as **George Coates,** Antenna Theatre, Soon 3, and others. He retired in 1991 to concentrate on directing, playwriting, and teaching.   MB

Welch, Deshler (1854–1920) Editor and author. After writing for Buffalo newspapers (1866–79) and the New York *Tribune* and *Star* (c. 1879–86), Welch became founding editor of *The Theatre* (1886–93), an illustrated weekly magazine on drama, music, and art. He also served as publicity manager for **Augustin Daly** (1887–91). His books include *The Life of Grover Cleveland* (1887).   TLM

Weller, Michael (1942–   ) New York–born playwright, educated at Brandeis and Manchester universities. After productions at the Edinburgh Festival Fringe and at **Charles Marowitz**'s Open Space (London) in 1969, he premiered *Cancer* at the Royal Court in 1970. Renamed ***Moonchildren,*** it opened at the **Arena Stage** in 1971, followed by productions both off and on Broadway in 1972. A popular critical success, *Moonchildren* depicts the hangups and idealism of the "children of the sixties," a subject Weller returned to with ***Loose Ends*** in 1979. Premiering at the Arena Stage prior to its Broadway debut, *Loose Ends* expresses the disillusionment of the 1970s as young people attempt to reconcile their ideals with the demands of careers, marriages, and families. Weller's other plays include *23 Years Later, Fishing, At Home, Spoils of War,* and *Lake No Bottom,* the last a 1990 study of the relationship of artist and critic. He also wrote the screenplays for *Hair* (1979) and *Ragtime* (1980).   TLM

Welles, (George) Orson (1915–85) Actor, playwright, and director whose place in history is ensured as a result of youthful accomplishments. By 1941 the protean Welles had established himself as a major actor and brilliant theatre director; had directed, cowritten, and starred in *Citizen Kane* (1940), one of the most influential films in cinema history; and had inadvertently created a national panic with his radio version of H. G. Wells's *The War of the Worlds* (1938). Welles's career began with an appearance at Dublin's Gate Theatre in 1931 as the Duke of Wurtemburg in *Jew Süss.* After touring with **Katharine Cornell** in 1933–4, he made his New York debut in 1934 in *Romeo and Juliet* (Chorus and Tybalt). In 1936, as director of the Negro People's Theatre, New York, he staged a controversial "voodoo" version of *Macbeth* with an all-black cast; in 1937, when appointed a director of the **Federal Theatre Project,** NYC, he directed notable productions of *Dr. Faustus* (and acted the title role) and *The Cradle Will Rock.* With **John Houseman** he cofounded the same year the **Mercury Theatre,** remembered primarily for its modern-dress production of *Julius Caesar.* Although Welles's theatre impact lessened after WW II, he is remembered for his direction of ***Native Son*** (1941); his 1946 version of ***Around the World in Eighty Days;*** his first appearance in London in 1951 as Othello, his adaptation and direction of *Moby Dick* (London 1955; New York, 1962); his direction and acting in *King Lear* (1956) at New York's City Center; and his direction at London's Royal Court Theatre of Ionesco's *Rhinoceros* (1960). Welles is the subject of two contradictory 1985 biographies by Barbara Leaming and Charles Higham, and a 1989 one by Frank Brady.   DBW

> *See:* R. France, *The Theatre of Orson Welles,* Lewisburg, PA, 1977; R. France, ed., *Orson Welles on Shakespeare,* Westport, CT, 1990; A. J. Tatomirovic, "The Theatre of Orson Welles, 1946–1960," PhD diss., New York U, 1991.

Wellman, Mac (1945–   ) Cleveland-born playwright (a "language-poet-playwright"), poet, novelist, and editor of two volumes of new American plays. His *Bad Penny* (1989) and *Crowbar* (1990; opening production of New York's Victoria Theatre) won Obie Awards. Other plays include *The Bad Infinity* (1988); *Terminal Hip* and *Sincerity Forever* – the latter, a 1990 source of controversy ("another NEA outrage"), being an angry work focused on "the eloquent ignoramuses of America"; and *7 Blowjobs* (1991), companion piece to *Sincerity Forever,* an exploration of the paranoia surrounding seven "obscene" photographs delivered to a U.S. senator's office.   BBW

Wemyss, Francis Courtney (1797–1859) English-born actor and manager who, a year after his first London appearance in 1821, made his American debut at the **Chestnut Street Theatre.** His forte was comedy and farce, and he excelled in roles such as Vapid in *The Dramatists,* Marplot in *The Busy Body,* and Rover in *Wild Oats.* He later acted in New York with **Charlotte Cushman,** William Macready, **Joseph Jefferson III,** and **Laura Keene.** In 1827 he turned to management, and was widely respected for his taste and integrity. He founded the Theatrical Fund to aid needy actors; edited 16 volumes of plays, published as the *Acting American Theatre;* and wrote an informative autobiography, *Twenty-six Years of the Life of an Actor and Manager* (1847).   TLM

West, Mae (1893–1980) Actress and playwright whose pose of unabashed but self-mocking sensuality made her a cult figure. A **vaudeville** headliner by 1911, she achieved notoriety in the lead role of her first play, *Sex* (1926), in which she was arrested [see **censorship**]. She continued to defy the censors with *The Drag* (1927), the first American drama to depict a homosexual party; *Diamond Lil* (1928), a melodramatic comedy about white slavery; and *The Constant Sinner* (1931). Her Hollywood career in the 1930s increased her fame, but the limitations forced on her by production codes brought her back to Broadway in *Catherine Was Great* (1944). West always located her insatiable, man-eating temptresses safely in past eras, and her own attitude was one of worldly bemusement. Her autobiography, *Goodness Had Nothing to Do with It,* was published in 1959.   LS

See: G. Eells & S. Musgrove, *Mae West,* New York, 1982; M. Leonard, *Mae West: Empress of Sex,* London, 1991.

West, Thomas Wade (1745–99) An English-born actor who emigrated in 1790, West founded the southern theatrical circuit extending from his theatre in Richmond, VA, to those he built in Norfolk, Alexandria, Fredericksburg, Petersburg, and Charleston. Known alternately as the Virginia Company and the South Carolina Company, West's actors appeared in well-mounted standard fare, for which he gained respect as comic actor, manager, and gentleman until his early death. The circuit continued to operate until the War of 1812.   RKB

See: *Theatre Survey* (Nov. 1972); *William and Mary Quarterly* (Jan. 1952).

Western, (Pauline) Lucille (1843–77) American actress. Born in New Orleans to comedian George Western and an actress later known as Mrs. Jane English, Lucille Western spent her childhood performing with her younger sister, Helen, in a piece designed to show off their dancing and farcical impersonations. As an adult, she excelled in emotional roles such as Lady Isabel in *East Lynne,* Marguerite Gautier in *Camille,* the title roles in *Lucretia Borgia* and *Leah, the Forsaken,* and her most popular role, Nancy in *Oliver Twist.* A dark-eyed beauty, she relied on inspiration more than art and gave the impression of being impulsive and untamed.   TLM

Western theatre see **Frontier theatre**

Weston, Jack (né Morris Weinstein) (c. 1922–) Stage, film, and television actor, accurately described in *The Filmgoer's Companion* as an "American roly-poly character actor" and by **Frank Rich** as an "old-school shtick artist." After a six-year stint in New York, which included supporting roles in *South Pacific* (1952) and *Bells Are Ringing* (1956), Weston pursued a career in film and television. He returned to Broadway to play Gaetano Proclo in *The Ritz* (1975) and created this role on film the following year. He received a Tony nomination for his performance as the small-time vaudeville agent involved in a fruitless relationship in *The Floating Light Bulb* (1981). He is married to actress Marge Redmond, with whom he has performed on occasion.   MR

West Side Story This updated musical version of *Romeo and Juliet,* with book by **Arthur Laurents,** music by **Leonard Bernstein,** and lyrics by **Stephen Sondheim,** opened at the **Winter Garden Theatre** on 26 September 1957. The rival families of Shakespeare's play were transformed by Laurents into gangs of white and Puerto Rican teenag-

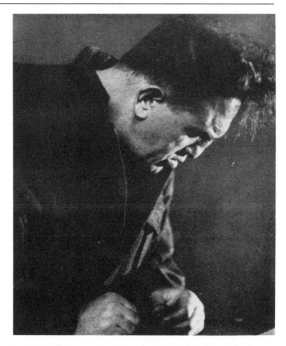

Louis Wolheim as Captain Flagg in *What Price Glory* (1924). Photo: Steichen. Courtesy: Don B. Wilmeth.

ers fighting for supremacy in Manhattan's decaying West Side. **Jerome Robbins,** the director and choreographer, created a series of frenetic dance sequences that stunningly articulated the gangs' restlessness and aggression. For the two young lovers, Tony and Maria (Larry Kert and Carol Lawrence), Bernstein and Sondheim wrote a series of expressive ballads including the soaring "Tonight" and the plaintive "Somewhere." At its opening, some critics complained that its violent story was inappropriate for the musical stage, while others praised it for expanding the boundaries of the musical in both plot and staging. Although its initial run was relatively short (732 performances), the musical has gained its stature over the years: The 1961 film version received an Academy Award for best picture; a 1980 revival directed by Robbins ran for 333 performances; the score has been played and recorded by philharmonic orchestras; and Bernstein shortly before his death conducted a recorded version featuring operatic voices.   MK

Wexler, Peter (1936–) Set, lighting, costume designer, and theatre consultant who has designed extensively for the Metropolitan and New York City Operas; his Met debut was with *Les Troyens* (1973). Broadway credits include *In the Matter of J. Robert Oppenheimer* and *Abe Lincoln in Illinois.* He was the first resident designer for the **Los Angeles Center Theatre,** and created the stage and decor for the New York Philharmonic Promenade Concerts in the 1960s and the stage for White House performances in 1961.   AA

What Price Glory by **Maxwell Anderson** and **Laurence Stallings** opened in New York on 3

September 1924, running for 299 performances. The large cast of this iconoclastic treatment of WW I included William Boyd as Sergeant Quirt and Louis Wolheim as Captain Flagg, the hard-boiled professional soldiers whose rivalry over sex, drinking, and fighting provides the main conflict; also Brian Donlevy, Fuller Mellish, Jr., and George Tobias as the young soldiers who become hardened and pragmatic under their tutelage. Presented as a realistic deflation of the romantic ideals of honor, bravery, and patriotism that had pervaded America's conception of war prior to the disillusionment of WW I, it replaced these ideals with admiration of the soldier's romantic sense of adventure and blind devotion to duty. It was written originally without the now familiar question mark at the end.   BCM

Wheatley, William (1816–76) Theatre manager and actor. Born into a theatrical family, Wheatley made his stage debut at age 10 in 1826 at the Park Theatre, New York, as young Albert in William Macready's production of *William Tell.* Following a tour with Macready, Wheatley returned to the Park and played the title role in *Tom Thumb,* establishing himself as a leading juvenile actor. After acting in small roles at the **Bowery Theatre** (1833), he returned to the Park (1834) as a "walking gentleman" to excel as Nicholas Nickleby, and as Charles in *London Assurance.* For the 1842–3 season, Wheatley acted with the **Walnut Street Theatre** company in **Philadelphia.** After a brief retirement from the stage, he returned to Philadelphia in 1853 to comanage the **Arch Street Theatre** with **John Drew.** He was sole manager in 1856, but two years later joined forces with **John Sleeper Clarke,** who ran it with him until the outbreak of the Civil War. In 1862 he returned to New York and leased **Niblo's Garden,** where he excelled in producing elaborate romantic dramas including *The Duke's Motto* and *Arrah-na-pogue.* His biggest hit came in 1866, however, when *The **Black Crook*** began its 475-performance run, creating a vogue for elaborate musical spectacle and making Wheatley a rich man. He retired from the stage in 1868.   TLM

Wheeler, Andrew Carpenter (1832–1903) Drama critic also known as Trinculo and Nym Crinkle. Born in New York, Wheeler began his career as a reporter on the *New York Times* in 1857. After traveling in the Midwest, he wrote for the *Milwaukee Daily Sentinel,* reported on the Civil War, and returned to New York to pursue a career in journalism. During 1869–76 he reviewed plays for the *Sunday World;* beginning in 1870 he replaced Henry Clapp, Jr., as drama critic of *The Leader;* for 1876–7, he followed Joseph Howard, Jr., on the *Sun;* his "Nym Crinkle's Feuilleton" graced the *New York Dramatic Mirror* during 1886–9; and in 1889 he added a regular column to **Deshler Welch's** *The Theatre.* Wheeler returned to the *World* in 1883 when Joseph Pulitzer purchased the paper. He was known also as a playwright, novelist, and essayist on nature (under the pen-name of J. P. Mowbray). Called by **James Huneker** "more brilliant than reliable," Wheeler popularized an aggressive style marked by devastating sarcasm. He opposed the Genteel Tradition, the aesthete views of **William Winter,** and the cultural shift of the country away from rugged individualism.   TLM

Wheeler, David (1925–) Director. A Harvard graduate who served as **José Quintero's** assistant (1958–61), he has been a major force in New England theatre since the early 1960s with well over 200 productions to his credit, including some 80 while artistic director (1963–77) of the Theatre Company of Boston, where numerous young actors worked under his tutelage (among them Robert Duvall, **Al Pacino,** Jon Voight, **Stockard Channing, Blythe Danner, Dustin Hoffman,** and Robert DeNiro). Since 1984 he has been resident director at the **American Repertory Theatre** (*True West,* 1982; De Lillo's *The Day Room,* 1986; *The Homecoming,* 1990; etc.) and, during the same period, frequent director for **Trinity Repertory.** On Broadway he directed Al Pacino in *The **Basic Training of Pavlo Hummel*** (1977) and *Richard III* (1979).   DBW

When You Comin' Back, Red Ryder? A suspense drama by **Mark Medoff** first presented at New York's **Circle Repertory Theatre** (November 1973) and subsequently moved to the Eastside Playhouse, opening 6 December 1973. This play provides a glimpse into the Southwest through a diner on a bypassed road in New Mexico. The character of Red Ryder is a pale youth who is among those terrorized and victimized by Teddy, a mysterious and ominous figure who comes to the diner with his girlfriend. The portrayal of this demonic character reflects a growing concern about sadistic violence in society, suggesting the menace of Pinter and the surrealism of **Sam Shepard.** Medoff received an Obie Award for distinguished playwriting and the Outer Critics' Circle Award as best playwright.   ER

White, Edgar (1947–) Born in Montserrat, West Indies, and brought to New York at age 5, White has contributed an original vision and allusive quality to **African-American theatre.** His plays explore themes of exile and reclamation of the self, of struggle and survival, with a strong sense of ritual. He was only 18 when his first drama, called *The Mummer's Play,* was produced at **Off-Broadway's Public Theater,** where six of his plays have now been staged. White has also had premieres in London, England, and in the West Indies. Among his published plays are *Underground: Four Plays* (1970); *The Crucificado: Two Plays* (1973); *Lament for Rastafari and Other Plays* (1983); and *Redemption Song and Other Plays* (1985).   EGH

White, George (1890–1968) Dancer and producer. As a producer of successful musical **revue**s in the 1920s, White provided stiff competition for **Florenz Ziegfeld.** He started out as a dancer in Bowery saloons, gradually working his way up to vaudeville with a dancing act. Between 1910 and 1918 he appeared as a dancer in a number of musicals, including the *Ziegfeld Follies of 1915.* In 1919 he produced the *Scandals of 1919,* the first in a series of 13 revues bearing the title of *Scandals.*

Because of his own background as a dancer, White emphasized dance in his revues, introducing black dance steps such as the Charleston and the black bottom to white audiences. His fast-paced revues were also noted for the jazz music of **George Gershwin** and **DeSylva, Brown, and Henderson.** White appeared as a dancer in several of the *Scandals,* and also contributed comedy sketches to several editions.   MK

White, Jane (1922–   ) African-American actress. A Smith College graduate, White came early to Broadway as the female lead in *Strange Fruit* (1945). Thereafter she played mostly in **Off-Broadway** and regional theatres, taking lead roles in *Blithe Spirit, The Taming of the Shrew,* and *Dark of the Moon* for the Hayloft Theatre in Allentown, PA, in 1948–9. In 1964 she appeared in three productions for the **New York Shakespeare Festival:** *Love's Labour's Lost, Troilus and Cressida,* and *Coriolanus,* for which she won an Obie Award as Volumnia. After engagements in Italy and France, she replaced Irene Pappas as Clytemnestra in the Off-Broadway *Iphigenia in Aulis* (1967). Her Goneril to **Morris Carnovsky**'s King Lear (1975) was hailed for its commanding intelligence, style, and rich contralto voice.   EGH

White, Richard Grant (1822–85) Journalist, philologist, critic, editor, and Shakespeare scholar. A graduate of New York University (1839), White wrote music and dramatic criticism for the New York *Courier and Enquirer,* serving as editor during 1854–9. He contributed essays on the theatre to *Atlantic, Putnam's,* and *Galaxy* magazines. He pursued Shakespeare as an avocation, writing/editing *Shakespeare's Scholar* (1854); the first edition in America of Shakespeare's plays from original sources (1857–63); *Studies in Shakespeare* (1866); and the Riverside edition of Shakespeare (1883). The first American Shakespeare scholar to gain an international reputation, White was the father of Stanford White, the architect.   TLM

Whitehead, Robert (1916–   ) Producer, born in Montréal and educated at Trinity College School in Canada, who began his producing career in 1947 with *Medea,* starring **Judith Anderson.** He was managing director for the **American National Theatre and Academy** (1951), joining **Roger Stevens** and others in forming the Producers Theatre (1953). He codirected the Repertory Theatre of **Lincoln Center** with **Elia Kazan** (1960–4), and has maintained a close association with the **John F. Kennedy Center.** His more than 50 New York productions include: *Member of the Wedding* (1950), *Bus Stop* (1955), *The Visit* (1958), *A Touch of the Poet* (1958), *A Man for All Seasons* (1961), *The Price* (1968), *Old Times* (1972), *A Texas Trilogy* (1976), *Betrayal* (1979), *Medea* (1982, starring his wife, **Zoë Caldwell**), *Death of a Salesman* (1984 revival), *Lillian* (1985, also with Caldwell), and *A Few Good Men* (1990).   TLM

White Slave, The A sentimental melodrama by **Bartley Campbell** that drew heavily on *The Octoroon, Uncle Tom's Cabin,* and *Kit, the Ar-*

kansas Traveller. It opened at New York's **Haverly**'s Theatre 3 April 1882 and ran two months. Although not a critical success, it remained a staple for touring companies until WW I. Judge Hardin hid the illegitimacy of his grandchild Lisa by having her raised by a black servant. After Hardin's death, Lisa was sold as a slave to Lacy, who lusted for her. In the play's most famous moment, Lisa spurned Lacy and defied his threat to make her a field hand, proclaiming: "Rags are royal raiment when worn for virtue's sake, and rather a hoe in my hands than self-contempt in my heart."   RAH

Whitman, Walt (1819–1892) Editor, journalist, and poet whose *Leaves of Grass* (1855) remains a major literary achievement of the 19th century. Whitman attended public schools and worked for numerous newspapers, including the *Brooklyn Daily Eagle* (1846–8), for which he contributed dramatic criticism. He faulted the "loud mouthed ranting style" of acting of the **Forrest** school (1846), and the vulgarity of New York theatres except the **Park,** which he thought "but a third-rate imitation of the best London theatres" (1847). His standards were high and his comments are among the most insightful of the age.   TLM

See: J. Kaplan, *Walt Whitman,* New York, 1980.

Who's Afraid of Virginia Woolf? by **Edward Albee** opened in New York on 13 October 1962, running for 664 performances. Directed by **Alan Schneider,** its cast included **Arthur Hill** as George, **Uta Hagen** as his wife and opponent Martha, and **George Grizzard** and Melinda Dillon as the young couple who stumble into the battle zone of their marriage. The play was made into a prize-winning film with Elizabeth Taylor, **Richard Burton,** George Segal, and Sandy Dennis, directed by **Mike Nichols.** It has been produced many times with actresses such as Glenda Jackson, **Kate Reid,** and **Colleen Dewhurst** as Martha. In three acts entitled "Fun and Games," "Walpurgisnacht," and "Exorcism," the play depicts the series of battle games with escalating stakes upon which George

Arthur Hill, George Grizzard, and Uta Hagen in *Who's Afraid of Virginia Woolf?* at the Billy Rose Theatre (NYC, 1962). Photo: Friedman–Abeles.

and Martha have built their marriage. When Martha wins at Humiliate the Host, George strikes back with Get the Guests, Martha ups the ante with Hump the Hostess, and George ends the night, and perhaps the games, by killing the fantasy son they have created as a "bean bag" between them. As George and Martha start a new day together without the buffer of games or fantasies, the young couple returns home with a greater understanding of their own marriage.   BCM

Why Marry? by **Jesse Lynch Williams.** This winner of the first Pulitzer Prize for Drama premiered 25 December 1917 at the Astor Theatre for a run of 120 performances (and later more than 500 performances in London). The play pits two womanly women against "a sexless freak with a scientific degree" (female), and progressive views of working women, sexual and economic equality, and useful careers, against repressive views of women as chattel and marriage as mercenary, habitual, and loveless. Faced with his own irrefutable arguments against marriage, Williams uses the liberated couple's public vows of love as a plighting of troth and weds them at play's end by default.   RKB

Wiest, Dianne (1948–) Actress and director who made her stage debut in Mack's *Esther* (1977) and on Broadway in *Frankenstein* (1981). Displaying a "combination of strength and vulnerability," she appeared with **Arena Stage** (1972–7), including *Our Town* and *Inherit the Wind* in the USSR (1973), and **Yale Repertory Theatre** (1980–1); recent productions include *Othello* (1982), *After the Fall* (1984), and **Tesich**'s *Square One* (1990). Wiest directed *Not About Heroes* **Off-Broadway** (1985). Among her numerous films are **Woody Allen**'s *The Purple Rose of Cairo* (1985), *Hannah and Her Sisters* (1986, Academy Award), *Radio Days* (1987), *September* (1987), and Foster's *Little Man Tate* (1991). She received 1979–80 Theatre World and **Clarence Derwent** awards and two Obies (*The Art of Dining,* 1979; **Lanford Wilson**'s *Serenading Louie* and Pinter's *A Kind of Alaska,* 1983).   REK

Wignell, Thomas (1753–1803) English-born actor-manager, he joined his cousin **Lewis Hallam**'s **American Company** in 1774 and soon became its leading man. Known primarily as a comedian, he played the role of Jonathan in the original production of **Royall Tyler**'s *The Contrast* and created the prototype of the **Yankee** character. In 1791 he left the company and teamed up with **Philadelphia** musician Alexander Reinagle to form the **Chestnut Street Theatre.** When their building was finally constructed three years later it was recognized as one of the finest playhouses in the nation. Wignell recruited many of his players from England, including **James Fennell, Mrs. Oldmixon, William Warren the elder,** and **Thomas A. Cooper.** For many years the company made Philadelphia the theatrical capital of America and developed a touring circuit encompassing Maryland, northern Virginia, and occasional visits to New York City. When Wignell died, his share in the company passed to his widow. Although she

and Reinagle were coowners, management of the company was assumed by actors Warren and **William B. Wood.** Warren eventually married Mrs. Wignell in 1806, and Wood joined him as owner of the company upon Reinagle's death in 1809. They finally disbanded in 1828.   RAS

Wilbur, Richard Purdy (1921–) A Pulitzer Prize–winning poet and translator, Wilbur has reclaimed the plays of Molière for the English-speaking stage. His translations include *The Misanthrope* (1955), *Tartuffe* (1963), *The School for Wives* (1971), and *The Learned Ladies* (1978), as well as Racine's *Andromache* (1982) and *Phaedra* (1986). Wilbur was a lyricist for the musical **Candide** (1956).   TLM

Wild West exhibition A re-creation of American frontier life and skills popular in the late 19th century. Occasional exhibits of broncobusting and Indian folkways were staged previously as museum attractions, but **P. T. Barnum** billed his Wild West extravaganza *Indian Life; or, A Chance for a Wife* in 1874 as a "thrilling arenic contest." The genre took its definitive shape under the guidance of **Col. William Frederick "Buffalo Bill" Cody,** a former Indian fighter and buffalo hunter, who starred in *Scouts of the Prairie,* a play written by the hack Ned Buntline and seen first in Chicago (1872) and in 1873 at New York's **Niblo's Garden.** The interest shown in a frontier fair he put on in North Platte, NE, in 1882 led him and crack-shot dentist Dr. W. F. Carver to organize a traveling show, *The Wild West,* which featured a program of shooting, roping, riding, and an attack on the Deadwood stagecoach. In his patent application Cody called it an "equestrian drama," for he disliked the term "show." In 1884 it went on the road under the ownership of Cody, the shrewd theatrical producer **Nate Salsbury,** and the sharpshooter A. H. Bogardus, who gave it a coherent dramatic structure, culminating in its absorption into **Steele Mac-Kaye**'s *Drama of Civilization* (Madison Square Garden, New York, 1885). From the first, it presented the white frontiersman as a civilizing factor in overcoming the savage elements of Nature and **Native Americans.** A European tour in 1887 (and again in 1903–6) made a deep impact, influencing the adventure novels of Karl May and, through him, the young **Bertolt Brecht.**

James A. Bailey took over Cody's Wild West in 1894 and used **circus** equipment and methods to enable it to make one-night stands; Cody added a "Congress of Rough Riders of the World," with Cossacks, gauchos, and Arabs bridging the gap between Sioux savagery and Plainsman nobility. The Buffalo Bill enterprise combined with Pawnee Bill's in 1909, but went into bankruptcy in 1913. A rival, the Miller Brothers and Edward Arlington's 101 Ranch Wild West Show – primarily a display of horsemanship minus the frontier-life romanticism – carried on during 1908–16, tried a revival in 1926 to no public interest, and folded in 1931. Motion pictures had taken over and expanded the depiction of cowboys and Indians, while authentic skills were relegated to the rodeo and circus "aftershows." One of Cody's stars, sharpshooter **Annie Oakley,** was to inspire the **Irving Berlin** musical comedy *Annie Get Your Gun* (1946). **Arthur Kopit**'s play *Indians* (1969) paints a sardonic picture of the relationship between Cody's exhibitions and the plight of the Native American.   LS

See: S. J. Blackstone, *Buckskins, Bullets and Business: A History of Buffalo Bill's Wild West,* Westport, CT, 1986; J. G. Rosa and R. May, *Buffalo Bill and His Wild West,* Lawrence, KS, 1989; D. Russell, *The Lives and Legends of Buffalo Bill,* Norman, OK, 1960; D. Russell, *The Wild West,* Fort Worth, TX, 1970.

Wilder, Clinton (1920–86) Producer, born in Irvine, PA, and educated at Princeton University; he began his professional career as a stage manager for *A Streetcar Named Desire* in 1947. He turned to producing with *Regina* (1949), *The Tender Trap* (1954), *Six Characters . . .* (1955), and *A Visit to a Small Planet* (1957). He joined with **Richard Barr** to form a production company, Theatre 1960 (later 1961, 1962, etc.), to present noncommercial, avant-garde plays. Their achievements include *The American Dream, The Death of Bessie Smith,* and *Happy Days* (1961); *Who's Afraid of Virginia Woolf?, Endgame, The Sandbox, Deathwatch,* and *Zoo Story* (1962). Joined by **Edward Albee** in 1963, they offered *The Dutchman* and *Tiny Alice* (1964); *Malcolm* and *The Long Christmas Dinner* (1966); *A Delicate Balance* (which won a Pulitzer Prize), *Rimers of Eldritch,* and *Everything in the Garden* (1967); and *Seascape* (1975).   TLM

Wilder, Thornton [Niven] (1897–1975) Novelist and playwright. While Wilder may be considered one of America's top 10 playwrights, his reputation rests upon three full-length plays and a half-dozen one-acts, beginning in 1931 with the publication of *The Long Christmas Dinner & Other Plays in One Act.* In 1938 his Pulitzer Prize–winning *Our Town* opened on Broadway, employing many of the experimental techniques Wilder had used in his one-acts: minimal scenery, narrative descriptions, and the like. *Our Town,* which has been called America's most read and most produced play, examines in the first act small-town life in Grover's Corners, NH, for a single day in 1901. Succeeding acts complete the cycle of marriage, birth, and death, ending with Emily Gibbs's conversation with the dead whom she has just joined.

Wilder's next play, *The Merchant of Yonkers,* closed after only 39 performances, but was a smash hit in 1964 as the musical *Hello, Dolly!* Of greater impact was *The Skin of Our Teeth* in 1942, a parable of the world's history centered around the Antrobus family. Act I is set in Excelsior, NJ, during the Ice Age; purposeful anachronisms mix with dinosaurs and refugees. Act II on the boardwalk at Atlantic City closes with Mr. Antrobus loading pairs of animals into his boat to avoid the Great Flood. Act III finds the Antrobus family coping with the aftereffects of a seven-year war, but finding hope in their very existence.   SMA

See: R. Goldstone and G. Anderson, *Thornton Wilder,* New York, 1982; G. Harrison, *The Enthusiast,* New Haven, 1983.

Wilkins, Edward G. P. (1829–61) A drama critic for the New York *Herald,* Wilkins wrote one

Bert Williams in blackface. Photo: Cavendish Morton, London. Courtesy: Laurence Senelick.

of the "merriest, brightest" and frequently produced contemporary comedies, *My Wife's Mirror* (1856). *Young New York* (1856), while reflecting local events, satirized society yet retained the positive approach of the heroine who followed Emerson's preachments.   WJM

Williams, Barney (né Bernard O'Flaherty) (1823–76) Irish-born actor whose first appearance on the New York stage was in 1836. In 1850 he married Maria Pray Mestayer (1828–1911), the widow of actor Charles Mestayer. For 20 years, the Williamses achieved considerable success, both in America and Great Britain, as a popular starring team in romantic Irish comedies such as *Born to Good Luck* and Samuel Lover's *Rory O'More.* Williams was regarded as unrivaled as the broadly comic, joking, hard-drinking, but appealing stage Irishman. For two seasons (1867–9) he managed the old **Wallack's Theatre** (by then the Broadway). His last appearance in *The Connie Soogah* and *The Fairy Circle* was at **Booth's Theatre** in New York on Christmas night, 1875.   DJW

Williams, Bert (né Egbert Austin Williams) (1874–1922) **African-American** comedian, born in Nassau, British West Indies, who began in **minstrel shows,** where he had to learn the standard "stage-darky" dialect and affect black-face to conceal his light complexion. From 1893 to 1908, he teamed with George Walker, who played the flashy free-spending urban sport to Williams's melancholy, shuffling fall-guy, both in **vaudeville** and a series of successful all-black musicals, including *Sons of Ham* (1900), *In Dahomey* (1902), and *Bandana Land* (1908). When Walker retired in 1909, the victim of advanced paresis, Williams went solo; already the first black comic to record for Victor (from 1901), he was known nationwide for such lugubrious songs as "I'm a Jonah Man" and "Nobody," and founded the first all-black actors' friendly society in 1906. Over protests from some of the white cast, Williams became the first black performer in *The* **Ziegfeld** *Follies,* in which he played annually during 1910–19 (missing only 1913 and 1918). "The funniest man I ever saw and the saddest man I ever knew," as **W. C. Fields** called him, played in tandem with **Leon Errol** and **Eddie Cantor,** and never failed with his one-man poker game.   LS

See: A. Charters, *Nobody: The Story of Bert Williams,* New York, 1970; M. Rowland, *Bert Williams, Son of Laughter,* New York, 1923, repr, 1964; E. L. Smith, *Bert Williams: A Biography of the Pioneer Black Comedian,* Jefferson, NC, 1992.

Williams, Jesse Lynch (1871–1929) Journalist, writer, and dramatist, remembered primarily as the winner of the first Pulitzer Prize for the best American play, **Why Marry?** (1917). Acted by amateurs and published in 1914 as *And So They Were Married* (1914), *Why Marry?* first questioned and then carefully defended the institution of marriage as the best that society can offer. *Why Not?* (1922) scrutinized divorce through two mismated couples and arrived at the same conclusion. As other plays reveal (e.g., *The Lovely Lady* [1925], concerned with parents and children), Williams's comedic solution to society's problems remained conventional.   WJM

Williams, John D. (1886?–1941) Producer and director, remembered today as the first producer to put **Eugene O'Neill** on the Broadway stage, having been persuaded by actor **Richard Bennett** to give **Beyond the Horizon** a trial matinee (1920). Williams had previously demonstrated that he was willing to produce controversial material with Galsworthy's *Justice* (1916), Maugham's *Our Betters* (1917), and **Augustus Thomas**'s *The Copperhead* (1918). He directed the long-running production of *Rain* (1922), adapted from the Maugham short story of a prostitute who resists reformation. He was, for a time, associated with **Charles Frohman,** and helped persuade **Maude Adams** to return to the stage (1931).   MR

Williams, Samm-Art (1946–) African-American actor and playwright from North Carolina. He joined the **Negro Ensemble Company** in 1973, played a number of prominent roles, and participated in its Playwrights' Workshop. Five of his plays were produced by the company, including *Home* (1979), about a black youth who leaves his southern farm for the urban North: Initially prosperous, he becomes embroiled in illegal dealings, loses everything, and decides to return home and rebuild his life. The play had an extended run at St. Mark's Playhouse and transferred to Broadway for 279 additional performances. It won Williams a 1981 Guggenheim Fellowship in playwriting.   EGH

Williams, Tennessee (1911–83) Playwright. From 1945, with his first success, *The* **Glass Menagerie,** Tennessee Williams has had a deep impact on the American theatre, bringing to it an original lyric voice and a new level of sexual frankness. The pleasure and the pain of sex was the great, inescapable subject of both his work and his life. In different moods and styles and with varying effectiveness, Williams returned repeatedly to the same neurotic conflicts embedded within the same character types: The spirits of Blanche Du Bois and Stanley Kowalski, the fierce antagonists of his masterpiece, *A* **Streetcar Named Desire** (1947), haunt practically all of his fables. Blanche is the lady of illusion and artifice, the fluttering Southern belle whose veneer of refinement masks emotional starvation and sexual rapacity. Desired and feared by Blanche as well as by Williams, Stanley is the muscled male whose potency contains the promise of both salvation and destruction.

As in *Streetcar,* the battle between repression and release, between the puritan and the cavalier, is at the heart of Williams's most vibrant work: **Summer and Smoke** (1948), *The Rose Tattoo* (1951), and *Battle of Angels* (1940, rewritten as *Orpheus Descending,* 1957). In some plays (*Battle of Angels, You Touched Me* [1945], **Sweet Bird of Youth** [1959]) lusty men reanimate languishing women; in others

Paul Newman, Geraldine Page, and Sidney Blackmer in Williams's *Sweet Bird of Youth,* directed by Elia Kazan at the Martin Beck Theatre (1959). Courtesy: Michael Gnat.

(***Cat on a Hot Tin Roof*** [1955], *The Milk Train Doesn't Stop Here Anymore* [1963]) the refusal of desirable males to satisfy deprived women provides the central conflict. Sometimes, as in *Cat on a Hot Tin Roof* and *Suddenly Last Summer* (1958), men withhold sex from women because they are homosexual; other times, as in *Milk Train,* because they want to transcend sexual desire. The source of Williams's profound sexual conflicts was the war between his fatally mismatched parents: his mother a rector's prudish daughter, his father a blustery womanizer who called his sensitive son "Miss Nancy." Unable in the American theatre of the 1950s and '60s to write openly about his own homosexual passion, Williams created nominally heterosexual dramas, transmuting tormented autobiography into artistic metaphor.

After *The **Night of the Iguana*** (1961), an uncharacteristic play of resolution and completion, Williams descended into a critical and commercial decline for the remaining 22 years of his life. Some of his later work, notably *The Gnädiges Fraulein* (1966), *In the Bar of a Tokyo Hotel* (1969), and *Outcry* (1973), chronicles the despair of creators who have lost control of their art. Other plays, such as *Small Craft Warnings* (1972) and especially *Vieux Carré* (1978), are attempts at self-restoration in which Williams returns to the delicacy of *The Glass Menagerie*. His Rabelaisian middle period is framed, as it were, by the directly autobiographical *Glass Menagerie* and *Vieux Carré*, in both of which Williams displays a healing compassion not only for others but also for himself as a young man. But neither the plays about disintegration nor the ones of partial affirmation have had the impact of his earlier work: Audiences and critics have generally found the dramas too private.

In his later years Williams's personal life seriously deteriorated: He became increasingly dependent on drugs and alcohol and required periods of institutional confinement. Yet he continued to write daily, rigorously devoting himself to his craft. Despite the blurred focus, the occasional self-parody, the lack of control in these later offerings, there remains much of value in passages that testify to Williams's powerful sense of theatre and to his melodic gifts. Even the least of his plays is a vehicle for bravura acting, for in good plays and bad Williams created wonderfully actable neurotics. Twisted by desire, plagued by anxiety, Williams's victims and outsiders speak a poetry of the dispossessed flavored with wit, irony, and gallantry.

Williams struggled through a long critical eclipse, but his reputation is now secure. Among American playwrights his achievement is equaled only by that of **Eugene O'Neill.**   FH

See: R. Boxill, *Tennessee Williams*, New York, 1987; A. J. Devlin, ed., *Conversations with Tennessee Williams*, Jackson, MS, 1986; R. F. Leavitt, *The World of Tennessee Williams*, New York, 1978; D. Spoto, *The Kindness of Strangers*, Boston, 1985; M. Van Antwerp and S. Johns, eds., *Dictionary of Literary Biography, Documentary Series, An Illustrated Chronicle. Vol. 4: Tennessee Williams*, Detroit, 1984; T. Williams, *Memoirs*, New York, 1975.

Williamstown (MA) Theatre Festival
Founded in 1955 by Yale Drama School professor Nikos Psacharopoulos, this festival has presented over 250 productions since its inception. Known for its appeal to established actors, many now primarily in films, as a place where they can return frequently to the stage, Williamstown also utilizes some of the best directors and designers in the U.S. and presents not only classics but avant-garde risks and unknown new plays. A rotating company of over 250 has been associated with the Festival, including the likes of **Christopher Reeve, Colleen Dewhurst,** Frank Langella, James Naughton, **Austin Pendleton, Richard Thomas, Olympia Dukakis, Blythe Danner, Geraldine Fitzgerald,** and Richard Chamberlain. A complex operation with at least six discrete production components, WTF has gained an international reputation and is considered by many the outstanding summer theatre establishment in the U.S. After Psacharopoulos's death in 1989, Peter Hunt, whose association with Williamstown began in 1958, was appointed artistic director.   DBW

Willis, Nathaniel Parker (1806–67) Playwright and essayist who began an intense but brief association with the theatre in 1837 with *Bianca Visconti,* the winner of **Josephine Clifton**'s $1,000 competition, and *The Kentucky Heiress,* also written for Clifton. Both plays failed in production. In 1839 Willis wrote *Tortesa the Usurer* for **James Wallack,** an appealing and well-dramatized story of a rich man who bargains for an aristocratic wife, who unfortunately loves another, but happily accepts an enchanting glover's daughter. Audiences, however, did not appreciate Willis's literary comedy, and starring actors did not want plays with several starring roles. Enjoying a reputation as the foremost essayist in America, Willis stopped writing plays.   WJM

See: H. A. Beers, *Nathaniel Parker Willis*, Boston, 1885.

Will Rogers Follies, The Musical play with book by **Peter Stone,** music by **Cy Coleman,** and lyrics by **Comden and Green;** opened 1 May 1991 at the refurbished **Palace Theatre** on Broadway, won six Tony Awards (including best musical) plus Drama Critics', Drama Desk, and Grammy awards, and settled in for a long run (still running as of summer 1992). Directed by **Tommy Tune** and starring Keith Carradine (replaced by Mac Davis after a year's run) as cowboy philosopher **Will Rogers,** this vehicle is a musical biography staged as one of **Ziegfeld**'s **revues.** Most critics complained that the format didn't work but praised the showmanship of Carradine, the spectacular staging and choreography of Tune, and the settings of **Tony Walton,** costumes of **Willa Kim,** and lighting of **Jules Fisher. David Richards** correctly predicted that the musical's "sumptuous production numbers, exquisite chorus girls, phosphorescent rope tricks in black light, a dog act, songs you actually want to hum, a stairway to paradise (or somewhere thereabouts), close harmony, and shapely legs in kaleidoscope patterns" were what audiences wanted to see.   TLM

Willson, Meredith (né Robert Meredith Reiniger) (1902–84) Composer, lyricist, and librettist, Willson studied at the New York Institute of Musical Art and played flute in John Philip Sousa's band and in the New York Philharmonic. For many years he worked as conductor and performer on NBC radio. In 1957 he turned his reminiscences of his Iowa boyhood into the hit Broadway musical *The Music Man,* surrounding the story of a fast-talking traveling salesman with patter songs, barbershop quartets, ragtime dance sequences, and Sousa-like marches. He returned to the same period and some of the same musical styles for *The Unsinkable Molly Brown* (1960). His final musical to reach Broadway, *Here's Love* (1963), was based on the film *Miracle on Thirty-fourth Street.* He wrote three autobiographical memoirs.   MK

Wilson, August (1945–) **African-American** playwright whose position in the theatre rose meteorically in less than a five-year period. Winner of the 1987 Pulitzer Prize for Drama for *Fences* and the 1990 Prize for *The Piano Lesson,* he has written a series of plays, each set in a different decade, that evolves into a cycle of dramas that he terms his "view of the black experience of the 20th century." Wilson has focused on what he perceives as the largest idea that confronted blacks in each decade, drawing heavily on his own experience growing up in the Hill district of Pittsburgh, PA, a black slum community. Wilson also is typical of an American playwright whose work has been fostered in the regions, with developmental work at the **Eugene O'Neill Theatre Center**'s **National Playwrights Conference** and premieres at the **Yale Repertory Theatre** under **Lloyd Richards**'s direction, beginning with *Ma Rainey's Black Bottom* (1984) and including *Fences, Joe Turner's Come and Gone* (1986), *The Piano Lesson* (1988), and *Two Trains Running* (1990; Broadway, 1992; with **Roscoe Lee Browne**). The latter, set in 1968 at a restaurant in Pittsburgh across the street from a funeral home and a meat market, focuses on disenfranchised characters looking back nostalgically and with some confusion at their limited "progress."

Wilson has won the Drama Desk Award, the New York Drama Critics' Circle Award, and a Tony Award for *Fences,* and Tony nominations for best play (*The Piano Lesson* and *Two Trains Running*). As of late 1991 Wilson was working on his '40s play for his decades cycle, tentatively titled *Moon Going Down* and set in a turpentine camp in Georgia. Likened by the Pulitzer board to **Eugene O'Neill,** Wilson has certainly emerged as the richest theatrical voice in the U.S. of the past decade and has managed to transcend the categorization of "black" playwright to speak through his dissection of black families and communities to a broad-based audience.   DBW

Wilson, Edwin (1927–) Drama critic and educator. Born in Nashville and educated at Vanderbilt, the University of Edinburgh, and Yale, Wilson has served as theatre critic for *The Wall Street Journal* since 1972. He has taught at Hofstra University (1958–60), Yale (1961–2), and Hunter College (1967–). Knowledgeable and demanding, Wilson holds the New York theatre to high standards, writes intelligently, and asks that playwrights have a point of view.   TLM

Wilson, Elizabeth (1921–) Actor. Prominent in stage, film, and television, Wilson has worked most often with **Mike Nichols, Alan Arkin,** and **Joseph Papp.** After 10 years in stock theatre, Wilson debuted on Broadway as Christine in *Picnic* (1953), the first of over 30 Broadway and **Off-Broadway** roles. Cast as spinsters, lonely mothers, and eccentrics, Wilson won both Tony and Obie awards for *Sticks and Bones* (Harriet, 1971), a Drama Desk Award for *Threepenny Opera* (Mrs. Peachum, 1976), an Obie for *Taken in Marriage* (Aunt Helen, 1979), and Drama Desk and Outer Critics' Circle awards for *Morning's at Seven* (Aaronetta, 1980).   TH-S

Wilson, Francis (1854–1935) Comedian and singer. After an apprenticeship as a utility actor and low comedian with a **stock company,** Wilson made his musical theatre debut in *Our Goblins* (1880). During 1885–9 he appeared in comic operas with the McCaull Opera Company, then established his own company. His greatest role was that of Cadeaux in *Erminie* (1886), a part he played nearly 1,300 times over 35 years. His other successes included *The Merry Monarch* (1890), *The Lion Tamer* (1891), *Half a King* (1896), and *The Toreador* (1902). From 1904 on, Wilson confined his efforts to comedy and drama. Because of his training in stock, Wilson brought to his musical roles the skills of a character actor, carefully preparing each move and gesture rather than trusting to improvisation. During 1913–21 he served as the first president of **Actors' Equity.** His entertaining autobiography was published in 1924.   MK

Wilson, Harry Leon (1867–1939) Playwright and writer. A collaborator with **Booth Tarkington** on *The Man from Home* (1907), Wilson had limited success in the theatre. Although the authors laughed at their hero, audiences laughed *with* him, and the play ran for five and a half years. Their nine subsequent plays together – including *Foreign Exchange, Your Humble Servant,* and *Cameo Kirby,* all in 1909 – were poorly received. Wilson also wrote the story from which **Kaufman** and **Connelly** created *Merton of the Movies* (1922).   WJM

Wilson, John Chapman (1899–1961) Producer and director. Born in New York and educated at Yale (1922), Wilson left a Wall Street career to become business manager for Noël Coward (1925). With *Design for Living* (1933), he began producing with Coward and **Lunt and Fontanne,** including *The Taming of the Shrew* (1935), *Tonight at 8:30* (1836), *Idiot's Delight,* and *Amphitryon 38* (1937). After 1938 he became an independent producer and director, presenting *Blithe Spirit* (1941), *A Connecticut Yankee* (1943), *Present Laughter* (1946), and *The Winslow Boy* (1947). He also directed *Kiss Me, Kate* (1948), which ran for 1,077 performances on Broadway. He retired in 1958.   TLM

Wilson, Lanford (1937–) Missouri-born playwright who began writing plays at the University of Chicago and then became part of a group of playwrights at the **Caffe Cino** in New York. There his first script was produced, *So Long at the Fair,* in 1963. Since then his plays have been produced at **La MaMa** in New York, the Mercury Theatre in London, most regional U.S. theatres, and on Broadway.

Among his more successful scripts are *The Madness of Lady Bright* (1964), *Balm in Gilead* and *This Is the Rill Speaking* (1965), *Rimers of Eldritch* (1966), *Lemon Sky* (1970), *The Great Nebula in Orion* (1971), *The **Hot l Baltimore*** (1973), *The **5th of July*** (1978), and ***Talley's Folly*** (1979), the last winning Wilson the Pulitzer Prize for Drama and the New York Drama Critics' Circle Award. His 1983 *Angel's Fall* was a critical, but not popular, success.

Wilson was one of the founders of the **Circle Repertory Company,** which staged several of his scripts. *The Hot l Baltimore,* involving various social outcasts in a condemned hotel, ran 1,166 performances, then the **Off-Broadway** record for a nonmusical American play.

Besides the Pulitzer Prize, Wilson has won the Drama Desk Vernon Rice Award for *The Rimers of Eldritch,* the New York Drama Critics' Circle Award, the Outer Circle Award, and an Obie for *The Hot l Baltimore,* and another Obie for *The Mound Builders.* In recent years Wilson has learned Russian in order to translate **Chekhov.** His ***Burn This*** appeared on Broadway in 1988 and two years later in London. Wilson's most recent play is *Redwood Curtain* (1992). SMA

See: G. Barnett, *Lanford Wilson,* New York, 1987; M. Busby, *Lanford Wilson,* Boise, ID, 1987.

Wilson, Robert (1941–) Director and designer whose training as a painter and architect is evident in his painterly theatre compositions. Wilson's work with brain-damaged children, using physical activity to influence mental activity, also influenced his dreamy pieces, especially their slow pace and repetition of simple movement. Christopher Knowles, an autistic adolescent, became a collaborator with Wilson on pieces like *A Letter to Queen Victoria* (1974) and *Einstein on the Beach* (1976), the latter also in collaboration with choreographers Andrew de Groat and Lucinda Childs and composer Philip Glass. Wilson was interested in Knowles's nondiscursive use of language and sought to create on stage his unusual way of structuring perceptions. Operatic in scale, Wilson's streams of visual and aural images lack plots and characters in any conventional sense and often employ massive scenery, animals, and complex lighting effects. *Nō*-like in tone, they take place in slow motion, altering the audience's sense of time; a simple action like crossing the stage can take an hour. *Deafman Glance* (1970) lasted eight hours, and *Overture to Ka Mountain,* created for the 1972 Shiraz Festival in Iran, lasted a week. In the 1980s Wilson began centering his work in Europe, where it was easier to find funding. There he created *The Man in the Raincoat* (1981, Cologne), *Great Day in the Morning* (1982, Paris), *The Golden Windows* (1982, Munich), *the CIVIL warS* (1983, five countries; the German section had its U.S. premiere at the **American Repertory Theatre,** 1985), and *The Black Rider:*

Robert Wilson's production of *When We Dead Awaken* at the American Repertory Theatre (1991). Set design by Wilson and John Conklin. Pictured are Mario Arrambide, Alvin Epstein, and Stephanie Roth. Photo: Dan Nutu. Courtesy: ART.

the casting of magic bullets (1990, Hamburg). In recent years, Wilson has been directing operas and plays from the classical repertory, among them *The Magic Flute* (1991, Paris) and *Parsifal* (1991, Houston). In conjunction with his direction of Ibsen's *When We Dead Awaken* at ART 1991, a major retrospective of his work was mounted at Boston's Museum of Fine Arts (seen later in Houston and San Francisco). AS

See: S. Brecht, *The Theatre of Visions: Robert Wilson,* New York, 1984; L. Shyer, *Robert Wilson and His Collaborators,* New York, 1989.

Wiman, Dwight Deere (1894–1951) Producer or coproducer of 56 plays and musicals. A native of Moline, IL, and an officer in the family agricultural implements firm, John Deere and Company, he produced several plays by **John Van Druten** and by **Paul Osborn,** and five musicals by **Richard Rodgers** and **Oscar Hammerstein II,** as well as *The Little Show* (1929), its offspring of 1930 and 1931, and **Street Scene** (1947). His production of Osborn's ***Morning's at Seven*** (1938) was his proudest achievement. He was director of entertainment for the American Red Cross in the United Kingdom (1942–6). WD

Winchell, Walter (1897–1972) Broadway columnist and drama critic. A native New Yorker, Winchell began as a reporter for *Vaudeville News* (1922), moving to the *New York Graphic* (1924–9) as drama critic and columnist. He became a national celebrity through his radio programs (1929–56) and through the syndication of his columns in Hearst's *New York Mirror* (1929–63). Winchell coined his own expressions ("cupiding" for romance and "mind your Winchell"). His fast-paced and staccato style gave a sense of excitement and importance to everything he covered. In his prime, he could turn a play or movie into a hit with a favorable notice. TLM

> See: J. Mosedale, *The Men Who Invented Broadway*, New York, 1981.

Windust, Bretaigne (1906–60) Paris-born director and actor who grew up in New York and attended Princeton University. In 1928 he co-founded the University Players at Falmouth, MA. He began his professional career in 1929 as assistant stage manager with the **Theatre Guild.** In 1932 he staged the London production of *Strange Interlude.* He made his New York acting debut in 1933 and received good notices although the play failed. The **Lunt**s noticed his work and hired him to play Tranio in *The Taming of the Shrew* (1935). His association with the Lunts continued in 1936 as he directed them in *Idiot's Delight* and a year later in *Amphitryon 38.* After staging a successful revival of *The Circle* with **Tallulah Bankhead** in 1938, Windust was to enjoy a decade of remarkable successes: *Life with Father* (1939), *Arsenic and Old Lace* (1941), *The Hasty Heart* (1945), *The State of the Union* (1945), and *Finian's Rainbow* (1947). Although he turned to films and television after 1947, Windust still enjoyed some success with *The Great Sebastians* (1956) and *The Girls in 509* (1958). His forte was comedy and his trademark was dramatic curtain calls and postcurtain tableaux. TLM

Winer, Linda (1946–   ) Critic who immediately after college began her career as theatre, dance, and music reviewer on the Chicago *Tribune* (1969–80). She then joined the entertainment staff of the New York *Daily News* as "cultural affairs specialist" (1982–6), before being named "New York Arts Critic" by the new *USA Today,* reviewing theatre and dance (1982–6). In 1987 she moved to New York *Newsday* as an arts columnist, becoming its chief theatre critic in 1988. In 1979, Winer was the first woman asked to participate for a full week as master critic at the National Critics Institute of the **Eugene O'Neill Theatre Center.** JD

Wings by **Arthur Kopit** was first produced at the **Yale Repertory Theatre** on 3 March 1978, and was moved to Broadway in 1979. Directed by John Madden, its original cast included **Constance Cummings** as Emily Stilson, the stroke victim whose subjective experience the play depicts, and Marianne Owen as Amy, her therapist. Originally written as a radio play, *Wings* uses sound, color, lighting effects, and experiments with dialogue to depict the long process Mrs. Stilson's consciousness goes through from the fragmentation caused by the stroke to an integrated perception through which she can again recognize herself, her memories, and her experience. In the course of it, she must struggle to maintain her sense of self against both her own confusion and the misunderstanding of others. BCM

Winter, William (1836–1917) Drama critic, theatre historian, and biographer. Born in Gloucester,

MA, and educated at Harvard University, Winter abandoned a law career for a literary one. Influenced by Henry Wadsworth Longfellow, Winter turned to writing poetry and reviewing books. In 1859 he moved to New York and worked as assistant editor and book reviewer for the *Saturday Press.* In 1860–1 he wrote briefly for *The Leader* before taking charge of the *Albion*'s dramatic department (1861–5), writing under the name of Mercutio. In 1865 he replaced Edward H. House as chief critic for the *New York Tribune,* a position he held until 1909, establishing himself as the foremost drama critic of his generation. The foundation of Winter's critical beliefs was essentially Aristotelian, tempered with 19th-century romantic idealism (later called "the Genteel Tradition"). He considered acting the primary art of theatre and the standard drama preferable to modern plays. He regarded the theatre as a temple of art to elevate and inspire humankind, and rejected the notion that art should depict real life. To Winter, beauty and morality were inseparable in art, and realism had banished both from the stage. Thus he saw Ibsenism as a "rank, deadly pessimism . . . a disease, injurious alike to the stage and to the public." Winter prepared acting versions of **Shakespeare**'s plays for **Edwin Booth** and **Augustin Daly.** He wrote lengthy biographies on Edwin Booth (1893), **Ada Rehan** (1898), **Richard Mansfield** (1910), **Joseph Jefferson** (1913), and **Tyrone Power** (1913). His more than 50 books provide a comprehensive record of the late-19th-century American stage. TLM

> See: R. M. Ludwig, "A Critical Biography of William Winter," PhD diss., Harvard U, 1950.

Winter Garden Theatre NYC theatre at 1634 Broadway, between 50th and 51st Streets. The Winter Garden, an important musical house, was designed for the **Shubert brothers** by architect William Swasey. It opened on 20 March 1911 with a double bill that included a curtain-raiser called *Bow Sing* and *La Belle Paree,* a **revue.** The Winter Garden was less a totally new theatre than an extensive remodeling of an existing building, the American Horse Exchange. The remodeled structure contained a cabaret, as well as a large theatre, which was decorated in a garden motif and contained an unusual feature for the time: a runway extending from the stage into the auditorium. In 1912 the Winter Garden became the home of *The Passing Show* (an annual Shubert revue designed to compete with **Florenz Ziegfeld**'s *Follies*), which continued to be presented regularly through 1924. During the 1910s and early '20s, the theatre was also the home of a number of light musicals conceived as vehicles for Shubert star **Al Jolson.** The Winter Garden was extensively remodeled during the 1920s by theatre architect Herbert Krapp. During the 1930s it housed such important musical attractions as the Shubert-produced editions of the *Ziegfeld Follies* and the long-running *Hellzapoppin',* starring **"Ole" Olsen and "Chick" Johnson.** From 1928 to 1933, and again during 1945–8, the Winter Garden was used for motion picture showings. Following its second reconversion to live performance, the theatre has been the home of such major musicals as *West Side Story* (1957), *Gypsy* (1959), and *Cats* (1982). The Winter Garden, which seats some 1,500 spectators, is owned by the **Shubert Organization.**   BMcN

Winterset by **Maxwell Anderson** was one of the author's most celebrated experiments in poetic writing, combining an "elevated language" with realistic, contemporary events. Based on the aftermath of the famous Sacco and Vanzetti trial, *Winterset* was written in blank verse and reflected Anderson's belief that theatre language must be poetic in order to explore universal truths. The play was produced by **Guthrie McClintic** in 1935 and featured a superb performance by **Burgess Meredith** and a spectacular set design by **Jo Mielziner.** It received mixed critical notices – although some of the praise was effusive – and ran for 178 performances. Considered by some to be Anderson's masterpiece, this contemporary poetic tragedy lost the Pulitzer Prize to *Idiot's Delight* but was the first play to be voted the prestigious Drama Critics' Circle Award.   BBW

Wisdom Bridge Theatre Founded on the northern edge of **Chicago** by David Beaird in 1974, and flourished under the artistic direction of **Robert Falls** (1977–85). Wisdom Bridge productions were marked by physical energy coupled with creative direction – such as a *Tartuffe* set on a plantation after the Civil War and Kabuki versions of western dramas directed by Shozo Sato. By 1985, prior to Falls's move to the **Goodman Theatre,** Wisdom Bridge had the second highest budget of a nonprofit Chicago theatre. Richard E. T. White's subsequent artistic direction was cut short by a falling out with long-time managing director Jeffrey Ortmann, who then assumed artistic control. In early 1992 staff payroll was suspended and the company's future was in peril.   SF

Wiseman, Joseph (1918–   ) Actor who has played a variety of roles from archbishop to rabbi, Nazi officer to Spanish statesman, beggar to lecherous cabbie. He made his stage debut in *Three Men on a Horse* (1936) and on Broadway in *Abe Lincoln in Illinois* (1938). Wiseman performed classical and contemporary roles at the **Mark Taper Forum, Arena Stage,** Pittsburgh Public Theater, **American Shakespeare Festival,** and **Circle in the Square;** productions include *Detective Story* (1949), *Golden Boy* (1952), *The Lark* (1955), *Incident at Vichy* (1964), Kipphardt's *In the Matter of J. Robert Oppenheimer* (1968), and Wiesel's *Zalmen, or the Madness of God* (1974). His films include *Detective Story* (1951), *Les Misérables* (1952), *Dr. No* (1962), *The Night They Raided Minsky*'s (1968), and *The Apprenticeship of Duddy Kravitz* (1974).   REK

Witching Hour, The Though produced by the **Shubert**s, playwright **Augustus Thomas** was able to control many of the arrangements for this production, which opened on 18 November 1907 for 212 performances and was followed by a lengthy tour. It is melodrama in the tradition of those plays that capitalize on subjects and devices of current interest – in this case, mental telepathy and hypnotism. John Mason played the good-hearted gambler who, after he utilizes telepathy to influence a jury and hypnotism to stop an assailant in his tracks, finally understands how he was able to win all those card games.   MR

Witham, Charles W. (1842–1926) was one of the first distinguished scenic artists of the American theatre [see **scenic design**]. He created the settings for all of **Edwin Booth**'s major productions in the late 1860s and '70s. He also was chief artist for **Augustin Daly** in the 1870s, and in the '80s he worked for **Edward Harrigan.**   AA

See: T. Marshall in *Anatomy of an Illusion: Studies in Nineteenth Century Design,* Amsterdam, 1969.

Wittstein, Ed (1929–   ) Set designer for theatre, television, and opera who studied at **Erwin Piscator**'s Dramatic Workshop, Parson's School of Design, and New York University. For television he designed the NBC Opera Productions, "Armstrong Circle Theatre," and the "Steve Allen Show." He designed several Broadway shows in the 1960s, including *The Knack* and *Enter Laughing,* as well as several seasons at the **American Shakespeare Festival.** He is best known, though, as the designer of the simple theatrical set for *The Fantasticks,* which has run **Off-Broadway** for over 30 years.   AA

Wiz, The Musical of L. Frank Baum's novel *The Wonderful Wizard of Oz,* with book by William F. Brown; opened 5 January 1975 at the **Majestic Theatre** in New York. Featuring an all-black cast, the familiar Oz story was retold in jive talk, with music and lyrics by Charlie Smalls that included rock, gospel, and soul music. The overall exotic style offered colorful and imaginative sets as the familiar characters appeared with a contemporary black twist, full of humor and satire. High-fashion costumes enhanced the spectacular dance numbers. The production appealed to a wide audience of all ages and ethnic groups.   ER

Wizard of Oz, The, by Paul Tietjens and A. Baldwin Sloane opened in Chicago 16 June 1902 and on Broadway 21 January 1903. Adapted by L. Frank Baum from his novel *The Wonderful Wizard of Oz* (1900), the libretto transformed Dorothy into a romantic ingenue who traveled through Oz with her pet cow, Imogene [see **animal impersonation**]. The production was known for its lavish scenery, including the Kansas Cyclone, the Wizard's Palace, and the Deadly Poppy Field. Vaudevillians **Montgomery and Stone** appeared as the Tin Man and the Scarecrow. The show toured the country for eight years, while Baum continued to adapt his Oz stories for the stage and wrote a total of 14 Oz books. He finally settled in Hollywood and founded the Oz Film Manufacturing Company (1914), which made half a dozen silent films during the single year of its existence. Other versions of Oz appeared on stage, film, and radio, and in 1939 MGM released the famous movie featuring Judy Garland, **Ray Bolger,** Jack Haley, and **Bert Lahr.**   JDM

See: J. Fricke, J. Scarfone, W. Stillman, *The Wizard of Oz,* New York, 1989.

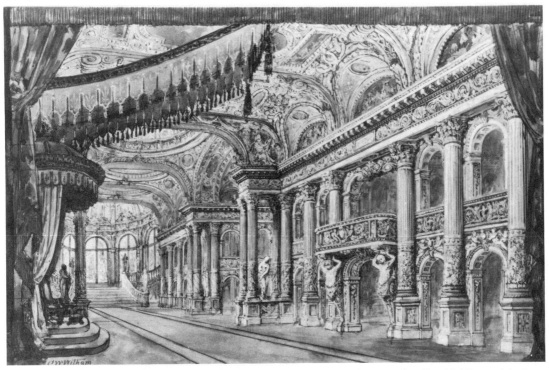

The last scene of *Richelieu*, designed by Charles Witham and presented by Edwin Booth at Booth's Theatre (1870). Courtesy: Theatre Collection, Museum of the City of New York.

Fred Stone as the Scarecrow and Dave Montgomery as the Tin Man in the musical comedy *The Wizard of Oz*. Courtesy: Laurence Senelick.

Wodehouse, P[elham] G[renville] (1881–1975) A successful London columnist and novelist, his song lyrics were first heard on the American stage in *Miss Springtime* (1916). He collaborated with librettist **Guy Bolton** and composer **Jerome Kern** on *Have a Heart* (1917) and *Leave It to Jane* (1917) and contributed lyrics and/or librettos to numerous other shows in the 1910s and '20s, notably *Oh, My Dear!* (1918), *Oh, Kay!* (1926), *Rosalie* (1928), and *The Three Musketeers* (1928). He was also a drama critic for the magazine *Vanity Fair*. His wry lyrics and witty librettos did much to improve the prestige of Broadway musicals. Other than working in the U.S. frequently, he lived in exile here only in the final three decades of his life.

MK

See: F. Donaldson, *P. G. Wodehouse: A Biography*, New York, 1982; D. A. Jasen, *The Theatre of P. G. Wodehouse*, London, 1979.

Wolfe, George C. (1955–) African-American playwright and director. College-trained Wolfe was twice winner at the American College Theatre Festival and spent four years writing and directing in Los Angeles. His first New York show, the musical *Paradise!* (1985) presented at **Playwrights**

Horizons, was unsuccessful, but he followed it with *The Colored Museum* (1986), a hilarious lampoon of black experience topics. Premiered at the **Crossroads Theatre** in New Brunswick, NJ, the play later ran for nine months at the **Public Theater** and moved to London. In 1990, in addition to directing the Public Theater's production of **Brecht**'s *The Caucasian Chalk Circle* set in Haiti, he was also selected as one of three resident directors at the **New York Shakespeare Festival.** His musical about Jelly Roll Morton, *Jelly's Last Jam,* premiered in Los Angeles (spring 1991) before opening on Broadway (spring 1992).   EGH

Women, The Biting social satire of Park Avenue elite women. This three-act play written by **Clare Boothe** Luce was one of the most successful comedies of the 1930s, with a run of 657 performances after its opening at the **Ethel Barrymore Theatre** on 26 December 1936. It subsequently was produced in many foreign countries and translated into several languages. No men appear in the play, although the group of indulged and malicious female characters are motivated almost exclusively by their relationships to men. Mary Haines, who is influenced by her catty crowd to divorce her husband because of his affair with a shopgirl, learns from them how to "sharpen her claws" and get him back. In 1939 MGM released an equally successful film version.   FB

Women's Project and Productions Producing group. Julia Miles founded The Women's Project in 1978 as part of the **American Place Theatre,** where she had been Associate Director since 1967. Initially funded by a Ford Foundation Grant, the Project became independent of American Place in 1987, with support from the Kentucky Foundation for Women. The project's mission is to identify, encourage, develop, and produce women playwrights and to help establish visibility for women directors. Miles frequently states that her goal will be met when women playwrights can be known just as playwrights. In its first 12 years, the Project produced over 50 plays, published four play anthologies, staged hundreds of rehearsed readings, and supported directors through a Directors Forum. The project now has over 290 artistic members, including many who have become leaders, including **Anne Bogart, Constance Congdon, Maria Irene Fornés, Emily Mann,** Sharon Ott, Carey Perloff, and Paula Vogel.   TH-S

See: J. Miles, ed., *The Women's Project: Seven Plays by Women,* New York, 1980.

Wonderful Town This musical, which reunited the team of **Leonard Bernstein** (music), **Betty Comden and Adolph Green** (lyrics), and director **George Abbott** (who had created *On the Town* in 1944), opened at the **Winter Garden Theatre** on 25 February 1953. It was based on the play *My Sister Eileen* by Joseph Fields and **Jerome Chodorov** (who also wrote the book for this show) and Ruth McKenney's stories. Set in New York's Greenwich Village in the 1930s, it told of two sisters, a writer and an actress, who come to New York to pursue their careers. After several adven-

tures the sisters achieve a measure of success, and, in traditional musical comedy fashion, fall in love. The role of the older sister, Ruth, was played by film star Rosalind Russell, whose stylish humor brightened such songs as "One Hundred Easy Ways to Lose a Man." Edith (Edie) Adams brought a strong singing voice to the part of the younger sister. A breezy, audience-pleasing musical, it broke no new ground in form or content.   MK

Wong, B. D. ("Bradd") (1962–) When he auditioned for the 1988 Broadway premiere of **David Henry Hwang**'s *M. Butterfly,* Wong was an obscure actor with few credits since his 1982 debut Off-Broadway. Cast in the showy role of Liling, a Chinese male spy masquerading as a woman, he turned the role into a career-launching *tour de force,* winning all major New York acting honors for 1988, including a Tony for featured actor. He has gone on to small roles in unmemorable films, but his vast talent remains largely untapped.   MB

Wood, Audrey (1905–85) **Agent.** A native New Yorker and the daughter of William H. Wood, first manager of the **Palace Theatre,** Wood began her career as reader for the Century Play Company, where she met William Liebling. Together they founded an artists' representative agency, Liebling–Wood, Inc., in 1937, and married in 1938. In 1954, the agency was sold to Music Corporation of America, where she remained until 1962, when she became head of the drama department at International Creative Management. A massive stroke in 1981 closed her successful career. Her most famous clients included **Tennessee Williams, Robert Anderson, William Inge, Arthur Kopit, Carson McCullers,** and Truman Capote.   MCH

See: A. Wood with M. Wilk, *Represented by Audrey Wood,* Garden City, NY, 1981.

Wood, Mrs. John (née Matilda Charlotte Vining) (1831–1915) Liverpool-born actress and manager who acted on provincial English stages for 12 years before marrying actor John Wood and coming to Boston in 1854. After their American debut at the **Boston Theatre** (September 1854), they appeared in New York at the Academy of Music (1856) before becoming regulars with the Boston Company. Mrs. Wood played a guest engagement at **Wallack's Theatre** in late 1856, creating the role of Minnehaha in **Charles Walcot**'s *Hiawatha.* At the end of the 1856–7 season, Mrs. Wood and her husband left for **San Francisco,** where she quickly became a star. After the couple separated, Mrs. Wood returned East to play starring engagements for the next four years. In 1863 she began a three-year stint as manager of the Olympic Theatre. She returned to England in 1866 and acted only once more (1872–3) in America. Saucy, impudent, and fun-loving, Mrs. Wood was called by Lawrence Hutton "one of the best burlesque actresses our stage has ever known."   TLM

Wood, [Margaret] Peggy (1892–1978) Actress and author who became an established musical and comedy star with the long-running *Maytime* (1917). Though eyebrows were raised when she replaced **Katharine Cornell** in **Shaw**'s *Candida* (1925), years later she was remembered in the *New York Times* as a "versatile artist . . . very much at home with Shakespeare, George Bernard Shaw, **Sigmund Romberg** and Noël Coward." Mama in the popular CBS-TV series "I Remember Mama" (1949–57), she received an Oscar nomination for Mother Superior in *The Sound of Music* (1965). In addition to a remembrance of **John Drew** (1928), she wrote several volumes of memoirs. MR

Wood, William Burke (1779–1861) Actor and manager, born of English parents in Montréal, Canada. As a young man he joined **Thomas Wignell**'s **Philadelphia** company, despite ill-health and lack of theatrical experience. Unsuccessful in tragic roles, Wood proved better suited to genteel comedy and ultimately found his niche in management. After the death of Wignell in 1803, he became assistant to the acting manager of the **Chestnut Street Theatre, William Warren the elder.** In 1804 he married Juliana Westray, a good actress who appeared under his management for many years. Warren and Wood shared a prosperous quarter-century together, bringing their Philadelphia, Baltimore, and Washington theatres to international eminence. Wood sold his shares back to Warren before the 1826 season, but remained as a company member. He left in 1828 to manage the new **Arch Street Theatre,** Philadelphia; and during 1829–46 he was at that city's **Walnut Street Theatre.** His reminiscences are recorded in *Personal Recollections,* published in 1855. DBW

Woodland Players see **Greet Players**

Woodruff, Robert (1947–) Free-lance director. With a graduate degree in theatre from San Francisco State University, Woodruff cofounded the **Eureka Theatre** and created the Bay Area Playwrights' Festival. He directed the premieres of **Sam Shepard**'s *Curse of the Starving Class* for the **New York Shakespeare Festival** and *Buried Child* and *True West* at the **Magic Theatre.** He also directed the Flying Karamazov Brothers in *A Comedy of Errors* at **Lincoln Center.** Often controversial, Woodruff has been one of our more imaginative avant-garde directors. JDM

Woods, A[ladore] H[erman] (1870–1951) Producer; he claimed that *Try and Get It* (1943) was his 409th production in all venues. At the peak of his success in the late 1920s, he had 23 plays running, some on Broadway, most on the road. Born in Budapest, Hungary, Woods grew up on NYC's Lower East Side. The operator of a Bowery nickelodeon, he turned in 1899 to producing low-budget melodramas, such as Theodore Kremer's *Bertha, the Sewing Machine Girl* (1906). In 1912 he built the Eltinge Theater in honor of **Julian Eltinge,** renowned female impersonator and star of his 1911 hit, *The Fascinating Widow.* His greatest Broadway hit was Bayard Veiller's melodrama *Within the Law* (1912), which ran 512 performances. His success was based on the timeless appeal of sex, as in *Up in*

Mabel's Room (1919); sentiment, as in *Eyes of Youth* (1917); lurid violence, as in *The Shanghai Gesture* (1926); and ethnic travesty, as in a Jewish-dialect series beginning with *Potash and Perlmutter* (1915). WD

Woodward, Charles, Jr. (19??–) Producer of avant-garde and mainstream plays, at times associated with **Richard Barr** and **Clinton Wilder.** *Johnny No-Trump* (1967) marked his New York debut, followed by *The Boys in the Band* (1969), *The Front Page* (1969), *Watercolor* and *CrissCrossing* (1970), *What the Butler Saw* (1970), *All Over* (1971), *The Grass Harp* (1971), *Noel Coward in Two Keys* (1974), *P.S. Your Cat is Dead!* (1975), *Seascape* (1975), *Sweeney Todd* (1979), and *Home Front* (1985), the last first produced in Dallas. TLM

Woodworth, Samuel (1785–1842) Playwright, best known for his song "The Old Oaken Bucket" and for *The Forest Rose* (1825, with music by John Davies), a light-hearted glorification of American farmers that became a vehicle for a host of "**Yankee**" actors for 40 years and is often called "the first American musical hit." He wrote seven other plays (e.g., *The Deed of Gift,* 1822; *LaFayette,* 1824; and *The Cannibals,* 1833), a patriotic novel, dedicatory addresses, and sentimental ballads, and edited numerous periodicals and newspapers, notably the New York *Mirror* (1823–42). He received small profit from his literary endeavors and died in poverty. RM

See: K. B. Taft, "Samuel Woodworth," PhD diss., U of Chicago, 1936.

Woollcott, Alexander (1887–1943) Drama critic who made his debut as a critic for the *New York Times* in 1914, replacing **Adolph Klauber.** His battles with the **Shubert**s in 1915 made him a celebrity. After military service in Paris (1917–19), he returned to the *Times,* and helped establish that witty "vicious circle" that met for lunch at the "Algonquin Round Table." In 1922 he was hired away by the *Herald,* and later reviewed for the *Sun* (1924–5) and the *World* (1925–8). In 1929 he established his "Shouts and Murmurs" column in the *New Yorker,* began his radio show (later commanding up to $3,500 per program for "The Town Crier"), and collaborated on two plays with **George S. Kaufman** (*The Channel Road* [1979]; *The Dark Tower* [1933]). He also appeared frequently as an actor, playing, according to **Brooks Atkinson,** "a sort of virtuoso fat man." Woollcott remains best known as the model for Sheridan Whiteside in Kaufman and **Hart**'s *The Man Who Came to Dinner.* Vitality and urbanity were his trademarks. TLM

See: M. U. Burns, *The Dramatic Criticism of Alexander Woollcott,* Metuchen, NJ, 1980; E. P. Hoyt, *Alexander Woollcott: The Man Who Came to Dinner,* New York, 1968.

Wooster Group, The New York ensemble formed in 1975 under the direction of **Elizabeth LeCompte;** successors to **Richard Schechner**'s **Performance Group.** Housed in SoHo's Performing Garage, Wooster Group's other members

The Wooster Group's *Brace Up!*, directed by Elizabeth LeCompte. Photo: Bob Van Dantzig. Courtesy: The Wooster Group.

are **James Clayburgh,** Willem Dafoe, **Spalding Gray,** Peyton Smith, Kate Valk, and Ron Vawter. The Group, recognized as "one of the most radically political, culturally radical theatres in the country, perhaps the world," composes "large ensemble multi-media theatre pieces," which join a repertoire.

The Wooster Group explores frequently unexamined, often suppressed and disturbing elements of society and culture, challenging unquestioned assumptions. Its material is derived from sources whose texts and images are quoted, reworked, and juxtaposed with fragments of disparate other elements. The Group aims "to create a 'theater reality' that incorporates life rather than represents it," habitually restructuring the spectator–performer relationship unconventionally.

Wooster Group pieces include the trilogies *Three Places in Rhode Island* (1975–9) and *The Road to Immortality* (1981–7), and an epilogue to the latter (*Brace Up!*, 1990). The Group produces films and videos including **Michael Kirby**'s *White Homeland Commando;* in 1990 they participated in the international Los Angeles Theatre Festival and in 1991 received an Obie for sustained achievement.   REK

See: D. Savran, *The Wooster Group, 1975–1985: Breaking the Rules,* Ann Arbor, MI, 1986.

Worth, Irene (1916–   ) American-born actress, known equally on both sides of the Atlantic. She has accumulated most major awards for her acting and has been especially praised for the musicality of her voice and her commanding stage presence; her talent is held in high esteem by both critics and colleagues. After teaching school for several years, she turned to the stage, making her professional debut with a touring company in 1942, then appeared a year later on Broadway with Elisabeth Bergner in *The Two Mrs. Carrolls*. Seeking classical training, she went to London in 1944 to study with Elsie Fogerty. Her first noteworthy appearance in London was as Ilona in Molnár's *The Play's the Thing* (1947). She appeared as Celia in the premiere of *The Cocktail Party* at the Edinburgh Festival (1949). After working with the Old Vic Company (1951–3), she helped found (with **Tyrone Guthrie** and Alec Guinness) the Stratford Festival in 1953. Following a succession of critically acclaimed portrayals in London, New York, and Stratford, ON, she joined the Royal Shakespeare Company, appearing as Goneril in Peter Brook's production of *King Lear* (1962). Other notable appearances in the past quarter of a century have included *Tiny Alice* (New York, 1964; Royal Shakespeare Company, 1970), Coward's *Suite in Three Keys* (London, 1966), *Heartbreak House* (Chichester, 1967), Brook's controversial *Oedipus* (National Theatre, 1968), *Hedda Gabler* (Stratford, ON, 1970), *The Seagull* (Chichester, 1973), *The Cherry Orchard* (NYC, 1977), *John Gabriel Borkman* (NYC, 1980), a "majestically unruffled" Volumnia in *Coriolanus* at London's National Theatre (1984), **Gurney**'s *The Golden Age* (NYC, 1984), and Grandma Kurnitz in **Lost in Yonkers** (NYC, 1991), for which she won her third Tony (the others being for *Tiny Alice* and a 1975 revival of **Sweet Bird of Youth**).   DBW

Wright, Garland (1946–   ) American director. Born in Midland, TX, Wright's earliest ambition was to be a painter. His theatre interests developed while he was attending Southern Methodist University, and his professional career began soon after when he joined the **American Shakespeare** Festival in Connecticut (1970). In 1974 he helped found New York's Lion Theatre and, coincidentally, began to work **Off-Broadway,** where he directed *Vanities* (1976). In 1980 he started a three-year stint as **Guthrie Theatre** Associate Director and further molded his craft there with notable productions like *Camille* (1980) and *Candide* (1982). During 1985–6 he held a similar position at **Arena Stage;** then in 1986 he was named Artistic Director of the Guthrie Theatre, the youngest in its history. He has distinguished himself since with productions of *The Misanthrope* (1987), *Richard III* (1988), *Henry IV (Parts 1 & 2),* and *Henry V* (1990).   KN

Wright, Richard (1908–60) **African-American** novelist and playwright. Born in Roxie, MS, Wright moved to Chicago at age 19 and taught himself to be a writer. In 1938 he published a book of short stories entitled *Uncle Tom's Children.* The following year the novel **Native Son** brought him international renown. It was dramatized by Wright and white playwright **Paul Green,** and directed by **Orson Welles** in 1941, featuring **Canada Lee** in the principal role. Wright's comedy *Daddy Goodness* was produced by the **Negro Ensemble Company** in 1968.   EGH

Wycherly, Margaret (DeWolfe) (1881–1956) London-born stage and film actress; student at Boston's Latin School and the **American Academy of Dramatic Arts,** she made her debut at 17 in *What Dreams May Come* with **Mme. Janauschek.** She married playwright Bayard Veiller, spent many years performing in **stock,** and toured with **Richard Mansfield.** She created the role of Lydia in **Bernard Shaw**'s *Cashel Byron's Profession* (1907) and performed for two years as Ada Lester in *Tobacco Road* (1933). In 1940 she went to Hollywood, where, in addition to *Sergeant York* (1941) and other films, she acted on television in the 1950s.   FHL

Wynn, Ed (né Isaiah Edwin Leopold) (1886–1966) Comedian who began in **vaudeville** in 1901, later teaming up with Jack Lewis as two collegians in the act "Rah, Rah, Boys." Starting with *The Ziegfeld Follies* of 1914 and 1915, he found a comfortable solo niche in musical comedy, including *The Perfect Fool* (1921), which became his nickname; *Simple Simon* (1930); *The Laugh Parade* (1931); and *Hurray for What?* (1937). Wynn's stage persona wore horn-rimmed glasses and tiny porkpie hats, spoke with a lisp, giggled, and walked with a mincing gait. Many of Wynn's gags were predicated on an inability to complete an anecdote or a piece of music; his insane inventions included a typewriter carriage for eating corn-on-the-cob and a cigarette lighter that pointed out the nearest matches. During 1932–7 Wynn was "The Fire Chief" on radio; in the 1950s and '60s he played dramatic roles in films and television.   LS

See: S. Green, *The Great Clowns of Broadway,* New York, 1984; K. Wynn, *Ed Wynn's Son,* New York, 1959.

Y

Yablokoff, Herman (1904–81) **Yiddish** actor. Born near Grodno (Belorussia), he was already a performer when he arrived in the U.S. in 1924. He starred in many musical productions, often directing and producing and even writing them himself. Among his best known works: *The Clown, The Dishwasher, My White Flower,* and the song "The Cigarette Peddler." He made many recordings and appeared for years on WEVD Yiddish-language radio. After WW II he toured DP camps. Although he rarely performed in the last few decades of his life, he was longtime president of the Hebrew Actors Union and the Yiddish National Theatre. NS

Yale Repertory Theatre An adjunct to the Yale School of Drama (established as a graduate school in 1955) in New Haven, CT, which in turn grew out of the Drama Department founded in 1925 by **George Pierce Baker,** this important **resident nonprofit professional theatre** was founded in 1966 by **Robert Brustein,** who served as artistic director until 1979. In 1968 it moved into a church converted into a theatre with a thrust stage and seating for 487. Central to each season under **Lloyd Richards,** who served as artistic director from 1979 to June 1991, were **Shakespeare, Athol Fugard** (seven plays in all), and especially **August Wilson,** as well as the Winterfest of New Plays. Richards was succeeded by Stan Wojewodski, Jr., formerly of Baltimore's **Center Stage.**

Among important new works premiered at Yale were **Eric Bentley**'s *Are You Now or Have You Ever Been . . . ?* (1972), **Robert Lowell's** version of *Prometheus Bound* (1967), **Kopit's** *Wings* (1978), three plays by Edward Bond (including *Bingo* in 1976), several by Fugard (including *A Lesson from Aloes, Master Harold . . .*, and *The Road to Mecca*), and all of Wilson's plays through 1991. DBW

Yankee theatre Yankee actors achieved their greatest popularity between 1825 and 1855, though Yankee characters appeared both earlier and later. The first notable "Jonathan" – the most common name (or nickname) – was in **Royall Tyler's** *The Contrast* (1787); the last, Joshua Whitcomb in **Denman Thompson's** *The Old Homestead* (1886). The stage Yankee possessed varying mixtures of the character attributes ascribed to rustic New Englanders ("down-easters"): simple, blundering, sentimental, parsimonious, patriotic, shrewd, critical of city folks, and devoted to tall tales and picturesque speech. This character was a storehouse of riches for eccentric comedians, many of whom began their careers as Yankee storytellers before appearing in plays.

The English comedian **Charles Mathews [Sr.]** was the first to discover the gold mine of good fun to be found in the Yankee in his *Trip to America* (1824) and *Jonathan in England* (1824). Four American actors quickly followed his lead:
1. **James H. Hackett** in his own *Sylvester Daggerwood* (1826), as Solomon Swap in *Jonathan in England* (1828), as Major Joe Bunker in *The Militia Muster* (1830), and as Lot Sap Sago in **Cornelius A. Logan**'s *Yankee Land* (1834);
2. **George Handel "Yankee" Hill,** often called "the most authentic," as John Bull disguised as Jonathan Doolittle in **William Dunlap's** *Trip to Niagara* (1828), as Jonathan in **Samuel Woodworth's** *The Forest Rose* (1832), in *Jonathan in England* (1932), as Jedediah Homebred in **J. S. Jones's** *The Green Mountain Boy* (1833), as Sy Saco in **John Augustus Stone's** *The Knight of the Golden Fleece; or, The Yankee in Spain* (1834), as Hiram Dodge in *The Yankee Pedlar* (Anon., 1835), as Abner Tanner in Jones's *The Adventurer; or, The Yankee in Tripoli* (1835), and as Solon Shingle in Jones's *The People's Lawyer* (1839);
3. **Danforth Marble** in E. H. Thompson and Marble's *Sam Patch* (1836), as Deuteronomy Dutiful in Logan's *The Vermont Wool Dealer* (1838), as Jacob Jewsharp in J. P. Addams's *The Maiden's Vow; or, The Yankee in Time* (1838), as Solon Shingle in Jones's *The People's Lawyer* (1839), and as Lot Sap Sago in Logan's *The Wag of Maine* (1842); and
4. Joshua Silsbee in *The Forest Rose* (1840), in *The Yankee Pedlar* (1841), in *The Green Mountain Boy* (1853), and in *The Vermont Wool Dealer* (1853).

In the 1830s and '40s, the Yankee actors were extremely popular in London, where critics found them not unlike "our own canny Yorkshire lads." RM

See: F. Hodge, *Yankee Theatre: The Image of America on the Stage, 1825–1850,* Austin, TX, 1964.

Yankowitz, Susan (1941–) Playwright. Using bold visual and verbal imagery, Yankowitz explores racism, sexism, and violence in avant-garde pieces, often created collaboratively. With the **Open Theatre,** she developed *Terminal* (1969, Drama Desk Award). Other major productions include *The Ha-Ha Play* (1970), *Slaughterhouse Play* (1971), *Boxes* (1972), *True Romances* (1978), and *Night Sky* (1991). TH-S

Yeargan, Michael (1946–) Scenic and costume designer, resident designer for the **Yale Repertory Theatre,** and a professor of stage design at Yale, where he had previously studied under **Donald Oenslager** and **Ming Cho Lee.** He has also designed extensively at the **Hartford Stage Company, American Repertory Theatre,** and the **Long Wharf Theatre,** as well as Broadway. In addition he has designed frequently for opera companies in Europe, the U.S., and Australia. Since a 1977 production of Strindberg's *Ghost Sonata* at Yale Rep, he has worked extensively with director **Andrei Serban,** including productions of *The Seagull* and *The Umbrellas of Cherbourg;* other collaborators have included **Mark Lamos, Arvin Brown,** and Elijah Moshinsky. His sets are typified by realistically detailed and textured romantic elements, but his theatricality and startling images place him in the postmodern school of design.   AA

Yellow Jacket by George C. Hazelton and J. Harry Benrimo introduced Western audiences to Chinese-style theatre; produced by William Harris, Jr., and the **Selwyn**s for an 80-performance run at the Fulton Theatre, opening 4 November 1912. Frequently revived, the original starred Saxone Morland as Chee Moo, concubine to the Emperor, and George Relph as Wu Hoo Git, her son, both condemned to death because she bore the emperor an ugly baby. The two are spared by a friendly farmer, but Chee Moo soon perishes. Encouraged by a loving Suey Sin Fah (Grace A. Barbour), Wuy Hoo defeats his step-brother and earns the right to wear the emperor's yellow jacket. Signor Perugini, functioning as a Greek chorus, narrates the drama, while a stagehand, recalling the visible Chinese property man, arranges settings.   GSA

Yiddish Art Theatre, The Maurice Schwartz's company, which opened at the Irving Place Theatre in New York in 1918. Rejecting the popular sentimental and melodramatic improvisations of *shund* (rubbish) theatre in favor of carefully rehearsed plays of quality, ensemble acting, and a high standard of presentation, its first successes came with **Peretz Hirshbein**'s earthy pastoral play *The Forgotten Nook,* followed by the same writer's *The Blacksmith's Daughter,* another delicate, idyllic play of village life. During its second year (its first as the YAT), 15 plays were added to the repertoire, including Sholom Aleichem's *Tevye the Milkman* and four of **Jacob Gordin**'s plays, including *God, Man and Devil,* based on the Faust legend. Inevitably "stars" were created, like **Bertha Gerstein, Ludwig Satz,** and Muni Weisenfreund (**Paul Muni**). Several productions in English translation transferred to Broadway, including Schwartz's greatest personal triumph: Israel Joshua Singer's *Yoshe Kalb.* The company continued active until the late 1930s.   AB

Yiddish theatre arrived in America early in the period of mass Eastern European immigration with a production of **Avrom Goldfadn**'s *Koldunye; or, The Witch* (1882) on New York's the Bowery. Because professional secular Yiddish-language theatre was still a new invention, many immigrant

Bessie Thomashefsky (Bracha Baumfeld-Kaufman, 1873–1962) as "The Green Boy." Courtesy: Laurence Senelick.

artists and audiences first encountered it in the U.S. Because of the relative security and prosperity of America's Jews, the U.S. (especially NYC's Lower East Side) is where Yiddish theatre flourished earliest, longest, and (at least, in the popular genres) most vigorously.

Yiddish theatres quickly proliferated in NYC, Boston, Detroit, Chicago, Baltimore, and elsewhere. By 1914 New York City had some 14 resident companies, as well as individual productions; troupes from there toured throughout the U.S., South America, and the Old Country. Companies developed structures dominated by a star-manager, repertory, or a family nucleus. A cluster of Yiddish theatrical unions organized in New York (and Buenos Aires), beginning with the Hebrew Actors Union Local One (1887).

Yiddish theatre has always been an important community institution, offering entertainment and escape, reminiscences of home and tradition, portrayals of immigrant life, and political forums. Translations of classics introduced immigrants to world literature; translations of mainstream hits helped them Americanize. Theatregoing was linked with activities of fraternal organizations; streets and cafés in theatre districts were thronged and sociable. In most Yiddish-speaking communities, amateur groups formed for aesthetic, social, and political purposes. Related industries also developed: cabarets, sheet music and recordings of show tunes, radio, and film. The Yiddish press printed related reviews, editorials, and gossip, and play texts were published for reading and amateur productions.

Stars, major community figures, commanded fierce fan (*patriotn*) loyalty. In the early years, the preferred acting style was grand and emotional. Comedy came out of broad character "types," and with music in most plays, all actors sang. Early stage idols included comic **Sigmund Mogulesko,** romantic baritone **Boris Thomashefsky,** dramatic actors **Jacob Adler** and **David Kessler,** and actresses Sara Adler, **Bertha Kalish, Keni Liptzin,** and Bessie Thomashefsky. Benefit performances honoring a specific star drew many fans, often supplying a major part of the actor's income.

People's tastes in theatre, from highbrow to low *shund,* served to define their positions in many other spheres. Play genres included music hall **revues,** costume operettas, domestic melodramas with music, and intellectual avant-garde. Playwrights included Avrom Goldfadn, "Professor" Moshe Ish HaLevi Hurwitz, Joseph Lateiner, Schomer, and – on a higher literary level – Sholom Aleichem (Sholem Rabinowitz), **Jacob Gordin,** and Leon Kobrin. Composers included Alexander Olshanetsky, Sholem Perlmutter, and Joseph Rumshinsky.

Because the more intellectual artists and audiences served as conduit for European (especially Russian) innovations, American Yiddish theatre fostered naturalism and expressionism, "art theatres," and Stanislavskian "method" acting before other U.S. theatres, and the Yiddish avant-garde was often reviewed in the intellectual English-language press. This, along with a vigorous musical tradition, a new benefit system (whereby charitable organizations could raise funds by selling blocks of seats), and a trained community of passionate and committed theatregoers, influenced mainstream American theatre.

After WW I, restricted immigration and demographic movement away from the old neighborhoods began to strangle Yiddish show business. Also, steady assimilation meant loss of Yiddish language and culture. English words crept into dialogue; American fads influenced Yiddish productions. Actually, playgoers were comfortable seeing English-language shows and films, and many of the younger generation preferred them.

Nevertheless, another generation of stars came to prominence: **Celia Adler, Jacob Ben-Ami, Joseph Buloff,** Pesach Burstein, **Bertha Gersten,** Samuel Goldenburg, Jennie Goldstein, Jacob Jacobs, Aaron Lebedeff, Michel Michalesko, Moyshe Oysher, **Molly Picon, Ludwig Satz, Rudolph Schildkraut, Maurice Schwartz,** Menashe Skulnik, and **Herman Yablokoff.** There were new popular playwrights, such as Z. Libin, H. Kalmanovitch, Max Gabel, William Segal, Anshel Shor, and Isidore Zolatarevsky, and composers such as Sholom Secunda. Little or art theatres – most notably Schwartz's **Yiddish Art Theatre,** Jacob Ben-Ami's **Jewish Art Theatre** (1919–20) and Irving Place Theatre (1926–7), and the **Artef** –

performed ambitious repertory by **Sholom Asch,** Osip Dimov (Joseph Perlman), **Peretz Hirshbein,** H. Leivick (Leyvik Halpern), and **David Pinski.** Acting styles ranged from broadly popular to abstract left-wing agitprop to Stanislavskian realism, according to the venue. Between 1935 and 1939, the **Federal Theatre Project** sponsored several Yiddish troupes, notably in New York and the Boston area.

Hitler and Stalin destroyed the Old World sources of Yiddish culture and Yiddish speakers. Continuing acculturation, movement to the suburbs, ascendence of Hebrew, and the spread of films and television all severely diminished audiences. Ages of performers and spectators rose, making the repertory and performance style seem old-fashioned, while new scripts and performances per season steadily decreased. Limited runs became the norm, with fewer than eight shows per week, including matinees for the convenience of the elderly.

Nevertheless, in the decades since WW II, most New York seasons have offered at least one locally mounted musical comedy; additionally, there has often been a touring company from Israel, Latin America, or Eastern Europe plus revues in various venues. Postwar stars have included Bruce Adler, Mina Bern, Ben Bonus, Reyzl Bozyk, Miriam Kressyn, Shifra Lehrer, Leon Leibgold, Jack Rechseit, Seymour Rexite, Eleanor Reissa, and Mary Soreanu. In New York, the Yiddish National Theatre sponsored by the Hebrew Actors Union mounts occasional productions, and the **Folksbiene,** the world's longest continuously performing Yiddish company, presents a new production annually. Around the country, scattered amateur groups, many of them affiliated with Jewish community centers or with universities, give readings and performances; Jewish centers also sponsor theatre-related events, such as exhibitions of theatre posters and memorabilia.

After the American Bicentennial in 1976 (and coincidentally also the centenary of professional secular Yiddish theatre), increased interest in ethnic roots fostered various innovative approaches to make Yiddish theatre accessible, including simultaneous translation devices, English-speaking narrators in the wings, and frequent English interpolations in dialogue and lyrics. Bilingual shows, like *The Golden Land* and *Songs of Paradise,* and English-language shows based on Yiddish theatre material, such as *Kuni-Leml,* attract non-Yiddish-speaking audiences. For many American Jews – including those who have never seen it – Yiddish theatre retains a romantic resonance and is integrated in their images of their forebears and cultural tradition. NS

See: I. Backalenick, *East Side Story,* Lanham, MD, 1988; D. Lifson, *Yiddish Theatre in America,* New York, 1965; J. A. Miller, *The Detroit Yiddish Theater,* Detroit, 1967; N. Sandrow, *Vagabond Stars: A World History of Yiddish Theater,* New York, 1977.

You Can't Take It with You Three-act comedy by **Moss Hart** and **George S. Kaufman;** opened at the **Booth Theatre,** 14 December 1936, and ran for 837 performances. Recipient of the Pulitzer Prize for drama in 1937, the play has been revived

You Can't Take It with You (1936), directed by George S. Kaufman, set by Donald Oenslager. Photo: Vandamm.

regularly since, most notably on Broadway in two productions directed by **Ellis Rabb** in 1965 and 1983, the latter at the **Plymouth Theatre** with an all-star cast headed by **Jason Robards, Jr., Elizabeth Wilson,** Bill McCutcheon, and **Colleen Dewhurst.**

The play presents lovable nonconformist characters of the Sycamore clan who are surviving the Depression by writing plays, making fireworks, playing the xylophone, and operating an amateur printing press. The most normal member of the family, Alice Sycamore, falls in love with the son of a Wall Street banker, and the play exploits the difference between these two worlds. The theme that money isn't everything was attractive in 1936 and has remained so since.   TLM

Youmans, Vincent (1899–1946) Composer who served in the Navy during WW I, then worked as a song plugger and rehearsal pianist before contributing songs to *Two Little Girls in Blue* (1921) and ultimately writing the scores for two of the most successful musicals of the 1920s: *No, No, Nanette* (1925) and *Hit the Deck* (1927). Songs by Youmans were also heard in *Great Day* (1929), *The 9:15 Revue* (1930), *Smiles* (1930), and *Take a Chance* (1932). Although Youmans's output was relatively small, many of his songs, such as "Tea for Two," "I Want to Be Happy," "Hallelujah," "More Than You Know," and "Time on My Hands," have become classics of the musical stage.   MK

See: G. Bordman, *Days to Be Happy, Years to Be Sad: The Life and Music of Vincent Youmans,* New York, 1982.

Young, Stark (1881–1963) Drama critic, translator, playwright, and director. Born in Mississippi, Young earned degrees in English at the University of Mississippi (1901) and at Columbia University (1902). After teaching in several universities, he became a contributing editor to *New Republic* in 1921 and an associate editor of *Theatre*

Arts magazine (1921–40). Young replaced Francis Hackett as chief drama critic of the *New Republic* in early 1922 and held the position (except for the 1924–5 season, when he reviewed for the *New York Times*) until his retirement in 1947. He was an advocate of the New Stagecraft movement and worked closely with **Eugene O'Neill, Kenneth Macgowan,** and **Robert Edmond Jones** at the Provincetown Playhouse. He staged the premiere of O'Neill's *Welded* in 1924. Young wrote several plays, none successful. He is better remembered for his translations of **Chekhov**'s plays, especially of *The Seagull* for the **Lunt**s in 1938. His books include *The Flower in Drama* (1923), *Glamour* (1925), *Theatre Practice* (1926), and *The Theatre* (1927).   TLM

See: J. Pilkington, ed., *Stark Young. A Life in the Arts: Letters, 1900–1962,* 2 vols., Baton Rouge, LA, 1975.

You're a Good Man, Charlie Brown Two-act musical comedy by Clark Gesner, opened 7 March 1967 at the **Off-Broadway** Theatre 80 St. Marks, running 1,597 performances. Based on Charles Schultz's popular "Peanuts" comic strip, this show began life as a children's record album. Expanded into a stage musical, its virtually nonnarrative book portrays, in a series of scenes much like a series of daily comic strips, a day in the life of Charlie Brown (Gary Burghoff) and the other familiar characters. Much of the charm came from director Joseph Hardy's playfully inventive staging, in which no attempt was made to make the characters resemble the original drawing except in costume (Snoopy was a plainly human actor) and scenes were created by assembling various geometric blocks. The consciously juvenile score contributed one pop hit: "Happiness Is."   JD

Yulin, Harris (1937–   ) Actor and director whose stage credits include **La MaMa, Hartford Stage, Circle in the Square, Mark Taper Forum,** the **Guthrie Theater,** and **Arena Stage.** A quiet,

thoughtful actor, he has performed classics at **New York Shakespeare Festival** (*Richard III*, 1966), premieres at **Yale Repertory** (*A Lesson from Aloes*, 1979), and a recent revival of *The Visit* with **Jane Alexander** for **Roundabout Theatre** (1992). Yu-lin directed **McNally**'s *Cuba Si* and Brecht's *The Guns of Carrar* (Theater de Lys, 1968), Molnár's *The Guardsman* (**Long Wharf**, 1982), and **Adele Shank**'s *Winterplay* (Second Stage, 1983). His films include *Scarface* (1983) and *Another Woman* (1988), and he appeared on television in "The Missiles of October" (1974) and the series "WIOU" (1990–1).
    REK

Yurka, Blanche (1893–1974) Czech-born actress, brought to the U.S. as an infant, who began acting in 1907 after training for opera. She applied to **David Belasco** successfully for work on the legitimate stage, her first leading role being in *Is Matrimony a Failure?* Over the next decade she shifted to tragedy, playing Gertrude to John Barrymore's [see **Drew–Barrymore**] Hamlet (1922), Gina in *The Wild Duck* (1925), and later a series of strong-willed female roles, winning praise for her emotional depth and vocal timbre. She was also an active member and organizer of **Actors' Equity,** being elected to a variety of positions in that organization. In 1955 she retired from the theatre, decrying the poverty of the theatre at that time, but soon returned to both films and Broadway. She often wrote (including an autobiography, *Bohemian Girl,* 1970) and lectured about the theatre.   SMA

Z

Zaks, Jerry (1946–) Educated at Dartmouth, Zaks began his theatrical career as an actor, appearing on Broadway in *Grease, Fiddler on the Roof,* and other shows. His directing credits include *Lend Me a Tenor,* (1989) for which he won Tony, Drama Desk, and Outer Critics' Circle awards. In the same year Zaks was called the outstanding director of comedy in the American theatre. He also restaged a successful *Anything Goes* in London after reviving it at **Lincoln Center.** During his tenure at Lincoln Center as director-in-residence, he also successfully directed *Six Degrees of Separation* in 1990, winning another Tony for his direction. In 1990 Zaks left Lincoln Center to work for the **Jujamcyn Theaters,** where his first effort was **Stephen Sondheim**'s musical *Assassins* at **Playwrights Horizons,** followed in 1992 by a critically acclaimed revival of *Guys and Dolls* on Broadway. SMA

Zeisler, Peter B. (1923–) Director since 1972 of **Theatre Communications Group,** the national organization for **resident nonprofit professional theatre.** Educated at Columbia University (1947), Zeisler worked as a production stage manager during 1948–59 and helped establish the **American Shakespeare Festival.** A cofounder of the **Guthrie Theatre,** he served as its managing director during 1963–7. He founded the League of Resident Theatres (LORT) in 1967 and became its first president. During 1971–3 he taught at the Yale School of Drama. The recipient of Fulbright and Ford Foundation Travel Grants to study European theatres, he has served as an arts consultant to Australia, China, and Japan. TLM

Ziegfeld, Florenz (1869–1932) Producer. Ziegfeld's first venture into show business was as manager of **Sandow,** a **vaudeville** strongman. After meeting singer **Anna Held** in Europe, Ziegfeld brought her to New York and presented her in several musicals. (They married in 1897, divorced in 1912.) At her suggestion, he created a Parisian-style **revue** called *Follies of 1907,* the first in a series that he continued to produce for the next quarter of a century. Initially presented on a modest scale, the *Follies* grew increasingly elaborate, eventually moving to the **New Amsterdam Theatre,** where designers such as **Joseph Urban** were given free reign to create ornate scenery and lavish costumes. In 1911 the show's title was changed to *The Ziegfeld Follies.* The motto "Glorifying the American Girl" underlines the *Follies*' emphasis on choruses of beautiful women in glittering production numbers.

Many of the shows also featured first-rate comedians such as **Bert Williams, Fanny Brice, W. C. Fields, Will Rogers,** and **Eddie Cantor,** and popular singers and dancers such as **Nora Bayes, Marilyn Miller,** and **Ina Claire.**

Besides producing annual editions of the *Follies,* Ziegfeld presented some of the most successful musical comedies and operettas of the 1920s, including *Sally* (1920), *Kid Boots* (1923), *Sunny* (1925), *Rio Rita* (1927), *Show Boat* (1927), *Rosalie* (1928), *The Three Musketeers* (1928), and *Whoopee* (1928). Rarely innovative in his choice of material or his production methods, Ziegfeld built his reputation as a producer on his ability to discover and nurture talented performers, and the care and expense with which he mounted his shows. MK

See: R. Carter, *The World of Flo Ziegfeld,* New York, 1974; C. Higham, *Ziegfeld,* London, 1973.

Ziegfeld Theatre Corner of Sixth Avenue and 54th Street, NYC [Architects: Thomas W. Lamb and **Joseph Urban**]. In 1927, **Florenz Ziegfeld** pushed the outer limits of the theatre district to Sixth Avenue when Hearst and Brisbane built him a theatre to house his productions. Its curved façade, egg-shaped auditorium, and Urban's mural "Lovers through History" were among its unusual features. One year after Ziegfeld's death, it was converted to movies, but in 1944 **Billy Rose** completely renovated it and returned it to legitimate status. During 1955–63 it was an NBC television studio, but again a theatre from 1963 until it was demolished in 1966. MCH

Zindel, Paul (1936–) Playwright. This former high-school chemistry teacher is chiefly known for two plays that continue to provide actresses with exceptionally challenging roles. The first, *The Effect of Gamma Rays on Man-in-the-Moon Marigolds* (1970), was produced in Houston before moving to New York, where it won the Pulitzer Prize and the Drama Critics' Circle Award. The less successful second, *And Miss Reardon Drinks a Little* (1971), continued his examination of fragile people who become a part of the madness surrounding them. Minimal theatrical success since *Miss Reardon* has led Zindel to turn to writing television plays and screenplays as well as highly praised novels for young adults. LDC

Zipprodt, Patricia (1925–) Costume designer who has been designing since the mid-1950s and became well known in the 1960s with such productions as *Fiddler on the Roof, Cabaret,* and *Pippin,* and the film *The Graduate.* She adapts her style to the demands of the script and the director, but if she has a trademark, it is textured clothes. Beginning with *Fiddler,* she developed a technique of creating layers of paint and dye that gave a vibrant or shimmering sense of color to costumes that would otherwise be drab. This approach continued through *Sunday in the Park with George* (1984), in which costumes were heavily textured with dye, paint, brocade, lace, and fabric.   AA

Zoo Story, The, by **Edward Albee** premiered **Off-Broadway** early in 1960 at the Provincetown Playhouse and was a sensational debut for the young writer. On a double bill with Beckett's *Krapp's Last Tape,* Albee's controversial one-act mimicked the "theatre of the absurd" while calling attention to discontent in contemporary American life. Directed by Milton Katselas and featuring George Maharis and **William Daniels,** the production ran for 582 performances and provoked a variety of articles and critiques about its "meaning." In 1963 it was revived with a production of Albee's *The American Dream* at the Cherry Lane Theatre, and since has had hundreds of amateur and professional productions.   BBW

Zoot Suit A **Chicano** drama by **Luis Valdéz** with music was commissioned by **Gordon Davidson** for the **Mark Taper Forum,** and first produced in 1978 by both **El Teatro Campesino** and the **Los Angeles Theatre Center** Group. Considered the first Hispanic-American play to reach Broadway, it opened at the **Winter Garden Theatre** 25 March 1979 in a revised version. Under the direction of Luis Valdéz, and featuring Edward James Olmos and Daniel Valdéz, this adaptation of real events that occurred in Los Angeles during WW II combines symbolism with **Living News-**

Edward James Olmos in Luis Valdéz's *Zoot Suit* (Hollywood, 1978). Photo: Joy Thompson. Courtesy: Mark Taper Forum.

paper techniques and agitprop theatre. The zoot suit serves as a symbol of protest and dignity about racial intolerance, injustice, and inequality. The play centers on gang leader Henry Reyna, who is arrested and convicted in a mass trial for a murder that occurred during a gang fight. The trial in court and through the press was so one-sided that the conviction was later overturned.   ER

Bibliography of Select Books on the American Theatre

This list of sources is intended as a supplement to sources cited throughout the guide and keyed to specific entries. Space limitation necessitates the exclusion of sources other than published books, although in consulting this checklist one should be aware that many authoritative efforts are to be found in theses and dissertations as well as in essays in periodicals. The following current serials most often contain research or criticism on American theatre and drama: *Theatre Survey, American Theatre, American Drama, Dramatists Quarterly, The Journal of Arts Management and Law, Journal of American Drama and Theatre, Theatre History Studies, Nineteenth Century Theatre, The Theatre Journal, Performance Arts Resources, Studies in American Drama 1945–Present, TheatreForum, Performing Arts Journal, Theater, The Drama Review, Theatre Three, Theatre Week, Variety, Back Stage, New York Theatre Critics' Reviews, Playbill,* and *Performance Art Journal.* Although American theatre is now defined broadly, including many variant forms of performance and venues, this bibliography concentrates on so-called legitimate theatre, especially since specific sources can be found under such headings as burlesque, vaudeville, circus, performance art, and so on. For those interested in more extensive bibliographies on popular entertainments, including the circus, various outdoor amusements, and musical theatre and the revue, three bibliographical essays by Wilmeth in M. Thomas Inge, ed., *Handbook of American Popular Culture,* 2d ed., Westport, CT, 1989, and his checklist in *Theatre History Studies* (1991) might prove helpful. Editions of plays are not listed. DBW

Part I: Reference

Appelbaum, Stanley, ed. *Great Actors and Actresses of the American Stage in Historic Photographs* [1850–1950]. New York: Dover, 1983.

—, ed. *The New York Stage: Famous Productions in Photographs* [1883–1939]. New York: Dover, 1976.

Arata, Esther S. *More Black American Playwrights.* Metuchen, NJ: Scarecrow, 1978.

Arata, Esther S., and Nicholas John Rotoli. *Black American Playwrights, 1800 to the Present: A Bibliography.* Metuchen, NJ: Scarecrow, 1976.

Archer, Stephen M. *American Actors and Actresses: A Guide to Information Sources.* Detroit: Gale Research, 1983.

Beckerman, Bernard, and Howard Siegman, eds. *On Stage: Selected Theater Reviews from The New York Times, 1920–1970.* New York: Arno, 1973.

Best Plays of [*1919–20–*]. Edited by Burns Mantle; John Chapman; Louis Kronenberger; Henry Hewes; Otis L. Guernsey, Jr. (since 1963). New York: Dodd, Mead, 1921–. [Excellent statistical and critical data; volumes published in 1933, 1944, and 1955 cover the period, 1894–1919]

Bloom, Ken. *Broadway: An Encyclopedia Guide to the History, People and Places of Times Square.* New York: Zeisler Group, 1991.

Blum, Daniel. *A Pictorial History of the American Theatre: 100 Years, 1860–1960.* New York: Bonanza Books, 1960; 4th ed. (1860–1976), ed. John Willis. New York: Crown, 1977.

—. *Great Stars of the American Stage.* New York: Greenberg, 1952.

Bordman, Gerald. *The Oxford Companion to American Theatre.* 2d ed. New York: Oxford UP, 1992.

Bronner, Edwin J. *The Encyclopedia of the American Theatre, 1900–1975.* San Diego/New York: A. S. Barnes, 1980.

Browne, Walter, and F. A. Austin, *Who's Who on the Stage.* New York: Walter Browne & F. A. Austin, 1906.

Browne, Walter, and E. DeRoy Koch. *Who's Who on the Stage, 1908.* New York: B. W. Dodge, 1908.

Bryan, George B. *Stage Lives: A Biographical and Index to Theatrical Biographies in English.* Westport, CT: Greenwood, 1985.

—. *Stage Deaths: A Biographical Guide to International Theatrical Obituaries, 1850 to 1990.* 2 vols. Westport, CT: Greenwood, 1991.

Coven, Brenda. *American Women Dramatists of the Twentieth Century: A Bibliography.* Metuchen, NJ: Scarecrow, 1982.

Csida, Joseph, and June Bundy Csida. *American Entertainment: A Unique History of Popular Show Business.* New York: Billboard–Watson Guptill, 1978.

Durham, Weldon B., ed. *American Theatre Companies, 1749–1887.* Westport, CT; Greenwood, 1986; . . . *1888–1930.* Greenwood, 1987; . . . *1931–1986.* Greenwood, 1989.

Eddleman, Floyd Eugene. *American Drama Criticism. Supplement II.* Hamden, CT: Shoe String, 1976.

Epstein, Lawrence, ed. *A Guide to Theatre in America.* New York: Macmillan, 1985.

France, Rachel. *A Century of Plays by American Women.* New York: Richards Rosen, 1979.

Franklin, Joe. *Joe Franklin's Encyclopedia of Comedians.* Secaucus, NJ: Citadel, 1979.

Frick, John W., and Carlton Ward. *Directory of Historic American Theatres.* Westport, CT: Greenwood, 1987.

Gohdes, Clarence. *Literature and Theater of the States*

and Regions of the USA: An Historical Bibliography. Durham, NC: Duke UP, 1967.

Griffiths, Trevor R., and Carole Woodis, eds. The Back Stage Theater Guide. New York: Back Stage Books (Watson-Guptill), 1991.

Guernsey, Otis L., Jr., ed./comp. Directory of the American Theater, 1894–1971. New York: Dodd, Mead, 1971.

Harris, Richard H. Modern Drama in America and England, 1950–1970. Detroit: Gale Research, 1982.

Hixon, Don L., and Dan A.Hennessee. Nineteenth-Century American Drama: A Finding Guide. Metuchen, NJ: Scarecrow, 1977.

Jewell, James C., with Thomas E. Howard. Broadway and the Tony Awards: The First Three Decades, 1947–1977. Washington, DC: UP of America, 1977.

Kaminsky, Laura J., ed. Nonprofit Repertory Theatre in North America, 1958–1975. Westport, CT: Greenwood, 1977.

Kaplan, Mike, ed. Variety Who's Who in Show Business. New York: Garland, 1983.

—. Variety Presents the Complete Book of Major U.S. Show Business Awards. New York: Garland, 1985.

Kaye, Phyllis Johnson, ed. National Playwrights Directory. Detroit: Gale Research, 1977.

Kolin, Philip C., ed. American Playwrights Since 1945: A Guide to Scholarship, Criticism, and Performance. Westport, CT: Greenwood, 1989.

Kullman, Colby H., and William C. Young, eds. Theatre Companies of the World: United States of America, Western Europe. Westport: Greenwood, 1986.

Lawliss, Chuck. The New York Theatre Sourcebook. New York: Fireside (Simon & Schuster), 1990.

Leavitt, Dinah L. Feminist Theatre Groups. Jefferson, NC: McFarland, 1980.

Leiter, Samuel L. Ten Seasons: New York Theatre in the Seventies. Westport, CT: Greenwood, 1986.

—, ed. The Encyclopedia of the New York Stage, 1920–1930. 2 vols. Westport, CT: Greenwood, 1985; . . . 1930–1940. Greenwood, 1989.

Leonard, William Torbert. Theatre: Stage to Screen to Television. 2 vols. Metuchen, NJ: Scarecrow 1981.

—. Broadway Bound: A Guide to Shows That Died Aborning. Metuchen, NJ: Scarecrow, 1983.

—. Masquerade in Black. Metuchen: Scarecrow, 1986.

—. Once Was Enough. Metuchen: Scarecrow, 1986.

Litto, Fredric M. American Dissertations on the Drama and the Theatre. Kent, OH: Kent State UP, 1969.

Loney, Glenn. Twentieth Century Theatre [Britain and the U.S.]. 2 vols. New York: Facts on File Publications, 1983.

Long, E. Hudson. American Drama from Its Beginning to the Present [bibliography]. New York: Appleton–Century–Crofts, 1970.

Lovell, John, Jr. Digests of Great American Plays. New York: Crowell, 1961.

McGill, Raymond D., ed. Notable Names in the American Theatre. Clifton, NJ: James T. White, 1976.

McGraw-Hill Encyclopedia of World Drama. Stanley Hochman, ed.-in-chief. 2d ed. 5 vols. New York: McGraw-Hill, 1984.

McNeil, Barbara, and Miranda C. Herbert, eds.

Performing Arts Biography Master Index. 2d ed. Detroit: Gale Research, 1981.

MacNicholas, John, ed. Twentieth-Century American Dramatists. 2 vols. Detroit: Gale Research, 1981.

Mapp, Edward. Directory of Blacks in the Performing Arts. Metuchen, NJ: Scarecrow, 1978.

Meserve, Walter J. American Drama to 1900: A Guide to Information Sources. Detroit: Gale Research, 1980.

Morrow, Lee Alan. The Tony Award Book: Four Decades of Great American Theater. New York: Abbeville, 1987.

Moyer, Ronald L. American Actors, 1861–1910: An Annotated Bibliography. Troy, NY: Whitston, 1979.

Mullin, Donald C. Victorian Actors and Actresses in Review: A Dictionary of Contemporary Views of Representative British and American Actors and Actresses, 1837–1901. Westport, CT: Greenwood, 1983.

New York Times Directory of the Theatre. Introd. by Clive Barnes. New York: Arno, 1973.

New York Times Theatre Reviews, 1870–1941. 10 vols. New York: New York Times–Arno, 1971–5.

Perry, Jeb H., ed. Variety Obits. Metuchen, NJ: Scarecrow, 1980.

Rigdon, Walter, ed. The Biographical Encyclopedia and Who's Who of the American Theatre. New York: James H. Heineman, 1966; 2d ed., Notable Names in the American Theatre. Clifton, NJ: James T. White, 1976.

Robinson, Alice M., Vera Mowry Roberts, and Milly S. Barranger. Notable Women in the American Theatre. Westport, CT: Greenwood, 1989.

Stanley, William T. Broadway in the West End. An Index of Reviews of American Theatre in London, 1950–1975. Westport, CT: Greenwood, 1978.

Stoddard, Richard. Stage Scenery, Machinery and Lighting: A Guide to Information Sources. Detroit: Gale Research, 1978.

—. Theatre and Cinema Architecture: A Guide to Information Sources. Detroit: Gale Research, 1978.

Stratman, Carl J. Bibliography of the American Theatre Excluding New York City. Chicago: Loyola UP, 1965.

—. American Theatrical Periodicals, 1798–1967. A Bibliographical Guide. Durham, NC: Duke UP, 1970.

Suskin, Steven. Opening Night on Broadway. New York: Schirmer Books, 1990.

Theatre Profiles. Published annually. New York: Theatre Communications Group.

Theatre World. Ed. Daniel Blum; John Willis. 1943–present. New York: Various publishers. [Copious illustrations and statistical matter on season]

Trapido, Joel, ed. An International Dictionary of Theatre Language. Westport, CT: Greenwood, 1985.

Wearing, J. P. American and British Theatrical Biography: A Directory. Metuchen, NJ: Scarecrow, 1979.

Wemyss, Francis Courtney. Chronology of the American Stage. New York, 1852. Reprint. NY: Benjamin Blom, 1968.

Who Was Who in the Theatre: 1912–1976. Detroit: Gale Research, 1978.

Who's Who in Entertainment. Wilmette, IL: Marquis, 1988.

Who's Who in the Theatre: 1912–1981. 17th ed. Ian Herbert, ed. Detroit: Gale Research, 1981.

Wilmeth, Don B. *The American Stage to World War I: A Guide to Information Sources*. Detroit: Gale Research, 1978.

—. *The Language of American Popular Entertainment: A Glossary of Argot, Slang, and Terminology*. Westport, CT: Greenwood, 1981.

—. *Variety Entertainment and Outdoor Amusements: A Reference Guide*. Westport, CT: Greenwood, 1982.

—. *American and English Popular Entertainment: A Guide to Information Sources*. Detroit: Gale Research, 1980.

Woll, Allen. *Dictionary of the Black Theatre: Broadway, Off-Broadway, and Selected Harlem Theatre*. Westport, CT: Greenwood, 1983.

Young, William C. *American Theatrical Arts: A Guide to Manuscripts and Special Collections in the United States and Canada*. Chicago: American Library Association, 1971.

—. *Famous Actors and Actresses on the American Stage: Documents of American Theater History*. 2 vols. New York: R. R. Bowker, 1975.

—. *Famous American Playhouses: Documents of American Theater History*. 2 vols. Chicago: American Library Association, 1973.

Part II: General History/Criticism (Including New York City)

Abramson, Doris E. *Negro Playwrights in the American Theatre, 1925–1959*. New York: Columbia UP, 1969.

Adler, Thomas P. *Mirror on the Stage: The Pulitzer Plays as an Approach to American Drama*. West Lafayette, IN: Purdue UP, 1987.

Alpert, Hollis. *Broadway*. New York: Arcade, 1991.

Anderson, John. *Box Office*. New York: Jonathan Cape and Harrison Smith, 1929.

—. *The American Theatre*. New York: Dial, 1938.

Atkinson, Brooks. *Broadway*. Rev. ed. New York: Macmillan, 1974.

Auster, Albert. *Actresses and Suffragists: Women in the American Theatre, 1890–1920*. New York: Praeger, 1984.

Banks, Ann, ed. *First-Person America*. New York: Alfred A. Knopf, 1980.

Barstow, Arthur. *The Director's Voice: Twenty-one Interviews*. New York: Theatre Communications Group, 1988.

Bartholomeusz, Dennis. *The Winter's Tale in Performance in England and America, 1611–1976*. Cambridge, UK: Cambridge UP, 1982.

Bauland, Peter. *The Hooded Eagle: Modern German Drama on the New York Stage*. Syracuse: Syracuse UP, 1968.

Bernheim, Alfred. *The Business of the Theatre*. New York, 1932. Reprint. NY: Benjamin Blom, 1964.

Bigsby, C. W. E. *A Critical Introduction to Twentieth-Century American Drama. Volume 1: 1900–1940*. Cambridge, UK: Cambridge UP, 1982; *Volume 2: Williams/Miller/Albee*. CUP, 1984; *Volume 3: Beyond Broadway*. CUP, 1985.

Birkmire, William H. *The Planning and Construction of American Theatres*. New York: John Wiley and Sons, 1901.

Birringer, Johannes. *Theatre, Theory, Postmodernism*. Bloomington: Indiana UP, 1991.

Blake, Ben. *The Awakening of the American Theatre*. New York: Tomorrow, 1935.

Blumenthal, George, as told to Arthur H. Menkin. *My 60 Years in Show Business: A Chronicle of the American Theater, 1874–1934*. New York: Frederick C. Osberg, 1936.

Bogard, Travis, Richard Moody, and Walter J. Meserve. *The Revels History of Drama in English. Volume VIII: American Drama*. London: Methuen, 1977.

Bond, Frederick W. *The Negro and the Drama*. Washington, DC: Associated, 1940.

Bost, James S. *Monarchs of the Mimic World or The American Theatre of the Eighteenth Century Through the Managers – The Men Who Made It*. Orono: U of Maine, 1977.

Bricker, Herschel L., ed. *Our Theatre Today*. New York: Samuel French, 1936.

Brown, John Mason. *Broadway in Review*. New York: W. W. Norton, 1940.

Brown, John Russell, and Bernard Harris, eds. *American Theatre*. London: Edward Arnold, 1967.

Brown, Thomas Allston. *History of the American Stage: Containing Biographical Sketches of Nearly Every Member of the Profession from 1733 to 1870*. New York: Dick and Fitzgerald, 1870.

Brown-Guillory, Elizabeth. *Their Place on the Stage: Black Women Playwrights in America*. Westport, CT: Greenwood, 1988.

Brustein, Robert. *Seasons of Discontent: Dramatic Opinion, 1959–1965*. New York: Simon & Schuster, 1965.

Burdick, Elizabeth B., Peggy C. Hansen, and Brenda Zanger, eds. *Contemporary Stage Design U.S.A.* New York: International Theatre Institute of the U.S. (dist. by Wesleyan UP), 1974.

Burge, James C. *Lines of Business: Casting Practice and Policy in the American Theatre, 1752–1899*. New York: Peter Lang, 1986.

Carter, Jean, and Jess Ogden. *Everyman's Drama: A Study of Noncommercial Theatre in the United States*. New York: American Association for Adult Education, 1938.

Chapman, John. *Theatre '53*. New York: Random House, 1953.

Cheney, Sheldon. *The New Movement in the Theatre*. New York: Mitchell Kennerley, 1914.

Chinoy, Helen Krich, and Linda Walsh Jenkins. *Women in American Theatre*. Rev. ed. New York: Theatre Communications Group, 1987.

Churchill, Allen. *The Great White Way: A Re-Creation of Broadway's Golden Era of Theatrical Entertainment*. New York: E. P. Dutton, 1962.

—. *The Theatrical 20s*. New York: McGraw-Hill, 1975.

Coad, Oral S. and Edwin Mims, Jr. *The American Stage*. New Haven, CT: Yale UP, 1929.

Cohn, Ruby. *Dialogue in American Drama*. Bloomington: Indiana UP, 1971.

—. *New American Dramatists*. 2d ed. New York: St. Martin's, 1991.

Coigney, Martha Wadsworth, ed. *Theatre 2: The American Theatre, 1968–1969*. New York: International Theatre Institute of U.S., 1970; *Theatre 3: 1969–70.* New York: Charles Scribner's Sons, 1970; *Theatre 4: 1970–71.* Scribner's, 1972; *Theatre 5: 1971–72.* Scribner's, 1973. [*See also* Gilder]

Cole, Toby, and Helen K. Chinoy, eds. *Actors on Acting.* New York: Crown, 1954.

Conolly, L. W., ed. *Theatrical Touring and Founding in North America.* Westport, CT: Greenwood, 1982.

Craig, E. Quita. *Black Drama of the Federal Theatre Era.* Amherst: U of Massachusetts, 1980.

Crawford, Mary Caroline. *The Romance of the American Theatre.* 2d rev. ed. New York: Halcyon House, 1940.

Daly, Charles P. *The First Theatre in America.* New York, 1896. Reprint. New York: Burt Franklin, 1970.

Daly, Frederic. *Henry Irving in England and America.* New York: R. Worthington, 1884.

Davidge, William P. *Footlight Flashes.* New York: American News Co., 1866.

Demastes, William W. *Beyond Naturalism: A New Realism in American Theatre.* Westport, CT: Greenwood, 1988.

Dickinson, Thomas H. *Playwrights of the New American Theatre.* New York: Macmillan Co., 1925.

Dimmick, Ruth Crosby. *Our Theatres Today and Yesterday.* New York: H. K. Fly Co., 1913.

Donohue, Joseph W., Jr., ed. *The Theatrical Manager in England and America.* Princeton, NJ: Princeton UP, 1971.

Downer, Alan S. *American Drama and Its Critics.* Chicago: U of Chicago, 1965.

—. *American Drama.* New York: Thomas Y. Crowell, 1960.

—. *Fifty Years of American Drama, 1900–1950.* Chicago: Regnery, 1951.

—, ed. *The American Theater Today.* New York: Basic Books, 1967.

Dukore, Bernard F. *American Dramatists 1918–1945.* New York: Grove, 1984.

Dunlap, William. *A History of the American Theatre.* New York, 1832. Reprint. NY: Burt Franklin, 1963.

Eaton, Walter Prichard. *At the New Theatre and Others: The American Stage, Its Problems and Performers, 1908–1910.* Boston: Small, Maynard, 1910.

—. *The American Stage of To-Day.* Boston: Small, Maynard, 1908.

Fabre, Geneviève. *Drumbeats, Masks, and Metaphor: Contemporary Afro-American Theatre.* Cambridge, MA: Harvard UP, 1983.

Fehl, Fred. *Stars of the Broadway Stage, 1940–1967.* New York: Dover, 1983.

—; text by William Stott with Jane Stott. *On Broadway: Performance Photographs by Fred Fehl.* Austin: U of Texas, 1978.

Fisher, Judith L., and Stephen Watt, eds. *When They Weren't Doing Shakespeare: Essays on Nineteenth-Century British & American Theatre.* Athens: U of Georgia, 1989.

Flexner, Eleanor. *American Playwrights, 1918–1938.* New York: Simon & Schuster, 1938.

Freedman, Morris. *American Drama in Social Context.* Carbondale: Southern Illinois UP, 1971.

Frenz, Horst, ed. *American Playwrights on Drama.* New York: Hill and Wang, 1965.

Frick, John W. *New York's First Theatrical Center: The Rialto at Union Square.* Ann Arbor: UMI Research, 1985.

Friedl, Bettina, ed. *On to Victory: Propaganda Plays of the Woman Suffrage Movement.* Boston: Northeastern UP, 1987.

Fyles, Franklin. *The Theatre and Its People.* New York: Doubleday, Page, 1900.

Gagey, Edmond McAdoo. *Revolution in American Drama.* New York: Columbia UP, 1947.

Gard, Robert E., Marston Balch, and Pauline Temkin. *Theatre in America: Appraisal and Challenge.* New York: Theatre Arts Books, 1968.

Gardner, R. H. *The Splintered Stage: The Decline of the American Theater.* New York: Macmillan, 1965.

Gassner, John. *The Theatre in Our Times.* New York: Crown, 1954.

—. *Theatre at the Crossroads.* New York: Holt, Rinehart and Winston, 1960.

Gergely, Emro Joseph. *Hungarian Drama in New York: American Adaptations, 1908–1940.* Philadelphia: U of Pennsylvania, 1947.

Gilder, Rosamond, ed. *Theatre 1.* New York: International Theatre Institute of the U.S. and DBS Publications, 1969. [*See also* Coigney]

Goldberg, Isaac. *The Drama of Transition.* Cincinnati: Stewart Kidd, 1922.

Golden, Joseph. *The Death of Tinker Bell: The American Theatre in the 20th Century.* Syracuse: Syracuse UP, 1967.

Goldman, William. *The Season: A Candid Look at Broadway.* New York: Harcourt, Brace & World, 1969.

Goldstein, Malcolm. *The Political Stage: American Drama and Theater of the Great Depression.* New York: Oxford UP, 1974.

Gottfried, Martin. *A Theater Divided: The Postwar American Stage.* Boston: Little, Brown, 1967.

—. *Opening Nights: Theater Criticism of the Sixties.* New York: Putnam's, 1969.

Gould, Thomas Ridgeway. *The Tragedian.* New York: Hurd and Houghton, 1868.

Grau, Robert. *The Business Man in the Amusement World.* New York: Broadway, 1910.

—. *The Stage in the Twentieth Century.* New York, 1912. Reprint. New York: Benjamin Blom, 1969.

Green, Stanley. *The Great Clowns of Broadway.* New York: Oxford UP, 1984.

Greenfield, Thomas A. *Work and Work Ethic in American Drama, 1920–1970.* Columbia: U of Missouri, 1982.

Grimsted, David. *Melodrama Unveiled: American Theater and Culture, 1800–1850.* Chicago: U of Chicago, 1968.

Guernsey, Otis L., Jr. *Curtain Time: The New York Theater, 1965–1987.* New York: Applause Books, 1987.

—. *Playwrights, Lyricists, Composers on Theater.* New York: Dodd, Mead, 1974.

Hamilton, Clayton. *The Theory of the Theatre.* New York: Henry Holt, 1910.

Hapgood, Norman. *The Changing Years: Reminiscences.* New York: Farrar and Rinehart, 1930.

—. *The Stage in America, 1897–1900*. New York: Macmillan, 1901.

Haring-Smith, Tori. *From Farce to Metadrama: A Stage History of The Taming of the Shrew, 1594–1983*. Westport, CT: Greenwood, 1985.

Hart, Lynda, ed. *Making a Spectacle: Feminist Essays on Contemporary Women's Theatre*. Ann Arbor: U of Michigan, 1989.

Haskins, James. *Black Theater in America*. New York: Thomas Y. Crowell, 1982.

Hatch, James V. *The Black Image on the American Stage*. New York: Drama Book Specialists, 1970.

Hatton, Joseph. *Henry Irving's Impressions of America*. Boston: James R. Osgood, 1884.

Henderson, Kathy. *First Stage: Profiles of the New American Actors*. New York: Quill, 1985.

Henderson, Mary C. *The City & the Theatre: New York Playhouses from Bowling Green to Times Square*. Clifton, NJ: James T. White, 1973.

—. *Theater in America: 200 Years of Plays, Players, and Productions*. New York: Harry N. Abrams, 1986.

Herron, Ima Honaker. *The Small Town in American Drama*. Dallas: Southern Methodist UP, 1969.

Hewitt, Barnard. *Theatre U.S.A., 1668–1957*. New York: McGraw-Hill, 1959.

Hill, Errol. *The Theatre of Black Americans*. 2 vols. Englewood Cliffs, NJ: Prentice-Hall, 1980.

Himmelstein, Morgan Y. *Drama Was a Weapon: The Left-Wing Theatre in New York, 1929–1941*. New Brunswick, NJ: Rutgers UP, 1963.

Hopgood, Norman. *The Stage in America, 1897–1900*. New York: Macmillan, 1901.

Hornblow, Arthur. *A History of the Theatre in America*. 2 vols. Philadelphia: J. B. Lippincott, 1919.

Houghton, Norris. *Advance from Broadway: 19,000 Miles of American Theatre*. New York: Harcourt, Brace, 1941.

Hoyt, Harlowe. *Town Hall Tonight*. New York: Bramhall House, 1955.

Hughes, Elinor. *Passing Through Broadway*. Boston: Waverly House, 1949.

Hughes, Glenn. *A History of the American Theatre, 1700–1950*. New York: Samuel French, 1951.

Hughes, Langston, and Milton Meltzer. *Black Magic: A Pictorial History of Black Entertainers in America*. New York: Bonanza Books, 1967.

Hutton, Laurence. *Curiosities of the American Stage*. New York: Harper & Brothers, 1891.

—. *Plays and Players*. New York: Hurd and Houghton, 1875.

Ireland, Joseph N. *Records of the New York Stage from 1750 to 1860*. 2 vols. New York: T. H. Morrell, 1866.

Isaacs, Edith J. R. *The Negro in the American Theatre*. New York: Theater Arts Books, 1947.

Jacobs, Susan. *On Stage: The Making of a Broadway Play*. New York: Alfred A. Knopf, 1967.

Johnson, Claudia D. *American Actress: Perspective on the Nineteenth Century*. Chicago: Nelson-Hall, 1984.

Johnson, Stephen Burge. *The Roof Gardens of Broadway Theatres, 1883–1942*. Ann Arbor: UMI Research, 1985.

Kazakoff, George. *Dangerous Theatre: The Federal Theatre Project as a Forum for New Plays*. New York: Peter Lang, 1989.

Kennedy, Harold J. *No Pickle, No Performance*. Garden City, NY: Doubleday, 1978.

Kerr, Walter. *God on the Gymnasium Floor and Other Theatrical Adventures*. New York: Simon & Schuster, 1970.

Kirby, Michael. *The New Theatre: Performance Documentation*. New York: New York UP, 1974.

Kostelanetz, Richard. *The Theatre of Mixed Means*. New York: Dial, 1968.

Krows, Arthur Edwin. *Play Production in America*. New York: Henry Holt, 1916.

Krutch, Joseph Wood. *The American Drama Since 1918*. New York: George Braziller, 1957.

Lahr, John. *Up Against the Fourth Wall*. New York: Grove, 1970.

Larson, Gary O. *The Reluctant Patron: The United States Government and the Arts, 1943–1965*. Philadelphia: U of Pennsylvania, 1983.

Laufe, Abe. *Anatomy of a Hit: Long-Run Plays on Broadway from 1900 to the Present Day*. New York: Hawthorn, 1966.

Leavitt, Dinah L. *Feminist Theatre Groups*. Jefferson, NC: McFarland, 1980.

Leiter, Samuel L. *Ten Seasons: New York Theatre in the Seventies*. Westport, CT: Greenwood, 1986.

—. *From Belasco to Brook: Representative Directors of the English-Speaking Stage*. Westport, CT: Greenwood, 1991.

Leman, Walter M. *Memories of an Old Actor*. San Francisco: A. Roman, 1886.

Leonard, William Torbert. *Theatre: Stage to Screen to Television*. 2 vols. Metuchen, NJ: Scarecrow, 1981.

Leslie, Amy. *Some Players*. Chicago and New York: Herbert S. Stone, 1899.

Leuchs, Frederick. *The Early German Theatre in New York, 1840–1872*. New York: Columbia UP, 1966.

Levine, Ira A. *Left-Wing Dramatic Theory in the American Theatre*. Ann Arbor: UMI Research, 1985.

Levine, Lawrence W. *Highbrow Lowbrow: The Emergence of Cultural Hierarchy in America*. Cambridge, MA: Harvard UP, 1988.

Lewis, Allan. *The Contemporary Theatre*. Rev. ed. New York: Crown, 1971.

—. *American Plays and Playwrights of the Contemporary Theatre*. New York: Crown, 1965.

Lewis, Emory. *Stages: The Fifty-Year Childhood of the American Theatre*. Englewood Cliffs, NJ: Prentice-Hall, 1969.

Lewisohn, Ludwig. *The Drama and the Stage*. New York: Harcourt, 1922.

Little, Stuart W., and Arthur Cantor. *The Playmakers*. New York: W. W. Norton, 1970.

—. *After the Fact: Conflict and Consensus – A Report on the First American Congress of Theatre*. New York: Arno, 1975.

Lowry, W. McNeil, ed. *The Performing Arts and American Society*. Englewood Cliffs, NJ: Prentice-Hall, 1978.

Lynes, Russell. *The Lively Audience: A Social History of the Visual and Performing Arts in America, 1890–1950*. New York: Harper & Row, 1985.

McArthur, Benjamin. *Actors and American Culture, 1880–1920*. Philadelphia: Temple UP, 1984.

McCarthy, Mary. *Mary McCarthy's Theatre Chronicles, 1937–1962*. New York: Farrar, Straus, 1963.

McCleery, Albert, and Carl Glick. *Curtains Going Up*. Chicago: Pitman, 1939.

McConachie, Bruce A. *Melodramatic Formations: American Theatre and Society, 1820–1870*. Iowa City: U of Iowa, 1992.

McConachie, Bruce A., and Daniel Friedman, eds. *Theatre for Working-Class Audiences in the United States, 1830–1980*. Westport, CT: Greenwood, 1985.

Macgowan, Kenneth. *Footlights Across America*. New York: Harcourt, Brace, 1929.

McKay, Frederic E., and Charles E. L. Wingate, eds. *Famous American Actors of Today*. New York: Thomas Y. Crowell, 1896.

McNamara, Brooks, ed. *American Popular Entertainments: A Collection of Jokes, Monologues & Comedy Routines*. New York: PAJ Publications, 1983.

Malpede, Karen, ed. *Women in Theatre: Compassion & Hope*. New York: Limelight, 1983.

Mantle, Burns. *Contemporary American Playwrights*. New York: Dodd, Mead, 1938.

Marks, Edward Bennett. *They All Had Glamour: From the Swedish Nightingale to the Naked Lady*. New York: J. Messner, 1944.

Marranca, Bonnie. *Theatrewritings*. New York: PAJ Publications, 1984.

Marranca, Bonnie, and Gautam Dasgupta. *American Playwrights: A Critical Survey*. New York: Drama Book Specialists, 1981.

Martin, Linda, and Kerry Segrave. *Women in Comedy: The Funny Ladies from the Turn of the Century to the Present*. Secaucus, NJ: Citadel, 1986.

Mason, Alexander. *The French Theatre in New York*. New York: Columbia UP, 1940.

Matlaw, Myron, ed. *American Popular Entertainment*. Westport, CT: Greenwood, 1979.

—, ed. *The Black Crook and Other Nineteenth-Century American Plays*. New York: Dutton, 1967. [Useful historical introduction]

Matthews, Brander, and Laurence Hutton, eds. *Actors and Actresses of Great Britain and the United States: From the Days of David Garrick to the Present Time*. 5 vols. New York: Cassell, 1886.

Mayorga, Margaret G. *A Short History of the American Drama*. New York: Dodd, Mead, 1932.

Meltzer, Milton. *Violins and Shovels*. New York: Delacorte, 1976.

Mersand, Joseph. *American Drama Since 1930*. New York: Modern Chapbooks, 1949.

Meserve, Walter J. *An Emerging Entertainment: The Drama of the American People to 1828*. Bloomington: Indiana UP, 1977.

—. *An Outline History of American Drama*. Totowa, NJ: Littlefield, Adams, 1965.

— *Heralds of Promise: The Drama of the American People in the Age of Jackson, 1829–1849*. Westport, CT: Greenwood, 1986.

—, ed. *Discussions of Modern American Drama*. Boston: D. C. Heath, 1965.

Miller, Jordan Y., ed. *American Dramatic Literature: Ten Modern Plays in Historical Perspective*. New York: McGraw-Hill, 1961. [Useful historical introduction]

Miller, Jordan Y., and Winifred L. Frazer. *American Drama Between the Wars: A Critical History*. Boston: Twayne, 1991.

Mills, John. *Hamlet on Stage: The Great Tradition*. Westport, CT: Greenwood, 1985.

Mitchell, Loften. *Voices of the Black Theatre*. Clifton, NJ: James T. White, 1975.

Moody, Richard, ed. *America Takes the Stage*. Bloomington: Indiana UP, 1955.

—. *Dramas from the American Theatre, 1762–1909*. Cleveland: World Publishing, 1966. [Excellent introductions and bibliographies]

Mordden, Ethan. *The American Theatre*. New York: Oxford UP, 1981.

Morehouse, Ward. *Forty-five Minutes Past Eight*. New York: Dial, 1939.

—. *Matinee Tomorrow: Fifty Years of Our Theater*. New York: Whittlesay House, 1949.

Morris, Lloyd R. *Curtain Time: The Story of the American Theatre*. New York: Random House, 1953.

Moses, Montrose J. *Famous Actor-Families in America*. New York: Thomas Y. Crowell, 1906.

—. *The American Dramatist*. Boston: Little, Brown, 1925.

Moskow, Michael H. *Labor Relations in the Performing Arts*. New York: Associated Council of the Arts, 1969.

Motherwell, Hiram Kelly. *The Theatre of Today*. New York: Dodd, Mead, 1914.

Moussinac, Leon. *The New Movement in the Theatre: A Survey of Recent Developments in Europe and America*. London: Batsford, 1931.

Murphy, Brenda. *American Realism and American Drama, 1880–1940*. Cambridge and New York: Cambridge UP, 1987.

Nannes, Caspar. *Politics in the American Drama*. Washington, DC: Catholic U of America, 1960.

Nathan, George G. *The Theatre Book of the Year, 1943–44* [through 1950–51]. New York: Knopf, 1944–51.

—. *Encyclopedia of the Theatre*. New York: Knopf, 1940.

—. *The Magic Mirror: Selected Writings on the Theatre*. New York: Alfred A. Knopf, 1960.

Netzer, Dick. *The Subsidized Muse: Public Support for the Arts in the United States*. Cambridge and New York: Cambridge UP, 1978.

Nightingale, Benedict. *Fifth Row Center: A Critic's Year On and Off Broadway*. New York: Times Books, 1986.

Northall, William K. *Before and Behind the Curtain; or, Fifteen Years Observations Among the Theatres of New York*. New York: W. F. Burgess, 1851.

Novick, Julius. *Beyond Broadway: The Quest for Permanent Theatres*. New York: Hill & Wang, 1968.

Nye, Russel Blaine. *Society and Culture in America, 1830–1860*. New York: Harper & Row, 1974.

Odell, George C. D. *Annals of the New York Stage*. 15 vols. New York: Columbia UP, 1927–49.

Ohringer, Frederic. *A Portrait of the Theatre*. Toronto: Merritt, 1979.

Olney, Julian. *Beyond Broadway* [Charles Laughton–Paul Gregory]. Ardmore, PA: Dorrance, 1979.

Orsmbee, Helen. *Backstage with Actors*. New York: Thomas Y. Crowell, 1938.

Parker, Dorothy, ed. *Essays on Modern American Drama: Williams, Miller, Albee, and Shepard*. Toronto: U of Toronto, 1987.

Peiss, Kathy. *Cheap Amusements: Working Women and Leisure in Turn-of-the-Century New York*. Philadelphia: Temple UP, 1986.

Performing Arts: Problems and Prospects (Rockefeller Panel Report). New York: McGraw-Hill, 1965.

Phelps, William Lyon. *Twentieth Century Theatre*. New York: Macmillan Co., 1918.

Pichel, Irving. *Modern Theatres*. New York: Harcourt, Brace, 1925.

Portraits of the American Stage, 1771–1971. Washington: Smithsonian Institution, 1971.

Postlewait, Thomas, and Bruce A. McConachie, eds. *Interpreting the Theatrical Past: Essays in the Historiography of Performance*. Iowa City: U of Iowa, 1989.

Power, Tyrone. *Impressions of America During the Years 1833, 1834, and 1835*. 2 vols. Philadelphia: Carey, Lea and Blandchard, 1836.

Quinn, Arthur Hobson. *A History of the American Drama from the Civil War to the Present*. Rev. ed. New York: Appleton–Century–Crofts, 1936.

—. *A History of the American Drama from the Beginning to the Civil War*. 2d ed. New York: Appleton–Century–Crofts, 1943.

Rabkin, Gerald. *Drama and Commitment: Politics in the American Theatre of the Thirties*. Bloomington: Indiana UP, 1964.

Rankin, Hugh F. *The Theater in Colonial America*. Chapel Hill: U of North Carolina, 1965.

Reed, Joseph Verner. *The Curtain Falls*. New York: Harcourt, Brace, 1935.

Reignolds-Winslow, Catherine. *Yesterdays with Actors*. Boston: Cupples, 1887.

Reynolds, R. C. *Stage Left: The Development of the American Social Drama in the Thirties*. Troy, NY: Whitston, 1986.

Ripley, John. *Julius Caesar on Stage in England and America, 1599–1973*. New York and Cambridge: Cambridge UP, 1980.

Rogoff, Gordon. *Theatre Is Not Safe: Theatre Criticism, 1962–1986*. Evanston: Northwestern UP, 1987.

Rydell, Robert W. *All the World's a Fair: Visions of Empire at American International Expositions, 1876–1916*. Chicago: U of Chicago, 1984.

Sampson, Henry T. *The Ghost Walks: A Chronological History of Blacks in Show Business, 1865–1910*. Metuchen, NJ: Scarecrow, 1988.

Samuel, Raphael, Ewan MacColl, and Stuart Cosgrove. *Theatres of the Left, 1880–1935: Workers' Theatre Movements in Britain and America*. London and Boston: Routledge & Kegan Paul, 1985.

Savran, David. *In Their Own Words. Contemporary American Playwrights*. New York: Theatre Communications Group, 1988.

Sayler, Oliver M. *Our American Theatre*. New York: Brentano's, 1923.

Sayre, Henry M. *The Object of Performance: The American Avant-Garde Since 1970*. Chicago: U of Chicago, 1989.

Scharine, Richard G. *From Class to Caste in American Drama: Political and Social Themes Since the 1930s*. Westport, CT: Greenwood, 1991.

Schechter, Joel. *Durov's Pig: Clowns, Politics and Theatre*. New York: Theatre Communications Group, 1985.

Schroeder, Patricia R. *The Presence of the Past in Modern American Drama*. Rutherford, NJ: Fairleigh Dickinson UP, 1989.

Seilhamer, George O. *History of the American Theatre, 1792–1797*. 3 vols. Philadelphia: Globe Printing House, 1888–91.

Sexton, R. W. *American Theatres of Today*. 2 vols. New York: Architectural Book Publishing, 1930.

Shacter, Susan, and Don Shewey. *Caught in the Act: New York Actors Face to Face*. New York: New American Library, 1986.

Shaw, Dale. *Titans of the American Stage: Edwin Forrest, the Booths, the O'Neills*. Philadelphia: Westminster, 1971.

Sielhamer, George O. *History of the New York Stage, From the First Performance in 1732 to 1901*. 3 vols. New York, 1903. Reprint. New York: Benjamin Blom, 1943.

Simon, John. *Uneasy Stages: A Chronicle of the New York Theater, 1963–1973*. New York: Random House, 1975.

Skinner, Otis. *Footlights and Spotlights*. Indianapolis, IN: Bobbs-Merrill Co., 1924.

Skinner, Richard Dana. *Our Changing Theatre*. New York: Dial, 1931.

Smiley, Sam. *The Drama of Attack: Didactic Plays of the American Depression*. Columbia: U of Missouri, 1972.

Smith, Michael. *Theatre Journal: Winter 1967*. Columbia: U of Missouri, 1968.

Sobel, Bernard. *Broadway Heartbeat: Memoirs of a Press Agent*. New York: Hermitage House, 1953.

Sper, Felix. *From Native Roots: A Panorama of Our Regional Drama*. Caldwell, ID: Caxton Printers, 1948.

Sponberg, Arvid F. *Broadway Talks: What Professionals Think About Commercial Theater in America*. Westport, CT: Greenwood, 1991.

Spritz, Kenneth. *Theatrical Evolution: 1776–1976*. Yonkers, NY: Hudson River Museum, 1976.

Steinberg, Mollie B. *The History of the Fourteenth Street Theatre*. New York: Dial, 1931.

Stevens, Ashton. *Actorviews*. Chicago: Covici-McGee Co., 1923.

Stevens, David H., ed. *Ten Talents in the American Theatre*. Norman: U of Oklahoma, 1957.

Stone, Henry Dickinson. *Personal Recollections of the Drama*. Albany, NY: C. Van Benthuysen, 1873.

Strang, Lewis C. *Famous Actresses of the Day in America*. Boston: L. C. Page, 1899.

—. *Famous Actors of the Day in America*. Boston: L. C. Page, 1900.

—. *Players and Plays of the Last Quarter Century*. 2 vols. Boston: L. C. Page, 1902.

Stratton, Clarence. *Theatron: An Illustrated Record*. New York: Holt, 1928.

Suskin, Steven. *Opening Night on Broadway*. New York: Schirmer Books, 1990.

Szilassy, Zoltán. *American Theater of the 1960s.* Carbondale: Southern Illinois UP, 1986.

Taubman, Howard. *The Making of the American Theatre.* New York: Coward McCann, 1965.

Taylor, Dwight. *Blood-and-Thunder* [on Charles A. Taylor]. New York: Atheneum, 1962.

Taylor, Karen Malpede. *People's Theatre in Amerika.* New York: Drama Book Specialists, 1972.

Toll, Robert C. *On with the Show: The First Century of Show Business in America.* New York: Oxford UP, 1976.

—. *The Entertainment Machine: American Show Business in the Twentieth Century.* New York: Oxford UP, 1982.

Toohey, John L. *A History of the Pulitzer Prize Plays.* New York: Citadel, 1967.

Towse, John Ranken. *Sixty Years in the Theatre.* New York: Funk and Wagnalls, 1916.

Urban, Joseph. *Theatres.* New York: Theatre Arts Books, 1929.

Valgemae, Mardi. *Accelerated Grimace: Expressionism in the American Drama of the 1920s.* Carbondale: Southern Illinois UP, 1972.

Vardac, A. Nicholas. *Stage to Screen.* Cambridge, MA: Harvard UP, 1949.

Vaughn, Jack A. *Early American Dramatists from the Beginning to 1900.* New York: Frederick Ungar, 1981.

Wagenknecht, Edward. *Merely Players.* Norman: U of Oklahoma, 1966.

Waldman, Max. *Waldman on Theater.* Garden City, NY: Doubleday, 1971.

Waldo, Lewis P. *The French Drama in America in the Eighteenth Century.* Baltimore, MD: Johns Hopkins UP, 1942.

Ware, Ralph H. *American Adaptations of French Plays on the New York and Philadelphia Stages from 1834 to the Civil War.* Philadelphia: U of Pennsylvania, 1930.

Weales, Gerald. *The Jumping-Off Place: American Drama in the 1960s, from Broadway to Off-Off Broadway to Happenings.* New York: Macmillan, 1969.

Wellwarth, George E. *The Theatre of Protest and Paradox: Developments in the Avant-Garde Drama.* Rev. ed. New York: New York UP, 1971.

Williams, Henry B., ed. *The American Theatre: A Sum of Its Parts.* New York: Samuel French, 1971.

Williams, Jay. *Stage Left.* New York: Scribner's, 1974.

Williams, Mance. *Black Theatre in the 1960s and 1970s: A Historical-Critical Analysis of the Movement.* Westport, CT: Greenwood, 1985.

Wilson, Garff B. *A History of American Acting.* Bloomington: Indiana UP, 1966.

— *Three Hundred Years of American Drama and Theatre.* Englewood Cliffs, NJ: Prentice-Hall, 1973.

Winter, William. *The Wallet of Time: Containing Personal, Biographical, and Critical Reminiscences of the American Theatre.* 2 vols. New York, 1913. Reprint. NY: Benjamin Blom, 1969.

Woollcott, Alexander. *Enchanted Aisles.* New York: G. P. Putnam's Sons, 1924.

Part III: Regional, Local, and Other Specific Studies

Arvold, Alfred G. *The Little Country Theatre.* New York: Macmillan, 1922.

Bishop, Mary, ed. *The Ohio Theatre, 1928–1979.* Columbus, OH: Columbus Association for the Performing Arts, 1978.

Bogdan, Robert. *Freak Show: Presenting Human Oddities for Amusement and Profit.* Chicago: U of Chicago, 1988.

Bowen, Elbert R. *Theatrical Entertainment in Rural Missouri Before the Civil War.* Columbia: U of Missouri, 1959.

Brede, Charles Frederic. *The German Drama in English on the Philadelphia Stage from 1794 to 1830.* Philadelphia: Americana Germanica, 1918.

Brett, Roger. *Temples of Illusion* [Providence, RI]. Providence: Brett Theatrical, 1976.

Brockman, C. Lance, curator. *The Twin City Scenic Collection: Popular Entertainment, 1895–1929.* Minneapolis: U Art Museum, 1987.

Bryer, Jackson, ed. *The Theatre We Worked For: Letters of Eugene O'Neill to Kenneth Macgowan.* New Haven, CT: Yale UP, 1982.

Campbell, Patricia J. *Passing the Hat: Street Performers in America.* New York: Delacorte, 1981.

Carson, William G. B. *Managers in Distress: The St. Louis Stage, 1840–1844.* St. Louis: St. Louis Historical Documents Foundation, 1949.

Cruise, Boyd, and Merle Harton. *Signor Faranta's Iron Theatre* [New Orleans]. New Orleans: Historic New Orleans Collection, 1982.

Davis, Susan G. *Parades and Power: Street Theatre in Nineteenth Century Philadelphia.* Philadelphia: Temple UP, 1986.

Dormon, James H., Jr. *Theater in the Ante Bellum South 1815–1861.* Chapel Hill: U of North Carolina, 1967.

Dunlap, William. *Memoirs of the Life of George Frederick Cooke.* 2 vols. New York: D. Longworth, 1813.

Durang, Charles. *The Philadelphia Stage, for the Years 1749–1855.* 7 vols. Philadelphia: Philadelphia Sunday Dispatch, 1854–55 (arr. and illust. by Thompson Westcott, 1868).

Eckey, Lorelei F., Maxine Allen Schoyer, and William T. Schoyer. *1,001 Broadways: Hometown Talent on Stage.* Ames: Iowa State UP, 1982.

Ernst, Alice Henson. *Trouping in the Oregon Country: A History of Frontier Theatre.* 1961. Reprint. Westport, CT: Greenwood, 1974.

Federal Theatre Project Collection. Washington, DC: Library of Congress, 1987.

Federal Theatre Project: A Catalog-Calendar of Productions. Compiled by staff of the Fenwick Library, George Mason University. Westport, CT: Greenwood, 1986.

Ford, Paul Leicester. *Washington and the Theatre* [George]. New York: Dunlap Society, 1899.

Free, William, and Charles Lower. *History into Drama: A Source Book on Symphonic Drama.* New York: Odyssey, 1963.

Furman, Evelyn E. Livingston. *The Tabor Opera House: A Captivating History.* Leadville, CO: np, 1972.

Gallegly, Joseph S. *Footlights on the Border: The*

Galveston and Houston Stage Before 1900. The Hague: Mouton, 1962.

Henderson, Myrtle. *History of the Theatre in Salt Lake City*. Salt Lake City: Deseret Book Co., 1941.

Hill, Errol. *The Jamaican Stage, 1655–1900: Profile of a Colonial Theatre*. Amherst: U of Massachusetts, 1992.

Hill, West T., Jr. *The Theatre in Early Kentucky, 1790–1820*. Lexington: U of Kentucky, 1971.

Hoole, W. S. *The Ante-Bellum Charleston Theatre*. Tuscaloosa: U of Alabama, 1946.

Hughes, Glenn. *The Penthouse Theatre: Its History and Technique*. New York: Samuel French, 1942.

Kendall, John S. *The Golden Age of the New Orleans Theatre*. Baton Rouge: Louisiana State UP, 1952.

Koenig, Linda Lee. *The Vagabonds: America's Oldest Little Theater* [Baltimore, MD]. Rutherford, NJ: Fairleigh Dickinson UP, 1983.

Koon, Helen Wickham. *How Shakespeare Won the West: Players and Performances in America's Gold Rush, 1849–1865*. Jefferson, NC: McFarland, 1989.

Larson, Carl F. W. *American Regional Theatre History to 1900: A Bibliography*. Metuchen, NJ: Scarecrow, 1979.

Lewis, Philip C. *Trouping: How the Show Came to Town*. New York: Harper & Row, 1973.

MacMinn, George R. *The Theater of the Golden Era in California*. Caldwell, ID: Caxton Printers, 1941.

Moore, Lester L. *Outside Broadway: A History of the Professional Theater in Newark, New Jersey, from the Beginning to 1867*. Metuchen, NJ: Scarecrow, 1970.

Murphy, Brenda. *Tennessee Williams and Elia Kazan: A Collaboration in the Theater*. Cambridge and New York: Cambridge UP, 1992.

O'Connor, John, and Lorraine Brown, eds. *Free, Adult, Uncensored: The Living History of the Federal Theatre Project*. Washington, DC: New Republic Books, 1978.

Patrick, J. Max. *Savannah's Pioneer Theatre from Its Origins to 1810*. Athens: U of Georgia, 1953.

Phelps, Henry Pitt. *Players of a Century: A Record of the Albany Stage*. 2d ed. Albany, NY: J. McDonough, 1890.

Poggi, Jack. *Theater in America: The Impact of Economic Forces, 1870–1967*. Ithaca: Cornell UP, 1968.

Pottlitzer, Joanne. *Hispanic Theater in the United States and Puerto Rico*. New York: Ford Foundation, 1988.

Pyper, George D. *The Romance of an Old Playhouse* [Salt Lake Theatre]. Salt Lake City, UT: Seagull, 1928.

Redfield, William. *Letters from an Actor*. New York: Viking, 1967.

Ritchey, David, compiler. *A Guide to the Baltimore Stage in the Eighteenth Century: A History and Day Book Calendar*. Westport, CT: Greenwood, 1982.

Ryan, Kate. *Old Boston Museum Days*. Boston: Little, Brown, 1915.

Rydell, Robert W. *All the World's a Fair: Visions of Empire at American International Expositions, 1876–1916*. Chicago: U of Chicago, 1984.

Shockley, Martin Staples. *The Richmond Stage, 1784–1812*. Charlottesville: UP of Virginia, 1977.

Skinner, Richard Dana. *Our Changing Theatre*. New York: Dial, 1931.

Slide, Anthony. *Selected Vaudeville Criticism*. Metuchen, NJ: Scarecrow, 1988.

Smith, Geddeth. *The Brief Career of Eliza Poe*. Rutherford: Fairleigh Dickinson UP, 1988.

Smither, Nelle. *A History of the English Theatre in New Orleans, 1806–1842*. Philadelphia, 1944. 2d ed. New York: Benjamin Blom, 1967.

Sobel, Bernard. *Broadway Heartbeat: Memoirs of a Press Agent*. New York: Hermitage House, 1953.

Sterne, Richard L. *John Gielgud Directs Richard Burton in Hamlet*. New York: Random House, 1967.

Stickney, Dorothy. *Openings and Closings*. Garden City, NY: Doubleday, 1979.

Vaughan, Stuart. *A Possible Theatre*. New York: McGraw-Hill, 1969.

Watson, Margaret G. *Silver Theatre: Amusements of Nevada's Mining Frontier, 1850 to 1864*. Glendale, CA: Arthur H. Clark Co., 1964.

Whitman, Willson. *Bread and Circuses: A Study of the Federal Theatre*. New York: Oxford UP, 1937.

Willard, George O. *History of the Providence Stage, 1762–1891*. Providence: Rhode Island News Co., 1891.

Willis, Eola. *The Charleston Stage in the XVIII Century*. Columbia, SC: State Company, 1924. Reprint. New York: Benjamin Blom, 1968.

Windham, Donald, ed. *Tennessee Williams' Letters to Donald Windham, 1940–1965*. New York: Holt, Rinehart & Winston, 1977.

Wright, Richardson. *Revels in Jamaica*. New York: Dodd, Mead, 1937.

Zivanovic, Judith K., ed. *Opera Houses of the Midwest*. np: Mid-America Theatre Conference, 1988.

Biographical Index

The following is an index to individuals mentioned in various entries who do not have entries of their own in this volume. (Asterisks refer the reader to entries in the *Cambridge Guide to World Theatre*.) Abbreviations are used to identify nationalities and fields of endeavor; these are followed by the titles (often shortened) of any entries where the individual is cited. The book's Introduction is referenced by section number: Intro(§1), Intro(§2), and so on.   DBW

Abbreviations

a	actor
adm	administrator
ag	agent
Alb	Albanian
arc	architect
art	artist (graphic)
Astl	Australian
Aus	Austrian
ba	banker
Bel	Belgian
Brit	British
Brz	Brazilian
c	critic
Can	Canadian
ch	choreographer
Chil	Chilean
Chn	Chinese
co	composer
Cub	Cuban
Cz	Czechoslovakian
d	director
da	dancer
Dan	Danish
de	designer
drm	dramaturg
Dut	Dutch
e	entertainer
ed	editor
edu	educator
en	entrepreneur
eq	equestrian
f	film
Fr	French
Ger	German
Gk	Greek
Hun	Hungarian
Ir	Irish
Isr	Israeli
It	Italian
Jp	Japanese
j	journalist
l	lyricist
Latv	Latvian
law	lawyer
lib	librettist
Lith	Lithuanian
ltg	lighting
m	manager
ma	magician
Mex	Mexican
mi	mime
mm	medicine man

mu	musician
Nor	Norwegian
p	producer
perf	performance artist
ph	photographer
pi	pioneer
pl	playwright
po	poet
Pol	Polish
pub	publisher
pug	pugilist
pup	puppeteer
R	Russian
rel	religious leader
Ro	Romanian
s	singer
SAf	South African
Sc	Scottish
sch	scholar
scpt	scene painter
scr	screenwriter
sh	showman
Sov	Soviet
Sp	Spanish
sr	social reformer
sto	storyteller
Swe	Swedish
t	theatre owner
tb	theatre builder
te	teacher
tech	technician
th	theorist
v	ventriloquist
w	writer
We	Welsh
WI	West Indian
Y	Yiddish
★	See entry in *Cambridge Guide to World Theatre*

Abady, Josephine (1950–   ) d; Cleveland Play House

Abbott, Bud (William) (1895/1900–74) e; burlesque

Abeles, Joseph (1911–91) ph; photographers

Abuba, Ernest (1947–   ) pl; Asian-American; Chang

Acosta, Iván (1943–   ) pl; Cuban-American

Adair, Jean (1873–1953) a; *Arsenic . . .*

Adams, Annie (1847–1916) a; Adams (M.)

Adams, Edith (Edie) (1929–   ) a, s; *Wonderful Town*

Adams, Franklin P. (1881–1960) en, w; *Dulcy*

Adams, Joey (1911–   ) e; Borscht belt

Adams, John Cranford (1903–86) sch, w; Oregon Shakespeare Festival

Adams, Lee (1924–   ) l; *Golden Boy;* Strouse

Addams, Augustus A. (?–1851) a; Intro(§1)

Addams, Jane (1860–1935) sr; community; Hull-House

Addams, John P. "Yankee" (1815–85) a, pl; Yankee

★Addison, Joseph (1672–1719) Brit, pl; Hallams; Intro(§1); Philadelphia

Adler, Dankmar (1844–1900) arc; architecture; McVicker's

Adler, Sara or Sarah (1865–1953) a; Adler (J.); ethnic; Yiddish

★Aeschylus (525/4–456/5 B.C.) Gk, pl; Jeffers; Lowell; *Mourning . . .*

Ailey, Alvin (1931–89) co; Nelson

Alam, Juan Shamsul (1946–   ) pl; Nuyorican

Alda, Alan (1936–   ) a, d, f d; Second City; Simon (N.)

Alda, Robert (1914–86) a; *Guys and Dolls*

Aldrich, Louis (Louis Lyon) (1843–1901) a; Campbell; *My Partner*

Aleichem, Sholom, *see* Rabinowitz, Solomon J.

Alessandro, Antonietta Pisanelli (1869–c. 1940) a; ethnic

Alexander, Mrs. John (Elizabeth) (1867–1947) de; costume

Alexander, Ronald (1917–   ) pl; Intro(§3); *Time Out for Ginger*

Alfred, William (1922–   ) pl, edu; *Hogan's Goat*

Algarín, Miguel (1941–   ) pl; Nuyorican

Ali, George (1866–1947) a; animal impersonation

Ali, Mohammed (Cassius Clay) (1942–   ) pug; Durham

Graham, Philip (1894–1967) edu, sch; showboats

Granger, Maude (1841/6–1928) a; *My Partner*

Grant, Cary (né Archibald Alexander Leach) (1904–86) a; *Holiday*

Grant, Lee (1929–   ) a, d; *Detective Story*

Grant, Micki (1941–   ) pl; Carroll

★Granville-Barker, Harley (1877–1946) Brit, a, c, d, pl; Intro(§2); Jones (R. E.); scenic design; Shakespeare

Gray, Amlin (1946–   ) pl; Intro(§4)

Gray, David (1870–1968) pl; Hopwood

Gray, Dolores (1924–   ) a; *Annie Get Your Gun*

★Gray, Simon (1936–   ) Brit, pl; Grimes; international; Intro(§4); Ivey (J.); Meadow; Ramsay; Richardson

Green, Schuyler (1880–1927) l; *Very Good Eddie*

Greenberg, Stanley R. (fl. 1960s) pl, w; Intro(§4)

Greenspan, David (1956–   ) d; New York Shakespeare Festival

Greenstreet, Sydney (1879–1954) a; Chekhov on . . .

Greenwich, Ellie (1940–   ) co; Heifner

Greif, Michael (1959–   ) d; New York Shakespeare Festival

★Greet, Ben (1857–1936) a, m; Greet Players; international

★Gregory, Lady Augusta Isabella (1852–1932) Brit, en, pl; community

Gregory, Montgomery (1887–c. 1940s) edu; Miller (May)

Gresham, Herbert (1853?–1921) Brit-born, d; Teal

Grey, Clifford (1887–1941) l; *Sally*

Gribble, Harry Wagstaff[e] (1896–1981) Brit, a, p, pl; *Anna Lucasta*

Grieg, Edvard (1843–1907) Nor, co; *Kismet*

Griffith, D. W. (1874/75–1948) a, d, f d; Loos

Griffith, Hugh (1912–80) Brit, a; *Look Homeward . . .*

Griffith, Robert E. (1907–61) p; Prince

★Grimaldi, Joseph (1778–1837) Brit, e; mime/pantomime

Grimke, Angelina Weld (1880–1958) pl; *Rachel*

Grimsley, Jim (1955–   ) pl; gay/lesbian

Grismer, Joseph (1849–1922) a; Warde

Groody, Louise (1897–1961) a, s; *No, No, Nanette*

Gros, Ernest (fl. 1900s) de; scenic design

Gross, Roger (1931–   ) edu, th; dramatic theory

★Grotowski, Jerzy (1933–   ) Pol, d; Clarke (M.); dramatic theory; feminist; international; Intro(§4); La MaMa; Maleczech; Off-Broadway; Performance Group; Schechner

★Grundy, Sidney (1848–1914) Brit, pl; Langtry

★Guilbert, Yvette (1865–1944) Fr, e; Neighborhood Playhouse

Guinan, Texas (1884–1933) a, en; nightclubs

★Guinness, Alec (1914–   ) Brit, a; Guthrie; international; Miller (G. H.); Reid; Worth

★Guitry, Sacha (1885–1957) Fr, a, pl; March

Guthrie, Kark (1933–   ) th; dramatic theory

Gwenn, Edmund (1875–1959) We-born, a; Chekhov on . . .

Gwynne, Fred (1926–   ) a; *Cat on a Hot Tin Roof*

Haas, Tom (1938–91) d; Indiana Rep

Haase, Friedrich (1811–86) Ger, a; Germania; Stadt Theater

Hackett, Albert (1900–   ) pl; *Diary of Anne Frank*

Hackett, Buddy (1924–   ) e; Intro(§3)

Hackett, Francis (1883–1962) c; Young

Hackman, Gene (1930–   ) a; *Any Wednesday*

Hagedorn, Jessica (c. 1950–   ) pl; Intro(§4)

Hailey, Oliver (1932–   ) pl; Moffat; Richardson

Haines, William Wister (1908–89) pl; Intro(§3)

Halbert, Delancey (1874–1904) c; Chicago

Halévy, Ludovic (1834–1908) Fr, pl; *Carmen Jones*

Haley, Jack (1899–1979) a; *Wizard of Oz*

Hall, Adelaide (1909/10–   ) a, s; musical

Hall, Albert (1937–   ) a; *Basic Training . . .*

Hall, Huntz (1920–   ) a; *Dead End*

★Hall, Peter (1930–   ) Brit, d, m; *Camino Real;* Channing (S.); Hoffman

Hallam, Adam (d. 1769) a; Hallam

Hallam, Mrs. Lewis (II) (née Eliza Tuke) (fl. 1785) a; Hallam

Hallam, Nancy (fl. 1759–61) a; Hallam

Halliday, Robert (1893–?) Sc-born, a, s; *Desert Song;* musical; *New Moon*

Halprin, Ann (1920–   ) ch, da; Intro(§4)

Hamburger, Richard (1951–   ) d, pl; Dallas Theater Center

Hamilton, John F. (1893–1967) a; *Of Mice and Men*

Hamlin, Fred (c. 1863–1904) p; *Babes in Toyland*

Hamlisch, Marvin (1944–   ) co; *Chorus Line*

Hammerstein, James (1931–   ) d; *Indian Wants the Bronx*

★Hampton, Christopher (1946–   ) Brit, pl; international; Maher

★Handke, Peter (1942–   ) Aus, pl; Chelsea Theatre

Haney, Carol (1924–64) a, da; Gennero

Hanford, Charles Barnum (1859–1926) a; Warde

Hanley, William (1931–   ) pl; Barr; *Slow Dance . . .*

Hansen, William (1911–75) a; *My Heart's . . .*

Hardwicke, Cedric (1893–1964) Brit, a; Aldrich; international

Hardy, Joseph (1929–   ) d; *You're a Good Man . . .*

Hardy, Thomas (1840–1928) pl, w; Cazuran; dramatic theory; *Marriage of Bette and Boo*

Hardy, William (1922–   ) pl; outdoor

★Hare, David (1947–   ) Brit, pl; Herrmann (E.); Hurt (M. B.); Intro(§4); New York Shakespeare Festival

Harewood, Dorian (1951–   ) a; *Streamers*

Harley, Margot (1935–   ) adm, p; Acting Company

Harling, Robert (1951–   ) a, pl; Off-Broadway

Harlow, Jean (1911–37) a; Bellamy; *Dinner at Eight*

Harmon, Mark (1951–   ) a; *Sweet Bird . . .*

Harper, Valerie (1940–   ) a; Second City

Harrigan, William (1894–1966) a; *Great God Brown;* Harrigan

Harrington, Jonathan (1809–81) ma; magic

Harris, Barbara (1935/7–   ) a; Off-Broadway; *Oh Dad, Poor Dad . . .*

Harris, Ed (1950–   ) a; *Fool for Love*

Harris, Henry B. (1866–1912) p; Helen Hayes Theatre

Harris, Richard (1933–   ) Ir, a; *Camelot*

Harrison, Charles (1883–1955) pl; tent show

Harrold, Orville (1878–1933) a, s; *Naughty Marietta*

Hart, Margie (1916–   ) e; Minsky

Hart, Roxanne (1952–   ) a; *Loose Ends*

Hart, Teddy (1897–1971) a; *Boys from Syracuse*

Hartinian, Linda (1948–   ) pl; Mabou Mines

Hartmann, Louis (1907–41) de; Belasco; scenic design; stage lighting

Harvey, Laurence (1928–73) a; *Summer and Smoke*

Hash, Burl (c. 1945–   ) d; Chelsea Theatre Center; Malpede

Hasso, Signe (1910/18–   ) Swe, a; Ibsen

Hastings, Edward (1931–   ) d; American Conservatory

Hastings, Thomas, see Carrère and Hastings

Hatton, Anne Kemble (fl. 1790s) Brit, pl; Native Americans portrayed

Hauptman, William (1942–   ) pl; Jujamcyn

★Hauptmann, Gerhart (1862–1946)

Scott, Seret (1949–) a; *Brothers*

Scott, Tommy (?) e; medicine shows

Scott, Walter (1771–1832) Sc, w; *Davy Crockett*

★Scribe, Augustin Eugène (1791–1861) Fr, pl; James; Modjeska

Scribner, Samuel A. (1859–1941) m; Syndicate

Secunda, Sholom (1895–1974) Y, co; Yiddish

Sefton, Joseph (c. 1811–81) a, m; Niblo

Segal, George (1934–) a; *Who's Afraid . . .*

Selbit, P. T. (1881–1938) Brit, ma; Goldin

Selz, Irma (1908–75) art; caricature

Selznick, Irene (1907–90) p; *Streetcar . . .*

Semans, William (1924–) d; Cricket Theatre

Sendak, Maurice (1928–) pl, w; Minneapolis

Sennett, Mack (1880–1960) f pio; Dressler

Seurat, Georges (1859–91) Fr, art; Patinkin

Seuss, [Dr.], *see* Geisel, Theodore

Seymour, Anne (1909–88) a; Davenport (E. L.)

Seymour, May Davenport (1883–1967) a, archivist; Davenport (E. L.); Seymour

Shafer, Robert (?–1956) a; *Damn Yankees*

★Shaffer, Peter Levin (1926–) Brit, pl; animal impersonation; Brisson; Dexter; Gill; Intro(§4); Rich

Shairp, Alexander Mordaunt (1887–1939) Brit, pl; gay/lesbian

Shapiro, Mel (1935–) d; *House of Blue Leaves*

Sharpe, Robert R. (fl. 1920s–30s) de; scenic design

★Shaw, [George] Bernard (1856–1950) Ir, c, pl; Aldrich; American Shakespeare Theatre; Ames; animal impersonation; Behrman; Bloodgood; Bosco; Brady (W. A.); Channing; community; Cornell; Coghlan (R.); criticism; Daly (Arnold); Derwent; Elliott (G.); ethnic; Fitzgerald; George; Harrison; Herrmann (E.); Huneker; Intro(§2,3); Hedgerow; Houdini; King (D.); Lahr (B.); Laughton; Lerner and Loewe; Lillie; Mansfield; Marbury; Massey; Mitchell (L. E.); musical; *My Fair Lady;* Nathan; Playhouse Theatre; Porter (S.); Preston; Russell (A.); San Francisco; *Servant in the House;* Shannon; Shaw and . . . ; *Tavern;* Theatre Guild; Wood (P.); Wycherly

Shaw, Peggy (1944–) a, d; gay/lesbian; Hughes; Split Britches

Shaw, Robert (1927–78) Brit, a, pl; Abraham

Shawn, Ted (1891–1972) ch, da; Brooklyn Academy; Cole (J.); nudity

Shean, Al (1868–1949) e; burlesque; Marx Bros.

Shearer, Norma (1900–83) a; *Idiot's Delight*

Sheen, Martin (Ramon Estevez) (1940–) a, d, p; *Subject Was Roses*

Shelley, Carole (1939–) Brit-born, a; Ibsen

Shepard, David (1926–) d; Chicago; Second City

Shepp, Archie (1937–) co; *Slave Ship*

★Sheridan, Richard Brinsley (1751–1816) Ir, m, pl; Clarke; Coghlan (C.); Crane; Dunlap; Freedman; Jeffersons; Murdoch (J. E.); Russell (A.); Russell (L.); Tyler (R.)

Sheridan, W(illiam) E(dward) (1839–87) a; Allen (V.)

Sherman, Hiram (1908–89) a; Mercury Theatre

Sherman, James (1939–) pl; Cantor

Sherman, Martin (1941?–) pl; Dukes; gay/lesbian

Sherman, Stuart (19??–) d, e, pl; Off-Off Broadway

★Sherriff, R. C. (1896–1975) Brit, pl; Miller (G. H.)

Sherwood, Madeleine (1926–) a; *Crucible*

Shevelove, Burt (1915–82) d, pl; *Funny Thing . . .* ; Gelbart; *No, No, Nanette*

★Shields, Ella (1879–1952) e, s; international

Shifflett, Jim (19??–) d; Body Politic

Shimono, Sab (c. 1942–) a; *Pacific Overtures*

Shiomi, R. A. (1947–) pl; Asian-American; Chang

Shipp, Cameron (1904?–61) w; Burke

Shipp, Jesse (fl. 1890s–1900s) pl; African-American

Shoemaker, Anne (1891–1975) a; *Great God Brown*

Shook, Sheridan (fl. 1870s) m; Palmer

Short, Martin (1951–) Can, a, e; Second City

Sickinger, Robert (fl. 1960s) d; Chicago; Hull-House

★Siddons, Sarah (1755–1831) Brit, a; Clifton; Cowell (Joe); Duff (M. A.); Holm; Warren (W., the elder)

Sierra, Rubén (19??–) pl; Chicano

Silsbee, Joshua (1813–55) a; *Forest Rose;* Intro(§1); Logan (C. A.); *Our American Cousin;* Yankee

Sil-Vara, G. (1876–1938) pl; Lunt and Fontanne

Silvera, Frank (1914–70) a; *Big White Fog; Camino Real*

Silverman, Sime (1872–1933) ed, w; periodicals; *Variety*

Simms, Hilda (1920–) a; *Anna Lucasta*

Simon, Danny (192?–) w; Simon (N.)

Simon, Paul (1941–) co, s; Lee (E.)

Simon, Roger Hendricks (1942–) Brit, d; *Moonchildren*

Sinatra, Frank (1915–) a, s; *On the Town; Our Town*

Sinclair, Catherine Norton (fl. 1837–59) a, m; Forrest; San Francisco

Sinclair, Upton (1878–1968) w; Klein

★Sinden, Donald (1923–) Brit, a; international

Singer, Israel J. (1893–1944) pl; Yiddish Art Theatre

Sinise, Gary (1953?–) a; *Grapes of Wrath; Landscape;* Steppenwolf; *True West*

Sklar, George (1908–88) pl; African-American; Seattle; *Stevedore;* Theatre Union

Sklar, Roberta (1940–) d, pl; feminist; Intro(§4)

Skulnik, Menashe (1892–1970) Y, a; Yiddish

Slattery, Charles (fl. 1930s) a; *Of Mice and Men*

Sloane, A. Baldwin (1872–1925) co; *Wizard of Oz*

Small, Philip (fl. 1920s) arc; Cleveland Play House

Smith, Anna Deavere (1950–) a, d, pl; Los Angeles Theatre Center; one-person

Smith, Art (1900–73) a; Group Theatre; *House of Connelly; Men in White; My Heart's . . .*

Smith, Bessie (1894–1937) e, s; Albee (E.); female/male

Smith, Derek (1927–) Brit, a; *Little Murders*

Smith, Evan (1967–) pl; gay/lesbian

Smith, Jack (1932–89) a, d, pl; gay/lesbian

Smith, Joseph (1805–44) rel; Rice (D.)

Smith, Lois (1930–) a; *Grapes of Wrath*

★Smith, Maggie (1934–) Brit, a; international

Smalls, Charlie (1943–87) co, l; *Wiz*

Smith, Michael (1935–) c; Caffe Cino

Smith, Michael (1951–) perf; performance art

Smith, Peyton (1948–) a; Wooster Group

Smith, Rex (1956–) a, s; Gilbert and Sullivan; Off-Broadway

Smith, Russell (1812–96) scpt; scenic design

Smith, William Neil (fl. 1920s–) arc; Nederlander Theatre

Snyder, Jacob (fl. mid-18th C.) scpt; scenic design

Snyder, Nancy (1949–) a; *Fifth of July*

Sokolow, Anna (1912/15–) co; Clarke (M.)

Solly, Bill (1931–) pl; gay/lesbian

Sonnenthal, Adolf Ritter von (1834–1909) Ger, a, m; Amberg; Shakespeare

Sontag, Karl (fl. mid-19th C.) Ger, a; Germania